CW01639186

HUGMAN'S FOOTBALL ANNUAL 1990

Ian Rush scores his first and Liverpool's second in the FA Cup Final win over Everton. Match Magazine

Edited by Barry J. Hugman

HUGMAN'S
SPORTING
PUBLICATIONS
LIMITED

© Hugman Enterprises Ltd 1989

First published in Great Britain in 1989 by
Hugman's Sporting Publications Ltd
24 Notting Hill Gate
London W11 3JQ

All rights reserved. No part of this publication may be reproduced, stored in a retrieval system, or transmitted, in any form or by any means, without the prior permission in writing of the publisher, nor be otherwise circulated in any form of binding or cover other than that in which it is published and without a similar condition including this condition being imposed on the subsequent publisher.

British Library Cataloguing in Publication Data
Hugman, Barry J. (Barry John)
Hugman's Football Annual 1990

ISBN 1 872290 00 0

Typeset by Area Graphics Ltd, Arden Press Way, Letchworth, Hertfordshire SG6 1LH
Printed in Great Britain by Cowells of Ipswich.

Contents

Acknowledgements

Once again the editor would like to thank the many various experts, without whose help this book would not have been possible to produce within the time allowed,

Alan Platt, the assistant editor, is a freelance transport planner whose most recent assignments have been overseas. Unlike many schoolboys he did not take an interest in soccer until the age of 14, but once involved, he was hooked. From 1960 onwards he has kept detailed records on all Football League clubs, and their players, and is happy to watch football at any level, "provided that there is something at stake and the players are trying". Mostly, he watches his beloved Liverpool, whom he has followed since 1961, and his local club Chesterfield, since 1983. And he contributed to the Chesterfield match programme from 1985 to 1986. We first met in 1981, following the publication of Football League Players' Records, when, after being impressed by the depth of research and immaculate attention to detail in that book, he volunteered his asssistance to all future editions. He is a most worthy member of the team where his vast expertise can be found among these pages.

Michael Featherstone is a keen sporting statistican and researcher, who works in the accounts department of a large public company. He started many years ago by collecting both cricket and soccer information, which he obtained from the Colindale National Newspaper Library. Several years later he joined Ray Spiller's Association of Football Statisticians after being introduced by his very good friend, the late Morley Farror. Following our first meeting in 1975, he began extensive research into post-war league footballers. This led to Football League Players' Records, first published in 1981, with the second edition released in 1984. He has also contributed to the British Boxing Yearbook, The Olympic Games, Complete Track and Field Results, 1896-1988, Cricket Who's Who and many other footballing publications.

Peter Arnold has been a sports enthusiast ever since he can remember. As a boy he would often be drawn to big sporting occasions and even played truant from school to watch the mighty Moscow Dynamos at Stamford Bridge in 1945. He has worked in publishing, editing many books on sports, games, leisure and pastimes, for over 30 years. Among the books he has written are: A History of Boxing, All-Time Greats of Boxing, A History of the Olympic Games, 100 Years of Test Cricket, World Soccer and an Encyclopedia of Gambling. Apart from producing various darts and snooker publications, he was my co-editor on The Olympic Games, Complete Track & Field Results, 1986-1988.

Steve Langbridge, who recently joined the team as my general assistant, has been well and truly baptized while working on this year's annual and my thanks go to him for his diligent help.

This year, we have formed an association with *Match Magazine*, through our very special relationship with the editor, Melvyn Bagnall. All the photographs used in this book were selected from their vast library, which was once again put at our disposal. And, as I said last year, it is easy to see how *Match* has such a vast circulation. Their appeal is in being able to satisfy both the older and younger fans alike. Once again the *Match* weekly club line-ups played an important role in our staff ascertaining match-by-match details, prior to auditing our records with the Football League, something which we have been doing successfully on behalf of Football League Players' Records since 1975.

Other special mentions must go to Maidstone's Mike Mercer, the secretary, and to Alan Brigden, a long serving fan, who supplied Vauxhall Conference information for last season's club performances.

My thanks go yet again to Mike Foster, of The Football League, who made the records available and to Sheila Murphy who lent her time and expertise to ensure that the information required was correct. I would also like to show appreciation for the support given by Gordon Taylor of the PFA and Trevor Phillips, the Commercial Director of the Football League.

Finally, as in all my other books, I must congratulate Edwin Cook and Ray Hedley for their expert handling in the area of picture layouts and design.

Preface

Sadly, everything memorable about events on the football field during the 1988–89 football season, was totally overshadowed by the appalling tragedy at Hillsborough Stadium, Sheffield on 15 April, when 94 Liverpool supporters were crushed to death at the start of the FA Cup semi-final between Liverpool and Nottingham Forest. While much could, and indeed should, be said about the causes of the disaster, and the responsibility for it, the authors of this book feel it inappropriate to pass judgement, in advance of the public inquiry, being conducted by Lord Justice Taylor. In the meantime we can do no more than extend our belated condolences to the bereaved.

Coming so soon after the misery of Bradford and Brussels, it is tempting, for some, to see a common thread and condemn football for all of society's ills. However, it is already clear that the cause of each of these disasters was different, even if certain elements were similar, and the end result depressingly so. All should be seen in the wider context of frequent tragedies in other spheres and an economic climate where the pursuit of profit and cost efficiency takes priority over public safety. Few would deny that a line must be drawn between cost and safety, but it does not seem that the line is yet in place.

The timing of the disaster was unfortunate, to say the least, since it followed, by one week, the provisional re-admission of English clubs to European competitions by UEFA, from 1990–91. One cannot help but feel that the decision was premature, since the reasons for the ban remain as valid in 1989 as they were in 1985.

The behaviour of some English supporters at the European Championships in West Germany, whilst execrable, was wildly exaggerated by some sections of the media. Nevertheless, it provoked a predictably "knee-jerk" reaction from the British government, who brought forward their long-threatened membership card scheme. Whilst this legislation will undoubtedly inconvenience, and in some cases effectively exclude, genuine law-abiding supporters from watching professional football, it is unclear how it can have any lasting effect on curbing or eliminating hooliganism. For membership cards to be confiscated, the hooligans must first be identified, prosecuted and convicted, something that the law enforcement agencies and courts have failed dismally to do for 20 years. Token fines and suspended prison sentences, far from deterring hooligans are, in effect, an encouragement to them, whilst the ambivalent attitude of some media, condemning them on one hand, whilst providing them with maximum publicity on the other, only elevates them to the status of "folk-hero" to their friends and followers. The membership card scheme may, as the government claim, or may not, break the link between football and hooliganism, at the possible cost of killing football as a spectator sport. What it will not do is stop hooliganism in general, which will continue to rise until the time that the government and the courts start getting tough with violent offenders.

Unfortunately Football League clubs earn little sympathy, for their claim that they cannot afford to implement the membership card scheme, when they are prepared to spend enormous sums on players. Once again, as in the late 1970s, clubs seem prepared to bankrupt themselves in auctions for players, often no better than those they already have. Only a few clubs with money to burn, can afford to buy players "off the peg" — the remainder would be better advised to pay more attention to the talent in their youth and reserve teams. The new League champions, Arsenal, are a shining example to the rest of the clubs in this respect. Rich enough to indulge in the orgy of spending, practised by most of their rivals, they signed only one player, for a modest £400,000, whilst upgrading nine youth team players to full professionals, and won the championship with a team, half of which was "home grown" and the remainder signed over a three year period for relatively modest fees. Newcastle United by contrast spent £5 million pounds on 14 players and were relegated with a team, which seemed a pale shadow of the previous season.

At a time when English football requires strong and clearheaded leadership to fight the government legislation on identity cards, and address the problems of stadium design and crown safety raised by the Hillsborough disaster, the Football League Management Committee seem only concerned with the distribution of television money and how to make more revenue by increasing the size of the League, along with the promotion of more and more meaningless cup competitions, which, quite rightly, the supporters ignore.

After laboriously reducing the size of the First Division from 22 to 20 clubs to ease fixture congestion and to allow time for national team managers to prepare for important international fixtures, without the risk of their squads being decimated by injuries, the Football League Mangement Committee now propose to restore the First Division to its former unwieldy size. It should be noted that last season, even with a reduced fixture list and a mild winter with few postponements, the First Division programme still had eight fixtures outstanding after the final Saturday of the season. This was only partly due to the hiatus following Hillsborough, as most of the postponements resulted from fixture clashes with the three cup competitions.

As for the football on the pitch, so dwarfed by

events off the field, the incredible climax to the First Division championship when Arsenal wrested the title from Liverpool's grasp in the final minute of the last game of the season, only partly redeemed a lack-lustre season in which only Arsenal, of the elite teams, showed any overall consistency. For much of the season Liverpool stuttered, plagued by injury to key players, and only from March onwards did they show the form of the previous season. A late charge, remarkable even by their own standards, of 13 victories and one draw in 14 games, narrowed Arsenal's lead from 18 points to parity. But the emotional trauma of Hillsborough, plus a difficult match with relegation threatened West Ham, left them mentally and physically jaded for the championship decider at Anfield, a few days later. Nevertheless, it was cruel luck to be denied the "double" with virtually the last kick of the season. All credit, however, to Arsenal, who topped the table for most of the season, but were "written off" by the media before the final game. Their overall record shows them to be worthy champions and they showed immense character in defying the odds to win it on the ground of the reigning champions. Once again it was shown that the enduring appeal of English football, for all of its shortcomings, is that there are no certainties.

Chelsea bestrode the Second Division like a colossus, winning the championship with such authority and conviction, that it would be surprising if they do not challenge the First Division elité in the forthcoming season. Manchester City accompanied them with far less conviction and, for all their youthful talent, it remains to be seen if they are ready. Wolves took one more step back towards the big time when winning the Third Division championship and Steve Bull, a throwback to the old fashioned 50s style centre-forwards, once again finished as the League's top scorer, with 54 goals in all competitions for his club. Not only that, but he scored on his international debut for England and became only the fourth player from the lower divisions to be selected for an England team. In the Fourth Division, it was heart warming to see two perenially struggling teams, Crewe Alexandra and Tranmere Rovers win promotion and their end of season meeting at Prenton Park attracted an astonishing attendance of 15,000, where 1,500 was the norm only three years ago.

The play-off system continues to provoke controversy, and rightly so, since its format is flawed. Where promotion and relegation are not automatic, the issues should be decided by games between teams from different divisions, not teams from the same division who have already played each other twice. The present system allows middle of the table teams with mediocre playing records, who finish sixth or seventh in their division, when winning a few fairly meaningless end of season games, to overtake the third placed team which has challenged hard for promotion all season, as happened with Aldershot in 1986–87 and Swansea City in 1987–88. When play-offs are also decided by away goals and extra time penalties, the result becomes a lottery and an arbitrary method of deciding important issues. Fortunately, this season, justice was done, as Crystal Palace, third in the Second Division, Port Vale, third in the Third Division and Leyton Orient from the Fourth Division, eventually prevailed. Although Orient finished sixth, two points behind Scunthorpe, who were fourth, they recovered well from an appalling start to the season, and with 86 goals, were arguably the most entertaining team in the division.

The "wooden spoon" race to decide which club lost its Football League place, was a close-run thing between Colchester and Darlington, neither team showing much fight until the closing weeks of the season. In the end Colchester saved their bacon by winning their last five games, including the vital one at Darlington, which condemned the north-eastern club to their demise. A qualified welcome go to their replacement, Maidstone United, worthy winners of the GM Vauxhall Conference, whose playing record was excellent, but who play at Dartford 20 miles away from their home town, with no realistic prospects of ever returning there. It is a depressing trend for football clubs to abandon their homes for financial gain and lose touch or break faith with their long time supporters and local community. Admittedly Bristol Rovers have made a great success of their enforced move to Bath, but happily Charlton Athletic have finally admitted to the folly of deserting The Valley and will return there during next season with, hopefully, 20,000 plus attendances to welcome them back.

If this preface reads more like an epilogue, it must be remembered that football is still the sport that attracts more interest and publicity in the country. Never was the emotional attachment and passion for the game shown more clearly than in the aftermath of the Hillsborough disaster, not only by the people of Liverpool, but by supporters all over the country. The governments identity card scheme will undoubtedly slash attendances and the Football League may well disintegrate as the top clubs desert to form a Super League or even, in time, a European League, while the lower division clubs resign to join an enlarged GM Vauxhall Conference. But football itself will survive because, for many people, the commitment to the club they love and their identification with its successes and failures are one of their few pleasures in life.

Introduction

The 1987–88 season ended with the First Division reduced from the 22 clubs that had comprised it since the First World War to 20 clubs, as the result of two seasons of play-off relegation/promotion matches. It was ironic that for years thoughtful fans had been arguing for a smaller First Division on the grounds that the top clubs with their European commitments were playing too many matches, and that now this had come about, English teams were out of European competition. Whether or not English teams would be allowed back into Europe was to be one of the main footballing topics of the summer, together with the argument about the desirability of identity cards for fans attending matches at home. The Government insisted on linking the two questions, making it clear that ministerial approval of re-entry into Europe was dependent on the clubs first organising a membership card scheme. Majority opinion in the game and the media and, indeed, of the police authorities, was that the identity card scheme would not in any way help to reduce violence and hooliganism associated with football.

Other topics likely to keep football in the news during the summer were the arrangements for football to be televised — the BBC, ITV and a new rival, British Satellite Broadcasting, were competing for rights — and, on the field, the European Championship.

Early administrative business to get out of the way was the Football League's Annual General Meeting, where Bobby Charlton was one of five candidates for four First Division places on the Management Committee (one arising because Ken Bates, the Chelsea chairman, lost his place when Chelsea lost First Division status). Alas, Charlton was the odd man out, finishing bottom of the poll. Two men re-elected were Philip Carter, of Everton, as League President for the next three years, and David Dein of Arsenal. However, few things run smoothly in football, and these two were to be in the centre of controversy later in the year when the competition for television rights became cut-throat. The most controversial motion before the AGM was a proposal to deduct points from clubs with poor records of discipline, coupled with longer suspensions for players who commit serious offences. This was seen as a determined move to clean up football. It was proposed by the Management Committee and supported by the FA and the Professional Footballers Association, but received only 18½ votes out of 60, thus confirming the League's apparent reluctance to deal with the characters who were spoiling the game.

Wimbledon, of course, remained the club who made most news of the disciplinary kind. The incident in which the Cup-holders bared their backsides to the crowd at Alan Cork's testimonial match at the end of the previous season came up for jurisdiction, and the club was fined £5,000, and the players £750 each.

The Football League lost its secretary after the AGM when it was announced that Graham Kelly had been appointed Chief Executive at the Football Association. This was a new post created

Liverpool: 1987-88 League Champions

Match Magazine

because of the impending retirement of Ted Croker, the General Secretary. Meanwhile, as the European Championship got under way in West Germany, the FA confirmed that it had not bid to stage the 1992 European Championship in England. England would have had a strong favourite's chance to host the tournament (the 1966 World Cup is the only major event to be staged in the country of the game's birth), but sadly the spectre of hooliganism had persuaded the FA to forego the chance.

England and the Republic of Ireland, drawn in the same group in the European Championship, began their campaigns with a match against each other, and the result was a surprising 1-0 victory to the Irish, an early headed goal by Ray Houghton doing the damage.

It was a bad day for England when they played their second match against Holland. First it became known that the report which the Minister of Sport, Colin Moynihan, had sent to UEFA regarding the state of hooliganism in England was unpromising, drawing attention to "disturbingly large numbers of hooligans". In the match at Dusseldorf, England did their utmost but the Dutch had an extra touch of class (and hat-trick man Marco van Basten) and won 3-1. It was Peter Shilton's 100th appearance for England. The Republic of Ireland's excellent 1-1 draw with the USSR meant that England were eliminated from the Championship. One result was that certain tabloid newspapers heightened their vicious campaign to get Bobby Robson sacked as England manager.

Violence in the streets of Stuttgart and Dusseldorf during the Championship were admitted by the West German authorities to be largely the work of local thugs, but any violence these days was bad news for England's chances of European rehabilitation at club level, and provided ammunition for the Government. The FA announced that they would withdraw their request to UEFA for English clubs to be re-admitted to Europe, but Bert Millichip, the Chairman, said that they would not withdraw England from competitions. This last remark was in answer to pressure from the Government, who seemed anxious to isolate England from world football altogether.

England lost their final match 3-1 to the USSR and Robson came home to the worst vilification ever heaped upon a football manager by the lower end of the tabloid newspaper market. Meanwhile the Republic of Ireland were desperately unlucky, being prevented from going into the semi-finals by a freakish goal in the 82nd minute which gave Holland a 1-0 victory over them. As Holland went on to win the Championship and prove themselves easily the best team in Europe, and the Irish had also drawn with the USSR, the other finalists, they did much better than anybody could have expected. Apart from three from Celtic, all their players were from the English First Division.

Hans Baengerter, the retiring General Secretary of UEFA, had his say in the re-entry discussions: "There is little chance of re-admission for English clubs unless the authorities take away the passports from hooligans." The FA Chairman, Bert Millichip, was elected to the executive of UEFA and pledged that he would do his best to keep England in international football.

Hooliganism won a small battle when a four-team Wembley spectacular involving Arsenal, Spurs, Bayern Munich and Milan, which had been planned to open the new season by bringing Dutch stars van Basten and Ruud Gullit to Wembley failed to get FA sanction on the grounds of "potential crowd disorder".

The television coverage saga began to hot up near the end of June when it was revealed that ITV had contacted top clubs in order to obtain exclusive rights to televise from their grounds. It was believed that ten clubs had been approached. Since 1978 the BBC and ITV had negotiated jointly with the football authorities, but the imminence of satellite TV and a big offer to the League from British Satellite Broadcasting had prompted the ITV move. ITV, by approaching clubs direct, were accused of attempting to split the League and create a "Super-league".

A split in the Management Committee itself became apparent when three of the eight-man committee — President Philip Carter (Everton), David Dein (Arsenal) and Gordon McKeag (Newcastle) found other members objecting to their "secret" talks with ITV on behalf of the "elite" ten clubs when they should be representing the interests of all 92 League clubs. The three were barred from a session of the committee at Plymouth, where legal advice was taken on their position. Gordon Taylor, the Professional Footballers' Association secretary, was also called into discussions because of threats of redundancies among players. Meanwhile the BBC had approached the League and the FA with counter-proposals.

Early July saw movement on the "hooligan front" when the FA changed its mind on the four-team Wembley Festival, planned for 13 and 14 August, on learning that the capacity at each game would be 60,000, all seated, and that no alcohol would be on sale within the ground. Less reassuring news for the game was an announcement that Minister of Sport Colin Moynihan would head a committee to monitor the introduction of a national identity card system for supporters.

On 12 July the law was invoked in the television battle when the Football League obtained an "injunction" against the "rebels" — Spurs, Manchester United, Arsenal, Everton and Liverpool — from signing any agreement with ITV within the next week without the consent of the Management Committee. ITV had hoped that a signing was imminent. Immediately there was a softening of rebel attitudes — ITV amended their offer so that all 92 clubs would benefit while Philip Carter claimed that a super-league had never been on the agenda.

Chelsea, meanwhile, were handed the heaviest FA fine ever, £75,000, and were ordered to keep their terraces closed for the first six matches of the forthcoming season for their failure to control their supporters at the play-off game with Middlesbrough at the end of the previous season. It was revealed that 102 spectators had been arrested and 25 policemen injured.

A long-running transfer saga was decided on 25 July when West Ham's Tony Cottee decided to join Everton rather than Arsenal at a fee of around £2.2 million. Another West Ham man decided to give up playing. Billy Bonds, two months short of his 42nd birthday, became youth team coach after over 1,000 games for the club and an MBE, awarded for services to football. The shadier side of football was exposed by a report prepared by Liverpool City council trading standards officers, who named 56 sources, including 12 First Division clubs, of overpriced tickets for the FA Cup final. Liverpool fans alone paid over £500,000 above published price for their tickets, the report alleged. The FA appointed a sub-committee to investigate.

The first week of August saw the TV wrangle resolved. ITV won the right to show League matches live for four seasons for £44 million — 18 League fixtures per season plus the final stages of the League Cup competition. The BBC and BSB arranged a £30 million five-year deal with the FA to show FA Cup ties and England matches. The winners appeared to be football. The 1986 two-year joint deal by BBC and ITV for 14 live games per season had been worth only £6.2 million. Indeed, a television attitude that football was becoming less worthy for screening seemed to have turned round completely with the companies now scrambling to pay huge fees to show football.

The weekend of 13-14 August at last saw some action on the pitch, instead of round the negotiating tables. The four-club Wembley Festival of Football was played, principally for the Italian television network Canale 5, in the same ownership as AC Milan, one of the four competing teams. On Saturday Milan beat Bayern Munich 1-0, so Italian TV viewers were pleased to see their team remain in contention for Sunday. Arsenal beat Spurs, for whom Terry Venables had spent £4 million on new players during the summer, 4-0 in an impressive display. On Sunday Arsenal played even better to beat Bayern Munich 3-0, while AC Milan beat Spurs 2-1. So Arsenal won the tournament on goal difference, they and Milan having won both their games.

As the new season approached, Wimbledon made the first disciplinary news. The club with the worst disciplinary record in the League, which had been given three months to "clean up its act", had Vinny Jones sent off in a pre-season friendly for elbowing in the face, a defender of the Shanklin, Isle of Wight, team. Manager Bobby Gould ruled him out of the FA Charity Shield match as punishment and banned him "indefinitely".

Big transfer news days before the new season concerned Ian Rush, whom Liverpool had sold a season or two earlier to Juventus for £3.2 million. After a year of comparative failure, he was bought back by Liverpool, who were still owed by Juventus half the original fee. The return fee was said to be £2.8 million.

Alan Smith scores for Arsenal in the 3-0 win over Bayern Munich during the Wembley Festival of Football

Match Magazine

On the day of the Charity Shield, the banned Vinny Jones was photographed wearing his new Simod boots, having been chosen to market them by the Italian sportswear manufacturers who sponsor the Simod Cup, perhaps bringing a new meaning to "bovver boots". Philip Carter, the League President, learned that on 18 October he would need some charity himself from certain club chairmen, because that was the date fixed for an Extraordinary General Meeting of the League at which he and David Dein of Arsenal would be called upon to resign because of their conduct during the TV negotiations, when some thought they were negotiating for their own clubs at the expense of the whole of the League, which they were supposed to represent.

Liverpool duly won the Charity Shield by beating Wimbledon 2-1, John Aldridge, who missed the vital penalty in the previous FA Cup Final, scoring both the goals. Ian Rush did not play, and there was a lot of discussion about the role of Aldridge, if any, when Rush returned to the team.

Finances having made much of the soccer news in the close season, there was more good news when Barclays Bank announced that prize money in the coming season would be doubled, and that runners-up in each division would benefit as well as the winners.

After one of the most eventful close seasons for a long time, the new season was awaited with eager anticipation.

Dave Beasant's magnificent penalty save against Liverpool in the 1988 FA Cup Final, along with Sanchez's goal, brought the Cup to Wimbledon for the first time

Match Magazine

FINAL
FOOTBALL LEAGUE TABLES
1987–88

FIRST DIVISION

			Home			Goals		Away			Goals		
		P	W	D	L	F	A	W	D	L	F	A	Pts
1	Liverpool	40	15	5	0	49	9	11	7	2	38	15	90
2	Manchester U.	40	14	5	1	41	17	9	7	4	30	21	81
3	Nottingham F.	40	11	7	2	40	17	9	6	5	27	22	73
4	Everton	40	14	4	2	34	11	5	9	6	19	16	70
5	Q.P.R.	40	12	4	4	30	14	7	6	7	18	24	67
6	Arsenal	40	11	4	5	35	16	7	8	5	23	23	66
7	Wimbledon	40	8	9	3	32	20	6	6	8	26	27	57
8	Newcastle U.	40	9	6	5	32	23	5	8	7	23	30	56
9	Luton T.	40	11	6	3	40	21	3	5	12	17	37	53
10	Coventry C.	40	6	8	6	23	25	7	6	7	23	28	53
11	Sheffield Wed.	40	10	2	8	27	30	5	6	9	25	36	53
12	Southampton	40	6	8	6	27	26	6	6	8	22	27	50
13	Tottenham H.	40	9	5	6	26	23	3	6	11	12	25	47
14	Norwich C.	40	7	5	8	26	26	5	4	11	14	26	45
15	Derby Co.	40	6	7	7	18	17	4	6	10	17	28	43
16	West Ham U.	40	6	9	5	23	21	3	6	11	17	31	42
17	Charlton Ath.	40	7	7	6	23	21	2	8	10	15	31	42
18	Chelsea*	40	7	11	2	24	17	2	4	14	26	51	42
19	Portsmouth*	40	4	8	8	21	27	3	6	11	15	39	35
20	Watford*	40	4	5	11	15	24	3	6	11	12	27	32
21	Oxford U.*	40	5	7	8	24	34	1	6	13	20	46	31

* relegated

Peter Beardsley (left) and Steve McMahon celebrate Liverpool's League Championship win, following the 1-0 victory over "Spurs"

Match Magazine

SECOND DIVISION

			Home			Goals		Away			Goals		
		P	W	D	L	F	A	W	D	L	F	A	Pts
1	Millwall†	44	15	3	4	45	23	10	4	8	27	29	82
2	Aston Villa†	44	9	7	6	31	21	13	5	4	37	20	78
3	Middlesbrough†	44	15	4	3	44	16	7	8	7	19	20	78
4	Bradford C.	44	14	3	5	49	26	8	8	6	25	28	77
5	Blackburn Rov.	44	12	8	2	38	22	9	6	7	30	30	77
6	Crystal Palace	44	16	3	3	50	21	6	6	10	36	38	75
7	Leeds U.	44	14	4	4	37	18	5	8	9	24	33	69
8	Ipswich T.	44	14	3	5	38	17	5	6	11	23	35	66
9	Manchester C.	44	11	4	7	50	28	8	4	10	30	32	65
10	Oldham Ath.	44	13	4	5	43	27	5	7	10	29	37	65
11	Stoke C.	44	12	6	4	34	22	5	5	12	16	35	62
12	Swindon T.	44	10	7	5	43	25	6	4	12	30	35	59
13	Leicester C.	44	12	5	5	35	20	4	6	12	27	41	59
14	Barnsley	44	11	4	7	42	32	4	8	10	19	30	57
15	Hull C.	44	10	8	4	32	22	4	7	11	22	38	57
16	Plymouth Arg.	44	12	4	6	44	26	4	4	14	21	41	56
17	Bournemouth	44	7	7	8	36	30	6	3	13	20	38	49
18	Shrewsbury T.	44	7	8	7	23	22	4	8	10	19	32	49
19	Birmingham C.	44	7	9	6	20	24	4	6	12	21	42	48
20	West Bromwich A.	44	8	7	7	29	26	4	4	14	21	43	47
21	Sheffield U.*	44	8	6	8	27	28	5	1	16	18	46	46
22	Reading*	44	5	7	10	20	25	5	5	12	24	45	42
23	Huddersfield T.*	44	4	6	12	20	38	2	4	16	21	62	28

* relegated † promoted

THIRD DIVISION

			Home			Goals		Away			Goals		
		P	W	D	L	F	A	W	D	L	F	A	Pts
1	Sunderland†	46	14	7	2	51	22	13	5	5	41	26	93
2	Brighton & H.A.†	46	15	7	1	37	16	8	8	7	32	31	84
3	Walsall†	46	15	6	2	39	22	8	7	8	29	28	82
4	Notts. Co.	46	14	4	5	53	24	9	8	6	29	25	81
5	Bristol C.	46	14	6	3	51	30	7	6	10	26	32	75
6	Northampton T.	46	12	8	3	36	18	6	11	6	34	33	73
7	Wigan Ath.	46	11	8	4	36	23	9	4	10	34	38	72
8	Bristol Rov.	46	14	5	4	43	19	4	7	12	25	37	66
9	Fulham	46	10	5	8	36	24	9	4	10	33	36	66
10	Blackpool	46	13	4	6	45	27	4	10	9	26	35	65
11	Port Vale	46	12	8	3	36	19	6	3	14	22	37	65
12	Brentford	46	9	8	6	27	23	7	6	10	26	36	62
13	Gillingham	46	8	9	6	45	21	6	8	9	32	40	59
14	Bury	46	9	7	7	33	26	6	7	10	25	31	59
15	Chester C.	46	9	8	6	29	30	5	8	10	22	32	58
16	Preston N.E.	46	10	6	7	30	23	5	7	11	18	36	58
17	Southend U.	46	10	6	7	42	33	4	7	12	23	50	55
18	Chesterfield	46	10	5	8	25	28	5	5	13	16	42	55
19	Mansfield T.	46	10	6	7	25	21	4	6	13	23	38	54
20	Aldershot	46	12	3	8	45	32	3	5	15	19	42	53
21	Rotherham U.*	46	8	8	7	28	25	4	8	11	22	41	52
22	Grimsby T.*	46	6	7	10	25	29	6	7	10	23	29	50
23	York C.*	46	4	7	12	27	45	4	2	17	21	46	33
24	Doncaster Rov.*	46	6	5	12	25	36	2	4	17	15	48	33

* relegated † promoted

FOURTH DIVISION

			Home			Goals		Away			Goals		
		P	W	D	L	F	A	W	D	L	F	A	Pts
1	Wolverhampton W.†	46	15	3	5	47	19	12	6	5	35	24	90
2	Cardiff C.†	46	15	6	2	39	14	9	7	7	27	27	85
3	Bolton W.†	46	15	6	2	42	12	7	6	10	24	30	78
4	Scunthorpe U.	46	14	5	4	42	20	6	12	5	34	31	77
5	Torquay U.	46	10	7	6	34	16	11	7	5	32	25	77
6	Swansea C.†	46	9	7	7	35	28	11	3	9	27	28	70
7	Peterborough U.	46	10	5	8	28	26	10	5	8	24	27	70
8	Leyton Orient	46	13	4	6	55	27	6	8	9	30	36	69
9	Colchester U.	46	10	5	8	23	22	9	5	9	24	29	67
10	Burnley	46	12	5	6	31	22	8	2	13	26	40	67
11	Wrexham	46	13	3	7	46	26	7	3	13	23	32	66
12	Scarborough	46	12	8	3	38	19	5	6	12	18	29	65
13	Darlington	46	13	6	4	39	25	5	5	13	32	44	65
14	Tranmere Rov.	46	14	2	7	43	20	5	7	11	18	33	64
15	Cambridge U.	46	10	6	7	32	24	6	7	10	18	28	61
16	Hartlepool U.	46	9	7	7	25	25	6	7	10	25	32	59
17	Crewe Alex.	46	7	11	5	25	19	6	8	9	32	34	58
18	Halifax T.	46	11	7	5	37	25	3	7	13	17	34	55
19	Hereford U.	46	8	7	8	25	27	6	5	12	16	32	54
20	Stockport Co.	46	7	7	9	26	26	5	8	10	18	32	51
21	Rochdale	46	5	9	9	28	34	6	6	11	19	42	48
22	Exeter C.	46	8	6	9	33	29	3	7	13	20	39	46
23	Carlisle U.	46	9	5	9	38	33	3	3	17	19	53	44
24	Newport Co.*	46	4	5	14	19	36	2	2	19	16	69	25

* replaced by Lincoln C. † promoted

A review of the 1988-89 English Football Season

AUGUST

Cottee and Aldridge Start With Hat Tricks

On the last Saturday in August the League programme started. Published on page 10 are the final League tables from the 1987-88 season. Of the 92 League clubs, 22, or nearly a quarter, would be beginning the new season in a new division. As it happened, the play-offs altered nothing this year with one exception — Swansea City won promotion from the Fourth Division to the Third despite finishing sixth. Scunthorpe was the unlucky club, finishing seven points higher than Swansea but losing out in the play-offs.

Many players were beginning the campaign with new clubs. Mention has been made of Ian Rush returning to Liverpool from Juventus — another to make the return trip after an expensive and unsuccessful spell on the continent was Mark Hughes, bought back by Manchester United from Barcelona for £1.5 million. The ex-England forward Gordon Cowans also returned to his former club, Aston Villa, from Bari in Italy, but at only £250,000. Paul Rideout, a former Villa player, left Bari for the same price, but for Southampton. Departing the country were Nico Claesen, the Belgian World Cup star whose stay at White Hart Lane had not been very successful — he left Spurs for Antwerp at £550,000 — Lee Chapman, sold by Sheffield Wednesday to Niort, in France (but he would be returning), and Johnny Metgod, former Forest and latterly Spurs player, who returned to Holland and Feyenoord. Kevin Moran, famous for being sent off in the Cup Final, left Manchester United for Sporting Gijon. England players Brian Stein of Luton and Graham Rix of Arsenal left the League to play for Caen in France.

On the domestic front, Cottee's move to Everton has been noted. Other famous names on the move were Paul Gascoigne and Paul Stewart, who both joined Spurs, the former from Newcastle for £2 million and the latter from Manchester City for £1.7 million. Gary Stevens, the England full-back, moved from Everton to Rangers for £1.2 million, to join international colleagues Terry Butcher and Chris Woods. As well as Cottee, Everton bought two men for just under £1 million each: Pat Nevin, from Chelsea for £925,000, and Stuart McCall, from Bradford for £850,000. For around these prices two of Wimbledon's FA Cup winning side were sold to Newcastle: Andy Thorn and Dave Beasant, the captain and goalkeeper who saved a Cup Final penalty. West Ham used some of their Cottee money to buy a replacement: Dave Kelly, a striker from Walsall.

Other interesting moves were Kevin Drinkell, from Norwich to Rangers; Steve Hodge, who because of homesickness returned to his first club, Nottingham Forest from Spurs; Neil McDonald, who moved from Newcastle to Everton; John Hendrie, from Bradford to Newcastle; Graham Roberts, the former Spurs and England player, from Rangers to Chelsea; Derek Mountfield, an Everton stalwart in their best days, to Aston Villa; Paul Goddard, from Newcastle to Derby (Liverpool had been

John Aldridge holds the Charity Shield aloft after scoring both goals in a 2-1 revenge win over Wimbledon

Match Magazine

Tony Cottee pictured after joining Everton from West Ham for a fee in excess of £2 million

Match Magazine

Welsh International, Peter Nicholas and English International, Graham Roberts sign for Chelsea in a bid to take the Londoners back to the First Division

Match Magazine

interested); Simon Barker from Blackburn to QPR; Steve Bould, from Stoke to Arsenal; and Peter Nicholas, from Aberdeen to Chelsea.

Well-known players who moved for more modest fees included Luton's Mark Stein, who joined QPR; Steve Williams, an international as recently as 1984, from Arsenal to Luton; Alan Harper, who performed excellently as a utility player in Everton's Championship years, to Sheffield Wednesday; Alan McKnight, a Northern Ireland international goalkeeper, from Celtic to West Ham; Mark Chamberlain, England winger in 1985, from Sheffield Wednesday to Portsmouth. Arthur Albiston went from Manchester United to West Brom, and another former United full-back favourite, John Gidman, was transferred from Manchester City to Stoke. George Burley, the former Ipswich and Scotland full back, left Sunderland for Gillingham, and Osvaldo Ardiles, World Cup winner, left Spurs for Queens Park Rangers.

The biggest spenders were Everton, Liverpool and Spurs, while Newcastle United had also experienced a major change of personnel. These teams were naturally watched with interest on the first day.

Perhaps the most satisfying individual performances were achieved by hat-trick men. Tony Cottee gave the supporters of his new club every encouragement with three of the four goals by which Everton beat Newcastle (not a good omen for the new keeper, Beasant). For other reasons, John Aldridge must have been pleased with his hat-trick in Liverpool's 3-0 win at Charlton. Ian Rush came on as a substitute in this match — for Beardsley, not Aldridge.

Other men to feel pleased were Paul Rideout, Southampton's import from Bari, who scored two in a 4-0 win over West Ham, Alan Smith, still comparatively new at Arsenal, who scored three in a 5-1 victory at Wimbledon and Paul Goddard, who scored the only goal for his new club Derby against Middlesbrough.

Millwall, in their first match in the First Division, drew 2-2 at Aston Villa, after leading 2-0, a satisfactory beginning. In the Second Division, perhaps the most satisfied team was Blackburn, who after missing promotion the previous season by being well beaten in the play-offs by Chelsea, won 2-1 at Stamford Bridge.

Of the ten promoted clubs, the only side to win was, ironically, Swansea, who won 3-2 at Gillingham. As well as Villa and Millwall, who drew with each other, Sunderland and Walsall also drew. Middlesbrough, Brighton, Wolves, Cardiff, Bolton and Lincoln, who were returning to the League as winners of the GM Vauxhall Conference after only one season away, all lost. Of the 12 relegated clubs, the picture was nearly as bad. Four won: Portsmouth, Watford, Sheffield United and Rotherham, but two of these wins were against other relegated clubs. One drew — Oxford — while seven lost: Chelsea, Reading, Huddersfield, Grimsby, York, Doncaster and Newport, who in the GM Vauxhall Conference had already lost their first three matches.

Trevor Hebberd of Derby rises above a Middlesbrough defender. The ball didn't hit the target on this occasion, but the "Rams" still won 1-0

Match Magazine

The most extraordinary event of the first day, however, was Spurs' postponement of their home match with Coventry six hours before kick-off because rubble from building work was blocking safety exits.

Midweek fixtures began on the Monday following the first Saturday, and featured the fag-end of the League's Centenary celebrations, a tournament for eight clubs called the Mercantile Credit Centenary Trophy. The biggest crowd for the three "quarter-finals" on this evening was 20,141 at Anfield, where Liverpool beat Nottingham Forest 4-1. The big story was the omission of Aldridge so that Rush could play. Rush failed to score. In the other matches, Manchester United beat Everton 1-0 at Old Trafford, and Newcastle won 1-0 after extra time against Wimbledon at St James's Park. The round was completed on Wednesday when Arsenal beat Queens Park Rangers 2-0 at Loftus Road.

There was a Second Division programme, where Watford and Portsmouth won again to begin their efforts to regain First Division status in the best way with two wins, and the Littlewoods Cup got under way with first round, first leg ties. In this competition the League's leading scorer of the previous season, Steve Bull, opened his account with two against Birmingham.

SEPTEMBER

The Left Hook Picked Up By Television News

The big match on the soccer season's second Saturday, 4 September, was at Anfield, where the opponents were Manchester United. Only five months earlier United manager Alex Ferguson had complained that Liverpool were always favoured by referees at Anfield, a remark that prompted a rude response from Liverpool manager Kenny Dalglish. This simmering feud together with the natural animosity which the two sets of fans had for each other led to the kick-off being brought forward to 12 o'clock, on the assumption that the spectators would not have had the opportunity to get drunk and cause disorder. Despite Liverpool having dominated the Championship for nine seasons, they had beaten United in League matches only twice in that period, a fact which rankled with Anfield fans. The match proved to be a fierce one. Strachan and McMahon went off early with injuries, and the fact that only four players went into the book said more for referee Hackett's lenience than anything else. At the end of the day Liverpool fans were happy with a 1-0 win, the goal, appropriately enough, coming from a penalty. Aldridge played as centre-forward, before being substituted by Rush 12 minutes from the end. PSV Eindhoven, hoping to cash in on Liverpool's embarrassment of strikers, offered £1 million for Aldridge, but were refused.

Liverpool joined Everton, Norwich and Southampton as First Division leaders with two wins in two matches. Cottee scored Everton's goal at Coventry to maintain his good start, but the victory owed more to a dazzling goalkeeping display by Neville Southall. At the other end of the table, Middlesbrough and West Ham had lost twice. Spurs, having missed the opening day because of "crowd rubble" began at Newcastle with a 2-2 draw (after being two down) and their £2 million signing, Gascoigne, was roundly booed and was taken off after 78 minutes in an undistinguished debut.

The Second Division, with most teams having played three matches, had Portsmouth and Watford at the head of affairs with nine points, Portsmouth, after a 4-0 defeat of Leeds, enjoying a 9-1 goal difference. Blackburn were also 100 per cent having played only two matches. Chelsea and Manchester City, two teams favoured for promotion, had each collected one point from three games.

Sheffield United and Fulham, clubs with traditions better suited to the higher levels of football, had begun well in the Third Division with two wins, while Rotherham, Wrexham, Burnley and Hartlepool had 100 per cent records in the Fourth. Lincoln, back in the League, had yet to score a goal.

Bryan Robson and Peter Shilton, two of England's most established internationals, were reprimanded by the FA for night-time flings

In a goalmouth scramble, Colin Clarke of Southampton, vainly searches for his first league goal of the season, while Gary Ablett of Liverpool challenges successfully. Liverpool won 3-1 at the Dell

Match Magazine

which they enjoyed just before the European Championships — incidents which the tabloid press had recently publicised. On the field, mid-week saw the settling of the Littlewoods Cup first round ties. There were no real shocks, Peterborough's elimination of West Brom being the biggest surprise. Meanwhile, Cardiff, being a Welsh club rather than English, played in Europe and drew 0-0 in the first round, first leg of the European Cup Winners Cup at Derry City (Eire). Ian Rush scored his first goal since returning to Liverpool — for the reserves in a win against Leeds. Somebody pointed out that Liverpool Reserves had never lost when Rush had scored . . .

On the third Saturday of the season, Liverpool and Everton dropped their first points with draws, leaving less fashionable Norwich and Southampton, narrow home winners over QPR and Luton respectively, isolated at the top of the First Division with three wins each. Only Middlesbrough, 1-0 losers at Old Trafford, remained without a point. Arsenal had a satisfying 3-2 win at White Hart Lane. Liverpool, who drew 1-1 at Aston Villa, played both Rush and Aldridge, omitting current England international Beardsley. Neither striker scored.

In the Second Division, Watford reigned supreme after their fourth straight win. Portsmouth, who played on Sunday, dropped their first point in a 1-1 draw at Swindon. Blackburn kept their 100 per cent record, winning at Stoke, while Birmingham and Brighton were the only two clubs pointless. Draws for Chelsea and Manchester City left them ten points off the pace after only four games.

In the two lower divisions, the only side with maximum points was Fourth Division Burnley, whose 6-0 defeat of York put them clear. No sides were pointless.

Qualifying matches for the 1990 World Cup took top billing in mid September. The two Irelands, Northern Ireland and the Republic, drew 0-0 in Belfast. Wales, after another great display by goalkeeper Neville Southall, were a trifle unlucky to lose 1-0 to Holland in Amsterdam, Ruud Gullit scoring seven minutes from time. Scotland won 2-1 in Norway. England, meanwhile, had a Wembley friendly with Denmark and won 1-0, Neil Webb scoring.

A Friday evening match in which Burnley dropped their first points in a 0-0 draw at Stockport saw 13 arrests as fighting broke out at half-time. Two policemen were injured.

Next day, Norwich, winning 2-0 at Newcastle, proudly led the First Division on their own, Southampton dropped two points, although a 2-2 draw at Highbury could not be called disappointing, except in its manner. The Saints were two up at half-time, and the equaliser came in the seventh of nine minutes added on for injury. The worst injury was to Southampton's Glenn Cockerill, whose jaw was broken. Although the incident in which it happened was missed by the officials, ITV showed in a news broadcast (and in slow motion) Arsenal's England player Paul Davis throwing a left hook at

Nigel Winterburn's expression says it all, as he scores for Arsenal in the "Gunner's" 3-2 win over local rivals, "Spurs"

Match Magazine

Cockerill. The FA promised that the film would be studied to see if disciplinary action should be taken, and also said that they would consider the criticism of the referee voiced by the Southampton manager Chris Nicholl over the prolonged injury time. Middlesbrough scored their first points with a 1-0 home victory over Wimbledon, but the best performance was that of fellow promotion winners Millwall, who beat Everton 2-1 at the Den for their third win since the opening day draw. They stood third in the table, naturally the highest in the club's history. Liverpool, again playing both Rush and Aldridge, obtained no goals from either, but Beardsley saved them in a 1-1 home draw with Spurs, the Londoners' best result to date. Spurs' centre back Fairclough was sent off for throwing a punch near the end.

Watford lost at Ipswich in the Second Division, and Blackburn dropped their first points with a home draw with Swindon. Manchester City at last won, but Chelsea could only draw at Barnsley and were still without a win after five games. City's victims were Brighton, one of the promoted teams, who still had to score a point. Bradford, by beating Oldham, moved into second place behind Watford as Portsmouth lost at home 3-1 to Hull.

David Rocastle, the young Arsenal player, made his debut for England in September

Match Magazine

This division looked as if it might become an awkward one to win.

Northampton went to the top of the Third Divison, but Sheffield United, in second place, impressed the most with a 6-1 defeat of Chester, Brian Deane and Tony Agana each getting a hat-trick. Port Vale were also 6-1 winners over Cardiff, and followed this up on Monday night with a 5-0 defeat of Chesterfield to go level on points with Northampton. Rotherham won 4-0 at Grimsby in the Fourth Division to head Burnley at the top on goal difference.

During the week it was learned that Liverpool's popular goalkeeper, Bruce Grobbelaar, had been taken to hospital with meningitis, and would be out of the game for some time. Arsenal, without Davis, banned by his manager, beat Liverpool, without Grobbelaar, 2-1 in the first semi-final of the Mercantile Credit Centenary Trophy. The following night Manchester United beat Newcastle 2-0 after extra time to join them in the final.

In mid-week Second Division games, Watford beat Bradford 2-0 to stay top, but Blackburn also won, at Hull, and Ipswich, showing good form, won 5–1 at Shrewsbury. Manchester City won 3-1 at Stamford Bridge, and any hopes Chelsea had of a quick return to the top flight appeared to be vanishing rapidly. In the Third Division Northampton, the leaders over the weekend, went down 4-0 at Sheffield United, who assumed top place with 18 goals in five matches. Rotherham kept ahead in the Fourth Division with a 4-1 defeat of Leyton Orient, and as Burnley and Cambridge both lost, their nearest rivals were now Hartlepool, 3-2 winners at bottom-placed York.

The long drawn-out and, in the view of most, boring Centenary celebrations ran into a snag when Manchester United announced themselves reluctant to postpone their Saturday fixture on 8 October in order to play the Centenary Trophy final against Arsenal on Sunday. United claimed their match with Sheffield Wednesday was heavily sponsored, and claimed there was little interest in the Centenary final anyway. The League insisted that the final go ahead at Villa Park, and that United stick to arrangements already made. A little light relief was brought to the season when Cyril Knowles resigned the managership of Torquay, saying: "There's no going back", only to go back 48 hours later. Nice one, Cyril.

Paul Davis and Vinny Jones were back in their respective teams on the last Saturday of September after bans by their managers. Both were on losing sides, Arsenal going down 2-1 at Sheffield Wednesday and Wimbledon losing 1-0 at home to Coventry. Wimbledon, with one point, were now firmly at the foot of the table. Norwich and Millwall drew 2-2 at Carrow Road to remain first and third in the table, with Liverpool moving up to second by changing places with Southampton, whom they beat 3-1 at The Dell. Aldridge scored, while Rush was on the bench.

In the Second Division, Blackburn won and went top on goal difference, as Watford only drew. Chelsea at last won — ironically at Leeds where they had previously failed to win in 23 attempts over 52 years. Brighton lost at Swindon and remained the only side in the League without a point.

Sheffield United would have been top scorers in the League even if they hadn't scored at all, but in fact they won 4-1 at Brentford and stayed impressively at the head of the Third Division. Port Vale, winners at Bristol City, kept up the chase, and Wolves, who won 5-2 at Swansea (Bull scored twice) stayed third. In the Fourth Division Rotherham won at Carlisle, Hartlepool beat Cambridge and Burnley beat Colchester to stay as the top three.

The Littlewoods Cup second round began on Tuesday 28 September. Sheffield United kept up their good League form by beating First Division rivals Newcastle 3-0. Blackpool beat Sheffield Wednesday 2-0, Burnley drew at Luton 1-1, Northampton and Notts County earned home draws with Charlton and Spurs, Scarborough drew at Portsmouth and Scunthorpe beat Chelsea 4-1. The following night the best performance was Tranmere's 0-0 draw at Middlesbrough. Lincoln held Southampton 1-1 (Jimmy Case was sent off after a clash with Gordon Hobson, transferred

Derby County's number ten, Trevor Hebberd, scores in the 1-1 draw at Nottingham Forest

Match Magazine

from Southampton to Lincoln earlier). Bristol City, in winning 4-2 at Oxford, ended a run of 27 home games without defeat in the "League Cup" for Oxford.

Off the field, Leeds sacked Billy Bremner as manager, the third in a row of the famous side of the early 1970s to lose the manager's job — Allan Clarke and Eddie Gray being his predecessors.

Another midfield player to do some heartsearching was Arsenal's Paul Davis. The FA disciplinary committee banned him for nine games and fined him £3000, the heaviest individual ban for many years, for his TV punch which broke Glenn Cockerill's jaw. The charge was bringing the game into disrepute. It was said that the ban might have been heavier but for Davis' previous good conduct. This "good" conduct amounted to 11 cautions in five years.

At Leicester University a meeting of 300 delegates to the "Football into the 1990s" conference made clear its overwhelming opposition to the government's proposed "blanket membership" solution to football's hooligan problem. Graham Kelly, the FA Chief Executive, estimated that forcing all spectators to hold a membership card of a particular club would mean a 25 per cent loss of revenue to the game.

September ended on a sad note with news of the death at 95 of Dick Pym, who was England's oldest international. He will probably be best remembered for keeping goal for Bolton Wanderers in three Wembley Cup finals in the 1920s, and not conceding a goal in three victories.

OCTOBER

Millwall Top the League With Spurs at the Bottom

The first of October was a Saturday, and it was a great day for Millwall. They beat Queens Park Rangers 3-2 and went to the top of the First Division in their first season in the top grade. A surprising 3-1 home defeat for Norwich by Charlton and an even bigger shock, a 2-1 defeat for Liverpool by Newcastle at Anfield, helped put them there. Liverpool seemed unable to sort out their strikers. Rush came on just before an hour elapsed and played alongside Aldridge, but the Liverpool goal came from defender Gillespie.

There were new leaders in the Second Division, too, Ipswich winning at West Brom and taking over the top spot. They were helped by Watford losing at home to Swindon and Blackburn losing at Manchester City. A win for Brighton gave them their first points and lifted them off the bottom.

The Third Division leaders, Sheffield United, lost at Bolton, but stayed on top as Port Vale and Wolves drew with each other at Molineux. Northampton came back into the picture with a 6-0 defeat of Aldershot, who were rooted at the bottom with two points.

The Fourth Division leaders, Rotherham, also lost (1-0 at home to Exeter) to complete a strange day for the pace-makers, but they, too, stayed top.

As every club had played at least six League

matches, it is a good time to look at the leaders to note the clubs which had got away to the best starts. The top six in each division on the evening of 1 October were as follows:

	P	W	D	L	F	A	Pts
First Division							
Millwall	6	4	2	0	13	7	14
Norwich C.	6	4	1	1	11	8	13
Liverpool	6	3	2	1	10	5	11
Southampton	6	3	2	1	10	6	11
Manchester U.	6	3	2	1	7	3	11
Arsenal	6	3	1	2	17	11	10
Second Division							
Ipswich T.	7	5	2	0	15	6	17
Blackburn Rov.	7	5	1	1	12	4	16
Watford	8	5	1	2	15	8	16
Bradford C.	8	4	3	1	9	5	15
Manchester C.	8	4	2	2	12	11	14
Portsmouth	8	3	3	2	15	10	12
Third Division							
Sheffield U.	7	5	0	2	22	8	15
Port Vale	7	4	2	1	19	7	14
Bolton W.	7	4	2	1	14	6	14
Wolvehampton W.	7	4	2	1	15	9	14
Northampton T.	7	4	1	2	13	7	13
Mansfield T.	7	3	4	0	9	5	13
Fourth Division							
Rotherham U.	7	5	1	1	17	4	16
Hartlepool U.	7	5	0	2	11	9	15
Scarborough	7	4	2	1	19	10	14
Burnley	7	4	2	1	13	5	14
Rochdale	7	4	1	2	13	10	13
Crewe Alex.	7	3	3	1	10	7	12

The only League game on Monday night saw Port Vale beat Huddersfield 2-0 and go to the top of the Third Division. There was a full programme on Tuesday and Wednesday, when European fixtures were continued. In these the Football League's representative, Cardiff, marched forward to the second round of the Cup Winners Cup with a 4-0 defeat of Derry City.

In the Second Division, new leaders Ipswich lost at Crystal Palace, and Watford went to the top with a 3-1 victory over Oldham. Manchester City continued their upward move with a 4-1 defeat of Portsmouth. Nobody could overtake Port Vale in the Third (Sheffield United did not play), but in the Fourth Division Rotherham lost 1-0 at Burnley, allowing Scarborough and Burnley to go above them.

Arsenal and Manchester United were absent from the programme on Saturday 8 October because of their Centenary final on Sunday, and Sheffield Wednesday and Millwall, their opponents, also took an enforced day off. This allowed Norwich to go back to the top of the First Division with a 1-0 win at Derby. Coventry, winning 3-0 at Newcastle, moved into third place as Liverpool lost 1-0 on Luton's plastic pitch, on which they have never been very happy.

Watford maintained their lead in the Second Division with a 2-0 defeat of Sunderland, but Blackburn kept right behind them with a last-minute winner to beat Crystal Palace 5-4 in a thrilling match. Ipswich also returned to winning form with a 1-0 defeat of challengers Manchester City. Port Vale, 2-0 winners at Wigan, and Sheffield United, with a useful 2-0 victory over rivals Wolves, continued to lead the way in the Third Division, while Burnley's 3-0 defeat of Exeter took them to the top of the Fourth again. Scarborough were very upset with their 0-0 draw with Leyton Orient which cost them the lead, and were talking of legal action over the incident in which their player-coach Colin Morris suffered a broken leg. Second thoughts persuaded them against it.

On Sunday Arsenal and Manchester United brought the protracted Centenary celebrations finally to an end with the final of the Mercantile Credit Trophy, which Arsenal won 2-1, their second trophy of the season so far.

Manager shuffles hit the news this week, with Howard Wilkinson, formerly at Hillsborough, leaving Wednesday for the post at Leeds, and Newcastle, who were the subject of a take-over bid by a group of wealthy shareholders called the Magpie Group, sacking Willie McFaul.

The Littlewoods Cup second round, second leg ties were played on 11 and 12 October. Of the clubs who created surprises in the first leg, Sheffield United held on to beat Newcastle 3-2 on aggregate (0-2 on the night), Blackpool lost 3-1 at Sheffield Wednesday but went through on the away goal, Burnley failed to eliminate Luton, losing the home leg 1-0, Northampton and Notts County went out at Charlton and Spurs, but only by the odd goal, Scarborough beat Portsmouth 3-1 (aggregate 5-3), Scunthorpe drew at Stamford Bridge to beat Chelsea 6-3 on aggregate, Tranmere won 1-0 at home to send Middlesbrough crashing, and Lincoln lost 3-1 at Southampton. Bristol City beat Oxford again for a 6-2 aggregate. Oldham overcame Darlington only after extra time, and Leyton Orient won 2-1 at Stoke to level the tie and then won on penalties. Barnsley won 1-0 at Wimbledon in the second leg, but had unfortunately for them lost at home by 2-0. Ian Rush, replacing Aldridge in Liverpool's forward line at Walsall, at last scored his first senior goal after ten games back in harness.

An expensive penalty miss as Paul Stewart of Tottenham hits the bar and allows Manchester United to leave White Hart Lane with a 2-2 draw

Match Magazine

Lineker goes close for England in the 0-0 draw against Sweden

Match Magazine

Off the field, Ron Atkinson decided to accept a lucrative proposition to manage Atletico Madrid and left West Bromwich Albion. His number two, Colin Addison, went with him, and a day or two later Brian Talbot, club captain and PFA Chairman, was appointed caretaker manager. Paul Davis lost his appeal against his disciplinary sentence despite Gordon Taylor, the PFA Chief Executive, describing him as an "unfortunate victim of circumstance" for breaking another player's jaw in front of TV cameras. Taylor also threw new light on today's accepted standards of behaviour when he described Davis' record of 14 cautions in more than 300 games as "virtually a model of good behaviour".

Back on League business on Saturday, the top game was Coventry's 0-0 draw with Millwall, as most First Division games were postponed in deference to England's forthcoming midweek World Cup match with Sweden. Blackburn gave their promotion prospects a lift with a 2-1 defeat of Barnsley, going to the top level with Watford, who only drew at home to bottom club Brighton. Manchester City climbed to fourth, and Chelsea entered the top six with a 4-1 win at Oldham. Port Vale, Sheffield United and Wolves all had 2-1 wins to stay in front in the Third Division, and Burnley, despite crashing 3-0 to Peterborough, kept ahead in the Fourth because Scarborough and Rotherham could only draw. Darlington, without a win in ten games and four points adrift at the foot, looked strong candidates to lose their League status. The performance of the day was Leyton Orient's 8-0 defeat of Colchester, their record victory and Colchester's worst defeat, which coincidentally had been 7-0 against Leyton Orient in 1952. The Colchester manager, Roger Brown, resigned.

There was Football League business to get settled in the third week of October, and it began on Monday with a commission taking two points away from Tottenham Hotspur for failing to play their opening match of the season against Coventry.

Paul Davis (8) scores for Arsenal in the 2-1 Mercantile Credit Trophy win over Manchester United

Match Magazine

Meanwhile Liverpool's Danish midfield star Jan Molby began a three-month jail sentence for driving at speeds of up to 100 mph through 30 mph zones when pursued by police. He admitted having been drinking, driving on the wrong side of the road and through red traffic lights. The Liverpool club announced they would consider the matter of his continuing his career with them.

On Tuesday, the League President, Philip Carter of Everton, together with David Dein of Arsenal, were emphatically voted off the League Management Committee over their involvement in the summer's TV negotiations, when it seemed that they had had talks about a TV deal to benefit their own clubs without notifying the Management Committee. Carter became the first President in the League's 100-year history to be voted out of office.

The big matches on 19 October were the World Cup qualifiers. England entered the fray with a very disappointing 0-0 draw with Sweden at Wembley. Wales, under the new managership of Terry Yorath, also disappointed with a 2-2 draw at Swansea with Finland. Scotland, in a group of five nations, which meant that they could finish second and qualify, could only draw 1-1 at Hampden Park with Yugoslavia. On reflection, the camp seemed moderately happy with a draw against the favourites in the group. Northern Ireland lost 1-0 in Hungary to a goal five minutes from time, a disappointing result which gave them a hard task to qualify. After the game Mal Donaghy was said to have been signed by Manchester United from Luton for £700,000, but decided he wanted to think about it. David Burrows, a 19-year-old West Brom defender, joined Liverpool for £500,000. Both buying clubs were suffering from a long injury list, and of course Liverpool were without Molby for a spell.

Down with the less affluent of the League, a Friday night score-line of Bournemouth 0 Shrewsbury 1 was not world-shattering, but it registered Shrewsbury's first win of the season, leaving Darlington as the only club yet to break its duck.

Saturday's games saw Burrows appear for Liverpool and Lee Chapman for Nottingham Forest, Chapman having just been bought from Niort of France, who could not ultimately pay the fee they had agreed with Sheffield Wednesday earlier in the year.

The FA looked into this last transaction — although in this case everybody had behaved honestly, it was noted that a move abroad and a buy-back was a method of avoiding the Transfer Tribunal. An unscrupulous club could, through this loophole, arrange to obtain a player cheaply.

Burrows had a disappointing debut — a 0-0 draw at home with Coventry. Rush was now starting games for Liverpool with Aldridge joining him late from the bench. Chapman would probably be better pleased with Forest's 2-2 draw at Millwall at the top of the table. Millwall remained the only unbeaten side in the division. In the Second Division Blackburn stayed top with a draw at Oxford, but of the top six only Chelsea won, a 5-0 beating of Plymouth lifting them to fifth. Talbot, the WBA manager, scored his side's goal in a 1-0 win — the team were creeping up the table since Atkinson departed.

In the Third Division Port Vale lost and were overtaken by Sheffield United. Wolves kept on their tail and Swansea were a threatening fourth. Rotherham overtook Burnley in the Fourth Division on goal difference with Scarborough and Rochdale a point behind.

Weekend transfer news was a family affair. Dean Saunders, who was once given a free transfer by Swansea and later cost Oxford £60,000 from Brighton, was sold by Oxford chairman Kevin Maxwell to dad Robert at Derby for £1 million, a record for both clubs. This deal was allegedly fixed without the knowledge of Oxford's manager Mark Lawrenson, who threatened to resign. For this he was dismissed, and his assistant Brian Horton was appointed in his place, despite Horton's expressed sympathy for Lawrenson. Newcastle were a club experiencing gross managerial difficulties — everybody they approached seemed reluctant to join them.

In an Everton attack on the Manchester United goal, Dave Watson (5) heads against the bar. The match ended in a 1-1 draw

Match Magazine

Derby County, who beat Wimbledon 4-1 at the Baseball Ground, are shown in the unusual position of having to defend their goal as the "Dons" go close

Match Magazine

Chairman McKeag flew to Spain to talk to Howard Kendall — and also to the holiday-making Chairman of Oldham regarding Joe Royle. Kendall and Royle, like the others, declined the invitation.

On the field, Monday evening seemed an inauspicious day for the Third Division leaders Port Vale and Sheffield United to shoot it out at Vale Park, but over 13,000 saw United go ahead and then salvage a 3-3 draw with two late goals. Less than 3,500 saw a remarkable game at Tranmere the same evening — the 75th minute goal that beat Lincoln 1-0 came when Tranmere were playing with nine men, two having been sent off.

A big League programme on Tuesday 25 October saw Blackburn, Chelsea and Ipswich all beaten without scoring in the Second Division, with Watford taking full advantage by beating Barnsley 4-0 to go clear, while Portsmouth's 1-0 win at Ipswich lifted them to third. Rotherham did themselves a good turn in the Fourth Division, with a 3-0 win, while their rivals were held to draws. Amid much talk of managers, Terry Venables completed his first year at Tottenham, where a 2-1 home defeat by Southampton meant only seven wins in 31 League games since he took over. Spurs were firmly at the foot of the table.

European football occupied Wednesday night, and Cardiff lost 2-1 to Aarhus of Denmark. In the First Division, Norwich had an excellent 2-1 win at Old Trafford to confirm their status as worthy leaders. Forest beat Liverpool 2-1 (Rush) and Newcastle, under caretaker manager Colin Suggett, lightened the gloom with a 3-0 defeat of neighbours Middlesbrough. In the Second Division West Brom beat Manchester City to maintain their advance.

The vacancies on the Football League Management Committee were filled by John Smith of Liverpool, a last-minute candidate, and Robert Chase of Norwich. Bobby Charlton, who seemed certain to be elected before the nomination of Smith, was again the unlucky loser.

The last Saturday of October saw Norwich draw at home with Southampton, but stay six points clear as Millwall lost 4-2 at Middlesbrough. Norwich midfielder Andy Townsend, who was bought from Southampton, was struck full in the face by a shot, and sent to hospital with a tube in his throat to help his breathing. He later recovered. Arsenal moved into second place with a game in hand, beating Coventry 2-0, while Liverpool's 2-0 win at West Ham moved them into fourth. Forest, Southampton and Middlesbrough came next. Middlesbrough's win was watched by their new signing, Peter Davenport, bought for £700,000 from Manchester United. Meanwhile Derby's new signing, Dean Saunders, scored twice in a 4-1 defeat of Wimbledon — while at his old club, Oxford, a mere 5,000 crowd called on the Maxwells to resign.

In the Second Division Watford won 1-0 at Walsall and went five points clear of Blackburn. The Lancashire side lost at home 2-1 to West Brom, who moved smoothly into third place, with Portsmouth, Chelsea, Manchester City and Barnsley following on.

Sheffield United won to keep on top in the Third Division, but Port Vale lost at Brentford and dropped to third. The team moving up was Wolves, 3-1 winners at Gillingham. Fulham, Reading, Preston and Swansea came next.

Burnley overtook Rotherham, who lost 1-0 at Scarborough, in the Fourth Division, Scarborough remaining third. Crewe moved into fourth, with Rochdale, who drew 2-2 at home to Darlington (still without a win) dropping to fifth, followed by Scunthorpe.

Next day, Sunday 30 October, was the big kick-off — ITV uncovered The Match, the big new soccer coverage. It was, of course, the same old soccer coverage with more cameras, including one in each goal net to give a too-close and unrealistic view of the ball entering the net. Other innovations were grabbing a player off the pitch for an "interview" (nothing of interest was ever said) and a half-time cocktail of all the goals of the day before (the half-time interval was extended to 15 minutes, for this and advertisements). There was also a "Player of the Match". The kick-off was an odd 3.05 pm (the programme started at 3.00 to avoid clashing with BBC's *EastEnders*).

ITV were unlucky in their first choice of game, in that Everton and Manchester United were two powerful clubs unfortunately slipping down the table at the time. In the event, it was not a bad match, improving in the second half when both goals came in the 1-1 draw. However at a cost of around £500,000 per match ITV possibly had too much invested in its success, and the efforts of Brian Moore and Ian St John to pretend either that the match was "tremendous", or was shortly going to become tremendous if everybody kept watching, were a trifle embarrassing.

Nevertheless, football was back on the telly, and all fans were pleased. The month ended with Newcastle's chairman, Gordon McKeag, continuing his desperate round-the-world search for a manager with a call to Glasgow and an invitation to former Celtic manager David Hay to apply. Keith Burkinshaw, who formerly knew great glory days as Spurs manager, took over Gillingham, whose record of having lost their last 11 games was even worse than that of the present-day Spurs.

NOVEMBER

Viv Anderson Gets Involved in Matters of Disrepute

The Littlewoods Cup third round began on 1 November. Ties were no longer on a two-leg basis, which did not help Spurs, who failed to beat Blackburn at home and faced a replay. There were no very big surprises, although Norwich lost 2-0 at Leicester and Scarborough drew at home with Southampton. Villa beat Millwall 3-1 and Wimbledon beat Manchester United 2-1 to get rid of two big guns. Arsenal drew 1-1 at Liverpool, having had the best of the game, so these two had to fight again. West Ham's 5-0 defeat of Derby, and Bristol City's 4-1 elimination of Crystal Palace were the two most emphatic wins. Wimbledon's match with United had a nasty end when United full back Viv Anderson was attacked, allegedly by a Wimbledon player, John Fashanu, in the tunnel after the game. Alex Ferguson, a witness, first reported the matter to police but tried to smooth it over later.

Newcastle announced that the caretaker manager, Colin Suggett, who was reserve team coach under Willie McFaul, would be the new permanent manager. The Magpie Group said the search for a manager had turned Newcastle into a laughing stock. Brian Talbot at the same time was confirmed as the new West Bromwich Albion manager in happier circumstances, as he had led them to four successive wins. However, even this had its sour side, as the club considered sueing Ron Atkinson for walking out on his contract, especially as Atletico showed no inclination to pay the £150,000 compensation Albion wanted. Perhaps Atletico thought the compensation should be theirs in view of Albion's improvement.

Tranmere, who beat Blackpool 1-0 in the Littlewoods Cup, found themselves in trouble through having barred Vicki Oysten, a director of Blackpool (and a woman) from the boardroom. A threat to report the club to the Equal Opportunities Commission, and another by the local Labour council to withdraw a loan, prompted a rapid apology and an explanation that it was a mistake.

On Guy Fawkes day, a Saturday, the biggest fireworks came at Plymouth, where Tommy Tynan, the much-travelled 33-year-old striker, scored all four in a 4-3 win over promotion hopefuls Blackburn. The best victory in that division, however, was Chelsea's 2-1 win at Watford, who continued to lead, but with West Brom and Chelsea edging a little closer.

The First Division leaders made no mistakes, however, Norwich winning 2-0 at Wimbledon to stay seven points clear of Millwall, who also won. Arsenal, with two games in hand, had been selected for the Match on Sunday, when they were visiting Forest. Liverpool stood third, with Rush and Aldridge both starting and both scoring in a 3-0 beating of Middlesbrough. Spurs, at the foot, lost 3-1 at home to Derby.

There were new leaders in the Third Division, with Wolves beating Southend 3-0 while Sheffield United lost 3-2 to Huddersfield.

On Sunday Arsenal, who won The Match 4-1 with a very good display, moved into second place in the First Division and singled themselves out as Norwich's most serious challengers. An English international playing for Rangers was in the news next day when Terry Butcher was fined £500 by the Scottish FA for bringing the game into disrepute. It seemed that after a game at Aberdeen he had kicked in a door and been interviewed by the police.

Nigel Clough, Nottingham Forest's young centre-forward, scored twice in the exciting 3-3 draw at West Ham

Match Magazine

European competition was scheduled for midweek, and Cardiff lost 4-0 at Aarhus, so the Football League's interest ended. However there was a mixture of League, Littlewoods Cup and Simod Cup matches to keep domestic fans relatively happy.

In the League, the most significant move came in the Third Division, where Wolves won 1-0 at Bristol City to confirm their leadership status. None of the first eight teams in the Fourth Division could win.

In the Littlewoods Cup third-round replays, Arsenal and Liverpool drew after extra time at Highbury, but Spurs won 2-1, also after extra time at Blackburn. Everton drew 1-1 at home to Oldham.

The first round of the Simod Cup saw Aston Villa beat neighbours Birmingham 6-0 and Chelsea beat Plymouth 6-2. There were few surprises: Sunderland won 1-0 at Charlton before 1,666 spectators, and Millwall needed a penalty shoot-out to beat Barnsley at the Den (a huge 3,300 saw this).

To stop crowds flocking to matches in such vast numbers the Government's membership scheme was announced in a white paper. The main proposals were that a new Football Membership Authority would run the scheme, each spectator would need a card carrying name, photo, club and number, that giving false information or attempting to gain entry without a card would be a criminal offence and that convicted fans would be banned for up to five years. Few concerned with football greeted the white paper with any enthusiasm. Some pointed to the scorers of Wolves three goals the previous Saturday: Downing, Streete, Bull.

Tommy Tynan, with four goals, was the hero of Plymouth Argyle's 4-3 victory over Blackburn Rovers

Match Magazine

Oxford were given a petition signed by about three-quarters of their average gate calling on the chairman to resign before the match with Birmingham.

There was more serious trouble on the field when Wimbledon's Vinny Jones tackled Spurs' Gary Stevens with the result that the Spurs man went to hospital for an operation on snapped knee ligaments. However Spurs won 3-2 to climb off the bottom of the table. The Littlewoods Cup replay win at Blackburn looked as if it might be a turning point for them. Norwich could only draw at home with Sheffield Wednesday, who equalised with two minutes left, and Arsenal's 1-0 win at Newcastle took them to within four points with a game in hand. Millwall, who had bought from Newcastle a new £300,000 winger, Paul Stephenson, a couple of days earlier, drew 1-1 at Liverpool, Stephenson being the scorer.

In the Second Division, Watford's 3-1 defeat at Manchester City brought them back closer to the chasing pack. Blackburn and Portsmouth won to be nearest, Chelsea drew and West Brom lost at Leeds. Ipswich and Manchester City were also in touch. In the Third Division Wolves, by beating Huddersfield 4-1 (Mutch, Streete, Bull were the scorers in a continuing comment on the Government) continued five points clear of Sheffield United. Scarborough struck the front for the first time in the Fourth Division as Rotherham were held at Cambridge, while Darlington won their first League match of the season, 2-1 at Carlisle.

In midweek, the publication of Viv Anderson's autobiography brought him into more conflict with the FA (the fracas with Fashanu was already awaiting investigation). In his book Anderson claimed that he would not hesitate to commit a "professional foul" on an opponent going through towards goal. He also criticised referees, and the FA promised to look at it all. Later they charged him with bringing the game into disrepute.

The Republic of Ireland played a World Cup match and lost 2-0 in Spain. It was disappointing, but not a bad setback, as Spain were always likely to be one of the two qualifiers from this group. England, meanwhile, accepted lots of Arab cash to play in Riyadh, and drew 1-1 with Saudi Arabia, a result which drew the tabloid's knives out again for sticking into Bobby Robson.

Two of the richer men in football indulged in a spate when Brian Clough ventured to suggest that Peter Shilton could be past his best for the 1990 World Cup. Derby chairman Robert Maxwell reacted fiercely on TV and called upon Derby supporters to give Clough a "thumbs down" at

Old Arsenal man, Lee Chapman, now with Nottingham Forest, is outjumped by Steve Bould in the home game against the "Gunners", who won 4-1

Match Magazine

every chance they had. Clough claimed to have started legal action over these intemperate outbursts. Sadly Jesper Olsen, one of the cleverest footballing imports, left Manchester United for Bordeaux for £400,000. He had never properly flourished in the physical Football League and had not enjoyed the confidence of some of the managers at Old Trafford.

Only the top two divisions were engaged in League football on 19 November, as it was FA Cup day. Arsenal moved nearer to Norwich by beating Middlesbrough 3-0 while the Canaries drew 1-1 at Goodison Park. The gap was two points, and Arsenal had a game in hand. Millwall and Liverpool won to keep up the chase.

Portsmouth went to the top of the Second Division by beating Barnsley 3-0. Watford, Chelsea and West Brom could only draw away, and Blackburn and Manchester City, who won away, remained third and fourth.

The most meritorious of all the non-League performances in the Cup first round came from Altrincham, who beat Lincoln 3-2, and Bognor, who beat Exeter 2-1. Brandon United drew at Doncaster and Fareham drew at Torquay. Non-League clubs who drew at home with their seniors were Enfield, Runcorn, Stafford Rangers and Telford.

The Football League elected Jack Dunnett of Notts County to be its new President. Dunnett had been President before Philip Carter and was clearly the choice of the Second Division clubs rather than the elite.

A mid-week hotch-potch on 22 November included League games, FA Cup replays, Littlewoods Cup replays, Simod Cup matches and Sherpa Van Trophy matches. The players likely to remember the day most were those of Runcorn, who won their Cup replay 3-2 at Wrexham, coming from behind. This set up a local derby with Crewe. Alas Brandon lost at home to Doncaster 2-1, while Telford and Stafford could not win away on League grounds. Transfer news concerned the Everton striker Adrian Heath, who moved to Espanol, Barcelona's second club, for £500,000.

The biggest match in a second mixed evening was the Littlewoods Cup, third round, second replay at Highbury, where Liverpool, in an exciting match, beat Arsenal 2-1. Fareham lost at home to Torquay in the FA Cup, but Enfield drew at Leyton Orient to force a second replay. Off the field, Viv Anderson learned for the second time in two days that he was to be charged with bringing the game into disrepute. He was to be co-defendant, rather than witness, in the case of the bundle in the Wimbledon tunnel. The FA also announced that Graeme Hogg, a former United player now at Portsmouth, was to be fined £2,000 for running down United in a Sunday newspaper.

The results on the last Saturday in November left clubs much as they were. Arsenal lost 2-1 at Derby, but Norwich, Millwall and Liverpool could not take advantage and only drew, the last 1-1 at home to Wimbledon. Fans were beginning to wonder if Liverpool's engine was running out of petrol at last.

Watford, Blackburn, Manchester City and Chelsea all won in the Second Division to overtake Portsmouth, who lost at Blackburn. West Brom, who beat Palace 5-3, kept in touch. Wolves continued to streak ahead in the Third Division, beating Preston 6-0 with Steve Bull scoring four. Sheffield United and Port Vale each won 3-0 to remain the nearest chasers. There were three teams with identical records separated by goal difference at the top of the Fourth Division: Rotherham, Scarborough and Crewe, in that order. None of them won, and the division was very open, with only seven points between the first club and the 15th. A run by anybody could gain promotion. On Friday night, Darlington won 2-1 at Colchester and relegated their opponents to last place and possible League extinction.

The Sunday television Match was Newcastle v Manchester United, billed as the battle of the strikers, Marandinha and Hughes. A poor game finished 0-0, and the fans waited patiently for the turn of Norwich and Millwall.

Monday night soccer saw Enfield win 1-0 at Leyton to go into the second round of the FA Cup with a home tie against Cardiff. At Newcastle, the Magpie Group obtained 10 per cent more shares and claimed to be approaching the 51 per cent needed for a take-over. The manager of another club with a spot of bother, Bobby Gould of Wimbledon, went in trepidation to the FA's offices after the expiry of the clubs 12-match "probationary period", imposed after a record £8,000 disciplinary fine in the summer. To his surprise, he was congratulated on the club's improved behaviour. Of course, the 30 bookings and one sending-off over the same period of the previous season could hardly be anything else but improved upon, but the club's record of "only" nine bookings in their last 12 games was apparently as good as all but seven other League clubs. Perhaps Paul Davis wasn't so bad after all. He had just served his nine-match ban and had played for Arsenal reserves the previous Saturday.

The Littlewoods, Simod, Sherpa Van Trophies progressed on the last day of November, and there was one startling result: West Ham 4 Liverpool 1 in the Littlewoods Cup fourth round. The match was a triumph for Paul Ince, who scored twice. Villa progressed to the next round (6-2 over Ipswich) but Leicester v Forest and QPR v Wimbledon could not produce a goal.

Spurs did well without playing. With the help of a Queen's Counsel they won an appeal against the Football League's docking of two points for their opening day mishap and leapt over Charlton and Luton to 15th place in the table.

A report commissioned by the League and prepared by Jimmy Hill, Ron Greenwood and Bertie Mee, had its main recommendations to improve the League game explained by Hill to 1,200 Barclays Bank managers at the Grosvenor Hotel. Instead of proposing a return to the sensible two points for a win one for a draw used by 95 per cent of all Leagues over the world, the great minds suggested more points for margin of victory, e.g. four for 3-1, five for 3-0 and a maximum six for 5-1 or better. It is to be hoped that the Bank managers greet this scheme with the same enthusiasm they'd show to a manufacturer of lead balloons seeking an overdraft.

DECEMBER

Arsenal and Norwich Begin to Draw Away

Crewe went to the top of the Fourth Division for the first time on Friday evening, 2 December, with a 1-0 win over Halifax. Of more importance to the other end of the League spectrum was Jan Molby's release from prison and assurance by Liverpool that he would have every chance to rehabilitate himself in the team.

With Arsenal and Liverpool reserved for Sunday, December's first Saturday saw Norwich crash 3-1 at Aston Villa and Millwall lose at home 1-0 to West Ham, whose Cup victory over Liverpool seemed to have inspired them. Manchester United won their fourth League game of the season by beating Charlton 3-0, and Everton scored a welcome win over Spurs, Cottee getting the only goal. Paul Bracewell, injured for 2½ years, returned for Everton.

In the Second Division, Chelsea won 3-0 at Stoke and moved to within a point of Watford, who drew at Sunderland. Blackburn lost, and

Manchester City, Portsmouth and West Brom all drew, the last two at Fratton Park.

On Sunday Arsenal and Liverpool drew 1-1 in The Match, a good game. Wolves also played on Sunday as if preparing for when they would be TV material again, but lost 3-1 at Northampton, a reminder to stay in their place for now.

Next day Newcastle appointed Jim Smith, who had been at Queens Park Rangers, as their new manager. Colin Suggett returned to coaching. Smith's first moves were to buy Kevin Brock from his old club for £300,000 and sell back John Robertson to Hearts. Robertson had cost £750,000 the previous April.

It was revealed that Liverpool had an embarrassment of riches at the back as well as a surfeit of strikers. Bruce Grobbelaar, who had recovered from meningitis and played for the reserves, asked for a transfer at not being able to get his place back from Mike Hooper, who had played well in Bruce's absence. Liverpool insisted on keeping Bruce.

The second round of the FA Cup was played on 10 December, with Kettering beating Bristol Rovers 2-1. Maidstone drew at Reading and Yeovil drew at home with Torquay. In the First Division, the big two met. Arsenal went to Norwich and drew 0-0, keeping nicely placed just behind. Millwall lost 2-0 at Tottenham and looked to be fading. Coventry went third by beating Manchester United 1-0. Jim Smith started with a win as Newcastle beat Wimbledon 2-1. They stayed bottom, but were now level on points with Wimbledon and West Ham.

In the Second Division, Chelsea and Portsmouth drew at Stamford Bridge and Watford drew at home to Oxford, allowing Manchester City to go top with a 4-0 defeat of Bradford. Blackburn, who beat Ipswich 1-0, were second and West Brom, who beat Hull 2-0, were fifth. These six had led the division for a little while now.

The Sunday Match was at Anfield, where Everton and Liverpool drew 1-1. Southall played well to keep Everton in the match, but the Blues were robbed when what appeared in replay to be a particularly good winner was disallowed.

The Sherpa Van and Simod tournaments gently meandered on in mid-December, while FA Cup replays saw Maidstone and Yeovil fall to Reading and Torquay. The Littlewoods Cup fourth round produced a shock for Everton, who were beaten 3-1 at Bradford. Queens Park Rangers won 1-0 at Wimbledon in a replay, but the big news from them was the appointment of former England international, Trevor Francis, as player-manager. Peter Shreeves, the caretaker manager for six days, was named as assistant manager, after being

Opposite: Norwich City, who were second in the First Division at the end of 1988, owed a lot to their fine midfielder, Mike Phelan

Match Magazine

Paul Allen (left) and Terry Fenwick (right) shown challenging West Ham's George Parris, during Tottenham's 2-0 win at Upton Park

Match Magazine

in charge of the Cup win earlier in the day.

Friday night football on 16 December saw Chelsea win 4-1 at Birmingham and go to the top of the Second Division — an amazing recovery from their poor start to the season. The lead was short-lived, as Blackburn beat Watford 2-1 on Saturday and went above them again. West Brom beat Stoke 6-0 on Sunday and moved up to third place.

The best Saturday performance was Norwich's 1-0 win at Liverpool, which kept them just in front of Arsenal, who beat Manchester United 2-1. Millwall returned to winning ways with a 1-0 defeat of Sheffield Wednesday, while Derby, on a good run, won 2-0 at Coventry and moved above them into fourth. Newcastle drew 3-3 with Southampton and at last moved off the bottom of the table, jumping Wimbledon and West Ham, while Trevor Francis picked himself for the QPR side which drew 0-0 with Everton. Wimbledon, however, played in the Sunday Match, winning 1-0 at Nottingham Forest and moved back up the table.

Wolves beat Mansfield 6-2 in the Third Division, Bull getting three, and resumed the gallop towards promotion. Port Vale were second but Sheffield United lost at home to Southend.

John Fashanu of Wimbledon, repeated last year's performance, when he scored in the 4-0 win over Luton at Plough Lane

Match Magazine

Spurs, who were not satisfied with the form of Bobby Mimms, their relatively new goalkeeper, signed the Norwegian international Erik Thorstvedt from IFK Gothenburg for £450,000.

The week leading up to Christmas saw FA disciplinary matters settled. A certain amount of seasonal goodwill was around when John Fashanu was fined £2,000 and banned for three matches for his assault on Viv Anderson in the Wimbledon tunnel incident. Most observers, with Paul Davis in mind, expected a heavier penalty. Anderson was fined £750 and banned for one game for his part, which was held to be provocative. The suspension was academic, as he was out with a back injury, which later necessitated a spinal disc removing.

Two days later Mark Dennis was the recipient of the goodwill. The Queens Park Rangers full back was charged with bringing the game into disrepute for the sixth time after spitting at a Fulham player in a reserve match. It was said that in his career Dennis had been sent off ten times, received two more red cards for after-match incidents and been booked 68 times. The previous year he had been suspended for eight games, and his club had said they would not support him in future actions. He must have thanked the Christmas spirit when he was merely fined £1,000, the committee regarding this, together with the automatic three-match suspension for the sending off, as sufficient punishment.

The identity-card scheme still provoked bitter arguments, with the Sports Minister tinkering with the proposals, but still fighting practically a lone battle. A remark that he would oppose English clubs' re-entry into Europe as long as football continued to obstruct his wishes, he admitted could be taken as blackmail. Several MPs called for his resignation, and football authorities and police once again pointed out errors in his statistics.

Northern Ireland suffered a big setback to their World Cup prospects when they lost 4-0 in Spain in their qualifying group. Three points from four matches meant little likelihood of going to the finals in 1990. Scotland lost a friendly in Italy 2-0, where a hotly disputed penalty put the Italians on their way.

Bristol City played a second and third replay of their FA Cup second round tie with Aldershot, before finally winning 1-0.

Some managers went Christmas shopping in the days before the holiday. Jim Smith signed Kenny Sansom, the much-capped England full back, who went to Newcastle after eight years at Arsenal for £300,000. Aston Villa manager Graham Taylor sold striker Gary Thompson to his old club, Watford, for £325,000.

The traditional nine-point holiday rush began on Boxing Day with a full programme, although First Division leaders Norwich did not play till next day, enabling Arsenal to go top for the first time with a 3-2 victory at Charlton. It was only a 24-hour lead, as Norwich beat the bottom club West Ham 2-1 to go back to the top, although Arsenal had a game in hand. Millwall lost and Liverpool won at Derby to go third. The first two had by now opened a gap of six points, however. At the other end, Newcastle won 2-1 at Sheffield Wednesday, and West Ham were beginning to get detached, three points adrift.

Chelsea, who beat Ipswich 3-0, went to the top of the Second Division on goal difference from West Brom, who won 3-1 at Oldham. Watford beat Portsmouth to stay only two points behind, but the overnight leaders Blackburn lost at Leeds, and Manchester City lost at Stoke. Oxford's Richard Hill scored four as his team won 5-1 at Walsall, who became the new bottom club as Birmingham drew at Shrewsbury.

Wolves were held 0-0 at Bristol Rovers, so Port Vale and Sheffield United, who both won away, closed the gap. These three were four points clear of Bury and Swansea.

In the Fourth Division there was a battle of the leaders, and Crewe won it, 2-1 at Rotherham. Wrexham slipped into second place with a 3-1 win at Burnley. Burnley and Rochdale, early contenders for leadership, had now slid halfway down the table. Scarborough and Scunthorpe, with draws, kept in touch. Darlington and Colchester, both home losers, were seven points adrift at the foot, and looked to face a private battle to avoid losing League status at the end of the season.

On the last day of 1988, Arsenal went top of the table again by winning 3-0 at Aston Villa. This time Norwich were held at home 0-0 by Middlesbrough, so Arsenal led on goal difference. Liverpool's match was the Sunday televised one, and they lost 3-1 at Manchester United, so the top two led by seven points from Millwall, who clung on with a 1-0 win at Derby. Spurs, beating Newcastle 2-0, had left the bottom of the table behind, and were now tenth.

Chelsea and West Brom drew 1-1 at Stamford Bridge in the top-of-the-table Second Division struggle and stayed in the first two places, Chelsea having slightly the better goal difference. Chelsea's last minute equaliser came from a penalty after Talbot handled. Watford won to join them at the top, but Blackburn and Portsmouth each lost 4-0 and Portsmouth were beginning to lose touch.

In the Third Division, Port Vale had spurned the chance of overnight leadership by losing 1-0 to lowly Gillingham on Friday evening. On Saturday, Sheffield United lost 2-0 at Preston, so Wolves 2-2 draw at Brentford increased their lead to four points.

Wrexham, 1-0 winners at Leyton Orient, went to the top of the Fourth Division for the first time as Crewe lost 2-1 at Scarborough, who regained third place. Rotherham also won, so four teams had opened a little gap.

As football moved into 1989 the top and bottom in each division on 1 January was as follows:

	P	W	D	L	F	A	Pts
First Division							
Arsenal	18	11	4	3	40	20	37
Norwich C.	19	10	7	2	28	19	37
Millwall	18	8	6	4	29	21	30
Everton	18	8	6	4	25	17	30
Liverpool	19	7	7	5	23	16	28
Manchester U.	19	6	9	4	25	17	27
Bottom							
Luton T.	19	4	8	7	17	22	20
Charlton Ath.	19	3	8	8	19	31	17
Newcastle U.	19	4	5	10	16	34	17
West Ham U.	19	3	5	11	15	33	14
Second Division							
Chelsea	23	11	8	4	44	24	41
West Bromwich A.	23	11	8	4	39	21	41
Watford	23	12	5	6	35	22	41
Manchester C.	23	11	7	5	33	23	40
Blackburn Rov.	23	12	3	8	36	32	39
Barnsley	23	10	6	7	32	29	36
Bottom							
Oldham Ath.	23	5	8	10	36	40	23
Shrewsbury T.	23	4	10	9	20	31	22
Birmingham C.	23	3	6	14	16	46	15
Walsall	23	2	8	13	19	34	14
Third Division							
Wolverhampton W.	21	13	5	3	49	25	44
Port Vale	20	12	4	4	44	20	40
Sheffield U.	20	12	2	6	46	25	38
Chester C.	21	10	6	5	35	32	36
Swansea C.	21	9	8	4	30	25	35
Bristol Rov.	21	9	7	5	38	28	34
Bottom							
Wigan Ath.	22	4	7	11	25	32	19
Gillingham	21	6	1	14	19	33	19
Aldershot	20	3	6	11	17	39	15
Chesterfield	20	3	3	14	14	50	12
Fourth Division							
Wrexham	21	10	8	3	39	27	38
Rotherham U.	21	10	7	4	35	17	37
Scarborough	21	10	7	4	35	24	37
Crewe Alex.	21	10	7	4	29	21	37
Torquay U.	21	10	4	7	27	24	34
Exeter C.	21	10	3	8	33	30	33
Bottom							
York C.	21	6	5	10	28	36	23
Carlisle U.	21	5	7	9	24	30	22
Darlington	21	2	9	10	21	40	15
Colchester U.	21	3	5	13	23	44	14

JANUARY

Sutton's Ups and Downs, Clough's Lefts and Rights

A full programme on Monday 2 January completed the Christmas struggle for points. In the First Division Arsenal won 2-0 against local rivals Spurs in a match played in the evening for the TV cameras, while Norwich had earlier achieved only a draw with Queens Park Rangers. So the Gunners' lead stretched to two points and they had a game in hand. Paul Davis returned as substitute for Arsenal. Millwall won to stay third, and Coventry beat Sheffield Wednesday 4-0 to go fourth. Early season challengers Southampton completed a poor holiday with a 6-1 defeat at Luton.

In the Second Division both Chelsea and West Brom won, but whereas Chelsea's win was 3-2 at Oxford, West Brom won 4-0 with four second-half goals against Shrewsbury. This was just enough to put West Brom top on goal difference. It was a remarkable turn-round in form since earlier in the season, equalling that of Chelsea. This was a great triumph for Brian Talbot. When Ron Atkinson left, the side was 18th in the table, with only two wins in ten matches. Of the 14

Tottenham's new goalkeeper, Erik Thorstvedt, made his debut against Nottingham Forest and, although on the losing side, remained in the "Spurs" team for the rest of the season

Match Magazine

League games under Talbot, ten had been won and only one lost to take them to the top. Blackburn recovered to win 4-3 after being 2-3 down at half-time to Stoke. Watford lost to drop to fourth.

The Third Division shock was Sheffield United's 3-1 home defeat by bottom club Chesterfield. They continued to lose ground to winners Wolves and Port Vale, and found themselves back with the chasing pack. The Bristol clubs attracted 23,000 to Ashton Gate to see Rovers win 1-0. The Fourth Division leading clubs also had an unimpressive day, although Crewe managed to beat lowly Carlisle 1-0 to go back on top. Wrexham, overnight leaders, needed a late penalty to draw 3-3 at home to Darlington, struggling for their League life. None of the others in the top six won, allowing Tranmere to creep into fifth.

Liverpool ended their Christmas programme a day late, with a 1-0 home win over Aston Villa. Molby made his first full appearance since his release. Gary Megson joined Manchester City from Sheffield Wednesday, where it was alleged players were queueing up to leave.

The big story of the FA Cup third round was the victory of Sutton United, who beat Coventry, the Cup winners of 1987, 2-1. Coventry, fifth in the Championship, were the highest side ever knocked out of the Cup by a non-League side. Of the other non-Leaguers, Kettering drew 1-1 with Halifax and Welling lost 1-0 to Blackburn.

The other surprises of the round were provided by Bradford, who beat Spurs 1-0, and Grimsby, who won 2-1 at Middlesbrough. On Sunday, Norwich won 3-1 at Port Vale, after being down at half-time, and West Ham drew with Arsenal.

Rotherham, already out of the Cup, won 3-0 at Peterborough to go to the top of the Fourth Division.

In a mixed bag of midweek games, pride of place went to Kettering, who won 3-2 at Halifax, and to West Ham, who won 1-0 at Highbury, both clubs going through to the fourth round of the FA Cup. Other Cup news concerned the Office of Fair Trading who were urged by Liverpool City Council to pursue their investigation into the FA's distribution of Cup Final tickets. It appeared that the OFT were still awaiting a reply from the FA to letters.

Dave Beasant became Chelsea's most expensive buy when they paid £725,000 to

David Platt, barely in the picture, scores Aston Villa's first goal in the 3-2 third round FA Cup win over Crewe

Match Magazine

Sutton United celebrate their first goal, through Rains, against Coventry City in the third round of the FA Cup. The Non-Leaguers won 2-1 and progressed to the next round

Match Magazine

Newcastle for the keeper who had left Wimbledon for £850,000 only months before. He had cost Wimbledon £1,000 from Edgware nine years earlier. Jock Wallace, twice a previous manager of Rangers and once of Seville, took over as manager of Colchester United, 92nd in the Football League. Colchester lost a 2-0 lead to go down 3-2 at home to Tranmere in Wallace's first match, a Friday night game.

On Saturday, Arsenal won 3-1 at Everton and Norwich crashed 2-1 at home to Coventry, so Arsenal led by five points with a game in hand. Coventry went third as Millwall lost and Liverpool could only draw, so things looked bright for the Gunners. West Ham, for the second time this season, were inspired by a good Cup win, and won 2-1 at Derby. They moved above Newcastle, who became the bottom club.

In the Second Division, West Brom lost 2-0 at Watford, so Chelsea went three points clear from these two clubs and Manchester City. Blackburn were a point behind, and then there was a six-point gap. Wolves and Port Vale won in the Third Division, but Swansea overtook Sheffield United, who could only draw, and had lost their impressive early season form. In the Fourth Division, Rotherham won to go three points clear of Crewe, who drew. At the foot Darlington won a point to open a two-point gap over Colchester.

Big names to get the boot in midweek were Ron Atkinson, after less than 100 days as manager at Atletico Madrid — his assistant, Colin Addison, took over — and Alan Ball, chief coach at Portsmouth, after already having been demoted from five years in the managerial seat earlier in the season.

A newcomer to English football made his debut for Ipswich reserves — Sergei Baltacha, 46 times

Dave Beasant became Chelsea's record signing when purchased from Newcastle for £725,000

Match Magazine

a Soviet international, whom Ipswich had bought for £200,000.

Amid a plethora of Simod and Sherpa Van matches in midweek, the most notable matches were Watford's 1-0 FA Cup victory over Newcastle in a third round, third replay, and the Littlewoods Cup quarter-finals. Bristol City, Nottingham Forest and West Ham proceeded to the semi-finals while Southampton drew at Luton. The Forest victory over Queens Park Rangers was notable for the behaviour of manager Brian Clough, who, when fans invaded the pitch, acted as a one-man clearing squad, clipping the ears of four fans and forcibly escorting two more from the pitch. Unfortunately for him, ITV cameras were present and his bout of fisticuffs was shown in the national news. Fortunately for him, on the other hand, nobody retaliated, or there could have been much more serious implications. Ossie Ardiles broke a bone in his leg in this match.

Millwall and Norwich provided the entertainment for ITV's The Match at the weekend, and excellent entertainment it was as Norwich won 3-2 with a late goal. This cut Arsenal's lead slightly at the top of the table as they had dropped two home points to Sheffield Wednesday on Saturday. Coventry, Liverpool, Nottingham Forest and Manchester United all won just behind them, and chased the leaders in this order.

Chelsea and Blackburn drew 1-1 at Blackburn in a top-of-the-Second Division clash, and Watford and Manchester City moved to within a point of Chelsea. Neighbours Birmingham and Walsall were losing touch at the bottom. Wolves could beat an improving Chesterfield only by 1-0 in the Third Division, but it took them ten points clear as Port Vale lost at home to Bury, who joined the fringe of the chasing clubs. Rotherham lost and were joined at the top of the Fourth Division by Crewe, with Wrexham and Scarborough heading the chasing pack.

The first Soviet to play in the Football League, Sergei Baltacha, opened the scoring for Ipswich against Stoke, and led his side to a 5-1 win.

On Monday night Manchester United beat Queens Park Rangers 3-0 in a second replay to go into the fourth round of the FA Cup. Luton Town did the trick on Wednesday, when they won their Littlewoods Cup quarter-final replay 2-1 at Southampton, when all the goals came in extra time.

On Saturday it was announced that Brian Clough had been charged by the FA with bringing the game into disrepute over his televised scrapping. Nottinghamshire police let it be known that they would not be bringing charges because of insufficient evidence (not enough millions of televiewers saw it).

Sutton United were in the Sunday paper headlines again after the FA Cup fourth round, but not as they would have wished. They were beaten 8-0 at Norwich. Kettering also went out, but only by 2-1 at Charlton. Altogether the games were free of surprises, although Brentford's 3-1 defeat of Manchester City was unexpected. Liverpool won 2-0 at Millwall's Den in Sunday's Match.

League action was confined to the lower divisions, where the most significant result was a 1-1 draw between Darlington and Fourth Division leaders Crewe. Darlington edged four points clear of Colchester at the bottom.

A surprising managerial casualty at the end of January was Bradford City's Terry Dolan, whose club had knocked Spurs out of the FA Cup three weeks earlier but had just been eliminated 2-1 at home by Hull. Bradford sought Terry Yorath as replacement.

Meanwhile Aston Villa snapped up the Bradford striker Ian Ormondroyd for £650,000. FA Cup replays were settled in midweek, but the last stories of January were sad ones. Proud Newcastle were revealed to be £3 million in debt, and Gerry Armstrong, a Northern Ireland World Cup hero in 1982, was charged with grievous bodily harm after allegedly butting a spectator while playing for Brighton reserves in a Sussex Cup match.

FEBRUARY

Forest Win Their Way to Wembley — Twice

February began with a mixture of midweek Cup games, West Ham and Grimsby fighting their way through to the fifth round of the FA Cup in replays. Managers and would-be managers made news. Trevor Francis of Queens Park Rangers spent £500,000 for Liverpool's Nigel Spackman and £425,000 for Aston Villa's under-21 international Andy Gray. Graham Taylor of

Villa, who were out of the Cups and looked to be on the slide, bought Nigel Callaghan for £550,000 from Derby, to add to his recent purchase of Ormondroyd. Terry Yorath walked out on Swansea for the Bradford City managership, but the Swansea chairman threatened to hold him to the remaining months of his contract, and also bar him from his part-time managership of Wales. Yorath had been commuting from Leeds for all his 2½-year spell in the hot seat at Swansea, and clearly wanted to get back to Yorkshire.

There was a minute concession from the Government on the identity-card controversy which had simmered all winter. Doubts were expressed about the new electronic turnstiles, and the Government hinted that if they were found not to work properly the date of implementing the scheme could be postponed until after the proposed spring of 1990.

Before the Saturday fixtures of 4 February, Swansea gained an injunction lasting a week against Terry Yorath taking over at Bradford, although the Yorkshire club had already announced his appointment.

On the pitch Arsenal and Norwich won to maintain their *status quo*, but the week's big spenders had mixed fortunes — Villa beat Sheffield Wednesday 2-0 but QPR lost at home 2-1 to Millwall. Vinny Jones spoiled Wimbledon's improving record of discipline by being sent off for butting Kevin Ratcliffe at Goodison Park — his second sending-off there in two seasons, and the 32nd Wimbledon sending-off in eight years. In the Second Division, Chelsea had a remarkable 7-0 away win over bottom club Walsall, Gordon Durie getting five. With Watford and West Bromwich Albion losing, Chelsea and Manchester City opened a little gap of three points over the chasing group of these two and Blackburn.

While Port Vale and Wolves drew at Vale Park in the Third Division, Sheffield United returned to form with a 4-0 victory over Bolton, but Wolves remained 11 points clear and looked good for a second promotion season in succession.

In the Fourth Division, Crewe had another narrow victory over a struggling side when they beat Hereford 2-1. This was enough to put them three points clear as their rivals continued to falter. The bottom club Colchester got a point at Scarborough.

Trevor Francis added to his squad at Queens Park Rangers in midweek by signing Peter Reid from Everton — but no money changed hands. The Department of Employment made a curious decision regarding a Yugoslavian player signed by Southampton — they refused him a work permit on the grounds that his skills would not enhance the English game. Southampton's manager, Chris Nicholl, had provisionally signed him for £250,000, so somebody's judgement was at fault somewhere.

There were World Cup games on 9 February and Scotland had a remarkable 3-2 win in Cyprus,

John Barnes, not in picture, scores for England in the 2-1 win over Greece

Match Magazine

after being 2-1 behind. The winning goal came after six minutes of injury time had been played. The referee was hit by a missile and later knocked out by a spectator as he left the field. Northern Ireland lost 2-0 to Spain in Belfast, which virtually ended their qualification chances. England and Wales meanwhile played friendlies, England winning 2-1 in Greece and Wales recovering to draw 3-3 in Israel.

A shock result at home was in the Welsh Cup, where Cardiff, earlier in the season the Football League's standard bearers in Europe, lost 3-1 at non-League Kidderminster Harriers.

An FA disciplinary commission examined the case of Brian Clough and the pitch invaders, and fined him £5,000 and banned him from the bench for the rest of the season. His good record and his contrition earned the comparatively lenient sentence. Meanwhile Paul Gascoigne and Terry Venables of Spurs appeared likely to have to face similar commissions over intemperate newspaper comments which appeared under their names.

In Friday night Fourth Division matches Crewe won 1-0 at Stockport to improve their promotion prospects, and another draw for Colchester, 2-2 with Burnley, kept alive their hopes of continued League existence — they were now two points behind Darlington.

On the same day, Terry Yorath won part two of his legal tussle with Swansea, when the injunction against him taking over at Bradford was lifted. He was in charge as Bradford drew at home 1-1 with Plymouth.

There was spice to the match at the City Ground, where Brian Clough was on the bench for the last time before his suspension, as the opponents were Queens Park Rangers — a repeat of the match which caused the trouble. This time TV cameras were banned. Rangers new manager Trevor Francis, was a fan of Clough, who had, ten years earlier to the week, made him Britain's first £1-million footballer. The clubs, both managed by "strikers", drew 0-0.

Bournemouth's Gerry Peyton fails to stop Mark Hughes from firing Manchester United into the sixth round of the FA Cup

Match Magazine

In other matches, Arsenal won 2-1 at Millwall to maintain their healthy gap over Norwich in the First Division. Chelsea beat Swindon 3-2 in the Second, in a match of three own goals (Chelsea 2 Swindon 1). Manchester City beat Ipswich 4-0, and these two now had six and five-point leads over the chasers, all of whom drew.

Wolves' Third Division lead stretched to 13 points with a 5-2 defeat of Fulham, Steve Bull scoring a hat-trick. Wolves were the only team in the top six to win. Scunthorpe moved into second place in the Fourth Division, while Darlington, second from bottom, sacked manager Dave Booth. Brian Little was appointed in his place.

The Sunday televised Match was a Littlewoods Cup semi-final first leg, and Luton Town appeared to make the second leg unnecessary by taking a 3-0 lead at West Ham.

Two strife-torn clubs were again in the news: Newcastle United, where a purchase of shares might or might not have given the Magpie Group control — when the dust settled it seemed that they hadn't quite got control but they were a lot nearer — and Sheffield Wednesday, where Imre Varadi asked for a transfer allegedly on the urging of his wife, and was promptly fined and suspended by the manager, Peter Eustace.

Mid-February saw the retirement from the Football Association of secretary Ted Croker after 16 years — he was only the fifth FA secretary in more than 100 years.

Midweek soccer saw the second Littlewoods Cup semi-final, first leg, and Bristol City, led by player-manager Joe Jordan, exceeded all expectations by holding Nottingham Forest 1-1 in Nottingham — indeed only a late own-goal saved Forest from defeat. Simod Cup and Sherpa Van Trophy quarter-final ties also took place, and in a friendly Arsenal beat France 2-0, as France prepared for a World Cup fixture with Scotland.

Sheffield Wednesday sacked Peter Eustace on St Valentine's Day and immediately welcomed a new love in Ron Atkinson, late of Manchester United, West Brom and Atletico Madrid.

Gerry Armstrong, who resigned from Brighton after the head-butting incident mentioned earlier, was ordered to pay £200 compensation and considered whether or not to stay in football. One who had no option was Port Vale's Phil Sproson, forced to retire through injury after 495 matches for the club, which began soon after his uncle, Roy Sproson, retired after 832 matches. The two Sprosons had served Vale almost continuously for 39 years.

The FA Cup fifth round was the main business on 18 February. The only surprise victory was Brentford's at Blackburn, by two late goals, but Bournemouth put up an excellent performance in holding Manchester United to a 1-1 draw, and actually missed a "winner" in the last minute by inches. Otherwise it was what-might-have-been for Hull, who led Liverpool 2-1 at half-time only to lose 3-2, and Grimsby, who were one up at

Wimbledon at half-time, only for Wimbledon to make it safe with an injury-time goal when Grimsby were pressing hard to get back on terms.

As Norwich were engaged on Cup duty (they won), Arsenal played their game in hand in the League, and drew 0-0 at Queens Park Rangers, so held a four-point lead with 24 games played. Manchester United were eight points further back, and Liverpool, with a game in hand, were 15 points behind Arsenal.

In the Second Division Chelsea kept a one-point lead over Manchester City as both won away, and there was now an eight-point gap to the next club. Wolves did not play, and Port Vale cut their Third Division lead to seven points. Crewe also did not play in the Fourth Division but their cause was helped by shock results from the bottom two clubs — Colchester won 3-2 at second-placed Scunthorpe, and Darlington, with their new manager, won 2-1 at third-placed Rotherham. There remained a big gap between these two and Peterborough, but the struggle to avoid League banishment looked like being an exciting one.

Forest won the Sunday Match 3-0 at Watford, and joined Everton, Brentford, West Ham, Liverpool, Norwich and Wimbledon in the sixth round of the Cup. Manchester United joined them in midweek with a 1-0 defeat of Bournemouth in their replay.

As the Identity Card scheme was debated in the House of Lords, it was revealed that about 15 Liverpool fans returning from Hull on the previous Saturday had fought with about 30 Tranmere fans returning from York, resulting in hospital treatment for three and much damage to a train. The Lords decided that the Government scheme should be phased-in gradually, and while the Government itself seemed determined not to heed their Lordships, a growing band of Tory MPs were beginning to question whether or not the whole idea might explode in the Government's face.

On Tuesday night, Arsenal lost 1-0 at Coventry, and Norwich lost 2-1 at Tottenham to renew the hopes of some of the other clubs, like Millwall, who won to move up to fifth, 12 points behind Arsenal. The following night Nottingham Forest beat Crystal Palace 3-1 in a Simod Cup semi-final to creep even nearer the achievement of appearing in three Wembley finals in one season.

The Newcastle annual general meeting passed peacefully enough for the board, as it transpired the Magpie Group lacked a majority of shares, but the Group's leader, John Hall, promised to continue the fight. The Football League were also having trouble finding a leader. After turning down all five candidates on a short list for chief executive, they decided to use the services of a head-hunting firm.

Paul Gascoigne was found guilty of bringing the game into disrepute by the FA for comments about the Newcastle board, but as he was partly replying to published comments by a former Newcastle chairman he received only a warning, and Terry Venables escaped censure over his newspaper comments.

Ron Atkinson made his first signing for Sheffield Wednesday when he purchased Carlton Palmer from West Bromwich Albion for £400,000 plus Colin West, which valued Palmer at around £750,000 — Palmer was a player at the Hawthorns when Atkinson was manager, while West had been a clubmate at Watford of Albion manager Brian Talbot.

Liverpool's winning goal and John Aldridge's second in the fifth round of the FA Cup against Hull City at Boothferry Park

Match Magazine

The last Saturday in February saw Arsenal and Norwich return to winning ways by beating Luton and Manchester United respectively, while Millwall beat Coventry to go third. Chelsea dropped two Second Division points following a home draw with Oldham, allowing Manchester City to lead by one point. Blackburn won to close the gap behind Chelsea to four points; Watford were a further six more points adrift. There was little change in the lower divisions as six games were abandoned through heavy rain, though on Friday night Colchester had drawn with Leyton Orient to climb to one point behind Darlington at the foot of the Fourth Division.

On Sunday, Forest won the second leg of their Littlewoods Cup semi-final 1-0 at Bristol City, the goal coming in extra time after a brave display by City. Colin Moynihan, the Minister of Sport, criticised an FA decision to seek the re-admission of English clubs to European competition, which the FA chief executive, Graham Kelly, interpreted as an attempt to keep up the pressure for his Identity Card scheme after its House of Lords rebuff.

On the last day of February, Everton beat QPR 1-0 to go into the Simod Cup final at Wembley, where Nottingham Forest awaited them. Next day Luton, the holders, beat West Ham 2-0 in the second leg of the Littlewoods Cup semi-final and also earned themselves a Wembley final with Forest. Arsenal were very fortunate to draw 0-0 at home with Millwall, thus missing a chance to open a seven-point gap at the top of the First Division. Liverpool won next day as if to remind Arsenal and Norwich that they couldn't slip up too often.

Chelsea won and Manchester City drew in Second Division games, so Chelsea again took the lead. Over 33,000 saw mid-table Leeds and Bradford draw 3-3 in a local derby. Colchester's 1-1 draw with Rotherham took them level with Darlington on points in their survival struggle.

Lee Chapman (left) of Nottingham Forest is challenged by Rob Hindmarch of Derby during the local derby at the Baseball Ground. Chapman and Hodge scored one apiece in Forest's 2-0 win

Match Magazine

MARCH

Liverpool Begin Their Move to Challenge Arsenal

The Identity Card and re-entry to Europe themes made news again at the beginning of March, with Graham Kelly, the FA chief executive, saying he would pursue the application for re-admission to Europe at the UEFA meeting in Madeira on 11 April, and the Minister of Sport, Colin Moynihan, saying it was inconceivable that clubs be re-admitted, as the FA and League had not come up with a single anti-hooligan measure in nine months. Moynihan continued to insist that his ID scheme be in place before the Government gave approval for English clubs to return to European competition, and UEFA president, Jacques George, went on record as saying that without that approval the clubs would remain outcasts. And so the ill-feeling continued.

Newport County were in the news, too, as the club was finally wound up with debts of £126,000. They had entered the League in 1921, were not re-elected in 1931, but returned in 1932. Their highest League position was 22nd in the Second Division in 1947 (they won the Third Division South in the last season before the Second World War). At the time of their dissolution they were two points adrift at the foot of the GM Vauxhall Conference. But within hours of their demise talks were under way to get a new company floated.

Wimbledon were fined £10,000 for making unauthorised loans to players after a League investigation into their books. Viv Anderson was reprimanded by an FA disciplinary commission for bringing the game into disrepute after admitting in his autobiography that he would willingly commit "professional" fouls. A more fundamental conflict seemed to be brewing when Gordon Taylor, the PFA secretary, said he intended to disrupt the FA's automatic suspension system unless the case of West Ham's Mark Ward was reviewed. Sent off for striking a Charlton player in an FA Cup tie, and therefore automatically suspended, Ward appeared to be a victim of the FA's inflexibility, as the TV playback seemed to show that Ward was innocent.

The first Saturday in March saw only one First Division game, as players were resting before England's World Cup match in Albania in midweek. In the match played at Hillsborough, Sheffield Wednesday beat Charlton 3-1 in a relegation clash, but the most significant news from Sheffield was that captain Mel Sterland had departed to Rangers for £800,000.

Chelsea didn't play, but retained Second Division leadership as Manchester City lost 1-0 at Watford. Blackburn also lost and Bournemouth appeared among the chasing group with a 3-2 win at Crystal Palace. There were no alarms for the leaders in the lower divisions on a quiet week-end.

The Wednesday World Cup programme went well for British teams. England won the tricky match in Tirana 2-0, with Barnes and Robson scoring the goals against Albania, and Scotland beat France by the same score, Johnston getting

both goals. The Republic of Ireland's 0-0 draw in Hungary was a satisfactory result, as they now faced four home matches and expected to climb the table.

On the domestic scene Chelsea received government approval to redevelop Stamford Bridge — a small victory in their efforts to keep football there in face of the owners' desire to demolish the stadium for housing. The same owners had similar plans for Craven Cottage, and the clubs were fighting hard to keep football in West London. Another West London Club, Queens Park Rangers, paid Southampton £800,000 for striker Colin Clarke in an effort to keep clear of the relegation zone.

Saturday saw the Championship suddenly looking open again, as Arsenal lost 3-1 at Highbury to Nottingham Forest. With only one win in five League games Arsenal were now only two points clear of Norwich, whose 1-0 defeat of Wimbledon kept them in the chase. Further back, Forest and Liverpool, who won 4-0 at Middlesbrough, looked to be stirring themselves for a late challenge. In the Second Division Manchester City went to the top as Chelsea only drew with Watford, and these two clubs were looking strong favourites for the automatic promotion places. Behind them at least another nine clubs were seeking some consistency to get a play-off place. City's Paul Lake swallowed his tongue after a collision in the match with Leicester, and play was held up for seven minutes while the club's physio and doctor gave treatment.

The case of Martin Allen of QPR made the women's pages of the newspapers after he was fined two weeks' wages and dropped by manager Trevor Francis. His crime was that he had left the team's hotel in Newcastle on the morning of the match to fly south to be present at the birth of his first child.

Arsenal's Saturday defeat looked more ominous on Tuesday night when Liverpool beat Luton 5-0 to make their intentions clear. Manchester City won 4-2 at Sunderland to move further ahead at the top of the Second Division. In a midweek fixture list curtailed by many flooded grounds, Wolves beat Gillingham 6-1 and galloped on towards promotion.

Newport County were finally wound up in the High Court, having failed to meet their debts, and their ground was padlocked. A Granada TV programme, "Out of Order", showed what happened to a referee in a First Division match. Mr David Elleray had been wired for sound before an Arsenal victory at The Den, and the PFA were upset at the result — a programme which showed several Arsenal players swearing at the referee or haranguing him as a cheat.

It was FA Cup quarter-final day on 14 March, and Liverpool and Forest maintained their "double" prospects with a 4-0 home win over Brentford, and a 1-0 away win over Manchester United respectively. West Ham and Norwich drew, and on Sunday's televised game Everton beat the holders, Wimbledon, 1-0.

In the Second Division, an impressive 3-2 win by Chelsea at Maine Road took them back above City at the top of the table. Wins by West Brom, Blackburn and Ipswich kept them the nearest of the play-off contenders. Wolves, Port Vale and

The Arsenal wall line up to defend a free-kick during their 3-1 defeat by Nottingham Forest at Highbury

Match Magazine

Alan Smith scores Arsenal's solitary goal in the game at home to Nottingham Forest

Match Magazine

Steve Hodge clears off the line from Manchester United's Brian McClair at Old Trafford. Nottingham Forest won this FA Cup quarter-final by the only goal of the game

Match Magazine

Sheffield United were well clear in the Third Division, with Wolves ten points ahead on their own, while Crewe, Rotherham and Scunthorpe were heading the Fourth.

Arsenal dropped further home points in midweek, drawing at home 2-2 with Charlton, while Liverpool won 3-1 at Coventry to close to eight points behind with two games in hand. Forest's run of 18 matches without defeat came to an end as they lost at home 2-1 to Spurs, so they probably resigned themselves to the prospect of winning three Cups. They were drawn to meet Liverpool in the FA Cup semi-final, and by beating West Ham 3-1 in a replay, Norwich City were matched with Everton in the other semi. Chelsea won again, at Sunderland, and looked to have the Second Division championship in their grasp.

In desperate transfer deals Frank McAvennie returned to West Ham, who because of Arsenal's interest had to pay Celtic £1.25 million, about half a million more than they had sold him for 18 months earlier, and Gordon Strachan left Manchester United for Leeds for £300,000. As the annual transfer deadline arrived (after which clubs may not use new players in important League games) there was a rush of spending, with Leeds, Portsmouth and West Brom well to the fore. The highest price paid was £500,000 by Leeds to Spurs for Chris Fairclough. A nostalgic touch was provided by Asa Hartford, who had made the headlines in 1971 when his transfer to Leeds, the most powerful team of the day, was cancelled on the discovery that he had a hole in his heart. Now, sacked as player-manager of Stockport County 18 years and several international caps later, he was snapped up on a free transfer by Oldham Athletic.

The Easter programme got under way on Saturday 25 March, and Norwich immediately signalled that they were not ready to be Champions by losing at home 2-0 to relegation contenders Newcastle United. Arsenal won 3-1 at Southampton, and Liverpool won the Sunday Match 2-1 at Tottenham, and these two seemed to be preparing for a private race to the line. Easter Monday's matches were notable for Wolves losing 1-0 to Bristol Rovers, and so sacrificing the last unbeaten home record of the season, and the affair of five penalties at Crystal Palace — four for Palace and one for Brighton. Palace scored only one of their four, but it proved the winner in a 2-1 win, and they moved closer to the play-off zone.

Liverpool ended their Easter programme on Wednesday and beat Derby 1-0, to be five points behind Arsenal. The match between the two scheduled for 23 April looked as if it might be the Championship decider, and Liverpool insisted they would play on this day for the TV cameras, despite it being only three days before England's World Cup return with Albania. A petition from 26,000 Merseyside fans opposed to the government's ID scheme was handed to Liverpool MP Eric Heffer during the Derby match. The first of these two items of news became redundant after tragic events in April, while the second took on deeper significance.

The month ended with a surprise result or two. Sheffield United lost 2-1 at Southend; Fourth Division leaders Crewe lost 2-1 at Torquay and bottom club Colchester improved their chances of staying in the League with a 3-0 defeat of Rochdale, their biggest win for over 15 months.

APRIL

Britain's Biggest Soccer Disaster at Hillsborough

On 1 April Liverpool won 1-0 at early pacemakers Norwich; Arsenal played on Sunday for the TV viewers and drew 1-1 at Old Trafford. So Arsenal were three points ahead while Liverpool had a game in hand. Goal difference was practically the same, so everything was to play for.

Chelsea's Second Division victory over Barnsley 5-3 took them ten points clear. Leeds' spending helped them to a 3-0 win over Bournemouth and took them into the promotion play-off zone. Shrewsbury, Walsall and Birmingham were firmly in the relegation zone.

In midweek, Leeds lost 2-1 at home before 25,600 spectators to Crystal Palace, who took their place in the top six. Fulham, Third Division promotion hopefuls, suffered a surprising 7-0 defeat at Chester, and a training injury appeared to jeopardise Arsenal's chances of the Championship when Alan Smith, the division's leading scorer, fractured a cheekbone in two places.

On 8 April, Arsenal beat Everton 2-0, but Liverpool did better with a 5-1 destruction of Sheffield Wednesday, enough to make their goal difference one better than Arsenal's. In the Second Division, Chelsea, with no goal difference problems, won 3-2 at West Bromwich Albion to give another promotion hopeful a setback.

The big match on Sunday was the final of the Littlewoods Cup, and the first of Nottingham Forest's three possible (and two already certain) Wembley finals. Forest beat Luton 3-1, despite being a goal down at half-time and having had a legitimate goal (proved by the slow-motion replay) disallowed for off-side.

On Tuesday night, 11 April, Liverpool went to the top of the First Division by winning their match in hand of Arsenal. They won 2-1 at Millwall, and their goal difference was 31 to Arsenal's 29. Among other games, Bolton beat Blackpool 1-0 in the first leg of the Sherpa Van Trophy final, Northern Section.

At an important UEFA meeting, it was decided that English clubs should be re-admitted to Europe in the the 1990-91 season, subject to support from the British Government. Liverpool, however, would have to wait for three further years before being allowed back. Meanwhile the EEC parliament passed a resolution in Strasbourg which might lead to an even bigger upheaval in British football. This was that there should be no transfer fees for players and that clubs in Europe should not be restricted in the number of foreign players they could use. This would allow players to move from club to club as other workers moved from company to company, and would mean, if and when implemented, a radical change in the professional game as it has been played in Britain for over 100 years. All the best players would be tempted to Europe for high salaries.

More midweek soccer saw Wolves take a 2-1 lead in the Southern Section of the Sherpa Van Trophy final by winning their away leg at Torquay.

Saturday 15 April was FA Cup semi-final day, and a day never to be forgotten in English Football. Tragedy struck at Hillsborough where

Peter Beardsley tries to thread his way through Norwich City's defence. The Liverpool striker failed to score on this occasion, leaving it to Ronnie Whelan to get the winner

Match Magazine

Liverpool were meeting Nottingham Forest. A crush outside the ground just before kick-off, caused by many Liverpool fans arriving late for various reasons, and many others arriving without a ticket, led to fears of a disaster. A decision was made to open a gate at the Leppings Lane end (the Liverpool end) and the crowd pressed in, but unfortunately poured through a tunnel into an area of the terracing already nearly full. The resultant pressure caused many fans to be crushed, either in the tunnel or against barriers, particularly the perimeter fence set up to prevent invasion of the pitch. It took a while for the scale of the tragedy to sink in, even after the game was stopped and some fans managed to get over the fence or were pulled up into the grandstand above. Even when it was clear that people were dying the police were unable to breach the perimeter fence and let the fans onto the pitch. At last, when all was calm, it was known that there were 94 deaths, with others likely from a large number of casualties in hospital. A full-scale enquiry was set up and it would be premature to comment further here.

Liverpool, of course, was a city in shock, and it was some time before football would resume there. The Anfield pitch was the repository of thousands of wreaths and messages, and scarves and tokens tied to stanchions and crash barriers made a moving display.

As this is a football annual, we must chronicle the football events which followed, even though there were those who wanted the season curtailed.

Everton won the other semi-final, a Pat Nevin goal against Norwich being enough to take them to Wembley. On the same day, Arsenal beat Newcastle (but only 1-0 at Highbury) to regain the League leadership. Birmingham found themselves with the unwanted distinction of being the first club to be relegated. Chelsea lost at Leicester to end a run of 27 unbeaten games — one short of Liverpool's Second Division record. Tranmere's draw at Hartlepool took them to the top of the Fourth Division, where all the leading clubs were showing a reluctance to put together a consistent run to take them clear. At the other end Darlington won 1-0 at Burnley to go two points clear of Colchester, who drew 1-1 at Lincoln and had a game in hand.

The PFA dinner on the day after the tragedy went ahead in muted fashion, as the first chance players had to pay their respects to the bereaved and injured. Mark Hughes was voted PFA player of the year, and Paul Merson young player of the year.

Amid the discussions about what matches should or should not go on, Arsenal showed their compassion by defying League instructions and calling off their Tuesday match with Wimbledon. Arsenal's responsible attitude meant a hiatus in the Championship struggle that was to last for the rest of the month.

Tony Cottee scores the second goal for Everton against Nottingham Forest in the Simod Cup Final

Match Magazine

Nottingham Forest pictured after their 4-3 Simod Cup Final win over Everton

Match Magazine

Cottee, hidden from view, gets in a non-scoring header during the Norwich-Everton FA Cup Semi-Final

Match Magazine

Queens Park Rangers followed Arsenal's lead on Wednesday, but a number of matches took place. The Sherpa Van Trophy finals, North and South, were decided. Bolton won the Northern by drawing at Blackpool 1-1 after extra time, the score after 90 minutes being 1-0 for Blackpool, and thus level on aggregate. In the Southern final Torquay pulled off a great surprise by winning 2-0 at Wolves, and taking the tie 3-2 on aggregate.

Anfield removed its fences before football resumed with a full programme on Saturday. At 3.06, the time the Hillsborough game had been stopped the week before, a minute's silence in respect and remembrance of the victims was observed at all League games.

Chelsea beat Leeds with a goal by Bumstead and assured themselves of the Second Division Championship and, of course, promotion to the First Division. Of the clubs behind them Crystal Palace won and looked the only team with a chance to catch Manchester City for the second automatic promotion place.

While Arsenal and Liverpool maintained the *status quo* in the First Division, Norwich could only draw at home with Villa, and more or less conceded the race to the giants from the North and London.

In the Third Division play-off places, Preston, with a 1-0 win at Chester, had a satisfactory day, joining Fulham, Bristol Rovers, Port Vale and Sheffield United (in ascending order) in the battle behind Wolves, who looked safe for an automatic promotion place. In the Fourth Division, Darlington beat promotion hopefuls Scarborough 2-1, and had a lead of four points over rivals Colchester at the foot (but Colchester had a game in hand).

The Hillsborough disaster continued to have a profound effect on the season. There were many recriminations and accusations about it, and the Government's ID plans became inextricably mixed in. Some clubs began dismantling perimeter fences: the Liverpool club itself took time to decide whether or not to proceed with the FA Cup campaign. A peculiar sense of waiting hung over

Wembley beckons Everton as Pat Nevin scores the only goal of their FA Cup Semi-Final against Norwich

Match Magazine

the programme. It was partly dispelled on 26 April, because World Cup ties were scheduled, and some players returned for the first time since Hillsborough to the fray. Two who declined to play were Liverpool's John Barnes and John Aldridge, who could not bring themselves to turn out for England and the Republic of Ireland respectively while there was comforting still to be done.

England helped their World Cup qualifying prospects with a smooth 5-0 defeat of Albania, Liverpool's Beardsley scoring two of the goals. Scotland had a surprisingly tight squeeze against Cyprus, winning only by 2-1, but with two to qualify from their group they looked as good as there already with nine points out of ten. The

Republic of Ireland scored their first goal in the competition, but it was enough to beat Spain 1-0. With four points from four games, their position was very much stronger than it looked, with their home fixtures to come. Northern Ireland won 2-0 in Malta, but in the same group as their neighbours had no real chance of qualifying. Wales lost a friendly to Sweden, 2-0 at Wrexham.

Birmingham City, doomed to Third Division football for next season, were bought by three Indian brothers who had made their fortunes with a Manchester fashion house. The Kumar brothers, keen footballers, promised the club would survive, with new facilities for families and children.

The last Saturday of April saw most First Division action at the foot of the table, although Spurs won 5-0 at Millwall to move into fifth place, an excellent recovery from their dismal early season form. The best performance in the lower divisions was Rotherham's 6-0 defeat of Hartlepool. Rotherham went top of the Fourth and looked as if they meant to stay there. A

Paul Walsh (7) is surrounded by his Tottenham team-mates after scoring the winner against Everton

Match Magazine

showdown match was played at the foot of the table, with Colchester, enjoying a late run, winning 2-1 at Darlington, and taking a two-point advantage over them.

On Sunday, 30 April, Liverpool played again. They won 4-0 at Parkhead, where Celtic played them in a charity match for the Hillsborough victims.

Forest, too, were in action, playing Everton in the Simod Cup Final. It was an excellent match which went to extra time when the teams stood at 2-2 at 90 minutes. Forest won 4-3 to take their second Cup of the season, and Brian Clough went up the steps to receive it himself.

MAY/JUNE

Arsenal's Incredible Victory

May was to be the month in which the long drawn-out season came to a climax, and it began impressively for Arsenal with a 5-0 hammering of Norwich. This not only took them six points clear of Liverpool (who had two games in hand), but considerably improved their goal difference, just in case the teams finished level on points.

In a full May Day programme in the lower divisions, Manchester City drew 1-1 at home with Crystal Palace, who remained the only side which could deprive them of the automatic promotion spot in second place. Watford lost at home to Sunderland, but, with Blackburn and Swindon,

Left hand column: Sheffield Wednesday's Steve Whitton (left) is beaten off by Nicol and Ablett of Liverpool as the "Reds" win 5-1 at Anfield and close in on Arsenal

Match Magazine

they seemed almost sure to fight out the play-offs with Palace. In the Third Division, Port Vale lost at home to Northampton, which more or less gave Sheffield United the second certain promotion place behind Wolves, condemning the "Valiants" to play-off for the other place.

Things were tightest at the top of the Fourth Division. Rotherham drew at Scunthorpe, these clubs remaining first and third, while Tranmere, in second place, lost at Hereford. Scarborough and Crewe were still in the running for one of the three automatic places, and Leyton Orient looked good for a play-off spot. There was a group chasing the last play-off place, with Wrexham and Cambridge leading the way. At the bottom, Colchester had a stroke of fortune, coming from 0-2 down to win 3-2 after the Halifax goalkeeper had been carried off. This took them five points clear of Darlington, who now looked strong favourites to drop out of the League. The team to replace them would be Maidstone United, who clinched the GM Vauxhall Conference title while playing in the Kent Senior Cup Final (they won), because Kettering were beaten. Maidstone had failed to gain election to the League in 1983 and 1984.

Playing their "Bank Holiday" game on 2 May, Darlington scored a big upset with a 3-1 win at Cambridge, thus proving they were not dead yet, and at the same time denting Cambridge's prospects of promotion. In the struggle to avoid relegation from the First Division, Southampton overtook Aston Villa by winning 2-1 at Villa Park, while Luton climbed above Charlton with a 5-2 victory. Southampton looked safe, but Villa, Middlesbrough, Luton, Sheffield Wednesday and Charlton had it still to fight for. Although not yet doomed, Newcastle and West Ham could hardly afford to drop another point in their desperate efforts to avoid the drop.

Liverpool returned to competitive football on 4 May, playing before the cameras at Goodison Park. It was an emotional evening, and the football was competitive enough. There were no goals, but everybody was satisfied with the match. The loss of two points by Liverpool gave Arsenal the advantage in the title race, but the Gunners had to visit Anfield at the end of the season, so Liverpool were still masters of their own fate. Steve Nicol was chosen by the Football Writers as Footballer of the Year.

Ecstasy is written all over the face of Liverpool's John Aldridge as he scores his second goal in the 3-1 FA Cup Semi-Final defeat of Nottingham Forest

Match Magazine

In the First Division relegation struggle, West Ham won 2-1 at Newcastle to keep their own slight hopes alive, and sentenced Newcastle to relegation.

On the first Saturday in May, Arsenal won 1-0 at Middlesbrough to open up an eight-point gap at the top, as Liverpool were engaged in their Cup semi-final replay on Sunday. In the relegation zone, West Ham beat Luton 1-0 to extend hopes of survival, while Charlton beat Wimbledon 1-0. Southampton won and were safe, but Villa lost and remained in the thick of the fight.

In the Second Division, Manchester City maintained an extraordinary diffidence about clinching promotion. They were 3-0 up at half-time against Bournemouth, but struggled to a 3-3 draw. However, Palace, too, only drew, and City were nearly there. In the Fourth Division, Colchester beat Exeter 4-0 on Friday night, so Darlington had to win at Scunthorpe to keep alive hopes of League football next season. Alas, they crashed 5-1, so were relegated to the GM Vauxhall Conference. Scunthorpe considerably helped their promotion prospects, as did Rotherham, who looked likely champions, and Wrexham, whose 2-1 win at Carlisle eased them into a one-point lead in the race for the last play-off place.

The replay of the FA Cup semi-final, so tragically cut short at Hillsborough, was at Old Trafford on 7 May. Liverpool won 3-1 with two goals from Aldridge, and played some excellent football. Forest's good season, therefore, saw them win two Cups, but miss out for the second year running to Liverpool in the FA Cup semi-final. The FA considered deciding the Cup Final on penalties, if it were drawn, but then rejected the idea, even though a replay would not be possible until well into June in this congested season.

Tuesday night's results ensured interest right to the end of the season. West Ham won 2-0 at Sheffield Wednesday. Both clubs were in the bottom three, but Villa, Charlton, Middlesbrough and Luton could all still be overtaken. Palace beat Stoke 1-0 in the Second Division, and with one game left could still pip Manchester City for the automatic promotion place, although they would need to win by a good score, while City lost. In the Fourth Division, Crewe, Tranmere, Wrexham and Cambridge all won to keep their respective promotion hopes alive.

In Wednesday's matches, a tired Liverpool beat Forest 1-0 at Anfield through an Aldridge penalty, to get within five points of Arsenal, and keep their double hopes high. Charlton, at the other end, beat Derby 3-0 and made themselves virtually safe. They were preparing to return to their original home at the Valley, after three seasons at Selhurst Park. In fact First Division football had not been seen at the Valley for 33 years.

Many clubs finished their seasons on Saturday, 13 May, and of course several issues were decided. But the outcome at the top of the First Division would not be settled for a while, although it took a big swing. Arsenal were surprisingly beaten 2-1 at home by Derby, while Liverpool, who were one down at half-time to Wimbledon, recovered to win 2-1. So the gap was reduced to two points, and Liverpool, with their game in hand, were in a good position with Arsenal having to visit Anfield.

At the foot, Sheffield Wednesday made themselves safe by beating Middlesbrough 1-0, thus relegating Middlesbrough after one season in the top flight. West Ham's run stumbled with a 3-1 defeat at Everton, while Villa drew with Coventry. So the final relegation place depended upon whether West Ham could win their last two games and overtake Villa, whose programme was over.

In the Second Division promotion race, the situation at half-time was that Manchester City were one down at Bradford, while Palace were four up against Birmingham. That gave them identical goal differences, so everything was possible in the second halves. It was City who came through by equalising five minutes from time, thus gaining the point which made goal difference irrelevant. Unfortunately, the situation had been too tense for some spectators at Selhurst Park as Birmingham fans climbed a fence and fought with Palace supporters. Fourteen people were treated in hospital, a sad incident in view of Hillsborough, and an indication that some hooligans might be utterly incurable. Palace, Watford, Blackburn and Swindon were set to play-off for the other promotion place. Champions Chelsea ended their season with a win at Portsmouth, giving them 99 points and 96 goals.

There were no surprises in the Third Division, where the issues had already been more or less settled. Southend won their last game but failed to escape relegation on goal difference, as Blackpool also won.

In the Fourth Division, Scunthorpe crashed 4-1 at Leyton Orient and were edged out of a certain promotion place by Tranmere and Crewe, who drew 1-1. Wrexham's 2-1 defeat of Rochdale guaranteed them the fourth play-off place — Scunthorpe, Scarborough and Leyton Orient being their competitors.

As the half-dozen or so outstanding League matches began to be played off in midweek, so Liverpool beat Queens Park Rangers 2-0 on Tuesday to head the table again by one point. The two leaders again had the same goal difference, and each had two games to play. On Wednesday, Arsenal seemed to throw their chance away with a 2-2 draw at Highbury with Wimbledon. They returned to the top on the strength of having scored more goals than Liverpool, but it looked now as if they might need to win their last match at Anfield to take the title — possibly by two goals.

The following day West Ham kept their flag flying with a splendid 2-1 victory at Nottingham Forest. They had now won five of their last six matches, and needed to win their last match to stay in the First Division. Unfortunately for them it was to be at Anfield.

Graham Kelly, the FA's chief executive, suggested a compromise scheme on identity cards: a 'partial' membership scheme for home supporters, and a 100 per cent scheme for away supporters. It was to be considered by the FA Council.

Midfield activity from the Liverpool-Nottingham Forest FA Cup Semi-Final

Match Magazine

Saturday, 20 May, was the day of the most emotional FA Cup Final since Manchester United's defeat in 1958. It was an excellent game, with much thoughtful football after Aldridge had given Liverpool a fourth-minute lead. The match really came to life with a last-minute equalizer by Everton substitute Stuart McCall. In extra time substitute Rush gave Liverpool the lead again, McCall equalized with his second, and Rush scored the winner. Liverpool there after kept possession with a lot of passing among the back four, which suggested a curious caution and lack of belief in the country's leading team. It was interesting that, even in the Cup Final, Liverpool should have substituted Rush for Aldridge — after a whole season it was still not certain who was first choice. More significant were two controversial incidents: the fans singing of "You'll Never Walk Alone" during the anthem, a snub to royalty who did not attend the services for Hillsborough victims, and a few pitch invasions, principally at Everton's first goal. The Wembley authorities announced that the perimeter fencing, which had

Steve McMahon (left) and Ronnie Whelan show off the FA Cup after Liverpool's great victory over local rivals, Everton

Match Magazine

Wolves—Champions of the Third Division

Match Magazine

been removed, would be back for the Rous Cup international. Thus Hillsborough had almost passed into memory.

On Sunday and Monday the League promotion play-offs began. Watford did well to draw 0-0 at Blackburn, and Palace would be satisfied with a 1-0 defeat at Swindon in the first legs. In the Third Division play-offs, Fulham held Bristol Rovers to 1-0 away, while Port Vale did better with a 1-1 draw at Preston. Home sides took a two-goal advantage in the Fourth Division play-offs, Leyton Orient beating Scarborough 2-0 and Wrexham beating Scunthorpe 3-1.

In midweek, West Ham's gallant efforts to maintain their status finally folded in a 5-1 defeat by Liverpool. Level at half-time, they were over-run in the last ten minutes, Liverpool's final goal meant that Arsenal would now have to win at Anfield in the final match by two clear goals to wrest the title.

England began the Rous Cup matches with a 0-0 draw with Chile. Two new caps appeared in the forward line: John Fashanu and Nigel Clough.

On Wednesday night, the Second and Fourth Division play-offs proceeded, and four clubs bowed out of the promotion chase. Palace beat Swindon 2-0 to go into the final, where surprisingly Blackburn Rovers would be their opponents. Rovers drew 1-1 at Watford, making the aggregates level, so extra time was played. When this produced no further goals, Rovers went through on the "away goals" principle.

Scarborough beat Leyton Orient 1-0, but Orient won the tie 2-1 on aggregate, while Wrexham beat Scunthorpe 2-0 away to achieve an easy 5-1 aggregate win. Coincidentally, Scunthorpe had finished fourth in the division the previous year, again with 77 points, one fewer than the promoted team, only to fail in the play-offs to a club which finished seven points below them, and this strange quirk of fate had now been repeated as Wrexham had finished six points below them. Scunthorpe lost three men through injury in the two games.

The Third Division matches were easily won. Four second-half goals saw Bristol Rovers win 4-0 at Craven Cottage, and 5-0 on aggregate, while Port Vale beat Preston 3-1 to go through 4-2 on aggregate.

Friday, 26 May, saw the most amazing conclusion ever to the First Division Championship. Only once before had the title been decided by the two contenders meeting in the last match — a virtual "final" — and on that occasion in 1962, Arsenal's task was impossible, to win by 7-0 at Manchester United. On this night they needed to win by 2-0 at Anfield, but hardly anybody gave them a chance. However, when Alan Smith gave them a 1-0 lead early in the second half, the excitement became intense. With about 20 minutes left, Michael Thomas missed an easy chance for a second. Then, in the second minute of injury time, the ball went from Arsenal's goalkeeper, John Lukic, through to Thomas again, with an almost identical chance to the one he missed earlier, and this time he made no mistake. Liverpool's stamina had run out at last, their fixture-packed final three weeks eventually catching up on them physically and psychologically. There is no doubt that Liverpool were England's strongest club. It must be said that, in a season in which the spotlight had been as much on spectators as players, the Liverpool fans were splendid and generous in their applause for Arsenal.

A sad note on this great day for football was the announcement of the death of Don Revie, the former England manager, and the manager of Leeds in the 1960s and 1970s, when, for a time, the club was almost as dominant as Liverpool today.

On Saturday, England beat Scotland 2-0 at Hampden Park, the second goal coming from substitute Steve Bull, the prolific Wolves scorer, whose goals over two seasons just exceeded 100.

As the season drew to an end, it was estimated that League attendances were well past 18 million, an increase of nearly half a million on the previous season, and the third consecutive season in which attendances had risen. It was, of course, impossible to predict what would happen in the future, with the whole question of membership schemes, identity cards and restrictions on away supporters still not decided.

The Sherpa Van Trophy final on Sunday, 28 May, drew 46,513 spectators to Wembley to see Third Division Bolton Wanderers revive memories of their great Wembley days in the 1920s and 1950s with a 4-1 defeat of Fourth Division Torquay United.

The Republic of Ireland beat Malta 2-0 in Dublin to remain on course for a World Cup place, with four Liverpool players, including substitute Aldridge, in the side, playing their fourth big game in nine days.

The Rous Cup concluded with Scotland defeating Chile 2-0 at Hampden Park, leaving England the winners.

The finals of the play-offs began on 30 May, with Leyton Orient visiting Wrexham in the Fourth Division final and gaining a 0-0 draw, which made them promotion favourites.

On the last day of May, Blackburn Rovers took a 3-1 lead over Crystal Palace in the Second Division play-off final, a last-minute goal giving them a useful advantage for the second leg, while Port Vale got a good 1-1 draw with a second-half equalizer at Bristol Rovers in the Third Division final.

World Cup qualifying matches were played at the end of the English domestic season, Wales beginning the home countries' involvement with a 0-0 draw with West Germany at Cardiff Arms Park — the first soccer international there since 1910. They had little hope of qualifying.

As the regular soccer season moved into June, so England beat Poland 3-0 at Wembley to send themselves into the summer break with a healthy lead in their qualifying group: seven points out of eight and a goal difference of 10-0. Peter Shilton equalled Bobby Moore's record of 108 England caps. An excellent performance by the Republic of Ireland, who beat Hungary 2-0 in Dublin, also put them into a good position for one of the qualifying places in their group.

It was 3 June before six clubs knew which division they would be starting the new season in eight weeks time. Crystal Palace led Blackburn 2-0 at the end of 90 minutes at Selhurst Park, and went into extra time. They clinched their First Division place with a third goal five minutes from the end.

Port Vale beat Bristol Rovers 1-0, to move up to the Second Division, which was justice as they had been in the top three nearly all season, and had finished third in the table, nine points clear of the fourth club. Leyton Orient, with a goal eight minutes from time against Wrexham, which gave them a 2-1 victory, won promotion to the Third Division. Ironically, just as in the previous season, only one club missed out on promotion through having to play-off, after having finished in what in the pre-play-off days would have been a promotion place.

The season ended with England drawing a friendly with Denmark 1-1 in Copenhagen, going through the season unbeaten. Peter Shilton won his 109th cap, a new record.

Alan Smith gets between two Liverpool defenders to score Arsenal's first goal in the "Gunners" dramatic League Championship winning game at Anfield

Match Magazine

Michael Thomas (left) and Alan Smith celebrate as Arsenal are proclaimed First Division Champions

Match Magazine

FINAL FOOTBALL LEAGUE TABLES 1988–89

FIRST DIVISION

			Home			Goals		Away			Goals		
		P	*W*	*D*	*L*	*F*	*A*	*W*	*D*	*L*	*F*	*A*	*Pts*
1	Arsenal	38	10	6	3	35	19	12	4	3	38	17	76
2	Liverpool	38	11	5	3	33	11	11	5	3	32	17	76
3	Nottingham F.	38	8	7	4	31	16	9	6	4	33	27	64
4	Norwich C.	38	8	7	4	23	20	9	4	6	25	25	62
5	Derby Co.	38	9	3	7	23	18	8	4	7	17	20	58
6	Tottenham H.	38	8	6	5	31	24	7	6	6	29	22	57
7	Coventry C.	38	9	4	6	28	23	5	9	5	19	19	55
8	Everton	38	10	7	2	33	18	4	5	10	17	27	54
9	Q.P.R.	38	9	5	5	23	16	5	6	8	20	21	53
10	Millwall	38	10	3	6	27	21	4	8	7	20	31	53
11	Manchester U.	38	10	5	4	27	13	3	7	9	18	22	51
12	Wimbledon	38	10	3	6	30	19	4	6	9	20	27	51
13	Southampton	38	6	7	6	25	26	4	8	7	27	40	45
14	Charlton Ath.	38	6	7	6	25	24	4	5	10	19	34	42
15	Sheffield Wed.	38	6	6	7	21	25	4	6	9	13	26	42
16	Luton T.	38	8	6	5	32	21	2	5	12	10	31	41
17	Aston Villa	38	7	6	6	25	22	2	7	10	20	34	40
18	Middlesbrough*	38	6	7	6	28	30	3	5	11	16	31	39
19	West Ham U.*	38	3	6	10	19	30	7	2	10	18	32	38
20	Newcastle U.*	38	3	6	10	9	28	4	4	11	13	35	31

* relegated

SECOND DIVISION

			Home			Goals		Away			Goals		
		P	*W*	*D*	*L*	*F*	*A*	*W*	*D*	*L*	*F*	*A*	*Pts*
1	Chelsea†	46	15	6	2	50	25	14	6	3	46	25	99
2	Manchester C.†	46	12	8	3	48	28	11	5	7	29	25	82
3	Crystal Palace†	46	15	6	2	42	17	8	6	9	29	32	81
4	Watford	46	14	5	4	41	18	8	7	8	33	30	78
5	Blackburn Rov.	46	16	4	3	50	22	6	7	10	24	37	77
6	Swindon T.	46	13	8	2	35	15	7	8	8	33	38	76
7	Barnsley	46	12	8	3	37	21	8	6	9	29	37	74
8	Ipswich T.	46	13	3	7	42	23	9	4	10	29	38	73
9	West Bromwich A.	46	13	7	3	43	18	5	11	7	22	23	72
10	Leeds U.	46	12	6	5	34	20	5	10	6	25	30	67
11	Sunderland	46	12	8	3	40	23	4	7	12	20	37	63
12	Bournemouth	46	13	3	7	32	20	5	5	13	21	42	62
13	Stoke C.	46	10	9	4	33	25	5	5	13	24	47	59
14	Bradford C.	46	8	11	4	29	22	5	6	12	23	37	56
15	Leicester C.	46	11	6	6	31	20	2	10	11	25	43	55
16	Oldham Ath.	46	9	10	4	49	32	2	11	10	26	40	54
17	Oxford U.	46	11	6	6	40	34	3	6	14	22	36	54
18	Plymouth Arg.	46	11	4	8	35	22	3	8	12	20	44	54
19	Brighton & H.A.	46	11	5	7	36	24	3	4	16	21	42	51
20	Portsmouth	46	10	6	7	33	21	3	6	14	20	41	51
21	Hull C.	46	7	9	7	31	25	4	5	14	21	43	47
22	Shrewsbury T.*	46	4	11	8	25	31	4	7	12	15	36	42
23	Birmingham C.*	46	6	4	13	21	33	2	7	14	10	43	35
24	Walsall*	46	3	10	10	27	42	2	6	15	14	38	31

* relegated † promoted

THIRD DIVISION

			Home			Goals		Away			Goals		
		P	*W*	*D*	*L*	*F*	*A*	*W*	*D*	*L*	*F*	*A*	*Pts*
1	Wolverhampton W.†	46	18	4	1	61	19	8	10	5	35	30	92
2	Sheffield U.†	46	16	3	4	57	21	9	6	8	36	33	84
3	Port Vale†	46	15	3	5	46	21	9	9	5	32	27	84
4	Fulham	46	12	7	4	42	28	10	2	11	27	39	75
5	Bristol Rov.	46	9	11	3	34	21	10	6	7	33	30	74
6	Preston N.E.	46	14	7	2	56	31	5	8	10	23	29	72
7	Brentford	46	14	5	4	36	21	4	9	10	30	40	68
8	Chester C.	46	12	6	5	38	18	7	5	11	26	43	68
9	Notts. Co.	46	11	7	5	37	22	7	6	10	27	32	67
10	Bolton W.	46	12	8	3	42	23	4	8	11	16	31	64
11	Bristol C.	46	10	3	10	32	25	8	6	9	21	30	63
12	Swansea C.	46	11	8	4	33	22	4	8	11	18	31	61
13	Bury	46	11	7	5	27	22	5	6	12	28	45	61
14	Huddersfield T.	46	10	8	5	35	25	7	1	15	28	48	60
15	Mansfield T.	46	10	8	5	32	22	4	9	10	16	30	59
16	Cardiff C.	46	10	9	4	30	16	4	6	13	14	40	57
17	Wigan Ath.	46	9	5	9	28	22	5	9	9	27	31	56
18	Reading	46	10	6	7	37	29	5	5	13	31	43	56
19	Blackpool	46	10	6	7	36	29	4	7	12	20	30	55
20	Northampton T.	46	11	2	10	41	34	5	4	14	25	42	54
21	Southend U.*	46	10	9	4	33	26	3	6	14	23	49	54
22	Chesterfield*	46	9	5	9	35	35	5	2	16	16	51	49
23	Gillingham*	46	7	3	13	25	32	5	1	17	22	49	40
24	Aldershot*	46	7	6	10	29	29	1	7	15	19	49	37

* relegated † promoted

FOURTH DIVISION

			Home			Goals		Away			Goals		
		P	*W*	*D*	*L*	*F*	*A*	*W*	*D*	*L*	*F*	*A*	*Pts*
1	Rotherham U.†	46	13	6	4	44	18	9	10	4	32	17	82
2	Tranmere Rov.†	46	15	6	2	34	13	6	11	6	28	30	80
3	Crewe Alex.†	46	13	7	3	42	24	8	8	7	25	24	78
4	Scunthorpe U.	46	11	9	3	40	22	10	5	8	37	35	77
5	Scarborough	46	12	7	4	33	23	9	7	7	34	29	77
6	Leyton Orient†	46	16	2	5	61	19	5	10	8	25	31	75
7	Wrexham	46	12	7	4	44	28	7	7	9	33	35	71
8	Cambridge U.	46	13	7	3	45	25	5	7	11	26	37	68
9	Grimsby T.	46	11	9	3	33	18	6	6	11	32	41	66
10	Lincoln C.	46	12	6	5	39	26	6	4	13	25	34	64
11	York C.	46	10	8	5	43	27	7	5	11	19	36	64
12	Carlisle U.	46	9	6	8	26	25	6	9	8	27	27	60
13	Exeter C.	46	14	4	5	46	23	4	2	17	19	45	60
14	Torquay U.	46	15	2	6	32	23	2	6	15	13	37	59
15	Hereford U.	46	11	8	4	40	27	3	8	12	26	45	58
16	Burnley	46	12	6	5	35	20	2	7	14	17	41	55
17	Peterborough U.	46	10	3	10	29	32	4	9	10	23	42	54
18	Rochdale	46	10	10	3	32	26	3	4	16	24	56	53
19	Hartlepool U.	46	10	6	7	33	33	4	4	15	17	45	52
20	Stockport Co.	46	8	10	5	31	20	2	11	10	23	32	51
21	Halifax T.	46	10	7	6	42	27	3	4	16	27	48	50
22	Colchester U.	46	8	7	8	35	30	4	7	12	25	48	50
23	Doncaster Rov.	46	9	6	8	32	32	4	4	15	17	46	49
24	Darlington*	46	3	12	8	28	38	5	6	12	25	38	42

* replaced by Maidstone U. † promoted

The English Football League Clubs

The complete Barclays League Record for Every Club During 1988-89.

Each club is portrayed match by match and includes the date, venue, opponent, result, half-time (H/T) score, League position (Lge Posn), attendance, full line-ups, substitutes and goalscorers. Maidstone United are also included as they join the Football League for 1989–90, following their championship win in the Vauxhall Conference, and their 1988–89 record in that League is recorded within these pages.

Please note that the League positions have been determined following each match and that the attendances shown are those which have been reported in the press.

In the Players: League Record table, the substitutes are denoted by an ★ and the players that they replaced are shown in **bold**.

Finally, it is worth noting that the "Play-Offs" are not recorded in this section, but are reported in the review of the 1988–89 season.

A jubilant Arsenal pictured with the 1988–89 League Championship Trophy, following their 2–0 victory over Liverpool at Anfield Match Magazine

IT'S NO GOOD SHOUTING AT THE REF!

YOU'RE BETTER OFF TALKING TO

BARCLAYS

Barclays Bank PLC
2 Circus Place
London Wall
London EC2M 5UN
Tel: 01-256 6111

ALDERSHOT (Division 4)

Team Manager Len Walker.
Club Address Recreation Ground, High Street, Aldershot GU11 1TW. Tel: (0252) 20211.
Current Ground Capacity 12,000.
Record Attendance 19,138 v Carlisle U., FA Cup 4th Round replay, 28 January 1970.
Year Formed 1926. Turned professional 1927.
Previous Names None.
Club Nickname "The Shots".
Club Colours Red shirts with blue trim, blue shorts, red stockings and two blue hoops.
Club Honours None.
League History 1932-58 Div. 3(S); 1958-73 Div. 4; 1973-76 Div. 3; 1976-87 Div. 4; 1987-89 Div. 3; 1989- Div. 4.
Most League Points in a Season (2 for a win) 57 in Div. 4, 1978-79. (3 for a win) 75 in Div. 4, 1983-84.
Most League Goals in a Season 83 in Div. 4, 1963-64.
Record Victory 8-1 v Gateshead in Div. 4, 13 September 1958.
Record Defeat 0-9 v Bristol C. in Div. 3(S), 28 December 1946.
Consecutive League Wins 6 in 1961.
Consecutive League Defeats 9 in 1965-66.
Record League Appearances Murray Brodie, 461 between 1970-83.
Record League Goalscorer—Career Jack Howarth, 171 between 1965-77.
Record League Goalscorer—Season John Dungworth, 26 in Div. 4, 1978-79.

Aldershot: League Record, 1988-89 (Division 3)

Match Number	Date	Venue	Opponents	Result	H/T	Lge Posn	Attend
1	27.8.88	A	Chesterfield	L 1-2	0-0		2327
2	3.9.88	H	Gillingham.	L 0-2	0-1	22	2477
3	10.9.88	A	Bristol Rov.	D 2-2	2-0	23	3382
4	17.9.88	H	Southend U.	D 2-2	0-1	23	2170
5	20.9.88	A	Wolverhampton W.	L 0-1	0-1	24	8991
6	24.9.88	H	Bolton W.	L 0-3	0-1	24	2126
7	1.10.88	A	Northampton T.	L 0-6	0-1	24	3477
8	4.10.88	H	Wigan Ath.	W 3-1	1-0	24	1527
9	9.10.88	H	Swansea C.	L 0-1	0-1	24	2809
10	15.10.88	A	Fulham	L 1-5	0-2	24	4573
11	22.10.88	H	Huddersfield T.	L 0-1	0-1	24	2155
12	25.10.88	A	Bristol C.	D 1-1	1-0	24	8685
13	29.10.88	H	Chester C.	D 1-1	1-1	24	1862
14	8.11.88	H	Sheffield U.	W 1-0	1-0	23	2934
15	12.11.88	A	Blackpool	L 0-4	0-2	23	2690
16	26.11.88	A	Mansfield T.	D 1-1	1-0	23	2715
17	3.12.88	H	Notts Co.	L 2-3	0-2	23	2191
18	18.12.88	H	Brentford	D 0-0	0-0	23	4012
19	26.12.88	A	Reading	L 1-3	0-1	23	6350
20	31.12.88	A	Bury	W 1-0	0-0	23	3186
21	2.1.89	H	Cardiff C.	L 0-1	0-0	23	2768
22	7.1.89	H	Preston N.E.	W 2-1	0-0	23	2135
23	14.1.89	A	Gillingham	D 1-1	0-1	24	3781
24	21.1.89	H	Bristol Rov.	L 1-3	0-2	24	3101
25	28.1.89	A	Southend U.	D 1-1	0-0	24	3014
26	4.2.89	H	Northampton T.	W 5-1	3-1	22	2244
27	11.2.89	A	Wigan Ath.	L 1-2	1-0	23	2132
28	13.2.89	A	Port Vale	L 0-3	0-1	23	5033
29	17.2.89	A	Swansea C.	L 0-1	0-0	23	4922
30	21.2.89	H	Bristol C.	L 0-1	0-1	23	1969
31	4.3.89	A	Huddersfield T.	L 1-2	1-1	23	4709
32	11.3.89	H	Port Vale	D 2-2	0-0	23	2397
33	15.3.89	A	Chester C.	D 1-1	1-0	23	2028
34	18.3.89	H	Chesterfield	W 2-0	0-0	23	1886
35	25.3.89	A	Cardiff C.	L 2-3	1-1	23	3251
36	27.3.89	H	Reading	D 1-1	0-0	23	4960
37	1.4.89	A	Brentford	L 1-2	0-0	24	5200
38	4.4.89	A	Preston N.E.	D 2-2	0-0	24	5977
39	8.4.89	H	Bury	W 4-1	0-1	23	1677
40	15.4.89	H	Wolverhampton W.	L 1-2	0-1	24	5465
41	22.4.89	A	Bolton W.	L 0-1	0-0	24	4407
42	25.4.89	H	Fulham	L 1-2	0-0	24	3841
43	29.4.89	H	Blackpool	W 1-0	1-0	24	1763
44	1.5.89	A	Sheffield U.	L 0-1	0-0	24	11737
45	6.5.89	A	Notts Co.	L 1-4	1-0	24	4261
46	13.5.89	H	Mansfield T.	D 0-0	0-0	24	1549

Players: League Record, 1988-89 (Division 3)

Match Number	1	2	3	4	5	6	7	8	9	10	11	12	13	14	15	16	17	18	19	20	21	22	23
Anderson, Darren		★		★[1]		★	9	9[1]	**9**				★			8	8	★	5	★		★	
Barnes, David	3	3	3	3	3	3	3	3	3	3	3	3	3	3	3	3	3[1]		3	3	3	3	3
Berry, Steve	2	2	2	2	2	2	2	2	2	2	2	2											
Brown, Kevan														2	2	2	2	2	2	2	2	2	2
Burvill, Glen	4	4	4[1]				4	4	**4**	4	**4**	4[1]	**4**	4		4	4[1]	**4**	**4**	4	**4**	**4**	4[1]
Chandler, Ian	**9**	**9**	9	**9**		★	★	**8**[1]	★										★[1]				
Claridge, Steve										9	9	9	9[1]	9[1]	9	9	9	9	9	9	9	9	9
Coombs, Paul																							
Devereux, James																			★				
Hewitt, Darren											★												
Holsgrove, Paul															★								
Lange, Tony	1	1	1	1	1	1	1	1	1	1	1	1	1	1	1	1	1	1	1	1	1	1	1
McDonald, Ian	10	10	10	10[1]	10	10	10	10	10	10	10	10	10	10	10	10[1]	10	10	10	**10**	10	10	10
Mazzon, Giorgio	11			4	4	**4**		★	★	★[1]	★		2	7	7	7	**7**	7	**7**	7	7	**7**	★
Osgood, Stephen																							
Phillips, Ian	7	7	7	7	7	7	7	7	7	7	7	7	7		11			3					
Puckett, David																							
Randall, Adrian					9	9	11	11[1]	11	**11**	**11**	11	11	11		11	11	11	11	11[1]	11	11	11
Riley, Glyn	8	8	8	8	8	8	**8**		8	8	8	8	**8**	8	8					8	8	8	8
Ring, Mike	★	11	11	11	11	**11**							★		**4**		★	8	8		★	★[1]	
Smith, Colin	5	5	5	5	5	5	5	5	5	5	5	5	5	5	5	5	5	5		5	5	5[1]	5
Stewart, Ian																							**7**
Wignall, Steve	6[1]	6	6	6	6	6	6	6	6	6	6	6	6	6	6	6	6	6	6	6	6	6	6
Own Goals			1																				

Match Number	24	25	26	27	28	29	30	31	32	33	34	35	36	37	38	39	40	41	42	43	44	45	46	Apps	Subs	Goals
Anderson, Darren	6	★		★		★		★	6	6	6	6	6	6	6	6	6	6	6	6	6	6	6	22	11	2
Barnes, David	3	3	3	3	3	3	3	3	3	3	**3**	3			11	11	3				7	7		39	0	1
Berry, Steve																								12	0	0
Brown, Kevan	2	2	2	2	2	2	2				★		2	2	2	2		2	2	2	2	2	2	27	1	0
Burvill, Glen	4	**4**	4	4	4	4	4	4	4[1]	4	4	4	4	4	4	4	4	4	4[1]	4	4	4[1]	**4**	42	0	7
Chandler, Ian																								5	4	2
Claridge, Steve	9	**9**	9[1]	**9**	9	**9**	9	9[1]	9	9[1]	9[1]	9	9	9[1]	9[1]	9[1]	9	9	**9**	9	**9**	9	9	37	0	9
Coombs, Paul																							7	1	0	0
Devereux, James																								0	1	0
Hewitt, Darren																							★	0	2	0
Holsgrove, Paul																								0	1	0
Lange, Tony	1	1	1	1	1	1	1	1	1	1	1	1	1	1	1	1	1	1		1	1	1	1	45	0	0
McDonald, Ian	10	10[1]	10	**10**[1]				10	10	10	**10**	10[1]	**10**	10	10	10[1]	10	10	10	10	10	**10**	10	43	0	6
Mazzon, Giorgio					**10**	**10**	10				★	★	★						★	★			3	18	10	1
Osgood, Stephen																			1					1	0	0
Phillips, Ian								2	2	2	2	2	3	3	3	3	2	3	3	3	3	3		30	0	0
Puckett, David		8	8[3]	8	8	8	8	8	8[1]	8	8[1]	8[1]	8[1]	8	8[1]	8[2]	8	8		8[1]	8	8	8	21	0	11
Randall, Adrian	**11**	11	11	11	11	11	**11**	**11**	11	**11**	11	**11**	11	11					8	**11**	11	11	11	37	0	2
Riley, Glyn	8	★		★	★	★	★	★		★							11	11	**11**					22	7	0
Ring, Mike	★[1]																							8	6	2
Smith, Colin	5	5	5	5	5	5	5	5	5	5	5	5	5	5	5	5	5[1]	5	5	5	5	5	5	45	0	2
Stewart, Ian	7	7	7	7	7	7	7	7	7	7	7	7	7	7	7	7	7	7	7	7		★		21	1	0
Wignall, Steve		6	6	6	6	6	6	**6**											★		★			30	2	1
Own Goals			1																							2

FA Cup: 1988-89: 1st Round: Hayes (H) 1-0; 2nd Round: Bristol C. (H) 1-1, Replay (A) 0-0, 2nd Replay (H) 2-2, 3rd Replay (A) 0-1.
Littlewoods Cup: 1988-89: 1st Round: Leyton Orient (A) 0-2, (H) 0-0.

HI-FI MIDI SYSTEMS · HI-FI COMPONENTS · PORTABLE AUDIO · CAR AUDIO · TELEVISION · ...PES ·

U 16
SCOTLAND '89
PRESENTED BY JVC

JVC MIDI W51CD
50w per channel 3-way speaker system
Compact disc player
Double cassette deck
Auto memory digital receiver
Built in 5-band graphic equaliser
Auto return turntable
Compu Link remote control
6 disc CD auto changer (optional)
Surround Sound speakers (optional)

JVC
FOUNDERS OF THE FUTURE

AUDIO TAPES · FLOPPY DISCS · CAR AUDIO ·

CAR AUDIO · VIDEO TAPES · AUDIO TAPES ·

· VIDEOMOVIE · TELEVISION · PORTABLE AUDIO · HI-FI COMPONENTS · HI-FI MIDI SYSTEMS · AUDIO/VIDEO ACCESSORIES ·

ARSENAL (Division 1)

Team Manager George Graham.
Club Address Arsenal Stadium, Highbury, London N5. Tel: 01-226 0304.
Current Ground Capacity 57,000.
Record Attendance 73,295 v Sunderland, Div. 1, 9 March 1935.
Year Formed 1886. Turned professional 1891.
Previous Names Dial Square, Royal Arsenal, Woolwich Arsenal.
Club Nickname "The Gunners".
Club Colours Red shirts with white sleeves, white shorts and red and white stockings.
Club Honours Football League: Div. 1 Champions 1930-31, 1932-33, 1933-34, 1934-35, 1937-38, 1947-48, 1952-53, 1970-71, 1988-89. FA Cup: Winners 1930, 1936, 1950, 1971, 1979. League Cup: Winners 1987. European Fairs Cup: Winners 1969-70.

League History 1893-1904 Div. 2; 1904-13 Div. 1; 1913-19 Div. 2; 1919- Div. 1.
Most League Points in a Season (2 for a win) 66 in Div. 1, 1930-31. (3 for a win) 76 in Div. 1, 1988-89.
Most League Goals in a Season 127 in Div. 1, 1930-31.
Record Victory 12-0 v Loughborough T. in Div. 2, 12 March 1900.
Record Defeat 0-8 v Loughborough T. in Div. 2, 12 December 1896.
Consecutive League Wins 9 in 1971.
Consecutive League Defeats 7 in 1977.
Record League Appearances George Armstrong, 500 between 1961-77.
Record League Goalscorer—Career Cliff Bastin, 150 between 1930-47.
Record League Goalscorer—Season Ted Drake, 42 in Div. 1, 1934-35.

Arsenal: League Record, 1988-89 (Division 1)

Match Number	Date	Venue	Opponents	Result	H/T	Lge Posn	Attend
1	27.8.88	A	Wimbledon	W 5-1	3-1		15710
2	3.9.88	H	Aston Villa	L 2-3	0-1	8	37417
3	10.9.88	A	Tottenham H.	W 3-2	3-2	6	32621
4	17.9.88	H	Southampton	D 2-2	0-2	5	31384
5	24.9.88	A	Sheffield Wed	L 1-2	0-1	7	17830
6	1.10.88	A	West Ham U.	W 4-1	2-1	6	27658
7	22.10.88	H	Q.P.R.	W 2-1	0-0	4	33202
8	25.10.88	A	Luton T.	D 1-1	1-0	3	10548
9	29.10.88	H	Coventry C.	W 2-0	1-0	2	31273
10	6.11.88	A	Nottingham F.	W 4-1	1-1	2	19038
11	12.11.88	A	Newcastle U.	W 1-0	0-0	2	24033
12	19.11.88	H	Middlesbrough	W 3-0	1-0	2	32294
13	26.11.88	A	Derby Co.	L 1-2	0-0	2	21209
14	4.12.88	H	Liverpool	D 1-1	0-0	2	31863
15	10.12.88	A	Norwich C.	D 0-0	0-0	2	23069
16	17.12.88	H	Manchester U.	W 2-1	2-0	2	37422
17	26.12.88	A	Charlton Ath.	W 3-2	1-0	2	18439
18	31.12.88	A	Aston Villa	W 3-0	2-0	1	32486
19	2.1.89	H	Tottenham H.	W 2-0	1-0	1	45129
20	14.1.89	A	Everton	W 3-1	0-0	1	34825
21	21.1.89	H	Sheffield Wed.	D 1-1	0-0	1	33490
22	4.2.89	H	West Ham U.	W 2-1	0-0	1	40139
23	11.2.89	A	Millwall	W 2-1	0-1	1	21854
24	18.2.89	A	Q.P.R.	D 0-0	0-0	1	20543
25	21.2.89	A	Coventry C.	L 0-1	0-0	1	21290
26	25.2.89	H	Luton T.	W 2-0	0-0	1	31012
27	28.2.89	H	Millwall	D 0-0	0-0	1	37524
28	11.3.89	H	Nottingham F.	L 1-3	1-3	1	39639
29	21.3.89	H	Charlton Ath.	D 2-2	2-1	1	30259
30	25.3.89	A	Southampton	W 3-1	1-0	1	19202
31	2.4.89	A	Manchester U.	D 1-1	0-0	1	37977
32	8.4.89	H	Everton	W 2-0	1-0	1	37608
33	15.4.89	H	Newcastle U.	W 1-0	0-0	1	38023
34	1.5.89	H	Norwich C.	W 5-0	2-0	1	28449
35	6.5.89	A	Middlesbrough	W 1-0	0-0	1	21803
36	13.5.89	H	Derby Co.	L 1-2	0-1	1	41008
37	17.5.89	H	Wimbledon	D 2-2	1-1	1	39132
38	26.5.89	A	Liverpool	W 2-0	0-0	1	41718

Players: League Record, 1988-89 (Division 1)

Match Number	1	2	3	4	5	6	7	8	9	10	11	12	13	14	15	16	17	18	19	20	21	22	23	24	25	26	27	28	29	30	31	32	33	34	35	36	37	38	Apps	Subs	Goals
Adams, Tony	6	6	6	6	6	6	6^{1}	6	6^{1}	6^{1}	6	6	6	6	6	6	6	6	6			6	6	6	6	6	6	6	6	6	6^{1}	6	6	6	6	6	6	6	36	0	4
Bould, Stephen	5					5	5	5	5	5^{1}	5^{1}	5	5	5	5	5	5	5	5			★	★	★	2	5	5	**2**			10	10	10	10	10	**10**	★	**10**	26	4	2
Caesar, Gus																				6	**6**																		2	0	0
Davis, Paul	8	8	8	**8**	8	8													★	4	4								4^{1}	4	**4**								11	1	1
Dixon, Lee	2	2	2	2	2	2	2	2	2	2	2	2	2	2	2	2				2	2	2	2	**2**			★	★	2	2	2	2^{1}	2	2	2	2	2	2	31	2	1
Groves, Perry		★	★		★	**10**	★		★				★					★^{1}	★	★	★	11^{1}				10^{1}	10	**10**	★	**10^{1}**			★			★	★	★	6	15	4
Hayes, Martin				★		★			★	★	10	★	11	★	★							★		★	★									★	★^{1}	★	**10**	★	3	14	1
Lukic, John	1	1	1	1	1	1	1	1	1	1	1	1	1	1	1	1	1	1	1	1	1	1	1	1	1	1	1	1	1	1	1	1	1	1	1	1	1	1	38	0	0
Marwood, Brian	11^{1}	11^{1}	**11^{1}**	11^{1}	11	11	11	11	11	11^{1}	11	**11**		**11**	11	11	11^{2}	11	**11**	**11**	11		11^{1}	11	**11**	11	11	11	11	11	**11**	**11**	11^{1}						31	0	9
Merson, Paul	10^{1}	10	10	**10**	**10**		**10**	10	**10**	**10**	★	10^{2}	10	10	**10**	10^{1}	10^{1}	**10**	10^{1}	**10^{1}**	10^{1}	**10**	10	**10**	10																
O'Leary, David		5	5	5	5												2	2	2	5	5	**5**	**5**	5	5	★	★	★	**10**	★^{1}	★	★	★	**11**	**11**	**11**	**11^{1}**	**11**	29	8	10
Quinn, Niall																										2	2	5	5	5	5	5	**5**	5	5	5	5	5	26	0	0
Richardson, Kevin			★	★			8	8	8	8	8	8	**8**	8	8	8	8	8	**8**	8^{1}	8	8	8	8	8							9^{1}	9	★					2	1	1
Rocastle, David	7	**7**	**7**	7	7	7^{1}	7	7	**7**	7	**7**	7^{1}	7	7	7	7	7	7^{1}	7	7	**7**	7	7	7	7	8	**8**	8	**8**	8	8	8	8	8	8	8	8	8	32	2	1
Smith, Alan	9^{3}	9^{1}	9^{1}	9^{1}	9^{1}	9^{2}	9^{1}	9^{1}	9	9^{1}	9	9	9	9^{1}	9	9	9	9^{1}	9	9^{1}	9	9^{1}	9^{1}	9	9	**7**	**7**	7	7^{1}	7^{1}	7	7	**7**	7^{1}	7	7	7	7	38	0	6
Thomas, Michael	4	4	4	4	4	4^{1}	4	4	4^{1}	4	4	4	4^{1}	4	4	4^{1}	4	4	4^{1}	★	★	4	4	4	4	9^{1}	9	9^{1}	9	9	9			**9^{2}**	9	9^{1}	9	9^{1}	36	0	23
Winterburn, Nigel	3	3	3^{1}	3	3	3	3	3	3	3	3	3	3	3	3	3	3	3	3	3	3	3	3	3	3	4	4	4	★		★	4	4	4^{1}	4	4	4	4^{1}	33	4	7
																										3	3	3	3	3	3	3	3	3^{1}	3	3	3^{1}	3	38	0	3
Own Goals																																									0

FA Cup: 1988-89: 3rd Round: West Ham U. (A) 2-2, Replay (H) 0-1.
Littlewoods Cup: 1988-89: 2nd Round: Hull C. (A) 2-1 (H) 3-0; 3rd Round: Liverpool (A) 1-1, Replay (H) 0-0, 2nd Replay 0-1.

ASTON VILLA (Division 1)

Team Manager Graham Taylor.
Club Address Villa Park, Trinity Road, Birmingham B6 6HE. Tel: 021-327 6604.
Current Ground Capacity 48,000.
Record Attendance 76,588 v Derby Co., FA Cup 6th Round, 2 March 1946.
Year Formed 1874. Turned professional 1885.
Previous Names None.
Club Nickname "The Villans".
Club Colours Claret and blue shirts, claret shorts and blue stockings.
Club Honours Football League: Div. 1 Champions 1893-94, 1895-96, 1896-97, 1898-99, 1899-1900, 1909-10, 1980-81; Div. 2 Champions 1937-38, 1959-60; Div. 3 Champions 1971-72. FA Cup: Winners 1887, 1895, 1897, 1905, 1913, 1920, 1957. Football League Cup: Winners 1961, 1975, 1977. European Cup: Winners 1982-83. European Super Cup: Winners 1982-83.
League History 1888-1936 Div. 1; 1936-38 Div. 2; 1938-59 Div. 1; 1959-60 Div. 2; 1960-67 Div. 1; 1967-70 Div. 2; 1970-72 Div. 3; 1972-75 Div. 2; 1975-87 Div. 1; 1987-88 Div. 2; 1988- Div. 1.
Most League Points in a Season (2 for a win) 70 in Div. 3, 1971-72. (3 for a win) 68 in Div. 1, 1982-83.
Most League Goals in a Season 128 in Div. 1, 1930-31.
Record Victory 13-0 v Wednesbury Old Athletic in FA Cup 1st Round, 1886.
Record Defeat 1-8 v Blackburn Rov. in FA Cup 3rd Round, 16 February 1889.
Consecutive League Wins 9 in 1897.
Consecutive League Defeats 11 in 1910 and 1963.
Record League Appearances Charlie Aitken, 561 between 1961-76.
Record League Goalscorer—Career Harry Hampton, 213 between 1904-20 and Billy Walker, 213 between 1919-34.
Record League Goalscorer—Season "Pongo" Waring, 49 in Div. 1, 1930-31.

Aston Villa: League Record, 1988-89 (Division 1)

Match Number	Date	Venue	Opponents	Result	H/T	Lge Posn	Attend
1	27.8.88	H	Millwall	D 2-2	2-2		22449
2	3.9.88	A	Arsenal	W 3-2	1-0	5	37417
3	10.9.88	H	Liverpool	D 1-1	1-0	8	41409
4	17.9.88	A	West Ham U.	D 2-2	2-0	10	19186
5	24.9.88	H	Nottingham F.	D 1-1	1-0	9	23029
6	1.10.88	A	Sheffield Wed.	L 0-1	0-1	11	18301
7	8.10.88	H	Wimbledon	L 0-1	0-0	16	15146
8	15.10.88	A	Charlton Ath.	D 2-2	0-1	15	7594
9	22.10.88	H	Everton	W 2-0	1-0	9	26636
10	29.10.88	H	Tottenham H.	W 2-1	0-0	9	26238
11	5.11.88	A	Manchester U.	D 1-1	0-1	8	44804
12	12.11.88	A	Southampton	L 1-3	1-1	12	16007
13	19.11.88	H	Derby Co.	L 1-2	0-0	13	23489
14	26.11.88	A	Coventry C.	L 1-2	0-1	14	20104
15	3.12.88	H	Norwich C.	W 3-1	1-1	14	19653
16	10.12.88	A	Middlesbrough	D 3-3	2-1	14	18096
17	17.12.88	A	Luton T.	D 1-1	0-1	15	8785
18	26.12.88	H	Q.P.R.	W 2-1	2-0	10	25106
19	31.12.88	H	Arsenal	L 0-3	0-2	16	32486
20	3.1.89	A	Liverpool	L 0-1	0-0	16	39014
21	14.1.89	H	Newcastle U.	W 3-1	1-1	12	21010
22	21.1.89	A	Nottingham F.	L 0-4	0-1	14	22662
23	4.2.89	H	Sheffield Wed.	W 2-0	2-0	11	19334
24	11.2.89	A	Wimbledon	L 0-1	0-1	12	6201
25	14.2.89	A	Everton	D 1-1	1-1	11	20142
26	25.2.89	H	Charlton Ath.	L 1-2	1-1	12	16481
27	1.3.89	A	Tottenham H.	L 0-2	0-1	13	19090
28	12.3.89	H	Manchester U.	D 0-0	0-0	12	28332
29	18.3.89	A	Millwall	L 0-2	0-1	12	13206
30	25.3.89	H	West Ham U.	L 0-1	0-1	14	22471
31	27.3.89	A	Q.P.R.	L 0-1	0-0	15	11378
32	1.4.89	H	Luton T.	W 2-1	2-1	14	15640
33	8.4.89	A	Newcastle U.	W 2-1	1-0	13	20329
34	22.4.89	A	Norwich C.	D 2-2	0-0	13	14551
35	29.4.89	H	Middlesbrough	D 1-1	0-0	13	18590
36	2.5.89	H	Southampton	L 1-2	0-2	14	15218
37	6.5.89	A	Derby Co.	L 1-2	1-1	14	18112
38	13.5.89	H	Coventry C.	D 1-1	1-0	17	29906

Players: League Record, 1988-89 (Division 1)

Match Number	1	2	3	4	5	6	7	8	9	10	11	12	13	14	15	16	17	18	19
Birch, Paul	**7**		★											★		★	★		
Butler, Lee																			
Callaghan, Nigel																			
Cowans, Gordon	10	10	10	10	10	10	10	10	10	10	10^{1}	10	10	10	10	10	10	10	10
Daley, Tony	★	7	**7**	7	7	7	7	7	7^{1}	7^{1}	7	7^{1}	7	**11**	11	11	**11**	11	11
Duffy, Darrell																			
Evans, Allan	5	5	5	**5**			★	4	4	4	4	4	4		5	5	5	5	5
Gage, Kevin	3		3	★	5^{1}	5	5	5	5	5	5	5	5	4	4^{2}	**4**	4	4	4
Gallacher, Bernard					★						11	11	**11**						
Gray, Andy	**4**	4^{1}	4	4	4	4	4					★	★	7	7	7^{1}	7	7	**7**
Gray, Stuart	11^{1}	11	11	11	**11**	11	11	11	11	11				3	3	3	3	3	3
Hunt, David																			
Keown, Martin	6	6	6	6	6	6	6	6	6	6	6	6	6	6	6	6	6		★
Lillis, Mark																			
McInally, Alan	9^{1}	9^{2}	9^{1}	9^{2}	**9**			$★^{1}$	9	9	9	9	9	9^{1}	9	9^{2}	9	9^{2}	9
Mountfield, Derek				3	3	3	3	3	3	3	3	3	3^{1}	5		★		6	6
Olney, Ian								**9**											
Ormondroyd, Ian																			
Platt, David	8	8	8	8	8	8	8	8^{1}	8^{1}	8	8	8	8	8	8^{1}	8	8	8	8
Price, Chris	2	2	2	2	2	2	2	2	2	2	2	2	2	2	2	2	2	2	2
Sims, Steve		3																	
Spink, Nigel	1	1	1	1	1	1	1	1	1	1	1	1	1	1	1	1	1	1	1
Thompson, Garry	★		★		★	9	**9**												
Williams, Gareth																			
Own Goals										1							1		

Match Number	20	21	22	23	24	25	26	27	28	29	30	31	32	33	34	35	36	37	38	Apps	Subs	Goals
Birch, Paul			7		★			7	7	**7**								★	7	6	6	0
Butler, Lee						1			1	1	1									4	0	0
Callaghan, Nigel				7^{1}	7	7	7	11	11	11	7	★	7	7	7	7	7	7	11	15	1	1
Cowans, Gordon	**10**	10	10	10	**10**	10	10^{1}	10		★	**10**		10	10	**10**				10	32	1	2
Daley, Tony	7	11^{1}	★				9				8	★	11^{1}			**10**	★	**10**		25	4	5
Duffy, Darrell																		2		1	0	0
Evans, Allan	5				6	6	**6**					**4**	4	4	4	4	4		4	26	1	0
Gage, Kevin	4	4	2	4	4	4	4	4	4	4										27	1	3
Gallacher, Bernard																				3	1	0
Gray, Andy	★	7^{1}	**4**																	15	3	3
Gray, Stuart	11	3	3	3	3	3	3	3	3	**3**	3	10	3	3^{1}	3	3^{1}	3^{1}	3	3	35	0	4
Hunt, David																		6		1	0	0
Keown, Martin	6	6	6	6			★	6	6	6	6	6	6	6	6	6	6		6	32	2	0
Lillis, Mark												**8**						4		2	0	0
McInally, Alan	**9**	9^{1}	9	9	9	9			9	9	**9**		9	9	9^{1}	9	**9**	9	**9**	32	1	14
Mountfield, Derek	3	5	5	5	5	5	5	5			★	3								22	2	1
Olney, Ian	★	★	11						★	★	★	9	$★^{1}$	11	11^{1}	11	11	**11**	★	8	7	2
Ormondroyd, Ian				11	11	11^{1}	11	9	**10**	10		11			★	★	10	★		9	3	1
Platt, David	8	8	8	8^{1}	8	8	8	8	8	8	4	7	8	8^{1}	8	8	8	8^{1}	8^{1}	38	0	7
Price, Chris	2	**2**		2	2	2	2	2	2	2	2	2	2	2	2	2	2		2	36	0	0
Sims, Steve									5	5	5	5	5	5	5	5	5	5	5	12	0	0
Spink, Nigel	1	1	1	1	1		1	1				1	1	1	1	1	1	1	1	34	0	0
Thompson, Garry																				2	3	0
Williams, Gareth											11									1	0	0
Own Goals																						2

FA Cup: 1988-89: 3rd Round: Crewe Alex (A) 3-2; 4th Round: Wimbledon (H) 0-1.

Littlewoods Cup: 1988-89: 2nd Round: Birmingham C. (A) 2-0 (H) 5-0; 3rd Round: Millwall (H) 3-1; 4th Round: Ipswich T. (H) 6-2; Quarter-Final: West Ham U. (A) 1-2.

Aston Villa keeps on running...

... so do Mita copiers

Year after year, Mita have proved they're top of the league in copiers.
With a range of machines that has re-defined reliability in the field.
And the kind of national support any team would envy!
(That's because Mita's teamwork makes other teams look as if they're standing still!)
Keep on running with Mita.
The cup-winners in the copier league!

ASTON VILLA F.C.
mita
keeps on running!

MITA COPYSTAR (UK) LTD.,
Mita House, Hamm Moor Lane,
Addlestone Surrey KT15 2SB.
Tel: 0932 858266

BARNSLEY (Division 2)

Team Manager Allan Clarke.
Club Address Oakwell Ground, Grove Street, Barnsley. Tel: (0226) 295353.
Current Ground Capacity 36, 864.
Record Attendance 40, 255 v Stoke C., FA Cup 5th Round, 15 February 1936.
Year Formed 1887. Turned professional 1888.
Previous Names Barnsley St Peter's.
Club Nickname "The Tykes" or "Colliers".
Club Colours Red shirts, white shorts and white stockings.
Club Honours Football League: Div. 3(N) Champions 1933-34, 1938-39, 1954-55. FA Cup: Winners 1912.
League History 1898-1932 Div. 2; 1932-34 Div. 3(N); 1934-38 Div. 2; 1938-39 Div 3(N); 1946-53 Div. 2; 1953-55 Div. 3(N); 1955-59 Div. 2; 1959-65 Div. 3; 1965-68 Div. 4; 1968-72 Div. 3; 1972-79 Div. 4; 1979-81 Div. 3; 1981- Div. 2.
Most League Points in a Season (2 for a win) 67 in Div. 3(N), 1938-39. (3 for a win) 74 in Div. 2, 1988-89.
Most League Goals in a Season 118 in Div. 3(N), 1933-34.
Record Victory 9-0 v Loughborough Town in Div. 2, 28 January 1899 and v Accrington Stanley in Div. 3(N), 3 February 1934.
Record Defeat 0-9 v Notts. County in Div. 2, 19 November 1927.
Consecutive League Wins 10 in 1955.
Consecutive League Defeats 9 in 1953.
Record League Appearances Barry Murphy, 513 between 1962-78.
Record League Goalscorer—Career Ernest Hine, 123 between 1921-38.
Record League Goalscorer—Season Cecil McCormack, 33 in Div. 2, 1950-51.

Barnsley: League Record, 1988-89 (Division 2)

Match Number	Date	Venue	Opponents	Result	H/T	Lge Posn	Attend
1	27.8.88	A	Oldham Ath.	D 1-1	0-1		6551
2	29.8.88	H	Swindon T.	D 1-1	1-0	9	6034
3	3.9.88	H	Stoke C.	W 1-0	0-0	6	5682
4	10.9.88	A	Hull C.	D 0-0	0-0	9	5654
5	17.9.88	H	Chelsea	D 1-1	1-1	10	6942
6	21.9.88	A	Leeds U.	L 0-2	0-0	13	17390
7	24.9.88	H	Manchester C.	L 1-2	0-0	16	9300
8	1.10.88	A	Birmingham C.	W 5-3	2-0	12	4892
9	5.10.88	A	Brighton & H.A.	W 1-0	0-0	8	7327
10	8.10.88	H	West Bromwich A.	W 2-1	0-1	5	5674
11	15.10.88	A	Blackburn Rov.	L 1-2	1-1	8	9316
12	22.10.88	H	Ipswich T.	W 2-0	2-0	7	6325
13	25.10.88	A	Watford	L 0-4	0-2	8	10356
14	29.10.88	H	Plymouth Arg.	W 3-1	1-0	7	5485
15	5.11.88	A	Crystal Palace	D 1-1	0-0	7	7768
16	12.11.88	H	Bradford C.	D 0-0	0-0	8	8838
17	19.11.88	A	Portsmouth	L 0-3	0-2	11	10001
18	26.11.88	H	Bournemouth	W 5-2	2-0	7	4937
19	3.12.88	A	Oxford U.	L 0-2	0-0	9	4449
20	10.12.88	H	Walsall	W 1-0	0-0	7	5173
21	17.12.88	H	Leicester C.	W 3-0	2-0	7	6477
22	26.12.88	A	Sunderland	L 0-1	0-0	8	21994
23	31.12.88	A	Shrewsbury T.	W 3-2	1-1	6	4401
24	2.1.89	H	Hull C.	L 0-2	0-2	7	9879
25	14.1.89	A	Swindon T.	D 0-0	0-0	9	10201
26	21.1.89	H	Oldham Ath.	W 4-3	1-0	8	7879
27	4.2.89	A	Brighton & H.A.	D 2-2	1-1	7	12498
28	11.2.89	A	West Bromwich A.	D 1-1	1-0	8	12650
29	21.2.89	A	Ipswich T.	L 0-2	0-1	10	9995
30	25.2.89	H	Blackburn Rov.	L 0-1	0-0	11	8777
31	28.2.89	H	Watford	D 2-2	1-0	13	6163
32	4.3.89	A	Bradford C.	W 2-1	1-0	11	11805
33	11.3.89	H	Crystal Palace	D 1-1	1-1	10	7055
34	19.3.89	H	Leeds U.	D 2-2	1-1	12	11578
35	25.3.89	A	Stoke C.	D 1-1	0-1	12	10209
36	27.3.89	H	Sunderland	W 3-0	1-0	12	8070
37	1.4.89	A	Chelsea	L 3-5	2-2	12	16023
38	8.4.89	H	Shrewsbury T.	W 1-0	1-0	11	5252
39	11.4.89	A	Leicester C.	W 1-0	1-0	8	7266
40	15.4.89	H	Birmingham C.	D 0-0	0-0	9	6464
41	22.4.89	A	Manchester C.	W 2-1	1-0	8	21274
42	25.4.89	A	Plymouth Arg.	W 2-1	1-1	8	5468
43	29.4.89	A	Bournemouth	L 2-3	1-1	8	5520
44	1.5.89	H	Oxford U.	W 1-0	0-0	8	5940
45	6.5.89	H	Portsmouth	W 1-0	0-0	7	5718
46	13.5.89	A	Walsall	W 3-1	1-0	7	3966

Players: League Record, 1988-89 (Division 2)

Match Number	1	2	3	4	5	6	7	8	9	10	11	12	13	14	15	16	17	18	19	20	21	22	23
Agnew, Steve	8	8	8[1]	8	8	8	8	**8**	8	8	**8**	★	★						★	★	8[1]	**8**	
Baker, Clive	1	1	1	1	1	1	1	1	1	1	1	1	1	1	1	1	1	1	1	1	1	1	1
Beresford, John	3	3	**3**	3	3	3	3	3[1]	3	3	3	3	3	3	**3**					3	3	3	8
Broddle, Julian			★					11[1]	11	11	11	11	11	11	11[1]	11	11	11	11	11[1]	11	11	11
Clarke, Michael			**11**																				
Cooper, Steve	9[1]	9	9	9	9	9	9		★	★	★	9[2]	9	9[1]	9	9				9	9	**9**	9
Currie, David	10	10	10	10		10	10	10[1]	10[1]	10[1]	10	**10**				**10**	10	10[4]	10	10	10[1]	10	10[1]
Dobbin, Jim	4	4	5	11	11[1]	11	11	★		★	★	8	8	8[1]	8	8	8	8[1]	8	8		★	
Foreman, Darren					★																		
Futcher, Paul	6	6	6	6	6	6	6				6	6	6	6	6	6	6	6	6	6	6	6	6
Joyce, Joe	2	2	2	2	2	2	2	2	2	2	2	2	2	2	2	2	2	2	2	2	2	2	2
Lowndes, Steve	**7**	7[1]	7	7	7	7	**7**	7[1]	7	**7**	**7**	★	**7**				9		★		7	7	7[1]
Macdonald, John	★		★		**10**									10	10	★		7	**7**				★
McGugan, Paul	5	5						6	6	**6**					★	3	3	3	3	**5**	5[1]	5	5
Marshall, Colin							★																
Rees, Tony								9[1]	**9**	9	9	**7**	10	7	7	7	7	**9**	**9**	**7**		★	
Robinson, Mark																		★		★			
Shotton, Malcolm				5	5	5	5[1]	5	5	5	5	5	5	5	5	5	5	5	5				**3**
Thomas, Gwyn	11	11	4	4	4	4	4	4	4	4[1]	4	4	4	4[1]	4	4	4	4	4	4	4	4	4
Tiler, Carl																							
Own Goals											1												1

Match Number	24	25	26	27	28	29	30	31	32	33	34	35	36	37	38	39	40	41	42	43	44	45	46	Apps	Subs	Goals
Agnew, Steve		7	8	8[1]	8	8	8	8	8	8	8[1]	8	8	8[1]	8	8	8	8[1]	8	8	8	8	8[1]	35	4	7
Baker, Clive	1	1	1	1	1	1	1	1	1	1	1	1	1	1	1	1	1	1	1	1	1	1	1	46	0	0
Beresford, John	3	3	**3**	3	3	3	3		3															27	0	1
Broddle, Julian	11			★	10	★	★	9	9	9	3	3	3	3	3	3	3	3	3	3	3	3	3	34	4	3
Clarke, Michael								3		**3**														3	0	0
Cooper, Steve	9	9	9	9[1]	9	9	9					★	★[1]	★	**9**	9	9			★	9	**9**		28	7	6
Currie, David	10	10	10[2]	10		10	10	10	10[1]	10	**10**	10[1]	**10**	10	10	10	**10**	10	10[1]	10	**10**	10[1]	10[1]	41	0	16
Dobbin, Jim	★	8	4			4	4	4	4	4	4	4	4[1]	4[1]	4	4	4	4	4	4	4	4	4	36	5	5
Foreman, Darren											★			★	★						★			0	5	0
Futcher, Paul	6	6	6	6	6	6	6	6	6	6	6	6	6	6		6	6	6	6	6		6	6	41	0	0
Joyce, Joe	2	2	2	2	2	2	2	2	2	2	2	2	2	2	2	2	2	2	2	2	2	2		45	0	0
Lowndes, Steve			7[1]		7[1]	**7**					9	9	9	9	6	7[1]	7	9	9	9		★	9	30	3	6
Macdonald, John	8	11	11	11	11	11	**11**	11[1]	11[1]	11[1]	11	11	11	**11**	11[1]	11	11	11	11	11	11	11	11[1]	28	4	5
McGugan, Paul	5	5	5	**5**	5	**5**																		19	1	1
Marshall, Colin																								0	1	0
Rees, Tony	**7**			7						★														15	2	1
Robinson, Mark							7	7	7	7	7[1]	**7**	7[1]	**7**	7		★	7	7	**7**	7	7	7	15	3	2
Shotton, Malcolm		4	★	4	4	★	5	5[1]	5	5			5	5	5	5	5	5[1]	5[1]	5[1]	5	5	5	35	2	5
Thomas, Gwyn	4																							24	0	2
Tiler, Carl											5	5										6[1]	2	4	0	1
Own Goals			1												1					1						5

FA Cup: 1988-89: 3rd Round: Chelsea (H) 4-0; 4th Round Stoke C. (A) 3-3, Replay (H) 2-1; 5th Round: Everton (H) 0-1.
Littlewoods Cup: 1988-89: 2nd Round: Wimbledon (H) 0-2, (A) 1-0.

BIRMINGHAM CITY (Division 3)

Team Manager Dave Mackay.
Club Address St Andrews, Birmingham B9 4NH. Tel: 021-772 0101/2689.
Current Ground Capacity 38,408.
Record Attendance 66,844 v Everton, FA Cup 5th Round, 11 February 1939.
Year Formed 1875. Turned professional 1885.
Previous Names Small Heath Alliance, Small Heath, Birmingham.
Club Nickname "The Blues".
Club Colours Royal blue shirts, white shorts and blue stockings with white hoops on turnover.
Club Honours Football League: Div. 2 Champions 1892-93, 1920-21, 1947-48, 1954-55. Football League Cup: Winners 1963.
League History 1892-94 Div. 2; 1894-96 Div. 1; 1896-1901 Div. 2; 1901-02 Div. 1; 1902-03 Div. 2; 1903-08 Div. 1; 1908-21 Div. 2; 1921-39 Div. 1; 1939-48 Div. 2; 1948-50 Div. 1; 1950-55 Div. 2; 1955-65 Div. 1; 1965-72 Div. 2; 1972-79 Div. 1; 1979-80 Div. 2; 1980-84 Div. 1; 1984-85 Div. 2; 1985-86 Div. 1; 1986-89 Div. 2; 1989-Div 3.
Most League Points in a Season (2 for a win) 59 in Div. 2, 1947-48. (3 for a win) 82 in Div. 2, 1984-85.
Most League Goals in a Season 103 in Div. 2, 1893-94.
Record Victory 12-0 v Walsall Town Swifts in Div. 2, 17 December 1892 and v Doncaster Rov. in Div. 2, 11 April 1903.
Record Defeat 1-9 v Sheffield Wed. in Div. 1, 13 December 1930 and v Blackburn Rov. in Div. 1, 5 January 1895.
Consecutive League Wins 13 in 1892-93.
Consecutive League Defeats 8 in 1978-79.
Record League Appearances Gil Merrick, 486 between 1946-60.
Record League Goalscorer—Career Joe Bradford, 249 between 1920-35.
Record League Goalscorer—Season Joe Bradford, 29 in Div. 1, 1927-28.

Birmingham City: League Record, 1988-89 (Division 2)

Match Number	Date	Venue	Opponents	Result	H/T	Lge Posn	Attend
1	27.8.88	A	Watford	L 0-1	0-1		12656
2	3.9.88	H	Leicester C.	L 2-3	2-2	22	7932
3	10.9.88	A	Oldham Ath.	L 0-4	0-1	24	5796
4	17.9.88	H	Sunderland	W 3-2	1-0	20	6871
5	20.9.88	A	Walsall	L 0-5	0-0	23	8780
6	24.9.88	A	Blackburn Rov.	L 0-3	0-3	23	7562
7	1.10.88	H	Barnsley	L 3-5	0-2	24	4892
8	4.10.88	H	Plymouth Arg.	L 0-1	0-0	24	4921
9	8.10.88	A	Bournemouth	W 1-0	1-0	22	6186
10	15.10.88	H	West Bromwich A.	L 1-4	1-2	22	10453
11	22.10.88	A	Manchester C.	D 0-0	0-0	24	20205
12	25.10.88	H	Stoke C.	L 0-1	0-0	24	6262
13	29.10.88	A	Swindon T.	L 1-2	0-1	24	6937
14	5.11.88	H	Portsmouth	D 0-0	0-0	24	5866
15	12.11.88	A	Oxford U.	L 0-3	0-1	24	5589
16	19.11.88	A	Hull C.	D 1-1	1-0	24	5134
17	22.11.88	H	Leeds U.	D 0-0	0-0	24	6168
18	26.11.88	H	Ipswich T.	W 1-0	1-0	24	5932
19	3.12.88	A	Bradford C.	D 2-2	1-1	24	9503
20	10.12.88	H	Crystal Palace	L 0-1	0-1	24	6523
21	16.12.88	H	Chelsea	L 1-4	0-1	24	7897
22	26.12.88	A	Shrewsbury T.	D 0-0	0-0	23	7347
23	31.12.88	A	Brighton & H.A.	L 0-4	0-0	23	9324
24	2.1.89	H	Oldham Ath.	D 0-0	0-0	23	5998
25	14.1.89	A	Leeds U.	L 0-1	0-0	23	21837
26	21.1.89	H	Watford	L 2-3	2-2	23	6396
27	4.2.89	A	Plymouth Arg.	W 1-0	1-0	23	7721
28	11.2.89	H	Bournemouth	L 0-1	0-0	23	6444
29	18.2.89	H	Manchester C.	L 0-2	0-1	23	11707
30	25.2.89	A	West Bromwich A.	D 0-0	0-0	23	16148
31	28.2.89	A	Stoke C.	L 0-1	0-1	24	7904
32	4.3.89	H	Oxford U.	D 0-0	0-0	24	4954
33	11.3.89	A	Portsmouth	L 0-1	0-0	24	8078
34	18.3.89	H	Walsall	W 1-0	0-0	23	6558
35	25.3.89	A	Leicester C.	L 0-2	0-1	24	9564
36	27.3.89	H	Shrewsbury T.	L 1-2	1-0	24	4964
37	1.4.89	A	Sunderland	D 2-2	0-1	24	10969
38	4.4.89	A	Chelsea	L 1-3	1-1	24	14796
39	8.4.89	H	Brighton & H.A.	L 1-2	1-2	24	4579
40	15.4.89	A	Barnsley	D 0-0	0-0	24	6464
41	18.4.89	H	Swindon T.	L 1-2	0-2	24	4026
42	22.4.89	H	Blackburn Rov.	W 2-0	0-0	24	5813
43	29.4.89	A	Ipswich T.	L 0-4	0-2	24	9975
44	1.5.89	H	Bradford C.	W 1-0	1-0	23	4735
45	6.5.89	H	Hull C.	W 1-0	0-0	23	4686
46	13.5.89	A	Crystal Palace	L 1-4	0-4	23	17581

Players: League Record, 1988-89 (Division 2)

Match Number	1	2	3	4	5	6	7	8	9	10	11	12	13	14	15	16	17	18	19	20	21	22	23	24	25	26	27	28	29	30	31	32	33	34	35	36	37	38	39	40	41	42	43	44	45	46	Apps	Subs	Goals
Ashley, Kevin															2							2	2		2	2	2	2	2	2	2	2	2	2	2	2											15	0	0
Atkins, Ian	4	4	4	4^{1}	4	4	4^{1}	4	4	4	4	4	4^{1}	4	4	4	4	4	4	4	4	4	4	4			4	4	4	4	4	4	4	4	4	4	4	4	4	4	4					4	40	0	3
Bird, Adrian	5	6	6			6		**6**	6	6		★		5		8			8			**8**																									11	1	0
Bremner, Des	7			7	7	7	★	7	7	7^{1}	7	7	7	7	7	7	7	7	7	7	7	7	7	7	7	7			7	7	7	7	7														28	1	1
Burton, Michael																																			★	★			★				★				0	4	0
Childs, Gary			★	8^{1}				★		**8**	**8**	8	★	8			**8**	**8**			★			11										8	**8**	8	8	8	8	8			★	9	★	★	16	7	1
Clarkson, Ian							6						**5**																		6										3	2	**2**	2	**2**	2	9	0	0
Fox, Matthew																														5				6							5						3	0	0
Frain, John		7	**7**	6	**6**				3^{1}	3	3	**3**			**8**	3											9	**9**		3	3	3	3	3	3	3	3^{1}	3	3	3		3	3	3^{1}	3	3	28	0	3
Godden, Tony	1	1	1	1	1	1	1																																								7	0	0
Hansbury, Roger																		1	1	1																											3	0	0
Hopkins, Robert																																			11	**11**			11		8	11	11	11	11	11	9	0	0
Langley, Kevin	8	8	**8**				$\mathbf{8}^{1}$	**8**					8	6	6	6^{1}	6	6	6	6	6	6	6	6	6	6	6	**6**			★		★	7	7	7	7	7	7	7	7	7	7	7	7	7	34	2	2
Morris, Ronnie			★		★		7	★		★										8	**8**							★				★				★											3	7	0
Overson, Vince		5	5	5	5	5	5	5	5	5	5	5			5	5	5	5	5	5	5	5	5	5	5	5	5	5	5		5	5	5	5	5	5	5	5	5	5		5	5	5	5	5	41	0	0
Peer, Dean									8	2	6	6	6					★							★					8	**8**						2	2		2	2^{1}	4	4		9	8	15	2	1
Ranson, Ray	2	2	2	2	2	2	2	2	2				2	2		2	2	2	2	2	2																										17	0	0
Richards, Carl										9	9	9	9		10	10	10	**10**	10^{1}	10	**10**	10	**10**	10					★				8	**9**			10	10^{1}									18	1	2
Roberts, Brian	3	3	3	3	3	3	**3**	3			2	2	3	3	3		3	3	3	3	3	3	3	2	4	4	7	7	6	**6**		6	**6**		6	6	6	6	6	6	6	6	6	6	6	6	41	0	0
Robinson, Colin	10	10^{1}	10	10^{1}	10	10	10^{1}	10	10	**10**	10	**10**	**10**								★		★		10	10	10^{1}	10	10	10	**10**	10	10	10	10	10			**9**	10		8^{1}	8	8	8		31	2	5
Sturridge, Simon										★	★	★		**10**	★											★				★	★	**8**		★	9	9^{1}	9	9	10^{1}		10	10	10	10	10	10^{1}	13	8	3
Tait, Paul							★							★				★						8		**8**	8	★	**8**											9	9						6	4	0
Thomas, Martin								1	1	1	1	1	1	1	1	1	1				1	1	1	1	1	1	1	1	1	1	1	1	1	1	1	1	1	1	1	1	1	1	1	1	1	1	36	0	0
Trewick, John	6				8	**8**																★	8	3	3	3	3	3	3																		10	1	0
Whitton, Steve	9	9	9	9	9	9	9	9	**9**								9	9^{1}	9^{1}	9	9^{1}	9	9	9	9	9^{2}		8	9	9	9																23	0	5
Wigley, Steve	11	11	11	11	11	11	11	11	11	11	11	11	11	11	11	11	11	11	11	11	11	11	11		11	11	11	11	11	11	11	11	11	11^{1}													33	0	1
Yates, Mark						★			★				★	9	9	9	★								**8**							9	9				11^{1}	11	2	11	11	9^{1}	**9**	4	4^{1}	**9**	16	4	3
Own Goals		1																																															1

FA Cup: 1988-89: 3rd Round: Wimbledon (H) 0-1.

Littlewoods Cup: 1988-89: 1st Round: Wolverhampton W (A) 2-3 (H) 1-0; 2nd Round: Aston Villa (H) 0-2 (A) 0-5.

BLACKBURN ROVERS (Division 2)

Team Manager Donald Mackay.
Club Address Ewood Park, Blackburn BB2 4JF. Tel: (0254) 55342.
Current Ground Capacity 18,600.
Record Attendance 61,783 v Bolton W., FA Cup 6th Round, 2 March 1929.
Year Formed 1875. Turned professional 1880.
Previous Names Blackburn Grammar School OB.
Club Nickname "The Blue and Whites".
Club Colours Blue and white halved shirts, white shorts and blue stockings with red and white tops.
Club Honours Football League: Div. 1 Champions 1911-12, 1913-14; Div. 2 Champions 1938-39; Div. 3 Champions 1974-75. FA Cup: Winners 1884, 1885, 1886, 1890, 1891, 1928.
League History 1888-1936 Div. 1; 1936-39 Div. 2; 1946-47 Div. 1; 1947-57 Div. 2; 1957-66 Div. 1; 1966-71 Div. 2; 1971-75 Div. 3; 1975-79 Div. 2; 1979-80 Div. 3; 1980- Div. 2.
Most League Points in a Season (2 for a win) 60 in Div. 3, 1974-75. (3 for a win) 77 in Div. 2, 1988-89.
Most League Goals in a Season 114 in Div. 2, 1954-55.
Record Victory 11-0 v Rossendale U. in FA Cup 1st Round, 1884-85.
Record Defeat 0-8 v Arsenal in Div. 1, 25 February 1933.
Consecutive League Wins 8 in 1980.
Consecutive League Defeats 7 in 1966.
Record League Appearances Derek Fazackerley, 596 between 1970-86.
Record League Goalscorer—Career Simon Garner, 144 between 1978-89.
Record League Goalscorer—Season Ted Harper, 43 in Div. 1, 1925-26.

Blackburn Rovers: League Record, 1988-89 (Division 2)

Match Number	Date	Venue	Opponents	Result	H/T	Lge Posn	Attend
1	27.8.88	A	Chelsea	W 2-1	1-1		8722
2	3.9.88	H	Oldham Ath.	W 3-1	2-0	5	10082
3	10.9.88	A	Stoke C.	W 1-0	1-0	3	8624
4	17.9.88	H	Swindon T.	D 0-0	0-0	5	7622
5	20.9.88	A	Hull C.	W 3-1	3-1	3	6681
6	24.9.88	H	Birmingham C.	W 3-0	3-0	1	7562
7	1.10.88	A	Manchester C.	L 0-1	0-0	2	22111
8	5.10.88	A	Bradford C.	D 1-1	1-0	2	13022
9	8.10.88	H	Crystal Palace	W 5-4	1-1	2	8022
10	15.10.88	H	Barnsley	W 2-1	1-1	1	9316
11	22.10.88	A	Oxford U.	D 1-1	1-0	1	6478
12	25.10.88	A	Sunderland	L 0-2	0-2	2	16601
13	29.10.88	H	West Bromwich A.	L 1-2	1-1	2	9503
14	5.11.88	A	Plymouth Arg.	L 3-4	0-3	4	7823
15	12.11.88	H	Brighton & H.A.	W 2-1	2-1	2	6980
16	19.11.88	A	Walsall	W 2-1	1-0	3	5848
17	22.11.88	H	Shrewsbury T.	L 0-1	0-1	3	6898
18	26.11.88	H	Portsmouth	W 3-1	1-1	2	8141
19	3.12.88	A	Bournemouth	L 1-2	0-0	3	8418
20	10.12.88	H	Ipswich T.	W 1-0	1-0	2	7258
21	17.12.88	H	Watford	W 2-1	2-0	1	8080
22	26.12.88	A	Leeds U.	L 0-2	0-2	3	31622
23	31.12.88	A	Leicester C.	L 0-4	0-2	5	10820
24	2.1.89	H	Stoke C.	W 4-3	2-3	3	11654
25	14.1.89	A	Shrewsbury T.	D 1-1	0-0	5	3879
26	21.1.89	H	Chelsea	D 1-1	0-1	5	11713
27	4.2.89	H	Bradford C.	W 2-1	0-1	4	9571
28	11.2.89	A	Crystal Palace	D 2-2	1-1	4	11270
29	21.2.89	H	Oxford U.	W 3-1	2-0	3	5724
30	25.2.89	A	Barnsley	W 1-0	0-0	3	8777
31	28.2.89	H	Sunderland	D 2-2	0-2	3	8288
32	4.3.89	A	Brighton & H.A.	L 0-3	0-0	3	8075
33	11.3.89	H	Plymouth Arg.	L 1-2	0-1	3	7462
34	15.3.89	A	West Bromwich A.	L 0-2	0-1	4	12821
35	18.3.89	H	Hull C.	W 4-0	1-0	4	5864
36	24.3.89	A	Oldham Ath.	D 1-1	0-1	4	11752
37	27.3.89	H	Leeds U.	W 2-0	0-0	4	11533
38	1.4.89	A	Swindon T.	D 1-1	0-0	4	8220
39	4.4.89	A	Watford	D 2-2	0-0	4	8667
40	8.4.89	H	Leicester C.	D 0-0	0-0	3	8080
41	15.4.89	H	Manchester C.	W 4-0	2-0	3	16927
42	22.4.89	A	Birmingham C.	L 0-2	0-0	5	5813
43	29.4.89	A	Portsmouth	W 2-1	0-0	5	6057
44	1.5.89	H	Bournemouth	W 2-0	1-0	5	9345
45	6.5.89	H	Walsall	W 3-0	0-0	3	8236
46	13.5.89	A	Ipswich T.	L 0-2	0-1	5	10861

Players: League Record, 1988-89 (Division 2)

Match Number	1	2	3	4	5	6	7	8	9	10	11	12	13	14	15	16	17	18	19	20	21	22	23
Ainscow, Alan	★	★	★				★	4	4	4	4	**4**	**4**	★									★
Atkins, Mark	2	2	2	2	2	2	2	2	2	2	2	2	2	2	2	2	2	**2**	2	2	2	2	2
Byrne, David																							
Collier, Darren																							
Curry, Sean						★	★					★	★	**9**									
Dawson, Alistair			★									★		4				★		3	**3**		
Diamond, Anthony																							
Finnigan, Tony	**4**	4	4	4	4	4	**4**															★	4
Garner, Simon	10	10^{3}	10	10	10^{2}	10^{1}	10	10	10^{2}	10	10^{1}	10	10	10^{1}	10	10	10	10	10^{1}	10	**10**	10	10
Gayle, Howard	9^{2}	9	9	9	9	**9**	9	9	7^{2}	**7^{1}**	7	9	9	7	7	7	7	7^{2}	**7**	7^{1}	7^{1}	7	**7**
Gennoe, Terry	1	1	1	1	1	1	1	1	1	1	1	1	1	1	1	1	1	1	1	1	1		
Hendry, Colin	5	5	5^{1}	5	5^{1}	5^{1}	5	5^{1}	5^{1}	5	5	5				5	5	5^{1}	5	5	5	5	5
Hildersley, Ron	8	**8**	**8**												4	4	4	4	8	8	8^{1}	**8**	8
Hill, Keith													5^{1}	5	5								★
Kennedy, Andy								★	9	9^{1}	**9**			★^{1}	9^{2}	9^{2}	9	**9**	9	9	9	**9**	
Mail, David	6	6	6	6	6	6	6	6	6	6	6	6	6	6	6	6	6	6	6	6	6	6	**6**
May, David																							
Millar, John	3	3	3	3	3	3	3	3	3	3	3	3	3	**3**	3	3	3	3	3		★	3	3
Miller, Ian	7	7	7	7	7	7	**7**	**7**		★	★	**7**	7					★	★		★	★	9
O'Keefe, Vince																						1	1
Reid, Nicky				8	8	8	8	8	8	8	8	8	8	8^{1}	8	8	8	8	4	4	4	4	
Sellars, Scott	11	11	**11**	11	11	11	11	11	11	11	11	11	11	11	11	11	11	11	11	11	11	11	11
Sulley, Chris																							
Own Goals						1																	

Match Number	24	25	26	27	28	29	30	31	32	33	34	35	36	37	38	39	40	41	42	43	44	45	46	Apps	Subs	Goals
Ainscow, Alan	★	★																					★	6	9	0
Atkins, Mark	2^{1}	2	2	2^{1}	2	2	2	2^{1}	2	2	2	2	2	2	2	2^{1}	2	2	2	2	2^{1}	2	2	46	0	5
Byrne, David							9	**9**	9	9														4	0	0
Collier, Darren																							1	1	0	0
Curry, Sean																					★	★		1	6	0
Dawson, Alistair																								3	3	0
Diamond, Anthony		★			★	★	★	★	★	**10**	★		★	★	★									1	10	0
Finnigan, Tony	4	**4**	4	4	4			★	★	★														13	4	0
Garner, Simon	10	10	10	10	**10**	10	**10^{1}**	10	**10**	★	10	10^{1}	10^{1}			**10**	**10**	10^{3}	10	10	10^{1}	10^{1}	10	43	1	19
Gayle, Howard	7^{1}		7	7^{1}	7^{1}	7	7	7	7	7	7	7^{2}	7	7^{1}	7^{1}	7^{1}	7	7	7	7^{2}	7	**7**	7	45	0	19
Gennoe, Terry	1	1	1	1	1	1	1	1	1	1	1	1	1	1	1	1	1	1	1	1	1	1		43	0	0
Hendry, Colin	5			5	5	5^{1}	5	5	**5**	5	5	5	**5**	5				5	5	5	5	5	5	38	0	7
Hildersley, Ron	8^{1}	8^{1}	8	8	8	8	8	8	8	8^{1}	**8**		★	★										23	2	4
Hill, Keith		5	5^{1}						6	**6**	★	6	6	6	5	5	5							13	2	2
Kennedy, Andy	9^{1}	**9**	**9**									9^{1}	9	**9^{1}**	**9**	9	9	9^{1}	9	**9**				23	2	10
Mail, David	**6**	6	6	6	6	6	6	6			**6**					6	6	6	6	6	6	6	6	40	0	0
May, David															6									1	0	0
Millar, John						3^{1}	3	**3**	3			8	8	**8**	8	8	8	8	8	8	8	8	8	37	1	1
Miller, Ian		7	★	9	9^{1}	**9**					9			10	10	★	★			★	**9**	9	9	21	10	1
O'Keefe, Vince																								2	0	0
Reid, Nicky						4	4	4	4	4	4	4	4	4	4	4	4	4	4	4	4	4	4	37	0	1
Sellars, Scott	11	11	11	11	11	11	11	11	11	11	11	11	**11**	11	11	11	11	11	11	11	11	11^{2}	11	46	0	2
Sulley, Chris	3	3	3	3	3					3	3	3	3	3	3	3	3	3	3	3	3	3	**3**	19	0	0
Own Goals						1		1																		3

FA Cup: 1988-89: 3rd Round: Welling (A) 1-0; 4th Round: Sheffield Wed. (H) 2-1; 5th Round: Brentford (H) 0-2.
Littlewoods Cup: 1988-89: 2nd Round: Brentford (H) 3-1, (A) 3-4; 3rd Round: Tottenham H. (A) 0-0 Replay (H) 1-2.

BLACKPOOL (Division 3)

Team Manager Jimmy Mullen.
Club Address Bloomfield Road Ground, Blackpool FY1 6JJ. Tel: (0253) 404331.
Current Ground Capacity 12,696.
Record Attendance 39,118 v Manchester U., Div. 1, April 1952.
Year Formed 1887. Turned professional 1887.
Previous Names South Shore.
Club Nickname "The Seasiders".
Club Colours All tangerine with white trim.
Club Honours Football League: Div. 2 Champions 1929-30. FA Cup: Winners 1953.
League History 1896-99 Div. 2; 1899 Failed re-election; 1900-30 Div. 2; 1930-33 Div. 1; 1933-37 Div. 2; 1937-67 Div. 1; 1967-70 Div. 2; 1970-71 Div. 1; 1971-78 Div. 2; 1978-81 Div. 3; 1981-85 Div. 4; 1985- Div. 3.

Most League Points in a Season (2 for a win) 58 in Div. 2, 1929-30. (3 for a win) 86 in Div. 4, 1984-85.
Most League Goals in a Season 98 in Div. 2, 1929-30.
Record Victory 10-0 v Lanerossi Vicenza in Anglo-Italian Tournament, 10 June 1972.
Record Defeat 1-10 v Small Heath in Div. 2, 2 March 1901 and v Huddersfield T. in Div. 1, 13 December 1930.
Consecutive League Wins 9 in 1936-37.
Consecutive League Defeats 8 in 1898-99.
Record League Appearances Jimmy Armfield, 568 between 1954-71.
Record League Goalscorer—Career Jimmy Hampson, 247 between 1927-38.
Record League Goalscorer—Season Jimmy Hampson, 45 in Div. 2, 1929-30.

Blackpool: League Record, 1988-89 (Division 3)

Match Number	Date	Venue	Opponents	Result	H/T	Lge Posn	Attend
1	27.8.88	A	Chester C.	D 1-1	0-1		3496
2	3.9.88	H	Notts Co.	L 0-1	0-0	20	4669
3	10.9.88	A	Preston N.E.	L 0-1	0-0	22	8779
4	17.9.88	H	Mansfield T.	D 1-1	0-1	22	4012
5	20.9.88	H	Bristol C.	D 2-2	1-2	20	3412
6	24.9.88	A	Chesterfield	W 2-0	0-0	17	2128
7	30.9.88	A	Wigan Ath.	L 1-2	0-1	20	4141
8	4.10.88	H	Northampton T.	W 3-1	1-0	17	3034
9	8.10.88	A	Bolton W.	D 2-2	1-1	18	7106
10	15.10.88	H	Sheffield U.	L 1-2	1-1	18	8471
11	22.10.88	H	Port Vale	W 3-2	1-2	16	7045
12	25.10.88	A	Wolverhampton W.	L 1-2	0-1	16	12104
13	29.10.88	H	Cardiff C.	W 1-0	0-0	16	3849
14	5.11.88	A	Fulham	D 1-1	0-0	16	4760
15	8.11.88	A	Gillingham	L 0-1	0-1	16	3541
16	12.11.88	H	Aldershot	W 4-0	2-0	15	2690
17	26.11.88	H	Swansea C.	D 0-0	0-0	16	3443
18	3.12.88	A	Huddersfield T.	D 1-1	0-0	16	5738
19	17.12.88	H	Bristol Rov.	D 1-1	0-0	16	3240
20	26.12.88	A	Brentford	L 0-1	0-0	17	6021
21	30.12.88	A	Reading	L 1-2	1-2	17	5554
22	2.1.89	H	Bury	D 2-2	1-0	18	4199
23	14.1.89	A	Notts Co.	D 1-1	1-0	17	4748
24	21.1.89	H	Preston N.E.	W 1-0	0-0	16	8951
25	28.1.89	A	Mansfield T.	W 1-0	0-0	15	2738
26	4.2.89	H	Wigan Ath.	W 2-0	0-0	12	4221
27	11.2.89	A	Northampton T.	L 2-4	1-2	15	3303
28	18.2.89	H	Bolton W.	W 2-0	0-0	11	5552
29	25.2.89	A	Sheffield U.	L 1-4	0-3	13	11317
30	28.2.89	H	Wolverhampton W.	L 0-2	0-0	15	6482
31	4.3.89	A	Port Vale	L 0-1	0-1	17	6306
32	11.3.89	H	Fulham	L 0-1	0-0	18	3014
33	18.3.89	H	Chester C.	D 1-1	0-0	19	2795
34	25.3.89	A	Bury	D 0-0	0-0	19	3717
35	27.3.89	H	Brentford	L 0-3	0-0	19	3053
36	1.4.89	A	Bristol Rov.	L 0-1	0-0	20	5355
37	4.4.89	A	Southend U.	L 1-2	1-1	21	2795
38	8.4.89	H	Reading	L 2-4	0-1	21	2792
39	15.4.89	A	Bristol C.	W 2-1	0-1	21	5090
40	22.4.89	H	Chesterfield	L 1-2	0-0	22	3221
41	29.4.89	A	Aldershot	L 0-1	0-1	22	1763
42	1.5.89	H	Gillingham	W 4-1	1-1	22	2152
43	6.5.89	H	Huddersfield T.	W 2-1	1-0	22	4070
44	9.5.89	H	Southend U.	W 3-2	3-0	20	3999
45	13.5.89	A	Swansea C.	W 2-1	1-1	19	3494
46	16.5.89	A	Cardiff C.	D 0-0	0-0	19	3426

Players: League Record, 1988-89 (Division 3)

Match Number	1	2	3	4	5	6	7	8	9	10	11	12	13	14	15	16	17	18	19	20	21	22	23
Burgess, David	3	3	2	2	2	2	2	2	2	2	2	2	2	2	2	2	2	2	2	2	2	2	2
Coughlin, Russell	10	10	10	**10**	**10**	10	10	10	10	10^1	10^1	**10**	10	10	10	10^1	10	10	10	10	10	10^1	10
Cunningham, Tony	8^1	8	8	8	**8**	8	8	8	8^1	8	8^1	8	8	8	8	8	8	8^1	8	8	8^1	8^1	8
Davies, Michael	7	7	7	7	7^1	7										7			★	7	7	7	7
Deary, John	4	4	4	4	4	4	4	4^1	4	4	4	4	4	4	4	4^1	**4**	4	4	4		★	
Elliott, Shaun	6	6	6	6	6	6	6	**6**			6	6	6	6	6	6	6	6	6	6	6	6	6
Garner, Andy	**9**	**9**	9	9^1	9	9^1	9	9	9	9	9	9	9^1	9^1	9	9^2	9	9	9^1	9	9	9	9
Gore, Ian	2	**2**							6	6	★	11	7	7	7								4
Kelly, Gary									1	1	1	1	1										
Madden, Craig								★	★	★	★^{1}	5	**11**				★	★	7	**11**			
Matthews, Neil							★	7	7		**7**	**7**					★						
Methven, Colin	5	5	**5**	5	5	5	5	5	5	5	**5**	★	5	5	5	**5**	5	5	5	5	5	5	5
Morgan, Stephen		11	3	**3**	3	**3**	3	3	3^1	3	3	3^1	3	3	**3**	3	3	3	**3**	**3**	3	3	3^1
O'Keefe, Vince																							
Rooney, Simon																							
Siddall, Barry	1	1	1	1	1	1	1	1						1	1	1	1	1	1	1	1	1	1
Taylor, Mark			11	11	11^1	**11**^{1}	11^1								★	**11**	11	**11**					
Thompson, Chris		★	★	★	★	★		★^{1}	**11**	**11**	11	★		11	**11**			★	11				
Walsh, Mick																	7	**7**		★	4	**4**	
Walwyn, Keith	★	★		★	★	★	**7**			7			★		★	★				★	★	★	11
Wright, Alan	11							**11**								★					**11**	**11**	
Own Goals								1															

Match Number	24	25	26	27	28	29	30	31	32	33	34	35	36	37	38	39	40	41	42	43	44	45	46	Apps	Subs	Goals
Burgess, David	2	2	2	2	2	2	2	2	2	2	2	2	2	2	2	2	2	2	2	2	2	2	2	46	0	0
Coughlin, Russell			★	6	6	4	4	4	4	4	4	4	4		4	4	10	10	10	**10**	10	10^1	10	42	1	5
Cunningham, Tony	8	8	8	8	8^1	8	8	8																31	0	7
Davies, Michael	7	7	**7**		★	★	11	11	11	11	**11**	11	★	7	7^1	7	7	7			★			25	5	2
Deary, John	10	5	5^2	7	7	7	7	7	7	7^1	7	7		4	10	10				★				35	2	2
Elliott, Shaun	6	6	6			6	6	6	6	6	6	6	6	6	6	6	6	6	6	**6**	6		6	41	0	0
Garner, Andy	9	9	9	9	9	9^1	9	9	9	9	9		9	9	9^1	9	9^1	9	9^1				★	41	1	11
Gore, Ian	4	4	4	**4**	**4**						10	**8**	**7**			11	11			★				19	2	0
Kelly, Gary																								5	0	0
Madden, Craig	11	11^1	11	**11**	**11**						8	9	8	8	8	8	4	★		9^1	9^1	9	9	20	7	4
Matthews, Neil												★				**3**		★	7^1	7	**7**	7	7	10	4	1
Methven, Colin	**5**			5	5	**5**	**5**	**5**	5	5	5	5	5	5^1	5	5		5	5	5	5	5		41	1	1
Morgan, Stephen	3	3	3	3	3	3	3	3	3	3	3	3	3	**3**	**3**		★	3	3	3	3	3	3	43	1	3
O'Keefe, Vince					1	1	1	1	1	1														6	0	0
Rooney, Simon														★										0	1	0
Siddall, Barry	1	1	1	1							1	1	1	1	1	1	1	1	1	1	1	1	1	35	0	0
Taylor, Mark																								8	1	3
Thompson, Chris	★^{1}	10	10	10^2	10^1	**10**	10	10	**10**	10	★	10	10	10	★		**5**	4	4	4^1	4^2	4	4	25	11	8
Walsh, Mick				★		★																6	5	6	3	0
Walwyn, Keith	★			★	★	11	★	★	8	8						★^{2}	8	**8**	8^1	8	8	8	**8**	13	17	3
Wright, Alan									★				11	11	11		3	**11**	11	11	11	11	11	14	2	0
Own Goals																			1			1				3

FA Cup: 1988-89: 1st Round: Scunthorpe U. (H) 2-1; 2nd Round: Bury (H) 3-0; 3rd Round: Bournemouth (H) 0-1.

Littlewoods Cup: 1988-89: 1st Round: Carlisle U. (A) 1-1 (H) 3-0; 2nd Round: Sheffield Wed. (H) 2-0 (A) 1-3; 3rd Round: Tranmere Rov. (A) 0-1.

BOLTON WANDERERS (Division 3)

Team Manager Phil Neal.
Club Address Burnden Park, Bolton BL3 2QR. Tel: (0204) 389200.
Current Ground Capacity 25,000.
Record Attendance 69,912 v Manchester C., FA Cup 5th Round, 18 February 1933.
Year Formed 1874. Turned professional 1880.
Previous Names Christ Church.
Club Nickname "The Trotters".
Club Colours White shirts, navy blue shorts and white stockings.
Club Honours Football League: Div. 2 Champions 1908-09, 1977-78. Div. 3 Champions 1972-73. FA Cup: Winners 1923, 1926, 1929, 1958.
League History 1888-99 Div. 1; 1899-1900 Div. 2; 1900-03 Div.1; 1903-05 Div. 2; 1905-08 Div. 1; 1908-09 Div. 2; 1909-10 Div. 1; 1910-11 Div. 2; 1911-33 Div. 1; 1933-35 Div. 2; 1935-64 Div 1; 1964-71 Div. 2; 1971-73 Div. 3; 1973-78 Div. 2; 1978-80 Div..1; 1980-83 Div. 2; 1983-87 Div. 3; 1987-88 Div. 4; 1988- Div.3.
Most League Points in a Season (2 for a win) 61 in Div. 3, 1972-73. (3 for a win) 78 in Div. 4, 1987-88.
Most League Goals in a Season 96 in Div. 2, 1934-35.
Record Victory 13-0 v Sheffield U. in FA Cup 2nd Round, 1 February 1890.
Record Defeat 0-7 v Manchester C. in Div. 1, 21 March 1936.
Consecutive League Wins 11 in 1904.
Consecutive League Defeats 10 in 1902-03.
Record League Appearances Eddie Hopkinson, 519 between 1956-70.
Record League Goalscorer—Career Nat Lofthouse, 255 between 1946-61.
Record League Goalscorer—Season Joe Smith, 38 in Div. 1, 1920-21.

Bolton Wanderers: League Record, 1988-89 (Division 3)

Match Number	Date	Venue	Opponents	Result	H/T	Lge Posn	Attend
1	27.8.88	A	Southend U.	L 0-2	0-1		4075
2	3.9.88	H	Cardiff C.	W 4-0	0-0	10	4831
3	10.9.88	A	Reading	D 1-1	0-0	10	4660
4	17.9.88	H	Bristol Rov.	D 1-1	1-0	10	4821
5	20.9.88	H	Fulham	W 3-2	1-1	7	4239
6	24.9.88	A	Aldershot	W 3-0	1-0	5	2126
7	1.10.88	H	Sheffield U.	W 2-0	1-0	3	9345
8	4.10.88	A	Swansea C.	L 0-1	0-0	3	3283
9	8.10.88	H	Blackpool	D 2-2	1-1	4	7106
10	15.10.88	A	Port Vale	L 1-2	1-1	9	7985
11	22.10.88	H	Wolverhampton W.	L 1-2	1-0	14	8174
12	25.10.88	A	Wigan Ath.	D 1-1	0-0	13	4438
13	29.10.88	H	Chesterfield	W 5-0	2-0	12	4757
14	5.11.88	A	Bristol C.	D 1-1	0-1	12	8807
15	8.11.88	A	Huddersfield T.	W 1-0	0-0	10	7802
16	12.11.88	H	Bury	L 2-4	0-2	12	7897
17	26.11.88	H	Northampton T.	W 2-1	0-1	9	4446
18	3.12.88	A	Brentford	L 0-3	0-1	12	4628
19	17.12.88	H	Chester C.	L 0-1	0-0	13	4318
20	26.12.88	A	Preston N.E.	L 1-3	0-2	15	12104
21	31.12.88	A	Notts Co.	L 0-2	0-2	15	5097
22	2.1.89	H	Mansfield T.	D 0-0	0-0	15	4935
23	6.1.89	H	Gillingham	W 2-1	1-0	15	4187
24	14.1.89	A	Cardiff C.	L 0-1	0-0	15	4212
25	21.1.89	H	Reading	D 1-1	0-0	15	5172
26	28.1.89	A	Bristol Rov.	L 0-2	0-1	16	5375
27	4.2.89	A	Sheffield U.	L 0-4	0-0	18	11162
28	11.2.89	H	Swansea C.	W 1-0	0-0	17	4178
29	18.2.89	A	Blackpool	L 0-2	0-0	17	5552
30	4.3.89	A	Wolverhampton W.	L 0-1	0-1	19	13516
31	11.3.89	H	Bristol C.	W 2-0	0-0	19	4423
32	14.3.89	A	Chesterfield	D 1-1	0-1	18	2877
33	18.3.89	H	Southend U.	D 0-0	0-0	17	3505
34	25.3.89	A	Mansfield T.	D 1-1	1-1	17	3253
35	27.3.89	H	Preston N.E.	W 1-0	1-0	17	10281
36	1.4.89	A	Chester C.	D 0-0	0-0	16	3225
37	4.4.89	A	Gillingham	W 1-0	1-0	16	3096
38	8.4.89	H	Notts Co.	D 3-3	0-3	16	4521
39	15.4.89	A	Fulham	D 1-1	0-0	16	4950
40	22.4.89	H	Aldershot	W 1-0	0-0	15	4407
41	25.4.89	H	Port Vale	D 1-1	1-0	15	5296
42	29.4.89	A	Bury	D 0-0	0-0	14	4393
43	1.5.89	H	Huddersfield T.	W 3-1	1-0	13	5511
44	6.5.89	H	Brentford	W 4-2	3-2	10	4627
45	9.5.89	H	Wigan Ath.	D 1-1	1-0	10	6166
46	13.5.89	A	Northampton T.	W 3-2	0-2	10	3655

Players: League Record, 1988-89 (Division 3)

Match Number	1	2	3	4	5	6	7	8	9	10	11	12	13	14	15	16	17	18	19	20	21	22	23	24	25	26	27	28	29	30	31	32	33	34	35	36	37	38	39	40	41	42	43	44	45	46	Apps	Subs	Goals
Barnes, Peter																									★	11	**11**																				2	1	0
Brookman, Nicky	7	4				★^{1}		★		8^1	5	11^1	7	5	5	5	4^1	4	10	★				★	4	4	4	7	**7**	7	**4**		★					11									20	5	4
Brown, Philip	2	2	2	2^1	2	2	2	2	2	2	2	2	2^2	2	2	2^1	2	2	2	2	2	2	2	2	2	2	2	2	2	2	2	2	2	2	2	2	2	2	2	2	2	2	2	2	2	2	46	0	4
Came, Mark	5	5																																													2	0	0
Chandler, Jeff																		★			7	★	11	11	**11**						7	★	★	7	7	11	7	7	**7**	**7**	7^1	**7**	7^1	**7**			16	4	2
Cowdrill, Barry	3	3	3	3	3	3							3	3	3	3	3	3	3	3	3	3	3	3	3	3	3	3	3	3	3	3	3	3	3	**3**			3	3	3	3	3	3	3	3	38	0	0
Crombie, Dean			7	★			3	3	3	3	**3**	3	★	7	7	7	5	5								★				5	5	5	5	5	5		5	6	5	5	5	5	5	5	5	**5**	28	3	0
Darby, Julian	4	11^2	11	11	11	11	11	11	11	11	11	5	11	11	11	11	11	11	11	11	11	11	4	4			7	11	11	11	11^2	11	11	11	11	5	11	5	11	11	11	11	11	11^1	11	11	44	0	5
Elliott, Steve	10	10		**10**																																											3	0	0
Felgate, David	1	1	1	1	1	1	1	1	1	1	1	1	1	1	1	1	1	1	1	1	1	1	1	1	1	1	1	1	1	1	1	1	1	1	1	1	1	1	1	1	1	1	1	1	1	1	46	0	0
Henshaw, Gary	★	7^1	4	4	7	7	7	**7**	7	7	7	7					★		**7**	**7**				★	7^1	**7**				★						7										★	16	5	2
Jeffrey, Michael																														**10**	10	**10**	10	**10**	10	**10**				★		★					7	2	0
Jemson, Nigel																				10	10	**10**	★	**10**																							4	1	0
Keeley, Glenn			5	5	5	5	5	5	5	5			5						5	5	5	5	5	5	5	5	5	5	5																		20	0	0
Morgan, Trevor			10	★	10^1	9	9	9	9^1	9	9^1	9	9^2	9^1	9^1	9	9	**9**	9	9	9	9	9	9	9	**9**	9	9	9					★	★	★		★^{1}	10^1	**10**	10	10	10^1	10	**10**	10	34	5	10
Neal, Phil											★					★											★			★						★	3	**3**	6								3	5	0
Savage, Rob	11				4^1	**4**	4	4	4	4	4	4	**4**	**4**	4	**4**		★	4	4^1	**4**	**4**				8	8	4^1	4	**4**		4	**4**	4^1	**4**	4	4	4	4	4^1	4	4	4	4^1	4	4	37	1	6
Stevens, Ian	**9**				★	10^2	10	10	**10**		★	10	10^1	10	**10**	10	10^1	10	★			★	**10^1**			★											10	**10**							★		15	6	5
Storer, Stuart				**7**									★	★	★	★	**7**	**7**			★	7	7	**7**					★		★	7	**7**		★			★	★	★		★		★	7^1	7^1	10	13	2
Thomas, John		9^1	9^1	9	**9**				★	10	**10**														10	10	10	10	10	9	9	9	9	9	**9**	9	9^1	9^1	9	9	9	**9**	9^1	9^2	9	9^2	28	1	9
Thompson, Steve	8	8	8	8	8^1	8	8^2	8	8^1		8	8	8	8	8	8^1	8	8	8	8	8	8	8^1	8	8			8	8	8	8	8^1	8	8	8^1	8	8	8^1	8	8	8	8	8	8	8	8	43	0	9
Winstanley, Mark	6	6	6	6	6	6	6	6	6	6	6	6	**6**	6	6	**6**	6	6	6	6	6	6	6	6	6	6	6	6	6	6	6	6	6	6	6	6	6			6	6	6	6	6	6	6	44	0	0
Own Goals																																																	0

FA Cup: 1988-89: 1st Round: Chesterfield (H) 0-0, Replay 3-2; 2nd Round: Port Vale (H) 1-2.
Littlewoods Cup: 1988-89: 1st Round: Chester C. (H) 1-0 (A) 1-3.

BOURNEMOUTH (Division 2)

Team Manager Harry Redknapp.
Club Address Dean Court Ground, Bournemouth. Tel: (0202) 35381.
Current Ground Capacity 12,708.
Record Attendance 28,799 v Manchester U., FA Cup 6th Round, 2 March 1957.
Year Formed 1899. Turned professional 1912.
Previous Names Boscombe St Johns, Boscombe, Bournemouth and Boscombe Ath.
Club Nickname "The Cherries".
Club Colours All red with white trim.
Club Honours Football League: Div. 3 Champions 1986-87.
League History 1923-58 Div. 3(S); 1958-70 Div. 3; 1970-71 Div. 4; 1971-75 Div. 3; 1975-82 Div. 4; 1982-87 Div. 3; 1987- Div. 2.
Most League Points in a Season (2 for a win) 62 in Div. 3, 1971-72. (3 for a win) 97 in Div. 3, 1986-87.
Most League Goals in a Season 88 in Div. 3(S), 1956-57.
Record Victory 11-0 v Margate in FA Cup 1st Round, 20 November 1971.
Record Defeat 0-9 v Lincoln C. in Div. 3, 18 December 1982.
Consecutive League Wins 7 in 1970.
Consecutive League Defeats 7 in 1955.
Record League Appearances Ray Bumstead, 414 between 1958-70.
Record League Goalscorer—Career Ron Eyre, 202 between 1924-33.
Record League Goalscorer—Season Ted MacDougall, 42 in Div. 4, 1970-71.

Bournemouth: League Record, 1988-89 (Division 2)

Match Number	Date	Venue	Opponents	Result	H/T	Lge Posn	Attend
1	27.8.88	A	Sunderland	D 1-1	1-1		17998
2	3.9.88	H	Chelsea	W 1-0	0-0	11	8763
3	10.9.88	A	Brighton & H.A.	W 2-1	2-0	8	8247
4	17.9.88	H	Leeds U.	D 0-0	0-0	7	7922
5	20.9.88	A	Swindon T.	L 1-3	1-2	8	8055
6	24.9.88	H	Oxford U.	W 2-1	1-0	7	6532
7	1.10.88	A	Stoke C.	L 1-2	0-1	10	7485
8	5.10.88	A	West Bromwich A.	D 0-0	0-0	11	7248
9	8.10.88	H	Birmingham C.	L 0-1	0-1	15	6186
10	15.10.88	A	Portsmouth	L 1-2	0-1	18	12801
11	21.10.88	H	Shrewsbury T.	L 0-1	0-1	20	5449
12	25.10.88	A	Oldham Ath.	L 0-2	0-1	20	4518
13	29.10.88	H	Ipswich T.	W 1-0	0-0	18	6648
14	5.11.88	A	Bradford C.	W 1-0	0-0	17	9067
15	12.11.88	H	Crystal Palace	W 2-0	1-0	13	8697
16	19.11.88	H	Manchester C.	L 0-1	0-1	15	9874
17	26.11.88	A	Barnsley	L 2-5	0-2	19	4937
18	29.11.88	H	Hull C.	W 5-1	0-0	13	5420
19	3.12.88	H	Blackburn Rov.	W 2-1	0-0	8	8418
20	10.12.88	A	Plymouth Arg.	D 1-1	0-0	11	10619
21	17.12.88	H	Walsall	W 2-1	1-0	8	6985
22	26.12.88	A	Leicester C.	W 1-0	0-0	7	13896
23	31.12.88	A	Watford	L 0-1	0-0	9	14006
24	2.1.89	H	Brighton & H.A.	W 2-1	0-1	6	10627
25	14.1.89	A	Hull C.	L 0-4	0-3	10	5690
26	21.1.89	H	Sunderland	L 0-1	0-1	12	8992
27	4.2.89	H	West Bromwich A.	W 2-1	1-1	11	11571
28	11.2.89	A	Birmingham C.	W 1-0	0-0	6	6444
29	25.2.89	H	Portsmouth	W 1-0	0-0	6	9959
30	28.2.89	H	Oldham Ath.	D 2-2	1-1	7	7783
31	4.3.89	A	Crystal Palace	W 3-2	2-0	5	10022
32	11.3.89	H	Bradford C.	W 3-0	1-0	5	8122
33	14.3.89	A	Ipswich T.	L 1-3	0-3	6	10747
34	18.3.89	H	Swindon T.	L 2-3	0-2	8	9752
35	25.3.89	A	Chelsea	L 0-2	0-0	9	22467
36	27.3.89	H	Leicester C.	W 2-1	2-0	6	8913
37	1.4.89	A	Leeds U.	L 0-3	0-1	8	21095
38	4.4.89	A	Walsall	D 1-1	1-1	9	3619
39	8.4.89	H	Watford	L 0-1	0-1	9	9766
40	11.4.89	A	Shrewsbury T.	L 0-1	0-0	10	2457
41	15.4.89	H	Stoke C.	L 0-1	0-0	12	6834
42	22.4.89	A	Oxford U.	L 1-3	0-2	12	5684
43	29.4.89	H	Barnsley	W 3-2	1-1	11	5520
44	1.5.89	A	Blackburn Rov.	L 0-2	0-1	12	9345
45	6.5.89	A	Manchester C.	D 3-3	0-3	12	30564
46	13.5.89	H	Plymouth Arg.	D 0-0	0-0	12	7230

Players: League Record, 1988-89 (Division 2)

Match Number	1	2	3	4	5	6	7	8	9	10	11	12	13	14	15	16	17	18	19	20	21	22	23	24	25	26	27	28	29	30	31	32	33	34	35	36	37	38	39	40	41	42	43	44	45	46	Apps	Subs	Goals
Aylott, Trevor	9	9	9	9	9	9^{1}	9	9		9	9	**9**	9	9	9^{1}	9	9^{1}	9^{1}	**9**	9	9^{1}	9	9	9	9	9	9	9				**9**	9	9	★	9	9	9	9	9	9	9^{1}	9		**9**		39	1	6
Barnes, David																																			7	7	7	7	7	7	**7**	7	7	7			10	0	0
Bishop, Ian	10	10	10	10	10	10	10	**10**	10	10	10	10	10^{1}	10	10	10	10	10	10	10	10	10	10	10	10	10	10	10	10	10	10	10^{1}	10	10	10	10	10	10			10	10	10	10	10	10	44	0	2
Blissett, Luther																	11^{1}	11^{4}	11^{1}	11^{1}	11^{1}	11	11	11^{1}	11	11	11	11	11	11^{2}	11	11^{2}	11^{1}	11^{1}	11	11^{1}	11	11	11	11	11	11	11^{2}	11	11^{1}	11	30	0	19
Bond, Kevin	4	4	4	4	4^{1}	4	4	4	4	4	4	4	4	4	4	**4**	4	4	4	4	4	4	4	4	**4**	4	4																				27	0	1
Brooks, Shaun	8	8	8^{1}	8	8	8	8^{1}	8	8	8	★	**8**		8^{1}	8	8	**8**	8	8	6	6	6	8	8	**8**	**8**								★	★			★	8	8	★	8	★	★	8	8	29	7	3
Clarke, Colin																			$★^{1}$	8	8	8^{1}																									3	1	2
Close, Shaun	11^{1}				★	★	★	★	**11**	11^{1}		11	11	11	11	11		★							★	★			9	9	9	★	★		**9**									9	★		13	10	2
Coleman, David											★	3	3														8^{1}	8					★							**2**				5	★		6	3	1
Cooke, Richard	7	$\mathbf{7}^{1}$							★		11					★									★	★	$\mathbf{7}^{1}$	7	7	7	7^{1}	7	**7**	7													11	4	3
Holmes, Matthew																																											8	8	$\mathbf{7}^{1}$	7	4	0	1
Morrell, Paul	3	3	3	3	3	3	3	3	3	**3**	**3**			3	3	3	3	3	3	3	3	3	3	3	3	3	3	3	3	3	3	3	**3**	3	3	3	3	3	3	3	3	3	3	**3**	3	3	44	0	0
Mundee, Denny												★																																		9	1	1	0
Newson, Mark	2	2	2^{1}	2	2	2^{1}	2	2		2	2		2	2	2	2	2	2	2				2	2^{1}	2	2	2	2^{1}	2^{1}	2	2	2	2	2^{1}	2	2	2	2	2		2	2	2^{1}	2	2	2	40	0	7
O'Connor, Mark			7	7	**7**	7	11	11		★		7	7	7	7^{1}	7	7	7	7	7	7	7	7	7	7	**7**			8	8	8^{1}	8	8	**8**	**8**		★		10	★	★						29	4	2
O'Driscoll, Sean		★			★			★	2	7	7	2	8	6	6	6	6	**6**	6	2	2	2	6	6	6	6	6	6	6	6	6	6	6	6	6	6	**6**	6	6	6	6	6	6	6	6	6	38	3	0
Peyton, Gerry	1	1	1	1	1	1	1	1	1	1	1	1	1	1	1	1	1	1	1	1	1	1	1	1	1	1	1	1	1	1	1	1	1	1	1	1	1	1			1						39	0	0
Puckett, David									9	★	8	★																																			2	2	0
Pulis, Tony											5	5	6																							8	8	8	5	5	5	5					10	0	0
Richards, Carl		11	11	11	11	**11**	7	**7**	7																																						8	0	0
Shearer, Peter																																								10	**8**				5^{1}	5	4	0	1
Smeulders, John																																							1	1		1	1	1	1	1	7	0	0
Teale, Shaun																											★	4	4	4	4	4	4	4	4	4	4	4	4	4	4	4	4	4	4	4	19	1	0
Whitlock, Mark	6	6	6	6	**6**	6	**6**	6	6	6	**6**	6					★																														12	1	0
Williams, John	5	5	5	5	5	5	5	5	5	**5**			5	5	5	5	5	5	5	5	5	5	5	5	5	5	5	5	5	5	5^{1}	5	5	5	5	5	5	$\mathbf{5}^{1}$					**5**				37	0	2
Own Goals																																				1													1

FA Cup: 1988-89: 3rd Round: Blackpool (A) 1-0; 4th Round: Hartlepool U. (A) 1-1, Replay (H) 5-2; 5th Round: Manchester U. (H) 0-1.
Littlewoods Cup: 1988-89: 1st Round: Bristol Rov. (H) 1-0 (A) 0-0; 2nd Round: Coventry C. (H) 0-4 (A) 1-3.

BRADFORD CITY (Division 2)

Team Manager Terry Yorath.
Club Address Valley Parade Ground, Bradford BD8 7DY. Tel: (0274) 306062.
Current Ground Capacity 16,072.
Record Attendance 39,146 v Burnley, FA Cup 4th Round, 11 March 1911.
Year Formed 1903. Turned professional 1903.
Previous Names None.
Club Nickname "The Bantams".
Club Colours Claret and amber shirts, black shorts and amber stockings.
Club Honours Football League: Div. 2 Champions 1904-08; Div. 3 Champions 1984-85; Div. 3(N) Champions 1928-29. FA Cup: Winners 1911.
League History 1903-08 Div. 2; 1908-22 Div. 1; 1922-27 Div. 2; 1927-29 Div. 3(N); 1929-37 Div. 2; 1937-61 Div. 3; 1961-69 Div. 4; 1969-72 Div. 3; 1972-77 Div. 4; 1977-78 Div. 3; 1978-82 Div. 4; 1982-85 Div. 3; 1985- Div. 2.
Most League Points in a Season (2 for a win) 63 in Div. 3(N), 1928-29. (3 for win) 94 in Div. 3, 1984-85.
Most League Goals in a Season 128 in Div. 3(N), 1928-29.
Record Victory 11-1 v Rotherham U. in Div. 3(N), 25 August 1928.
Record Defeat 1-9 v Colchester U. in Div. 4, 30 December 1961.
Consecutive League Wins 10 in 1983-84.
Consecutive League Defeats 8 in 1933.
Record League Appearances Cec Podd, 502 between 1970-84.
Record League Goalscorer—Career Bobby Campbell, 121 between 1981-86.
Record League Goalscorer—Season David Layne, 34 in Div. 4, 1961-62.

Bradford City: League Record, 1988-89 (Division 2)

Match Number	Date	Venue	Opponents	Result	H/T	Lge Posn	Attend
1	27.8.88	A	Brighton & H.A.	W 3-1	1-1		10190
2	29.8.88	H	Stoke C.	D 0-0	0-0	4	11918
3	3.9.88	H	Shrewsbury T.	W 1-0	1-0	3	9765
4	10.9.88	A	Sunderland	D 0-0	0-0	4	16286
5	17.9.88	H	Oldham Ath.	W 2-0	2-0	2	12325
6	20.9.88	A	Watford	L 0-2	0-0	5	12296
7	24.9.88	A	Ipswich T.	D 1-1	0-0	5	13024
8	1.10.88	H	Portsmouth	W 2-1	2-1	4	11208
9	5.10.88	H	Blackburn Rov.	D 1-1	0-1	2	13022
10	8.10.88	A	Plymouth Arg.	L 1-3	0-3	6	6855
11	15.10.88	H	Crystal Palace	L 0-1	0-1	9	11098
12	22.10.88	A	West Bromwich A.	L 0-1	0-0	12	8989
13	26.10.88	H	Leeds U.	D 1-1	0-1	15	13048
14	29.10.88	A	Oxford U.	W 4-3	1-1	10	5303
15	5.11.88	H	Bournemouth	L 0-1	0-0	13	9067
16	12.11.88	A	Barnsley	D 0-0	0-0	12	8838
17	19.1.88	H	Chelsea	D 2-2	1-0	12	11442
18	26.11.88	A	Leicester C.	L 0-1	0-1	16	9553
19	3.12.88	H	Birmingham C.	D 2-2	1-1	19	9503
20	10.12.88	A	Manchester C.	L 0-4	0-1	20	20129
21	17.12.88	H	Swindon T.	D 2-2	1-2	18	9462
22	26.12.88	A	Hull C.	D 1-1	0-0	18	8791
23	31.12.88	A	Walsall	W 1-0	1-0	17	5366
24	21.1.89	H	Sunderland	W 1-0	0-0	17	12186
25	14.1.89	A	Stoke C.	L 1-2	1-2	18	9919
26	21.1.89	H	Brighton & H.A.	L 0-1	0-1	18	8183
27	4.2.89	A	Blackburn Rov.	L 1-2	1-0	18	9571
28	11.2.89	H	Plymouth Arg.	D 1-1	0-1	19	8693
29	18.2.89	H	West Bromwich A.	W 2-0	1-0	18	11047
30	25.2.89	A	Crystal Palace	L 0-2	0-1	18	7455
31	1.3.89	A	Leeds U.	D 3-3	2-2	19	33325
32	4.3.89	H	Barnsley	L 1-2	0-1	21	11805
33	11.3.89	A	Bournemouth	L 0-3	0-1	21	8122
34	15.3.89	H	Oxford U.	D 0-0	0-0	21	7553
35	18.3.89	H	Watford	W 2-1	0-0	19	10003
36	25.3.89	A	Shrewsbury T.	W 3-1	1-0	16	4575
37	27.3.89	H	Hull C.	D 1-1	1-1	17	11802
38	1.4.89	A	Oldham Ath.	D 1-1	0-0	16	8589
39	4.4.89	A	Swindon T.	L 0-1	0-1	19	6476
40	8.4.89	H	Walsall	W 3-1	1-1	18	8763
41	15.4.89	H	Ipswich T.	D 2-2	2-1	18	9691
42	22.4.89	A	Portsmouth	W 2-1	1-0	16	6909
43	29.4.89	H	Leicester C.	W 2-1	0-0	14	8703
44	1.5.89	A	Birmingham C.	L 0-1	0-1	14	4735
45	6.5.89	A	Chelsea	L 1-3	0-1	14	18003
46	13.5.89	H	Manchester C.	D 1-1	1-0	14	12479

Players: League Record, 1988-89 (Division 2)

Match Number	1	2	3	4	5	6	7	8	9	10	11	12	13	14	15	16	17	18	19	20	21	22	23
Abbott, Greg					★		**10**		★	★	★	7	4^{1}	4	**4**	**2**	★						
Banks, Ian	4^{1}	4	4	4	4	4	4	4	4	4	4	**4**			★	4	**4**	**4**	**4**	4	4	4	4
Campbell, David																							
Chapman, Gary											★		**7**										
Costello, Peter																			3	★			
Duxbury, Lee																							
Ellis, Mark																							
Evans, David	6	6	6	6	6	6	6	6	**6**		6	6	6	6						3	6	6	6
Evans, Mark																							
Goddard, Karl	3	3	3	3						3	**3**			3		3	3	3			**3**	**3**	
Graham, James																							
Jackson, Peter					**3**	3	3	3	3	6	5	3	3	5^{1}	5	**6**	6	6	6	**6**			3
Jewell, Paul	**11**	**11**	11	**11**		★		★	★	11^{1}	11	★	★	7	**7**				★^{1}	★	★^{1}	★	★
Kennedy, Mick	10	10	10	10	10	10		10	10	10	10	**10**	10	10^{1}	10	10	10	10	10	10	10	10	10
Leonard, Mark	★	★	★	★	11	11	11	**11**	11			11	11	11^{1}	11	11	11	11	11^{1}	**11**	11	11	**11^{1}**
Litchfield, Peter													1	1	1								
Mitchell, Brian	2	2	2	2	2	**2**	2^{1}	2	2	2	2	2	2	2	2	★	2	2	2	2	2	2	2
Oliver, Gavin	5	5	5	5	5	5	5	5	5	5		5	5		6	5	5	5	5	5	5	5	5
Ormondroyd, Ian	9^{1}	9	9^{1}	9	9	9	9	9	**9**	9	9	9	9	**9**	9	9	9^{2}	9	9	9	9	9	9
Palin, Leigh							★					★		8^{1}	8	7	7	7	7	7	7^{1}	7^{1}	7
Quinn, Jimmy																							
Sinnott, Lee	8	8	8	8	8	8	8	8^{1}	8	8	8	8	8		3	8	8	8	8	8	8	8	8
Thomas, Andy	7^{1}	7	**7**	7	7^{2}	7	7	7^{1}	7^{1}	**7**	**7**			★	★	★		★					
Tinnion, Brian																							
Tomlinson, Paul	1	1	1	1	1	1	1	1	1	1	1	1				1	1	1	1	1	1	1	1
Own Goals																							

Match Number	24	25	26	27	28	29	30	31	32	33	34	35	36	37	38	39	40	41	42	43	44	45	46	Apps	Subs	Goals
Abbott, Greg	3	**3**		4^{1}	4	4^{1}			4	4	4	4^{1}	4	4	4	4	4	4				11	11	23	5	4
Banks, Ian	4	**4^{1}**		★	★	11^{1}	4	4			★	**6**												26	4	3
Campbell, David												11	**6^{1}**	6	6	6	7	7	7	7	**7**	7	**7**	12	0	1
Chapman, Gary																								1	1	0
Costello, Peter			★		★^{1}	★	★	**7^{1}**	**7**															3	5	2
Duxbury, Lee																							★	0	1	0
Ellis, Mark																		★	11	**11**	**11**		8^{1}	4	1	1
Evans, David	6	6	**6**	**6**	6	6	**6**		★	**6**	6						6	6	6	6	6	6	6	33	1	0
Evans, Mark					1														1			1		3	0	0
Goddard, Karl				**10**	**10**			★		★		★	**11**	**11**	**11**	**11**				★	★			18	5	0
Graham, James							★																	0	1	0
Jackson, Peter	5	5	5	5	5	5	5	5^{1}	5	5			★						★	5^{1}	5		5	30	2	3
Jewell, Paul	★	★	9	11	11	10	11	11	11	11	11		★	★	★	★	11^{1}	**11**	8^{1}	8	8	★		22	17	5
Kennedy, Mick	**10**	10	10				10	10	10	10	10													30	0	1
Leonard, Mark	11^{1}	11	11	9	9	**9**	9	9	9^{1}	9	9	9^{1}	9	9	9	9	9	9^{1}	9	9	9	9	9	40	4	7
Litchfield, Peter																				1	1			5	0	0
Mitchell, Brian	2	2	2	2	2	2	2	2	2	2	2	2	2	2	2	2	2	2	2	2		2	2	44	1	1
Oliver, Gavin		★	3	3	**3**	3	3	3	**3**		**5**	5	5	5	5	5	5	5^{1}	**5**			5		38	1	1
Ormondroyd, Ian	9	9																						25	0	4
Palin, Leigh	7	7	7	7				**6**	6	7	7	7	7	7	7	7			4^{1}	4	4	4	4	28	2	4
Quinn, Jimmy												10	10^{2}	10^{1}	10^{1}	10	10^{1}	10	10	10^{1}	10	10^{1}	10	12	0	7
Sinnott, Lee	8	8	8	8	8	8	8	8^{1}	8	8	8	8	8	8	8	8	8	8			2	**8**		42	0	2
Thomas, Andy			4	★	7	7	**7**	★	★												★			15	8	5
Tinnion, Brian										3	3	3	3	3	3	3	3^{1}	3	3	3	3	3	3	14	0	1
Tomlinson, Paul	1	1	1	1		1	1	1	1	1	1	1	1	1	1	1	1	1					1	38	0	0
Own Goals																										0

FA Cup: 1988-89: 3rd Round: Tottenham H. (H) 1-0; 4th Round: Hull C. (H) 1-2.

Littlewoods Cup: 1988-89: 2nd Round: Reading (A) 1-1, (H) 2-1; 3rd Round: Scunthorpe U. (H) 1-1, Replay (A) 1-0; 4th Round: Everton (H) 3-1; Quarter-Final: Bristol C. (H) 0-1.

BRENTFORD (Division 3)

Team Manager Steve Perryman.
Club Address Griffin Park, Braemer Road, Brentford, Middlesex TW8 0NT. Tel: 01-847 2511.
Current Ground Capacity 12,041.
Record Attendance 39,626 v Preston N.E., FA Cup 6th Round, 5 March 1938.
Year Formed 1889. Turned professional 1899.
Previous Names None.
Club Nickname "The Bees".
Club Colours Red and white striped shirts, black shorts and red stockings with white tops.
Club Honours Football League: Div. 2 Champions 1934-35; Div. 3(S) Champions 1932-33; Div. 4 Champions 1962-63.
League History 1920-33 Div. 3(S); 1933-35 Div. 2; 1935-47 Div. 1; 1947-54 Div. 2; 1954-62 Div. 3(S); 1962-63 Div. 4; 1963-66 Div. 3; 1966-72 Div. 4; 1972-73 Div. 3; 1973-78 Div. 4; 1978- Div. 3.
Most League Points in a Season (2 for a win) 62 in Div. 3(S), 1932-33 and in Div. 4, 1962-63. (3 for a win) 68 in Div. 3, 1981-82 and in Div. 3, 1987-88.
Most League Goals in a Season 98 in Div. 4, 1962-63.
Record Victory 9-0 v Wrexham in Div. 3, 15 October 1963.
Record Defeat 0-7 v Swansea T. in Div. 3(S), 8 November 1924 and v Walsall in Div. 3(S), 19 January 1957.
Consecutive League Wins 9 in 1932.
Consecutive League Defeats 9 in 1925 and 1928.
Record League Appearances Ken Coote, 513 between 1949-64.
Record League Goalscorer—Career Jim Towers, 153 between 1954-61.
Record League Goalscorer—Season Jack Holliday, 38 in Div. 3(S), 1932-33.

Brentford: League Record, 1988-89 (Division 3)

Match Number	Date	Venue	Opponents	Result	H/T	Lge Posn	Attend
1	27.8.88	H	Huddersfield T.	W 1-0	0-0		5632
2	3.9.88	A	Northampton T.	L 0-1	0-1	14	4488
3	10.9.88	H	Wigan Ath.	D 1-1	1-0	13	4081
4	17.9.88	A	Swansea C.	D 1-1	0-0	14	5015
5	21.9.88	A	Bristol Rov.	W 2-1	0-0	9	3836
6	24.9.88	H	Sheffield U.	L 1-4	1-1	11	6577
7	1.10.88	H	Gillingham	W 1-0	0-0	8	4839
8	5.10.88	A	Chester C.	L 2-3	2-3	16	2004
9	9.10.88	H	Southend U.	W 4-0	0-0	8	5106
10	15.10.88	A	Bury	L 1-3	1-2	14	2359
11	22.10.88	H	Preston N.E.	L 0-2	0-0	15	5584
12	25.10.88	A	Chesterfield	D 2-2	0-0	15	1876
13	29.10.88	H	Port Vale	W 2-1	0-0	13	5212
14	5.11.88	A	Reading	D 2-2	2-1	15	7974
15	8.11.88	H	Notts Co	W 2-1	1-0	11	4013
16	12.11.88	A	Mansfield T.	L 0-1	0-1	14	3181
17	25.11.88	A	Cardiff C.	L 0-1	0-1	15	3405
18	3.12.88	H	Bolton W.	W 3-0	1-0	14	4628
19	18.12.88	A	Aldershot	D 0-0	0-0	15	4012
20	26.12.88	H	Blackpool	W 1-0	0-0	12	6021
21	31.12.88	H	Wolverhampton W.	D 2-2	1-1	12	8020
22	2.1.89	A	Fulham	D 3-3	2-2	12	8120
23	14.1.89	H	Northampton T.	D 2-0	2-0	10	6043
24	21.1.89	A	Wigan Ath.	D 1-1	1-1	10	2514
25	4.2.89	A	Gillingham	D 0-0	0-0	11	4002
26	11.2.89	H	Chester C.	L 0-1	0-0	12	5748
27	25.2.89	H	Bury	D 2-2	1-0	14	6077
28	28.2.89	H	Chesterfield	W 1-0	0-0	13	4192
29	4.3.89	A	Preston N.E.	L 3-5	2-2	13	8186
30	11.3.89	H	Reading	W 3-2	2-1	11	6866
31	13.3.89	A	Port Vale	L 2-3	0-1	12	5577
32	24.3.89	H	Fulham	L 0-1	0-0	14	10851
33	27.3.89	A	Blackpool	W 3-0	0-0	14	3053
34	1.4.89	H	Aldershot	W 2-1	0-0	14	5200
35	4.4.89	H	Bristol C.	W 3-0	2-0	11	4627
36	8.4.89	A	Wolverhampton W.	L 0-2	0-1	13	14196
37	11.4.89	A	Bristol C.	W 1-0	0-0	9	4339
38	15.4.89	H	Bristol Rov.	W 2-1	0-1	8	7558
39	18.4.89	A	Southend U.	D 1-1	0-0	7	4119
40	22.4.89	A	Sheffield U.	D 2-2	0-1	7	12613
41	25.4.89	A	Huddersfield T.	W 2-1	0-0	7	3538
42	29.4.89	H	Mansfield T.	W 1-0	1-0	7	5231
43	1.5.89	A	Notts Co.	L 0-3	0-2	7	4989
44	6.5.89	A	Bolton W.	L 2-4	2-3	9	4627
45	9.5.89	H	Swansea C.	D 1-1	0-1	9	4415
46	13.5.89	H	Cardiff C.	D 1-1	0-1	7	4865

Players: League Record, 1988-89 (Division 3)

Match Number	1	2	3	4	5	6	7	8	9	10	11	12	13	14	15	16	17	18	19	20	21	22	23	24	25	26	27	28	29	30	31	32	33	34	35	36	37	38	39	40	41	42	43	44	45	46	Apps	Subs	Goals
Ansah, Andrew																																★							★		64		★	10^{2}	**7**	**9**	3	4	2
Bates, Jamie		2	★	2	2	2	2	2	2	2	5	3	2	2	2	2	2										★	★	2^{1}	**2**	★	2	4	4	4	4	4	4	4	2	2	**2**	2	2	**2**	★	31	5	1
Birch, Paul	★	★																																													0	2	0
Blissett, Gary	10	10	10^{1}	10	10	10	10	10^{1}	10	10		10	10	**10**	10	10	10	10						★	10	10	10^{1}			10	10	10	10	10	10	10	10	10^{1}	10	10	10^{1}	10			10^{1}	10	35	1	6
Booker, Bob		★		**6**	6	**6**	**6**	**6**		★	★																																				5	3	0
Buttigieg, John															4	4	**11**	6	2			★							**9**				★	★	2	2		2	2			★	★	7	★	2	12	6	0
Cadette, Richard	**9**	**9**	9	9	9^{2}	9	9	9^{1}	9	9	9	9^{2}	9	9	**9^{2}**	9	9	9^{2}	9	9	9	9^{1}	9^{1}	9	9	9	**9**	9^{1}		9	**9**												**11**			★	31	1	12
Cockram, Allan	6^{1}	**6**	6				★	★	6^{1}	**6^{1}**							★	2	6	6	6	**6**	**6**	6	6	6	★	10	10	★	★	6	6^{2}	6	6^{1}	**6**	6	6	6	6	**6**	6^{1}	6	6	6	6	31	6	7
Driscoll, Andrew																																												★			0	1	0
Evans, Terry	5	5	**5**	5	5	5	5	5	5^{1}	5		**5**	5	5	5	**5**	5	5^{1}	5	5	5	5	5	5	5	5	5	5	5	5^{1}	5	5	**5**	5	5	5	5^{1}	5	5	5	5	5	5	5	5	5^{1}	45	0	5
Feeley, Andy	2		2				3	**3**	★	11	**2**	★	**6**	6	6	6	6			2	2	2	2	**2**	2	**2**	**2**	2			2	7	2	**2**		★	2					8	8	**8**	8	**7**	30	3	0
Gayle, Marcus											★								★							★																					0	3	0
Godfrey, Kevin													**11**				★	11	**10**	10	10^{1}	10^{1}	10	**10**			11^{1}	11	11^{1}	11	11^{1}	11	**11^{1}**	**11**	★	★	★	★	9	9^{1}	9^{1}	9	10	11	11	11	24	5	8
Holdsworth, Dean										★	10	11	$★^{1}$	★	★	★																															2	5	1
Jones, Keith	7	7	7	7	7	7	7	7	7	7	7	7	7^{1}	7	7	7	7	7	7	7	7^{1}	7	7	7			7	7	7	7	7		7	7^{1}	7	7	7	7	7	7	7	7	**7**				40	0	3
Lee, Colin												★																				4															1	1	0
Millen, Keith	4	4	4	4^{1}	4	4	4	4	4	4	4	4	4	4			4	4	4	4	4	4	4	4	4	4	4	4	4	4^{1}	4^{1}									4	4	4	4	4	4	4	36	0	3
Parks, Tony	1	1	1	1	1	1	1	1											1	1	1	1	1	1	1	1				1	1	1	1	1	1	1	1	1	1	1	1	1	1	1	1	1	33	0	0
Pearce, Graham											11	2		11	11	11		3							★				★			9	9		★		★	★			★	★	9	3	3		11	7	0
Perryman, Steve				★		★					**6**	**6**	★																																		2	3	0
Purdie, Jon																																	★	9	**9**	**9**	**9**	**9**									5	1	0
Ratcliffe, Simon																							★	★	7	7	6	6	6^{1}	6	**6**																7	2	1
Roberts, Jeremy																	1	1									1	1	1																		5	0	0
Sealy, Tony																																8	8	8^{1}	8^{2}	8	8	8	**8**	8^{1}	**8**				★	8	11	1	4
Sinton, Andy	8	8	8	8	8	8^{1}	8^{1}	8	8^{2}	8	8	8	8	8^{1}	8	8	8	**8**	8	8^{1}	8	8^{1}	8	8^{1}	8	8	8	8	8	8^{1}	8																31	0	9
Smeulders, John									1	1	1	1	1	1	1	1																															8	0	0
Smillie, Neil	11	11	11	11	11	11	11	11	11									★	11	11	11	11	11	11	11	11			★					★	11	11	11	11^{1}	11^{1}	11	11	**11**					25	3	2
Stanislaus, Roger	3	3	3	3	3	3		★	**3**	**3**	3		3	3	3	3	**3**		3	3	3	3	3^{1}	3	**3**	3	3	**3**	3	3	3	**3**	3	3	**3**	3	**3**	**3**	3	3	3	3	3	9	9	3	42	1	1
Own Goals														1																																			1

FA Cup: 1988-89: 1st Round: Halesowen (H) 2-0; 2nd Round: Peterborough U. (A) 0-0, Replay (H) 3-2; 3rd Round: Walsall (A) 1-1, Replay (H) 1-0; 4th Round: Manchester C. (H) 3-1; 5th Round: Blackburn Rov. (A) 2-0; Quarter-Final: Liverpool (A) 0-4.
Littlewoods Cup: 1988-89: 1st Round: Fulham (A) 2-2 (H) 1-0; 2nd Round: Blackburn Rov. (A) 1-3 (H) 4-3.

BRIGHTON & HOVE ALBION (Division 2)

Team Manager Barry Lloyd.
Club Address Goldstone Ground, Old Shoreham Road, Hove, Sussex BN3 7DE. Tel: (0273) 739535.
Current Ground Capacity 26,000.
Record Attendance 36,747 v Fulham, Div. 2, 27 December 1958.
Year Formed 1900. Turned professional 1900.
Previous Names Brighton and Hove Rangers.
Club Nickname "The Seagulls".
Club Colours Blue and white striped shirts, blue shorts and blue stockings.
Club Honours Football League: Div. 3(S) Champions 1957-58; Div. 4 Champions 1964-65.
League History 1920-58 Div. 3(S); 1958-62 Div. 2; 1962-63 Div. 3; 1963-65 Div. 4; 1965-72 Div. 3; 1972-73 Div. 2; 1973-77 Div. 3; 1977-79 Div. 2; 1979-83 Div. 1; 1983-87 Div. 2; 1987-88 Div. 3; 1988- Div. 2.

Most League Points in a Season (2 for a win) 65 in Div. 3(S), 1955-56 and in Div. 3, 1971-72. (3 for a win) 84 in Div. 3, 1987-88.
Most League Goals in a Season 112 in Div. 3(S), 1955-56.
Record Victory 10-1 v Wisbech in FA Cup 1st Round, 13 November 1965.
Record Defeat 0-9 v Middlesbrough in Div. 2, 23 August 1958.
Consecutive League Wins 9 in 1926.
Consecutive League Defeats 12 in 1972-73.
Record League Appearances "Tug" Wilson, 509 between 1922-36.
Record League Goalscorer—Career Tommy Cook, 113 between 1922-29.
Record League Goalscorer—Season Peter Ward, 32 in Div. 3, 1976-77.

Brighton & Hove Albion: League Record, 1988-89 (Division 2)

Match Number	Date	Venue	Opponents	Result	H/T	Lge Posn	Attend
1	27.8.88	H	Bradford C.	L 1-3	1-1.		10190
2	3.9.88	A	Oxford U.	L 2-3	0-2	24	6004
3	10.9.88	H	Bournemouth	L 1-2	0-2	23	8247
4	17.9.88	A	Manchester C.	L 1-2	0-1	24	16033
5	21.9.88	H	West Bromwich A.	L 0-1	0-0	24	7395
6	24.9.88	A	Swindon T.	L 0-3	0-1	24	6585
7	1.10.88	H	Leeds U.	W 2-1	0-1	22	7109
8	5.10.88	H	Barnsley	L 0-1	0-0	23	7327
9	8.10.88	A	Leicester C.	L 0-1	0-0	24	9201
10	15.10.88	A	Watford	D 1-1	0-0	24	12126
11	22.10.88	H	Oldham Ath.	W 2-0	2-0	23	7699
12	26.10.88	H	Walsall	D 2-2	1-2	23	8311
13	29.10.88	A	Chelsea	L 0-2	0-1	23	15406
14	5.11.88	H	Shrewsbury T.	W 3-1	0-0	23	7365
15	12.11.88	A	Blackburn Rov.	L 1-2	1-2	23	6980
16	19.11.88	A	Ipswich T.	W 3-2	1-2	22	12386
17	26.11.88	H	Sunderland	W 3-0	1-0	21	10038
18	3.12.88	A	Hull C.	L 2-5	1-3	21	5686
19	6.12.88	A	Plymouth Arg.	L 0-3	0-1	22	8133
20	10.12.88	H	Stoke C.	D 1-1	0-1	22	7443
21	17.12.88	A	Portsmouth	L 0-2	0-1	22	12467
22	26.12.88	H	Crystal Palace	W 3-1	2-0	22	13515
23	31.12.88	H	Birmingham C.	W 4-0	0-0	20	9324
24	2.1.89	A	Bournemouth	L 1-2	1-0	21	10627
25	14.1.89	H	Plymouth Arg.	D 2-2	1-1	20	8504
26	21.1.89	A	Bradford C.	W 1-0	1-0	20	8183
27	4.2.89	A	Barnsley	D 2-2	1-1	20	12498
28	11.2.89	H	Leicester C.	D 1-1	0-1	20	9572
29	18.2.89	A	Oldham Ath.	L 1-2	1-2	21	5918
30	25.2.89	H	Watford	W 1-0	1-0	20	9522
31	28.2.89	A	Walsall	L 0-1	0-0	21	4613
32	4.3.89	H	Blackburn Rov.	W 3-0	0-0	20	8075
33	11.3.89	A	Shrewsbury T.	D 1-1	1-0	20	4029
34	15.3.89	H	Chelsea	L 0-1	0-1	20	12600
35	18.3.89	A	West Bromwich A.	L 0-1	0-0	21	11586
36	25.3.89	H	Oxford U.	W 2-1	0-1	21	9077
37	27.3.89	A	Crystal Palace	L 1-2	0-2	21	14384
38	1.4.89	H	Manchester C.	W 2-1	1-0	20	12072
39	5.4.89	H	Portsmouth	W 2-1	1-0	18	10100
40	8.4.89	A	Birmingham C.	W 2-1	2-1	17	4579
41	15.4.89	A	Leeds U.	L 0-1	0-1	17	14915
42	22.4.89	H	Swindon T.	L 0-2	0-0	18	9510
43	29.4.89	A	Sunderland	L 0-1	0-1	20	12856
44	1.5.89	H	Hull C.	D 1-1	0-0	19	6750
45	6.5.89	H	Ipswich T.	L 0-1	0-0	20	8616
46	13.5.89	A	Stoke C.	D 2-2	1-1	19	5841

Players: League Record, 1988-89 (Division 2)

Match Number	1	2	3	4	5	6	7	8	9	10	11	12	13	14	15	16	17	18	19	20	21	22	23
Armstrong, Gerry		★^{1}	9						9	9			★										
Bissett, Nicky																				5	5	5	5
Bremner, Kevin				9^{1}	9	9	9^{1}	9			9	9^{1}	9	9	9	9^{1}	9^{1}	9^{1}	9	9	9	9^{1}	9^{3}
Brown, Kevan	2					★		3															
Chapman, Ian											3												
Chivers, Gary	3	2^{1}	2^{1}	2	2	2	2	2	2	2	2	2	2	2^{1}	2	2	2^{1}	2	2	2	2	2^{1}	2^{1}
Codner, Robert			11	11	**11**	11	11	11	11	11	11	11	11	11	11				★	11	11	**11**	
Coles, David																							
Cooper, Geoff																						★	**11**
Crumplin, John					★										10			★	**11**	10			
Curbishley, Alan	4	4	**4**	4	4			★			8	8^{1}	8	8	8^{1}	8^{1}	8	**8**	8	8	8	8	8
Digweed, Perry					**1**																		
Dublin, Keith		3	3	3	3	3	3		3	3		3	3	3	3	3	3	3	3	3	3	3	3
Fearon, Ron						1	1	1	1	1	1	1											
Gatting, Steve	6	6	6	6	6	6	6	6	6	6	6^{1}	6	6	6	6	6	6	6^{1}	6	6^{1}	6	6	6
Isaac, Robert	5	5	5	5	5	5	4	**4**	4														
Keeley, John	1	1	1	1									1	1	1	1	1	1	1	1	1	1	1
May, Larry							5	5	5	5	5^{1}	5	5	5	5	5^{1}	5	5	5				
Nelson, Gary	7^{1}	7	7	7	7	7	7^{1}	7	7	7	7	7	7	7^{1}	7	7	7	7	7	7	7	7^{1}	7
Owers, Adrian	8	8	8	8	8	**8**	★				★					10	10	10	**10**				
Penney, Steve	11	**11**	★													11	11^{1}	**11**			10	10	10
Trusson, Mike							**8**	8	8	8													
Wilkins, Dean	10	10	**10**	**10**	10	10		★		4	4	4	4	4	4	4	4	4	4	4	4	4	4
Wood, Paul	9	9	★	★	★	4	10	**10**	10	10	**10**	10	**10**	10^{1}				★	★				★
Own Goals										1													

Match Number	24	25	26	27	28	29	30	31	32	33	34	35	36	37	38	39	40	41	42	43	44	45	46	Apps	Subs	Goals
Armstrong, Gerry																								3	2	1
Bissett, Nicky	5					6	6	6	6							5	5	5	5	5	5	5		16	0	0
Bremner, Kevin	9	9^{1}	9	9^{1}	9	9	9^{1}	9	9^{1}	9	9	9	9	9	9	9^{1}	9	9	9	9	9	9	9	41	0	15
Brown, Kevan																								2	1	0
Chapman, Ian					★		5	5	5	6	6	6	6	6	6	6	6	6	6	6	6	6	6	18	1	0
Chivers, Gary	2	2	2	2	2	2	2	2	2	2	2	2	2	2	2	2	2	2	2	2	2	2	2	46	0	6
Codner, Robert													★	★	★	★	★	**8**	**8**	8	8^{1}	8	8	22	6	1
Coles, David										1														1	0	0
Cooper, Geoff	**11**	★																	★					2	3	0
Crumplin, John		★						★	11	11	**11**	11						★						9	5	0
Curbishley, Alan	8	8			★	★	★				★	10	10^{1}	10^{1}	10^{1}	10	10	10	10	10	10	10	10	32	5	6
Digweed, Perry																								1	0	0
Dublin, Keith	3	3	3	3	3	3	3	3	3	3	3	3	3	3	3	3	3	3	3	3	3	3	3	43	0	0
Fearon, Ron																								7	0	0
Gatting, Steve	6	6	6	6	**6**																		5	29	0	3
Isaac, Robert																								9	0	0
Keeley, John	1	1	1	1	1	1	1	1	1		1	1	1	1	1	1	1	1	1	1	1	1	1	37	0	0
May, Larry		5^{1}	5	5	5	5				5	5	5	5	5	**5**									24	0	3
Nelson, Gary	7^{1}	7	7	7^{1}	7^{1}	7	7	7	7^{2}	7^{1}	7	7	7^{1}	7	7	7^{1}	7^{2}	7	7	7	7	7	7^{1}	46	0	15
Owers, Adrian		**10**	10^{1}	10	10	10^{1}	10	10	10	10	10							★	4					21	3	2
Penney, Steve	10																							9	1	1
Trusson, Mike			8	8	**8**	**8**	**8**	8	8	8	**8**	8	**8**	8	8	**8**	**8**				★	11	11	21	1	0
Wilkins, Dean	4	4	4	4	4	4	4	4	4	4	4	4	4	4	4	4	4	**4**		4	4	4	4^{1}	42	1	1
Wood, Paul	★	**11**	11	11	11	11	11	**11**			★		11	**11**	11	11	11	11	11	11	**11**			27	8	1
Own Goals															1											2

FA Cup: 1988-89: 3rd Round: Leeds U. (H) 1-2.

Littlewoods Cup: 1988-89: 1st Round: Southend U. (A) 0-2, (H) 0-1.

BRISTOL CITY (Division 3)

Team Manager Joe Jordan.
Club Address Ashton Gate, Bristol BS3 2EJ. Tel: (0272) 632812.
Current Ground Capacity 30,868.
Record Attendance 43,335 v Preston N.E., FA Cup 5th Round, 16 February 1935.
Year Formed 1894. Turned professional 1897.
Previous Names Bristol South End.
Club Nickname "The Robins".
Club Colours Red shirts, white shorts and red stockings.
Club Honours Football League: Div. 2 Champions 1905-06; Div. 3(S) Champions 1922-23, 1926-27, 1954-55.
League History 1901-06 Div. 2; 1906-11 Div. 1; 1911-22 Div. 2; 1922-23 Div. 3(S); 1923-24 Div. 2; 1924-27 Div. 3(S); 1927-32 Div. 2; 1932-55 Div. 3(S); 1955-60 Div. 2; 1960-65 Div. 3; 1965-76 Div. 2; 1976-80 Div. 1; 1980-81 Div. 2; 1981-82 Div. 3; 1982-84 Div. 4; 1984- Div. 3.
Most League Points in a Season (2 for a win) 70 in Div. 3(S), 1954-55. (3 for a win) 82 in Div. 4, 1983-84.
Most League Goals in a Season 104 in Div. 3(S), 1926-27.
Record Victory 11-0 v Chichester in FA Cup 1st Round, 5 November 1960.
Record Defeat 0-9 v Coventry C. in Div. 3(S), 28 April 1934.
Consecutive League Wins 14 in 1905.
Consecutive League Defeats 7 in 1931 and 1970.
Record League Appearances John Atyeo, 596 between 1951-66.
Record League Goalscorer—Career John Atyeo, 314 between 1951-66.
Record League Goalscorer—Season Don Clark, 36 in Div. 3(S), 1946-47.

Bristol City: League Record, 1988-89 (Division 3)

Match Number	Date	Venue	Opponents	Result	H/T	Lge Posn	Attend
1	27.8.88	A	Notts Co.	D 0-0	0-0		6280
2	3.9.88	H	Chesterfield	W 4-0	1-0	2	7547
3	10.9.88	A	Chester C.	L 0-2	0-0	11	2823
4	17.9.88	H	Preston N.E.	D 1-1	1-1	12	7913
5	20.9.88	A	Blackpool	D 2-2	2-1	12	3412
6	24.9.88	H	Port Vale	L 0-1	0-1	16	7235
7	1.10.88	H	Swansea C.	W 2-0	1-0	12	7786
8	4.10.88	A	Gillingham	W 1-0	1-0	7	3102
9	8.10.88	H	Fulham	L 1-5	0-2	11	8160
10	15.10.88	A	Huddersfield T.	W 1-0	0-0	11	5952
11	22.10.88	A	Northampton T.	W 3-1	0-1	7	3668
12	25.10.88	H	Aldershot	D 1-1	0-1	8	8685
13	29.10.88	A	Mansfield T.	D 2-2	2-1	11	3800
14	5.11.88	H	Bolton W.	D 1-1	1-0	9	8807
15	8.11.88	H	Wolverhampton W.	L 0-1	0-0	12	11336
16	12.11.88	A	Wigan Ath	W 1-0	0-0	10	2675
17	26.11.88	A	Sheffield U.	L 0-3	0-1	12	11248
18	3.12.88	H	Reading	W 2-1	0-1	10	8045
19	17.12.88	H	Cardiff C.	W 2-0	1-0	7	7493
20	26.12.88	A	Bury	L 1-2	1-1	10	3368
21	31.12.88	A	Southend U.	W 2-1	1-0	9	4012
22	2.1.89	H	Bristol Rov.	L 0-1	0-0	10	23191
23	14.1.89	A	Chesterfield	L 0-1	0-0	11	3488
24	21.1.89	H	Chester C.	L 0-1	0-0	13	9586
25	28.1.89	A	Preston N.E.	L 0-2	0-0	13	6080
26	3.2.89	A	Swansea C.	D 1-1	1-0	14	6523
27	11.2.89	H	Gillingham	W 1-0	0-0	11	7319
28	18.2.89	A	Fulham	L 1-3	1-1	13	4408
29	21.2.89	A	Aldershot	W 1-0	1-0	11	1969
30	4.3.89	H	Northampton T.	W 3-1	3-0	12	7197
31	11.3.89	A	Bolton W.	L 0-2	0-0	14	4423
32	18.3.89	H	Notts Co	L 0-4	0-1	14	6407
33	21.3.89	H	Mansfield T.	W 2-0	1-0	11	5065
34	25.3.89	A	Bristol Rov	D 1-1	1-1	11	8676
35	27.3.89	H	Bury	W 3-0	1-0	10	8496
36	1.4.89	A	Cardiff C.	D 1-1	0-1	11	6152
37	4.4.89	A	Brentford	L 0-3	0-2	13	4627
38	8.4.89	H	Southend U.	L 0-2	0-1	14	6213
39	11.4.89	H	Brentford	L 0-1	0-0	14	4339
40	15.4.89	H	Blackpool	L 1-2	1-0	14	5090
41	18.4.89	H	Huddersfield T.	W 6-1	5-0	13	4542
42	21.4.89	A	Port Vale	W 1-0	0-0	13	6923
43	29.4.89	H	Wigan Ath.	L 0-1	0-0	13	5156
44	1.5.89	A	Wolverhampton W.	L 0-2	0-1	14	17351
45	5.5.89	A	Reading	W 2-1	1-1	12	3620
46	13.5.89	H	Sheffield U.	W 2-0	0-0	11	10769

Players: League Record, 1988-89 (Division 3)

Match Number	1	2	3	4	5	6	7	8	9	10	11	12	13	14	15	16	17	18	19	20	21	22	23	24	25	26	27	28	29	30	31	32	33	34	35	36	37	38	39	40	41	42	43	44	45	46	Apps	Subs	Goals
Bailey, John										3	3	3	3	3	3	3	3	3	3	3	3	3	3	3	3	3	3	3	3	3	3	3	3	3	3	3	3	3	3	3	3	3	3	3			35	0	0
Bromage, Russell	3	3	3	3¹	3	3	3	3																														8	8	8					3	3	13	0	1
Caldwell, Tony	11																																														1	0	0
Carter, Tim				1	1	1																																									3	0	0
Dolan, Eamonn																											8	7	7																		3	0	0
Eaton, Jason																																											★	★			0	2	0
Fitzpatrick, Paul		★																																													0	1	0
Galliers, Steve	8	8	8	8	8	8	8	8	8	8	8	8	8		8	8	8	8			★		11	7	7	7	7					★	7	7			★				8	8	7	7	7	7	30	3	0
Gavin, Mark								7¹	7		11		11	11	11	11¹	11	11	11	11	11	11	9	11	11	★	★	9			★	7							6	6	6¹	6	8	8	8	8	26	3	3
Hawkins, Nigel		11			★	★	11	11	11							★	★	★¹	★¹	★		★											9	★				9		★				11			7	10	2
Honor, Christian	★			★																2	2	2	2	2	2	2	2	2	2	2	2	2	2	2	2	2	2	2			2	2	2		2	2	24	2	0
Humphries, Glenn	4								★	4	4	4	4	4	4	4	4	4	4														4	4	4	4	4	4	4	4			★	2			20	2	0
Jordan, Joe								★	★	11	★	11											★				★¹		★				★														2	7	1
Leaning, Andy							1	1	1	1	1																																			1	6	0	0
Llewellyn, Andy	2	2¹	2	2	2	2	2	2	2	2				2	★	★			★											7	7																13	3	0
McClaren, Steve	6	6	6	6	6	6	6	6	6	6	6	6	6	6	6		6	6	6	6	6	6	6	6	6	★	11	8	8	8	8	8	8	8	7	7	7	7	7	7	7¹	7	6	6	6	6	44	1	1
McGarvey, Scott			11	11	11²	11	★	9	9	★	9²	9¹	9¹	★	★	7	7	7	7	7¹	7¹	7	7	★		9	9	11¹										★									20	6	9
Mardon, Paul		4	4	4			★	★	3	★																6	6	6	★	6	6	6	★	★	8	8	8	★									13	7	0
Milne, Ralph	7		★	7	7	7	7¹				7¹	7	7	7	7																																10	1	2
Newman, Rob	9	7¹	7	9	4	4	4	4	4¹	7	2	2	2	8¹	2	2	5	2	2¹	4	4	4	4	4	4	4	4	4	4	4	4	4	6²	6	6	6	6	6	2	2	4	4	4	4	4	4	46	0	6
Pender, John	5	5	5	5	5	5	5	5	5	5	5	5	5	5	5	5		5	5	5	5	5	5	5	5	5	5	5	5	5	5	5	5	5	5	5	5	5	5	5	5	5	5	5	5¹	5	45	0	1
Shepherd, Anthony																						★	8	8																							2	1	0
Shutt, Carl		9	9	★	9	9	9			9		★	★	9	9	9	9	9	9	9	9	9		9	9				9	9¹	9	9															21	3	1
Stanley, Gary																6	2		8	8	8	8				11		★	6	★																	8	2	0
Taylor, Bob																																		9	9¹	9¹	9		9	9¹	9³	9¹	9	9	9	9¹	12	0	8
Turner, Robert																									8	8¹			11	11¹	11	11	11	11	11²	11	11	11	11	11	11	11	11		11¹	11¹	19	0	6
Walsh, Alan	10	10²	10	10	10	10	10¹	10	10	10¹	10	10	10¹	10	10	10	10	10¹	10	10	10¹	10	10	10	10	10	10	10	10¹	10¹	10	10	10	10¹	10	10	10	10	10	10	10¹	10	10	10	10	10	46	0	11
Waugh, Keith	1	1	1									1	1	1	1	1	1	1	1	1	1	1	1	1	1	1	1	1	1	1	1	1	1	1	1	1	1	1	1	1	1	1	1	1	1		37	0	0
Own Goals																																																	0

FA Cup: 1988-89: 1st round: Southend U. (H) 3-1; 2nd Round: Aldershot (A) 1-1, Replay (H) 0-0, 2nd Replay (A) 2-2, 3rd Replay (H) 1-0; 3rd Round: Hartlepool U. (A) 0-1.
Littlewoods Cup: 1988-89: 1st Round: Exeter C. (H) 1-0 (A) 1-0; 2nd Round: Oxford U. (A) 4-2 (H) 2-0; 3rd Round: Crystal Palace (H) 4-1; 4th Round: Tranmere Rov. (H) 1-0; Quarter-Final: Bradford C. (A) 1-0; Semi-Final: Nottingham F. (A) 1-1 (H) 0-1.

BRISTOL ROVERS (Division 3)

Team Manager Gerry Francis.
Club Address Twerton Park, Twerton, Bath (shared with Bath City). Tel: (0225) 23087.
Current Ground Capacity 9,100.
Record Attendance 38,472 v Preston N.E., FA Cup 4th Round, 30 January 1960.
Year Formed 1883. Turned professional 1897.
Previous Names Black Arabs, Eastville Rovers, Bristol Eastville Rovers.
Club Nickname "The Pirates".
Club Colours Blue and white quartered shirts, white shorts and blue stockings with two white rings on top.
Club Honours Football League: Div. 3(S) Champions 1952-53.
League History 1921-53 Div 3(S); 1953-62 Div. 2; 1962-74 Div. 3; 1974-81 Div. 2; 1981- Div. 3.
Most League Points in a Season (2 for a win) 64 in Div. 3(S), 1952-53. (3 for a win) 79 in Div. 3, 1983-84.
Most League Goals in a Season 92 in Div. 3(S), 1952-53.
Record Victory 7-0 v Swansea T. in Div. 2, 2 October 1954, v Brighton & H.A. in Div. 3(S), 29 November 1952 and v Shrewsbury T. in Div. 3, 21 March 1964.
Record Defeat 0-12 v Luton T. in Div. 3(S), 13 April 1936.
Consecutive League Wins 12 in 1952-53.
Consecutive League Defeats 8 in 1961.
Record League Appearances Stuart Taylor, 546 between 1965-80.
Record League Goalscorer—Career Geoff Bradford, 242 between 1949-64.
Record League Goalscorer—Season Geoff Bradford, 33 in Div. 3(S), 1952-53.

Bristol Rovers: League Record, 1988-89 (Division 3)

Match Number	Date	Venue	Opponents	Result	H/T	Lge Posn	Attend
1	27.8.88	H	Wigan Ath.	W 3-2	1-2		4080
2	3.9.88	A	Sheffield U.	L 1-4	1-2	15	9586
3	10.9.88	H	Aldershot	D 2-2	0-2	16	3382
4	17.9.88	A	Bolton W.	D 1-1	0-1	16	4821
5	21.9.88	H	Brentford	L 1-2	0-0	17	3836
6	24.9.88	A	Northampton T.	W 2-1	0-0	10	3886
7	1.10.88	A	Cardiff C.	D 2-2	2-0	14	5038
8	5.10.88	H	Preston N.E.	W 1-0	1-0	9	3689
9	8.10.88	A	Mansfield T.	L 1-2	1-1	12	3381
10	15.10.88	H	Notts Co.	W 2-0	1-0	12	4183
11	22.10.88	H	Chester C.	W 4-1	2-1	6	3811
12	26.10.88	A	Reading	L 1-3	1-2	9	7150
13	29.10.88	H	Huddersfield T.	W 5-1	3-1	8	4460
14	5.11.88	A	Chesterfield	W 3-0	1-0	6	2480
15	8.11.88	A	Southend U.	D 2-2	1-1	5	2453
16	12.11.88	H	Gillingham	W 2-0	0-0	4	4826
17	26.11.88	H	Bury	L 1-3	0-2	6	4251
18	3.12.88	A	Fulham	W 2-0	1-0	4	4461
19	17.12.88	A	Blackpool	D 1-1	0-0	5	3240
20	26.12.88	H	Wolverhampton W.	D 0-0	0-0	6	8480
21	31.12.88	H	Swansea C.	D 1-1	1-1	6	4803
22	2.1.89	A	Bristol C.	W 1-0	0-0	5	23191
23	14.1.89	H	Sheffield U.	D 1-1	0-0	5	6623
24	21.1.89	A	Aldershot	W 3-1	2-0	5	3101
25	28.1.89	H	Bolton W.	W 2-0	1-0	3	5375
26	4.2.89	H	Cardiff C.	L 0-1	0-0	6	5815
27	11.2.89	A	Preston N.E.	D 1-1	1-0	5	7365
28	18.2.89	H	Mansfield T.	D 0-0	0-0	7	4669
29	25.2.89	A	Notts Co.	L 0-1	0-1	7	5176
30	1.3.89	H	Reading	D 1-1	1-0	8	4573
31	4.3.89	A	Chester C.	W 2-0	0-0	6	3082
32	11.3.89	H	Chesterfield	W 2-1	2-0	6	4686
33	14.3.89	A	Huddersfield T.	D 3-2	1-2	5	4105
34	25.3.89	H	Bristol C.	D 1-1	1-1	5	8676
35	27.3.89	A	Wolverhampton W.	W 1-0	1-0	4	20913
36	1.4.89	H	Blackpool	W 1-0	0-0	4	5355
37	5.4.89	H	Port Vale	D 2-2	1-1	4	6869
38	8.4.89	A	Swansea C.	D 1-1	1-1	4	5645
39	15.4.89	A	Brentford	L 1-2	1-0	4	7558
40	22.4.89	H	Northampton T.	D 1-1	0-1	4	5568
41	28.4.89	A	Gillingham	W 3-2	0-1	4	4004
42	1.5.89	H	Southend U.	D 1-1	0-1	5	6250
43	3.5.89	A	Wigan Ath.	L 0-3	0-1	5	2529
44	6.5.89	H	Fulham	D 0-0	0-0	5	7302
45	9.5.89	A	Port Vale	L 0-1	0-0	5	6136
46	13.5.89	A	Bury	D 0-0	0-0	5	3073

Players: League Record, 1988-89 (Division 3)

Match Number	1	2	3	4	5	6	7	8	9	10	11	12	13	14	15	16	17	18	19	20	21	22	23
Alexander, Ian		2	2	2	2	2	**2**	2	2	2	2	2	2	2	2				2	2	2	2	2
Bailey, Dennis																							
Clark, Billy	4	4	4	4	4		6	4	4		4	4											
Dryden, Richard				★																			
Hazel, Ian																							
Hibbitt, Kenny																							
Holloway, Ian	7	7^{1}	7	7	7	7	7^{1}	7	7	7	7	7	7^{1}	7	7	7	7	7	7	7	7	7	7^{1}
Jones, Vaughan	6	**6**	6	6	6	6		6	6	6^{1}	6	6	6	6	6	6	6	6	6	6	6	6	6
McClean, Christian					★						★^{1}	★		9	9	9^{1}	★		★		★	★	★
Martyn, Nigel	1	1	1	1	1	1	1	1	1	1	1	1	1	1	1	1	1	1	1	1	1	1	1
Mehew, David	5	5	5	5				5	5	5	**5**^{1}	5	5	5^{2}	5^{1}	5	**5**^{1}	5^{1}	5				
Nixon, Paul																							
Penrice, Gary	10^{2}	10	**10**		10^{1}	10^{1}	10^{1}	10^{1}	10^{1}	10^{1}	10	10	10^{1}	10	10	10	10	10^{1}	10	10	10	10^{1}	10
Purnell, Philip	11	11	11	**11**	11	11	11	11	11	11	11	11	11^{2}	11^{1}	11^{1}	11	11	11	11^{1}	11	11^{1}	11	11
Reece, Andy	8	8	8	8	**8**	8	8	8	8	8	8^{2}	8^{1}	8^{1}	8	8	8^{1}	8	8	8	8	8	8	8
Smith, Paul		★	★	10	5	5^{1}	5													5	5	**5**	**5**
Stapleton, Simon	2						★									2	2	2					
Twentyman, Geoff	3	3	3	3^{1}	3	3	3	3	3	3	3	3	3	3	3	3	3	3	3	3	3	3	3
Viney, Keith						4	4			★													
White, Devan	9^{1}	9	9^{2}	9	9	9	9	9	9	9	9	**9**	9				9	9	**9**	9	**9**	9	9
Yates, Steven										**4**			4	4	4	4	4	4	4	4	4	4	4
Own Goals																							

Match Number	24	25	26	27	28	29	30	31	32	33	34	35	36	37	38	39	40	41	42	43	44	45	46	Apps	Subs	Goals
Alexander, Ian	2	**2**	2	2	2	2	2	2	2	2	2	2	2	2	2	2	2	2	2	2	2	2	2	42	0	0
Bailey, Dennis							8^{1}	**8**^{1}	8^{1}	8^{2}	8	8^{1}	8	8	8^{1}	8^{1}	8^{1}	8	8	8	8	**8**	8	17	0	9
Clark, Billy		★																						10	1	0
Dryden, Richard																								0	1	0
Hazel, Ian							5	5	**5**															3	0	0
Hibbitt, Kenny									★															0	1	0
Holloway, Ian	7^{1}	7	7	7	7	7	7	7			7	7	7	7	7	7	7	7^{1}	7	7	7	7	7	44	0	6
Jones, Vaughan	6	6	6	6	6	6	6	6	6	6^{1}	6	6	6	6	6	6	6	6	6	6	6	6	6	45	0	2
McClean, Christian		10	★		★	★	9	9	9	9	9	**9**	**9**	★	9	**9**					**9**	9	**9**	16	12	2
Martyn, Nigel	1	1	1	1	1	1	1	1	1	1	1	1	1	1	1	1	1	1	1	1	1	1	1	46	0	0
Mehew, David						**5**			7	5		11	11	**11**	**5**	5	5	5	**5**^{1}	**5**	5	5	5	31	0	7
Nixon, Paul																	★							0	1	0
Penrice, Gary	10^{2}		10	10^{1}	10	10	10	10	10^{1}	10	10^{1}	10	10	10^{1}	10^{1}	10	10	10^{2}	10	10	10	10		43	0	20
Purnell, Philip	11	11	11	11	11	11	11	11^{1}	11	11	**11**								★	★			10	35	2	7
Reece, Andy	8	8^{1}	8	8	8					7	5	5	5	5^{1}	11	11	11	11	11	11	11	11	11	42	0	7
Smith, Paul	5	5	**5**	5	**5**	8																		14	2	1
Stapleton, Simon																								4	1	0
Twentyman, Geoff	3	3	3	3	3	3	3	3	3	3	3	3	3	3	3	3	3	3	3	3	3	3	3	46	0	1
Viney, Keith																								2	1	0
White, Devan	9	9^{1}	9	9	9	9		★			★	★	★^{1}	9	★	★	**9**	9	9	9	★	★	★	31	9	5
Yates, Steven	4	4	4	4	4	4	4	4	4	4	4	4	4	4	4	4	4	4	4	4	4	4	4	35	0	0
Own Goals																										0

FA Cup: 1988-89: 1st Round: Fisher Ath. (H) 3-0; 2nd Round: Kettering T. (A) 1-2.
Littlewoods Cup: 1988-89: 1st Round: Bournemouth (A) 0-1, (H) 0-0.

BURNLEY (Division 4)

Team Manager Frank Casper.
Club Address Turf Moor, Burnley BB10 4BX. Tel: (0282) 27777/38021.
Current Ground Capacity 25,000.
Record Attendance 54,775 v Huddersfield T., FA Cup 3rd Round, 23 February 1924.
Year Formed 1882. Turned professional 1883.
Previous Names Burnley Rovers.
Club Nickname "The Clarets".
Club Colours Claret shirts with light blue sleeves, white shorts and stockings.
Club Honours Football League: Div. 1 Champions 1920-21, 1959-60; Div. 2 Champions 1897-98, 1972-73; Div. 3 Champions 1981-82. FA Cup: Winners 1914.
League History 1888-97 Div. 1; 1897-98 Div. 2; 1898-1900 Div. 1; 1900-13 Div. 2; 1913-30 Div. 1; 1930-47 Div. 2; 1947-71 Div. 1; 1971-73 Div. 2; 1973-76 Div. 1; 1976-80 Div. 2; 1980-82 Div. 3; 1982-83 Div. 2; 1983-85 Div. 3; 1985- Div. 4.
Most League Points in a Season (2 for a win) 62 in Div. 2, 1972-73. (3 for a win) 80 in Div. 3, 1981-82.
Most League Goals in a Season 102 in Div. 1, 1960-61.
Record Victory 9-0 v Darwen in Div. 1, 9 January 1892, v Crystal Palace in FA Cup replay, 1908-09, v New Brighton in FA Cup 4th Round, 26 January 1957 and v Penrith in FA Cup 1st Round, 17 November 1984.
Record Defeat 0-10 v Aston Villa in Div. 1, 29 August 1925, and v Sheffield U. in Div. 1, 19 January 1929.
Consecutive League Wins 10 in 1912-13.
Consecutive League Defeats 8 in 1889-90, 1895.
Record League Appearances Jerry Dawson, 530 between 1906-29.
Record League Goalscorer—Career George Beel, 178 between 1923-32.
Record League Goalscorer—Season George Beel, 35 in Div. 1, 1927-28.

Burnley: League Record, 1988-89 (Division 4)

Match Number	Date	Venue	Opponents	Result	H/T	Lge Posn	Attend
1	27.8.88	H	Rochdale	W 2-1	1-0		7510
2	3.9.88	A	Halifax T.	W 2-1	1-0	3	3371
3	10.9.88	H	York C.	W 6-0	2-0	1	7239
4	16.9.88	A	Stockport Co.	D 0-0	0-0	2	6500
5	20.9.88	A	Torquay U.	L 0-2	0-1	3	3021
6	24.9.88	H	Colchester U.	W 2-0	1-0	3	7177
7	1.10.88	A	Darlington	D 1-1	0-0	4	3409
8	4.10.88	H	Rotherham U.	W 1-0	0-0	1	9283
9	8.10.88	H	Exeter C.	W 3-0	1-0	1	7889
10	15.10.88	A	Peterborough U.	L 0-3	0-1	1	5023
11	22.10.88	H	Leyton Orient	D 2-2	0-1	2	8502
12	25.10.88	A	Carlisle U.	D 0-0	0-0	2	4543
13	29.10.88	H	Cambridge U.	W 2-0	1-0	1	8670
14	5.11.88	A	Scunthorpe U.	L 1-2	0-0	4	6358
15	8.11.88	H	Lincoln C.	L 1-4	1-1	4	8740
16	12.11.88	A	Scarborough	L 0-1	0-0	5	5501
17	26.11.88	A	Doncaster Rov.	L 0-1	0-0	9	2724
18	3.12.88	H	Hartlepool U.	D 0-0	0-0	9	6281
19	17.12.88	A	Hereford U.	D 0-0	0-0	9	2442
20	26.12.88	H	Wrexham	L 1-3	1-1	12	9174
21	31.12.88	H	Grimsby T.	W 1-0	0-0	10	7367
22	2.1.89	A	Tranmere Rov.	L 1-2	0-1	14	7974
23	14.1.89	H	Halifax T.	W 2-1	1-0	12	8297
24	21.1.89	A	Rochdale	L 1-2	1-0	13	5799
25	28.1.89	H	Stockport Co.	W 1-0	0-0	9	6942
26	4.2.89	H	Torquay U.	W 1-0	0-0	8	6626
27	10.2.89	A	Colchester U.	D 2-2	2-0	8	3809
28	18.2.89	A	Exeter C.	L 0-3	0-1	10	3672
29	25.2.89	H	Peterborough U.	D 1-1	0-0	9	6848
30	4.3.89	A	Leyton Orient	L 0-3	0-0	11	3974
31	11.3.89	H	Scunthorpe U.	L 0-1	0-1	14	6813
32	14.3.89	A	Cambridge U.	L 1-2	0-1	17	3100
33	18.3.89	A	York C.	D 0-0	0-0	18	3164
34	21.3.89	H	Carlisle U.	D 0-0	0-0	17	5258
35	25.3.89	H	Tranmere Rov.	D 2-2	0-1	15	6838
36	27.3.89	A	Wrexham	L 2-4	1-2	18	3956
37	1.4.89	H	Hereford U.	D 3-3	1-1	18	5534
38	4.4.89	H	Crewe Alex.	W 1-0	1-0	17	5677
39	8.4.89	A	Grimsby T.	L 0-1	0-0	17	4856
40	15.4.89	H	Darlington	L 0-1	0-0	17	5578
41	22.4.89	A	Rotherham U.	L 1-3	1-3	17	5726
42	29.4.89	H	Doncaster Rov.	W 3-0	1-0	16	4211
43	1.5.89	A	Lincoln C.	W 3-2	2-0	16	3594
44	6.5.89	A	Hartlepool U.	D 2-2	1-0	16	2174
45	9.5.89	A	Crewe Alex	L 0-4	0-1	16	2963
46	13.5.89	H	Scarborough	L 0-1	0-0	16	6206

Players: League Record, 1988-89 (Division 4)

Match Number	1	2	3	4	5	6	7	8	9	10	11	12	13	14	15	16	17	18	19	20	21	22	23
Atkinson, Paul		11	11^1	11	11	11	**11**	11	11	11							**11**	**11**	11	**11**			
Britton, Ian	7	7	7^1	7	7	7	7	7	7	7	**11**						4	4	4	4	4	4^1	4
Comstive, Paul	10^1	10^1	10^2	10	10	10	10	10	10	10	10^1	10	10	10	10^1	10	10	10	10	10	10	10	**10**
Daniel, Peter	2	2	2	2	2	2	2	2	2	2	2	2	2	2									
Davis, Steve	5	5	5	5	5	5	5				6	6			6	5	5	5	5	5	5	5	5
Deakin, Ray	3	3	3	3	3	**3**																	
Farrell, Andrew	4^1	4	4	4	4	4	3	3	3	3	4	4	4	4	4	4	3	3	3	3	3	2	3
Gardner, Stephen	6	6	6	6	6	6	6	6	6	6	3		6	6	2	6	6	6	6	6	6	6	6
Grewcock, Neil																							
Hardy, Jason																							
Hooper, Stuart																							
Hoskin, Ashley												★								★	11	**11**	
James, Leighton	9																						11
Jones, David																							
McGrory, Shaun												3	3	3	**3**	3					★	3	
Measham, Ian																2	2	2	2	2	**2**		2
Miller, David																							
Monington, Mark																							
Morley, Tony													11	11	11	11	7						
O'Connell, Brendan	★	9^1	9^1	9	9	9^1	9^1	9	9^1	9	9^1	9	9^1	9^1	9	9	9	9	9	9^1	9	9	9
Oghani, George	8	8	8^1	8	8	8	8	8^1	8^1	8	8	8	8^1	8	8	8	**8**	**8**	8	8	8^1	8	8^2
Pearce, Chris	1	1	1	1	1	1	1	1	1	1	1	1	1	1	1	1	1	1	1	1	1	1	1
Rowell, Gary	**11**					$★^1$	4	4	4	4	★	**11**			★		★	★					
Taylor, Steve							★											★				★	
White, Winston											7	7	7	7	7	7	★	7	7	7	7	7	7
Williams, David																							
Zelem, Peter								5	5^1	5	5	5	5	5	5								★
Own Goals																							

Match Number	24	25	26	27	28	29	30	31	32	33	34	35	36	37	38	39	40	41	42	43	44	45	46	Apps	Subs	Goals
Atkinson, Paul								★																13	1	1
Britton, Ian	4	4^1	4	4	4	4	4	4	4	4	4	4	**4**	4	4	4	4	★					**10**	36	1	3
Comstive, Paul	10	10	10	10	**10**				**10**	10	10	10^2	10	**10**					$★^1$	10	10	**10**		37	1	9
Daniel, Peter																								14	0	0
Davis, Steve	5	5	5	5	5	5	5	5	5	5					5	5	5	5	5	5	5	5	5	37	0	0
Deakin, Ray				11	11	11													11	11	11	11	11	14	0	0
Farrell, Andrew	3^1	3	3	**3**	★		3	7										4^1	4	4	4^1	**4**	4	35	1	4
Gardner, Stephen	6	6	6	6		3	10	6	6	6	6	6	6	**6**	6	6	6	6	6	6	6	6	6	44	0	0
Grewcock, Neil										★	11	11	11^1	7	7	7	7	**7**	7	7	7	7		12	1	1
Hardy, Jason							★	3	3	3	3	3	3	3	3^1	3	3	3	3	3	3	3	3	16	1	1
Hooper, Stuart																		★						0	1	0
Hoskin, Ashley			★																					2	3	0
James, Leighton	**11**	11	**11**			★	11	11	★				★	11^2	11	11	**11**	11			9^1	★	**7**	14	4	3
Jones, David							9	**9**								**8**	**8**							4	0	0
McGrory, Shaun	★		★		**3**								$★^1$	★	10	10	10	**10**	**10**			★	★	12	7	1
Measham, Ian	2	2	2	2	2	2^1	2	2	2	2	2	2	2	2	2	2	2	2	2	2	2	2	2	30	0	1
Miller, David					6	6	6	**10**																4	0	0
Monington, Mark									11	11	5	5	5	5^1			★						★	6	2	1
Morley, Tony																								5	0	0
O'Connell, Brendan	9	9	9^1	9	9	9			9	9	9	9	9	9	9	9	9	9	9^2	9^1		9	9	42	1	13
Oghani, George	8	8	8	8	8	8	**8**	8	**8**	8	**8**	8		8	8									37	0	7
Pearce, Chris	1	1	1	1	1	1	1	1	1	1	1	1	1	1	1								1	39	0	0
Rowell, Gary				★	★	**10**	★		★		★		8											8	10	1
Taylor, Steve																								0	3	0
White, Winston	7	7	**7**	7^2	7	7	**7**	★	7^1	**7**	7	7	**7**	★		★	★	8	8	8^2	8	8	8	30	5	5
Williams, David																1	1	1	1	1	1	1		7	0	0
Zelem, Peter																								8	1	1
Own Goals																										0

FA Cup: 1988-89: 1st Round: Chester C. (H) 0-2.
Littlewoods Cup: 1988-89: 1st Round: Rochdale (A) 3-3 (H) 2-1; 2nd Round: Luton T. (A) 1-1 (H) 0-1.

BURY (Division 3)

Team Manager Sam Ellis.
Club Address Gigg Lane, Bury BL9 9HR. Tel: 061-764 4881/2.
Current Ground Capacity 8,000.
Record Attendance 35,000 v Bolton W., FA Cup 3rd Round, 9 January 1960.
Year Formed 1885. Turned professional 1885.
Previous Names None.
Club Nickname "The Shakers".
Club Colours White shirts, royal blue shorts and white stockings.
Club Honours Football League: Div. 2 Champions 1894-95. Div. 3 Champions 1960-61. FA Cup: Winners 1900, 1903.
League History 1894-95 Div. 2; 1895-1912 Div. 1; 1912-24 Div. 2; 1924-29 Div. 1; 1929-57 Div 2; 1957-61 Div. 3; 1961-67 Div. 2; 1967-68 Div. 3; 1968-69 Div. 2, 1969-71 Div. 3; 1971-74 Div. 4; 1974-80 Div. 3; 1980-85 Div. 4; 1985- Div. 3.
Most League Points in a Season (2 for a win) 68 in Div. 3, 1960-61. (3 for a win) 84 in Div. 4, 1984-85.
Most League Goals in a Season 108 in Div. 3, 1960-61.
Record Victory 12-1 v Stockton in FA Cup 1st Round replay, 1896-97.
Record Defeat 0-10 v Blackburn Rov. in FA Cup preliminary Round, 1st October 1887 and v West Ham U. in Milk Cup, 2nd Round, 2nd leg, 25 October 1983.
Consecutive League Wins 9 in 1960.
Consecutive League Defeats 6 in 1953 and 1967.
Record League Appearances Norman Bullock, 506 between 1920-35.
Record League Goalscorer—Career Craig Madden, 129 between 1977-86.
Record League Goalscorer—Season Craig Madden, 35 in Div. 4, 1981-82.

Bury: League Record, 1988-89 (Division 3)

Match Number	Date	Venue	Opponents	Result	H/T	Lge Posn	Attend
1	27.8.88	H	Wolverhampton W.	W 3-1	2-0		4314
2	3.9.88	A	Swansea C.	D 1-1	0-1	3	5141
3	10.9.88	H	Port Vale	D 0-0	0-0	6	2978
4	17.9.88	A	Fulham	D 0-1	0-1	13	3754
5	24.9.88	H	Mansfield T.	L 0-1	0-0	20	2412
6	1.10.88	A	Chesterfield	W 2-1	1-1	16	1837
7	4.10.88	H	Reading	W 2-1	1-1	9	2027
8	8.10.88	A	Preston N.E	L 0-1	0-0	14	5863
9	15.10.88	H	Brentford	W 3-1	2-1	13	2359
10	22.10.88	A	Gillingham	W 4-3	3-1	10	2850
11	25.10.88	H	Southend U.	W 3-1	0-0	6	2419
12	29.10.88	A	Sheffield U.	L 1-2	0-2	9	12348
13	1.11.88	A	Cardiff C.	L 0-3	0-0	11	2411
14	5.11.88	H	Notts Co.	D 1-1	0-1	10	2692
15	8.11.88	H	Chester C.	W 2-1	1-0	9	2497
16	12.11.88	A	Bolton W.	W 4-2	2-0	8	7897
17	26.11.88	A	Bristol Rov.	L 3-1	2-0	4	4251
18	3.12.88	H	Wigan Ath.	W 1-1	1-0	5	3121
19	17.12.88	A	Huddersfield T.	L 2-3	1-2	6	5150
20	26.12.88	H	Bristol C.	W 2-1	1-1	4	3368
21	31.12.88	H	Aldershot	L 0-1	0-0	8	3186
22	2.1.89	A	Blackpool	D 2-2	0-1	7	4199
23	7.1.89	A	Northampton T.	L 0-2	0-1	8	3463
24	14.1.89	H	Swansea C.	W 1-0	0-0	6	2608
25	21.1.89	A	Port Vale	W 3-1	1-1	6	5783
26	28.1.89	H	Fulham	W 3-1	1-0	5	3582
27	4.2.89	H	Chesterfield	W 2-1	1-1	3	3844
28	11.2.89	A	Reading	D 1-1	0-1	3	3804
29	18.2.89	H	Preston N.E.	D 1-1	0-0	3	6977
30	25.2.89	A	Brentford	D 2-2	0-1	3	6077
31	28.2.89	A	Southend U.	D 1-1	0-1	3	2479
32	4.3.89	H	Gillingham	W 1-0	1-0	3	4313
33	11.3.89	A	Notts Co.	L 0-3	0-1	5	5757
34	14.3.89	H	Sheffield U.	L 1-2	0-1	6	5334
35	18.3.89	A	Wolverhampton W.	L 0-4	0-1	7	14828
36	25.3.89	H	Blackpool	D 0-0	0-0	8	3717
37	27.3.89	A	Bristol C.	L 0-3	0-1	8	8496
38	1.4.89	H	Huddersfield T.	L 0-6	0-2	8	4145
39	4.4.89	H	Northampton T.	L 0-1	0-1	9	1965
40	8.4.89	A	Aldershot	L 1-4	1-0	10	1677
41	15.4.89	H	Cardiff C.	W 1-0	1-0	10	2124
42	22.4.89	A	Mansfield T.	D 1-1	0-1	10	2826
43	29.4.89	H	Bolton W.	D 0-0	0-0	10	4393
44	1.5.89	A	Chester C.	L 0-2	0-1	10	2110
45	6.5.89	A	Wigan Ath.	L 0-1	0-0	13	3045
46	13.5.89	H	Bristol Rov.	D 0-0	0-0	13	3073

Players: League Record, 1988-89 (Division 3)

Match Number	1	2	3	4	5	6	7	8	9	10	11	12	13	14	15	16	17	18	19	20	21	22	23
Atkin, Paul																							
Bishop, Charlie	11^1	11	3	3	3	3	3	3		3^1	3	3	3	3	3	3	3	3		3	**3**	3	**3**
Brotherston, Noel			11	**11**																			
Clements, Kenny		★	5	5		6	**6**	6	6	6	6	6	6	6	6	6	6	6	6	6	6	6	6
Eli, Roger																							
Elliott, Steve						9	9^1	9	9^1	9	9	9	**9**	9	9	9^2	9^2	9	9^1	9	9	9^1	9
Entwistle, Wayne			★	★																			
Farnworth, Simon	1	1	1	1	1	1	1	1	1	1	1	1	1	1	1	1	1	1		1	1	1	1
Fazackerley, Derek																					★	5	★
Godden, Tony																			1				
Greenwood, Nigel								★		★			★		★^{1}			★			★		★
Higgins, Mark	6	6	6	6	6																		
Hill, Andy	2	2	2	2	2	2	2	2	2	2	2	2	**2**	2	2	2	2	2	2	2	2	2	2
Hoyland, Jamie	9^1	9	9	9	9	4	4	4	4	4	4	4	4	4^1	4^1	4	4	4	4	4^1	4	4	4
Hulme, Kevin																							
Jones, David					★																		
Lee, David	7	7^1	7	7	7	7	7^1	7	7	**7**	7^1	7	7	7	7	7	7	7	7	7	7	7	7
Leonard, Gary	4	4			★		★	8					★		★	10^1							
McIlroy, Sammy	10	10	10	10	10	10	10	**10**	10^1	10	10	10	10	10	**10**		10	10	10	10	10	10	**10**
Parkinson, Philip			**4**	4	**4**	★			3	★	11	11	11	11	11	11	11	11	11	11	11	11	11
Pashley, Terry	3	3			**11**	**11**	11	11	11	**11**													
Robinson, Liam	8^1	8	8	8	8	8^1	8		8^1	8^3	8^2	8^1	8	8	8	8^1	8	**8^1**	8^1	8^1	8	8^1	8
Valentine, Peter	5	**5**			5	5^1	5	5	5	5	5	5	5	5	5	5	5	5	5	5	**5**		5
Wassall, Darren																							
Windridge, David																			3				
Own Goals																	1						

Match Number	24	25	26	27	28	29	30	31	32	33	34	35	36	37	38	39	40	41	42	43	44	45	46	Apps	Subs	Goals
Atkin, Paul														★										0	1	0
Bishop, Charlie	3	3	3	3	3	3^1	3	3	3	3	3	3	3	3	3				11		★			37	1	3
Brotherston, Noel																								2	0	0
Clements, Kenny	6	6	6	6	6	6	6	6	6	6	6	6	6	6	6	6	6	6	6	6	6	**6**	6	43	1	0
Eli, Roger			★				★																	0	2	0
Elliott, Steve	**9**	9	9	**9**	**9**	9	9^1	**9^1**			9	**9**				9	9	9^1						31	0	11
Entwistle, Wayne																								0	2	0
Farnworth, Simon	1	1	1	1	1	1	1	1	1	1	1	1	1	1	1	1	1	1	1	1	1	1	1	45	0	0
Fazackerley, Derek				★		5	5	5	★	★		★				5	**5**		★			7		7	7	0
Godden, Tony																								1	0	0
Greenwood, Nigel	★			★	★			★	9	**9**			9	★	9	★	8		9	9	9	9	**9**	10	13	1
Higgins, Mark																								5	0	0
Hill, Andy	2	2	2	2	2	2	2	2		2	2	2	2			2	2	2	**2**	2	2	2	2	43	0	0
Hoyland, Jamie	4	4	4^1	4	4^1	4	4^1	4	4^1	4	4	4	4	4	4	4	4	4	4^1	4	4	4	4	46	0	9
Hulme, Kevin													8	**9**							★	11	★	3	2	0
Jones, David																								0	1	0
Lee, David	7	7^1	7	7	7	7	7	7	7	7	7	7	7	7	7	7	7	7	7	7	**7**		7	45	0	4
Leonard, Gary					★																			4	5	1
McIlroy, Sammy	10	10	10	10^1	10	10	10	10	10	10	10	10	10	**10**	10	10	10	10	10	10	10	10	10	45	0	2
Parkinson, Philip	11	11	11	11	11			11	11	11	11	11	11	11	11	11	11	11		11	**11**	★	11	36	3	0
Pashley, Terry				**5**	**5**	11	**11**		**2**	★		★		2	2	3	3^1	3	3	3	3	3	3	23	2	1
Robinson, Liam	8^1	8^2	8^2	8^1	8	8	8	8	8	8	8	**8**		8	8	**8**		8	8	8	8	8	8	43	0	20
Valentine, Peter	5	5	**5**														★	5	5	5	5	5	5	29	1	1
Wassall, Darren									5	**5**	5^1	5	5	5	5									7	0	1
Windridge, David																								1	0	0
Own Goals																										1

FA Cup: 1988-89: 1st Round: Guisborough (A) 1-0; 2nd Round: Blackpool (A) 0-3.
Littlewoods Cup: 1988-89: 1st Round: Wrexham (H) 2-1 (A) 2-2; 2nd Round: Everton (A) 0-3 (H) 2-2.

CAMBRIDGE UNITED (Division 4)

Team Manager Chris Turner.
Club Address Abbey Stadium, Newmarket Road, Cambridge. Tel: (0223) 241237.
Current Ground Capacity 10,150.
Record Attendance 14,000 v Chelsea, Friendly, 1 May 1970.
Year Formed 1919. Turned professional 1946.
Previous Names Abbey United.
Club Nickname "United".
Club Colours Black and amber striped shirts, black shorts and stockings.
Club Honours Football League: Div. 4 Champions 1976-77.
League History 1970-73 Div. 4; 1973-74 Div. 3; 1974-77 Div. 4; 1977-78 Div. 3; 1978-84 Div. 2; 1984-85 Div. 3; 1985- Div. 4.
Most League Points in a Season (2 for a win) 65 in Div. 4, 1976-77. (3 for a win) 68 in Div. 4, 1987-88.
Most League Goals in a Season 87 in Div. 4, 1976-77.
Record Victory 6-0 v Darlington in Div. 4, 18 September 1971 and v Hartlepool U. in Div. 4, 11 February 1989.
Record Defeat 0-6 v Aldershot in Div. 3, 13 April 1974, v Darlington in Div. 4, 28 September 1974 and v Chelsea in Div. 2, 15 January 1983.
Consecutive League Wins 7 in 1977 and 1984.
Consecutive League Defeats 7 in 1983, 1984-85, 1985.
Record League Appearances Steve Fallon, 410 between 1974-86.
Record League Goalscorer—Career Alan Biley, 74 between 1975-86.
Record League Goalscorer—Season David Crown, 24 in Div. 4, 1985-86.

Cambridge United: League Record, 1988-89 (Division 4)

Match Number	Date	Venue	Opponents	Result	H/T	Lge Posn	Attend
1	27.8.88	H	Grimsby T.	W 4-1	2-1		2290
2	3.9.88	A	Hereford U.	L 2-4	1-3	9	1711
3	10.9.88	H	Stockport Co	W 1-0	1-0	5	1911
4	16.9.88	A	Tranmere Rov.	W 2-1	2-1	3	3248
5	20.9.88	H	Lincoln C.	L 2-3	0-1	4	2776
6	24.9.88	A	Hartlepool U.	L 2-3	1-2	9	2385
7	30.9.88	H	Carlisle U.	W 3-2	1-1	7	2043
8	4.10.88	A	Crewe Alex.	L 0-2	0-1	8	1588
9	8.10.88	H	Halifax T.	W 2-1	0-0	6	1800
10	15.10.88	A	Scunthorpe U.	L 0-1	0-0	8	3514
11	21.10.88	A	Colchester U.	W 2-1	0-0	7	2138
12	25.10.88	H	Scarborough	D 2-2	1-1	6	2673
13	29.10.88	A	Burnley	L 0-2	0-1	8	8670
14	4.11.88	H	Exeter C.	W 2-0	0-0	7	2063
15	8.11.88	A	Darlington	D 1-1	0-1	9	1467
16	12.11.88	H	Rotherham U.	D 1-1	1-0	8	2882
17	26.11.88	H	Leyton Orient	D 2-2	1-0	11	2675
18	2.12.88	A	Torquay U.	L 1-3	0-3	12	1992
19	16.12.88	A	Wrexham	L 1-3	1-2	15	1728
20	26.12.88	H	Doncaster Rov.	D 0-0	0-0	17	2673
21	30.12.88	H	Rochdale	W 2-0	0-0	11	2319
22	3.1.89	A	Peterborough U.	W 5-1	3-1	9	4622
23	14.1.89	H	Hereford U.	W 2-1	2-1	9	2193
24	21.1.89	A	Grimsby T.	L 0-4	0-2	10	3653
25	28.1.89	H	Tranmere Rov.	D 1-1	1-0	11	2239
26	4.2.89	A	Lincoln C.	L 0-3	0-0	11	3239
27	11.2.89	H	Hartlepool U.	W 6-0	2-0	9	2300
28	17.2.89	A	Halifax T.	D 0-0	0-0	9	1531
29	25.2.89	H	Scunthorpe U.	L 0-3	0-1	10	2563
30	1.3.89	A	Scarborough	L 1-2	0-0	14	2011
31	5.3.89	H	Colchester U.	W 3-1	2-1	9	4205
32	11.3.89	A	Exeter C.	W 3-0	1-0	7	3180
33	14.3.89	H	Burnley	W 2-1	1-0	7	3100
34	17.3.89	A	Stockport Co.	D 0-0	0-0	7	2521
35	25.3.89	H	Peterborough U.	W 2-1	1-0	8	4215
36	27.3.89	A	Doncaster Rov.	D 1-1	0-0	8	1937
37	31.3.89	H	Wrexham	W 2-0	0-0	8	3072
38	4.4.89	H	York C.	D 1-1	0-1	8	2400
39	8.4.89	A	Rochdale	L 1-2	1-2	8	1314
40	15.4.89	A	Carlisle U.	D 1-1	0-0	7	2579
41	22.4.89	H	Crewe Alex.	D 1-1	0-1	7	3512
42	29.4.89	A	Leyton Orient	D 1-1	1-1	8	5057
43	2.5.89	H	Darlington	L 1-3	0-0	8	3310
44	6.5.89	H	Torquay U.	W 3-0	1-0	8	2163
45	9.5.89	A	York C.	W 2-1	2-0	8	2336
46	13.5.89	A	Rotherham U.	D 0-0	0-0	8	9567

Players: League Record, 1988-89 (Division 4)

Match Number	1	2	3	4	5	6	7	8	9	10	11	12	13	14	15	16	17	18	19	20	21	22	23
Allen, Greg	**6**		10	10	10																		
Anderson, Doug							11	11	11	11	11^2	11	**11**	**11**									
Bailie, Colin	2	2	2	2	2	2	2	2	2	2	2	2	2	2^1	2	2	2	2	2	2	2	2	**2**
Bastock, Paul	1	1																					
Beck, John	7	6		★	★	★	6	6	6	6	6	**6^1**	6	6	6	6	6	6	**6**				
Bull, Gary		★										★						★	★				
Byrne, David			**6**	**6**	6	**6**																	
Chapple, Philip	5	5	5	5	5	5^1	5^1	5	5	5	5	5	5	5	5	5	5	5	5	5	5	5	5
Clayton, Gary	★	7	7	7	7	7	7^1	7	7	7	7	7	7	7	7	7	7	7	7	7	7	7	7
Croft, Brian												★	★	$★^1$	11	11^1	11	11	11	11	**11**	**11**	11
Daish, Liam																			4	4	4	4	4
Dearden, Kevin																							
Dennis, Anthony																							
Dublin, Dion																			★	★	9	9^3	9^1
Hamilton, Ian	10		★			10	10	10	10	10	10	10	10	10	**10**	10	10	10					
Holmes, Micky																							
Howard, Mark																							
Kimble, Alan	3	3	3	3^1	3	3	3	3	3	3	3	3	3	3	3	3	3	3	3	3	3^1	3^1	3
Leadbitter, Chris	11	11	11	11	**11**	**11**															★	$★^1$	★
Poole, Gary																							
Reilly, George	9^2	9^1	9	9	9^1	9	9^1	**9**	9	9	9		9	9	**9**	9	9^2	9	**9**	**9**			
Ryan, Laurie	8^2		8^1	8^1	8	8	**8**	8	**8**			**9**	★	★	8	**8**	8	**8**	8^1	8	8^1	8^1	8^1
Smith, Lindsay	4	4	4	4	4^1	4	4	4	4^1	4	4	4	4	4	4^1	4	4	4^1					
Taylor, John		**8**				$★^1$	★	★	$★^1$	8	8	8^1	**8**	**8**	★	★			10	10	10	10	10
Turner, Paul		10													★					6	6	6	6
Vaughan, John			1	1	1	1	1	1	1	1	1	1	1	1	1	1	1	1	1	1	1	1	1
Own Goals		1																					

Match Number	24	25	26	27	28	29	30	31	32	33	34	35	36	37	38	39	40	41	42	43	44	45	46	Apps	Subs	Goals
Allen, Greg																								4	0	0
Anderson, Doug																								8	0	2
Bailie, Colin																								23	0	1
Bastock, Paul																								2	0	0
Beck, John	★	2^1	2	2	2	★		8	8^1	8	8	8	8	8^1	8	8	8	8	8	**8**	8	8	8	35	5	4
Bull, Gary	★	★	8	9^1	9	**9**																		4	6	1
Byrne, David																								4	0	0
Chapple, Philip	5	5	5	5^1	5	5	5	5	5	5	5	5	5	5	5	5	5	5	5	5	5	5	5	46	0	3
Clayton, Gary	7	7	7	7	7	2	2	2	2	2	2	2	2	2	2	2	2	2	2	2	2	2	2	45	1	1
Croft, Brian	**11**	**11**	11				★	★																12	5	2
Daish, Liam	4	4	6	6	6	6	6	6	6	6	6	6	6	6	6	6	6	6	6	6	6	6	6	28	0	0
Dearden, Kevin									1	1	1	1	1	1	1	1	1	1	1	1	1	1	1	15	0	0
Dennis, Anthony						7	7^1	7	**7**	**7**	7	7^1	7	7	7	**7**	7^1	7	7	7	7	7	7	18	0	3
Dublin, Dion	9	9	★						★	★	★	★		★	★		4	**4**	4	4	4^1	4^1	4	12	9	6
Hamilton, Ian																								14	1	0
Holmes, Micky				8	8	**8**	8		★							★		★		★	9	9	9	7	4	0
Howard, Mark																★				★				0	2	0
Kimble, Alan	3	3		3	3	3	3	3	3	3^1	3	3^1	3	3	3^1	3	3	3	3	3	3^1	3	3	45	0	6
Leadbitter, Chris		★	3	11^1	11	11	11	11^1	11^1	11	11	11	11	11	11	11	11	11^1	11	**11**	11^1	11	11	27	4	6
Poole, Gary	2																							1	0	0
Reilly, George			**9**																					20	0	7
Ryan, Laurie	**8**	**8**	★		★	★	**9**	9^1	**9**	9	**9**	**9**	9^1	**9**	**9**	9^1	9	9	9	9^1				34	5	12
Smith, Lindsay																								18	0	4
Taylor, John	10	10	10	10^3	10	10	10	10^1	10^1	10^1	10	10	10	10^1	10	10	10	10	10^1	10	10	10^1	10	34	6	12
Turner, Paul	6	6	4	4	4	4	4	4	4	4	4	4	4	4	4	**4**								21	1	0
Vaughan, John	1	1	1	1	1	1	1	**1**																29	0	0
Own Goals																										1

FA Cup: 1988-89: 1st Round: Woking (A) 4-1; 2nd Round: Bognor Regis T. (A) 1-0; 3rd Round: Plymouth Arg. (A) 0-2.
Littlewoods Cup: 1988-89: 1st Round: Gillingham (H) 1-2, (A) 1-3.

CARDIFF CITY (Division 3)

Team Manager Frank Burrows.
Club Address Ninian Park, Cardiff CF1 8SX. Tel: (0222) 398636/7/8.
Current Ground Capacity 39,900.
Record Attendance 61,566 Wales v England, 14 October 1961.
Year Formed 1899. Turned professional 1910.
Previous Names Riverside, Riverside Albion, Cardiff.
Club Nickname "The Bluebirds".
Club Colours Royal blue shirts, white shorts and royal blue stockings.
Club Honours Football League: Div. 3(S) Champions 1946-47. FA Cup: Winners 1927.
League History 1920-21 Div. 2; 1921-29 Div. 1; 1929-31 Div. 2; 1931-47 Div. 3(S); 1947-52 Div. 2; 1952-57 Div. 1; 1957-60 Div. 2; 1960-62 Div. 1; 1962-75 Div. 2; 1975-76 Div. 3; 1976-82 Div. 2; 1982-83 Div. 3, 1983-85 Div. 2; 1985-86 Div. 3; 1986-88 Div. 4; 1988- Div. 3.
Most League Points in a Season (2 for a win) 66 in Div. 3(S), 1946-47. (3 for a win) 86 in Div. 3, 1982-83.
Most League Goals in a Season 93 in Div. 3(S), 1946-47.
Record Victory 9-2 v Thames in Div. 3(S), 6 February 1932.
Record Defeat 2-11 v Sheffield U. in Div. 1, 1 January 1926.
Consecutive League Wins 9 in 1946.
Consecutive League Defeats 7 in 1933.
Record League Appearances Phil Dwyer, 471 between 1972-85.
Record League Goalscorer—Career Len Davies, 128 between 1920-31.
Record League Goalscorer—Season Stan Richards, 31 in Div. 3(S), 1946-47.

Cardiff City: League Record, 1988-89 (Division 3)

Match Number	Date	Venue	Opponents	Result	H/T	Lge Posn	Attend
1	27.8.88	H	Fulham	L 1-2	1-0		6024
2	3.9.88	A	Bolton W.	L 0-4	0-0	24	4831
3	10.9.88	H	Huddersfield T.	W 3-0	3-0	17	3891
4	17.9.88	A	Port Vale	L 1-6	1-3	20	4280
5	23.9.88	A	Southend U.	D 0-0	0-0	22	3199
6	1.10.88	H	Bristol Rov.	D 2-2	0-2	22	5038
7	8.10.88	H	Reading	L 1-2	1-0	23	4057
8	15.10.88	A	Chester C.	D 0-0	0-0	22	2796
9	22.10.88	A	Mansfield T.	D 2-2	1-0	22	3566
10	29.10.88	A	Blackpool	L 0-1	0-0	21	3849
11	1.11.88	H	Bury	W 3-0	0-0	21	2411
12	5.11.88	H	Gillingham	W 1-0	0-0	20	3658
13	12.11.88	H	Northampton T.	W 1-0	1-0	17	3280
14	25.11.88	H	Brentford	W 1-0	1-0	17	3405
15	3.12.88	A	Preston N.E.	D 3-3	0-2	17	4926
16	17.12.88	A	Bristol C.	L 0-2	0-1	18	7493
17	26.12.88	H	Swansea C.	D 2-2	2-2	18	10675
18	30.12.88	H	Wigan Ath.	D 2-2	0-1	19	4621
19	2.1.89	A	Aldershot	W 1-0	0-0	17	2768
20	10.1.89	A	Wolverhampton W.	L 0-2	0-2	17	14870
21	14.1.89	H	Bolton W.	W 1-0	0-0	16	4212
22	21.1.89	A	Huddersfield T.	L 0-1	0-1	17	4869
23	28.1.89	H	Port Vale	W 3-0	1-0	17	4507
24	4.2.89	A	Bristol Rov.	W 1-0	0-0	13	5815
25	11.2.89	H	Sheffield U.	D 0-0	0-0	14	5772
26	18.2.89	A	Reading	L 1-3	0-2	16	4359
27	28.2.89	A	Notts Co.	L 0-2	0-1	18	4266
28	4.3.89	H	Mansfield T.	D 0-0	0-0	18	3217
29	11.3.89	A	Gillingham	W 2-1	2-0	16	2927
30	18.3.89	A	Fulham	L 0-2	0-1	18	4261
31	21.3.89	A	Chesterfield	L 0-4	0-2	18	2888
32	25.3.89	H	Aldershot	W 3-2	1-1	17	3251
33	27.3.89	A	Swansea C.	D 1-1	1-0	18	9201
34	1.4.89	H	Bristol C.	D 1-1	1-0	18	6152
35	4.4.89	H	Wolverhampton W.	D 1-1	0-1	18	7219
36	7.4.89	A	Wigan Ath.	L 0-1	0-0	18	2083
37	11.4.89	A	Sheffield U.	W 1-0	1-0	17	11618
38	15.4.89	A	Bury	L 0-1	0-1	17	2124
39	18.4.89	H	Notts Co.	L 0-1	0-1	18	3079
40	22.4.89	H	Southend U.	W 2-0	1-0	17	3268
41	29.4.89	A	Northampton T.	L 0-3	0-1	18	3194
42	1.5.89	H	Chesterfield	L 0-1	0-1	18	3244
43	5.5.89	H	Preston N.E.	D 0-0	0-0	19	3196
44	9.5.89	H	Chester C.	W 2-0	0-0	16	3002
45	13.5.89	A	Brentford	D 1-1	1-0	17	4865
46	16.5.89	H	Blackpool	D 0-0	0-0	16	3426

Players: League Record, 1988-89 (Division 3)

Match Number	1	2	3	4	5	6	7	8	9	10	11	12	13	14	15	16	17	18	19	20	21	22	23
Abrahams, Gareth								3		6	6	6	6	5	5	5	5	5	5	5	5	**5**	
Bartlett, Kevin	★	★				★[1]	**8**	8	8	8	★[1]	8[1]	8[1]	8	8[2]	8	8	**8**[1]	**8**	**8**	8[1]	8	8[1]
Bater, Phil	2			★	★	**10**	2	2	2				★	★	★	★				★	6	6	3
Boyle, Terry	6	6	6	**6**	6	6	6	6	6					6	6	6	6	6	6	6	★	★	5
Curtis, Alan	7	7		7	8	8	7[1]				7	7	7	7	7	**7**	7	7[1]	7[1]	**7**	**7**		
Fry, Chris																							
Gibbins, Roger																							
Gilligan, Jimmy	9	9	9	9[1]	9	9[1]	9	9	9	9	9[1]	9	9	9[1]	9[1]	9	9[2]	9	9	9	9	9	9[2]
Gummer, Jason		**10**	10	10	**10**											10	**10**						
Haig, Richard																							
Holmes, Matthew																							
Kelly, Mark	11	11	11		11	11	11		4	4	8	11	11				★	10	10	10	**10**	10	**10**
Ketteridge, Steve								10	10[1]	10	10[1]	10	10										
Lynex, Steve	**4**	★	7	11	7	**7**		11	11	11	**11**			**11**	11	11	11	11	11	11	11	**11**	11
McDermott, Brian	10			8		★	10		7[1]	★													
Morgan, Jonathan							4	4															★
Platnauer, Nicky	3	**3**	3	3	3	3	3			3	3	3	3	3	3	3						7	7
Roberts, Jonathan																							
Rodgerson, Ian	★	2	2	2	2	2			3	2	2	2	2	2	2	**2**	2	2	2	2	2	2	2
Stevenson, Nigel	5	5	**5**[1]	5	5	5	5	5	5	5	5	5	**5**				3	3	3	3	3	3	6
Tupling, Stephen			★												10	**10**							
Walsh, Ian	**8**[1]	8	8[2]																				
Wheeler, Paul							★	7								★		★	★	★	★	★	
Wimbleton, Paul		4	4	4	4	4				**7**	4	4	4	4	4	4	4	4	4	4	4	4	4
Wood, George	1	1	1	1	1	1	1	1	1	1	1	1	1	1	1	1	1	1	1	1	1	1	1
Own Goals																							

Match Number	24	25	26	27	28	29	30	31	32	33	34	35	36	37	38	39	40	41	42	43	44	45	46	Apps	Subs	Goals
Abrahams, Gareth		7	6	**6**	6	6	6	6						5[1]	5	5	5[1]	5	5	5	**5**	5	5	31	0	2
Bartlett, Kevin	**8**	8																						18	4	9
Bater, Phil	3	6	**8**	8	8	★	★	**11**	8	8	8		8	8	8	2	2	6	8	8	2		**8**	27	9	0
Boyle, Terry	5	5	5	5	5	5[1]	5	5	5	5	5	5	5							6	6[1]	6	6	34	2	2
Curtis, Alan			**7**	7	7	7	7	7	7[1]	7		7	**7**		★	7	7	7	7	7	7		**7**	34	1	4
Fry, Chris															★	★	**11**	★	**11**	**11**	**11**	**11**	★	5	4	0
Gibbins, Roger												★	★	7	7	★	10	10	10	10	10	10	4	9	3	0
Gilligan, Jimmy	9[1]	9	9	9	9	9[1]	9	9	9[1]	9[1]	9	9	9	9	9	9	9[1]	9	9	9	9[1]	9	9	46	0	15
Gummer, Jason																			★	★	8	8[1]	10	9	2	1
Haig, Richard																						★		0	1	0
Holmes, Matthew									★															0	1	0
Kelly, Mark	10	10	★		★	8	**8**	★			7					**11**		**11**						24	4	0
Ketteridge, Steve																								6	0	2
Lynex, Steve	11	11	11	11	11	11	**11**	★	**11**	11	11	11	11	11	**11**								11	34	2	0
McDermott, Brian																								4	2	1
Morgan, Jonathan	★					★	★	**8**			4	**8**		4	4	4	4	4	4	4	4	★	★	13	6	0
Platnauer, Nicky	7	3	3	3	3	3	3	3	3	3	3[1]	3[1]	3	3	3	3	3	3	3	3	3	3	3	39	0	2
Roberts, Jonathan																						1		1	0	0
Rodgerson, Ian	2	2	2	2	2	2	2	2	2	2	2	2	2	2	2			**2**	2	**2**			**2**	39	1	0
Stevenson, Nigel	**6**								6	6	6	6	6	6	6	6	6	★	**6**					31	1	1
Tupling, Stephen																						2		3	1	0
Walsh, Ian			★[1]	★	★					★	★	★	**10**				★							4	7	4
Wheeler, Paul	★		10	10	**10**	**10**	10	10	10[1]	**10**	**10**	**10**	★	10	**10**	**10**			★	★	★	**7**		15	12	1
Wimbleton, Paul	4	4	4	4	**4**	**4**	4	4	4	4		4	4			8	8	8			★	4		35	1	0
Wood, George	1	1	1	1	1	1	1	1	1	1	1	1	1	1	1	1	1	1	1	1	1		1	45	0	0
Own Goals																										0

FA Cup: 1988-89: 1st Round: Hereford U. (H) 3-0; 2nd Round: Enfield (A) 4-1; 3rd Round: Hull C. (H) 1-2.
Littlewoods Cup: 1988-89: 1st Round: Swansea C. (H) 0-1 (A) 2-0; 2nd Round: Q.P.R. (A) 0-3 (H) 1-4.

CARLISLE UNITED (Division 4)

Team Manager Clive Middlemass.
Club Address Brunton Park, Carlisle CA1 1LL. Tel: (0228) 26237.
Current Ground Capacity 18,035.
Record Attendance 27,500 v Birmingham C., FA Cup 3rd Round, 5 January 1957 and v Middlesbrough, FA Cup 5th Round, 7 February 1970.
Year Formed 1904. Turned professional 1921.
Previous Names Carlisle Red Rose.
Club Nickname "The Cumbrians" or "Blues".
Club Colours All blue with red and white trim.
Club Honours Football League: Div. 3 Champions 1964-65.
League History 1928-58 Div. 3(N); 1958-62 Div. 4; 1962-63 Div. 3; 1963-64 Div. 4; 1964-65 Div. 3; 1965-74 Div. 2; 1974-75 Div. 1; 1975-77 Div. 2; 1977-82 Div. 3; 1982-86 Div. 2; 1986-87 Div. 3; 1987- Div. 4.

Most League Points in a Season (2 for a win) 62 in Div. 3(N), 1950-51. (3 for a win) 80 in Div. 3, 1981-82.
Most League Goals in a Season 113 in Div. 4, 1963-64.
Record Victory 8-0 v Hartlepool U. in Div. 3(N), 1 September 1928 and v Scunthorpe U. in Div. 3(N), 25 December 1952.
Record Defeat 1-11 v Hull C. in Div. 3(N), 14 January 1939.
Consecutive League Wins 6 in 1937 and 1981-82.
Consecutive League Defeats 8 in 1935.
Record League Appearances Alan Ross, 466 between 1963-79.
Record League Goalscorer—Career Jimmy McConnell, 126 between 1928-32.
Record League Goalscorer—Season Jimmy McConnell, 42 in Div. 3(N), 1928-29.

Carlisle United: League Record, 1988-89 (Division 4)

Match Number	Date	Venue	Opponents	Result	H/T	Lge Posn	Attend
1	27.8.88	H	Peterborough U.	D 2-2	1-1		2650
2	3.9.88	A	York C.	D 1-1	1-0	15	2303
3	10.9.88	H	Tranmere Rov.	D 1-1	0-0	15	2384
4	16.9.88	A	Halifax T.	D 3-3	3-1	14	1546
5	20.9.88	A	Scunthorpe U.	D 1-1	0-1	18	3113
6	24.9.88	H	Rotherham U.	L 0-2	0-0	19	2862
7	30.9.88	A	Cambridge U.	L 2-3	1-1	20	2043
8	4.10.88	H	Colchester U.	L 1-2	0-0	22	2193
9	8.10.88	A	Hereford U.	L 1-2	1-1	23	2127
10	15.10.88	H	Torquay U.	W 2-1	0-0	23	2164
11	22.10.88	A	Exeter C.	L 0-3	0-1	23	2235
12	25.10.88	H	Burnley	D 0-0	0-0	23	4543
13	29.10.88	A	Lincoln C.	W 2-0	0-0	22	3727
14	5.11.88	H	Scarborough	L 0-1	0-1	22	2617
15	8.11.88	A	Leyton Orient	L 0-2	0-0	22	2869
16	12.11.88	H	Darlington	L 1-2	0-2	23	2194
17	26.11.88	H	Grimsby T.	W 2-1	0-1	22	2175
18	3.12.88	A	Wrexham	L 1-2	1-2	22	1892
19	17.12.88	A	Hartlepool U.	W 2-0	2-0	22	1974
20	26.12.88	H	Rochdale	W 1-0	0-0	22	1013
21	31.12.88	H	Stockport Co.	D 1-1	1-0	22	3774
22	2.1.89	A	Crewe Alex.	W 0-1	0-1	22	4626
23	10.1.89	A	Doncaster Rov.	W 3-1	1-0	21	2128
24	14.1.89	H	York C.	D 0-0	0-0	21	3462
25	21.1.89	A	Peterborough U.	W 4-1	2-0	20	2537
26	28.1.89	H	Halifax T.	W 3-1	0-0	16	3007
27	4.2.89	H	Scunthorpe U.	L 0-3	0-1	18	2627
28	11.2.89	A	Rotherham U.	L 1-2	1-1	19	4111
29	18.2.89	H	Hereford U.	W 3-0	1-0	18	2548
30	4.3.89	H	Exeter C.	W 1-0	0-0	17	2601
31	11.3.89	A	Scarborough	W 1-0	0-0	13	2354
32	14.3.89	H	Lincoln C.	W 2-1	2-0	11	2691
33	17.3.89	A	Tranmere Rov.	D 0-0	0-0	11	5143
34	21.3.89	A	Burnley	D 0-0	0-0	10	5258
35	25.3.89	H	Crewe Alex.	L 0-1	0-1	12	4866
36	27.3.89	A	Rochdale	D 0-0	0-0	13	2145
37	1.4.89	H	Hartlepool U.	W 2-1	2-0	11	3158
38	4.4.89	H	Doncaster Rov.	L 0-1	0-1	12	2991
39	7.4.89	A	Stockport Co.	D 1-1	0-1	14	2543
40	15.4.89	H	Cambridge U.	D 1-1	0-0	14	2579
41	21.4.89	A	Colchester U.	D 1-1	1-0	14	3906
42	29.4.89	A	Grimsby T.	D 0-0	0-0	14	3837
43	1.5.89	H	Leyton Orient	W 2-1	2-1	13	2401
44	3.5.89	A	Torquay U.	L 0-1	0-1	14	1603
45	6.5.89	H	Wrexham	L 1-2	0-1	14	2427
46	13.5.89	A	Darlington	W 3-2	3-1	12	3049

Players: League Record, 1988-89 (Division 4)

Match Number	1	2	3	4	5	6	7	8	9	10	11	12	13	14	15	16	17	18	19	20	21	22	23	24	25	26	27	28	29	30	31	32	33	34	35	36	37	38	39	40	41	42	43	44	45	46	Apps	Subs	Goals
Butler, Martin																						7																									1	0	0
Clark, Jonathan	6	6	6^{1}	6	6	6	6	6																																							8	0	1
Dalziel, Ian	3	3	3	3	3	3	**3**		3	3	3	3	3	3	3	3^{1}		3	3	3	3	3	3	3	3	3	3	3	3	3	3	3	3	3	3	3			3	3	3	3	3	3	3	3	42	0	1
Fitzpatrick, Paul								10	10	6	6	6	6	6	6	6	6				6	6	6	**6**	6	6	6	6	6	6	6	6	6	6	6	6	6	**6**	6	6	6				**6**		32	0	0
Fyfe, Tony				★		★				9^{1}	**9**							★	10	**10**	10		**9**	★	★	★	★	9	9^{2}	★	**9**	9^{1}	**9**	9	**9**	9	9	9				9					17	8	4
Gorman, Paul	8	8	8	8	8^{1}	8	8	8	8	8	8	8	8	8	8	**8**	8	8	8	8	8	8	8^{3}	8	8	8^{1}	8	8	8			8	8	8	**8**	8	8	8	8	8	8	8		8	8	8^{1}	43	0	6
Graham, Mike			2	2	2	2	2	2	2	2	2	2	2	2	2	2	2	2	2	2	2	2	2	2	2^{1}	2	2	2^{1}	2	2	2	2	2	2	2	2	2	2	2	2	2	**6**	6	6	2	2	44	0	2
Halpin, John	11		**11**													10	11	11	11^{1}	11	11	11	11	11	11^{1}	11^{2}	11	11	11	11	11	11^{1}	11	11	11	11	11^{2}	11	11	**11**	11	11	11	11	11	11	33	0	7
Harkness, Steven																													10	8	10	7	7	7	7		7	7	**7**				8		★	7	12	1	0
Hetherington, Brent	10^{2}	**10**	★	**10^{1}**	10	10	10	7	7^{1}	10^{1}	10	10	10^{2}				10^{1}	10	7	7	7	10	10	10	10^{2}	10	10	10			★	10	10	10	★	★		★	★	★		★	10^{1}	★	**7**	★	29	10	11
Jeffels, Simon																★	**5**			5	5	5	5	5	5	5	5	5	**5**	5	5	5	5	5	5	5	5	5	**5**	5	5	5	5	5	5	5	28	1	0
McKellar, David										1	1	1	1	1	1	1	1	1				1	1	1	1	1	1	1	1	1	1	1	1	1	1	1	1	1	1	1	1	1	1	1	1	1	34	0	0
Marshall, Gary	7	11	7	7^{1}	11	11	11	11	11	11	11	11	11	11	11	11	7^{1}	7											★															★	★		18	3	2
Nuttell, Michael														★	10	★																															1	2	0
Ogley, Mark	4	5	5	5	5	5	5	5	5	5	5	5	5	5	5	**5**		5	5												7						4				4	4	4	4	4	6	26	0	0
Proudlock, Paul																																			10	10	10	10	10	10	10^{1}			10	10	**10^{2}**	10	0	3
Prudhoe, Mark	1	1	1	1	1	1	1	1	1										1	1	1																										12	0	0
Robertson, James	2	2					★										★																									2	2	**2**			5	2	0
Saddington, Nigel	5	4	4	4	4	4	4^{1}	4	4	4	4	4	4	4	4	4	4	4	4^{1}	4	4	4	4	4	4	4	4	4	4	4	4^{1}	4	4	4	4	**4**		4	4^{1}	4						4	40	0	4
Sendall, Richard	9	9	9	9^{1}	9	9	9	9^{1}	9		★		★	10			★		★	★	9	9	★	★						10^{1}	**8**								9	**9^{1}**	9	10	9^{1}	9	9^{1}	9	22	7	6
Stephens, Archie		★	**10**									9	**9**	**9**	9	9	**9**	**9**	**9**	9^{1}				**9**	**9**	**9**	**9**			**9**	★		★														15	3	1
Stonehouse, Kevin																																			★				★	★							0	3	0
Walsh, Derek		7^{1}	★	11	7	**7**	7^{1}	3	6	7	7	7	7	7	7	7	3	6	6	6			7	7	7	7	7	7	7^{1}	7						7	3	3		7	7	7	7	**7**			34	1	3
Own Goals																		1			1																												2

FA Cup: 1988-89: 1st Round: Telford U. (A) 1-1, Replay (H) 4-1; 2nd Round: Scarborough (A) 1-0; 3rd Round: Liverpool (H) 0-3.
Littlewoods Cup: 1988-89: 1st Round: Blackpool (H) 1-1 (A) 0-3.

SUCCESSFUL TEAMWORK

THE WOOLWICH AND CHARLTON

WOOLWICH
EQUITABLE BUILDING SOCIETY

ANYTHING'S POSSIBLE WITH THE WOOLWICH

CHARLTON ATHLETIC (Division 1)

Team Manager Lennie Lawrence.
Club Address The Valley, Floyd Road, London SE7 8AW. Tel: 01-858 3711/2.
Current Ground Capacity 30,000.
Record Attendance 75,031 v Aston Villa, FA Cup 5th Round, 12 February 1938.
Year Formed 1905. Turned professional 1920.
Previous Names None.
Club Nickname "The Haddicks", "Robins", or "Valiants".
Club Colours Red shirts, white shorts and white stockings.
Club Honours Football League: Div. 3(S) Champions 1928-29, 1934-35. FA Cup: Winners 1947.
League History 1921-29 Div. 3(S); 1929-33 Div.2; 1933-35 Div. 3(S); 1935-36 Div. 2; 1936-57 Div. 1; 1957-72 Div. 2; 1972-75 Div. 3; 1975-80 Div. 2; 1980-81 Div. 3; 1981-86 Div. 2; 1986- Div. 1.

Most League Points in a Season (2 for a win) 61 in Div. 3(S), 1934-35. (3 for a win) 77 in Div. 2, 1985-86.
Most League Goals in a Season 107 in Div. 2, 1957-58.
Record Victory 8-1 v Middlesbrough in Div. 1, 12 September 1953.
Record Defeat 1-11 v Aston Villa in Div. 2, 14 November 1959.
Consecutive League Wins 7 in 1980.
Consecutive League Defeats 9 in 1957.
Record League Appearances Sam Bartram, 583 between 1934-56.
Record League Goalscorer—Career Stuart Leary, 153 between 1951-62.
Record League Goalscorer—Season Ralph Allen, 32 in Div. 3(S), 1934-35.

Charlton Athletic: League Record, 1988-89 (Division 1)

Match Number	Date	Venue	Opponents	Result	H/T	Lge Posn	Attend
1	27.8.88	H	Liverpool	L 0-3	0-1		21389
2	3.9.88	A	West Ham U.	W 3-1	1-0	10	19566
3	10.9.88	H	Millwall	L 0-3	0-2	12	13375
4	17.9.88	A	Coventry C.	L 0-3	0-0	16	11890
5	24.9.88	H	Newcastle U.	D 2-2	1-0	16	6088
6	1.10.88	A	Norwich C.	W 3-1	1-1	13	11470
7	8.10.88	H	Tottenham H.	D 2-2	1-0	14	14384
8	15.10.88	H	Aston Villa	D 2-2	1-0	12	7594
9	22.10.88	A	Derby Co.	D 0-0	0-0	13	14106
10	29.10.88	H	Sheffield Wed.	W 2-1	1-0	11	5933
11	5.11.88	A	Southampton	L 0-2	0-0	14	12826
12	12.11.88	H	Everton	L 1-2	1-2	15	8627
13	19.11.88	A	Wimbledon	D 1-1	0-0	15	5631
14	26.11.88	H	Nottingham F.	L 0-1	0-1	16	6411
15	3.12.88	A	Manchester U.	L 0-3	0-1	15	31173
16	10.12.88	H	Q.P.R.	D 1-1	0-1	17	6012
17	17.12.88	A	Middlesbrough	D 0-0	0-0	17	16065
18	26.12.88	H	Arsenal	L 2-3	0-1	19	18439
19	31.12.88	H	West Ham U.	D 0-0	0-0	18	11084
20	2.1.89	A	Millwall	L 0-1	0-0	18	17025
21	14.1.89	H	Luton T.	W 3-0	3-0	18	5212
22	21.1.89	A	Newcastle U.	W 2-0	1-0	17	19076
23	4.2.89	H	Norwich C.	L 1-2	0-0	17	7518
24	11.2.89	A	Tottenham H.	D 1-1	1-0	17	22803
25	25.2.89	A	Aston Villa	W 2-1	1-1	17	16481
26	1.3.89	A	Liverpool	L 0-2	0-1	17	30283
27	4.3.89	A	Sheffield Wed.	L 1-3	1-1	17	16081
28	11.3.89	H	Southampton	D 2-2	1-0	17	6377
29	21.3.89	A	Arsenal	D 2-2	1-2	18	30259
30	25.3.89	H	Coventry C.	D 0-0	0-0	15	6728
31	1.4.89	H	Middlesbrough	W 2-0	1-0	15	6696
32	10.4.89	A	Everton	L 2-3	1-1	17	16316
33	22.4.89	H	Manchester U.	W 1-0	1-0	17	12055
34	29.4.89	A	Q.P.R.	L 0-1	0-1	17	13432
35	2.5.89	A	Luton T.	L 2-5	0-4	18	10024
36	6.5.89	H	Wimbledon	W 1-0	1-0	15	7230
37	10.5.89	H	Derby Co.	W 3-0	1-0	14	7448
38	13.5.89	A	Nottingham F.	L 0-4	0-3	14	17637

Players: League Record, 1988-89 (Division 1)

Match Number	1	2	3	4	5	6	7	8	9	10	11	12	13	14	15	16	17	18	19	20	21	22	23	24	25	26	27	28	29	30	31	32	33	34	35	36	37	38	Apps	Subs	Goals
Bennett, Michael						7	7	7	7	7	**7**	**7**	7	7	7	**7**																							11	0	0
Bolder, Bob	1	1	1	**1**	1	1	1	1	1	1	1	1	1	1	1	1	1	1	1	1	1	1	1	1	1	1	1	1	1	1	1	1	1	1	1	1	1	1	38	0	0
Campbell, David				★										★	**8**	★	7	7	7							★	7												5	4	0
Caton, Tommy													5	5	5	5	5	5							5[1]	5	5	5					4	**4**	**4**				13	0	1
Crooks, Garth															★	**8**	8	**8**			**11**[1]	11	11[1]	11	**11**		★	11		★				★	**11**				10	4	2
Gritt, Steve	7	9	**9**	9	9	9	**9**	**9**[1]				6	6	6	6	6[1]	6	6	**6**		**3**	3	**10**	**8**										**6**		6			22	0	2
Humphrey, John	2	2	2	2	2	2	2	2	2	2	2	2	2	2	2	2	2	2	2	2	2	2	2	2	2	2	2	2	2	2	2[1]	2	2	2	2	2	2	2	38	0	1
Jones, Andy					★		★[1]	★			★	★																							★[2]	★	11[1]	11	2	7	4
Leaburn, Carl	9	10	10	10	**10**	10	10	**10**	10	10	9	**10**	10	10	10	10	10	10	**10**	10	★		★		★	11	**11**		11	11	11	11	11	11		**11**[1]			29	3	1
Lee, Robert	8	7	7	7	7[1]			★		★	★	★	★[1]	8				★	8	7	7	7[2]	7	7	7	7		7[1]	7	7	7	7	7	7	7	7	7	7	25	6	5
Mackenzie, Steve	10	4	4	4	4	4	4	4	4	4	8	4	4	4	4			★[2]	9	6	9	9	9	9	9	**9**	**9**	9	9[1]	9	9	9	9	9	9	9	9	9	35	1	3
Miller, Paul	6	6	6	6	6																																		5	0	0
Minto, Scott																★				11	★																		1	2	0
Mortimer, Paul			★			11[1]	11	11	11	11	11	11	11	11	11	11	11	11	11		10[1]	10	★	★	8	8	8	10	10[1]	10	10[1]	10[1]	10	10	10	**10**	10	**10**	30	3	5
Pates, Colin								6	6	6	6								5	5	5	5	5	5			★		5	5	5	5	5	5	5	5	5	5	20	1	0
Peake, Andy	4			★		6	6[1]		9	9	4	9	9	9	9	9	9	**9**	★	9	6	6	6	6	6	6	6	6	6	**6**	6	6	6				6	6	29	2	1
Reid, Mark	3	3	3	3	3	3	3	3	3	3	3	3	3	**3**	3	3	3	3	3	3			**3**	3	3	3	3	3	3	3	3	3	3[1]	3	3	3	3	3	36	0	1
Shirtliff, Peter	5	5	5	5	5	5	5	5	5	5[1]	5	5				4	4	4	4	4	4	4	4	4	4	4	4	4	4	4	4	4		★	6	4	4[1]	4	33	1	2
Stuart, Mark		11	11	**11**	11																																		4	0	0
Walsh, Colin	11																													★					8	★		★	2	3	0
Williams, Paul		8[2]	8	8	8[1]	8[2]	8	8[1]	8	**8**[1]	**10**	8[1]	**8**						★	8	8[1]	8	8	10[1]	10	10	10[1]	8[1]	8	**8**	8	8	8	8	★	8	8[1]	8	30	2	13
Own Goals		1																							1							1									3

FA Cup: 1988-89: 3rd Round: Oldham Ath. (H) 2-1; 4th Round: Kettering T. (H) 2-1; 5th Round: West Ham U. (H) 0-1.
Littlewoods Cup: 1988-89: 2nd Round: Northampton T. (A) 1-1 (H) 2-1; 3rd Round: Q.P.R. (A) 1-2.

CHELSEA (Division 1)

Team Manager Bobby Campbell.
Club Address Stamford Bridge, London SW6. Tel: 01-385 5545/6.
Current Ground Capacity 43,900.
Record Attendance 82,905 v Arsenal, Div. 1, 12 October 1935.
Year Formed 1905. Turned professional 1905.
Previous Names None.
Club Nickname "The Blues".
Club Colours All royal blue.
Club Honours Football League: Div. 1 Champions 1954-55. Div. 2 Champions 1983-84. 1988-89 FA Cup: Winners 1970. Football League Cup: Winners 1965. European Cup-Winners Cup: Winners 1970-71.
League History 1905-07 Div. 2; 1907-10 Div. 1; 1910-12 Div. 2; 1912-24 Div. 1; 1924-30 Div. 2; 1930-62 Div. 1; 1962-63 Div. 2; 1963-75 Div. 1; 1975-77 Div. 2; 1977-79 Div. 1; 1979-84 Div. 2; 1984-88 Div. 1; 1988-89 Div. 2; 1989- Div. 1.
Most League Points in a Season (2 for a win) 57 in Div 2, 1906-07. (3 for a win) 99 in Div. 2, 1988-89.
Most League Goals in a Season 98 in Div. 1, 1960-61.
Record Victory 13-0 v Jeunesse Hautcharage in European Cup-Winners Cup 1st Round, 29 September 1971.
Record Defeat 1-8 v Wolverhampton W. in Div. 1, 26 September 1953.
Consecutive League Wins 8 in 1927 and 1989.
Consecutive League Defeats 7 in 1952.
Record League Appearances Ron Harris, 655 between 1962-80.
Record League Goalscorer—Career Bobby Tambling, 164 between 1958-70.
Record League Goalscorer—Season Jimmy Greaves, 41 in Div. 1, 1960-61.

Chelsea: League Record, 1988-89 (Division 2)

Match Number	Date	Venue	Opponents	Result	H/T	Lge Posn	Attend
1	27.8.88	H	Blackburn Rov.	L 1-2	1-1		8722
2	30.8.88	A	Crystal Palace	D 1-1	1-0	14	17490
3	3.9.88	A	Bournemouth	L 0-1	0-0	16	8763
4	10.9.88	H	Oxford U.	D 1-1	0-0	15	7587
5	17.9.88	A	Barnsley	D 1-1	1-1	16	6942
6	20.9.88	H	Manchester C.	L 1-3	1-1	19	8856
7	24.9.88	A	Leeds U.	W 2-0	2-0	17	26080
8	1.10.88	H	Leicester C.	W 2-1	0-0	13	7050
9	4.10.88	H	Walsall	W 2-0	0-0	14	6747
10	9.10.88	A	Swindon T.	D 1-1	0-0	10	11346
11	15.10.88	A	Oldham Ath.	W 4-1	2-1	6	7817
12	22.10.88	H	Plymouth Arg.	W 5-0	4-0	5	12658
13	25.10.88	A	Hull C.	L 0-3	0-1	7	6953
14	29.10.88	H	Brighton & H.A.	W 2-0	1-0	5	15406
15	5.11.88	A	Watford	W 2-1	2-1	3	17631
16	12.11.88	H	Sunderland	D 1-1	0-1	4	19210
17	19.11.88	A	Bradford C.	D 2-2	0-1	5	11442
18	26.11.88	H	Shrewsbury T.	W 2-0	2-0	4	11595
19	3.12.88	A	Stoke C.	W 3-0	1-0	2	12288
20	10.12.88	H	Portsmouth	D 3-3	2-1	4	20221
21	16.12.88	A	Birmingham C.	W 4-1	1-0	2	7897
22	26.12.88	H	Ipswich T.	W 3-0	2-0	1	17621
23	31.12.88	H	West Bromwich A.	D 1-1	0-1	1	25906
24	2.1.89	A	Oxford U.	W 3-2	2-1	2	11427
25	14.1.89	H	Crystal Palace	W 1-0	1-0	1	24184
26	21.1.89	A	Blackburn Rov.	D 1-1	1-0	1	11713
27	4.2.89	A	Walsall	W 7-0	4-0	1	6860
28	11.2.89	H	Swindon T.	W 3-2	3-2	1	17829
29	18.2.89	A	Plymouth Arg.	W 1-0	1-0	1	13180
30	25.2.89	H	Oldham Ath.	D 2-2	2-1	2	13261
31	28.2.89	H	Hull C.	W 2-1	0-0	1	11407
32	11.3.89	H	Watford	D 2-2	2-2	2	22188
33	15.3.89	A	Brighton & H.A.	W 1-0	1-0	2	12600
34	18.3.89	A	Manchester C.	W 3-2	2-0	1	40070
35	21.3.89	A	Sunderland	W 2-1	1-1	1	14714
36	25.3.89	H	Bournemouth	W 2-0	0-0	1	22467
37	28.3.89	A	Ipswich T.	W 1-0	0-0	1	22950
38	1.4.89	H	Barnsley	W 5-3	2-2	1	16023
39	4.4.89	H	Birmingham C.	W 3-1	1-1	1	14796
40	8.4.89	A	West Bromwich A.	W 3-2	3-2	1	22858
41	15.4.89	A	Leicester C.	L 0-2	0-0	1	19468
42	22.4.89	H	Leeds U.	W 1-0	0-0	1	30337
43	29.4.89	A	Shrewsbury T.	D 1-1	0-0	1	5588
44	1.5.89	H	Stoke C.	W 2-1	1-1	1	14946
45	6.5.89	H	Bradford C.	W 3-1	1-0	1	18003
46	13.5.89	A	Portsmouth	W 3-2	0-1	1	12051

Players: League Record, 1988-89 (Division 1)

Match Number	1	2	3	4	5	6	7	8	9	10	11	12	13	14	15	16	17	18	19	20	21	22	23
Beasant, Dave																							
Bumstead, John	11	11			11	**6**	11^1	11	11	11												★	**8**
Clarke, Stephen	2	2	2	2	2	2	2	2	2			2	2	2	2	**2**							
Dixon, Kerry						9	9	9	9^1	9^1	9	9^1	9	**9**^{1}	**9**^{1}	9	9	9^1	9	9^1	9^2	9^1	9
Dodds, Billy			★	★																			
Dorigo, Tony						3	3	3	3^1	3	3	3^1	3	3	3	3	3	3^1	3	3	3	**3**	3
Durie, Gordon	10	10	10	10	**10**	10	**10**^{1}					10^2	10	10	10^1	10	10	10		**10**^{1}	10^2	10^1	10
Freestone, Roger		1		1	1		1	1	1	1	1	1	1	1	1	1	1	1	1	1	1	1	1
Hall, Gareth		7	**7**	**7**	★			★		2	2						2	2	2	2	2	2	2
Hazard, Mike																							
Hitchcock, Kevin	1		1			1																	
Le Saux, Graeme																							
Lee, David								★^{1}	6	6			★		★	★	5^1	5	5	5	5	**8**^{1}	
McAllister, Kevin	7		11	11^1	7	7	7	7	7		7^1	**7**	**7**	★		★	★		10^1	★		★	★
MacLaughlin, Joe	5										5	5	5	5	5	5						5	5
Mitchell, David																							
Monkou, Ken																							
Nicholas, Peter	8	8	8	8	8	8	8	**8**	8	8	8^1	8	8	8	8	8	8	8	8	8^1	8		
Pates, Colin	6	5	5	5	5	5^1	5	5	5	5													
Roberts, Graham	**4**	4	4	4	4^1	4	4	4^1	4	4	4	4^1	4	4	4	4	4	4	4^1	4	4	4	4^1
Wilson, Clive	3	3	3	3	3	11	6				11	★	★	11	11	11	11	11	11^1	11	11	11	11
Wilson, Kevin	9^1	9^1	9	9	9	★	★	10	10	10	10^1	11	11	7^1	7	7^1	7^1	7	7	7	7	7	7
Wood, Darren	★	6	6	6	6			**6**		7	6^1	6	**6**	6	6	**6**	**6**	6	6	6	6	6	6
Own Goals																							

Match Number	24	25	26	27	28	29	30	31	32	33	34	35	36	37	38	39	40	41	42	43	44	45	46	Apps	Subs	Goals
Beasant, Dave		1	1	1	1	1	1	1	1	1	1	1	1	1	1	1	1	1	1	1	1	1	1	22	0	0
Bumstead, John	★			6	6	6	6	6	6	6	6	6	6	6	6	6	6	**6**	6^1	6	6			27	2	2
Clarke, Stephen		2	2	2	2	2	2	2	2	2	2	2	2	2	2	2	2	2	2	2	2	2	**2**	36	0	0
Dixon, Kerry	9^2	9	9^1			9^1	9	9^1	9	9	9^1	9	9	9	9^4	9^1	9	9	9	9^1	9^1	9^2	**9**	39	0	25
Dodds, Billy																								0	2	0
Dorigo, Tony	3	3^1	3		3	3	3	3	3^1	3	3^1	3	3	3	3	3	3	3	3	3	3	3	3	40	0	6
Durie, Gordon	**10**			10^5	10^1	**10**					**10**	10	10^1	10^1	10^1	10	10	10	10	**10**				32	0	17
Freestone, Roger	1																							21	0	0
Hall, Gareth	2	★	6														★			★	10	6	6	17	5	0
Hazard, Mike				11	11	**11**	11																	4	0	0
Hitchcock, Kevin																								3	0	0
Le Saux, Graeme																							★	0	1	0
Lee, David	**8**	10	10			★									★	★	5^1	★						12	8	4
McAllister, Kevin	★						★	7	7	7	7	7	7	7	7	7	7^1	7	7	7	7	7	7^2	28	8	6
MacLaughlin, Joe	5	5	5	5	5	5	5	5	5	5	5	5	5	5	5	**5**		5	5	5	**5**	5	5	31	0	0
Mitchell, David		8	8	9	9	7	**10**																	6	0	0
Monkou, Ken																					★		★	0	2	0
Nicholas, Peter				8	8	8	8	8	8	8	8	8	8	8	8	8	**8**	8	8			8	8	39	0	2
Pates, Colin																								10	0	1
Roberts, Graham	4	**4**	4	4^1	4	4	4^2	4	4^1	4	4	4^1	4^1	4	**4**	4^1	4^1	4	4	4	4^1	4^1	4	46	0	15
Wilson, Clive	11^1	11	11	3				11	11	11	★									8	8	10	10^1	29	3	3
Wilson, Kevin	7	7	7	7^1	7	★	7	10^1	10	10^1	11^1	11^1	11	11	11	11^1	11	11	11	11	11	11	11	43	3	12
Wood, Darren	6	6																						21	1	1
Own Goals					2																					2

FA Cup: 1988-89: 3rd Round: Barnsley (A) 0-4

Littlewoods Cup: 1988-9: 2nd Round: Scunthorpe U. (A) 1-4 (H) 2-2.

CHESTER CITY (Division 3)

Team Manager Harry McNally.
Club Address The Stadium, Sealand Road, Chester CH1 4LW. Tel: (0244) 371376.
Current Ground Capacity 22,000.
Record Attendance 20,500 v Chelsea, FA Cup 3rd Round replay, 16 January 1952.
Year Formed 1884. Turned professional 1902.
Previous Names Chester.
Club Nickname "The Blues".
Club Colours Royal blue shirts with white pinstripe, white shorts and stockings.
Club Honours None.
League History 1931-58 Div. 3(N); 1958-75 Div. 4; 1975-82 Div. 3; 1983-86 Div. 4; 1986- Div. 3.

Most League Points in a Season (2 for a win) 56 in Div. 3(N), 1946-47 and in Div. 4, 1964-65. (3 for a win) 84 in Div. 4, 1985-86.
Most League Goals in a Season 119 in Div. 4, 1964-65.
Record Victory 12-0 v York C. in Div. 3(N), 1 February 1936.
Record Defeat 2-11 v Oldham Ath. in Div. 3(N), 19 January 1952.
Consecutive League Wins 8 in 1934, 1936 and 1978.
Consecutive League Defeats 7 in 1955, 1956 and 1982.
Record League Appearances Ray Gill, 406 between 1951-62.
Record League Goalscorer—Career Gary Talbot, 83 between 1963-69.
Record League Goalscorer—Season Dick Yates, 36 in Div. 3(N), 1946-47.

Chester City: League Record, 1988-89 (Division 3)

Match Number	Date	Venue	Opponents	Result	H/T	Lge Posn	Attend
1	27.8.88	H	Blackpool	D 1-1	1-0		3496
2	3.9.88	A	Port Vale	W 2-1	2-0	6	4213
3	10.9.88	H	Bristol C.	W 2-0	0-0	2	2823
4	17.9.88	A	Sheffield U.	L 1-6	0-3	8	8675
5	20.9.88	A	Preston N.E.	D 3-3	1-1	9	5415
6	24.9.88	H	Huddersfield T.	W 3-0	2-0	6	3319
7	1.10.88	A	Reading	L 1-3	0-2	7	4376
8	5.10.88	H	Brentford	W 3-2	3-2	7	2004
9	9.10.88	A	Notts Co.	D 2-2	1-1	6	5772
10	15.10.88	H	Cardiff C.	D 0-0	0-0	8	2796
11	22.10.88	A	Bristol Rov.	L 1-4	1-2	13	3811
12	26.10.88	H	Mansfield T.	D 0-0	0-0	13	1805
13	29.10.88	A	Aldershot	D 1-1	1-1	14	1862
14	5.11.88	H	Swansea C.	W 3-1	2-0	11	2263
15	8.11.88	A	Bury	L 1-2	0-1	13	2497
16	12.11.88	H	Chesterfield	W 3-1	1-1	11	2099
17	26.11.88	H	Southend U.	L 2-4	1-1	13	2050
18	3.12.88	A	Gillingham	W 2-0	1-0	11	3329
19	17.12.88	A	Bolton W.	W 1-0	0-0	9	4318
20	26.12.88	H	Wigan Ath.	W 1-0	0-0	8	3262
21	31.12.88	H	Northampton T.	W 2-1	0-1	4	2733
22	2.1.89	A	Wolverhampton W.	L 1-3	1-3	6	21901
23	7.1.89	A	Fulham	L 1-4	0-3	7	4196
24	14.1.89	H	Port Vale	L 1-2	1-0	9	4891
25	21.1.89	A	Bristol C.	W 1-0	0-0	8	9586
26	4.2.89	H	Reading	W 3-0	1-0	7	2364
27	11.2.89	A	Brentford	W 1-0	0-0	7	5748
28	18.2.89	H	Notts Co	W 1-0	0-0	5	3157
29	28.2.89	A	Mansfield T.	L 0-2	0-0	7	2796
30	4.3.89	H	Bristol Rov.	L 0-2	0-0	8	3082
31	11.3.89	A	Swansea C.	D 1-1	1-1	8	4311
32	15.3.89	H	Aldershot	D 1-1	0-1	9	2028
33	18.3.89	A	Blackpool	D 1-1	0-0	8	2795
34	25.3.89	H	Wolverhampton W.	D 1-1	1-1	9	8236
35	27.3.89	A	Wigan Ath.	L 0-3	0-1	10	3132
36	1.4.89	H	Bolton W.	D 0-0	0-0	9	3225
37	5.4.89	H	Fulham	W 7-0	2-0	8	2121
38	8.4.89	A	Northampton T.	W 2-0	0-0	7	2845
39	15.4.89	A	Huddersfield T.	L 1-3	0-1	7	6109
40	19.4.89	H	Sheffield U.	L 0-1	0-1	7	4282
41	22.4.89	H	Preston N.E.	L 0-1	0-0	9	4617
42	29.4.89	A	Chesterfield	W 2-1	0-0	8	3529
43	1.5.89	H	Bury	W 2-0	1-0	8	2110
44	6.5.89	H	Gillingham	W 2-0	1-0	7	2106
45	9.5.89	A	Cardiff C.	L 0-2	0-0	7	3002
46	13.5.89	A	Southend U.	L 0-1	0-0	8	4089

Players. League Record, 1988-89 (Division 3)

Match Number	1	2	3	4	5	6	7	8	9	10	11	12	13	14	15	16	17	18	19	20	21	22	23
Abel, Graham	5	5	5	5	5	5	5	5	5	5	5	5	5	**5^{1}**		5		5	5	5	5^{1}	**5**	5
Barrow, Graham		8	8	8	8	8	8	8^{1}	8^{1}	8	8	8	8	8	8	8	8	8	8	8			8
Benjamin, Ian	**9**	9	9^{1}	9	★	★	★		9^{1}	**9**	9^{1}	9	9	9	9	**9**	9	9	9	9	★	10	9
Bennett, Gary	11			★				★		★	★		★	10									
Butler, Barry	8				6							4	4	★	5	2	5	2	6	6	2	2	2
Dale, Carl	★		$★^{1}$		9^{2}	9	**9**	9^{1}		11	★	11	**11**	**11^{2}**	**11**	11^{2}	11	11^{1}	11^{1}	11	11^{1}	11	11
Glenn, David	2	2	2	2	2	**2**	2	2	2	2	2	2		2					2	**2**			
Graham, Milton																				★	**10**	★	10
Hawtin, Craig													2^{1}		2		2						
Hinnigan, Joe	4	4	4	4	**4**				4		4			4	4	4	4	4	4	4	4	4	**4**
Jakub, Joe	7	7	7	7	7	7	7	7^{1}	7	7	7	7	7	7	7	7	7	7	7	7	7	7	7
Johnson, Steve	10^{1}	10^{1}	10	10	10^{1}	10^{1}	10	10	10	10	10	10	10	★	**10**	★	10^{2}	10^{1}	10		9	9^{1}	★
Kelly, Tony						4	4	4	11	4													
Lane, Martin																							
Lightfoot, Chris	6	6	6	**6^{1}**		6	6	6	6	6	**6**	6	6	6	6	6	6	6		$★^{1}$	6	6	6^{1}
Lundon, Sean					11						11				★			**3**			8	**8**	
Newhouse, Aiden	★	11	**11**	11		11^{1}	11	**11**							$★^{1}$	10				**10**		★	
O'Keefe, Eamon																							
Painter, Peter																							
Stewart, Billy	1	1	1	1	1	1	1	1	1	1	1	1	1	1	1	1	1	1	1	1	1	1	1
Woodthorpe, Colin	3	3^{1}	3	3	3	3	3^{1}	3	3	3	**3**	3	3	3	3	3	3		3	3	3	3	3
Wynne, Darren																		★					
Own Goals						1										1							

Match Number	24	25	26	27	28	29	30	31	32	33	34	35	36	37	38	39	40	41	42	43	44	45	46	Apps	Subs	Goals
Abel, Graham	5	5	5	5	5	5	5	5	5	5	5^{1}	5		**9**			8	9	9	4	4	3		40	0	3
Barrow, Graham	8	8	8	8	8	8	8	8	8	8	8							8	8	8^{1}	**8**			35	0	3
Benjamin, Ian																								18	4	3
Bennett, Gary																								2	5	0
Butler, Barry	2	**2**	2	2	2	2	2	2	2	2	2		2	2	2	**2**	2		2	2	2	2	**2**	34	1	0
Dale, Carl	11^{1}	11	11^{2}	11^{1}	11	11	11	11^{1}	11^{1}	11	11		11	11^{3}	**11**		11	11	11^{1}	11	11^{1}	11	11	38	3	22
Glenn, David					★							2						2						17	1	0
Graham, Milton	10	**10**	★				10	10	10	**10**	★	8	9	10^{1}	10	10	10	**10**	10	10	10	10	10	20	4	1
Hawtin, Craig																								3	0	1
Hinnigan, Joe	4	4	4^{1}	4	4	4	**4**	4	**4**	4	**4**	**4**	4	4^{1}	4	4	4	4	**4**		★	**4**	4	38	1	2
Jakub, Joe	7	7	7	7	7	7	7	7	7	7	7	7	7	7	7	7	7					8	8	42	0	1
Johnson, Steve	9	9^{1}	9	9	9^{1}	9	9	9	9	9	9	9				**9**	**9**					9	**9**	35	3	10
Kelly, Tony																								5	0	0
Lane, Martin	6	6	6	6	6	6	6	6	6	6	6	6	6	6	6	6	6	6	6	6	6	6	6	23	0	0
Lightfoot, Chris		★		★							★	★	5	5	5^{1}	5	5	5	5^{1}	5^{1}	5	5	5	31	5	6
Lundon, Sean																								5	1	0
Newhouse, Aiden		★	**10**	**10**	**10**	10	★		★			11	**10**		★	★		★				★	★	14	11	2
O'Keefe, Eamon										$★^{1}$	**10**	**10**	8	8^{1}	8^{1}	8	★	★	7	**7**	7^{1}	7	7	11	3	4
Painter, Peter													★	★	9	11^{1}		**7**	★	9	**9**			5	3	1
Stewart, Billy	1	1	1	1	1	1	1	1	1	1	1	1	1	1	1	1	1	1	1	1	1	1	1	46	0	0
Woodthorpe, Colin	3	3	3	3	3	3	3	3	3	3	3	3	3	3^{1}	3	3	3	3	3	3	3		3	44	0	3
Wynne, Darren												★				★				★	★		★	0	6	0
Own Goals																										2

FA Cup: 1988-89: 1st Round: Burnley (A) 2-0; 2nd Round: Huddersfield T. (A) 0-1.
Littlewoods Cup: 1988-89: 1st Round: Bolton W. (A) 0-1 (H) 3-1; 2nd Round: Nottingham F. (A) 0-6 (H) 0-4.

CHESTERFIELD (Division 4)

Team Manager Paul Hart.
Club Address Recreation Ground, Chesterfield S40 4SX. Tel: (0246) 31535.
Current Ground Capacity 11,210.
Record Attendance 30,968 v Newcastle U., Div. 2. 7th April 1939.
Year Formed 1866. Turned professional 1891.
Previous Names Chesterfield Town, Chesterfield Municipal.
Club Nickname "The Blues" or "Spireites".
Club Colours Royal blue shirts with white pinstripe, white shorts with blue side stripes and white stockings.
Club Honours Football League: Div. 3(N) Champions 1930-31, 1935-36; Div. 4 Champions 1969-70, 1984-85.
League History 1908-09 Div. 2; 1909 Failed re-election; 1921-31 Div. 3(N); 1931-33 Div. 2; 1933-36 Div. 3(N); 1936-51 Div. 2; 1951-58 Div. 3(N); 1958-61 Div. 3; 1961-70 Div. 4; 1970-83 Div. 3; 1983-85 Div. 4; 1985-89 Div. 3; 1989- Div. 4.
Most League Points in a Season (2 for a win) 64 in Div. 4, 1969-70. (3 for a win) 91 in Div. 4, 1984-85.
Most League Goals in a Season 102 in Div. 3(N), 1930-31.
Record Victory 10-0 v Glossop N.E. in Div. 2, 17 January 1903.
Record Defeat 0-10 v Gillingham in Div. 3, 5 September 1987.
Consecutive League Wins 10 in 1933.
Consecutive League Defeats 9 in 1960.
Record League Appearances Dave Blakey, 617 between 1948-67.
Record League Goalscorer—Career Ernie Moss, 161 between 1969-86.
Record League Goalscorer—Season Jimmy Cookson, 44 in Div. 3(N), 1925-26.

Chesterfield: League Record, 1988-89 (Division 3)

Match Number	Date	Venue	Opponents	Result	H/T	Lge Posn	Attend
1	27.8.88	H	Aldershot	W 2-1	0-0		2327
2	3.9.88	A	Bristol C.	L 0-4	0-1	17	7547
3	10.9.88	H	Wolverhampton W.	L 0-3	0-2	20	4217
4	17.9.88	A	Northampton T.	L 0-3	0-2	21	4520
5	19.9.88	A	Port Vale	L 0-5	0-3	21	4469
6	24.9.88	H	Blackpool	L 0-2	0-0	23	2128
7	1.10.88	H	Bury	L 1-2	1-1	23	1837
8	4.10.88	A	Notts Co.	L 0-4	0-2	24	4519
9	8.10.88	A	Gillingham	W 1-0	1-0	22	2901
10	15.10.88	H	Preston N.E.	L 0-3	0-2	23	2813
11	22.10.88	A	Southend U.	L 1-3	0-3	23	2662
12	25.10.88	H	Brentford	D 2-2	0-0	23	1876
13	29.10.88	A	Bolton W.	L 0-5	0-2	24	4757
14	5.11.88	H	Bristol Rov.	L 0-3	0-1	24	2480
15	12.11.88	A	Chester C.	L 1-3	1-1	24	2099
16	26.11.88	A	Reading	D 0-0	0-0	24	4775
17	3.12.88	H	Mansfield T.	L 1-3	1-1	24	4236
18	17.12.88	A	Swansea C.	L 0-2	0-1	24	3656
19	26.12.88	H	Huddersfield T.	D 1-1	1-1	24	5539
20	31.12.88	H	Fulham	W 4-1	2-0	24	3086
21	2.1.89	A	Sheffield U.	W 3-1	2-1	24	15769
22	7.1.89	A	Wigan Ath.	W 2-0	2-0	24	2249
23	14.1.89	H	Bristol C.	W 1-0	0-0	22	3488
24	21.1.89	A	Wolverhampton W.	L 0-1	0-0	22	15049
25	28.1.89	H	Northampton T.	D 1-1	0-1	22	3920
26	4.2.89	A	Bury	L 1-2	1-1	23	3844
27	11.2.89	H	Notts Co.	W 3-0	2-0	22	4943
28	18.2.89	H	Gillingham	W 3-1	1-0	22	3432
29	25.2.89	A	Preston N.E.	L 0-6	0-4	22	7074
30	28.2.89	A	Brentford	L 0-1	0-0	22	4192
31	4.3.89	H	Southend U.	W 2-1	0-1	21	3261
32	11.3.89	A	Bristol Rov.	L 1-2	0-2	21	4686
33	14.3.89	H	Bolton W.	D 1-1	1-0	21	2877
34	18.3.89	A	Aldershot	L 0-2	0-0	21	1886
35	21.3.89	H	Cardiff C.	W 4-0	2-0	21	2888
36	25.3.89	H	Sheffield U.	W 2-1	1-0	20	10991
37	27.3.89	A	Huddersfield T.	D 1-1	1-1	20	5819
38	1.4.89	H	Swansea C.	W 2-0	0-0	19	3349
39	4.4.89	H	Wigan Ath.	D 1-1	0-1	19	3179
40	8.4.89	A	Fulham	L 1-2	0-0	20	4252
41	15.4.89	H	Port Vale	L 1-2	0-2	20	5895
42	22.4.89	A	Blackpool	W 2-1	0-0	20	3221
43	29.4.89	H	Chester C.	L 1-2	0-0	21	3529
44	1.5.89	A	Cardiff C.	W 1-0	1-0	20	3244
45	6.5.89	A	Mansfield T.	L 1-3	0-2	21	4767
46	13.5.89	H	Reading	L 2-4	2-0	22	3107

Players: League Record, 1988-89 (Division 3)

Match Number	1	2	3	4	5	6	7	8	9	10	11	12	13	14	15	16	17	18	19	20	21	22	23
Alleyne, Robert			★	9	9	9	9^1	9	9	9	**9**	9^2	9	8	8	8	8	★	**7**	**8**	★		
Arnott, Kevin	8	8	8	8	8	8	8	**8**	8	8	8	8	8	4	10	10						★	8
Astbury, Mike	1		1	1	1																	1	
Bloomer, Rob		★		3	3	11	★	★	4	4	4	4	4	10	4^1	2	2	8	8^1	10^2	10^1	10	10^1
Brien, Tony																		5	5	5^1	5	5	5
Brown, Jim		1				1	1	1	1	1	1	1	1	1	1	1							
Cherry, Steve																	1	1	1	1	1		1
Dempsey, Mark							11	11	11														
Eley, Kevin	7	7	7	7	7	7	**7**	7		★	11	11		7	7	**7**	7	7	★	7	7	**7**	**7**
Gormley, Eddie																4	10	10	10				
Henderson, Mick	4	4	4	4	4	4	4	**4**		11							★	**4**					
Hewitt, Jamie	2	2	2	2	2	2	2	2	2	2	2	2	2	**2**	2					2	2	2	2
Hoole, David														★									
Hunter, Les	6	**6**	6	6												5	5						
Leonard, Mike																							
McDonald, Gavin											★				★					★^{1}	**8**		★
McGeeney, Pat	3	**3**	3		6			★	7	**7**	7	7	7				**4**						
Morris, Andy	10^1	10	10	10	10	10	10	10	10	10	10^1	10	10	9	9	9	11	11	11	11	11^2	11	11
Prindiville, Stephen				11	11	3	3	3	3^1	3	3	3	3	3	3	3	3	3	3	3	3	3	3
Rogers, Lee	5	5	★															2	2	6	6	6	6
Rolph, Andrew																							
Shaw, Adrian																			4	4	4	4	4
Slack, Trevor						6	6	6	6	6	6	6	6	6	5								
Thompson, Nigel	11	11	**11**										11	**11**		★							
Waller, David	9^1	9	9											★	**11**	11	9^1	9	9	9	9	9	9
Wood, Darren		★	5	5	5	5	5	5	5	5	5	5	5	5	6	6	6	6	6			8^1	
Own Goals																						1	

Match Number	24	25	26	27	28	29	30	31	32	33	34	35	36	37	38	39	40	41	42	43	44	45	46	Apps	Subs	Goals
Alleyne, Robert				8	8				★	10	**10**				★	11				★	★	**8**	★	22	8	3
Arnott, Kevin	★	★	4	4	4	4	4	4	4						★	4	4	4	4	4	4	4	4	32	4	0
Astbury, Mike					1	1	1																	8	0	0
Bloomer, Rob	10	**10**	**10**	10	10^1	**10**	10	2^1	2	2	4	4^1	4	4	4	**2**	11	11	10	10	10	10	10^1	41	3	10
Brien, Tony	5	5	5	5	5	5	5	5	5	5	5	5	5	5	5	5	5	5	5	5	5	5	5	29	0	1
Brown, Jim																								12	0	0
Cherry, Steve	1	1	1	1																				10	0	0
Dempsey, Mark																								3	0	0
Eley, Kevin	7	7	7	**7**				10	**10**	**7**	**7**	**7**	7	**7**	7	7	7	7	7	**7**	7	**7**		38	2	0
Gormley, Eddie																								4	0	0
Henderson, Mick																								10	1	0
Hewitt, Jamie	2	2	2	2	2	2	**2**		★	4	2	2	10	10^1	10	10	10	**10**	2	2	2	2		39	1	1
Hoole, David		★	8			★	★				★	10	**2**	2	**2**	★	**2**					★		6	7	0
Hunter, Les																								6	0	0
Leonard, Mike								1	1	1	1	1	1	1	1	1	1	1	1	1	1	1	1	16	0	0
McDonald, Gavin	**8**	**8**	★		★	★	7	**7**																5	7	1
McGeeney, Pat																								10	1	0
Morris, Andy	11	11	11^1	11	11	11	11	11	11	11	11	11^3	11	11					11	11	11	11	11^1	42	0	9
Prindiville, Stephen	3	3	3	3	3	3	3	3	3	3	3	3	3	3	3	3	3	3	3	3	3	3	3	43	0	1
Rogers, Lee	6	6	6	6	6	6	6	6	6	6	6		★				6	2					2	22	2	0
Rolph, Andrew				★	7^1	**7**	★	★	**7**	★	★	★					★	★					**7**	4	8	1
Shaw, Adrian	4	4				8	**8**	8	8^1	8	8	8	8	8	8	8	8	**8**	8	8	**8**	★	8	24	1	1
Slack, Trevor												6	6	6	6	6		6	6	6	6	6	6	21	0	0
Thompson, Nigel																								5	1	0
Waller, David	9	9^1	9	9^1	9^1	9	9	9^1	9	9^1	9	9	9^2	9	9^1	9^1	9^1	9^1	9^2	9^1	9^1	9^1	9	35	1	18
Wood, Darren														★	**11**			★						19	3	1
Own Goals				2											1											4

FA Cup: 1988-89: 1st Round: Bolton W. (A) 0-0, Replay (H) 2-3.
Littlewoods Cup: 1988-89: 1st Round: Port Vale (A) 2-3 (H) 1-1.

COLCHESTER UNITED (Division 4)

Team Manager Jock Wallace.
Club Address Layer Road Ground, Colchester. Tel: (0206) 574042.
Current Ground Capacity 6,500.
Record Attendance 19,072 v Reading, FA Cup 1st Round, 27 November 1948.
Year Formed 1937. Turned professional 1937.
Previous Names None.
Club Nickname "The U's".
Club Colours Royal blue shirts, white shorts and royal blue stockings.
Club Honours None.
League History 1950-58 Div. 3(S); 1958-61 Div. 3; 1961-62 Div. 4; 1962-65 Div. 3; 1965-66 Div. 4; 1966-68 Div. 3; 1968-74 Div. 4; 1974-76 Div. 3; 1976-77 Div. 4; 1977-81 Div. 3; 1981- Div. 4.
Most League Points in a Season (2 for a win) 60 in Div. 4, 1973-74. (3 for a win) 81 in Div. 4, 1982-83.
Most League Goals in a Season 104 in Div. 4, 1961-62.
Record Victory 9-1 v Bradford C. in Div. 4, 30 December 1961.
Record Defeat 0-8 v Leyton Orient in Div. 4, 15 October 1988.
Consecutive League Wins 7 in 1968-69.
Consecutive League Defeats 8 in 1954.
Record League Appearances Mickey Cook, 613 between 1969-84.
Record League Goalscorer—Career Martyn King, 131 between 1956-65.
Record League Goalscorer—Season Bobby Hunt, 37 in Div. 4, 1961-62.

Colchester United: League Record, 1988-89 (Division 4)

Match Number	Date	Venue	Opponents	Result	H/T	Lge Posn	Attend
1	27.8.88	H	York C.	W 1-0	0-0		1644
2	2.9.88	A	Tranmere Rov.	D 0-0	0-0	8	3401
3	9.9.88	H	Doncaster Rov.	L 0-1	0-0	12	1726
4	16.9.88	A	Wrexham	D 2-2	1-0	13	2873
5	20.9.88	H	Scarborough	W 3-1	1-0	11	1424
6	24.9.88	A	Burnley	L 0-2	0-1	12	7177
7	1.10.88	H	Lincoln C.	L 1-3	1-1	16	1529
8	4.10.88	A	Carlisle U.	W 2-1	0-0	11	2193
9	8.10.88	H	Scunthorpe U.	L 1-2	1-1	17	1299
10	15.10.88	A	Leyton Orient	L 0-8	0-4	21	3412
11	21.10.88	H	Cambridge U.	L 1-2	0-0	22	2138
12	25.10.88	A	Rotherham U.	L 0-2	0-0	22	4066
13	28.10.88	H	Stockport Co.	D 1-1	1-0	23	1643
14	4.11.88	A	Crewe Alex.	L 1-3	1-1	23	2787
15	8.11.88	A	Halifax	L 2-3	1-2	23	2176
16	11.11.88	H	Torquay U.	D 2-2	1-0	22	1926
17	25.11.88	H	Darlington.	L 1-2	0-1	24	1550
18	3.12.88	A	Exeter C.	L 2-4	1-2	24	2132
19	16.12.88	A	Rochdale	D 1 1	0-1	24	1258
20	26.12.88	H	Peterborough U.	L 1-2	0-1	24	2828
21	30.12.88	H	Hartlepool U.	L 1-2	1-0	24	2359
22	2.1.89	A	Grimsby T.	D 2-2	1-2	24	4472
23	14.1.89	H	Tranmere Rov.	L 2-3	1-0	24	3458
24	21.1.89	A	York C.	L 0-2	0-1	24	2119
25	4.2.89	A	Scarborough.	D 0-0	0-0	24	1913
26	10.2.89	H	Burnley	D 2-2	0-2	24	3809
27	18.2.89	A	Scunthorpe U.	W 3-2	2-0	24	4286
28	24.2.89	H	Leyton Orient	W 1-0	1-0	24	4269
29	28.2.89	H	Rotherham U.	D 1-1	0-1	24	3671
30	5.3.89	A	Cambridge U.	L 1-3	1-2	24	4205
31	10.3.89	H	Crewe Alex.	W 2-1	1-1	24	3088
32	13.3.89	A	Stockport Co.	L 0-1	0-0	24	2027
33	18.3.89	A	Doncaster Rov.	L 1-3	1-2	24	1237
34	24.3.89	H	Grimsby T.	D 0-0	0-0	24	4507
35	27.3.89	A	Peterborough U.	L 0-3	0-1	24	3529
36	31.3.89	H	Rochdale	W 3-0	0-0	24	3631
37	4.4.89	H	Hereford U.	D 1-1	1-1	24	2862
38	8.4.89	A	Hartlepool U.	L 1-2	0-0	24	1501
39	12.4.89	A	Hereford U.	D 1-1	1-0	24	2015
40	15.4.89	A	Lincoln C.	D 1-1	0-0	24	3519
41	21.4.89	H	Carlisle U.	D 1-1	0-1	24	3906
42	25.4.89	H	Wrexham	W 2-1	1-1	24	2918
43	29.4.89	A	Darlington	W 2-1	1-1	23	7126
44	1.5.89	H	Halifax T.	W 3-2	0-1	23	5065
45	5.5.89	H	Exeter C.	W 4-0	2-0	23	5256
46	13.5.89	A	Torquay U.	W 3-1	0-0	22	2066

Players: League Record, 1988-89 (Division 4)

Match Number	1	2	3	4	5	6	7	8	9	10	11	12	13	14	15	16	17	18	19	20	21	22	23
Allinson, Ian																			11	11	11	11[1]	11
Barnett, David	4	4			4	4	4	4	4	4	4				11	11	11		8	8	8	8	8
Bedford, Kevin		★	★	11	11	11					3	3	3	3	3	3	3	3	3	3	3	3	3
Bennett, Gary											★						8						
Cartwright, Stephen	3	3	3	3	3	3	3	3	3	3													
Chatterton, Nick																	★	8					
Coleman, Philip																							
Coombe, Mark																1	1	1					
Daniels, Scott														★	★	★	★	6	5	5	5	7	7
English, Tony		2	2								8[1]	8	8	8	8	8[1]	6		7	7	7[1]	2	2
Grenfell, Stephen	11	11	11								11	11		★									
Hedman, Rudi	2			2	2	2	2	2	2[1]	2	2	2	2	2	2	2	2	7	2				
Hetzke, Steve	5	5																★	★	6	6	6	6
Hicks, Stuart			5	5	5	5	5	5	5	5	5	5	5	5	5	5	5	5		★		5	5
Hill, Colin	6	6	6	6	6	6	6	6	6	6	6	6	6	6	6	6		2	6	2	2		★
Hunter, Lee			★	★			7	7	7	7			★										
Kelly, Tony												4	4	4	4[1]	4[1]	4	4	4	4	4	4	4
McAlister, Tom																							
McGee, Paul																							
Pollard, Kelly																							
Radford, Mark			4	4	★	★	★		★	★	★	★	11	11		★	7[1]	11			★	★	
Scott, Robert																							
Stafford, Clive																							
Swindlehurst, Dave	10	10	10	10[1]	10[1]	10	10[1]	10[1]	10	10		10						9[1]					
Taylor, Les																							★
Tempest, Dale	9[1]	9	9	9[1]	9[1]	9	9	9[1]	9	9	9	9	9[1]	9	9	9	9	★[1]	★	★	★	★	9
Walsh, Mario											10	★	10	10[1]	10	10	10	10	10[1]	10[1]	10	10	10[2]
Walton, Mark	1	1	1	1	1	1	1	1	1	1	1	1	1	1	1				1	1	1	1	1
Warner, John																							
White, Winston	7	7	7	7	7	7	8	8	8	8													
Wilkins, Richard	8	8	8	8	8[1]	8	11	11	11	11	7	7	7	7	7[1]	7			9	9	9	9[1]	
Own Goals																							

Match Number	24	25	26	27	28	29	30	31	32	33	34	35	36	37	38	39	40	41	42	43	44	45	46	Apps	Subs	Goals
Allinson, Ian	11	11	7[1]	7	7[1]	7[1]				9	7	9	★	10	11	11	11	11	11[1]	11	11[1]	11[1]	11	24	1	7
Barnett, David		7	★		8																			19	1	0
Bedford, Kevin	3	3	3	3	3	3					11	11												24	2	0
Bennett, Gary					★	★	7	7					7[1]	7	7									6	3	1
Cartwright, Stephen																								10	0	0
Chatterton, Nick																								1	1	0
Coleman, Philip	2							2	2	2		2			★	★	★		2		★			6	4	0
Coombe, Mark																								3	0	0
Daniels, Scott	7			★			★	5	5			★	2	2	5	5	5	5	★	2		2	2	18	8	0
English, Tony	8	8	8	8[1]		8	8	8[2]	7	7	2	7	8	8[1]	8	8	8	8	3	8	8	8[1]	8	36	0	8
Grenfell, Stephen																								5	1	0
Hedman, Rudi																								17	0	1
Hetzke, Steve	6	5	5	5	5	5	5				5	5	5	5					5[1]	5	5	5	5[1]	22	2	2
Hicks, Stuart	5	2	2	2	2	2	2	10	8	5	8	4	★	★	2	2	2	2						34	3	0
Hill, Colin	★	6	6	6	6	6	6	6	6	6	6	6	6	6	6	6	6	6	6	6	6	6	6	42	2	0
Hunter, Lee																		★						4	4	0
Kelly, Tony	4																							13	0	2
McAlister, Tom		1	1	1	1	1	1	1	1	1	1	1	1	1	1	1	1	1	1	1	1			20	0	0
McGee, Paul			11	11	11																			3	0	0
Pollard, Kelly																						★[1]	★	0	2	1
Radford, Mark							★	4	11	11			4	4	4	★	★		8	★	2	4	4	16	14	1
Scott, Robert											9	8	9[1]	9	9[1]	9[1]	9	9[1]	9	9[1]	9	9		12	0	5
Stafford, Clive							3	3	3	3	3	3	3	3	3	3	3	3		3	3	3	3	16	0	0
Swindlehurst, Dave																								12	0	5
Taylor, Les	★	4	4	4	4	4	4			4	4					4	4	4	4	4	4			14	2	0
Tempest, Dale	9					9	10	★	4							10	10	★	10				★[1]	25	8	7
Walsh, Mario	10	10	10[1]	10						10[1]	10	10	10					10	★	10[1]	10	10[1]	10	25	2	9
Walton, Mark	1																					1	1	23	0	0
Warner, John				★[1]	10	10	9	9	9	★	★	★		★	10					★	★[1]	★	9[1]	7	8	3
White, Winston																								10	0	0
Wilkins, Richard		9	9	9[1]	9	11	11[1]	11	10	8			11[1]	11	★	7	7[1]	7	7	7	7[1]	7	7	39	1	8
Own Goals																										0

FA Cup: 1988-89: 1st Round: Fulham (A) 1-0; 2nd Round: Swansea C. (H) 2-2, Replay (A) 3-1; 3rd Round: Shrewsbury T. (A) 3-0; 4th Round: Sheffield U. (A) 3-3, Replay (H) 0-2.
Littlewoods Cup: 1988-89: 1st Round: Northampton T. (H) 0-0 (A) 0-5.

COVENTRY CITY (Division 1)

Team Manager John Sillett.
Club Address Highfield Road Stadium, King Richard Street, Coventry CV2 4FW. Tel: (0203) 57171.
Current Ground Capacity 28,273.
Record Attendance 51,455 v Wolverhampton W., Div. 2, 29 April 1967.
Year Formed 1883. Turned professional 1893.
Previous Names Singers.
Club Nickname "The Sky Blues".
Club Colours All sky blue.
Club Honours Football League: Div. 2 Champions 1966-67; Div. 3 Champions 1963-64; Div. 3(S) Champions 1935-36. FA Cup: Winners 1987.
League History 1919-25 Div. 2; 1925-26 Div. 3(N); 1926-36 Div. 3(S); 1936-52 Div. 2; 1952-58 Div. 3(S); 1958-59 Div. 4; 1959-64 Div. 3; 1964-67 Div. 2; 1967- Div. 1.
Most League Points in a Season (2 for a win) 60 in Div. 4, 1958-59 and in Div. 3, 1963-64. (3 for a win) 63 in Div. 1, 1986-87.
Most League Goals in a Season 108 in Div. 3(S), 1931-32.
Record Victory 9-0 v Bristol C. in Div. 3(S), 28 April 1934.
Record Defeat 2-10 v Norwich C. in Div. 3(S), 15 March 1930.
Consecutive League Wins 6 in 1964.
Consecutive League Defeats 9 in 1919.
Record League Appearances George Curtis, 486 between 1956-70.
Record League Goalscorer—Career Clarrie Bourton, 171 between 1931-37.
Record League Goalscorer—Season Clarrie Bourton, 49 in Div. 3(S), 1931-32.

Coventry City: League Record, 1988-89 (Division 1)

Match Number	Date	Venue	Opponents	Result	H/T	Lge Posn	Attend
1	3.9.88	H	Everton	L 0-1	0-1		18625
2	10.9.88	A	Sheffield Wed.	W 2-1	0-0	11	15633
3	17.9.88	H	Charlton Ath.	W 3-0	0-0	9	11890
4	24.9.88	A	Wimbledon	W 1-0	1-0	6	4474
5	1.10.88	H	Middlesbrough	L 3-4	1-3	8	14527
6	8.10.88	A	Newcastle U.	W 3-0	3-0	3	22896
7	15.10.88	H	Millwall	D 0-0	0-0	3	19369
8	22.10.88	A	Liverpool	D 0-0	0-0	6	38742
9	29.10.88	A	Arsenal	L 0-2	0-1	8	31273
10	5.11.88	H	West Ham U.	D 1-1	0-1	7	14651
11	12.11.88	H	Luton T.	W 1-0	1-0	6	12631
12	19.11.88	A	Nottingham F.	D 0-0	0-0	7	17250
13	23.11.88	A	Tottenham H.	D 1-1	0-1	6	21961
14	26.11.88	H	Aston Villa	W 2-1	1-0	5	20104
15	3.12.88	A	Q.P.R.	L 1-2	0-1	6	9853
16	10.12.88	H	Manchester U.	W 1-0	0-0	3	19936
17	17.12.88	H	Derby Co.	L 0-2	0-0	5	17229
18	26.12.88	A	Southampton	D 2-2	2-0	6	16008
19	31.12.88	A	Everton	L 1-3	1-2	7	30790
20	2.1.89	H	Sheffield Wed.	W 5-0	2-0	5	15191
21	14.1.89	A	Norwich C.	W 2-1	0-0	3	14399
22	21.1.89	H	Wimbledon	W 2-1	1-1	3	12472
23	4.2.89	A	Middlesbrough	D 1-1	1-1	3	17352
24	11.2.89	H	Newcastle U.	L 1-2	0-0	5	16577
25	21.2.89	H	Arsenal	W 1-0	0-0	3	21290
26	25.2.89	A	Millwall	L 0-1	0-0	4	13021
27	11.3.89	A	West Ham U.	D 1-1	1-0	6	15205
28	18.3.89	H	Tottenham H.	D 1-1	1-0	6	17156
29	22.3.89	H	Liverpool	L 1-3	1-2	6	23807
30	25.3.89	A	Charlton Ath.	D 0-0	0-0	7	6728
31	27.3.89	H	Southampton	W 2-1	1-1	6	11734
32	1.4.89	A	Derby Co.	L 0-1	0-0	7	15175
33	8.4.89	H	Norwich C.	W 2-1	1-1	6	12740
34	15.4.89	A	Luton T.	D 2-2	0-0	7	8610
35	22.4.89	H	Q.P.R.	L 0-3	0-2	8	11319
36	29.4.89	A	Manchester U.	W 1-0	0-0	6	29799
37	13.5.89	A	Aston Villa	D 1-1	0-1	7	29906
38	15.5.89	H	Nottingham F.	D 2-2	0-0	7	14003

Players: League Record, 1988-89 (Division 1)

Match Number	1	2	3	4	5	6	7	8	9	10	11	12	13	14	15	16	17	18	19	20	21	22	23	24	25	26	27	28	29	30	31	32	33	34	35	36	37	38	Apps	Subs	Goals
Bannister, Gary	10	10	10^1	10^1	10	10	10	10	10	**10**	10						★	9^1	$\mathbf{9}^1$				8	8			10	10^1	10^1	10				★	10	10^1	10^1		22	0	8
Bennett, David																			★	7				★	10	10	7	7											5	2	0
Borrows, Brian	2	2	2	2	2	2	2	2	2	2	2	2	2	2	2	2	2	2	2	2	2	2	2	2	2	2	2	2	2	2	2^1	2	2	2	2	2	2	2	38	0	1
Clark, Howard										7	7	**7**									★						★	★		★	**7**							$★^1$	4	5	1
Dobson, Tony																							3	3	3	3	3	3	3	3	3	3	3	3	3	3	3	3	16	0	0
Downs, Greg	3	3	3	3	3	3	3	3	3	3	3	3	3	3	**3**	3	3	3	**3**															6	★			★	20	2	0
Emerson, Dean										**5**								6	6		7	7	7	7	7	7			4	4	4	4	4	**4**		4	4	4	18	0	0
Gynn, Micky	**7**	7	7	7	7	7^1	7	**7**																															8	0	1
Houchen, Keith									11	★		10	10^1	10^1	10	10	10	10	10										★	★	9								10	3	2
Kilcline, Brian	5	5	5	5	**5**	5	5				5	5	5	5	5	5	**5**	5	5	5^1	5	5^1	5	**5**	5^1	5	5^1	5	5	5	5	5	5			5	5	5	33	0	4
Livingstone, Stephen																																						10	1	0	0
McGrath, Lloyd														★	★					10	**10**	10	10	**10**				**4**											6	2	0
Ogrizovic, Steve	1	1	1	1	1	1	1	1	1	1	1	1	1	1	1	1	1	1	1	1	1	1	1	1	1	1	1	1	1	1	1	1	1	1	1	1	1	1	38	0	0
Peake, Trevor	6	6	6	6	6	6	6	6	6			6	6	6	6	6				6	6	6	6	6	6	6	6	6	6	6	6	6	6		6	6	6	**6**	32	0	0
Phillips, David	★				★			★	7			★	7	7	7	7	**7**	7^1	7	3	3	3					4	8	**7**	**7**		7	7^1	7	7	7	7	**7**	22	4	2
Regis, Cyrille	9	9^1	9	9	9	9^1	9	9	9	9	9	9	9	$\mathbf{9}^1$	9	9^1	9			9	9	9	9^1	9	9	9	**9**		9	**9**		9	9	9^1	9	9	9	9^1	34	0	7
Rodger, Graham								5	5	6	6^1				11		6																	5	5				8	0	1
Sedgley, Stephen	4	4	4	4	4	4	4	4	4	4	4	4	4	4	4	4	4	4	4	4^1	4	4	4	4	4	4					10	10	10	10	**4**				31	0	1
Smith, David	11	11	11^2	11	11	11	11	11		11	11	11	11	11		11	11		★	11	11	11	11	11	11	11	11	11	**11**	11	11	**11**	11	11^1	**11**	11	11	11	34	1	3
Speedie, David	8	8^1	8	8	8^3	8^1	8	8	8	8	8	8	8	8	8^1	8	8	8	8	8^3	8^2	8^1			8	8	8	9	8	8	8^1	8	8^1	8	8	8	8	8	36	0	14
Thompson, Keith										$★^1$							★	11	11					★					★		★	★			★				2	7	1
Own Goals																								1																	1

FA Cup: 1988-89: 3rd Round: Sutton U. (A) 1-2.

Littlewoods Cup: 1988-89; 2nd Round: Bournemouth (A) 4-0 (H) 3-1; 3rd Round: Nottingham F. (A) 2-3.

CREWE ALEXANDRA (Division 3)

Team Manager Dario Gradi.
Club Address Football Ground, Gresty Road, Crewe. Tel: (0270) 213014.
Current Ground Capacity 4,500.
Record Attendance 20,000 v Tottenham H., FA Cup 4th Round, 30 January 1960.
Year Formed 1877. Turned professional 1893.
Previous Names None.
Club Nickname "The Railwaymen".
Club Colours Red shirts, white shorts and red stockings.
Club Honours None.
League History 1892-96 Div. 2; 1896 Failed re-election; 1921 Re-entered Div. 3(N); 1958-63 Div. 4; 1963-64 Div. 3; 1964-68 Div. 4; 1968-69 Div. 3; 1968-89 Div. 4; 1989- Div. 3.
Most League Points in a Season (2 for a win) 59 in Div. 4, 1962-63. (3 for a win) 78 in Div. 4, 1988-89.
Most League Goals in a Season 95 in Div. 3(N), 1931-32.
Record Victory 8-0 v Rotherham U. in Div. 3(N), 1 October 1932.
Record Defeat 2-13 v Tottenham H. in FA Cup 4th Round replay, 3rd February 1960.
Consecutive League Wins 7 in 1928-29 and 1986-87.
Consecutive League Defeats 10 in 1923, 1957-58 and 1979.
Record League Appearances Tommy Lowry, 436 between 1966-78.
Record League Goalscorer—Career Bert Swindells, 126 between 1928-37.
Record League Goalscorer—Season Terry Harkin, 34 in Div. 4, 1964-65.

Crewe Alexandra: League Record, 1988-89 (Division 4)

Match Number	Date	Venue	Opponents	Result	H/T	Lge Posn	Attend
1	27.8.88	A	Leyton Orient	D 0-0	0-0		3992
2	3.9.88	H	Scunthorpe U.	W 3-2	2-1	7	1514
3	10.9.88	A	Lincoln C.	D 2-2	1-1	9	2651
4	17.9.88	H	Darlington	W 2-0	1-0	7	1711
5	21.9.88	A	Hereford U.	W 1-0	0-0	4	1981
6	23.9.88	H	Stockport Co.	D 1-1	1-0	4	2975
7	1.10.88	A	Rochdale	L 1-2	1-0	6	2227
8	4.10.88	H	Cambridge U.	W 2-0	1-0	4	1588
9	8.10.88	A	Wrexham.	D 0-0	0-0	5	2689
10	15.10.88	H	Doncaster Rov.	L 0-2	0-0	5	2180
11	22.10.88	A	Hartlepool U.	W 3-0	1-0	5	1972
12	25.10.88	H	Grimsby T.	D 2-2	1-2	4	2311
13	29.10.88	A	Exeter C.	W 2-1	2-0	4	2567
14	4.11.88	H	Colchester U.	W 3-1	1-1	3	2787
15	8.11.88	A	York C.	L 0-3	0-0	3	1980
16	12.11.88	H	Tranmere Rov.	W 2-1	0-1	3	3293
17	25.11.88	H	Peterborough U.	D 1-1	1-0	3	2645
18	2.12.88	A	Halifax T.	W 1-0	0-0	2	2026
19	16.12.88	H	Torquay U.	D 0-0	0-0	2	3269
20	26.12.88	A	Rotherham U.	W 2-1	1-0	1	7165
21	31.12.88	A	Scarborough	L 1-2	0-1	4	3088
22	2.1.89	H	Carlisle U.	W 1-0	1-0	2	4626
23	14.1.89	A	Scunthorpe U.	D 2-2	1-0	2	4032
24	21.1.89	H	Leyton Orient	W 2-1	1-0	2	2933
25	28.1.89	A	Darlington	D 1-1	0-0	1	1902
26	4.2.89	H	Hereford U.	W 2-1	2-1	1	2987
27	10.2.89	A	Stockport Co.	W 1-0	1-0	1	5015
28	17.2.89	H	Wrexham	D 2-2	1-2	1	5627
29	24.2.89	A	Doncaster Rov.	W 1-0	0-0	1	1713
30	28.2.89	A	Grimsby T.	D 0-0	0-0	1	5044
31	4.3.89	H	Hartlepool U.	W 3-0	0-0	1	3981
32	10.3.89	A	Colchester U.	L 1-2	1-1	1	3088
33	14.3.89	H	Exeter C.	W 2-1	0-0	1	3156
34	18.3.89	H	Lincoln C.	W 2-0	1-0	1	3106
35	25.3.89	A	Carlisle U.	W 1-0	1-0	1	4866
36	27.3.89	H	Rotherham U.	L 1-3	0-0	2	5994
37	31.3.89	A	Torquay U.	L 1-2	1-0	3	3087
38	4.4.89	A	Burnley	L 0-1	0-1	4	5677
39	8.4.89	H	Scarborough	D 1-1	1-1	4	3243
40	14.4.89	H	Rochdale	W 3-1	1-0	2	4144
41	22.4.89	A	Cambridge U	D 1-1	1-0	2	3512
42	29.4.89	A	Peterborough U.	L 2-3	1-1	4	3546
43	1.5.89	H	York C.	L 1-2	0-1	5	3693
44	6.5.89	H	Halifax T.	D 2-2	1-0	4	3476
45	9.5.89	H	Burnley	W 4-0	1-0	4	2963
46	13.5.89	A	Tranmere Rov.	D 1-1	0-1	3	15286

Players: League Record, 1988-89 (Division 4)

Match Number	1	2	3	4	5	6	7	8	9	10	11	12	13	14	15	16	17	18	19	20	21	22	23	24	25	26	27	28	29	30	31	32	33	34	35	36	37	38	39	40	41	42	43	44	45	46	Apps	Subs	Goals
Billing, Peter	6			4	5	5					★	6	4	4	4	4	4	4	4	4	4	4	4	4	4	4^1	4	4	4	4	4	4	4	4				4	4	4	4	4	4	4	4	4	36	1	1
Callaghan, Aaron	4	4	4		4	4	4	4	4	4	4	4	★	6^1	6	6^1	7	7	7	7	7	7	7	7	5	5	5				★	5	5	5^1	5	5^1	5	5	5	5	5	5		5	5	5	39	2	4
Clayton, Paul																									9	9	9	9^1	9	9	9	9	9	9	9	9	9	9	9	9			8	8^1	8^3	8^1	20	0	6
Cronin, Dennis	★				★	9	9^1	9	9	9	9	9	9	9	9	9	9^1							★																							12	3	2
Cutler, Chris	9	9^2																									★																				2	1	2
Doyle, Maurice													★																									6	6^1	6^1							3	1	2
Edwards, Paul																													1	1	1	1	1	1	1	1	1	1									10	0	0
Edwards, Paul R		3	3	3	3	3	3	3	3	3	3	3	3	3^1	3	3	3	3^1	3	3	3	3	3	3	3	3	3	3	3^1	3	3	3	3	3	3	3	3	3	3	3	3	3	3	3	3^1	3	45	0	4
Edwards, Robert				★															★	★			★																								0	4	0
Elliott, Lee																		9																													1	0	0
Fishenden Paul	11	11	11^1	11^1	11	11	11	11^1	11	11	11^1	11	11^1	11	11	11	11	11	11	11^1	11	11^1	11^1	11	11^1	11	11	11^1	11	11	11	11	11^1	11^1	11	11	11^1	11	11	11^1	11^1	11	11^1	11	11	11	46	0	16
Gage, Wakely																★	6	6	6	★	★	6	6							★		★			★	★							5			★	6	8	0
Gardiner, Mark	3								2		10^1	10	10	10^1	10	10^1	10	10	10	10^1	10	★	10^1	10^1	10	10^1	10^1	10	10	10	10^1	10	10	10	10^1	10	10	10	10	10	10	10	10	10^1	10	10	37	1	11
Goodison, Wayne	2	2	2	2			6	2		2					★		2	2	2	2	2	2	2	2^1											8	8	8	2	2	2	2	2	2				24	1	1
Greygoose, Dean	1	1	1	1	1	1	1	1	1	1	1	1	1	1	1	1	1	1	1	1	1	1	1	1	1	1	1	1											1	1	1	1	1	1	1	1	36	0	0
Harrison, Wayne																			9	9	9																										3	0	0
Hignett, Craig									8																																						1	0	0
Jasper, Dale	7	7	7	7	7	7^1	7	7	7	7	7	7	7	7	7	7								★	7	7	7	7	7	7	7	7	7	7	7	7	7	7	7	7	7	7	7	7	7	7	38	1	1
Jones, Rob		6	6	6^1	6	6	★	8	6	8	6		6		★	★	★	★	5					8												★									★		12	7	1
Macowat, Ian	5	5	5	5	★	★	5	5	5	5	5	5^1	5	5	5	5		★		5	5			6	6	★		5	5	5	5				4	4	4	★									25	5	1
Morton, Neil		★	★				★			★		★																																			0	5	0
Murphy, Aidan	8	8	8	8	8	8	8			★	8^1	8^1	8	8	8	8	8	8	8	8	8	8	8		★	8	8	8	8	8	8	8^1	8^1	8							8	8^1	★	★			31	4	5
Sussex, Andy	10	10^1	10	10	10	10	10	10^1	10	10																			★	★	★	★	★	★			★	★		★^{1}	9	9^1	9	9	9	9	16	9	4
Swain, Kenny				★	2	2	2	6		6	2	2	2	2	2	2	5	5		6	6	5	5	5	2	2	2	2	2	2	2	2	2	2	2	2	2	8	8	8	6	6	6	2	2	2	40	1	0
Wakenshaw, Robbie																					★	9																									1	1	0
Walters, Steven																						10	9	9	8	6	6	6	6	6	6^1	6	6	6	6	6	6				★	★	★	6	6	6	19	3	1
Wilkinson, Stephen			9^1	9	9^1	★			★																																						3	2	2
Own Goals													1								1											1																	3

FA Cup: 1988-89: 1st Round: Stafford R. (A) 2-2, Replay (H) 3-2; 2nd Round: Runcorn (A) 3-0; 3rd Round: Aston Villa (H) 2-3.
Littlewoods Cup: 1988-89: 1st Round: Lincoln C. (H) 1-1 (A) 1-2.

Soar like the Eagles.

Virgin offers you the best flights across the big pond.

Virgin atlantic

For details and reservations telephone Virgin Atlantic on **0293 38222** or see your local travel agent.

CRYSTAL PALACE (Division 1)

Team Manager Steve Coppell.
Club Address Selhurst Park, London SE25 6PU. Tel: 01-653 4462.
Current Ground Capacity 36,000.
Record Attendance 51,482 v Burnley, Div. 2, 11 May 1979.
Year Formed 1905. Turned professional 1905.
Previous Names None.
Club Nickname "The Eagles".
Club Colours Red and blue striped shirts, red shorts and red stockings.
Club Honours Football League: Div. 2 Champions 1978-79, Div. 3(S) Champions 1920-21.
League History 1920-21 Div. 3(S); 1921-25 Div. 2; 1925-58 Div. 3(S); 1958-61 Div. 4; 1961-64 Div. 3; 1964-69 Div. 2; 1969-73 Div. 1; 1973-74 Div. 2; 1974-77 Div. 3; 1977-79 Div. 2; 1979-81 Div. 1; 1981-89 Div. 2; 1989- Div. 1.
Most League Points in a Season (2 for a win) 64 in Div. 4, 1960-61. (3 for a win) 81 in Div. 2, 1988-89.
Most League Goals in a Season 110 in Div. 4, 1960-61.
Record Victory 9-0 v Barrow in Div. 4, 10 October 1959.
Record Defeat 4-11 v Manchester C. in FA Cup 5th Round, 20 February 1926.
Consecutive League Wins 8 in 1921.
Consecutive League Defeats 8 in 1925.
Record League Appearances Jim Cannon, 571 between 1973-88.
Record League Goalscorer—Career Peter Simpson, 154 between 1930-36.
Record League Goalscorer—Season Peter Simpson, 46 in Div. 3(S), 1930-31.

Crystal Palace: League Record, 1988-89 (Division 2)

Match Number	Date	Venue	Opponents	Result	H/T	Lge Posn	Attend
1	30.8.88	H	Chelsea	D 1-1	1-1		17490
2	3.9.88	H	Watford	L 0-2	0-1	18	10474
3	10.9.88	A	Walsall	D 0-0	0-0	16	6525
4	17.9.88	H	Shrewsbury T.	D 1-1	0-1	18	7006
5	20.9.88	A	Sunderland	D 1-1	1-0	17	13150
6	24.9.88	A	Portsmouth	D 1-1	0-1	20	11249
7	1.10.88	H	Plymouth Arg.	W 4-1	3-1	18	8047
8	4.10.88	H	Ipswich T.	W 2-0	2-0	11	10325
9	8.10.88	A	Blackburn Rov.	L 4-5	1-1	17	8022
10	15.10.88	A	Bradford C.	W 1-0	1-0	12	11098
11	22.10.88	H	Hull C.	W 3-1	1-1	8	8464
12	25.10.88	H	Oxford U.	W 1-0	0-0	5	10114
13	29.10.88	A	Stoke C.	L 1-2	0-1	8	9118
14	5.11.88	H	Barnsley	D 1-1	0-0	9	7768
15	12.11.88	A	Bournemouth	L 0-2	0-1	11	8697
16	19.11.88	H	Leicester C.	W 4-2	1-1	9	8843
17	26.11.88	A	West Bromwich A.	L 3-5	0-1	11	11099
18	3.12.88	H	Manchester C.	D 0-0	0-0	13	12444
19	10.12.88	A	Birmingham C.	W 1-0	1-0	10	6523
20	17.12.88	H	Leeds U.	D 0-0	0-0	10	9847
21	26.12.88	A	Brighton & H.A.	L 1-3	0-?	14	13515
22	30.12.88	A	Oldham Ath.	W 3-2	1-0	12	6562
23	2.1.89	H	Walsall	W 4-0	3-0	8	9352

Match Number	Date	Venue	Opponents	Result	H/T	Lge Posn	Attend
24	14.1.89	A	Chelsea	L 0-1	0-1	12	24184
25	21.1.89	H	Swindon T.	W 2-1	0-1	9	8109
26	4.2.89	A	Ipswich T.	W 2-1	2-1	6	14569
27	11.2.89	H	Blackburn Rov.	D 2-2	1-1	7	11270
28	25.2.89	H	Bradford C.	W 2-0	1-0	7	7455
29	1.3.89	A	Oxford U.	L 0-1	0-0	9	6020
30	4.3.89	H	Bournemouth	L 2-3	0-2	12	10022
31	11.3.89	A	Barnsley	D 1-1	1-1	11	7055
32	18.3.89	H	Sunderland	W 1-0	0-0	10	9108
33	24.3.89	A	Watford	W 1-0	0-0	10	15095
34	27.3.89	H	Brighton & H.A.	W 2-1	2-0	7	14384
35	1.4.89	A	Shrewsbury T.	L 1-2	1-2	9	4160
36	5.4.89	A	Leeds U.	W 2-1	2-1	6	25604
37	8.4.89	H	Oldham Ath.	W 2-0	1-0	5	9089
38	11.4.89	A	Hull C.	W 1-0	1-0	5	5050
39	15.4.89	H	Portsmouth	W 2-0	0-0	4	12358
40	22.4.89	A	Plymouth Arg.	W 2-0	1-0	4	8492
41	25.4.89	A	Swindon T.	L 0-1	0-1	4	11045
42	29.4.89	H	West Bromwich A.	W 1-0	0-0	4	13728
43	1.5.89	A	Manchester C.	D 1-1	0-1	4	33456
44	6.5.89	A	Leicester C.	D 2-2	1-1	5	9917
45	9.5.89	H	Stoke C.	W 1-0	1-0	3	12159
46	13.5.89	H	Birmingham C.	W 4-1	4-0	3	17581

Players: League Record, 1988-89 (Division 2)

Match Number	1	2	3	4	5	6	7	8	9	10	11	12	13	14	15	16	17	18	19	20	21	22	23	24	25	26	27	28	29	30	31	32	33	34	35	36	37	38	39	40	41	42	43	44	45	46	Apps	Subs	Goals
Barbor, Philip	★	★	11	11	11	11	11	11	11	11	11^{2}	11	11	11	11	11^{2}	11	11	11	11	11	11	11	11	11	11	11	11	11	11	11	11	11^{1}	11	11	11	11^{1}	11	11	11	11	11	11	11	11	11	44	2	6
Bright, Mark	9	9	9	9	9	9	9^{1}	9^{1}	9^{1}	9	9	9	9^{1}	9^{1}	9	9^{1}	9	9	9	9	9	9	9^{3}	9	9^{2}	9	9^{1}	9^{2}	9	9	9	9^{1}	9	9^{1}	9	9	9^{1}	9	9^{1}	9^{2}	9	9	9	9	9	9	46	0	20
Burke, David	3	3	3	3	3	3	3	3	3	3	3	3	3					3	3	3	3	3	3	3	3	3	3	3	3	3				★	3	3	3	3	3	3	3	3	3	3	3	3	38	1	0
Dyer, Alex															★	7	7^{1}	7	7^{1}	7	7																										6	1	2
Harris, Mark																																									★		★				0	2	0
Hedman, Rudi																					★		★																					★	2	★	1	4	0
Hone, Mark								2																																							1	0	0
Hopkins, Jeff			5	5	5	5	5	5	5	5	5	5	5	5	5	5	5	5	5	5	5	5	5	5	5	5	5		5	5	5	5	5	5	5	5	5	5	5	5	5	5	5	5	5	5	43	0	0
McGoldrick, Eddie																								7	7	7	7	7	7	7	7	7	7	7	7	7	7	7	7			★	7	7	7	7	20	1	0
Madden, David		★																											★	4	4	4	4	4	4^{1}	4^{1}	4	4	4	4	4	4	4	4^{2}	4^{1}	4	17	2	5
Nebbeling, Gavin	5															6	6^{1}	6	6	6	6	6	6	6	6																			6	6	6	14	0	1
O'Reilly, Gary	6	6	6	6	6^{1}	6	6	6	6^{1}	6	6	6	6	6	6											6	6	6	6	6	6	6	6	6	6	6	6	6	6	6	6	6					32	0	2
Pardew, Alan	★	5	4	4	4	4	4^{1}	4	4	4	4	4	4	4	4	4	4	4	4	4	4	★	8	8	8	8	8	8	8	8	8	8	8	8	8	8	8	8	8	8	8	8	8	8	8		43	2	1
Parkin, Brian			1	1	1	1	1	1	1	1	1	1	1	1	1	1	1	1	1	1	1																										19	0	0
Pemberton, John	2	2	2	2	2	2	2		2	2	2	2	2	2	2		2	2	2	2	2	2	2	2	2	2	2	2	2	2^{1}	2	2	2	2	2	2	2	2	2	2	2	2	2			2	42	0	1
Pennyfather, Glenn	4	4														3	3				★	4	4	4	4	4	4	4	4		★															8	13	2	0
Powell, Chris															3	3	★																														2	1	0
Redfearn, Neil	7^{1}	7	7	7	7	7	7	7	7	7	7	7^{1}	7	7	7																																15	0	2
Salako, John	11	11		★	★			★	★		★	10	10	10		★	★	★				7	7	★			★	10	10				★		★			★	★	7	7	7		★		★	12	16	0
Shaw, Richard										★			★			2	★											5			3	3	3	3			★			★		★	6	2			8	6	0
Suckling, Perry	1	1																				1	1	1	1	1	1	1	1	1	1	1	1	1	1	1	1	1	1	1	1	1	1	1	1	1	27	0	0
Thomas, Geoff	8	8	8	8	8	8	8^{1}	8	8^{1}	8	8	8	8	8	8	8^{1}	8^{1}	8	8	8	8	8^{1}																									22	0	5
Wright, Ian	10	10	10	10^{1}	10	10^{1}	10^{1}	10^{1}	10^{1}	10^{1}	10^{1}			★	10	10	10	10	10	10	10^{1}	10^{2}	10^{1}	10	10	10^{2}	10^{1}			10^{1}	10^{1}	10	10	10^{1}	10	10^{1}	10	10^{1}	10^{1}	10	10	10^{1}	10^{1}	10	10	10^{3}	41	1	25
Own Goals																																														1			1

FA Cup: 1988-89: 3rd Round: Stoke C. (A) 0-1.
Littlewoods Cup: 1988-89: 2nd Round: Swindon T. (A) 2-1 (H) 2-0; 3rd Round: Bristol C. (A) 1-4.

I·S·L

Industrial Scaffolding Limited

SPECIALISTS IN SCAFFOLDING ERECTION FOR:

* *PETRO-CHEMICAL COMPLEXES*
* *POWER STATIONS*
* *STEELWORKS*
* *ALL CIVIL WORK*
* *OFFSHORE CONTRACTS*

A COMPLETE SCAFFOLDING SERVICE

HAREWOOD WORKS THORNABY CLEVELAND

Telephone 615631

A MEMBER OF B.E.T. PLANT SERVICES LTD.

OFFICIAL SPONSORS OF DARLINGTON FOOTBALL CLUB

DARLINGTON (Vauxhall Conference)

Team Manager Brian Little.
Club Address Feethams Ground, Darlington. Tel: (0325) 465097.
Current Ground Capacity 13,511.
Record Attendance 21,023 v Bolton W., League Cup 3rd Round, 14 November 1960.
Year Formed 1883. Turned professional 1908.
Previous Names None.
Club Nickname "The Quakers".
Club Colours All white with black trim.
Club Honours Football League: Div. 3(N) Champions 1924-25.
League History 1921-25 Div. 3(N); 1925-27 Div. 2; 1927-58 Div. 3(N); 1958-66 Div. 4; 1966-67 Div. 3; 1967-85 Div. 4; 1985-87 Div. 3; 1987-89 Div. 4; 1989- Vauxhall Conference.

Most League Goals in a Season 108 in Div. 3(N), 1929-30.
Most League Points in a Season (2 for a win) 59 in Div. 4, 1965-66. (3 for a win) 85 in Div. 4, 1984-85.
Record Victory 9-2 v Lincoln C. in Div. 3(N), 7 January 1928.
Record Defeat 0-10 v Doncaster Rov. in Div. 4, 25 January 1964.
Consecutive League Wins 5 in 1922, 1924, 1928, 1975 and 1985.
Consecutive League Defeats 8 in 1985.
Record League Appearances Ron Greener, 442, between 1955-67.
Record League Goalscorer—Career Alan Walsh, 87 between 1978-84.
Record League Goalscorer—Season David Brown, 39 in Div. 3(N), 1924-25.

Darlington: League Record, 1988-89 (Division 4)

Match Number	Date	Venue	Opponents	Result	H/T	Lge Posn	Attend
1	27.8.88	H	Stockport Co.	L 1-4	0-2		1794
2	3.9.88	A	Hartlepool U.	L 1-2	0-0	23	2843
3	10.9.88	H	Peterborough U.	D 2-2	1-1	22	1521
4	17.9.88	A	Crewe Alex.	L 0-2	0-1	23	1711
5	20.9.88	H	Exeter C.	D 2-2	1-0	22	1216
6	23.9.88	A	Leyton Orient	L 0-1	0-0	24	2755
7	1.10.88	H	Burnley	D 1-1	0-0	24	3409
8	5.10.88	A	Scarborough	L 2-3	1-2	24	2442
9	8.10.88	H	Rotherham U.	D 1-1	0-0	24	1746
10	15.10.88	A	York C.	L 1-4	0-2	24	2851
11	22.10.88	A	Lincoln C.	L 2-3	0-0	24	3705
12	25.10.88	H	Torquay U.	D 0-0	0-0	24	1374
13	29.10.88	A	Rochdale	D 2-2	1-1	24	2476
14	5.11.88	H	Doncaster Rov.	L 1-3	0-1	24	1625
15	8.11.88	H	Cambridge U.	D 1-1	1-0	24	1467
16	12.11.88	A	Carlisle U.	W 2-1	2-0	24	2194
17	25.11.88	A	Colchester U.	W 2-1	1-0	23	1550
18	3.12.88	H	Scunthorpe U.	D 3-3	1-1	23	1745
19	16.12.88	A	Tranmere Rov.	L 0-2	0-2	23	2981
20	26.12.88	H	Halifax T.	L 0-2	0-1	23	2131
21	31.12.88	H	Hereford U.	D 0-0	0-0	23	1755
22	2.1.89	A	Wrexham	D 3-3	1-2	23	6016
23	14.1.89	H	Hartlepool U.	D 0-0	0-0	23	3521
24	21.1.89	A	Stockport Co.	D 0-0	0-0	23	2889
25	28.1.89	H	Crewe Alex.	D 1-1	0-0	23	1902
26	4.2.89	A	Exeter C.	L 1-2	1-0	23	2687
27	11.2.89	H	Leyton Orient	L 1-3	1-2	23	1833
28	14.2.89	A	Grimsby T.	D 0-0	0-0	23	4628
29	18.2.89	A	Rotherham U.	W 2-1	0-0	23	4228
30	25.2.89	H	York C.	D 2-2	0-0	23	2504
31	28.2.89	A	Torquay U.	L 0-1	0-0	23	1627
32	4.3.89	H	Lincoln C.	W 2-1	1-0	23	2169
33	10.3.89	A	Doncaster Rov.	L 0-1	0-0	23	1538
34	14.3.89	H	Rochdale	L 1-2	1-1	23	1867
35	18.3.89	A	Peterborough U.	D 1-1	0-0	23	2484
36	25.3.89	H	Wrexham	W 2-1	1-1	23	2281
37	27.3.89	A	Halifax T.	L 0-1	0-0	23	1849
38	1.4.89	H	Tranmere Rov	L 1-2	0-1	23	2492
39	4.4.89	H	Grimsby T.	D 1-1	1-0	23	1840
40	8.4.89	A	Hereford U.	D 1-1	0-0	23	2009
41	15.4.89	A	Burnley	W 1-0	0-0	23	5578
42	22.4.89	H	Scarborough	W 2-1	1-0	23	2850
43	29.4.89	H	Colchester U.	L 1-2	1-1	24	7126
44	2.5.89	A	Cambridge U.	W 3-1	0-0	24	3310
45	6.5.89	A	Scunthorpe U.	L 1-5	0-1	24	5296
46	13.5.89	H	Carlisle U.	L 2-3	1-3	24	3049

Players: League Record, 1988-89 (Division 4)

Match Number	1	2	3	4	5	6	7	8	9	10	11	12	13	14	15	16	17	18	19	20	21	22	23	24	25	26	27	28	29	30	31	32	33	34	35	36	37	38	39	40	41	42	43	44	45	46	Apps	Subs	Goals
Anderson, Dale	★	10				★	★	9	★	7	★																						★					10									4	6	0
Batch, Nigel					1	1	1	1	1	1	1	1	1	1	1	1	1	1	1	1	1	1	1	1	1	1	1	1	1	1	1	1	1	1													30	0	0
Bonnyman, Phil	3																★																			10	10		8	8	8	8	8^{1}	8^{1}	8	8	11	1	2
Caizley, Kevin	8	★	10		10		7												4											★	★									★				7^{1}	7	7	8	4	1
Clayton, Paul	10			10	8		10	10		★						9	9	9		9																											9	1	0
Dyson, Paul																																			5	5	5	5	5	5^{1}	5^{1}	5	5	5	5	5^{1}	12	0	3
Emson, Paul	7	7	7	7	7	7		7^{1}	7		7	★	★	★	★	11^{1}	11	11	11	11	★								10^{1}	10	10	10	10	9	9^{1}	11^{1}	11	11	★	9				10	10	★	27	7	5
Gidman, John																														8	8	8	8	8^{1}	8	8	8	8		4	4	4	4				13	0	1
Hine, Mark	4	4	4	4	4	4	4	4^{1}	4	4	4	4	4	4	4			4			4	4^{1}	4	4	4	4	4	4	4	4	4	4	4	4	4	4	4	4	4			★	★	4	4	4	38	2	2
Hyde, Gary		★	★	★	★	10	8	8	8	8	8	8	8	8	8	8	8		9	7	11	11^{1}	11	11	11	11		7	7^{1}	7^{1}	7	7	7	7	7	7	7	7								★	31	5	3
McAndrew, Tony																	4	8	8	8	8	8		8	8	8	8	11																			11	0	0
McAughtrie, David	6	6	6	6	6	6	5					7	7	7			7	7	7	4								5	5	5	5	5			★												19	1	0
Macdonald, Gary	9	9	9	9	9^{1}	9	9	6	9	9	9^{1}	9	9^{1}	9	9				★	★	9		8	7	7	7	7	9	9	9	9		5	5	★	★	★	★^{1}	11^{1}	11	11	11	11	11	11	11	35	6	5
McJannet, Les																					2	2	2	2	2	2	2	2	2	2	2	2	2	2	2	2^{1}	2	2	2	2	2	2	2	2	2	2	26	0	1
Moore, David	5	5	5	5	5	5			5	5	5	5	5	5	5	5	5	5	5	5		★	5	5	5	5	5^{1}	8	8										★	★	★		★				25	5	1
Morgan, Gary		3	3	3	3	3	3	3	3	3	3	3	3	3	3	3	3	3	3	3	3	3	3	3	3	3^{1}	3	3	3	3	3					3	3	3	3		3	3	3	3			38	0	1
Prudhoe, Mark																																			1	1	1	1	1	1	1	1	1	1	1	1	12	0	0
Robinson, Michael	★																																														0	1	0
Robinson, Neil	2	8	8	8	2	8	2	2	2	2	2	2	2	2	2	2	2	2	2	2	7	7	7						11	11^{1}	11	11	11	11	11			★	7	7	7	7	7	★	3		36	2	1
Rodwell, James				2																																											1	0	0
Shearer, David																						9	9	9	9	9	9	★																			6	1	0
Smallwood, Neil	1	1	1	1																																											4	0	0
Smith, Alan									10	★			★	★	7	4					5	5	★								★	3	3	3	3					3							10	5	0
Stephens, Archie																																				9	9	9	9		9	9^{2}	9	9^{1}	9	9^{1}	10	0	4
Stonehouse, Kevin	11^{1}	11^{1}	11^{1}	11	11	11	11^{1}	11	11^{1}	11	11	11	11	11^{1}	11	7			★	★	★	★	★	★	★		11			6	6	9^{1}	9	★													21	8	7
Willis, Jim		2	2^{1}			2	6	5	6	6	6	6	6	6	6	6	6	6	6	6	6	6	6	6	6	6	6	6	6			6^{1}	6	6	6	6	6	6	6	6	6	6	6	6	6	6	41	0	2
Willis, Paul																																													★^{1}	10	1	1	1
Worthington, Gary								★		10^{1}	10^{1}	10	10^{1}	10	10^{1}	10^{1}	10^{2}	10^{3}	10	10	10	10^{1}	10	10	10^{1}	10	10	10					10	10	★	★			10	10	10	10	10		★	3	27	4	12
Own Goals					1																																												1

FA Cup: 1988-89: 1st Round: 1988-89: Notts Co. (H) 1-2.
Littlewoods Cup: 1988-89: 1st Round: Doncaster Rov. (A) 1-1 (H) 2-0; 2nd Round: Oldham Ath. (H) 2-0 (A) 0-4.

DERBY COUNTY (Division 1)

Team Manager Arthur Cox.
Club Address Baseball Ground, Shaftesbury Crescent, Derby DE3 8NB. Tel: (0332) 40105.
Current Ground Capacity 26,500.
Record Attendance 41,826 v Tottenham H., Div. 1, 20 September 1969.
Year Formed 1884. Turned professional 1884.
Previous Names None.
Club Nickname "The Rams".
Club Colours White shirts, blue shorts and blue stockings.
Club Honours Football League: Div 1. Champions 1971-72, 1974-75. Div. 2 Champions 1911-12, 1914-15, 1968-69, 1986-87; Div. 3(N) Champions 1956-57. FA Cup: Winners 1946.
League History 1888-1904 Div. 1; 1904-12 Div. 2; 1912-14 Div. 1; 1914-15 Div. 2; 1915-21 Div. 1; 1921-26 Div. 2; 1926-53 Div. 1; 1953-55 Div. 2; 1955-57 Div. 3(N); 1957-69 Div. 2; 1969-80 Div. 1; 1980-84 Div. 2; 1984-86 Div. 3; 1986-87 Div. 2; 1987- Div. 1.
Most League Points in a Season (2 for a win) 63 in Div. 2, 1968-69, in Div. 3(N) 1955-56 and 1956-57. (3 for a win) 84 in Div. 3, 1985-86 and in Div. 2, 1986-87.
Most League Goals in a Season 111 in Div. 3(N), 1956-57.
Record Victory 12-0 v Finn Harps in UEFA Cup 3rd Round 1st Leg, 15 September 1976.
Record Defeat 2-11 v Everton in FA Cup 1st Round, 1889-90.
Consecutive League Wins 9 in 1969.
Consecutive League Defeats 8 in 1965 and 1988.
Record League Appearances Kevin Hector, 486 between 1966-82.
Record League Goalscorer—Career Steve Bloomer, 291 between 1892-1914.
Record League Goalscorer—Season Jack Bowers, 37 in Div. 1, 1930-31 and Ray Straw, 37 in Div. 3(N), 1956-57.

Derby County: League Record, 1988-89 (Division 1)

Match Number	Date	Venue	Opponents	Result	H/T	Lge Posn	Attend
1	27.8.88	H	Middlesbrough	W 1-0	0-0		19432
2	3.9.88	A	Millwall	L 0-1	0-1	9	13060
3	10.9.88	H	Newcastle U.	W 2-0	0-0	7	16014
4	17.9.88	A	Nottingham F.	D 1-1	0-0	7	24818
5	24.9.88	H	Q.P.R.	L 0-1	0-1	10	14008
6	1.10.88	A	Southampton	D 0-0	0-0	9	13285
7	8.10.88	H	Norwich C.	L 0-1	0-0	12	14117
8	22.10.88	H	Charlton Ath.	D 0-0	0-0	15	14106
9	29.10.88	H	Wimbledon	W 4-1	1-1	13	15050
10	5.11.88	A	Tottenham H.	W 3-1	1-1	6	22868
11	12.11.88	H	Manchester U.	D 2-2	1-1	8	24080
12	19.11.88	A	Aston Villa	W 2-1	0-0	6	23489
13	26.11.88	H	Arsenal	W 2-1	0-0	7	21209
14	3.12.88	A	Sheffield Wed.	D 1-1	0-1	5	20609
15	10.12.88	H	Luton T.	L 0-1	0-1	7	15228
16	17.12.88	A	Coventry C.	W 2-0	0-0	4	17229
17	26.12.88	H	Liverpool	L 0-1	0-1	7	25213
18	31.12.88	H	Millwall	L 0-1	0-0	8	16154
19	2.1.89	A	Newcastle U.	W 1-0	0-0	7	30555
20	14.1.89	H	West Ham U.	L 1-2	1-2	8	16796
21	21.1.89	A	Q.P.R.	W 1-0	0-0	8	9516
22	4.2.89	H	Southampton	W 3-1	1-0	7	13758
23	11.2.89	A	Norwich C.	L 0-1	0-0	8	17227
24	25.2.89	H	Everton	W 3-2	1-1	6	17103
25	1.3.89	A	Wimbledon	L 0-4	0-3	8	4207
26	11.3.89	H	Tottenham H.	D 1-1	1-0	8	18306
27	18.3.89	A	Middlesbrough	W 1-0	1-0	7	16580
28	25.3.89	H	Nottingham F.	L 0-2	0-1	8	25174
29	29.3.89	A	Liverpool	L 0-1	0-1	9	42518
30	1.4.89	H	Coventry C.	W 1-0	0-0	9	15175
31	8.4.89	A	West Ham U.	D 1-1	1-1	9	16560
32	15.4.89	A	Manchester U.	W 2-0	1-0	8	34145
33	22.4.89	H	Sheffield Wed.	W 1-0	0-0	6	17529
34	29.4.89	A	Luton T.	L 0-3	0-1	7	8507
35	6.5.89	H	Aston Villa	W 2-1	1-1	6	18112
36	10.5.89	A	Charlton Ath.	L 0-3	0-1	6	7448
37	13.5.89	A	Arsenal	W 2-1	1-0	5	41008
38	15.5.89	A	Everton	L 0-1	0-1	5	17826

Players: League Record, 1988-89 (Division 1)

Match Number	1	2	3	4	5	6	7	8	9	10	11	12	13	14	15	16	17	18	19
Blades, Paul	6	6	6	6	6	6	6	6	6	6	6	6	6	6	6	2	2	2	2
Callaghan, Nigel	11	11	11	11	11				**11**	11	**11**	**11**	11^{1}	11^{1}	11	11	**11**	**11**	11
Chiedozie, John	8	**8**																	
Cross, Steve			★	★	**8**					4							★	★	
Forsyth, Mike	3	3	3	3	3	3	3	3	3	3	3	3	3	3	3	3	3	3	3
Gee, Philip		★	**8**	**8**									9^{1}	**9**	★				
Goddard, Paul	9^{1}	9	9^{1}	9	9	9	9	9	9	9	9	9^{1}			**9**	9	**9**	9	9
Hebberd, Trevor	10	10	10^{1}	10^{1}	10	10	10	10	10	10	10^{1}	10	10	10	10	10	10	**10**	10
Hindmarch, Rob								5	5							6	6	6	6
McMinn, Ted			**7**	7	**7**	7	7	7	7	7^{2}	7	7	7	7	7	7^{1}	7	7	7
Micklewhite, Gary	7	**7**			★				$★^{1}$		★	★		★			★	★	
Patterson, Mark															2				
Penney, David						8	8	8											
Pickering, Nick		★	★		★	11	11	11											
Sage, Mel	2	2	2	2	2	2	2	2	2^{1}	2	2	2	2	2					
Saunders, Dean									8^{2}	8^{1}	8^{1}	8^{1}	8	8	8	8^{1}	8	8	8
Shilton, Peter	1	1	1	1	1	1	1	1	1	1	1	1	1	1	1	1	1	1	1
Williams, Geraint	4	4	4	4	4	4	4	4	4		4	4	4	4	4	4	4	4	4
Wright, Mark	5	5	5	5	5	5	5			5	5	5	5	5	5	5	5	5	5^{1}
Own Goals																			

Match Number	20	21	22	23	24	25	26	27	28	29	30	31	32	33	34	35	36	37	38	Apps	Subs	Goals
Blades, Paul	2	2	6	2	2	2	2	2	2	2	2^{1}	2	2	2	2	2	2	5	5	38	0	1
Callaghan, Nigel	11	**11**																		18	0	2
Chiedozie, John																				2	0	0
Cross, Steve	★	★	2	★		★	★	10	★	9		★			★			7	7	7	12	0
Forsyth, Mike	3	3	3	3	3	3	3	3	3	3	3	3	3	3	3	3	3	3	3	38	0	0
Gee, Philip	**9**	9						9	**9**						★				★	8	4	1
Goddard, Paul			9^{1}	9	9^{2}	9	**9**				9	**9**	9^{1}	9	**9**	9	9	9	**9**	31	0	7
Hebberd, Trevor	10	10	10^{1}	**10**	10	**10**	10		10	**10**	10	10	10	10	**10**	10^{1}	10	10	10	37	0	5
Hindmarch, Rob	6	6	5	6	6	6	6	6	6	6	6	6	6	6	6	6	6	6	6	25	0	0
McMinn, Ted	**7**	7	7	7			7	7^{1}	7	7	7	7	7	7	7	7	**7**			32	0	4
Micklewhite, Gary			11	11	7	**7**	11	11	11	11	11	11^{1}	11^{1}	11	11	11	11	11	**11**	19	7	3
Patterson, Mark																				1	0	0
Penney, David	★			★		★				★							★		★	3	6	0
Pickering, Nick					11	11														5	3	0
Sage, Mel																		2	2	16	0	1
Saunders, Dean	8^{1}	8	8^{1}	**8**	8^{1}	8	8^{1}	8	8	8	8	8	8	8^{1}	8	8^{1}	8	8^{2}	8	30	0	14
Shilton, Peter	1	1	1	1	1	1	1	1	1	1	1	1	1	1	1	1	1	1	1	38	0	0
Williams, Geraint	4	4^{1}	4	4	4	4	4	4	4	4	4	4	4	4	4	4	4	4	4	37	0	1
Wright, Mark	5	5		5	5	5	5	5	5	5	5	5	5	5	5	5	5			33	0	1
Own Goals																						0

FA Cup: 1988-89: 3rd Round: Southampton (H) 1-1. Replay (A) 2-1; 4th Round: Watford (A) 1-2.

Littlewoods Cup: 1988-89: 2nd Round: Southend U. (H) 1-0 (A) 2-1; 3rd Round: West Ham U. (A) 0-5.

DONCASTER ROVERS (Division 4)

Team Manager Joe Kinnear.
Club Address Belle Vue Ground, Doncaster. Tel: (0302) 539441.
Current Ground Capacity 7,500.
Record Attendance 37,149 v Hull C., Div. 3(N), 2 October 1948.
Year Formed 1879. Turned professional 1885.
Previous Names None.
Club Nickname "Rovers".
Club Colours Red shirts, white shorts and red stockings.
Club Honours Football League: Div. 3(N) Champions 1934-35, 1946-47, 1949-50, Div. 4 Champions 1965-66, 1968-69.
League History 1901-03 Div. 2; 1903 Failed re-election; 1904-05 Div. 2; 1905 Failed re-election; 1923-35 Div. 3(N); 1935-37 Div. 2; 1937-47 Div. 3(N); 1947-48 Div. 2; 1948-50 Div. 3(N); 1950-58 Div. 2; 1958-59 Div. 3; 1959-66 Div. 4; 1966-67 Div. 3; 1967-69 Div. 4; 1969-71 Div. 3; 1971-81 Div. 4; 1981-83 Div. 3; 1983-4 Div. 4; 1984-88 Div. 3; 1988- Div. 4.
Most League Points in a Season (2 for a win) 72 in Div. 3(N), 1946-47. (3 for a win) 85 in Div. 4, 1983-84.
Most League Goals in a Season 123 in Div. 3(N), 1946-47.
Record Victory 10-0 v Darlington in Div. 4, 25 January 1964.
Record Defeat 0-12 v Small Heath in Div. 2, 11 April 1903.
Consecutive League Wins 10 in 1947.
Consecutive League Defeats 9 in 1905.
Record League Appearances Fred Emery, 406 between 1925-36.
Record League Goalscorer—Career Tom Keetley, 180 between 1923-29.
Record League Goalscorer—Season Clarrie Jordan, 42 in Div. 3(N), 1946-47.

Doncaster Rovers: League Record, 1988-89 (Division 4)

Match Number	Date	Venue	Opponents	Result	H/T	Lge Posn	Attend
1	27.8.88	A	Rotherham U.	L 0-3	0-1		4497
2	3.9.88	H	Exeter C.	W 2-1	1-1	13	1525
3	9.9.88	A	Colchester U.	W 1-0	0-0	7	1726
4	16.9.88	H	Torquay U.	L 1-2	0-1	11	2220
5	20.9.88	A	Rochdale	L 0-2	0-0	17	1645
6	24.9.88	H	Wrexham	D 2-2	1-0	15	1712
7	1.10.88	A	Stockport Co.	L 0-2	0-1	18	1959
8	4.10.88	H	Hereford U.	W 3-2	2-1	14	1281
9	8.10.88	H	Hartlepool U.	W 1-0	1-0	11	2091
10	15.10.88	A	Crewe Alex.	W 2-0	0-0	6	2180
11	21.10.88	H	Halifax T.	L 1-4	1-4	9	3038
12	25.10.88	A	York C.	D 1-1	1-1	12	2957
13	29.10.88	H	Leyton Orient	W 1-0	0-0	7	2182
14	5.11.88	A	Darlington	W 3-1	1-0	6	1625
15	8.11.88	A	Grimsby T.	L 0-5	0-2	8	3300
16	12.11.88	H	Peterborough U.	L 2-3	0-1	13	2224
17	26.11.88	H	Burnley	W 1-0	0-0	8	2724
18	2.12.88	A	Tranmere Rov.	D 2-2	2-0	8	3412
19	17.12.88	H	Scunthorpe U.	D 2-2	1-1	8	3381
20	26.12.88	A	Cambridge U.	D 0-0	0-0	9	2673
21	28.12.88	A	Lincoln C.	L 1-3	1-1	12	5213
22	2.1.89	H	Scarborough	W 3-1	2-1	11	3053
23	10.1.89	H	Carlisle U.	L 1-3	0-1	11	2128
24	14.1.89	A	Exeter C.	L 0-3	0-2	13	2540
25	21.1.89	H	Rotherham U.	W 1-0	0-0	11	4432
26	28.1.89	A	Torquay U.	L 2-3	2-1	12	2103
27	4.2.89	H	Rochdale	D 1-1	0-0	12	1868
28	11.2.89	A	Wrexham	D 1-1	1-0	13	3244
29	18.2.89	A	Hartlepool U.	L 1-2	0-0	14	1922
30	24.2.89	H	Crewe Alex.	L 0-1	0-0	15	1713
31	28.2.89	H	York C.	L 1-2	0-0	16	1526
32	3.3.89	A	Halifax T.	L 0-2	0-0	20	1675
33	10.3.89	H	Darlington	W 1-0	0-0	18	1538
34	14.3.89	A	Leyton Orient	L 0-4	0-1	19	2824
35	18.3.89	H	Colchester U.	W 3-1	2-1	17	1237
36	25.3.89	A	Scarborough	L 0-2	0-1	18	2792
37	27.3.89	H	Cambridge U.	D 1-1	0-0	19	1937
38	1.4.89	A	Scunthorpe U.	L 1-2	1-2	19	5334
39	4.4.89	A	Carlisle U.	W 1-0	1-0	18	2991
40	8.4.89	H	Lincoln C.	L 0-1	0-0	18	2124
41	14.4.89	H	Stockport Co.	D 2-2	0-1	18	1363
42	22.4.89	A	Hereford U.	L 1-3	0-1	18	1804
43	29.4.89	A	Burnley	L 0-3	0-1	21	4211
44	1.5.89	H	Grimsby T.	L 2-3	1-2	22	2183
45	6.5.89	H	Tranmere Rov.	D 0-0	0-0	22	2268
46	13.5.89	A	Peterborough U.	L 0-2	0-1	23	2984

Players: League Record, 1988-89 (Division 4)

Match Number	1	2	3	4	5	6	7	8	9	10	11	12	13	14	15	16	17	18	19	20	21	22	23
Ashurst, Jack																5	5	5	5	5	5	5	5
Beattie, Stuart		5	5	5	5	5^{1}	5	5	5	5	5	5	5	5	5	2	2	2					
Brevett, Rufus																			2	3			★
Brockie, Vincent																				2	2	2	2
Daly, Gerry	8	8				8	8	8	8	8	8	8	8	8^{1}	8		8	8	8^{1}	8	8	8	8
Dobson, Paul	10	10^{2}	10	10	10	10			10	10^{2}	10	10^{1}	10	10	10	$★^{2}$	10	10^{1}	10^{1}	★	10	10	10^{1}
Douglas, Colin	2	2	2	2	2	2	2	10^{1}	2	2	2	2	2	2	2	10	11^{1}	11	11	11	4	11	11
Gaughan, Steve	★	★	8	★	8	★							★	★		8	★	★	7				
Gorman, Paul	★			★	★		★	★			★		★	$★^{1}$		★							
Hall, Mark																							
Jones, Gary																							
Kimble, Garry	11	11	11	11	11	11	11	11	11	11	11	11	11	11	11	11							
Malcolm, Paul	1	1	1				1	1	1	1	1	1	1	1	1	1	1	1	1	1	1	1	1
Peckett, Andy					★														★		★		★
Powell, Cliff																							
Raffell, Stephen	5		4	4	4	4	4	2			★												
Rankine, Mark	9	9	9^{1}	9	9	9^{1}	9	9^{1}	9^{1}	9	9	9	9^{1}	9	9	9	9	9^{1}	9	9	9	9^{1}	9
Raven, Paul	6	6	6	6	6	6	6	6	6	6	6	6	6	6^{1}	6	6	6	6	6	6	6	6	6
Robinson, Leslie	7	7	7	7	7	7	7	7	7	7	7	7	7	7	7	7	7	7		7	7	7^{1}	7
Robinson, Ronnie	3	3	3	3^{1}	3	3	3	3^{1}	3	3	3^{1}	3	3	3	3	3	3	3	3	4	3	3^{1}	3
Samways, Mark				1	1	1																	
Stewart, Robert							10																
Trotter, Michael																	4	4	4				
Turnbull, Lee	4	4		8				4	4	4	4	4	4	4	4	4							
Ward, Tony																				10	11	4	4
Own Goals																					1		

Match Number	24	25	26	27	28	29	30	31	32	33	34	35	36	37	38	39	40	41	42	43	44	45	46	Apps	Subs	Goals
Ashurst, Jack		5	5^{1}	5	5	5	5	5	5	5	5	5	5	5	5	5	5	5	5	5	5	5	5	30	0	1
Beattie, Stuart																								17	0	1
Brevett, Rufus	3	3	3	3	3	3	3	3	3				3	3	3	3	3	3	3	3	3	3	3	22	1	0
Brockie, Vincent	4	4	4	4^{1}	4^{1}	4	4				4	4	4	2	2	4	4		2	4	4	4	4	23	0	2
Daly, Gerry	8	8	8	8	8	8	8	8	8	8^{1}	8	8		8^{1}	8	8	8	8	8	★	★			37	2	4
Dobson, Paul	10	10	10																					22	2	10
Douglas, Colin	5	2	2	2	2	2	2	2	2	2	2	2	6	6	6	6	6	6	6	2	2	2	2	46	0	2
Gaughan, Steve	11	11^{1}	11^{1}	11	11	11	11	11	11	11	★	3	★	4	4	11	11	★	4	11	11		★	22	12	2
Gorman, Paul																								0	9	1
Hall, Mark	2																							1	0	0
Jones, Gary			★	10		$★^{1}$	7	7	★			$★^{1}$	8	★	★		★	4	★	10	10	10	10	9	8	2
Kimble, Garry							★	★	★	3	11	11	11	11	11			11	11	★	★	11	11	26	5	0
Malcolm, Paul	1	1	1	1								1	1	1	1	1	1	1	1	1	1			34	0	0
Peckett, Andy	★	★																					★	0	7	0
Powell, Cliff													2			2	2	2						4	0	0
Raffell, Stephen																		★		6	6	6	6	11	2	0
Rankine, Mark	9	9	9	9	9	9	9	9	9	9	9	9^{2}	9	9	9^{1}	9^{1}	9	9	9	9	9	9	9	46	0	11
Raven, Paul	6	6	6	6	6	6	6	6	6	6	6	6												35	0	1
Robinson, Leslie	7	7	7	7	7	7			7	7	7	7	7	7	7	7	7	7^{1}	7	7	7^{1}	7	7	43	0	3
Robinson, Ronnie				★			★	4	4	4	3													27	2	4
Samways, Mark					1	1	1	1	1	1	1											1	1	12	0	0
Stewart, Robert																								1	0	0
Trotter, Michael																								3	0	0
Turnbull, Lee				★	10	10	10	10^{1}	10	10	10	10	10	10	10	10	10	10^{1}	10^{1}	8	8^{1}	8	8	31	1	4
Ward, Tony																								4	0	0
Own Goals																										1

A Cup: 1988-89: 1st Round: Brandon (H) 0-0, Replay (A) 2-1; 2nd Round: Sheffield U. (H) 1-3.
ttlewoods Cup: 1988-89: 1st Round: Darlington (H) 1-1 (A) 0-2.

EVERTON (Division 1)

Team Manager Colin Harvey.
Club Address Goodison Park, Liverpool L4 4EL. Tel: 051-521 2020.
Current Ground Capacity 50,059.
Record Attendance 78,299 v Liverpool, Div. 1, 18 September 1948.
Year Formed 1878. Turned professional 1885.
Previous Names St Domingo.
Club Nickname "The Toffeemen".
Club Colours Royal blue shirts, white shorts and blue stockings with white turnovers.
Club Honours Football League: Div. 1 Champions 1890-91, 1914-15, 1927-28, 1931-32, 1938-39, 1962-63, 1969-70, 1984-85, 1986-87; Div. 2 Champions 1930-31. FA Cup: Winners 1906, 1933, 1966, 1984. European Cup-Winners Cup: 1984-85.
League History 1888-1930 Div. 1; 1930-31 Div. 2; 1931-51 Div. 1; 1951-54 Div. 2; 1954- Div. 1.
Most League Points in a Season (2 for a win) 66 in Div. 1, 1969-70. (3 for a win) 90 in Div. 1, 1984-85.
Most League Goals in a Season 121 in Div. 2, 1930-31.
Record Victory 11-2 v Derby Co. in FA Cup 1st Round, 1889-90.
Record Defeat 4-10 v Tottenham H. in Div. 1, 11 October 1958.
Consecutive League Wins 12 in 1894.
Consecutive League Defeats 6 in 1929-30, 1958 and 1972.
Record League Appearances Ted Sagar, 465 between 1929-53.
Record League Goalscorer—Career "Dixie" Dean, 349 between 1925-37.
Record League Goalscorer—Season "Dixie" Dean, 60 in Div. 1, 1927-28 (League record).

Everton: League Record, 1988-89 (Division 1)

Match Number	Date	Venue	Opponents	Result	H/T	Lge Posn	Attend
1	27.8.88	H	Newcastle U.	W 4-0	2-0		41560
2	3.9.88	A	Coventry C.	W 1-0	1-0	1	18625
3	10.9.88	H	Nottingham F.	D 1-1	0-1	3	34003
4	17.9.88	A	Millwall	L 1-2	0-2	6	17507
5	24.9.88	H	Luton T.	L 0-2	0-0	8	26017
6	1.10.88	A	Wimbledon	L 1-2	0-2	10	6367
7	8.10.88	H	Southampton	W 4-1	1-1	8	25356
8	22.10.88	A	Aston Villa	L 0-2	0-1	11	26636
9	30.10.88	H	Manchester U.	D 1-1	0-0	14	27005
10	5.11.88	A	Sheffield Wed.	D 1-1	0-0	15	21761
11	12.11.88	A	Charlton Ath.	W 2-1	2-1	10	8627
12	19.11.88	H	Norwich C.	D 1-1	0-0	10	28118
13	26.11.88	A	West Ham U.	W 1-0	0-0	9	22176
14	3.12.88	H	Tottenham H.	W 1-0	1-0	8	29657
15	11.12.88	A	Liverpool	D 1-1	0-1	8	42372
16	17.12.88	A	Q.P.R.	D 0-0	0-0	8	10067
17	26.12.88	H	Middlesbrough	W 2-1	2-1	5	32651
18	31.12.88	H	Coventry C.	W 2-1	2-1	4	30790
19	2.1.89	A	Nottingham F.	W 0-2	0-1	6	26008
20	14.1.89	H	Arsenal	L 1-3	0-0	7	34825
21	21.1.89	A	Luton T.	L 0-1	0-1	9	9013
22	4.2.89	H	Wimbledon	D 1-1	1-1	9	23365
23	11.2.89	A	Southampton	D 1-1	0-1	9	15845
24	14.2.89	H	Aston Villa	D 1-1	1-1	9	20142
25	25.2.89	A	Derby Co.	L 2-3	1-1	10	17103
26	11.3.89	H	Sheffield Wed.	W 1-0	1-0	11	22524
27	22.3.89	A	Newcastle U.	L 0-2	0-1	11	20933
28	25.3.89	H	Millwall	D 1-1	0-1	11	27062
29	27.3.89	A	Middlesbrough	D 3-3	2-1	11	21351
30	1.4.89	H	Q.P.R.	W 4-1	2-0	11	23028
31	8.4.89	A	Arsenal	L 0-2	0-1	11	37608
32	10.4.89	H	Charlton Ath.	W 3-2	1-1	11	16316
33	22.4.89	A	Tottenham H.	L 1-2	0-0	12	28568
34	3.5.89	H	Liverpool	D 0-0	0-0	12	45994
35	6.5.89	A	Norwich C.	L 0-1	0-0	12	13239
36	10.5.89	A	Manchester U.	W 2-1	1-1	12	26722
37	13.5.89	H	West Ham U.	W 3-1	1-1	11	21694
38	15.5.89	H	Derby Co.	W 1-0	1-0	8	17826

Players: League Record, 1988-89 (Division 1)

Match Number	1	2	3	4	5	6	7	8	9	10	11	12	13	14	15	16	17	18	19
Bracewell, Paul														6	**6**	6	6	6^{1}	6
Clarke, Wayne				★	★									★	9^{1}	9	★		
Cottee, Tony	10^{3}	10^{1}	10	10	10	10	10^{2}	10	10^{1}	10	10	10	10	10^{1}	10	10	**10**^{1}	10	10
Ebbrell, John																			
Heath, Adrian			★^{1}	7	7	7^{1}	7	7	**7**										
McCall, Stuart	8	8	8	**8**	8	8	8	8	8	8	8	8	8	8	8	8	8		
McDonald, Neil	2	2	2	2	**2**	2													
Nevin, Pat	11	7	**7**													**11**	9	9	**9**
Pointon, Neil	3	3	3	3		3		★									3	★	3
Ratcliffe, Kevin							4	4	4	4	4	4	4	4	4	4		4	4
Reid, Peter	6	6	6	6	6	6	6	6	6	6	6^{1}	6	6		★		★	8	8
Sharp, Graeme	9^{1}	9	9	9	9	9	9	9	9	9	9^{1}	9	9	**9**					
Sheedy, Kevin	★	11	**11**	**11**	11	11										★	**11**	11^{2}	11
Snodin, Ian	4	4	4	4	4	4	2	2	2	2	2	2	2	2	2	2	2	2	2
Southall, Neville	1	1	1	1	1	1	1	1	1	1	1	1	1	1	1	1	1	1	1
Steven, Trevor	**7**						11^{1}	**11**	11	7^{1}	7	7^{1}	7^{1}	7	7	7	7^{1}	7	7
Van Den Hauwe, Pat				★		5	3	**3**	3	3	3	3	3	3	3	3	4	**3**	
Watson, David	5	5	5	5	5		5^{1}	5	5	5	5	5	5	5	5	5	5	5	5
Wilson, Ian			★		3			★	★	11	11	11	11	11	11				★
Own Goals				1															

Match Number	20	21	22	23	24	25	26	27	28	29	30	31	32	33	34	35	36	37	38	Apps	Subs	Goals
Bracewell, Paul	6	6			6		6	6	6	6	6	6	6	**6**	6	6		6^{1}		20	0	2
Clarke, Wayne	9	9		★		10^{1}	9	★	**10**	9	9^{1}	9	10	★		9			★	12	8	3
Cottee, Tony	10	10	10	**10**	10^{1}		10^{1}	**10**	★	**10**^{1}	10^{1}	10		10	10	10	10	10	10	35	1	13
Ebbrell, John			★									★	★						8	1	3	0
Heath, Adrian																				6	1	2
McCall, Stuart	★	**8**	8	8	8	8	8	**8**	★			5	8	★	★	7	6		6	29	4	0
McDonald, Neil	★	★	2	2	2	2	★	2	2	2	2	2	2	2^{1}	2	2	2	2	2	22	3	1
Nevin, Pat	7	**7**	7	★	★	★	★	★	8	8^{1}	8	8	**7**^{1}	7	7		7	7	7	20	5	2
Pointon, Neil	3	3				3	3	3	3	3	3	3	3			3	★	3	3	20	3	0
Ratcliffe, Kevin	4	4	4	4	4	4	4	4	4	4	4		4	4	4	4	4	4	4	30	0	0
Reid, Peter	**8**																			16	2	1
Sharp, Graeme			9^{1}	9	9	**9**^{1}		9	9				9^{1}	9	9		9^{2}	9	**9**	26	0	7
Sheedy, Kevin	**11**	11		11^{1}	11	11	**11**	11	**11**^{1}	11^{1}	11^{1}	11	11^{1}	**11**	**11**	11		**11**^{1}		24	2	8
Snodin, Ian	2	2				6	**2**													23	0	0
Southall, Neville	1	1	1	1	1	1	1	1	1	1	1	1	1	1	1	1	1	1	1	38	0	0
Steven, Trevor			6	7	7	7	7	7	7	7	7^{1}	**7**		8	8	8	8	8		29	0	6
Van Den Hauwe, Pat			3	3	**3**			5	5	5		4	5	3	3		**3**			24	1	0
Watson, David	5^{1}	5	5	5	5	5	5				5			5	5	5	5	5^{1}	5	32	0	3
Wilson, Ian		★	**11**	**6**						★							11	★	11^{1}	11	7	1
Own Goals																						1

FA Cup: 1988-89: 3rd Round: West Bromwich A. (A) 1-1, Replay (H) 1-0; 4th Round: Plymouth Arg. (A) 1-1, Replay (H) 4-0; 5th Round: Barnsley (A) 1-0; Quarter-Final: Wimbledon (H) 1-0; Semi-Final: Norwich C. 1-0; Final: Liverpool 2-3.
Littlewoods Cup: 1988-89: 2nd Round: Bury (H) 3-0 (A) 2-2; 3rd Round: Oldham Ath. (H) 1-1, Replay (A) 2-0; 4th Round: Bradford C. (A) 1-3.

)ave Watson (Everton & England) Match Magazine

EXETER CITY (Division 4)

Team Manager Terry Cooper.
Club Address St James Park, Exeter EX4 6PX. Tel: (0392) 54073.
Current Ground Capacity 9,500.
Record Attendance 20,984 v Sunderland, FA Cup 6th Round replay, 4 March 1931.
Year Formed 1904. Turned professional 1908.
Previous Names None.
Club Nickname "The Grecians".
Club Colours Red and white striped shirts, black shorts and black stockings with red turnovers.
Club Honours None.
League History 1920-58 Div. 3(S); 1958-64 Div. 4; 1964-66 Div. 3; 1966-77 Div. 4; 1977-84 Div. 3; 1984- Div. 4.
Most League Points in a Season (2 for a win) 62 in Div. 4, 1976-77. (3 for a win) 60 in Div. 4, 1988-89.
Most League Goals in a Season 88 in Div. 3(S), 1932-33.
Record Victory 8-1 v Coventry C. in Div. 3(S), 4 December 1926 and v Aldershot in Div. 3(S), 4 May 1935.
Record Defeat 0-9 v Notts Co. in Div. 3(S), 16 October 1948 and v Northampton T. in Div. 3(S), 12 April 1958.
Consecutive League Wins 7 in 1977.
Consecutive League Defeats 7 in 1936 and 1984.
Record League Appearances Arnold Mitchell, 493 between 1952-66.
Record League Goalscorer—Career Tony Kellow, 128 between 1976-88.
Record League Goalscorer—Season Fred Whitlow, 34 in Div 3(S), 1932-33.

Exeter City: League Record, 1988-89 (Division 4)

Match Number	Date	Venue	Opponents	Result	H/T	Lge Posn	Attend
1	27.8.88	H	Wrexham	L 0-2	0-1		2504
2	3.9.88	A	Doncaster Rov.	L 1-2	1-1	20	1525
3	10.9.88	H	Halifax T.	W 4-1	1-0	14	1725
4	17.9.88	A	Rochdale	L 1-2	1-1	18	1216
5	20.9.88	A	Darlington	D 2-2	0-1	20	1216
6	24.9.88	H	Scunthorpe U.	D 2-2	1-0	18	1876
7	1.10.88	A	Rotherham U.	W 1-0	0-0	15	4075
8	5.10.88	H	Torquay U.	W 3-0	0-0	12	4243
9	8.10.88	A	Burnley	L 0-3	0-1	15	7889
10	15.10.88	H	Grimsby T.	W 2-1	1-0	14	2232
11	22.10.88	H	Carlisle U.	W 3-0	1-0	8	2235
12	25.10.88	A	Leyton Orient	L 0-4	0-0	11	3873
13	29.10.88	H	Crewe Alex.	L 1-2	0-2	14	2567
14	4.11.88	A	Cambridge U.	L 0-2	0-0	16	2063
15	9.11.88	H	Scarborough	W 1-0	0-0	13	2351
16	12.11.88	A	Lincoln C.	L 0-2	0-1	18	3461
17	26.11.88	A	Hartlepool U.	D 2-2	0-0	18	2125
18	3.12.88	H	Colchester U.	W 4-2	2-1	14	2132
19	17.12.88	A	Peterborough U.	W 1-0	0-0	12	3149
20	26.12.88	H	Hereford U.	W 3-1	1-1	7	3229
21	31.12.88	H	York C.	W 2-0	1-0	6	3092
22	2.1.89	A	Stockport Co.	L 0-4	0-2	8	2936
23	14.1.89	H	Doncaster Rov.	W 3-0	2-0	7	2540
24	21.1.89	A	Wrexham	L 0-3	0-0	8	2514
25	28.1.89	H	Rochdale	W 5-1	2-1	7	2428
26	4.2.89	H	Darlington	W 2-1	0-1	6	2687
27	11.2.89	A	Scunthorpe U.	L 0-2	0-1	7	4102
28	18.2.89	H	Burnley	W 3-0	1-0	7	3672
29	25.2.89	A	Grimsby T.	L 1-2	0-1	7	4684
30	1.3.89	H	Leyton Orient	D 1-1	0-0	8	2890
31	4.3.89	A	Carlisle U.	L 0-1	0-0	8	2601
32	11.3.89	H	Cambridge U.	L 0-3	0-1	9	3180
33	14.3.89	A	Crewe Alex.	L 1-2	0-0	10	3156
34	17.3.89	A	Halifax T.	W 3-0	1-0	9	1473
35	20.3.89	A	Tranmere Rov.	L 0-2	0-1	9	3885
36	25.3.89	H	Stockport Co.	D 2-2	0-2	7	3058
37	27.3.89	A	Hereford U.	L 0-1	0-0	9	2735
38	1.4.89	H	Peterborough U.	W 3-1	2-0	9	2522
39	5.4.89	H	Tranmere Rov.	L 0-1	0-1	10	2956
40	8.4.89	A	York C.	L 1-3	0-1	10	2052
41	15.4.89	H	Rotherham U.	D 0-0	0-0	10	2594
42	22.4.89	A	Torquay U.	W 4-0	1-0	9	2939
43	29.4.89	H	Hartlepool U.	W 2-1	1-1	10	2380
44	1.5.89	A	Scarborough	L 1-2	1-2	11	2513
45	5.5.89	A	Colchester U.	L 0-4	0-2	12	5256
46	13.5.89	H	Lincoln C.	L 0-1	0-1	13	2249

Players: League Record, 1988-89 (Division 4)

Match Number	1	2	3	4	5	6	7	8	9	10	11	12	13	14	15	16	17	18	19	20	21	22	23
Banks, Chris	**2**	2	2	2	2	2	2	2	2	2	2	2	2	2	2	2	2	2	2	2	2	2	2
Batty, Paul			9	9	9	9	9	9^{1}	9	9	9	9	9	**9**	9	9			3				
Benjamin, Ian																							
Cooper, Richard	6	6	6	**6**	6	6	6	6	6	6	6	6	6	6			6	6	6	6^{1}	6	6	6
Dryden, Richard						**3**	3	3	3	3	3												
Gwinnett, Mel	1	1	1	1	1	1	1	1	1	1	1	1	1	1	1	1	1						
Harris, Carl																					★	8	11
Harris, Jamie	★	9															★	★				★	
Harrower, Steven	11	**11**	11	11	11	11	11	11	11	11	11	11	11	11	11	11	11	11					
Heath, Herbert																							
Hiley, Scott	8	8	8	8^{1}	8	8	8	8	**8**	**8**	**8**		8		8	8	8	8^{1}	8	8	**8**	★	8
Jones, Mark														3	3	3	3	**3**					
Langley, Tommy	9			★	★^{1}	★				★	★^{1}	8	**3**	8	★	★	**10**		11	11	11	**11**	
McDermott, Brian																							
Miller, Kevin																							
Neville, Steve	10	10^{1}	10^{1}	10	10	10^{1}	10	10^{1}	10	10^{1}	10	10	10^{1}	10	10	10		10^{1}	10^{1}	10	10^{1}	**10**	10^{1}
Parker Martin																							
Roberts, Paul																				3	3	3	
Rogers, Lee	4	4	4	4	4	4	4	4	4	4	4	4	4	4	4	4	4	4	4	4	4	4	4
Rowbotham, Darren	7	7	7^{1}	7	7^{1}	7	7	7^{1}	7	7	7^{2}	7	7	7	7^{1}	7	7^{1}	7^{1}	7	7^{1}	7^{1}	7	7^{2}
Smith, Keith																							
Taylor, Shaun	5	5	5	5	5	5^{1}	5	5	5	5^{1}	5	5	5	5	5	5	5^{1}	5^{1}	5	5^{1}	5	5	5
Tupling, Stephen																							3
Viney, Keith	3	3															**9**						
Vinnicombe, Chris		★										3	★				★	9	9	9	9	9	9
Walter, Dave																		1	1	1	1	1	1
Withey, Graham			3^{2}	3	**3**				★					★	**6**	**6**							
Young, Richard																							
Own Goals							1																

Match Number	24	25	26	27	28	29	30	31	32	33	34	35	36	37	38	39	40	41	42	43	44	45	46	Apps	Subs	Goals
Banks, Chris	2	2	2	2	2	2	2	2	2	2	2		2	★	2^{1}	2	2	2	2	2	2	★	2	43	2	1
Batty, Paul																								15	0	1
Benjamin, Ian			**8**	8	8^{1}	8	8	8	8	8	8	8	8	8	8	8	8	8	8	8^{1}	8^{1}	8		20	0	3
Cooper, Richard	6	6	6	★	★	★	★	10																25	4	1
Dryden, Richard									3	3	3	3	3	3	3	3	**3**	3	3	3	3	3	3	21	0	0
Gwinnett, Mel																								17	0	0
Harris, Carl	★	**11**	**11**	11	**11**^{1}	**11**	11	**11**										**7**		**9**	★	★	★	11	5	1
Harris, Jamie																								1	4	0
Harrower, Steven																								18	0	0
Heath, Herbert			★	**6**				★				2		**2**										3	2	0
Hiley, Scott	8								**11**	11^{1}	11	11	11	**11**	11	**11**	11^{1}	11	11	11^{1}	**11**	11	11	36	1	5
Jones, Mark																								5	0	0
Langley, Tommy	**11**											9	9	9	**9**									14	7	2
McDermott, Brian					6	6	6	6	6	6	6	6	**6**	6	6	6	6	6	6^{1}	6	6	**6**	6	19	0	1
Miller, Kevin																		1	1	1				3	0	0
Neville, Steve	**10**	10^{1}	10^{1}	**10**	10^{1}	**10**	10								10^{1}	10	10	10	10	10	**10**	10	10	38	0	14
Parker Martin		★																						0	1	0
Roberts, Paul																								3	0	0
Rogers, Lee	4	4	4	4	4	4	4	4	4	4	4	4	4	4	4	4	4	4	4	4		4	4	45	0	0
Rowbotham, Darren	7	7^{1}	7^{1}	7	7	7^{1}	7^{1}	7	7	7	7^{1}	7	7^{2}	7	7	7	7		7^{1}	7	7	7	7	45	0	20
Smith, Keith	★	8^{2}	★	★		★		3	★	★	★		★	★		★	★	★			★			2	13	2
Taylor, Shaun	5	5	5	5	5	5	5	5	5	5	5^{1}	5	5	5	5	5	5	5	5	5	5	5	5	46	0	6
Tupling, Stephen	3	3^{1}	3	3	3	3	**3**		★															8	1	1
Viney, Keith																								3	0	0
Vinnicombe, Chris	9	9	9	9	9	9	9	9	**9**	9	**9**									★	4	**2**	8	21	4	0
Walter, Dave	1	1	1	1	1	1	1	1	1	1	1	1	1	1	1	1	1				1	1	1	26	0	0
Withey, Graham																								5	2	2
Young, Richard									10	**10**	10^{1}	10	10	10	★^{1}	9	9	9	9^{2}		9	9	**9**	13	1	4
Own Goals																										1

FA Cup: 1988-89: 1st Round: Bognor Regis T. (A) 1-2.
Littlewoods Cup: 1988-89: 1st Round: Bristol C. (A) 0-1 (H) 0-1.

FULHAM (Division 3)

Team Manager Ray Lewington.
Club Address Craven Cottage, Stevenage Road, London SW6. Tel: 01-736 6561.
Current Ground Capacity 25,680.
Record Attendance 49,335 v Millwall, Div. 2, 8 October 1938.
Year Formed 1879. Turned professional 1898.
Previous Names Fulham St Andrew's.
Club Nickname "The Cottagers".
Club Colours White shirts with black collar, black shorts and white stockings with three black hoops on turnover.
Club Honours Football League: Div. 2 Champions 1948-49; Div. 3(S) Champions 1931-32.
League History 1907-28 Div. 2; 1928-32 Div. 3(S); 1943-49 Div. 2; 1949-52 Div. 1; 1952-59 Div. 2; 1959-68 Div. 1; 1968-69 Div. 2; 1969-71 Div. 3; 1971-80 Div. 2; 1980-82 Div. 3; 1982-86 Div. 2; 1986- Div. 3.
Most League Points in a Season (2 for a win) 60 in Div. 2, 1958-59 and in Div. 3, 1970-71. (3 for a win) 78 in Div. 3, 1981-82.
Most League Goals in a Season 111 in Div. 3(S), 1931-32.
Record Victory 10-1 v Ipswich T. in Div. 1, 26 December 1963.
Record Defeat 0-10 v Liverpool in League Cup 2nd Round 1st leg, 23 September 1986.
Consecutive League Wins 8 in 1963.
Consecutive League Defeats 11 in 1961-62.
Record League Appearances Johnny Haynes, 594 between 1952-70.
Record League Goalscorer—Career Bedford Jezzard, 154 between 1948-56.
Record League Goalscorer—Season Frank Newton, 43 in Div. 3(S), 1931-32.

Fulham: League Record, 1988-89 (Division 3)

Match Number	Date	Venue	Opponents	Result	H/T	Lge Posn	Attend
1	27.8.88	A	Cardiff C.	W 2-1	0-1		6024
2	3.9.88	H	Southend U.	W 1-0	0-0	7	4754
3	10.9.88	A	Mansfield T.	L 1-3	0-2	7	2734
4	17.9.88	H	Bury	W 1-0	1-0	3	3754
5	20.9.88	A	Bolton W.	L 2-3	1-1	6	4239
6	24.9.88	H	Wigan Ath.	D 1-1	0-1	7	3431
7	1.10.88	A	Huddersfield T.	L 0-2	0-0	11	4576
8	5.10.88	H	Wolverhampton W.	D 2-2	0-1	13	4828
9	8.10.88	A	Bristol Rov.	W 5-1	2-0	6	8160
10	15.10.88	H	Aldershot	W 5-1	2-0	4	4573
11	22.10.88	A	Swansea C.	L 0-2	0-1	9	4737
12	25.10.88	H	Northampton T.	W 3-2	1-1	7	4644
13	29.10.88	A	Notts Co.	W 1-0	1-0	4	5514
14	5.11.88	H	Blackpool	D 1-1	0-0	8	4760
15	8.11.88	H	Reading	W 2-1	1-1	6	6934
16	12.11.88	A	Sheffield U.	L 0-1	0-1	7	11087
17	26.11.88	A	Port Vale	L 0-3	0-1	8	5079
18	3.12.88	H	Bristol Rov.	L 0-2	0-1	9	4461
19	17.12.88	H	Preston N.E.	W 2-1	1-0	8	3858
20	26.12.88	A	Gillingham	W 1-0	0-0	7	5871
21	31.12.88	A	Chesterfield	L 1-4	0-2	10	3086
22	2.1.89	H	Brentford	D 3-3	2-2	9	8120
23	7.1.89	H	Chester C.	W 4-1	3-0	6	4196
24	13.1.89	A	Southend U.	D 0-0	0-0	7	4844
25	21.1.89	H	Mansfield T.	D 1-1	1-1	7	4148
26	28.1.89	A	Bury	L 1-3	0-1	8	3582
27	4.2.89	H	Huddersfield T.	L 1-2	0-0	10	4081
28	11.2.89	A	Wolverhampton W.	L 2-5	1-4	10	15621
29	18.2.89	H	Bristol C.	W 3-1	1-1	9	4408
30	28.2.89	A	Northampton T.	L 1-2	1-2	10	3948
31	4.3.89	H	Swansea C.	W 1-0	0-0	9	4710
32	11.3.89	A	Blackpool	W 1-0	0-0	9	3014
33	14.3.89	H	Notts Co.	W 2-1	1-0	7	3402
34	18.3.89	H	Cardiff C.	W 2-0	1-0	6	4261
35	24.3.89	A	Brentford	W 1-0	0-0	6	10851
36	27.3.89	H	Gillingham	L 1-2	0-0	7	6476
37	1.4.89	A	Preston N.E.	W 4-1	2-1	5	8190
38	5.4.89	A	Chester C.	L 0-7	0-2	6	2121
39	8.4.89	H	Chesterfield	W 2-1	0-0	5	4252
40	15.4.89	H	Bolton W.	D 1-1	0-0	5	4950
41	22.4.89	A	Wigan Ath.	W 1-0	0-0	5	3056
42	25.4.89	A	Aldershot	W 2-1	0-0	4	3841
43	29.4.89	H	Sheffield U.	D 2-2	1-1	5	7794
44	1.5.89	A	Reading	W 1-0	1-0	4	5152
45	6.5.89	A	Bristol Rov.	D 0-0	0-0	4	7302
46	13.5.89	H	Port Vale	L 1-2	1-0	4	6257

Players: League Record, 1988-89 (Division 3)

Match Number	1	2	3	4	5	6	7	8	9	10	11	12	13	14	15	16	17	18	19	20	21	22	23	24	25	26	27	28	29	30	31	32	33	34	35	36	37	38	39	40	41	42	43	44	45	46	Apps	Subs	Goals
Barnett, Gary	9	**9**	7	7	7	7	7	7	11	11[1]	11	11[1]	7	7	7[1]	**7**	**7**	7	7	7	**7**	**7**	7[1]	**7**	**7**	**7[1]**	7	7																			28	0	5
Batty, Laurence																																				1											1	0	0
Cawley, Peter																			5		5	5	★	★																							3	2	0
Cole, Michael	10	**10**	10	10[1]	10	**10**	**10**											★	9	9	9	9	9	9	9	**9**	**9**	9	**9**	**9**	9	9	9	9	9[1]	9	9	9	9	**9**	9	**9**	**9**	9	9	9[1]	35	1	3
Davies, Gordon		★[1]			★	★	★	10						★					10	10[1]	10	10[2]	**10[1]**	10	10[1]	10	10	10[1]	10[1]	10	10	10	10[2]	10	**10**	10	10[2]	10	**10**	10	10	**10[1]**	10[1]	10	**10**	**10**	29	5	14
Donnellan, Leo																							★	★	★				★																		0	4	0
Eckhardt, Jeff	2	3	5	5	5	5	5	5	5[1]	5[1]	5	5	6	6	6	6	6	6	6	6	6	6	6	6	6	6	6				6	6	6	6	6	6	6	6	6	6	6	6	6	6	6	6	43	0	2
Elkins, Gary	3[1]	5	3	3	3	3												★	3	3	3	3	3	3	3	3	3	3	3	3									5						★	2	20	2	1
Gordon, Colin									**10**	10	10	10	10	10[1]	10	10	10	**10**								★	★			64					★	★	3[1]	**3**									12	5	2
Gore, Shaun							3						5	5	5		5	5																													6	0	0
Hoddy, Kevin		★	★																																												0	2	0
Kerrins, Wayne													★				3	3												**11**																	3	1	0
Langley, Richard	6	2	2	2	2	2			3	3	**3**	**3**													5				2	2	2	2	2	2	2	2											19	0	0
Marshall, John				★			★	3	7[1]	7[1]	7	7	2	2	2	2	2	2	2	2	2	2	2	2	2	2	2	2	7[1]	7	7[1]	7	7	7[1]	7	7[1]	7	7	7[1]	7	7	7	7	7	7	7	39	2	7
Mauge, Ronald						11	**11**	11	★																												2	2	2	2	2	2	2	2	2		12	1	0
Peters, Gary					★[1]	★	2	2	2[1]	2	2	2				5																															7	2	2
Rougvie, Doug																												6[1]	5	5	5	5	5	5	5	5	5	5		5	5	5	5	5	5	5	18	0	1
Sayer, Andy	7[1]	8	9[1]	9	9[1]	**9[1]**	9	9	9[2]	9[2]	9	9	**9**	**9**	9[1]	9	9	9			★	★								★	11					★			★[1]	★		★	★			★	19	9	10
Scott, Peter					**11**			★			★	★	8	8	8	8	8	8	8	8	8	8[1]	8[1]	8	8	8	8	8	8	8	8	8	8	8	8		8	8	8	8	8	8	8[1]	8	8	8	34	3	3
Skinner, Justin	4	7	8	8	**8**	8	8	**8[1]**	8	8	**8**	**8[1]**				★	★		4[1]	4	4	**4**				★	★		4	4[1]	4	4[1]	4	4[1]	4	4	4	**4**	4	4[1]	4	4	4	4[1]	4	4	34	4	8
Stannard, Jim	1	1	1	1	1	1	1	1	1	1	1	1	1	1	1	1	1	1	1	1	1	1	1	1	1	1	1	1	1	1	1	1	1	1	1		1	1	1	1	1	1	1	1	1	1	45	0	0
Thomas, Glen	5	6	6	6	6	6	6	6	6	6	6	6	3	3	3	3				5		★	5	**5**		5	5	5	6	6	3	3	3	3	3	3		★	3	3	3[1]	3	3	3	3	3	38	2	1
Walker, Clive	11	11	**11**	**11**							★	★	11[1]	11	11	11	11	11	11[1]	11	11[1]	11	11[1]	11	11	11	11[1]	11	11[1]			11	11	11	11	**11**	11[1]	11	11	11	11	11[1]	11	11	11	11	36	2	8
Wilson, Robert	8	4	4	4	4	4	4	4[1]	4	4	4	4	4	4	4	4	4	**4**					**4**	4	4	4	**4**	4								**8**		★				★					25	2	1
Own Goals												1																																					1

FA Cup: 1988-89: 1st Round: Colchester U. (H) 0-1.
Littlewoods Cup: 1988-89: 1st Round: Brentford (H) 2-2 (A) 0-1.

GILLINGHAM (Division 4)

Team Manager Damien Richardson.
Club Address Priestfield Stadium, Gillingham. Tel: (0634) 51854.
Current Ground Capacity 19,581.
Record Attendance 23,002 v Q.P.R., FA Cup 3rd Round, 10 January 1948.
Year Formed 1893. Turned professional 1894.
Previous Names New Brompton.
Club Nickname "The Gills".
Club Colours Royal blue shirts, white shorts and stockings with blue trim.
Club Honours Football League: Div. 4 Champions 1963-64.
League History 1920-38 Div. 3(S); 1938 Failed re-election; 1938-44 Southern League; 1944-46 Kent League; 1946-50 Southern League; 1950-58 Div. 3(S); 1958-64 Div. 4; 1964-71 Div. 3; 1971-74 Div. 4; 1974-89 Div. 3; 1989- Div. 4.

Most League Points in a Season (2 for a win) 62 in Div. 4, 1973-74. (3 for a win) 83 in Div. 3, 1984-85.
Most League Goals in a Season 90 in Div. 4, 1973-74.
Record Victory 10-0 v Chesterfield in Div. 3, 5 September 1987.
Record Defeat 2-9 v Nottingham F. in Division 3(S), 18 November 1950.
Consecutive League Wins 7 in 1954-55.
Consecutive League Defeats 10 in 1988.
Record League Appearances John Simpson, 571 between 1957-72.
Record League Goalscorer-Career Brian Yeo, 135 between 1963-75.
Record League Goalscorer—Season Ernie Morgan, 31 in Div. 3(S), 1954-55 and Brian Yeo, 31 in Div. 4, 1973-74.

Gillingham: League Record, 1988-89 (Division 3)

Match Number	Date	Venue	Opponents	Result	H/T	Lge Posn	Attend
1	27.8.88	H	Swansea C.	L 2-3	1-1		4437
2	3.9.88	A	Aldershot	W 2-0	1-0	11	2477
3	10.9.88	H	Sheffield U.	W 2-1	1-1	5	5041
4	17.9.88	A	Huddersfield T.	D 1-1	0-0	6	4688
5	20.9.88	A	Mansfield T.	L 1-2	0-0	10	3153
6	24.9.88	H	Reading	L 0-1	0-1	13	4469
7	1.10.88	A	Brentford	L 0-1	0-0	18	4839
8	4.10.88	H	Bristol C.	L 0-1	0-1	20	3102
9	8.10.88	H	Chesterfield	L 0-1	0-1	20	2901
10	15.10.88	A	Southend U.	L 1-2	0-1	21	3200
11	22.10.88	H	Bury	L 3-4	1-3	21	2850
12	25.10.88	A	Preston N.E.	L 0-5	0-2	21	6390
13	29.10.88	H	Wolverhampton W.	L 1-3	0-1	22	5288
14	5.11.88	A	Cardiff C.	L 0-1	0-0	22	3658
15	8.11.88	H	Blackpool	W 1-0	1-0	22	3541
16	12.11.88	A	Bristol Rov.	L 0-2	0-0	22	4826
17	26.11.88	A	Notts Co.	W 2-1	1-1	22	4611
18	3.12.88	H	Chester C.	L 0-2	0-1	22	3329
19	18.12.88	A	Northampton T.	W 2-1	0-0	22	3829
20	26.12.88	H	Fulham	L 0-1	0-0	22	5871
21	30.12.88	H	Port Vale	W 1-0	0-0	22	4706
22	2.1.89	A	Wigan Ath.	L 0-3	0-2	22	3090
23	6.1.89	A	Bolton W.	L 1-2	0-1	22	4187
24	14.1.89	H	Aldershot	D 1-1	1-0	23	3781
25	21.1.89	A	Sheffield U.	L 2-4	0-3	23	9336
26	28.1.89	H	Huddersfield T.	L 1-2	1-1	23	3530
27	4.2.89	H	Brentford	D 0-0	0-0	24	4002
28	11.2.89	A	Bristol C.	L 0-1	0-0	24	7319
29	18.2.89	A	Chesterfield	L 1-3	0-1	24	3432
30	25.2.89	H	Southend U.	D 1-1	1-0	24	3574
31	28.2.89	H	Preston N.E.	L 1-3	1-0	24	3031
32	4.3.89	A	Bury	L 0-1	0-1	24	4313
33	11.3.89	H	Cardiff C.	L 1-2	0-2	24	2927
34	14.3.89	A	Wolverhampton W.	L 1-6	0-4	24	12574
35	19.3.89	A	Swansea C.	L 2-3	0-2	24	4252
36	24.3.89	H	Wigan Ath.	W 2-1	0-1	24	3244
37	27.3.89	A	Fulham	W 2-1	0-0	24	6476
38	1.4.89	H	Northampton T.	W 1-0	0-0	23	3466
39	4.4.89	H	Bolton W.	L 0-1	0-1	23	3096
40	8.4.89	A	Port Vale	L 1-2	0-1	24	5358
41	15.4.89	H	Mansfield T.	W 3-0	0-0	23	2594
42	22.4.89	A	Reading	W 2-1	1-0	23	3511
43	28.4.89	H	Bristol Rov.	L 2-3	1-0	23	4004
44	1.5.89	A	Blackpool	L 1-4	1-1	23	2152
45	6.5.89	A	Chester C.	L 0-2	0-1	23	2106
46	13.5.89	H	Notts Co.	W 2-1	2-0	23	2877

Players: League Record, 1988-89 (Division 3)

Match Number	1	2	3	4	5	6	7	8	9	10	11	12	13	14	15	16	17	18	19	20	21	22	23	24	25	26	27	28	29	30	31	32	33	34	35	36	37	38	39	40	41	42	43	44	45	46	Apps	Subs	Goals
Beadle, Peter																																	★	11													1	1	0
Burley, George	2	2	2	2	2	2	2	2	2	2	2	2	2	2	2^{1}	2	2	2	2	2	2	2	2	2	2	2	2	2	2	2	2^{1}	2	2	2	2	2	2	2	2	2	2	2	2	2	2	2	46	0	2
Clarke, Brian	5	**5**		6	6		5	5	5	5	5		5																																		10	0	0
Cooper, Mark	**10**	★					10	★		11	11^{1}	**7**			★	★	7	7	8	8	8^{1}	**8**	**8**		8^{1}	9																					14	4	3
Docker, Ian						★			★				**11**	10	10	10	10	5	10	10	**10**	10	10	10	**10**		10	8	8	10	10	10	10	10	10	10	10	10	10	10	10	10	**3**	★	3	3	32	3	0
Eeles, Anthony																										**8**							7	**7**													3	0	0
Gavin, Patrick																																		9^{1}	9^{1}	9^{1}	9	9^{1}	9	9	**9^{1}**	**9^{1}**	9	**9**	9	9^{1}	13	0	7
Guscott, Lindon																																		★			★										0	2	0
Haines, Ivan														★	5	5	5		5	5	5	5	**5**		★	6																				6	10	2	0
Haylock, Paul	3	3	3	3	3	3	**3**	3	3	3	3	3	3	3	3	3	3	3	3	3	3	3	3	3	7	10	★		10													★		3	★		28	3	0
Hillyard, Ron	1	1	1	1	1	1																												1	1	1	1	1	1	1	1	1	1	1	1	1	19	0	0
Joseph, Francis																															7	7	8	8	**8**	8	8	8	8	**8**	$★^{1}$	★	★	★	★		10	5	1
Kite, Phil							1	1	1	1	1	1	1	1	1	1	1	1	1	1	1	1	1	1	1	1	1	1	1	1	1	1	1														27	0	0
Lillis, Jason	★	**10**	**10^{1}**	10	10	**10**			★	★	**7^{1}**	★	**8**	7	**7**	8	★	★									★	**10**	★		★	**8**			$★^{1}$												12	10	3
Lovell, Steve	9^{1}	9^{1}	9^{1}	9^{1}	9^{1}	9	9	9	9	9^{1}	9^{1}	9	9^{1}	9	9	9	**9**	**9**	9^{2}	9	9	9	9	9	**9**		9	9	**9^{1}**	9	9	9	**9**							$★^{1}$	8	8^{1}	8^{1}	8	8	8	38	1	14
Manuel, Billy																												6	★			5	5	5	5	**5**	★	★	★	**7**	7	7	7	7	7	7^{1}	13	4	1
O'Shea, Timothy																											8	7	7	7	8				4	4	5	5	5	5	5	**5**	5	5	**5**	10	17	0	0
Peacock, Gavin	4^{1}	4	4	4	4	4	4	4	4	4	4	4	4	4	4	4	4	4	4	4	4	4	4^{1}	4^{1}	4	4^{1}	**4**		4	4	**4**	4	4	**4**		$★^{1}$	4^{2}	4	4	4	4^{1}	4	4	4^{1}	4	4	43	1	9
Pearson, Richard																																							★						10	5	2	1	0
Perry, Andy				★	★	7	7	7	**7**	**7**				★	8										★	7				8		★															8	5	0
Quow, Trevor	8	8	8	8	8	8	8	**8**	**8**	8	8	8	★	**8**			8^{1}	8		★	★	11	★																								16	4	1
Reeves, Alan																												4	6	6	6	6	6	6	6	6	6	6	**6**	6	6	6	6	6	6		18	0	0
Shipley, George	7	7^{1}	**7**													**7**		10	7	**7**	7	7	7	8		★	**7**	★																			12	2	1
Smith, David	11	11	11	**11**	11	11	★	11	11			11	★	11	11	11	11^{1}	11	11	11	11		11	11	11	11	11	11	11	11	11	11	11		11	11	11	11	11	11	11	11	11^{1}	11	**11**	11	40	2	2
Stimson, Mark																									3	3	3	3	3	3	3	3	3	3	3	3	3	3	3	3	3	3					18	0	0
Walford, Steve																			6	6	6	**6**																									4	0	0
Walker, Alan	6	6	6			6	6	6	6	6	6	6	6	6	6	6	6	6							6		6	5	**5**	5^{1}	5																22	0	1
Weatherly, Mark		★	★	7	**7**		11	10	10	10	10	**10**	10	**5**								★	6	6																			10	**10**			14	3	0
West, Gary			5	5	5	5						5											★	5	5^{1}	5	5																				9	1	1
Williams, Jeremy			★								★	★	7									★		7										★	7	7	**7**	**7**	**7**	★							7	6	0
Own Goals																																	1																1

FA Cup: 1988-89: 1st Round: Peterborough U. (H) 3-3, Replay (A) 0-1.
Littlewoods Cup: 1988-89: 1st Round: Cambridge U. (A) 2-1 (H) 3-1; 2nd Round: Millwall (A) 0-3 (H) 1-3.

GRIMSBY TOWN (Division 4)

Team Manager Alan Buckley
Club Address Blundell Park, Cleethorpes, South Humberside DN35 7PY. Tel: (0472) 697111.
Current Ground Capacity 20,865.
Record Attendance 31,651 v Wolverhampton W., FA Cup 5th Round, 20 February 1937.
Year Formed 1878. Turned professional 1890.
Previous Names Grimsby Pelham.
Club Nickname "The Mariners".
Club Colours Black and white vertical striped shirts, black shorts and white stockings.
Club Honours Football League: Div. 2 Champions 1900-01, 1933-34; Div. 3(N) Champions 1925-26, 1955-56; Div. 3 Champions 1979-80; Div. 4 Champions 1971-72.
League History 1892-1901 Div. 2; 1901-03 Div. 1; 1903-10 Div 2; 1910 Failed re-election; 1911-20 Div. 2; 1920-21 Div. 3; 1921-26 Div. 3(N); 1926-29 Div. 2; 1929-32 Div. 1; 1932-34 Div. 2; 1934-48 Div. 1; 1948-51 Div. 2; 1951-56 Div. 3(N); 1956-59 Div. 2; 1959-62 Div. 3; 1962-64 Div. 2; 1964-68 Div. 3; 1968-72 Div. 4; 1972-77 Div. 3; 1977-79 Div. 4; 1979-80 Div. 3; 1980-87 Div. 2; 1987-88 Div. 3; 1988- Div. 4.
Most League Points in a Season (2 for a win) 68 in Div. 3(N), 1955-56. (3 for a win) 70 in Div. 2, 1983-84.
Most League Goals in a Season 103 in Div. 2, 1933-34.
Record Victory 9-2 v Darwen in Div. 2, 15 April 1899.
Record Defeat 1-9 v Arsenal in Div. 1, 28 January 1931.
Consecutive League Wins 11 in 1952.
Consecutive League Defeats 9 in 1907-08.
Record League Appearances Keith Jobling, 448 between 1953-69.
Record League Goalscorer—Career Pat Glover, 182 between 1930-39.
Record League Goalscorer—Season Pat Glover, 42 in Div. 2, 1933-34.

Grimsby Town: League Record, 1988-89 (Division 4)

Match Number	Date	Venue	Opponents	Result	H/T	Lge Posn	Attend
1	27.8.88	A	Cambridge U.	L 1-4	1-2		2290
2	3.9.88	H	Torquay U.	W 1-0	0-0	14	2857
3	10.9.88	A	Scunthorpe U.	D 1-1	1-1	11	6037
4	17.9.88	H	Rotherham U.	L 0-4	0-3	17	3697
5	20.9.88	A	Wrexham	W 2-1	2-1	14	2267
6	24.9.88	H	Rochdale	L 1-3	1-1	16	2939
7	1.10.88	A	Hereford U.	L 1-2	1-0	19	1888
8	4.10.88	H	Tranmere Rov.	D 0-0	0-0	20	2288
9	8.10.88	H	Peterborough U.	D 0-0	0-0	20	2820
10	15.10.88	A	Exeter C.	L 1-2	0-1	22	2232
11	22.10.88	H	York C.	W 2-0	2-0	21	2825
12	25.10.88	A	Crewe Alex	D 2-2	2-1	21	2311
13	29.10.88	H	Halifax T.	W 3-2	0-1	18	3260
14	5.11.88	A	Stockport Co.	L 1-3	0-1	19	2064
15	8.11.88	H	Doncaster Rov.	W 5-0	2-0	16	3300
16	12.11.88	A	Hartlepool U.	L 1-2	0-0	20	1782
17	26.11.88	A	Carlisle U.	L 1-2	1-0	20	2175
18	3.12.88	H	Scarborough	W 2-1	1-0	20	3887
19	17.12.88	H	Leyton Orient	D 2-2	0-0	20	3446
20	26.12.88	A	Lincoln C.	D 2-2	0-1	19	8038
21	31.12.88	A	Burnley	L 0-1	0-0	19	7367
22	2.1.89	H	Colchester U.	D 2-2	2-1	20	4472
23	14.1.89	A	Torquay U.	D 2-2	0-1	20	2251
24	21.1.89	H	Cambridge U.	W 4-0	2-0	19	3653
25	4.2.89	H	Wrexham	L 0-1	0-1	20	5038
26	11.2.89	A	Rochdale	W 2-0	2-0	16	1621
27	14.2.89	H	Darlington	D 0-0	0-0	19	4628
28	25.2.89	H	Exeter C.	W 2-1	1-0	16	4684
29	28.2.89	H	Crewe Alex.	D 0-0	0-0	15	5044
30	4.3.89	A	York C.	W 3-0	1-0	13	3481
31	7.3.89	A	Rotherham U.	L 0-1	0-0	14	4888
32	11.3.89	H	Stockport Co.	W 2-0	0-0	11	4685
33	14.3.89	A	Halifax T.	L 1-2	0-2	13	1609
34	18.3.89	H	Scunthorpe U.	D 1-1	0-0	14	9796
35	24.3.89	A	Colchester U.	D 0-0	0-0	14	4507
36	27.3.89	H	Lincoln C.	W 1-0	0-0	12	8618
37	1.4.89	A	Leyton Orient	L 0-5	0-1	13	4149
38	4.4.89	A	Darlington	D 1-1	0-1	13	1840
39	8.4.89	H	Burnley	W 1-0	0-0	12	4856
40	15.4.89	H	Hereford U.	D 1-1	0-0	11	4036
41	25.4.89	A	Peterborough U.	W 2-1	0-1	11	2937
42	29.4.89	H	Carlisle U.	D 0-0	0-0	11	3837
43	1.5.89	A	Doncaster Rov.	W 3-2	2-1	10	2183
44	6.5.89	A	Scarborough	W 3-2	2-1	9	3923
45	9.9.89	A	Tranmere Rov.	L 2-3	2-2	9	6938
46	13.5.89	H	Hartlepool U.	W 3-0	1-0	9	3400

Players: League Record, 1988-89 (Division 4)

Match Number	1	2	3	4	5	6	7	8	9	10	11	12	13	14	15	16	17	18	19	20	21	22	23	24	25	26	27	28	29	30	31	32	33	34	35	36	37	38	39	40	41	42	43	44	45	46	Apps	Subs	Goals
Agnew, Paul	3	3	3	3	3	3	3	3	3	3	3	3	3			★	3	3	3	3	3	3	3	3	3	3	3	3	3					★	3	3	3				3	3	**3**				32	2	0
Alexander, Keith		**11**	11^{1}	11	11	11	**11**	**11**	11	11^{1}	11^{1}	11	11	11	11^{1}	11	**11**	11^{1}	11	11^{1}	11	**11^{1}**	11^{1}	11	11	11^{2}	11	11	**11**		★	11	11	11	11	11	11	11	11	11	11^{1}	11	★	11^{2}	11	11^{1}	42	2	14
Banton, Dale																																				**7**			9	★		★	11^{1}	★	★	★	3	5	1
Caldwell, Tony			**10**	**10**		★																																									2	1	0
Cockerill, John	5			6			★			★	10^{1}			3	10^{1}	10	10^{1}	10^{1}	10			★	10	10	10	10	10	10							10	10	10	10		★	★	10	10	10	10^{1}	10^{1}	24	5	6
Cunningham, Shaun	6	6	6	8	6	6	6	6	6	6	6	6	6	6	6	6	6	6	6			6	6	6^{1}	6	6	6	6	6	6	6	6	6	6	6	6	6	6	6	6	6	6	6	6	6	6	44	0	1
Dixon, Andrew	**2**				2	2	**2**			★																																					4	1	0
Gilbert, David																																				8	8	8	8	8^{1}	8	8	8	**8**	8^{1}	8^{1}	11	0	3
Grocock, Chris	★			2	10	**10**		★	★	10				★		★				★	★																										4	7	0
Jobling, Kevin	7	7	7	7	7^{1}	7	7	7	**7**	**7**									★	10	10	**10**	**7**		2	7	**7**		10	10	10	10^{1}	10	10	7	2	7	7^{1}	10	**10**	10^{1}	**7**					31	1	4
Lever, Mark		2	2					5	5	5	5	5	5	5	5	5	5	5	5^{1}	5	5	5	5	5	**5**	5	5	5^{1}	5	5	5	5	5	5	5	5	**5**		5	**5**				5	5	**5**	37	0	2
McDermott, John	**8**	★		★			10	2	2	2	7	2	7	7^{1}	2	2	2	2	2	2	2	2	2	2				2	2	2	2	2	2	2	2		2	2		9	2	2	2	9	3	2	36	2	1
North, Marc	11	9^{1}	8		8^{1}	8^{1}	8	8	8	**8**	★	7					7	7	7	**7**	7	★	9^{1}	7	7	2	2	7	7	7^{1}	7	7^{1}	7	7													27	2	6
O'Kelly, Richard	9	8	9	**9**	9	9	9^{1}	9	9	9	9	9	9^{1}	9	9	**9**	9	9	**9**	9	**9**	9^{1}		9^{1}	9	9	9	9^{1}	9	9^{1}	9	9	9^{1}	9^{1}	9	9^{1}	**9**				**9**	★	9^{1}				38	1	10
Reece, Paul		1	1	1	1	1											1			1	1	1	1	1	1														1	1							14	0	0
Saunders, Steve			★	★			★	10	10		8	8^{2}	8^{2}	8	8^{1}	8	8	8	8^{1}	8	8	8	8	8^{1}	8	8	8	8	8	8^{1}	8	8	8	8	8	★	★	9	7^{1}	7	7	9	**7**	7^{1}	9	9	36	5	10
Sherwood, Steve	1						1	1	1	1	1	1	1	1	1	1		1	1							1	1	1	1	1	1	1	1	1	1	1	1	1			1	1	1	1	1	1	32	0	0
Smaller, Paul																																														★	0	1	0
Stephenson, Geoffrey															3	**3**														3	3	3	**3**	**3**			★	3	3	3				**3**	★	3	12	2	0
Stoutt, Stephen	10^{1}	10																																													2	0	1
Tillson, Andy	★	5	5	5	5	5	5	4	4	4	4	4	4	4	4	4	4	4	4	4	4	4	4	4^{1}	4	4	4	4	4	4	4	4	4	4	4	4	4	4	4	4	4	4	4^{1}	4	**4**		44	1	2
Watson, Tommy												10	10	10	7^{2}	7^{1}	★			6^{1}	6	7	★		★		★		★	11	**11**		★						★				★	★	**7**	**7**	12	9	4
Williams, Tommy	4	4	4	4	4	4	4				**2**		2	**2**																								5	2	2	5	**5**	5	2	2	4	19	0	0
Own Goals																																																	0

FA Cup: 1988-89: 1st Round: Wolverhampton W. (H) 1-0; 2nd Round: Rotherham U. (H) 3-2; 3rd Round: Middlesbrough (A) 2-1; 4th Round: Reading (H) 1-1, Replay (A) 2-1; 5th Round: Wimbledon (A) 1-3.
Littlewoods Cup: 1988-89: 1st Round: Rotherham U. (H) 0-1 (A) 0-1.

HALIFAX TOWN (Division 4)

Team Manager Billy Ayre.
Club Address Shay Ground, Halifax HX1 2YS. Tel: (0422) 53423.
Current Ground Capacity 4,275.
Record Attendance 36,885 v Tottenham H, FA Cup 5th Round, 14 February 1953.
Year Formed 1911. Turned professional 1911.
Previous Names None.
Club Nickname "The Shaymen".
Club Colours Blue and white striped shirts, white shorts with blue trim and blue stockings with white tops.
Club Honours None.
League History 1921-58 Div. 3(N); 1958-63 Div 3; 1963-69 Div. 4; 1969-76 Div. 3; 1976- Div. 4.
Most League Points in a Season (2 for a win) 57 in Div. 4, 1968-69. (3 for a win) 60 in Div. 4, 1982-83.
Most League Goals in a Season 83 in Div. 3(N), 1957-58.
Record Victory 7-0 v Bishop Auckland in FA Cup 2nd Round replay, 10 January 1967.
Record Defeat 0-13 v Stockport Co. in Div. 3(N), 6 January 1934.
Consecutive League Wins 7 in 1964.
Consecutive League Defeats 8 in 1946-47.
Record League Appearances John Pickering, 367 between 1965-74.
Record League Goalscorer—Career Ernest Dixon, 129 between 1922-30.
Record League Goalscorer—Season Albert Valentine, 34 in Div. 3(N), 1934-35.

Halifax Town: League Record, 1988-89 (Division 4)

Match Number	Date	Venue	Opponents	Result	H/T	Lge Posn	Attend
1	27.8.88	A	Torquay U.	W 2-0	1-0		2769
2	3.9.88	H	Burnley	L 1-2	0-1	11	3371
3	10.9.88	A	Exeter C.	L 1-4	0-1	18	1725
4	16.9.88	H	Carlisle U.	D 3-3	1-3	15	1546
5	19.9.88	A	Stockport Co.	D 1-1	0-1	14	2206
6	24.9.88	H	Tranmere Rov.	L 2-3	1-0	20	1662
7	1.10.88	A	York C.	L 3-5	1-3	21	2238
8	4.10.88	H	Wrexham	W 4-0	3-0	18	1199
9	8.10.88	A	Cambridge U.	L 1-2	0-0	21	1800
10	14.10.88	H	Rochdale	W 4-1	2-0	19	2553
11	21.10.88	A	Doncaster Rov.	W 4-1	4-1	16	3038
12	25.10.88	H	Peterborough U.	W 5-0	0-0	10	2248
13	29.10.88	A	Grimsby T.	L 2-3	1-0	13	3260
14	4.11.88	H	Hartlepool U.	W 1-0	1-0	10	2182
15	8.11.88	H	Colchester U.	W 3-2	2-1	7	2176
16	12.11.88	A	Hereford U.	L 1-3	0-2	10	1929
17	26.11.88	A	Lincoln C.	L 1-2	1-1	13	3379
18	2.12.88	H	Crewe Alex.	L 0-1	0-0	17	2026
19	17.12.88	H	Scarborough	L 0-2	0-1	18	1890
20	26.12.88	A	Darlington	W 2-0	1-0	15	2131
21	31.12.88	A	Rotherham U.	L 0-2	0-0	18	5258
22	2.1.89	H	Scunthorpe U.	W 5-1	2-0	15	2650
23	14.1.89	A	Burnley	L 1-2	0-1	16	8297
24	20.1.89	H	Torquay U.	W 2-0	2-0	15	1830
25	28.1.89	A	Carlisle U.	L 1-3	0-0	15	3007
26	4.2.89	H	Stockport Co.	D 2-2	1-0	15	1938
27	10.2.89	A	Tranmere Rov.	L 0-2	0-0	16	4674
28	14.2.89	H	Leyton Orient	D 2-2	0-0	16	1477
29	17.2.89	H	Cambridge U.	D 0-0	0-0	17	1531
30	1.3.89	A	Peterborough U.	L 1-2	0-0	18	2159
31	3.3.89	H	Doncaster Rov.	W 2-0	0-0	16	1675
32	11.3.89	A	Hartlepool U.	L 0-2	0-1	20	1786
33	14.3.89	H	Grimsby T.	W 2-1	2-0	16	1609
34	17.3.89	H	Exeter C.	L 0-3	0-1	20	1473
35	25.3.89	A	Scunthorpe U.	D 0-0	0-0	19	4591
36	27.3.89	H	Darlington	W 1-0	0-0	16	1849
37	1.4.89	A	Scarborough	L 1-3	0-1	17	2365
38	4.4.89	A	Leyton Orient	L 0-2	0-0	18	3288
39	7.4.89	H	Rotherham U.	D 1-1	1-0	19	2947
40	14.4.89	H	York C.	D 0-0	0-0	19	1875
41	21.4.89	A	Wrexham	L 0-3	0-1	20	1782
42	25.4.89	A	Rochdale	D 1-1	0-0	17	1388
43	29.4.89	H	Lincoln C.	L 0-1	0-0	20	1261
44	1.5.89	A	Colchester U.	L 2-3	1-0	21	5065
45	5.5.89	A	Crewe Alex.	D 2-2	0-1	21	3476
46	13.5.89	H	Hereford U.	D 2-2	1-1	21	1082

Players: League Record, 1988-89 (Division 4)

Match Number	1	2	3	4	5	6	7	8	9	10	11	12	13	14	15	16	17	18	19	20	21	22	23
Allison, Wayne	10^{1}	10	10		10	10	10^{2}	**10^{1}**			10	10	10	10^{1}	10	10	10^{1}	10	10	10	10	10^{2}	10^{1}
Barr, Billy	2	2	2	2	2	**2^{1}**	2	3	3	3^{1}	3	3	3	3	3	3	★	**9**	9	2	2	2	2
Barr, Robert				3	5	5																	
Blain, Colin	7				3	**3**	**3**													★	★	**4**	**9**
Bramhall, John	5^{1}	5	5	5					5	5	6	6	6^{1}	6	6	6	6	6	6	6	6	6	6
Broadbent, Graham																							
Donnelly, Paul																							
Fleming, Craig																						★	
Fleming, Paul																							★
Harrison, Frank																							
Hedworth, Chris								2	2	2	2	**2**				**2**	2	2	2				
Henry, Liburd		★	★	10	★	★																	
Horner, Philip	8	8	8	8	8	8	8^{1}	6^{1}	6	**6**						★^{1}	3	3	3	3	3	3	3
Logan, David	3	3	**3**																				
McPhillips, Terry		★^{1}	9	9^{3}	**9**	9^{1}	9	9^{1}	9^{1}	9^{2}	9^{2}	9^{1}	9	9	9^{2}	9	9			9^{2}	9	9	
Martin, Dean			**7**	7	7^{1}	7	**7**	7	7	7	7	7	7	7	7^{1}	**7**			7	**7**	7	7	7
Matthews, Mike	4	4	4				4	4	4	4	4	4	4^{1}	4	4	4	4	4					
Matthews, Neil	9						★	11^{1}	11	11^{1}	11^{1}	11^{2}	11	11	11		11	11	11	11	11	11^{1}	11
Paterson, Toby																							
Pullan, Chris																							
Richardson, Lee	11	11	11	11	11	11	11	★	10	10	★	★^{1}	2	2	2	11	7	7	4	4	**4**		4
Richardson, Nick																							
Robinson, David							5	5			5	5	5	5	5	5	5	5	5	**5**	5	5^{1}	5
Roche, Pat	1	1	1	1				1	1	1	1	1	1	1	1	1	1	1	1				
Sinclair, Ronnie																				1			
Smith, Gareth						★																	
Watson, Andy		**9**	★	4	4	4	★	8	8	8	**8^{1}**	8^{1}	8	8	8	8	**8**	8	8	8	8	8^{1}	8
Whitehead, Alan	6	6	6^{1}	6	6	6	6													★			
Whitehead, Philip					1	1	1														1	1	1
Willis, Paul		**7**								★						★		★					
Own Goals																							

Match Number	24	25	26	27	28	29	30	31	32	33	34	35	36	37	38	39	40	41	42	43	44	45	46	Apps	Subs	Goals
Allison, Wayne	10^{2}	10			10^{1}	10	10	10	10	10^{1}	10	10	10	10	10	10	10	10	10	10	10	10^{1}	10	41	0	14
Barr, Billy	2	2	2	2	2	2	2	2	2	2		11	11^{1}	**11**	5			**7**	7^{1}	7	7	**7**	7	42	1	4
Barr, Robert																		5						4	0	0
Blain, Colin				10	★	★	11	11	8	4	4			5					5	**5**		3		16	4	0
Bramhall, John	6	6^{1}	6				6	6	6	6	6	6	6	6	6	6	6	6	6	**6**	6	6	**6**	39	0	3
Broadbent, Graham						★	★	★^{1}	★		★			★			★	★		★	9	★^{1}	11	2	10	2
Donnelly, Paul																							★	0	1	0
Fleming, Craig																								0	1	0
Fleming, Paul	**9**	**9**	10	6	6	6	7	7	7	7	2	2	2	2	2	2	2	2	2	2	2	**2**		22	1	0
Harrison, Frank										3	3	3	3	3	3	3	3	3	3	3	3		3	13	0	0
Hedworth, Chris																						5	2	11	0	0
Henry, Liburd																								1	4	0
Horner, Philip	3	3	3	3	3	3			3		★	4	4	4	4	4	4	4	4	4	4	4	4	36	2	3
Logan, David																								3	0	0
McPhillips, Terry		★	9^{1}	9	9	9	**9**	9	**9**	9^{1}	9	9	9	9^{1}	9	9^{1}	**9**	9	9	9	★^{1}	★	9^{2}	37	4	23
Martin, Dean	7	7	7	7	7	7					7	7	7	7	7	7	7							32	0	2
Matthews, Mike																								15	0	1
Matthews, Neil	11	11	11	11	**11^{1}**	**11**			11	11	**11**				11	11	11		11	11	11	11	★	32	2	7
Paterson, Toby																		★						0	1	0
Pullan, Chris				4	4	**4**	4^{1}	**4**																5	0	1
Richardson, Lee	4	4	4																					22	3	1
Richardson, Nick	★							★										**11**		★	5	9	**5**	4	3	0
Robinson, David	5	5	5	5	5	5	5	5	5	5	5	5	5			5	5							30	0	1
Roche, Pat												1	1	1	1		1	1	1	1	**1**			25	0	0
Sinclair, Ronnie			1	1	1	1	1	1	1	1	1													10	0	0
Smith, Gareth																								0	1	0
Watson, Andy	8	8	8^{1}	8	8	8	8	**8^{1}**	★	8	**8**	8	8	8	8	8	8	8	8	8	8	8	8	42	3	5
Whitehead, Alan							3	3	**4**															10	1	1
Whitehead, Philip	1	1													1							1	1	11	0	0
Willis, Paul																								1	3	0
Own Goals																					1					1

FA Cup: 1988-89: 1st Round: York C. (H) 1-0; 2nd Round: Altrincham (A) 3-0; 3rd Round: Kettering T. (A) 1-1, Replay (H) 2-3.

Littlewoods Cup: 1988-89: 1st Round: Scarborough (A) 1-1 (H) 2-2.

HARTLEPOOL UNITED (Division 4)

Team Manager Bobby Moncur.
Club Address The Victoria Ground, Clarence Road, Hartlepool. Tel: (0429) 272584.
Current Ground Capacity 6,620.
Record Attendance 17,426 v Manchester U., FA Cup 3rd Round, 5 January 1957.
Year Formed 1908. Turned professional 1908.
Previous Names Hartlepools United, Hartlepool.
Club Nickname "The Pool".
Club Colours Blue shirts, white shorts and blue stockings.
Club Honours None.
League History 1921-58 Div. 3(N); 1958-68 Div. 4; 1968-69 Div. 3; 1969- Div. 4.

Most League Points in a Season (2 for a win) 60 in Div. 4, 1967-68. (3 for a win) 70 in Div. 4, 1985-86.
Most League Goals in a Season 90 in Div. 3(N), 1956-57.
Record Victory 10-1 v Barrow in Div. 4, 4 April 1959.
Record Defeat 1-10 v Wrexham in Div. 4, 3 March 1962.
Consecutive League Wins 7 in 1956 and 1968.
Consecutive League Defeats 8 in 1950.
Record League Appearances Wattie Moore, 448 between 1948-60.
Record League Goalscorer—Career Ken Johnson, 98 between 1949-64.
Record League Goalscorer—Season William Robinson, 28 in Div. 3(N), 1927-28.

Hartlepool United: League Record, 1988-89 (Division 4)

Match Number	Date	Venue	Opponents	Result	H/T	Lge Posn	Attend
1	27.8.88	A	Lincoln C.	W 1-0	1-0		3361
2	3.9.88	H	Darlington	W 2-1	0-0	4	2843
3	10.9.88	A	Torquay U.	L 0-2	0-0	6	2027
4	17.9.88	H	Leyton Orient	W 1-0	0-0	4	1823
5	20.9.88	A	York C.	W 3-2	2-1	2	2611
6	24.9.88	H	Cambridge U.	W 3-2	2-1	2	2385
7	30.9.88	A	Tranmere Rov.	L 1-2	1-2	2	3624
8	4.10.88	H	Rochdale	L 0-1	0-0	5	2483
9	8.10.88	A	Doncaster Rov.	L 0-1	0-1	8	2091
10	15.10.88	H	Wrexham	L 1-3	1-2	12	2235
11	22.10.88	H	Crewe Alex.	L 0-3	0-1	15	1972
12	24.10.88	A	Stockport Co.	L 0-3	0-2	18	2098
13	29.10.88	H	Hereford U.	D 1-1	1-0	19	1593
14	4.11.88	A	Halifax T.	L 0-1	0-1	20	2182
15	9.11.88	A	Peterborough U.	W 1-0	0-0	17	3148
16	12.11.88	H	Grimsby T.	W 2-1	0-0	15	1782
17	26.11.88	H	Exeter C.	D 2-2	0-0	15	2125
18	3.12.88	A	Burnley	D 0-0	0-0	16	6284
19	17.12.88	H	Carlisle U.	L 0-2	0-2	17	1974
20	26.12.88	A	Scunthorpe U.	D 1-1	0-0	18	4595
21	30.12.88	A	Colchester U.	W 2-1	0-1	14	2359
22	2.1.89	H	Rotherham U.	D 1-1	0-0	16	3370
23	14.1.89	A	Darlington	D 0-0	0-0	15	3521
24	21.1.89	H	Lincoln C.	W 3-2	2-0	14	2860
25	4.2.89	H	York C.	D 0-1	0-0	17	2863
26	11.2.89	A	Cambridge U.	L 0-6	0-2	17	2300
27	18.2.89	H	Doncaster Rov.	W 2-1	0-0	17	1922
28	28.2.89	H	Stockport Co.	D 2-2	1-0	16	1692
29	4.3.89	A	Crewe Alex.	L 0-3	0-0	19	3981
30	7.3.89	A	Wrexham	L 3-4	2-3	19	2449
31	11.3.89	H	Halifax T.	W 2-0	1-0	17	1786
32	15.3.89	A	Hereford U.	L 0-2	0-1	18	2157
33	18.3.89	H	Torquay U.	L 0-1	0-1	21	1516
34	21.3.89	A	Leyton Orient	L 3-4	1-1	21	3406
35	25.3.89	A	Rotherham U.	L 0-4	0-3	21	4915
36	27.3.89	H	Scunthorpe U.	L 0-2	0-0	21	1923
37	1.4.89	A	Carlisle U.	L 1-2	0-2	21	3158
38	5.4.89	A	Scarborough	L 0-2	0-2	21	2155
39	8.4.89	H	Colchester U.	W 2-1	0-0	21	1501
40	11.4.89	H	Scarborough	W 3-1	0-0	21	1897
41	15.4.89	H	Tranmere Rov.	D 2-2	1-0	21	2496
42	22.4.89	A	Rochdale	D 0-0	0-0	19	1406
43	29.4.89	A	Exeter C.	L 1-2	1-1	22	2380
44	1.5.89	H	Peterborough U.	W 2-1	0-0	19	1643
45	6.5.89	H	Burnley	W 2-2	0-1	18	2174
46	13.5.89	A	Grimsby T.	L 0-3	0-1	19	3400

Players: League Record, 1988-89 (Division 4)

Match Number	1	2	3	4	5	6	7	8	9	10	11	12	13	14	15	16	17	18	19	20	21	22	23
Allon, Joe													9	9	9	9		9	**9**	9[1]			9
Atkinson, Patrick					A												★		★				
Baker, Paul							★	5	5	10[1]	10	10	10	10	6	6	6	6	6	6	6	6	6
Barras, Anthony																							
Barratt, Tony	11	11	11	2	2	2	2	2	2	2	★	2	2[1]	2	11	11	**11**		4	11	11	11	11
Borthwick, John	**10**	**10**	10		★												9		★	★	9[1]	9	
Dalton, Paul																							
Dixon, Kevin	9	9	**9**	9	9[1]	9[2]	9[1]	9	9	9	9	9			**4**	4							
Doig, Russell			★	11	11[1]	11	11	11	**11**	**11**	11			★	★		4	4					
Grayson, Simon	★	★	★	10	**10**	10	10	10	**10**	★				★	10[1]	10[1]	10[1]	10	10	10	10	10[1]	10
Haigh, Paul	2	2	2						★	5	**2**	11	11	11	2	2							
Hepple, John																							
Honour, Brian	7	7	7	7	7[1]	7	7	7	7	7	7	7	7	7	7	7	7	7	7	7	7	7	7
Locker, Stephen																							
McAndrew, Tony																							
McKellar, David	1	1	1	1	1																		
McKinnon, Robert	3	3	**3**	3	3	3	3	3	3	3	3	3	3	3	3	3	3	3	3	3	3	3	3
Moverley, Robert																					1	1	1
Muggleton, Carl													1	1	1	1	1	1	1	1			
Nobbs, Keith																	2	2	2	2	2	2	2
Norton, Paul											1	1											
Ogden, Paul									★									11	**11**				
Plaskett, Stephen																							
Smith, Tony	5	5[1]	5	5	5	5	5				5	5	5	5	5	5	5[1]	5					
Stokes, Wayne	6	6	6	6	6	6	6	6	6	6	6	6	6	6					5	5	5[1]	5	5
Tinkler, John	4	4	4	4[1]	4	4	**4**	4	4	4	4	4	4	**4**						4	4	4	4
Toman, Andy	8[1]	8[1]	8	8	8	8[1]	8	8	8	8	8	8	8	8	8	8[1]	8	8	8	**8**	8	8	8
Tunks, Roy						1	1	1	1	1													
Own Goals																							

Match Number	24	25	26	27	28	29	30	31	32	33	34	35	36	37	38	39	40	41	42	43	44	45	46	Apps	Subs	Goals
Allon, Joe	9	9	9	**9**										7	7	7	7[1]	7	7	7[1]	7	7[1]		21	0	4
Atkinson, Patrick	11[2]	11			11	11					★[1]	/				★			★			★	7	6	7	3
Baker, Paul	6	6	6	6	6	6	6[1]	6	6	6	6[1]	9	9	9	9	9[1]	9[1]	9[1]	9	9	9	9	9	39	1	6
Barras, Anthony								★		★	10													1	2	0
Barratt, Tony	2	2	11	11	2	2	2	2	2	2														31	1	1
Borthwick, John				★	9	**9**	9	9	**9**	9	9											★	6	14	5	1
Dalton, Paul							11	11	11	11	11	11	11	11	11	11	11[1]	11	11	11	11[1]	11	11	17	0	2
Dixon, Kevin																								14	0	4
Doig, Russell			★	★	★	★			★	**10**														11	8	1
Grayson, Simon	10[1]	10	**10**	10[1]	10[1]	10	10[2]	10[1]	10			**10**	10	10[1]	10	**10**	10	10	10	10	10[1]	10	10	36	5	12
Haigh, Paul																								10	1	0
Hepple, John												★											2	1	1	0
Honour, Brian	7	7	7	7	7	7	7	7	7	7	**7**													34	0	1
Locker, Stephen																							★	0	1	0
McAndrew, Tony												6	6	6	6									4	0	0
McKellar, David																								5	0	0
McKinnon, Robert	3	3	3	3	3	3	3	3	3	3	3	3	3	3	3	3	3	3[1]	3	3	3	3[1]	**3**	46	0	2
Moverley, Robert	1	1	1	1	1	1	1	1	1	1	1	1				1	1	1	1	1	1	1	1	23	0	0
Muggleton, Carl																								8	0	0
Nobbs, Keith			2	**2**		★		5								6	6	6	6	6	6	6		17	1	0
Norton, Paul													1	1	1									5	0	0
Ogden, Paul	8											★	7							★	4	**4**	4	7	3	0
Plaskett, Stephen											2	2	2	2	2	2	2	2	2	2	2	2		12	0	0
Smith, Tony																				5	5	**5**	5	19	0	2
Stokes, Wayne	5	5	5	5	5	5	5		5	5	5[1]	5	5	5	5	5	5	5	**5**					37	0	2
Tinkler, John	4	4	4	4[1]	4	4	4	4	4	4	4	**4**	4	4	4	4[1]	4	4	4	**4**				38	0	3
Toman, Andy		8	8	8	8[1]	8	8	8[1]	8	8	8	8	8	8	8	8	8	8	8	8	8	8	8	45	0	6
Tunks, Roy																								5	0	0
Own Goals																										0

FA Cup: 1988-89: 1st Round: Wigan Ath. (H) 2-0; 2nd Round: Notts Co. (H) 1-0; 3rd Round: Bristol C. (H) 1-0; 4th Round: Bournemouth (H) 1-1, Replay (A) 2-5.
Littlewoods Cup: 1988-89: 1st Round: Sheffield U. (H) 2-2 (A) 0-2.

HEREFORD UNITED (Division 4)

Team Manager Ian Bowyer.
Club Address Edgar Street, Hereford. Tel: (0432) 276666.
Current Ground Capacity 12,500.
Record Attendance 18,114 v Sheffield Wed., FA Cup 3rd Round, 4 January 1958.
Year Formed 1924. Turned professional 1924.
Previous Names None.
Club Nickname "United".
Club Colours White shirts with black pinstripe, black shorts and white stockings.
Club Honours Football League: Div. 3 Champions 1975-76.
League History 1972-73 Div. 4; 1973-76 Div. 3; 1976-77 Div. 2; 1977-78 Div. 3; 1978- Div. 4.
Most League Points in a Season (2 for a win) 63 in Div. 3, 1975-76. (3 for a win) 77 in Div. 4, 1984-85.
Most League Goals in a Season 86 in Div. 3, 1975-76.
Record Victory 11-0 v Thynnes in FA Cup Preliminary Round, September 1947.
Record Defeat 0-6 v Rotherham U. in Div. 4, 29 April 1989.
Consecutive League Wins 5 in 1984.
Consecutive League Defeats 7 in 1976.
Record League Appearances Chris Price, 330 between 1976-86.
Record League Goalscorer—Career Dixie McNeil, 88 between 1974-83.
Record League Goalscorer—Season Dixie McNeil, 35 in Div 3, 1975-76.

Hereford United: League Record, 1988-89 (Division 4)

Match Number	Date	Venue	Opponents	Result	H/T	Lge Posn	Attend
1	27.8.88	A	Scunthorpe U.	L 1-3	0-0		3663
2	3.9.88	H	Cambridge U.	W 4-2	3-1	12	1711
3	10.9.88	A	Leyton Orient	W 3-1	2-0	4	3087
4	17.9.88	H	Scarborough	L 1-3	0-1	9	2359
5	21.9.88	H	Crewe Alex.	L 0-1	0-0	15	1981
6	24.9.88	A	Lincoln C.	L 0-2	0-1	17	2915
7	1.10.88	H	Grimsby T.	W 2-1	0-1	14	1888
8	4.10.88	A	Doncaster Rov.	L 2-3	1-2	16	1281
9	8.10.88	H	Carlisle U.	W 2-1	1-1	13	2127
10	15.10.88	A	Stockport Co.	W 2-1	1-1	10	2035
11	22.10.88	A	Peterborough U.	L 1-2	0-1	13	3460
12	26.10.88	H	Rochdale	D 4-4	2-3	14	2071
13	29.10.88	A	Hartlepool U.	D 1-1	0-1	15	1593
14	5.11.88	H	Wrexham	D 0-0	0-0	14	2372
15	7.11.88	A	Tranmere Rov.	L 0-1	0-1	14	3587
16	12.11.88	H	Halifax T.	W 3-1	2-0	16	1929
17	26.11.88	H	Rotherham U.	D 1-1	1-0	16	2058
18	3.12.88	A	York C.	L 1-4	0-1	19	1698
19	17.12.88	H	Burnley	D 0-0	0-0	19	2442
20	26.12.88	A	Exeter C.	L 1-3	1-1	20	3229
21	31.12.88	A	Darlington	D 0-0	0-0	20	1755
22	2.1.89	H	Torquay U.	D 1-1	1-0	21	2356
23	14.1.89	A	Cambridge U.	L 1-2	1-2	22	2193
24	21.1.89	H	Scunthorpe U.	L 1-2	0-0	22	2024
25	28.1.89	A	Scarborough	W 2-0	0-0	21	2199
26	4.2.89	A	Crewe Alex.	L 1-2	1-2	22	2987
27	11.2.89	H	Lincoln C.	W 3-2	1-0	21	2113
28	18.2.89	A	Carlisle U.	L 0-3	0-1	21	2548
29	25.2.89	H	Stockport Co.	W 2-1	2-0	20	2015
30	28.2.89	A	Rochdale	D 2-2	2-1	20	1060
31	4.3.89	H	Peterborough U.	W 4-0	0-0	18	2094
32	11.3.89	A	Wrexham	D 1-1	1-0	19	2960
33	15.3.89	H	Hartlepool U.	W 2-0	1-0	17	2157
34	18.3.89	H	Leyton Orient	D 1-1	1-0	16	2063
35	25.3.89	A	Torquay U.	L 0-1	0-0	17	2542
36	27.3.89	H	Exeter C.	W 1-0	0-0	15	2735
37	1.4.89	A	Burnley	D 3-3	1-1	16	5534
38	4.4.89	A	Colchester U.	D 1-1	1-1	16	2862
39	8.4.89	H	Darlington	D 1-1	0-0	16	2009
40	12.4.89	H	Colchester U.	D 1-1	0-1	16	2015
41	15.4.89	A	Grimsby T.	D 1-1	0-0	15	4036
42	22.4.89	H	Doncaster Rov.	W 3-1	1-0	11	1804
43	29.4.89	A	Rotherham U.	L 0-6	0-2	15	5334
44	1.5.89	H	Tranmere Rov.	W 2-1	1-1	14	2844
45	6.5.89	H	York C.	L 1-2	0-1	15	1819
46	13.5.89	A	Halifax T.	D 2-2	1-1	15	1082

Players: League Record, 1988-89 (Division 4)

Match Number	1	2	3	4	5	6	7	8	9	10	11	12	13	14	15	16	17	18	19	20	21	22	23
Benbow, Ian	★		8		★	★	★	11		10	**10**		6		**6**			★		★	7	7	**7**
Bowyer, Ian	★	6	6	6	★	★				6	6				★								
Bradley, Russell																	5	5	5	5		5	
Campbell, Michael	**7**																						
Crane, Andy	3	3	3	3	3	3	**3**	3		3	3	3	3	3	3	3	3	3	3	**3**	3	3	3
Devine, Steve	10	5	5	5	5	5	5	5	3	5	5	5		5	5	5	★		7	4	4	4	5
Elliott, Anthony																							1
Jones, Mark	2	2	2				2	2	2	2	2	2	2	2		2	2	2	2	2	2	2	2
Jones, Richard	**8**				6	6	6	6	6			4	4	4		6	6	6	6	6	6	6	6
Lamb, Alan																							
McLoughlin, Paul	11^{1}	11^{2}	11	11	**11**	11	11		9^{1}	9	9	11	11	11	11	11	11	11	11	11	11	**11**	11
Maddy, Paul	6	8^{1}		8	8	**8**	**8**	8	10		★	6		6		★	7	**7**					
Mardenborough, Steve		7	7	7	7	**7**	7	7	7	7	7	7	7	**7**	7	7				7		★	10
Narbett, Jonathan									8	8	8	8	8^{1}	8	8	8^{2}	8	8	8	**8**	8	8	8
Peacock, Darren																							
Pejic, Mel	4						★		5^{1}														★
Rose, Kevin	1	1	1	1	1	1	1	1	1	1	1	1	1	1	1	1	1	1	1	1	1	1	
Stant, Philip	9	9^{1}	9^{2}	9^{1}	**9**	9	9^{1}	9^{2}				9^{3}	9	9	9	**9**^{1}	9^{1}	9^{1}	9	9^{1}	9	9^{1}	9^{1}
Stevens, Gary	5	4	4	4	4	4	4	4	4	4^{2}	4^{1}		5	★	4	4	4	4	4	★	5		4
Tester, Paul		10	10^{1}	10	10	10	10^{1}	10	11	11	11	10^{1}	10	10	10	10	**10**	10	10	10	10	10	
Williams, Robert				2	2	2									2								
Own Goals																							

Match Number	24	25	26	27	28	29	30	31	32	33	34	35	36	37	38	39	40	41	42	43	44	45	46	Apps	Subs	Goals
Benbow, Ian			7	7	**7**	7	7	**7**		7	**7**	7	7	7	7	**7**		★^{1}	**9**	9	7	**7**	6	27	7	1
Bowyer, Ian																								5	4	0
Bradley, Russell												4	4	4	4^{1}	4	5	5						12	0	1
Campbell, Michael																								1	0	0
Crane, Andy	**3**	7	3					3			3				**3**	3				★	★	3		30	2	0
Devine, Steve	6	3		3	3	3	3	4	3	3		3	3	3	5	5	3	3	3	3	**3**		3	40	1	0
Elliott, Anthony	1	1	1	1	1	1	1	1	1	1	1	1	1	1	1	1	1	1	1	1	1	1		23	0	0
Jones, Mark	2	2		2	2	2	2	2	2	2	2	2	2	2	2	2	2	2	2	2	2	2	2	41	0	0
Jones, Richard	7^{1}	6	6	6		6	6		6	6	6	6	6	6	6	6	6	6	5	5	5	4	4	38	0	1
Lamb, Alan												8	10^{1}	10^{1}	9	10	10	10	7	7		★		9	1	2
McLoughlin, Paul	11	11	11	11	11	11^{1}	11^{2}	11^{1}	11	11	11	★	**11**	11^{2}	**11**	**11**	11^{1}	11	11^{2}	11	11	11	11	44	1	13
Maddy, Paul					6			6	★		★	11	8	8			★	★	6	6	6	6		21	6	1
Mardenborough, Steve	10				★			★	7			★	★		★							★	7	20	7	0
Narbett, Jonathan	8	8^{2}	8	8	8	8	8	8	8	8	8			★	8	8	8	8	8	8	8^{1}	8	8^{1}	35	1	7
Peacock, Darren															★	★		4	4	4	4	5	5	6	2	0
Pejic, Mel	5	5	5	5^{1}	5	5	5	5	5	5	5^{1}	5	5	**5**										16	2	3
Rose, Kevin																							1	23	0	0
Stant, Philip	9	9	9^{1}	9^{1}	9	9^{1}	9	9^{3}	**9**	9^{1}	9	**9**	**9**	**9**		9^{1}	9	**9**	★^{1}		9^{1}	9^{1}	9^{1}	40	1	28
Stevens, Gary	4	4	4	4	4	4	4	★	4	4	4						**4**							30	3	3
Tester, Paul	★	10	10	10^{1}	10	10	10	**10**	10^{1}	10^{1}	10	**10**	★	★	10	★	7	**7**	10	**10**	10	**10**	10	40	4	6
Williams, Robert			2																					5	0	0
Own Goals																										0

FA Cup: 1988-89: 1st Round: Cardiff C. (A) 0-3.
Littlewoods Cup: 1988-89: 1st Round: Plymouth Arg. (H) 0-3 (A) 2-3.

HUDDERSFIELD TOWN (Division 3)

Team Manager Eoin Hand.
Club Address Leeds Road, Huddersfield HD1 6PE. Tel: (0484) 20335/6.
Current Ground Capacity 32,000.
Record Attendance 67,037 v Arsenal, FA Cup 6th Round, 27 February 1932.
Year Formed 1908. Turned professional 1908.
Previous Names None.
Club Nickname "The Terriers".
Club Colours Blue and white striped shirts, white shorts and white stockings.
Club Honours Football League: Div.1 Champions 1923-24, 1924-25, 1925-26; Div. 2 Champions 1969-70; Div. 4 Champions 1979-80. FA Cup: Winners 1922.
League History 1910-20 Div. 2; 1920-52 Div. 1; 1952-53 Div. 2; 1953-56 Div. 1; 1956-70 Div. 2; 1970-72 Div. 1; 1972-73 Div. 2; 1973-75 Div. 3; 1975-80 Div. 4; 1980-83 Div. 3; 1983-88 Div. 2; 1988- Div. 3.
Most League Points in a Season (2 for a win) 66 in Div. 4, 1979-80. (3 for a win) 82 in Div. 3, 1982-83.
Most League Goals in a Season 101 in Div. 4, 1979-80.
Record Victory 10-1 v Blackpool in Div. 1, 13 December 1930.
Record Defeat 0-8 v Middlesbrough in Div. 1, 30 September 1950.
Consecutive League Wins 11 in 1920.
Consecutive League Defeats 7 in 1913-14, 1955.
Record League Appearances Billy Smith, 520 between 1914-34.
Record League Goalscorer—Career George Brown, 142 between 1921-29 and Jimmy Glazzard, 142 between 1946-56.
Record League Goalscorer—Season Sam Taylor, 35 in Div. 2, 1919-20 and George Brown, 35 in Div. 1, 1925-26.

Huddersfield Town: League Record, 1988-89 (Division 3)

Match Number	Date	Venue	Opponents	Result	H/T	Lge Posn	Attend
1	27.8.88	A	Brentford	L 0-1	0-0		5632
2	3.9.88	H	Preston N.E.	W 2-0	2-0	13	5622
3	10.9.88	A	Cardiff C.	L 0-3	0-3	18	3891
4	17.9.88	H	Gillingham	D 1-1	0-0	18	4688
5	20.9.88	H	Notts Co.	W 3-1	1-1	11	5655
6	24.9.88	A	Chester C.	L 0-3	0-2	14	3319
7	1.10.88	H	Fulham	W 2-0	0-0	10	4576
8	3.10.88	A	Port Vale	L 0-2	0-2	11	5938
9	8.10.88	A	Northampton T.	W 3-1	3-0	10	3975
10	15.10.88	H	Bristol C.	L 0-1	0-0	16	5952
11	22.10.88	A	Aldershot	W 1-0	1-0	12	2155
12	25.10.88	H	Swansea C.	D 1-1	0-0	12	5711
13	29.10.88	A	Bristol Rov.	L 1-5	1-3	15	4460
14	5.11.88	H	Sheffield U.	W 3-2	2-1	14	10400
15	8.11.88	H	Bolton W.	L 0-1	0-0	15	7802
16	12.11.88	A	Wolverhampton W.	L 1-4	1-1	16	12697
17	26.11.88	A	Wigan Ath.	W 2-0	1-0	14	2779
18	3.12.88	H	Blackpool	D 1-1	0-0	15	5738
19	17.12.88	H	Bury	W 3-2	2-1	12	5150
20	26.12.88	A	Chesterfield	D 1-1	1-1	13	5630
21	31.12.88	A	Mansfield T.	L 0-1	0-0	14	4638
22	2.1.89	H	Southend U.	W 3-2	1-0	14	6403
23	14.1.89	A	Preston N.E.	L 0-1	0-0	14	6959
24	21.1.89	H	Cardiff C.	W 1-0	1-0	11	4869
25	28.1.89	A	Gillingham	W 2-1	1-1	10	3530
26	4.2.89	A	Fulham	W 2-1	0-0	9	4081
27	11.2.89	H	Port Vale	D 0-0	0-0	9	8004
28	18.2.89	H	Northampton T.	L 1-2	1-1	10	5802
29	4.3.89	H	Aldershot	W 2-1	1-1	10	4709
30	7.3.89	H	Reading	D 2-2	1-1	10	4933
31	11.3.89	A	Sheffield U.	L 1-5	0-1	10	15000
32	14.3.89	H	Bristol Rov.	L 2-3	2-1	10	4105
33	22.3.89	A	Swansea C.	L 0-1	0-1	12	4075
34	25.3.89	A	Southend U.	W 4-2	2-0	10	3582
35	27.3.89	H	Chesterfield	D 1-1	1-1	11	5819
36	1.4.89	A	Bury	W 6-0	2-0	10	4145
37	5.4.89	A	Reading	L 1-2	0-1	11	3802
38	8.4.89	H	Mansfield T.	W 2-0	0-0	9	5327
39	15.4.89	H	Chester C.	W 3-1	1-0	9	6109
40	18.4.89	A	Bristol C.	L 1-6	0-5	9	4542
41	22.4.89	A	Notts Co.	L 0-3	0-1	12	5499
42	25.4.89	H	Brentford	L 1-2	0-0	12	3538
43	29.4.89	H	Wolverhampton W.	D 0-0	0-0	12	8757
44	1.5.89	A	Bolton W.	L 1-3	0-1	12	5511
45	6.5.89	A	Blackpool	L 1-2	0-1	14	4070
46	13.5.89	H	Wigan Ath.	D 1-1	1-0	14	4225

Players: League Record, 1988-89 (Division 3)

Match Number	1	2	3	4	5	6	7	8	9	10	11	12	13	14	15	16	17	18	19	20	21	22	23
Barham, Mark	11																						
Bent, Junior							★	11	11^1	11	11	★	★		★	★	2	2	2^1	2^1	2	8^1	2
Brown, Malcolm			7																				
Bryne, Micky			**9**	★	9^2	9	**9**				★	11	11	11^1	11	**11**	**11**	★	**9**	9	9	9^1	**11**
Cecere, Michele																9	9^1	9	★	★	★	11	9
Duggan, Andrew																							
France, Paul							6	6															
Hardwick, Steve	1	1	1	1	1	1	1	1	1	1	1	1	1	1	1	1	1	1	1	1	1	1	1
Holmes, Micky	**4**	4	★	★	★	★	8																
Hutchings, Chris	3	3	3	3^1	3	3		8	3^1	3	3^1	3^1	3^1	3	3	3	3	3	3	3	3	3	3
McInerney, Ian						**11**	**11**																
Marsden, Chris		11	11	11	**11**				★	★									11	**11**	**11**		
Maskell, Craig	10	10^1	10	10	10^1	10	10^2	10	10^1	10	10	**10**	10	10^2	10	10^1	10^1	10^1	10^1	10	10	10^1	10
May, Andy	8		8	4	4	**4**	4	4	4	4	4	4	4	4	4	**4**	4	4	4	4	4	4	4
Mitchell, Graham	★	7	6	8	**8**	8	7	7	6	6	6	6	**6**	6	6	6	6	6	6	6	6	6	6
O'Doherty, Ken		**5**		5	5	5	5	5	5	5	5	5	5	5	5	5	5	5	5	5	5	5	
O'Regan, Kieran	7	8	4	**7**	7	7	3	3	7	7	7	7	7	7	**7**	7	7	7	7^1	7	7	7	7
Shotton, Malcolm	6	6^1																					
Smith, Mark																							
Trevitt, Simon	2	2	2	2	2	2	2	2	2	2	2	2	2	2	2	2						2	★
Tucker, Gordon	5	★	5	6	6	6																	5
Ward, Peter	★						★	9	★														
Winter, Julian									8	8	8	8	8	8	8	8	8	8	8	8	8		8
Withe, Peter	9	9	★	**9**	★	★			**9**	9	9	9	9	9	9	★	★	**11**					★
Own Goals																							

Match Number	24	25	26	27	28	29	30	31	32	33	34	35	36	37	38	39	40	41	42	43	44	45	46	Apps	Subs	Goals
Barham, Mark																								1	0	0
Bent, Junior	2^1	2				7	★		★			★												14	8	5
Brown, Malcolm																								1	0	0
Bryne, Micky	**11**	**11**	★	★	★	★^{1}	7		**7**	7	7^1	7	7^1	**7**	7	**7**	**7**	**7**				★	7	29	8	7
Cecere, Michele	9	9	9^1	9	9	9	9	9	9^1	9	9	**9**	9^1	9	**9**	9	9	9	9	**9**	9	**9**	9	28	3	4
Duggan, Andrew						6	6^1	2	6	6	6^1	6	6	6		6	6	6				5	5	14	0	2
France, Paul					★																			2	1	0
Hardwick, Steve	1	1	1	1	1	1	1	1	1	1	1	1	1	1	1	1	1	1	1	1	1	1	1	46	0	0
Holmes, Micky																								3	4	0
Hutchings, Chris	3	3	3	3	3			3	3	3	3	3	3	3	3	3			3	3	3	3	3	41	0	5
McInerney, Ian														★	★^{1}	★	★		11	★	11	7		5	5	1
Marsden, Chris					6			**6^1**					★			★			8					10	4	1
Maskell, Craig	10	10^1	10	10	10^1	10	10^1	10	10^1	10	10^2	10^1	10^3	10	10^1	10	10^1	10	10^1	10	10^1	10^1	10^1	46	0	28
May, Andy	4	4	4	4	4	4	4	4	4	4	4	4	4	4^1	**4**	4^1	4	4	**4**	4	4	4	4	45	0	2
Mitchell, Graham	6	6	6	6													3	3	6	6	6	6	6	33	1	0
O'Doherty, Ken	5	5	5^1	5	5	5	5	5	5	5		5	5	5	5	5	5	5						37	0	1
O'Regan, Kieran	7	7^1	7	7	7	3	3	7	2										7	7	7	2		36	0	2
Shotton, Malcolm																								2	0	1
Smith, Mark				★	**11**	**11**	**11**	11	11	11	11	11	11^1	11	11	11^1	11	11	★	11	★	11	11	17	3	2
Trevitt, Simon		★	2	2	2	2	2	★		2	2	2	2	2	2	2	2	2	2	2	2	★	2	35	4	0
Tucker, Gordon											5				6				5	5	5			11	1	0
Ward, Peter																								1	3	0
Winter, Julian	8	8	8	**8**		**8^1**	8	**8**	8	8	8	**8**	8	8	8	8^1	8		8	8	8	8	8	35	0	2
Withe, Peter	★	★	**11**	**11**	**8**	★	★	★										★						14	12	0
Own Goals																										0

FA Cup: 1988-89: 1st Round: Rochdale (H) 1-1, Replay (A) 4-3; 2nd Round: Chester C. (H) 1-0; 3rd Round: Sheffield U. (H) 0-1.
Littlewoods Cup: 1988-89: 1st Round: Scunthorpe U. (A) 2-3 (H) 2-2.

HULL CITY (Division 2)

Team Manager Colin Appleton.
Club Address Boothferry Park, Hull HU4 6EU. Tel: (0482) 51119/563750.
Current Ground Capacity 28,000.
Record Attendance 55,019 v Manchester U., FA Cup 6th Round, 26 February 1949.
Year Formed 1904. Turned professional 1905.
Previous Names None.
Club Nickname "The Tigers".
Club Colours Amber shirts with red and black trim, black shorts with amber and red stripe down side and red stockings.
Club Honours Football League: Div. 3(N) Champions 1932-33, 1948-49; Div. 3 Champions 1965-66.
League History 1905-30 Div. 2; 1930-33 Div. 3(N); 1933-36 Div. 2; 1936-49 Div. 3(N); 1949-56 Div. 2; 1956-58 Div. 3(N); 1958-59 Div. 3; 1959-60 Div. 2; 1960-66 Div. 3; 1966-78 Div. 2; 1978-81 Div. 3; 1981-83 Div. 4; 1983-85 Div. 3; 1985- Div. 2.
Most League Points in a Season (2 for a win) 69 in Div. 3, 1965-66. (3 for a win) 90 in Div. 4, 1982-83.
Most League Goals in a Season 109 in Div. 3, 1965-66.
Record Victory 11-1 v Carlisle U. in Div. 3(N), 14 January 1939.
Record Defeat 0-8 v Wolverhampton W. in Div. 2, 4 November 1911.
Consecutive League Wins 10 in 1948 and 1966.
Consecutive League Defeats 8 in 1934.
Record League Appearances Andy Davidson, 520 between 1952-67.
Record League Goalscorer—Career Chris Chilton, 193 between 1960-71.
Record League Goalscorer—Season Bill McNaughton, 39 in Div. 3(N), 1932-33.

Hull City: League Record, 1988-89 (Division 2)

Match Number	Date	Venue	Opponents	Result	H/T	Lge Posn	Attend
1	27.8.88	H	Manchester C.	W 1-0	0-0		11653
2	29.8.89	A	Oxford U.	L 0-1	0-1	7	5772
3	3.9.88	A	Plymouth Arg.	L 0-2	0-0	13	8202
4	10.9.88	H	Barnsley	D 0-0	0-0	12	5654
5	17.9.88	A	Portsmouth	W 3-1	2-0	11	11599
6	20.9.88	H	Blackburn Rov.	L 1-3	1-3	13	6681
7	24.9.88	A	Oldham Ath.	D 2-2	0-2	14	6319
8	1.10.88	H	Walsall	D 0-0	0-0	14	4845
9	4.10.88	H	Leicester C.	D 2-2	1-1	17	5079
10	8.10.88	A	Shrewsbury T.	W 3-1	2-0	11	3287
11	15.10.88	H	Sunderland	D 0-0	0-0	15	8261
12	22.10.88	A	Crystal Palace	L 1-3	1-1	15	8464
13	25.10.88	H	Chelsea	W 3-0	1-0	11	6953
14	29.10.88	A	Leeds U.	L 1-2	0-1	15	17536
15	5.11.88	H	Swindon T.	W 1-0	1-0	12	5192
16	13.11.88	A	Stoke C.	L 0-4	0-1	17	10505
17	19.11.88	H	Birmingham C.	D 1-1	0-1	16	5134
18	26.11.88	A	Watford	L 0-2	0-2	18	10404
19	29.11.88	A	Bournemouth	L 1-5	0-0	19	5420
20	3.12.88	H	Brighton & H.A.	W 5-2	3-1	17	5686
21	10.12.88	A	West Bromwich A.	L 0-2	0-0	18	10094
22	26.12.88	H	Bradford C.	D 1-1	0-0	19	8791
23	31.12.88	H	Ipswich T.	D 1-1	1-0	19	7800
24	2.1.89	A	Barnsley	W 2-0	2-0	18	9879
25	14.1.89	H	Bournemouth	W 4-0	3-0	17	5690
26	21.1.89	A	Manchester C.	L 1-4	0-3	17	20485
27	4.2.89	A	Leicester C.	W 2-0	1-0	16	9996
28	11.2.89	H	Shrewsbury T.	W 3-0	2-0	14	11472
29	25.2.89	A	Sunderland	L 0-2	0-0	15	14719
30	28.2.89	A	Chelsea	L 1-2	0-0	15	11407
31	4.3.89	H	Stoke C.	L 1-4	0-4	17	5915
32	11.3.89	A	Swindon T.	L 0-1	0-1	18	7090
33	14.3.89	H	Leeds U.	L 1-2	1-0	19	8887
34	18.3.89	A	Blackburn Rov.	L 0-4	0-1	20	5864
35	25.3.89	H	Plymouth Arg.	W 3-0	2-0	19	5851
36	27.3.89	A	Bradford C.	D 1-1	1-1	20	11802
37	1.4.89	H	Portsmouth	D 1-1	0-0	21	5325
38	4.4.89	H	Oxford U.	L 1-2	0-2	21	6260
39	8.4.89	A	Ipswich T.	D 1-1	0-1	21	10191
40	11.4.89	H	Crystal Palace	L 0-1	0-1	21	5050
41	15.4.89	A	Walsall	D 1-1	0-0	21	3935
42	22.4.89	H	Oldham Ath.	D 1-1	0-1	21	6748
43	29.4.89	H	Watford	L 0-3	0-1	21	5225
44	1.5.89	A	Brighton & H.A.	D 1-1	0-0	21	6750
45	6.5.89	A	Birmingham C.	L 0-1	0-0	21	4686
46	13.5.89	H	West Bromwich A.	L 0-1	0-1	21	5217

Players: League Record, 1988-89 (Division 2)

Match Number	1	2	3	4	5	6	7	8	9	10	11	12	13	14	15	16	17	18	19	20	21	22	23
Askew, Billy									7														
Bell, Doug																							
Brown, Nicky																							
Buckley, Neil																			2			6	6
Calvert, Mark																							
Daniel, Ray				11	11	**11**			3	3	**7**	7	7	7			3	3	3	3^{1}	3	3	3
De Mange, Ken				★	★	★	★	★	★^{1}	4	**4**		★	★	8	8	8	8	8			10	10
Dyer, Alex	7	7	7	7	7^{1}	7	11	11	11	11	11	11^{1}	11	11	11								
Edwards, Keith	10^{1}	10	10	10	10^{2}	10^{1}	10	10	10^{1}	10^{2}	10	10	10^{2}	10	10	10	10^{1}	10	10	10	10		
Hesford, Iain																							1
Hotte, Tim												★											
Jacobs, Wayne	3	3	3	3	**3**			**3**			3	3	**3**	3	3	3							
Jenkinson, Leigh																11	★			11	**11**		
Jobson, Richard	2	2	2	5	5	5	5	5	5	5	5	5	5	5	5	5	5	5	5	5	5	5	5
Kelly, Gavin							1																
McParland, Ian																							
Moore, John	9	9	9	9		★		★	9	9	9				9^{1}	9	**9**	★	**9**				
Mudd, Paul																							
Murray, Malcolm																							
Norman, Tony	1	1	1	1	1	1		1	1	1	1	1	1	1	1	1	1	1	1	1	1	1	
Palmer, Charlie	★			2	2	**2**	2	2	**2**			2	2	2^{1}	2	2	2	2		2	2	2	2
Payton, Andrew			★		9	9	9	**9**			★			★		★	11	11	11^{1}	7^{2}	7	7^{1}	7
Roberts, Gareth	8	8	8	8	**8**	8	8	8	8	8^{1}	8				7	**7**	7	7	7	8	8	8	8
Saville, Andy	11	11	**11**		★				★	7		9	9	**9**			★	**9**	★	9^{1}	9	9	★
Skipper, Peter	5	5	5																				
Smith, Michael							7				★	**8**	8^{1}	**8**							★	11	**11**
Swan, Peter																							
Terry, Steve	6	6	6	6	6	6	6^{1}	6	6	6	6	6	6	6	6	6	6	6	6	6	6		
Thompson, Leslie						3	**3**	7															
Warren, Lee	**4**	4	4	**4**	4	4	4	4	4	2	2	4	4	4	4	4	**4**	4	4	4	4	4	4
Whitehurst, Billy																							9^{1}
Own Goals							1													1			

Match Number	24	25	26	27	28	29	30	31	32	33	34	35	36	37	38	39	40	41	42	43	44	45	46	Apps	Subs	Goals
Askew, Billy		**11**	11	11	11	11	11	7	7	7					8	8	8		**11**	11			6	16	0	0
Bell, Doug												11	11	11	**11**									4	0	0
Brown, Nicky	2	2	2	2	2	2	2	2	2				2	2	2	2								13	0	0
Buckley, Neil	6	6	6	6	6	6	6	6	**6**											5				13	0	0
Calvert, Mark									**11**											**8**	8	8	**8**	5	0	0
Daniel, Ray	**11**						7	11												6	6	6	3	23	0	1
De Mange, Ken	4	4	4	4	4	**4**	4	4			★							★	★	★	11	11	★	19	13	1
Dyer, Alex																								15	0	2
Edwards, Keith	10^{2}	10^{3}	10^{1}	10^{2}	10^{2}	10	10	10	10	**10**	**10**	10^{1}	10^{1}	10^{1}	10	10	**10**	10^{1}	10	10	10^{1}	10	10	44	0	25
Hesford, Iain	1	1	1	1	1	1	1	1	1	1	1	1	1	1	1	1	1	1	1	1			1	22	0	0
Hotte, Tim																								0	1	0
Jacobs, Wayne	3	3	3	3	3	3	3	3	3	3	3	3	3	3	3	3	3	3	3	3	3			33	0	0
Jenkinson, Leigh										11	**11**	★		★	★				★				11	6	5	0
Jobson, Richard	5	5	5	5	5	5	5	5	4	4	4	5^{1}	5	5	5	5	5	5	5	2	2	2	2	46	0	1
Kelly, Gavin																					1	1		3	0	0
McParland, Ian												7	7	7	7	7	7	**7**	7^{1}	7	7	7		11	0	1
Moore, John																								11	3	1
Mudd, Paul																						3		1	0	0
Murray, Malcolm									★	2	2	**2**					2	2	2				★	6	2	0
Norman, Tony																								21	0	0
Palmer, Charlie																								17	1	1
Payton, Andrew	**7**	7	7	7	7	7			★	★	★	★					★				★	9		18	10	4
Roberts, Gareth	**8**	8	8	8	8	8	8^{1}	8	8	8^{1}	8	**8**					11	11	8					35	0	3
Saville, Andy	★								9	6	9													14	6	1
Skipper, Peter																								3	0	0
Smith, Michael						★					7					11							**7**	9	3	1
Swan, Peter												4	4	4	4^{1}	**4**		4	4	4	4	4	4	11	0	1
Terry, Steve									5	5	5	6	6	6	6	6	6				5	5	5	33	0	1
Thompson, Leslie													8	**8**		★		8						6	1	0
Warren, Lee	★										6						4	6	**6**					27	1	0
Whitehurst, Billy	9	9^{1}	9	9	9^{1}	9	9	9^{1}		9		9	9	9	9	9^{1}	9	9	9	9	**9**		9	21	0	5
Own Goals												1														3

FA Cup: 1988-89: 3rd Round: Cardiff C. (A) 2-1; 4th Round: Bradford C. (A) 2-1; 5th Round: Liverpool (H) 2-3.
Littlewoods Cup: 1988-89: 2nd Round: Arsenal (H) 1-2 (A) 0-3.

IPSWICH TOWN (Division 2)

Team Manager John Duncan.
Club Address Portman Road, Ipswich, Suffolk IP1 2DA. Tel: (0473) 219211.
Current Ground Capacity 37,000.
Record Attendance 38,010 v Leeds U., FA Cup 6th Round, 8 March 1975.
Year Formed 1878. Turned professional 1936.
Previous Names None.
Club Nickname "The Blues" or "Town".
Club Colours Blue shirts with red band and white trim, white shorts and blue stockings.
Club Honours Football League: Div. 1 Champions 1961-62; Div. 2 Champions 1960-61, 1967-68; Div. 3(S) Champions 1953-54, 1956-57. FA Cup: Winners 1978. UEFA Cup: Winners 1980-81.
League History 1938-54 Div. 3(S); 1954-55 Div. 2; 1955-57 Div. 3(S); 1957-61 Div. 2; 1961-64 Div. 1; 1964-68 Div. 2; 1968-86 Div. 1; 1986- Div. 2.
Most League Points in a Season (2 for a win) 64 in Div. 3(S), 1953-54 and in 1955-56. (3 for a win) 83 in Div. 1, 1981-82.
Most League Goals in a Season 106 in Div. 3(S), 1955-56.
Record Victory 10-0 v Floriana in European Cup 1st Round, 25 September 1962.
Record Defeat 1-10 v Fulham in Div. 1, 26 December 1963.
Consecutive League Wins 8 in 1953.
Consecutive League Defeats 10 in 1954.
Record League Appearances Mick Mills, 591 between 1966-82.
Record League Goalscorer—Career Ray Crawford, 204 between 1958-69.
Record League Goalscorer—Season Ted Phillips, 41 in Div. 3(S), 1956-57.

Ipswich Town: League Record, 1988-89 (Division 2)

Match Number	Date	Venue	Opponents	Result	H/T	Lge Posn	Attend
1	27.8.88	A	Stoke C.	D 1-1	0-1		8639
2	3.9.88	H	Sunderland	W 2-0	1-0	8	12835
3	10.9.88	A	Leicester C.	W 1-0	1-0	7	10816
4	17.9.88	H	Watford	W 3-2	1-1	4	14644
5	20.9.88	A	Shrewsbury T.	W 5-1	3-1	2	4154
6	24.9.88	H	Bradford C.	D 1-1	0-0	3	13024
7	1.10.88	A	West Bromwich A.	W 2-1	1-0	1	9357
8	4.10.88	A	Crystal Palace	L 0-2	0-2	2	10325
9	8.10.88	H	Manchester C.	W 1-0	1-0	3	15521
10	15.10.88	H	Oxford U.	L 1-2	0-2	3	13039
11	22.10.88	A	Barnsley	L 0-2	0-2	4	6325
12	25.10.88	H	Portsmouth	L 0-1	0-0	6	14796
13	29.10.88	A	Bournemouth	L 0-1	0-0	9	6648
14	5.11.88	H	Leeds U.	L 0-1	0-1	11	11755
15	8.11.88	H	Walsall	W 3-1	1-0	6	9067
16	12.11.88	A	Swindon T.	W 3-2	0-1	6	7246
17	19.11.88	H	Brighton & H.A.	L 2-3	2-1	8	12386
18	26.11.88	A	Birmingham C.	L 0-1	0-1	9	5932
19	3.12.88	H	Plymouth Arg.	D 2-2	1-2	7	9929
20	10.12.88	A	Blackburn Rov.	L 0-1	0-1	13	7258
21	16.12.88	H	Oldham Ath.	W 2-1	0-1	9	8982
22	26.12.88	A	Chelsea	L 0-3	0-2	13	17621
23	31.12.88	A	Hull C.	D 1-1	0-1	14	7800
24	2.1.89	H	Leicester C.	W 2-0	1-0	12	14037
25	14.1.89	A	Walsall	W 4-2	0-0	8	4623
26	21.1.89	H	Stoke C.	W 5-1	0-0	7	14699
27	4.2.89	H	Crystal Palace	L 1-2	1-2	9	14569
28	11.2.89	A	Manchester C.	L 0-4	0-2	12	22145
29	21.2.89	H	Barnsley	W 2-0	1-0	7	9995
30	25.2.89	A	Oxford U.	D 1-1	0-1	9	6086
31	28.2.89	A	Portsmouth	W 1-0	0-0	6	7145
32	4.3.89	H	Swindon T.	L 1-2	0-0	9	11542
33	11.3.89	A	Leeds U.	W 4-2	1-0	9	19639
34	14.3.89	H	Bournemouth	W 3-1	3-0	6	10747
35	18.3.89	H	Shrewsbury T.	W 2-0	0-0	5	10913
36	25.3.89	A	Sunderland	L 0-4	0-1	5	13859
37	28.3.89	H	Chelsea	L 0-1	0-0	5	22950
38	1.4.89	A	Watford	L 2-3	0-2	7	12054
39	4.4.89	A	Oldham Ath.	L 0-4	0-2	10	5182
40	8.4.89	H	Hull C.	D 1-1	1-0	8	10191
41	15.4.89	A	Bradford C.	D 2-2	1-2	10	9691
42	22.4.89	H	West Bromwich A.	W 2-1	0-0	9	12047
43	29.4.89	H	Birmingham C.	W 4-0	2-0	9	9975
44	1.5.89	A	Plymouth Arg.	W 1-0	1-0	9	6484
45	6.5.89	A	Brighton & H.A.	W 1-0	0-0	8	8616
46	13.5.89	H	Blackburn Rov.	W 2-0	1-0	8	10861

Players: League Record, 1988-89 (Division 2)

Match Number	1	2	3	4	5	6	7	8	9	10	11	12	13	14	15	16	17	18	19	20	21	22	23
Atkinson, Dalian	10	10^1	10^1	10^1	10	10^1	10	10	10	10	10	10	**10**	★	10	10^1	10	10	10	10		**10**	
Baltacha, Sergei																							
Cheetham, Micky																							
D'Avray, Mich	**9**	9	9	**9**		9	6	6	6		★	5	5	**9**					$★^1$	★	★		
Dozzell, Jason	8	8^1	8	8	8^1	8	8^1	8	8^1	8^1	8	8	8	8	8	8^1	8	8	8	8	8^1	8	8
Fearon, Ron																							1
Forrest, Craig	1	1	1	1	1	1	1	1	1	1	1	1	1	1	1	1	1	1	1	1	1	1	
Gregory, David																						★	
Harbey, Graham						6					★		★	3	3	3	3	3				3	3
Hill, David	3	3	3	3	3	3	3	3	3	3	3	3	3						4	4	4		10
Humes, Tony	5^1	**5**	5	5	5	**5**	5	**5**	5	5	5			5	5	**5**							
Johnson, Gavin																							
Juryeff, Ian																							
Kiwomya, Chris						★				★	**11**	**11**	★		★	★					**10**	★	
Linighan, David	6	6	6	6	6			★	11	6				6	6	6	**6**	6	6	6	6	6	6
Lowe, David	7	7	7	7^1	7	7	7^1	7	7	7	7	7	7	7	**7**	7	7^1	7	7^1	**7**	7	7	7
Milton, Simon	★	★		11^1	9^3		9	9	9	**9**	**9**	★	**9**	★		★	**5**	4		★	★	**9**	
O'Donnell, Chris																	★	2					
Redford, Ian																	★	5	**5**	**5**	**5**	5	5^1
Stockwell, Mike				★	4	4				11	6	6	6	**11**	11^1	**11**	11^1	11	11	11	11	11	11
Wark, John	11	11	11		11	11	11	11				9	11	10	9^2	9	9	9	9	9	9^1		9
Woods, Neil						★																	
Yallop, Frank	2	2	2	2	2^1	2	2	2	2	2	2	2	2	2	2	2	2		2	2	2	2	2
Zondervan, Romeo	4	4	4	4			4	4	4	4	4	4	4	4	4	4^1	4		3	3	3	4	4
Own Goals																							

Match Number	24	25	26	27	28	29	30	31	32	33	34	35	36	37	38	39	40	41	42	43	44	45	46	Apps	Subs	Goals
Atkinson, Dalian					10	**10**	10	10	**10**	10^1	10^2	10^2	10	10	10	**10**	10							33	1	10
Baltacha, Sergei			11^1	11	**11**	11	11	11	11	**5**		★	2	5	5	**5**	5	**2**	2	2	2	2	2	19	1	1
Cheetham, Micky																				★		★	10	1	2	0
D'Avray, Mich		★	★				8	8	8	8	5	5	5		★	★		5^1	5	5	5	5^1	**5**	24	8	3
Dozzell, Jason	8	8^1	8^2	8	8	**8^1**																		29	0	11
Fearon, Ron	1	1	1	1	1	1	1	1	1	1	1	1	1	1	1	1	1							18	0	0
Forrest, Craig																		1	1	1	1	1	1	28	0	0
Gregory, David		★																						0	2	0
Harbey, Graham	3	**3**	3	3	3			★									★	11	**3**	3	3	3	3	19	4	0
Hill, David	10	10	10	10	4	4	4	4	4	11	11	11	11	11	11	11	**11**					4	★	35	1	0
Humes, Tony										2	2	2	3	3	**3**	3		3	11^1	11	11^1	**11**		26	0	3
Johnson, Gavin						3	3	**3**	3															4	0	0
Juryeff, Ian					★	★																		0	2	0
Kiwomya, Chris	7	7^1	7^1	7	7	★			★	★	8	8	8	8	**8**	8	8		★			**7**		16	10	2
Linighan, David	6^1	6	6	6	6	6	6^1	6	6	6	6	6	6	6	6	6	6	6	6	6	6	6	6	40	1	2
Lowe, David													★		★	7	7	7	7	7^2	7		7	30	2	6
Milton, Simon	11^1			★		7^1	7	7^1	7^1	7^1	7	7	**7**	7	7^1			10	**10**	**10**		★	★	25	10	10
O'Donnell, Chris																								1	1	0
Redford, Ian	5	5^1	5	**5**	5	5	5	5	5							★	3	8	8	8	8	8	8	22	2	2
Stockwell, Mike		**11**																	★	★	10	10	11	20	3	2
Wark, John	9	9^1	**9**	9^1	9	9	9	9	9	9^2	9^1	9	9	9	9^1	9	9	9	9^1	**9^1**	9	9	9^2	41	0	13
Woods, Neil																								0	1	0
Yallop, Frank	2	2	2^1	2	2	2	2	2	2	3	3	**3**		2	2	2	2	★			★			38	2	2
Zondervan, Romeo	4	4	4	4						4	4	4	4	4	4	4	4	4^1	4	4^1	**4**		**4**	37	0	3
Own Goals																	1									1

FA Cup: 1988-89: 3rd Round: Nottingham F. (A) 0-3.

Littlewoods Cup: 1988-89: 2nd Round: Port Vale (A) 0-1 (H) 3-0; 3rd Round: Leyton Orient (H) 2-0; 4th Round: Aston Villa (A) 2-6.

TOP MAN
TM
DESIGN FOR MEN

TOP MAN

LEEDS UNITED (Division 2)

Team Manager Howard Wilkinson.
Club Address Elland Road, Leeds LS11 0ES. Tel: (0532) 716037.
Current Ground Capacity 40,176.
Record Attendance 57,892 v Sunderland, FA Cup 5th Round replay, 15 March 1967.
Year Formed 1919. Turned professional 1920.
Previous Names None.
Club Nickname "The Whites".
Club Colours All white with blue and yellow trim.
Club Honours Football League: Div. 1 Champions 1968-69, 1973-74; Div. 2 Champions 1923-24, 1963-64. FA Cup: Winners 1972. Football League Cup: Winners 1968. European Fairs Cup: Winners 1967-68, 1970-71.
League History 1920-24 Div. 2; 1924-27 Div. 1; 1927-28 Div.2; 1928-31 Div.1; 1931-32 Div.2; 1932-47 Div. 1; 1947-56 Div 2; 1956-60 Div. 1; 1960-64 Div. 2; 1964-82 Div 1; 1982- Div. 2.
Most League Points in a Season (2 for a win) 67 in Div. 1, 1968-69. (3 for a win) 69 in Div. 2, 1984-85.
Most League Goals in a Season 98 in Div. 2, 1927-28.
Record Victory 10-0 v Lyn Oslo in European Cup 1st Round 1st Leg, 17 September 1969.
Record Defeat 1-8 v Stoke C. in Div. 1, 27 August 1934.
Consecutive League Wins 9 in 1931.
Consecutive League Defeats 6 in 1947.
Record League Appearances Jack Charlton, 628 between 1953-73.
Record League Goalscorer—Career Peter Lorimer, 168 between 1962-86.
Record League Goalscorer—Season John Charles, 42 in Div. 2, 1953-54.

Leeds United: League Record, 1988-89 (Division 2)

Match Number	Date	Venue	Opponents	Result	H/T	Lge Posn	Attend
1	27.8.88	H	Oxford U.	D 1-1	1-1		20697
2	3.9.88	A	Portsmouth	L 0-4	0-2	21	15263
3	10.99.88	H	Manchester C.	D 1-1	0-0	20	23122
4	17.9.88	A	Bournemouth	D 0-0	0-0	19	7922
5	21.9.88	H	Barnsley	W 2-0	0-0	16	17390
6	24.9.88	H	Chelsea	L 0-2	0-2	18	26080
7	1.10.88	A	Brighton & H.A.	L 1-2	1-0	21	7109
8	4.10.88	A	Sunderland	L 1-2	0-1	21	12671
9	8.10.88	H	Watford	L 0-1	0-0	21	15657
10	16.10.88	A	Swindon T.	D 0-0	0-0	21	9234
11	22.10.88	H	Leicester C.	D 1-1	1-0	21	17263
12	26.10.88	A	Bradford C.	D 1-1	1-0	22	13048
13	29.10.88	H	Hull C.	W 2-1	1-0	21	17536
14	5.11.88	A	Ipswich T.	W 1-0	1-0	20	11755
15	12.11.88	H	West Bromwich A.	W 2-1	2-1	19	20442
16	19.11.88	A	Oldham Ath.	D 2-2	1-1	20	8824
17	22.11.88	A	Birmingham C.	D 0-0	0-0	19	6168
18	26.11.88	H	Stoke C.	W 4-0	2-0	14	19933
19	3.12.88	A	Walsall	W 3-0	1-0	11	6885
20	10.12.88	H	Shrewsbury T.	L 2-3	0-2	14	19967
21	17.12.88	A	Crystal Palace	D 0-0	0-0	14	9847
22	26.12.88	H	Blackburn Rov.	W 2-0	2-0	11	31622
23	31.12.88	H	Plymouth Arg.	W 2-0	0-0	11	24043

Match Number	Date	Venue	Opponents	Result	H/T	Lge Posn	Attend
24	2.1.89	A	Manchester C.	D 0-0	0-0	11	33034
25	14.1.89	H	Birmingham C.	W 1-0	0-0	7	21837
26	21.1.89	A	Oxford U.	L 2-3	2-2	11	7926
27	4.2.89	H	Sunderland	W 2-0	1-0	8	31985
28	11.2.89	A	Watford	D 1-1	0-1	9	13439
29	18.2.89	A	Leicester C.	W 2-1	2-1	6	14151
30	25.2.89	H	Swindon T.	D 0-0	0-0	8	22651
31	1.3.89	H	Bradford C.	D 3-3	2-2	8	33325
32	5.3.89	A	West Bromwich A.	L 1-2	1-2	10	15964
33	11.3.89	H	Ipswich T.	L 2-4	0-1	12	19639
34	14.3.89	A	Hull C.	W 2-1	0-1	10	8887
35	19.3.89	A	Barnsley	D 2-2	1-1	10	11578
36	25.3.89	H	Portsmouth	W 1-0	0-0	8	27049
37	27.3.89	A	Blackburn Rov.	L 0-2	0-0	10	11533
38	1.4.89	H	Bournemouth	W 3-0	1-0	6	21095
39	5.4.89	H	Crystal Palace	L 1-2	1-2	7	25604
40	9.4.89	A	Plymouth Arg.	L 0-1	0-0	11	9365
41	15.4.89	H	Brighton & H.A.	W 1-0	1-0	7	14915
42	22.4.89	A	Chelsea	L 0-1	0-0	10	30337
43	29.4.89	A	Stoke C.	W 3-2	1-2	10	9051
44	1.5.89	H	Walsall	W 1-0	0-0	10	13280
45	6.5.89	H	Oldham Ath.	D 0-0	0-0	10	14459
46	13.5.89	A	Shrewsbury T.	D 3-3	2-2	10	4693

Players: League Record, 1988-89 (Division 2)

Match Number	1	2	3	4	5	6	7	8	9	10	11	12	13	14	15	16	17	18	19	20	21	22	23	24	25	26	27	28	29	30	31	32	33	34	35	36	37	38	39	40	41	42	43	44	45	46	Apps	Subs	Goals
Adams, Micky	3	3	**3**	3	3	3	3	3	3								★										4	4	4	4	**4**	**4**[1]															15	1	1
Aizlewood, Mark	4	4	4	4	**4**		**4**			4	4	4	4	4	4[1]	4	4	4	4	4	4	4	4	4	4	4			★	★	★	★	4	4	4[1]	4	4	4	4		3	4	**4**	**4**[1]			34	4	3
Andews, Ian																					1																										1	0	0
Ashurst, Jack	6	6	6	6	6	6				★																																					6	1	0
Aspin, Neil			★					★	2	2	2	2	2	2	2	2	2	2	2	2	2	2	2	2	2	2	2	**2**	2	2	2			6	6	2	2	2	2	2		**2**					31	2	0
Baird, Ian	9	9	9		9	**9**	9[1]	**9**	9	9	9	**9**	9[1]	9	9[1]	9	9	9[2]	9	**9**	9	9[1]	9[1]	**9**	9	**9**	9	9	**9**	**9**	9[1]	9	9	9[1]		9[1]	9	9	9	9		9	**9**	9	9	**9**	43	0	10
Batty, David			7	7	7	7	7	7	7	**7**	**7**	7	7	7	7	**7**		★						★			7	7	7	7	7	7	7	7			★			8			★	★	8	8	25	5	0
Blake, Noel	5	5	5[1]	5	5	5	5	5	5	5	5	5	5	5	5	5	5	5	5	5	5	5	5	5	5	5[1]	5	5	5	5	5[1]	5	5[1]		5	5	5	5		5	5	5	5	5	5	5	44	0	4
Davison, Bobby	★	★	**10**	10	10[1]	10		10[1]	**10**	**10**	**10**	10[1]	**10**	10	**10**	**10**[2]	**10**	10[1]	10[2]	10[1]	**10**	**10**[1]	**10**	10	**10**	10	10[1]	**10**	10[1]	10	10	**10**	**10**	**10**[1]	**10**	**10**					10	10	10[1]	**10**			37	2	14
Day, Mervyn	1	1	1	1	1	1	1	1	1	1	1	1	1	1	1	1	1	1	1	1		1	1	1	1	1	1	1	1	1	1	1	1	1	1	1	1	1	1	1	1	1	1	1	1	1	45	0	0
Fairclough, Chris																																				6	6	6	6	6	6	6	6	6	6	6	11	0	0
Haddock, Peter	2	2		★	★	**4**		**2**																											2						**2**		★	★	2	2	8	4	0
Hilaire, Vince	8	11	11	11	11[1]	11	11	11	11	11	11[1]	11	**11**	**11**	11	11	11	11	**11**	11	**11**	**11**	11	**11**	11[1]	11[1]	11	11	11	11	11[1]	11	11[1]	**11**	**11**	11	**11**		**11**				11	11	11	11	42	0	6
Kerr, Dylan																																									★	**3**				★	1	2	0
Mumby, Peter																																													★		0	1	0
Ormsby, Brendan																																														4	1	0	0
Pearson, John	**10**	10	★	★		★	10	★	★	★	★	★	★	★	★	★						★	★	★	★	★		★[1]	★	★		★	★	★	9	★	10		★	★	9	★					6	27	1
Rennie, David	★						6	6	6	6	6	6	6	6	6	6	6	6	6	6	6	6	6	6	6	6	6	6	6	6	6	6	**6**						5	★	★				**4**	10[1]	30	3	1
Sheridan, John			8	**8**	8	8	★	8	8	8	8	**8**	8[1]	**8**[1]	8	8	8	**8**[1]	8	8[1]	8	8	8	8		8	8[1]	8	**8**	8	8	8	8	8	8[1]	**8**	**8**	8	8		8	★	8[1]	8			38	2	7
Shutt, Carl																																						10[3]	10[1]	**10**							3	0	4
Snodin, Glynn	11[1]					★	8		★	3	3	3	3	3	**3**	3	3	3	3	3	3	3	3[1]	3	3	3	3	3	3[1]	**3**	3	3	3	3	3	3	3	**3**	3	**3**							33	2	3
Speed, Gary																																													10		1	0	0
Stiles, John	**7**	8						4	**4**		★	★	★	★																															★	★	4	6	0
Strachan, Gordon																																				7	7	7	7	7	7	7	7[1]	7	7	7[2]	11	0	3
Swan, Peter																																		5													1	0	0
Taylor, Bob		**7**		**9**													★			★	★														★												2	4	0
Whitlow, Mike																		7	7[1]	7	7	7	7	7	7	**7**							★	★	7			11		11	**11**	11	3	3	**3**	**3**	18	2	1
Williams, Andy															★	★	**7**		★		★	★			8	★		★							★	★	★	★		4	4[1]	8	2	2			7	11	1
Williams, Gary			2	2	2	2	2																									2	2	2													8	0	0
Own Goals																																																	0

FA Cup: 1988-89: 3rd Round: Brighton & H.A. (A) 2-1; 4th Round: Nottingham F. (A) 0-2.
Littlewoods Cup: 1988-89: 2nd Round: Peterborough U. (A) 2-1) (H) 3-1; 3rd Round: Luton T. (H) 0-2.

Gary McAllister (Leicester City) Match Magazine

LEICESTER CITY (Division 2)

Team Manager David Pleat.
Club Address City Stadium, Filbert Street, Leicester LE2 7FL. Tel: (0533) 555000.
Current Ground Capacity 31,000.
Record Attendance 47,298 v Tottenham H., FA Cup 5th Round, 18 February 1928.
Year Formed 1884. Turned professional 1894.
Previous Names Leicester Fosse.
Club Nickname "The Filberts" or "Foxes".
Club Colours Blue shirts with white pinstripe, white shorts and stockings with blue trim.
Club Honours Football League: Div. 2 Champions 1924-25, 1936-37, 1953-54, 1956-57, 1970-71, 1979-80. Football League Cup: Winners 1964.
League History 1894-1908 Div. 2; 1908-09 Div. 1; 1909-25 Div. 2; 1925-35 Div. 1; 1935-37 Div. 2; 1937-39 Div. 1; 1946-54 Div. 2; 1954-55 Div. 1; 1955-57 Div. 2; 1957-69 Div. 1; 1969-71 Div. 2; 1971-78 Div. 1; 1978-80 Div. 2; 1980-81 Div. 1; 1981-83 Div. 2; 1983-87 Div. 1; 1987- Div. 2.
Most League Points in a Season (2 for a win) 51 in Div. 2, 1956-57. (3 for a win) 70 in Div. 2, 1982-83.
Most League Goals in a Season 109 in Div. 2, 1956-57.
Record Victory 10-0 v Portsmouth in Div. 1, 20 December 1928.
Record Defeat 0-12 v Nottingham F. in Div. 1, 21 April 1909.
Consecutive League Wins 7 in 1908, 1925 and 1962-63.
Consecutive League Defeats 7 in 1931-32.
Record League Appearances Adam Black, 528 between 1920-35.
Record League Goalscorer—Career Arthur Chandler, 259 between 1923-35.
Record League Goalscorer—Season Arthur Rowley, 44 in Div. 2, 1956-57.

Leicester City: League Record, 1988-89 (Division 2)

Match Number	Date	Venue	Opponents	Result	H/T	Lge Posn	Attend
1	27.8.88	H	West Bromwich A.	D 1-1	0-0		13082
2	29.8.88	A	Portsmouth	L 0-3	0-1	20	10737
3	3.9.88	A	Birmingham C.	W 3-2	2-2	12	7932
4	10.9.88	H	Ipswich T.	L 0-1	0-1	13	10816
5	17.9.88	A	Oxford U.	D 1-1	1-0	14	6610
6	21.9.88	H	Plymouth Arg.	W 1-0	0-0	11	9117
7	24.9.88	H	Watford	D 2-2	1-1	11	10957
8	1.10.88	A	Chelsea	L 1-2	0-0	15	7050
9	4.10.88	A	Hull C.	D 2-2	1-1	18	5079
10	8.10.88	H	Brighton & H.A.	W 1-0	0-0	12	9201
11	15.10.88	H	Stoke C.	W 2-0	1-0	10	10312
12	22.10.88	A	Leeds U.	D 1-1	0-1	11	17263
13	26.10.88	H	Swindon T.	D 3-3	0-3	10	9271
14	29.10.88	A	Shrewsbury T.	L 0-3	0-1	14	5178
15	5.11.88	H	Manchester C.	D 0-0	0-0	16	14080
16	12.11.88	A	Walsall	W 1-0	1-0	10	6895
17	19.11.88	A	Crystal Palace	L 2-4	1-1	13	8843
18	26.11.88	H	Bradford C.	W 1-0	1-0	10	9553
19	3.12.88	A	Oldham Ath.	D 1-1	0-0	12	5789
20	10.12.88	H	Sundorland	W 3-1	2-0	9	11093
21	17.12.88	A	Barnsley	L 0-3	0-2	12	6477
22	26.12.88	H	Bournemouth	L 0-1	0-0	16	13896
23	31.12.88	H	Blackburn Rov.	W 4-0	2-0	13	10820
24	2.1.89	A	Ipswich T.	L 0-2	0-1	15	14037
25	14.1.89	H	Portsmouth	W 2-1	1-1	14	10567
26	21.1.89	A	West Bromwich A.	D 1-1	0-0	14	15792
27	4.2.89	H	Hull C.	L 0-2	0-1	15	9996
28	11.2.89	A	Brighton & H.A.	D 1-1	1-0	17	9572
29	18.2.89	H	Leeds U.	L 1-2	1-2	17	14151
30	25.2.89	A	Stoke C.	D 2-2	2-2	16	9666
31	28.2.89	A	Swindon T.	L 1-2	1-0	16	7456
32	4.3.89	H	Walsall	W 1-0	0-0	15	9375
33	11.3.89	A	Manchester C.	L 2-4	0-0	15	22266
34	15.3.89	H	Shrewsbury T.	D 1-1	1-1	15	7750
35	18.3.89	A	Plymouth Arg.	D 1-1	0-1	15	6703
36	25.3.89	H	Birmingham C.	W 2-0	1-0	15	9564
37	27.3.89	A	Bournemouth	L 1-2	0-2	15	8913
38	1.4.89	H	Oxford U.	W 1-0	1-0	13	8187
39	8.4.89	A	Blackburn Rov.	D 0-0	0-0	13	8080
40	11.4.89	H	Barnsley	L 0-1	0-1	13	7266
41	15.4.89	H	Chelsea	W 2-0	0-0	13	19468
42	22.4.89	A	Watford	L 1-2	1-1	15	11262
43	29.4.89	A	Bradford C.	L 1-2	0-0	16	8703
44	1.5.89	H	Oldham Ath.	L 1-2	0-1	16	7223
45	6.5.89	H	Crystal Palace	D 2-2	1-1	16	9917
46	13.5.89	A	Sunderland	D 2-2	0-0	15	15819

Players: League Record, 1988-89 (Division 2)

Match Number	1	2	3	4	5	6	7	8	9	10	11	12	13	14	15	16	17	18	19	20	21	22	23
Brien, Tony																	5						
Brown, Grant	6		6	6	6	6	6	6		6	6	6	**6**										
Charles, Gary																							
Cooper, Paul		1	1	1	1	1	1	1	1	1	1	1	1	1	1	1	1	1	1	1	1	1	1
Cross, Nicky	8	**8**	**8**^{1}	8	**8**^{1}	8	8	8	8	8	8	8	8	8	8	8	8			★^{1}	8	★	8^1
Eccles, Peter																							
Groves, Paul										★	4	**4**							5	5	**5**		★
Hodge, Martin	1																						
Kennedy, Mick																							
McAllister, Gary	10	10	10	10	10	10	10	10	10^1	10	10	10	10^2	10	10	10	10^1	10	10	10	10	10	10^1
Mauchlen, Alistair	2^1	2	2	**2**	2	**2**	2	2	4	4				4	4	4	4	4	4	**4**			**2**
Mills, Gary																							
Morgan, Simon						★	3	3	3	3	3			6	6	6	6	6	6	**6**	6	6	6
Muggleton, Carl																							
Newell, Mike	9	9	9^1	9	9	9^1	9	9	9	9	9^2	9	9	9	9	9^1	9^1	9	9	9^1	9	9	9^1
North, Marc																							
Paris, Alan		6							2	**2**	2	2	2	2	2	2	2	2	2	2	2	2	
Puttnam, David																							
Quinn, Jimmy	★	★	11^1	11	11	11		★^{1}	6	★^{1}		★^{1}	4	★	★	★	11	11^1	11^1	11	★	11	★
Ramsey, Paul	4	**4**	4	4	4	4	4	4														**4**	4
Reid, Paul	**7**	★	7	**7**	★		7^1	7	7	7	7	7	7	7	7	7	7	7	7	7^1	7	7	7
Russell, Martin								**11**				★	★	★	**11**	**11**		8		8	★	**8**	
Spearing, Tony	3	3	3	3	3	3						3	3	3	3	3	3	3			3	3	3
Turner, Philip	11	7		★															3	3	**4**	★	11^1
Walsh, Steve	5	5	5	5	5	5	5^1	5	5	5	5	5	5	5	5	5		5				5	**5**
Weir, Peter		11	★	★	7	7	11				**11**	**11**	11	**11**									
Wilkinson, Stephen																							
Williams, Darren									11^1	**11**	★								8	★	11		
Own Goals													1										

Match Number	24	25	26	27	28	29	30	31	32	33	34	35	36	37	38	39	40	41	42	43	44	45	46	Apps	Subs	Goals
Brien, Tony																								1	0	0
Brown, Grant																							6	12	0	0
Charles, Gary													★	2	3	2	**2**		★		★	2		5	3	0
Cooper, Paul	1	1																						24	0	0
Cross, Nicky	8	8	8			8^1	8	8	8^1	8	8	8^1	**8**	★	**8**	8	8	8^1	**8**	8	**8**	★^{1}		37	4	9
Eccles, Peter																**5**								1	0	0
Groves, Paul	★		★		**8**	★	★	**4**	★													★		7	8	0
Hodge, Martin						1	1	1	1	1	1	1	1	1	1	1	1	1	1	1	1	1	1	19	0	0
Kennedy, Mick												4	4	**4**	4			4	**4**	4	4		8	9	0	0
McAllister, Gary	10	10	10	10	10^1	**10**	10	10	10	10^1	10^1	10	10	10^1	10^1	10	10	10	10	10	10	10	10^1	46	0	11
Mauchlen, Alistair	2	2	2	2	4	2	2	2	**2**	2	2	2	2^2	8	2		4	2	2	2	2			38	0	3
Mills, Gary									11	11	11	11	11	11	11	11	11	11	11	11	**11**			13	0	0
Morgan, Simon	**6**	6	6	6	6					6			3	**3**		★	5	5	5	5	5	5	5	30	2	0
Muggleton, Carl			1	1	1																			3	0	0
Newell, Mike	9		9	9	9	9	9	9^1	9	9^1	9	9	9	9	9	9	9	9	9^1	9	9^1	9	9^1	45	0	13
North, Marc													★	★	★	★	★		★		★	**8**^{1}		1	7	1
Paris, Alan	5	5	5	5	2	6	6	6	6		6	6	**6**	6	6	6	6	6	6	6^1	6	6	2	37	0	1
Puttnam, David																	★					11	**11**	2	1	0
Quinn, Jimmy	★	9	★	8	★	★	★	★		★	★													13	18	6
Ramsey, Paul	**4**	4	**4**	4		4	**4**		4	4	4					**4**						**4**	4	22	0	0
Reid, Paul	7	7^1	**7**^{1}	7	7	7	7^1	7	7	7	**7**	7	7	7	7	7	**7**	7^1	7	7	7	7	7	43	2	6
Russell, Martin																								6	4	0
Spearing, Tony	3	3	3	3	3	3	3	3	3	**3**	3	3				3	3	3	3	3	3	3	3	36	0	0
Turner, Philip	11	11^1	11	11	11	**11**	**11**	11																14	2	2
Walsh, Steve					5	5	5^1	5	5	5	5	5	5	5	5									30	0	2
Weir, Peter																								8	2	0
Wilkinson, Stephen																							★	0	1	0
Williams, Darren																								4	2	1
Own Goals																										1

FA Cup: 1988-89: 3rd Round: Manchester C. (A) 0-1.
Littlewoods Cup: 1988-89: 2nd Round: Watford (H) 4-1 (A) 2-2; 3rd Round: Norwich C. (H) 2-0; 4th Round: Nottingham F. (H) 0-0, Replay (A) 1-2.

LEYTON ORIENT (Division 3)

Team Manager Frank Clark.
Club Address Leyton Stadium, Brisbane Road, Leyton, London E10 5NE. Tel: 01-539 2223/4.
Current Ground Capacity 26,500.
Record Attendance 34,345 v West Ham U., FA Cup 4th Round, 25 January 1964.
Year Formed 1881. Turned professional 1903.
Previous Names Glyn Cricket and Football Club, Eagle Football Club, Orient Football Club, Clapton Orient, Orient.
Club Nickname "The O's".
Club Colours All red.
Club Honours Football League: Div. 3 Champions 1969-70; Div.3(S) Champions 1955-56.
League History 1905-29 Div. 2; 1929-56 Div. 3(S); 1956-62 Div. 2; 1962-63 Div. 1; 1963-66 Div. 2; 1966-70 Div. 3; 1970-82 Div. 2; 1982-85 Div. 3; 1985-89 Div. 4; 1989- Div. 3.
Most League Points in a Season (2 for a win) 66 in Div. 3(S), 1955-56. (3 for a win) 75 in Div. 4, 1988-89.
Most League Goals in a Season 106 in Div. 3(S), 1955-56.
Record Victory 8-0 v Colchester U. in Div. 4, 15 October 1988.
Record Defeat 0-8 v Aston Villa in FA Cup 4th Round, 30 January 1929.
Consecutive League Wins 10 in 1956.
Consecutive League Defeats 8 in 1927-28.
Record League Appearances Peter Allen, 430 between 1965-78.
Record League Goalscorer—Career Tom Johnston, 119 between 1956-61.
Record League Goalscorer—Season Tom Johnston, 35 in Div. 2, 1957-58.

Leyton Orient: League Record, 1988-89 (Division 4)

Match Number	Date	Venue	Opponents	Result	H/T	Lge Posn	Attend
1	27.8.88	H	Crewe Alex.	D 0-0	0-0		3992
2	3.9.88	A	Stockport Co.	D 0-0	0-0	16	1947
3	10.9.88	H	Hereford U.	L 1-3	0-2	19	3087
4	17.9.88	A	Hartlepool U.	L 0-1	0-0	21	1823
5	20.9.88	A	Rotherham U.	L 1-4	0-2	23	4289
6	23.9.88	H	Darlington	W 1-0	0-0	21	2755
7	1.10.88	A	Torquay U.	L 0-3	0-2	22	2526
8	4.10.88	H	York C.	W 4-0	2-0	19	2467
9	8.10.88	A	Scarborough	D 0-0	0-0	19	2376
10	15.10.88	H	Colchester U.	W 8-0	4-0	17	3412
11	22.10.88	A	Burnley	D 2-2	1-0	18	8502
12	25.10.88	H	Exeter C.	W 4-0	0-0	13	3873
13	29.10.88	A	Doncaster Rov.	L 0-1	0-0	16	2182
14	5.11.88	H	Peterborough U.	L 1-2	1-1	18	3695
15	8.11.88	H	Carlisle U.	W 2-0	0-0	13	2869
16	12.11.88	A	Scunthorpe U.	D 2-2	1-1	17	4239
17	26.11.88	A	Cambridge U.	D 2-2	0-1	17	2675
18	3.12.88	H	Lincoln C.	W 3-1	2-0	13	3093
19	17.12.88	A	Grimsby T.	D 2-2	0-0	14	3446
20	26.12.88	H	Tranmere Rov.	W 2-0	0-0	10	4249
21	31.12.88	H	Wrexham	L 0-1	0-0	13	4025
22	2.1.89	A	Rochdale	W 3-0	1-0	12	2036
23	14.1.89	H	Stockport Co.	L 1-2	0-1	14	3828
24	21.1.89	A	Crewe Alex.	L 1-2	0-1	16	2933
25	4.2.89	H	Rotherham U.	W 3-1	0-1	14	3290
26	11.2.89	A	Darlington	W 3-1	2-1	12	1833
27	14.2.89	A	Halifax T.	D 2-2	0-0	12	1477
28	18.2.89	H	Scarborough	L 2-3	2-0	12	3877
29	24.2.89	A	Colchester U.	L 0-1	0-1	12	4269
30	1.3.89	A	Exeter C.	D 1-1	0-0	13	2890
31	4.3.89	H	Burnley	W 3-0	0-0	9	3974
32	11.3.89	A	Peterborough U.	W 1-0	0-0	10	3306
33	14.3.89	H	Doncaster Rov.	W 4-0	1-0	8	2824
34	18.3.89	A	Hereford U.	D 1-1	0-1	8	2063
35	21.3.89	H	Hartlepool U.	W 4-3	1-1	7	3406
36	25.3.89	H	Rochdale	W 3-0	1-0	6	4591
37	27.3.89	A	Tranmere Rov.	L 0-3	0-1	7	6872
38	1.4.89	H	Grimsby T.	W 5-0	1-0	6	4149
39	4.4.89	H	Halifax T.	W 2-0	0-0	6	3288
40	8.4.89	A	Wrexham	W 1-0	1-0	6	2437
41	15.4.89	H	Torquay U.	W 3-1	1-0	6	4642
42	22.4.89	A	York C.	D 1-1	1-0	6	2744
43	29.4.89	H	Cambridge U.	D 1-1	1-1	5	5657
44	1.5.89	A	Carlisle U.	L 1-2	1-2	6	2401
45	6.5.89	A	Lincoln C.	W 1-0	0-0	6	3579
46	13.5.89	H	Scunthorpe U.	W 4-1	2-0	6	6366

Players: League Record, 1988-89 (Division 4)

Match Number	1	2	3	4	5	6	7	8	9	10	11	12	13	14	15	16	17	18	19	20	21	22	23
Baker, Steve	7	7	7	7	7	7	7	7	7	7^{1}	7	7	**7**	7	7^{1}	7	11	9	9	9	9	9	**9**
Campbell, Kevin																							
Carter, Darren																							
Castle, Stephen																							★
Comfort, Alan	11	11	11	11	11	11	11	11^{1}	11	11^{1}	11^{1}	11^{1}	11	11	11^{1}	11^{1}			11^{1}	11	11	11	11
Cooper, Mark																							
Corner, David	5	5	5												6								
Day, Keith	6	6		5	5	5	5	5	5	5^{1}	5	5	5	5	5	5	5	5	5	5	5	5	5
Dickenson, Kevin	3	3	3	3	3	3	3	3	3	3	3	3^{1}	3	3			3	3	3	3	**3**		
Hales, Kevin	4	4	4	4	4	4	4	4^{1}	4	4^{1}		4	4	4	4	4	4^{1}	4^{1}	4	**4**			
Harvey, Lee				8	8	8							★	6		★^{1}	7	7	7	7	7	7^{2}	
Heald, Paul																			1	1	1	1	1
Howard, Terry	2	2	2	2	2	2	2	2	2	2	2	2	2	2	2	2	2	2	2	2^{1}	2	2	2^{1}
Hull, Alan	★	9	9^{1}	9			★		9	9^{3}	9	9^{1}	9	9	9	**9**	9						
Jones, David																					★	★	
Juryeff, Ian	10	**10**	10	**10**	10	10^{1}	10	10^{1}	10	10	10^{1}	10^{1}	10	10^{1}	10	10	10^{1}	10^{1}	10^{1}	10	10	**10**^{1}	10
Kerrins, Wayne																							
Ketteridge, Steve			**6**	6	6^{1}	6												11					
Nugent, Kevin			★				**9**																7
O'Shea, Timothy											4			★	3	3				★^{1}	4	4	4
Shinners, Paul	**9**	★		★	9	9		9															
Sitton, John							6	6^{1}	6	6^{1}	6	6	6			6	6	6	6	6		6	6
Smalley, Mark																					6	3	3
Ward, Paul	8	8	8				8	8	8	8	8	8	8	8	**8**	8	8	8^{1}	8	8	8	8	8
Wells, Peter	1	1	1	1	1	1	1	1	1	1	1	1	1	1	1	1	1	1					
Own Goals																							

Match Number	24	25	26	27	28	29	30	31	32	33	34	35	36	37	38	39	40	41	42	43	44	45	46	Apps	Subs	Goals
Baker, Steve	9	7	7	7	7	7	7	7	7	7	7	7	7	7	7	7	7	7^{1}	7	7	7	7	7	46	0	3
Campbell, Kevin	7^{1}	9^{2}	10	10	10^{1}	10	10^{1}	10^{1}	10	10^{1}	10	10^{1}	10	10	**10**^{1}	10								16	0	9
Carter, Darren																							★	0	1	0
Castle, Stephen	★	4	4	4	4^{1}	4	4	4	4	8^{1}	8	8	8^{1}	8	8	8	8	8	8	8	8^{1}	8^{1}	8^{1}	22	2	6
Comfort, Alan	11	11^{1}	11^{1}	11^{2}	11	11	11	11^{2}	11	11^{1}	11^{1}	11	11^{1}	11	11^{1}	11	11^{1}	11^{1}	11	11	11	11	**11**	44	0	19
Cooper, Mark		★	9^{1}	9	9	**9**	**9**	9	★		★			★			10	10				10	10^{3}	10	4	4
Corner, David																								4	0	0
Day, Keith	5	5	5	5	5	5	5	5	5	5	5	5^{1}	5	5	5	5	5	5	5	5	5	5	5	45	0	2
Dickenson, Kevin	3	3	3	3	3	3	3		3	3	3	3	3	3	3	3	3	**3**			★	3	3	38	1	1
Hales, Kevin								3	8	4	**4**	4	4^{1}	**4**	4	4^{2}	4	4^{1}	4	4^{1}	**4**	4	4	35	0	9
Harvey, Lee							★	★	**9**	9^{1}	9	9	9	9	9^{2}	9	9	9	9	9	9	9	**9**	25	4	6
Heald, Paul	1	1	1	1	1	1	1	1	1	1	1	1	1	1	1	1	1	1	1	1	1	1	1	28	0	0
Howard, Terry	2	2	2^{1}	2	2	2	2	2	2^{1}	2	2	2^{1}	2	2	2	2	2	2	2	2	2	2	2	46	0	5
Hull, Alan						★									★						★			12	5	5
Jones, David																								0	2	0
Juryeff, Ian	10	**10**																	10	10	**10**		★	28	1	9
Kerrins, Wayne																			3	3	3			3	0	0
Ketteridge, Steve																								5	0	1
Nugent, Kevin																								2	1	0
O'Shea, Timothy	**4**																							7	2	1
Shinners, Paul																								4	2	0
Sitton, John	6	6	6	6	6	6	6	6	6	6	6	6^{1}	6	6	6	6	6	6	6^{1}	6	6	6	6	37	0	4
Smalley, Mark																		★						3	1	0
Ward, Paul	8	8	8	8	8	8	8	**8**																28	0	1
Wells, Peter																								18	0	0
Own Goals																										1

FA Cup: 1988-89: 1st Round: Enfield (A) 1-1, Replay (H) 2-2, 2nd Replay (H) 0-1.
Littlewoods Cup: 1988-89: 1st Round: Aldershot (H) 2-0 (A) 0-0; 2nd Round: Stoke C. (H) 1-2 (A) 2-1; 3rd Round: Ipswich T. (A) 0-2.

LINCOLN CITY (Division 4)

Team Manager Colin Murphy.
Club Address Sincil Bank, Lincoln LN5 8LD. Tel: (0522) 22224.
Current Ground Capacity 9,500.
Record Attendance 23,196 v Derby Co., Football League Cup, 4th Round, 15 November 1967.
Year Formed 1884. Turned professional 1892.
Previous Names None.
Club Nickname "The Imps".
Club Colours Red and white striped shirts, black shorts and red stockings.
Club Honours Football League: Div. 3(N) Champions 1931-32, 1947-48, 1951-52; Div. 4 Champions 1975-76. Vauxhall Conference Champions 1987-88.
League History 1892-1921 Div. 2; 1921-32 Div. 3(N); 1932-34 Div. 2; 1934-48 Div. 3(N); 1948-49 Div. 2; 1949-52 Div. 3(N); 1952-61 Div. 2; 1961-62 Div. 3; 1962-76 Div. 4; 1976-79 Div. 3; 1979-81 Div. 4; 1981-86 Div. 3; 1986-87 Div. 4; 1987-88 Vauxhall Conference; 1988- Div. 4.
Most League Points in a Season (2 for a win) 74 in Div. 4, 1975-76. (3 for a win) 77 in Div. 3, 1981-82.
Most League Goals in a Season 121 in Div. 3(N), 1951-52.
Record Victory 11-1 v Crewe Alex. in Div. 3(N), 29 September 1951.
Record Defeat 3-11 v Manchester C. in Div. 2, 23 March 1895.
Consecutive League Wins 10 in 1930-31 and 1974-75.
Consecutive League Defeats 12 in 1896-97.
Record League Appearances Tony Emery, 402 between 1946-59.
Record League Goalscorer—Career Andy Graver, 144 between 1950-61.
Record League Goalscorer—Season Allan Hall, 42 in Div. 3(N), 1931-32.

Lincoln City: League Record, 1988-89 (Division 4)

Match Number	Date	Venue	Opponents	Result	H/T	Lge Posn	Attend
1	27.8.88	H	Hartlepool U.	L 0-1	0-1		3361
2	3.9.88	A	Wrexham	L 0-3	0-0	24	2312
3	10.9.88	H	Crewe Alex.	D 2-2	1-1	23	2651
4	17.9.88	A	Peterborough U.	D 1-1	0-0	22	4256
5	20.9.88	A	Cambridge U.	W 3-2	1-0	19	2776
6	24.9.88	H	Hereford U.	W 2-0	1-0	13	2915
7	1.10.88	A	Colchester U.	W 3-1	1-1	10	1529
8	5.10.88	H	Scunthorpe U.	W 1-0	1-0	7	5443
9	8.10.88	A	Torquay U.	L 0-1	0-1	9	2105
10	15.10.88	H	Scarborough	D 2-2	2-1	7	4535
11	22.10.88	H	Darlington	W 3-2	0-0	6	3705
12	24.10.88	A	Tranmere Rov.	L 0-1	0-0	12	3498
13	29.10.88	H	Carlisle U.	L 0-2	0-0	12	3727
14	5.11.88	A	Rotherham U.	L 0-2	0-2	15	4506
15	8.11.88	A	Burnley	W 4-1	1-1	12	8740
16	12.11.88	H	Exeter C.	W 2-0	1-0	7	3461
17	26.11.88	H	Halifax T.	W 2-1	1-1	5	3379
18	3.12.88	A	Leyton Orient	L 1-3	0-2	6	3093
19	17.12.88	A	Stockport Co.	L 0-1	0-0	11	2355
20	26.12.88	H	Grimsby T.	D 2-2	1-0	11	8038
21	28.12.88	H	Doncaster Rov.	W 3-1	1-1	9	5213
22	2.1.89	A	York C.	L 1-2	1-0	11	3589
23	7.1.89	A	Rochdale	D 2-2	1-1	10	1515
24	14.1.89	H	Wrexham	W 4-3	2-1	10	3860
25	21.1.89	A	Hartlepool U.	L 2-3	0-2	9	2860
26	28.1.89	H	Peterborough U.	D 1-1	0-0	10	4150
27	4.2.89	H	Cambridge U.	W 3-0	0-0	9	3239
28	11.2.89	A	Hereford U.	L 2-3	0-1	10	2113
29	18.2.89	H	Torquay U.	W 1-0	1-0	8	3423
30	25.2.89	A	Scarborough	D 1-1	0-1	8	3293
31	1.3.89	H	Tranmere Rov.	W 2-1	0-0	7	3560
32	4.3.89	A	Darlington	L 1-2	0-1	7	2169
33	11.3.89	H	Rotherham U.	L 0-1	0-1	8	5186
34	14.3.89	A	Carlisle U.	L 1-2	0-2	9	2691
35	18.3.89	A	Crewe Alex.	L 0-2	0-1	10	3106
36	25.3.89	H	York C.	W 2-1	1-1	10	3710
37	27.3.89	A	Grimsby T.	L 0-1	0-0	10	8618
38	1.4.89	H	Stockport Co.	D 0-0	0-0	12	3400
39	5.4.89	H	Rochdale	W 4-1	3-0	9	2034
40	8.4.89	A	Doncaster Rov.	W 1-0	0-0	9	2124
41	15.4.89	H	Colchester U.	D 1-1	0-0	9	3519
42	22.4.89	A	Scunthorpe U.	D 0-0	0-0	8	5729
43	29.4.89	A	Halifax T.	W 1-0	0-0	9	1261
44	1.5.89	H	Burnley	L 2-3	0-2	9	3594
45	6.5.89	H	Leyton Orient	L 0-1	0-0	10	3579
46	13.5.89	A	Exeter C.	W 1-0	1-0	10	2249

Players: League Record, 1988-89 (Division 4)

Match Number	1	2	3	4	5	6	7	8	9	10	11	12	13	14	15	16	17	18	19	20	21	22	23
Bowling, Ian																							
Bressington, Graham	5	5	5	5	5	5	5	5	5	5	5	5	5	5	5	5	5	5			5	5	5
Brown, Phil	9	9	9	4	4	4	4	4	4	4	4	4	4	4	10	10	10	10	10	10		★	★
Casey, Paul																			4		7		
Clarke, David	**4**	**4**				★	10	3	3	8¹	**8**	8	8	8	8	8		★					
Cook, Mark																							
Cumming, Bobby	**8**	**8**			8	**8**	8	8									8¹	8¹	8	8	8	8	8¹
Davis, Darren	7	7	7	7	7	7	7	7	7	7	7	7	7	7	7	7	7	**7**	7	3	3	3	3
Dunkley, Malcolm																							
Evans, Clive	2	2	2¹	2	2	2	2	2	2	2	2	2	2	2	2	2	2	2	2	2	2	2	2
Franklin, Neil															★								
Gamble, Willie	★	★	4	★	10	10¹		10¹	10	10¹	10¹	10	**10**	★				64	★				
Hobson, Gordon				9	9¹	9¹	9²	9	9	9	9		9	9	9³	9²	9	9		9¹	9	9	9
James, Anthony		★	8	8			★		8		★	9	★	**10**		6			5	5		★	
McGinley, John																					★	**11**	**11**
Matthewson, Trevor	6	6	6	6	6	6	6	6	6	6	6	6	6	6	**6**		6¹	6	6	6	6¹	6	6
Nicholson, Shane	3	3	3	3	3	3	**3**			3	3¹	3	3	3	3	3	3	3	3	4	11	**4**	4
Ranshaw, Richard	★																						
Schofield, John															4	4	4	**4**			4	7	7
Scott, Chris																							
Sertori, Mark	11	11	11	11	11²	11	11	11	11	11	11¹	11	11	11	11	11	11	11	11	11			★
Smith, Paul	10	10	10¹	**10**¹															9	7¹	10²	10¹	**10**¹
Wallington, Mark	1	1	1	1	1	1	1	1	1	1	1	1	1	1	1	1	1	1	1	1	1	1	1
Own Goals							1																

Match Number	24	25	26	27	28	29	30	31	32	33	34	35	36	37	38	39	40	41	42	43	44	45	46	Apps	Subs	Goals
Bowling, Ian											1	1						1	1	1	1	1	1	8	0	0
Bressington, Graham	5			8	**7**	8¹	**7**													8	5	5	**5**	30	0	1
Brown, Phil	7	7¹	7¹	7	11	7	★	7	7	★					7	7		★		★¹	★		8	31	7	3
Casey, Paul					★														★	2	2	2	2	6	2	0
Clarke, David		★	3	3	3	3	3¹	3¹	3	3	11	**11**	11	11	11	11¹	3	11	3	3	3	11	11	33	3	4
Cook, Mark																							7	1	0	0
Cumming, Bobby	8¹	8	8				8	8	8	8	8	8	8				11¹	8	8	11	11	8		29	0	5
Davis, Darren	3	**3**									3	3	3	3	3	3	5	3	6	★	6¹	3	3¹	37	1	2
Dunkley, Malcolm				10²	10¹	10	10	10	10¹	10	10	**10**	★	★										9	2	4
Evans, Clive	2	2	2	2	2	2	2	2	2	**2**	2	2	2	2	2	2¹	2	**2**	**2**					42	0	2
Franklin, Neil																								0	1	0
Gamble, Willie									★								7	7	7	7	7¹	**7**		15	7	5
Hobson, Gordon	9²	9	9	9¹	9¹					9	9¹	9	**9**	9	9	9						9	9	32	0	15
James, Anthony				5	5		5	5	5	5	5	5	5	5	5	**5**		5	5	**5**				23	5	0
McGinley, John	**10**	10	10	11		11	★	11	**11**	11		★	7	**7**		★	9	9¹	9			★		15	5	2
Matthewson, Trevor	6	6	6	6	6	6	6	6	6	6	6	6	**6**	6	6	6	6	6		**6**		6	6	43	0	2
Nicholson, Shane	11	11	11				**11**						★	8	8	8	8	4	11		8		★	32	2	1
Ranshaw, Richard																								0	1	0
Schofield, John	4¹	4	4	4	8	4	4	4	4	4	4	4	4	4	4	**4**¹	4		4	4	4	4	4	29	0	2
Scott, Chris		5	5		**4**	5																		4	0	0
Sertori, Mark	★											★				★				9	**9**			22	4	4
Smith, Paul					★	9	9	9	9	7	7	7	10²	10	10	10¹	10	10	10	10	10	10	10	27	1	10
Wallington, Mark	1	1	1	1	1	1	1	1	1	1			1	1	1	1	1							38	0	0
Own Goals								1																		2

FA Cup: 1988-89: 1st Round: Altrincham (A) 2-3.
Littlewoods Cup: 1988-89: 1st Round: Crewe Alex. (A) 1-1 (H) 2-1; 2nd Round: Southampton (H) 1-1 (A) 1-3.

LIVERPOOL (Division 1)

Team Manager Kenny Dalglish.
Club Address Anfield Road, Liverpool 4. Tel: 051-263 2361.
Current Ground Capacity 45,485.
Record Attendance 61,905 v Wolverhampton W., FA Cup 4th Round, 2 February 1952.
Year Formed 1892. Turned professional 1892.
Previous Names None.
Club Nickname "The Reds" or "Pool".
Club Colours All red with white trim.
Club Honours Football League: Div. 1 Champions 1900-01, 1905-06, 1921-22, 1922-23, 1946-47, 1963-64, 1965-66, 1972-73, 1975-76, 1976-77, 1978-79, 1979-80, 1981-82, 1982-83, 1983-84, 1985-86, 1987-88, Div. 2 Champions 1893-94, 1895-96, 1904-05, 1961-62. FA Cup: Winners 1965, 1974, 1986, 1989. Football League Cup: Winners 1981, 1982, 1983, 1984. League Super Cup: Winners 1985-86, European Cup: Winners 1976-77, 1977-78, 1980-81, 1983-84. UEFA Cup: Winners 1972-73, 1975-76. Super Cup: Winners 1977.

League History 1893-94 Div. 2; 1894-95 Div. 1; 1895-96; Div. 2; 1896-1904 Div. 1; 1904-05 Div. 2; 1905-54 Div. 1; 1954-62 Div. 2; 1962-Div. 1.
Most League Points in a Season (2 for a win) 68 in Div. 1, 1978-79. (3 for a win) 90 in Div. 1, 1987-88.
Most League Goals in a Season 106 in Div. 2, 1895-96.
Record Victory 11-0 v Stromsgodset in European Cup Winners Cup 1st Round 1st Leg, 17 September 1974.
Record Defeat 1-9 v Birmingham C. in Div. 2, 11 December 1954.
Consecutive League Wins 11 in 1982.
Consecutive League Defeats 9 in 1899.
Record League Appearances Ian Callaghan, 640 between 1960-78.
Record League Goalscorer—Career Roger Hunt, 245 between 1959-69.
Record League Goalscorer—Season Roger Hunt, 41 in Div. 2, 1961-62.

Liverpool: League Record, 1988-89 (Division 1)

Match Number	Date	Venue	Opponents	Result	H/T	Lge Posn	Attend
1	27.8.88	A	Charlton Ath.	W 3-0	1-0		21389
2	3.9.88	H	Manchester U.	W 1-0	1-0	3	42026
3	10.9.88	A	Aston Villa	D 1-1	0-1	5	41409
4	17.9.88	H	Tottenham H.	D 1-1	0-0	4	40929
5	24.9.88	A	Southampton	W 3-1	1-1	2	21046
6	1.10.88	H	Newcastle U.	L 1-2	1-1	3	39139
7	8.10.88	A	Luton T.	L 0-1	0-1	4	12117
8	22.10.88	H	Coventry C.	D 0-0	0-0	6	38742
9	26.10.88	A	Nottingham F.	L 1-2	0-0	7	29755
10	29.10.88	A	West Ham U.	W 2-0	0-0	4	30198
11	5.11.88	H	Middlesbrough	W 3-0	1-0	3	39489
12	12.11.88	H	Millwall	D 1-1	1-1	5	41966
13	19.11.88	A	Q.P.R	W 1-0	1-0	4	20065
14	26.11.88	H	Wimbledon	D 1-1	0-0	4	36188
15	4.12.88	A	Arsenal	D 1-1	0-0	4	31863
16	11.12.88	H	Everton	D 1-1	1-0	4	42372
17	17.12.88	H	Norwich C.	L 0-1	0-0	6	34325
18	26.12.88	A	Derby Co	W 1-0	1-0	3	25213
19	1.1.89	A	Manchester U.	L 1-3	0-0	5	44475
20	3.1.89	H	Aston Villa	W 1-0	0-0	4	39014
21	14.1.89	A	Sheffield Wed.	D 2-2	0-2	5	31524
22	21.1.89	H	Southampton	W 2-0	0-0	4	35565
23	4.2.89	A	Newcastle U.	D 2-2	1-1	5	30966
24	1.3.89	H	Charlton Ath.	W 2-0	1-0	6	30283
25	11.3.89	A	Middlesbrough	W 4-0	2-0	4	25197
26	14.3.89	H	Luton T.	W 5-0	2-0	4	31447
27	22.3.89	A	Coventry C.	W 3-1	2-1	4	23807
28	26.3.89	A	Tottenham H.	W 2-1	0-0	3	30012
29	29.3.89	H	Derby Co.	W 1-0	1-0	3	42518
30	1.4.89	A	Norwich C.	W 1-0	1-0	2	26338
31	8.4.89	H	Sheffield Wed	W 5-1	2-0	2	39672
32	11.4.89	A	Millwall	W 2-1	2-1	2	22130
33	3.5.89	A	Everton	D 0-0	0-0	2	45994
34	10.5.89	H	Nottingham F.	W 1-0	0-0	2	39793
35	13.5.89	A	Wimbledon	W 2-1	0-1	2	14730
36	16.5.89	H	Q.P.R.	W 2-0	1-0	2	38368
37	23.5.89	H	West Ham U.	W 5-1	1-1	1	41855
38	26.5.89	H	Arsenal	L 0-2	0-0	2	41718

Players: League Record, 1988-89 (Division 1)

Match Number	1	2	3	4	5	6	7	8	9	10	11	12	13	14	15	16	17	18	19	20	21	22	23	24	25	26	27	28	29	30	31	32	33	34	35	36	37	38	Apps	Subs	Goals
Ablett, Gary				3	11	3	★	2	2	2	2	2	2	2	2	2	2	2	2	2	2	2	2	2	2	2	2	2	2	2	2	2	2	2	2	2	2	2	34	1	0
Aldridge, John	8^3	**8**	8	8	8^1	8		★	★	8	8^1	8	**8^1**	★	8	**8**			8	8	$★^1$	8^1	8^1	8^1	8^1	8^3	8^1	8^1	8	8	8	8^1	**8**	8^1	8^1	**8^1**	**8^1**	8	31	4	21
Barnes, John	10	10	**10**				10	10	10	10	10	10			10^1	10	10	10	10^1	10	10	10	10	10	10	**10**	10^1	10	10^1	10	10^1	10^1	10	10	10^1	10	10^1	10	33	0	8
Beardsley, Peter	**7**	7	★	7^1	7^1	7	7	7	7	7^1	7^1	7	7	7	7	7	7	7	7	7	7	7	★	7^1	7^1	7^1	7	7^1	7	7	7^2	7	7	**7**		7	★	★	33	4	10
Burrows, David								6	6	6	6	3	3		★	6	6	6	6	3	3	3	3	3		★					★			3		★	★		16	5	0
Gillespie, Gary	2	2	2	2	2	2^1	**2**																	5	6	**6**	6	6	6	6	**6**								15	0	1
Grobbelaar, Bruce	1	1	1	1																		1	1	1	1	1	1	1	1	1	1	1	1	1	1	1	1	1	21	0	0
Hansen, Alan																																	6	6	6	6	**6**	6	6	0	0
Hooper, Michael					1	1	1	1	1	1	1	1	1	1	1	1	1	1	1	1	1																		17	0	0
Houghton, Ray	9	9	7^1	10	9	9	8	8	8	11	11	9	10	10^1	9	9^1	8	8	9	9	8	11	7	9	9^1	9	9	9	9	9	9^1	9	9	9	9	9	7^2	7	38	0	7
McDonald, Kevin					6		11	**11**																															3	0	0
McMahon, Steve	11	**11**									★	11	11	11	11	11	11	11	11	11	**11**		**11**	11	11^1	11^1	11	11	11	11	11^1	11	11	11	11	11	11	11	28	1	3
Marsh, Michael																								★															0	1	0
Molby, Jan	6	6^1	6	**6**	10^1	10	6												★	6	6	6	6	**6**															12	1	2
Nicol, Steve	4	4	4	4	4	4	4	4	4	4	4	4^1	4	4	4	4	4	4	4	4	4^1	4	4	4	4	4	4	4	4	4	4	4	4	4	4	4	4	4	38	0	2
Rush, Ian	★	★	9	9		★	9	9	9^1	9^1	**9^1**		9	**9**	★	9	9^1				9	9^1	9^1										★	★	★	★	9^1	**9**	16	8	7
Spackman, Nigel		★	11	11		6			**11**	★	★	6	6	6	6		★																						8	4	0
Staunton, Steve				★	★	**11**					★	★		8	**3**			3	**3**						3	3	3	3	3	3	**3**	3	3		3	**3**		3	17	4	0
Venison, Barry	3	3	3		**3**		3	3	3	3	**3**			3		3	**3**														★	6					3		14	1	0
Watson, Alex																										★									**7**				1	1	0
Whelan, Ronnie	5	5	5	5	5	5	5	5	5	**5**	5	**5**	5	5	5	5	5	5	5	5^1	5	5	5		5	5	5^1	5	5	5^1	5	5	5	5	5	5^1	5	5	37	0	4
Own Goals																																									0

FA Cup: 1988-89: 3rd Round: Carlisle U. (A) 3-0; 4th Round: Millwall (A) 2-0; 5th Round: Hull C. (A) 3-2; Quarter-Final : Brentford (H) 4-0; Semi-Final: Nottingham F. 3-1; Final: Everton 3-2 (winners).
Littlewoods Cup: 1988-89: 2nd Round: Walsall (H) 1-0 (A) 3-1; 3rd Round: Arsenal (H) 1-1, Replay (A) 0-0, 2nd Replay 2-1; 4th Round: West Ham U. (A) 1-4.

As usual, only one team will clean up this season.

CANDY AND LIVERPOOL F.C.
THE WINNING TEAM

CANDY DOMESTIC APPLIANCES LIMITED / NEW CHESTER ROAD / BROMBOROUGH / WIRRAL / MERSEYSIDE L62 3PE

LUTON TOWN (Division 1)

Team Manager Ray Harford.
Club Address 70-72 Kenilworth Road, Luton. Tel: (0582) 411622.
Current Ground Capacity 14,000.
Record Attendance 30,069 v Blackpool, FA Cup 6th Round replay, 4 March 1959.
Year Formed 1885. Turned professional 1890.
Previous Names None.
Club Nickname "The Hatters".
Club Colours White shirts with navy and orange trim, navy shorts and white stockings with orange and navy turnovers.
Club Honours Football League: Div. 2 Champions 1981-82; Div. 3(S) Champions 1936-37; Div. 4 Champions 1967-68. Football League Cup: Winners 1988.
League History 1897-1900 Div. 2; 1900 Failed re-election, 1920-37 Div. 3(S); 1937-55 Div. 2; 1955-60 Div. 1; 1960-63 Div. 2; 1963-65 Div. 3; 1965-68 Div 4; 1968-70 Div. 3; 1970-74 Div. 2; 1974-75 Div. 1; 1975-82 Div. 2; 1982- Div. 1.
Most League Points in a Season (2 for a win) 66 in Div. 4, 1967-68. (3 for a win) 88 in Div. 2, 1981-82.
Most League Goals in a Season 103 in Div. 3(S), 1936-37.
Record Victory 12-0 v Bristol Rov. in Div. 3(S), 13 April 1936.
Record Defeat 0-9 v Small Heath in Div. 2, 12 November 1898.
Consecutive League Wins 9 in 1977.
Consecutive League Defeats 8 in 1899-1900.
Record League Appearances Bob Morton, 494 between 1948-64.
Record League Goalscorer—Career Gordon Turner, 243 between 1950-64.
Record League Goalscorer—Season Joe Payne, 55 in Div. 3(S), 1936-37.

Luton Town: League Record, 1988-89 (Division 1)

Match Number	Date	Venue	Opponents	Result	H/T	Lge Posn	Attend
1	27.8.88	A	Sheffield Wed.	L 0-1	0-0		16433
2	3.9.88	H	Wimbledon	D 2-2	1-1	12	8067
3	10.9.88	A	Southampton	L 1-2	0-1	16	13214
4	17.9.88	H	Manchester U.	D 0-2	0-1	18	11010
5	24.9.88	A	Everton	W 2-0	0-0	15	26017
6	1.10.88	A	Nottingham F.	D 0-0	0-0	17	15340
7	8.10.88	H	Liverpool	W 1-0	1-0	13	12117
8	22.10.88	A	Middlesbrough	L 1-2	0-2	16	17792
9	25.10.88	H	Arsenal	D 1-1	0-1	16	10548
10	29.10.88	H	Q.P.R.	D 0-0	0-0	16	8453
11	5.11.88	A	Millwall	L 1-3	0-3	16	12511
12	12.11.88	A	Coventry C.	L 0-1	0-1	16	12631
13	19.11.88	H	West Ham U.	W 4-1	3-0	16	9378
14	26.11.88	A	Norwich C.	D 2-2	1-1	15	13541
15	3.12.88	H	Newcastle U.	D 0-0	0-0	15	8338
16	10.12.88	A	Derby Co.	W 1-0	1-0	15	15228
17	17.12.88	H	Aston Villa	D 1-1	1-0	16	8785
18	26.12.88	A	Tottenham H.	D 0-0	0-0	16	27377
19	31.12.88	A	Wimbledon	L 0-4	0-2	17	4899
20	2.1.89	H	Southampton	W 6-1	2-0	15	8637
21	14.1.89	A	Charlton Ath.	L 0-3	0-3	16	5212
22	21.1.89	H	Everton	W 1-0	1-0	13	9013
23	4.2.89	H	Nottingham F.	L 2-3	2-2	14	10465
24	18.2.89	H	Middlesbrough	W 1-0	0-0	13	8187
25	25.2.89	A	Arsenal	L 0-2	0-0	14	31012
26	11.3.89	H	Millwall	L 1-2	0-2	15	7838
27	14.3.89	A	Liverpool	L 0-5	0-2	15	31447
28	18.3.89	H	Sheffield Wed.	L 0-1	0-0	16	7776
29	21.3.89	A	Q.P.R.	D 1-1	0-0	15	9372
30	25.3.89	A	Manchester U.	L 0-2	0-2	17	36335
31	28.3.89	H	Tottenham H.	L 1-3	1-0	17	11146
32	1.4.89	A	Aston Villa	L 1-2	1-2	18	15640
33	15.4.89	H	Coventry C.	D 2-2	0-0	18	8610
34	22.4.89	A	Newcastle U.	D 0-0	0-0	18	18493
35	29.4.89	H	Derby Co.	W 3-0	1-0	18	8507
36	2.5.89	H	Charlton Ath.	W 5-2	4-0	16	10024
37	6.5.89	A	West Ham U.	L 0-1	0-1	17	18686
38	13.5.89	H	Norwich C.	W 1-0	0-0	16	10862

Players: League Record, 1988-89 (Division 1)

Match Number	1	2	3	4	5	6	7	8	9	10	11	12	13	14	15	16	17	18	19	20	21	22	23	24	25	26	27	28	29	30	31	32	33	34	35	36	37	38	Apps	Subs	Goals
Allinson, Ian	★				★	★				**8**					★																								1	4	0
Beaumont, David																								6	6	6	6	6	6	6	6	6	6	6	6	6	6	6	15	0	0
Black, Kingsley	11	11^1	11	11	11^1	11	11	11	11^1	11	11	11	11^2	11	11	11	11		★	11^1	11	**11**	11^1	11	11	11	11	11	11	11	11	11	11	**11**	11^1	**11**	**11**	11	36	1	8
Breacker, Tim	2				★			★	3												★	2	2	2	2	2	2	2	2	2	2	2	2	2	2	2	2	2	19	3	0
Chamberlain, Alec																																	1	1	1	1	1	1	6	0	0
Cooke, Richard																														★	★		★		★	★	★		0	6	0
Donaghy, Mal	6	6	6		6	6	6																																6	0	0
Dowie, Iain																					★	★				★	★	★	★	★	**8**								1	7	0
Dreyer, John	3			3	3	3	3	3		3	3											6	6			★						★	3^1	3	3	3	3	3	16	2	1
Foster, Steve	5	5	5^1	5	5	5	5	5	5	5	5	5	5	5	5	5	5	5	5	5	5	5	5	5^1	5			5	5	5	5^1	5	5	5	5	5	5	5	36	0	3
Grimes, Ashley		3	3									3	3									3	**3**	3		3	3	**3**			3	**3**							12	0	0
Harford, Mick	9	9	9	9	9	**9**	9^1	9	9			9	9	9		9^1	9	9	9	9^2		9	9^1	9	9	9	9	9	9	9	9	9		9	9^1	9^1	9	9	33	0	7
Harvey, Richard														3	3	3	3	3	3	3	**3**				3			★	3	3									11	1	0
Hill, Ricky				10	**10**	10	10	10	10	10	10	10			10	10	10	10	10	10^1	10	10	10	10	10	10	10	10	10^1	10	10	10^1	10	10	10	10	10	10	33	0	3
James, Julian											**2**																												1	0	0
Johnson, Marvin				6				6	6	6	6	6	6	6	6	6	6	6	6	6	6						5												16	0	0
Johnson, Robert		2	2	2	2	2	2	**2**	2	2	★	2	2	2	2	2	2	2	2	2	2	★																	19	2	0
McDonough, Darren								**4**	**4**																	5	8	8	4	4	7	**7**		★					9	1	0
Meade, Raphael																													**8**			★	**9**	★					2	2	0
Oldfield, David	10	10	8	**8**	**8^1**	8	**8**	8	★	★	8	★	10	10	**9**	★		11	11		**9**		★		★														15	6	1
Preece, David		8	**10**										4	4	4	4	4	4	4	4	4	4	4	4	**4**	**4**	**4**	**4**		**8**	4		4	4	4	4	4	4	26	0	0
Sealey, Les	1	1	1	1	1	1	1	1	1	1	1	1	1	1	1	1	1	1	1	1	1	1	1	1	1	1	1	1	1	1	1	1							32	0	0
Wegerle, Roy	**8**		★	★			★	★	8	9	9	8	8^1	8^2	8	**8**	8^1	8	**8**	8^2	8	8^1	8	8	8	**8**						8	8	**8**	8	8^1	8	8	26	4	8
Williams, Steve	4	4	4	4	4	4	4			4	4	**4**																											10	0	0
Wilson, Danny	7	7	7	7	7	7	7	7^1	7	7	7^1	7	7^1	7	7	7	7	7	7	7	7	**7**	7	7	7	7^1	7	7	7	**7**		4	7^1	7	**7^1**	7^2	7	7^1	37	0	9
Own Goals		1																																		1					2

FA Cup: 1988-89: 3rd Round: Millwall (A) 2-3.

Littlewoods Cup: 1988-89: 2nd Round: Burnley (H) 1-1 (A) 1-0; 3rd Round: Leeds U. (A) 2-0; 4th Round: Manchester C. (H) 2-1; Quarter-Final: Southampton (H) 1-1, Replay (A) 2-1; Semi-Final: West Ham U. (A) 3-0 (H) 2-0; Final: Nottingham F. 1-3.

David Preece (Luton Town) Match Magazine

MAIDSTONE UNITED (Division 4)

Team Manager Keith Peacock.
Club Address Watling Street, Dartford (shared with Dartford).
Current Ground Capacity 4,000.
Record Attendance 10,951 v Charlton Ath., FA Cup 3rd Round replay, 15 February 1979.
Year Formed 1897. Turned professional 1897-1927. 1971-.
Previous Names None.
Club Nickname "The Stones".
Club Colours Gold shirts, black shorts and black stockings with gold trim
Club Honours None.
League History 1989-Div. 4.
Record Victory 12-1 v Chislet C.W. in Kent Senior Cup, 4 October 1952, 11.0 v Swanscombe in Kent League, 8 December 1900, and v Dartford in Kent League, 12 April 1902.
Record Defeat 1-12 v Northfleet in Kent League, 13 February 1932, 0-11 v Margate in Kent League, 15 February 1936, v Northfleet in Kent League, 4 March 1936, and v Bromley in Kent Amateur Cup, 11 February 1950.

Maidstone United: League Record, 1988-89 (Vauxhall Conference)

Match Number	Date	Venue	Opponents	Result	H/T	Lge Posn	Attend
1	20.8.88	A	Cheltenham T.	W 4-0	1-0	1	1321
2	23.8.88	A	Wycombe W.	W 3-2	1-2	1	1674
3	27.8.88	H	Altrincham	W 7-2	3-1	1	624
4	29.8.88	H	Runcorn	D 2-2	1-0	3	1005
5	3.9.88	A	Boston U.	W 4-1	2-0	1	2701
6	7.9.88	H	Welling U.	W 3-0	1-0	1	1322
7	10.9.88	H	Kidderminster Har.	L 0-3	0-1	3	910
8	13.9.88	A	Enfield	D 1-1	1-0	3	815
9	17.9.88	A	Macclesfield T.	L 3-4	1-3	3	1342
10	24.9.88	H	Telford U.	L 1-3	0-1	6	548
11	28.9.88	H	Aylesbury U.	D 1-1	0-1	7	559
12	8.10.88	A	Northwich Vic.	L 0-2	0-1	8	700
13	15.10.88	H	Chorley	W 2-0	0-0	5	506
14	22.10.88	H	Yeovil T.	W 5-0	1-0	5	638
15	5.11.88	A	Kettering T.	D 3-3	2-1	5	2010
16	12.11.88	H	Stafford R..	W 3-0	0-0	4	636
17	26.11.88	A	Chorley	W 3-1	2-0	4	607
18	3.12.88	H	Barnet	W 3-2	1-0	4	1110
19	17.12.88	A	Altrincham	W 1-0	1-0	5	1017
20	26.12.88	H	Sutton U.	D 1-1	0-0	6	1063
21	31.12.88	H	Wycombe W.	L 1-3	0-2	6	1127
22	2.1.89	A	Sutton U.	D 1-1	1-1	6	1179
23	7.1.89	A	Telford U.	W 2-1	0-0	5	1146
24	21.1.89	H	Macclesfield T.	D 3-3	3-2	5	768
25	28.1.89	A	Aylesbury U.	W 2-1	2-1	4	1202
26	18.2.89	A	Fisher Ath.	W 2-0	0-0	5	743
27	1.3.89	H	Fisher Ath.	W 1-0	1-0	2	638
28	4.3.89	H	Cheltenham T	W 2-0	0-0	1	842
29	11.3.89	A	Yeovil T.	W 2-1	1-1	1	2235
30	18.3.89	H	Kettering T.	D 0-0	0-0	1	2861
31	25.3.89	H	Enfield	W 3-1	2-0	1	1341
32	27.3.89	A	Welling U.	D 0-0	0-0	2	2541
33	1.4.89	H	Boston U.	W 3-0	3-0	2	1033
34	8.4.89	A	Kidderminster Har.	W 6-3	3-1	2	1749
35	18.4.89	A	Weymouth	W 3-1	2-0	2	956
36	22.4.89	A	Stafford R.	W 2-0	1-0	2	1253
37	26.4.89	A	Northwich Vic.	W 4-1	2-0	1	1350
38	29.4.89	H	Weymouth	W 3-0	1-0	1	1851
39	3.5.89	A	Barnet	L 1-2	0-1	1	2650
40	6.5.89	A	Runcorn	W 1-0	1-0	1	1097

Players: League Record, 1988-89 (Vauxhall Conference)

Match Number	1	2	3	4	5	6	7	8	9	10	11	12	13	14	15	16	17	18	19	20
Ashford, Noel	9	9	9	9	**9**						9	9	9^1	9						
Beattie, Andy	5	5^1	5	5	5	5	5	5		**5**										
Beeney, Mark	1	1	1	1	1	1	1	1	1	1	1	1	1	1	1	1	1	1	1	1
Berry, Les	2	2	2	2	2	2	2	2	2	2	2	2	2	2	2	2	2	2	2	2
Butler, Steve			10^3	10^1	10^2	10	10	10	10^1	10^1	10^1	10	10	10^2	10	10	10^2	10	10	10
Charlery, Ken																				
Collins, Paul											★	6	6	**6**	6	6	6	**6**		
Cooper, Gary																				
Docker, John	★	★	$★^1$	3	3	3	3	9	9	9	**8**			★						
Gall, Mark	10^3	10^1	11^2	11^1	11^2	11^2	11	11^1	11^1	11	**11**		11	11^3	11^3	11^1	**11**	11^2	11	11
Golley, Mark	7^1	7	7	7	7	7	7	7	7	7	7	7	7	7	7	7^1	7	7	7	7
Goyette, Paul	**6**	**6**												★		8		★		
Hill, Mark	3	3	$\mathbf{3}^1$					3	3	3		3	3	3	3	3	3	**3**	3	3^1
Jacques, David				★	★	★	★				3		5	5			★	9	6	6
Mehmet, Dave																				
Pamphlett, Tony									5	4	5	4	4	4	4	4	4	4	5	4
Roast, Jesse	4	4	4	4	4	4	4	4	4	8	4	**5**			5	5	5^1	5	4	5
Rogers, Tony	11					**9**	**9**		★	★	★	11					★	$★^1$		**8**
Scotting, Allen															★					★
Sorrell, Tony		11	6	6	6	6	6	6	6^1	6	6	★			9	9^1	9		9^1	9
Stewart, Malcolm	8	8^1	8	**8**	8	8^1	8	8	**8**			8	8^1	**8**	**8**		**8**	8	8	
Own Goals																				

Match Number	21	22	23	24	25	26	27	28	29	30	31	32	33	34	35	36	37	38	39	40	Apps	Subs	Goals
Ashford, Noel		8	9	9	9^1	9	9	9		9	9^1	9	11	11	11	11^1	11	11	11	11	27	0	4
Beattie, Andy						6	6	6	6	6			6	6	6	6	6	6	**6**	6	22	0	1
Beeney, Mark	1	1	1	1	1	1	1	1	1	1	1	1	1	1	1	1	1	1	1	1	40	0	0
Berry, Les	2	2	2	2^1	2	2	2	2	2	2	2	2	2	2	2	2	2	2	2	2	40	0	1
Butler, Steve	10	10	10	10^2	10	10^1	10^1	10	10	10	10	10	10^2	10^3	10^1	10	10^2	10^1	10	10	38	0	26
Charlery, Ken								★	**11**	**11**	$\mathbf{11}^1$	11	9^1	9	9^1	9^1	$\mathbf{9}^1$		9		10	1	5
Collins, Paul	11	6	6^1	6	5																12	1	1
Cooper, Gary											6	6									2	0	0
Docker, John																					8	4	1
Gall, Mark	★	11	**11**	★		★	**11**	**11**	★	★	★						★	9^2	$★^1$	9^1	25	8	26
Golley, Mark	7	7	7	7	7	7	7	7^1	7^1	7	7^1	7	7	7^1	7	7	7^1	**7**	7	7	40	0	7
Goyette, Paul																					3	2	0
Hill, Mark	3			★	3	3	3	3^1	3	3	3	3	3	3	3^1	3	3	3		**3**	31	1	4
Jacques, David	**6**		★	8	6	8	8	8	8	5	5	5	5	5	5	5	5	5	5	5	24	6	0
Mehmet, Dave									9^1	8	8	8	**8**	**8**	**8**	**8**	8				9	0	1
Pamphlett, Tony	4	4^1	4	4	4^1	4^1	4	4	4	4	4	4	4	4^1	4	4	4	4	4	4	32	0	4
Roast, Jesse	5	5	**5**	5	★	5	5	5	5				★	$★^1$	★	★		★	3	★	27	7	2
Rogers, Tony	8^1		$★^1$	11	11	**11**	★														9	7	3
Scotting, Allen		3	3	**3**																	3	2	0
Sorrell, Tony	9	9	8		**8**													★	**8**		20	2	3
Stewart, Malcolm																		**8**	★	8	18	1	3
Own Goals																							0

FA Cup: 1988-89: 1st Round: Newport Co. (A) 2-1; 2nd Round: Reading (A) 1-1, Replay (H) 1-2.

MANCHESTER CITY (Division 1)

Team Manager Mel Machin.
Club Address Maine Road, Moss Side, Manchester M14 7WN. Tel: 061-226 1191/2.
Current Ground Capacity 52,600.
Record Attendance 84,569 v Stoke C., FA Cup 6th Round, 3 March 1934.
Year Formed 1887. Turned professional 1887.
Previous Names Ardwick.
Club Nickname "City" or "The Blues".
Club Colours Sky blue shirts with white trim, white shorts and navy blue stockings.
Club Honours Football League: Div. 1 Champions 1936-37, 1967-68; Div. 2 Champions 1898-99, 1902-03, 1909-10, 1927-28, 1946-47, 1965-66. FA Cup: Winners 1904, 1934, 1956, 1969, Football League Cup: Winners 1970, 1976. European Cup-Winners Cup: Winners 1969-70,
League History 1892-99 Div. 2; 1899-1902 Div. 1; 1902-03 Div. 2; 1903-09 Div. 1; 1909-10 Div. 2; 11910-26 Div. 1; 1926-28 Div. 2; 1928-38 Div. 1; 1938-47 Div. 2; 1947-50 Div. 1; 1950-51 Div. 2; 1951-63 Div. 1; 1963-66 Div. 2; 1966-83 Div. 1; 1983-85 Div. 2, 1985-87 Div. 1; 1987-89 Div. 2; 1989- Div. 1.
Most League Points in a Season (2 for a win) 62 in Div. 2, 1946-47. (3 for a win) 82 in Div. 2, 1988-89.
Most League Goals in a Season 108 in Div. 2, 1926-27.
Record Victory 11-3 v Lincoln C. in Div. 2, 23 March 1895.
Record Defeat 1-9 v Everton in Div. 1, 3 September 1906.
Consecutive League Wins 9 in 1912.
Consecutive League Defeats 6 in 1910 and 1960.
Record League Appearances Alan Oakes, 564 between 1959-76.
Record League Goalscorer—Career Tommy Johnson, 158 between 1919-30.
Record League Goalscorer—Season Tommy Johnson, 38 in Div. 1, 1928-29.

Manchester City: League Record, 1988-89 (Division 2)

Match Number	Date	Venue	Opponents	Result	H/T	Lge Posn	Attend
1	27.8.88	A	Hull C.	L 0-1	0-0		11653
2	29.8.88	H	Oldham Ath.	L 1-4	0-2	24	22594
3	3.9.88	H	Walsall	D 2-2	0-1	20	17104
4	10.9.88	A	Leeds U.	D 1-1	0-0	19	23122
5	17.9.88	H	Brighton & H.A.	W 2-1	1-0	13	16033
6	20.9.88	A	Chelsea	W 3-1	1-1	9	8856
7	24.9.88	A	Barnsley	W 2-1	0-0	8	9300
8	1.10.88	H	Blackburn Rov.	W 1-0	0-0	5	22111
9	5.10.88	H	Portsmouth	W 4-1	3-1	4	17202
10	8.10.88	A	Ipswich T.	L 0-1	0-1	4	15521
11	15.10.88	A	Plymouth Arg.	W 1-0	0-0	4	10158
12	22.10.88	H	Birmingham C.	D 0-0	0-0	3	20205
13	26.10.88	A	West Bromwich A.	L 0-1	0-1	4	14258
14	29.10.88	H	Sunderland	D 1-1	1-1	6	22398
15	5.11.88	A	Leicester C.	D 0-0	0-0	6	14080
16	12.11.88	H	Watford	W 3-1	0-1	7	21142
17	19.11.88	A	Bournemouth	W 1-0	1-0	4	9874
18	26.11.88	H	Oxford U.	W 2-1	0-1	3	20145
19	3.12.88	A	Crystal Palace	D 0-0	0-0	4	12444
20	10.12.88	H	Bradford C.	W 4-0	1-0	1	20129
21	17.12.88	H	Shrewsbury T.	D 2-2	0-2	3	19613
22	26.12.88	A	Stoke C.	L 1-3	1-0	5	24056
23	31.12.88	A	Swindon T.	W 2-1	1-0	4	10776
24	2.1.89	H	Leeds U.	D 0-0	0-0	5	33034
25	14.1.89	A	Oldham Ath.	W 1-0	1-0	4	19200
26	21.1.89	H	Hull C.	W 4-1	3-0	3	20485
27	4.2.89	A	Portsmouth	W 1-0	1-0	2	13207
28	11.2.89	H	Ipswich T.	W 4-0	2-0	2	22145
29	18.2.89	A	Birmingham C.	W 2-0	1-0	2	11707
30	25.2.89	H	Plymouth Arg.	W 2-0	1-0	1	22451
31	1.3.89	H	West Bromwich A.	D 1-1	0-0	2	25109
32	4.3.89	A	Watford	L 0-1	0-1	2	15747
33	11.3.89	H	Leicester C.	W 4-2	0-0	1	22266
34	14.3.89	A	Sunderland	W 4-2	3-1	1	16101
35	18.3.89	H	Chelsea	L 2-3	0-2	2	40070
36	25.3.89	A	Walsall	D 3-3	2-2	2	7562
37	27.3.89	H	Stoke C.	W 2-1	1-0	2	28303
38	1.4.89	A	Brighton & H.A.	L 1-2	0-1	2	12072
39	4.4.89	A	Shrewsbury T.	W 1-0	0-0	2	8271
40	8.4.89	H	Swindon T.	W 2-1	1-1	2	22663
41	15.4.89	A	Blackburn Rov.	L 0-4	0-2	2	16927
42	22.4.89	H	Barnsley	L 1-2	0-1	2	21274
43	29.4.89	A	Oxford U.	W 4-2	0-2	2	7762
44	1.5.89	H	Crystal Palace	D 1-1	1-0	2	33456
45	6.5.89	H	Bournemouth	D 3-3	3-0	2	30564
46	13.5.89	A	Bradford C.	D 1-1	0-1	2	12479

Players: League Record, 1988-89 (Division 2)

Match Number	1	2	3	4	5	6	7	8	9	10	11	12	13	14	15	16	17	18	19	20	21	22	23
Beckford, Jason											★			★				★		★		★	**9**
Biggins, Wayne	8	8						5¹	5¹	5	5	5	11	**11**	11	11²	11	11	11		★	**11**	11
Bradshaw, Carl													★	9					★				
Brightwell, Ian	5	5	5	5	5¹	5²	5					★	5	5	5	5	5	5	5	5²	5	5	5
Cooper, Paul																							
Dibble, Andy	1	1	1	1	1	1	1	1	1	1	1	1	1	1	1	1	1	1	1	1	1	1	1
Gayle, Brian	4	4	4	4	4	4	4	4	4	4	4¹	4	4	4	4	4	4	4	4	4	4	4	4¹
Gleghorn, Nigel	11		**11**								2	**2**	2	8				★	★	11	**11**	8¹	★
Hinchcliffe, Andy	3	3	3	3	3	3	3	3	3	3	3	3	3	3¹	3	3	3			3	3²	3	3
Hughes, Michael											**11**												
Lake, Paul	2	2¹	7	11	11	11	11	11	11¹	11		11						**3**	**3**	★	10	10	8
McNab, Neil	**10**	10	10¹	10¹	10	10	10	10	10	10	10	10	10	10	10	10	10	**10**	10	10			10
Megson, Gary																							
Morley, Trevor	9	9	9¹	9	9	9	9¹	9	9	9	9	9	**9**		9	9	9	9¹	9	9	9	9	
Moulden, Paul			★	8	8¹	8¹	8	8	8¹	8	8	**8**	8		8	8¹	8¹	8	**8**	8²	8	★	
Oldfield, David																							
Redmond, Steve	6	6	6	6	6	6	6	6	6	6	6	6	6	6	6	6	6	6¹	6	6	6	6	6
Scott, Ian																							
Seagraves, Mark		★	2	2	2	2	2	2	2	**2**		★		2	2	2	2	2	2	**2**	2	2	2
Simpson, Paul		**11**																					
Taggart, Gerald																							
Varadi, Imre	★	★	**8**																				
White, David	7	**7**	★	7	7	7	7¹	7	7¹	7	7	7	7	7	7	7	7	7	7	**7**	7	**7**	7¹
Williams, Bill										★													
Own Goals																							

Match Number	24	25	26	27	28	29	30	31	32	33	34	35	36	37	38	39	40	41	42	43	44	45	46	Apps	Subs	Goals
Beckford, Jason	**9**									★														2	6	0
Biggins, Wayne	11	11	11²	11	11²	11	**11¹**	11	11	**11**						11	11	**11**	★		★			29	3	9
Bradshaw, Carl													★			★								1	4	0
Brightwell, Ian	5	★													**2**					5¹	5	5	5	24	2	6
Cooper, Paul														1	1	1	1	1	1			1	1	8	0	0
Dibble, Andy	1	1	1	1	1	1	1	1	1	1	1	1	**1**							1	**1**			38	0	0
Gayle, Brian	4	4	4	4	4¹	4	4	4	4	4	4	4	4	4		4	4	4	4					41	0	3
Gleghorn, Nigel	★	★		9¹	9	9¹	9	**9**	**9**	9¹	9¹	**9**	9	★	★	9			**11**	11¹	11¹	11	11	25	7	7
Hinchcliffe, Andy	3	3	3				★	★	3	3	3			3¹	3	3	3¹	3	3	3	3	3	3	37	2	5
Hughes, Michael																								1	0	0
Lake, Paul	**8**	9	9	2	2	2	2	2	2	**2**		2	2	2	4	2	**2**		2¹	2	2	2	2	37	1	3
McNab, Neil	10	10	10	10	10	10¹	10¹	10	10	10	10	10¹	10	10			10	10	10	10	10	10	10	42	0	5
Megson, Gary		**5¹**	5	5	5	5	5	5	5	5	5	5	5	5	5	5	5	5	5	4	4	4	4	22	0	1
Morley, Trevor	★			8	8¹	8	8	8	8	8³	8¹	8		11	11¹	8¹	9	8		9	9	9¹	9¹	39	1	12
Moulden, Paul		**8**	8¹				★	★¹	★	7		★	8²	8	8		8	★	8	8	**8**	**8²**	8	29	7	13
Oldfield, David											11	11	11¹	**9¹**	9	**10**	★¹	9	9		★	★		8	3	3
Redmond, Steve	6	6	6	6	6	6	6	6	6	6	6	6	6	6	6	6	6	6	6	6	6	6	6	46	0	1
Scott, Ian															**10**									1	0	0
Seagraves, Mark	2	2	2																					21	2	0
Simpson, Paul																								1	0	0
Taggart, Gerald				3	3	3	**3**	**3**		★	2	3¹	3		★			2						9	2	1
Varadi, Imre																								1	2	0
White, David	7	7	7¹	7	7	7	7	7	7		7²	7	7	7	7	7	7	7	7	7¹	7	7	7	44	1	7
Williams, Bill																								0	1	0
Own Goals																				1						1

FA Cup: 1988-89: 3rd Round: Leicester C. (H) 1-0; 4th Round: Brentford (A) 1-3.
Littlewoods Cup: 1988-89: 2nd Round: Plymouth Arg. (H) 1-0 (A) 6-3; 3rd Round: Sheffield U. (H) 4-2; 4th Round: Luton T. (A) 1-2.

MANCHESTER UNITED (Division 1)

Team Manager Alex Ferguson.
Club Address Old Trafford, Manchester M16 0RA. Tel: 061-872 1661/2.
Current Ground Capacity 56,385.
Record Attendance 76,962 Wolverhampton W. v Grimsby T., FA Cup Semi-final, 25 March 1939.
Year Formed 1878. Turned professional 1885.
Previous Names Newton Heath.
Club Nickname "The Red Devils".
Club Colours Red shirts with red, white and black trim, white shorts and black stockings with red tops with three white bands.
Club Honours Football League: Div. 1 Champions 1907-08, 1910-11, 1951-52, 1955-56, 1956-57, 1964-65, 1966-67; Div. 2 Champions 1935-36, 1974-75. FA Cup: Winners 1909, 1948, 1963, 1977, 1983, 1985. European Cup: Winners 1967-68.
League History 1892-94 Div. 1; 1894-1906 Div. 2; 1906-22 Div. 1; 1922-25 Div. 2; 1925-31 Div. 1; 1931-36 Div. 2; 1936-37 Div. 1; 1937-38 Div. 2; 1938-74 Div. 1; 1974-75 Div. 2; 1975- Div. 1.
Most League Points in a Season (2 for a win) 64 in Div. 1, 1956-57. (3 for a win) 81 in Div. 1, 1987-88.
Most League Goals in a Season 103 in Div. 1, 1956-57 and in 1958-59.
Record Victory 10-0 v Anderlecht in European Cup preliminary round, 26 September 1956.
Record Defeat 0-7 v Blackburn Rov. in Div. 1, 10 April 1926, v Aston Villa in Div. 1, 27 December 1930 and v Wolverhampton W. in Div. 2, 26 December 1931.
Consecutive League Wins 14 in 1904-05.
Consecutive League Defeats 14 in 1930.
Record League Appearances Bobby Charlton, 606 between 1956-73.
Record League Goalscorer—Career Bobby Charlton, 199 between 1956-73.
Record League Goalscorer—Season Dennis Viollet, 32 in Div. 1, 1959-60.

Manchester United: League Record, 1988-89 (Division 1)

Match Number	Date	Venue	Opponents	Result	H/T	Lge Posn	Attend
1	27.8.88	H	Q.P.R.	D 0-0	0-0		46377
2	3.9.88	A	Liverpool	L 0-1	0-1	14	42026
3	10.9.88	H	Middlesbrough	W 1-0	0-0	10	40422
4	17.9.88	A	Luton T.	W 2-0	1-0	8	11010
5	24.9.88	H	West Ham U.	W 2-0	1-0	5	39941
6	1.10.88	A	Tottenham H.	D 2-2	1-1	5	29318
7	22.10.88	A	Wimbledon	D 1-1	1-0	7	12143
8	26.10.88	H	Norwich C.	L 1-2	0-0	12	36998
9	30.10.88	A	Everton	D 1-1	0-0	10	27005
10	5.11.88	H	Aston Villa	D 1-1	1-0	11	44804
11	12.11.88	A	Derby Co.	D 2-2	1-1	11	24080
12	19.11.88	H	Southampton	D 2-2	1-1	11	37277
13	23.11.89	H	Sheffield Wed.	D 1-1	0-0	12	30867
14	27.11.88	A	Newcastle U.	D 0-0	0-0	11	20350
15	3.12.88	H	Charlton Ath.	W 3-0	1-0	9	31173
16	10.12.88	A	Coventry C.	L 0-1	0-0	10	19936
17	17.12.88	A	Arsenal	L 1-2	0-2	10	37422
18	26.12.88	H	Nottingham F.	W 2-0	1-0	9	39582
19	1.1.89	H	Liverpool	W 3-1	0-0	6	44475
20	2.1.89	A	Middlesbrough	L 0-1	0-0	9	24411
21	14.1.89	H	Millwall	W 3-0	2-0	6	40931
22	21.1.89	A	West Ham U.	W 3-1	1-1	6	29822
23	5.2.89	H	Tottenham H.	W 1-0	0-0	5	41423
24	11.2.89	A	Sheffield Wed.	W 2-0	1-0	3	34820
25	25.2.89	A	Norwich C.	L 1-2	0-2	5	23155
26	12.3.89	A	Aston Villa	D 0-0	0-0	8	28332
27	25.3.89	H	Luton T.	W 2-0	2-0	6	36335
28	27.3.89	A	Nottingham F.	L 0-2	0-1	7	30092
29	2.4.89	H	Arsenal	D 1-1	0-0	10	37977
30	8.4.89	A	Millwall	D 0-0	0-0	10	17523
31	15.4.89	H	Derby Co.	L 0-2	0-1	10	34145
32	22.4.89	A	Charlton Ath.	L 0-1	0-1	10	12055
33	29.4.89	H	Coventry C.	L 0-1	0-0	11	29799
34	2.5.89	H	Wimbledon	W 1-0	0-0	10	23368
35	6.5.89	A	Southampton	L 1-2	0-1	10	17012
36	8.5.89	A	Q.P.R.	L 2-3	2-1	11	10070
37	10.5.89	H	Everton	L 1-2	1-1	11	26722
38	13.5.89	H	Newcastle U.	W 2-0	0-0	10	30379

Players: League Record, 1988-89 (Division 1)

Match Number	1	2	3	4	5	6	7	8	9	10	11	12	13	14	15	16	17	18	19	20	21	22	23	24	25	26	27	28	29	30	31	32	33	34	35	36	37	38	Apps	Subs	Goals
Anderson, Viv		2				★																						2	2	2	**2**								5	1	0
Beardsmore, Russell					★		★										★	5	5[1]	**8**	**5**		★	★	★	**2**	**8**	8	**8**	8	**8**	8	8	8	8[1]	8	8	8	17	6	2
Blackmore, Clayton	2	3	3	3	2		2	2	3	2	3	5	**5**	3	5	5	**5**				8[1]	5	5	5	**2**	★	3[1]	3	★							5[1]	**5**	**5**	26	2	3
Brazil, Derek																																					★		0	1	0
Bruce, Steve	4	4	4	4	4	4	4	4	4	4[1]	4	4	4	4	4	4	4	4	4	4	4	4	4	4	4	4	4	4	4	4	4	4	4	4	4	4[1]	4	4	38	0	2
Davenport, Peter	**9**	★	8	8[1]	11[1]	**11**	**11**	**11**																															7	1	2
Donaghy, Mal									6	6	6	6	6	6	6	6	6	6	6	6	6	6	6	6	6	6	6	6	3	3	6	3	3	3	3	6	6	6	30	0	0
Duxbury, Mike		6	6	6	6	6	6	6	**5**	★	**5**																				★	2	2	2	2	2	**2**	2	16	2	0
Garton, Billy		★	2	2	**5**	**2**	5	5	2		2	2	2	2	2	**2**																							13	1	0
Gibson, Colin									★	**3**																													1	1	0
Gill, Tony												★	★	5		★	★			**2**	7[1]	2						★											4	5	1
Hughes, Mark	10	10	10	10	10[1]	10[1]	10[1]	10[1]	10[1]	10	10[1]	10[1]	10[1]	10	10[1]	10	10[1]	10[1]	10[1]	10	10[1]	10	10	**10**	10	10	10	10	10	10	10	10	10	10	10	10	10[1]	10	38	0	14
Leighton, Jim	1	1	1	1	1	1	1	1	1	1	1	1	1	1	1	1	1	1	1	1	1	1	1	1	1	1	1	1	1	1	1	1	1	1	1	1	1	1	38	0	0
McClair, Brian	6	9	9	9	9	9[1]	9	9	9	9	9[1]	9	9	9	9[1]	9	9	9	9[1]	9	9	9[1]	9[1]	9[2]	9	9	9	9	9	9	9	9	9	9[1]	9	9	9	9[1]	38	0	10
McGrath, Paul	5	**5**	5	5		5													★	5			★	3	5[1]	5	5	**5**	5	**5**	5	5	5	5	5				18	2	1
Maiorana, Giuliano																					★						★		**11**	★	11			★					2	4	0
Martin, Lee	3													★	3	3	**2**	2	**2**		2	3[1]	2	2	★	**3**	2	★	★	11	3		**11**	11	**11**	11	11	3	20	4	1
Milne, Ralph												11	11	**8**	11[1]	★	11	11[1]	11	11	**11**	11	11	11	**11**	★	11[1]	**11**				**11**			★	7	7	**11**	19	3	3
O'Brien, Liam	★								★	5																													1	2	0
Olsen, Jesper	11	11	11	11	★	★		★	11	11	★																												6	4	0
Robins, Mark							★							★					★	★											7	★	★			★	★	★	1	9	0
Robson, Bryan	7	7	7[1]	7[1]	7	7	7	7	7	7	7	7[1]	7	7	7	7	7	7	7	7		7	7	7	7	7	7	7	7	7		7	7	7	**7**			7[1]	34	-0	4
Sharpe, Lee					**3**	3	3	3			11	**3**	3	**11**		11	3	3	3	3	3	★	**3**		3	11									★	**3**	3	★	19	3	0
Strachan, Gordon	8	**8**			8	8	**8**	8	**8**	8	8	8	**8**		8	8	8	8	**8**			**8[1]**	**8**	8	8	8													21	0	1
Whiteside, Norman																													6	6		6	6	**6**	6				6	0	0
Wilson, David													★							★	★										★								0	4	0
Own Goals																													1												1

FA Cup: 1988-89: 3rd Round: Q.P.R. (H) 0-0. Replay (A) 2-2, 2nd Replay (H) 3-0; 4th Round: Oxford U. (H) 4-0; 5th Round: Bournemouth (A) 1-0; Quarter-Final: Nottingham F. (H) 0-1.
Littlewoods Cup: 1988-89: 2nd Round: Rotherham U. (A) 1-0 (H) 5-0; 3rd Round: Wimbledon (A) 1-2.

Norman Whiteside (Manchester United & Northern Ireland) Match Magazine

MANSFIELD TOWN (Division 3)

Team Manager George Foster.
Club Address Field Mill Ground, Quarry Lane, Mansfield. Tel: (0623) 23567.
Current Ground Capacity 10,468.
Record Attendance 24,467 v Nottingham F., FA Cup 3rd Round, 10 January 1963.
Year Formed 1905. Turned professional 1905.
Previous Names None.
Club Nickname "The Stags".
Club Colours All amber with blue trim.
Club Honours Football League: Div. 3 Champions 1976-77; Div. 4 Champions 1974-75.
League History 1931-32 Div. 3(S); 1932-37 Div. 3(N); 1937-47 Div. 3(S); 1947-58 Div. 3(N); 1958-60 Div. 3; 1960-63 Div. 4; 1963-72 Div. 3; 1972-75 Div. 4; 1975-77 Div. 3; 1977-78 Div. 2; 1978-80 Div. 3; 1980-86 Div. 4; 1986- Div. 3.

Most League Points in a Season (2 for a win) 68 in Div. 4, 1974-75. (3 for a win) 81 in Div. 4, 1985-86.
Most League Goals in a Season 108 in Div. 4, 1962-63.
Record Victory 9-2 v Rotherham U. in Div. 3(N), 27 December 1932 and v Hounslow T. in FA Cup 1st Round replay, 5 November 1962.
Record Defeat 1-8 v Walsall in Div. 3(N), 19 January 1933.
Consecutive League Wins 7 in 1962.
Consecutive League Defeats 7 in 1947.
Record League Appearances Sandy Pate, 413 between 1967-78.
Record League Goalscorer—Career Harry Johnson, 104 between 1931-36.
Record League Goalscorer—Season Ted Harston, 55 in Div. 3(N), 1936-37.

Mansfield Town: League Record, 1988-89 (Division 3)

Match Number	Date	Venue	Opponents	Result	H/T	Lge Posn	Attend
1	27.8.88	H	Northampton T.	D 1-1	0-0		4042
2	3.9.88	A	Wigan Ath.	D 0-0	0-0	18	2514
3	10.9.88	H	Fulham	W 3-1	2-0	9	2734
4	17.9.88	A	Blackpool	D 1-1	1-0	9	4012
5	20.9.88	H	Gillingham	W 2-1	0-0	5	3153
6	24.9.88	A	Bury	W 1-0	0-0	4	2412
7	1.10.88	H	Notts Co.	D 1-1	0-0	6	5907
8	4.10.88	A	Southend U.	D 1-1	0-1	5	2436
9	8.10.88	H	Bristol Rov.	W 2-1	1-1	3	3381
10	15.10.88	A	Reading	L 0-1	0-1	5	6604
11	22.10.88	H	Cardiff C.	D 2-2	0-1	5	3566
12	26.10.88	A	Chester C.	D 0-0	0-0	6	1805
13	29.10.88	H	Bristol C.	D 2-2	1-2	10	3800
14	5.11.88	A	Preston N.E.	L 0-2	0-1	13	6434
15	8.11.88	A	Swansea C.	L 1-3	0-0	14	3526
16	12.11.88	H	Brentford	W 1-0	1-0	13	3181
17	26.11.88	H	Aldershot	D 1-1	0-1	11	2715
18	3.12.88	A	Chesterfield	W 3-1	1-1	8	4236
19	17.12.88	A	Wolverhampton W.	L 2-6	1-4	11	12134
20	26.12.88	H	Port Vale	L 0-1	0-0	14	5218
21	31.12.88	H	Huddersfield T.	W 1-0	0-0	13	4638
22	2.1.89	A	Bolton W.	D 0-0	0-0	13	4935
23	14.1.89	H	Wigan Ath.	L 0-1	0-1	13	2788
24	21.1.89	A	Fulham	D 1-1	1-1	14	4148
25	28.1.89	H	Blackpool	L 0-1	0-0	14	2738
26	4.2.89	A	Notts Co.	L 1-2	1-2	16	5924
27	11.2.89	H	Southend U.	W 4-0	2-0	13	2414
28	18.2.89	A	Bristol Rov.	D 0-0	0-0	15	4669
29	25.2.89	H	Reading	W 2-1	0-0	12	3012
30	28.2.89	H	Chester C.	W 2-0	0-0	9	2796
31	4.3.89	A	Cardiff C.	D 0-0	0-0	11	3217
32	11.3.89	H	Preston N.E.	L 0-3	0-0	13	4706
33	18.3.89	A	Northampton T.	L 1-2	1-0	13	2821
34	21.3.89	A	Bristol C.	L 0-2	0-1	14	5065
35	25.3.89	H	Bolton W.	D 1-1	1-1	13	3253
36	27.3.89	A	Port Vale	W 2-1	1-1	13	8198
37	1.4.89	H	Wolverhampton W.	W 3-1	1-1	13	9205
38	4.4.89	H	Sheffield U.	L 0-1	0-0	15	8524
39	8.4.89	A	Huddersfield T.	L 0-2	0-0	15	5327
40	15.4.89	A	Gillingham	L 0-3	0-0	15	2594
41	22.4.89	H	Bury	D 1-1	1-0	16	2826
42	25.4.89	A	Sheffield U.	W 2-1	1-0	14	11638
43	29.4.89	A	Brentford	L 0-1	0-1	15	5231
44	2.5.89	H	Swansea C.	D 0-0	0-0	15	2550
45	6.5.89	H	Chesterfield	W 3-1	2-0	15	4767
46	13.5.89	A	Aldershot	D 0-0	0-0	15	1549

Players: League Record, 1988-89 (Division 3)

Match Number	1	2	3	4	5	6	7	8	9	10	11	12	13	14	15	16	17	18	19	20	21	22	23	24	25	26	27	28	29	30	31	32	33	34	35	36	37	38	39	40	41	42	43	44	45	46	Apps	Subs	Goals
Anderson, Nick															**2**																																1	0	0
Beasley, Andy																																								1	1	1	1	1	**1**		6	0	0
Cassells, Keith	10	10	10[2]	10	10[1]	10[1]	10	10			10[2]	10	**10**						10	10	10	10	10	10[1]	10	10[1]	10[2]	10	10	10	10	10	10	10	**10**	10	10[2]	**10**	10	10	10	**10[1]**			10[1]	★	36	1	14
Chambers, Stephen			4						4	4								★																												★	3	2	0
Charles, Steve	11[1]	11	11	11	11	11	11	11	11[2]	**11**	**11**	11	11[1]	11	11	**11[1]**	★	8	8	11	11	11	11	11	11	11	8[1]	8	8	8[1]	8	8	8	8	8	8	8	8	8	8	8	11	8	11	8	8	45	1	7
Christie, Trevor																																			9[1]	9	9	9	9	9	9	9	9	9	9	**9**	12	0	1
Coleman, Simon	6	6	6	6	6	6	6	6	6	6	6	6	6	6	6	6	6[1]	6[2]	6[1]	6	6	6	6	6	6	6	6	6	6	6	6	**6**	6	6	6	6[1]	6	6	6		6	6	6	6	6	6	45	0	5
Cox, Brian	1	1	1	1	1	1	1	1	1	1	1	1	1	1	1	1	1	1	1	1	1	1	1	1	1	1	1	1	1	1	1	1	1	1	1	1	1	1	1								39	0	0
Foster, George	5	5	5	5	5	5	5	5	5	5	5	5	5	5	5	5	5	5	5	5	5	5	5	5	5	5	5	5	5				5	5	5	5	5	5	5	5	5	5		5	5	5	42	0	0
Garner, Paul										★	3								★																												1	2	0
Graham, Mike	2																																														1	0	0
Gray, Kevin																																													7		1	0	0
Hathaway, Ian																																★	★	7			★		**11**	★	★	★	★	★	11[1]	**11**	4	8	1
Hodges, David		9	9[1]	9	9	9	9[1]	9[1]	9	9	**9**	9	9	**9**	9[1]	9	**9**	9	**7**	4	4	4	4	4	4	4	4	4	4	4	4	4	4	**4**	★			★	**3**	**11**			10			10	37	2	4
Kearney, Mark	8	8	8	8	8	8	8	8	8	8	8	8	8	**8**	8	★	11	11	11	8	8	8	8	8	8	3	3	3	3	3[1]	3	3	3	3	3	3	3	3		3	3	3	3	3	3[1]	3	44	1	2
Kent, Kevin	9					★	★	★	10	**10**	4	4	4[1]	10	**10**	10	10	10		7	7	9	**9**	9	9	9	9[1]	9	9	9	**9**			9	4	4	4[1]	4	4	4	**4[1]**	8[1]	4	4	4	4	36	3	5
Kenworthy, Tony	3	3	3	3	3	**3**	**3**							★		8	3	3	3	3	3	3	3	3						5	5	5															19	1	0
Leishman, Graham																			★[1]	**9**	**9**				3	**8**	★	★		★	7	★	**9**						★								6	6	1
Lowery, Tony	4	4				**4**	4	**4**						4	4	4	**4**	4	4			★																									11	1	0
McKernon, Craig		2	2	2	2	2	2	2	2	2	2	2	2	2		2	2	**2**	2	2	2	2	2	2	2	2	2	2			2	2	2	2	2	2	2	2	2	2	2	2	2	2	2	2	42	0	0
Owen, Gordon	7	7	7	7[1]	7	7	7	7	7	7	7	7	7	7	7	7	7	**7**			★[1]	**7**	7	7	**7**	7	**7**	**7**	7[2]	**7**		**7**	7	★	7	7[1]	**7**	7	7	7	7	7	7	7			39	2	5
Pearcey, Jason																																														1	1	0	0
Place, Mark								3	3	3					★					★									2	2	★	9								6	11	**4**	5	**8**			11	3	0
Ryan, John	★			4	**4**					★	★	3	3	3	3	3	8		**9**				★		★	★	11	11	11	11	11	11	11	11	11	11	11	11				★	**11**	10			23	7	0
Stringfellow, Ian					★[1]	★					★		★	★	★		★	★																													0	8	1
Williams, Steven																																							★						★	7	1	2	0
Own Goals																		1															1																2

FA Cup: 1988-89: 1st Round: Sheffield U. (H) 1-1, Replay (A) 1-2.
Littlewoods Cup: 1988-89: 1st Round: Notts Co. (A) 0-5 (H) 1-0.

MIDDLESBROUGH (Division 2)

Team Manager Bruce Rioch.
Club Address Ayresome Park, Middlesbrough, Cleveland TS1 4PB. Tel: (0642) 819659/815996.
Current Ground Capacity 30,000.
Record Attendance 53,596 v Newcastle U., Div. 1, 27 December 1949.
Year Formed 1876. Turned professional 1889.
Previous Names None.
Club Nickname "The Boro".
Club Colours Red shirts with white shoulders and sleeves, white shorts and red stockings with white and blue hooped turnovers.
Club Honours Football League: Div. 2 Champions 1926-27, 1928-29, 1973-74.
League History 1899-1902 Div. 2; 1902-24 Div. 1; 1924-27 Div. 2; 1927-28 Div. 1; 1928-29 Div. 2; 1929-54 Div. 1; 1954-66 Div. 2; 1966-67 Div. 3; 1967-74 Div. 2; 1974-82 Div. 1; 1982-86 Div. 2; 1986-87 Div. 3; 1987-88 Div. 2; 1988-89 Div. 1; 1989- Div. 2.
Most League Points in a Season (2 for a win) 65 in Div. 2, 1973-74. (3 for a win) 94 in Div. 3, 1986-87.
Most League Goals in a Season 122 in Div. 2, 1926-27.
Record Victory 9-0 v Brighton & H.A. in Div. 2, 23 August 1958.
Record Defeat 0-9 v Blackburn Rov. in Div. 2, 6 November 1954.
Consecutive League Wins 9 in 1974.
Consecutive League Defeats 8 in 1954.
Record League Appearances Tim Williamson, 563 between 1902-23.
Record League Goalscorer—Career George Camsell, 326 between 1925-39.
Record League Goalscorer—Season George Camsell, 59 in Div. 2, 1926-27 (Div. 2 record).

Middlesbrough: League Record, 1988-89 (Division 1)

Match Number	Date	Venue	Opponents	Result	H/T	Lge Posn	Attend
1	27.8.88	A	Derby Co.	L 0-1	0-0		19432
2	3.9.88	H	Norwich C.	L 2-3	1-2	19	18259
3	10.9.88	A	Manchester U.	L 0-1	0-0	20	40422
4	17.9.88	H	Wimbledon	W 1-0	1-0	15	17709
5	24.9.88	A	Tottenham H.	L 2-3	1-1	18	23427
6	1.10.88	A	Coventry C.	W 4-3	3-1	15	14527
7	8.10.88	H	West Ham U.	W 1-0	1-0	10	19608
8	22.10.88	H	Luton T.	W 2-1	2-0	8	17792
9	26.10.88	A	Newcastle U.	L 0-3	0-1	10	23927
10	29.10.88	H	Millwall	W 4-2	1-2	7	19788
11	5.11.88	A	Liverpool	L 0-3	0-1	10	39489
12	12.11.88	H	Q.P.R.	W 1-0	1-0	7	20565
13	19.11.88	A	Arsenal	L 0-3	0-1	8	32294
14	26.11.89	H	Sheffield Wed.	L 0-1	0-1	11	19310
15	3.12.88	A	Nottingham F.	D 2-2	0-0	12	17742
16	10.12.88	H	Aston Villa	D 3-3	1-2	12	18096
17	17.12.88	H	Charlton Ath.	D 0-0	0-0	13	16065
18	26.12.88	A	Everton	L 1-2	1-2	14	32651
19	31.12.88	A	Norwich C.	D 0-0	0-0	15	16021
20	2.1.89	H	Manchester U.	W 1-0	0-0	13	24411
21	14.1.89	A	Southampton	W 3-1	0-1	11	13157
22	21.1.89	H	Tottenham H.	D 2-2	1-1	10	23692
23	4.2.89	H	Coventry C.	D 1-1	1-1	10	17352
24	18.2.89	A	Luton T.	L 0-1	0-0	12	8187
25	21.2.89	A	Millwall	L 0-2	0-1	13	11394
26	26.2.89	H	Newcastle U.	D 1-1	0-1	12	24385
27	11.3.89	H	Liverpool	L 0-4	0-2	12	25197
28	18.3.89	H	Derby Co.	L 0-1	0-1	13	16580
29	25.3.89	A	Wimbledon	D 1-1	1-1	13	5275
30	27.3.89	H	Everton	D 3-3	1-2	13	21351
31	1.4.89	A	Charlton Ath.	L 0-2	0-1	16	6696
32	8.4.89	H	Southampton	D 3-3	1-0	15	16983
33	11.4.89	A	West Ham U.	W 2-1	0-1	14	16217
34	15.4.89	A	Q.P.R.	D 0-0	0-0	13	10313
35	22.4.89	H	Nottingham F.	L 3-4	1-2	14	20778
36	29.4.89	A	Aston Villa	D 1-1	0-0	14	18590
37	6.5.89	H	Arsenal	L 0-1	0-0	16	21803
38	13.5.89	A	Sheffield Wed.	L 0-1	0-0	18	20582

Players: League Record, 1988-89 (Division 1)

Match Number	1	2	3	4	5	6	7	8	9	10	11	12	13	14	15	16	17	18	19	20	21	22	23	24	25	26	27	28	29	30	31	32	33	34	35	36	37	38	Apps	Subs	Goals
Barham, Mark																													11	11	**11**						★		3	1	0
Brennan, Mark	8	8	8	8	8	8	8	8	8	8	8	8[1]	8	8	8[1]	8[1]	8	8	8	8		**8**	8	**8**		8	**8**												25	0	3
Burke, Mark	★	11[1]	11			9[1]	**9**	**9**	9	9[1]	9	**9**	**9**	★	11	**11**	11			★	★[1]	★	9	★		★		11				★[1]	10	10	10	**11**	**11**	**11**	21	8	5
Cooper, Colin	3	3	3	3	3	3	3	3[1]	3	3	3	3	3	3	3	3	3	3	3	3	3	3[1]	3	3	3	3	3	3	3	3	3	3	3	3	**3**				35	0	2
Davenport, Peter											10	**10**	10	10	10	10	**10**	10	10	10[1]	10	10			10	10	10	10	10	10[1]	10	**10**			★[1]	10[1]	10	10	23	1	4
Gill, Gary	★																				**8**		★	**9**					8	8	8	**8**							6	2	0
Glover, Dean	11						★		★			★	★	9	9	9	9	**9**[1]	9	9																			8	4	1
Hamilton, Gary	**5**	5	5	5[1]	5	5	5	5	5	5	5	5	**5**	**5**	5	5[1]	5	5	5	5	5	5	5	5	5	5	5	5			★	11[1]	11	11	**11**	9	9	9	35	1	3
Kernaghan, Alan	6	★	★			4	★	★	★	★		★	★			★	★	★						★	9					★	★	★	8	8		★	★	★	5	18	0
Kerr, Paul			**10**	10	10	10	**10**	10	**10**	**10**								★			9[1]	9	**10**	10	8	**9**	9	8					★		8			8	18	2	1
Mohan, Nicky																					2		2												★	3	3	3	5	1	0
Mowbray, Tony	4	4[1]	4	4	4[1]		4	4	4	4	4	4	4	4	4	4[1]	4	4	4	4	4	4	4	4	4	4	4	4	4	4	4	4	4	4	4	4	4	4	37	0	3
Pallister, Gary		6	6	6	6	6	6[1]	6	6	6	6	6	6	6	6	6	6	6	6	6	6	6	6	6	6	6	6	6	6	6	6	6	6	6	6	6	6	6	37	0	1
Parkinson, Gary	2	2	2	2	2	2	2	2	2	2[1]	2	2	2	2	2	2	2	2	2	**2**		2		2	2	2	2	2	2	2[1]	2	2	2	2	2	2	2	2	36	0	2
Pears, Steve	1	1	1	1	1	1	1	1	1	1	1	1	1	1	1	1	1	1	1	1	1	1					1	1	1	1									26	0	0
Poole, Kevin																							1	1	1	1					1	1	1	1	1	1	1	1	12	0	0
Proctor, Mark																													5	5	5	5	5	5	5	5	5	5	10	0	0
Proudlock, Paul																											★												0	1	0
Ripley, Stuart	10	10	9	11	11	11	11	11	**11**	11[1]	11	11	11	11	7[1]	**7**		**11**	11	11	11	11[1]	11	11	11	11	11	9	9	**9**	9	9	**9**	9	9[1]	8	**8**		36	0	4
Senior, Trevor	**9**	**9**		9	9																																		4	0	0
Slaven, Berrie	7	7	7	7	7[1]	7[3]	7	7[1]	7	7[1]	7	7	7	7		★	7	7	7	7	7[1]	7	7[1]	7	7	7[1]	7	7	7[1]	7[1]	**7**	7[1]	7[2]	7	7[1]	7	7	7	36	1	15
Own Goals																																									0

FA Cup: 1988-89: 3rd Round: Grimsby T. (H) 1-2.
Littlewoods Cup: 1988-89: 2nd Round: Tranmere Rov. (H) 0-0 (A) 0-1.

MILLWALL (Division 1)

Team Manager John Docherty.
Club Address The Den, Cold Blow Lane, London SE14 5RH. Tel: 01-639 3143/4.
Current Ground Capacity 22,290.
Record Attendance 48,672 v Derby Co., FA Cup 5th Round, 20 February 1937.
Year Formed 1885. Turned professional 1893.
Previous Names Millwall Rovers, Millwall Athletic.
Club Nickname "The Lions".
Club Colours Blue shorts, white shorts and blue stockings.
Club Honours Football League: Div. 2 Champions 1987-88; Div. 3(S) Champions 1927-28, 1937-38; Div. 4 Champions 1961-62.
League History 1920-28 Div. 3(S); 1928-34 Div. 2; 1934-38 Div. 3(S); 1938-48 Div. 2; 1948-58 Div. 3(S); 1958-62 Div. 4; 1962-64 Div. 3; 1964-65 Div. 4; 1965-66 Div. 3; 1966-75 Div. 2; 1975-76 Div. 3; 1976-79 Div. 2; 1979-85 Div. 3; 1985-88 Div. 2; 1988- Div. 1.
Most League Points in a Season (2 for a win) 65 in Div. 3(S), 1927-28, and in Div. 3, 1965-66. (3 for a win) 90 in Div. 3, 1984-85.
Most League Goals in a Season 127 in Div. 3(S), 1927-28.
Record Victory 9-1 v Torquay U. in Div. 3(S), 29 August 1927, and Coventry C. in Div. 3(S), 19 November 1927.
Record Defeat 1-9 v Aston Villa in FA Cup 4th Round, 28 January 1946.
Consecutive League Wins 10 in 1928.
Consecutive League Defeats 11 in 1929.
Record League Appearances Barry Kitchener, 523 between 1967-82.
Record League Goalscorer—Career Derek Possee, 79 between 1967-73.
Record League Goalscorer—Season Richard Parker, 37 in Div. 3(S), 1926-27.

Millwall: League Record, 1988-89 (Division 1)

Match Number	Date	Venue	Opponents	Result	H/T	Lge Posn	Attend
1	27.8.88	A	Aston Villa	D 2-2	2-2		22449
2	3.9.88	H	Derby Co.	W 1-0	1-0	6	13060
3	10.9.88	A	Charlton Ath.	W 3-0	2-0	4	13375
4	17.9.88	H	Everton	W 2-1	2-0	3	17507
5	24.9.88	A	Norwich C.	D 2-2	0-0	3	16616
6	1.10.88	H	Q.P.R.	W 3-2	3-1	1	14103
7	15.10.88	A	Coventry C.	D 0-0	0-0	2	19369
8	22.10.88	H	Nottingham F.	D 2-2	0-1	2	16874
9	29.10.88	A	Middlesbrough	L 2-4	2-1	3	19788
10	5.11.88	H	Luton T.	W 3-1	3-0	2	12511
11	12.11.88	A	Liverpool	D 1-1	1-1	4	41966
12	19.11.88	H	Newcastle U.	W 4-0	2-0	3	15767
13	26.11.88	A	Southampton	D 2-2	1-1	3	15925
14	3.12.88	H	West Ham U.	L 0-1	0-1	3	20105
15	10.12.88	A	Tottenham H.	L 0-2	0-1	5	27660
16	17.12.88	H	Sheffield Wed.	W 1-0	0-0	3	11917
17	26.12.88	A	Wimbledon	L 0-1	0-0	4	11398
18	31.12.88	A	Derby Co.	W 1-0	0-0	3	16154
19	2.1.89	H	Charlton Ath.	W 1-0	0-0	3	17025
20	14.1.89	A	Manchester U.	L 0-3	0-2	4	40931
21	22.1.89	H	Norwich C.	L 2-3	2-2	7	13687
22	4.2.89	A	Q.P.R.	W 2-1	0-0	6	12381
23	11.2.89	H	Arsenal	L 1-2	1-0	7	21854
24	21.2.89	H	Middlesbrough	W 2-0	1-0	5	11394
25	25.2.89	H	Coventry C.	W 1-0	0-0	3	13021
26	28.2.89	A	Arsenal	D 0-0	0-0	3	37524
27	11.3.89	A	Luton T.	W 2-1	2-0	3	7838
28	18.3.89	H	Aston Villa	W 2-0	1-0	3	13206
29	25.3.89	A	Everton	D 1-1	1-0	4	27062
30	27.3.89	H	Wimbledon	L 0-1	0-0	4	13679
31	1.4.89	A	Sheffield Wed.	L 0-3	0-1	4	18358
32	8.4.89	H	Manchester U.	D 0-0	0-0	5	17523
33	11.4.89	H	Liverpool	L 1-2	1-2	6	22130
34	22.4.89	A	West Ham U.	L 0-3	0-3	7	16603
35	29.4.89	H	Tottenham H.	L 0-5	0-2	8	16551
36	3.5.89	A	Nottingham F.	L 1-4	0-1	8	15928
37	6.5.89	A	Newcastle U.	D 1-1	1-0	8	14435
38	13.5.89	H	Southampton	D 1-1	0-1	9	12011

Players: League Record, 1988-89 (Division 1)

Match Number	1	2	3	4	5	6	7	8	9	10	11	12	13	14	15	16	17	18	19	20	21	22	23	24	25	26	27	28	29	30	31	32	33	34	35	36	37	38	Apps	Subs	Goals
Anthrobus, Stephen																																				11	11	11	3	0	0
Briley, Les	8	8	8^{1}	8	8			8	8	8	8	8	8	8	8	8	8	8	8			8	8	8^{1}	8	8	8	8	8	8	8	8	8	8	8				31	0	2
Carter, Jimmy		★		★		★														7	7^{1}	7^{1}	7^{1}	7	7	7	7^{2}	7	7	7	7			4	11	★	★	★	14	6	5
Cascarino, Tony	10^{2}	10	10^{1}	10^{2}	10^{1}	10^{2}	10	10	10^{1}	10	10	10^{1}	10	10	10	10	10	10	10	10	10^{1}	10^{1}	10	10	10^{1}	10	10	10	10	10	10	10	10	10	10	10	10	10	38	0	13
Dawes, Ian	3	3	3	3	3	3	3	3	3	3^{1}	3	3	3	3	3	3	3	3	3	★	3	3	3									3	3	3	3	★	★	3	27	3	1
Horne, Brian	1	1	1	1	1	1	1	1	1	1	1	1	1	1	1	1	1	1	1	1	1	1	1	1	1	1	1	1	1	1	1	1	1	1	1	1	1	1	38	0	0
Horrix, Dean																	★					9								★	★	9	9	9	9				5	3	0
Hurlock, Terry	4	4	4	4	4	4^{1}	4	4	4		4	4^{1}	4	4	4	4	4	4	4	4	4	4	4			4	4	4^{1}	4	4	4	4	4		4	4	4	4	34	0	3
Lawrence, George	7	7	7	7	7	7		7	7	7																								★	7				10	1	0
McLeary, Alan	6	6	6	6	6	6	6	6	6	6	6	6^{1}	6	6	6	6	6	6	6	6	6	6	2	2	2	2	2	2	2	2	2	6	6	6	2	6	6	6	38	0	1
Morgan, Darren						8	8			4	★									8	8			4	4														7	1	0
O'Callaghan, Kevin	11	11	11	11	11^{1}	11	11	11	11	11^{1}	11	11^{1}	11^{1}	11	11	11	11	11	11	11	11	11	11	11	11	11	11	11^{1}	11	11	11	11	11	11					34	0	5
Reid, Wesley																																						7	1	0	0
Ruddock, Neil								$★^{1}$	★																														0	2	1
Salman, Danis	2	2	2	2			7	★	5		★				★				★	3	2			★	★					★	★	7	7^{1}	7					11	8	1
Sheringham, Edward	9	9^{1}	9^{1}	9	9	9	9	9^{1}	9^{1}	9^{1}	9	9	9^{1}	9	9	9^{1}	9	9^{1}	9	9	9		9	9	9	9	9	9	9^{1}	9	9					9	9^{1}	9^{1}	33	0	11
Sparham, Sean																								3	3	3	3	3	3	3	3		★		★	3	3		10	2	0
Stephenson, Paul											7^{1}	7	7	7	7	7	7	7	7	★																7	7		11	1	1
Stevens, Keith				★	2	2	2	2	2	2	2	2	2	2	2	2	2	2	2	2												2	2	2		2	2	2	22	1	0
Thompson, David	5									5									$★^{1}$			2	5	5	5	5	5	5	5	5	5			★	5				13	2	1
Treacy, Darren																																				8	8	8	3	0	0
Wood, Steve		5	5	5	5	5	5	5			5	5	5	5	5	5	5	5	5	5	5	5	6	6	6	6	6	6	6	6	6	5	5	5	6	5	5	5	35	0	0
Own Goals																								1												1					2

FA Cup: 1988-89: 3rd Round: Luton T. (H) 3-2; 4th Round: Liverpool (H) 0-2.
Littlewoods Cup: 1988-89: 2nd Round: Gillingham (H) 3-0 (A) 3-1; 3rd Round: Aston Villa (A) 1-3.

Terry Hurlock (Millwall), left, is beaten to the ball by Nigel Spackman (Q.P.R.), during last season's local derby. Match Magazine

NEWCASTLE UNITED (Division 2)

Team Manager Jim Smith.
Club Address St James' Park, Newcastle-upon-Tyne NE1 4ST. Tel: (091) 232 8361.
Current Ground Capacity 37,637.
Record Attendance 68,386 v Chelsea, Div. 1, 3rd September 1930.
Year Formed 1882. Turned professional 1889.
Previous Names Newcastle East End, Newcastle West End.
Club Nickname "The Magpies".
Club Colours Black and white striped shirts, black shorts and black stockings with two white hoops on the top.
Club Honours Football League: Div. 1 Champions 1904-05, 1906-07, 1908-09, 1926-27; Div. 2 Champions 1964-65. FA Cup: Winners 1910, 1924, 1932, 1951, 1952, 1955. European Fairs Cup: Winners 1968-69.
League History 1893-98 Div. 2; 1898-1934 Div. 1; 1934-48 Div. 2; 1948-61 Div. 1; 1961-65 Div. 2; 1965-78 Div. 1; 1978-84 Div. 2; 1984-89 Div. 1; 1989-Div. 2.
Most League Points in a Season (2 for a win) 57 in Div. 2, 1964-65. (3 for a win) 80 in Div. 2, 1983-84.
Most League Goals in a Season 98 in Div. 1, 1951-52.
Record Victory 13-0 v Newport Co. in Div. 2, 5 October 1946.
Record Defeat 0-9 v Burton Wanderers in Div. 2, 15 April 1895.
Consecutive League Wins 7 in 1904, 1909 and 1964-65.
Consecutive League Defeats 10 in 1977.
Record League Appearances Jim Lawrence, 432 between 1904-22.
Record League Goalscorer—Career Jackie Milburn, 177 between 1946-57.
Record League Goalscorer—Season Hughie Gallacher, 36 in Div. 1, 1926-27.

Newcastle United: League Record, 1988-89 (Division 1)

Match Number	Date	Venue	Opponents	Result	H/T	Lge Posn	Attend
1	27.8.88	A	Everton	L 0-4	0-2		41560
2	3.9.88	H	Tottenham H.	D 2-2	2-0	17	32977
3	10.9.88	A	Derby Co.	L 0-2	0-0	19	16014
4	17.9.88	H	Norwich C.	L 0-2	0-1	20	22801
5	24.9.88	A	Charlton Ath.	D 2-2	0-1	19	6088
6	1.10.88	A	Liverpool	W 2-1	1-1	18	39139
7	8.10.88	H	Coventry C.	L 0-3	0-3	19	22896
8	22.10.88	A	West Ham U.	L 0-2	0-0	20	17765
9	26.10.88	H	Middlesbrough	W 3-0	1-0	18	23927
10	29.10.88	H	Nottingham F.	L 0-1	0-0	18	24765
11	5.11.88	A	Q.P.R.	L 0-3	0-2	19	11013
12	12.11.88	H	Arsenal	L 0-1	0-0	20	24033
13	19.11.88	A	Millwall	L 0-4	0-2	20	15767
14	27.11.89	H	Manchester U.	D 0-0	0-0	20	20350
15	3.12.88	A	Luton T.	D 0-0	0-0	20	8338
16	10.12.88	A	Wimbledon	W 2-1	1-0	20	20146
17	17.12.88	H	Southampton	D 3-3	1-2	18	19986
18	26.12.88	H	Sheffield Wed.	W 2-1	2-1	18	25573
19	31.12.88	A	Tottenham H.	L 0-2	0-2	19	27739
20	2.1.89	H	Derby Co.	L 0-1	0-0	19	30555
21	14.1.89	A	Aston Villa	L 1-3	1-1	20	21010
22	21.1.89	H	Charlton Ath.	L 0-2	0-1	20	19076
23	4.2.89	H	Liverpool	D 2-2	1-1	19	30966
24	11.2.89	A	Coventry C.	W 2-1	0-0	19	16577
25	26.2.89	A	Middlesbrough	D 1-1	2-0	19	24385
26	11.3.89	H	Q.P.R.	L 1-2	0-0	19	21577
27	15.3.89	A	Nottingham F.	D 1-1	0-1	19	20800
28	22.3.89	H	Everton	W 2-0	1-0	19	20933
29	25.3.89	A	Norwich C.	W 2-0	1-0	19	22440
30	27.3.89	H	Sheffield Wed.	L 1-3	1-2	19	31040
31	1.4.89	A	Southampton	L 0-1	0-0	19	16175
32	8.4.89	H	Aston Villa	L 1-2	0-1	19	20329
33	15.4.89	A	Arsenal	L 0-1	0-0	19	38023
34	22.4.89	H	Luton T.	D 0-0	0-0	19	18493
35	29.4.89	A	Wimbledon	L 0-4	0-1	19	5206
36	3.5.89	H	West Ham U.	L 1-2	1-1	20	14202
37	6.5.89	H	Millwall	D 1-1	0-1	20	14435
38	13.5.89	A	Manchester U.	L 0-2	0-0	20	30379

Players: League Record, 1988-89 (Division 1)

Match Number	1	2	3	4	5	6	7	8	9	10	11	12	13	14	15	16	17	18	19	20	21	22	23	24	25	26	27	28	29	30	31	32	33	34	35	36	37	38	Apps	Subs	Goals
Anderson, John	2	**2**	2	2		2	2	2	2	2	2	2	2	2	2	2						5	5	5												**2**	2^{1}	2	21	0	1
Beasant, Dave	1	1	1	1	1	1	1	1	1	1	1	1	1	1	1	1	1	1	1	1																			20	0	0
Bogie, Ian		8	8	8	★			★									★																						3	3	0
Brazil, Gary																								11	★	9	**9**	★	★	★									3	4	0
Brock, Kevin																11	11^{1}	11	11	11	11	11	11		11	11	11^{1}	11	11	11	11	11		11	11	11	11	11	21	0	2
Cornwell, John					**2**		★		6	6		5	**5**	5	5	5																							8	1	0
Craig, Albert		★																																					0	1	0
Gourlay, Archie															★																								0	1	0
Hendrie, John	7	7	7	7	7	7^{1}	7	8	8	8	8	8	8	7	7	7^{2}	7	7	7	7	7	7	7	7^{1}	7	**7**	7	7	7	7	7	7	7	7					34	0	4
Howey, Stephen																																						★	0	1	0
Jackson, Darren	★	10^{1}	10	10	10^{1}	8	8	10	4	4	10	10	★		10	**9**																							13	2	2
Jackson, Peter	5																																						1	0	0
Kelly, Gary																											1	1	1	1	1	1	1	1	1				9	0	0
Kristensen, Bjorn																																8	2	**2**	**2**	★			4	1	0
Lormor, Anthony																																				10^{1}	7	**7**	3	0	1
McCreery, David	4	4	4	4	4	4	4	**4**			4	4	4	4	4	4	4	**4**	**4**	4	4	**4**	4	4	4	4	4	4	4	4	4	4	4	4	4	4	4	4	36	0	0
McDonald, Robert													9	9		★	8	8^{1}	8	8													★		★	★			6	4	1
Mirandinha, Francisco	**9**				9	9^{1}	9	9	9^{2}	9		9	★	10	**9**	**10**	**9**	★	★	**9**	9^{1}	★	9^{1}	**9^{1}**	**9**	★		**9^{1}**	**9^{1}**	9^{1}	**9**	**9**		★					22	6	9
O'Brien, Liam													7	8	8	8	2	★	★	★	6	9	10	10	10^{1}	**10**	10	10^{1}	10^{1}	10	10	10							17	3	3
O'Neill, Michael	11	9	9	**9**		**10**	**10**	11	10	10	**11**						$★^{2}$	**9^{1}**	**9**	★		★		★		★	★	★	★	★	★		10	**10**	10		10	**10**	17	10	3
Payne, Lee									**11**	**11**	★	11		**11**	11						**8**																		6	1	0
Pingel, Frank																					★	8	8^{1}	8	8	8	**8**	**8**	**8**	**8**	**8**		**8**		**7**	**7**			13	1	1
Ranson, Ray																		2	2	2	2	2			2	2^{1}	2	2	2	**2**	2	2			★				13	1	1
Robertson, John	8	11	11	11	**11**	★	★	★	★	★	9	**7**																											7	5	0
Robinson, David												★																											0	1	0
Roche, David																																	★					★	0	2	0
Roeder, Glenn													10				6	6	6	6		6	6	6	6	6					6	6^{1}	6	6	6	6	6	6	18	0	1
Sansom, Kenny																		3	3	3	3	3	3	3	3	3	3	3	3	3	3	3	3	3	3	3		3	20	0	0
Scott, Kevin		5	5	5	5	5	5	5	5	5	5								5	5	5		2	2	5	5	5	5	5	5	5	5	5	5	5	5	5	5	29	0	0
Stephenson, Paul				★	8	11	11	7	7	7	7																												7	1	0
Sweeney, Paul																															★	★	**11**	8	8	8	3	8	6	2	0
Thorn, Andy	6	6^{1}	6	6	6	6	**6**	**6**			6	6	6	6	6	6	5	5									6	6	6	6			9	9	9	9	9	9	26	0	1
Tinnion, Brian	3			3	$★^{1}$			3	3	3	3	3	3	3	3	3	**3**																						12	1	1
Wharton, Kenny	10	3	3		3	3	3						**11**	★		★	10	10	10	**10**	10	**10**					★							★			8		14	4	0
Wright, Tommy																					1	1	1	1	1	1										1	1	1	9	0	0
Own Goals									1																																1

FA Cup: 1988-89: 3rd Round: Watford (H) 0-0, Replay (A) 2-2, 2nd Replay (H) 0-0, 3rd Replay (A) 0-1.
Littlewoods Cup: 1988-89: 2nd Round: Sheffield U. (A) 0-3 (H) 2-0.

NORTHAMPTON TOWN (Division 3)

Team Manager Graham Carr.
Club Address County Ground, Abington Avenue, Northampton NN1 4PS. Tel: (0604) 721103/39500.
Current Ground Capacity 12,000.
Record Attendance 24,523 v Fulham, Div. 1, 23 April 1966.
Year Formed 1897. Turned professional 1901.
Previous Names None.
Club Nickname "The Cobblers".
Club Colours Claret shirts with white trim, white shorts and claret stockings.
Club Honours Football League: Div. 3 Champions 1962-63; Div. 4 Champions 1986-87.
League History 1920-58 Div. 3(S); 1958-61 Div. 4; 1961-63 Div. 3; 1963-65 Div. 2; 1965-66 Div. 1; 1966-67 Div. 2; 1967-69 Div 3; 1969-76 Div 4; 1976-77 Div. 3; 1977-87 Div. 4; 1987- Div 3.
Most League Points in a Season (2 for a win) 68 in Div. 4, 1975-76. (3 for a win) 99 in Div. 4, 1986-87.
Most League Goals in a Season 109 in Div.3, 1962-63, and in Div. 3(S), 1952-53.
Record Victory 10-0 v Walsall in Div. 3(S), 5 November 1927.
Record Defeat 0-10 v Bournemouth in Div. 3(S), 2 September 1939.
Consecutive League Wins 8 in 1960.
Consecutive League Defeats 8 in 1935.
Record League Appearances Tommy Fowler, 521 between 1946-61.
Record League Goalscorer—Career Jack English, 135 between 1947-60.
Record League Goalscorer—Season Cliff Holton, 36 in Div. 3, 1961-62.

Northampton Town: League Record, 1988-89 (Division 3)

Match Number	Date	Venue	Opponents	Result	H/T	Lge Posn	Attend
1	27.8.88	A	Mansfield T.	D 1-1	0-0		4042
2	3.9.88	H	Brentford	W 1-0	1-0	8	4488
3	10.9.88	A	Notts Co.	W 1-0	0-0	3	6084
4	17.9.88	H	Chesterfield	W 3-0	2-0	1	4520
5	20.9.88	A	Sheffield U.	L 0-4	0-2	4	11904
6	24.9.88	H	Bristol Rov.	L 1-2	0-0	8	3886
7	1.10.88	H	Aldershot	W 6-0	1-0	5	3477
8	4.10.88	A	Blackpool	L 1-3	0-1	6	3034
9	8.10.88	H	Huddersfield T.	L 1-3	0-3	8	3975
10	15.10.88	A	Swansea C.	L 0-1	0-1	15	4583
11	22.10.88	H	Bristol C.	L 1-3	1-0	17	3668
12	25.10.88	A	Fulham	L 2-3	1-1	17	4644
13	29.10.88	H	Reading	L 1-3	0-2	18	4355
14	5.11.88	A	Wigan Ath.	W 3-1	2-1	17	2472
15	8.11.88	H	Port Vale	L 1-3	1-1	17	3796
16	12.11.88	A	Cardiff C.	L 0-1	0-1	18	3280
17	26.11.88	A	Bolton W.	L 1-2	1-0	19	4446
18	4.12.88	H	Wolverhampton W.	W 3-1	2-1	18	6494
19	18.12.88	H	Gillingham	L 1-2	0-0	20	3829
20	26.12.88	A	Southend U.	L 1-2	1-2	20	5034
21	31.12.88	A	Chester C.	L 1-2	1-0	20	2733
22	2.1.89	H	Preston N.E.	W 1-0	0-0	21	4219
23	7.1.89	H	Bury	W 2-0	1-0	16	3463
24	14.1.89	A	Brentford	L 0-2	0-2	19	6043
25	21.1.89	H	Notts Co.	L 1-3	0-1	20	3704
26	28.1.89	A	Chesterfield	D 1-1	1-0	20	3920
27	4.2.89	A	Aldershot	L 1-5	1-3	21	2244
28	11.2.89	H	Blackpool	W 4-2	2-1	20	3303
29	18.2.89	A	Huddersfield T.	W 2-1	1-1	18	5802
30	25.2.89	H	Swansea C.	W 1-0	0-0	17	3900
31	28.2.89	H	Fulham	W 2-1	2-1	16	3948
32	4.3.89	A	Bristol C.	L 1-3	0-3	16	7197
33	11.3.89	H	Wigan Ath.	D 1-1	0-0	17	3443
34	15.3.89	A	Reading	D 1-1	1-1	16	3746
35	18.3.89	H	Mansfield T.	W 2-1	0-1	15	2821
36	25.3.89	A	Preston N.E.	L 2-3	1-1	16	9137
37	27.3.89	H	Southend U.	D 2-2	0-0	16	3707
38	1.4.89	A	Gillingham	L 0-1	0-0	17	3466
39	4.4.89	A	Bury	W 1-0	1-0	16	1965
40	8.4.89	H	Chester C.	L 0-2	0-0	17	2845
41	15.4.89	H	Sheffield U.	L 1-2	1-1	19	5030
42	22.4.89	A	Bristol Rov.	D 1-1	1-0	19	5568
43	29.4.89	H	Cardiff C.	W 3-0	1-0	17	3194
44	1.5.89	A	Port Vale	W 2-1	1-0	16	6604
45	6.5.89	A	Wolverhampton W.	L 2-3	0-2	16	15259
46	13.5.89	H	Bolton W.	L 2-3	2-0	20	3655

Players: League Record, 1988-89 (Division 3)

Match Number	1	2	3	4	5	6	7	8	9	10	11	12	13	14	15	16	17	18	19	20	21	22	23
Adcock, Tony	10	10	10	10^{3}	10	10^{1}	10^{2}	10	10	10	10	10^{1}	10	10^{1}	10	10	10	10^{1}	10	10^{1}	10	10	10
Anderson, Doug																				11	11	11	**11**
Berry, Steve													11	7^{1}	2	7	7	7	2	2	2	2	2
Blair, Andy													7	★		★							
Bodley, Mike																							
Cobb, Gary										**11**													
Collins, Darren																							
Craig, Albert																							
Culpin, Paul		★	8^{1}	8	8	**8**	8^{3}	**8**				8^{1}	8	8^{1}	8^{1}	8	8^{1}	8	**8**	**8**	8^{1}	8	8^{1}
Donald, Warren	4	4	4	4	4	4	4	4	4	4	4	4	**4**	4	4	**4**	4	4	4		4	4	4
Donegal, Glenville	11^{1}	**11**			★	★			**8**	8									★	★			
Flexney, Paul		5	5	5	**5**	5	5	5	5		5		5	**5**			5						
Garwood, Jason			11	11	**11**	11	**11**		★														
Gilbert, David	**9**	9	9	9	9	9	9^{1}	9^{1}	9	9	9	9	9	9	9	9	9	9	9^{1}	9	9	9	9
Gleasure, Peter	1	1	1	1	1	1	1	1	1	1	1	1	1	1	1	1	1	1	1	1	1	1	1
Johnson, Ian											★	5			5								
Longhurst, David	**8**							★															
McGoldrick, Eddie	5	2	2	2	2	2	2	2	2	2	2^{1}	2	2^{1}	2		2	11	5	5	5	5	5	5
McPherson, Keith	6						6	6	6	6	6	6	6	6	6	6	6	6	6	6	6	6	6
Preece, Andy																			★				
Quow, Trevor																							
Reed, Graham	2	6	6	6	6	6				**5**	**8**												
Sandeman, Bradley	★							★	★	★	**11**	7	★		7	★			**7**	7			★^{1}
Singleton, Martin	7	7	7	7	7	7	7	7	7^{1}	7	7												
Thomas, Dean	3	3	3	3	3	3	3	3	3	3	3	3	3	3	3	3	3	3^{1}	3	3	7	3^{1}	3
Wilcox, Russell																							
Williams, Wayne																5	2	2^{1}					
Wilson, Paul	★	8^{1}			★		★	**11**	**11**	★	★	11		11	11	**11**		11	11	4	3	7	7
Own Goals																							

Match Number	24	25	26	27	28	29	30	31	32	33	34	35	36	37	38	39	40	41	42	43	44	45	46	Apps	Subs	Goals
Adcock, Tony	10	10^{1}	10	10	10^{1}	10	10	10	10	10^{1}	10	10	10^{1}	10^{1}	10	10	10	10	10^{1}	10	10	10	10^{1}	46	0	17
Anderson, Doug		★																						4	1	0
Berry, Steve	11	11	11	11	11^{1}	11	11	11	11	11	11	11	11	11	11	11	11	11	8	7^{1}	7	**7**	7	34	0	3
Blair, Andy																								1	2	0
Bodley, Mike	5	5	5	5	5	5	5	5	**5**				8	8	8	3	3	**3**	3	3	3	**3**	3	20	0	0
Cobb, Gary																								1	0	0
Collins, Darren				★				8	**8**	8		★			★		★	**8**						4	4	0
Craig, Albert			7^{1}	**7**																				2	0	1
Culpin, Paul	**8**	8	8		8	8^{1}	8		★	★	8	**8**		★^{1}	**7**	8	**8**	★	★	8	8^{1}	8	8^{1}	33	6	14
Donald, Warren	4	4									5	5^{1}	5	5	5	5	5	5	5	5	5	5	5	37	0	1
Donegal, Glenville																						★^{1}		4	5	2
Flexney, Paul																								12	0	0
Garwood, Jason																								5	1	0
Gilbert, David	**9**	**9**		8	9^{2}	9^{1}	9	9^{1}	9	9	9	9												34	0	7
Gleasure, Peter	1	1	1	1	1	1	1	1	1	1	1	1	1	1	1	1	1	1	1	1	1	1	1	46	0	0
Johnson, Ian																								2	1	0
Longhurst, David																								1	1	0
McGoldrick, Eddie																								22	0	2
McPherson, Keith	6	6	6	6	6	6	6	6	6	6	6^{1}	6	6	6	6	6	6	6^{1}	6	6	6	6	6	41	0	2
Preece, Andy																								0	1	0
Quow, Trevor	★	7	9	9	7	7	7	7	7	7	7	7	7	**7**		7^{1}	7	7	7					17	1	1
Reed, Graham																								8	0	0
Sandeman, Bradley	★		★	★	4	4			★	**5**				★	★							★		8	14	1
Singleton, Martin																								11	0	1
Thomas, Dean	3		4	4			4^{1}	4^{1}	4	4	4	4^{1}	4^{1}	4	4	4	4	4	4	4^{2}	4^{1}	4	4	43	0	9
Wilcox, Russell													9	**9**	9	9	9	9	9	9	9	9^{1}	9	11	0	1
Williams, Wayne	2	2	2	**2**	2	2	2	2	2	2	2	2	2	2	2	2	2	2	**2**	2	2	2	2	26	0	1
Wilson, Paul	7	3	**3**	3	3	3	3	3	3	3	3	3	3	3	**3**			★	11	11	11	11	11	33	6	1
Own Goals				1					1																	2

FA Cup: 1988-89: 1st Round: Swansea C. (A) 1-3.
Littlewoods Cup: 1988-89: 1st Round: Colchester U. (A) 0-0 (H) 5-0; 2nd Round: Charlton Ath. (H) 1-1 (A) 1-2.

NORWICH CITY (Division 1)

Team Manager Dave Stringer.
Club Address Carrow Road, Norwich NR1 1JE. Tel: (0603) 612131.
Current Ground Capacity 26,812.
Record Attendance 43,984 v Leicester C., FA Cup 6th Round, 30 March 1963.
Year Formed 1905. Turned professional 1905.
Previous Names None.
Club Nickname "The Canaries".
Club Colours Yellow shirts with green pinstripe, green shorts with yellow trim and yellow stockings.
Club Honours Football League: Div. 2 Champions 1971-72, 1985-86; Div. 3(S) Champions 1933-34; Football League Cup: Winners 1962, 1985.
League History 1920-34 Div. 3(S); 1934-39 Div. 2; 1946-60 Div. 3; 1960-72 Div. 2; 1972-74 Div. 1; 1974-75 Div. 2; 1975-81 Div. 1; 1981-82 Div. 2; 1982-85 Div. 1; 1985-86 Div. 2; 1986- Div. 1.
Most League Points in a Season (2 for a win) 64 in Div. 3(S), 1950-51. (3 for a win) 84 in Div. 2, 1985-86.
Most League Goals in a Season 99 in Div. 3(S), 1952-53.
Record Victory 10-2 v Coventry C. in Div. 3(S), 15 March 1930.
Record Defeat 2-10 v Swindon T. in Southern League, 5 September 1908.
Consecutive League Wins 9 in 1985-86.
Consecutive League Defeats 7 in 1935 and 1957.
Record League Appearances Ron Ashman, 592 between 1947-64.
Record League Goalscorer—Career Johnny Gavin, 122 between 1948-58.
Record League Goalscorer—Season Ralph Hunt, 31 in Div. 3(S), 1955-56.

Norwich City: League Record, 1988-89 (Division 1)

Match Number	Date	Venue	Opponents	Result	H/T	Lge Posn	Attend
1	27.8.88	H	Nottingham F.	W 2-1	2-0		13488
2	3.9.88	A	Middlesbrough	W 3-2	2-1	4	18259
3	10.9.88	H	Q.P.R.	W 1-0	0-0	2	11174
4	17.9.88	A	Newcastle U.	W 2-0	1-0	1	22801
5	24.9.88	H	Millwall	D 2-2	0-0	1	16616
6	1.10.88	H	Charlton Ath.	L 1-3	1-1	1	11470
7	8.10.88	A	Derby Co.	W 1-0	0-0	1	14117
8	22.10.88	H	Tottenham H.	W 3-1	2-0	1	20330
9	26.10.88	A	Manchester U.	W 2-1	0-0	1	36998
10	29.10.88	H	Southampton	D 1-1	0-0	1	14808
11	5.11.88	A	Wimbledon	W 2-0	1-0	1	5853
12	12.11.88	H	Sheffield Wed.	D 1-1	1-0	1	14353
13	19.11.88	A	Everton	D 1-1	0-0	1	28118
14	26.11.88	H	Luton T.	D 2-2	1-1	1	13541
15	3.12.88	A	Aston Villa	L 1-3	1-1	1	19653
16	10.12.88	H	Arsenal	D 0-0	0-0	1	23069
17	17.12.88	A	Liverpool	W 1-0	0-0	1	34325
18	27.12.88	H	West Ham U.	W 2-1	0-0	1	17491
19	31.12.88	H	Middlesbrough	D 0-0	0-0	2	16021
20	2.1.89	A	Q.P.R.	D 1-1	0-0	2	12461
21	14.1.89	H	Coventry C.	L 1-2	0-0	2	14399
22	22.1.89	A	Millwall	W 3-2	2-2	2	13687
23	4.2.89	A	Charlton Ath.	W 2-1	0-0	2	7518
24	11.2.89	H	Derby Co.	W 1-0	0-0	2	17227
25	21.2.89	A	Tottenham H.	L 1-2	0-1	2	19120
26	25.2.89	H	Manchester U.	W 2-1	2-0	2	23155
27	11.3.89	H	Wimbledon	W 1-0	0-0	2	15159
28	25.3.89	H	Newcastle U.	L 0-2	0-1	2	22440
29	27.3.89	A	West Ham U.	W 2-0	0-0	2	27265
30	1.4.89	H	Liverpool	L 0-1	0-1	3	26338
31	5.4.89	A	Nottingham F.	L 0-2	0-2	3	19872
32	8.4.89	A	Coventry C.	L 1-2	1-1	3	12740
33	19.4.89	A	Southampton	D 0-0	0-0	3	14403
34	22.4.89	H	Aston Villa	D 2-2	0-0	3	14551
35	1.5.89	A	Arsenal	L 0-5	0-2	4	28449
36	6.5.89	H	Everton	W 1-0	0-0	3	13239
37	13.5.89	A	Luton T.	L 0-1	0-0	4	10862
38	17.5.89	A	Sheffield Wed.	D 2-2	0-0	4	16230

Players: League Record, 1988-89 (Division 1)

Match Number	1	2	3	4	5	6	7	8	9	10	11	12	13	14	15	16	17	18	19	20	21	22	23	24	25	26	27	28	29	30	31	32	33	34	35	36	37	38	Apps	Subs	Goals
Allen, Malcolm	★	★		★		★	★				★[1]	9	9[1]	**9**	9	★							9[1]	9	9	9[1]	9	9	9[1]	**9**	**9**		8	8			★		15	8	5
Bowen, Mark	3[1]	3	3	3	3	**3**	3	3	3	3	3	3	3	3	3	3	3	3	3	3	3	3[1]	3	**3**	3	3	3	3	3	3	3	3		3	3			3	35	0	2
Butterworth, Ian	4	4	4	4	4	4	4	4	4	4	4	4	4	4	4	4		★	★	4	4	4[1]	4	4	**4**	4[1]	4	4	4	4	4	4	4	4	4	4	4	4	35	2	2
Coney, Dean																													★	8	8	8	9	9[1]	9		★		6	2	1
Cook, Paul																																	★			11	11	11	3	1	0
Crook, Ian	6	6	**6**	6	6[1]	6	**6**	6	**6**	6					★		4	4	4	6				★	★			★	★		★	★	10	10		3	3	10	19	7	1
Culverhouse, Ian	2	2	2	2	2	2	2	2	2	2	2	2	2	2	2	2	2	2	2	2	2	2	2	2	2	2	2	**2**	2	2	**2**	2	2	2	2	2	2	2	38	0	0
Fleck, Robert	**8**[1]	**8**[1]	8	8[1]	8	**8**	**8**	8[1]	8	8[1]	**8**	**8**	**8**	8	**8**	**8**	8	8	**8**	★	8	8[1]	8	8[1]				★	**8**	★	★	9[1]			8	8	8	8[1]	29	4	9
Fox, Ruel									★	★																							**11**	★					1	3	0
Gordon, Dale	7	**7**	7	7[1]	7	7	7	7	7	7	7	7	7	7[1]	**7**	7	7	7[1]	7	7	7[1]	7	7	7	7	7	7	7	7	7	7	7	7	**7**	7	7[1]	**7**	7	38	0	5
Gunn, Bryan	1	1	1	1	1	1	1	1	1	1	1	1	1	1	1	1	1	1	1	1	1	1	1	1	1	1	1	1	1	1	1	1	1		1	1	1	1	37	0	0
Linighan, Andy	5	5	5	5	5	5[1]	5	5[1]	5	5	5[1]	5	5	5	5	5	5	5	5	**5**	5	5	5	5	5	5	5	5	5[1]	5	5	5	5	5	5	**5**		5	37	0	4
Phelan, Mike	10	10	10[1]	10	10	10	10	10	10[1]	10	10	10	10	10	10	10	10	10	10	10	10	10	10	10	10	10	10	10	**10**	10	10	**10**	★	11	10	10	**10**		36	1	2
Putney, Trevor	11	11	11	11	**11**	11	11				11	11[1]	11	11	11[1]	11	11	11	**11**	★	11	11	11	11	11[1]	11	11[1]	11	11	11	11	11	**3**		11	★	5		31	2	4
Rosario, Robert	9	9[1]	9	**9**	9[1]	9	9	9[1]	9	9	9			★	★	9	9	9	9	**9**	9	9			8	8	8	**8**								9	9	9[1]	25	2	4
Sheffield, Jonathan																																		1					1	0	0
Taylor, Alan												★	★						★	8[1]																			1	3	1
Townsend, Andy		★	★		★	★	★	11	11[1]	**11**	6	6	6	6	6	6	6[1]	**6**[1]	6	11	6	6	6[1]	6	6	6	6	6	6	6	6	6	6	6[1]	6	6	6	6	31	5	5
Own Goals		1					1							1																											3

FA Cup: 1988-89: 3rd Round: Port Vale (A) 3-1; 4th Round: Sutton U. (H) 8-0; 5th Round: Sheffield U. (H) 3-2; Quarter-Final: West Ham U. (A) 0-0, Replay (H) 3-1; Semi-Final: Everton 0-1.
Littlewoods Cup: 1988-89: 2nd Round: Preston N.E. (H) 2-0 (A) 3-0; 3rd Round: Leicester C. (A) 0-2.

NOTTINGHAM FOREST (Division 1)

Team Manager Brian Clough.
Club Address City Ground, Nottingham NG2 5FJ. Tel: (0602) 822202.
Current Ground Capacity 35,000.
Record Attendance 49,945 v Manchester U., Div. 1, 28 October 1967.
Year Formed 1865. Turned professional 1889.
Previous Names None.
Club Nickname "The Reds".
Club Colours Red shirts with white pinstripe, white shorts and red stockings.
Club Honours Football League: Div. 1 Champions 1977-78; Div. 2 Champions 1906-07, 1921-22; Div. 3(S) Champions 1950-51. FA Cup: Winners 1898, 1959. Football League Cup: Winners 1978, 1979, 1989. European Cup: Winners 1978-79, 1979-80. Super Cup: Winners 1979-80.
League History 1892-1906 Div. 1; 1906-1907 Div. 2; 1907-1911 Div. 1; 1911-22 Div. 2; 1922-25 Div. 1; 1925-49 Div. 2; 1949-51 Div. 3(S); 1951-57 Div. 2; 1957-72 Div. 1; 1972-77 Div. 2; 1977- Div. 1.
Most League Points in a Season (2 for a win) 70 in Div. 3(S), 1950-51. (3 for a win) 74 in Div. 1, 1983-84.
Most League Goals in a Season 110 in Div. 3(S), 1950-51.
Record Victory 14-0 v Clapton in FA Cup 1st Round, 1890-91.
Record Defeat 1-9 v Blackburn Rov. in Div. 2, 10 April 1937.
Consecutive League Wins 7 in 1892, 1906, 1921 and 1979.
Consecutive League Defeats 14 in 1913.
Record League Appearances Bob McKinlay, 614 between 1951-70.
Record League Goalscorer—Career Grenville Morris, 199 between 1898-1913.
Record League Goalscorer—Season Wally Ardron, 36 in Div. 3(S), 1950-51.

Nottingham Forest: League Record, 1988-89 (Division 1)

Match Number	Date	Venue	Opponents	Result	H/T	Lge Posn	Attend
1	27.8.88	A	Norwich C.	L 1-2	0-2		13488
2	3.9.88	H	Sheffield Wed.	D 1-1	1-0	13	18963
3	10.9.88	A	Everton	D 1-1	1-0	14	34003
4	17.9.88	H	Derby Co.	D 1-1	0-0	14	24818
5	24.9.88	A	Aston Villa	D 1-1	0-1	14	23029
6	1.10.88	H	Luton T.	D 0-0	0-0	16	15340
7	8.10.88	A	Q.P.R.	W 2-1	1-1	11	11205
8	22.10.88	A	Millwall	D 2-2	1-0	14	16874
9	26.10.88	H	Liverpool	W 2-1	0-0	9	29755
10	29.10.88	A	Newcastle U.	W 1-0	0-0	5	24765
11	6.11.88	H	Arsenal	L 1-4	1-1	9	19038
12	12.11.88	A	West Ham U.	D 3-3	3-2	9	21682
13	19.11.88	H	Coventry C.	D 0-0	0-0	9	17250
14	26.11.88	A	Charlton Ath.	W 1-0	1-0	8	6411
15	3.12.88	H	Middlesbrough	D 2-2	0-0	10	17742
16	10.12.88	A	Southampton	D 1-1	0-1	9	15259
17	18.12.88	H	Wimbledon	L 0-1	0-0	9	16427
18	26.12.88	A	Manchester U.	L 0-2	0-1	12	39582
19	31.12.88	A	Sheffield Wed.	W 3-0	3-0	11	20407
20	2.1.89	H	Everton	W 2-0	1-0	8	26008
21	15.1.89	A	Tottenham H.	W 2-1	2-1	6	16903
22	21.1.89	H	Aston Villa	W 4-0	1-0	5	22662
23	4.2.89	A	Luton T.	W 3-2	2-2	4	10465
24	11.2.89	H	Q.P.R.	D 0-0	0-0	4	19690
25	11.3.89	A	Arsenal	W 3-1	3-1	5	39639
26	15.3.89	H	Newcastle U.	D 1-1	1-0	5	20800
27	22.3.89	H	Tottenham H.	L 1-2	0-0	5	23098
28	25.3.89	A	Derby Co.	W 2-0	1-0	5	25174
29	27.3.89	H	Manchester U.	W 2-0	1-0	5	30092
30	1.4.89	A	Wimbledon	L 1-4	1-2	5	7867
31	5.4.89	H	Norwich C.	W 2-0	2-0	4	19872
32	12.4.89	H	Southampton	W 3-0	2-0	4	18948
33	22.4.89	A	Middlesbrough	W 4-3	2-1	4	20778
34	3.5.89	H	Millwall	W 4-1	1-0	4	15928
35	10.5.89	A	Liverpool	L 0-1	0-0	4	39793
36	13.5.89	H	Charlton Ath.	W 4-0	3-0	3	17637
37	15.5.89	A	Coventry C.	D 2-2	0-0	3	14003
38	18.5.89	H	West Ham U.	L 1-2	1-2	3	20843

Players: League Record, 1988-89 (Division 1)

Match Number	1	2	3	4	5	6	7	8	9	10	11	12	13	14	15	16	17	18	19	20	21	22	23	24	25	26	27	28	29	30	31	32	33	34	35	36	37	38	Apps	Subs	Goals
Carr, Franz	★		★	★	★^{1}	★	7								7	7	7	7	**7**	**7**	7	**7**	7	7	7^1	7	7							7	**7**	7^1	7		18	5	3
Chapman, Lee								10	10	10^1	10	**10**	10	**10**	10^2	10	10	**10**	10	10	10	10	10	**10**	10	10	10	10^1	10^1	10	**10**	10	10^2		10	**10**	10	10^1	30	0	8
Charles, Gary											**7**																												1	0	0
Chettle, Stephen	2^1	2	2	2	2	2	2	2	2	2	2	2	2	2	2	4	**2**				★	4	4	4				★	★	2	2		★			★^{1}		5	23	5	2
Clough, Nigel	9	9	9	9	9	9	9^1	9	9	9	9^1	9^2	9	9	9	9^1	9	**9**			9^1	9	9^2	9	9^1	9^1	9	9	9	9^1	9^1	**9**^{1}	9	9	9	9	9^1	9	36	0	14
Crosby, Gary	7	7	**7**	7	7	7	11	7	7	7		★	**7**									★																	11	2	0
Crossley, Mark									1	1																													2	0	0
Foster, Colin	5	5	5	5^1	5	5	5^1	5	5	5	5	5	5	5	5	5	5														★								17	1	2
Gaynor, Tommy			10	**10**	**10**	**10**	10	11										★	9^1	9^1								**7**	7	7	7	7^1	**7**	10^1	★	★		7	16	3	4
Hodge, Steve	10	10	6	6	6	6	6	6^2	6	6	6	6^1	6	6	6		★	6	6^1	6	6	6^1	6	6	6	6	6	6^1	6	6	6	6	6	6^1				6	33	1	7
Laws, Brian												★				2	★	2	2	2	2	2^1	2	2	2	2	2	2	2			2	2	2	2	2	2	2	20	2	1
Parker, Gary																6	**6**		11	11^1	11^1	11^1	11^1	11	11	11	11^1	11	11	11	11	11	11^1	11^1	11	**11**	11	11	22	0	7
Pearce, Stuart	3	3	3	3	3	3	3	3	3	3	3	**3**	3	3^1	3	3			3	3	3	3^1	3	3	3^1	3	3	3	**3**^{1}	3	3^1	3^1	3	3	3	3	3	3	36	0	6
Rice, Brian	**11**	11	11	11	11	11			11^1	11	11	11	11	11	11	11	11	11														★			6	6	6		19	1	1
Starbuck, Philip											★	7		7				★	★	★				★															2	5	0
Sutton, Steve	1	1	1	1	1	1	1	1			1	1	1	1	1	1	1	1	1	1	1	1	1	1	1	1	1	1	1	1	1	1	1	1	1	1	1	1	36	0	0
Walker, Des	4	4	4	4	4	4	4	4	4	4	4	4	4	4	4		4	4	4	4	**4**				4	4	4	4	4	4	4	4	4	4	4	4	4	4	34	0	0
Webb, Neil	8	8	8^1	8	8	8	8	8	8^1	**8**			8	8	8	8	8	8	8^1	8	8	8	8	8	8	8	8	8	8	8	8	8	8^1	8	8	8^1	8^1	8	36	0	6
Williams, Brett																	3	3																					2	0	0
Wilson, Terry	6	6								★	8	8	★	★				5	5	5	5	5	5	5	5	5	5	5	5	5	5	5	5	5	5	5^1	5		24	3	1
Own Goals		1																																1							2

FA Cup: 1988-89: 3rd Round: Ipswich T. (H) 3-0; 4th Round: Leeds U. (H) 2-0; 5th Round: Watford (A) 3-0; Quarter-Final: Manchester U. (A) 1-0; Semi-Final: Liverpool 1-3.

Littlewoods Cup: 1988-89: 2nd Round: Chester C. (H) 6-0 (A) 4-0; 3rd Round: Coventry C. (H) 3-2; 4th Round: Leicester C. (A) 0-0, Replay (H) 2-1; Quarter-Final: Q.P.R. (H) 5-2; Semi-Final: Bristol C. (H) 1-1 (A) 1-0; Final: Luton T. 3-1 (Winners).

NOTTS COUNTY (Division 3)

Team Manager Neil Warnock.
Club Address County Ground, Meadow Lane, Nottingham NG2 3HJ. Tel: (0602) 861155.
Current Ground Capacity 24,045.
Record Attendance 47,310 v York C., FA Cup 6th Round, 12 March 1955.
Year Formed 1862. Turned professional 1885.
Previous Names None.
Club Nickname "The Magpies".
Club Colours Black and white striped shirts, black shorts with white stripe down the side and white stockings with black hoops
Club Honours Football League: Div. 2 Champions 1896-97, 1913-14, 1922-23; Div. 3(S) Champions 1930-31, 1949-50; Div. 4 Champions 1970-71. FA Cup: Winners 1894.
League History 1888-93 Div. 1; 1893-97 Div. 2; 1897-1913 Div. 1; 1913-14 Div. 2; 1914-20 Div. 1; 1920-23 Div. 2; 1923-26 Div. 1; 1926-30 Div. 2; 1930-31 Div. 3(S); 1931-35 Div. 2; 1935-50 Div. 3(S); 1950-58 Div. 2; 1958-59 Div. 3; 1959-60 Div. 4; 1960-64 Div. 3; 1964-71 Div. 4; 1971-73 Div. 3; 1973-81 Div. 2; 1981-84 Div. 1; 1984-85 Div. 2; 1985- Div. 3.
Most League Points in a Season (2 for a win) 69 in Div. 4, 1970-71. (3 for a win) 81 in Div. 3, 1987-88.
Most League Goals in a Season 107 in Div. 4, 1959-60.
Record Victory 15-0 v Thornhill U., FA Cup 1st Round, 24 October 1885.
Record Defeat 1-9 v Blackburn Rov. in Div. 1, 16 November 1889, v Aston Villa in Div. 1, 29 September 1888 and v Portsmouth in Div. 2, 9 April 1927.
Consecutive League Wins 8 in 1914.
Consecutive League Defeats 7 in 1888-89, 1912, 1933 and 1983.
Record League Appearances Albert Iremonger, 564 between 1904-26.
Record League Goalscorer—Career Les Bradd, 125 between 1967-78.
Record League Goalscorer—Season Tom Keetley, 39 in Div. 3(S), 1930-31.

Notts County: League Record, 1988-89 (Division 3)

Match Number	Date	Venue	Opponents	Result	H/T	Lge Posn	Attend
1	27.8.88	H	Bristol C.	D 0-0	0-0		6280
2	3.9.88	A	Blackpool	W 1-0	0-0	9	4669
3	10.9.88	H	Northampton T.	L 0-1	0-0	14	6084
4	17.9.88	A	Wolverhampton W.	D 0-0	0-0	15	10870
5	20.9.88	A	Huddersfield T.	L 1-3	1-1	17	5655
6	24.9.88	H	Preston N.E.	D 0-0	0-0	18	4965
7	1.10.88	A	Mansfield T.	D 1-1	0-0	19	5907
8	4.10.88	H	Chesterfield	W 4-0	2-0	17	4519
9	9.10.88	H	Chester C.	D 2-2	1-1	17	5772
10	15.10.88	A	Bristol Rov.	L 0-2	0-1	17	4183
11	22.10.88	H	Reading	D 3-3	1-3	18	5170
12	29.10.88	H	Fulham	L 0-1	0-1	19	5514
13	5.11.88	A	Bury	D 1-1	1-0	18	2692
14	8.11.88	A	Brentford	L 1-2	0-1	19	4013
15	12.11.88	H	Southend U.	D 1-1	1-0	19	5037
16	26.11.88	H	Gillingham	L 1-2	1-1	20	4611
17	3.12.88	A	Aldershot	W 3-2	2-0	19	2191
18	18.12.88	A	Wigan Ath.	W 1-0	0-0	18	3010
19	26.12.88	H	Sheffield U.	L 1-4	1-0	19	11590
20	31.12.88	H	Bolton W.	W 2-0	2-0	18	5097
21	2.1.89	A	Port Vale	L 0-1	0-0	19	7084
22	7.1.89	A	Swansea C.	L 0-2	0-1	19	5808
23	14.1.89	H	Blackpool	D 1-1	0-1	21	4748
24	21.1.89	A	Northampton T.	W 3-1	1-0	18	3704
25	29.1.89	H	Wolverhampton W.	D 1-1	1-0	18	9058
26	4.2.89	H	Mansfield T.	W 2-1	2-1	17	5924
27	11.2.89	A	Chesterfield	L 0-3	0-2	18	4943
28	18.2.89	A	Chester C.	L 0-1	0-0	19	3157
29	25.2.89	H	Bristol Rov.	W 1-0	1-0	19	5176
30	28.2.89	H	Cardiff C.	W 2-0	1-0	17	4266
31	4.3.89	A	Reading	W 3-1	1-1	14	4153
32	11.3.89	H	Bury	W 3-0	1-0	12	5757
33	14.3.89	A	Fulham	L 1-2	0-1	12	3402
34	18.3.89	A	Bristol C.	W 4-0	1-0	10	6407
35	25.3.89	H	Port Vale	L 1-4	0-2	12	7328
36	27.3.89	A	Sheffield U.	D 1-1	1-1	12	13039
37	1.4.89	H	Wigan Ath.	W 1-0	1-0	12	4929
38	4.4.89	H	Swansea C.	W 1-0	1-0	10	3940
39	8.4.89	A	Bolton W.	D 3-3	3-0	11	4521
40	15.4.89	A	Preston N.E.	L 0-3	0-1	12	6735
41	18.4.89	A	Cardiff C.	W 1-0	1-0	12	3079
42	22.4.89	H	Huddersfield T.	W 3-0	1-0	8	5499
43	28.4.89	A	Southend U.	D 1-1	0-1	9	3931
44	1.5.89	H	Brentford	W 3-0	2-0	9	4989
45	6.5.89	H	Aldershot	W 4-1	0-1	8	4261
46	13.5.89	A	Gillingham	L 1-2	0-2	9	2877

Players: League Record, 1988-89 (Division 3)

Match Number	1	2	3	4	5	6	7	8	9	10	11	12	13	14	15	16	17	18	19	20	21	22	23	24	25	26	27	28	29	30	31	32	33	34	35	36	37	38	39	40	41	42	43	44	45	46	Apps	Subs	Goals
Barnes, Paul										**8**		★	★													★	★	8	**8^{1}**	8	**8^{3}**	**8^{1}**	**8**	**8^{2}**	8	8	8										11	4	7
Birtles, Garry	9	**9**	9	9	**9**		9	9	9^{2}	9	9	**9**	9	9	6	**6**		**6**		6	6	**6**													★												19	1	2
Cherry, Steve																												1	1	1	1	1	1	1	1	1	1	1	1		1	1	1	1	1	1	18	0	0
Davison, Aidan																																								1							1	0	0
Draper, Mark				**11**													8							$★^{1}$	10	10	10	11	11					11^{1}	11	★	**10**	★	★	**8**		8^{1}	**8**	8	8	8	16	4	3
Fairclough, Wayne							★				2							11	11	11	**11**	11	11	2			★							★		10	★	**8**		3	8	10	10		★	★	14	6	0
Johnson, Tommy						★																				★							★							★	10	11^{2}	11^{1}	**11**	11^{1}	11	6	4	4
Kevan, David						★	4	4	4	4	**4**				10	4	4^{1}							6	**6**					11^{1}	11	11	**11**						8		4			★			16	2	2
Law, Nicky	6	6	6	6	6	6	6	6	6	6	6^{1}	6	6	6		★	5	5	**5**	5^{1}	5	★	6		2	2	2	6	6	6	6	6	6	6	6	6	**6**	6	6	6	6	6	6	6	6^{1}	6^{1}	42	2	4
Leonard, Mike	1	1	1	1	1	1	1	1	1	1	1	1	1	1	1	1	1	1	1	1	1	1	1	1	1	1	1																				27	0	0
Lund, Gary	★	★			★	**9**		8		★	★	8	8^{1}	8	9	9	9^{1}	9	9	9^{1}	9	9	9^{1}	9	9	**9**	**9**	9	9	9	9	9^{1}	9	9	**9**	9	9	9^{1}	9	9	9	9	9	9^{1}	9^{1}	9	37	5	8
McParland, Ian	**8**	8	8	8	8	8	8^{1}		8		**8**						★	8^{1}	8	8	8	8	8	8^{2}	8	**8**	8		★			$★^{1}$	$★^{1}$														19	4	6
McStay, Willie			★	★		10	2	2^{1}	2	2			★	2	2		7	★	2	2	2	**2**	2						2	2	★	2	2	2	2	2	2	2	2	2			★	10	10	10	27	6	1
Mills, Gary	7	7^{1}	7	7	7	7	7	7	7	7	7^{1}	7	7	7	7^{1}	7		7	7	7	7	7	7	7	7	7	7	7	7	**7**																	29	0	3
Norton, David	2	2	2	2	2	2						2	**2**																																		8	0	0
O'Riordan, Donal	4	4	4	4	4	**4**				★	★	4	4	4^{1}	4	2	6	4	4	4	4	4	4	4	4^{1}	4	**4**	4	5	5	4	4	4	4^{1}	4	4	4	4	4	5	★	4	4	**4**	4	**4**	40	3	3
Palmer, Charlie																												2	4	4	**2**									4	2	2	2	2	2	**2**	11	0	0
Pike, Geoff	10	10	10	10	10		10	10^{1}	10	**10**	10	10	10	10		10		10	10^{1}	10	10	10	**10**	**10**	★	6^{1}	6	10	10	10	10	10	10	**10**	**10**		★	10	10	10							34	2	3
Rimmer, Stuart															8	8^{1}	10^{1}		★																												3	1	2
Thorpe, Adrian	11	11	**11**		11	11	11	11^{1}	11	11	11^{1}	11	**11**	11	11	11	**11**		★		★	★	★	11	11	11	11			★	★			★	★	**11**	11^{1}	11	11^{1}	11	**11**			★		★	26	10	4
Turner, Philip																															7	7	7	7	7	7	7	7	7^{1}	7	7	7	7	7	7^{1}	7	16	0	2
Withe, Chris	3	3	3	3	3	3	**3**	3	3	3	3	3	3	3	3	3	3	3	3	3	3	3	3	3	3	3	3	3	3	3^{1}	3	3	3	3	3	3	3	3	**3**		3	3	3	**3**	3	3	45	0	1
Yates, Dean	5	5	5	5	5^{1}	5	5	5^{1}	5	5	5	5	5	5	5	5	2	2	**6**			5	5	5	5	5	5	5			5	5	5	5	5^{1}	5^{1}	5	5	5		5^{1}	5	5	5^{1}	5	5	41	0	6
Own Goals																										1													1					1					3

FA Cup: 1988-89: 1st Round: Darlington (A) 2-1; 2nd Round: Hartlepool U. (A) 0-1.
Littlewoods Cup: 1988-89: 1st Round: Mansfield T. (H) 5-0; 2nd Round: Tottenham H. (H) 1-1 (A) 1-2.

OLDHAM ATHLETIC (Division 2)

Team Manager Joe Royle.
Club Address Boundary Park, Oldham. Tel: 061-624 4972.
Current Ground Capacity 21,962.
Record Attendance 47,671 v Sheffield Wed., FA Cup 4th Round, 25 January 1930.
Year Formed 1894. Turned professional 1899.
Previous Names Pine Villa.
Club Nickname "The Latics".
Club Colours All blue.
Club Honours Football League: Div. 3(N) Champions 1952-53; Div. 3 Champions 1973-74.
League History 1907-10 Div. 2; 1910-23 Div. 1; 1923-35 Div. 2; 1935-53 Div. 3(N); 1953-54 Div. 2; 1954-58 Div. 3; 1958-63 Div. 4; 1963-69 Div. 3; 1969-71 Div. 4; 1971-74 Div. 3; 1974- Div. 2.
Most League Points in a Season (2 for a win) 62 in Div. 3, 1973-74. (3 for a win) 75 in Div. 2, 1986-87.
Most League Goals in a Season 95 in Div. 4, 1962-63.
Record Victory 11-0 v Southport in Div. 4, 26 December 1962.
Record Defeat 4-13 v Tranmere Rov. in Div. 3(N), 26 December 1935.
Consecutive League Wins 10 in 1974.
Consecutive League Defeats 8 in 1932-33, 1934-35.
Record League Appearances Ian Wood, 525 between 1966-80.
Record League Goalscorer—Career Eric Gemmell, 110 between 1947-54.
Record League Goalscorer—Season Tom Davis, 33 in Div. 3(N), 1936-37.

Oldham Athletic: League Record, 1988-89 (Division 2)

Match Number	Date	Venue	Opponents	Result	H/T	Lge Posn	Attend
1	27.8.88	H	Barnsley	D 1-1	1-0		6551
2	29.8.88	A	Manchester C.	W 4-1	2-0	3	22594
3	3.9.88	A	Blackburn Rov.	L 1-3	0-2	9	10082
4	10.9.88	H	Birmingham C.	W 4-0	1-0	6	5796
5	17.9.88	A	Bradford C.	L 0-2	0-2	8	12325
6	20.9.88	H	Oxford U.	W 3-0	2-0	6	5847
7	24.9.88	H	Hull C.	D 2-2	2-0	6	6319
8	1.10.88	A	Sunderland	L 2-3	2-2	9	12529
9	4.10.88	A	Watford	L 1-3	0-2	10	10038
10	8.10.88	H	Stoke C.	D 2-2	2-0	13	6600
11	15.10.88	H	Chelsea	L 1-4	1-2	17	7817
12	22.10.88	A	Brighton & H.A.	L 0-2	0-2	19	7699
13	25.10.88	H	Bournemouth	W 2-0	1-0	16	4518
14	29.10.88	A	Portsmouth	D 1-1	1-1	17	11310
15	5.11.88	H	Walsall	W 3-0	3-0	14	5760
16	11.11.88	A	Shrewsbury T.	D 0-0	0-0	15	4701
17	19.11.88	H	Leeds U.	D 2-2	1-1	14	8824
18	26.11.88	A	Plymouth Arg.	L 0-3	0-2	17	7829
19	3.12.88	H	Leicester C.	D 1-1	0-0	20	5789
20	10.12.88	A	Swindon T	D 2-2	0-1	19	5540
21	16.12.88	A	Ipswich T.	L 1-2	1-0	20	8982
22	26.12.88	H	West Bromwich A.	L 1-3	0-2	20	9827
23	30.12.88	H	Crystal Palace	L 2-3	0-1	21	6562
24	2.1.89	A	Birmingham C.	D 0-0	0-0	20	5988
25	14.1.89	H	Manchester C.	L 0-1	0-1	21	19200
26	21.1.89	A	Barnsley	L 3-4	0-1	21	7879
27	4.2.89	H	Watford	W 3-1	2-0	21	6364
28	11.2.89	A	Stoke C.	D 0-0	0-0	21	10992
29	18.2.89	H	Brighton & H.A.	W 2-1	2-1	20	5918
30	25.2.89	A	Chelsea	D 2-2	1-2	21	13261
31	28.2.89	A	Bournemouth	D 2-2	1-1	20	7783
32	3.3.89	H	Shrewsbury T.	W 3-0	1-0	19	6014
33	11.3.89	A	Walsall	D 2-2	0-1	19	5576
34	14.3.89	H	Portsmouth	W 5-3	2-0	16	5773
35	18.3.89	A	Oxford U.	D 1-1	1-1	16	4588
36	24.3.89	H	Blackburn Rov.	D 1-1	1-0	17	11752
37	27.3.89	A	West Bromwich A.	L 1-3	0-0	19	13812
38	1.4.89	H	Bradford C.	D 1-1	0-0	19	8589
39	4.4.89	H	Ipswich T.	W 4-0	2-0	17	5182
40	8.4.89	A	Crystal Palace	L 0-2	0-1	19	9089
41	15.4.89	H	Sunderland	D 2-2	1-2	20	5944
42	22.4.89	A	Hull C.	D 1-1	1-0	20	6748
43	29.4.89	H	Plymouth Arg.	D 2-2	2-1	19	4614
44	1.5.89	H	Leicester C.	W 2-1	1-0	17	7223
45	6.5.89	A	Leeds U.	D 0-0	0-0	17	14459
46	13.5.89	H	Swindon T.	D 2-2	1-2	16	5676

Players: League Record, 1988-89 (Division 2)

Match Number	1	2	3	4	5	6	7	8	9	10	11	12	13	14	15	16	17	18	19	20	21	22	23	24	25	26	27	28	29	30	31	32	33	34	35	36	37	38	39	40	41	42	43	44	45	46	Apps	Subs	Goals
Adams, Neil																									11	11	11	11	11	11	11	**11**	11														9	0	0
Barlow, Andrew	3	3	**3**	3	3	3	3	3										**3**			10	★	6	6	**6**																	5					14	1	0
Barrett, Earl	2	2	2	2	2	4	4	4	4	4	3	3	3	3	3	3	3	2	3	3	3	3	3	3	3	3	3	3	3	3			3	3	3	3	3	3	3	3	3	3	3	3	3	3	44	0	0
Blundell, Chris									3	3																																					2	0	0
Bramwell, Steven																																					★										0	1	0
Bunn, Frankie	10[1]	10	10	10[1]	10	**10**	**10[2]**	10[2]	10[1]	9[1]	9	9	9[1]	9[1]	9	9	9[1]		9	**9**												★	★[1]	9	9				9	9	9	9	**9**				26	2	12
Cecere, Michele	9	**9**	**9**	9[2]	9	9	9	★		★	★	**11**	★	**10**																																	9	4	2
Donachie, Willie			★	★	★			★	★	2	6	6	6																																		4	5	0
Flynn, Michael	4	4	4	4	**4**									★		5	5	**5**																													8	1	0
Gayle, Andrew																																														★	0	1	0
Hallworth, Jonathan																											1	1	1	1	1	1	1	1	1	1	1	1	1	1	1		1				16	0	0
Hartford, Asa																																					★	4	★	★			★	9	9		3	4	0
Henry, Nicky																						★	★	11	★	6	★								5	9	9	9	4	4	4	4	4	4	4	4	14	4	0
Holden, Andy																									5	5	**6**		6[1]	6	6	6	6[1]	6[1]									6	6	6	6[1]	13	0	4
Irwin, Dennis					★	2	2	2	**2**		2	2	2	2	2	2	2	9	2	2	2	**2**	2	2	2	2	2[1]	2	2	2	2	2	2	2	2	2	2	2	2	2	2	2	2[1]	2	2	2	40	1	2
Kelly, John	8	8	8	**8**	8	8	8	**8**	8	8[1]	8	8	8	8	8	8	8	8	8	8[1]	8[1]	8	8	8			4	4	4	4	4[1]	4	4	4	4	4[1]	4			★	8	8	8	8[1]	8	**8**	41	1	6
Kelly, Norman																								64																							0	1	0
Litchfield, Peter									1	1	1																																				3	0	0
Marshall, Ian	5	5	5[1]	5[1]	5	5	5	5	5	5	5	5	5[1]	5	5[1]				5	5	5	5	5	5	9	9	5	5	5	5	5	5	5	5		5	5	5	5	5	5		5	5	5	5	41	0	4
Milligan, Michael	6	6[1]	6	6	**6**	6	6	6	**6**						6	6	6	6	6	6	6	6			10	10	10	10	10	10	10[1]	10	10	10[1]	10	10	10	10[1]	10[1]	10	10[1]	10	10	10	10	10	39	0	6
Morgan, Stephen																								**9**																							1	0	0
Palmer, Roger	7	7[3]	7	7	7	7[2]	7	7	7	7	7[1]	**7**	7	7	7[1]	7	7[1]	7	7	7[1]	7	7	7	7	7	7[1]	7	7	7	7[1]	7	7[1]	7	7	7	7	**7**	7	7[2]	7	7	7	7	7	7	7[1]	46	0	15
Philliskirk, Tony		★	★								★	★	**10**	★				★		★		10[1]	**10**																								3	7	1
Rhodes, Andy	1	1	1	1	1	1	1	1				1	1	1	1	1	1	1	1	1	1	1	1	1	1	1																1		1	1	1	27	0	0
Ritchie, Andy							★	9	9	10	**11**				10[1]	10	10	10	10[1]	10	11	9	11[1]		8	8[2]	8[2]	8	8	8[1]	8	8[2]	8	8[1]	8[1]	8	8[1]	8	8[1]	**8**						9	30	1	14
Skipper, Peter											4	4	4	4	4	4	4	4	4	4	4	4	4[1]	4	4	**4**		6			3	3			6	6	6	6	6	6	6	6					27	0	1
Warhurst, Paul														**6**				★					★	10																							2	2	0
Williams, Gary						★[1]			★	**6**	**10**	★	★																																		2	4	1
Wright, Tommy	11	11	11	11	11	11	11	11	11	11		10	**11**	11	11	11	11	11	11	11	9	**11**	**9**			★	9	9	9[1]	9	9	9	**9**	11[2]	11	11	**11**	11	**11**	**11**	11[1]	11[1]	11[1]	11[1]	11	11	42	1	7
Own Goals																																																	0

FA Cup: 1988-89: 3rd Round: Charlton Ath. (A) 1-2.

Littlewoods Cup: 1988-89: 2nd Round: Darlington (A) 0-2 (H) 4-0; 3rd Round: Everton (A) 1-1, Replay (H) 0-2.

100% Teamwork.

Wang are famous for getting different types of Integrated Technology to work together as a team.

Valuing effective team work as we do, sponsoring Oxford United Football Club was an obvious move.

OXFORD UNITED

Because in the same way that we're helping to build British business for the future, we want British sport to have a strong future too. Wang The Number 1 IT Sponsor of Sport.

WANG

Integrated Business Solutions

Contact: Caroline Peden, Wang (U.K.) Ltd., 1000 Great West Road, Brentford, Middlesex TW8 9HL. 01-568 4444.

OXFORD UNITED (Division 2)

Team Manager Brian Horton.
Club Address Manor Ground, Headington, Oxford. Tel: (0865) 61503.
Current Ground Capacity 14,374.
Record Attendance 22,730 v Preston N.E., FA Cup 6th Round, 29 February 1964.
Year Formed 1896. Turned professional 1949.
Previous Names Headington United.
Club Nickname "The U's".
Club Colours Yellow shirts with blue trim, blue shorts and blue stockings.
Club Honours Football League: Div. 2 Champions 1984-85; Div. 3 Champions 1967-68, 1983-84. Football League Cup: Winners 1986.
League History 1962-65 Div. 4; 1965-68 Div. 3; 1968-76 Div. 2; 1976-84 Div. 3; 1984-85 Div. 2; 1985-88 Div. 1; 1988- Div. 2.
Most League Points in a Season (2 for a win) 61 in Div. 4, 1964-65. (3 for a win) 95 in Div. 3, 1983-84.
Most League Goals in a Season 91 in Div. 3, 1983-84.
Record Victory 7-0 v Barrow in Div. 4, 19 December 1964.
Record Defeat 0-6 v Liverpool in Div. 1, 22 March 1986.
Consecutive League Wins 6 in 1968, 1982-83 and 1985.
Consecutive League Defeats 6 in 1968-69 and 1975.
Record League Appearances John Shuker, 480 between 1962-77.
Record League Goalscorer—Career Graham Atkinson, 75 between 1962-73.
Record League Goalscorer—Season John Aldridge, 30 in Div. 2, 1984-85.

Oxford United: League Record, 1988-89 (Division 2)

Match Number	Date	Venue	Opponents	Result	H/T	Lge Posn	Attend
1	27.8.88	A	Leeds U.	D 1-1	1-1		20697
2	29.8.88	H	Hull C.	W 1-0	1-0	5	5772
3	3.9.88	H	Brighton & H.A.	W 3-2	2-0	4	6004
4	10.9.88	A	Chelsea	D 1-1	0-0	5	7587
5	17.9.88	H	Leicester C.	D 1-1	0-1	6	6610
6	20.9.88	A	Oldham Ath.	L 0-3	0-2	7	5847
7	24.9.88	A	Bournemouth	L 1-2	0-1	12	6532
8	1.10.88	H	Shrewsbury T.	W 4-1	2-1	8	4385
9	5.10.88	H	Swindon T.	D 1-1	0-0	7	9398
10	8.10.88	A	Portsmouth	L 1-2	1-1	10	9567
11	15.10.88	A	Ipswich T.	W 2-1	2-0	7	13039
12	22.10.88	H	Blackburn Rov.	D 1-1	0-1	10	6478
13	25.10.88	A	Crystal Palace	L 0-1	0-0	12	10114
14	29.10.88	H	Bradford C.	L 3-4	1-1	16	5303
15	2.11.88	H	Sunderland	L 2-4	1-3	16	6270
16	5.11.88	A	West Bromwich A.	W 2-3	1-1	19	11643
17	12.11.88	H	Birmingham C.	W 3-0	1-0	17	5589
18	19.11.88	H	Plymouth Arg.	L 0-1	0-1	18	5429
19	26.11.88	A	Manchester C.	L 1-2	1-0	20	20145
20	3.12.88	H	Barnsley	W 2-0	0-0	18	4449
21	10.12.88	A	Watford	D 1-1	1-0	17	10473
22	26.12.88	A	Walsall	W 5-1	0-1	17	6332
23	31.12.88	A	Stoke C.	L 0-1	0-1	18	10552
24	2.1.89	H	Chelsea	L 2-3	1-2	19	11427
25	14.1.89	A	Sunderland	L 0-1	0-1	19	12853
26	21.1.89	H	Leeds U.	W 3-2	2-2	19	7926
27	5.2.89	A	Swindon T.	L 0-3	0-1	19	10229
28	11.2.89	H	Portsmouth	W 1-0	1-0	17	6156
29	21.2.89	A	Blackburn Rov.	L 1-3	0-2	19	5724
30	25.2.89	H	Ipswich T.	D 1-1	1-0	19	6086
31	1.3.89	H	Crystal Palace	W 1-0	0-0	17	6020
32	4.3.89	A	Birmingham C.	D 0-0	0-0	16	4954
33	11.3.89	H	West Bromwich A.	D 1-1	1-1	17	7581
34	15.3.89	A	Bradford C.	D 0-0	0-0	17	7553
35	18.3.89	H	Oldham Ath.	D 1-1	1-1	17	4588
36	25.3.89	A	Brighton & H.A.	L 1-2	1-0	18	9077
37	27.3.89	H	Walsall	W 1-0	1-0	16	5101
38	1.4.89	A	Leicester C.	L 0-1	0-1	18	8187
39	4.4.89	A	Hull C.	W 2-1	2-0	16	6260
40	8.4.89	H	Stoke C.	W 3-2	2-1	15	5297
41	15.4.89	A	Shrewsbury T.	D 2-2	1-0	15	3583
42	22.4.89	H	Bournemouth	W 3-1	2-0	14	5684
43	29.4.89	H	Manchester C.	L 2-4	2-0	15	7762
44	1.5.89	A	Barnsley	L 0-1	0-0	15	5940
45	6.5.89	A	Plymouth Arg.	L 1-3	0-0	15	4989
46	13.5.89	H	Watford	L 0-4	0-1	17	6573

Players: League Record, 1988-89 (Division 2)

Match Number	1	2	3	4	5	6	7	8	9	10	11	12	13	14	15	16	17	18	19	20	21	22	23
Bardsley, David	2	2	2	2	2	2	2	2	2	2[1]	2	2[1]	2	7	7	2	2[1]	2	2	2	2[1]	2	2
Beauchamp, Joseph																							
Briggs, Gary								5	5	5	**5**	5	5	5	5	5	5	5	5				
Durnin, John																							
Evans, Ceri																							
Ford, Michael																							
Foyle, Martin	8[1]	8	8	8	8	8	8	8[1]	8	8	8[1]	8	8	8[1]	8[2]	8[1]	8[2]	8	8	8	8	8[1]	8
Greenall, Colin	6	6	6[1]	6	6	6	6	6	6	6	6	6	6	6	6	6	6	6	6	6	6	6	6
Heath, Philip	7	7	7[1]	7	7	7	7							**11**	★	★		★					★
Hill, Richard	5	5	5	5	5	5	5		★	★	★		9	10[1]	**10**			★	9[1]	9	9	9[4]	9
Hucker, Peter	1	1	1	1	1	1	1																
Judge, Alan								1	1	1	1	1	1	1	1	1	1	1	1	1	1	1	1
Lewis, Micky	4	4	4	4	4	**4**	**4**									**10**	10	10		5	5	5	5
Leworthy, David				★[1]	**9**									9	9								★
Mustoe, Robbie	10	10	**10**	10	10	**10**	★[1]	10[1]	**10**	10	10	**10**	**10**		★	★	11	4			★		
Nogan, Lee													★										
Phillips, Jimmy	3	3	3	**3**	3	3		3[1]	3	3	3[1]	3	3	3	3	3	3	3	3	3[1]	3	3	3
Phillips, Lee						★	10	4	4	4	4	4	4	4[1]	4	4			4	4	4	4	**4**
Purdie, Jon			★	9	★	★		7	7	7		★	★				★	**11**					
Reck, Sean											7	7	**7**			7	**7**	**7**					
Rhoades-Brown, Peter	**11**	**11**		★			★	11	11	**11**													
Saunders, Dean	9	9[1]	9[1]			9	9	9[1]	9[1]	9	9	9											
Shelton, Gary	★	★	11	**11**	11[1]	11	**11**							★			4		10	10	10	10	10
Simpson, Paul															11	9[1]	9	9	11	11[1]	**11**	11	**11**
Slatter, Neil											11	11	11	2	**2**	11							
Smart, Gary							3												7	7	7	7	7
Own Goals																							

Match Number	24	25	26	27	28	29	30	31	32	33	34	35	36	37	38	39	40	41	42	43	44	45	46	Apps	Subs	Goals
Bardsley, David	2	2	2	2	7	7	7	7[1]	**7**										7	7[1]	7	7	7	37	0	6
Beauchamp, Joseph																							★	0	1	0
Briggs, Gary																7	7	7[1]						15	0	1
Durnin, John					9	9	9	9	9	10	10	10	10	10[1]	10	10[1]	10[1]	10	10	10	10	10	10	19	0	3
Evans, Ceri															5						6	6	6	4	0	0
Ford, Michael		★	★	★	10	**10**	**10**							11	**11**							★[1]	**11**	6	4	1
Foyle, Martin	8[1]	8	8[1]	8	8	8	8	8	8	8[1]	8	8	8[1]	8	8	8	**8**							40	0	14
Greenall, Colin	6	6	6	6	6				6	6	6	6	6	6	6	6	6	6[1]	6	6				40	0	2
Heath, Philip	★											★							★			★		8	8	1
Hill, Richard	9[1]	9	9	9	11	**11**	11[1]	11	11	7	7	7	7		★	11	11[2]	**11**			11	11	★	33	6	10
Hucker, Peter	1				1	1	1	1	1	1	1	1	1	1	1	1	1	1	1	1	1	1		26	0	0
Judge, Alan		1	1	1																			1	20	0	0
Lewis, Micky	5	5	5	5	5	5	5	5	5	5	5	5	5	5		5	5	5	5	5	5	5	5	36	0	0
Leworthy, David	★	★		★									★				★	★		★				3	9	1
Mustoe, Robbie	4								★	9	9	9	9	9	9	9[1]	9	9	**9**	9	9	**9**		28	5	3
Nogan, Lee																						8	**9**	2	1	0
Phillips, Jimmy	3	3	3	3	3	3	3	3	3	3	3	3	3	3	3	3	3	3	3	3	3	3	3	45	0	3
Phillips, Lee			**4**[1]	4	4[1]	4	4	4	4	4	4	**4**[1]												25	1	4
Purdie, Jon																								5	6	0
Reck, Sean																								6	0	0
Rhoades-Brown, Peter																								5	2	0
Saunders, Dean																								10	0	4
Shelton, Gary	10	10	10	**10**		★	★	10	10				4	4	4	4	4	4	4	4	4	4	4	28	5	1
Simpson, Paul	**11**	**11**	11[1]	**11**		★[1]				11	11	11	11	7	7			8	8[3]	8[1]	8		8	24	1	8
Slatter, Neil		4	7	7	2	6	6	6	2	2	2	**2**	2	2	2			2	2	2	2	**2**		25	0	0
Smart, Gary	**7**	**7**				2	2	2				★				2	2		11	**11**			2	16	1	0
Own Goals																										0

FA Cup: 1988-89: 3rd Round: Sunderland (A) 1-1, Replay (H) 2-0; 4th Round: Manchester U. (A) 0-4.
Littlewoods Cup: 1988-89: 2nd Round: Bristol C. (H) 2-4 (A) 0-2.

PETERBOROUGH UNITED (Division 4)

Team Manager Mick Jones.
Club Address London Road Ground, Peterborough PE2 8AL. Tel: (0733) 63947.
Current Ground Capacity 17,129.
Record Attendance 30,096 v Swansea T., FA Cup 5th Round, 20 February 1965.
Year Formed 1923. Turned professional 1934.
Previous Names Peterborough and Fletton United.
Club Nickname "The Posh".
Club Colours Blue shirts, white shorts and blue stockings.
Club Honours Football League: Div. 4 Champions 1960-61.
League History 1960-61 Div. 4; 1961-68 Div. 3; 1968-74 Div. 4; 1974-79 Div. 3; 1979- Div. 4.
Most League Points in a Season (2 for a win) 66 in Div. 4, 1960-61. (3 for a win) 82 Div. 4, 1981-82.
Most League Goals in a Season 134 in Div. 4, 1960-61.
Record Victory 8-1 v Oldham Ath. in Div. 4, 26 November 1969.
Record Defeat 1-8 v Northampton T. in FA Cup 2nd Round 2nd replay, 18 December 1946.
Consecutive League Wins 7 in 1960-61, 1973.
Consecutive League Defeats 5 in 1988-89.
Record League Appearances Tommy Robson, 482 between 1968-81.
Record League Goalscorer—Career Jim Hall, 122 between 1967-75.
Record League Goalscorer—Season Terry Bly, 52 in Div. 4, 1960-61.

Peterborough United: League Record, 1988-89 (Division 4)

Match Number	Date	Venue	Opponents	Result	H/T	Lge Posn	Attend
1	27.8.88	A	Carlisle U.	D 2-2	1-1		2650
2	3.9.88	H	Scarborough	L 1-4	1-1	19	3956
3	10.9.88	A	Darlington	D 2-2	1-1	20	1521
4	17.9.88	H	Lincoln C.	D 1-1	0-0	20	4256
5	19.9.88	A	Tranmere Rov.	L 0-1	0-1	21	2597
6	24.9.88	H	York C.	L 0-1	0-0	23	2756
7	1.10.88	A	Wrexham	D 1-1	1-0	23	1826
8	5.10.88	H	Stockport Co.	W 1-0	1-0	21	2572
9	8.10.88	A	Grimsby T.	D 0-0	0-0	22	2820
10	15.10.88	H	Burnley	W 3-0	1-0	20	5023
11	22.10.88	H	Hereford U.	W 2-1	1-0	17	3460
12	25.10.88	A	Halifax T.	L 0-5	0-0	19	2248
13	29.10.88	H	Scunthorpe U.	L 1-2	1-1	20	3532
14	5.11.88	A	Leyton Orient	W 2-1	1-1	17	3695
15	9.11.88	H	Hartlepool U.	L 0-1	0-0	19	3148
16	12.11.88	A	Doncaster Rov.	W 3-2	1-0	19	2224
17	25.11.88	A	Crewe Alex.	D 1-1	0-1	19	2645
18	3.12.88	H	Rochdale	W 1-0	0-0	15	3273
19	17.12.88	H	Exeter C.	L 0-1	0-0	16	3149
20	26.12.88	A	Colchester U.	W 2-1	1-0	14	2828
21	31.12.88	A	Torquay U.	L 0-1	0-0	17	2877
22	3.1.89	H	Cambridge U.	L 1-5	1-3	18	4622
23	7.1.89	H	Rotherham U.	L 0-3	0-0	18	3368
24	14.1.89	A	Scarborough	L 1-2	0-0	19	2279
25	21.1.89	H	Carlisle U.	L 1-4	0-2	21	2537
26	28.1.89	A	Lincoln C.	D 1-1	0-0	22	4150
27	4.2.89	H	Tranmere Rov.	D 1-1	0-0	21	2744
28	11.2.89	A	York C.	L 1-5	0-2	22	2438
29	25.2.89	A	Burnley	D 1-1	0-0	22	6848
30	1.3.89	H	Halifax T.	W 2-1	0-0	22	2159
31	4.3.89	A	Hereford U.	L 0-4	0-0	22	2094
32	11.3.89	H	Leyton Orient	L 0-1	0-0	22	3306
33	14.3.89	A	Scunthorpe U.	L 0-3	0-1	22	3983
34	18.3.89	H	Darlington	D 1-1	0-0	22	2484
35	25.3.89	A	Cambridge U.	L 1-2	0-1	22	4215
36	27.3.89	H	Colchester U.	W 3-0	1-0	22	3529
37	1.4.89	A	Exeter C.	L 1-3	0-2	22	2522
38	4.4.89	A	Rotherham U.	D 1-1	1-1	22	4762
39	8.4.89	H	Torquay U.	W 3-1	0-0	22	2614
40	15.4.89	H	Wrexham	W 1-0	1-0	22	3067
41	21.4.89	A	Stockport Co.	W 2-1	2-0	21	2091
42	25.4.89	H	Grimsby T.	L 1-2	1-0	22	2937
43	29.4.89	H	Crewe Alex.	W 3-2	1-1	18	3546
44	1.5.89	A	Hartlepool U.	L 1-2	0-0	20	1643
45	6.5.89	A	Rochdale	D 0-0	0-0	20	1430
46	13.5.89	H	Doncaster Rov.	W 2-0	1-0	17	2984

Players: League Record, 1988-89 (Division 4)

Match Number	1	2	3	4	5	6	7	8	9	10	11	12	13	14	15	16	17	18	19	20	21	22	23
Andrews, Gary				7	7		7	7	7	7	7	7	7	7	7	7	7	7					2
Butterworth, Gary																			★				
Carr, Ashley																	★						
Collins, Steve	3	3	3			3	★	★	2				★	2^{1}	**2**	2	2	2	2	2	2	2	★
Crichton, Paul														1	1	1	1	1	1	1			1
Cusack, Nicky	9	9	9^{2}	9	9	9	9^{1}	9	9	9^{1}	9^{1}	9	9	9	9	9	9^{1}	9	9	9			11
Genovese, Domenico	7	**7**	**7**	**10^{1}**	**10**		★																
Goldsmith, Craig		★	★	11	11	11	11	11^{1}	11	11^{1}	11	11	11	11	11	11	11	11	11	11	11	11	★
Gooding, Mick	4^{2}	4^{1}	4																				
Gunn, Bryn	10	10	10	3	3	10	3	3	3	3	3	3	3	3	3	3^{2}	3	3	3	3^{1}	3	3	3
Halsall, Mike	8	8	8	8	8	8	8	8	8	8	8	8	8	8	8	8	8	8	8	**8**	8	8	8
Harle, David																							
Langan, David	2	2	2	2	2	2	**2**	**2**		2	2	2	**2**		★				4	7	7	7	7
Longhurst, David									10	10	10^{1}	10	10	10^{1}	10	**10**	10	10	10	10	10	10	**10**
Luke, Noel	11	11	11	4	4	4	4	4	4	4	4	4	4^{1}	4	4	4	4	4		4	4	4	4
McElhinney, Gerry	5	5	5	5	5	5	5	5	5	5	5	5	5	5	5	5	**5**	5	**5**	5^{1}	5	5	**5**
Madrick, Carl				★	★	7	**10**	10							★	★			★				
Neenan, Joe	1	1	1	1	1	1	1	1	1	1	1	1	1								1	1	
Oakes, Keith	6	6	6	6	6	6	6	6	6	6^{1}	6	6	6	6	6	6	6	6^{1}	6	6	6	6	6
Osborne, Steven																							
Philpott, Lee																			**7**	★			
Pollard, Gary																							
Sterling, Worrell																							
Swindlehurst, Dave																					9	9^{1}	9
Walsh, Colin																							
Own Goals																							

Match Number	24	25	26	27	28	29	30	31	32	33	34	35	36	37	38	39	40	41	42	43	44	45	46	Apps	Subs	Goals
Andrews, Gary	7	5	7	5	7	7	7	7	7	7	**7**				6	6	**4**			5	**5**	6	**6**	33	0	0
Butterworth, Gary		4	4		★	4	4	4	**4**															6	2	0
Carr, Ashley																								0	1	0
Collins, Steve	★	3	3	3	**3**					11	4	4		8	8	8	8			★	4	4	4	28	6	1
Crichton, Paul	1	1	1	1	1	1	1	1	1	1	1	1	1	1	1	1	1	1	1	1	1	1	1	31	0	0
Cusack, Nicky	11^{1}	9	9	9	9	9	9^{1}	9	9	9	9	9	**9**	9	9	**9**	9^{1}	9	9	9	9	9	9	44	0	10
Genovese, Domenico		10			★	★			★	4	★			★		★	★							7	8	1
Goldsmith, Craig	★	11	11^{1}	11	11				**11**		11	11^{1}	11	**11**	11^{1}	**11**	**11**	11	11		★	★	11^{1}	34	6	6
Gooding, Mick																								3	0	3
Gunn, Bryn	3	2	5	2	**5**	3^{1}	3	3	3	3	3	3	3	3	3	3	3	3^{1}	3	3^{1}	3^{1}	3	3	46	0	7
Halsall, Mike	8	8^{1}	8	8	8	8	8	8	8	8	8	8	8					8	8	8	8	8	8	42	0	1
Harle, David													4	4	4	4		4	4	**4**				7	0	0
Langan, David	2																							18	1	0
Longhurst, David	10		10	10	10	**10**	10	10	10	10	10^{1}	10	10^{2}	**10**	10	10^{2}	10	10	10	10	10	10	10	37	0	7
Luke, Noel	4	7	2	7	2	2	2	2	2	2	2	2	2	2	2	2	2	2^{1}	2	2^{1}	2	2	2	45	0	3
McElhinney, Gerry	**5**												5	5	5	5	5	5	**5**			5	5	33	0	1
Madrick, Carl																								3	5	0
Neenan, Joe																								15	0	0
Oakes, Keith	6	6	6	6^{1}		6	6^{1}	6	6	6	6	6	6	6^{1}			6	6	6	6	6			41	0	5
Osborne, Steven													★	★		★	★		$★^{1}$	11	11	**11**	★	3	6	1
Philpott, Lee									★															1	2	0
Pollard, Gary					6	5	5	5	5	5	5	5												8	0	0
Sterling, Worrell												7	7	7	7	7^{1}	7	7	7	7^{1}	7	7	7^{1}	12	0	3
Swindlehurst, Dave	**9**																							4	0	1
Walsh, Colin				4	4^{1}	11	11	11																5	0	1
Own Goals													1													1

FA Cup: 1988-89: 1st Round: Gillingham (A) 3-3, Replay (H) 1-0; 2nd Round: Brentford (H) 0-0, Replay (A) 2-3.
Littlewoods Cup: 1988-89: 1st Round: West Bromwich A. (A) 3-0 (H) 0-2; 2nd Round: Leeds U. (H) 1-2 (A) 1-3.

PLYMOUTH ARGYLE (Division 2)

Team Manager Ken Brown.
Club Address Home Park, Plymouth, Devon PL2 3DQ. Tel: (0752) 562561/2/3.
Current Ground Capacity 26,500.
Record Attendance 43,596 v Aston Villa, Div. 2, 10 October 1936.
Year Formed 1886. Turned professional 1903.
Previous Names Argyle Athletic Club.
Club Nickname "The Pilgrims".
Club Colours Green shirts with black trim, black shorts and white stockings.
Club Honours Football League: Div. 3(S) Champions 1929-30, 1951-52; Div. 3 Champions 1958-59.
League History 1920-30 Div. 3(S); 1930-50 Div. 2; 1950-52 Div. 3(S); 1952-56 Div. 2; 1956-58 Div. 3(S); 1958-59 Div. 3; 1959-68 Div. 2; 1968-75 Div. 3; 1975-77 Div. 2; 1977-86 Div. 3; 1986- Div. 2.
Most League Points in a Season (2 for a win) 68 in Div. 3(S), 1929-30. (3 for a win) 87 in Div. 3, 1985-86.
Most League Goals in a Season 107 in Div. 3(S), 1925-26 and 1951-52.
Record Victory 8-1 v Millwall in Div. 2, 16 January 1932.
Record Defeat 0-9 v Stoke C. in Div. 2, 17 December 1960.
Consecutive League Wins 9 in 1930 and 1986.
Consecutive League Defeats 9 in 1947.
Record League Appearances Sammy Black, 470 between 1924-38.
Record League Goalscorer—Career Sammy Black, 180 between 1924-38.
Record League Goalscorer—Season Jack Cock, 32 in Div. 3(S), 1925-26.

Plymouth Argyle: League Record, 1988-89 (Division 2)

Match Number	Date	Venue	Opponents	Result	H/T	Lge Posn	Attend
1	27.8.88	A	Walsall	D 2-2	2-0		6178
2	3.9.88	H	Hull C.	W 2-0	0-0	7	8202
3	10.9.88	A	Watford	L 0-3	0-1	11	12040
4	17.9.88	H	Stoke C.	W 4-0	2-0	9	7823
5	21.9.88	A	Leicester C.	L 0-1	0-0	12	9117
6	24.9.88	H	West Bromwich A.	D 1-1	0-0	13	8539
7	1.10.88	A	Crystal Palace	L 1-4	1-3	19	8047
8	4.10.88	A	Birmingham C.	W 1-0	0-0	13	4921
9	8.10.88	H	Bradford C.	W 3-1	3-0	8	6855
10	15.10.88	H	Manchester C.	L 0-1	0-0	14	10158
11	22.10.88	A	Chelsea	L 0-5	0-4	16	12658
12	25.10.88	H	Shrewsbury T.	D 0-0	0-0	18	6298
13	29.10.88	A	Barnsley	L 1-3	0-1	19	5485
14	5.11.88	H	Blackburn Rov.	W 4-3	3-0	18	7823
15	12.11.88	A	Portsmouth	L 0-2	0-2	20	11572
16	19.11.88	A	Oxford U.	W 1-0	1-0	17	5429
17	26.11.88	H	Oldham Ath.	W 3-0	2-0	13	7829
18	3.12.88	A	Ipswich T.	D 2-2	2-1	16	9929
19	6.12.88	H	Brighton & H.A.	W 3-0	1-0	7	8133
20	10.12.88	H	Bournemouth	D 1-1	0-0	8	10619
21	18.12.88	H	Sunderland	L 1-4	0-2	11	13498
22	26.12.88	A	Swindon T.	L 0-1	0-1	15	7883
23	31.12.88	A	Leeds U.	L 0-2	0-0	16	24043
24	2.1.89	H	Watford	W 1-0	0-0	16	12142
25	14.1.89	A	Brighton & H.A.	D 2-2	1-1	16	8504
26	21.1.89	H	Walsall	W 2-0	0-0	15	11505
27	4.2.89	H	Birmingham C.	L 0-1	0-1	14	7721
28	11.2.89	A	Bradford C.	D 1-1	1-0	16	8693
29	18.2.89	H	Chelsea	L 0-1	0-1	16	13180
30	25.2.89	A	Manchester C.	L 0-2	0-1	17	22451
31	28.2.89	A	Shrewsbury T.	L 0-2	0-1	18	2978
32	4.3.89	H	Portsmouth	L 0-1	0-0	18	8131
33	11.3.89	A	Blackburn Rov.	W 2-1	1-0	16	7462
34	18.3.89	H	Leicester C.	D 1-1	1-0	18	6703
35	25.3.89	A	Hull C.	L 0-3	0-2	20	5851
36	27.3.89	H	Swindon T.	W 4-1	3-0	18	8487
37	1.4.89	A	Stoke C.	D 2-2	0-2	17	8363
38	4.4.89	A	Sunderland	L 1-2	0-2	20	8003
39	9.4.89	H	Leeds U.	W 1-0	0-0	19	9365
40	15.4.89	A	West Bromwich A.	D 2-2	0-1	19	11358
41	22.4.89	H	Crystal Palace	L 0-2	0-1	19	8492
42	25.4.89	H	Barnsley	L 1-2	1-1	19	5468
43	29.4.89	A	Oldham Ath.	D 2-2	1-2	18	4614
44	1.5.89	H	Ipswich T.	L 0-1	0-1	20	6484
45	6.5.89	H	Oxford U.	W 3-1	0-0	18	4989
46	13.5.89	A	Bournemouth	D 0-0	0-0	18	7230

Players: League Record, 1988-89 (Division 2)

Match Number	1	2	3	4	5	6	7	8	9	10	11	12	13	14	15	16	17	18	19	20	21	22	23	24	25	26	27	28	29	30	31	32	33	34	35	36	37	38	39	40	41	42	43	44	45	46	Apps	Subs	Goals
Barlow, Martin																																													★		0	1	0
Brimacombe, John	2	2	2	11	11	11	11[1]	11	11	11	11	11	**11**		6	5	5	5	4	4	4																						8	3	3	3	24	0	1
Brown, Ken				2	2	2	2	2	2	2	2	2	2	2	2	2	2	2	2	2	2	2	2	2			2	2	2	2	2	2	2			2	2	2	2	2[1]	2	2	2	2	2	2	39	0	1
Burrows, Adrian	4	4	4	4	**4**	4	4	4	4	4	4	4	4	4	4	4	4	4				4	4	4	4	4	4	4	4	4	4	4	4	4	4	4	4	4	4	4	4	4	4	4	4[1]	4	43	0	1
Bryne, David																																		8	10	10	**7**	7	7	7	7	7[1]	7	7	**7**	**7**	13	0	1
Campbell, David																																	10														1	0	0
Campbell, Greg															★		10[1]	10[1]	10	**10**	10				★	★	★	★								★							★[1]			8	6	7	3
Cherry, Steve	1	1	1	1	1	1	1		1	1	1	1	1	1	1	1																															15	0	0
Cooper, Leigh	3	3	3	3	3	3	3	3	3	3	3	3	3	3	**3**																																15	0	0
Evans, Stewart	★	7					★																																								1	2	0
Garner, Darren																																													**10**		1	0	0
Hodges, Kevin	7										★	7	7		8	7	8[1]	8	8	8	8	8	8	8	8	8	**10**	10	10	10	10	10		★			★	★	★	11	★		★	10		★	23	8	1
McCarthy, Sean	10	**10**	10	10	10	10	10	10	10[1]	10	10	10	10	10	**10**					★		10	10	10	**10**	**10**	8	8[1]	8	**8**	8	**8**	8		8	8[2]	8[1]	8	8[1]	8[1]	8	8		8	8[1]		37	1	8
Marker, Nick	5[1]	5	5	5[1]	5	5	5	5	5	5	5	5	5[1]	5				★	5	5	5	5	5	5	5	5[1]	5	5	5	5	5	5	5	5	5	5[1]	5	5	5	5	5	5	5[1]	5	5	5	42	1	6
Matthews, John	8	8	8	8	8	8	**8**	8	8	**8**	**8**				★	8											7	**7**	**7**	7	**7**	**7**	7	**7**	7	7	10	**10**	**10**	10	**10**	10	**10**				29	1	0
Miller, Allan																	1	1	1	1	1	1	1	1	1	1	1	1	1																		13	0	0
Morrison, Andrew																																													6	6	2	0	0
Penhaligon, Gary								1																																							1	0	0
Pickard, Owen																																★		10													1	1	0
Plummer, Calvin			7	7	7	7	7	7	7	7	**7**			7	7	10	7	**7**	7[1]	7	7							★	★	★	★	★														★	17	6	1
Rowbotham, Jason																									2	2						3		2	2												5	0	0
Smith, Mark	6	6	6	6	6	6	6	6	6		6	6	6									7	7	6	6	6	6	6	6	6	6	6	6	6	6	6	6	6	6	6	6	6	6	6			35	0	0
Stuart, Mark														11	11	11	11	11[1]	11	11	11	11	11	11	11[1]	11	11	11	11	11	11	11	11[1]	11[1]	11	11	11	11	11		11	11	11	11	11[1]	11	32	0	5
Summerfield, Kevin	11	11	11		★		★			★		8	8	8		6	6	6	6	6[1]	6	6	6	7[1]	7	7																					17	3	2
Tynan, Tommy	**9**[1]	9[1]	9	9[3]	9	9[1]	**9**	9[1]	9[2]	9	9	9	9	9[4]	9	9[1]	9[1]	9	9[2]	9	9[1]	9	9	9	9[1]	9[1]	9	**9**	9	9	9	9	9[1]	9	9	**9**[1]	9[1]	9[1]	9	9	9	9	9	9	9	9	46	0	24
Uzzell, John		★								6	★		★	6	5	3	3	3	3	3	3	3	3	3	3	3	3	3	3	3	3		3	3	3	3	3	3	3	3	3	3	**3**				30	3	0
Whiston, Peter																																													★	**10**	1	1	0
Wilmot, Rhys																														1	1	1	1	1	1	1	1	1	1	1	1	1	1	1	1	1	17	0	0
Own Goals		1																																															1

FA Cup: 1988-89: 3rd Round: Cambridge U. (H) 2-0; 4th Round: Everton (H) 1-1, Replay (A) 0-4.
Littlewoods Cup: 1988-89: 1st Round: Hereford U. (A) 3-0 (H) 3-2; 2nd Round: Manchester C (A) 0-1 (H) 3-6.

PORTSMOUTH (Division 2)

Team Manager John Gregory.
Club Address Fratton Park, Frogmore Road, Portsmouth PO4 8RA. Tel: (0705) 731204.
Current Ground Capacity 28,000.
Record Attendance 51,385 v Derby Co., FA Cup 6th Round, 26 February 1949.
Year Formed 1896. Turned professional 1898.
Previous Names RA Portsmouth.
Club Nickname "Pompey".
Club Colours Royal blue shirts with white collar and cuffs, white shorts and red stockings.
Club Honours Football League: Div. 1 Champions 1948-49, 1949-50; Div. 3(S) Champions 1923-24; Div. 3 Champions 1961-62, 1982-83. FA Cup: Winners 1939.
League History 1920-24 Div. 3(S); 1924-27 Div. 2; 1927-59 Div. 1; 1959-61 Div. 2; 1961-62 Div. 3; 1962-76 Div. 2; 1976-78 Div. 3; 1978-80 Div. 4; 1980-83 Div. 3; 1983-87 Div. 2; 1987-88 Div. 1; 1988- Div. 2.
Most League Points in a Season (2 for a win) 65 in Div. 3, 1961-62. (3 for a win) 91 in Div. 3, 1982-83.
Most League Goals in a Season 91 in Div. 4, 1979-80.
Record Victory 9-1 v Notts Co. in Div. 2, 9 April 1927.
Record Defeat 0-10 v Leicester C. in Div. 1, 20 October 1928.
Consecutive League Wins 7 in 1980 and 1983.
Consecutive League Defeats 9 in 1959-60, 1960, 1963 and 1975.
Record League Appearances Jimmy Dickinson, 764 between 1946-65.
Record League Goalscorer—Career Peter Harris, 194 between 1946-60.
Record League Goalscorer—Season Billy Haines, 40 in Div. 2, 1926-27.

Portsmouth: League Record, 1988-89 (Division 2)

Match Number	Date	Venue	Opponents	Result	H/T	Lge Posn	Attend
1	27.8.88	A	Shrewsbury T.	W 2-1	1-1		5333
2	29.8.88	H	Leicester C.	W 3-0	1-0	1	10737
3	3.9.88	H	Leeds U.	W 4-0	2-0	1	15263
4	11.9.88	A	Swindon T.	D 1-1	1-0	2	11443
5	17.9.88	H	Hull C.	L 1-3	0-2	3	11599
6	20.9.88	A	Stoke C.	D 2-2	1-1	4	7025
7	24.9.88	H	Crystal Palace	D 1-1	1-0	4	11249
8	1.10.88	A	Bradford C.	L 1-2	1-2	6	11208
9	5.10.88	A	Manchester C.	L 1-4	1-3	9	17202
10	8.10.88	H	Oxford U.	W 2-1	1-1	7	9567
11	15.10.88	H	Bournemouth	W 2-1	1-0	5	12801
12	22.10.88	A	Walsall	D 1-1	1-0	6	5626
13	25.10.88	A	Ipswich T.	W 1-0	0-0	3	14796
14	29.10.88	H	Oldham Ath.	D 1-1	1-1	4	11310
15	5.11.88	A	Birmingham C.	D 0-0	0-0	5	5866
16	12.11.88	H	Plymouth Arg.	W 2-0	2-0	3	11572
17	19.11.88	H	Barnsley	W 3-0	2-0	1	10001
18	26.11.88	A	Blackburn Rov.	L 1-3	1-1	5	8141
19	3.12.88	H	West Bromwich A.	D 0-0	0-0	6	12779
20	10.12.88	A	Chelsea	D 3-3	1-2	6	20221
21	17.12.88	H	Brighton & H.A.	W 2-0	1-0	5	12467
22	26.12.88	A	Watford	L 0-1	0-0	6	15224
23	31.12.88	A	Sunderland	L 0-4	0-2	7	21556

Match Number	Date	Venue	Opponents	Result	H/T	Lge Posn	Attend
24	2.1.89	H	Swindon T	L 0-2	0-1	9	11681
25	14.1.89	A	Leicester C.	L 1-2	1-1	13	10567
26	21.1.89	H	Shrewsbury T.	W 2-0	1-0	10	8446
27	4.2.89	H	Manchester C.	L 0-1	0-1	14	13207
28	11.2.89	A	Oxford U.	L 0-1	0-1	13	6156
29	18.2.89	H	Walsall	D 1-1	0-1	14	7310
30	25.2.89	A	Bournemouth	L 0-1	0-0	14	9959
31	28.2.89	H	Ipswich T.	L 0-1	0-0	14	7145
32	4.3.89	A	Plymouth Arg.	W 1-0	0-0	14	8131
33	11.3.89	H	Birmingham C.	W 1-0	0-0	13	8078
34	14.3.89	A	Oldham Ath.	L 3-5	0-2	13	5773
35	18.3.89	H	Stoke C.	D 0-0	0-0	13	7624
36	25.3.89	A	Leeds U.	L 0-1	0-0	14	27049
37	27.3.89	H	Watford	D 2-2	2-0	13	9364
38	1.4.89	A	Hull C.	D 1-1	0-0	14	5325
39	5.4.89	A	Brighton & H.A.	L 1-2	1-0	15	10100
40	8.4.89	H	Sunderland	W 2-0	1-0	13	7724
41	15.4.89	A	Crystal Palace	L 0-2	0-0	16	12358
42	22.4.89	H	Bradford C.	L 1-2	0-1	17	6909
43	29.4.89	H	Blackburn Rov.	L 1-2	0-0	17	6057
44	1.5.89	A	West Bromwich A.	L 0-3	0-1	18	9506
45	6.5.89	A	Barnsley	L 0-1	0-0	19	5718
46	13.5.89	H	Chelsea	L 2-3	1-1	20	12051

Players: League Record, 1988-89 (Division 2)

Match Number	1	2	3	4	5	6	7	8	9	10	11	12	13	14	15	16	17	18	19	20	21	22	23	24	25	26	27	28	29	30	31	32	33	34	35	36	37	38	39	40	41	42	43	44	45	46	Apps	Subs	Goals
Aspinall, Warren				★	★	9^1	8^1	9^1	9^1	9^1	9	9	9	9^1	9	9	**9**	9	9	9	9^1	9	9	**9**		10^1	10	10	10			★	10	10^1	10	10	10^1	10	10	10	10	10^1	10	**10**	10	★	36	4	11
Awford, Andy																																									6	6	6	★			3	1	0
Ball, Kevin											6	6	6	6	6	6	6	6	6	6^1	6	6	6	6																							14	0	1
Beresford, John																																				★	3										1	1	0
Chamberlain, Mark			7^1	7^1	**7**	7	7		7		7^1	7	7	7	7	7^1	7	7^1	7	7	7	**7**	**7**					7	7	7	7	7	7^1	7	7	**7**											28	0	6
Connor, Terry	10^1	10^2	10^1	10	10^1	10	10	10	**10**	**7**	**10**																			**10**	10	**10**															14	0	5
Dillon, Kevin	4	4	4	4	4	4	4			★							★	★	★	8	8	8	11	7			8	**8**		★	4	4	4	4	**4**							4	4	4	4	10	24	5	0
Fillery, Mike																									**11**		★	**6**	6					★	**11**	★	7	7	7^1	7	7	7	7^1	7	7	7	14	3	2
Gilbert, Billy	6	6	**6**	6	6			4	6			5									4																						★	★		★	9	3	0
Gosney, Andrew																															1	1	1	1	1	1	1	1	1	1	1	1	1	**1**			14	0	0
Hardyman, Paul	3	3	3	3	3	3	**3**	3	3	3	3	**3**				11		**11**		11	11^1	**11**	★	11		3	**3**							2					★		9	**9**					23	2	1
Hogg, Graeme	5	5	5	5	5	5	5	5	5	5	5		5	5	5	5	5	5	5	5	5		5	5	5	5^1	5	5	5	5	5	5	5	5	5	5	5	5	5				5	5	5	5	41	0	1
Horne, Barry	8	8	**8**	8	8	8^1	2	8	8	8	8	8	8^1	8	8	8	8^2	8	8			★	8	8	8	8			8	8	8	8	8	8	8												30	1	4
Kelly, Mark	$★^1$		★			11	11	**11**	11	11	11	**11**	11	11	**11**	★	**11**		**11**			★	★	★	★	★	★	★			★	11	11	**11**	★						★						15	13	1
Knight, Alan	1	1	1	1	1	1	1	1	1	1	1	1	1	1	1	1	1	1	1	1	1	1	1	1	1	1	1	1	1	1															1	1	32	0	0
Kuhl, Martin								7	4	4	4	4	4	4	4	4	4	4	4	4^1		4	4	4	10	11	11	11	11	**4**					★	4	4	4	4	4	4			9	9	4	31	1	1
Maguire, Gavin																									4	4	4	4	4	6	6	6	6	6	6	6	6		6	6				6	6	6	18	0	0
Moncur, John																																				8	8	8	**8**	8	**8**	8					7	0	0
Moran, Paul																									7	**7**	**7**																				3	0	0
Neill, Warren	2	2	2	2	**2**			**2**	2	2	2	2	2	2	2	2	2	2	2	2	2	2	2	2	2	2	2	2	2	2	2	2	2		2	2	2	2	2	2	2	2	2	2	2	2	43	0	0
Powell, Darryl																								★						9	**9**																2	1	0
Quinn, Mike	9	9^1	9^1	**9**	9		9	★	★	10^1	$★^1$	10^1	10	10	10	10^1	10^1	10	10	10^1	10	10	10	10	9^1	9	9	9	9^1			9^1	9	9^2	9	9	9^1	9^1	9	9^2			**9**			9^1	36	3	18
Ross, Michael																														★																	0	1	0
Russell, Lee							★																																			★					0	2	0
Sandford, Lee	11	11	11	11	11	2		★				★	3	3	3	**3**	3	3	3	3	3	3	**3**	**3**				★		11	11							3		5	5	5	8	8	8	**8**	28	3	0
Symons, Chris																									6	6																					2	0	0
Whitehead, Clive	**7**	7	★		★	6	6	6		6		★			★		★					5			3		6	3	3	3	3	3	3	3	**3**		6	3	3	3	3	3	3	3	3	3	27	5	0
Wigley, Steve																																				11	11	11	11	11	11	11	11	11	11	**11**	11	0	0
Own Goals			1																																											1			2

FA Cup: 1988-89: 3rd Round: Swindon T. (H) 1-1, Replay (A) 0-2.
Littlewoods Cup: 1988-89: 2nd Round: Scarborough (H) 2-2 (A) 1-3.

PORT VALE (Division 2)

Team Manager John Rudge.
Club Address Vale Park, Burslem, Stoke on Trent. Tel: (0782) 814134.
Current Ground Capacity 16,800.
Record Attendance 50,000 v Aston Villa, FA Cup 5th Round, 20 February 1960.
Year Formed 1876. Turned professional 1885.
Previous Names Burslem Port Vale.
Club Nickname "The Valiants".
Club Colours White shirts with black trim, black shorts and white stockings.
Club Honours Football League: Div 3(N) Champions 1929-30, 1953-54; Div. 4 Champions 1958-59.
League History 1892-96 Div. 2; 1896 Failed re-election; 1898-1907 Div. 2; 1907 Resigned; 1919-29 Div. 2; 1929-30 Div. 3(N); 1930-36 Div. 2; 1936-38 Div. 3(N); 1938-52 Div. 3(S); 1952-54 Div. 3(N); 1954-57 Div. 2; 1957-58 Div. 3(S); 1958-59 Div. 4; 1959-65 Div. 3; 1965-70 Div. 4; 1970-78 Div. 3; 1978-83 Div. 4; 1983-84 Div. 3; 1984-86 Div. 4; 1986-89 Div. 3; 1989- Div. 2.
Most League Points in a Season (2 for a win) 69 in Div. 3(N), 1953-54. (3 for a win) 88 in Div. 4, 1982-83.
Most League Goals in a Season 110 in Div. 4, 1958-59.
Record Victory 9-1 v Chesterfield in Div. 2, 24 September 1932.
Record Defeat 0-10 v Sheffield U. in Div. 2, 10 December 1892 and v Notts Co. in Div. 2, 26 February 1895.
Consecutive League Wins 8 in 1893.
Consecutive League Defeats 9 in 1957.
Record League Appearances Roy Sproson, 761 between 1950-72.
Record League Goalscorer—Career Wilf Kirkham, 154 between 1923-33.
Record League Goalscorer—Season Wilf Kirkham, 38 in Div. 2, 1926-27.

Port Vale: League Record, 1988-89 (Division 3)

Match Number	Date	Venue	Opponents	Result	H/T	Lge Posn	Attend
1	27.8.88	A	Preston N.E.	W 3-1	1-0		6718
2	3.9.88	H	Chester C.	L 1-2	0-2	12	4213
3	10.9.88	A	Bury	D 0-0	0-0	12	2978
4	17.9.88	H	Cardiff C.	W 6-1	3-1	5	4280
5	19.9.88	H	Chesterfield	W 5-0	3-0	1	4469
6	24.9.88	A	Bristol C.	W 1-0	1-0	2	7235
7	1.10.88	A	Wolverhampton W.	D 3-3	2-1	2	14018
8	3.10.88	H	Huddersfield T.	W 2-0	2-0	1	5938
9	8.10.88	A	Wigan Ath.	W 2-0	0-0	1	3976
10	15.10.88	H	Bolton W.	W 2-1	1-1	1	7985
11	22.10.88	A	Blackpool	L 2-3	2-1	2	7045
12	24.10.88	H	Sheffield U.	D 3-3	0-1	2	13246
13	29.10.88	A	Brentford	L 1-2	0-0	3	5212
14	8.11.88	A	Northampton T.	W 3-1	1-1	4	3796
15	12.11.88	H	Swansea C.	W 2-1	2-1	3	6248
16	26.11.88	H	Fulham	W 3-0	1-0	3	5079
17	2.12.88	A	Southend U.	D 1-1	1-1	3	3245
18	17.12.89	H	Reading	W 3-0	1-0	2	4779
19	26.12.88	A	Mansfield T	W 1-0	0-0	2	5218
20	30.12.88	A	Gillingham	L 0-1	0-0	2	4706
21	2.1.89	H	Notts Co.	W 1-0	0-0	2	7084
22	14.1.89	A	Chester C.	W 2-1	0-1	2	4891
23	21.1.89	H	Bury	L 1-3	1-1	2	5783
24	28.1.89	A	Cardiff C.	L 0-3	0-1	2	4507
25	4.2.89	H	Wolverhampton W.	D 0-0	0-0	2	16362
26	11.2.89	A	Huddersfield T.	D 0-0	0-0	2	8004
27	13.2.89	H	Aldershot	W 3-0	1-0	2	5033
28	18.2.89	H	Wigan Ath.	W 2-1	1-0	2	6100
29	28.2.89	A	Sheffield U.	D 0-0	0-0	2	18787
30	4.3.89	H	Blackpool	W 1-0	1-0	2	6306
31	11.3.89	A	Aldershot	D 2-2	0-0	2	2397
32	13.3.89	H	Brentford	W 3-2	1-0	2	5577
33	18.3.89	H	Preston N.E.	D 1-1	0-1	2	8584
34	25.3.89	A	Notts Co.	W 4-1	2-0	2	7328
35	27.3.89	H	Mansfield T.	L 1-2	1-1	2	8198
36	1.4.89	A	Reading	L 0-3	0-1	2	4501
37	5.4.89	A	Bristol Rov.	D 2-2	1-1	2	6869
38	8.4.89	H	Gillingham	W 2-1	1-0	2	5358
39	15.4.89	A	Chesterfield	W 2-1	2-0	2	5895
40	21.4.89	H	Bristol C.	L 0-1	0-0	3	6923
41	25.4.89	A	Bolton W.	D 1-1	0-1	3	5296
42	29.4.89	A	Swansea C.	D 0-0	0-0	3	4229
43	1.5.89	H	Northampton T.	L 1-2	0-1	3	6604
44	6.5.89	H	Southend U.	W 2-0	2-0	3	4516
45	9.5.89	H	Bristol Rov.	W 1-0	0-0	3	6136
46	13.5.89	A	Fulham	D 2-1	0-1	3	6257

Players: League Record, 1988-89 (Division 3)

Match Number	1	2	3	4	5	6	7	8	9	10	11	12	13	14	15	16	17	18	19	20	21	22	23	24	25	26	27	28	29	30	31	32	33	34	35	36	37	38	39	40	41	42	43	44	45	46	Apps	Subs	Goals
Atkinson, Paul	11^2	11														11^1	11																														4	0	3
Beckford, Darren	10^1	10	10	10^1	10^3	10	10	10	10^1	10	10	10	10	10^1	10^1	10^2	10	10^1	10	10	10^1	10^1	10	10		10	10^2	10	10	10	10	10	10	10^3	10	10		★	10^2	10	10	10	10	10			41	1	20
Earle, Robbie	8	8	8	8^1	8	8	8^1	8	8^1	8			8^1	8^1	8	8	8	8	8^1	8	8	8^1	8	8	8	8	8	8^1	8	8	8^1	8	8	8	8^1	8	8^1	8	8	8	8^1	8	8	8	8^1	8	44	0	13
Finney, Kevin	★			★	★		4	4			★	8	★	★	★		★																											★	10	10^1	5	9	1
Ford, Gary	7	7	7	7	7^2	7	7	7^1	7	7	7	7^2	7	7				7								7					★	7^1	7^1	7	7	7											21	1	7
Futcher, Ron	9	9^1	9	9^2	9	9	9^1	9^1	9	9	9^2	9^1	9	9^1	9^1			9	9	9	9	9	9^1	9	9			9^1	9	9^1	9^1	9^1	9	9	9	9	9	9		★	9	9	9^1	9^1	9	★	39	2	17
Glover, Dean																									6	6	6	6	6	6	6	6	6	6	6	6	6	6	6	6	6	6	6	6	6	6	22	0	0
Grew, Mark	1	1	1	1	1	1	1		1	1								1	1	1	1	1	1	1	1	1	1	1	1	1	1	1	1	1	1	1	1	1	1	1	1	1	1	1	1		37	0	0
Harper, Stephen				★	★									★		★								★		★	★																				0	7	0
Hazell, Bob	5	5	5	5						5	5	5	5	5	5	5	5	5	5	5	5	5																									17	0	0
Hughes, Darren			3	3	3	3	3	3	3	3	3	3	3	3	3	3	3	3	3	3	3	3	3	3	3	3	3	3	3	3	3	3	3	3	3	3	3	3	3	3	3	3	3	3	3	3	44	0	0
Jeffers, John																				★	7	7	7	7													★	★	7	7	7	★	7	7	7	7	11	4	0
Jepson, Ronnie																																							★							9	1	1	0
Jones, Andy																									10	9	9^1		★	★	★	$★^1$	★	★	★	★	10^1	10	9	9	★	11					8	9	3
Mills, Simon	2	2			5	5	5	5	5	2	6	2	2	2	7	7	7	2	2	2		4	5	5	2	2	2	2	2	2	2	2	2	2	2	2	2	2	2	2	2	2	2	2	2	2	43	0	0
Porter, Andrew											8												★	6	7	★	7	7		7							7	7					11	11^1	11	11	12	2	1
Riley, David		★	11	11^1	11	11	11	11	11	11^1	11	11	11	11	11	9	9	11^1	11	11	11	11	11	11	11	11	11	11	11	11	11	11	11	11	11	11	11	11	11	11	11						39	1	3
Sproson, Phil	6	6	6	6	6	6	6^1	6	6	6		6			6	6	6^1	6	6	6	6	6	6																								20	0	2
Stowell, Mike											1	1	1	1	1	1	1																														7	0	0
Walker, Ray	4	4	4	4^1	4	4^1			4	4^1	4	4	4	4	4	4	4	4	4	4	4		4	4	4	4	4	4	4	4	4	4	4	4^1	4	4	4	4^1	4	4	4	4	4	4	4	4	43	0	5
Webb, Alan	3	3	2	2	2	2	2	2	2		2		6	6	2	2	2		7	7	2	2	2	2	5	5	5	5	5		5				★	★	5	5	5	5	5	5	5	5			35	2	0
West, Gary																													7	5	7	5	5	5	5	5					★	7	★	★	5	5^1	11	3	1
Wood, Trevor								1																																						1	2	0	0
Own Goals																		1																				1											2

FA Cup: 1988-89: 1st Round: Southport (A) 2-0; 2nd Round: Bolton W. (A) 2-1; 3rd Round: Norwich C. (H) 1-3.
Littlewoods Cup: 1988-89: 1st Round: Chesterfield (H) 3-2 (A) 1-1; 2nd Round: Ipswich T. (H) 1-0 (A) 0-3.

PRESTON NORTH END (Division 3)

Team Manager John McGrath.
Club Address Deepdale, Preston, PR1 6RU. Tel: (0772) 795919.
Current Ground Capacity 19,000.
Record Attendance 42,684 v Arsenal, Div. 1, 23 April 1938.
Year Formed 1881. Turned professional 1885.
Previous Names None.
Club Nickname "The Lilywhites" or "North End".
Club Colours All white.
Club Honours Football League: Div. 1 Champions 1888-89, 1889-90; Div. 2 Champions 1903-04, 1912-13, 1950-51; Div. 3 Champions 1970-71. FA Cup: Winners 1889, 1938.
League History 1888-1901 Div. 1; 1901-04 Div. 2; 1904-12 Div. 1; 1912-13 Div. 2; 1913-14 Div. 1; 1914-15 Div. 2; 1919-25 Div. 1; 1925-34 Div. 2; 1934-49 Div. 1; 1949-51 Div. 2; 1951-61 Div. 1; 1961-70 Div. 2; 1970-71 Div. 3; 1971-74 Div. 2; 1974-78 Div. 3; 1978-81 Div. 2; 1981-85 Div. 3; 1985-87 Div. 4; 1987- Div. 3.
Most League Points in a Season (2 for a win) 61 in Div. 3, 1970-71. (3 for a win) 90 in Div. 4, 1986-87.
Most League Goals in a Season 100 in Div. 2, 1927-28 and in Div. 1, 1957-58.
Record Victory 26-0 v Hyde in FA Cup 1st Series, 1st Round, 15 October 1887.
Record Defeat 0-7 v Blackpool in Div. 1, 1 May 1948.
Consecutive League Wins 14 in 1950-51.
Consecutive League Defeats 8 in 1983.
Record League Appearances Alan Kelly, 447 between 1961-74.
Record League Goalscorer—Career Tom Finney, 187 between 1946-60.
Record League Goalscorer—Season Ted Harper, 37 in Div. 2, 1932-33.

Preston North End: League Record, 1988-89 (Division 3)

Match Number	Date	Venue	Opponents	Result	H/T	Lge Posn	Attend
1	27.8.88	H	Port Vale	L 1-3	0-1		6718
2	3.9.88	A	Huddersfield T.	L 0-2	0-2	23	5622
3	10.9.88	H	Blackpool	W 1-0	0-0	19	8779
4	17.9.88	A	Bristol C.	D 1-1	1-1	19	7913
5	20.9.88	H	Chester C.	D 3-3	1-1	18	5415
6	24.9.88	A	Notts Co.	D 0-0	0-0	19	4965
7	1.10.88	H	Southend U.	W 3-2	0-2	15	5348
8	5.10.88	A	Bristol Rov.	L 0-1	0-1	19	3689
9	8.10.88	H	Bury	W 1-0	0-0	13	5863
10	15.10.88	A	Chesterfield	W 3-0	2-0	10	2813
11	22.10.88	A	Brentford	W 2-0	0-0	8	5584
12	25.10.88	H	Gillingham	W 5-0	2-0	4	6390
13	29.10.88	A	Swansea C.	D 1-1	1-0	6	5370
14	5.11.88	H	Mansfield T.	W 2-0	1-0	3	6434
15	8.11.88	H	Wigan Ath.	D 2-2	1-2	7	8396
16	12.11.88	A	Reading	D 2-2	1-1	6	6225
17	26.11.88	A	Wolverhampton W.	L 0-6	0-3	7	13180
18	3.12.88	H	Cardiff C.	D 3-3	2-0	7	4926
19	17.12.88	A	Fulham	L 1-2	0-1	10	3858
20	26.12.88	H	Bolton W.	W 3-1	2-0	9	12104
21	31.12.88	H	Sheffield U.	W 2-0	0-0	7	11005
22	2.1.89	A	Northampton T.	L 0-1	0-0	8	4219
23	7.1.89	A	Aldershot	L 1-2	0-0	9	2135
24	14.1.89	H	Huddersfield T.	W 1-0	0-0	8	6959
25	21.1.89	A	Blackpool	L 0-1	0-0	9	8951
26	28.1.89	H	Bristol C.	W 2-0	0-0	7	6080
27	3.2.89	A	Southend U.	L 1-2	0-2	8	2948
28	11.2.89	H	Bristol Rov.	D 1-1	0-1	8	7365
29	18.2.89	A	Bury	D 1-1	0-0	8	6977
30	25.2.89	H	Chesterfield	W 6-0	4-0	8	7074
31	28.2.89	A	Gillingham	W 3-1	0-1	5	3031
32	4.3.89	H	Brentford	W 5-3	2-2	5	8186
33	11.3.89	A	Mansfield T.	W 3-0	0-0	4	4706
34	14.3.89	H	Swansea C.	D 1-1	1-0	4	8975
35	18.3.89	A	Port Vale	D 1-1	1-0	4	8584
36	25.3.89	H	Northampton T.	W 3-2	1-1	4	9137
37	27.3.89	A	Bolton W.	L 0-1	0-1	5	10281
38	1.4.89	H	Fulham	L 1-4	1-2	6	8190
39	4.4.89	H	Aldershot	D 2-2	0-0	5	5977
40	8.4.89	A	Sheffield U.	L 1-3	0-0	6	12718
41	15.4.89	H	Notts Co.	W 3-0	1-0	6	6735
42	22.4.89	A	Chester C.	W 1-0	0-0	6	4617
43	29.4.89	H	Reading	W 2-1	2-0	6	7003
44	1.5.89	A	Wigan Ath.	D 1-1	1-0	6	5671
45	5.5.89	A	Cardiff C.	D 0-0	0-0	6	3196
46	13.5.89	H	Wolverhampton W.	D 3-3	1-1	6	14126

Players: League Record, 1988-89 (Division 3)

Match Number	1	2	3	4	5	6	7	8	9	10	11	12	13	14	15	16	17	18	19	20	21	22	23
Allardyce, Sam		6		6	6	6	6	6			★	**6**				6	6	6					**5**
Atkins, Robert	4	4	4	4	4	4	4	4	4	4	4	4	4	4	4	4	4	4					
Bogie, Ian																							
Brazil, Gary	10	10	10	10	10	10	10^2	10			★^{2}	10^2	10	10	10^1	10	10	7^1	9	10	10	10	10
Brown, David	1	1	1	1	1	1	1	1	1	1	1	1	1	1	1	1	1						
Ellis, Tony	9	★	9	9	9^1	9	**9**	9	9^1	9^1	9	9^2	9^1	9	9	9^1	9	9^2		9^1	9	**9**	9
Fitzpatrick, Paul																		10	10				
Harper, Stephen																							
Hughes, Adrian									6	6	**6**		6	6	6		★	5	5	6^1	6	6	6
Jemson, Nigel																							
Jones, Alex	5	5	5	5	5	5	5	**5**				★							4	4	4	4	4
Joyce, Warren		★	8	8	8				10	8	8	8^1	8	8	8	8	8	8	8	8^1	8^1	8	8^1
McAteer, Andy	3		3	3	3	3	3^1												3	3	3	**3**	★
Miller, David	2	2	7	7	**7**	**7**	★	2	**2**			11	★									★	
Mooney, Brian		7				★	7	7	7	7^1	7	7	7	7^1	7	7	7		7	7	7	7	7
Patterson, Mark	**11**	11	11^1	11	11^2	11	11	11	11	11	11		**11**	11	11^1	11^1	11	11	11^1	11	11^1	11	11
Philliskirk, Tony																							
Rathbone, Mike	★	3	2	2^1	2	2	2	3	3	3	3	3	3	3^1	3	3	3	3				★	**3**
Swann, Gary	8	**8**			★	8	8	**8**	★	10^1	**10**												
Tunks, Roy																		1	1	1	1	1	1
Williams, Neil	7^1	**9**						★	8	2	2	2	2	2	2	2	2	2	2	2	2	2	2
Wrightson, Jeff	6		6					★	5	5	5	5	5	5	5	5	**5**		6	5	5	5	★
Own Goals																							

Match Number	24	25	26	27	28	29	30	31	32	33	34	35	36	37	38	39	40	41	42	43	44	45	46	Apps	Subs	Goals
Allardyce, Sam															3		4							13	1	0
Atkins, Robert			6	6	6	6	6	6	6	6	6	6	6	6	6	6	6	4	4	4	4	4	4	39	0	0
Bogie, Ian					9	9	9	9	9	9	**9**	★		★	★	**7^1**	7		★					9	4	1
Brazil, Gary	10	10	10	★																				23	2	8
Brown, David																		1	1	1	1	1	1	23	0	0
Ellis, Tony	9	9	9	9	★	8	8^3	8^2	8^1	8^1	8	8^1	8	8	8	**8**	8	8^1	8	8	8	8	8^2	43	2	21
Fitzpatrick, Paul																								2	0	0
Harper, Stephen															★	★	11		**11**		★			2	3	0
Hughes, Adrian	6	6														5	5	6	6	6	6	6	6	22	1	1
Jemson, Nigel														★		★	**10**	10	10^1	10	**10^1**	★	**10**	6	3	2
Jones, Alex	4	4	4	4	4	4	4	4	4	4	4	4	4	4	4	4								29	1	0
Joyce, Warren	8	8	8	8	**8**	★	★		★^{2}		★	9	9^2	9	9	9	9	9^1	9	9	9	9	9	35	5	9
McAteer, Andy		★		**10**																				11	2	1
Miller, David																								9	3	0
Mooney, Brian	7	7	7^2	7^1	7^1	7	**7**	7	7	7	7	7	7	7	**7**		★	7	7	7	7	7	7	38	2	6
Patterson, Mark	11^1	11	11	11	11	11	11^1	11^1	11^1	11	11	11	11^1	11		11		11		11^2	11	11	11^1	42	0	15
Philliskirk, Tony					10	**10**	10^2	10	**10^1**	10^1	10	**10**	10	**10**	10^1	10^1						**10**	★	13	1	6
Rathbone, Mike	3	**3**	3	3	3	3	3	3	3	3	3	3	3	**3**										32	2	2
Swann, Gary															**11**	3	3	3^1	3	3	3	3	3	16	2	2
Tunks, Roy	1	1	1	1	1	1	1	1	1	1	1	1	1	1	1	1	1							23	0	0
Williams, Neil	2	2	2	2	2	2^1	2	2	2	2	2	2	2	2	2	2	2	2	2	2	2	2	2	40	1	2
Wrightson, Jeff	5	5	5	5	5	5	5	5	5	5	5	5	5	5	5			5	5	5	5	5	5	36	2	0
Own Goals										1	1						1									3

FA Cup: 1988-89: 1st Round: Tranmere Rov. (H) 1-1, Replay (A) 0-3.
Littlewoods Cup: 1988-89: 1st Round: Wigan Ath. (A) 0-0 (H) 1-0; 2nd Round: Norwich C. (A) 0-2 (H) 0-3.

QUEENS PARK RANGERS (Division 1)

Team Manager Trevor Francis.
Club Address South Africa Road, London W12 7PA. Tel: 01-743 0262/3/4/5.
Current Ground Capacity 27,000.
Record Attendance 35,353 v Leeds U., Div. 1, 27 April 1974.
Year Formed 1885. Turned professional 1898.
Previous Names St Jude's Institute.
Club Nickname "Rangers" or "The R's".
Club Colours Blue and white hooped shirts, white shorts and white stockings with three blue bands at top.
Club Honours Football League: Div. 2 Champions 1982-83; Div 3(S) Champions 1947-48; Div. 3 Champions 1966-67. Football League Cup: Winners 1967.
League History 1920-48 Div. 3(S); 1948-52 Div. 2; 1952-58 Div. 3(S); 1958-67 Div. 3; 1967-68 Div. 2; 1968-69 Div. 1; 1969-73 Div. 2; 1973-79 Div. 1; 1979-83 Div. 2; 1983- Div. 1.
Most League Points in a Season (2 for a win) 67 in Div. 3, 1966-67. (3 for a win) 85 in Div. 2, 1982-83.
Most League Goals in a Season 111 in Div. 3, 1961-62.
Record Victory 9-2 v Tranmere Rov. in Div. 3, 3 December 1960.
Record Defeat 1-8 v Mansfield T. in Div. 3, 15 March 1965 and v Manchester U. in Div. 1, 19 March 1969.
Consecutive League Wins 8 in 1931.
Consecutive League Defeats 9 in 1969.
Record League Appearances Tony Ingham, 514 between 1950-63.
Record League Goalscorer—Career George Goddard, 172 between 1926-34.
Record League Goalscorer—Season George Goddard, 37 in Div. 3(S), 1929-30.

Queens Park Rangers: League Record, 1988-89 (Division 1)

Match Number	Date	Venue	Opponents	Result	H/T	Lge Posn	Attend
1	27.8.88	A	Manchester U.	D 0-0	0-0		46377
2	3.9.88	H	Southampton	L 0-1	0-1	15	9053
3	10.9.88	A	Norwich C.	L 0-1	0-0	17	11174
4	17.9.88	H	Sheffield Wed.	W 2-0	1-0	11	8011
5	24.9.88	A	Derby Co.	W 1-0	1-0	5	14008
6	1.10.88	A	Millwall	L 2-3	1-3	12	14103
7	88.10.88	H	Nottingham F.	L 1-2	1-1	17	11205
8	15.10.88	H	West Ham U.	W 2-1	0-1	9	14566
9	22.10.88	A	Arsenal	L 1-2	0-0	12	33202
10	29.10.88	A	Luton T.	D 0-0	0-0	14	8453
11	5.11.88	H	Newcastle U.	W 3-0	2-0	12	11013
12	12.11.88	A	Middlesbrough	L 0-1	0-1	14	20565
13	19.11.88	H	Liverpool	L 0-1	0-1	14	20065
14	26.11.88	A	Tottenham H.	D 2-2	2-0	13	26698
15	3.12.88	H	Coventry C.	W 2-1	1-0	13	9853
16	10.12.88	A	Charlton Ath.	D 1-1	1-0	13	6012
17	17.12.88	H	Everton	D 0-0	0-0	14	10067
18	26.12.88	A	Aston Villa	L 1-2	0-2	15	25106
19	31.12.88	A	Southampton	W 4-1	0-0	12	15086
20	2.1.89	H	Norwich C.	D 1-1	0-0	14	12461
21	14.1.89	A	Wimbledon	L 0-1	0-1	15	7118
22	21.1.89	H	Derby Co.	L 0-1	0-0	16	9516
23	4.2.89	H	Millwall	L 1-2	0-0	16	12381
24	11.2.89	A	Nottingham F.	D 0-0	0-0	16	19690
25	18.2.89	H	Arsenal	D 0-0	0-0	16	20543
26	25.2.89	A	West Ham U.	D 0-0	0-0	16	17371
27	11.3.89	A	Newcastle U.	W 2-1	0-0	13	21577
28	21.3.89	H	Luton T.	D 1-1	0-0	12	9372
29	25.3.89	A	Sheffield Wed.	W 2-0	0-0	12	18804
30	27.3.89	H	Aston Villa	W 1-0	0-0	12	11378
31	1.4.89	A	Everton	L 1-4	0-2	12	23028
32	8.4.89	H	Wimbledon	W 4-3	3-1	12	9569
33	15.4.89	H	Middlesbrough	D 0-0	0-0	12	10313
34	22.4.89	A	Coventry C.	W 3-0	2-0	11	11319
35	29.4.89	H	Charlton Ath.	W 1-0	1-0	10	13432
36	8.5.89	H	Manchester U.	W 3-2	1-2	9	10070
37	13.5.89	H	Tottenham H.	W 1-0	0-0	8	21873
38	16.5.89	A	Liverpool	L 0-2	0-1	9	38368

Players: League Record, 1988-89 (Division 1)

Match Number	1	2	3	4	5	6	7	8	9	10	11	12	13	14	15	16	17	18	19
Allen, Bradley																			
Allen, Martin	7	7	7	7	7	7^{1}	7	3	3	3	3^{1}	**3**	3	3	3	3			11^{1}
Ardiles, Osvaldo	6	6	★									★	★	**5**					★
Barker, Simon	11	11	**8**		11	★		2	2	**2**	**2**	2	**2**	**2**			**11**	11	★^{1}
Brock, Kevin	8	**8**	**11**	11		**11**	11	**11**	11	11	★	★	11	11	11				
Channing, Justin																			
Clarke, Colin																			
Coney, Dean			9		★		10	★		★					2		10	10	10
Dennis, Mark	3	3	3	3	3	**3**	**3**								★		**3**		
Falco, Mark	9	9	★			★		7	7^{1}	7	7^{1}	7	7	7^{1}	7^{1}	7	7	7	7^{2}
Fereday, Wayne	2	2	2	9	9	9	9	9	9	9	9	9	9	9	9	9	9	**9**	
Fleming, Mark																			
Francis, Trevor	**10**	**10**		8^{2}	8	8^{1}	8	8	**8**	**8**	8	8	**8**	8^{1}	8^{1}	8^{1}	8	8^{1}	8
Gray, Andy																			
Herrera, Roberto																			
Johns, Nicky						1	1	1											
Kerslake, David					2	2		★	★	★	★		★	★		11	★	6	
Law, Brian				2															3
McDonald, Alan	5	5	5	5	5	5	5	5	5	5	5	5	5			2	2	2	2
Maddix, Danny		★	6	6	6		2	6^{1}	6	6	6^{1}	6	6	6	6	6	6	★	6
Maguire, Gavin						6	6				11	11		★	5	5		**3**	
Parker, Paul	4	4	4	4	4	4	4	4	4	4	4	4	4	4	**4**	4	4	4	4
Pisanti, David													10	10	10	10	5	5	**5**
Reid, Peter																			
Seaman, David	1	1	1	1	1				1	1	1	1	1	1	1	1	1	1	1
Sinton, Andy																			
Spackman, Nigel																			
Stein, Mark	★	★	10	10	**10^{1}**	10	★^{1}	**10^{1}**	10	10	**10**	**10**					★	★	**9**
Own Goals																			

Match Number	20	21	22	23	24	25	26	27	28	29	30	31	32	33	34	35	36	37	38	Apps	Subs	Goals
Allen, Bradley		★																		0	1	0
Allen, Martin	11								11	11^{1}	**7**	**7**	7	7	★	★		3	3	26	2	4
Ardiles, Osvaldo		2																		4	4	0
Barker, Simon	10	8	8	★	9	**7**	7		★									10	2	21	4	1
Brock, Kevin																				12	2	0
Channing, Justin					2	2	2						**2**	2	2^{1}	2	2	**2**		9	0	1
Clarke, Colin								9^{1}	9^{1}	**9**	9	9	9^{1}	9	9^{2}	9	9	9	9	12	0	5
Coney, Dean		10	10	10	10	10	★	★												11	5	0
Dennis, Mark						**3**	**3**	3		3	3	3	3	3						16	1	0
Falco, Mark	7^{1}			9^{1}		9	**9**			★^{1}	**8**	8^{1}	**8^{1}**	**8**				★^{1}	★	22	5	12
Fereday, Wayne		9	**9**	**11**				2	3	2	2	2	★	★	3	3	**3**			29	2	0
Fleming, Mark			2																	1	0	0
Francis, Trevor	8																			19	0	7
Gray, Andy				8	**8**	8	8	**7**	**7**						**7**	**7**	7^{2}	7	**7**	11	0	2
Herrera, Roberto		★	★																	0	2	0
Johns, Nicky																				3	0	0
Kerslake, David	★	**11**	11		★	★									8	8	8	**8**	8	11	10	0
Law, Brian	5	5	5	**3**																6	0	0
McDonald, Alan	2			5			5	5	5	5	5	5	5	**5**			★	★	★	27	3	0
Maddix, Danny	6	6	6	2	5	5	10	★	2	★	★				5	5	5	5	5	28	5	2
Maguire, Gavin																				7	1	0
Parker, Paul	4	4	4	4	4			4	4	4	4	4	4	4	4	4	4	4	4	36	0	0
Pisanti, David	3	**3**	3	★	3	11	★	**11**												13	2	0
Reid, Peter					11	4	4	10	10	10	10	10	10^{1}	10	10	**10**	**10**		**10**	14	0	1
Seaman, David	1	1	1	1	1	1	1	1	1	1	1	1	1	1	1	1	1	1	1	35	0	0
Sinton, Andy										7	11^{1}	11	11	11	11	11^{1}	11^{1}	11	11	10	0	3
Spackman, Nigel				6	6	6	6	6	6	6	6	6	6^{1}	6	6	6	6	6	6	16	0	1
Stein, Mark	**9**	7	7	7	7	★	11	8^{1}	8	**8**	★	★	★	★		★	★			19	12	4
Own Goals																						0

FA Cup: 1988-89: 3rd Round: Manchester U. (A) 0-0, Replay (H) 2-2, 2nd Replay (A) 0-3.
Littlewoods Cup: 1988-89: 2nd Round: Cardiff C. (H) 3-0 (A) 4-1; 3rd Round: Charlton Ath. (H) 2-1; 4th Round: Wimbledon (H) 0-0, Replay (A) 1-0; Quarter-Final: Nottingham F. (A) 2-5.

READING (Division 3)

Team Manager Ian Branfoot.
Club Address Elm Park, Norfolk Road, Reading. Tel: (0734) 507878/9/0.
Current Ground Capacity 17,100.
Record Attendance 33,042 v Brentford, FA Cup 5th Round, 19 February 1927.
Year Formed 1871. Turned professional 1895.
Previous Names None.
Club Nickname "The Royals".
Club Colours Sky blue shirts with white centre panel, sky blue shorts and navy stockings.
Club Honours Football League: Div. 3 Champions 1985-86; Div. 3(S) Champions 1925-26; Div. 4 Champions 1978-79.
League History 1920-26 Div. 3(S); 1926-31 Div. 2; 1931-58 Div. 3(S); 1958-71 Div. 3; 1971-76 Div. 4; 1976-77 Div. 3; 1977-79 Div. 4; 1979-83 Div. 3; 1983-84 Div. 4; 1984-86 Div. 3; 1986-88 Div. 2; 1988- Div. 3.
Most League Points in a Season (2 for a win) 65 in Div. 4, 1978-79. (3 for a win) 94 in Div. 3, 1985-86.
Most League Goals in a Season 112 in Div. 3(S), 1951-52.
Record Victory 10-2 v Crystal Palace in Div. 3(S), 4 September 1946.
Record Defeat 0-18 v Preston N.E. in FA Cup 1st Round, 1893-94.
Consecutive League Wins 13 in 1985.
Consecutive League Defeats 6 in 1971 and 1989.
Record League Appearances Steve Death, 471 between 1969-82.
Record League Goalscorer—Career Ronnie Blackman, 158 between 1947-54.
Record League Goalscorer—Season Ronnie Blackman, 39 in Div. 3(S), 1951-52.

Reading: League Record, 1988-89 (Division 3)

Match Number	Date	Venue	Opponents	Result	H/T	Lge Posn	Attend
1	27.8.88	H	Sheffield U.	L 1-3	0-2		5512
2	3.9.88	A	Wolverhampton W.	L 1-2	1-0	21	10513
3	10.9.88	H	Bolton W.	D 1-1	0-0	24	4660
4	17.9.88	A	Wigan Ath.	L 0-3	0-1	24	2534
5	21.9.88	H	Southend U.	W 4-0	2-0	19	4062
6	24.9.88	A	Gillingham	W 1-0	1-0	12	4469
7	1.10.88	H	Chester C.	W 3-1	2-0	9	4376
8	4.10.88	A	Bury	L 1-2	1-1	13	2027
9	8.10.88	A	Cardiff C.	W 2-1	0-1	9	4057
10	15.10.88	H	Mansfield T.	W 1-0	1-0	7	6604
11	22.10.88	A	Notts Co.	D 3-3	3-1	11	5170
12	26.10.88	H	Bristol Rov.	W 3-1	2-1	4	7150
13	29.10.88	A	Northampton T.	W 3-1	2-0	5	4355
14	5.11.88	H	Brentford	D 2-2	1-2	7	7974
15	8.11.88	A	Fulham	L 1-2	1-1	8	6934
16	12.11.88	H	Preston N.E.	D 2-2	1-1	9	6225
17	26.11.88	H	Chesterfield	D 0-0	0-0	10	4775
18	3.12.88	A	Bristol C.	L 1-2	1-0	13	8045
19	17.12.88	A	Port Vale	L 0-3	0-1	14	4779
20	26.12.88	H	Aldershot	W 3-1	1-0	11	6350
21	30.12.88	H	Blackpool	W 2-1	2-1	11	5554
22	2.1.89	A	Swansea C.	L 0-2	0-0	11	6772
23	14.1.89	H	Wolverhampton W.	L 0-2	0-2	12	9353
24	21.1.89	A	Bolton W.	D 1-1	0-0	12	5172
25	4.2.89	A	Chester C.	L 0-3	0-1	15	2364
26	11.2.89	H	Bury	D 1-1	1-0	16	3804
27	18.2.89	H	Cardiff C.	W 3-1	2-0	12	4359
28	25.2.89	A	Mansfield T.	L 1-2	0-0	15	3012
29	1.3.89	A	Bristol Rov.	D 1-1	0-1	14	4573
30	4.3.89	H	Notts Co.	L 1-3	1-1	15	4153
31	7.3.89	A	Huddersfield T.	D 2-2	1-1	15	4933
32	11.3.89	A	Brentford	L 2-3	1-2	15	6866
33	15.3.89	H	Northampton T.	D 1-1	1-1	15	3746
34	18.3.89	A	Sheffield U.	L 0-1	0-0	16	11867
35	25.3.89	H	Swansea C.	W 2-0	1-0	15	4367
36	27.3.89	A	Aldershot	D 1-1	0-0	15	4960
37	1.4.89	H	Port Vale	W 3-0	1-0	15	4501
38	5.4.89	H	Huddersfield T.	W 2-1	1-0	14	3802
39	8.4.89	A	Blackpool	W 4-2	1-0	12	2792
40	14.4.89	A	Southend U.	L 1-2	0-1	13	4625
41	19.4.89	H	Wigan Ath.	L 0-3	0-2	14	3821
42	22.4.89	H	Gillingham	L 1-2	0-1	14	3511
43	29.4.89	A	Preston N.E.	L 1-2	0-2	16	7003
44	1.5.89	H	Fulham	L 0-1	0-1	17	5152
45	5.5.89	H	Bristol C.	L 1-2	1-1	18	3620
46	13.5.89	A	Chesterfield	W 4-2	0-2	17	3107

Players: League Record, 1988-89 (Division 3)

Match Number	1	2	3	4	5	6	7	8	9	10	11	12	13	14	15	16	17	18	19	20	21	22	23	24	25	26	27	28	29	30	31	32	33	34	35	36	37	38	39	40	41	42	43	44	45	46	Apps	Subs	Goals
Beavon, Stuart	4		8	4	4^1	4	4	4	4	**4**^{1}			4	4	4	**4**					★	★	4	4	4	4	4	4	4	4^1	4	4	4	4	4	4^1	4^1	4	4^1	4	4	4	4^1	4	4	4^2	37	2	9
Conroy, Michael								★	9^1		10	10^2	10^1	**10**	**10**				10		★	10	**10**		★				★																		9	4	4
Curle, Keith	2	6	6	6	6	6	6	6	6	6																																					10	0	0
Elsey, Karl	★	2	2	2	8	8	8	8	8	8	8^1	8	3	3	2	8	4	4	4	4	**4**	**4**	★	8	8	8	8	8	8^1	**8**	★			8	8	8	8	8	8^1	8	8	8	8	8	8	8	41	3	3
Francis, Steve	1	1	1	1	1	1	1	1	1	1	1	**1**																									1	1	1	1	1	1	1	1	1	1	22	0	0
Franklin, Paul	6			7	★	2	2	2	2	**2**				2		2	★	2	2		2	2																								2	14	2	0
Gernon, Irvin					3	3	3	3	3	★	6	3	6	6	3		3		6	3	3	3	3	★	6														★			★		3			18	4	0
Gilkes, Michael	11^1	11	11	11	11	11	11	11	11^1	11	11^1	11	11^1	11	11	11	11	11	11	11	11	11	11	11	11	11	11^1	11	11	11	11	3	3	10	10	10	10^1	10	10^1	10^1	10	3^1	10	10	10	10	46	0	9
Gordon, Colin	★			9	9^1	9																																									3	1	1
Hicks, Martin	5	5	5	5	5^1	5	5	5		5	5	5	5	5	5	5	5	5	5	5	5	5	5	5^1	5	5	5	5	5	5	5	5	5	5	5	5	5	5	5	5	5	5	5	5	5^1	5	45	0	3
Jones, Linden	**7**	7	7					★	★	7		7	7^1	**7**^{1}	**7**	7								7	2	2	2	2	2	2	7	7^1	**7**	2	2	2	2	2	2	2					**2**		27	2	3
King, Andrew				★																																											0	1	0
Knight, Keith					**7**^{1}	7	7^2	**7**	**7**		7	★^{1}		★^{1}	★		7	7	7	7^1	7^1	**7**	7										★	7	**7**	**7**	**7**	**7**	**7**	**7**	7	7	7	**7**	**7**		25	4	7
Moran, Steve	**10**	10	10	**10**	10	10^1	10	**10**	10	★				★	★	10^1	**10**	10					★	10	**10**	10^1	10^1	10	**10**	10	10	10	10		★	★	★	★		★		**10**		★	★		23	11	4
Payne, Lee																																11	11^1	11	**11**	11	11	11	11^1	11	11	11	11	11	11	11^1	15	0	3
Phillips, Gary													1	1	1	1	1	1	1	1	1	1	1	1	1	1	1	1	1	1	1	1	1	1	1	1											24	0	0
Richardson, Steve	3	3	3	3	**2**					3	3	2	2			3	2	3	3	2		★	2	3	3	3	3	3	3	3	3	2	2	3	3	3	3	3	3	3	3	2	3	2	3	3	38	1	0
Senior, Trevor										9	9^1	9	9	9	9^1	9^1	9	9^1	9	9	9^1	9	9	9	9	9	9^1	9^1	9	9	9^2	9^1	9	9	9^2	9	9^1	9^1	9	9	9	9	9	9	9	9^1	37	0	15
Tait, Mick	9	4	4				9^1	9^1	5	10		6			6	6	6	**8**	8	10^2	**10**		**8**		7	7	7	7	7	7	8	8	8	6	6	6	6	6^1		6	6	6	6	**6**		6	36	0	5
Taylor, Les	8	8		**8**							4	4	8	8	8	★	8	★		8	8	8																									12	2	0
Taylor, Scott				★	★																																							★			0	3	0
Whitehurst, Billy		9^1	9^1																																												2	0	2
Whitlock, Mark																		6		6	6	6	6	**6**		6	6	6	6	6	6	6	6		★				6						6		16	1	0
Williams, Adrian											2													2						★	**2**										2		2		★	7	6	2	0
Own Goals																																																	0

FA Cup: 1988-89: 1st Round: Hendon (H) 4-2; 2nd Round: Maidstone U. (H) 1-1, Replay (A) 2-1; 3rd Round: Tranmere Rov. (A) 1-1, Replay (H) 2-1; 4th Round: Grimsby T. (A) 1-1, Replay (H) 1-2.
Littlewoods Cup: 1988-89: 1st Round: Torquay U. (A) 1-0 (H) 3-1; 2nd Round: Bradford C. (H) 1-1 (A) 1-2.

ROCHDALE (Division 4)

Team Manager Terry Dolan.
Club Address Spotland, Wilbutts Lane, Rochdale OL11 5DS. Tel: (0706) 44648/9.
Current Ground Capacity 12,500.
Record Attendance 24,231 v Notts. Co., FA Cup 2nd Round, 10 December 1949.
Year Formed 1907. Turned professional 1907.
Previous Names None.
Club Nickname "The Dale".
Club Colours White shirts, navy shorts and white stockings.
Club Honours None.
League History 1921-58 Div. 3(N); 1958-59 Div. 3; 1959-60 Div. 4; 1969-74 Div. 3; 1974- Div. 4.
Most League Points in a Season (2 for a win) 65 in Div. 4, 1978-79. (3 for a win) 55 in Div. 4, 1985-86.
Most League Goals in a Season 105 in Div. 3(N), 1926-27.
Record Victory 8-1 v Chesterfield in Div. 3(N), 18 December 1926.
Record Defeat 0-8 v Wrexham in Div. 3(N), 28 December 1929 and 1-9 v Tranmere Rov. in Div. 3(N), 25 December 1931.
Consecutive League Wins 8 in 1969.
Consecutive League Defeats 17 in 1931-32.
Record League Appearances Graham Smith, 317 between 1966-74.
Record League Goalscorer—Career Reg Jenkins, 119 between 1964-73.
Record League Goalscorer—Season Albert Whitehurst, 44 in Div. 3(N), 1926-27.

Rochdale: League Record, 1988-89 (Division 4)

Match Number	Date	Venue	Opponents	Result	H/T	Lge Posn	Attend
1	27.8.88	A	Burnley	L 1-2	0-1		7510
2	3.9.88	H	Rotherham U.	L 0-2	0-2	21	2107
3	10.9.88	A	Scarborough	D 3-3	1-0	21	2456
4	17.9.88	H	Exeter C.	W 2-1	1-1	16	1216
5	20.9.88	H	Doncaster Rov.	W 2-0	0-0	13	1645
6	24.9.88	A	Grimsby T.	W 3-1	1-1	6	2939
7	1.10.88	H	Crewe Alex.	W 2-1	0-1	5	2227
8	4.10.88	A	Hartlepool U.	W 1-0	0-0	3	2483
9	8.10.88	H	Stockport Co.	D 1-1	1-1	4	3021
10	14.10.88	A	Halifax T.	L 1-4	0-2	4	2553
11	22.10.88	H	Scunthorpe U.	W 1-0	0-0	4	2250
12	26.10.88	A	Hereford U.	D 4-4	3-2	4	2071
13	29.10.88	H	Darlington	D 2-2	1-1	5	2476
14	4.11.88	A	Tranmere Rov.	L 0-2	0-1	8	3740
15	8.11.88	A	Torquay U.	L 0-1	0-1	11	1931
16	12.11.88	H	Wrexham	D 3-3	0-1	12	2280
17	26.11.88	H	York C.	W 2-0	0-0	7	1880
18	3.12.88	A	Peterborough U.	L 0-1	0-0	11	3273
19	16.12.88	H	Colchester U.	D 1-1	1-0	10	1258
20	26.12.88	A	Carlisle U.	L 0-1	0-0	13	1013
21	30.12.88	A	Cambridge U.	L 0-2	0-0	16	2319
22	2.1.89	H	Leyton Orient	L 0-3	0-1	18	2036
23	7.1.89	H	Lincoln C.	D 2-2	1-1	17	1515
24	14.1.89	A	Rotherham U.	L 1-3	1-2	17	4541
25	21.1.89	H	Burnley	W 2-1	0-1	17	5799
26	28.1.89	A	Exeter C.	L 1-5	1-2	18	2428
27	4.2.89	A	Doncaster Rov.	D 1-1	0-0	19	1868
28	11.2.89	H	Grimsby T.	L 0-2	0-2	20	1621
29	17.2.89	A	Stockport Co.	L 0-3	0-2	20	2858
30	28.2.89	H	Hereford U.	D 2-2	1-2	21	1060
31	4.3.89	A	Scunthorpe U.	L 0-4	0-2	21	4098
32	11.3.89	H	Tranmere Rov.	W 3-1	0-1	21	2158
33	14.3.89	A	Darlington	W 2-1	1-1	20	1876
34	18.3.89	H	Scarborough	W 2-1	2-0	19	1636
35	25.3.89	A	Leyton Orient	L 0-3	0-1	20	4591
36	27.3.89	H	Carlisle U.	D 0-0	0-0	20	2145
37	31.3.89	A	Colchester U.	L 0-3	0-0	20	3631
38	5.4.89	A	Lincoln C.	L 1-4	0-3	20	2034
39	8.4.89	H	Cambridge U.	W 2-1	2-1	20	1314
40	14.4.89	A	Crewe Alex.	L 1-3	0-1	21	4144
41	22.4.89	H	Hartlepool U.	D 0-0	0-0	22	1406
42	25.4.89	H	Halifax T.	D 1-1	0-0	22	1388
43	29.4.89	A	York C.	D 3-3	1-2	19	1920
44	1.5.89	H	Torquay U.	W 2-1	1-0	17	1239
45	6.5.89	H	Peterbrough U.	D 0-0	0-0	17	1430
46	13.5.89	A	Wrexham	L 1-2	0-1	18	3125

Players: League Record, 1988-89 (Division 4)

Match Number	1	2	3	4	5	6	7	8	9	10	11	12	13	14	15	16	17	18	19	20	21	22	23
Alford, Carl																							
Armitage, Andrew	3	3	3				3	3	3	3	3		3			★	4	★	3	3	3		3
Beaumont, Chris		**9**								★		9[1]	10	10	10	10[1]	10[1]	10	**9**	9	7	★	
Brown, Malcolm																							
Copeland, Simon	**2**	2	2	2	2	2	2	2	2	2				2	2	2	2	2	6			★	2
Edmonds, Neil				9	7[1]	7	7[1]	7	7	★	9[1]	3	9[2]	9	7	9	9		10	10	**10**	10	10
Fothergill, Ashley																							
Frain, David	11[1]	11	11	11[1]	11[1]	**11**		11	11	11	11	11[2]	11	11	11	11[1]	11	11	11	**11**	11	11	11
Harris, Carl	7	**7**	7[1]	**7**					★	**7**	7	**7**	7	**7**									
Jones, Paul																							
Lomax, Geoff	4	4			6	**6**					2	2	2	3	3	3	**3**		2	7	6	**3**	6
Lucketti, Chris																							
McIntyre, Joseph																							
Mellish, Stuart			★			★[1]	11											**9**		2		6	7
Mycock, David				3	3	3												3					
O'Shaughnessy, Steve	10	10	10[1]	10	10	10	10	10	**10**	10	10	10			★	**7**	7	4	7[1]	4	4	4	
Reid, Shaun	8	6	6	6		★	6	6	6[1]	6	6	6	6	6	6	6[1]	6	6	4				
Roberts, William																							
Smart, Jason	6	★	4	4	4	4	4	4	4	4	4	4	4	4	4	4				6	2	2	4
Smith, Mark	9	8	**8**	8[1]	8	8[2]	8[1]	8	8	8[1]	8	8	8	8	8	★	8[1]	8	8	8	8	8	8[1]
Sutton, David	5	5	5[1]	5	5	5	5	5	5	5	5	5[1]	5	5	5	5	5	5	5	5	5	5	5
Taylor, Steve																							
Walling, Dean	★	★	9	★	9	9	9	9	9	**9**		★		★	**9**	**8**			★		9	9	9[1]
Welch, Keith	1	1	1	1	1	1	1	1	1	1	1	1	1	1	1	1	1	1	1	1	1	1	1
Windridge, David																							
Wood, Paul																	★	7		★	★	**7**	
Own Goals								1															

Match Number	24	25	26	27	28	29	30	31	32	33	34	35	36	37	38	39	40	41	42	43	44	45	46	Apps	Subs	Goals
Alford, Carl			★		★																	★	★	0	4	0
Armitage, Andrew	3	3	3	3	3			3	★	3	3	3	3	3	3	3	3	3	**3**		3	3	3	33	3	0
Beaumont, Chris	★	9[1]	9[1]	9[1]	9	9	9	9	**7**[1]	7	7	7	**7**	7	7	7		7	7	7	**7**		7	31	3	7
Brown, Malcolm							4						2	2	2	2	**2**	2		2	2	2	2	11	0	0
Copeland, Simon	**2**	2	2	2	2	2	2	2											6	**6**				27	1	0
Edmonds, Neil	10	7	7	7	7	★			10	10	10	10	10	10	10[1]	10[1]	7	**11**	★	★[1]	★	**7**		34	5	8
Fothergill, Ashley						7	7	10	2	2	2	2						★	**2**					8	1	0
Frain, David	11[1]	11[1]	11	11	11	11			11	11	11	11	11	11	11	11[1]	11[1]		11[1]	11	11[1]	11	11	42	0	12
Harris, Carl																								9	1	1
Jones, Paul									5	5	5[2]	5	5	5	5	5	5		5	5	5	5	5	14	0	2
Lomax, Geoff			★	6		5	5	5	**3**					6	6	6	10	**10**						26	1	0
Lucketti, Chris																		5						1	0	0
McIntyre, Joseph							11	**11**	★				★											2	2	0
Mellish, Stuart	7			★	6			7							**8**	8	8	8						12	3	1
Mycock, David						3	3												★	3	6	6	**6**	10	1	0
O'Shaughnessy, Steve	6	6	**6**		★	6	10[1]	6	6[2]	6	6	6	6		★	4	6	6	8	8[1]	8	8	8	38	3	6
Reid, Shaun																								17	1	2
Roberts, William						**8**																		1	0	0
Smart, Jason	4	4	4	4	4	4	6	4	4	4	4	4	4	4	4		4	4	4	4	4	4	4	41	1	0
Smith, Mark	8	8	8	8																				26	1	7
Sutton, David	5	5	5	**5**	**5**																			28	0	2
Taylor, Steve							8[1]	8	8	8[1]	8	8	8	8	9	9	9	★	10	10	9[1]	9	9[1]	16	1	4
Walling, Dean	9				**8**			★	9	9[1]	9	9	9	9			★	9	9	9[1]	10	10	10	26	8	3
Welch, Keith	1	1	1	1	1	1	1	1	1	1	1	1	1	1	1	1	1	1	1	1	1	1	1	46	0	0
Windridge, David		10	**10**	10	10	10																		5	0	0
Wood, Paul																								2	3	0
Own Goals																										1

FA Cup: 1988-89: 1st Round: Huddersfield T. (A) 1-1, Replay (H) 3-4.
Littlewoods Cup: 1988-90: 1st Round: Burnley (H) 3-3 (A) 1-2.

ROTHERHAM UNITED (Division 3)

Team Manager Billy McEwan.
Club Address Millmoor Ground, Rotherham. Tel: (0709) 562434.
Current Ground Capacity 18,000.
Record Attendance 25,000 v Sheffield U., Div. 2, 13 December 1952 and v Sheffield Wed., Div. 2, 26 January 1952.
Year Formed 1884. Turned professional 1905.
Previous Names Thornhill United, Rotherham Town, Rotherham County.
Club Nickname "The Merry Millers".
Club Colours Red shirts, white collar and sleeves, white shorts and white stockings.
Club Honours Football League: Div. 3 Champions 1980-81; Div. 3(N) Champions 1950-51, Div. 4 Champions 1988-89.
League History 1893-96 Div. 2; 1896 Failed re-election; 1919-23 Div. 2; 1923-51 Div. 3(N); 1951-68 Div. 2; 1968-73 Div. 3; 1973-75 Div. 4; 1975-81 Div. 3; 1981-83 Div. 2; 1983-88 Div. 3; 1988-89 Div. 4; 1989- Div. 3.
Most League Points in a Season (2 for a win) 71 in Div. 3(N), 1950-51. (3 for a win) 82 in Div. 4, 1988-89.
Most League Goals in a Season 114 in Div. 3(N), 1946-47.
Record Victory 8-0 v Oldham Ath. in Div. 3(N), 26 May 1947.
Record Defeat 1-11 v Bradford C. in Div. 3(N), 25 August 1928.
Consecutive League Wins 9 in 1982.
Consecutive League Defeats 8 in 1956.
Record League Appearances Danny Williams, 459 between 1946-60.
Record League Goalscorer—Career Gladstone Guest, 130 between 1946-56.
Record League Goalscorer—Season Wally Ardron, 38 in Div. 3(N), 1946-47.

Rotherham United: League Record, 1988-89 (Division 4)

Match Number	Date	Venue	Opponents	Result	H/T	Lge Posn	Attend
1	27.8.88	H	Doncaster Rov.	W 3-0	1-0		4497
2	3.9.88	A	Rochdale	W 2-0	2-0	1	2107
3	10.9.88	H	Wrexham	D 2-2	1-1	2	4367
4	17.9.88	A	Grimsby T.	W 4-0	3-0	1	3697
5	20.9.88	H	Leyton Orient	W 4-1	2-0	1	4289
6	24.9.88	A	Carlisle U.	W 2-0	0-0	1	2862
7	1.10.88	H	Exeter C.	L 0-1	0-0	1	4075
8	4.10.88	A	Burnley	L 0-1	0-0	2	9283
9	8.10.88	A	Darlington	D 1-1	0-0	3	1746
10	15.10.88	H	Tranmere Rov.	D 0-0	0-0	3	4133
11	22.10.88	A	Torquay U.	W 2-1	2-0	1	2228
12	25.10.88	H	Colchester U.	W 2-0	0-0	1	4066
13	29.10.88	A	Scarborough	L 0-1	0-1	2	4106
14	5.11.88	H	Lincoln C.	W 2-0	2-0	1	4506
15	8.11.88	H	Scunthorpe U.	D 3-3	2-1	1	5923
16	12.11.88	A	Cambridge U.	D 1-1	0-1	2	2882
17	26.11.88	A	Hereford U.	D 1-1	0-1	1	2058
18	3.12.88	H	Stockport Co.	W 2-1	1-1	1	4105
19	16.12.88	A	York C.	D 1-1	0-0	1	2650
20	26.12.88	H	Crewe Alex.	L 1-2	0-1	3	7165
21	31.12.88	H	Halifax T.	W 2-0	0-0	2	5258
22	2.1.89	A	Hartlepool U.	D 1-1	0-0	3	3370
23	7.1.89	A	Peterborough U.	W 3-0	0-0	1	3368
24	14.1.89	H	Rochdale	W 3-1	2-1	1	4541
25	21.1.89	A	Doncaster Rov.	L 0-1	0-0	1	4432
26	4.2.89	A	Leyton Orient	L 1-3	1-0	4	3290
27	11.2.89	H	Carlisle U.	W 2-1	1-1	3	4111
28	18.2.89	H	Darlington	L 1-2	0-0	4	4228
29	25.2.89	A	Tranmere Rov.	D 0-0	0-0	4	6509
30	28.2.89	A	Colchester U.	D 1-1	1-0	5	3671
31	4.3.89	H	Torquay U.	W 1-0	1-0	4	3791
32	7.3.89	H	Grimsby T.	W 1-0	0-0	2	4888
33	11.3.89	A	Lincoln C.	W 1-0	1-0	2	5186
34	14.3.89	H	Scarborough	D 1-1	1-1	3	6010
35	18.3.89	A	Wrexham	W 4-1	1-1	2	2929
36	25.3.89	H	Hartlepool U.	W 4-0	3-0	2	4915
37	27.3.89	A	Crewe Alex.	W 3-1	0-0	1	5994
38	1.4.89	H	York C.	L 0-1	0-0	1	5926
39	4.4.89	H	Peterborough U.	D 1-1	1-1	1	4762
40	7.4.89	A	Halifax T.	D 1-1	0-1	2	2947
41	15.4.89	A	Exeter C.	D 0-0	0-0	3	2594
42	22.4.89	H	Burnley	W 3-1	3-1	1	5726
43	29.4.89	H	Hereford U.	W 6-0	2-0	1	5334
44	1.5.89	A	Scunthorpe U.	D 0-0	0-0	1	8775
45	6.5.89	A	Stockport Co.	W 3-1	1-1	1	4313
46	13.5.89	H	Cambridge U.	D 0-0	0-0	1	9567

Players: League Record, 1988-89 (Division 4)

Match Number	1	2	3	4	5	6	7	8	9	10	11	12	13	14	15	16	17	18	19	20	21	22	23
Ash, Mark																							
Barnsley, Andy																			11	11	5	5	5
Buckley, John			7	7	7^{1}	7	**7**	★	★	7	7	7	7					★	★^{1}	★	7^{1}	11	**7**
Crosby, Philip	3	3	3	**3**	3	3	3	3	**3**	6	6^{1}	6				6	6	6	**6**		6	6	6
Dempsey, Mark														★	★	8^{1}	8	**8**	8	8	**8**		8
Evans, Stewart																10	10	10	10	10	**10**		10^{2}
Goodwin, Shaun	★	★		★	★		4		★	4	4^{1}	4	4	7	7^{1}	**7**		11		3	11	8	★
Grealish, Tony	**4**	4	4	4	**4^{1}**	4		4	8^{1}			★	★	4	**4**	4	4^{1}	4	4	4	4	4	4
Green, John	6	6	6	6	6	6	6	6	6	5	5	5^{1}	6	6	6	5	5	5	5	**5**			
Haycock, Paul	**10**	10	10	**10**	10	10^{1}	**10**	10		10	10	10	**10**					9^{1}	9	**9**			
Hazel, Desmond	7	**7**					★	**7**	10	11	11	**11**	11	**11**	11^{1}	11	7	7^{1}	7	7	★	7	11
Heard, Pat	11^{1}	11	11	11^{1}	11^{1}	11	11	11	7	3	3	3	3	3	3	3	3	3	3	6	3	3	3
Johnson, Nigel	5	5^{1}	5	5	5	5	5	5	5				5	5	5								
Mendonca, Clive	★			★			★		**11**					10^{1}	10		**9**				★	10	★
O'Hanlon, Kelham	1	1	1	1	1	1	1	1	1	1	1	1	1	1	1	1	1	1	1	1	1	1	1
Pepper, Nigel																★	11						
Russell, Billy	2^{1}	2	2	2	2	2	2	2	2	2	2	2	2	2	2	2	2	2	2	2	2^{1}	2	2
Scott, Martin																							
Thompson, Simon																	★						
Williams, Andy	8	8	8	8^{1}	8^{1}	8	8	8	4	8	8	8	8	8^{1}	8								
Williamson, Bobby	9^{1}	9^{1}	9^{2}	9^{2}	9	9^{1}	9	9	9	9	9	9^{1}	9	9	9	9				★^{1}	9	9^{1}	**9^{1}**
Own Goals															1								

Match Number	24	25	26	27	28	29	30	31	32	33	34	35	36	37	38	39	40	41	42	43	44	45	46	Apps	Subs	Goals
Ash, Mark				5																				1	0	0
Barnsley, Andy	5	5	5	2	5	5	5	5	3	3	**3**		4	4	4	4	5	6	**6**	6	6	6	6	27	0	0
Buckley, John	**7**	7	11	★	7		★	★	★		★	★	★		★	★	★	★	7	7^{2}		★	4	19	17	5
Crosby, Philip	6^{1}	6	6	6	6	6	6	6	6	6	6	3	3	3	3	3	6		★					36	1	2
Dempsey, Mark	8	**8**				7	7	7	7	7	7	7	7	7	**7**		**7**	**7**		★	7	7	7	24	3	1
Evans, Stewart	10	**10**	**10**	10	**10**				10	10	10	★^{2}	10^{2}	10	10	**10**			★	★	★	★	★	19	6	6
Goodwin, Shaun	★	★	8	8	8	8	**8**	**8**	**8**	8	8	8	**8**	8	8	8	8	8	8	8^{1}	8	8^{1}	**8**	33	8	4
Grealish, Tony	4	4	4	4	**4**	4	4^{1}	4	4	4		4				**7**	4	4	4	**4**	4	**4**	★	36	3	4
Green, John			2																					21	0	1
Haycock, Paul		★	★	9^{1}	★	10	10	10				**10**	★		★	★	10	10	**10**	10^{1}	**10**	**10**	**10**	27	6	4
Hazel, Desmond	11	11	★	7	11	11	11	11	11	11	11^{1}	**11**	**11**	11	11	11	11	11	11	**11^{1}**	11	11^{2}	11	39	3	6
Heard, Pat	3	3	**7**	**11^{1}**	★				★		**4**													28	2	4
Johnson, Nigel									5^{1}	5	5	5	5	5	5	5		5	5	5	5	5	5	26	0	2
Mendonca, Clive																								5	5	1
O'Hanlon, Kelham	1	1	1	1	1	1	1	1	1	1	1	1	1	1	1	1	1	1	1	1	1	1	1	46	0	0
Pepper, Nigel																								1	1	0
Russell, Billy	2	2			2	2	2	2	2	2	2	2	2	2	2	2	2	2	2	2	2	2	2	44	0	2
Scott, Martin			3	3	3	3	3	3			★	6	6	6	6	6	3	3	3^{1}	3	3	3	3	18	1	1
Thompson, Simon																								0	1	0
Williams, Andy																								15	0	3
Williamson, Bobby	9^{2}	9	9^{1}		9^{1}	9	9	9^{1}	**9**	9	9	9^{2}	9^{1}	9^{3}	**9**	9^{1}	9^{1}	9	9^{2}	9^{1}	9	9	9	41	1	27
Own Goals										1			1													3

FA Cup: 1988-89: 1st Round: Barrow (H) 3-1; 2nd Round: Grimsby T. (A) 2-3.
Littlewoods Cup: 1988-89: 1st Round: Grimsby T. (A) 1-0 (H) 1-0; 2nd Round: Manchester U. (H) 0-1 (A) 0-5.

SCARBOROUGH (Division 4)

Team Manager Colin Morris.
Club Address The Athletic Ground, Seamer Road, Scarborough YO12 4HF. Tel: (0723) 375094.
Current Ground Capacity 10,000.
Record Attendance 11,130 v Luton T., FA Cup 3rd Round, 1938.
Year Formed 1879. Turned professional 1926.
Previous Names None.
Club Nickname "The Boro".
Club Colours All red.
Club Honours None.
League History 1987- Div. 4.
Most League Points in a Season (3 for a win) 77 in Div. 4, 1988-89.
Most League Goals in a Season 67 in Div. 4, 1988-89.

Record Victory 16-1 v Leeds Amateurs in FA Amateur Cup, 9 November 1907.
Record Defeat 1-16 v Southbank in Northern League, 15 November 1919.
Consecutive League Wins 3 in August-September 1987, September-October 1987 and September-October 1988.
Consecutive League Defeats 4 in December 1987-January 1988.
Record League Appearances Neil Thompson, 87 between 1987-89.
Record League Goalscorer—Career Neil Thompson, 15 between 1987-89.
Record League Goalscorer—Season Gary Brook, 12 in Div. 4, 1988-89.

Scarborough: League Record, 1988-89 (Division 4)

Match Number	Date	Venue	Opponents	Result	H/T	Lge Posn	Attend
1	27.8.88	H	Tranmere Rov.	D 0-0	0-0		2893
2	3.9.88	A	Peterborough U.	W 4-1	1-1	5	3956
3	10.9.88	H	Rochdale	D 3-3	0-1	8	2456
4	17.9.88	A	Hereford U.	W 3-1	1-0	5	2359
5	20.9.88	A	Colchester U.	L 1-3	0-1	8	1424
6	24.9.88	H	Torquay U.	W 5-2	2-1	5	1986
7	1.10.88	A	Scunthorpe U.	W 3-0	1-0	3	4167
8	5.10.88	H	Darlington	W 3-2	2-1	1	2442
9	8.10.88	H	Leyton Orient	D 0-0	0-0	2	2376
10	15.10.88	A	Lincoln C.	D 2-2	1-2	2	4535
11	22.10.88	H	Stockport Co.	D 1-1	1-1	3	2449
12	25.10.88	A	Cambridge U.	D 2-2	1-1	3	2673
13	29.10.88	H	Rotherham U.	W 1-0	1-0	3	4106
14	5.11.88	A	Carlisle U.	W 1-0	1-0	2	2617
15	9.11.88	A	Exeter C.	L 0-1	0-0	2	2351
16	12.11.88	H	Burnley	W 1-0	0-0	1	5501
17	26.11.88	H	Wrexham	L 0-3	0-1	2	3689
18	3.12.88	A	Grimsby T.	L 1-2	0-1	3	3887
19	17.12.88	A	Halifax T.	W 2-0	1-0	3	1890
20	26.12.88	H	York C.	D 0 0	0 0	4	6067
21	31.12.88	H	Crewe Alex.	W 2-1	1-0	3	3088
22	2.1.89	A	Doncaster Rov.	L 1-3	1-2	4	3053
23	14.1.89	H	Peterborough U.	W 2-1	0-0	3	2279
24	21.1.89	A	Tranmere Rov.	D 1-1	1-0	4	4538
25	28.1.89	H	Hereford U.	L 0-2	0-0	5	2199
26	4.2.89	H	Colchester U.	D 0-0	0-0	5	1913
27	11.2.89	A	Torquay U.	W 1-0	0-0	5	2442
28	18.2.89	A	Leyton Orient	W 3-2	0-2	2	3877
29	25.2.89	H	Lincoln C.	D 1-1	1-0	3	3293
30	1.3.89	H	Cambridge U.	W 2-1	0-0	2	2011
31	4.3.89	A	Stockport Co.	D 2-2	0-2	3	2648
32	11.3.89	H	Carlisle U.	L 0-1	0-0	5	2354
33	14.3.89	A	Rotherham U.	D 1-1	1-1	5	6010
34	18.3.89	A	Rochdale	L 1-2	0-2	6	1636
35	25.3.89	H	Doncaster Rov.	W 2-0	1-0	5	2792
36	27.3.89	A	York C.	D 0-0	0-0	5	4872
37	1.4.89	H	Halifax T.	W 3-1	1-0	5	2365
38	5.4.89	H	Hartlepool U.	W 2-0	2-0	5	2155
39	8.4.89	A	Crewe Alex.	D 1-1	1-1	5	3243
40	11.4.89	A	Hartlepool U.	L 1-3	0-0	5	1897
41	15.4.89	H	Scunthorpe U.	W 1-0	0-0	5	4456
42	22.4.89	A	Darlington	L 1-2	0-1	6	2850
43	29.4.89	A	Wrexham	W 1-0	0-0	5	1940
44	1.5.89	H	Exeter C.	W 2-1	2-1	4	2513
45	6.5.89	H	Grimsby T.	L 2-3	1-2	5	3923
46	13.5.89	A	Burnley	W 1-0	0-0	5	6206

Players: League Record, 1988-89 (Division 4)

Match Number	1	2	3	4	5	6	7	8	9	10	11	12	13	14	15	16	17	18	19	20	21	22	23	24	25	26	27	28	29	30	31	32	33	34	35	36	37	38	39	40	41	42	43	44	45	46	Appe	Subs	Goals
Adams, Steve			★			★[1]	**7[1]**	**7**	★									★	★	**7**	7	7[1]	**7**	★	★	★						**7**		★	**7**	★	★		★								8	12	3
Bennyworth, Ian	6	6[1]	6	6	6	6	6	6	6	6	**6[1]**	6	6	6	6	6	6	6	6	6	6	**6**	6	6	6	**6**	6	6	6	6	**6**	6	6	6												6	35	0	2
Blackwell, Kevin	1	1	1	1	1				1	1	1	1	1	1	1	1	1	1																													15	0	0
Brook, Gary	10	10	10[1]	10	**10**	10[1]	10	10	10	10	10	10	10	10	10	10[1]	10	10[1]	10	10	10	10	10	10	10	10	10	10[1]	10[1]	10[1]	10[1]			10	10[1]	10	10[1]	10[1]	10	**10**	10	10	**10[1]**	10	10	10	44	0	12
Brotherston, Noel													7	**7**	**7**	**7**	**7**																														5	0	0
Charlton, Kevin						1	1	1																																							3	0	0
Cook, Mitchell	8	8[1]	8[1]	8[1]	8[1]	8	8	8	8	8	8	8	8	8	8	8	8	8		★		★	9[1]	9	9	8	8	8	8	8	8	8	8	8	★	★	★	★	★	★	9	9	★	★		7	33	10	5
Dobson, Paul																											9	9[1]	9	**9**	9[1]	9	9	9[1]	9	9	**9**	**9**	**7[1]**	7[1]	7	**7**	**7**	**7**			18	0	5
Graham, Tommy	11	11	11	11	11	11	11	11	11	11	11	11	11	11[1]	11	11	11	11	11	11	11[1]	11	11	**11**	11	11				★	★	10	10	★	**8**	8	**8**	8	8	8	8	8	8	8[1]	8	8[1]	40	3	4
Ironside, Ian																			1	1	1	1	1	1	1	1	1	1	1	1	1	1	1	1	1	1	1	1	1	1	1	1	1	1	1	1	28	0	0
Kamara, Alan	2	2	2	2	2	2	2	2	2	2	2	2	**2**	2	2	2	**2**	2	2	2	2	2	2	2[1]	2	2	2	2	2	2	2	2	2	**2**	2	2	2	2	2	2	2	2			2	2	44	0	1
McJannet, Les												★	★				★																														0	3	0
Matthews, Mike																			8[1]	8	8	8	8	8	**8**																						7	0	1
Mell, Stewart				★	★							★								**9**		★																									1	4	0
Morris, Colin	7	7	7[1]	7	7	7[1]			**7**										**7**				★[1]	7	7	7	7	7	7	7	7		7	**7**						★			9	★	7		20	3	3
Norris, Steve	9	9[1]	**9**	**9[1]**	9	**9**	9[1]	9[2]	9	9	9	9	9[1]	9	9	9	9	9	**9[1]**													★			★	**7**	7[1]	7	**9**	**9**		★	★	**9**	9[1]	9	27	4	9
Olsson, Paul							★	★		7	7	**7[1]**		★	★	★	★	**7**	★							9	4	4[1]	4	4	4	4	4	4	4[1]	4	4	4	4	4	4[1]	4	4	4	4	4	25	7	4
Outhart, Anthony											★																																				0	1	0
Richards, Steve	5	5	5	5[1]	5	5	5	5	5	5	5	**5**	5	5	5	5	5	5	5	5	5	5	5	5	5	5	5	5	5	5	**5**				5	**5**	5	5	5	5	5	5	5	5	5		42	0	1
Russell, Martin																											11[1]	11	11	11[1]	11	11	11	11	11	11	11	11	11	11	11	11	11	11	11	11	20	0	2
Short, Chris																																											2	2			2	0	0
Short, Craig	4	4	4	4	4	4	4	4[1]	4	4[1]	4	4[1]	4	4	4	4	4	4	4	4	4	4	4	4	4	4					★	5	5	5	6	6	6	6	6	6	6	6[1]	6	6[1]	6	6	41	1	5
Thompson, Leslie																				★	9[1]	**9**																									2	1	1
Thompson, Neil	3	3[1]	3	3	3	3[2]	3[1]	3	3	3[1]	3	3	3	3	3	3	3	3	3	3	3	3	3	3	3	3	3	3	3	3	3	3	3[1]	3	3	3	3[1]	3[1]	3	3	3	3	3	3	3[1]	3	46	0	9
Own Goals																																																	0

FA Cup: 1988-89: 1st Round: Stockport Co. (H) 2-1; 2nd Round: Carlisle U. (H) 0-1.

Littlewoods Cup: 1988-89: 1st Round: Halifax T. (H) 1-1 (A) 2-2; 2nd Round: Portsmouth (A) 2-2 (H) 3-1; 3rd Round: Southampton (H) 2-2, Replay (A) 0-1.

SCUNTHORPE UNITED (Division 4)

Team Manager Mike Buxton.
Club Address Old Show Ground, Scunthorpe, South Humberside. Tel: (0724) 848077.
Current Ground Capacity 10,800.
Record Attendance 23,935 v Portsmouth, FA Cup 4th Round, 30 January 1954.
Year Formed 1904. Turned professional 1912.
Previous Names Scunthorpe, Lindsay United, Scunthorpe and Lindsay United.
Club Nickname "The Iron".
Club Colours All claret and blue.
Club Honours Football League: Div. 3(N) Champions 1957-58.
League History 1950-58 Div. 3(N); 1958-64 Div. 2; 1964-68 Div. 3; 1968-72 Div 4; 1972-73 Div. 3; 1973-83 Div. 4; 1983-84 Div. 3; 1984- Div. 4.

Most League Points in a Season (2 for a win) 66 in Div. 3(N), 1957-58. (3 for a win) 83 in Div. 4, 1982-83.
Most League Goals in a Season 88 in Div. 3(N), 1957-58.
Record Victory 9-0 v Boston U. in FA Cup 1st Round, 21 November 1953.
Record Defeat 0-8 v Carlisle U. in Div. 3(N), 25 December 1952.
Consecutive League Wins 6 in 1954 and 1965.
Consecutive League Defeats 7 in 1973.
Record League Appearances Jack Brownsword, 595 between 1950-65.
Record League Goalscorer—Career Steve Cammack, 110 between 1979-86.
Record League Goalscorer—Season Barrie Thomas, 31 in Div. 2, 1961-62.

Scunthorpe United: League Record, 1988-89 (Division 4)

Match Number	Date	Venue	Opponents	Result	H/T	Lge Posn	Attend
1	27.8.88	H	Hereford U.	W 3-1	0-0		3663
2	3.9.88	A	Crewe Alex.	L 2-3	1-2	10	1514
3	10.9.88	H	Grimsby T.	D 1-1	1-1	11	6037
4	17.9.88	A	York C.	W 2-1	1-0	8	2735
5	20.9.88	H	Carlisle U.	D 1-1	1-0	10	3113
6	24.9.88	A	Exeter C.	D 2-2	0-1	8	1876
7	1.10.88	H	Scarborough	L 0-3	0-1	13	4167
8	5.10.88	A	Lincoln C.	L 0-1	0-1	15	5443
9	8.10.88	A	Colchester U.	W 2-1	1-1	12	1299
10	15.10.88	H	Cambridge U.	W 1-0	0-0	9	3514
11	22.10.88	A	Rochdale	L 0-1	0-0	12	2250
12	25.10.88	H	Wrexham	W 3-1	1-1	9	2999
13	29.10.88	A	Peterborough U.	W 2-1	1-1	6	3532
14	5.11.88	H	Burnley	W 2-1	0-0	5	6358
15	8.11.88	A	Rotherham U.	D 3-3	1-2	5	5923
16	12.11.88	H	Leyton Orient	D 2-2	1-1	4	4239
17	26.11.88	H	Torquay U.	W 1-0	1-0	4	3359
18	3.12.88	A	Darlington.	D 3-3	1-1	4	1745
19	17.12.88	A	Doncaster Rov.	D 2-2	1-1	5	3381
20	26.12.88	H	Hartlepool U.	D 1-1	0-0	5	4595
21	31.12.88	H	Tranmere Rov.	L 0-1	0-1	8	4154
22	2.1.89	A	Halifax T.	L 1-5	0-2	8	2650
23	7.1.89	A	Stockport Co.	W 2-1	1-0	7	2656
24	14.1.89	H	Crewe Alex.	D 2-2	0-1	8	4032
25	21.1.89	A	Hereford U.	W 2-1	0-0	6	2024
26	28.1.89	H	York C.	W 4-2	3-1	4	4196
27	4.2.89	A	Carlisle U.	W 3-0	1-0	3	2627
28	11.2.89	H	Exeter C.	W 2-0	1-0	2	4102
29	18.2.89	H	Colchester U.	L 2-3	0-2	3	4286
30	25.2.89	A	Cambridge U.	W 3-0	1-0	2	2563
31	28.2.89	A	Wrexham	L 0-2	0-2	3	2609
32	4.3.89	H	Rochdale	W 4-0	2-0	2	4098
33	11.3.89	A	Burnley	W 1-0	1-0	3	6813
34	14.3.89	H	Peterborough U.	W 3-0	1-0	2	3983
35	18.3.89	A	Grimsby T.	D 1-1	0-0	3	9796
36	25.3.89	H	Halifax T..	D 0-0	0-0	3	4591
37	27.3.89	A	Hartlepool U.	W 2-0	0-0	3	1923
38	1.4.89	H	Doncaster Rov.	W 2-1	2-1	2	5334
39	4.4.89	H	Stockport Co.	D 1-1	0-1	2	3958
40	7.4.89	A	Tranmere Rov.	L 1-2	0-2	3	10465
41	15.4.89	A	Scarborough	L 0-1	0-0	4	4456
42	22.4.89	H	Lincoln C.	D 0-0	0-0	4	5729
43	28.4.89	A	Torquay U.	W 2-0	0-0	3	2544
44	1.5.89	H	Rotherham U.	D 0-0	0-0	3	8775
45	6.5.89	H	Darlington	W 5-1	1-0	2	5296
46	13.5.89	A	Leyton Orient	L 1-4	0-2	4	6366

Players: League Record, 1988-89 (Division 4)

Match Number	1	2	3	4	5	6	7	8	9	10	11	12	13	14	15	16	17	18	19	20	21	22	23
Brown, David																							1
Brown, Tony	6	6	6		**6**	6	6	★	11	11	6						★	11	6	6	6	6	
Cork, David																							
Cotton, Perry																							
Cowling, David	11^1	11	11	11	**11**	**11**					11	11	11	11	11	11	11		**11**	**11**	11		★
Daws, Tony	★^{1}	9	9	9^2	9	9^1	9	9	9	9	9	9^1	9	9	9	9^2	9^1	9^1	9	9	**9**	**9**	9^1
Flounders, Andy	10	10^1	10	10	10^1	10	10	10	**10**^{1}	10	10	10^1	10	10^1	10^1	10	**10**	10	10^1	10	10	★	10^1
Hamilton, Ian																				★	★	10^1	11
Harle, David							8	8	8	8	8	8	8^1	8	8	8	8	8	8	8^1	8	8	8
Hodkinson, Andy	7	7	7	7	7	7	7	7	7	7	7	7^1	7^1	7	7^1	**7**	7	7	7^1	**7**	7	7	**7**
Lister, Steve	5	5^1	5^1	5	5	5	5	5	5	5	5	5	5	5^1	5^1	5	5	5^1	5	5	5	5	5
Longden, Paul	2	**2**	2	2	2	2			★	3	3	3	3	3	3	3	3	3	3	3	3	3	3
Money, Richard					★								4	4	4	**4**							
Musselwhite, Paul	1	1	1	1	1	1	1	1	1	1	1	1	1	1	1	1	1	1	1	1	1	1	
Nicol, Paul																							★
Richardson, Ian		★			★	★	11	**11**	★^{1}							★			★				
Rumble, Paul	3		3	3	3	3^1	3	3	**3**														
Shearer, David	**9**																						
Smalley, Paul							2	2	2	2	2	2	2	2	2	2	2	2^1		2	**2**	2	2
Stevenson, Andrew		3		6	8	8		6	6	6		6	6	6	6	6	6	6	2	★	★	11	**6**
Taylor, Kevin	4^1	4	4	4	4	4	4	4	4	4^1	4	4				★	4	4	4	4	4	4	4
Winter, Julian	8	8	8	8																			
Own Goals																							

Match Number	24	25	26	27	28	29	30	31	32	33	34	35	36	37	38	39	40	41	42	43	44	45	46	Apps	Subs	Goals
Brown, David	1	1	1	1																				5	0	0
Brown, Tony	★	6	6^1	6	6	6	6	6	6^1	6	6	6	6	6	6			6						29	3	2
Cork, David						★			★	4	4	**4**		★	★	★	★	★	6	6	**6**	6	6	8	7	0
Cotton, Perry																★								0	1	0
Cowling, David	**3**	8	8	8	8^1	8	8	8	**8**	8	8	8	8	8	8	8	8	8	8	**8**		8	8	38	1	2
Daws, Tony	9^2	9^1	9^2	9	9	9	9^1	9	9^2	9	9	9	9	9^1	9	9	9^1	9	9	9^1	9	9^3	9	45	1	24
Flounders, Andy	10	10	10	10^1	10	**10**	10^1	10	10	10	10^3	10^1	10	10^1	10	10	10	10	10	10	10	10^1	10	45	1	16
Hamilton, Ian	11	11	11	11	11	11	11	11	11	11	11	11	**11**	11	11	11	11	11	11	11	11	11	11	25	2	1
Harle, David	**8**																							18	0	2
Hodkinson, Andy	7	7^1	7			★	3	**5**	5^1				★	7	**7**^{1}	**7**	★	**7**	7	7^1	7	7	7	38	3	8
Lister, Steve	5			7^1	7^1	7^1	7	7	7	7^1	7	7	7											34	0	9
Longden, Paul	★	3	3	3				3	**3**	3	3	3	3	3	3	3	3	3	3	3	3	3	3	39	2	0
Money, Richard																	**7**							5	1	0
Musselwhite, Paul					1	1	1	1	1	1	1	1	1	1	1	1	1	1	1	1	1	1	1	41	0	0
Nicol, Paul		5	5	5	5	5^1	5	★	★	5	5	5	5	5	5	5	5	5	5	5	5	5	5	20	3	1
Richardson, Ian																					★			2	7	1
Rumble, Paul																								8	0	1
Shearer, David																								1	0	0
Smalley, Paul	2	2	2	2	2	2	2	2	2	2	2	2	2	2	2	**2**	**2**	2	2	2	2	2	2	39	0	1
Stevenson, Andrew	6				3	**3**										6	6			★	8			23	3	0
Taylor, Kevin	4	4	4	4^1	4	4	4^1	4	4			★	4	**4**	4^1	4^1	4	4	4	4	4	4^1	4^1	39	2	8
Winter, Julian																								4	0	0
Own Goals			1																							1

FA Cup: 1988-89: 1st Round: Blackpool (A) 1-2.
Littlewoods Cup: 1988-89: 1st Round: Huddersfield T. (H) 3-2 (A) 2-2; 2nd Round: Chelsea (H) 4-1 (A) 2-2; 3rd Round: Bradford C. (A) 1-1, Replay (H) 0-1.

SHEFFIELD UNITED (Division 2)

Team Manager Dave Bassett.
Club Address Bramall Lane Ground, Sheffield S2 4SU. Tel: (0742) 738955/6/7.
Current Ground Capacity 44,010.
Record Attendance 68,287 v Leeds U., FA Cup 5th Round, 15 February 1936.
Year Formed 1889. Turned professional 1889.
Previous Names None.
Club Nickname "The Blades".
Club Colours Red and white striped shirts, black shorts and red stockings.
Club Honours Football League: Div. 1 Champions 1897-98; Div. 2 Champions 1952-53; Div. 4 Champions 1981-82. FA Cup: Winners 1899, 1902, 1915, 1925.
League History 1892-93 Div. 2; 1893-1934 Div. 1; 1934-39 Div. 2; 1946-49 Div. 1; 1949-53 Div. 2; 1953-56 Div. 1; 1956-61 Div. 2; 1961-68 Div. 1; 1968-71 Div. 2; 1971-76 Div. 1; 1976-79 Div. 2; 1979-81 Div. 3; 1981-82 Div 4; 1982-84 Div. 3; 1984-88 Div. 2; 1988-89 Div. 3; 1989- Div. 2.
Most League Points in a Season (2 for a win) 60 in Div. 2, 1952-53. (3 for a win) 96 in Div. 4, 1981-82.
Most League Goals in a Season 102 in Div. 1, 1925-26.
Record Victory 10-0 v Port Vale in Div. 2, 10 December 1892 and v Burnley in Div. 1, 19 January 1929.
Record Defeat 0-13 v Bolton W., FA Cup 2nd Round, 1 February 1890.
Consecutive League Wins 8 in 1893, 1903, 1958 and 1960.
Consecutive League Defeats 7 in 1975.
Record League Appearances Joe Shaw, 629 between 1948-66.
Record League Goalscorer—Career Harry Johnson, 205 between 1919-30.
Record League Goalscorer—Season Jimmy Dunne, 41 in Div. 1, 1930-31.

Sheffield United: League Record, 1988-89 (Division 3)

Match Number	Date	Venue	Opponents	Result	H/T	Lge Posn	Attend
1	27.8.88	A	Reading	W 3-1	2-0		5512
2	3.9.88	H	Bristol Rov.	W 4-1	2-1	1	9586
3	10.9.88	A	Gillingham	L 1-2	1-1	4	5041
4	17.9.88	H	Chester C.	W 6-1	3-0	2	8675
5	20.9.88	H	Northampton T.	W 4-0	2-0	2	11904
6	24.9.88	A	Brentford	W 4-1	1-1	1	6577
7	1.10.88	A	Bolton W.	L 0-2	0-1	1	9345
8	8.10.88	H	Wolverhampton W.	W 2-0	1-0	2	14272
9	15.10.88	A	Blackpool	W 2-1	1-1	2	8471
10	22.10.88	H	Wigan Ath.	W 2-1	1-0	1	11763
11	24.10.88	A	Port Vale	D 3-3	1-0	1	13246
12	29.10.88	H	Bury	W 2-1	2-0	1	12348
13	5.11.88	A	Huddersfield T.	L 2-3	1-2	2	10400
14	8.11.88	A	Aldershot	L 0-1	0-1	2	2934
15	12.11.88	H	Fulham	W 1-0	1-0	2	11087
16	26.11.88	H	Bristol C.	W 3-0	1-0	2	11248
17	3.12.88	A	Swansea C.	D 2-2	1-0	2	5676
18	17.12.88	H	Southend U.	L 1-2	0-0	3	9556
19	26.12.88	A	Notts Co.	W 4-1	0-1	3	11590
20	31.12.88	A	Preston N.E.	L 0-2	0-0	3	11005
21	2.1.89	H	Chesterfield	L 1-3	1-2	4	15769
22	14.1.89	A	Bristol Rov.	D 1-1	0-0	4	6623
23	21.1.89	H	Gillingham	W 4-2	3-0	4	9336
24	4.2.89	H	Bolton W.	W 4-0	0-0	4	11162
25	11.2.89	A	Cardiff C.	D 0-0	0-0	4	5772
26	25.2.89	H	Blackpool	W 4-1	3-0	4	11317
27	28.2.89	H	Port Vale	D 0-0	0-0	4	18787
28	4.3.89	A	Wigan Ath.	W 2-1	1-1	4	3966
29	11.3.89	H	Huddersfield T.	W 5-1	1-0	3	15000
30	14.3.89	A	Bury	W 2-1	1-0	3	5334
31	18.3.89	H	Reading	W 1-0	0-0	3	11867
32	25.3.89	A	Chesterfield	L 1-2	0-1	3	10991
33	27.3.89	H	Notts Co.	D 1-1	1-1	3	13039
34	31.3.89	A	Southend U.	L 1-2	1-1	3	4584
35	4.4.89	A	Mansfield T.	W 1-0	0-0	3	8524
36	8.4.89	H	Preston N.E.	W 3-1	0-0	3	12718
37	11.4.89	H	Cardiff C.	L 0-1	0-1	3	11618
38	15.4.89	A	Northampton T.	W 2-1	1-1	3	5030
39	19.4.89	A	Chester C.	W 1-0	1-0	2	4282
40	22.4.89	H	Brentford	D 2-2	1-0	2	12613
41	25.4.89	H	Mansfield T.	L 1-2	0-1	2	11638
42	29.4.89	A	Fulham	D 2-2	1-1	2	7794
43	1.5.89	H	Aldershot	W 1-0	0-0	2	11737
44	6.5.89	H	Swansea C.	W 5-1	2-0	2	15383
45	9.5.89	A	Wolverhampton W.	D 2-2	0-1	2	24321
46	13.5.89	A	Bristol C.	L 0-2	0-0	2	10769

Players: League Record, 1988-89 (Division 3)

Match Number	1	2	3	4	5	6	7	8	9	10	11	12	13	14	15	16	17	18	19	20	21	22	23
Agana, Tony	★	9^1	9	9^3	9^1	9^2	9	9^1	9	9	9	9	9^2	9	9	9^1	9^1	9	9	9	9^1	9^1	9
Barnsley, Andy			2										★				★						
Benstead, Graham	1	1	1	1	1	1	1	1	1	1	1	1	1	1	1	1	1	1	1	1	1	1	1
Booker, Bob																4	4	4	4	4	4	4	4^1
Bryson, Ian	11	11^2	11^1	11	11^2	11	11						11			11	11	11	11	11	11	11	11
Carr, Darren													5									6	6^1
Deane, Brian	10^1	10	10	10^3	10^1	10	10	10^1	10	10^1	10^1	10^1	10	10	10^1	10^2	10^1		10	10	10		
Dickinson, Martin						★																	
Downes, Chris													4	4									
Duffield, Peter		★	7	7	★		★	11	★	★	$★^1$	★	7	7	4		★	7	7^1	7	★	★	7^1
Francis, John				★				★			★				11			10^1			★		★
Gannon, John																							
Joseph, Francis	9^1						★		★	★	11^1	11	★	11	★			★		★		★	10^1
Moore, John																							
Pike, Martin	3	3	3	3	3	3	3	3	3^1	3	3	3	3	3	3	3	3	3	3^2	3	3		3
Powell, Cliff	2																						
Roberts, Alan	7	7^1			7	7^1	7	7	7	7	7	7		★	7	7	7	★		★	7	7	
Ryan, Vaughan																						2	2
Smith, Brian	6	6	6	6	6	6	6	6	6	6	6	6	6	6	6	6	6	6	6	6	6		★
Stancliffe, Paul	5^1	5	5	5	5	5	5	5	5	5	5	5		5	5	5	5	5	5	5	5	5	
Thompson, Steve																							5
Todd, Mark	8	8	8	8	8	8^1	8	8	8	8	8	8	8	8	8	8	8	8	8^1	8	8	8	8
Tracey, Simon																							
Webster, Simon	4	4	4	4	4	4	4	4	4^1	4^1	4	4											
Whitehouse, Dane									11	11												3	
Wilder, Chris		2		2	2	2	2	2	2	2	2	2^1	2	2	2	2	2	2	2	2	2		
Williams, Paul			★																			10	
Own Goals																							

Match Number	24	25	26	27	28	29	30	31	32	33	34	35	36	37	38	39	40	41	42	43	44	45	46	Apps	Subs	Goals
Agana, Tony	9^1	9	9	9	9	9	9	9	9	9	★	9	9^1	9	9	9^1	9^1	9^1	9^1	9	9^3	9^1	9	44	2	24
Barnsley, Andy																								1	2	0
Benstead, Graham	1	1	1	1	1		1	1	1	1	1	1	1	1	1	1	1							39	0	0
Booker, Bob			4	4	4	4	4	4	4	4	4^1	4	4	4	4	4		4	6	6	6			26	0	2
Bryson, Ian	11	11	11	11	11	11^1	11	11	11^1	11	11	11	11	11			★	11	11^1	11	11	11	11	36	1	8
Carr, Darren	6	6		★												8	4					6	6	9	1	1
Deane, Brian	10	10	10	10	10^2	10^1	10^1	10^1	10	10^1	10	10	10^1	10	10^1	10	10	10	10	10^1	10	10	10	43	0	22
Dickinson, Martin																								0	1	0
Downes, Chris																								2	0	0
Duffield, Peter	8^2	8	7^1	7	7	7^2	7^1	7	7		7	7^1	7^1	7	7		$★^1$	7	★	★				25	13	12
Francis, John	★		★	★	★	★		★	★	★	9	★	★	★	★			★			★			3	19	1
Gannon, John			$★^1$		★		★	★		★	★		★	★	11	11	11	8	8	8	8	8		8	8	1
Joseph, Francis																								5	8	3
Moore, John																		★		4	4	4	4	4	1	0
Pike, Martin	3	3	3^1	3	3	3	3	3	3	3	3	3	3	3	3	3	3	3	3	3	3^1	3	3	45	0	5
Powell, Cliff																				5	★		★	2	2	0
Roberts, Alan	7	7								7					★	7	7		7	7	7	7	7	25	4	2
Ryan, Vaughan		★																						2	1	0
Smith, Brian	2	2	2	2	2	2	2	2	2	2	2	2	2											34	1	0
Stancliffe, Paul	5	5	5	5	5	5	5	5	5	5	5	5	5	5	5	5	5	5			5^1	5^1	5	42	0	3
Thompson, Steve	4	4	6	6	6	6	6	6	6	6	6	6	6	6	6^1	6	6	6	5					20	0	1
Todd, Mark			8^1	8	8	8	8	8	8	8	8	8	8	8	8		8		4				8	39	0	3
Tracey, Simon						1												1	1	1	1	1	1	7	0	0
Webster, Simon																								12	0	2
Whitehouse, Dane																			★	★				3	2	0
Wilder, Chris														2	2	2	2	2	2	2	2	2	2	29	0	1
Williams, Paul																								1	1	0
Own Goals	1					1																				2

FA Cup: 1988-89: 1st Round: Mansfield T. (A) 1-1, Replay (H) 2-1; 2nd Round: Doncaster Rov. (A) 3-1; 3rd Round: Huddersfield T. (A) 1-0; 4th Round: Colchester U. (H) 3-3, Replay (A) 2-0; 5th Round: Norwich C. (A) 2-3.

Littlewoods Cup: 1988-89: 1st Round: Hartlepool. U. (A) 2-2 (H) 2-0; 2nd Round: Newcastle U. (H) 3-0 (A) 0-2; 3rd Round: Manchester C. (A) 2-4.

SHEFFIELD WEDNESDAY (Division 1)

Team Manager Ron Atkinson.
Club Address Hillsborough, Sheffield S6 1SW. Tel: (0742) 343122.
Current Ground Capacity 54,281.
Record Attendance 72,841 v Manchester C., FA Cup 5th Round, 17 February 1934.
Year Formed 1867. Turned professional 1887.
Previous Names The Wednesday.
Club Nickname "The Owls".
Club Colours Blue and white striped shirts, white shorts and stockings.
Club Honours Football League: Div. 1 Champions 1902-03, 1903-04, 1928-29, 1929-30; Div. 2 Champions 1899-1900, 1925-26, 1951-52, 1955-56, 1958-59. FA Cup: Winners 1896, 1907, 1935.
League History 1892-99 Div. 1; 1899-1900 Div. 2; 1900-20 Div. 1; 1920-26 Div. 2; 1926-37 Div. 1; 1937-50 Div. 2; 1950-51 Div. 1; 1951-52 Div. 2; 1952-55 Div. 1; 1955-56 Div. 2; 1956-58 Div. 1; 1958-59 Div. 2; 1959-70 Div. 1; 1970-75 Div. 2; 1975-80 Div. 3; 1980-84 Div. 2; 1984- Div. 1.
Most League Points in a Season (2 for a win) 62 in Div. 2, 1958-59. (3 for a win) 88 in Div. 2, 1983-84.
Most League Goals in a Season 106 in Div. 2, 1958-59.
Record Victory 12-0 v Halliwell in FA Cup 1st Round, 17 January 1891.
Record Defeat 0-10 v Aston Villa in Div. 1, 5 October 1912.
Consecutive League Wins 9 in 1904.
Consecutive League Defeats 7 in 1893.
Record League Appearances Andy Wilson, 502 between 1900-20.
Record League Goalscorer—Career Andy Wilson, 200 between 1900-20.
Record League Goalscorer—Season Derek Dooley, 46 in Div. 2, 1951-52.

Sheffield Wednesday: League Record, 1988-89 (Division 1)

Match Number	Date	Venue	Opponents	Result	H/T	Lge Posn	Attend
1	27.8.88	H	Luton T.	W 1-0	0-0		16433
2	3.9.88	A	Nottingham F.	D 1-1	0-1	7	18963
3	10.9.88	H	Coventry C.	L 1-2	0-0	9	15633
4	17.9.88	A	Q.P.R.	L 0-2	0-1	12	8011
5	24.9.88	H	Arsenal	W 2-1	1-0	12	17830
6	1.10.88	H	Aston Villa	W 1-0	1-0	7	18301
7	22.10.88	A	Southampton	W 2-1	1-1	5	12725
8	29.10.88	A	Charlton Ath.	L 1-2	0-1	10	5933
9	5.11.88	H	Everton	D 1-1	0-0	13	21761
10	12.11.88	A	Norwich C.	D 1-1	0-1	13	14353
11	20.11.88	H	Tottenham H.	L 0-2	0-0	13	15386
12	23.11.88	A	Manchester U.	D 1-1	0-0	12	30867
13	26.11.88	A	Middlesbrough	W 1-0	1-0	10	19310
14	3.12.88	H	Derby Co.	D 1-1	1-0	11	20609
15	10.12.88	A	West Ham U.	D 0-0	0-0	11	16676
16	17.12.88	A	Millwall	L 0-1	0-0	12	11917
17	26.12.88	H	Newcastle U.	L 1-2	1-2	13	22573
18	31.12.88	H	Nottingham F.	L 0-3	0-3	16	20407
19	2.1.89	A	Coventry C.	L 0-5	0-2	17	15191
20	14.1.89	H	Liverpool	D 2-2	2-0	17	31524
21	21.1.89	A	Arsenal	D 1-1	0-0	18	33490
22	4.2.89	A	Aston Villa	L 0-2	0-2	18	19334
23	11.2.89	H	Manchester U.	L 0-2	0-1	18	34280
24	18.2.89	H	Southampton	D 1-1	0-0	18	16677
25	25.2.89	A	Wimbledon	L 0-1	0-1	18	4384
26	4.3.89	H	Charlton Ath.	W 3-1	1-1	18	16081
27	11.3.89	A	Everton	L 0-1	0-1	18	22542
28	18.3.89	A	Luton T.	W 1-0	0-0	15	7776
29	25.3.89	H	Q.P.R.	L 0-2	0-0	17	18804
30	27.3.89	A	Newcastle U.	W 3-1	2-1	14	31040
31	1.4.89	H	Millwall	W 3-0	1-0	13	18358
32	5.4.89	H	Wimbledon	D 1-1	0-0	13	15777
33	8.4.89	A	Liverpool	L 1-5	0-2	14	39672
34	12.4.89	A	Tottenham H.	D 0-0	0-0	14	17270
35	22.4.89	A	Derby Co.	L 0-1	0-0	16	17529
36	9.5.89	H	West Ham U.	L 0-2	0-0	18	19905
37	13.5.89	H	Middlesbrough	W 1-0	0-0	16	20582
38	17.5.89	H	Norwich C.	D 2-2	0-0	15	16230

Players: League Record, 1988-89 (Division 1)

Match Number	1	2	3	4	5	6	7	8	9	10	11	12	13	14	15	16	17	18	19
Barrick, Dean																			
Bennett, David																			
Bradshaw, Carl			★	★	11														
Cranson, Ian			★	6	6	6	6	6	6	4	4	4	4	4	4	4	4	4	
Fee, Greg																			
Galvin, Tony	11	11	11	11	★	★													★
Gregory, Tony																★		7	★
Harper, Alan	6	6	6											★	10	10			2
Hirst, David	★	★	8[1]	8	8	8[1]				★	★	10	10	10	8	8	8[1]	8	
Hodgson, David							★	★[1]	10	11	11	11	★		9	★			8
Jonsson, Siggi	10	10	10	10	10	10			★	6	7	7	7	8	6	11	11	11	11
Knight, Ian																			4
McCall, Steve																			
Madden, Lawrie	5	5	5	5	5	5	5	5	5		6	6	6	6		6	6	6	6
Megson, Gary	7	7	7	7	7[1]	7	7	7	7	7		★	11	7	7	7	7	★	7
Palmer, Carlton																			
Pearson, Nigel	4	4	4	4	4[1]	4	4	4	4	5	5	5	5	5	5	5	5	5	5
Pressman, Kevin	1	1	1	1	1	1									1	1	1		
Proctor, Mark	8	8					11	11	11	8	8	8	8	11	11	2	2	2	3
Reeves, David					9	9	8[1]	8	★	10	10			★				★	
Rostron, Wilf																			
Sterland, Mel	2[1]	2[1]	2	2	2	2	2	2	2[1]	2[1]	2	2	2[1]	2[1]	2		10		
Turner, Chris							1	1	1	1	1	1	1	1				1	1
Varadi, Imre						11	9[1]	9	9			★	★		★	9	9	9	9
West, Colin	9	9	9	9	★	★	10	10	8	9	9	9[1]	9	9			★	10	10
Whitton, Steve																			
Wood, Darren																			
Worthington, Nigel	3	3	3	3	3	3	3	3	3	3	3	3	3	3	3	3	3	3	
Own Goals																			

Match Number	20	21	22	23	24	25	26	27	28	29	30	31	32	33	34	35	36	37	38	Apps	Subs	Goals
Barrick, Dean											11[1]	11	11	11[1]	11	11	11	11		8		
Bennett, David																					0	2
Bradshaw, Carl										7	7	7	7	7	7	7	7	7	7	10	0	0
Cranson, Ian	4	4	4	4	4	6														1	2	0
Fee, Greg							6			6	6	6								25	1	0
Galvin, Tony	★				7	11					8	8	8	8	8		8	8	8	8	0	0
Gregory, Tony							11[1]	11	★	★	★						★	★	11	9	9	1
Harper, Alan		11	11	11	11															1	2	0
Hirst, David			10	10	8	10	2	2	2	2	2	2	2	2	2	2	2	2	2	23	1	0
Hodgson, David		★					10[1]	10	10[1]	10	10[1]	10	10[1]	10	10	10	10	10	10	28	4	7
Jonsson, Siggi	11		8	8	9															6	5	1
Knight, Ian		6					8[1]	8		11		★	6	6				★		25	3	1
McCall, Steve																				2	0	0
Madden, Lawrie	6		6	6		3			8	8										2	0	0
Megson, Gary								6	6							8	6	6	6	27	0	0
Palmer, Carlton						4														16	2	1
Pearson, Nigel	5	5	5	5	5	5		4	4	4	4	4[1]	4	4	4	4	4	4	4	13	0	1
Pressman, Kevin							5	5	5	5	5[1]	5	5		5	5	5	5	5	37	0	2
Proctor, Mark	7[1]	7	7	7	6[1]	7														9	0	0
Reeves, David	8	8		★	★	★	7	7	7											24	0	2
Rostron, Wilf	3	3	3	3	3			★									★		★[1]	8	9	2
Sterland, Mel	2	2	2	2	2	2			11					5						7	0	0
Turner, Chris	1	1	1	1	1	1														22	0	6
Varadi, Imre	10[1]	10[1]	★	9	10	9	1	1	1	1	1	1	1	1	1	1	1	1	1	29	0	0
West, Colin	9	9	9				★		★							9				14	6	3
Whitton, Steve																				17	3	1
Wood, Darren		★				8	9	9	9	9	9	9[2]	9	9	9		9	9[1]	9	12	0	3
Worthington, Nigel							4				3				6	6		3	3	7	1	0
							3	3	3	3		3	3	3	3	3	3			28	0	0
Own Goals																			1			1

FA Cup: 1988-89: 3rd Round: Torquay U. (H) 5-1; 4th Round: Blackburn Rov. (A) 1-2.
Littlewoods Cup: 1988-89: 2nd Round: Blackpool (A) 0-2 (H) 3-1.

SHREWSBURY TOWN (Division 3)

Team Manager Ian McNeill.
Club Address Gay Meadow, Shrewsbury. Tel: (0743) 60111.
Current Ground Capacity 16,000.
Record Attendance 18,917 v Walsall, Div. 3, 26 April 1961.
Year Formed 1886. Turned professional 1905.
Previous Names None.
Club Nickname "Town".
Club Colours White shirts with blue trim, blue shorts, white stockings with blue trim.
Club Honours Football League: Div. 3 Champions 1978-79.
League History 1950-51 Div. 3(N); 1951-58 Div. 3(S); 1958-59 Div. 4; 1959-74 Div. 3; 1974-75 Div. 4; 1975-79 Div. 3; 1979-89 Div. 2; 1989- Div. 3.
Most League Points in a Season (2 for a win) 62 in Div. 4, 1974-75. (3 for a win) 70 in Div. 2, 1981-82.
Most League Goals in a Season 101 in Div. 4, 1958-59.
Record Victory 7-0 v Swindon T. in Div. 3(S), 6 May 1955.
Record Defeat 1-8 v Norwich C. in Div. 3(S), 1952-53 and v Coventry C. in Div. 3, 22 October 1963.
Consecutive League Wins 7 in 1950 and 1955.
Consecutive League Defeats 7 in 1951-52.
Record League Appearances Colin Griffin, 405 between 1975-88.
Record League Goalscorer—Career Arthur Rowley, 152 between 1958-65.
Record League Goalscorer—Season Arthur Rowley, 38 in Div. 4, 1958-59.

Shrewsbury Town: League Record, 1988-89 (Division 2)

Match Number	Date	Venue	Opponents	Result	H/T	Lge Posn	Attend
1	27.8.88	H	Portsmouth	L 1-2	1-1		5333
2	3.9.88	A	Bradford C.	L 0-1	0-1	23	9765
3	10.9.88	H	West Bromwich A.	D 1-1	0-0	22	5851
4	17.9.88	A	Crystal Palace	D 1-1	1-0	21	7006
5	20.9.88	H	Ipswich T.	L 1-5	1-3	21	4154
6	24.9.88	H	Sunderland	D 0-0	0-0	22	4195
7	1.10.88	A	Oxford U	L 1-4	1-2	23	4385
8	4.10.88	A	Stoke C.	D 0-0	0-0	22	8075
9	8.10.88	H	Hull C.	L 1-3	0-2	23	3287
10	15.10.88	H	Walsall	D 0-0	0-0	23	5026
11	21.10.88	A	Bournemouth	W 1-0	1-0	22	5449
12	25.10.88	A	Plymouth Arg.	D 0-0	0-0	21	6298
13	29.10.88	H	Leicester C.	W 3-0	1-0	22	5178
14	5.11.88	A	Brighton & H.A.	L 1-3	0-0	22	7365
15	11.11.88	H	Oldham Ath.	D 0-0	0-0	22	4701
16	19.11.88	H	Watford	D 1-1	1-0	23	4621
17	22.11.88	A	Blackburn Rov.	W 1-0	1-0	21	6898
18	26.11.88	A	Chelsea	L 0-2	0-2	22	11595
19	3.12.88	H	Swindon T.	L 0-1	0-1	22	3524
20	10.12.88	A	Leeds U.	W 3-2	2-0	21	19967
21	17.12.88	A	Manchester C.	D 2-2	2-0	21	19613
22	26.12.88	H	Birmingham C.	D 0-0	0-0	21	7347
23	31.12.88	H	Barnsley	L 2-3	1-1	22	4401
24	2.1.89	A	West Bromwich A.	L 0-4	0-0	22	18411
25	14.1.88	H	Blackburn Rov.	D 1-1	0-0	22	3879
26	21.1.89	A	Portsmouth	L 0-2	0-1	22	8446
27	4.2.89	H	Stoke C.	L 1-2	1-0	22	6646
28	11.2.89	A	Hull C.	L 0-3	0-2	22	11472
29	25.2.89	A	Walsall	D 1-1	1-1	22	5871
30	28.2.89	H	Plymouth Arg.	W 2-0	1-0	22	2978
31	3.3.89	A	Oldham Ath.	L 0-3	0-1	22	6014
32	11.3.89	H	Brighton & H.A.	D 1-1	0-1	22	4029
33	15.3.89	A	Leicester C.	D 1-1	1-1	22	7750
34	18.3.89	A	Ipswich T.	L 0-2	0-0	22	10913
35	25.3.89	H	Bradford C.	L 1-3	0-1	22	4575
36	27.3.89	A	Birmingham C.	W 2-1	0-1	22	4964
37	1.4.89	H	Crystal Palace	W 2-1	2-1	22	4160
38	4.4.89	H	Manchester C.	L 0-1	0-0	22	8271
39	8.4.89	A	Barnsley	L 0-1	0-1	22	5252
40	11.4.89	H	Bournemouth	W 1-0	0-0	22	2457
41	15.4.89	H	Oxford U.	D 2-2	0-1	22	3583
42	22.4.89	A	Sunderland	L 1-2	0-1	22	9427
43	29.4.89	H	Chelsea	D 1-1	0-0	22	5588
44	1.5.89	A	Swindon T.	L 0-1	0-1	22	8698
45	6.5.89	A	Watford	D 0-0	0-0	22	10052
46	13.5.89	H	Leeds U.	D 3-3	2-2	22	4693

Players: League Record, 1988-89 (Division 2)

Match Number	1	2	3	4	5	6	7	8	9	10	11	12	13	14	15	16	17	18	19	20	21	22	23
Bell, Doug				★	**4**		8	7	7	4	4	**4**		8	8	8	8	8	8	8	8	**8**	8^1
Brown, Michael	11	7	11	11	7	10		★	★	7	7	7	7	7	★	9	**9**		★	★			7
Finley, Alan	6	6	6	6	6	6	6	6	6	6	6	6	6^1	6	6	6	6	6				★	6
Geddis, David		★	9^1	★		4	9	9	9	9	9												
Green, Richard	5	5	5	5	3	3	3	3	3^1	2	2	2	2	2^1	2	2	2	2	2	2	2	2	2
Green, Ron							1	1	1	1	1	1	1	1	1	1	1	1	1	1	1	1	1
Griffin, Colin	★																						
Griffiths, Carl							★	**10**	10		★	★	8	★	9			★	★	9^2	9^2	9	9
Hughes, Ken																							
Irvine, Alan	9	10	**10**	10	9	**9**	10		★	10	**10^1**	10	10^2	10	10	10	10^1	10		10	10	10	10^1
Kasule, Victor	7	★	★	**7**	11	7	**7**						★	★				9	**9**				
Kelly, Tony																							
McGinlay, John																							
McNally, Bernard	8^1	8	8	8	8	**8**		8															
Melrose, Jim	★	9	★	**9**	★						★	9	**9**	**9**					**10**				
Moyes, David						★	4^1	4	**4**		5	5	5	5	5	5	5	5	5	5	5	5	5
Osbourne, Gary																★	★			7	7	7	
Perks, Stephen	1	1	1	1	1	1																	
Pittman, Stephen																							
Pratley, Richard																		★	6	6	6	6	
Priest, Philip	**4**		**7**							8	8	**8**	4	4	**4**	**4**	4	**4**	4	**4**	**4**	**4**	
Rougvie, Doug		**4**	4	4^1	5^1	5	5	5	5	5		★	3	3	3	3	3	3	3	3^1	3	3	3
Steele, Timothy					★	★			8	★					7	7^1	7	**7**	7	★	★	★	
Thomas, Micky	**10**	11			**10**	11	11	11	11	11	**11**	11	**11**	11	11	11	11	11	11	**11**	11	11	11
Williams, Brian	3	3	3	3			★			3	3	3	★										4
Williams, Wayne	2	2	2	2	2	2	**2**	2	**2**														
Worsley, Graeme																							
Own Goals																							

Match Number	24	25	26	27	28	29	30	31	32	33	34	35	36	37	38	39	40	41	42	43	44	45	46	Apps	Subs	Goals
Bell, Doug	8			11	11		4	4	**4**										7	**7**				25	1	1
Brown, Michael	7	7	**7**	7	7	7	7	7	7	7	7	7	7	7	7	7	7	7		★	7	7	7	35	6	0
Finley, Alan	6		★		2	6	6	6	6	6	6			6	6	6	6	**6**						32	2	1
Geddis, David																								7	2	1
Green, Richard	**2**	2	2	**2**		2^1	2	2				2	2	2	2	2				★	★	9	2	37	2	3
Green, Ron																								17	0	0
Griffin, Colin																								0	1	0
Griffiths, Carl	**9**	9	9	9	★	10	10	10		★	★	**9**		★								★	9^2	17	11	6
Hughes, Ken	1	1	1	1	1	1										1								7	0	0
Irvine, Alan	10	10	10	10					10	10	**10**	**10**				★	**9**							29	2	5
Kasule, Victor	★	8^1	8	8	**8**				★				★		★	★	**11**							12	9	1
Kelly, Tony				★	10	8	8^1	8	8^1	4	4	4^1	4^1	**4^1**	4	4	4	4	4	4	4	4	4	19	1	5
McGinlay, John						★	**9^1**	**9**	**9**	**9**	9		**9**	**9^1**	9	**9**		$★^1$	10^1	10^1	10	10	10	14	2	5
McNally, Bernard									★	8	8	8	8	8	8	8	8	8	8	8	8	8	8^1	21	1	2
Melrose, Jim					9	**9**							10	10	10	**10**	$★^1$	9^1	9	9	**9**			16	5	2
Moyes, David	5	5	5	5	5						★	6	6	★			★	★	6	6	6	6	6	28	5	1
Osbourne, Gary							★	★																3	4	0
Perks, Stephen							1	1	1	1	1	1	1	1	1		1	1	1	1	1	1	1	22	0	0
Pittman, Stephen												★	3	3	3	3	3	3	**3**	3	3	**3**	3	11	1	0
Pratley, Richard	★	6	6	6	6	5	5	5	5	5	5	5	5	5	5	5	5	5	5	5	5	5	5	26	2	0
Priest, Philip		4	4	**4^1**	**4**	4		★	2	2	2	★				11	10	**10**						26	2	1
Rougvie, Doug																								20	1	3
Steele, Timothy			★	★	★																			6	9	1
Thomas, Micky	11	11	**11**			11	11	**11**	11	11	**11**	11	11^1	11	**11**			11	11	**11**	11	11	11	40	0	1
Williams, Brian	4	3	3	3	3	3	3	3	3	3^1	3	3							★					20	3	1
Williams, Wayne	3																							10	0	0
Worsley, Graeme																	2	2	2	2	2	2		6	0	0
Own Goals																										0

FA Cup: 1988-89: 3rd Round: Colchester U. (H) 0-3.
Littlewoods Cup: 1988-89: 1st Round: Walsall (H) 2-2 (A) 0-3.

SOUTHAMPTON (Division 1)

Team Manager Chris Nicholl.
Club Address The Dell, Milton Road, Southampton SO9 4XX. Tel: (0703) 220505.
Current Ground Capacity 25,000.
Record Attendance 31,044 v Manchester U., Div. 1, 8 October 1969.
Year Formed 1885. Turned professional 1894.
Previous Names Southampton St Mary's.
Club Nickname "The Saints".
Club Colours Red shirts with black trim and white vertical band on chest, black shorts and white stockings with two red hoops on turnovers.
Club Honours Football League: Div. 3(S) Champions 1921-22; Div. 3 Champions 1959-60. FA Cup: Winners 1976.
League History 1920-22 Div. 3(S); 1922-53 Div. 2; 1953-58 Div. 3(S); 1958-60 Div. 3; 1960-66 Div. 2; 1966-74 Div. 1; 1974-78 Div. 2; 1978- Div. 1.
Most League Points in a Season (2 for a win) 61 in Div. 3(S), 1921-22 and in Div. 3, 1959-60. (3 for a win) 77 in Div. 1, 1983-84.
Most League Goals in a Season 112 in Div. 3(S), 1957-58.
Record Victory 14-0 v Newbury in F A Cup 1st qual. Round, 10 September 1894.
Record Defeat 0-8 v Tottenham H. in Div. 2, 28 March 1936 and v Everton in Div. 1, 20 November 1971.
Consecutive League Wins 6 in 1964.
Consecutive League Defeats 5 in 1927, 1957 and 1967-68 and 1988-89.
Record League Appearances Terry Paine, 713 between 1956-74.
Record League Goalscorer—Career Mike Channon, 182 between 1966-82.
Record League Goalscorer—Season Derek Reeves, 39 in Div. 3, 1959-60.

Southampton: League Record, 1988-89 (Division 1)

Match Number	Date	Venue	Opponents	Result	H/T	Lge Posn	Attend
1	27.8.88	H	West Ham U.	W 4-0	2-0		18407
2	3.9.88	A	Q.P.R.	W 1-0	1-0	2	9053
3	10.9.88	H	Luton T.	W 2-1	1-0	1	13214
4	17.9.88	A	Arsenal	D 2-2	2-0	2	31384
5	24.9.88	H	Liverpool	L 1-3	1-1	4	21046
6	1.10.88	H	Derby Co.	D 0-0	0-0	4	13285
7	8.10.88	A	Everton	L 1-4	1-1	6	25356
8	22.10.88	H	Sheffield Wed.	L 1-2	1-1	10	12725
9	25.10.88	A	Tottenham H.	W 2-1	0-1	5	19517
10	29.10.88	A	Norwich C.	D 1-1	0-0	6	14808
11	5.11.88	H	Charlton Ath.	W 2-0	0-0	4	12826
12	12.11.88	H	Aston Villa	W 3-1	1-1	3	16007
13	19.11.88	A	Manchester U.	D 2-2	1-1	5	37277
14	26.11.88	H	Millwall	D 2-2	1-1	6	15925
15	3.12.88	A	Wimbledon	L 1-2	1-1	7	6040
16	10.12.88	H	Nottingham F.	D 1-1	1-0	6	15259
17	17.12.88	A	Newcastle U.	D 3-3	2-1	7	19986
18	26.12.88	H	Coventry C.	D 2-2	0-2	8	16008
19	31.12.88	H	Q.P.R.	L 1-4	0-0	9	15086
20	2.1.89	A	Luton T.	L 1-6	0-2	10	8637
21	14.1.89	H	Middlesbrough	L 1-3	1-0	13	13157
22	21.1.89	A	Liverpool	L 0-2	0-0	15	35565
23	4.2.89	A	Derby Co.	L 1-3	0-1	15	13758
24	11.2.89	H	Everton	D 1-1	1-0	14	15845
25	18.2.89	A	Sheffield Wed.	D 1-1	0-0	14	16667
26	25.2.89	H	Tottenham H.	L 0-2	0-1	15	16702
27	11.3.89	A	Charlton Ath.	D 2-2	0-1	16	6377
28	25.3.89	H	Arsenal	L 1-3	0-1	18	19202
29	27.3.89	A	Coventry C.	L 1-2	1-1	18	11734
30	1.4.89	H	Newcastle U.	W 1-0	0-0	17	16175
31	8.4.89	A	Middlesbrough	D 3-3	0-1	17	16983
32	12.4.89	A	Nottingham F.	L 0-3	0-2	17	18948
33	15.4.89	A	West Ham U.	W 2-1	1-1	16	14766
34	19.4.89	H	Norwich C.	D 0-0	0-0	16	14403
35	22.4.89	H	Wimbledon	D 0-0	0-0	15	13805
36	2.5.89	A	Aston Villa	W 2-1	2-0	13	15218
37	6.5.89	H	Manchester U.	W 2-1	1-0	13	17012
38	13.5.89	A	Millwall	D 1-1	1-0	13	12011

Players: League Record, 1988-89 (Division 1)

Match Number	1	2	3	4	5	6	7	8	9	10	11	12	13	14	15	16	17	18	19
Adams, Micky																			
Baker, Graham					8	8	8	**8**	4	4	10^1	10	10	10^2			10	10	**10**
Benali, Francis						★	★	★	10	10									
Blake, Mark							5												
Burridge, John	1	1	1	1	1	1	1	1	1	1	1	1	1	1	1				
Case, Jimmy	4	4	4	4	4	4	4				4	4	4	4	4	4	4	4	4
Clarke, Colin	9	9	9	9	9	9	9	9	**9**										
Cockerill, Glenn	8^1	8	8	8				4	8^2	8	8	8	8	8	8	8	8	**8**	**8**
Cook, Andy																			
Flowers, Tim																1	1	1	1
Forrest, Gerry	2	2	2	2	2	2	2												2
Horne, Barry																			
Le Tissier, Matt	★^{1}	11^1	**11**	11^1		★	★	★	★	**9**	9	9^2	9^1	9	9	9	**9**^{2}	9	9^1
Maddison, Neil									★	★					10^1	10^1			
Moore, Kevin	5	5	5	5	5	**5**		5	5	5	5	5	5	5	5	5	5	5^1	5
Osman, Russell	6	6	6	6	6	6	6	6	6	6	6	6	6	6	6	6	6	6	6
Rideout, Paul	10^2	**10**	10^1	10	**10**	10	10	10									★	★	★
Ruddock, Neil																			
Shearer, Alan		★			★														
Statham, Derek	3	3	3	3	3^1	3	3	3^1	3	3	3	3	3	3	3	3	3	3	3
Wallace, Danny	**11**		★	★	11	11	**11**^{1}	**11**	11	11^1	11^1	11	11	11	11	11	11	11	11
Wallace, Raymond								2	2	2	2	2	2	2	2	2	2	2	★
Wallace, Rodney	7	7	7^1	7^1	7	**7**	**7**	7	7	7	7	7^1	7	7	7	7	7^1	7^1	7
Own Goals													1						

Match Number	20	21	22	23	24	25	26	27	28	29	30	31	32	33	34	35	36	37	38	Apps	Subs	Goals
Adams, Micky									3	3	3	3	3	3	3	3				8	0	0
Baker, Graham	10	**10**	10	2	8	8	**8**		★											20	1	3
Benali, Francis				★				**11**												3	4	0
Blake, Mark		4	**4**																	3	0	0
Burridge, John	1	1	1	1	1	1	1				1	1	1	1	1	1	1	1	1	31	0	0
Case, Jimmy	4	8	8	4	4	4	4	4		4	4	4	4	4	4	4	4	4	4	34	0	0
Clarke, Colin																				9	0	0
Cockerill, Glenn		★	7	8	10	10	10	8	8^1	8	8	8	8	8	8	8	8	8^1	8^1	33	1	6
Cook, Andy		★	3	3																2	1	0
Flowers, Tim								1	1	1										7	0	0
Forrest, Gerry	2	2			2	2	2		★				★				3	3		15	2	0
Horne, Barry									4	10	10	10	**10**	10	10	10	10	10	10	11	0	0
Le Tissier, Matt	9	7		**7**								★	★		11	11	11	11	11	21	7	9
Maddison, Neil	8																			3	2	2
Moore, Kevin	5	5^1	5	5	5^1					5				5						25	0	3
Osman, Russell	6		6	6	6	6	6	6	**6**		6	6	6	6	6	6	6	6	6	36	0	0
Rideout, Paul		9	9	10			★	10^1	**10**				**9**	9^1	9	9	9^1	9	9	20	4	6
Ruddock, Neil						5	5	5	5	6	5^1	5^2	5		5	5	5	5	5	13	0	3
Shearer, Alan					9	9	9	9	9	9	9	9								8	2	0
Statham, Derek	3	**3**			3	3	3	3											3	26	0	2
Wallace, Danny	11		★	9^1	11	11	11	★	11	11^1	11	11	11	11						27	4	5
Wallace, Raymond		6	2					2	2	2	2	2	2	2	2	2	2	2	2	25	1	0
Wallace, Rodney	7^1	11	11	11	7	7^1	7	7^1	7	7	7	**7**^{1}	7	7^1	7	7	7^1	7^1	7	38	0	12
Own Goals																						1

FA Cup: 1988-89: 3rd Round: Derby Co. (A) 1-1, Replay (H) 1-2.

Littlewoods Cup: 1988-89: 2nd Round: Lincoln C. (A) 1-1 (H) 3-1; 3rd Round: Scarborough (A) 2-2, Replay (H) 1-0; 4th Round: Tottenham H. (H) 2-1; Quarter-Final: Luton T. (A) 1-1, Replay (H) 1-2.

SOUTHEND UNITED (Division 4)

Team Manager David Webb.
Club Address Roots Hall Ground, Victoria Avenue, Southend-on-Sea. Tel: (0702) 340707.
Current Ground Capacity 10,753.
Record Attendance 31,090 v Liverpool, FA Cup 3rd Round, 10 January 1979.
Year Formed 1906. Turned professional 1906.
Previous Names None.
Club Nickname "The Shrimpers".
Club Colours Blue shirts, yellow shorts and blue stockings.
Club Honours Football League: Div. 4 Champions 1980-81.
League History 1920-58 Div. 3(S); 1958-66 Div. 3; 1966-72 Div. 4; 1972-76 Div. 3; 1976-78 Div. 4; 1978-80 Div. 3; 1980-81 Div. 4; 1981-84 Div. 3; 1984-87 Div. 4; 1987-89 Div. 3; 1989- Div. 4.
Most League Points in a Season (2 for a win) 67 in Div. 4, 1980-81. (3 for a win) 80 in Div. 4, 1986-87.
Most League Goals in a Season 92 in Div. 3(S), 1950-51.
Record Victory 10-1 v Golders Green in FA Cup 1st Round, 24 November 1934 and v Brentwood in FA Cup 2nd Round, 7 December 1968.
Record Defeat 1-9 v Brighton & H.A. in Div. 3, 27 November 1965.
Consecutive League Wins 6 in 1932, 1972, 1978 and 1980.
Consecutive League Defeats 6 in 1931-32 and 1955.
Record League Appearances Sandy Anderson, 451 between 1950-63.
Record League Goalscorer—Career Roy Hollis, 122 between 1953-60.
Record League Goalscorer—Season Jim Shankly, 31 in Div. 3(S), 1928-29 and Sammy McCrory 31 in Div. 3(S), 1957-58.

Southend United: League Record, 1988-89 (Division 3)

Match Number	Date	Venue	Opponents	Result	H/T	Lge Posn	Attend
1	27.8.88	H	Bolton W.	W 2-0	1-0		4075
2	3.9.88	A	Fulham	L 0-1	0-0	4	4754
3	9.9.88	H	Swansea C.	L 0-2	0-1	16	4357
4	17.9.88	A	Aldershot	D 2-2	1-0	17	2170
5	21.9.88	A	Reading	L 0-4	0-2	20	4062
6	23.9.88	H	Cardiff C.	D 0-0	0-0	21	3199
7	1.10.88	A	Preston N.E.	L 2-3	2-0	21	5348
8	4.10.88	H	Mansfield T.	D 1-1	1-0	21	2436
9	9.10.88	A	Brentford	L 0-4	0-0	21	5106
10	15.10.88	H	Gillingham	W 2-1	1-0	20	3200
11	22.10.88	H	Chesterfield	W 3-1	3-0	19	2662
12	25.10.88	A	Bury	L 1-3	0-0	19	2419
13	28.10.88	H	Wigan Ath.	L 1-2	0-1	20	3120
14	5.11.88	A	Wolverhampton W.	L 0-3	0-2	21	10432
15	8.11.88	H	Bristol Rov.	D 2-2	1-1	21	2453
16	12.11.88	A	Notts Co.	D 1-1	0-1	21	5037
17	26.11.88	A	Chester C.	W 4-2	1-1	18	2050
18	2.12.88	H	Port Vale	D 1-1	1-1	18	3245
19	10.12.88	A	Wigan Ath.	L 0-3	0-1	20	2027
20	17.12.88	A	Sheffield U	W 2-1	0-0	17	9556
21	26.12.88	H	Northampton T.	W 2-1	2-1	16	5034
22	31.12.88	H	Bristol C.	L 1-2	0-1	16	4012
23	2.1.89	A	Huddersfield T.	L 2-3	0-1	19	6403
24	13.1.89	H	Fulham	D 0-0	0-0	20	4844
25	21.1.89	A	Swansea C.	L 0-2	0-1	21	3388
26	28.1.89	H	Aldershot	D 1-1	0-0	21	3014
27	3.2.89	H	Preston N.E.	W 2-1	2-0	19	2948
28	11.2.89	A	Mansfield T.	L 0-4	0-2	21	2414
29	25.2.89	A	Gillingham	D 1-1	0-1	20	3574
30	28.2.89	H	Bury	D 1-1	1-0	20	2479
31	4.3.89	A	Chesterfield	L 1-2	1-0	20	3261
32	10.3.89	H	Wolverhampton W.	W 3-1	2-0	20	5924
33	18.3.89	A	Bolton W.	D 0-0	0-0	20	3505
34	25.3.89	H	Huddersfield T.	L 2-4	0-2	21	3582
35	27.3.89	A	Northampton T.	D 2-2	0-0	21	3707
36	31.3.89	H	Sheffield U.	W 2-1	1-1	21	4584
37	4.4.89	H	Blackpool	W 2-1	1-1	20	2795
38	8.4.89	A	Bristol C.	W 2-0	1-0	19	6213
39	14.4.89	H	Reading	W 2-1	1-0	18	4625
40	18.4.89	H	Brentford	D 1-1	0-0	18	4119
41	22.4.89	A	Cardiff C.	L 0-2	0-1	18	3268
42	28.4.89	H	Notts Co.	D 1-1	1-0	19	3931
43	1.5.89	A	Bristol Rov.	D 1-1	1-0	19	6250
44	6.5.89	H	Port Vale	L 0-2	0-2	20	4516
45	9.5.89	A	Blackpool	L 2-3	0-3	21	3999
46	13.5.89	H	Chester C.	W 1-0	0-0	21	4089

Players: League Record, 1988-89 (Division 3)

Match Number	1	2	3	4	5	6	7	8	9	10	11	12	13	14	15	16	17	18	19	20	21	22	23	24	25	26	27	28	29	30	31	32	33	34	35	36	37	38	39	40	41	42	43	44	45	46	Apps	Subs	Goals
Bennett, Gary																10	10^{1}	10	10	10	10	10^{1}	10	10		10	10	10				11	10	11			4				★						16	1	2
Brush, Paul	6	6	6	6	6	5	5	5	5	6	6	6	6	6					5	6	6	6	6					6										6	6	6	6	6	6	6		6	28	0	0
Butler, Peter	7	7	7	7	7	7	7	7	7	4	4	4								4	7	4	4	6	6	6				★	7^{1}	4	4	4	4	4		4	4	4	4	4	4	4	4^{1}	4	34	1	2
Clark, Paul										7	7	7	7	7	7	7								7	7	7	7					7	7	7	7											7	16	0	0
Crown, David	9^{1}	9	9	9^{1}	9	9	9^{1}	9	9	9^{1}	9^{2}	9^{1}	9	9	9^{2}	9^{1}	9^{1}	9	9	9		9	9^{1}	9	9	9^{1}	9^{1}	9	9^{1}	9^{1}	9	9^{2}	9	9^{2}	9^{1}	9	9	9	9^{2}	9		9^{1}	9	9	9^{1}	9	44	0	25
Edinburgh, Justin						2	2	2	2					2	2	2	2	2	2		★	8						3	3	3																	14	1	0
Edwards, Andrew																			4																												1	0	0
Hall, Derek	8	8	8	8	8	8	8^{1}	8	8	8	8	8	8	★	6	6				★	8	7	7	8	8	8	8^{1}	7	7	7		8	8	8	8	8	8^{1}	8	8	8	8	8	8	8			38	2	3
Johnson, Peter	3	3	3	3	3	3	3	3	3	3	3	3	3	3	3	3	3	3	3	3	3	3	3	3	3	3	3				3	3	3	3	3	3	3	3	3	3	3	3	3	3	3	3	43	0	0
Jones, Matthew															★																																0	1	0
Ling, Martin	11	11	11	11^{1}	11	11	11	11^{1}	11	11^{1}	11	11	11	11	11	11	11^{1}	11	11	11	11	11	11	11	11	11	11	11	11	11	11		11	★	11	11	11	11^{2}	11	11	11	11		★	7	11	42	2	6
McDonough, Roy	10	10	10	10	10	10	10	10	10	10	10^{1}	10	10	★	10				★	5	9^{1}	★	8^{1}		10		★	5	10	10	10	10		10	10	10^{1}	10^{1}	10	10	10	10	10	10	10	10	10	36	4	5
Martin, David	4	4	4	4	4	4	4	4	4			★		4	4	4	4	4			4^{1}	2	2	4	4	4	4	4	4	4	4			★	★	7	7	7	7	7	7	7	7	7			34	3	1
Matthews, David			★	★	★	★			★					8																																	1	5	0
Newell, Paul																								1																					1		2	0	0
O'Shea, Danny	2^{1}	2	2	2	2	6	6		★	2	2	2	2				6	6	6	2	2								6	6	6																19	1	1
Prior, Spencer																													5	5	5					6	6	5	5	5	5	5	5	5	5	5^{1}	14	0	1
Roberts, Paul																								2	2	2	2	2	2	2	2	2	2	2	2	2	2	2	2	2	2	2	2	2	2	2	23	0	0
Robinson, Martin												★	$★^{1}$	10	8	8	8^{1}	8^{1}	8	8^{1}					★		6	8							$★^{1}$					★	★	★	11^{1}	11	11		12	7	6
Sansome, Paul	1	1	1	1	1	1	1	1	1	1	1	1	1	1	1	1	1	1	1	1	1	1	1		1	1	1	1	1	1	1	1	1	1	1	1	1	1	1	1	1	1	1	1		1	44	0	0
Smith, Nick			★			★		6	6				4		★		7	7	7	7								★																			7	4	0
Tilson, Steven																												★	8	8	8	6^{1}	6	6	6		★			$★^{1}$	9	★	★	★	8	8	10	6	2
Westley, Shane	5	5	5	5	5					5	5	5	5	5	5	5	5	5			5	5	5	5	5	5	5					5	5	5	5	5	5								6		28	0	0
Young, Richard	★																				★																										0	2	0
Own Goals																				1																1													2

FA Cup: 1988-89: 1st Round: Bristol C. (A) 1-3.
Littlewoods Cup: 1988-89: 1st Round: Brighton & H.A. (H) 2-0 (A) 1-0; 2nd Round: Derby Co. (A) 0-1 (H) 1-2.

STOCKPORT COUNTY (Division 4)

Team Manager Danny Bergera.
Club Address Edgeley Park, Hardcastle Road, Stockport, Cheshire SK3 9DD. Tel: 061-480 8888.
Current Ground Capacity 7,800.
Record Attendance 27,833 v Liverpool, FA Cup 5th Round, 11 February 1950.
Year Formed 1883. Turned professional 1891.
Previous Names Heaton Norris Rovers, Heaton Norris.
Club Nickname "County" or "The Hatters".
Club Colours White shirts, blue shorts and white stockings.
Club Honours Football League: Div. 3(N) Champions 1921-22, 1936-37; Div. 4 Champions 1966-67.
League History 1900-04 Div. 2; 1904 Failed re-election; 1905-21 Div. 2; 1921-22 Div. 3(N); 1922-26 Div. 2; 1926-37 Div. 3(N); 1937-38 Div. 2; 1938-58 Div. 3(N); 1958-59 Div. 3; 1959-67 Div. 4; 1967-70 Div. 3; 1970- Div. 4.
Most League Points in a Season (2 for a win) 64 in Div. 4, 1966-67. (3 for a win) 64 in Div. 4, 1985-86.
Most League Goals in a Season 115 in Div. 3(N), 1933-34.
Record Victory 13-0 v Halifax T. in Div. 3(N), 6 January 1934.
Record Defeat 1-8 v Chesterfield in Div. 2, 19 April 1902 and 0-7 v Sheffield Wed. in League Cup 2nd Round 2nd leg, 6 October 1986.
Consecutive League Wins 8 in 1927-28.
Consecutive League Defeats 9 in 1908-09.
Record League Appearances Bob Murray, 465 between 1952-63.
Record League Goalscorer—Career Jack Connor, 132 between 1951-56.
Record League Goalscorer—Season Alf Lythgoe, 46 in Div. 3(N), 1933-34.

Stockport County: League Record, 1988-89 (Division 4)

Match Number	Date	Venue	Opponents	Result	H/T	Lge Posn	Attend
1	27.8.88	A	Darlington	W 4-1	2-0		1794
2	3.9.88	H	Leyton Orient	D 0-0	0-0	6	1947
3	10.9.88	A	Cambridge U.	L 0-1	0-1	10	1911
4	16.9.88	H	Burnley	D 0-0	0-0	12	6500
5	19.9.88	H	Halifax T.	D 1-1	1-0	8	2206
6	23.9.88	A	Crewe Alex.	D 1-1	0-1	14	2975
7	1.10.88	H	Doncaster Rov.	W 2-0	1-0	12	1959
8	5.10.88	A	Peterborough U.	L 0-1	0-1	13	2572
9	8.10.88	A	Rochdale	D 1-1	1-1	14	3021
10	15.10.88	H	Hereford U.	L 1-2	1-1	18	2035
11	22.10.88	A	Scarborough	D 1-1	1-1	20	2449
12	24.10.88	H	Hartlepool U.	W 3-0	2-0	15	2098
13	28.10.88	A	Colchester U.	D 1-1	0-1	17	1643
14	5.11.88	H	Grimsby T.	W 3-1	1-0	12	2064
15	8.11.88	A	Wrexham	L 0-2	0-1	14	1865
16	11.11.88	H	York C.	W 3-2	2-2	14	2477
17	25.11.88	H	Tranmere Rov.	D 1-1	0-1	14	2952
18	3.12.88	A	Rotherham U.	L 1-2	1-1	18	4105
19	17.12.88	H	Lincoln C.	W 1-0	0-0	13	2355
20	26.12.88	A	Torquay U.	L 1-2	0-1	16	2838
21	31.12.88	A	Carlisle U.	D 1-1	0-1	15	3774
22	2.1.89	H	Exeter C.	W 4-0	2-0	12	2936
23	7.1.89	H	Scunthorpe U.	L 1-2	0-1	13	2656
24	14.1.89	A	Leyton Orient.	W 2-1	1-0	11	3828
25	20.1.89	H	Darlington	D 0-0	0-0	12	2889
26	28.1.89	A	Burnley	L 0-1	0-0	13	6942
27	4.2.89	A	Halifax T.	D 2-2	0-1	13	1938
28	10.2.89	H	Crewe Alex.	L 0-1	0-1	15	5015
29	17.2.89	H	Rochdale	W 3-0	2-0	13	2858
30	25.2.89	A	Hereford U.	L 1-2	0-2	13	2015
31	28.2.89	A	Hartlepool U.	D 2-2	0-1	14	1692
32	4.3.89	H	Scarborough	D 2-2	2-0	12	2648
33	11.3.89	A	Grimsby T.	L 0-2	0-0	15	4685
34	13.3.89	H	Colchester U.	W 1-0	0-0	12	2027
35	17.3.89	H	Cambridge U.	D 0-0	0-0	13	2521
36	25.3.89	A	Exeter C.	D 2-2	2-0	13	3058
37	27.3.89	H	Torquay U.	D 0-0	0-0	14	2808
38	1.4.89	A	Lincoln C	D 0-0	0-0	15	3400
39	4.4.89	A	Scunthorpe U	D 1-1	1-0	15	3958
40	7.4.89	H	Carlisle U.	D 1-1	1-0	15	2543
41	14.4.89	A	Doncaster Rov.	D 2-2	1-0	16	1363
42	21.4.89	H	Peterborough U.	L 1-2	0-2	16	2091
43	28.4.89	A	Tranmere Rov.	L 0-1	0-0	17	6270
44	1.5.89	H	Wrexham	D 2-2	0-1	18	2118
45	6.5.89	H	Rotherham U.	L 1-3	1-1	19	4313
46	13.5.89	A	York C.	L 0-2	0-1	20	2327

Players: League Record, 1988-89 (Division 4)

Match Number	1	2	3	4	5	6	7	8	9	10	11	12	13	14	15	16	17	18	19	20	21	22	23	24	25	26	27	28	29	30	31	32	33	34	35	36	37	38	39	40	41	42	43	44	45	46	Apps	Subs	Goals
Angell, Brett											9	8^1	8	8	**8**	9^1	**9**	9	9	**9**		★			★	★	★		9^2	9			★	★	★	10					★	★	9	9^1	9	9	17	9	5
Batch, Nigel																																			1	1	1	1	1	1	1	1	1	1	1	1	12	0	0
Bullock, Steven		9	★	★	★	★		★	★							★	★	4	4	4	2	4	4	4	4	4																	6	**2**	2	★	13	9	0
Butler, Brian	2	2	2	2	2	2^1	2	2	2	2	2	2	2	2	2	**2**	2	2	2	**2**		2	2			2	**2**	2	11	11^1	2	2									4	7	7				32	0	2
Caldwell, Tony									9	9	8	9		9^1	9					★	9^1	**9^1**	9	9	9	9	9^1	9	10	10	7^1	7	7	10	**10**						9^1	**9**					23	1	6
Colville, Robert		8		8									★		★	8^1	8	8	8	8^1	8	**8^1**	8	8^1	8	8	8	8	8	8	8	8^1	8	8	8	**8**	8	8	8	8				★	★		27	4	5
Cooke, John			10	10	10	10	10^1	10	10	10	11	**11^1**							10	10	4	10^1	10	11	11	11	11^1	11			11	11	11	**11^1**	**11**		★	10	10^1	10		★	★	10	10	10	31	3	6
Coyle, Tony	4^1	4				11	**4**	4	4	4			9	4^1	4	4	**4**																	7	7	7^1	7	7	7	7	**11**	**11**	11	11			23	0	3
Dooner, Gary																																														11	1	0	0
Gorton, Andy	1	1	1	1	1	1	1	1	1	1	1	1	1	1	1	1	1	1	1	1	1	1	1	1	1	1	1	1	1	1	1	1	1	1													34	0	0
Hancock, Tony																				★	★	$★^1$	$★^1$	★	★	**10**	10	10			9^1	9^1	9	**9**	9	★	**10**				10^1	10	**10**	★	★	★	12	10	5
Hart, Nigel	3	3	3	**3**	3	3	3	3	3	3	3^1	3	3	3	3	3^1	3	3	3	3	3	3	**3**							★			5	5	5	5	5	5	5	5	5	5	5	5	5	5	37	1	2
Hartford, Asa	**10**										**10**	**10**	**10**	10	10	**10**					**10**			**10**	**10**						**10**	10		★	★												12	2	0
Hendrie, Paul	8	10	8	4	8	8	8	8	8								10	**10**																													11	0	0
Howard, Mark	11^1	11	11	11	**11**		★	**11**		★		★	11	★	★	6	★							2^1	**2**																						10	6	2
Leonard, Gary																																				11	11	11	11	11	8	8	8	**8**	**8^1**	8	11	0	1
Logan, David											4	4	4	**11**	11	11	11	11	11	11	11	11	11		3	**3**	3	3	3	3	3	3	3	3	3	3	3	3	3	3	3	3	3	3	3	3	35	0	0
McKenzie, Ian					4	4	11	9	11	11	★	★		★		★								3		★	★				★		**10**	2	2												10	7	0
Matthews, Mike																											4	4	4	4	4	4	4	4	4	4	4	4	4		4	4	4	4^1	4	**4**	19	0	1
Payne, Mark	9^1		9	9	9	**9**	9			**6**			★				6		7	7	7		★	7	7	7	**7**	7	**7**	**7**															**11**	**7**	20	2	1
Pickering, Mike																		★	5	5	5	5	**5**						5	**5**																	7	1	0
Scott, Ian	★							6	**6**	8	6	6	6	**6**	**6**																																8	1	0
Stapleton, John			**4**																																												1	0	0
Thorpe, Andy	5	5	5	5	5	5	5	5	5	5	5	5	5	5	5	5	5	5				7	7	5	5	5	5	5	2	2	5	5	2			2	2	2	2	2	2	2	2	7	7	2	41	0	0
Williams, Bill	6	6	6	6	6	6	6											6	6^1	6	6	6	6	6	6	6	6	6	6	6	6	6	6	6	6	6	6	6	6	6	6	6^1		6	6	6	35	0	2
Wylde, Rodger	7^1	7	7	7	7^1	7	7^1	7	7^1	7^1	7	7^1	**7**	7^1	7	7	7^1	7^1											$★^1$	★						9^1	9	9	9	9^1			7				24	2	12
Own Goals													1																																				1

FA Cup: 1988-89: 1st Round: Scarborough (A) 1-2.
Littlewoods Cup: 1988-89: 1st Round: Tranmere Rov. (H) 0-1 (A) 1-1.

STOKE CITY (Division 2)

Team Manager Mick Mills.
Club Address Victoria Ground, Stoke on Trent. Tel: (0782) 413511.
Current Ground Capacity 35,812.
Record Attendance 51,380 v Arsenal, Div.1, 29 March 1937.
Year Formed 1863. Turned professional 1885.
Previous Names Stoke.
Club Nickname "The Potters".
Club Colours Red and white striped shirts, white shorts and stockings.
Club Honours Football League: Div. 2 Champions 1932-33, 1962-63; Div. 3(N) Champions 1926-27. Football League Cup: Winners 1972.
League History 1888-90 Div. 1; 1890 Not re-elected; 1891-1907 Div. 1; 1907-08 Div. 2; 1908 Resigned; 1919-22 Div. 2; 1922-23 Div. 1; 1923-26 Div. 2; 1926-27 Div. 3(N); 1927-33 Div. 2; 1933-53 Div. 1; 1953-63 Div. 2; 1963-77 Div. 1; 1977-79 Div. 2; 1979-85 Div. 1; 1985- Div. 2.
Most League Points in a Season (2 for a win) 63 in Div. 3(N), 1926-27. (3 for a win) 59 in Div. 2, 1988-89.
Most League Goals in a Season 92 in Div. 3(N), 1926-27.
Record Victory 10-3 v West Bromwich A. in Div. 1, 14 September 1889.
Record Defeat 0-10 v Preston N.E. in Div. 1, 14 September 1889.
Consecutive League Wins 7 in 1905 and 1947.
Consecutive League Defeats 11 in 1985.
Record League Appearances Eric Skeels, 506 between 1959-76.
Record League Goalscorer—Career Freddie Steele, 142 between 1934-49.
Record League Goalscorer—Season Freddie Steele, 33 in Div. 1, 1936-37.

Stoke City: League Record, 1988-89 (Division 2)

Match Number	Date	Venue	Opponents	Result	H/T	Lge Posn	Attend
1	27.8.88	H	Ipswich T.	D 1-1	1-0		8639
2	29.8.88	A	Bradford C.	D 0-0	0-0		11918
3	3.9.88	A	Barnsley	L 0-1	0-0	15	5682
4	10.9.88	H	Blackburn Rov.	L 0-1	0-1	17	8624
5	17.9.88	A	Plymouth Arg.	L 0-4	0-2	23	7823
6	20.9.88	H	Portsmouth	D 2-2	1-1	22	7025
7	24.9.88	A	Walsall	W 2-1	1-1	19	7795
8	1.10.88	H	Bournemouth	W 2-1	1-0	16	7485
9	4.10.88	H	Shrewsbury T.	D 0-0	0-0	19	8075
10	8.10.88	A	Oldham Ath.	D 2-2	0-2	19	6600
11	15.10.88	A	Leicester C.	L 0-2	0-1	20	10312
12	22.10.88	H	Watford	W 2-0	1-0	17	7878
13	25.10.88	A	Birmingham C.	W 1-0	0-0	14	6262
14	29.10.88	H	Crystal Palace	W 2-1	1-0	11	9118
15	5.11.88	A	Sunderland	D 1-1	1-0	10	17923
16	13.11.88	H	Hull C.	W 4-0	1-0	8	10505
17	19.11.88	H	Swindon T.	W 2-1	0-0	7	9339
18	26.11.88	A	Leeds U.	L 0-4	0-2	8	19933
19	3.12.88	H	Chelsea	W 0-3	0-1	10	12288
20	10.12.88	A	Brighton & H A	D 1-1	1-0	12	7443
21	18.12.88	A	West Bromwich A.	L 0-6	0-2	14	17634
22	26.12.88	H	Manchester C.	W 3-1	0-1	10	24056
23	31.12.88	H	Oxford U.	W 1-0	1-0	10	10552
24	2.1.89	A	Blackburn Rov.	L 3-4	3-2	13	11654
25	14.1.89	H	Bradford C.	W 2-1	2-1	11	9919
26	21.1.89	A	Ipswich T.	D 1-5	0-0	13	14699
27	4.2.89	A	Shrewsbury T.	W 2-1	0-1	12	6646
28	11.2.89	H	Oldham Ath.	D 0-0	0-0	10	10992
29	25.2.89	H	Leicester C.	D 2-2	2-2	12	9666
30	28.2.89	H	Birmingham C.	W 1-0	1-0	10	7904
31	4.3.89	A	Hull C.	W 4-1	4-0	7	5915
32	11.3.89	H	Sunderland	W 2-0	1-0	7	12489
33	18.3.89	A	Portsmouth	D 0-0	0-0	9	7624
34	25.3.89	H	Barnsley	D 1-1	1-0	10	10209
35	27.3.89	A	Manchester C.	L 1-2	0-1	11	28303
36	1.4.89	H	Plymouth Arg.	D 2-2	2-0	11	8363
37	4.4.89	H	West Bromwich A.	D 0-0	0-0	11	11151
38	8.4.89	A	Oxford U.	L 2-3	1-2	12	5297
39	11.4.89	A	Watford	L 2-3	1-2	12	9086
40	15.4.89	A	Bournemouth	W 1-0	0-0	11	6834
41	22.4.89	H	Walsall	L 0-3	0-2	11	8132
42	29.4.89	H	Leeds U.	L 2-3	2-1	13	9051
43	1.5.89	A	Chelsea	L 1-2	1-1	13	14946
44	6.5.89	A	Swindon T.	L 0-3	0-0	13	9543
45	9.5.89	A	Crystal Palace	L 0-1	0-1	13	12159
46	13.5.89	H	Brighton & H.A.	D 2-2	1-1	13	5841

Players: League Record, 1988-89 (Division 2)

Match Number	1	2	3	4	5	6	7	8	9	10	11	12	13	14	15	16	17	18	19	20	21	22	23	24	25	26	27	28	29	30	31	32	33	34	35	36	37	38	39	40	41	42	43	44	45	46	Apps	Subs	Goals
Bamber, Dave																						9	9	9	9	9^{1}		9	9^{1}	9		9	9	**9**	9	**9^{1}**	9	9^{1}	9	9	**9**	9^{2}	**9**	9	9	9	23	0	6
Barrett, Scott											1																1	1	1	1	1	1	1	1	1	1	1	1	1	1	1	1					17	0	0
Beagrie, Peter	11	11	11	11	11	11	11	11^{1}	11	11	11	11^{1}	11	**11**	11	11^{1}	11	11	11	9^{1}	11	11	11	11	11	11	11	11	11^{1}	11	11	11^{1}	11	11	11						11	11	11	11	11	11^{1}	41	0	7
Beeston, Carl	5	**5**		5	5				3	3									★	5		6	6								4^{2}	5	8	4	**8**	8		11	11	8	5	10	6	**6**			22	1	2
Derry, George											6	6	6	6	6	6	6^{1}	6	**6**	6	6	5^{1}	5	6	6	6	6	6	6	6^{1}	6	6	6	6^{1}	6	6	6		6		6	6		★	6	6	32	1	4
Butler, John																						2	2	2	2	2	2	2	2	2	2	2	2	2	2^{1}	2	2	2	2	2	2	2	2	2	2	2	25	0	1
Carr, Cliff		★	3	3	3	3	3				3	3	3	3	3	3^{1}	3	3	**3**	3	3	3	3	3	3		3	3	3	3	3	3	3	3	3	3	3	3	3	3	3	3	3	**3**	3	3	40	1	1
Ford, Tony	8		8	8	8	2	2	2	2	2	2	2	2	2	2	2	2	2	2	7	10	10	10			7	9	**8**	4	8																	27	0	0
Fox, Peter	1	1	1	1	1	1	1	1	1	1		1	1	1	1	1	1	1	1	1	1	1	1	1	1	1																	1	1	1	1	29	0	0
Gidman, John	2	2	5	2	**2**					★				★	★					2	2																										7	3	0
Hackett, Gary	**7**	7	7	7	7	7^{1}	7	7	7	7	7	7	7	7	7	7^{1}	7	**7**	7	11	7	7	7	7	7^{1}	★	7	7	7	7	7^{1}	7^{1}	7	7	7	7	7	7	7	7	7	7	7	7	7	7	45	1	5
Hemming, Chris						5	5	3																														6									4	0	0
Henry, Tony	6	6	6	6	6	6	6	6	6	6	4	8	8	8^{1}	8	8^{1}	8	8	8		5	★	8^{1}	8	8^{1}	8	**8**	★		4					★	11^{1}	11	8^{1}	8	6	8	**8**	8	8	8	8	37	3	6
Higgins, Mark								5	5	5	5	5	5	5	5	5	5	5	5					5	5	5	5	5	5	5	5		5	5	5	**5**	5	5	5	5		5	5^{1}	5	5	5	33	0	1
Kamara, Chris	4^{1}	**4**	4	4	4	4	4	4	4	4^{1}		4	4	4	4	4	4	4	4	4	4	4^{2}	4	4	4	4	4	4				4	4		4	4	4	4	4	4	4	4	4				38	0	4
Morgan, Nick	★	9	9		★	9	9^{1}	**9**																					★		10^{1}			★		★			10^{2}	10	10		★	★	10	10^{1}	11	7	5
Parkin, Steve	3	3	2																							3																					4	0	0
Saunders, Carl	10	10	10	10	10	8	8	8	8	8	9	9				9	**9**	9	★	8				10^{2}	10	**10**	★	★	8		8	8	★	8	★	10	8	**10**					★	10			27	6	2
Shaw, Graham	9	★		9	★			$★^{1}$	9	**9**	★		9	9^{1}	9^{1}	★	$★^{1}$	★	9		9						10^{1}	**10**	**10**	10	9	10	**10**	10	**10**	★	10	★									19	9	5
Stainrod, Simon					**9**	10^{1}	10^{1}	10	10	10^{1}	10	10	10^{1}	10	**10**	**10**	10	10	10	10																											16	0	4
Ware, Paul		8									**8**										8	**8**																		11^{1}	★	★	**10**	4	4	4	9	2	1
Own Goals												1												1			1																						3

FA Cup: 1988-89: 3rd Round: Crystal Palace (H) 1-0; 4th Round: Barnsley (H) 3-3, Replay (A) 1-2.
Littlewoods Cup: 1988-89: 2nd Round: Leyton Orient (A) 2-1 (H) 1-2.

SUNDERLAND (Division 2)

Team Manager Denis Smith.
Club Address Roker Park Ground, Sunderland. Tel: (0783) 5140332
Current Ground Capacity 37,887.
Record Attendance 75,118 v Derby Co., FA Cup 6th Round replay, 8 March 1933.
Year Formed 1879. Turned professional 1886.
Previous Names Sunderland and District Teachers.
Club Nickname "The Rokerites".
Club Colours Red and white striped shirts, black shorts and white stockings.
Club Honours Football League: Div. 1 Champions 1891-92, 1892-93, 1894-95, 1901-02, 1912-13, 1935-36; Div. 2 Champions 1975-76; Div. 3 Champions 1987-88. FA Cup: Winners 1937, 1973.
League History 1890-1958 Div. 1; 1958-64 Div. 2; 1964-70 Div. 1; 1970-76 Div. 2; 1976-77 Div. 1; 1977-80 Div. 2; 1980-85 Div. 1; 1985-87 Div. 2; 1987-88 Div. 3; 1988- Div. 2.
Most League Points in a Season (2 for a win) 63 in Div. 3(N), 1926-27. (3 for a win) 93 in Div. 3, 1987-88.
Most League Goals in a Season 109 in Div. 1, 1935-36.
Record Victory 11-1 v Fairfield in FA Cup 1st Round, 1894-95.
Record Defeat 0-8 v West Ham U. in Div. 1, 19 October 1968 and v Watford in Div. 1, 25 September 1982.
Consecutive League Wins 13 in 1891-92.
Consecutive League Defeats 9 in 1976-77.
Record League Appearances Jim Montgomery, 537 between 1962-77.
Record League Goalscorer—Career Charlie Buchan, 209 between 1911-25.
Record League Goalscorer—Season Dave Halliday, 43 in Div. 1, 1928-29.

Sunderland: League Record, 1988-89 (Division 2)

Match Number	Date	Venue	Opponents	Result	H/T	Lge Posn	Attend
1	27.8.88	H	Bournemouth	D 1-1	1-1		17998
2	3.9.88	A	Ipswich T.	L 0-2	0-1	19	12835
3	10.9.88	H	Bradford C.	D 0-0	0-0	18	16286
4	17.9.88	A	Birmingham C.	L 2-3	0-1	22	6871
5	20.9.88	H	Crystal Palace	D 1-1	0-1	18	13150
6	24.9.88	A	Shrewsbury T.	D 0-0	0-0	21	4195
7	1.10.88	H	Oldham Ath.	W 3-2	2-2	20	12529
8	4.10.88	H	Leeds U.	W 2-1	1-0	15	12671
9	8.10.88	A	Walsall	L 0-2	0-0	20	6150
10	15.10.88	A	Hull C.	D 0-0	0-0	19	8261
11	22.10.88	H	Swindon T.	W 4-0	2-0	14	13520
12	25.10.88	H	Blackburn Rov.	W 2-0	2-0	10	16601
13	29.10.88	A	Manchester C.	D 1-1	1-1	13	22398
14	2.11.88	A	Oxford U.	W 4-2	3-1	8	6270
15	5.11.88	H	Stoke C.	D 1-1	0-1	8	17923
16	12.11.88	A	Chelsea	D 1-1	1-0	9	19210
17	19.11.88	H	West Bromwich A.	D 1-1	0-1	10	18141
18	26.11.88	A	Brighton & H.A.	L 0-3	0-1	12	10038
19	3.12.88	H	Watford	D 1-1	0-1	14	16330
20	10.12.88	A	Leicester C.	L 1-3	0-2	16	11093
21	18.12.88	A	Plymouth Arg.	W 4-1	2-0	13	13498
22	26.12.88	H	Barnsley	W 1-0	0-0	9	21994
23	31.12.88	H	Portsmouth	W 4-0	2-0	8	21566
24	2.1.89	A	Bradford C.	L 0-1	0-0	10	12186
25	14.1.89	H	Oxford U.	W 1-0	1-0	6	12853
26	21.1.89	A	Bournemouth.	W 1-0	1-0	6	8992
27	4.2.89	A	Leeds U.	L 0-2	0-1	10	31985
28	11.2.89	H	Walsall	L 0-3	0-1	11	14203
29	18.2.89	A	Swindon T.	L 1-4	1-3	13	7432
30	25.2.89	H	Hull C.	W 2-0	0-0	10	14719
31	28.2.89	A	Blackburn Rov.	D 2-2	2-0	12	8288
32	11.3.89	A	Stoke C.	L 0-2	0-1	14	12489
33	14.3.89	H	Manchester C.	L 2-4	1-3	14	16101
34	18.3.89	A	Crystal Palace	L 0-1	0-0	14	9108
35	21.3.89	H	Chelsea	L 1-2	1-1	14	14714
36	25.3.89	H	Ipswich T.	W 4-0	1-0	14	13859
37	27.3.89	A	Barnsley	L 0-3	0-1	14	8070
38	1.4.89	H	Birmingham C.	D 2-2	1-0	15	10969
39	4.4.89	H	Plymouth Arg.	W 2-1	2-0	13	8003
40	8.4.89	A	Portsmouth	L 0-2	0-1	14	7724
41	15.4.89	A	Oldham Ath.	D 2-2	2-1	14	5944
42	22.4.89	H	Shrewsbury T.	W 2-1	1-0	13	9427
43	29.4.89	H	Brighton & H.A.	W 1-0	1-0	12	12856
44	1.5.89	A	Watford	W 1-0	1-0	11	13499
45	6.5.89	A	West Bromwich A.	D 0-0	0-0	11	10451
46	13.5.89	H	Leicester C.	D 2-2	0-0	11	15819

Players: League Record, 1988-89 (Division 2)

Match Number	1	2	3	4	5	6	7	8	9	10	11	12	13	14	15	16	17	18	19	20	21	22	23
Agboola, Reuben	3	3			3	3	3	3	3	3	3	3	3	3	**3**			3	3	3			★
Armstrong, Gordon	8	8	8	**8**	8	8	8	8	8	8	8	8	8^{1}	8^{1}	8	8	8	8	8	8	8^{1}	8	8^{1}
Atkinson, Brian																							
Barnes, Peter																							
Bennett, Gary	4^{1}	4	4	4	4	4					★			★	★	4	4^{1}	4	4	**4**	2	2	2
Carter, Tim																					1	1	
Cornforth, John			★	★		★																	★
Cullen, Anthony																							
Doyle, Steve	6	6	6	6	6	6	6	6	6	6	6	6	6	6	6^{1}	**6**	**6**	**6**	6	6	6	6	**6**
Gabbiadini, Marco	10	10	**10**		★		9^{1}	9^{1}	9	9	9^{2}	9^{1}	9	9^{1}	9	**9^{1}**	9	9	9	9	10^{1}	10	10
Gates, Eric	**9**	9	9	9	**9**	**9**			★	★						★	★	★		★	9^{1}	9	9^{1}
Gray, Frank		★	3	3	★		2	2	2	2	**2**	2	2	2	2	2	2	**2**	2	2	3	3	**3**
Hauser, Thomas																							
Hawke, Warren																							
Hay, Alan																							
Hesford, Iain	1	1	1	1	1	1	1	1	1	1	1	1	1	1	1	1	1	1	1	1			
Kay, John	2	2	2	2	2	2										7							
Lemon, Paul	7	**7**																					
Lynch, Tommy																3	3						
MacPhail, John	5	**5**	5	5	5	5	5^{1}	5	5	5	5	5	5	5^{1}	5	5	5	5	5^{1}	5	5	5	5
Norman, Tony																							1
Ogilvie, Gary																★							
Ord, Richard		★					4	4	4	4	4	4	4	**4**	4			★		★	4	4	4^{1}
Owers, Gary	★		7	7	**7**	7	7	7	7	7	7^{1}	7	7	7	7		7	7	7	7	7	7	7
Pascoe, Colin	11	11	11	11^{2}	11^{1}	11	11^{1}	11	11	11	11	11	11	11	11	11	11	11	11	11^{1}	11^{1}	11	11^{1}
Wharton, Sean																							
Whitehurst, Billy				10	10	10	10	10^{1}	**10**	**10**	10^{1}	10	10	10^{1}	10	10	10	10	10	**10**			
Williams, Paul																							
Own Goals												1										1	

Match Number	24	25	26	27	28	29	30	31	32	33	34	35	36	37	38	39	40	41	42	43	44	45	46	Apps	Subs	Goals
Agboola, Reuben		★	★		**7**	★	4	4	4	4	**4**										3	3	3	25	4	0
Armstrong, Gordon	8	8	8	8	8	8^{1}	8	8	8	8	8	8	8	8	8	8^{2}	8		8^{1}	8	8	11	11	45	0	8
Atkinson, Brian																**11**	11	★						2	1	0
Barnes, Peter						**7**																		1	0	0
Bennett, Gary	2	2	2	2	2	2	2	2	2	2	2	2	2	2	5	2	2	2	2	2	2	2	2^{1}	37	3	3
Carter, Tim																								2	0	0
Cornforth, John		10	**6**	10	10	10	★											4	4	10	**4**		**8**	10	5	0
Cullen, Anthony					★	★	7	7	**7**	★					★									3	4	0
Doyle, Steve	6			6	6	6	6	6	6	**6**	6			**4**			7					8		35	0	1
Gabbiadini, Marco	10		10				**10^{1}**	10^{2}	10	10^{1}	10	10^{1}	10^{3}	10	10^{1}	10					10^{1}	10	10	35	1	18
Gates, Eric	9	9	9^{1}	9	9	9	**9**	**9**	**9**	9^{1}	**9**		★	★	9	9	10	10	**10**	★	**9**	**9**	★	27	10	4
Gray, Frank	3	3	3	3	3	3	3	3	3	**3**	3	3	3	3	3	3	★	3		★				36	4	0
Hauser, Thomas							★	★	★	★	★	9	**9**	**9**	★			9^{1}	9^{1}			★	9	6	7	2
Hawke, Warren																	★		★	**9**	★			1	3	0
Hay, Alan													**4**											1	0	0
Hesford, Iain																								20	0	0
Kay, John															2		3		3	**3**				11	0	0
Lemon, Paul	7	7		★							★	11	★	★	4^{1}	4	**4**	7	7	4	★	4	★	12	6	1
Lynch, Tommy												4						**11**						4	0	0
MacPhail, John	5	**5**	5	5	5	5	5	5	5	5	5	5	5	5		5	5	5^{1}	5	5	5	5	5	45	0	4
Norman, Tony	1	1	1	1	1	1	1	1	1	1	1	1	1	1	1	1	1	1	1	1	1	1	1	24	0	0
Ogilvie, Gary																								0	1	0
Ord, Richard	4	4	4	4	4	**4**					11	6	6	6	6	6	6	6	6	6	6	6	**6**	31	3	1
Owers, Gary	11	6^{1}	7	**7**					★	7	7	7	7^{1}	7	7	7		8	11	7	7		4	36	2	3
Pascoe, Colin		11	11	11	11	11	11^{1}	11	11	11			11	11	**11**					11^{1}	11	7	7^{1}	39	0	10
Wharton, Sean																	**9**							1	0	0
Whitehurst, Billy																								17	0	3
Williams, Paul																★								0	1	0
Own Goals																										2

FA Cup: 1988-89: 3rd Round: Oxford U. (H) 1-1, Replay (A) 0-2.
Littlewoods Cup: 1989-89: 1st Round: York C. (A) 0-0 (H) 4-0; 2nd Round: West Ham U. (H) 0-3 (A) 1-2.

SWANSEA CITY (Division 3)

Team Manager Ian Evans.
Club Address Vetch Field, Swansea. Tel: (0792) 51311.
Current Ground Capacity 26,237.
Record Attendance 32,796 v Arsenal, FA Cup 4th Round, 17 February 1968.
Year Formed 1900. Turned professional 1912.
Previous Names Swansea Town.
Club Nickname "The Swans".
Club Colours All white.
Club Honours Football League: Div. 3(S) Champions 1924-25, 1948-49.
League History 1920-25 Div. 3(S); 1925-47 Div. 2; 1947-49 Div. 3(S); 1949-65 Div. 2; 1965-67 Div. 3; 1967-70 Div. 4; 1970-73 Div. 3; 1973-78 Div. 4; 1978-79 Div. 3; 1979-81 Div. 2; 1981-83 Div. 1; 1983-84 Div. 2; 1984-86 Div. 3; 1986-88 Div. 4; 1988- Div. 3.
Most League Points in a Season (2 for a win) 62 in Div. 3(S), 1948-49. (3 for a win) 70 in Div. 4, 1987-88.
Most League Goals in a Season 90 in Div. 2, 1956-57.
Record Victory 12-0 v Sliema Wanderers in European Cup Winners Cup 1st Round, 1st leg, 15 September 1982.
Record Defeat 1-8 v Fulham in Div. 2, 22 January 1938.
Consecutive League Wins 8 in 1961.
Consecutive League Defeats 6 in 1935 and 1957.
Record League Appearances Wilfred Milne, 585 between 1919-37.
Record League Goalscorer—Career Ivor Allchurch, 166 between 1949-68.
Record League Goalscorer—Season Cyril Pearce, 35 in Div. 2, 1931-32.

Swansea City: League Record, 1988-89 (Division 3)

Match Number	Date	Venue	Opponents	Result	H/T	Lge Posn	Attend
1	27.8.88	A	Gillingham	W 3-2	1-1		4437
2	3.9.88	H	Bury	D 1-1	1-0	5	5141
3	9.9.88	A	Southend U.	W 2-0	1-0	1	4357
4	17.9.88	H	Brentford	D 1-1	0-0	4	5015
5	24.9.88	H	Wolverhampton W.	L 2-5	1-3	9	5240
6	1.10.88	A	Bristol C.	L 0-2	0-1	17	7786
7	4.10.88	H	Bolton W.	W 1-0	0-0	15	3283
8	9.10.88	A	Aldershot	W 1-0	1-0	9	2809
9	15.10.88	H	Northampton T.	W 1-0	1-0	6	4583
10	22.10.88	H	Fulham	W 2-0	1-0	4	4737
11	25.10.88	A	Huddersfield T.	D 1-1	0-0	5	5711
12	29.10.88	H	Preston N.E.	D 1-1	0-1	7	5370
13	1.11.88	A	Wigan Ath.	W 2-1	1-1	3	2432
14	5.11.89	A	Chester C.	L 1-3	0-2	4	2263
15	8.11.88	H	Mansfield T.	W 3-1	0-0	3	3526
16	12.11.88	A	Port Vale	L 1-2	1-2	5	6248
17	26.11.88	A	Blackpool	D 0-0	0-0	5	3443
18	3.12.88	H	Sheffield U.	D 2-2	0-1	6	5676
19	17.12.88	H	Chesterfield	W 2-0	1-0	4	3656
20	26.12.88	A	Cardiff C.	D 2-2	2-2	5	10675
21	31.12.88	A	Bristol Rov.	D 1-1	1-1	5	4803
22	2.1.89	H	Reading	W 2-0	0-0	4	6772
23	7.1.89	H	Notts Co.	W 2-0	1-0	3	5808
24	14.1.89	A	Bury	L 0-1	0-0	3	2608
25	21.1.89	H	Southend U.	W 2-0	1-0	3	3388
26	3.2.89	H	Bristol C.	D 1-1	0-1	5	6523
27	11.2.89	A	Bolton W.	L 0-1	0-0	6	4178
28	17.2.89	H	Aldershot	W 1-0	0-0	4	4922
29	25.2.89	A	Northampton T.	L 0-1	0-0	5	3900
30	4.3.89	A	Fulham	L 0-1	0-0	7	4710
31	11.3.89	H	Chester C.	D 1-1	1-1	7	4311
32	14.3.89	A	Preston N.E.	D 1-1	0-1	9	8975
33	19.3.89	H	Gillingham	W 3-2	2-0	8	4252
34	22.3.89	H	Huddersfield T.	W 1-0	1-0	6	4075
35	25.3.89	A	Reading	L 0-2	0-1	7	4367
36	27.3.89	H	Cardiff C.	D 1-1	0-1	6	9201
37	1.4.89	A	Chesterfield	L 0-2	0-0	7	3349
38	4.4.89	A	Notts Co.	L 0-1	0-1	7	3940
39	8.4.89	H	Bristol Rov.	D 1-1	1-1	8	5645
40	15.4.89	H	Wigan Ath.	L 1-2	0-1	11	3719
41	22.4.89	A	Wolverhampton W.	D 1-1	0-1	11	13921
42	29.4.89	H	Port Vale	D 0-0	0-0	11	4229
43	2.5.89	A	Mansfield T.	D 0-0	0-0	11	2550
44	6.5.89	A	Sheffield U.	L 1-5	0-2	11	15383
45	9.5.89	A	Brentford	D 1-1	1-0	11	4415
46	13.5.89	H	Blackpool	L 1-2	1-1	12	3494

Players: League Record, 1988-89 (Division 3)

Match Number	1	2	3	4	5	6	7	8	9	10	11	12	13	14	15	16	17	18	19	20	21	22	23
Allon, Joe				★		**8**																	
Bodak, Peter						10	10	**10**	10	10	**10**	★		★	7^1	**7**			10^1				
Bracey, Lee																	1	1	1	1	1	1	1
Coleman, Christopher	3	3	3	3	3		3	3	3	3	3	3	3	3	3	3	3	3	3	3	3	3	
D'Auria, David				★	11	★	4	4^1	4^1	4	**4**	**4**											
Davey, Simon							**7**	7	**7**														
Davies, Alan	10	10	10	10	**8**					8^1	8^1	6	6	10	10^1	6	6	10	**6^1**	6^1	6	6	8
Holdsworth, Dean	★	8	8	8	9^1																		
Hough, David	2	2	2	2	2	2	2	2			★	★	4	**4**	**4**	**4**	4	4	4	4	4	4	4
Hutchison, Tommy		★	9	**9**	★		9	9	9	9^1	9	9	9^1	9	9	9	9	9	9	9	9	9	10
James, Robbie	6^2	6^1	6	6	6	6	6^1	6	6	6	6		8	6	6	8	8	6	8	8	8	8^1	6^1
Knill, Alan	5^1	5	5	5	5	5	5	5	5	5	5	5	5	5	5	5			5	5	5	5	5
Legg, Andrew						3																	
Lewis, Dudley						11	11	11	11	11	11	11	11	11	11	11	11	11	11	11	11	11	11
Love, Ian	9	9				★	8	8	8			**8**		★	★	★	★		★	11			
Melville, Andrew	4	4	4^1	4^1	4^1	**4**		★	2	2	2	2^1	2^1	2^1	2	2^1	2	2^1	2	2	2	2	2
Phillips, Stuart																							9
Puckett, David																	5	5		10^1	10^1	10	**7**
Raynor, Paul	11	**11**	11^1	11		9																	
Thorner, Steve	7	7	7	**7**	7	7				7	7	7	7	**7**		★	7	7	7	7	7	**7**	★
Wade, Bryan	**8**				10		★		★		★	10	10	8	8^1	10	**10**	8^1				$★^1$	3^1
West, Colin																							
Wilmot, Rhys	1	1	1	1	1	1	1	1	1	1	1	1	1	1	1	1							
Own Goals																							

Match Number	24	25	26	27	28	29	30	31	32	33	34	35	36	37	38	39	40	41	42	43	44	45	46	Apps	Subs	Goals
Allon, Joe																								1	1	0
Bodak, Peter		**7**			7^1		7	★	10	7^1	**7**	**7**					★	★		★				10	6	4
Bracey, Lee	1	1	1	1	1	1	1	1	1	1	1	1	1	1	1	1	1	1	1	1	1	1	1	30	0	0
Coleman, Christopher		3	3	3	3	3	3	3	3	3	3	3	**3**	3	3	3	3	3	3	3	3	**3**	**3**	43	0	0
D'Auria, David	★	★		**7**		**7**	★																	9	5	2
Davey, Simon																								3	0	0
Davies, Alan	8	8	8	8	8	8	8	8	8	8	8	8	8	**8**	8	8	8	8	8	8	8	8	8	42	0	5
Holdsworth, Dean																								4	1	1
Hough, David	4	4	★	**2**	2	2	2			★	★	★	7	**7**	7	★	7	**7**			★	★	★	30	10	0
Hutchison, Tommy	10	10	11	11	11	11	**11**	11	11	**11**	11	**11**	11	11	11	11	11	11	11	11	11	**11**	11	42	2	3
James, Robbie	6	6	6^1	6	6	6	6	6	6	6	6^1	6	6	6		7	6				$★^1$	★	★	38	3	9
Knill, Alan	5	5	5	5		5	5	5	5^1	5	5	5	5	5	5	5	5	5	5	5	5	5	5	43	0	2
Legg, Andrew																			7	7	**7**	**7**	7	6	0	0
Lewis, Dudley	11		2	4	4	4	4	4	4	4	4	4	4	4	4	4	4	4	4	4	4	4	4	40	0	0
Love, Ian						★																		7	7	0
Melville, Andrew	2	2	4	9	5	10	10	2^1	2	2	2	2	2	2	2	2^1	2	2	2	2	2	2	2	44	1	10
Phillips, Stuart	9		9	★	9											★								4	2	0
Puckett, David	★	9^1																						7	1	3
Raynor, Paul		$★^1$	★	★		9	9	9	9	9^1	9	9	9^1	9	9	**9**	9	9	9	9	**9**	9	9^1	23	3	5
Thorner, Steve	7		**7**										★	★	6	6		6	6	6	6	6	6	27	4	0
Wade, Bryan	**3**		10	10	10		**7**	10	10			★	★	★	★									17	8	4
West, Colin										10^1	10	10	**10**	10	**10**	**10**	**10^1**	10^1	10	**10**	10	10	10	14	0	3
Wilmot, Rhys																								16	0	0
Own Goals																										0

FA Cup: 1st Round: Northampton T. (H) 3-1; 2nd Round: Colchester U. (A) 2-2, Replay (H) 1-3.
Littlewoods Cup: 1988-89: 1st Round: Cardiff C. (A) 1-0 (H) 0-2.

SWINDON TOWN (Division 2)

Team Manager Lou Macari.
Club Address County Ground, Swindon, Wiltshire. Tel: (0793) 642984.
Current Ground Capacity 20,000.
Record Attendance 32,000 v Arsenal, FA Cup 3rd Round, 15 January 1972.
Year Formed 1881. Turned professional 1894.
Previous Names None.
Club Nickname "The Robins".
Club Colours Red shirts with white pinstripe, white shorts and red stockings.
Club Honours Football League: Div. 4 Champions 1985-86. Football League Cup: Winners 1969.
League History 1920-58 Div. 3(S); 1958-63 Div. 3; 1963-65 Div. 2; 1965-69 Div. 3; 1969-74 Div. 2; 1974-82 Div. 3; 1982-86 Div. 4; 1986-87 Div. 3; 1987- Div. 2.
Most League Points in a Season (2 for a win) 64 in Div. 3, 1968-69. (3 for a win) 102 in Div. 4, 1985-86.
Most League Goals in a Season 100 in Div. 3(S), 1926-27.
Record Victory 10-1 v Farnham United in FA Cup 1st Round, 28 November 1925.
Record Defeat 1-10 v Manchester C. in FA Cup 4th Round replay, 25 January 1930.
Consecutive League Wins 8 in 1926 and 1986.
Consecutive League Defeats 6 in 1967 and 1980.
Record League Appearances John Trollope, 770 between 1960-80.
Record League Goalscorer—Career Harry Morris, 216 between 1926-33.
Record League Goalscorer—Season Harry Morris, 47 in Div. 3(S), 1926-27.

Swindon Town: League Record, 1988-89 (Division 2)

Match Number	Date	Venue	Opponents	Result	H/T	Lge Posn	Attend
1	27.8.88	A	Barnsley	D 1-1	0-1		6034
2	3.9.88	A	West Bromwich A.	L 1-3	1-3	17	7518
3	11.9.88	H	Portsmouth	D 1-1	0-1	15	11443
4	17.9.88	A	Blackburn Rov.	D 0-0	0-0	17	7622
5	20.9.88	H	Bournemouth	W 3-1	2-1	15	8055
6	24.9.88	H	Brighton & H.A.	W 3-0	1-0	10	6585
7	1.10.88	A	Watford	W 3-2	2-1	7	11657
8	5.10.88	A	Oxford U.	D 1-1	0-0	9	9398
9	9.10.88	H	Chelsea	D 1-1	0-0	11	11346
10	16.10.88	H	Leeds U.	D 0-0	0-0	11	9234
11	22.10.88	A	Sunderland	L 0-4	0-2	13	13520
12	26.10.88	A	Leicester C.	D 3-3	3-0	16	9271
13	29.10.88	H	Birmingham C.	W 2-1	1-0	12	6937
14	5.11.88	A	Hull C.	L 0-1	0-1	15	5192
15	12.11.88	H	Ipswich T.	L 2-3	1-0	18	7246
16	19.11.88	A	Stoke C.	L 1-2	0-0	19	9339
17	26.11.88	H	Walsall	W 1-0	0-0	15	5328
18	3.12.88	A	Shrewsbury T.	W 1-0	1-0	15	3524
19	10.12.88	H	Oldham Ath.	D 2-2	1-0	15	5540
20	17.12.88	A	Bradford C.	D 2-2	2-1	15	9462
21	26.12.88	H	Plymouth Arg.	W 1-0	1-0	12	7883
22	31.12.88	H	Manchester C.	L 1-2	0-1	15	10776
23	2.1.89	A	Portsmouth	W 2-0	1-0	14	11681
24	14.1.89	H	Barnsley	D 0-0	0-0	15	10201
25	21.1.89	A	Crystal Palace	L 1-2	1-0	16	8109
26	5.2.89	H	Oxford U.	W 3-0	1-0	14	10229
27	11.2.89	A	Chelsea	L 2-3	2-3	15	17829
28	18.2.89	H	Sunderland	W 4-1	3-1	11	7432
29	25.2.89	A	Leeds U.	D 0-0	0-0	13	22651
30	28.2.89	H	Leicester C.	W 2-1	0-1	11	7456
31	4.3.89	A	Ipswich T.	W 2-1	0-0	8	11542
32	11.3.89	H	Hull C.	W 1-0	1-0	8	7090
33	18.3.89	A	Bournemouth	W 3-2	2-0	7	9752
34	25.3.89	H	West Bromwich A.	D 0-0	0-0	6	12240
35	27.3.89	A	Plymouth Arg	L 1-4	0-3	9	8487
36	1.4.89	H	Blackburn Rov.	D 1-1	0-0	10	8220
37	4.4.89	H	Bradford C.	W 1-0	1-0	7	6476
38	8.4.89	A	Manchester C.	L 1-2	1-1	7	22663
39	15.4.89	H	Watford	D 1-1	1-0	8	9828
40	18.4.89	A	Birmingham C.	W 2-1	2-0	7	4026
41	22.4.89	A	Brighton & H.A.	W 2-0	0-0	7	9510
42	25.4.89	H	Crystal Palace	W 1-0	1-0	6	11045
43	29.4.89	A	Walsall	D 2-2	1-1	6	5288
44	1.5.89	H	Shrewsbury T.	W 1-0	1-0	6	8698
45	6.5.89	H	Stoke C.	W 3-0	0-0	6	9543
46	13.5.89	A	Oldham Ath.	D 2-2	2-1	6	5676

Players: League Record, 1988-89 (Division 2)

Match Number	1	2	3	4	5	6	7	8	9	10	11	12	13	14	15	16	17	18	19	20	21	22	23	24	25	26	27	28	29	30	31	32	33	34	35	36	37	38	39	40	41	42	43	44	45	46	Apps	Subs	Goals
Barnard, Leigh									★		9																																				1	1	0
Barnes, Bobby	11	11	11	11	11^1	11^1	11^1	11	**11**	11	11	**11**	11	11	11	**11**			10																												17	0	3
Bodin, Paul		7	**8**		★																			3	3	3	3^1	3	3	3	3	3	3	3	3	**3**											15	1	1
Calderwood, Colin	8	8	5	8	5^1	8^1	8	8	8	8	**8**	8	8	8		8	6	6	6	6			6	5	5	5^1	5	5	5	5	6	6	6	6	5	5	5	5	6	6	6	6	6^1	6	6	6	43	0	4
Cornwell, John																						★	11	10	6	11	**11**																				5	1	0
Coyne, Peter		★																																													0	1	0
Digby, Fraser	1	1	1	1	1	1	1	1	1	1	1	1	1	1	1	1	1	1	1	1	1	1	1	1	1	1	1	1	1	1	1	1	1	1	1	1	1	1	1	1	1	1	1	1	1	1	46	0	0
Foley, Steve			7^1	7	7	7	7	7	7	7	7	7	7	7	7	7	7^1	7	7	7	7	7	**7**	7	7^1	7	7			7	7	7	7^2	7	7	7^1	7	7	7		**7^2**	7	7	7	7		40	0	8
Geddis, David													★				11	11^1	11	11^1	11		9^1	11	11		★																				8	2	3
Gittens, John	6	6	6	6	6	6	6	6	6	6	6	6	6	6	6^1	6					6	**6**			8	6	6	6	6	6					6	6	6	6								5	29	0	1
Henry, Charlie	★	★	★		★		★			★	★	9^1	**9**	9	9^1	9	9	**9**	9^1	9	9	9	★	**9**	9			★																			13	9	3
Hockaday, David	2	2	2	2	2	2	2	2	2	2	2	2	2	2	2	2	2	2	2	2	2	2	2			2	2	2	2	2	2	2	2	2	2	2	2	2	2	2	2	2	2	2	2	2	44	0	0
Jones, Tom							4^1	4	4	4	4	4	4	4	4	4^1	4	4	**4**	4	4	4	4	4	4	4	4	4	4	4^1	4	4	4^1	4	4^1	4	4	4	4	4	4	4	4	4	4^1	4	40	0	6
King, Philip	3	3	3	3	3	3	3	3	3	3	3	3^1	3	3	3	3	3	3	3	3	3	3	3						11	★	★			★			3	3	3	3	3	3	3	3^1	3	3	34	3	2
MacLaren, Ross	4	4	4	4	4^1	4									8		10	10	8	10	10	10	10	6	10	10^1	10	10	10	**10**	10	10	10	10	10	10	10	10	10	10^2	10	10	10	10	10	10	37	0	4
McLoughlin, Alan	**7**								5			★												2	2	9^1	9	8^1	8	8	**8**	9	9	9	9	9	9	9	9	9	9	9	9	9	9	9^1	25	1	3
Parkin, Tim	5	**5**		5	8	5	5	5^1		5	5	5	5	5	5	5	5	5	5	5	5	5	**5**								5	5	5	**5**					5	5	5	5	5	5	5		32	0	1
Shearer, Duncan	9	**9**	9	9	**9**	9	9^1	9	9^1	**9**				★		★		★		8^1	8^1	11	8^1					7^2	7	9^1	9	8^1	8	8	8	8	8^1	8^1	8	8	8	8	8^1	8	8^2	8	33	3	14
Simpson, Fitzroy																		★						★				**11**								★				7	★					7	3	4	0
White, Steve	10^1	10^1	10	10	**10**	10^1	**10**	10	10	10	10	10^1	10^2	**10**	10	10	8	**8**	★			8^1	★	8		8	8	9^1	9	11	11^2	11	11	11	11	11	11	11	11^1	11	11	11^1	11	11	11	11^1	41	2	13
Own Goals																			1								1																						2

FA Cup: 1988-89: 3rd Round: Portsmouth (A) 1-1, Replay, (H) 2-0; 4th Round: West Ham U. (H) 0-0, Replay (A) 0-1.
Littlewoods Cup: 1988-89: 2nd Round: Crystal Palace (H) 1-2 (A) 0-2.

TORQUAY UNITED (Division 4)

Team Manager Cyril Knowles.
Club Address Plainmoor Ground, Torquay, Devon TQ1 3PS. Tel: (0803) 38666.
Current Ground Capacity 4,999.
Record Attendance 21,908 v Huddersfield T., FA Cup 4th Round, 29 January 1955.
Year Formed 1898. Turned professional 1921.
Previous Names Torquay Town.
Club Nickname "The Gulls".
Club Colours Yellow shirts, royal blue shorts and stockings.
Club Honours None.
League History 1927-58 Div. 3(S); 1958-60 Div. 4; 1960-62 Div. 3; 1962-66 Div. 4; 1966-72 Div. 3; 1972 - Div. 4.
Most League Points in a Season (2 for a win) 60 in Div. 4, 1959-60. (3 for a win) 77 in Div. 4, 1987-88.
Most League Goals in a Season 89 in Div. 3(S), 1956-57.
Record Victory 9-0 v Swindon T. in Div. 3(S), 8 March 1952.
Record Defeat 2-10 v Fulham in Div. 3(S), 7 September 1931 and v Luton T. in Div. 3(S), 2 September 1933.
Consecutive League Wins 6 in 1953.
Consecutive League Defeats 8 in 1948 and 1971.
Record League Appearances Dennis Lewis, 443 between 1947-59.
Record League Goalscorer—Career Sammy Collins, 203 between 1948-58.
Record League Goalscorer—Season Sammy Collins, 40 in Div. 3(S), 1955-56.

Torquay United: League Record, 1988-89 (Division 4)

Match Number	Date	Venue	Opponents	Result	H/T	Lge Posn	Attend
1	27.8.88	H	Halifax T.	L 0-2	0-1		2769
2	3.9.88	A	Grimsby T.	L 0-1	0-0	22	2857
3	10.9.88	H	Hartlepool U.	W 2-0	0-0	17	2027
4	16.9.88	A	Doncaster Rov.	W 2-1	1-0	10	2220
5	20.9.88	H	Burnley	W 2-0	1-0	5	3021
6	24.9.88	A	Scarborough	L 2-5	1-2	11	1986
7	1.10.88	H	Leyton Orient	W 3-0	2-0	8	2526
8	5.10.88	A	Exeter C.	L 0-3	0-0	11	4243
9	8.10.88	H	Lincoln C.	W 1-0	1-0	7	2105
10	15.10.888	A	Carlisle U.	L 1-2	0-0	11	2164
11	22.10.88	H	Rotherham U.	L 1-2	0-2	14	2228
12	25.10.88	A	Darlington	D 0-0	0-0	14	1374
13	29.10.88	H	Tranmere Rov.	W 3-2	1-1	9	2038
14	5.11.89	A	York C.	D 1-1	0-0	11	2007
15	8.11.88	H	Rochdale	W 1-0	1-0	10	1931
16	11.11.88	A	Colchester U.	D 2-2	0-1	9	1926
17	26.11.88	A	Scunthorpe U.	L 0-1	0-1	12	3359
18	2.12.88	H	Cambridge U.	W 3-1	3-0	7	1992
19	16.12.88	A	Crewe Alex.	D 0-0	0-0	7	3269
20	26.12.88	H	Stockport Co.	W 2-1	1-0	6	2838
21	31.12.88	H	Peterborough U.	W 1-0	0-0	5	2877
22	2.1.89	A	Hereford U.	D 1-1	0-1	6	2356
23	14.1.89	H	Grimsby T.	D 2-2	1-0	6	2251

Match Number	Date	Venue	Opponents	Result	H/T	Lge Posn	Attend
24	20.1.89	A	Halifax T.	L 0-2	0-2	7	1830
25	28.1.89	H	Doncaster Rov.	W 3-2	1-2	8	2103
26	4.2.89	A	Burnley	L 0-1	0-0	10	6626
27	11.2.89	H	Scarborough	L 0-1	0-0	11	2442
28	18.2.89	A	Lincoln C.	L 0-1	0-1	11	3423
29	28.2.89	H	Darlington	W 1-0	0-0	9	1627
30	4.3.89	A	Rotherham U.	L 0-1	0-1	10	3791
31	13.3.89	A	Tranmere Rov.	L 0-3	0-1	15	3558
32	18.3.89	A	Hartlepool U.	W 1-0	1-0	12	1516
33	25.3.89	H	Hereford U.	W 1-0	0-0	11	2542
34	27.3.89	A	Stockport Co.	D 0-0	0-0	11	2808
35	31.3.89	H	Crewe Alex.	W 2-1	0-1	10	3087
36	4.4.89	H	Wrexham	D 0-0	0-0	11	2421
37	8.4.89	A	Peterborough U.	L 1-3	0-0	11	2614
38	15.4.89	A	Leyton Orient	L 1-3	0-1	13	4642
39	22.4.89	H	Exeter C.	L 0-4	0-1	15	2939
40	25.4.89	H	York C.	W 2-0	1-0	12	2015
41	28.4.89	H	Scunthorpe U.	L 0-2	0-0	12	2544
42	1.5.89	A	Rochdale	L 1-2	0-1	15	1239
43	3.5.89	H	Carlisle U.	W 1-0	1-0	13	1603
44	6.5.89	A	Cambridge U.	L 0-3	0-1	13	2163
45	9.5.89	A	Wrexham	L 0-1	0-0	14	2056
46	13.5.89	H	Colchester U.	L 1-3	0-0	14	2066

Players: League Record, 1988-89 (Division 4)

Match Number	1	2	3	4	5	6	7	8	9	10	11	12	13	14	15	16	17	18	19	20	21	22	23
Airey, Carl																							
Bastow, Ian																							
Cole, David	5		5	5	5	**5**	5	**5**	6^{1}	5	5	5	5	5	5	5	5	5	5	5	5	5	**5**
Coombe, Mark																							
Crichton, Paul	1	1	1	1	1	1	1	1	1	1	1	1	1										
Davies, Andrew																							
Dawkins, Derek		10	10	10	10				★	★	★	4	★		★	★	2						
Edwards, Dean	9	**9**	9	9	9^{2}	9^{1}	$\mathbf{9}^{1}$	9	9	9	**9**	★	9	9	★	**9**	★	★	★	★	★^{1}	7	★
Elliott, Matthew																							
Gibbins, Roger	11	11	**11**	11^{1}	11	11	11	11	**11**	**11**	11	11	11^{1}		**7**		★	10	10	10	10	**10**	10^{1}
Gummer, Jason																							
Haslegrave, Sean		★															**9**						
Hirons, Paul																							
Holmes, Paul	2	2	2	2	2	2	2	2		2	2	2		★		2		★	9			★	★
Joyce, Sean	6	**6**	**6**	6^{1}	**6**	6	6^{1}	**6**	6	6	6	★	6	6	6	6	6		★	11	11	11	11
Kelly, Tom	3	3	3	3	3	3	3	3	3	3	3	3	3	3	3	3	3	3	3	3	3	3	3
Leyden, Darren																							
Lloyd, Philip	8	8	8^{1}	8	8	8	8^{1}	8	8	8^{1}	8	8	8^{1}	8	8	8	8	8	8	8	8	8	8
Loram, Mark	10	5							★		★	**6**	★	★	9	10^{2}	10	**6**	6	6^{1}	6	6^{1}	6
Love, Ian																							
McNichol, Jim	**4**	4	4^{1}	4	4	4^{1}	4	4	4	4				4	4	4	4	4	4	4^{1}	4	4	4^{1}
Morrison, John	★																					★	
Pugh, Daral	7	7	7	7	7	7	7	7	7	7	7	7	7	**7**				2	2	2	2	**2**	2
Smith, James		★	★			★	★	★	2	★	**4**		2^{1}	2^{1}	2	7	**7**	7^{1}	**7**	7	**7**		7
Smith, Paul																							
Thompson, Richard	★											9	**10**	**10**	$\mathbf{10}^{1}$	★		$\mathbf{9}^{2}$		**9**	9	9	**9**
Tupling, Stephen						**10**	★	★															
Veysey, Kenny														1	1	1	1	1	1	1	1	1	1
Weston, Ian			★		★	★	**10**	10	**10**	**10**	10^{1}	**10**	**4**	11	11	**11**	11	11	**11**				
Own Goals																							

Match Number	24	25	26	27	28	29	30	31	32	33	34	35	36	37	38	39	40	41	42	43	44	45	46	Apps	Subs	Goals
Airey, Carl	★	★	★	**9**	7	★	11	11	10	**9**	★	★^{1}	2	★^{1}	7	7	$\mathbf{7}^{1}$							10	7	3
Bastow, Ian															★					**10**				1	1	0
Cole, David			4	**5**	5	5	5	5	★	★					6		11	**11**	11		★			32	3	1
Coombe, Mark																1	1	1	1	1	1	1	1	8	0	0
Crichton, Paul																								13	0	0
Davies, Andrew																				4	4	**4**		3	0	0
Dawkins, Derek																								6	6	0
Edwards, Dean	9	2^{1}	9	2		9^{1}	9		$\mathbf{9}^{1}$				**9**		**9**	9	★	**7**	★	9	**9**	9	9	30	10	8
Elliott, Matthew											5	5	5	5	5	5	5^{1}	5	**5**	5^{1}	5	5	5	13	0	2
Gibbins, Roger																								20	1	3
Gummer, Jason								9	11	11	11	11^{1}	11	11										7	0	1
Haslegrave, Sean																								1	1	0
Hirons, Paul				★						★			★		★	11								1	4	0
Holmes, Paul	**2**		2				4	4	5	2			★	★										19	6	0
Joyce, Sean	11	11^{1}	11	11	11	**11**															**6**		★	27	3	3
Kelly, Tom	3	3	3	3		3	3	3	3	3	3	3	3	3	3	**3**	3	3	3	★		3	3	43	1	0
Leyden, Darren	5	5	5	★	2	★													4	**2**	2			7	2	0
Lloyd, Philip	8	8	**8**	8	**8**	8	8	8	8	8	8	8	8	8	8	8	8	8	8	8	8	8	8	46	0	4
Loram, Mark	6	6	6	6	6	6	6	6	6	6	6	6	6	6		6	6	6	6^{1}	6		6	6	33	4	5
Love, Ian										5	9	9		**9**			9	9	**9**		11	★		8	1	0
McNichol, Jim	4	4		4	4	4			4	4	4	4	4	4	4	4	4	4					**4**	36	0	4
Morrison, John	★		★		3	2	2	2	2		2				2	2	2	2	2		★	11	11	13	5	0
Pugh, Daral				★								**2**		2				★	★	3	3	2	2	26	3	0
Smith, James	7	7	7	7	★	**7**	**7**		★						11^{1}		10	10	7	11	7	**7**	**7**	26	8	4
Smith, Paul								7	**7**	$\mathbf{7}^{1}$	**7**	7	7	7		★				7		★	★	8	3	1
Thompson, Richard		**9**			**9**		★	★																11	4	3
Tupling, Stephen																								1	2	0
Veysey, Kenny	1	1	1	1	1	1	1	1	1	1	1	1	1	1	**1**									25	0	0
Weston, Ian	**10**	10^{1}	**10**	10	10	10	10	**10**		10	10	10	**10**	**10**	10	10		★	10	★	10	10	10	32	5	2
Own Goals																							1			1

FA Cup: 1988–89: 1st Round: Fareham T. (H) 2-2, Replay (A) 3-2; 2nd Round: Yeovil T. (A) 1-1, Replay (H) 1-0; 3rd Round: Sheffield Wed. (A) 1-5.
Littlewoods Cup: 1988-89: 1st Round: Reading (H) 0-1 (A) 1-3.

·HOLSTEN·
Pils

PROUD SPONSORS OF
TOTTENHAM HOTSPUR.

TOTTENHAM HOTSPUR (Division 1)

Team Manager Terry Venables.
Club Address 748 High Road, Tottenham, London N17. Tel: 01-801 3411.
Current Ground Capacity 34,000.
Record Attendance 75,038 v Sunderland, FA Cup 6th Round, 5 March 1938.
Year Formed 1882. Turned professional 1895.
Previous Names Hotspur.
Club Nickname "The Spurs".
Club Colours White Shirts, navy blue shorts and white stockings.
Club Honours Football League: Div. 1 Champions 1950-51, 1960-61. Div. 2 Champions 1919-20, 1949-50. FA Cup: Winners 1901, 1921, 1961, 1962, 1967, 1981, 1982. Football League Cup: Winners 1971, 1973. European Cup Winners Cup: Winners 1962-63. UEFA Cup: Winners 1971-72, 1983-84.
League History 1908-09 Div. 2; 1909-15 Div. 1; 1919-20 Div. 2; 1920-28 Div. 1; 1928-33 Div. 2; 1933-35 Div. 1; 1935-50 Div. 2; 1950-77 Div. 1; 1977-78 Div. 2; 1978- Div. 1.
Most League Points in a Season (2 for a win) 70 in Div. 2, 1919-20. (3 for a win) 77 in Div. 1, 1984-85.
Most League Goals in a Season 115 in Div. 1, 1960-61.
Record Victory 13-2 v Crewe Alex. in FA Cup 4th Round replay, 3 February 1960.
Record Defeat 0-7 v Liverpool in Div. 1, 2 September 1978.
Consecutive League Wins 13 in 1960.
Consecutive League Defeats 5 in 1912, 1955 and 1975.
Record League Appearances Steve Perryman, 655 between 1969-86.
Record League Goalscorer—Career Jimmy Greaves, 220 between 1961-70.
Record League Goalscorer—Season Jimmy Greaves, 37 in Div. 1, 1962-63.

Tottenham Hotspur: League Record, 1988-89 (Division 1)

Match Number	Date	Venue	Opponents	Result	H/T	Lge Posn	Attend
1	3.9.88	A	Newcastle U.	D 2-2	0-2		32977
2	10.9.88	H	Arsenal	L 2-3	2-3	15	32621
3	17.9.88	A	Liverpool	D 1-1	0-0	17	40929
4	24.9.88	H	Middlesbrough	W 3-2	1-1	13	23427
5	1.10.88	H	Manchester U.	D 2-2	1-1	14	29318
6	8.10.88	A	Charlton Ath.	D 2-2	0-1	15	14384
7	22.10.88	A	Norwich C.	L 1-3	0-2	19	20330
8	25.10.88	H	Southampton	L 1-2	1-0	19	19517
9	29.10.88	A	Aston Villa	L 1-2	0-0	20	26238
10	5.11.88	H	Derby Co.	L 1-3	1-1	20	22868
11	12.11.88	H	Wimbledon	W 3-2	1-1	18	23587
12	20.11.88	A	Sheffield Wed.	W 2-0	0-0	17	15386
13	23.11.88	H	Coventry C.	D 1-1	1-0	17	21961
14	26.11.88	H	Q.P.R.	D 2-2	0-2	17	26698
15	3.12.88	A	Everton	L 0-1	0-1	16	29657
16	10.12.88	H	Millwall	W 2-0	1-0	16	27660
17	17.12.88	A	West Ham U.	W 2-0	1-0	11	28365
18	26.12.88	H	Luton T.	D 0-0	0-0	11	27377
19	31.12.88	H	Newcastle U.	W 2-0	2-0	10	27739
20	2.1.89	A	Arsenal	L 0-2	0-1	11	45129
21	15.1.89	H	Nottingham F.	L 1-2	1-2	14	16903
22	21.1.89	A	Middlesbrough	D 2-2	1-1	12	23692
23	5.2.89	A	Manchester U.	L 0-1	0-0	13	41423
24	11.2.89	H	Charlton Ath.	D 1-1	0-1	13	22803
25	21.2.89	H	Norwich C.	W 2-1	1-0	11	19120
26	25.2.89	A	Southampton	W 2-0	1-0	11	16702
27	1.3.89	H	Aston Villa	W 2-0	1-0	10	19090
28	11.3.89	A	Derby Co.	D 1-1	0-1	10	18306
29	18.3.89	A	Coventry C.	D 1-1	0-1	9	17156
30	22.3.89	A	Nottingham F.	W 2-1	0-0	8	23098
31	26.3.89	H	Liverpool	L 1-2	0-0	10	30012
32	28.3.89	A	Luton T.	W 3-1	0-1	6	11146
33	1.4.89	H	West Ham U.	W 3-0	1-0	6	28375
34	12.4.89	H	Sheffield Wed.	D 0-0	0-0	6	17270
35	15.4.89	A	Wimbledon	W 2-1	1-0	5	12366
36	22.4.89	H	Everton	W 2-1	0-0	5	28568
37	29.4.89	A	Millwall	W 5-0	2-0	5	16551
38	13.5.89	A	Q.P.R.	L 0-1	0-0	6	21873

Players: League Record, 1988-89 (Division 1)

Match Number	1	2	3	4	5	6	7	8	9	10	11	12	13	14	15	16	17	18	19	20	21	22	23	24	25	26	27	28	29	30	31	32	33	34	35	36	37	38	Apps	Subs	Goals
Allen, Paul	11	11	11	11	11	5¹	11	11	**11**	**11**		★	★	11	11	11	11	11	11	11	11	11	11	11	11	11	11	11	11	11	11	11	11	11	11	**11**	11	**11**	35	2	1
Bergsson, Gudni																		5	8	8	8	5	**5**	5										1					8	0	0
Butters, Guy											★¹	2	2	2	2	2	2	2	2	2	2	2	2	2	2	2	2	2	2	2	2	2	2	2	2	2	2	2	27	1	1
Fairclough, Chris	5	5	5	5			5¹	5	5	5	5	5	5	5	5	5	5		5	5	5					5	5												20	0	1
Fenwick, Terry	4¹	4	4¹	4¹	4	4¹	4	4	4¹	4	4¹	4	4	4	4	4	4	4	4	4	4	4	4	4			4	4	4	4	4¹	4	4¹		4	4	**4**		34	0	8
Gascoigne, Paul	**8**	8¹	8	8	**8**	8	8	8	8	8	8	**8**	8	8¹	8	8¹	**8**	**8**			★	**8**	8	8	8¹			8¹	**8**			8¹	8	8	8	**8**	8	**8**	31	1	6
Gray, Philip														★																									0	1	0
Howells, David	★	★	★	★¹	★	★	★		**7**	★		★							★		★	**7**	**7**	**7**	★	★			★	8¹	8	5¹	★	5	5	5	5	5	12	15	3
Hughton, Chris	3		★		5																**3**	3	3	3	3	3	3	3	3	3	3	3	3	3	3	3	3	3	20	1	0
Mabbutt, Gary	6	6	6	6	6	6	6	6	6	6	6	6	6	6	6	6	6¹	6	6	6	6	6	6	6	6	6	6	6	6	6	6	6	6	6	6	6	6	6	38	0	1
Mimms, Bob	1	1	1	1	1	1	1	1	1	1	1	1	1	1	1	1	1	1	1	1																			20	0	0
Moncur, John									★																														0	1	0
Moran, Paul	★	★		★						**7**	7	**7**	**7**					★																					4	4	0
Nayim Amor, Mohamed																									4	4¹	8	**5**	5	**5**	**5**		5¹			★	★	★	8	3	2
Polston, Jonathan																	★														★							★	0	3	0
Robson, Mark																	★								**10**	**10**	10	★											3	2	0
Samways, Vincent		**10**	10	10	10	10	**10**			★	11¹	11	**11**	★	7			★												★¹	★			10		★	★¹	4	12	7	3
Statham, Brian	2	**2**	2	**2**	2	2																																	6	0	0
Stevens, Gary							2	2	2	2	**2**																												5	0	0
Stewart, Paul					★	11	7	10	10	10¹	10	10²	10¹	10	10	10	10	10	10	10	10	10²	10	10¹				10	10	10	10	10	10¹		10¹	10	10³	10	29	1	12
Stimson, Mark									★																														0	1	0
Thomas, Mitchell	10	3	3	3	3	3	3	3	3	3	3	3	3	**3**	3	3	3¹	3	3	3		★	★		5	8		★											22	3	1
Thorstvedt, Erik																					1	1	1	1	1	1	1	1	1	1	1	1	1	1	1	1	1	1	18	0	0
Waddle, Chris	9¹	9¹	**9**	9¹	**9¹**	9	9	9	9	9	9	9	9	9¹	9	9¹	9	9	9¹	9	9¹	9	9	9	9¹	9¹	9²	9	9¹	9	9	9	9	9	9¹	9	**9**	9	38	0	14
Walsh, Paul	**7**	7	**7**	**7**	7¹	**7**		7					★	**7**	★	7	**7**	**7**	**7¹**	7	**7**	★	★	★	7	7	7	**7**	7	7	**7**	7¹	7	7	7	7²	7¹	7	28	5	6
Own Goals								1																																	1

FA Cup: 3rd Round: Bradford C. (A) 0-1.
Littlewoods Cup: 1988-89: 2nd Round: Notts Co. (A) 1-1 (H) 2-1; 3rd Round: Blackburn Rov. (H) 0-0, Replay (A) 2-1; 4th Round: Southampton (A) 1-2.

TRANMERE ROVERS (Division 3)

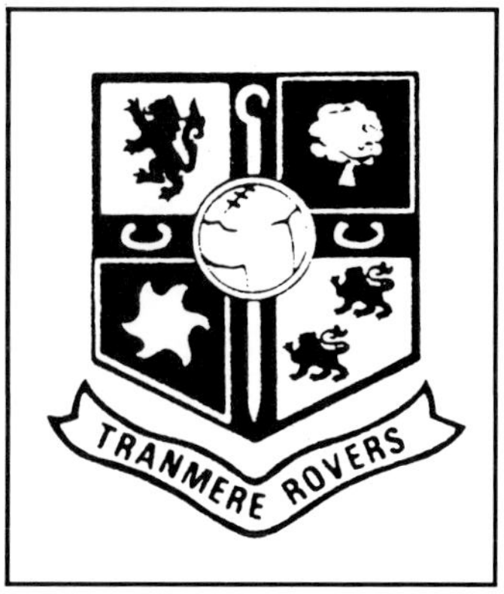

Team Manager John King.
Club Address Prenton Park, Prenton Road West, Birkenhead. Tel: 051-608 3677/4194.
Current Ground Capacity 12,000
Record Attendance 24,424 v Stoke C., FA Cup 4th Round, 5 February 1972.
Year Formed 1883. Turned professional 1912.
Previous Names Belmont.
Club Nickname "Rovers".
Club Colours All white.
Club Honours Football League: Div. 3(N) Champions 1937-38.
League History 1921-38 Div. 3(N); 1938-39 Div. 2; 1946-58 Div. 3(N); 1958-61 Div. 3; 1961-67 Div. 4; 1967-75 Div. 3; 1975-76 Div. 4; 1976-79 Div. 3; 1979-89 Div. 4; 1989- Div. 3.

Most League Points in a Season (2 for a win) 60 in Div. 4, 1964-65. (3 for a win) 80 in Div. 4, 1988-89.
Most League Goals in a Season 111 in Div. 3(N), 1930-31.
Record Victory 13-4 v Oldham Ath. in Div. 3(N), 26 December 1935.
Record Defeat 1-9 v Tottenham H. in FA Cup 3rd Round replay, 14 January 1953.
Consecutive League Wins 8 in 1964.
Consecutive League Defeats 8 in 1938.
Record League Appearances Harold Bell, 595 between 1946-59.
Record League Goalscorer—Career Bunny Bell, 104 between 1931-36.
Record League Goalscorer—Season Bunny Bell, 35 in Div. 3(N), 1933-34.

Tranmere Rovers: League Record, 1988-89 (Division 4)

Match Number	Date	Venue	Opponents	Result	H/T	Lge Posn	Attend
1	27.8.88	A	Scarborough	D 0-0	0-0		2893
2	2.9.88	H	Colchester U.	D 0-0	0-0	17	3401
3	10.9.88	A	Carlisle U.	D 1-1	0-0	16	2384
4	16.9.88	H	Cambridge U.	L 1-2	1-2	19	3248
5	19.9.88	H	Peterborough U.	W 1-0	1-0	12	2597
6	24.9.88	A	Halifax T.	W 3-2	0-1	10	1662
7	30.9.88	H	Hartlepool U.	W 2-1	2-1	9	3624
8	4.10.88	A	Grimsby T.	D 0-0	0-0	7	2288
9	7.10.88	H	York C.	L 0-1	0-1	10	3054
10	15.10.88	A	Rotherham U.	D 0-0	0-0	15	4133
11	22.10.88	A	Wrexham	D 3-3	0-2	11	3334
12	24.10.88	H	Lincoln C.	W 1-0	0-0	6	3498
13	29.10.88	A	Torquay U.	L 2-3	1-1	11	2038
14	4.11.88	H	Rochdale	W 2-0	1-0	9	3740
15	7.11.88	H	Hereford U.	W 1-0	1-0	5	3587
16	12.11.88	A	Crewe Alex.	L 1-2	1-0	6	3293
17	25.11.88	A	Stockport Co.	D 1-1	1-0	10	2952
18	2.12.88	H	Doncaster Rov.	D 2-2	0-2	10	3412
19	16.12.88	H	Darlington	W 2-0	2-0	6	2981
20	26.12.88	A	Leyton Orient	L 0-2	0-0	8	4249
21	31.12.88	A	Scunthorpe U.	W 1-0	1-0	7	4154
22	2.1.89	H	Burnley	W 2-1	1-0	5	7974
23	14.1.89	A	Colchester U.	W 3-2	0-1	5	3458

Match Number	Date	Venue	Opponents	Result	H/T	Lge Posn	Attend
24	21.1.89	H	Scarborough	D 1-1	0-1	5	4538
25	28.1.89	A	Cambridge U.	D 1-1	0-1	6	2239
26	4.2.89	A	Peterborough U.	D 1-1	0-0	7	2744
27	10.2.89	H	Halifax T.	W 2-0	0-0	6	4674
28	18.2.89	A	York C.	W 1-0	1-0	6	2923
29	25.2.89	H	Rotherham U.	D 0-0	0-0	5	6509
30	1.3.89	A	Lincoln C.	L 1-2	0-0	6	3560
31	3.3.89	H	Wrexham	W 2-1	0-1	5	7353
32	11.3.89	A	Rochdale	L 1-3	1-0	6	2158
33	13.3.89	H	Torquay U.	W 3-0	1-0	6	3558
34	17.3.89	H	Carlisle U.	D 0-0	0-0	4	5143
35	20.3.89	H	Exeter C.	W 2-0	1-0	4	3885
36	25.3.89	A	Burnley	D 2-2	1-0	4	6838
37	27.3.89	H	Leyton Orient	W 3-0	1-0	4	6872
38	1.4.89	A	Darlington	W 2-1	1-0	4	2492
39	5.4.89	A	Exeter C.	W 1-0	1-0	3	2956
40	7.4.89	H	Scunthorpe U.	W 2-1	2-0	1	10465
41	15.4.89	A	Hartlepool U.	D 2-2	0-1	1	2496
42	28.4.89	H	Stockport Co.	W 1-0	0-0	2	6270
43	1.5.89	A	Hereford U.	L 1-2	1-1	2	2844
44	6.5.89	A	Doncaster Rov.	D 0-0	0-0	3	2268
45	9.5.89	A	Grimsby T.	W 3-2	2-2	2	6938
46	13.5.89	H	Crewe Alex.	D 1-1	1-0	2	15286

Players: League Record, 1988-89 (Division 4)

Match Number	1	2	3	4	5	6	7	8	9	10	11	12	13	14	15	16	17	18	19	20	21	22	23
Bishop, Eddie					**4**^{1}	**4**	4	4	**4**	4	4^1	4	**4**	4^1	4	4^1		8	★	★			★
Collings, Paul																	1						
Harvey, Jimmy	8	8	8	8	8	8	**8**	8	8	8	8^2	8	8	8	**8**		**8**		**8**	8	8	8	8^1
Higgins, David	2	2	2	2	2	2^1	2	**2**	2	2	2	2	2	2	2	2	2	2		2	**2**	2	2
Hughes, Mark			5	**5**	5	5	5	5	5	5	5	5	5	5					2				**5**
McCarrick, Mark				3	3	3	3	3	3	3	3	3	3	**3**		3	3	3^1	3	3	3	3	3^1
McKenna, Ken				★																			
Malkin, Chris								★	★								★			★	★		7
Martindale, David	4	4	4	**4**		★	★		★				★	★	★	8	4	4	4	**4**	4	4^1	4
Moore, Ronnie	5	5													5	5	5	**5**	5	**5**	5	5	
Morrisey, John Jnr	7	7	7	7	7	7	7	7	**7**	**7**	7	7	**7**	7^1	7	7	**7**	7^1	7	7	7	7	
Muir, Ian	10	10	10	10^1	10	10^2	10^1	10	10	10	10	10^1	10^1	10	10^1	10	10^1	10	10^2	10	10	10	10
Mungall, Steve	11	11	11	11	11	11	11	11	11	11	11	11	11	11	11	11	11	11	11	11	11	11	11
Murray, Edward										★			★										
Nixon, Eric	1	1	1	1	1	1	1	1	1	1	1	1	1	1	1	1		1	1	1	1	1	1
Smith, John					★										3								
Steel, Jim	9	9	9^1	9	9	9	9^1	9	9	9	9	9	9^1	9	9	9	9	9	9	9	9	9^1	9
Thomas, Tony																							
Vickers, Stephen	6	6	6	6	6	6	6	6	6	6	6	6	6	6	6	6	6	6	6	6	6	6	6^1
Williams, Gary	3	3	3	★													★	★					
Own Goals																					1		

Match Number	24	25	26	27	28	29	30	31	32	33	34	35	36	37	38	39	40	41	42	43	44	45	46	Apps	Subs	Goals
Bishop, Eddie	★^{1}		★	4^1	4	4	4	4	**4**	4	4	★	4^2				★	8	4	**4**	4	★	★	26	9	8
Collings, Paul																								1	0	0
Harvey, Jimmy	8	8	8	8	**8**	8	8	8	8	8		8	8	8^1	8	8	**8**		**8**	8	**8**	8	8	42	0	4
Higgins, David	2	2			2	2	2	2	2	2	2	2	2	2	2	2	2	2	2	2	2	2	2	43	0	1
Hughes, Mark	5	5	**5**	**5**	5	**5**	**5**	5	**5**	5	**5**	5	5	5	5	5	5	**5**	5	5	**5**	5^1	5	37	0	1
McCarrick, Mark	3	3	3	3	3	3	3	3	3	3	3	3	3	3	3	3	3	3	3	3	3	3^1	3	42	0	3
McKenna, Ken																								0	1	0
Malkin, Chris		★	9^1	★		★	★		7^1	7^2	7	★					★	★		★	9	★		6	14	4
Martindale, David	**4**	4	**4**		★				★		8	**4**				★		4	★	★	★	**4**	**4**	20	12	1
Moore, Ronnie																								10	0	0
Morrisey, John Jnr	7	7^1	7	7	7	7	7	7				**7**	7	7	**7**	7	7^1	**7**	7	**7**	7	7	7	42	0	4
Muir, Ian	10	10	10	10	10^1	10	10^1	10^1	10	10	10	10^2	10	10	10	10	10^1	10^1	10^1	10^1	10	10^1	10^1	46	0	21
Mungall, Steve	11	11	11	11	11	11	11	11	11	11	11	11	11	11^1	11	11	**11**					11	11	42	0	1
Murray, Edward									★		★				★			★			★			0	7	0
Nixon, Eric	1	1	1	1	1	1	1	1	1	1	1	1	1	1	1	1	1	1	1	1	1	1	1	45	0	0
Smith, John																								1	1	0
Steel, Jim	9	**9**		9	9	9	9	9^1	9	9	9	9	9	9^1	9	9	9	9^1	9	9		**9**	9	44	0	7
Thomas, Tony			★											4	4^1	**4**^{1}	4	11	11	11	11			8	1	2
Vickers, Stephen	6	6	6	6^1	6	6	6	6	6	6	6	6	6	6	6^1	6	6	6	6	6	6	6	6	46	0	3
Williams, Gary			2	2																				5	3	0
Own Goals										1																2

FA Cup: 1988-89: 1st Round: Preston N.E. (A) 1-1, Replay (H) 3-0; 2nd Round: Northwich Vic. (A) 2-1; 3rd Round: Reading (H) 1-1, Replay (A) 1-2.
Littlewoods Cup: 1988-89: 1st Round: Stockport Co. (A) 1-0 (H) 1-1; 2nd Round: Middlesbrough (A) 0-0 (H) 1-0, 3rd Round: Blackpool (H) 1-0; 4th Round: Bristol C. (A) 0-1.

WALSALL (Division 3)

Team Manager Tommy Coakley.
Club Address Fellows Park, Walsall. Tel: (0922) 22791.
Current Ground Capacity 16,018.
Record Attendance 24,453 v Newcastle U., Div. 2, 29 August 1961.
Year Formed 1888. Turned professional 1888.
Previous Names Walsall Swifts, Walsall Town, Walsall Town Swifts.
Club Nickname "The Saddlers".
Club Colours White shirts with red trim, red shorts and white stockings.
Club Honours Football League: Div. 4 Champions 1959-60.
League History 1892-95 Div. 2; 1895 Failed re-election; 1921-27 Div. 3(N); 1927-31 Div. 3(S); 1931-36 Div. 3(N); 1936-58 Div. 3(S); 1958-60 Div. 4; 1960-61 Div. 3; 1961-63 Div. 2; 1963-79 Div. 3; 1979-80 Div. 4; 1980-88 Div. 3; 1988- Div. 2.
Most League Points in a Season (2 for a win) 65 in Div. 4, 1959-60. (3 for a win) 82 in Div. 3, 1987-88.
Most League Goals in a Season 102 in Div. 4, 1959-60.
Record Victory 10-0 v Darwen in Div. 2, 4 March 1899.
Record Defeat 0-12 v Small Heath in Div. 2, 17 December 1892 and v Darwen in Div. 2, 26 December 1896.
Consecutive League Wins 7 in 1933 and 1959.
Consecutive League Defeats 15 in 1988-89.
Record League Appearances Colin Harrison, 467 between 1964-82.
Record League Goalscorer—Career Tony Richards, 184 between 1954-63.
Record League Goalscorer—Season Gilbert Alsop, 40 in Div. 3(N), 1933-34 and 1934-35.

Walsall: League Record, 1988-89 (Division 2)

Match Number	Date	Venue	Opponents	Result	H/T	Lge Posn	Attend
1	27.8.88	H	Plymouth Arg.	D 2-2	0-2		6178
2	3.9.88	A	Manchester C.	D 2-2	1-0	14	17104
3	10.9.88	H	Crystal Palace	D 0-0	0-0	14	6525
4	17.9.88	A	West Bromwich A.	D 0-0	0-0	15	13977
5	20.9.88	H	Birmingham C.	W 5-0	0-0	10	8780
6	24.9.88	H	Stoke C.	L 1-2	1-1	15	7795
7	1.10.88	A	Hull C.	D 0-0	0-0	17	4845
8	4.10.88	A	Chelsea	L 0-2	0-0	20	6747
9	8.10.88	H	Sunderland	W 2-0	0-0	16	6150
10	15.10.88	A	Shrewsbury T.	D 0-0	0-0	16	5026
11	22.10.88	H	Portsmouth	D 1-1	0-1	18	5626
12	26.10.88	A	Brighton & H.A.	D 2-2	2-1	19	8311
13	29.10.88	H	Watford	L 0-1	0-0	20	6682
14	5.11.88	A	Oldham Ath.	L 0-3	0-3	21	5760
15	8.11.88	A	Ipswich T.	L 1-3	0-1	21	9067
16	12.11.88	H	Leicester C.	L 0-1	0-1	21	6895
17	19.11.88	H	Blackburn Rov.	L 1-2	0-1	21	5848
18	26.11.88	A	Swindon T.	L 0-1	0-0	23	5328
19	3.12.88	H	Leeds U.	L 0-3	0-1	23	6885
20	10.12.88	A	Barnsley	L 0 1	0 0	23	5173
21	17.12.88	A	Bournemouth	L 1-2	0-1	23	6985
22	26.12.88	H	Oxford U.	L 1-5	1-0	24	6332
23	31.12.88	H	Bradford C.	L 0-1	0-1	24	5366
24	2.1.89	A	Crystal Palace	L 0-4	0-3	24	9352
25	14.1.89	H	Ipswich T.	L 2-4	0-0	24	4623
26	21.1.89	A	Plymouth Arg.	L 0-2	0-0	24	11505
27	4.2.89	H	Chelsea	L 0-7	0-4	24	6860
28	11.2.89	A	Sunderland	W 3-0	1-0	24	14203
29	18.2.89	A	Portsmouth	D 1-1	1-0	24	7310
30	25.2.89	H	Shrewsbury T.	D 1-1	1-1	24	5871
31	28.2.89	H	Brighton & H.A.	W 1-0	0-0	23	4613
32	4.3.89	A	Leicester C.	L 0-1	0-0	23	9375
33	11.3.89	H	Oldham Ath.	D 2-2	1-0	23	5576
34	18.3.89	A	Birmingham C.	L 0-1	0-0	24	6558
35	25.3.89	H	Manchester C.	D 3-3	2-2	23	7562
36	27.3.89	A	Oxford U.	L 0-1	0-1	23	5101
37	1.4.89	H	West Bromwich A.	D 0-0	0-0	23	9520
38	4.4.89	H	Bournemouth	D 1-1	1-1	23	3619
39	8.4.89	A	Bradford C.	L 1-3	1-1	23	8763
40	15.4.89	H	Hull C.	D 1-1	0-0	23	3935
41	18.4.89	A	Watford	L 0-5	0-4	23	9777
42	22.4.89	A	Stoke C.	W 3-0	2-0	23	8132
43	29.4.89	H	Swindon T.	D 2-2	1-1	23	5288
44	1.5.89	A	Leeds U.	L 0-1	0-0	24	13280
45	6.5.89	A	Blackburn Rov.	L 0-3	0-0	24	8236
46	13.5.89	H	Barnsley	L 1-3	0-1	24	3966

Players: League Record, 1988-89 (Division 2)

Match Number	1	2	3	4	5	6	7	8	9	10	11	12	13	14	15	16	17	18	19	20	21	22	23	24	25	26	27	28	29	30	31	32	33	34	35	36	37	38	39	40	41	42	43	44	45	46	Apps	Subs	Goals
Banton, Dale													10	10	10	**10**	**10**	10					★	**10**		**9**			**10**																		9	1	0
Barber, Fred	1	1	1	1	1	1	1	1	1	1	1	1	1	1	1	1	1	1	1	1	1	1	1	1	1	1	1	1	1	1	1	1	1	1	1	1	1	1	1	1	1	1	1	1			44	0	0
Bertschin, Keith							8	**8**	★	11	**8**				★	★	★	9	9	**9**	**9**				9	10		**10**												★		★		★	★	★	11	9	0
Callaghan, Willie					**10**	10^{1}																																									2	0	1
Christie, Trevor	10	10	10	10				10	**10^{1}**	10	10	10	8	8	9^{1}	9	9		10	10	10	10	**10**		**10**	★	9	★		9	9	9	9	9													26	2	2
Dornan, Andy	2	2	2	2	2	2	3										7	2	2	2	2	2	2	2	2	2	2	2	2	2	2	2	2	2	2												26	0	0
Forbes, Graeme	5	5	5	5	5^{1}	5	5	5	5	5	5	5	5	5	5	5	5	5	5	5	5	5	5	5	5	5	5	5	5	5	5	5	5	5	5	5		5	5	5	5	5	5	5	5	5	45	0	1
Goldsmith, Martin																									★				★																		0	2	0
Goodwin, Mark	8	8	**8**	8	8	**8**													8	**8**	8	8	8	8	8	**8**	★	8	8	10	10	10	10	10	10	10	10	10	10	**10**	**10**		★	10	10		30	2	0
Green, Ron																																													1	1	2	0	0
Hart, Peter	6	6	6	6	6	6	6	6	6	6	6	6	6	6	6	6	6	6	★	6	6	6	6	6	6	6	**6**																				26	1	0
Hawker, Phil	★	★	7				7	7	7	7	7^{1}	7	7			7			**6**							11	**11**					★	3^{1}	3	3	3	6	6	6	6	3	10	**10**				23	3	2
Jones, Paul								★	**8**		★			9	8	8	8	8	11	11	11	9	9			★	10																			10	13	3	0
Marsh, Chris			★	7			★					★	★	★	**7**	★					★		★	★	**11**																					★	3	10	0
Mower, Kenny					7	7		3	3	3	3	3	3	3	3	3	**3**	7	**7**					9	3	3	3	3	**3**	3	3	**3**				6					★	3	3	3	**3**		28	1	0
Naughton, Willie	11	11^{2}	11	11	11^{1}	11	11	★	11	★	**11**	11^{1}	**11**	**11**	**11**					★		11^{1}	11	11							11^{1}	★	11	11	11	**11**	11	11	11^{1}	11	11	11	11	**11**	**11**	**11**	31	4	7
Pritchard, Howard	7	**7**				★	**10**	11	★^{1}	**8**	★	**8^{1}**		7	★	**11**	11	**11**	★	7	7	7	**7**	7	7^{1}		7	7	7	7^{1}	7	7	7	**7**	**7**	7	7	7	7	7	7	7	7^{1}	7	7	7^{1}	36	5	6
Rees, Mark					★^{1}	★											★	★		★					★	7	★	11	11	11		**11**		★	★	2	2	2	2	2	2	2	2	2	2	2	16	9	1
Rimmer, Stuart																											8	9^{3}	9^{1}	8	8	8	8	8	8^{1}	8	8	8	8	8^{1}	8	**8^{1}**	8^{1}	8	8	**8**	20	0	8
Saville, Andy																																			9^{2}	9	9	9	9	9	9	9^{2}	9	**9**	9	9	12	0	4
Shakespeare, Craig	**4**	4	4	4	4^{1}	**4**	4	4	4	4	4	4	4	4	4	4	4	4	4	4	4^{1}	4	4	4		4	4	4	4	4	4	4	4	4	4	4	4	4^{1}	4	4	4	4	4	4	4	4	45	0	3
Smith, Dean																												6	6	6	6	6	6	6	6		5				6	6	6	6	6	6	15	0	0
Taylor, Alex	9^{2}	9	9	9	9^{1}	9	9	**9**	9	9	9	9	9																																		13	0	3
Taylor, Mark	3	3	3	3	3	3	2	2	2	2	2	2	2	2	2	2	2	3	3	3	3	3	3	3	4^{1}				★							★	3	3	3	3				★	★	3	30	4	1
Own Goals																	1																1																2

FA Cup: 1988-89: 3rd Round: Brentford (H) 1-1, Replay (A) 0-1.
Littlewoods Cup: 1988-89: Shrewsbury T. (A) 2-2 (H) 3-0; 2nd Round: Liverpool (A) 0-1 (H) 1-3.

WATFORD (Division 2)

Team Manager Steve Harrison.
Club Address Vicarage Road Stadium, Watford WD1 8ER. Tel: (0923) 30933.
Current Ground Capacity 26,996.
Record Attendance 34,099 v Manchester U., FA Cup 4th Round, 3 February 1969.
Year Formed 1891. Turned professional 1897.
Previous Names Hertfordshire Rangers, Watford Rovers, West Herts, Watford St Mary's.
Club Nickname "The Hornets".
Club Colours Yellow shirts with black and red facings, black shorts and red stockings with black and yellow tops.
Club Honours Football League: Div. 3 Champions 1968-69; Div. 4 Champions 1977-78.
League History 1920-58 Div. 3(S); 1958-60 Div. 4; 1960-69 Div. 3; 1969-72 Div. 2; 1972-75 Div. 3; 1975-78 Div. 4; 1978-79 Div. 3; 1979-82 Div. 2; 1982-88 Div. 1; 1988- Div. 2.
Most League Points in a Season (2 for a win) 71 in Div. 4, 1977-78. (3 for a win) 80 in Div. 2, 1981-82.
Most League Goals in a Season 92 in Div. 4, 1959-60.
Record Victory 10-1 v Lowestoft T. in FA Cup 1st Round, 27 November 1926.
Record Defeat 0-10 v Wolverhampton W. in FA Cup 1st Round replay, 13 January 1912.
Consecutive League Wins 7 in 1934 and 1977-78.
Consecutive League Defeats 9 in 1972-73.
Record League Appearances Duncan Welbourne, 411 between 1963-74.
Record League Goalscorer—Career Luther Blissett, 149 between 1975-88.
Record League Goalscorer—Season Cliff Holton, 42 in Div. 4, 1959-60.

Watford: League Record, 1988-89 (Division 2)

Match Number	Date	Venue	Opponents	Result	H/T	Lge Posn	Attend
1	27.8.88	H	Birmingham C.	W 1-0	1-0		12656
2	29.8.88	A	West Bromwich A.	W 1-0	1-0	2	10042
3	3.9.88	A	Crystal Palace	W 2-0	1-0	2	10474
4	10.9.88	H	Plymouth Arg.	W 3-0	1-0	1	12040
5	17.9.88	A	Ipswich T.	L 2-3	1-1	1	14644
6	20.9.88	H	Bradford C.	W 2-0	0-0	1	12296
7	24.9.88	A	Leicester C.	D 2-2	1-1	2	10957
8	1.10.88	H	Swindon T.	L 2-3	1-2	3	11657
9	4.10.88	H	Oldham Ath.	W 3-1	2-0	1	10038
10	8.10.88	A	Leeds U.	W 1-0	0-0	1	15657
11	15.10.88	H	Brighton & H.A.	D 1-1	0-0	2	12126
12	22.10.88	A	Stoke C.	L 0-2	0-1	2	7878
13	25.10.88	H	Barnsley	W 4-0	2-0	1	10356
14	29.10.88	A	Walsall	W 1-0	0-0	1	6682
15	5.11.88	H	Chelsea	L 1-2	1-2	1	17631
16	12.11.88	A	Manchester C.	L 1-3	1-0	1	21142
17	19.11.88	A	Shrewsbury T.	D 1-1	0-1	2	4621
18	26.11.88	H	Hull C.	W 2-0	2-0	1	10404
19	3.12.88	A	Sunderland	D 1-1	1-0	1	16330
20	10.12.88	H	Oxford U.	D 1-1	0-1	3	10473
21	17.12.88	A	Blackburn Rov.	L 1-2	0-2	4	8080
22	26.12.88	H	Portsmouth	W 1-0	0-0	4	15224
23	31.12.88	H	Bournemouth	W 1-0	0-0	3	14006
24	2.1.89	A	Plymouth Arg.	L 0-1	0-0	4	12142
25	14.1.89	H	West Bromwich A.	W 2-0	1-0	3	15168
26	21.1.89	A	Birmingham C.	W 3-2	2-2	2	6396
27	4.2.89	A	Oldham Ath.	L 1-3	0-2	3	6364
28	11.2.89	H	Leeds U.	D 1-1	1-0	3	13439
29	25.2.89	A	Brighton & H.A.	L 0-1	0-1	4	9522
30	28.2.89	A	Barnsley	D 2-2	0-1	4	6163
31	4.3.89	H	Manchester C.	W 1-0	1-0	4	15747
32	11.3.89	A	Chelsea	D 2-2	2-2	4	22188
33	18.3.89	A	Bradford C.	L 1-2	0-0	6	10003
34	24.3.89	H	Crystal Palace	L 0-1	0-0	7	15095
35	27.3.89	A	Portsmouth	D 2-2	0-2	8	9364
36	1.4.89	H	Ipswich T.	W 3-2	2-0	5	12054
37	4.4.89	H	Blackburn Rov.	D 2-2	0-0	5	8667
38	8.4.89	A	Bournemouth	W 1-0	1-0	6	9766
39	11.4.89	H	Stoke C.	W 3-2	2-1	6	9086
40	15.4.89	A	Swindon T.	D 1-1	0-1	6	9828
41	18.4.89	H	Walsall	W 5-0	4-0	3	9777
42	22.4.89	H	Leicester C.	W 2-1	1-1	3	11262
43	29.4.89	A	Hull C.	W 3-0	1-0	3	5225
44	1.5.89	H	Sunderland	L 0-1	0-1	3	13499
45	6.5.89	H	Shrewsbury T.	D 0-0	0-0	4	10052
46	13.5.89	A	Oxford U.	W 4-0	1-0	4	6753

Players: League Record, 1988-89 (Division 2)

Match Number	1	2	3	4	5	6	7	8	9	10	11	12	13	14	15	16	17	18	19	20	21	22	23	24	25	26	27	28	29	30	31	32	33	34	35	36	37	38	39	40	41	42	43	44	45	46	Apps	Subs	Goals
Bamber, Dave	9^{1}	8	9	9^{1}	9	9	**9**	9		★	★		**9**	9	**9**	9	9^{1}	9	9	**9**																											16	2	3
Blissett, Luther									9^{1}	9		9																																			3	0	1
Coton, Tony	1	1	1	1	1	1	1	1	1	1	1	1	1	1	1	1	1	1	1	1	1	1	1	1	1	1	1	1	1	1	1	1	1	1	1	1	1	1	1	1	1	1	1	1	1	1	46	0	0
Falconer, Willie	3			3	3	3	3	3					3^{1}	3	3	3	3			★			10	10	10	10	10	10		★	3	3	3	**3**			★	4	4^{1}	4	4	4	4^{1}	4	4	4^{2}	30	3	5
Gibbs, Nigel	2	2^{1}	2	2	2	2	2	2	2	2	2	2	2	2	2	2	2	2	2	2	2	2	2	2	2	2	2	2	2	2	2	2	2	2	2	2	2	2	2	2	2	2	2	2	2	2	46	0	1
Henry, Liburd																																										**9**					1	0	0
Hodges, Glyn	7	7	7	**7**				★	7	7^{1}						7	★	11	11	11	11								11	11^{1}	11	11	11	11	11^{1}	11^{1}	11	11	11^{1}	11	11	**11**					25	2	5
Holden, Richard	11	11	11	11	11	11^{2}	11	11^{1}	11	**11**	**11**	11	11^{1}	11	11	11	**11**					11	11^{1}	**11**	11^{1}	11	**11**	**11**	7	7	7	7	**7**	**7**									11	**11**			32	0	6
Holdsworth, David		5	5	5	5	5	5	5	5	5	5	5	5	5	5	★	5	5	5	5				★		5	5	5	5	5^{1}	5	5	5	5	★				★			★		★			27	6	1
Holdsworth, Dean																					$★^{1}$														★	9	9	★	★	★	★	$★^{1}$			★		2	8	2
Jackett, Kenny	4	4	3	4	4	4	4	4	4	4	4	4	4	4	4	**4**	4	3	3	3	3	3			3	3	3	3	3	3		★	★	★		3	3	3	3	3	3	3	3	3	3	3	39	3	0
McClelland, John	6	6	6	6	6	6	6	6	6	6	6	6				6	6	6	6	6	6	6	6	6	6	6	6	6	6	6	6	6	6	6	6	6	6	6	6	6	6	6	6	6	6	6	43	0	0
Miller, Paul													6	6	6	**5**					5	5	5	5	5											5	5	5	5	5^{1}	5	5	5	**5**	5	5	20	0	1
Morris, Mark	**5**																																		**5**												2	0	0
Porter, Gary	10	10	10^{1}	10^{1}	10	10	10^{1}	10^{1}	10	10	10^{1}	10	10	**10**	10	10^{1}	10	10	10	**10**	10	10	★	★					10	10	10	10	10	10	10	10^{1}	10	10	10^{1}	10	10^{2}	10	10	10	10	10	40	2	10
Pullan, Chris																																			3												1	0	0
Redfearn, Neil																		7	7	7	7	7^{1}	**7**	7	7	7	7^{1}	7																		11	12	0	2
Richardson, Lee																													4	**4**	4	**4**	4	4	4	4	**4**										9	0	0
Rimmer, Stuart											**9**																																				1	0	0
Roberts, Iwan					$\mathbf{7}^{2}$	7	★	**7**				★	$★^{1}$		★		★			★	9	8	★			★	★	★	8	9	9^{1}	$\mathbf{9}^{1}$	9	9												$★^{1}$	11	11	6
Rostron, Wilf		3							3	**3**	3	3											3	3																							7	0	0
Sherwood, Timothy			4							★	★			★		★	**7**	4^{1}	4^{1}	4	4	4	4	**4**	4	4	4	4																★	11		14	5	2
Sterling, Worrell							7				7	**7**																																			3	0	0
Thomas, Rod	★			★	★									7	7	7																			7	7	7^{1}	**7**	**7**	**7**	$\mathbf{7}^{1}$	7	7	7	7	7	15	3	2
Thompson, Garry																						9	9	9	9^{1}	$\mathbf{9}^{2}$	9	9	**9**		★	★		★	**9**		$★^{1}$	9^{1}	9	9	9^{1}		9^{1}	9	**9**	**9**	17	4	7
Wilkinson, Paul	8	9	8^{1}	8^{1}	8	8	8^{1}	8	8^{2}	8	8	8	8^{1}	8^{1}	8^{1}	8	8	8^{1}	8	8^{1}	**8**		**8**	8	8	8^{1}	8	8^{1}	★	8	**8**	8^{1}	8^{1}	8	8	8^{1}	**8**	8	**8**	8	8^{1}	8^{1}	8^{1}	8	8	8^{1}	45	1	19
Own Goals																																			1														1

FA Cup: 1988-89: 3rd Round: Newcastle U. (A) 0-0, Replay (H) 2-2, 2nd Replay (A) 0-0; 3rd Replay (H) 1-0; 4th Round: Derby Co. (H) 2-1; 5th Round: Nottingham F. (H) 0-3.
Littlewoods Cup: 1988-89: 2nd Round: Leicester C. (A) 1-4 (H) 2-2.

WEST BROMWICH ALBION (Division 2)

Team Manager Brian Talbot.
Club Address The Hawthorns, West Bromwich B71 4LF. Tel: 021-525 8888.
Current Ground Capacity 38,400.
Record Attendance 64,815 v Arsenal, FA Cup 6th Round, 6 March 1937.
Year Formed 1879. Turned professional 1885.
Previous Names West Bromwich Strollers.
Club Nicknames "The Throstles", "Baggies" or "Albion".
Club Colours Navy blue and white striped shirts, navy shorts and white stockings.
Club Honours Football League: Div. 1 Champions 1919-20; Div. 2 Champions 1901-02, 1910-11. FA Cup: Winners 1888, 1892, 1931, 1954, 1968. Football League Cup: Winners 1966.
League History 1888-1901 Div. 1; 1901-02 Div. 2; 1902-04 Div. 1; 1904-11 Div. 2; 1911-27 Div. 1; 1927-31 Div. 2; 1931-38 Div. 1; 1938-49 Div. 2; 1949-73 Div. 1; 1973-76 Div. 2; 1976-86 Div. 1; 1986- Div. 2.
Most League Points in a Season (2 for a win) 60 in Div. 1, 1919-20. (3 for a win) 72 in Div. 2, 1988-89.
Most League Goals in a Season 105 in Div. 2, 1929-30.
Record Victory 12-0 v Darwen in Div. 1, 4 April 1892.
Record Defeat 3-10 v Stoke C. in Div. 1, 4 February 1937.
Consecutive League Wins 11 in 1930.
Consecutive League Defeats 9 in 1985.
Record League Appearances Tony Brown, 574 between 1963-80.
Record League Goalscorer—Career Tony Brown, 218 between 1963-80.
Record League Goalscorer—Season William Richardson, 39 in Div. 1, 1935-36.

West Bromwich Albion: League Record, 1988-89 (Division 2)

Match Number	Date	Venue	Opponents	Result	H/T	Lge Posn	Attend
1	27.8.88	A	Leicester C.	D 1-1	0-0		13082
2	29.8.88	H	Watford	L 0-1	0-1	20	10042
3	3.9.88	H	Swindon T.	W 3-1	3-1	10	7518
4	10.9.88	A	Shrewsbury T.	D 1-1	0-0	10	5851
5	17.9.88	H	Walsall	D 0-0	0-0	12	13977
6	21.9.88	A	Brighton & H.A.	W 1-0	0-0	7	7395
7	24.9.88	A	Plymouth Arg.	D 1-1	0-0	9	8539
8	1.10.88	H	Ipswich T.	L 1-2	0-1	11	9357
9	5.10.88	H	Bournemouth	D 0-0	0-0	14	7248
10	8.10.88	A	Barnsley	L 1-2	1-0	18	5674
11	15.10.88	A	Birmingham C.	W 4-1	2-1	13	10453
12	22.10.88	H	Bradford C.	W 1-0	0-0	9	8989
13	26.10.88	H	Manchester C.	W 1-0	1-0	6	14258
14	29.10.88	A	Blackburn Rov.	W 2-1	1-1	3	9503
15	5.11.88	H	Oxford U.	W 3-2	1-1	2	11643
16	12.11.88	A	Leeds U.	L 1-2	1-2	5	20442
17	19.11.88	A	Sunderland	D 1-1	1-0	6	18141
18	26.11.88	H	Crystal Palace	W 5-3	1-0	6	11099
19	3.12.88	A	Portsmouth	D 0-0	0-0	6	12779
20	10.12.88	H	Hull C.	W 2-0	0-0	5	10094
21	18.12.88	H	Stoke C.	W 6-0	2-0	3	17634
22	26.12.88	A	Oldham Ath.	W 3-1	2-0	2	9827
23	31.12.88	A	Chelsea	D 1-1	1-0	2	25906
24	2.1.89	H	Shrewsbury T.	W 4-0	0-0	1	18411
25	14.1.89	A	Watford	L 0-2	0-1	2	15168
26	21.1.89	H	Leicester C.	D 1-1	0-0	4	15792
27	4.2.89	A	Bournemouth	L 1-2	1-1	5	11571
28	11.2.89	H	Barnsley	D 1-1	0-1	5	12650
29	18.2.89	A	Bradford C.	L 0-2	0-1	5	11047
30	25.2.89	H	Birmingham C.	D 0-0	0-0	5	16148
31	1.3.89	A	Manchester C.	D 1-1	0-0	5	25109
32	5.3.89	H	Leeds U.	D 2-1	2-1	5	15964
33	11.3.89	A	Oxford U.	D 1-1	1-1	6	7581
34	15.3.89	H	Blackburn Rov.	W 2-0	1-0	4	12821
35	18.3.89	H	Brighton & H.A.	W 1-0	0-0	3	11586
36	25.3.89	A	Swindon T.	D 0-0	0-0	3	12240
37	27.3.89	H	Oldham Ath.	W 3-1	0-0	3	13812
38	1.4.89	A	Walsall	D 0-0	0-0	3	9520
39	4.4.89	A	Stoke C.	D 0-0	0-0	3	11151
40	8.4.89	H	Chelsea	L 2-3	2-3	4	22858
41	15.4.89	H	Plymouth Arg.	D 2-2	1-0	5	11358
42	22.4.89	A	Ipswich T.	L 1-2	0-0	6	12047
43	29.4.89	A	Crystal Palace	L 0-1	0-0	7	13728
44	1.5.89	H	Portsmouth	W 3-0	1-0	7	9506
45	6.5.89	H	Sunderland	D 0-0	0-0	9	10451
46	13.5.89	A	Hull C.	W 1-0	1-0	9	5217

Players: League Record, 1988-89 (Division 2)

Match Number	1	2	3	4	5	6	7	8	9	10	11	12	13	14	15	16	17	18	19	20	21	22	23
Albiston, Arthur	3	3	3	3		2	2	2	2	2	2	3	3	3	3	3	3	3	3	3	3	3	3
Anderson, Colin	11	11	11	11	11	11	11	11	11	11	11	11	11	11^{1}	11^{1}		11	11	11	11	11	11	11^{1}
Banko, Ian																							
Bartlett, Kevin																							
Bradley, Darren	2	2	4	★						★	★	2				2	2	2	7	**7**			
Bradshaw, Paul																							
Burrows, David			★	★	3	3	3	3	3	3	3												
Cartwright, Neil																							
Cork, David					★	★	★			**8**													
Dobbins, Wayne													2	2	2						7	4	
Durnin, John												9	8^{1}	**8**	**8**	8^{1}							
Dyson, Paul	5	5	**5**^{1}																				
Ford, Tony																							
Goodman, Don	8		8^{1}	8	8	8^{1}	8	8	8					★	★^{1}	11	8	8^{3}	8	8^{2}	8^{2}	8^{1}	8
Gray, Andy		8	★	**9**																			
Hodson, Simeon			2	2	**2**														2	2	2	2	2
Hopkins, Robert	7	7	7	7	7	7	7	7	7	**7**	**7**^{2}	7	7	7	7^{1}	7	7	7^{1}				7^{1}	7
Naylor, Stuart	1	1	1	1	1	1	1	1	1	1	1	1	1	1	1	1	1	1	1	1	1	1	1
North, Stacey	6	6	6	6	6	6	6	6	6	6	6	6	6	6	6	6	6	6	6	6	6	6	6
Palmer, Carlton	10	10	10	10	10	10	**10**	10	10	10	10	10	10	10	10	10	10	10	10	10			
Paskin, John	9^{1}	9	**9**^{1}		**9**	**9**										★	★	★^{1}	★	★	10^{2}	10	10
Phillips, Stuart							9^{1}	9	9	9	9^{1}												
Raven, Paul																							
Rice, Brian																							
Robinson, Ronnie																							
Robson, Gary			4^{1}	★						★	8^{1}	8	9	9	9	**9**	**9**^{1}	9	**9**	9	9^{2}	9^{1}	9
Talbot, Brian	4	4			4	4	4	4	4	4^{1}	4	4^{1}	4	4	4	4	4	**4**	4	4	4		4
Walford, Steve																							
West, Colin																							
Whyte, Chris				5	5	5	5	5^{1}	5	5	5	5	5	5^{1}	5	5	5	5	5	5	5	5	5
Own Goals																							

Match Number	24	25	26	27	28	29	30	31	32	33	34	35	36	37	38	39	40	41	42	43	44	45	46	Apps	Subs	Goals
Albiston, Arthur	3^{1}	3	3	3^{1}	3	3	3	**3**	**3**		3	3	3	3	3	3	3	3	3	3	3	3		43	0	2
Anderson, Colin	11				11	11	11	11	11	11	11	11	11	11^{1}	11	11	11^{1}	11	11	**11**	11^{1}	11	11	42	0	6
Banko, Ian														★		★	10		4					2	2	0
Bartlett, Kevin						9	★	10	10	10	10	10^{1}	★	★^{1}	8	8	★	★	**7**		★	★	**8**^{1}	10	7	3
Bradley, Darren		11	**2**				2	2	7	7	2	2	2	2	2	2	6	**2**						23	3	0
Bradshaw, Paul	1	1																						2	0	0
Burrows, David																								7	2	0
Cartwright, Neil			★																					0	1	0
Cork, David																								1	3	0
Dobbins, Wayne	★	**2**	★	2	2			★	2	2							2		★	2				12	4	0
Durnin, John																								5	0	2
Dyson, Paul																								3	0	1
Ford, Tony													7	7	7	7	7^{1}	7	2	7	7	7	7	11	0	1
Goodman, Don	8^{1}				8^{1}	8	**8**	8	8^{2}	8	8	8	**8**	**8**			**8**	8	**8**	★	★	★	★	30	6	15
Gray, Andy																								2	1	0
Hodson, Simeon	**2**																							9	0	0
Hopkins, Robert	7	7	7	7	7	7	7	7				★												28	1	5
Naylor, Stuart			1	1	1	1	1	1	1	1	1	1	1	1	1	1	1	1	1	1	1	1	1	44	0	0
North, Stacey	6	6	6	6	6	6	6	6	6	6	6	6	6	6	6	6	5	6	6	6	6	6	6	46	0	0
Palmer, Carlton	10	10	10	10	10	10																		26	0	0
Paskin, John	★	8	**8**	8	★				★							★			★	8	**8**	**8**	★	14	11	5
Phillips, Stuart																								5	0	2
Raven, Paul																					2	2	2	3	0	0
Rice, Brian		★	11	11																				2	1	0
Robinson, Ronnie																							3	1	0	0
Robson, Gary	**9**^{1}	9	9^{1}	9	9	2	10	4	**4**	4	7	**7**	10	10	10	**10**		10	10	10	10	**10**	10	36	2	8
Talbot, Brian	4	4	4	4	**4**	4	4				4	4	4	**4**	4	4	4	4		4	4	4	**4**	39	0	2
Walford, Steve									★	3			5		5									3	1	0
West, Colin							9	9	9	9^{1}	9^{2}	9	9	9^{1}	9	9	9	9^{1}	9^{1}	9	**9**^{2}	9	9	17	0	8
Whyte, Chris	5	5	5	5	5	5	5	5^{1}	5	5	5	5		5		**5**		5	5	5	5	5	5	40	0	3
Own Goals	1																	1								2

FA Cup: 1988-89: 3rd Round: Everton (H) 1-1, Replay (A) 0-1.
Littlewoods Cup: 1988-89: 1st Round: Peterborough U. (H) 0-3 (A) 2-0.

WEST HAM UNITED (Division 2)

Team Manager
Club Address Boleyn Ground, Green Street, Upton Park, London E13. Tel: 01-472 2740.
Current Ground Capacity 35,510.
Record Attendance 42,322 v Tottenham H., Div. 1, 17 October 1970.
Year Formed 1895. Turned professional 1900.
Previous Names Thames Ironworks.
Club Nickname "The Hammers".
Club Colours Claret shirts with single blue hoop, white shorts and stockings.
Club Honours Football League: Div. 2 Champions 1957-58, 1980-81. FA Cup: Winners 1964, 1975, 1980. European Cup-Winners Cup: Winners 1964-65.
League History 1919-23 Div. 2; 1923-32 Div. 1; 1932-58 Div. 2; 1958-78 Div. 1; 1978-81 Div. 2; 1981-89 Div. 1; 1989-Div. 2.

Most League Points in a Season (2 for a win) 66 in Div. 2, 1980-81. (3 for a win) 84 in Div. 1, 1985-86.
Most League Goals in a Season 101 in Div. 2, 1957-58.
Record Victory 10-0 v Bury in Milk Cup 2nd Round 2nd Leg, 25 October 1983.
Record Defeat 2-8 v Blackburn Rov. in Div. 1, 26 December 1963.
Consecutive League Wins 9 in 1985.
Consecutive League Defeats 9 in 1932.
Record League Appearances Billy Bonds, 663 between 1967-88.
Record League Goalscorer—Career Vic Watson, 306 between 1920-35.
Record League Goalscorer—Season Vic Watson, 41 in Div. 1, 1929-30.

West Ham United: League Record, 1988-89 (Division 1)

Match Number	Date	Venue	Opponents	Result	H/T	Lge Posn	Attend
1	27.8.88	A	Southampton	L 0-4	0-2		18407
2	3.9.88	H	Charlton Ath.	L 1-3	0-1	20	19566
3	10.9.88	A	Wimbledon	W 1-0	1-0	13	7730
4	17.9.88	H	Aston Villa	W 2-2	0-2	13	19186
5	24.9.88	A	Manchester U.	L 0-2	0-1	17	39941
6	1.10.88	H	Arsenal	L 1-4	1-2	20	27658
7	8.10.88	A	Middlesbrough	L 0-1	0-1	20	19608
8	15.10.88	A	Q.P.R.	L 1-2	1-0	20	14566
9	22.10.88	H	Newcastle U.	W 2-0	0-0	18	17765
10	29.10.88	H	Liverpool	L 0-2	0-0	19	30198
11	5.11.88	A	Coventry C.	D 1-1	1-0	18	14651
12	12.11.88	H	Nottingham F.	D 3-3	2-3	17	21682
13	19.11.88	A	Luton T.	L 1-4	0-3	18	9378
14	26.11.88	H	Everton	L 0-1	0-0	19	22176
15	3.12.88	A	Millwall	W 1-0	1-0	19	20105
116	10.12.88	H	Sheffield Wed.	D 0-0	0-0	19	16676
17	17.12.88	H	Tottenham H.	L 0-2	0-1	20	28365
18	27.12.88	A	Norwich C.	L 1-2	0-0	20	17491
19	31.12.88	A	Charlton Ath.	D 0-0	0-0	20	11084
20	2.1.89	H	Wimbledon	L 1-2	1-1	20	18346
21	14.1.89	A	Derby Co	W 2-1	2-1	19	16796
22	21.1.89	H	Manchester U.	L 1-3	1-1	19	29822
23	4.2.89	A	Arsenal	L 1-2	0-0	20	40139
24	25.2.89	H	Q.P.R.	D 0-0	0-0	20	17371
25	11.3.89	H	Coventry C.	D 1-1	0-1	20	15205
26	25.3.89	A	Aston Villa	W 1-0	1-0	20	22471
27	27.3.89	H	Norwich C.	L 0-2	0-0	20	27265
28	1.4.89	A	Tottenham H.	L 0-3	0-1	20	28375
29	8.4.89	H	Derby Co.	D 1-1	1-1	20	16560
30	11.4.89	H	Middlesbrough	L 1-2	1-0	20	16217
31	15.4.89	H	Southampton	L 1-2	1-1	20	14766
32	22.4.89	H	Millwall	W 3-0	3-0	20	16603
33	3.5.89	A	Newcastle U.	W 2-1	1-1	20	14202
34	6.5.89	H	Luton T.	W 1-0	1-0	19	18686
35	9.5.89	A	Sheffield Wed.	W 2-0	0-0	19	19905
36	13.5.89	A	Everton	L 1-3	1-1	19	21694
37	18.5.89	A	Nottingham F.	W 2-1	2-1	19	20843
38	23.5.89	A	Liverpool	L 1-5	1-1	19	41885

Players: League Record, 1988-89 (Division 1)

Match Number	1	2	3	4	5	6	7	8	9	10	11	12	13	14	15	16	17	18	19
Brady, Liam												★	8	8	7	7	7	7	7
Devonshire, Alan		★	★	★	★	★	6	6	6	6				★	6	6	6	6	
Dickens, Alan	★	4	10	10	10	10^1	10	10	10^1	10	10	10	10	10	10	10	10	10	10
Dicks, Julian	3	3	3	3	3	3	3	3	3	3	3	3	3	3	3				3
Gale, Tony	4						4	4	4	4	4	4	4	4	4	4	4	4	4
Hilton, Paul	★		4		5	4	5	5					★						
Ince, Paul		★	6	6	6	6	11	11	11	11	11	11	11	11	11^1	11	11	11	
Keen, Kevin	6	6^1					★	★	★		6	6	6	6			★	★	11
Kelly, David	10	10	8	8^1	8	8	8	8^1	8	8	8^1	8^2			8	8	8	8	8
McAlister, Tom	1	1																	
McAvennie, Frank																			
McKnight, Allen			1	1	1	1	1	1	1	1	1	1	1	1	1	1	1	1	1
McQueen, Tommy																			
Martin, Alvin	5	5	5	5		5			5	5	5	5	5^1	5	5	5	5	5	5
Parkes, Phil																			
Parris, George	8	8	2	2	2	2	9					★	★			3	3	3	★
Potts, Steven	2	2					2	2			2	2	2	2	2	2	2	2	2
Robson, Stewart	11	11	11	11	11	11													
Rosenior, Leroy			9	9	9	9		9		★	9	9^1	9	9	9	9	9	9	9
Slater, Stuart	9	9							9	9									
Stewart, Ray									2^1	2								$★^1$	6
Strodder, Gary				4	4	★													
Ward, Mark	7	7	7^1	7	7	7	7	7	7	7	7	7	7	7					
Own Goals				1															

Match Number	20	21	22	23	24	25	26	27	28	29	30	31	32	33	34	35	36	37	38	Apps	Subs	Goals
Brady, Liam	7	7^1	7^1	10	10	10	10	10	10	10	10	10^1						11	10	21	1	3
Devonshire, Alan		6	6	6	6	6	6													14	6	0
Dickens, Alan	10	10		8	8	8	★	6	★	6	6	6	6^1	6	6^1	6^1	6	6	6	34	3	5
Dicks, Julian	3	3	3	3^1	3	3	3	3	3	3	3		3^1	3	3	3	3	3	3	34	0	2
Gale, Tony	4	4	4	4	4	4	4	4	4	4			4	4	4	4	4	4	4	31	0	0
Hilton, Paul							5	5			5	5								9	2	0
Ince, Paul		11	11	11	11	11^1	11^1	11	11	11		11	11	11	11	11	11		11	32	1	3
Keen, Kevin	11	★	★								11^1	3	10	10^1	10	10	10	10	★	16	8	3
Kelly, David	8	8^1	8	★		7								★	★		★			21	4	6
McAlister, Tom																				2	0	0
McAvennie, Frank							8	8	8	8	8	8	8	8					★	8	1	0
McKnight, Allen	1	1	1	1														1	1	23	0	0
McQueen, Tommy												★	★							0	2	0
Martin, Alvin	5		5		5	5				5				5	5	5	5	5	5	27	0	1
Parkes, Phil					1	1	1	1	1	1	1	1	1	1	1	1	1			13	0	0
Parris, George					★		2	2	2	2	2	2	2^1	2	2	2	2	2	2	23	4	1
Potts, Steven	2	5	2	2	2	2			6	★	4	4	5		★	★	★	★		23	5	0
Robson, Stewart																				6	0	0
Rosenior, Leroy	9^1	9	9	9				★		9^1	9	9			9	9^1	9	9^2	9^1	26	2	7
Slater, Stuart					9	9	9	9	9	★		★	9	9	8	8	8^1	8	8	16	2	1
Stewart, Ray	6	2																		5	1	2
Strodder, Gary		★	★	5					5											4	3	0
Ward, Mark			10	7	7		7	7	7	7	7	7	7^1	7	7	7	7	7	7	30	0	2
Own Goals																						1

FA Cup: 1988-89: 3rd Round: Arsenal (H) 2-2, Replay (A) 1-0; 4th Round: Swindon T. (A) 0-0, Replay (H) 1-0; 5th Round: Charlton Ath. (A) 1-0; Quarter-Final: Norwich C. (H) 0-0, Replay (A) 1-3.
Littlewoods Cup: 1988-89: 2nd Round: Sunderland (A) 3-0 (H) 2-1; 3rd Round: Derby Co. (H) 5-0; 4th Round: Liverpool (H) 4-1; Quarter-Final: Aston Villa (H) 2-1; Semi-Final: Luton T. (H) 0-3 (A) 0-2.

WIGAN ATHLETIC (Division 3)

Team Manager Brian Hamilton.
Club Address Springfield Park, Wigan. Tel: (0942) 44,433.
Current Ground Capacity 12,500.
Record Attendance 27,500 v Hereford U., FA Cup, 12 December 1953.
Year Formed 1932. Turned Professional 1932.
Previous Names None.
Club Nickname "The Latics".
Club Colours Royal blue shirts and shorts and white stockings.
Club Honours None.
League History 1978-82 Div. 4; 1982- Div.3.
Most League Points in a Season (2 for a win) 55 in Div 4, 1978-79 and in 1979-80. (3 for a win) 91 in Div. 4, 1981-82.
Most League Goals in a Season 80 in Div. 4, 1981-82.
Record Victory 7-2 v Scunthorpe U. in Div. 4, 12 March 1982.
Record Defeat 0-5 v Bristol Rov. in Div. 3, 26 February 1983 and v Chelsea in FA Cup 3rd Round replay, 26 January 1985.
Consecutive League Wins 6 in 1985 and 1986-87.
Consecutive League Defeats 5 in 1983.
Record League Appearances Colin Methven, 296 between 1979-86.
Record League Goalscorer—Career Peter Houghton, 62 between 1978-84.
Record League Goalscorer—Season Les Bradd, 19 in Div. 4, 1981-82.

Wigan Athletic: League Record, 1988-89 (Division 3)

Match Number	Date	Venue	Opponents	Result	H/T	Lge Posn	Attend
1	27.8.88	A	Bristol Rov.	L 2-3	2-1		4080
2	3.9.88	H	Mansfield T.	D 0-0	0-0	19	2514
3	10.9.88	A	Brentford	D 1-1	0-1	21	4081
4	17.9.88	H	Reading	W 3-0	1-0	11	2534
5	24.9.88	A	Fulham	D 1-1	1-0	15	3431
6	30.9.88	H	Blackpool	W 2-1	1-0	13	4141
7	4.10.88	A	Aldershot	L 1-3	0-1	16	1527
8	8.10.88	H	Port Vale	L 0-2	0-0	19	3976
9	15.10.88	A	Wolverhampton W.	L 1-2	1-2	19	10320
10	22.10.88	A	Sheffield U.	L 1-2	0-1	20	11763
11	25.10.88	H	Bolton W.	D 1-1	0-0	20	4438
12	28.10.88	A	Southend U.	W 2-1	1-0	17	3120
13	1.11.88	H	Swansea C.	L 1-2	1-1	17	2432
14	5.11.88	H	Northampton T.	L 1-3	1-2	19	2472
15	8.11.88	A	Preston N.E.	D 2-2	2-1	18	8396
16	12.11.88	H	Bristol C.	L 0-1	0-0	20	2675
17	26.11.88	H	Huddersfield T.	L 0-2	0-1	21	2779
18	3.12.88	A	Bury	D 1-1	0-1	21	3121
19	10.12.88	H	Southend U.	W 3-0	1-0	19	2027
20	18.12.88	H	Notts Co.	L 0-1	0-0	21	3010
21	26.12.88	A	Chester C.	L 0-1	0-0	21	3262
22	30.12.88	A	Cardiff C.	D 2-2	1-0	21	4621
23	2.1.89	H	Gillingham	W 3-0	2-0	20	3090
24	7.1.89	H	Chesterfield	L 0-2	0-2	21	2249
25	14.1.89	A	Mansfield T.	W 1-0	1-0	18	2788
26	21.1.89	H	Brentford	D 1-1	1-1	19	2514
27	4.2.89	A	Blackpool	L 0-2	0-0	20	4221
28	11.2.89	H	Aldershot	W 2-1	0-1	19	2132
29	18.2.89	A	Port Vale	L 1-2	0-1	20	6100
30	4.3.89	H	Sheffield U.	L 1-2	0-1	22	3966
31	11.3.89	A	Northampton T.	D 1-1	0-0	22	3443
32	24.3.89	A	Gillingham	L 1-2	1-0	22	3244
33	27.3.89	H	Chester C.	W 3-0	1-0	22	3132
34	1.4.89	A	Notts Co.	L 0-1	0-1	22	4929
35	4.4.89	A	Chesterfield	D 1-1	1-0	22	3179
36	7.4.89	H	Cardiff C.	W 1-0	0-0	22	2083
37	15.4.89	A	Swansea C.	W 2-1	1-0	22	3719
38	19.4.89	A	Reading	W 3-0	2-0	20	3821
39	22.4.89	H	Fulham	L 0-1	0-0	21	3056
40	29.4.89	A	Bristol C.	W 1-0	0-0	20	5156
41	1.5.89	H	Preston N.E.	D 1-1	0-1	21	5671
42	3.5.89	H	Bristol Rov.	W 3-0	1-0	20	2529
43	6.5.89	H	Bury	W 1-0	0-0	17	3045
44	9.5.89	A	Bolton W.	D 1-1	0-1	17	6166
45	13.5.89	A	Huddersfield T.	D 1-1	0-1	18	4225
46	16.5.89	H	Wolverhampton W.	D 1-1	0-1	18	5531

Players: League Record, 1988-89 (Division 3)

Match Number	1	2	3	4	5	6	7	8	9	10	11	12	13	14	15	16	17	18	19	20	21	22	23	24	25	26	27	28	29	30	31	32	33	34	35	36	37	38	39	40	41	42	43	44	45	46	Apps	Subs	Goals
Adkins, Nigel										1	1	1	1	1	1	1	1	1	1	1	1	1	1	1	1	1	1	1	1	1								1	1	1	1	1	1	1	1	1	30	0	0
Ainscow, Andrew																	11	11	10	10	10			★																			★				5	2	0
Atherton, Peter	2					2	2	2	★	★^{1}	2	2	2	2			4	2	2	2	2	**2**	2	2	2	2	**2**	2	2	2	2	2	2	2	4	4	4	4	4	4	4	4	4	4	4	4	38	2	1
Beesley, Paul	5	5	5	5	5	5	5	**5**	5	5	5	5	5	5	5	5	3	5	5	5	5	5	5	5		6	6	6	6	6	5	5	5	5	5^{1}	5		5	5	5	5^{1}	5	5	5	5	5	44	0	2
Butler, John	4	4	4	4	4^{1}	4^{1}	4	4	2	2	9	8^{1}	8	8	8	8	8	3	3	3																											20	0	3
Diamond, Anthony												10	10^{1}	10	10^{1}	10	10																														6	0	2
Entwistle, Wayne										10	10^{1}	9	9	**9**^{1}	9	9	9	9^{1}	9	**9**	9	9^{1}	9^{1}	**9**	9	9	9	9	**9**	**9**				★	★		★		★	9				★	10^{1}	10	24	5	6
Fallon, Shaun																																														**8**	1	0	0
Griffiths, Bryan														**11**					11^{1}	11	11	11^{1}	11	11	11	11	11	11^{1}	11^{1}	11	11	11^{1}	**11**^{1}	11	11	11	**11**	11	11	11	11	11^{1}	**11**	11	**11**	11^{1}	29	0	8
Hamilton, David					★	10	10	10	4	4	4	**4**^{1}				4				★	4	4	4^{1}	4			★	★	**4**																		13	4	2
Hemming, Chris																										5	5	5	5																		4	0	0
Hilditch, Mark	9	9	9	9^{1}	9	**9**			**9**^{1}	**9**								10		★	8	10	10^{1}	10	10					★	6	6	6	6	6	6	6	6	6								23	2	3
Holden, Andy	6	6	6	6	6	6	6	6	6	6	6	6	6	6	6		5	6	6^{1}	6	6	6	6	6																							23	0	1
Hughes, Philip	1	1	1	1	1	1	1	1	1																						1	1	1	1	1	1	1										16	0	0
Johnson, Alan																									5		★		★	**5**							5						★^{1}	8		★	4	4	1
McEwan, Stan								★						★		6	6																											★	8		3	3	0
Page, Don																																10	10	**10**	10	10	10^{1}	10^{1}	10	10	10	10	10	**10**	★	★	13	2	2
Parkinson, Joseph						★																			4^{1}	4	**4**	4	★	4	4		★	★	2	2											8	4	1
Pilling, Andrew	7	8	8	8	8	8	8	8	8	8	8	★	4	4	4		**7**	8	8	**8**		8	8	8	8	8	8	8	8	8	8^{1}	8	8	8						6	6	6^{1}	6	**6**	6	6	38	1	2
Ramage, Craig																															9	**9**	9^{1}	**9**	**9**	9^{1}	9	9	**9**		**9**						10	0	2
Rimmer, Neill	11^{1}	11	11^{1}	11	11	11^{1}	11	11	11	11	11	11	**11**	★	11	11																			8	8	8	8	8	8	8	8	**8**				24	1	3
Russell, Colin	10^{1}	10	10	10^{2}	**10**		7	7	10																																						8	0	3
Senior, Steve	8	2	2	2	2		9	9	3	3	3	3	3	3	2	2	2	4	4	4	3	3	3		6	10	10	10	10	10^{1}	10	4	4^{1}	4	3	3	2	2	2	2	2	2	2	2	2	2	44	0	2
Tankard, Allen	3	3	3	3	3	3	3	3					★		3	3						★		3	3	3	3	**3**	3	3	3	3	3	3			3	3	3	3^{1}	3	3	3	3	3	3	31	2	1
Thompson, David		7	7	7	7	7			7	7	7	7	7	7	7^{1}	7		7	7^{1}	7	7	7	7	7	7	7^{1}	7	7^{1}	7	7	7	7	7	7	7	7	7	7^{1}	7	7	7	7^{1}	7	7^{1}	7	7	42	0	7
Wilson, Andrew																	★																														0	1	0
Woods, Ray																														★		★									★	9	9	9	9	**9**	5	3	0
Own Goals							1																														1	1											3

FA Cup: 1988-89: 1st Round: Hartlepool U. (A) 0-2.
Littlewoods Cup: 1988-89: 1st Round: Preston N.E. (H) 0-0 (A) 0-1.

WIMBLEDON (Division 1)

Team Manager Bobby Gould.
Club Address Plough Lane Ground, Durnsford Road, Wimbledon, London SW19. Tel: 01-946 6311.
Current Ground Capacity 16,000
Record Attendance 18,000 v HMS Victory, FA Amateur Cup 3rd Round, 1934-35.
Year Formed 1889. Turned professional 1964.
Previous Names Wimbledon Old Centrals.
Club Nickname "The Dons".
Club Colours Royal blue shirts with yellow trim, blue shorts with yellow trim and blue stockings.
Club Honours Football League: Div. 4 Champions 1982-83. FA Cup: Winners 1988.
League History 1977-79 Div. 4; 1979-80 Div. 3; 1980-81 Div. 4; 1981-82 Div. 3; 1982-83 Div. 4; 1983-84 Div. 3; 1984-86 Div. 2; 1986- Div. 1.
Most League Points in a Season (2 for a win) 61 in Div. 4, 1978-79. (3 for a win) 98 in Div. 4, 1982-83.
Most League Goals in a Season 97 in Div. 3, 1983-84.
Record Victory 15-2 v Polytechnic in FA Cup Preliminary Round, 7 February 1929.
Record Defeat 0-8 v Everton in League Cup 2nd Round, 29 August 1978.
Consecutive League Wins 7 in 1983.
Consecutive League Defeats 4 in 1982.
Record League Appearances Alan Cork, 341 between 1978-89.
Record League Goalscorer—Career Alan Cork, 133 between 1978-89.
Record League Goalscorer—Season Alan Cork, 29 in Div. 3, 1983-84.

Wimbledon: League Record, 1988-89 (Division 1)

Match Number	Date	Venue	Opponents	Result	H/T	Lge Posn	Attend
1	27.8.88	H	Arsenal	W 1-5	1-3		15710
2	3.9.88	A	Luton T.	D 2-2	1-1	16	8067
3	10.9.88	H	West Ham U.	L 0-1	0-1	18	7730
4	17.9.88	A	Middlesbrough	L 0-1	0-1	19	17709
5	24.9.88	H	Coventry C.	L 0-1	0-1	20	4474
6	1.10.88	H	Everton	W 2-1	2-0	19	6367
7	8.10.88	A	Aston Villa	W 1-0	0-0	18	15146
8	22.10.88	H	Manchester U.	D 1-1	0-1	17	12143
9	29.10.88	A	Derby Co.	L 1-4	1-1	17	15050
10	5.11.88	H	Norwich C.	L 0-2	0-1	17	5853
11	12.11.88	A	Tottenham H.	L 2-3	1-1	19	23587
12	19.11.88	H	Charlton Ath.	D 1-1	0-0	17	5631
13	26.11.88	A	Liverpool	D 1-1	0-0	18	36188
14	3.12.88	H	Southampton	W 2-1	1-1	18	6040
15	10.12.88	A	Newcastle U.	L 1-2	0-1	18	20146
16	18.12.88	A	Nottingham F.	W 1-0	0-0	17	16427
17	26.12.88	H	Millwall	W 1-0	0-0	17	11398
18	31.12.88	H	Luton T.	W 4-0	2-0	14	4899
19	2.1.89	A	West Ham U.	W 2-1	1-1	12	18346
20	14.1.89	H	Q.P.R.	W 1-0	1-0	10	7118
21	21.1.89	A	Coventry C.	L 1-2	1-1	11	12472
22	4.2.89	A	Everton	D 1-1	1-1	12	23365
23	11.2.89	H	Aston Villa	W 1-0	1-0	10	6201
24	25.2.89	H	Sheffield Wed.	W 1-0	1-0	9	4384
25	1.3.89	H	Derby Co.	W 4-0	3-0	9	4207
26	11.3.89	A	Norwich C.	L 0-1	0-0	9	15159
27	25.3.89	H	Middlesbrough	D 1-1	1-1	10	5275
28	27.3.89	A	Millwall	W 1-0	0-0	9	13679
29	1.4.89	H	Nottingham F.	W 4-1	2-1	8	7867
30	5.4.89	A	Sheffield Wed.	D 1-1	0-0	8	15777
31	8.4.89	A	Q.P.R.	L 3-4	1-3	8	9569
32	15.4.89	H	Tottenham H.	L 1-2	0-1	9	12366
33	22.4.89	A	Southampton	D 0-0	0-0	9	13805
34	29.4.89	H	Newcastle U.	W 4-0	1-0	9	5206
35	2.5.89	A	Manchester U.	L 0-1	0-0	9	23368
36	6.5.89	A	Charlton Ath.	L 0-1	0-1	9	7230
37	13.5.89	H	Liverpool	L 1-2	1-0	12	14730
38	17.5.89	A	Arsenal	D 2-2	1-1	12	39132

Players: League Record, 1988-89 (Division 1)

Match Number	1	2	3	4	5	6	7	8	9	10	11	12	13	14	15	16	17	18	19	20	21	22	23	24	25	26	27	28	29	30	31	32	33	34	35	36	37	38	Apps	Subs	Goals
Brooke, Gary		★	★	**11**		7	7	**7**	★			★																			★	**7**							5	5	0
Cawley, Peter	**6**																																						1	0	0
Clement, Andy					3	3	3	3	3				★											★					3	3	3				3				9	2	0
Cork, Alan	★		10	★	★	8[1]	8	8	**8**	★	★	**8**	★	★		★			★	9			★	★				★		★				★	★	9	★	**10**[1]	9	16	2
Cotterill, Steve																																	★	★[1]	★	★			0	4	1
Curle, Keith								★		★	7	6	6	6	6	6	6	6	6	6	6	6	6	6	6	**6**													16	2	0
Fairweather, Carlton	8	8[1]	8	8	**8**			★	7	**11**	★	7	**7**	7[1]	7	7	7[1]	7	7	**7**	7	7	7	**7**	7	7						★				**7**			23	3	3
Fashanu, John	**9**[1]	9[1]	9	9	9	9[1]	**9**		9	9	**9**	9[1]	9			9	9	9[1]	9			9	9[1]	9[1]	9[1]	9	9	9[1]	9[1]	9[1]	9[1]	9	9				9	9	30	0	12
Fiore, Mark																																		**5**					1	0	0
Gayle, John																																		**9**	**9**				2	0	0
Gibson, Terry	7	**7**	7	7	**7**					8	8[2]		**8**	8[1]	8[1]	**8**	8	8[1]	**8**	8	8	**8**																	17	0	5
Green, Ron		1	1	1	1																																		4	0	0
Hazel, Ian				4																																			1	0	0
Jones, Vince					4	4	4	4	4[1]	4	4	4	4	4	**4**	4	4	4[1]	4	4	4	4	4				4	4	4	4	4	4	4	4[1]	4	4	4	4	31	0	3
Joseph, Roger	2	2	2	2	2	2	2	2	2	2	2	**2**	2	**2**						★			5	5	5	5	6	6	6	6	**6**	2	2	2	2	2	**2**	2	30	1	0
Kruszynski, Zbigniew																			★			★		4	4	4	7	7	7	7	**7**		7	7	7	★	7	7	13	3	0
McGee, Paul																																						8[1]	1	0	1
Miller, Paul															9						9		**8**	**8**	8[3]	8	8	**8**	8[1]	8	8	8	**8**	8[1]	**8**	8	8	★	17	1	5
Phelan, Terry	3	3	3	3						3	3	3		★	2	2	3	3	3	3	3	3	3	3	3	3	3	3			★	3	3	3		3	3	**3**	27	2	0
Quamina, Mark																																					**10**		1	0	0
Ryan, Vaughan	4	4	**4**											10	★																								4	1	0
Sanchez, Lawrie	10	**10**		10	10	10	10	10	10	10	10	10	10		10	10[1]	10	10	10	10	10	10[1]	10	10	**10**	10	10	10	10[2]	10	10[1]	10	10	10	10	**10**	★	★	34	2	5
Scales, John	★	6	6	6	6	6	6[1]	6	6	6	6	★	3	3	3	3	2	2[1]	2	2[1]	2[1]	2	2	2	2	2	2[1]	2	2	2	2	6	6	6	6	6	6	6	36	2	5
Segers, Hans						1	1	1	1	1	1	1	1	1	1	1	1	1	1	1	1	1	1	1	1	1	1	1	1	1	1	1	1	1	1	1	1	1	33	0	0
Tracey, Simon	1																																						1	0	0
Turner, Robert		★			★		★	**9**						**9**						★																			2	4	0
Wise, Dennis	11	11	11		11	11	11	11[1]	11	**7**	**11**	11	11	11	11	11	11	11	**11**[1]	11	11	11	11	11	11	11	11	11	11	11	11[1]	11	11	11[1]	11	11	11	11	37	0	4
Young, Eric	5	5	5	5	5	5	5	5	5	5	5	5	5	5	5	5	5	5	5	**5**	5	5			★	★	5	5	5	**5**	5	5[1]	5		5	5	5	5	33	2	1
Own Goals													1						1																		1				3

FA Cup: 1988-89: 3rd Round: Birmingham C. (A) 1-0; 4th Round: Aston Villa (A) 1-0; 5th Round: Grimsby T. (H) 3-1; Quarter-Final: Everton (A) 0-1.
Littlewoods Cup: 1988-89: 2nd Round: Barnsley (A) 2-0 (H) 0-1; 3rd Round: Manchester U. (H) 2-1; 4th Round: Q.P.R. (A) 0-0; Replay (H) 0-1.

Carlton Fairweather (Wimbledon) Match Magazine

Manders

PROFESSIONAL PRIDE PRODUCT PERFORMANCE

Professional pride and product performance have long been the hallmark of Manders Group of Companies in all aspects of manufacture and distribution whether it be ink or paint coatings or property. A pride which has indeed made Manders the independent Company they are today.

Progressive investment of over £2 million into upgrading factory and warehouse space for Manders Paints has recently taken place at the head office site at Heath Town.

Future investment plans for Mander Kidd inks in modernising plant will create dramatic differences to production and their stock capacity.

Recent investment of over £4 million upon refurbishment of the Mander Centre development in the centre of Wolverhampton provides local shoppers with an attractive up to date shopping environment. Further investment continues and is planned for Mander Domolac Industrial Division at Ruabon upgrading warehouse and production areas.

Business development and further acquisitions have created professional business growth enhanced by Manders continued local sponsorship of 3rd Division Champions Wolverhampton Wanderers Football Club and co-sponsorship of Worcestershire County Cricket Club.

Technical and manufacturing expertise, distribution and pride in investment and product performance give the quality that makes Manders Group of Companies a SHADE MORE PROFESSIONAL.

MAIN SPONSORS

Manders
Manders
Manders
Manders

Manders Holdings plc.
P.O. Box 186, Old Heath Road, Wolverhampton WV1 2QT.
Telephone: (0902) 53122. Telex: 338354. Fax: (0902) 52435

a BSI Registered Firm in accordance with BS 5750.

WOLVERHAMPTON WANDERERS (Division 2)

Team Manager Graham Turner.
Club Address Molineux Grounds, Wolverhampton WV1 4QR. Tel: (0902) 712181.
Current Ground Capacity 28,051.
Record Attendance 61,315 v Liverpool, FA Cup 5th Round, 11 February 1939.
Year Formed 1877. Turned professional 1888.
Previous Names St Luke's, Blakenhall, The Wanderers.
Club Nickname "Wolves".
Club Colours Old gold shirts, black collar and cuffs and shorts and old gold stockings.
Club Honours Football League: Div. 1 Champions 1953-54, 1957-58, 1958-59; Div. 2 Champions 1931-32, 1976-77; Div. 3(N) Champions 1923-24; Div. 3 Champions 1988-89; Div. 4 Champions 1987-88. FA Cup: Winners 1893, 1908, 1949, 1960. Football League Cup: Winners 1974, 1980.
League History 1888-1906 Div. 1; 1906-23 Div. 2; 1923-24 Div. 3(N); 1924-32 Div. 2; 1932-65 Div. 1; 1965-67 Div. 2; 1967-76 Div. 1; 1976-77 Div. 2; 1977-82 Div. 1; 1982-83 Div.2; 1983-84 Div 1; 1984-85 Div. 2; 1985-86 Div. 3; 1986-88 Div. 4; 1988-89 Div. 3; 1989- Div. 2.
Most League Points in a Season (2 for a win) 64 in Div. 1, 1957-58. (3 for a win) 92 in Div. 3, 1988-89.
Most League Goals in a Season 115 in Div. 2, 1931-32.
Record Victory 14-0 v Crosswell's Brewery in FA Cup 2nd Round, 1886-87.
Record Defeat 1-10 v Newton Heath in Div. 1, 15 October 1892.
Consecutive League Wins 8 in 1915, 1967, 1987 and 1988.
Consecutive League Defeats 8 in 1981-82.
Record League Appearances Derek Parkin, 501 between 1967-82.
Record League Goalscorer—Career Bill Hartill, 164 between 1928-35.
Record League Goalscorer—Season Dennis Westcott, 37 in Div. 1, 1946-47, and Steve Bull, 37 in Div. 3, 1988-89.

Wolverhampton Wanderers: League Record, 1988-89 (Division 3)

Match Number	Date	Venue	Opponents	Result	H/T	Lge Posn	Attend
1	27.8.88	A	Bury	L 1-3	0-2		4314
2	3.9.88	H	Reading	W 2-1	0-1	15	10513
3	10.9.88	A	Chesterfield	W 3-0	2-0	6	4217
4	17.9.88	H	Notts Co.	D 0-0	0-0	7	10870
5	20.9.88	H	Aldershot	W 1-0	1-0	3	8991
6	24.9.88	A	Swansea C.	W 5-2	3-1	3	5240
7	1.10.88	H	Port Vale	D 3-3	1-2	4	14018
8	5.10.88	A	Fulham	D 2-2	1-0	3	4828
9	8.10.88	A	Sheffield U.	L 0-2	0-1	5	14272
10	15.10.88	H	Wigan Ath.	W 2-1	2-1	3	10320
11	22.10.88	A	Bolton W.	W 2-1	0-1	3	8174
12	25.10.88	H	Blackpool	W 2-1	1-0	3	12104
13	29.10.88	A	Gillingham	W 3-1	1-0	2	5288
14	5.11.88	H	Southend U.	W 3-0	2-0	1	10432
15	8.11.88	A	Bristol C.	W 1-0	0-0	1	11336
16	12.11.88	H	Huddersfield T.	W 4-1	1-1	1	12697
17	26.11.88	H	Preston N.E.	W 6-0	3-0	1	13180
18	4.12.88	A	Northampton T.	L 1-3	1-2	1	6494
19	17.12.88	H	Mansfield T.	W 6-2	4-1	1	12134
20	26.12.88	A	Bristol Rov.	D 0-0	0-0	1	8480
21	31.12.88	A	Brentford	D 2-2	1-1	1	8020
22	2.1.89	H	Chester C.	W 3-1	3-1	1	21901
23	10.1.89	H	Cardiff C.	W 2-0	2-0	1	14870
24	14.1.89	A	Reading	W 2-0	2-0	1	9353
25	21.1.89	H	Chesterfield	W 1-0	0-0	1	15049
26	29.1.89	A	Notts Co.	D 1-1	0-1	1	9058
27	4.2.89	A	Port Vale	D 0-0	0-0	1	16362
28	11.2.89	H	Fulham	W 5-2	4-1	1	15621
29	28.2.89	A	Blackpool	W 2-0	0-0	1	6482
30	4.3.89	H	Bolton W.	W 1-0	1-0	1	13516
31	10.3.89	A	Southend U.	L 1-3	0-2	1	5924
32	14.3.89	H	Gillingham	W 6-1	4-0	1	12574
33	18.3.89	H	Bury	W 4-0	1-0	1	14828
34	25.3.89	A	Chester C.	D 1-1	1-1	1	8236
35	27.3.89	H	Bristol Rov.	L 0-1	0-1	1	20913
36	1.4.89	A	Mansfield T.	L 1-3	1-1	1	9205
37	4.4.89	A	Cardiff C.	D 1-1	1-0	1	7219
38	8.4.89	H	Brentford	W 2-0	1-0	1	14196
39	15.4.89	A	Aldershot	W 2-1	1-0	1	5465
40	22.4.89	H	Swansea C.	D 1-1	1-0	1	13921
41	29.4.89	A	Huddersfield T.	D 0-0	0-0	1	8757
42	1.5.89	H	Bristol C.	W 2-0	1-0	1	17351
43	6.5.89	H	Northampton T.	W 3-2	2-0	1	15259
44	9.5.89	H	Sheffield U.	D 2-2	1-0	1	24321
45	13.5.89	A	Preston N.E.	D 3-3	1-1	1	14126
46	16.5.89	A	Wigan Ath.	D 1-1	1-0	1	5531

Players: League Record, 1988-89 (Division 3)

Match Number	1	2	3	4	5	6	7	8	9	10	11	12	13	14	15	16	17	18	19	20	21	22	23
Bellamy, Gary	2	2	2	2	2	2	2	2	2	2	2	2	2	2	2	2	2	2	2	2	2	2	2
Bennett, Tommy														★			★						
Bull, Stephen	9	9	9	9	9^1	9^2	9^2	9	9	9^1	9^1	9	9^1	9^1	9	9^2	9^4	9	9^3	9	9^1	9^1	9^1
Chard, Philip	8	8^1	8^1	8	8	8^1	8	8	**8**	8	8	**8**											
Clarke, Nick					4	5	4	4	4											5	5		
Dennison, Robbie	11	11^1	**11**^{1}	11	11	11^1	11	11	11	11	11^1	11	11	11	11	11	11	11^1	**11**				★
Downing, Keith											★	★	8	8^1	8	8	**8**	8	★	11	11	11	**11**
Gallagher, Jackie			★						★	7^1	7	7	7	★			★						
Gooding, Mick					7	7	7	7^1	7									★	8^1	8	8	8^1	**8**
Hansbury, Roger																							
Kelly, Robert																							★
Kendall, Mark	1	1	1	1	1	1	1	1	1	1	1	1	1	1	1	1	1	1	1	1	1	1	1
Mutch, Andy	10	10	10	10	10	10	10	10^1	10	10	10	10^2	10^1	10	10^1	10^1	10^1	10	10^1	10	10^1	10^1	10^1
Robertson, Alistair	5	5	5	5	5		5	**5**				4	4	**5**	5	5	5	5	**5**			5	5
Robinson, Philip	6	6	6^1	6	6	6^1	6	6	6	6	6	6	6^1	6	6	6		6	6	6	**6**		
Steele, Timothy																							
Stowell, Mike																							
Streete, Floyd	4^1	4	4	**4**						4	**4**			**4**^{1}	4	4^1	4	4	4	4	4	4	4
Thompson, Andrew	3	3	3	3	3	3	3^1	3	3	3	3	3	3	7	7	7	7	**7**	7^1	7	7	7	7
Vaughan, Nigel	7	7	7	7													**6**^{1}		★		★	6	6
Venus, Mark				★		4		★	5	5	5	5	5	3	3	3	3	3	3	3	3	3	3
Own Goals																							

Match Number	24	25	26	27	28	29	30	31	32	33	34	35	36	37	38	39	40	41	42	43	44	45	46	Apps	Subs	Goals
Bellamy, Gary	2	2	2	2	2	2	2	2	2	2	2	2	2				2	2	2	2	2	2^1	2	43	0	1
Bennett, Tommy																								0	2	0
Bull, Stephen	9	9	9	9	9^3	9^1	9^1	9	9^1	9^3	9	9	9^1	9	9^1	9^1	9	9	9^2	9^1	9^1	9		45	0	37
Chard, Philip								★	**3**						★	★		★		★			9	14	5	3
Clarke, Nick																4								8	0	0
Dennison, Robbie	★	11	11	11	11	11	**11**	**11**	11^1	**11**	11	11	11	11	11	**11**^{1}	11	11	11	11	11^1	11	11	41	2	8
Downing, Keith	11		5	5	5	5	5	5		★		★	★	★	**8**	8	8	**8**	8	8	8	8		25	7	1
Gallagher, Jackie																								4	4	1
Gooding, Mick	**8**	8	8	8	8	8	8	8	**8**	8	8	**8**				7	**7**	**7**	7	**7**	7	7	7^1	30	1	4
Hansbury, Roger																	1	1	1					3	0	0
Kelly, Robert					★																			0	2	0
Kendall, Mark	1	1	1	1	1	1	1	1	1											1	1	1	1	36	0	0
Mutch, Andy	10^2	10	10^1	10	**10**	10	10	10	10^2	10^1	10^1	10	10	10	**10**	10	10	10	10	10^1	10	10^2		45	0	21
Robertson, Alistair	5	5											3	5	5	5	5	5	5	5	5	5	5	30	0	0
Robinson, Philip					★				★	★			**8**	**8**	★	★		★		★			8	23	7	3
Steele, Timothy							★	★	5^1	5	5	5	**5**	7	7		★						★	7	4	1
Stowell, Mike										1	1	1	1	1	1	1								7	0	0
Streete, Floyd	4	4	4	4	4	4	4	4^1	4	4	4	4	4	4	4^1		4	4	4	4	4	4	4	38	0	5
Thompson, Andrew	7	7	7	7	7^1	7	7	**7**	7^1	7	7	7	7	2^1	2	2	3	3	3	3^1	3	3	3	46	0	6
Vaughan, Nigel	6	6^1	6	6	**6**	6^1	6	6	6	**6**	6	6	6	6	6	**6**	6^1	6	6	**6**	6	6	**6**	30	2	4
Venus, Mark	3	3	3	3	3	3	3	3	★	3	3	3	64	3	3	3							10	31	4	0
Own Goals					1																					1

FA Cup: 1988-89: 1st Round: Grimsby T. (A) 0-1.
Littlewoods Cup: 1988-89: 1st Round: Birmingham C. (H) 3-2 (A) 0-1.

WREXHAM (Division 4)

Team Manager Dixie McNeil.
Club Address Racecourse Ground, Mold Road, Wrexham: Tel: (0978) 262129.
Current Ground Capacity 22,500.
Record Attendance 34,445 v Manchester U., FA Cup 4th Round, 26 January 1957.
Year Formed 1873. Turned professional 1912.
Previous Names Wrexham Olympic.
Club Nickname "The Robins".
Club Colours Red shirts with white trim, white shorts with red trim and red stockings with white hoops on turnovers.
Club Honours Football League: Div. 3 Champions 1977-78
League History 1921-58 Div. 3(N); 1958-60 Div. 3; 1960-62 Div. 4; 1962-64 Div. 3; 1964-70 Div. 4; 1970-78 Div.3; 1978-82 Div. 3; 1983- Div. 4.

Most League Points in a Season (2 for a win) 61 in Div. 4, 1969-70 and in Div. 3, 1977-78. (3 for a win) 71 in Div. 4, 1988-89.
Most League Goals in a Season 106 in Div. 3(N), 1932-33.
Record Victory 10-1 v Hartlepool U. in Div. 4, 3 March 1962.
Record Defeat 0-9 v Brentford in Div. 3, 15 October 1963.
Consecutive League Wins 7 in 1961 and 1978.
Consecutive League Defeats 9 in 1963.
Record League Appearances Arfon Griffiths, 592 between 1959-79.
Record League Goalscorer—Career Tom Bamford, 175 between 1928-34.
Record League Goalscorer—Season Tom Bamford, 44 in Div. 3(N), 1933-34.

Wrexham: League Record, 1988-89 (Division 4)

Match Number	Date	Venue	Opponents	Result	H/T	Lge Posn	Attend
1	27.8.88	A	Exeter C.	W 2-0	1-0		2504
2	3.9.88	H	Lincoln C.	W 3-0	0-0	2	2312
3	10.9.88	A	Rotherham U.	D 2-2	1-1	2	4367
4	16.9.88	H	Colchester U.	D 2-2	0-1	6	2873
5	20.9.88	H	Grimsby T.	L 1-2	1-2	7	2267
6	24.9.88	A	Doncaster Rov.	D 2-2	0-1	7	1712
7	1.10.88	H	Peterborough U.	D 1-1	0-1	11	1826
8	4.10.88	A	Halifax T.	L 0-4	0-3	13	1199
9	8.10.88	H	Crewe Alex.	D 0-0	0-0	16	2689
10	15.10.88	A	Hartlepool U.	W 3-1	2-1	13	2235
11	22.10.88	H	Tranmere Rov.	D 3-3	2-0	10	3334
12	25.10.88	A	Scunthorpe U.	L 1-3	1-1	16	2999
13	29.10.88	H	York C.	W 2-1	1-1	10	2014
14	5.11.88	A	Hereford U.	D 0-0	0-0	13	2372
15	8.11.88	H	Stockport Co.	W 2-0	1-0	15	1865
16	12.11.88	A	Rochdale	D 3-3	1-0	11	2280
17	26.11.88	A	Scarborough	W 3-0	1-0	6	3689
18	3.12.88	H	Carlisle U.	W 2-1	2-1	5	1892
19	16.12.88	H	Cambridge U.	W 3-1	2-1	4	1728
20	26.12.88	A	Burnley	W 3-1	1-1	2	9174
21	31.12.88	A	Leyton Orient	W 1-0	0-0	1	4025
22	2.1.89	H	Darlington	D 3-3	2-1	3	6016
23	14.1.89	A	Lincoln C.	L 3-4	1-2	4	3860
24	21.1.89	H	Exeter C.	W 3-0	0-0	3	2514
25	4.2.89	A	Grimsby T.	W 1-0	1-0	2	5038
26	11.2.89	H	Doncaster Rov.	D 1-1	0-1	4	3244
27	17.2.89	A	Crewe Alex.	D 2-2	2-1	5	5627
28	28.2.89	H	Scunthorpe U.	W 2-0	2-0	4	2609
29	3.3.89	A	Tranmere Rov.	L 1-2	1-0	6	7353
30	7.3.89	H	Hartlepool U.	W 4-3	3-2	4	2449
31	11.3.89	H	Hereford U.	D 1-1	0-1	4	2960
32	14.3.89	A	York C.	L 0-1	0-0	4	2006
33	18.3.89	H	Rotherham U.	L 1-4	1-1	5	2929
34	25.3.89	A	Darlington	L 1-2	1-1	7	2281
35	27.3.89	H	Burnley	W 4-2	2-1	6	3956
36	31.3.89	A	Cambridge U.	L 0-2	0-0	7	3072
37	4.4.89	A	Torquay U.	D 0-0	0-0	7	2421
38	8.4.89	H	Leyton Orient	L 0-1	0-1	7	2437
39	15.4.89	A	Peterborough U.	L 0-1	0-1	8	3067
40	21.4.89	H	Halifax T.	W 3-0	1-0	7	1782
41	25.4.89	A	Colchester U.	L 1-2	1-1	7	2918
42	29.4.89	H	Scarborough	L 0-1	0-0	7	1948
43	1.5.89	A	Stockport Co.	D 2-2	1-0	7	2118
44	6.5.89	A	Carlisle U.	W 2-1	1-0	7	2427
45	9.5.89	H	Torquay U.	W 1-0	0-0	7	2056
46	13.5.89	H	Rochdale	W 2-1	1-0	7	3125

Players: League Record, 1988-89 (Division 4)

Match Number	1	2	3	4	5	6	7	8	9	10	11	12	13	14	15	16	17	18	19	20	21	22	23	24	25	26	27	28	29	30	31	32	33	34	35	36	37	38	39	40	41	42	43	44	45	46	Apps	Subs	Goals
Beaumont, Nigel	5	5	5	5	5	**5**	5	5																				3	3	5	3	6	★	6							6	6	6	5	5	5	20	1	0
Bowden, Jon	4	4	4	**4**	4	**4**	4	4	**4**		★		4^{1}	11	11^{1}	11	11^{2}	11	11	11^{1}	**11**	11		**7^{1}**	7^{1}	7	7^{1}	7	11	11	11	11	11	11^{1}	11	11	11	11	11	11	11	11	11	**11**		11^{1}	41	1	10
Buxton, Steve	★	9	9	9	9	9	9	9	**9**	9		★				★		★	9^{1}	9	9	9	7	9	9	9	9	**9**											★	9^{2}	9	9	**9**	9	9^{1}		25	5	4
Carter, Mike		★	★		★				★	★														★		★				7^{1}	7	7	**7**	**7**											11		6	7	1
Cooper, Graham	11^{1}	11^{2}	11	11^{1}	11	11	11	11	★	**11^{1}**	11^{2}	11	11			★					★		11^{1}	11	11	**11**	11	11	9^{1}	9^{1}	9^{1}	9	9	9	**7**	**7**	7	**7**	★		★	★	**7**			★	29	7	11
Filson, Robert																																											★				0	1	0
Flynn, Brian	★	**7**	**7**	7	**7**		★	★	11	4	**4**	**4**	8	8	8	8	8	8	8^{1}	8	8	8	**8**	8	8	8	8	8	8	8	**8**	8	8	**8**					7	8	8	8	8	8	8	8	38	3	1
Hunter, Geoff			★	$★^{1}$	8^{1}	8^{1}	8	**8**	8	8	8	8					4	4	4	4^{1}	4	**4**	4	4			4	4	4	**4**	4	4	4	4	4	4	4	4	4	4	4	4	4	4	4	4	36	2	4
Jones, Joey	6	6	6^{1}	6	6	6	6	6	6	6^{1}	6	6	6	6	6	6^{2}	6	6^{2}	6	6	6	6	6^{1}	6	6	6	6	6^{1}	6	6	6		6		6	6	6	6	6	6				6	6	6	41	0	8
Jones, Paul																																			8	8	8	8	**8**								5	0	0
Kearns, Ollie	**9**													★			9^{1}	**9**		$★^{1}$		★	**9**										★	★	9^{1}	9	9	9	**9**				★		★	9^{1}	10	7	4
Lane, Martin									5	5	5	5	5	5																																	6	0	0
Morris, Mark																							1												1	1											3	0	0
Preece, Roger	7			★	**2**	7	**7**	7	7	7^{1}	7^{1}	7	7	7	7	7^{1}	7	7	7	**7**	7	7^{1}	★					★	7						★	★	★	★		7^{1}	**7**	**7**		★			23	8	5
Raynor, Paul											9	9	9	**9**	9	9																															6	0	0
Russell, Kevin	10^{1}	10^{1}	10	10	10	10^{1}	10^{1}	10	10	10	10	10	10^{1}	10	10	**10**	10	10	10^{1}	10	10^{1}	10^{2}	10^{1}	10^{1}	10	10	10^{1}	10^{1}	10	10^{2}	10	10	10^{1}	10	10^{3}	10	**10**	10	10	10	10^{1}	10	10^{1}	10^{1}	10	10	46	0	22
Salathiel, Neil	2	2	2	2	3	2	**2**	2						2	2	2	2	2	2	2	2	2	2	2	2	2	2	2	2	2	2	2	3	2	**2**							★	5	2	2	2	34	1	0
Salmon, Mike	1	1	1	1	1	1	1	1	1	1	1	1	1	1	1	1	1	1	1	1	1	1		1	1	1	1	1	1	1	1	1	1	1			1	1	1	1	1	1	1	1	1	1	43	0	0
Taylor, Jason						★																																									0	1	0
Thackeray, Andy	**8**	8	**8**	8	★	3	★		2	2	2	2	2	4	4^{1}	**4**			★				★		4	4				★	★		2	★	★	2	2	2	2	2	2	2	2	7^{1}	**7**	**7**	27	8	2
Williams, Mike															5	5	5	5	**5**	5	5	5	5	5	5	5	5	5	5		5	5	**5**	5	5	5	5	5	5	5	5	**5**					27	0	0
Wrench, Mark						★	3	3																								3															3	1	0
Wright, Darren	3	3	3^{1}	**3**					3	3	3	3	3	3	3	3	3	3	3	3	3	3	3	3	3	3^{1}	3			3				3	3	3	3	3	3	3	3	3	3^{1}	3	3	3	37	0	3
Own Goals												1												1																									2

FA Cup: 1988-89: 1st Round: Runcorn (A) 2-2, Replay (H) 2-3.
Littlewoods Cup: 1988-89: 1st Round: Bury (A) 1-2 (H) 2-2.

YORK CITY (Division 4)

Team Manager John Bird.
Club Address Bootham Crescent, York. Tel: (0904) 24447.
Current Ground Capacity 14,109.
Record Attendance 28,123 v Huddersfield T., FA Cup 6th Round, 5 March 1938.
Year Formed 1903. Turned professional 1922.
Previous Names None.
Club Nickname "The Minstermen".
Club Colours Red shirts, navy blue shorts and white stockings.
Club Honours Football League: Div. 4 Champions 1983-84.
League History 1929-58 Div. 3(N); 1958-59 Div. 4; 1959-60 Div. 3; 1960-65 Div. 4; 1965-66 Div. 3; 1966-71 Div. 4; 1971-74 Div. 3; 1974-76 Div. 2; 1976-77 Div. 3; 1977-84 Div. 4; 1984-88 Div. 3; 1988- Div. 4.
Most League Points in a Season (2 for a win) 62 in Div. 4, 1964-65. (3 for a win) 101 in Div. 4, 1983-84.
Most League Goals in a Season 96 in Div. 4, 1983-84.
Record Victory 9-1 v Southport in Div. 3(N), 2 February 1957.
Record Defeat 0-12 v Chester C. in Div. 3(N), 1 February 1936.
Consecutive League Wins 7 in 1964.
Consecutive League Defeats 6 in 1966.
Record League Appearances Barry Jackson, 482 between 1958-70.
Record League Goalscorer—Career Norman Wilkinson, 125 betwen 1954-66.
Record League Goalscorer—Season Bill Fenton, 31 in Div. 3(N), 1951-52, Arthur Bottom, 31 in Div. 3(N), 1954-55 and 1955-56.

York City: League Record, 1988-89 (Division 4)

Match Number	Date	Venue	Opponents	Result	H/T	Lge Posn	Attend
1	27.8.88	A	Colchester U.	L 0-1	0-0		1644
2	3.9.88	H	Carlisle U.	D 1-1	0-1	18	2303
3	10.9.88	A	Burnley	L 0-6	0-2	24	7239
4	17.9.88	H	Scunthorpe U.	L 1-2	0-1	24	2735
5	20.9.88	H	Hartlepool U.	L 2-3	1-2	24	2611
6	24.9.88	A	Peterborough U.	W 1-0	0-0	22	2756
7	1.10.88	H	Halifax T.	W 5-3	3-1	17	2238
8	4.10.88	A	Leyton Orient	L 0-4	0-2	21	2467
9	7.10.88	A	Tranmere Rov.	W 1-0	1-0	18	3054
10	15.10.88	H	Darlington	W 4-1	2-0	16	2851
11	22.10.88	A	Grimsby T.	L 0-2	0-2	19	2825
12	25.10.88	H	Doncaster Rov.	D 1-1	1-1	20	2957
13	29.10.88	A	Wrexham	L 1-2	1-1	21	2014
14	5.11.88	H	Torquay U.	D 1-1	0-0	21	2007
15	8.11.88	H	Crewe Alex.	W 3-0	0-0	18	1980
16	11.11.88	A	Stockport Co.	L 2-3	2-2	21	2477
17	26.11.88	A	Rochdale	L 0-2	0-0	21	1880
18	3.12.88	H	Hereford U.	W 4-1	1-0	21	1698
19	16.12.88	H	Rotherham U.	D 1-1	0-0	21	2650
20	26.12.88	A	Scarborough	D 0-0	0-0	21	5057
21	31.12.88	A	Exeter C.	L 0-2	0-1	21	3092
22	2.1.89	H	Lincoln C.	W 2-1	0-1	19	3589
23	14.1.89	A	Carlisle U.	D 0-0	0-0	21	3462
24	21.1.89	H	Colchester U.	W 2-0	1-0	18	2119
25	28.1.89	A	Scunthorpe U.	L 2-4	1-3	19	4196
26	4.2.89	A	Hartlepool U.	W 1-0	0-0	16	2863
27	11.2.89	H	Peterborough U.	W 5-1	2-0	14	2438
28	18.2.89	H	Tranmere Rov.	L 0-1	0-1	15	2923
29	25.2.89	A	Darlington	D 2-2	0-0	14	2504
30	28.2.89	A	Doncaster Rov.	W 2-1	0-0	12	1526
31	4.3.89	H	Grimsby T.	L 0-3	0-1	15	3481
32	14.3.89	H	Wrexham	W 1-0	0-0	13	2006
33	18.3.89	H	Burnley	D 0-0	0-0	15	3164
34	25.3.89	A	Lincoln C.	L 1-2	1-1	16	3710
35	27.3.89	H	Scarborough	D 0-0	0-0	17	4872
36	1.4.89	A	Rotherham U.	W 1-0	0-0	14	5926
37	4.4.89	A	Cambridge U.	D 1-1	1-0	14	2400
38	8.4.89	H	Exeter C.	W 3-1	1-0	13	2052
39	14.4.89	A	Halifax T.	D 0-0	0-0	12	1875
40	22.4.89	H	Leyton Orient	D 1-1	0-1	12	2744
41	25.4.89	A	Torquay U.	L 0-2	0-1	14	2015
42	29.4.89	H	Rochdale	D 3-3	2-1	13	1920
43	1.5.89	A	Crewe Alex.	W 2-1	1-0	12	3693
44	6.5.89	A	Hereford U.	W 2-1	1-0	11	1819
45	9.5.89	H	Cambridge U.	L 1-2	0-2	11	2336
46	13.5.89	H	Stockport Co.	W 2-0	1-0	11	2327

Players: League Record, 1988-89 (Division 4)

Match Number	1	2	3	4	5	6	7	8	9	10	11	12	13	14	15	16	17	18	19	20	21	22	23
Banton, Dale	10	10^{1}	10	10	10^{1}	10	10^{1}	10	10	10^{1}	10												
Barratt, Tony																							
Bradshaw, Darren	2		4	4	2^{1}	2	2^{1}	2	2	2	2	2	2	2	2	2		4	4	2	2	2	2
Branagan, Jim		2	2	2	3	3	3	3	3	3	3	3	3			★			2				
Butler, Martin		★	★	★	7	7	7^{1}	7	7	7^{2}	7	7	7										
Canham, Tony	★	4			11	11	11^{1}	11	11^{1}	11^{1}	11	11	11	11	11	11	7	11^{1}	11	11	11	11	11
Clegg, Tony		3	8		★						5												
Dixon, Kevin																	10	10	10	10	10	10^{1}	10
Dunn, Iain										★	★	9^{1}	9	10	10^{1}	10^{1}						★	7
Eli, Roger														$★^{1}$	7	7	8						
Endersby, Scott																							
Fazackerley, Derek	5	6	6	6	6	6	6	6	6	6	6	6	6	6	6	6							
Greenough, Ricky																	2	2	5	5	5	5	5
Hall, Wayne																							
Hay, Alan																			3				
Helliwell, Ian	9	9	9	9	9	9^{1}	9	9	9	9	9						9	9^{2}	9	9	9	9	9
Himsworth, Gary	11	11	11	11								10	10	7		★	11	7^{1}	7	7	7	7	
Hotte, Tim				8		★																	
Howlett, Gary	7	7	7	7^{1}	8	8	8^{1}	8	8	8	8												
Hurlstone, Gary																							
Johnson, Paul	3		3	3	4	4	4	4	4	4	4	4	4	3	3^{1}	3	3	3		3	3	3	3
McMillan, Andy												★	★										
Marples, Chris	1	1	1	1	1	1	1	1	1	1	1	1	1	1	1	1	1	1	1	1	1	1	1
Morris, Neil														9	9	9	★						
Reid, Shaun																				4	4	4	4
Shaw, Adrian												8	8	4	4	4							
Smith, Kevin	6		5			5		★				5	5^{1}	5	5	5^{1}	5	5	6	6	6	6^{1}	6
Spooner, Steve	8	8																8	8^{1}	8	8	8	8
Tutill, Stephen		5		5	5		5	5	5	5							6	6					
Wilson, Phil	4		★							★	★	★	★	8	8^{1}	8	4						
Own Goals																							

Match Number	24	25	26	27	28	29	30	31	32	33	34	35	36	37	38	39	40	41	42	43	44	45	46	Apps	Subs	Goals
Banton, Dale																								11	0	4
Barratt, Tony												7	7	2	2	2	2	2	2	2	2	2	2	12	0	0
Bradshaw, Darren	2	2	2	2	2	2	2	2	2	2	2	2	2											34	0	2
Branagan, Jim																								13	1	0
Butler, Martin																								9	3	3
Canham, Tony	11	11^{2}	11	11^{1}	11	11	11				11	11	11^{1}	11	11	11	11	11	11^{1}	11	11	11	11	40	1	9
Clegg, Tony																								3	1	0
Dixon, Kevin	10^{1}	10	10	10^{1}	10	10^{1}	10	10	10	10	10			★										18	1	4
Dunn, Iain	7				★			★	11	★		★	★	7	7^{1}	7	7^{1}	7	7^{1}	7	7	7	7	18	8	6
Eli, Roger																								3	1	1
Endersby, Scott									1															1	0	0
Fazackerley, Derek																								16	0	0
Greenough, Ricky	5	5	5	5	5	5	5^{1}	5	5	5	5	5	5	5	5	5	5	5	5					26	0	1
Hall, Wayne																						★	★	0	2	0
Hay, Alan																								1	0	0
Helliwell, Ian	9	9	9^{1}	9^{2}	9	9^{1}	9	9	9	9	9	9	9	9	9^{1}	9	9	9	9	9^{1}	9	9	9^{2}	41	0	11
Himsworth, Gary		★	7	7	7	7	7	7	7	7	7^{1}	10	10	10	10	10	10	10	10					30	2	2
Hotte, Tim																								1	1	0
Howlett, Gary	$★^{1}$	7		4	4	4		11										★	★	10	10^{1}	10	10	20	3	4
Hurlstone, Gary									★	11														1	1	0
Johnson, Paul	3	3	3	3	3	3	3	3	3	3	3	3	3	3	3	3	3	3	3	3	3	3	3	44	0	1
McMillan, Andy																								0	2	0
Marples, Chris	1	1	1	1	1	1	1	1		1	1	1	1	1	1	1	1	1	1	1	1	1	1	45	0	0
Morris, Neil																								3	1	0
Reid, Shaun	4	4	4				4	4	4	4	4	4	4	4^{1}	4	4	4	4	4	4^{1}	4	4	4	24	0	2
Shaw, Adrian																								5	0	0
Smith, Kevin	6	6	6	6	6	6	6^{1}	6	6	6	6									5	5^{1}	5	5	30	1	5
Spooner, Steve	8	8	8	8^{1}	8	8	8	8	8^{1}	8	8	8	8	8	8^{1}	8	8	8	8	8	8	8^{1}	8	31	0	5
Tutill, Stephen								★				6	6	6	6	6	6	6	6^{1}	6	6	6	6	21	1	1
Wilson, Phil																								5	5	1
Own Goals																										0

FA Cup: 1988-89: 1st Round: Halifax T. (A) 0-1.
Littlewoods Cup: 1988-89: 1st Round: Sunderland (H) 0-0 (A) 0-4.

THE WINNER
MATCH
Your up-to-date football weekly
OUT ON WEDNESDAY

A–Z of English Football League Players

The Career Record of Every Footballer who Played in the Barclays League During 1988–89.

The criteria for inclusion is as follows: Every player who played in the Football League during 1988-89. All players registered with Football League clubs at the close of 1988–89, who did not appear last season, but played in 1987–88. Also included are specially selected players currently playing abroad or in the Scottish League, plus the players of Maidstone United, who have appeared in the League when with other clubs.

Key to Reading the Entries

Players' Names: Surname shown first, followed by leading Christian name, plus any initials.

Birthplace: For players born outside the British Isles and Ireland, only the name of the country is given.

Date: Birthdate by day, month and year.

Source: This column indicates a player's origins, whether from outside the F.L. or within the ranks of the League. For the latter the following code is used:

- Jnrs = Junior players signed from school/college without serving an apprenticeship or trainee period.
- App = Apprentice signing prior to 1986.
- YTS = Trainee. This rank was introduced in 1986 and includes players sponsored by the Government's Youth Training Scheme.
- Tr = Transfers (including free transfers).
- L = Loan signing, or temporary transfer, shown only when the player made an appearance.

League Club: All clubs who have been members of the Football League. Where the club name is followed by the following codes: (Am) = Amateur; (App) = Apprentice; (N/C) = Non-contract; (Sch) = Schoolboy — indicates that the player did not, or has not, signed a professional contract with the club.

Date Signed: The date given by month/year is when the player signed professional forms. In the case of non-contract players and apprentices who did not turn professional, the date of signing is that of the status indicated. N/L denotes that the player was signed while the club in question was outside the League. For players signed first on loan before a permanent transfer was arranged, the date of signing is that of the loan transfer, except when the player returned to his former club and made further appearances.

Seasons Played: The years that are shown indicate the first year of a season.

Career Record: Only Football League matches are shown and do not include the "play-offs". Figures for substitutes are only given when the player took part in the match and does not include non-playing subs.

Pos.: Position. As many players fill more than one position during their career, only their principal role is shown here. Since 1970 most teams adopted a 4–3–3 or 4–4–2 formation. In the late 1980s, many clubs played with a fifth defender known as a "Sweeper", but as few players can claim to be a specialist, the term is not used.

- (CD) = Central Defender.
- (M) = Midfield (central).
- (RM/LM) = Right or Left Midfield, primarily defensive.
- (RW/LW) = Right or Left Wing, auxiliary forwards.

Misc: The miscellaneous column records other information including: International honours at Schoolboy (Sch), Youth (Yth), Under 21/23 and Full, plus Semi-Professional (Semi-Pro). For the four home countries: England (E), Northern Ireland (NI), Scotland (S) and Wales (W), plus the Irish Republic (IR), international appearances are updated up to and including 11 June, 1989. Playing substitutes are used in the totals.

General Note: Player's records shown span Football League careers only.

Tony Adams (Arsenal & England) Match Magazine

John Aldridge (Liverpool & Eire) Match Magazine

Malcolm Allen (Norwich City & Wales) Match Magazine

Players Names	Birthplace	Date	Previous Club	League Club	Date Sign'd	Seasons Played	Career Record Apps	Sub	Gls	Pos.	Misc
ABBOTT, Greg S.	Coventry	14.12.63	App	**Coventry C.**	12.81					(M/FB)	
			Tr	**Bradford C.**	09.82	1982-88	200	20	35		
ABEL, Graham	Runcorn	17.09.60	Northwich Vic.	**Chester C.**	10.85	1985-88	149	0	8	(CD)	
ABLETT, Gary I.	Liverpool	19.11.65	App	**Liverpool**	11.83	1986-88	54	3	1	(D)	E U21-1
			L	**Derby Co.**	01.85	1984	3	3	0		
			L	**Hull C.**	09.86	1986	5	0	0		
ABRAHAM, Gareth J.	Merthyr Tydfil	13.02.69	YTS	**Cardiff C.**	07.87	1987-88	33	0	3	(CD)	
ACHAMPONG, Kenny	Kilburn	26.06.66	App	**Fulham**	06.84	1984-87	68	13	15	(F)	
ADAMS, Micky R.	Rotherham	08.11.61	App	**Gillingham**	11.79	1979-82	85	7	4	(LB)	E Yth Int
			Tr	**Coventry C.**	07.83	1983-86	85	5	9		
			Tr	**Leeds U.**	01.87	1986-87	72	1	2		
			Tr	**Southampton**	03.89	1988	8	0	0		
ADAMS, Neil J.	Stoke	23.11.65		**Stoke C.**	06.85	1985	31	1	4	(M)	E U21-1
			Tr	**Everton**	06.86	1986-87	17	3	0		
			L	**Oldham Ath.**	01.89	1988	9	0	0		
ADAMS, Steve	Sheffield	07.09.59	Worksop T.	**Scarborough**	09.87	1987-88	25	23	5	(W)	
ADAMS, Tony A.	Romford	10.10.66	App	**Arsenal**	01.84	1983-88	145	1	13	(CD)	E Yth Int/E U21-5/E-17
ADCOCK. A.C. (Tony)	Bethnal Green	27.02.63	App	**Colchester U.**	02.81	1980-86	192	18	98	(F)	
			Tr	**Manchester C.**	06.87	1987	12	3	5		
			Tr	**Northampton T.**	01.88	1987-88	64	0	27		
ADKINS, Nigel H.	Birkenhead	11.03.65	App	**Tranmere Rov.**	03.83	1982-85	86	0	0	(G)	E Sch Int
			Tr	**Wigan Ath.**	07.86	1986-88	40	0	0		
AGANA, P.A. (Tony)	Bromley	02.10.63	Weymouth	**Watford**	08.87	1987	12	3	1	(F)	E Semi-Pro Int 1986
			Tr	**Sheffield U.**	02.88	1987-88	55	3	26		
AGBOOLA, Reuben O.F.	Camden	30.05.62	App	**Southampton**	04.80	1980-84	89	1	0	(D)	
			Tr	**Sunderland**	01.85	1984-88	93	5	0		
			L	**Charlton Ath.**	10.86	1986	1	0	0		
AGNEW, Paul	Lisburn (NI)	15.08.65	Cliftonville	**Grimsby T.**	02.84	1983-88	126	4	1	(LB)	NI Yth Int
AGNEW, Steve M.	Shipley	09.11.65	App	**Barnsley**	11.83	1983-88	102	8	14	(M)	
AINSCOW, Alan	Bolton	15.07.53	App	**Blackpool**	07.71	1971-77	178	14	28	(M)	
			Tr	**Birmingham C.**	07.78	1978-80	104	4	16		
			Tr	**Everton**	08.81	1981-82	24	4	3		
			L	**Barnsley**	11.82	1982	2	0	0		
			Hong Kong	**Wolverhampton W.**	08.84	1984-85	56	2	5		
			Tr	**Blackburn Rov.**	12.85	1985-88	42	23	5		
AINSCOW, Andrew P.	Orrell	01.10.68	App	**Wigan Ath.**	10.86	1987-88	14	8	4	(F)	E Yth Int
AIREY, Carl	Wakefield	06.02.65	App	**Barnsley**	02.83	1982-83	30	8	5	(F)	
			L	**Bradford C.**	10.83	1983	4	1	0		
			Tr	**Darlington**	08.84	1984-85	72	3	28		
			Charleroi (Belgium)	**Chesterfield**	12.86	1986	24	2	4		
			Tr	**Rotherham U.**	08.87	1987	25	7	11		
				Torquay U. (N/C)	01.89	1988	10	7	3		
AIZLEWOOD, Mark	Newport	01.10.59	App	**Newport Co.**	10.77	1975-77	35	3	1	(M)	W Sch Int/W U21-2/W-13/ Brother of Steve
			Tr	**Luton T.**	04.78	1978-81	90	8	3		
			Tr	**Charlton Ath.**	11.82	1982-86	152	0	9		
			Tr	**Leeds U.**	02.87	1986-88	65	5	3		
ALBISTON, Arthur R.	Edinburgh	14.07.57	App	**Manchester U.**	07.74	1974-87	364	15	6	(LB)	S Sch Int/SU21-5/S-14
			Tr	**West Bromwich A.**	08.88	1988	43	0	2		
ALDRIDGE, John W.	Liverpool	18.09.58	South Liverpool	**Newport Co.**	04.79	1979-83	159	11	69	(F)	IR-24
			Tr	**Oxford U.**	03.84	1983-86	111	3	72		
			Tr	**Liverpool**	01.87	1986-88	69	12	49		
ALEXANDER, Ian	Glasgow	26.01.63	Leicester Juv.	**Rotherham U.**	10.81	1981-82	5	6	0	(RB)	
			Cyprus	**Bristol Rov.**	08.86	1986-88	107	2	2		
ALEXANDER, Keith	Nottingham	14.11.58	Barnet	**Grimsby T.**	07.88	1988	42	2	14	(W)	
ALFORD, Carl P.	Manchester	11.02.72	YTS	**Rochdale** (YTS)	11.88	1988	0	4	0		
ALLARDYCE, Sam	Dudley	19.10.54	App	**Bolton W.**	11.71	1973-79	180	4	21	(CD)	
			Tr	**Sunderland**	07.80	1980	24	1	2		
			Tr	**Millwall**	09.81	1981-82	63	0	2		
			Tr	**Coventry C.**	09.83	1983	28	0	1		
			Tr	**Huddersfield T.**	07.84	1984	37	0	0		
			Tr	**Bolton W.**	07.85	1985	14	0	0		
			Tr	**Preston N.E.**	08.86	1986-88	88	2	2		
ALLEN, Bradley J.	Romford	13.09.71	Jnrs	**Q.P.R.**	09.88	1988	0	1	0	(F)	E Yth Int
ALLEN, Clive D.	Stepney	20.05.61	App	**Q.P.R.**	09.78	1978-79	43	6	32	(F)	Son of Les/E Sch Int/E Yth Int/E E U21-3/E-5/FWA & FPA Footballer of Year 1986-87
			Tr	**Arsenal**	06.80						
			Tr	**Crystal Palace**	08.80	1980	25	0	9		
			Tr	**Q.P.R.**	06.81	1981-83	83	4	40		
			Tr	**Tottenham H.**	08.84	1984-87	97	8	60		to Bordeaux (France) 6.88
ALLEN, Greg F.	West Ham	18.10.67	App	**Arsenal**	07.85					(M)	
			Dagenham	**Cambridge U.** (N/C)	08.88	1988	4	0	0		
ALLEN, Kenny R.	Thornaby	12.01.52	Jnrs	**Hartlepool U.** (Am)	08.68	1968	7	0	0	(G)	
			South Africa	**West Bromwich A.**	12.72						
			Bath C.	**Bournemouth**	08.78	1978-82	152	0	0		
			Bury (N/C)	**Peterborough U.** (N/C)	12.83						
			Tr	**Torquay U.**	03.84	1983-85	58	0	0		
			Tr	**Swindon T.**	09.85	1985-86	45	0	0		
			Tr	**Torquay U.**	12.86	1986-87	74	0	0		
			Bath C.	**Torquay U.**	03.89						
ALLEN, Malcolm	Caernarfon	21.03.67	App	**Watford**	03.85	1985-87	27	12	5	(F)	W-4
			L	**Aston Villa**	09.87	1987	4	0	0		
			Tr	**Norwich C.**	08.88	1988	15	8	5		
ALLEN, Martin J.	Reading	14.08.65	App	**Q.P.R.**	05.83	1984-88	126	8	16	(M)	E Yth Int/E U21-2
ALLEN, Paul K.	Aveley	28.08.62	App	**West Ham U.**	08.79	1979-84	149	3	6	(M)	E Yth Int/E U21-3/E 'B'
			Tr	**Tottenham H.**	06.85	1985-88	137	9	8		
ALLEYNE, Robert A.	Dudley	27.09.68		**Leicester C.**	01.87	1986	1	2	0	(F)	
			L	**Wrexham**	10.87	1987	7	3	2		
			Tr	**Chesterfield**	03.88	1987-88	32	8	5		

Players Names	Birthplace	Date	Previous Club	League Club	Date Sign'd	Seasons Played	Career Record Apps	Sub	Gls	Pos.	Misc
ALLINSON, Ian J.R.	Hitchin	01.10.57	App	**Colchester U.**	10.75	1974-82	291	17	69	(W)	
			Tr	**Arsenal**	10.83	1983-86	60	23	16		
			Tr	**Stoke C.**	06.87	1987	6	3	0		
			Tr	**Luton T.**	10.87	1987-88	24	8	3		
			Tr	**Colchester U.**	12.88	1988	24	1	7		
ALLISON, Wayne	Huddersfield	16.10.68	YTS	**Halifax T.**	06.87	1986-88	74	10	21	(F)	
ALLON, Joe B.	Gateshead	12.11.66	YTS	**Newcastle U.**	11.84	1984-86	9	0	2	(F)	E Yth Int
			Tr	**Swansea C.**	07.87	1987-88	27	7	12		
			Tr	**Hartlepool U.**	10.88	1988	21	0	4		
ANDERSON, Colin R.	Newcastle	26.04.62	App	**Burnley**	04.80	1980-81	3	3	0	(W)	
			North Shields	**Torquay U.**	09.82	1982-84	107	2	11		
			Tr	**West Bromwich A.**	03.85	1985-88	96	8	8		
ANDERSON, Dale	Newton Aycliffe	23.08.70	YTS	**Darlington**	09.88	1986-88	4	11	0	(F)	
ANDERSON, Darren I.	Merton	06.09.66	Coventry C.(App)	**Charlton Ath.**	03.84	1983-84	10	0	1	(CD)	E Yth Int
			L	**Crewe Alex.**	10.85	1985	5	0	0		
			Tr	**Aldershot**	07.86	1986-88	59	23	3		
ANDERSON, Doug E.	Hong Kong	29.08.63	Port Glasgow	**Oldham Ath.**	09.80	1981-83	4	5	0	(W)	
			Tr	**Tranmere Rov.**	08.84	1984-86	125	1	15		
			Tr	**Plymouth Arg.**	08.87	1987	17	2	1		
			L	**Cambridge U.**	09.88	1988	8	0	2		
			L	**Northampton T.**	12.88	1988	4	1	0		
ANDERSON, John C.P.	Dublin	07.11.59	App	**West Bromwich A.**	11.77					(RB)	IR U21-1/IR-16
			Tr	**Preston N.E.**	08.79	1979-81	47	4	0		
			Tr	**Newcastle U.**	09.82	1982-88	227	8	9		
ANDERSON, Nick J.	Lincoln	29.03.69	YTS	**Mansfield T.**	01.87	1986-88	9	11	0	(M)	
ANDERSON, Viv A.	Nottingham	29.08.56	App	**Nottingham F.**	08.74	1974-83	323	5	15	(RB)	E U21-1/E-30/EF Lge Rep
			Tr	**Arsenal**	07.84	1984-86	120	0	9		
			Tr	**Manchester U.**	05.87	1987-88	35	2	2		
ANDREWS, Gary M.	Nottingham	12.05.68	App	**Nottingham F.**	09.85					(D)	
			Tr	**Peterborough U.**	08.88	1988	33	0	0		
ANDREWS, Ian E.	Nottingham	01.12.64	App	**Leicester C.**	12.82	1983-87	126	0	0	(G)	E Yth Int/E U21-1
			L	**Swindon T.**	01.84	1983	1	0	0		
			Glasgow Celtic (L)	**Leeds U.**	12.88	1988	1	0	0		
ANGELL, Brett	Marlborough	20.08.68	YTS	**Portsmouth** (N/C)	08.86					(F)	Brother of Darren
			Cheltenham T.	**Derby Co.**	02.88						
			Tr	**Stockport Co.**	10.88	1988	17	9	5		
ANGELL, Darren J.	Marlborough	19.01.67	Newbury T.	**Portsmouth**	06.85					(D)	Brother of Brett
			L	**Colchester U.**	12.87	1987	1	0	0		
			Cheltenham T.	**Lincoln C.**	07.88						
ANSAH, Andrew	Lewisham	19.03.69	Dorking	**Brentford**	03.89	1988	3	4	2	(F)	
ANTHROBUS, Stephen A.	Lewisham	10.11.68	YTS	**Millwall**	08.86	1987-88	6	0	0	(W)	
ARDILES, Osvaldo C.	Argentina	03.08.52	Huracan (Arg)	**Tottenham H.**	07.78	1978-87	221	16	16	(M)	Argentine Int
			L	**Blackburn Rov.**	03.88	1987	5	0	0		
			Tr	**Q.P.R.**	08.88	1988	4	4	0		
ARMITAGE, Andrew M.	Leeds	17.10.68	YTS	**Leeds U.** (N/C)	08.87					(D)	
			Tr	**Rochdale**	07.88	1988	33	3	0		
ARMSTRONG, Gerry J.	Belfast	23.05.54	Bangor (NI)	**Tottenham H.**	11.75	1976-80	65	19	10	(F)	NI-63
			Tr	**Watford**	11.80	1980-82	50	26	12		
			Real Mallorca (Spain)	**West Bromwich A.**	08.85	1985	7	1	0		
			L	**Chesterfield**	01.86	1985	12	0	1		
			Tr	**Brighton & H.A.**	07.86	1986-88	30	17	6		
			L	**Millwall**	01.87	1987	7	0	0		
ARMSTRONG, Gordon I.	Newcastle	15.07.67	App	**Sunderland**	07.85	1984-88	137	4	20	(M)	
ARNOTT, Kevin W.	Gateshead	28.09.58	App	**Sunderland**	09.76	1976-81	132	1	16	(M)	
			L	**Blackburn Rov.**	11.81	1981	17	0	2		
			Tr	**Sheffield U.**	06.82	1982-86	120	1	11		
			L	**Blackburn Rov.**	11.82	1982	11	1	1		
			L	**Rotherham U.**	03.83	1982	9	0	2		
			Vasalund (Sweden)	**Chesterfield**	11.87	1987-88	51	4	1		
ASH, Mark C.	Sheffield	22.01.68	App	**Rotherham U.**	01.86	1986-88	14	6	0	(RB)	
ASHLEY, Kevin M.	Birmingham	31.12.68	App	**Birmingham C.**	12.86	1986-88	22	1	0	(FB)	
ASHURST, Jack	Coatbridge	12.10.54	App	**Sunderland**	10.71	1972-79	129	11	4	(CD)	
			Tr	**Blackpool**	10.79	1979-80	53	0	3		
			Tr	**Carlisle U.**	08.81	1981-85	194	0	2		
			Tr	**Leeds U.**	07.86	1986-88	88	1	1		
			Tr	**Doncaster Rov.**	11.88	1988	30	0	1		
ASKEW, W. (Billy)	Lumley	02.10.59	App	**Middlesbrough**	10.77	1979-81	10	2	0	(M)	
			Gateshead	**Hull C.**	09.82	1982-88	215	6	18		
ASPIN, Neil	Gateshead	12.04.65	App	**Leeds U.**	10.82	1981-88	203	4	5	(D)	
ASPINALL, Warren	Wigan	13.09.67	App	**Wigan Ath.**	08.85	1984-85	39	12	22	(F)	E Yth Int
			Tr	**Everton**	05.86	1985-86	0	7	0		
			Tr	**Aston Villa**	02.87	1986-87	40	4	14		
			Tr	**Portsmouth**	08.88	1988	36	4	11		
ASTBURY, Mike J.	Leeds	22.01.64	App	**York C.**	01.82	1980-85	48	0	0	(G)	
			L	**Peterborough U.**	01.86	1985	4	0	0		
			Tr	**Darlington**	03.86	1985-86	38	0	0		
			Tr	**Chester C.**	07.87	1987	5	0	0		
			Tr	**Chesterfield**	07.88	1988	8	0	0		
ATHERTON, Peter	Orrell	06.04.70	YTS	**Wigan Ath.**	02.88	1987-88	53	3	1	(FB)	
ATKIN, Paul A.	Nottingham	03.09.69	YTS	**Notts Co.**	07.87					(D)	E Yth Int
			Tr	**Bury**	03.89	1988	0	1	0		
ATKINS, Ian L.	Birmingham	16.01.57	App	**Shrewsbury T.**	01.75	1975-81	273	5	58	(M/CD)	
			Tr	**Sunderland**	08.82	1982-83	76	1	6		
			Tr	**Everton**	11.84	1984-85	6	1	1		
			Tr	**Ipswich T.**	09.85	1985-87	73	4	4		
			Tr	**Birmingham C.**	03.88	1987-88	48	0	4		
ATKINS, Mark N.	Doncaster	14.08.68	Jnrs	**Scunthorpe U.**	07.86	1984-87	45	5	2	(D)	
			Tr	**Blackburn Rov.**	06.88	1988	46	0	5		

Paul Allen (Tottenham Hotspur) Match Magazine

Mark Atkins (Blackburn Rovers) Match Magazine

Dave Beasant (Chelsea) Match Magazine

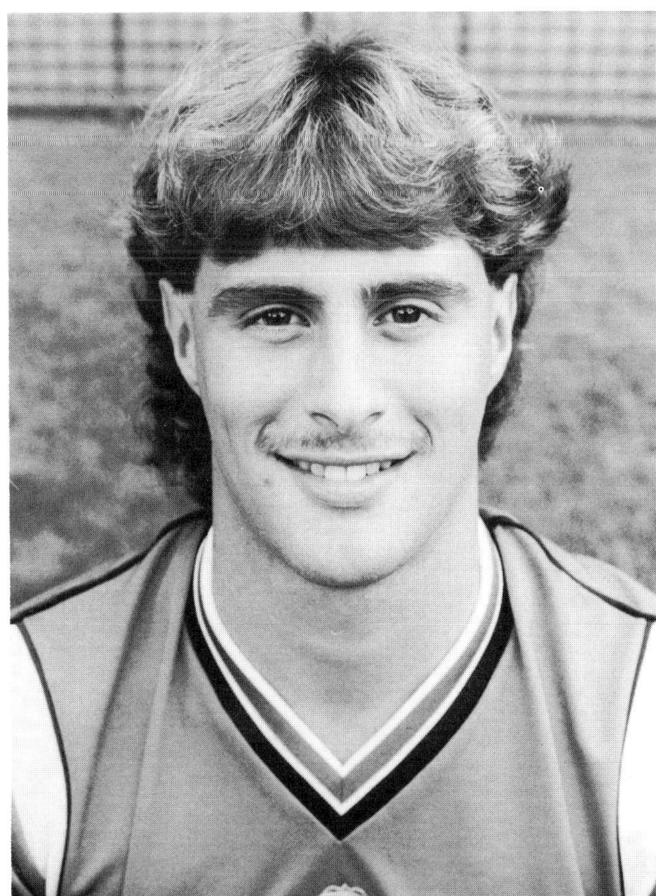

Clayton Blackmore (Manchester United & Wales) Match Magazine

Players Names	Birthplace	Date	Previous Club	League Club	Date Sign'd	Seasons Played	Career Record Apps	Sub	Gls	Pos.	Misc
ATKINS, Robert G.	Leicester	16.10.62	Enderby T.	Sheffield U.	07.82	1982-84	36	4	3	(CD)	
			Tr	Preston N.E.	02.85	1984-88	171	1	4		
ATKINSON, Brian	Darlington	19.01.71	YTS	Sunderland (YTS)	07.87	1988	2	1	0	(M)	
ATKINSON, Dalian R.	Shrewsbury	21.03.68	App	Ipswich T.	06.85	1985-88	49	11	18	(F)	
ATKINSON, Patrick D.	Singapore	22.05.70	Sheffield U. (YTS)	Hartlepool U.	08.88	1988	6	7	3	(F)	
ATKINSON, Paul	Chester-le-Street	19.01.66	App	Sunderland	11.83	1983-87	46	14	5	(W)	E Yth Int
			Tr	Port Vale	06.88	1988	4	0	3		
ATKINSON, Paul G.	Pudsey	14.08.61	App	Oldham Ath.	08.79	1979-82	139	4	11	(W)	Son of Charles
			Tr	Watford	07.83	1983	8	3	0		
			Tr	Oldham Ath.	08.85	1985-87	29	4	1		
			L	Swansea C.	12.86	1986	6	0	1		
			L	Bolton W.	02.87	1986	2	1	0		
			L	Swansea C.	03.87	1986	12	0	2		
			Tr	Burnley	07.88	1988	13	1	1		
AWFORD, Andy T.	Worcester	14.07.72	YTS	Portsmouth (YTS)	07.88	1988	3	1	0	(D)	
AYLOTT, Trevor K.C.	Bermondsey	26.11.57	App	Chelsea	07.76	1977-79	26	3	2	(F)	
			Tr	Barnsley	11.79	1979-81	93	3	26		
			Tr	Millwall	08.82	1982	32	0	5		
			Tr	Luton T.	03.83	1982-83	32	0	10		
			Tr	Crystal Palace	07.84	1984-85	50	3	12		
			L	Barnsley	02.86	1985	9	0	0		
			Tr	Bournemouth	08.86	1986-88	119	1	25		
BAILEY, Dennis L.	Lambeth	13.11.65	Barking	Fulham(N/C)	11.86					(F)	
			Farnborough T.	Crystal Palace	12.87	1987	0	5	1		
			L	Bristol Rov.	02.89	1988	17	0	9		
BAILEY, John A.	Liverpool	01.04.57	App	Blackburn Rov.	04.75	1975-78	115	5	1	(LB)	
			Tr	Everton	07.79	1979-85	171	0	3		
			Tr	Newcastle U.	10.85	1985-87	39	1	0		
			Tr	Bristol C.	09.88	1988	35	0	0		
BAILIE, Colin J.	Belfast	31.03.64	App	Swindon T.	03.82	1981-84	105	2	4	(FB)	
			Tr	Reading	07.85	1985-87	83	1	1		
			Tr	Cambridge U.	08.88	1988	23	0	1		
BAIRD, Ian J.	Rotherham	01.04.64	App	Southampton	04.82	1982-84	20	2	5	(F)	E Sch Int
			L	Cardiff C.	11.83	1983	12	0	6		
			L	Newcastle U.	12.84	1984	4	1	1		
			Tr	Leeds U.	03.85	1984-86	84	1	33		
			Tr	Portsmouth	06.87	1987	20	0	1		
			Tr	Leeds U.	03.88	1987-88	53	0	13		
BAKER, Clive E.	North Walsham	14.03.59	Jnrs	Norwich C.	07.77	1977-80	14	0	0	(G)	
			Tr	Barnsley	08.84	1984-88	208	0	0		
BAKER, Graham E.	Southampton	03.12.58	App	Southampton	12.76	1977-81	111	2	22	(M)	E U21-2
			Tr	Manchester C.	08.82	1982-86	114	3	19		
			Tr	Southampton	06.87	1987-88	55	2	8		
BAKER, D. Paul	Newcastle	05.01.63	Bishop Auckland	Southampton	06.84					(F/CD)	
			Tr	Carlisle U.	06.85	1985-86	66	5	11		
			Tr	Hartlepool U.	07.87	1987-88	77	2	25		
BAKER, Steve	Newcastle	02.12.61	App	Southampton	12.79	1980-87	61	12	0	(FB/M)	
			L	Burnley	02.84	1983	10	0	0		
			Tr	Leyton Orient	03.88	1987-88	55	0	5		
BALL, Kevin A.	Hastings	12.11.64	Coventry C.(App)	Portsmouth	10.82	1983-88	60	9	2	(CD)	
BALTACHA, Sergei	U.S.S.R.	17.02.58	Dinamo Kiev	Ipswich T.	01.89	1988	19	1	1	(CD)	Russian Int
BAMBER, J. Dave	St. Helens	01.02.59	Manchester Univ.	Blackpool	09.79	1979-82	81	5	29	(F)	
			Tr	Coventry C.	06.83	1983	18	1	3		
			Tr	Walsall	03.84	1983-84	17	3	7		
			Tr	Portsmouth	12.84	1984	4	0	1		
			Tr	Swindon T.	11.85	1985-87	103	3	31		
			Tr	Watford	06.88	1988	16	2	3		
			Tr	Stoke C.	12.88	1988	23	0	6		
BANKS, Chris	Stone	12.11.65	Jnrs	Port Vale	12.82	1984-87	50	15	1	(FB)	
			Tr	Exeter C.	06.88	1988	43	2	1		
BANKS, Ian F.	Mexborough	09.01.61	App	Barnsley	01.79	1978-82	158	6	37	(M)	
			Tr	Leicester C.	06.83	1983-86	78	15	14		
			Tr	Huddersfield T.	09.86	1986-87	78	0	17		
			Tr	Bradford C.	07.88	1988	26	4	3		
			Tr	West Bromwich A.	03.89	1988	2	2	0		
BANNISTER, Gary	Warrington	22.07.60	App	Coventry C.	05.78	1978-80	17	5	3	(F)	E U21-1
			Tr	Sheffield Wed.	08.81	1981-83	117	1	55		
			Tr	Q.P.R.	08.84	1984-87	136	0	56		
			Tr	Coventry C.	03.88	1987-88	29	3	9		
BANTON, Dale C.	Kensington	15.05.61	App	West Ham U.	05.79	1979-81	2	3	0	(F)	
			Tr	Aldershot	08.82	1982-84	105	1	47		
			Tr	York C.	11.84	1984-88	129	9	49		
			Tr	Walsall	10.88	1988	9	1	0		
			L	Grimsby T.	03.39	1988	3	5	1		
BARBER, Fred	Ferryhill	26.08.63	App	Darlington	08.81	1982-85	135	0	0	(G)	
			Tr	Everton	03.86						
			Tr	Walsall	10.86	1986-88	126	0	0		
BARBER, Philip A.	Tring	10.06.65	Aylesbury U.	Crystal Palace	02.84	1983-88	169	16	33	(W)	
BARDSLEY, David J.	Manchester	11.09.64	App	Blackpool	09.82	1981-83	45	0	0	(RB)	E Yth Int
			Tr	Watford	11.83	1983-87	97	3	7		
			Tr	Oxford U.	09.87	1987-88	71	0	7		
BARHAM, Mark F.	Folkestone	12.07.62	App	Norwich C.	04.80	1979-86	169	8	23	(W)	E Yth Int/E-2
			Tr	Huddersfield T.	07.87	1987-88	25	2	1		
			Tr	Middlesbrough	11.88	1988	3	1	0		
BARKER, Simon	Farnworth	04.11.64	App	Blackburn Rov.	11.82	1983-87	180	2	35	(M)	E U21-4
			Tr	Q.P.R.	07.88	1988	21	4	1		
BARLOW, Andrew J.	Oldham	24.11.65	Jnrs	Oldham Ath.	07.84	1984-88	117	12	2	(D/M)	
BARLOW, Martin D.	Plymouth	25.06.71	YTS	Plymouth Arg. (YTS)	08.88	1988	0	1	0	(F)	

Players Names	Birthplace	Date	Previous Club	League Club	Date Sign'd	Seasons Played	Career Record Apps	Sub	Gls	Pos.	Misc
BARNARD, Leigh K.	Worsley	29.10.58	App	**Portsmouth**	10.76	1977-81	71	8	8	(W)	
			L	**Peterborough U.**	03.82	1981	1	3	0		
			Tr	**Swindon T.**	07.82	1982-88	207	5	21		
			L	**Exeter C.**	02.85	1984	6	0	2		
BARNES, David	Paddington	16.11.61	App	**Coventry C.**	05.79	1979-81	9	0	0	(LB)	E Yth Int
			Tr	**Ipswich T.**	05.82	1982-83	16	1	0		
			Tr	**Wolverhampton W.**	10.84	1984-87	86	2	4		
			Tr	**Aldershot**	08.87	1987-88	68	1	1		
BARNES, David O. (Bobby)	Kingston	17.12.62	App	**West Ham U.**	09.80	1980-85	31	12	5	(W)	
			L	**Scunthorpe U.**	11.85	1985	6	0	0		
			Tr	**Aldershot**	03.86	1985-87	49	0	26		
			Tr	**Swindon T.**	10.87	1987-88	43	2	13		
			Tr	**Bournemouth**	03.89	1988	10	0	0		
BARNES, John C.B.	Jamaica (WI)	07.11.63	Sudbury Court	**Watford**	07.81	1981-86	232	1	65	(F)	E U21-2/E-47/FWA/PFA
			Tr	**Liverpool**	06.87	1987-88	71	0	23		Player of Year 1987-88
BARNES, Paul L.	Leicester	16.11.67	App	**Notts Co.**	11.85	1985-88	26	14	13	(F)	
BARNES, Peter S.	Manchester	10.06.57	App	**Manchester C.**	08.74	1974-78	108	7	15	(W)	E Yth Int/E U21-9/E-22/
			Tr	**West Bromwich A.**	07.79	1979-80	76	1	23		FL Rep/Son of Ken H.
			Tr	**Leeds U.**	08.81	1981	31	0	1		
			Real Betis (Spain)	**Leeds U.**	08.83	1983	25	2	4		
			Tr	**Coventry C.**	10.84	1984	18	0	2		
			Tr	**Manchester U.**	07.85	1985-86	19	1	2		
			Tr	**Manchester C.**	01.87	1986	8	0	0		
			L	**Bolton W.**	10.87	1987	2	0	0		
			L	**Port Vale**	12.87	1987	3	0	0		
			Tr	**Hull C.**	03.88	1987	11	0	0		
			Farense (Portugal)	**Bolton W.**	11.88	1988	2	1	0		
			Tr	**Sunderland**	02.89	1988	1	0	0		
BARNETT, David K.	Birmingham	16.04.67	Windsor & Eton	**Colchester U.**	08.88	1988	19	1	0	(M)	
BARNETT, Gary L.	Stratford	11.03.63	App	**Coventry C.**	01.81					(W)	
			Tr	**Oxford U.**	07.82	1982-85	37	8	9		
			L	**Wimbledon**	02.83	1982	5	0	1		
			L	**Fulham**	12.84	1984	0	2	1		
			Tr	**Fulham**	09.85	1985-88	143	5	29		
BARNSLEY, Andy	Sheffield	09.06.62	Denaby U.	**Rotherham U.**	06.85	1985	28	0	0	(D)	
			Tr	**Sheffield U.**	07.86	1986-88	73	4	0		
			Tr	**Rotherham U.**	12.88	1988	27	0	0		
BARR, Robert A.	Halifax	05.12.69	YTS	**Halifax T.**	06.88	1986-88	4	1	0	(CD)	
BARR, W.J. (Billy)	Halifax	21.01.69	YTS	**Halifax T.**	07.87	1987-88	67	6	4	(FB)	
BARRAS, Anthony	Billingham	29.03.71	YTS	**Hartlepool U.** (YTS)	07.87	1988	1	2	0		
BARRATT, A. (Tony)	Salford	18.10.65	Billingham T.	**Grimsby T.**	08.85	1985	20	2	0	(RB)	
			Billingham T.	**Hartlepool U.**	12.86	1986-88	93	5	4		
			Tr	**York C.**	03.89	1988	12	0	0		
BARRETT, Earl D.	Rochdale	28.04.67	App	**Manchester C.**	04.85	1985-86	2	1	0	(D)	
			L	**Chester C.**	03.86	1985	12	0	0		
			Tr	**Oldham Ath.**	11.87	1987-88	60	2	0		
BARRETT, Scott	Ilkeston	02.04.63	Ilkeston T.	**Wolverhampton W.**	09.84	1984-86	30	0	0	(G)	
			Tr	**Stoke C.**	07.87	1987-88	44	0	0		
BARRICK, Dean	Hemsworth	30.09.69	YTS	**Sheffield Wed.**	05.88	1988	8	0	2	(M)	
BARROW, Graham	Chorley	13.06.54	Altrincham	**Wigan Ath.**	07.81	1981-85	173	6	36	(M)	
			Tr	**Chester C.**	07.86	1986-88	114	0	12		
BARTLETT, Kevin F.	Portsmouth	12.10.62	App	**Portsmouth**	10.80	1980-81	0	3	0	(F)	
			Fareham T.	**Cardiff C.**	09.86	1986-88	60	22	25		
			Tr	**West Bromwich A.**	02.89	1988	10	7	3		
BARTRAM, Vince L.	Birmingham	07.08.68	Jnrs	**Wolverhampton W.**	08.85	1986	1	0	0	(G)	
BASTOCK, Paul A.	Leamington	19.05.70	Coventry C. (YTS)	**Cambridge U.**	03.88	1987-88	12	0	0	(G)	
BASTOW, Ian J.	Torquay	12.08.71	YTS	**Torquay U.**	03.89	1988	1	1	0		
BATCH, Nigel A.	Huddersfield	09.11.57	Derby Co.(App)	**Grimsby T.**	07.76	1976-86	348	0	0	(G)	
			Tr	**Lincoln C.**	(N/L)						
			Tr	**Darlington**	09.88	1988	30	0	0		
			L	**Stockport Co.**	03.89	1988	12	0	0		
BATER, Phil T.	Cardiff	26.10.55	App	**Bristol Rov.**	10.73	1974-80	211	1	2	(FB)	W U21-2
			Tr	**Wrexham**	09.81	1981-82	73	0	1		
			Tr	**Bristol Rov.**	09.83	1983-85	90	8	1		
			Tr	**Brentford**	05.86	1986	19	0	2		
			Tr	**Cardiff C.**	07.87	1987-88	67	9	0		
BATES, Jamie A.	Croydon	24.02.68	YTS	**Brentford**	08.86	1986-88	71	12	3	(CD)	
BATTY, David	Leeds	02.12.68	YTS	**Leeds U.**	07.87	1987-88	42	6	1	(M)	E U21-3
BATTY, Laurence W.	Westminster	15.02.64	Maidenhead U.	**Fulham**	08.84	1985-88	5	0	0	(G)	
BATTY, Paul W.	Doncaster	09.01.64	App	**Swindon T.**	01.82	1982-84	102	6	7	(M)	
			Tr	**Chesterfield**	07.85	1985	24	2	0		
			Tr	**Exeter C.**	07.86	1986-88	74	6	9		
BEADLE, Peter C.	Lambeth	13.05.72	YTS	**Gillingham** (YTS)	06.88	1988	1	1	0	(F)	
BEAGRIE, Peter S.	Middlesbrough	28.11.65	Jnrs	**Middlesbrough**	09.83	1984-85	24	9	2	(W)	E U21-2
			Tr	**Sheffield U.**	08.86	1986-87	81	3	11		
			Tr	**Stoke C.**	06.88	1988	41	0	7		
BEARDSLEY, Peter A.	Newcastle	18.01.61	Wallsend B.C.	**Carlisle U.**	08.79	1979-81	93	11	22	(F)	E-34
			Vancouver W. (Can.)	**Manchester U.**	09.82						
			Vancouver W. (Can.)	**Newcastle U.**	09.83	1983-86	146	1	61		
			Tr	**Liverpool**	07.87	1987-88	69	6	25		
BEARDSMORE, Russell P.	Wigan	28.09.68	App	**Manchester U.**	09.86	1988	17	6	2	(M)	E U 21-4
BEASANT, Dave	Willesden	20.03.59	Edgware T.	**Wimbledon**	08.79	1979-87	340	0	0	(G)	E 'B'
			Tr	**Newcastle U.**	06.88	1988	20	0	0		
			Tr	**Chelsea**	01.89	1988	22	0	0		
BEASLEY, Andy	Sedgley	05.02.64	App	**Luton T.**	02.82					(G)	
			Tr	**Mansfield T.**	07.84	1984-88	17	0	0		
			L	**Peterborough U.**	07.86	1986	7	0	0		
			L	**Scarborough**	03.88	1987	4	0	0		

Players Names	Birthplace	Date	Previous Club	League Club	Date Sign'd	Seasons Played	Career Record Apps	Sub	Gls	Pos.	Misc
BEATTIE, Andy H.	Liverpool	09.02.64	App	**Cambridge U.**	02.82	1983-87	94	3	2	(CD)	
BEATTIE, Stuart R.	Stevenston	10.07.67	Glasgow Rangers	**Doncaster Rov.**	01.87	1986-88	26	0	1	(CD)	
BEAUCHAMP, Joseph D.	Oxford	13.03.71	YTS	**Oxford U.**(YTS)	07.87	1988	0	1	0		
BEAUMONT, Chris P.	Sheffield	05.12.65	Denaby U.	**Rochdale**	07.88	1988	31	3	7	(F)	
BEAUMONT, David A.	Edinburgh	10.12.63	Dundee U.	**Luton T.**	01.89	1988	15	0	0	(CD)	S Yth Int/S U21-1
BEAUMONT, Nigel	Hemsworth	11.02.67	YTS	**Bradford C.**	07.85	1985	2	0	0	(D)	
			Tr	**Wrexham**	07.88	1988	20	1	0		
BEAVON, M. Stuart	Wolverhampton	30.11.58	App	**Tottenham H.**	07.76	1978-79	3	1	0	(M)	Son of Cyril
			L	**Notts. Co.**	12.79	1979	6	0	0		
			Tr	**Reading**	07.80	1980-88	351	13	41		
BECK, John A.	Edmonton	25.05.54	App	**Q.P.R.**	05.72	1972-75	32	8	1	(M)	
			Tr	**Coventry C.**	06.76	1976-78	60	9	6		
			Tr	**Fulham**	10.78	1978-81	113	1	12		
			Tr	**Bournemouth**	09.82	1982-85	132	5	13		
			Tr	**Cambridge U.**	07.86	1986-88	103	7	11		
BECKFORD, Darren R.	Manchester	12.05.67	App	**Manchester C.**	08.84	1984-86	7	4	0	(F)	E Yth Int/Brother of Jason
			L	**Bury**	10.85	1985	12	0	5		
			Tr	**Port Vale**	03.87	1986-88	86	7	33		
BECKFORD, Jason N.	Manchester	14.02.70	YTS	**Manchester C.**	08.87	1987-88	7	6	0	(W)	Brother of Darren/E Yth Int
BEDFORD, Kevin E.	Carshalton	26.12.68	App	**Wimbledon**	11.86	1987	4	0	0	(LB)	
			L	**Aldershot**	02.88	1987	16	0	0		
			Tr	**Colchester U.**	07.88	1988	24	2	0		
BEENEY, Mark R.	Tunbridge Wells	30.12.67	YTS	**Gillingham**	08.85	1986	2	0	0	(G)	
BEESLEY, Paul	Liverpool	21.07.65	Altrincham	**Wigan Ath.**	09.84	1984-88	142	2	3	(CD)	
BEESTON, Carl F.	Stoke	30.06.67	App	**Stoke C.**	06.85	1984-88	39	4	2	(M/D)	E U21-1
BEGLIN, Jim M.	Waterford (Ire)	29.07.63	Shamrock Rov.	**Liverpool**	05.83	1984-86	64	0	2	(LB)	IR-15
BELL, Doug	Paisley	05.09.59	Hibernian	**Shrewsbury T.**	12.87	1987-88	38	3	3	(M)	S U21-2
			L	**Hull C.**	03.89	1988	4	0	0		
BELLAMY, Gary	Worksop	04.07.62	App	**Chesterfield**	06.80	1980-86	181	3	7	(CD)	
			Tr	**Wolverhampton W.**	07.87	1987-88	67	0	3		
BENALI, Frances V.	Southampton	30.12.68	App	**Southampton**	12.86	1988	3	4	0	(F)	
BENBOW, Ian R.	Hereford	09.01.69	YTS	**Hereford U.**	07.87	1987-88	39	16	3	(M)	
BENJAMIN, Ian T.	Nottingham	11.12.61	App	**Sheffield U.**	05.79	1978-79	4	1	3	(F)	Brother of Triston/E Yt Int
			Tr	**West Bromwich A.**	08.79	1980	1	1	0		
			Tr	**Notts. Co.**	02.82						
			Tr	**Peterborough U.**	08.82	1982-83	77	3	14		
			Tr	**Northampton T.**	08.84	1984-87	147	3	58		
			Tr	**Cambridge U.**	10.87	1987	20	5	2		
			Tr	**Chester C.**	07.88	1988	18	4	3		
			Tr	**Exeter C.**	02.89	1988	20	0	3		
BENNETT, David A.	Manchester	11.07.59	Jnrs	**Manchester C.**	06.77	1978-80	43	9	9	(W)	Brother of Gary E.
			Tr	**Cardiff C.**	09.81	1981-82	75	2	18		
			Tr	**Coventry C.**	07.83	1983-88	157	15	25		
			Tr	**Sheffield Wed.**	03.89	1988	10	0	0		
BENNETT, Gary	Enfield	13.11.70	YTS	**Colchester U.**	11.88	1988	6	3	1	(F)	
BENNETT, Gary E.	Manchester	04.12.61	Ashton U.	**Manchester C.**	09.79					(CD)	Brother of David A.
			Tr	**Cardiff C.**	09.81	1981-83	85	2	11		
			Tr	**Sunderland**	07.84	1984-88	181	3	15		
BENNETT, Gary M.	Kirkby	20.09.62		**Wigan Ath.**	10.84	1984	10	10	3	(F)	
			Tr	**Chester C.**	08.85	1985-88	109	17	36		
			Tr	**Southend U.**	11.88	1988	16	1	2		
BENNETT, Martyn	Birmingham	04.08.61	App	**West Bromwich A.**	08.78	1978-87	180	1	9	(CD)	E Sch Int
BENNETT, Michael	Bolton	24.12.62	App	**Bolton W.**	01.80	1979-82	62	3	1	(LB)	E Yth Int
			Tr	**Wolverhampton W.**	06.83	1983	6	0	0		
			Tr	**Cambridge U.**	03.84	1983-85	76	0	0		
			Tr	**Preston N.E.**	09.86	1986-87	75	1	1		
BENNETT, Michael R.	Lambeth	27.07.69	App	**Charlton Ath.**	04.87	1986-88	22	7	1	(W)	
BENNETT, Tommy M.	Falkirk	12.12.69	App	**Aston Villa**	12.87						
			Tr	**Wolverhampton W.**	07.88	1988	0	2	0		
BENNYWORTH, Ian R.	Hull	15.01.62	App	**Hull C.**	01.80	1979	1	0	0	(CD)	
			Nuneaton Bor.	**Scarborough**	(N/L)	1987-88	73	1	3		
BENSTEAD, Graham M.	Aldershot	20.08.63	App	**Q.P.R.**	07.81					(G)	E Yth Int
			Tr	**Norwich C.**	03.85	1984-87	16	0	0		
			L	**Colchester U.**	08.87	1987	18	0	0		
			L	**Sheffield U.**	03.88	1987	8	0	0		
			Tr	**Sheffield U.**	07.88	1988	39	0	0		
BENT, Junior A.	Huddersfield	01.03.70	YTS	**Huddersfield T.**	12.87	1987-88	19	10	5	(W)	
BERESFORD, John	Sheffield	04.09.66	App	**Manchester C.**	09.83					(M/LB)	E Sch Int/E Yth Int
			Tr	**Barnsley**	07.86	1986-88	79	9	5		
			Tr	**Portsmouth**	03.89	1988	1	1	0		
BERGSSON, Gudni	Iceland	21.07.65	Valur (Iceland)	**Tottenham H.**	12.88	1988	8	0	0	(D)	Iceland Int
BERNAL, Andrew S.	Australia	16.05.66	Sporting Gijon (Spain)	**Ipswich T.**	09.87	1987	4	5	0	(D)	
BERRY, George F.	West Germany	19.11.57	App	**Wolverhampton W.**	11.75	1976-81	124	0	4	(CD)	W-5
			Tr	**Stoke C.**	08.82	1982-88	214	7	26		
			L	**Doncaster Rov.**	08.84	1984	1	0	0		
BERRY, Les D.	Plumstead	04.05.56	App	**Charlton Ath.**	03.74	1975-85	352	6	11	(CD)	
			Tr	**Brighton & H.A.**	08.86	1986	22	1	0		
			Tr	**Gillingham**	03.87	1986-87	26	5	0		
BERRY, Steve A.	Gosport	04.04.63	App	**Portsmouth**	01.81	1981-82	26	2	2	(M)	
			L	**Aldershot**	03.84	1983	5	2	0		
			Tr	**Sunderland**	07.84	1984-85	32	3	2		
			Tr	**Newport Co.**	12.85	1985-86	60	0	6		
			Tr	**Swindon T.**	03.87	1986-87	4	0	0		
			Tr	**Aldershot**	10.87	1987-88	48	0	6		
			Tr	**Northampton T.**	10.88	1988	34	0	3		

Steve Bould (Arsenal) Match Magazine

Tim Breaker (Luton Town) Match Magazine

Ian Brightwell (Manchester City) Match Magazine

Les Briley (Millwall) Match Magazine

Players Names	Birthplace	Date	Previous Club	League Club	Date Sign'd	Seasons Played	Career Record Apps	Sub	Gls	Pos.	Misc
BERTSCHIN, Keith E.	Enfield	25.08.56	Barnet	**Ipswich T.**	10.73	1975-76	19	13	8	(F)	E Yth Int/E U21-3
			Tr	**Birmingham C.**	07.77	1977-80	113	5	29		
			Tr	**Norwich C.**	08.81	1981-84	112	2	29		
			Tr	**Stoke C.**	11.84	1984-86	82	6	29		
			Tr	**Sunderland**	03.87	1986-87	25	11	7		
			Tr	**Walsall**	08.88	1988	11	9	0		
BIGGINS, Wayne	Sheffield	20.11.61	App	**Lincoln C.**	11.79	1980	8	0	1	(F)	
			Matlock T.	**Burnley**	02.84	1983-85	78	0	29		
			Tr	**Norwich C.**	10.85	1985-87	66	13	16		
			Tr	**Manchester C.**	07.88	1988	29	3	9		
BILLING, Peter G.	Liverpool	24.10.64	South Liverpool	**Everton**	01.86	1985	1	0	0	(CD)	
			Tr	**Crewe Alex.**	12.86	1986-88	83	5	1		
BIRCH, Paul	Birmingham	20.11.62	App	**Aston Villa**	07.80	1983-88	141	12	16	(M)	Brother of Alan
BIRCH, Paul A.	Reading	03.12.68	Arsenal (App)	**Portsmouth**	01.87					(F)	
			Tr	**Brentford**	12.87	1987-88	13	5	2		
BIRD, Adrian L.	Bristol	08.07.69	App	**Birmingham C.**	07.87	1986-88	23	4	0	(CD)	
BIRTLES, Garry	Nottingham	27.07.56	Long Eaton U.	**Nottingham F.**	12.76	1976-80	87	0	32	(F)	E U21-2/E-3/E 'B'
			Tr	**Manchester U.**	10.80	1980-81	57	1	11		
			Tr	**Nottingham F.**	09.82	1982-86	122	3	38		
			Tr	**Notts. Co.**	06.87	1987-88	62	1	9		
BISHOP, D. Charlie	Nottingham	16.02.68	Stoke C.(App)	**Watford**	04.86					(FB)	
			Tr	**Bury**	08.87	1987-88	50	5	3		
BISHOP, Eddie M.	Liverpool	28.11.62	Runcorn	**Tranmere Rov.**	03.88	1987-88	28	12	9	(M)	
BISHOP, Ian W.	Liverpool	29.05.65	App	**Everton**	05.83	1983	0	1	0	(M)	
			L	**Crewe Alex.**	03.84	1983	4	0	0		
			Tr	**Carlisle U.**	10.84	1984-87	131	1	14		
			Tr	**Bournemouth**	07.88	1988	44	0	2		
BISSET, Nicky	Fulham	05.04.64	Barnet	**Brighton & H.A.**	09.88	1988	16	0	0	(CD)	
BLACK, Kingsley	Luton	22.06.68	Jnrs	**Luton T.**	07.86	1987-88	46	4	8	(W)	NI-6/NIU21-1
BLACKMORE, Clayton G.	Neath	23.09.64	App	**Manchester U.**	09.82	1983-88	65	11	10	(FB)	W U21-3/W-21/W Yth Int
BLACKWELL, Kevin P.	Luton	21.12.58	Barnet	**Scarborough**	(N/L)	1987-88	36	0	0	(G)	
BLADES, Paul A.	Peterborough	05.01.65	App	**Derby Co.**	12.82	1982-88	139	8	1	(D)	E Yth Int
BLAIN, Colin A.	Urmston	07.03.70	YTS	**Halifax T.**	06.88	1987-88	18	5	0	(M)	
BLAIR, Andy	Kirkcaldy	18.12.59	App	**Coventry C.**	10.77	1978-80	90	3	6	(M)	S U21-5
			Tr	**Aston Villa**	08.81	1981-83	24	9	0		
			L	**Wolverhampton W.**	10.83	1983	10	0	0		
			Tr	**Sheffield Wed.**	08.84	1984-85	58	0	3		
			Tr	**Aston Villa**	03.86	1985-87	19	2	1		
			L	**Barnsley**	03.88	1987	6	0	0		
			Tr	**Northampton T.**	10.88	1988	1	2	0		
BLAKE, Mark C.	Portsmouth	17.12.67	App	**Southampton**	12.85	1985-88	18	0	2	(CD)	E Yth Int
BLAKE, Noel L.G.	Jamaica (WI)	12.01.62	Sutton Coldfield	**Aston Villa**	08.79	1979-81	4	0	0	(CD)	
			L	**Shrewsbury T.**	03.82	1981	6	0	0		
			Tr	**Birmingham C.**	09.82	1982-83	76	0	5		
			Tr	**Portsmouth**	08.84	1984-87	144	0	10		
			Tr	**Leeds U.**	07.88	1988	44	0	4		
BLISSETT, Gary P.	Manchester	29.06.64	Altrincham	**Crewe Alex.**	08.83	1983-86	112	10	38	(F)	
			Tr	**Brentford**	03.87	1986-88	85	2	20		
BLISSETT, Luther L.	Jamaica (WI)	01.02.58	Jnrs	**Watford**	07.75	1975-82	222	24	95	(F)	E U21-4/E-14
			A.C. Milan (Italy)	**Watford**	08.84	1984-88	113	14	44		
			Tr	**Bournemouth**	11.88	1988	30	0	19		
BLOOMER, R. (Bob)	Sheffield	21.06.66	Jnrs	**Chesterfield**	08.85	1985-88	105	14	14	(FB/M)	
BLUNDELL, Chris K.	Wigan	07.12.69	YTS	**Oldham Ath.**	07.88	1987-88	2	1	0	(D)	
BODAK, Peter J.	Birmingham	12.08.61	App	**Coventry C.**	05.79	1980-81	30	2	5	(M)	
			Tr	**Manchester U.**	08.82						
			Tr	**Manchester C.**	12.82	1982	12	2	1		
			Antwerp (Belgium)	**Crewe Alex.**	12.86	1986-87	49	4	7		
			Tr	**Swansea C.**	03.88	1987-88	25	6	4		
BODIN, Paul J.	Cardiff	13.09.64	Newport Co.(N/C)	**Cardiff C.**	08.82	1982-84	68	7	4	(M)	WU21-1
			Bath C.	**Newport Co.**	01.88	1987	6	0	1		
			Tr	**Swindon T.**	03.88	1987-88	18	3	2		
BODLEY, Mike J.	Hayes	14.09.67	App	**Chelsea**	09.85	1987	6	0	1	(CD)	
			Tr	**Northampton T.**	01.89	1988	20	0	0		
BOGIE, Ian	Newcastle	06.12.67	App	**Newcastle U.**	12.85	1986-88	7	7	0	(M)	E Sch Int
			Tr	**Preston N.E.**	02.89	1988	9	4	1		
BOLDER, R.J. (Bob)	Dover	02.10.58	Dover T.	**Sheffield Wed.**	03.77	1977-82	196	0	0	(G)	
			Tr	**Liverpool**	08.83						
			Tr	**Sunderland**	09.85	1985	22	0	0		
			Tr	**Charlton Ath.**	08.86	1986-88	99	0	0		
BOND, Kevin J.	West Ham	22.06.57	Bournemouth(App)	**Norwich C.**	06.75	1975-80	137	5	12	(CD)	Son of John
			Seattle S. (USA)	**Manchester C.**	09.81	1981-84	108	2	11		
			Tr	**Southampton**	09.84	1984-87	139	1	6		
			Tr	**Bournemouth**	08.88	1988	27	0	1		
BONNYMAN, Phil	Glasgow	06.02.54	Hamilton Acad.	**Carlisle U.**	03.76	1975-79	149	3	26	(M)	
			Tr	**Chesterfield**	03.80	1979-81	98	1	25		
			Tr	**Grimsby T.**	08.82	1982-86	146	5	15		
			L	**Stoke C.**	03.86	1985	7	0	0		
			Tr	**Darlington**	07.87	1987-88	49	1	5		
BOOKER, R. (Bob)	Watford	25.01.58	Bedmond S.C.	**Brentford**	10.78	1978-88	207	44	42	(M)	
			Tr	**Sheffield U.**	11.88	1988	26	0	2		
BORROWS, Brian	Liverpool	20.12.60	Jnrs	**Everton**	04.80	1981-82	27	0	0	(RB)	
			Tr	**Bolton W.**	03.83	1982-84	95	0	0		
			Tr	**Coventry C.**	06.85	1985-88	152	1	2		
BORTHWICK, John R.	Hartlepool	24.03.64	Owton MSC	**Hartlepool U.**	12.82	1982-88	96	21	15	(F)	
BOULD, Stephen A.	Stoke	16.11.62	App	**Stoke C.**	11.80	1981-87	179	4	6	(CD)	
			L	**Torquay U.**	10.82	1982	9	0	0		
			Tr	**Arsenal**	06.88	1988	26	4	2		

Players Names	Birthplace	Date	Previous Club	League Club	Date Sign'd	Seasons Played	Career Record Apps	Sub	Gls	Pos.	Misc
BOWDEN, Jon L.	Stockport	21.01.63	Jnrs	**Oldham Ath.**	01.80	1981-84	73	9	5	(M)	
			Tr	**Port Vale**	09.85	1985-86	64	6	7		
			Tr	**Wrexham**	07.87	1987-88	61	7	11		
BOWEN, R. Mark	Neath	07.12.63	App	**Tottenham H.**	12.81	1983-86	14	3	2	(FB)	W Sch/Yth Int/W U21-3/W-7
			Tr	**Norwich C.**	07.87	1987-88	58	1	3		
BOWLING, Ian	Sheffield	27.07.65	Gainsborough Trin.	**Lincoln C.**	10.88	1988	8	0	0	(G)	
BOWYER, Ian	Ellesmere Port	06.06.51	App	**Manchester C.**	08.68	1968-70	42	8	13	(M)	
			Tr	**Leyton Orient**	06.71	1971-72	75	3	18		
			Tr	**Nottingham F.**	10.73	1973-80	222	17	49		
			Tr	**Sunderland**	01.81	1980-81	15	0	1		
			Tr	**Nottingham F.**	01.82	1981-86	203	3	19		
			Tr	**Hereford U.**	07.87	1987-88	33	5	1		
BOYLE, Terry D.J.	Ammanford	29.10.58	App	**Tottenham H.**	11.75					(CD)	W Sch Int/W U21-1/W-2
			Tr	**Crystal Palace**	01.78	1977-80	24	2	1		
			L	**Wimbledon**	09.81	1981	5	0	1		
			Tr	**Bristol C.**	10.81	1981-82	36	1	0		
			Tr	**Newport Co.**	11.82	1982-85	165	1	11		
			Tr	**Cardiff C.**	08.86	1986-88	126	2	7		
BRACEWELL, Paul W.	Heswall	19.07.62	App	**Stoke C.**	02.80	1979-82	123	6	5	(M)	E U21-13/E-3
			Tr	**Sunderland**	07.83	1983	38	0	4		
			Tr	**Everton**	05.84	1984-88	95	0	7		
BRACEY, Lee M.I.	Barking	11.09.68	YTS	**West Ham U.**	07.87					(G)	
			Tr	**Swansea C.**	08.88	1988	30	0	0		
BRADLEY, Darren M.	Birmingham	24.11.65	App	**Aston Villa**	11.83	1984-85	16	4	0	(M)	E Yth Int
			Tr	**West Bromwich A.**	03.86	1985-88	62	7	1		
BRADLEY, Russell	Birmingham	28.03.66	Dudley T.	**Nottingham F.**	05.88					(CD)	
			L	**Hereford U.**	11.88	1988	5	0	0		
			L	**Hereford U.**	03.89	1988	7	0	1		
BRADSHAW, Carl	Sheffield	02.10.68	App	**Sheffield Wed.**	08.86	1986-88	16	16	4	(F)	E Yth Int
			L	**Barnsley**	08.86	1986	6	0	1		
			Tr	**Manchester C.**	09.88	1988	1	4	0		
BRADSHAW, Darren S.	Sheffield	19.03.67	Matlock T.	**Chesterfield**	08.87	1987	18	0	0	(M)	E Yth Int
			Matlock T.	**York C.**	11.87	1987-88	58	1	3		
BRADSHAW, Mark	Ashton-u-Lyne	07.06.69	YTS	**Blackpool**	12.87	1986-87	16	4	0	(D)	
BRADSHAW, Paul W.	Altrincham	28.04.56	App	**Blackburn Rov.**	07.73	1973-77	78	0	0	(G)	E Yth Int/E U21-4
			Tr	**Wolverhampton W.**	09.77	1977-83	200	0	0		
			Vancouver W. (Can)	**West Bromwich A.**	04.85	1985	8	0	0		
				Bristol Rov (N/C)	03.87	1986	5	0	0		
			Tr	**Newport Co.** (N/C)	07.87	1987	23	0	0		
			Tr	**West Bromwich A.**	08.88	1988	2	0	0		
BRADY, W. Liam	Dublin	13.02.56	App	**Arsenal**	08.73	1973-79	227	8	43	(M)	IR-70/PFA Player of Year 1979
			Ascoli (It.)	**West Ham U.**	03.87	1986-88	54	2	6		
BRAMHALL, John	Warrington	20.11.56	Stockton Heath	**Tranmere Rov.**	07.76	1976-81	164	6	7	(CD)	
			Tr	**Bury**	03.82	1981-85	165	2	17		
			L	**Chester C.**	11.85	1985	4	0	0		
			Tr	**Rochdale**	08.86	1986-87	86	0	13		
			Tr	**Halifax T.**	08.88	1988	39	0	3		
BRAMWELL, Steven	Stockport	09.10.70	YTS	**Oldham Ath.** (YTS)	07.87	1988	0	1	0	(F)	
BRANAGAN, Jim P.S.	Urmston	03.07.55	Jnrs	**Oldham Ath.**	07.73	1974-76	24	3	0	(FB)	Son of Ken
			Cape Town C.(SA)	**Huddersfield T.**	11.77	1977-78	37	1	0		
			Tr	**Blackburn Rov.**	10.79	1979-86	290	4	5		
			Tr	**Preston N.E.**	05.87	1987	3	0	0		
			Tr	**York C.**	10.87	1987-88	40	2	1		
BRANAGAN, Keith G.	Fulham	10.07.66	Jnrs	**Cambridge U.**	08.83	1983-87	110	0	0	(G)	
			Tr	**Millwall**	03.88						
BRAY, Ian M.	Neath	06.12.62	App	**Hereford U.**	12.80	1981-84	105	3	4	(LB)	
			Tr	**Huddersfield T.**	07.85	1985-87	74	1	1		
BRAZIL, Derek M.	Dublin	14.12.68	Rivermount B.C.	**Manchester U.**	03.86	1988	0	1	0	(CD)	
BRAZIL, Gary N.	Tunbridge Wells	19.09.62	Crystal Palace(App)	**Sheffield U.**	08.80	1980-84	39	23	9	(F)	
			L	**Port Vale**	08.84	1984	6	0	3		
			Tr	**Preston N.E.**	02.85	1984-88	163	3	56		
			Tr	**Newcastle U.**	02.89	1988	3	4	0		
BREACKER, Tim S.	Bicester	02.07.65	App	**Luton T.**	05.83	1983-88	158	6	2	(RB)	E U21-2
BREMNER, Des G.	Banff	07.09.52	Hibernian	**Aston Villa**	09.79	1979-84	170	4	9	(M)	S U23-9/S-1/Brother of Kevin
			Tr	**Birmingham C.**	09.84	1984-88	167	1	5		
BREMNER, Kevin J.	Banff	07.10.57	Keith	**Colchester U.**	10.80	1980-82	89	6	31	(F)	Brother of Des
			L	**Birmingham C.**	10.82	1982	3	1	1		
			L	**Wrexham**	12.82	1982	4	0	1		
			L	**Plymouth Arg.**	01.83	1982	5	0	1		
			Tr	**Millwall**	02.83	1982-84	87	9	33		
			Tr	**Reading**	08.85	1985-86	60	4	21		
			Tr	**Brighton & H.A.**	07.87	1987-88	83	2	23		
BRENNAN, Mark R.	Rossendale	04.10.65	App	**Ipswich T.**	04.83	1983-87	165	3	19	(M)	E Yth Int/E U21-5
			Tr	**Middlesbrough**	07.88	1988	25	0	3		
BRESSINGTON, Graham	Windsor	08.07.66	Wycombe W.	**Lincoln C.**	(N/L)	1988	30	0	1	(M)	
BREVETT, Rufus E.	Derby	24.09.69	YTS	**Doncaster Rov.**	06.88	1987-88	38	2	0	(LB)	
BRIEN, A.J. (Tony)	Dublin	10.02.69	App	**Leicester C.**	02.87	1987-88	12	4	1	(CD)	
			Tr	**Chesterfield**	12.88	1988	29	0	1		
BRIGGS, Gary	Leeds	21.06.59	App	**Middlesbrough**	05.77					(CD)	
			Tr	**Oxford U.**	01.78	1977-88	418	2	18		
BRIGHT, Mark A.	Stoke	06.06.62	Leek T.	**Port Vale**	10.81	1981-83	18	11	10	(F)	
			Tr	**Leicester C.**	07.84	1984-86	26	16	6		
			Tr	**Crystal Palace**	11.86	1986-88	112	0	51		
BRIGHTWELL, Ian R.	Lutterworth	09.04.68	Jnrs	**Manchester C.**	05.86	1986-88	68	7	12	(M)	E Yth Int/E U 21-2
BRILEY, Les	Lambeth	02.10.56	App	**Chelsea**	06.74					(M)	
			Tr	**Hereford U.**	05.76	1976-77	60	1	2		
			Tr	**Wimbledon**	02.78	1977-79	59	2	2		
			Tr	**Aldershot**	03.80	1979-83	157	0	3		
			Tr	**Millwall**	05.84	1984-88	179	1	10		

Steve Bull (Wolverhampton Wanderers & England) Match Magazine

Guy Butters (Tottenham Hotspur) Match Magazine

Tony Cascarino (Millwall & Eire) Match Magazine

Lee Chapman (Nottingham Forest) Match Magazine

Players Names	Birthplace	Date	Previous Club	League Club	Date Sign'd	Seasons Played	Career Record Apps	Sub	Gls	Pos.	Misc
BRIMACOMBE, John	Plymouth	25.11.58	Saltash U.	**Plymouth Arg.**	08.85	1985-88	75	3	3	(RB)	
BRITTON, Ian	Dundee	19.05.54	App	**Chelsea**	07.71	1972-81	253	10	33	(W)	
			Dundee U.	**Blackpool**	12.83	1983-85	100	6	15		
			Tr	**Burnley**	08.86	1986-88	102	6	10		
BROADBENT, Graham	Halifax	20.12.58	Emley	**Halifax T.** (N/C)	09.88	1988	2	10	2	(F)	
BROCK, Kevin S.	Bicester	09.09.62	App	**Oxford U.**	09.79	1979-86	229	17	26	(W)	E Sch Int/E U21-4
			Tr	**Q.P.R.**	08.87	1987-88	38	2	2		
			Tr	**Newcastle U.**	12.88	1988	21	0	2		
BROCKIE, Vincent	Greenock	02.02.69	YTS	**Leeds U.**	07.87	1987	2	0	0	(RB)	
			Tr	**Doncaster Rov.**	12.88	1988	23	0	2		
BRODDLE, Julian R.	Laughton	01.11.64	App	**Sheffield U.**	11.82	1981	1	0	0	(W)	
			Tr	**Scunthorpe U.**	08.83	1983-87	126	18	32		
			Tr	**Barnsley**	09.87	1987-88	43	14	4		
BROMAGE, Russell	Stoke	09.11.59	App	**Port Vale**	11.77	1977-86	339	8	13	(LB)	
			L	**Oldham Ath.**	10.83	1983	2	0	0		
			Tr	**Bristol C.**	08.87	1987-88	41	2	1		
BROOK, Gary	Dewsbury	09.05.64	Frickley Ath.	**Newport Co.**	12.87	1987	14	0	2	(F)	
			Tr	**Scarborough**	03.88	1987-88	49	0	12		
BROOKE, Gary J.	Bethnal Green	24.11.60	App	**Tottenham H.**	10.78	1980-84	49	24	15	(W)	
			Tr	**Norwich C.**	07.85	1985-86	8	6	2		
			Groningen (Neth)	**Wimbledon**	08.88	1988	5	5	0		
BROOKMAN, Nicky A.	Manchester	28.10.68	Wrexham (N/C)	**Bolton W.**	11.86	1986-88	47	8	10	(M)	
BROOKS, Shaun	Reading	09.10.62	App	**Crystal Palace**	10.79	1979-83	47	7	4	(M)	E Sch Int/E Yth Int/Son of John
			Tr	**Leyton Orient**	10.83	1983-86	140	8	26		
			Tr	**Bournemouth**	06.87	1987-88	62	11	9		
BROTHERSTON, Noel	Belfast	18.11.56	App	**Tottenham H.**	04.74	1975	1	0	0	(W)	NI U21-1/NI-27
			Tr	**Blackburn Rov.**	07.77	1977-86	307	10	40		
			Tr	**Bury**	06.87	1987-88	32	6	4		
			L	**Scarborough**	10.88	1988	5	0	0		
BROWN, A.J. (Tony)	Bradford	17.09.58	Thackley	**Leeds U.**	03.83	1982-84	24	0	1	(CD)	
			L	**Doncaster Rov.**	11.84	1984	5	0	0		
			Tr	**Doncaster Rov.**	03.85	1984-86	80	2	2		
			Tr	**Scunthorpe U.**	07.87	1987-88	46	8	2		
BROWN, David J.	Hartlepool	28.01.57	Horden CW	**Middlesbrough**	02.77	1977	10	0	0	(G)	
			L	**Plymouth Arg.**	08.79	1979	5	0	0		
			Tr	**Oxford U.**	10.79	1979-80	21	0	0		
			Tr	**Bury**	09.81	1981-84	146	0	0		
			Tr	**Preston N.E.**	06.86	1986-88	74	0	0		
			L	**Scunthorpe U.**	01.89	1988	5	0	0		
BROWN, Grant A.	Sunderland	19.11.69	YTS	**Leicester C.**	07.88	1987-88	14	0	0	(CD)	
BROWN, Jim G.	Coatbridge	11.05.52	Albion Rovers	**Chesterfield**	12.72	1972-73	47	0	0	(G)	S U23-4/S-1
			Tr	**Sheffield U.**	03.74	1973-77	170	0	0		
			Washington D.(USA)	**Cardiff C.**	12.82	1982	3	0	0		
			Kettering T.	**Chesterfield**	07.83	1983-88	135	0	1		
BROWN, Ken J.	Barking	11.07.67	App	**Norwich C.**	07.85	1986-87	24	1	0	(RB)	Son of Ken
			Tr	**Plymouth Arg.**	08.88	1988	39	0	1		
BROWN, Kevan	Andover	02.01.66	Jnrs	**Southampton**	07.84					(RB)	
			Tr	**Brighton & H.A.**	02.87	1986-88	52	1	0		
			Tr	**Aldershot**	11.88	1988	27	1	0		
BROWN, Malcolm	Salford	13.12.56	App	**Bury**	12.74	1973-76	10	1	0	(RB)	
			Tr	**Huddersfield T.**	05.77	1977-82	256	0	16		
			Tr	**Newcastle U.**	08.83	1984	39	0	0		
			Tr	**Huddersfield T.**	06.85	1985-88	93	3	2		
			Tr	**Rochdale** (N/C)	02.89	1988	11	0	0		
BROWN, Michael A.	Birmingham	08.02.68	App	**Shrewsbury T.**	02.86	1986-88	89	15	7	(F)	
BROWN, Nicky L.	Hull	16.10.66	YTS	**Hull C.**	08.85	1985-88	22	2	0	(FB)	
BROWN, Phil J.	Sheffield	16.01.66	App	**Chesterfield**	10.83	1982-86	82	5	19	(W)	Twin brother of Neil
			Tr	**Stockport Co.**	12.86	1986	23	0	1		
			Tr	**Lincoln C.**	(N/L)	1988	31	7	3		
BROWN, Philip	South Shields	30.05.59	Jnrs	**Hartlepool U.**	07.78	1979-84	210	7	8	(RB)	
			Tr	**Halifax T.**	07.85	1985-87	135	0	19		
			Tr	**Bolton W.**	06.88	1988	46	0	4		
BRUCE, Steve R.	Corbridge	31.12.60	App	**Gillingham**	10.78	1979-83	203	2	29	(CD)	E Yth Int/E-'B'
			Tr	**Norwich C.**	08.84	1984-87	141	0	14		
			Tr	**Manchester U.**	12.87	1987-88	59	0	4		
BRUSH, Paul	Plaistow	22.02.58	App	**West Ham U.**	02.76	1977-84	144	7	1	(FB)	
			Tr	**Crystal Palace**	09.85	1985-87	50	0	3		
			Tr	**Southend U.**	01.88	1987-88	41	1	1		
BRYSON, Ian C.	Kilmarnock	26.11.62	Kilmarnock	**Sheffield U.**	08.88	1988	36	1	8	(LW)	
BUCKLE, Paul J.	Hatfield	16.12.70	YTS	**Brentford** (YTS)	07.87	1987	0	1	0	(M)	
BUCKLEY, John W.	East Kilbride	10.05.62	Partick Thistle	**Doncaster Rov.**	07.84	1984-85	79	5	11	(W)	
			Tr	**Leeds U.**	06.86	1986-87	6	4	1		
			L	**Leicester C.**	03.87	1986	1	4	0		
			L	**Doncaster Rov.**	10.87	1987	6	0	0		
			Tr	**Rotherham U.**	11.87	1987-88	43	19	5		
BUCKLEY, Neil A.	Hull	25.09.68	YTS	**Hull C.**	12.86	1986-88	14	0	0	(D)	
BULL, Gary W.	Tipton	12.06.66	Paget Rangers	**Southampton**	10.86					(F)	
			Tr	**Cambridge U.**	03.88	1987-88	13	6	4		
BULL, Stephen G.	Tipton	28.03.65	Tipton T.	**West Bromwich A.**	08.85	1985-86	2	2	2	(F)	E-2/E U 21-3/E 'B'
			Tr	**Wolverhampton W.**	11.86	1986-88	119	0	86		
BULLOCK, Steven	Stockport	05.10.66	Jnrs	**Oldham Ath.**	07.84	1984-85	10	8	0	(D)	
			Tr	**Tranmere Rov.**	08.86	1986	25	5	1		
			Tr	**Stockport Co.**	08.87	1987-88	54	7	0		
BUMSTEAD, John	Rotherhithe	27.11.58	App	**Chelsea**	11.76	1978-88	285	12	35	(M)	
BUNN, Frankie S.	Birmingham	06.11.62	App	**Luton T.**	05.80	1980-84	52	7	9	(F)	
			Tr	**Hull C.**	07.85	1985-87	89	6	23		
			Tr	**Oldham Ath.**	12.87	1987-88	47	2	21		

Players Names	Birthplace	Date	Previous Club	League Club	Date Sign'd	Seasons Played	Career Record Apps	Sub	Gls	Pos.	Misc
BURGESS, David J.	Liverpool	20.01.60		Tranmere Rov.	08.81	1981-85	217	1	1	(D)	
			Tr	Grimsby T.	08.86	1986-87	66	3	0		
			Tr	Blackpool	07.88	1988	46	0	0		
BURKE, David I.	Liverpool	06.08.60	App	Bolton W.	08.77	1978-80	65	4	1	(LB)	E Yth Int
			Tr	Huddersfield T.	06.81	1981-87	189	0	3		
			Tr	Crystal Palace	10.87	1987-88	69	1	0		
BURKE, Mark S.	Solihull	12.02.69	App	Aston Villa	02.87	1986-87	5	2	0	(W)	E Yth Int
			Tr	Middlesbrough	12.87	1987-88	29	16	5		
BURLEY, George E.	Cumnock	03.06.56	App	Ipswich T.	06.73	1973-85	394	0	6	(RB)	S Sch Int/S U21-5/S-11
			Tr	Sunderland	09.85	1985-86	54	0	0		
			Tr	Gillingham	07.88	1988	46	0	2		
BURRIDGE, John	Workington	03.12.51	App	Workington	12.69	1968-70	27	0	0	(G)	
			Tr	Blackpool	04.71	1970-75	134	0	0		
			Tr	Aston Villa	09.75	1975-76	65	0	0		
			L	Southend U.	01.78	1977	6	0	0		
			Tr	Crystal Palace	03.78	1977-79	88	0	0		
			Tr	Q.P.R.	12.80	1980-81	39	0	0		
			Tr	Wolverhampton W.	08.82	1982-83	74	0	0		
			L	Derby Co.	09.84	1984	6	0	0		
			Tr	Sheffield U.	10.84	1984-86	109	0	0		
			Tr	Southampton	08.87	1987-88	62	0	0		
BURROWS, Adrian M.	Sutton-in-Ashfield	16.01.59		Mansfield T.	05.79	1979-81	77	1	5	(CD)	
			Tr	Northampton T.	08.82	1982-83	88	0	4		
			Tr	Plymouth Arg.	07.84	1984-88	127	2	5		
			L	Southend U.	09.87	1987	6	0	0		
BURROWS, David	Dudley	25.10.68	App	West Bromwich A.	10.86	1985-88	37	9	1	(LB)	E U 21-4
			Tr	Liverpool	10.88	1988	16	5	0		
BURTON, Michael J.	Birmingham	05.11.69	YTS	Birmingham C.	07.88	1988	0	4	0	(W)	
BURVILL, Glen	Canning Town	26.10.62	App	West Ham U.	09.80					(M)	
			Tr	Aldershot	08.83	1983-84	57	8	15		
			Tr	Reading	03.85	1984-85	24	6	0		
			L	Fulham	03.86	1985	9	0	2		
			Tr	Aldershot	07.86	1986-88	113	8	18		
BUTCHER, Terry I.	Singapore	28.12.58	Jnrs	Ipswich T.	08.76	1977-85	271	0	16	(CD)	E U21-7/E-63/to Glasgow Rangers 7.86
BUTLER, Barry	Farnworth	04.06.62	Atherton L.R.	Chester C.	12.85	1985-88	103	6	0	(M)	
BUTLER, Brian F.	Salford	04.07.66	App	Blackpool	07.84	1985-87	58	16	5	(FB)	
			Tr	Stockport Co.	07.88	1988	32	0	2		
BUTLER, John E.	Liverpool	07.02.62	Prescot Cables	Wigan Ath.	01.82	1981-88	238	7	15	(RB/M)	
			Tr	Stoke C.	12.88	1988	25	0	1		
BUTLER, Lee S.	Sheffield	30.06.66	Harworth Colly.	Lincoln C.	06.86	1986	30	0	0	(G)	
			Tr	Aston Villa	08.87	1988	4	0	0		
BUTLER, Martin	Hull	03.03.66	YTS	York C.	10.84	1984-88	40	25	9	(F)	Son of Ian
			L	Aldershot	12.85	1985	2	0	1		
			L	Exeter C.	02.87	1986	4	0	1		
			L	Carlisle U.	12.88	1988	1	0	0		
BUTLER, Peter J.	Halifax	27.08.66	App	Huddersfield T.	08.84	1984-85	0	5	0	(W)	
			L	Cambridge U.	01.86	1985	14	0	1		
			Tr	Bury	07.86	1986	9	2	0		
			Tr	Cambridge U.	12.86	1986-87	55	0	9		
			Tr	Southend U.	02.88	1987-88	49	1	5		
BUTLER, Steven	Birmingham	27.01.62	Wokingham T.	Brentford	12.84	1984-85	18	3	3	(F)	
BUTTERS, Guy	Hillingdon	30.10.69	YTS	Tottenham H.	07.88	1988	27	1	1	(D)	E U21-1
BUTTERWORTH, Gary J.	Whittlesey	08.09.69	YTS	Peterborough U.	06.88	1986-88	12	8	0	(F)	
BUTTERWORTH, Ian S.	Crewe	25.01.64	App	Coventry C.	08.81	1981-84	80	10	10	(CD)	E U21-8
			Tr	Nottingham F.	06.85	1985-86	26	1	0		
			L	Norwich C.	09.86	1986	4	0	0		
			Tr	Norwich C.	12.86	1986-88	93	3	2		
BUTTIGIEG, John	Malta	05.10.63	Sliema W. (Malta)	Brentford	11.88	1988	12	6	0	(D)	
BUXTON, Steve C.	Birmingham	13.03.60	Jnrs	Wrexham	07.78	1977-83	93	16	21	(F)	
			Tr	Stockport Co.	07.84	1984	12	6	1		
			Altrincham	Wrexham	10.85	1985-88	70	30	21		
BYRNE, David S.	Hammersmith	05.03.61	Kingstonian	Gillingham	07.85	1985	18	5	3	(W)	
			Tr	Millwall	07.86	1986-87	52	11	6		
			L	Cambridge U.	09.88	1988	4	0	0		
			L	Blackburn Rov.	02.89	1988	4	0	0		
			Tr	Plymouth Arg.	03.89	1988	13	0	1		
BYRNE, John F.	Manchester	01.02.61	App	York C.	01.79	1979-84	167	8	55	(F)	IR-13
			Tr	Q.P.R.	10.84	1984-87	108	8	30		to Le Harve (Fr.) 6.88
BYRNE, Micky	Dublin	14.01.60	Shamrock Rov.	Huddersfield T.	09.88	1988	29	8	7	(F)	
CADETTE, Richard R.	Hammersmith	21.03.65	Wembley	Leyton Orient	08.84	1984	19	2	4	(F)	
			Tr	Southend U.	08.85	1985-86	90	0	49		
			Tr	Sheffield U.	07.87	1987	26	2	7		
			Tr	Brentford	07.88	1988	31	1	12		
CAESAR, Gus C.	Haringey	05.03.66	App	Arsenal	02.84	1985-88	27	14	0	(CD)	E U21-3
CAIZLEY, Kevin	Jarrow	02.12.68	YTS	Newcastle U.	08.87					(M)	
			Tr	Darlington	07.88	1988	8	4	1		
CALDERWOOD, Colin	Stranraer	20.01.65	Jnrs	Mansfield T.	03.82	1981-84	97	3	1	(CD)	
			Tr	Swindon T.	06.85	1985-88	168	1	8		
CALDWELL, A. (Tony)	Salford	21.03.58	Horwich RMI	Bolton W.	06.83	1983-86	131	8	58	(F)	
			Tr	Bristol C.	07.87	1987	9	8	3		
			L	Chester C.	01.88	1987	4	0	0		
			Tr	Grimsby T.	09.88	1988	2	1	0		
			Tr	Stockport Co.	10.88	1988	23	1	6		
CALLAGHAN, Aaron J.	Dublin	08.10.66	App	Stoke C.	10.84	1984-86	10	5	0	(D)	IR Yth Int
			L	Crewe Alex.	11.85	1985	8	0	0		
			Tr	Oldham Ath.	10.86	1986-87	11	5	2		
			Tr	Crewe Alex.	05.88	1988	39	2	4		

Players Names	Birthplace	Date	Previous Club	League Club	Date Sign'd	Seasons Played	Career Record Apps	Sub	Gls	Pos.	Misc
CALLAGHAN, Nigel C.	Singapore	12.09.62	App	**Watford**	07.80	1980-86	209	13	41	(W)	E U21-9
			Tr	**Derby Co.**	02.87	1986-88	76	0	10		
			Tr	**Aston Villa**	02.89	1988	15	1	1		
CALLAGHAN, Willie T.	Dunfermline	23.03.67	Dumfermline Ath. (L)	**Walsall**	09.88	1988	2	0	1	(F)	
CALVERT, Mark R.	Consett	11.09.70	YTS	**Hull C.** (YTS)	07.87	1988	5	0	0	(W)	
CAME, Mark R.	Exeter	14.09.61	Winsford U.	**Bolton W.**	04.84	1984-88	144	2	7	(CD)	
CAMPBELL, David A.	Derry (NI)	02.06.65	App	**Nottingham F.**	06.83	1983-87	35	6	3	(W)	NI-9
			L	**Notts Co.**	02.87	1986	18	0	2		
			Tr	**Charlton Ath.**	10.87	1987-88	26	4	1		
			L	**Plymouth Arg.**	03.89	1988	1	0	0		
			Tr	**Bradford C.**	03.89	1988	12	0	1		
CAMPBELL, Greg R.	Portsmouth	13.07.65	App	**West Ham U.**	10.82	1984-85	3	2	0	(F)	Son of Robert
			L	**Brighton & H.A.**	02.87	1986	0	2	0		
			Sparta Rott'dam (Neth)	**Plymouth Arg.**	11.88	1988	6	7	3		
CAMPBELL, Kevin J.	Lambeth	04.02.70	YTS	**Arsenal**	02.88	1987	0	1	0	(F)	
			L	**Leyton Orient**	01.89	1988	16	0	9		
CAMPBELL, Michael J.	Oban	19.11.66	Army	**Hereford U.**(N/C)	08.88	1988	1	0	0	(M)	
CANHAM, A. (Tony)	Leeds	08.06.60	Harrogate RI	**York C.**	01.85	1984-88	132	9	34	(LW)	
CARR, Ashley	Crowland	15.08.68	Jnrs	**Peterborough U.**	08.86	1986-88	9	6	0	(M)	
CARR, Cliff P.	Hackney	19.06.64	App	**Fulham**	06.82	1982-86	136	9	14	(LB)	E U21-1
			Tr	**Stoke C.**	07.87	1987-88	79	3	1		
CARR, Darren J.	Bristol	04.09.68	YTS	**Bristol Rov.**	08.86	1985-87	26	3	0	(CD)	
			Tr	**Newport Co.**	10.87	1987	9	0	0		
			Tr	**Sheffield U.**	03.88	1987-88	12	1	1		
CARR, Franz A.	Preston	24.09.66	App	**Blackburn Rov.**	07.84					(W)	E Yth Int/E U21-9
			Tr	**Nottingham F.**	08.84	1985-88	99	5	14		
CARTER, Darren S.	Hackney	29.06.69		**Leyton Orient**	07.88	1988	0	1	0		
CARTER, Jimmy W.C.	Hammersmith	09.11.65	App	**Crystal Palace**	11.83					(W)	
			Tr	**Q.P.R.**	09.85						
			Tr	**Millwall**	03.87	1986-88	51	7	6		
CARTER, Lee R.	Dartford	22.03.70	YTS	**Northampton T.**(N/C)	07.88	1987	0	1	0	(CD)	
CARTER, Mike	Warrington	18.04.60	App	**Bolton W.**	07.77	1979-81	37	12	8	(W)	
			L	**Mansfield T.**	03.79	1978	18	0	4		
			L	**Swindon T.**	03.82	1981	4	1	0		
			Tr	**Plymouth Arg.**	08.82	1982	6	6	1		
			Tr	**Hereford U.**	03.83	1982-86	91	6	11		
			Tr	**Wrexham**	07.87	1987-88	25	9	7		
CARTER, Tim D.	Bristol	05.10.67	App	**Bristol Rov.**	10.85	1985-87	47	0	0	(G)	E Yth Int
			L	**Newport Co.**	12.87	1987	1	0	0		
			Tr	**Sunderland**	12.87	1987-88	3	0	0		
			L	**Carlisle U.**	03.88	1987	4	0	0		
			L	**Bristol C.**	09.88	1988	3	0	0		
CARTWRIGHT, Neil A.	Stourbridge	20.02.71	YTS	**West Bromwich A.**	07.89	1988	0	1	0	(F)	
CARTWRIGHT, Stephen. R.	Tamworth	08.01.65	Tamworth	**Colchester U.**	08.88	1988	10	0	0	(FB)	
CASCARINO, A.G. (Tony)	Orpington	01.09.62	Crockenhill	**Gillingham**	01.82	1981-86	209	10	78	(F)	IR-15
			Tr	**Millwall**	06.87	1987-88	77	0	33		
CASE, Jimmy R.	Liverpool	18.05.54	South Liverpool	**Liverpool**	05.73	1974-80	170	16	23	(M)	E U23-1
			Tr	**Brighton & H.A.**	08.81	1981-84	124	3	10		
			Tr	**Southampton**	03.85	1984-88	156	1	6		
CASEY, Paul	Worksop	06.10.61	App	**Sheffield U.**	06.79	1979-81	23	2	1	(FB)	
			Boston U.	**Lincoln C.**	(N/L)	1988	6	2	0		
CASSELLS, Keith B.	Islington	10.07.57	Wembley	**Watford**	11.77	1978-80	6	6	0	(F)	
			L	**Peterborough U.**	01.80	1979	8	0	0		
			Tr	**Oxford U.**	11.80	1980-81	43	2	13		
			Tr	**Southampton**	03.82	1981-82	13	6	4		
			Tr	**Brentford**	02.83	1982-84	80	6	28		
			Tr	**Mansfield T.**	08.85	1985-88	162	1	52		
CASTLE, Stephen C.	Barkingside	17.05.66	App	**Leyton Orient**	05.84	1984-88	125	9	26	(W)	
CATON, Tommy S.	Liverpool	06.10.62	App	**Manchester C.**	10.79	1979-83	164	1	8	(CD)	E Sch Int/E Yth Int/E U21-14
			Tr	**Arsenal**	12.83	1983-85	81	0	2		
			Tr	**Oxford U.**	02.87	1986-87	50	3	3		
			Tr	**Charlton Ath.**	11.88	1988	13	0	1		
CAWLEY, Peter	Walton-on-Thames	15.09.65	Chertsey T.	**Wimbledon**	01.87	1988	1	0	0	(CD)	
			L	**Bristol Rov.**	02.87	1986	9	1	0		
			L	**Fulham**	12.88	1988	3	2	0		
CECERE, Michele J.	Chester	04.01.68	App	**Oldham Ath.**	01.86	1986-88	35	17	8	(F)	
			Tr	**Huddersfield T.**	11.88	1988	28	3	4		
CHAMBERLAIN, Alec F.R.	March	20.06.64	Ramsey T.	**Ipswich T.**	07.81					(G)	
			Tr	**Colchester U.**	08.82	1982-86	188	0	0		
			Tr	**Everton**	07.87						
			L	**Tranmere Rov.**	11.87	1987	15	0	0		
			Tr	**Luton T.**	07.88	1988	6	0	0		
CHAMBERLAIN, Mark V.	Stoke	19.11.61	App	**Port Vale**	04.79	1978-81	90	6	17	(W)	E Sch Int/E U21-3/E-8/ Brother of Neville
			Tr	**Stoke C.**	08.82	1982-85	110	2	17		
			Tr	**Sheffield Wed.**	09.85	1985-87	32	34	8		
			Tr	**Portsmouth**	08.88	1988	28	0	6		
CHAMBERS, Stephen	Worksop	27.07.68	Sheffield Wed(App)	**Mansfield T.**	11.86	1986-88	8	10	0	(M)	
CHANDLER, Ian	Sunderland	20.03.68	Jnrs	**Barnsley**	08.86	1986	8	4	4	(F)	E Sch Int
			L	**Stockport Co.**	08.87	1987	4	1	0		
			Tr	**Aldershot**	08.88	1988	5	4	2		
CHANDLER, Jeff G.	Hammersmith	19.06.59	App	**Blackpool**	08.76	1977-78	31	6	7	(W)	IR U21-1/IR-2
			Tr	**Leeds U.**	09.79	1979-80	21	5	2		
			Tr	**Bolton W.**	10.81	1981-84	152	5	36		
			Tr	**Derby Co.**	07.85	1985-86	45	1	9		
			L	**Mansfield T.**	11.86	1986	6	0	0		
			Tr	**Bolton W.**	07.87	1987-88	18	5	4		
CHANNING, Justin A.	Reading	19.11.68	App	**Q.P.R.**	08.86	1986-88	18	7	2	(D)	E Yth Int

Glenn Cockerill (Southampton) Match Magazine

Alan Cork (Wimbledon) Match Magazine

Tony Coton (Watford) Match Magazine

Tony Daley (Aston Villa) Match Magazine

Players Names	Birthplace	Date	Previous Club	League Club	Date Sign'd	Seasons Played	Apps	Sub	Gls	Pos.	Misc
CHAPMAN, Gary A.	Leeds	01.05.64	Ossett A.	**Bradford C.**	08.88	1988	1	1	0	(W)	
CHAPMAN, Ian R.	Brighton	31.05.70	YTS	**Brighton & H.A.**	06.87	1986-88	23	1	0	(LB)	
CHAPMAN, Lee R.	Lincoln	05.12.59	Jnrs	**Stoke C.**	06.78	1979-81	95	4	34	(F)	Son of Roy/E U21-1
			L	**Plymouth Arg.**	12.78	1978	3	1	0		
			Tr	**Arsenal**	08.82	1982-83	15	8	4		
			Tr	**Sunderland**	12.83	1983	14	1	3		
			Tr	**Sheffield Wed.**	08.84	1984-87	147	2	63		
			Niort (France)	**Nottingham F.**	10.88	1988	30	0	8		
CHAPMAN, Les	Oldham	27.09.48	Huddersfield T. (Am.)	**Oldham Ath.**	01.67	1966-69	75	1	9	(M)	
			Tr	**Huddersfield T.**	09.69	1969-74	120	13	8		
			Tr	**Oldham Ath.**	12.74	1974-78	186	1	11		
			Tr	**Stockport Co.**	05.79	1979	32	0	1		
			Tr	**Bradford C.**	02.80	1979-82	137	2	3		
			Tr	**Rochdale**	06.83	1983-84	87	1	0		
			Tr	**Stockport Co.**	07.85	1985	38	0	3		
			Tr	**Preston N.E.**	07.86	1986-87	50	3	1		
CHAPPLE, Philip R.	Norwich	26.11.66	YTS	**Norwich C.**	07.85					(CD)	
			Tr	**Cambridge U.**	03.88	1987-88	50	2	4		
CHARD, Philip, J.	Corby	16.10.60	Corby T.	**Peterborough U.**	01.79	1978-84	153	19	18	(M)	
			Tr	**Northampton T.**	08.85	1985-87	113	2	27		
			Tr	**Wolverhampton W.**	03.88	1987-88	22	6	5		
CHARLES, Gary A.	Newham	13.04.70	YTS	**Nottingham F.**	11.87	1988	1	0	0	(D)	E U21-2
			L	**Leicester C.**	03.89	1988	5	3	0		
CHARLES, Steve	Sheffield	10.05.60	Sheffield Univ.	**Sheffield U.**	01.80	1979-84	112	11	10	(M)	
			Tr	**Wrexham**	10.84	1984-86	111	2	37		
			Tr	**Mansfield T.**	07.87	1987-88	91	1	19		
CHARLTON, Kevin P.	Tamworth	12.09.54	App	**Wolverhampton W.**	09.72					(G)	E Semi-pro Int 1985
			Tr	**Bournemouth**	12.73	1973-74	21	0	0		
			Tr	**Hereford U.**	06.75	1975-77	52	0	0		
			Telford U. (L)	**Scarborough**(N/C)	09.88	1988	3	0	0		
CHATTERTON, Nick J.	Norwood	18.05.54	Jnrs	**Crystal Palace**	03.72	1973-78	142	9	31	(M)	
			Tr	**Millwall**	11.78	1978-85	258	6	56		
			Tr	**Colchester U.**	09.86	1986-88	47	2	8		
CHEETHAM, Micky M.	Amsterdam (Neth)	30.06.67	Basingstoke T.	**Ipswich T.**	10.88	1988	1	2	0	(F)	
CHERRY, Steve R.	Nottingham	05.08.60	App	**Derby Co.**	03.78	1979-83	77	0	0	(G)	E Yth Int
			L	**Port Vale**	11.80	1980	4	0	0		
			Tr	**Walsall**	08.84	1984-85	71	0	0		
			Tr	**Plymouth Arg.**	10.86	1986-88	73	0	0		
			L	**Chesterfield**	12.88	1988	10	0	0		
			Tr	**Notts Co.**	02.89	1988	18	0	0		
CHETTLE, Stephen	Nottingham	27.09.68	App	**Nottingham F.**	08.86	1987-88	51	7	2	(RB)	E U21-6
CHIEDOZIE, John O.	Nigeria	18.04.60	App	**Leyton Orient**	04.77	1976-80	131	14	20	(W)	Nigerian Int
			Tr	**Notts Co.**	08.81	1981-83	110	1	15		
			Tr	**Tottenham H.**	08.84	1984-86	45	8	12		
			Tr	**Derby Co.**	08.88	1988	2	0	0		
CHILDS, Gary P.C.	Birmingham	19.04.64	App	**West Bromwich A.**	02.82	1981-83	2	1	0	(W)	E Yth Int
			Tr	**Walsall**	10.83	1983-86	120	11	17		
			Tr	**Birmingham C.**	07.87	1987-88	39	16	2		
CHIVERS, Gary P.S.	Stockwell	15.05.60	App	**Chelsea**	07.78	1978-82	128	5	4	(D)	
			Tr	**Swansea C.**	08.83	1983	10	0	0		
			Tr	**Q.P.R.**	02.84	1984-86	58	2	0		
			Tr	**Watford**	09.87	1987	14	0	0		
			Tr	**Brighton & H.A.**	03.88	1987-88	56	0	6		
CHRISTIE, Trevor	Newcastle	28.02.59	App	**Leicester C.**	12.76	1977-78	28	3	8	(F)	
			Tr	**Notts Co.**	06.79	1979-83	158	29	64		
			Tr	**Nottingham F.**	07.84	1984	14	0	5		
			Tr	**Derby Co.**	02.85	1984-85	65	0	22		
			Tr	**Manchester C.**	08.86	1986	9	0	3		
			Tr	**Walsall**	10.86	1986-88	91	8	22		
			Tr	**Mansfield T.**	03.89	1988	12	0	1		
CLARIDGE, Steve E.	Portsmouth	10.04.66	Fareham T.	**Bournemouth**	09.84	1984-85	3	4	1	(F)	
			Weymouth	**Crystal Palace**	08.88						
			Tr	**Aldershot**	10.88	1988	37	0	9		
CLARK, Howard W.	Coventry	19.09.68	App	**Coventry C.**	09.86	1988	4	5	1	(W)	
CLARK, Jonathan	Swansea	12.11.58	App	**Manchester U.**	11.75	1976	0	1	0	(M)	W Sch Int/W U21-2
			Tr	**Derby Co.**	09.78	1978-80	48	5	3		
			Tr	**Preston N.E.**	08.81	1981-86	107	3	10		
			Tr	**Bury**	12.86	1986	13	1	1		
			Tr	**Carlisle U.**	08.87	1987-88	48	1	2		
CLARK, Paul P.	Benfleet	14.09.58	App	**Southend U.**	07.76	1976-77	29	4	1	(CD)	E Sch Int/E Yth Int
			Tr	**Brighton & H.A.**	11.77	1977-80	69	10	9		
			L	**Reading**	10.81	1981	2	0	0		
			Tr	**Southend U.**	08.82	1982-88	205	6	3		
CLARK, W.R. (Billy)	Christchurch	19.05.67	YTS	**Bournemouth**	09.84	1984-87	4	0	0	(CD)	
			Tr	**Bristol Rov.**	10.87	1987-88	41	1	1		
CLARKE, Brian R.	Eastbourne	10.10.68	YTS	**Gillingham**	06.87	1988	10	0	0	(CD)	
CLARKE, Colin J.	Newry (NI)	30.10.62	App	**Ipswich T.**	10.80					(F)	NI-21
			Tr	**Peterborough U.**	07.81	1981-83	76	6	18		
			L	**Gillingham**	03.84	1983	8	0	1		
			Tr	**Tranmere Rov.**	07.84	1984	45	0	22		
			Tr	**Bournemouth**	06.85	1985	46	0	26		
			Tr	**Southampton**	06.86	1986-88	82	0	36		
			L	**Bournemouth**	12.88	1988	3	1	2		
			Tr	**Q.P.R.**	03.89	1988	12	0	5		
CLARKE, David A.	Nottingham	03.12.64	App	**Notts Co.**	12.82	1982-86	113	10	7	(LW)	E Yth Int
			Tr	**Lincoln C.**	(N/L)	1988	33	3	4		
CLARKE, Michael D.	Birmingham	22.12.67	Birmingham C.(App)	**Barnsley**	11.86	1986-88	37	3	3	(LW)	
CLARKE, Nick J.	Walsall	20.08.67	Jnrs	**Wolverhampton W.**	02.85	1985-88	59	4	1	(CD)	
CLARKE, Stephen	Saltcoats	29.08.63	St. Mirren	**Chelsea**	01.87	1986-88	89	1	1	(D)	S U21-8/S-5

Players Names	Birthplace	Date	Previous Club	League Club	Date Sign'd	Seasons Played	Career Record Apps	Sub	Gls	Pos.	Misc
CLARKE, Wayne	Wolverhampton	28.02.61	App	**Wolverhampton W.**	03.78	1977-83	129	19	30	(F)	E Sch Int/E Yth Int/Brother of Allan, Derek, Frank and Kelvin
			Tr	**Birmingham C.**	08.84	1984-86	92	0	38		
			Tr	**Everton**	03.87	1986-88	46	11	17		
CLARKSON, Ian S.	Solihull	04.12.70	YTS	**Birmingham C.**	12.88	1988	9	0	0	(CD)	
CLAYTON, Gary	Sheffield	02.02.63	Burton Albion	**Doncaster Rov.**	08.86	1986	34	1	5	(M)	E Semi-pro Int 1986
			Tr	**Cambridge U.**	06.87	1987-88	90	1	6		
CLAYTON, John	Elgin	20.08.61	App	**Derby Co.**	12.78	1978-81	21	3	4	(F)	
			Hong Kong	**Chesterfield**	06.83	1983	25	8	5		
			Tr	**Tranmere Rov.**	07.84	1984-85	47	0	35		
			Tr	**Plymouth Arg.**	08.85	1985-87	68	9	22		To Fortuna Sittard (Neth.) 6.88
CLAYTON, Paul S.	Dunstable	04.01.65	App	**Norwich C.**	01.83	1983-85	8	5	0	(F)	
			Tr	**Darlington**	03.88	1987-88	20	2	3		
			Tr	**Crewe Alex.**	01.89	1988	20	0	6		
CLEGG, A. (Tony)	Keighley	08.11.65	App	**Bradford C.**	11.83	1983-86	41	7	2	(D)	
			Tr	**York C.**	08.87	1987-88	38	3	3		
CLEMENT, Andy D.	Cardiff	12.11.67	App	**Wimbledon**	10.85	1986-88	14	12	0	(FB)	W Yth Int
			L	**Bristol Rov.**	03.87	1986	5	1	0		
			L	**Newport Co.**	12.87	1987	5	0	1		
CLEMENTS, Kenny H.	Manchester	09.04.55	Groundstaff	**Manchester C.**	07.75	1975-78	116	3	0	(CD)	
			Tr	**Oldham Ath.**	09.79	1979-84	204	2	2		
			Tr	**Manchester C.**	03.85	1984-87	104	2	1		
			Tr	**Bury**	03.88	1987-88	52	1	1		
CLOSE, Shaun C.	Islington	08.09.66	YTS	**Tottenham H.**	08.84	1986-87	3	6	0	(F)	
			Tr	**Bournemouth**	01.88	1987-88	28	11	8		
CLOUGH, Nigel H.	Sunderland	19.03.66	Jnrs	**Nottingham F.**	09.84	1984-88	157	3	63	(F)	Son of Brian/E U21-11/E-1
COBB, Gary E.	Luton	06.08.68	App	**Luton T.**	08.86	1986-87	6	3	0	(M)	
			L	**Northampton T.**	10.88	1988	1	0	0		
COCKERILL, Glenn	Grimsby	25.08.59	Louth U.	**Lincoln C.**	11.76	1976-79	65	6	10	(M)	Son of Ron/Brother of John
			Tr	**Swindon T.**	12.79	1979-80	23	3	1		
			Tr	**Lincoln C.**	08.81	1981-83	114	1	25		
			Tr	**Sheffield U.**	03.84	1983-85	62	0	10		
			Tr	**Southampton**	10.85	1985-88	140	5	22		
COCKERILL, John	Grimsby	12.07.61	Stafford R.	**Grimsby T.**	08.88	1988	24	5	6	(M)	Son of Ron/Brother of Glenn
COCKRAM, Allan C.	Kensington	08.10.63	App	**Tottenham H.**	01.81	1983	2	0	0	(W)	
			Tr	**Bristol Rov.**	08.85	1985	1	0	0		
			St Albans C.	**Brentford**	03.88	1987-88	38	6	9		
CODNER, Robert A.G.	Walthamstow	23.01.65	Tottenham H. (Jnr)	**Leicester C.**	09.83					(M)	
			Barnet	**Brighton & H.A.**	09.88	1988	22	6	1		
COLE, David A.	Barnsley	28.09.62		**Sunderland**	10.83					(CD)	
			Tr	**Swansea C.**	09.84	1984	7	1	0		
			Tr	**Swindon T.**	02.85	1984-86	69	0	3		
			Tr	**Torquay U.**	11.86	1986-88	107	3	6		
COLE, Michael W.	Stepney	03.09.66	App	**Ipswich T.**	11.83	1984-87	24	14	3	(F)	
			L	**Port Vale**	01.88	1987	4	0	1		
			Tr	**Fulham**	03.88	1987-88	44	1	4		
COLEMAN, Christopher	Swansea	10.06.70	Manchester C. (Jnr)	**Swansea C.**	08.87	1987-88	72	1	0	(LB)	W Yth Int
COLEMAN, David H.	Salisbury	08.04.67	Jnrs	**Bournemouth**	09.84	1985-88	11	5	1	(LB)	
			L	**Colchester U.**	02.88	1987	6	0	1		
COLEMAN, Nicky	Crayford	06.05.66	App	**Millwall**	01.84	1984-87	84	1	0	(LB)	
			L	**Swindon T.**	09.85	1985	13	0	4		
COLEMAN, Philip	Woolwich	08.09.60	App	**Millwall**	08.78	1978-80	23	13	1	(D)	
			Tr	**Colchester U.**	02.81	1980-83	82	4	6		
			L	**Wrexham**	09.83	1983	17	0	2		
			Chelmsford C.	**Exeter C.** (N/C)	12.84	1984	6	0	0		
			Tr	**Aldershot**	02.85	1984-85	45	0	5		
			Dulwich Hamlet	**Millwall**	09.86	1986	8	2	0		
			Finland	**Colchester U.** (N/C)	12.88	1988	6	4	0		
COLEMAN, Simon	Worksop	13.03.68	Jnrs	**Mansfield T.**	07.85	1986-88	91	0	7	(CD)	
COLES, David A.	Wandsworth	15.06.64	App	**Birmingham C.**	04.82					(G)	
			Tr	**Mansfield T.**	03.83	1982	3	0	0		
			Tr	**Aldershot**	08.83	1983-87	120	0	0		
			L	**Newport Co.**	01.88	1987	14	0	0		
			Sweden	**Brighton & H.A.**	02.89	1988	1	0	0		
COLLIER, Darren	Stockton	01.12.67	Middlesbrough (N/C)	**Blackburn Rov.**	12.87	1988	1	0	0	(G)	
COLLINGS, Paul W.	Liverpool	30.09.68		**Tranmere Rov.**	08.88	1988	1	0	0	(G)	
COLLINS, Darren	Winchester	24.05.67	Petersfield U.	**Northampton T.**	01.89	1988	4	4	0	(F)	
COLLINS, Paul	West Ham	11.08.66	App	**Gillingham**	08.84	1984-86	30	7	3	(M)	E Yth Int
COLLINS, Steve M.	Stamford	21.03.62	App	**Peterborough U.**	08.79	1978-82	92	2	1	(LB)	
			Tr	**Southend U.**	08.83	1983-84	51	0	0		
			Tr	**Lincoln C.**	03.85	1984-85	24	0	0		
			Tr	**Peterborough U.**	12.85	1985-88	114	8	2		
COLVILLE, Robert J.	Nuneaton	27.04.63	Rhos U.	**Oldham Ath.**	02.84	1983-86	22	10	4	(F)	
			Tr	**Bury**	10.86	1986-87	5	6	1		
			Tr	**Stockport Co.**	09.87	1987-88	67	4	18		
COMFORT, Alan	Aldershot	08.12.64	App	**Q.P.R.**	10.82					(LW)	E Yth Int
			Tr	**Cambridge U.**	09.84	1984-85	61	2	5		
			Tr	**Leyton Orient**	03.86	1985-88	145	5	46		
COMSTIVE, Paul T.	Southport	25.11.61	Jnrs	**Blackburn Rov.**	10.79	1980-82	3	3	0	(M)	
			L	**Rochdale**	09.82	1982	9	0	2		
			Tr	**Wigan Ath.**	08.83	1983-84	35	0	2		
			Tr	**Wrexham**	11.84	1984-86	95	4	8		
			Tr	**Burnley**	07.87	1987-88	81	1	17		
CONEY, Dean H.	Dagenham	18.09.63	App	**Fulham**	05.81	1980-86	209	2	56	(F)	E U21-9
			Tr	**Q.P.R.**	06.87	1987-88	36	12	7		
			Tr	**Norwich C.**	03.89	1988	6	2	1		
CONNOR, Terry F.	Leeds	09.11.62	App	**Leeds U.**	11.79	1979-82	83	13	19	(F)	E Yth Int/E U21-1
			Tr	**Brighton & H.A.**	03.83	1982-86	153	3	51		
			Tr	**Portsmouth**	06.87	1987-88	33	0	9		

Mervyn Day (Leeds United) Match Magazine

Kerry Dixon (Chelsea & England) Match Magazine

Lee Dixon (Arsenal) Match Magazine

Tony Dorigo (Chelsea) Match Magazine

Players Names	Birthplace	Date	Previous Club	League Club	Date Sign'd	Seasons Played	Career Record Apps	Sub	Gls	Pos.	Misc
CONROY, Michael K.	Glasgow	31.12.65	St. Mirren	**Reading**	09.88	1988	9	4	4	(F)	
COOK, Andy C.	Romsey	10.08.69	App	**Southampton**	06.87	1987-88	4	1	0	(LB)	
COOK, Mark R.	Boston	07.08.70	YTS	**Lincoln C.**	08.88	1988	1	0	0	(M)	
COOK, Mitchell C.	Scarborough	15.10.61	Scarborough	**Darlington**	08.84	1984-85	34	0	4	(M)	
			Tr	**Middlesbrough**	09.85	1985	3	3	0		
			Tr	**Scarborough**	(N/L)	1987-88	61	20	10		
COOK, Paul	Liverpool	22.02.67	Jnrs	**Wigan Ath.**	07.84	1984-87	77	6	14	(M)	
			Tr	**Norwich C.**	05.88	1988	3	1	0		
COOKE, John	Salford	25.04.62	App	**Sunderland**	11.79	1979-84	42	13	4	(W)	E Yth Int
			L	**Carlisle U.**	11.84	1984	5	1	2		
			Tr	**Sheffield Wed.**	06.85						
			Tr	**Carlisle U.**	10.85	1985-87	105	1	11		
			Tr	**Stockport Co.**	07.88	1988	31	3	6		
COOKE, Richard E.	Islington	04.09.65	App	**Tottenham H.**	05.83	1983-85	9	2	2	(W)	E Yth Int/EU21-1
			L	**Birmingham C.**	09.86	1986	5	0	0		
			Tr	**Bournemouth**	01.87	1986-88	63	9	15		
			Tr	**Luton T.**	03.89	1988	0	6	0		
COOMBE, Mark A.	Torquay	17.09.68	Bournemouth (YTS)	**Bristol C.**	08.87					(G)	
				Colchester U. (N/C)	10.88	1988	3	0	0		
			Tr	**Torquay U.**	12.88	1988	8	0	0		
COOMBS, Paul A.	Bristol	04.09.70	YTS	**Aldershot** (YTS)	07.87	1988	1	0	0		
COOPER, Colin T.	Hartlepool	28.02.67	Jnrs	**Middlesbrough**	06.84	1985-88	133	2	4	(LB)	E U21-7
COOPER, Geoff V.	Kingston	27.12.60	Bognor Regis T.	**Brighton & H.A.**	12.87	1987-88	2	5	0	(W)	
COOPER, Graham	Huddersfield	22.05.62	Emley	**Huddersfield T.**	03.84	1983-87	61	13	13	(W)	
			Tr	**Wrexham**	08.88	1988	29	7	11		
COOPER, Leigh V.	Reading	07.05.61	App	**Plymouth Arg.**	05.79	1979-88	314	7	17	(LB)	
COOPER, Mark D.	Watford	05.04.67	App	**Cambridge U.**	10.84	1983-86	62	9	17	(F)	
			Tr	**Tottenham H.**	03.87						
			L	**Shrewsbury T.**	09.87	1987	6	0	2		
			Tr	**Gillingham**	10.87	1987-88	38	11	11		
			Tr	**Leyton Orient**	02.89	1988	10	4	4		
COOPER, Paul D.	Brierley Hill	21.12.53	App	**Birmingham C.**	07.71	1971-73	17	0	0	(G)	
			Tr	**Ipswich T.**	03.74	1973-86	447	0	0		
			Tr	**Leicester C.**	06.87	1987-88	56	0	0		
			Tr	**Manchester C.**	03.89	1988	8	0	0		
COOPER, Richard D.	Brent	07.05.65	App	**Sheffield U.**	05.83	1982-84	2	4	0	(M)	
			Tr	**Lincoln C.**	08.85	1985-86	57	4	2		
			Tr	**Exeter C.**	07.87	1987-88	55	7	2		
COOPER, Steve B.	Birmingham	22.06.64	Moor Green	**Birmingham C.**	11.83					(F)	
			L	**Halifax T.**	12.83	1983	7	0	1		
			Tr	**Newport Co.**	09.84	1984	38	0	11		
			Tr	**Plymouth Arg.**	08.85	1985-87	58	15	15		
			Tr	**Barnsley**	08.88	1988	28	7	6		
COPELAND, Simon D.	Sheffield	10.10.68	YTS	**Sheffield U.**	06.87					(RB)	
			Tr	**Rochdale**	07.88	1988	27	1	0		
CORK, Alan G.	Derby	04.03.59	Jnrs	**Derby Co.**	07.77					(F)	
			L	**Lincoln C.**	09.77	1977	5	0	0		
			Tr	**Wimbledon**	02.78	1978-88	319	36	133		
CORK, David	Doncaster	28.10.62	App	**Arsenal**	06.80	1983	5	2	1	(F)	
			Tr	**Huddersfield T.**	07.85	1985-87	104	6	25		
			L	**West Bromwich A.**	09.88	1988	1	3	0		
			Tr	**Scunthorpe U.**	02.89	1988	8	7	0		
CORNER, David E.	Sunderland	15.05.66	App	**Sunderland**	04.84	1984-87	33	0	1	(CD)	E Yth Int
			L	**Cardiff C.**	09.85	1985	6	0	0		
			L	**Peterborough U.**	03.88	1987	9	0	0		
			Tr	**Leyton Orient**	07.88	1988	4	0	0		
CORNFORTH, John M.	Whitley Bay	07.10.67	App	**Sunderland**	10.85	1984-88	19	9	2	(M)	
			L	**Doncaster Rov.**	11.86	1986	6	1	0		
CORNWELL, John A.	Bethnal Green	13.10.64	App	**Leyton Orient**	10.82	1981-86	193	9	35	(M)	
			Tr	**Newcastle U.**	07.87	1987-88	28	5	1		
			Tr	**Swindon T.**	12.88	1988	5	1	0		
COSTELLO, Peter	Halifax	31.10.69	YTS	**Bradford C.**	07.88	1988	3	5	2	(F)	
COTON, A.P. (Tony)	Tamworth	19.05.61	Mile Oak Rov.	**Birmingham C.**	10.78	1980-84	94	0	0	(G)	
			Tr	**Watford**	09.84	1984-88	187	0	0		
COTTEE, A.R. (Tony)	West Ham	11.07.65	App	**West Ham U.**	09.82	1982-87	203	9	92	(F)	E Yth Int/E U21-8/E-6
			Tr	**Everton**	08.88	1988	35	1	13		
COTTERILL, Steve	Cheltenham	20.07.64	Burton A.	**Wimbledon**	02.89	1988	0	4	1	(F)	
COTTON, Perry	Chislehurst	11.11.65	New Zealand	**Scunthorpe U.** (N/C)	12.88	1988	0	1	0		
COUGHLIN, Russell	Swansea	15.02.60	App	**Manchester C.**	02.78					(M)	
			Tr	**Blackburn Rov.**	03.79	1978-80	22	2	0		
			Tr	**Carlisle U.**	10.80	1980-83	114	16	13		
			Tr	**Plymouth Arg.**	07.84	1984-87	128	2	18		
			Tr	**Blackpool**	12.87	1987-88	66	1	7		
COWANS, Gordon S.	Cornforth (Dm)	27.10.58	App	**Aston Villa**	09.76	1975-84	276	10	42	(M)	E Yth Int/E U21-5/E-9
			Bari (Italy)	**Aston Villa**	07.88	1988	32	1	2		
COWDRILL, Barry J.	Birmingham	03.01.57	Sutton Coldfield T.	**West Bromwich A.**	04.79	1979-87	127	4	0	(FB)	
			L	**Rotherham U.**	10.85	1985	2	0	0		
			Tr	**Bolton W.**	07.88	1988	38	0	0		
COWLING, David R.	Doncaster	27.11.58	App	**Mansfield T.**	11.76					(LW)	
			Tr	**Huddersfield T.**	08.77	1978-87	331	9	43		
			L	**Scunthorpe U.**	11.87	1987	1	0	0		
			L	**Reading**	12.87	1987	2	0	0		
			Tr	**Reading**	03.88	1987	7	1	1		
			Tr	**Scunthorpe U.**	08.88	1988	38	1	2		
COX, Brian R.	Sheffield	07.05.61	App	**Sheffield Wed.**	02.79	1978-80	22	0	0	(G)	
			Tr	**Huddersfield T.**	03.82	1981-87	213	0	0		
			Tr	**Mansfield T.**	08.88	1988	39	0	0		

Players Names	Birthplace	Date	Previous Club	League Club	Date Sign'd	Seasons Played	Career Record Apps	Sub	Gls	Pos.	Misc
COYLE, A. (Tony)	Glasgow	17.01.60	Albion Rovers	**Stockport Co.**	12.79	1979-85	215	4	28	(W)	
			Tr	**Chesterfield**	06.86	1986-87	71	5	4		
			Tr	**Stockport Co.**	08.88	1988	23	0	3		
COYNE, Peter D.	Hartlepool	13.11.58	App	**Manchester U.**	11.75	1975	1	1	1	(F)	
			Ashton U.	**Crewe Alex.**	08.77	1977-80	113	21	47		
			Hyde U.	**Swindon T.**	08.84	1984-88	99	11	30		
CRAIG, Albert H.	Glasgow	03.01.62	Hamilton Acad.	**Newcastle U.**	02.87	1986-88	6	4	0	(W)	
			L	**Northampton T.**	01.89	1988	2	0	1		
CRANE, Andy D.	Ipswich	03.01.67	App	**Ipswich T.**	04.84					(LB)	
			Tr	**Shrewsbury T.**	06.87						
			Tr	**Hereford U.**	07.88	1988	30	2	0		
CRANSON, Ian	Easington	02.07.64	App	**Ipswich T.**	07.82	1983-87	130	1	4	(CD)	E U21-5
			Tr	**Sheffield Wed.**	03.88	1987-88	29	1	0		
CRICHTON, Paul A.	Pontefract	03.10.65	Jnrs	**Nottingham F.**	05.86					(G)	
			L	**Notts. Co.**	09.86	1987	5	0	0		
			L	**Darlington**	01.87	1986	5	0	0		
			L	**Peterborough U.**	03.87	1986	4	0	0		
			L	**Darlington**	09.87	1987	3	0	0		
			L	**Swindon T.**	12.87	1987	4	0	0		
			L	**Rotherham U.**	03.88	1987	6	0	0		
			L	**Torquay U.**	08.88	1988	13	0	0		
			Tr	**Peterborough U.**	11.88	1988	31	0	0		
CROFT, Brian G.A.	Chester	27.09.67	YTS	**Chester C.**	07.86	1985-87	36	23	3	(W)	
			Tr	**Cambridge U.**	10.88	1988	12	5	2		
CROMBIE, Dean M.	Lincoln	09.08.57	Ruston Sports	**Lincoln C.**	02.77	1976-77	33	0	0	(D)	
			Tr	**Grimsby T.**	08.78	1978-86	316	4	3		
			Tr	**Bolton W.**	08.87	1987-88	52	3	0		
CRONIN, Dennis	Manchester	30.10.67	App	**Manchester U.**	10.85					(F)	
			Tr	**Stockport Co.**	08.87	1987	11	4	1		
			Tr	**Crewe Alex.**	08.88	1988	12	3	2		
CROOK, Ian S.	Romford	18.01.63	App	**Tottenham H.**	08.80	1981-85	10	10	1	(W)	
			Tr	**Norwich C.**	06.86	1986-88	66	16	7		
CROOKS, Garth A.	Stoke	10.03.58	App	**Stoke C.**	03.76	1975-79	141	6	48	(F)	E U21-4
			Tr	**Tottenham H.**	07.80	1980-84	121	4	48		
			L	**Manchester U.**	11.83	1983	6	1	2		
			Tr	**West Bromwich A.**	08.85	1985-86	39	1	16		
			Tr	**Charlton Ath.**	03.87	1986-88	39	10	14		
CROSBY, Gary	Sleaford	08.05.64	Lincoln Utd.	**Lincoln C.** (N/C)	08.86	1986	6	1	0	(W)	
			Grantham	**Nottingham F.**	12.87	1987-88	23	4	1		
CROSBY, Philip A.	Leeds	09.11.62	App	**Grimsby T.**	09.80	1979-82	34	5	1	(LB)	E Yth Int
			Tr	**Rotherham U.**	08.83	1983-88	181	2	2		
CROSS, Nicky J.R.	Birmingham	07.02.61	App	**West Bromwich A.**	02.79	1980-84	68	37	15	(F)	
			Tr	**Walsall**	08.85	1985-87	107	2	45		
			Tr	**Leicester C.**	01.88	1987-88	64	4	15		
CROSS, Paul	Barnsley	31.10.65	App	**Barnsley**	10.83	1982-87	78	2	0	(LB)	
CROSS, Steve C.	Wolverhampton	22.12.59	App	**Shrewsbury T.**	12.77	1976-85	240	22	34	(M)	
			Tr	**Derby Co.**	06.86	1986-88	21	19	3		
CROSSLEY, Mark G.	Barnsley	16.06.69	YTS	**Nottingham F.**	07.87	1988	2	0	0	(G)	
CROWN, David I.	Enfield	16.02.58	Walthamstow Ave.	**Brentford**	07.80	1980-81	44	2	8	(F)	
			Tr	**Portsmouth**	10.81	1981-82	25	3	2		
			L	**Exeter C.**	03.83	1982	0	1	3		
			Tr	**Reading**	08.83	1983-84	87	1	15		
			Tr	**Cambridge U.**	07.85	1985-87	106	0	44		
			Tr	**Southend U.**	11.87	1987-88	72	0	42		
CRUMPLIN, John L.	Bath	26.05.67	Bognor Regis T.	**Brighton & H.A.**	02.88	1986-88	31	12	2	(W)	
CULLEN, Anthony	Gateshead	30.09.69	Newcastle U. (YTS)	**Sunderland**	09.88	1988	3	1	0	(CD)	
CULPIN, Paul	Kirkby Muxloe	08.02.62	Jnrs	**Leicester C.**	05.81					(F)	E Semi-pro Int 1984-85
			Nuneaton Bor.	**Coventry C.**	06.85	1985-86	5	4	2		
			Tr	**Northampton T.**	10.87	1987-88	51	8	24		
CULVERHOUSE, Ian B.	Bishop's Stortford	22.09.64	App	**Tottenham H.**	09.82	1983	1	1	0	(RB)	E Yth Int
			Tr	**Norwich C.**	10.85	1985-88	126	0	0		
CUMMING, R. (Bobby)	Airdrie	07.12.55	Baillieston Jnrs	**Grimsby T.**	03.74	1974-86	338	27	56	(W/FB)	
			Tr	**Lincoln C.**	(N/L)	1988	29	0	5		
CUNNINGHAM, A.E. (Tony)	Jamaica (WI)	12.11.59	Stourbridge	**Lincoln C.**	05.79	1979-82	111	12	32	(F)	
			Tr	**Barnsley**	09.82	1982-83	40	2	11		
			Tr	**Sheffield Wed.**	11.83	1983	26	2	5		
			Tr	**Manchester C.**	07.84	1984	16	2	1		
			Tr	**Newcastle U.**	02.85	1984-86	37	10	4		
			Tr	**Blackpool**	07.87	1987-88	71	0	17		
CUNNINGTON, Shaun G.	Bourne	04.01.66	Jnrs	**Wrexham**	01.84	1982-87	196	3	12	(M)	
			Tr	**Grimsby T.**	02.88	1987-88	59	0	3		
CURBISHLEY L.C. (Alan)	Forest Gate	08.11.57	App	**West Ham U.**	07.75	1974-78	78	7	5	(M)	E Sch Int/E Yth Int/E U21-1
			Tr	**Birmingham C.**	07.79	1979-82	128	2	11		
			Tr	**Aston Villa**	03.83	1982-84	34	2	1		
			Tr	**Charlton Ath.**	12.84	1984-86	62	1	6		
			Tr	**Brighton & H.A.**	08.87	1987-88	66	5	12		
CURLE, Keith	Bristol	14.11.63	App	**Bristol Rov.**	11.81	1981-82	21	11	4	(CD)	
			Tr	**Torquay U.**	11.83	1983	16	0	5		
			Tr	**Bristol C.**	03.84	1983-87	113	8	1		
			Tr	**Reading**	10.87	1987-88	40	0	0		
			Tr	**Wimbledon**	10.88	1988	16	2	0		
CURRIE, David N.	Stockton	27.11.62		**Middlesbrough**	02.82	1981-85	94	19	31	(F)	
			Tr	**Darlington**	06.86	1986-87	76	0	33		
			Tr	**Barnsley**	02.88	1987-88	56	0	23		
CURRY, Sean P.	Liverpool	13.11.66	App	**Liverpool**	07.84					(F)	
			Tr	**Blackburn Rov.**	01.87	1986-88	25	13	7		

Players Names	Birthplace	Date	Previous Club	League Club	Date Sign'd	Seasons Played	Career Record Apps	Sub	Gls	Pos.	Misc
CURTIS, Alan T.	Rhondda	16.04.54	Jnrs	**Swansea C.**	07.72	1972-78	244	4	72	(F/M)	W U23-1/W U21-1/W-35/ Nephew of Roy Paul
			Tr	**Leeds U.**	06.79	1979-80	28	0	5		
			Tr	**Swansea C.**	12.80	1980-83	82	8	21		
			Tr	**Southampton**	11.83	1983-85	43	7	5		
			L	**Stoke C.**	03.86	1985	3	0	0		
			Tr	**Cardiff C.**	07.86	1986-88	114	3	10		
CUSACK, Nicky J.	Maltby	24.12.65	Alvechurch	**Leicester C.**	06.87	1987	5	11	1	(F)	
			Tr	**Peterborough U.**	07.88	1988	44	0	10		
CUTLER, Chris P.	Manchester	07.04.64	Jnrs	**Bury**	08.81	1981-84	8	15	3	(M/F)	
			Tr	**Crewe Alex.**	08.85	1985-88	92	10	19		
DAISH, Liam S.	Portsmouth	23.09.68	App	**Portsmouth**	09.86	1986	1	0	0	(CD)	
			Tr	**Cambridge U.** (N/C)	07.88	1988	28	0	0		
DALE, Carl	Colwyn Bay	24.09.66	Bangor C.	**Chester C.**	05.88	1988	38	3	22	(F)	
DALEY, A.M. (Tony)	Birmingham	18.10.67	App	**Aston Villa**	05.85	1984-88	80	24	13	(W)	E Yth Int
DALTON, Paul	Middlesbrough	25.04.67	Brandon U.	**Manchester U.**	05.88					(W)	
			Tr	**Hartlepool U.**	03.89	1988	17	0	2		
DALY, Gerry A.	Dublin	30.04.54	Bohemians	**Manchester U.**	04.73	1973-76	107	4	23	(M)	IR U21-1/IR-46
			Tr	**Derby Co.**	03.77	1976-79	111	1	31		
			Tr	**Coventry C.**	08.80	1980-83	82	2	15		
			L	**Leicester C.**	01.83	1982	17	0	1		
			Tr	**Birmingham C.**	08.84	1984-85	31	1	1		
			Tr	**Shrewsbury T.**	10.85	1985-86	55	0	8		
			Tr	**Stoke C.**	03.87	1986-87	17	5	1		
			Tr	**Doncaster Rov.**	07.88	1988	37	2	4		
DALZIEL, Ian	South Shields	24.10.62	App	**Derby Co.**	10.79	1981-82	22	0	4	(FB)	
			Tr	**Hereford U.**	05.83	1983-87	137	13	8		
			Tr	**Carlisle U.**	07.88	1988	42	0	1		
DANIEL, Peter W.	Hull	12.12.55	Jnrs	**Hull C.**	09.73	1974-77	113	0	9	(M/RB)	E U23-3/E U21-7
			Tr	**Wolverhampton W.**	05.78	1978-83	157	0	13		
			Tr	**Sunderland**	08.84	1984-85	33	1	0		
			Tr	**Lincoln C.**	11.85	1985-86	55	0	2		
			Tr	**Burnley**	07.87	1987-88	40	1	0		
DANIEL, Ray C.	Luton	10.12.64	App	**Luton T.**	09.82	1982-85	14	8	4	(M)	
			L	**Gillingham**	09.83	1983	5	0	0		
			Tr	**Hull C.**	06.86	1986-88	55	3	3		
DANIELS, Scott	Benfleet	22.11.69	YTS	**Colchester U.**	06.88	1987-88	18	9	0	(D)	
DARBY, Julian T.	Bolton	03.10.67	YTS	**Bolton W.**	07.86	1985-88	104	5	7	(M)	E Sch Int
DARBY, Lee A.	Salford	20.09.69	YTS	**Portsmouth**	10.86	1987	1	0	0	(M)	
D'AURIA, David A.	Swansea	26.03.70	YTS	**Swansea C.**	07.88	1987-88	9	9	2	(CD)	
DAVENPORT, Peter	Birkenhead	24.03.61	Cammell Laird	**Nottingham F.**	01.82	1981-85	114	4	54	(F)	E-'B'/E-1
			Tr	**Manchester U.**	03.86	1985-88	73	19	22		
			Tr	**Middlesbrough**	11.88	1988	23	1	4		
DAVEY, Simon	Swansea	01.10.70	YTS	**Swansea C.** (YTS)	08.87	1986-88	7	1	0	(F)	
DAVIES, Alan	Manchester	05.12.61	App	**Manchester U.**	12.78	1981-83	6	1	0	(W)	W U21-3/W-7
			Tr	**Newcastle U.**	08.85	1985-86	20	1	1		
			L	**Charlton Ath.**	03.86	1985	1	0	0		
			L	**Carlisle U.**	11.86	1986	4	0	1		
			Tr	**Swansea C.**	07.87	1987-88	84	0	8		
DAVIES, Andrew J.	Wolverhampton	06.06.72	YTS	**Torquay U.** (YTS)	07.88	1988	3	0	0	(CD)	
DAVIES, Gordon J.	Merthyr Tydfil	08.08.55	Merthyr Tydfil	**Fulham**	03.78	1977-84	244	3	114	(F)	W Sch Int/W-18
			Tr	**Chelsea**	11.84	1984-85	11	2	6		
			Tr	**Manchester C.**	10.85	1985-86	31	0	9		
			Tr	**Fulham**	10.86	1986-88	82	12	33		
DAVIES, Michael J.	Stretford	19.01.66	App	**Blackpool**	01.84	1983-88	151	15	13	(RB/W)	
DAVIES, Steven E.	Liverpool	16.07.60	Congleton T.	**Port Vale**	12.87	1987	1	5	0	(W)	
DAVIS, Darren J.	Sutton-in-Ashfield	05.02.67	App	**Notts Co.**	02.85	1983-87	90	2	1	(LB)	E Yth Int
			Tr	**Lincoln C.**	08.88	1988	37	1	2		
DAVIS, Paul V.	Camberwell	09.12.61	App	**Arsenal**	07.79	1979-88	245	14	25	(M)	E U21-11
DAVIS, Steve P.	Birmingham	26.07.65	Stoke C.(App)	**Crewe Alex.**	08.83	1983-87	140	5	1	(CD)	E Yth Int.
			Tr	**Burnley**	10.87	1987-88	70	0	5		
DAVISON, Aidan J.	Sedgefield (Dm)	11.05.68	Billingham Synth.	**Notts Co.**	03.88	1988	1	0	0	(G)	
DAVISON, R. (Bobby)	South Shields	17.07.59	Seaham CW	**Huddersfield T.**	07.80	1980	1	1	0	(F)	
			Tr	**Halifax T.**	08.81	1981-82	63	0	29		
			Tr	**Derby Co.**	12.82	1982-87	203	3	83		
			Tr	**Leeds U.**	11.87	1987-88	52	3	20		
D'AVRAY, J. Mich	South Africa	19.02.62	App	**Ipswich T.**	05.79	1979-88	162	37	36	(F)	E U21-2
			L	**Leicester C.**	02.87	1986	3	0	0		
DAWES, Ian R.	Croydon	22.02.63	App	**Q.P.R.**	12.80	1981-87	229	0	3	(LB)	E Sch Int
			Tr	**Millwall**	08.88	1988	27	3	1		
DAWKINS, Derek A.	Edmonton	29.11.59	App	**Leicester C.**	11.77	1977	3	0	0	(FB)	
			Tr	**MansfieldT.**	12.78	1978-80	73	0	0		
			Tr	**Bournemouth**	08.81	1981-82	4	4	0		
			Weymouth	**Torquay U.**	02.84	1983-88	153	22	7		
DAWS, A. (Tony)	Sheffield	10.09.66	App	**Notts Co.**	09.84	1984-85	6	2	1	(F)	E Yth Int
			Tr	**Sheffield U.**	08.86	1986	7	4	3		
			Tr	**Scunthorpe U.**	06.87	1987-88	53	3	27		
DAWSON, Alistair J.	Glasgow	25.02.58	Glasgow Rangers	**Blackburn Rov.**	08.87	1987-88	23	5	0	(CD)	S Yth Int/S U21-8/S-5
DAY, Keith	Grays	29.11.62	Aveley	**Colchester U.**	08.84	1984-86	113	0	12	(CD)	
			Tr	**Leyton Orient**	07.87	1987-88	86	0	5		
DAY, Mervyn R.	Chelmsford	26.06.55	App	**West Ham U.**	03.73	1973-78	194	0	0	(G)	E Yth Int/E U23-5
			Tr	**Leyton Orient**	07.79	1979-82	170	0	0		
			Tr	**Aston Villa**	08.83	1983-84	30	0	0		
			Tr	**Leeds U.**	01.85	1984-88	181	0	0		
DE MANGE, Ken J.P.	Dublin	03.09.64	Home Farm	**Liverpool**	08.83					(M)	IR Youth Int/IR-1
			L	**Scunthorpe U.**	12.86	1986	3	0	2		
			Tr	**Leeds U.**	09.87	1987	14	1	1		
			Tr	**Hull C.**	03.88	1987-88	27	14	1		

Gordon Durie (Chelsea & Scotland) Match Magazine

Mike Duxbury (Manchester United & England) Match Magazine

Tim Flowers (Southampton) Match Magazine

Simon Garner (Blackburn Rovers) Match Magazine

Players Names	Birthplace	Date	Previous Club	League Club	Date Sign'd	Seasons Played	Career Record Apps	Sub	Gls	Pos.	Misc
DEAKIN, Ray J.	Liverpool	19.06.59	App	Everton	06.77					(LB)	
			Tr	Port Vale	08.81	1981	21	2	6		
			Tr	Bolton W.	08.82	1982-84	104	1	2		
			Tr	Burnley	07.85	1985-88	143	0	6		
DEANE, Brian C.	Leeds	07.02.68	Jnrs	Doncaster Rov.	12.85	1985-87	59	7	12	(F)	
			Tr	Sheffield U.	07.88	1988	43	0	22		
DEARDEN, Kevin C.	Luton	08.03.70	YTS	Tottenham H.	07.88					(G)	
			L	Cambridge U.	03.89	1988	15	0	0		
DEARY, John S.	Ormskirk	18.10.62	App	Blackpool	03.80	1980-88	285	18	43	(M)	
DEEHAN, John M.	Birmingham	06.08.57	App	Aston Villa	04.75	1975-79	107	3	41	(F)	E Yth Int/E U21-7
			Tr	West Bromwich A.	09.79	1979-81	44	3	5		
			Tr	Norwich C.	12.81	1981-85	158	4	62		
			Tr	Ipswich T.	06.86	1986-87	45	4	11		
			Tr	Manchester C.	07.88						
DEMPSEY, Mark J.	Manchester	14.01.64	App	Manchester U.	01.82	1985	1	0	0	(M)	
			L	Swindon T.	01.85	1984	5	0	0		
			Tr	Sheffield U.	08.86	1986-87	60	3	8		
			L	Chesterfield	09.88	1988	3	0	0		
			Tr	Rotherham U.	10.88	1988	24	3	1		
DENNIS, J. Anthony	Maidenhead	01.12.63	App	Plymouth Arg.	12.81	1981-82	7	2	0	(W)	
			Tr	Exeter C.	08.83	1983	3	1	0		
			Slough T.	Cambridge U.	02.89	1988	18	0	3		
DENNIS, Mark E.	Streatham	02.05.61	App	Birmingham C.	08.78	1978-82	130	0	1	(LB)	E Yth Int/E U21-3
			Tr	Southampton	11.83	1983-86	95	0	2		
			Tr	Q.P.R.	05.87	1987-88	26	2	0		
DENNISON, Robbie	Banbridge (NI)	30.04.63	Glenavon	West Bromwich A.	09.85	1985-86	9	7	1	(W)	NI-6
			Tr	Wolverhampton W.	03.87	1986-88	94	2	14		
DENTON, Edward J.	Oxford	18.05.70	YTS	Oxford U.	07.88	1987	0	2	0	(M)	
DEVEREUX, James A.	Aldershot	20.02.70	YTS	Aldershot	07.88	1988	0	1	0	(F)	Son of Tony
DEVINE, Steve B.	Strabane (NI)	11.12.64	App	Wolverhampton W.	12.82					(D)	
			Tr	Derby Co.	03.83	1983-84	10	1	0		
			Tr	Stockport Co.	08.85	1985	2	0	0		
			Tr	Hereford U.	10.85	1985-88	131	5	2		
DEVONSHIRE, Alan E.	Park Royal	13.04.56	Southall	West Ham U.	10.76	1976-88	342	9	29	(M)	Son of Les/E-8
DIAMOND, Anthony J.	Rochdale	23.08.68	YTS	Blackburn Rov.	06.86	1986-88	9	17	2	(F)	NI U21-1
			L	Wigan Ath.	10.88	1988	6	0	2		
DIBBLE, Andy G.	Cwmbran	08.05.65	App	Cardiff C.	08.82	1981-83	62	0	0	(G)	W Yth Int/W U21-2/W-3
			Tr	Luton T.	07.84	1984-87	30	0	0		
			L	Sunderland	02.86	1985	12	0	0		
			L	Huddersfield T.	03.87	1986	5	0	0		
			Tr	Manchester C.	06.88	1988	38	0	0		
DICKENS, Alan W.	Plaistow	03.09.64	App	West Ham U.	08.82	1982-88	173	19	23	(M)	E Yth Int/E U21-1
DICKENSON, Kevin J.	Hackney	24.11.62	Tottenham H.(App)	Charlton Ath.	04.80	1979-84	72	3	1	(LB)	
			Tr	Leyton Orient	07.85	1985-88	145	1	3		
DICKINSON, Martin J.	Leeds	14.03.63	App	Leeds U.	05.80	1979-85	100	3	2	(CD)	
			Tr	West Bromwich A.	02.86	1985-87	46	4	2		
			Tr	Sheffield U.	07.88	1988	0	1	0		
DICKS, Julian A.	Bristol	08.08.68	App	Birmingham C.	03.86	1985-87	83	6	1	(LB)	Son of Alan/E U21-4
			Tr	West Ham U.	03.88	1987-88	42	2	0		
DIGBY, Fraser C.	Sheffield	23.04.67	App	Manchester U.	04.85					(G)	E Yth Int/E U21-4
			Tr	Swindon T.	09.86	1986-88	116	0	0		
DIGWEED, Perry M.	Westminster	26.10.59	App	Fulham	08.77	1976-80	15	0	0	(G)	
			Tr	Brighton & H.A.	01.81	1980-88	102	0	0		
			L	Chelsea	02.88	1987	3	0	0		
DILLON, Kevin P.	Sunderland	18.12.59	App	Birmingham C.	07.77	1977-82	181	5	15	(M)	E Yth Int/E U21-1
			Tr	Portsmouth	03.83	1982-88	206	9	45		
DIXON, Andrew	Louth	19.04.68	YTS	Grimsby T.	05.86	1986-88	35	3	0	(FB)	
DIXON, Kerry M.	Luton	24.07.61	Chesham U.	Tottenham H.	07.78					(F)	Son of Mike/E U21-1/E-8
			Dunstable T.	Reading	07.80	1980-82	110	6	51		
			Tr	Chelsea	08.83	1983-88	228	1	112		
DIXON, Kevin L.	Consett	27.07.60	Tow Law T.	Carlisle U.	08.83	1983	5	4	0	(W)	
			L	Hartlepool U.	10.83	1983	6	0	3		
			Tr	Hartlepool U.	08.84	1984-86	103	4	26		
			L	Scunthorpe U.	01.86	1985	14	0	2		
			Tr	Scunthorpe U.	08.87	1987	37	4	4		
			Tr	Hartlepool U.	06.88	1988	14	0	4		
			Tr	York C.	11.88	1988	18	1	4		
DIXON, Lee M.	Manchester	17.03.64	Jnrs	Burnley	07.82	1982-83	4	0	0	(FB)	
			Tr	Chester C.	02.84	1983-84	56	1	1		
			Tr	Bury	07.85	1985	45	0	6		
			Tr	Stoke C.	07.86	1986-87	71	0	5		
			Tr	Arsenal	01.88	1987-88	37	2	1		
DOBBIN, Jim	Dunfermline	17.09.63	Glasgow Celtic	Doncaster Rov.	03.84	1983-86	56	8	9	(M)	
			Tr	Barnsley	09.86	1986-88	80	7	11		
DOBBINS, L. Wayne	Bromsgrove	30.08.68	App	West Bromwich A.	08.86	1986-88	20	12	0	(M/FB)	
DOBSON, A.J. (Tony)	Coventry	02.02.69	App	Coventry C.	07.86	1986-88	18	0	0	(LB)	E U21-3
DOBSON, Paul	Hartlepool	17.12.62	Newcastle U.(Jnr)	Hartlepool U.	11.81	1981-82	23	8	8	(F)	
			Horden Colliery	Hartlepool U.	12.83	1983-85	60	20	24		
			Tr	Torquay U.	07.86	1986-87	63	14	38		
			Tr	Doncaster Rov.	08.88	1988	22	2	10		
			Tr	Scarborough	02.89	1988	18	0	5		
DOCKER, Ian	Norwich	12.09.69	YTS	Gillingham	09.87	1987-88	32	4	0	(M)	
DODDS, W. (Billy)	New Cumnock	05.02.69	App	Chelsea	05.86	1986-88	0	3	0	(F)	
DOIG, Russell	Millport	17.01.64	East Stirling	Leeds U.	07.86	1986-87	3	3	0	(W)	
			L	Peterborough U.	10.86	1986	7	0	0		
			Tr	Hartlepool U.	03.88	1987-88	20	8	1		
DOLAN, Eamonn J.	Dagenham	20.09.67	App	West Ham U.	03.85	1986-87	1	4	0	(F)	IR Yth Int
			L	Bristol C.	02.89	1988	3	0	0		

Players Names	Birthplace	Date	Previous Club	League Club	Date Sign'd	Seasons Played	Career Record Apps	Sub	Gls	Pos.	Misc
DONACHIE, Willie	Glasgow	05.10.51	Jnrs	**Manchester C.**	12.68	1969-79	347	4	2	(LB)	S U23-2/S-35
			Portland Timb. (USA)	**Norwich C.**	09.81	1981	11	0	0		
			Portland Timb. (USA)	**Burnley**	11.82	1982-84	60	0	3		
			Tr	**Oldham Ath.**	07.84	1984-88	139	6	3		
DONAGHY, Mal	Belfast	13.09.57	Larne T.	**Luton T.**	06.78	1978-88	410	0	16	(CD)	NI U21-1/NI-62
			Tr	**Manchester U.**	10.88	1988	30	0	0		
DONALD, Warren R.	Hillingdon	07.10.64	App	**West Ham U.**	10.82	1983	1	1	0	(M)	E Sch Int
			L	**Northampton T.**	03.85	1984	11	0	2		
			Tr	**Northampton T.**	10.85	1985-88	149	1	9		
DONEGAL, Glenville	Northampton	20.06.69	YTS	**Northampton T.**	08.87	1987-88	6	13	3	(F)	
DONNELLAN, Leo J.	Brent	19.01.65	App	**Chelsea**	08.82					(M)	IR U21-1/Brother of Gary
			L	**Leyton Orient**	12.84	1984	6	0	0		
			Tr	**Fulham**	08.85	1985-88	46	22	4		
DONNELLY, Paul A.	Liverpool	23.12.71	YTS	**Halifax T.** (YTS)	07.88	1988	0	1	0		
DONOWA, B. Louie	Ipswich	24.09.64	App	**Norwich C.**	09.82	1982-85	56	6	11	(W)	E U21-3/to La Coruna (Sp.) 2.86
			L	**Stoke C.**	12.85	1985	4	0	1		
DOONER, Gary J.	St. Helens	14.09.70	YTS	**Stockport Co.** (YTS)	09.87	1988	1	0	0	(W)	
DORIGO, A.R. (Tony)	Australia	31.12.65	App	**Aston Villa**	07.83	1983-86	106	5	1	(LB)	E U21-11/E 'B'
			Tr	**Chelsea**	05.87	1987-88	80	0	6		
DORNAN, Andy	Aberdeen	19.08.61	Motherwell	**Walsall**	08.86	1986-88	99	1	0	(RB)	
DOUGLAS, Colin F.	Kilmarnock	09.09.62	Glasgow Celtic(Jnr)	**Doncaster Rov.**	11.81	1981-85	202	10	48	(FB/F)	
			Tr	**Rotherham U.**	07.86	1986-87	82	1	4		
			Tr	**Doncaster Rov.**	08.88	1988	46	0	2		
DOWIE, Iain	Hatfield	09.01.65	Hendon	**Luton T.**	12.88	1988	1	7	0	(F)	NI U21-1
DOWNES, Chris B.	Sheffield	17.01.69	YTS	**Sheffield U.**	06.87	1988	2	0	0	(FB)	
			L	**Scarborough**	03.88	1987	2	0	0		
DOWNING, Keith G.	Oldbury	23.07.65	Mile Oak Rovers	**Notts. Co.**	05.84	1984-86	23	0	1	(W)	
			Tr	**Wolverhampton W.**	07.87	1987-88	52	14	2		
DOWNS, Greg	Nottingham	13.12.58	App	**Norwich C.**	12.76	1977-84	162	7	7	(LB)	
			L	**Torquay U.**	11.77	1977	1	0	1		
			Tr	**Coventry C.**	07.85	1985-88	126	3	4		
DOYLE, Maurice	Ellesmere Port	17.10.69	YTS	**Crewe Alex.**	07.88	1987-88	6	2	0	(M)	
			Tr	**Q.P.R.**	04.89						
DOYLE, Steve C.	Neath	02.06.58	App	**Preston N.E.**	06.75	1974-81	178	19	8	(M)	W U21-2
			Tr	**Huddersfield T.**	09.82	1982-86	158	3	6		
			Tr	**Sunderland**	09.86	1986-88	99	1	2		
DOZZELL, Jason A.W.	Ipswich	09.12.67	App	**Ipswich T.**	12.84	1983-88	153	17	20	(M)	EYth Int/E U21-7
DRAPER, Mark A.	Long Eaton	11.11.70	YTS	**Notts Co.**	12.88	1988	16	4	3	(W)	
DREYER, John B.	Alnwick	11.06.63	Wallingford T.	**Oxford U.**	01.85	1986-87	57	3	2	(D)	
			L	**Torquay U.**	12.85	1985	5	0	0		
			L	**Fulham**	03.86	1985	12	0	2		
			Tr	**Luton T.**	06.88	1988	16	2	1		
DRINKELL, Kevin S.	Grimsby	18.06.60	App	**Grimsby T.**	06.78	1976-84	242	28	89	(F)	
			Tr	**Norwich C.**	08.85	1985-87	121	0	50		to Glasgow Rangers 7.88
DRISCOLL, Andrew	Staines	21.10.71	YTS	**Brentford** (YTS)	07.88	1988	0	1	0	(RW)	
DRYDEN, Richard A.	Stroud	14.06.69	YTS	**Bristol Rov.**	07.88	1986-88	12	1	0	(LB)	
			L	**Exeter C.**	09.88	1988	6	0	0		
			Tr	**Exeter C.**	03.89	1988	15	0	0		
DUBLIN, Dion	Leicester	22.04.69		**Norwich C.**	03.88					(F)	
			Tr	**Cambridge U.** (N/C)	08.88	1988	12	9	6		
DUBLIN, Keith B.L.	High Wycombe	29.01.66	App	**Chelsea**	01.84	1983-86	50	1	0	(LB)	E Yth Int
			Tr	**Brighton & H.A.**	08.87	1987-88	89	0	5		
DUFFIELD, Peter	Middlesbrough	04.02.69	App	**Middlesbrough**	11.86					(W)	
			Tr	**Sheffield U.**	08.87	1987-88	32	17	13		
			L	**Halifax T.**	03.88	1987	12	0	6		
DUFFY, Darrell G.	Birmingham	18.01.71	YTS	**Aston Villa** (YTS)	06.87	1988	1	0	0	(D)	
DUGGAN, Andrew J.	Bradford	19.09.67	YTS	**Barnsley**	07.85	1986	1	1	0	(CD)	
			L	**Rochdale**	11.87	1987	3	0	0		
			Tr	**Huddersfield T.**	09.88	1988	14	0	2		
DUNKLEY, Malcolm	Wolverhampton	12.07.61	Bromsgrove Rov.	**Lincoln C.**	02.89	1988	9	2	4	(F)	
DUNN, Iain G.W.	York	01.04.70	Jnrs	**York C.**	07.88	1988	18	8	6	(F)	E Yth Int
DURIE, Gordon S.	Paisley	06.12.65	Hibernian	**Chelsea**	04.86	1985-88	77	7	34	(F)	S U21-3/S-2
DURNIN, John P.	Bootle	18.08.65	Waterloo Dock	**Liverpool**	03.86					(F)	
			L	**West Bromwich A.**	10.88	1988	5	0	2		
			Tr	**Oxford U.**	02.89	1988	19	0	3		
DUXBURY, Lee E.	Skipton	07.10.69	YTS	**Bradford C.**	07.88	1988	0	1	0	(M)	
DUXBURY, Mike	Accrington	01.09.59	App	**Manchester U.**	10.76	1980-88	262	18	6	(D/M)	E U21-7/E-10
DYER, Alex C.	West Ham	14.11.65	Watford(App)	**Blackpool**	10.83	1983-86	101	7	19	(W)	
			Tr	**Hull C.**	02.87	1986-88	59	1	14		
			Tr	**Crystal Palace**	11.88	1988	6	1	2		
DYSON, Paul I.	Birmingham	27.12.59	App	**Coventry C.**	06.77	1978-82	140	0	5	(CD)	E U21-4
			Tr	**Stoke C.**	07.83	1983-85	106	0	5		
			Tr	**West Bromwich A.**	03.86	1985-88	64	0	5		
			Tr	**Darlington**	03.89	1988	12	0	3		
EARLE, Robbie	Newcastle-u-Lyme	27.01.65	Jnrs	**Port Vale**	07.82	1982-88	207	9	54	(M)	
EATON, Jason C.	Bristol	29.01.69	Jnrs	**Bristol Rov.**	06.87	1987	0	3	0	(F)	
			Clevedon	**Bristol C.**	03.89	1988	0	2	0		
EBBRELL, John K.	Bromborough	01.10.69	YTS	**Everton**	11.86	1988	1	3	0	(M)	E Yth Int/E U21-2
ECCLES, Peter	Dublin	24.08.62	Dundalk	**Leicester C.**	10.88	1988	1	0	0	(CD)	IR-1
ECKHARDT, Jeff E.	Sheffield	07.10.65	Jnrs	**Sheffield U.**	08.84	1984-87	73	1	2	(D)	
			Tr	**Fulham**	11.87	1987-88	72	0	3		
EDINBURGH, Justin C.	Brentwood	18.12.69	YTS	**Southend U.**	07.88	1988	14	1	0	(FB)	
EDMONDS, Neil A.	Accrington	18.10.68	YTS	**Oldham Ath.**	06.86	1986-87	3	2	0	(W)	
			Tr	**Rochdale**	09.88	1988	34	5	8		

Billy Garton (Manchester United) Match Magazine

Terry Gibson (Wimbledon) Match Magazine

Gary Gill (Middlesbrough) Match Magazine

Gary Gillespie (Liverpool & Scotland) Match Magazine

Players Names	Birthplace	Date	Previous Club	League Club	Date Sign'd	Seasons Played	Career Record Apps	Sub	Gls	Pos.	Misc
EDWARDS, Andrew D.	Epping	17.09.71	YTS	**Southend U.** (YTS)	07.88	1988	1	0	0	(CD)	
EDWARDS, Dean S.	Wolverhampton	25.02.62	App	**Shrewsbury T.**	02.80	1979-81	7	6	1	(F)	
			Telford U.	**Wolverhampton W.**	10.85	1985-86	28	3	9		
			Tr	**Exeter C.**	03.87	1986-87	51	3	17		
			Tr	**Torquay U.**	08.88	1988	30	10	8		
EDWARDS, Keith	Stockton	16.07.57	Jnrs	**Sheffield U.**	08.75	1975-77	64	6	29	(F)	
			Tr	**Hull C.**	08.78	1978-81	130	2	57		
			Tr	**Sheffield U.**	09.81	1981-85	183	8	114		
			Tr	**Leeds U.**	08.86	1986-87	28	10	6		
			Aberdeen	**Hull C.**	03.88	1987-88	53	0	28		
EDWARDS, Paul	Liverpool	22.02.65	Leek T.	**Crewe Alex.** (N/C)	02.89	1988	10	0	0	(G)	
EDWARDS, Paul R.	Birkenhead	23.12.63	Altrincham	**Crewe Alex.**	01.88	1987-88	55	3	5	(FB)	
EDWARDS, Robert	Manchester	23.02.70	YTS	**Crewe Alex.**	07.88	1987-88	4	6	1	(M)	
EELES, Anthony G.	Chatham	15.11.70	YTS	**Gillingham** (YTS)	07.87	1988	3	0	0	(F)	
ELEY, Kevin	Mexborough	04.03.68	App	**Rotherham U.**	03.86	1983-86	3	10	0	(W)	
			Tr	**Chesterfield**	08.87	1987-88	68	8	2		
ELI, Roger	Bradford	11.09.65	App	**Leeds U.**	09.83	1984-85	1	1	0	(M)	
			Tr	**Wolverhampton W.**	01.86	1985-86	16	2	0		
			Cambridge U. (N/C)	**Crewe Alex.** (N/C)	09.87	1987	20	7	1		
			Pontefract Colly.	**York C.** (N/C)	11.88	1988	3	1	1		
			Tr	**Bury**	12.88	1988	0	2	0		
ELKINS, Gary	Wallingford	04.05.66	App	**Fulham**	12.83	1984-88	91	3	1	(D)	E Yth Int
ELLIOTT, Anthony R.	Nuneaton	30.11.69	YTS	**Birmingham C.**	12.86					(G)	E Yth Int
			Tr	**Hereford U.**	12.88	1988	23	0	0		
ELLIOTT, Lee	Ormskirk	05.05.70	Everton (YTS)	**Crewe Alex.**	06.88	1988	1	0	0	(F)	
ELLIOTT, Matthew S.	Wandsworth	01.11.68	Epsom & Ewell	**Charlton Ath.**	05.88					(CD)	
			Tr	**Torquay U.**	03.89	1988	13	0	2		
ELLIOTT, Paul M.	Lewisham	18.03.64	App	**Charlton Ath.**	03.81	1981-82	61	2	1	(CD)	E Yth Int/E U21-3/to Pisa (It.) 7.8
			Tr	**Luton T.**	03.83	1982-85	63	3	4		
			Tr	**Aston Villa**	12.85	1985-86	56	1	7		
ELLIOTT, Shaun	Haydon Bridge	26.01.57	App	**Sunderland**	01.75	1976-85	316	5	11	(CD)	E 'B'
			Tr	**Norwich C.**	08.86	1986-87	29	2	2		
			Tr	**Blackpool**	08.88	1988	41	0	0		
ELLIOTT, Steve B.	Haltwhistle	15.09.58	App	**Nottingham F.**	09.76	1978	4	0	0	(F)	
			Tr	**Preston N.E.**	03.79	1978-83	202	6	70		
			Tr	**Luton T.**	07.84	1984	12	0	3		
			Tr	**Walsall**	12.84	1984-85	68	1	21		
			Tr	**Bolton W.**	07.86	1986-88	57	3	10		
			Tr	**Bury**	09.88	1988	31	0	11		
ELLIS, A.J. (Tony)	Salford	20.10.64	Horwich RMI	**Oldham Ath.**	08.86	1986-87	5	3	0	(F)	
			Tr	**Preston N.E.**	10.87	1987-88	63	6	25		
ELLIS, Mark E.	Bradford	06.01.62	Jnrs	**Bradford C.**	08.80	1980-88	187	25	30	(W)	
ELSEY, Karl W.	Swansea	20.11.58	Pembroke Bor.	**Q.P.R.**	01.79	1978-79	6	1	0	(M)	
			Tr	**Newport Co.**	07.80	1980-83	114	9	15		
			Tr	**Cardiff C.**	09.83	1983-84	59	0	5		
			Tr	**Gillingham**	08.85	1985-87	126	2	13		
			Tr	**Reading**	08.88	1988	41	3	3		
EMERSON, Dean	Salford	27.12.62		**Stockport Co.**	02.82	1981-84	156	0	7	(M)	
			Tr	**Rotherham U.**	07.85	1985-86	55	0	8		
			Tr	**Coventry C.**	10.86	1986-88	56	1	0		
EMSON, Paul D.	Lincoln	22.10.58	Brigg T.	**Derby Co.**	09.78	1978-82	112	15	13	(W)	
			Tr	**Grimsby T.**	08.83	1983-85	90	7	15		
			Tr	**Wrexham**	07.86	1986-87	42	7	5		
			Tr	**Darlington**	08.88	1988	27	7	5		
ENDERSBY, Scott A.G.	Lewisham	20.02.62	App	**Ipswich T.**	03.79					(G)	E Yth Int
			Tr	**Tranmere Rov.**	07.81	1981-82	79	0	0		
			Tr	**Swindon T.**	08.83	1983-85	85	0	0		
			Tr	**Carlisle U.**	11.85	1985-86	52	0	0		
			Tr	**York C.**	07.87	1987-88	35	0	0		
			L	**Cardiff C.**	12.87	1987	4	0	0		
ENGLISH, A.K.(Tony)	Luton	19.10.66	Coventry C.(App)	**Colchester U.**	12.84	1984-88	176	2	30	(M/D)	Brother of Tom/E Yth Int
ENTWISTLE, Wayne P.	Bury	06.08.58	App	**Bury**	08.76	1976-77	25	6	7	(F)	E Yth Int
			Tr	**Sunderland**	11.77	1977-79	43	2	13		
			Tr	**Leeds U.**	10.79	1979	7	4	2		
			Tr	**Blackpool**	11.80	1980-81	27	5	6		
			Tr	**Crewe Alex.**	03.82	1981	11	0	0		
			Tr	**Wimbledon**	07.82	1982	4	5	3		
			Grays Ath.	**Bury**	08.83	1983-84	80	3	32		
			Tr	**Carlisle U.**	06.85	1985	8	1	2		
			Tr	**Bolton W.**	10.85	1985	5	3	0		
			L	**Burnley**	08.86	1986	6	2	2		
			Tr	**Stockport Co.**	10.86	1986-87	38	11	8		
			Tr	**Bury** (N/C)	08.88	1988	0	2	0		
			Tr	**Wigan Ath.**	10.88	1988	24	5	6		
EVANS, Allan	Dunfermline	12.10.56	Dunfermline Ath.	**Aston Villa**	05.77	1977-88	374	6	51	(CD)	S-4
EVANS, Ceri L.	New Zealand	02.10.63		**Oxford U.**	02.89	1988	6	4	1	(CD)	
EVANS, A. Clive	Birkenhead	01.05.57	App	**Tranmere Rov.**	05.75	1976-80	175	3	27	(W/FB)	
			Tr	**Wigan Ath.**	07.81	1981	29	3	2		
			Tr	**Crewe Alex.**	08.82	1982	26	2	7		
			Tr	**Stockport Co.**	08.83	1983-87	158	2	23		
			Tr	**Lincoln C.**	(N/L)	1988	42	0	2		
EVANS, David G.	West Bromwich	20.05.58	App	**Aston Villa**	02.76	1978	2	0	0	(CD)	
			Tr	**Halifax T.**	06.79	1979-83	218	0	9		
			Tr	**Bradford C.**	06.84	1984-88	198	1	3		
EVANS, Gareth J.	Coventry	14.01.67	App	**Coventry C.**	01.85	1985-86	5	2	0	(F)	
			Tr	**Rotherham U.**	10.86	1986-87	62	1	13		to Hibernian 2.88
EVANS, Mark	Leeds	24.08.70	YTS	**Bradford C.**	07.88	1988	3	0	0	(G)	

Players Names	Birthplace	Date	Previous Club	League Club	Date Sign'd	Seasons Played	Career Record Apps	Sub	Gls	Pos.	Misc
EVANS, Stewart J.	Maltby	15.11.60	App	**Rotherham U.**	11.78					(F)	
			Gainsborough Trin.	**Sheffield U.**	11.80						
			Tr	**Wimbledon**	03.82	1981-85	165	10	50		
			Tr	**West Bromwich A.**	08.86	1986	13	1	1		
			Tr	**Plymouth Arg.**	03.87	1986-88	36	9	10		
			Tr	**Rotherham U.**	11.88	1988	19	6	6		
EVANS, Terry W.	Hammersmith	12.04.65	Hillingdon Bor	**Brentford**	07.85	1985-88	93	1	10	(CD)	
FAIRCLOUGH, Chris H.	Nottingham	12.04.64	App	**Nottingham F.**	10.81	1982-86	102	5	1	(CD)	E U21-7/Brother of Wayne R.
			Tr	**Tottenham H.**	08.87	1987-88	60	0	5		
			Tr	**Leeds U.**	03.89	1988	11	0	0		
FAIRCLOUGH, Wayne R.	Nottingham	27.04.68	App	**Notts. Co.**	04.86	1985-88	34	29	0	(FB)	Brother of Chris
FAIRWEATHER, Carlton	Camberwell	22.09.61	Tooting & Mitcham	**Wimbledon**	12.84	1984-88	89	17	24	(W)	
FALCO, Mark P.	Hackney	22.10.60	App	**Tottenham H.**	07.78	1978-86	162	12	68	(F)	E Yth Int
			L	**Chelsea**	11.82	1982	3	0	0		
			Tr	**Watford**	10.86	1986	33	0	14		
			Glasgow Rangers	**Q.P.R.**	12.87	1987-88	37	9	17		
FALCONER, Willie	Aberdeen	05.04.66	Aberdeen	**Watford**	06.88	1988	30	3	5	(LB/M)	
FALLON, Shaun	Widnes	10.09.70	YTS	**Wigan Ath.**	07.87	1988	1	0	0	(M)	
FARNWORTH, Simon	Chorley	28.10.63	App	**Bolton W.**	09.81	1983-85	113	0	0	(G)	
			L	**Stockport Co.**	09.86	1986	10	0	0		
			L	**Tranmere Rov.**	01.87	1986	7	0	0		
			Tr	**Bury**	03.87	1986-88	98	0	0		
FARRELL, Andrew J.	Colchester	07.10.65	App	**Colchester U.**	09.83	1983-86	98	7	5	(W)	
			Tr	**Burnley**	08.87	1987-88	80	1	7		
FARRELL, Sean P.	Watford	28.02.69	App	**Luton T.**	02.87					(F)	
			L	**Colchester U.**	03.88	1987	4	5	1		
FASHANU, John	Kensington	18.09.62	Cambridge U.(Jnr)	**Norwich C.**	10.79	1981-82	6	1	1	(F)	Brother of Justin/E-2
			L	**Crystal Palace**	08.83	1983	1	0	0		
			Tr	**Lincoln C.**	09.83	1983-84	31	5	11		
			Tr	**Millwall**	11.84	1984-85	50	0	12		
			Tr	**Wimbledon**	03.86	1985-88	113	1	40		
FAZACKERLEY, Derek W.	Preston	05.11.51	App	**Blackburn Rov.**	10.69	1970-86	593	3	24	(CD)	
			Tr	**Chester C.**	01.87	1986-87	66	0	0		
			Tr	**York C.**	07.88	1988	16	0	0		
			Tr	**Bury**	12.88	1988	7	7	0		
FEARON, Ron T.	Romford	19.11.60	Dover T.	**Reading**	02.80	1980-82	61	0	0	(G)	
			Sutton U.	**Ipswich T.**	08.87	1987-88	28	0	0		
			L	**Brighton & H.A.**	09.88	1988	7	0	0		
FEE, Greg P.	Halifax	24.06.64	YTS	**Bradford C.**	05.83	1982-83	6	1	0	(CD)	
			Boston U.	**Sheffield Wed.**	08.87	1987-88	15	9	0		
FEELEY, Andy J.	Hereford	30.09.61	App	**Hereford U.**	08.79	1978-79	50	1	3	(FB)	
			Trowbridge T.	**Leicester C.**	02.84	1983-86	74	2	0		
			Tr	**Brentford**	08.87	1987-88	57	10	0		
FELGATE, David W.	Blaenau Ffestiniog	04.03.60	Jnrs	**Bolton W.**	08.78					(G)	W Sch Int/W-1
			L	**Rochdale**	10.78	1978	35	0	0		
			L	**Crewe Alex**	09.79	1979	14	0	0		
			L	**Rochdale**	03.80	1979	12	0	0		
			Tr	**Lincoln C.**	09.80	1980-84	198	0	0		
			L	**Cardiff C.**	11.84	1984	4	0	0		
			Tr	**Grimsby T.**	02.85	1984-86	36	0	0		
			L	**Bolton W.**	02.86	1985	15	0	0		
			Tr	**Bolton W.**	02.87	1986-88	112	0	0		
FENWICK, Terry W.	Seaham	17.11.59	App	**Crystal Palace**	12.76	1977-80	62	8	0	(D)	E Yth Int/E U21-11/E-20
			Tr	**Q.P.R.**	12.80	1980-87	256	0	33		
			Tr	**Tottenham H.**	12.87	1987-88	51	0	8		
FERDINAND, Leslie	Paddington	18.12.66	Hayes	**Q.P.R.**	04.87	1986-87	1	2	0	(F)	
			L	**Brentford**	03.88	1987	3	0	0		
FEREDAY, Wayne	Warley	16.06.63	App	**Q.P.R.**	09.80	1980-88	167	30	21	(W)	E U21-5
FIFE, Adrian	Peterborough	13.09.69	YTS	**Peterborough U.**(N/C)	07.88	1986-87	1	1	0	(F)	
FILLERY, Mike C.	Mitcham	17.09.60	App	**Chelsea**	08.78	1978-82	156	5	32	(M)	E Sch Int/E Yth Int
			Tr	**Q.P.R.**	08.83	1983-86	95	2	9		
			Tr	**Portsmouth**	07.87	1987-88	31	4	2		
FILSON, Robert M.	St. Helens	25.06.68		**Wrexham** (N/C)	02.89	1988	0	1	0		
FINLEY, Alan J.	Oxford	10.12.67	Marine	**Shrewsbury T.**	06.88	1988	32	2	1	(CD)	
FINNEY, Kevin	Newcastle-u-Lyme	19.10.69	YTS	**Port Vale**	06.87	1987-88	16	13	1	(M)	
FINNIGAN, A. (Tony)	Wimbledon	17.10.62	App	**Fulham**	10.80					(M)	E Yth Int
			Corinthian Casuals	**Crystal Palace**	02.85	1984-87	94	11	10		
			Tr	**Blackburn Rov.**	07.88	1988	13	4	0		
FIORE, Mark J.	Southwark	18.11.69	YTS	**Wimbledon**	07.88	1988	1	0	0	(M)	
FISHENDEN, Paul A.	Hillingdon	02.08.63	App	**Wimbledon**	10.81	1981-85	57	18	25	(F)	
			L	**Fulham**	12.85	1985	3	0	0		
			L	**Millwall**	09.86	1986	3	0	1		
			L	**Leyton Orient**	10.86	1986	4	0	0		
			Tr	**Crewe Alex.**	02.88	1987-88	61	0	19		
FITZPATRICK, Paul J.	Oxford	05.10.65	Tranmere Rov.(YTS)	**Bolton W.**	03.85	1984-85	13	1	0	(M)	
			Tr	**Bristol C.**	08.86	1986-88	40	4	7		
			Tr	**Carlisle U.**	10.88	1988	32	0	0		
			L	**Preston N.E.**	12.88	1988	2	0	0		
FLECK, Robert	Glasgow	11.08.65	Glasgow Rangers	**Norwich C.**	12.87	1987-88	47	4	16	(F)	S Yth Int/S U21-7
FLEMING, Craig	Calder	06.10.71	YTS	**Halifax T.** (YTS)	07.88	1988	0	1	0		
FLEMING, J. Gary	Derry (NI)	17.02.67	App	**Nottingham F.**	11.84	1984-87	71	3	0	(RB)	NI-9
FLEMING, Mark J.	Hammersmith	11.08.69	YTS	**Q.P.R.**	01.88	1987-88	1	2	0	(D)	
FLEMING, Paul	Halifax	06.09.67	YTS	**Halifax T.**	09.85	1985-88	56	4	0	(LB)	
FLEXNEY, Paul	Glasgow	18.01.65	Clyde	**Northampton T.**	08.88	1988	12	0	0	(CD)	to Kilmarnock 12.88
FLOUNDERS, Andy J.	Hull	13.12.63	App	**Hull C.**	12.81	1980-86	126	33	54	(F)	
			Tr	**Scunthorpe U.**	03.87	1986-88	105	1	46		

Players Names	Birthplace	Date	Previous Club	League Club	Date Sign'd	Seasons Played	Career Record Apps	Sub	Gls	Pos.	Misc
LOWERS, Tim D.	Kenilworth	03.02.67	App	**Wolverhampton W.**	08.84	1984-85	63	0	0	(G)	Son of Ron/E Yth Int/E U21-3
			Tr	**Southampton**	06.86	1986-88	25	0	0		
			L	**Swindon T.**	03.87	1986	2	0	0		
			L	**Swindon T.**	11.87	1987	5	0	0		
LYNN, Brian	Port Talbot	12.10.55	App	**Burnley**	10.72	1973-77	115	5	8	(M)	W Sch Int/W U23-2/W-66
			Tr	**Leeds U.**	11.77	1977-82	152	2	11		
			L	**Burnley**	03.82	1981	2	0	0		
			Tr	**Burnley**	11.82	1982-84	76	4	11		
			Tr	**Cardiff C.**	11.84	1984-85	32	0	0		
			Tr	**Doncaster Rov.**	11.85	1985	27	0	0		
			Tr	**Bury**	07.86	1986	19	0	0		
			Limerick C.(Ire)	**Doncaster Rov.** (N/C)	08.87	1987	18	6	1		
			Tr	**Wrexham**	02.88	1987-88	55	3	2		
LYNN, Michael A.	Oldham	23.02.69	App	**Oldham Ath.**	02.87	1987-88	37	3	1	(CD)	
			Tr	**Norwich C.**	12.88						
OLEY, Steve	Liverpool	04.10.62	App	**Liverpool**	09.80					(M)	
			L	**Fulham**	12.83	1983	2	1	0		
			Tr	**Grimsby T.**	08.84	1984	31	0	2		
			Tr	**Sheffield U.**	08.85	1985-86	56	10	14		
			Tr	**Swindon T.**	06.87	1987-88	75	0	12		
ORBES, Graeme S.A.	Forfar	29.07.58	Motherwell	**Walsall**	09.86	1986-88	129	0	7	(CD)	
ORD, Gary	York	08.02.61	App	**York C.**	02.79	1978-86	359	7	52	(W)	
			Tr	**Leicester C.**	06.87	1987	15	1	2		
			Tr	**Port Vale**	12.87	1987-88	44	1	10		
ORD, Michael P.	Bristol	09.02.66	App	**Leicester C.**	02.84					(CD)	Son of Anthony
			Devizes T.	**Cardiff C.**	09.84	1984-87	144	1	13		
			Tr	**Oxford U.**	06.88	1988	6	4	1		
ORD, Tony	Grimsby	14.05.59	App	**Grimsby T.**	05.77	1975-85	321	33	54	(W)	E 'B'
			L	**Sunderland**	03.86	1985	8	1	1		
			Tr	**Stoke C.**	07.86	1986-88	112	0	13		
			Tr	**West Bromwich A.**	03.89	1988	11	0	1		
OREMAN, Darren	Southampton	12.02.68	Jnrs	**Barnsley**	08.86	1986-88	22	8	5	(F)	E Sch Int
ORREST, Craig L.	Canada	30.09.67	App	**Ipswich T.**	08.85	1988	28	0	0	(G)	
			L	**Colchester U.**	03.88	1987	11	0	0		
ORREST, Gerry	Stockton	21.01.57	South Bank	**Rotherham U.**	02.77	1977-85	357	0	8	(RB)	
			Tr	**Southampton**	12.85	1985-88	111	3	0		
ORSYTH, Mike E.	Liverpool	20.03.66	App	**West Bromwich A.**	11.83	1983-85	28	1	0	(LB)	E Yth Int/E U21-1
			Tr	**Derby Co.**	03.86	1986-88	118	0	4		
OSTER, Colin J.	Chislehurst	16.07.64	App	**Leyton Orient**	02.82	1981-86	173	1	10	(CD)	
			Tr	**Nottingham F.**	02.87	1986-88	62	4	5		
OSTER, George W.	Plymouth	26.09.56	App	**Plymouth Arg.**	09.74	1973-81	201	11	6	(CD)	
			L	**Torquay U.**	10.76	1976	6	0	3		
			L	**Exeter C.**	12.81	1981	28	0	0		
			Tr	**Derby Co.**	06.82	1982	30	0	0		
			Tr	**Mansfield T.**	08.83	1983-88	263	0	0		
OSTER, Steve B.	Portsmouth	24.09.57	App	**Portsmouth**	09.75	1975-78	101	8	6	(CD)	E U21-1/E-3
			Tr	**Brighton & H.A.**	07.79	1979-83	171	1	6		
			Tr	**Aston Villa**	03.84	1983-84	15	0	3		
			Tr	**Luton T.**	11.84	1984-88	163	0	11		
OSTER, Wayne P.	Leigh	11.09.63	App	**Bolton W.**	08.81	1981-84	92	13	13	(M)	E Yth Int
			Tr	**Preston N.E.**	06.85	1985	25	6	3		to Hearts 8.86
OTHERGILL, Ashley G.	Harrogate	03.10.69	Middlesbrough (YTS)	**Rochdale**	10.88	1988	0	1	0	(M)	
OWLER, Lee E.	Nottingham	26.01.69	YTS	**Stoke C.**	07.88	1987	0	1	0	(FB)	
OX, Matthew C.	Birmingham	13.07.71	YTS	**Birmingham C.** (YTS)	07.87	1988	3	0	0	(CD)	
OX, Peter D.	Scunthorpe	05.07.57	App	**Sheffield Wed.**	06.75	1972-76	49	0	0	(G)	
			L	**Barnsley**	12.77	1977	1	0	0		
			Tr	**Stoke C.**	03.78	1978-88	317	0	0		
OX, Ruel A.	Ipswich	14.01.68	App	**Norwich C.**	01.86	1986-88	35	6	2	(W)	
OYLE, Martin J.	Salisbury	02.05.63	App	**Southampton**	08.80	1982-83	6	6	1	(F)	
			Tr	**Aldershot**	07.84	1984-86	98	0	35		
			Tr	**Oxford U.**	03.87	1986-88	73	4	24		
RAIN, David	Sheffield	11.10.62	Dronfield U.	**Sheffield U.**	09.85	1985-87	35	9	6	(W)	
			Tr	**Rochdale**	07.88	1988	42	0	12		
RAIN, John W.	Birmingham	08.10.68	App	**Birmingham C.**	10.86	1985-88	43	5	6	(M)	
RANCE, M. Paul	Holmfirth	10.09.68	YTS	**Huddersfield T.**	06.87	1987-88	7	4	0	(CD)	
RANCIS, John A.	Dewsbury	21.11.63	Emley	**Halifax T.** (N/C)	02.85	1984	1	3	0	(F)	
			Emley	**Sheffield U.**	09.88	1988	3	19	1		
RANCIS, Steve S.	Billericay	29.05.64	App	**Chelsea**	04.82	1981-85	71	0	0	(G)	E Yth Int
			Tr	**Reading**	02.87	1986-88	70	0	0		
RANCIS, Trevor J.	Plymouth	19.04.54	App	**Birmingham C.**	05.71	1970-78	278	2	118	(F)	E-43/E U23-5/E Yth Int
			Tr	**Nottingham F.**	02.79	1978-81	69	1	28		
			Tr	**Manchester C.**	09.81	1981	26	0	12		
			Glasgow Rangers	**Q.P.R.**	03.88	1987-88	27	1	7		
RANKLIN, Neil J.	Lincoln	10.03.69	YTS	**Lincoln C.** (YTS)	09.86	1986	15	0	0	(FB)	
			Sweden	**Lincoln C.** (N/C)	10.88	1988	0	1	0		
RANKLIN, Paul L.	Hainault	05.10.63	App	**Watford**	08.81	1982-86	32	0	0	(CD)	
			L	**Shrewsbury T.**	10.86	1986	6	0	0		
			L	**Swindon T.**	11.86	1986	5	0	1		
			Tr	**Reading**	06.87	1987-88	17	3	0		
REESTONE, Roger	Caerleon	19.08.68	YTS	**Newport Co.**	04.86	1986	13	0	0	(G)	
			Tr	**Chelsea**	04.87	1986-88	42	0	0		
RY, Chris D.	Cardiff	23.10.69	YTS	**Cardiff C.**	07.88	1988	5	4	0	(LW)	W Yth Int
UTCHER, Paul	Chester	25.09.56	App	**Chester C.**	01.74	1972-73	20	0	0	(CD)	Twin Brother of Ron/E U21-11/ Brother of Graham
			Tr	**Luton T.**	06.74	1974-77	131	0	1		
			Tr	**Manchester C.**	06.78	1978-79	36	1	0		
			Tr	**Oldham Ath**	08.80	1980-82	98	0	1		
			Tr	**Derby Co.**	01.83	1982-83	35	0	0		
			Tr	**Barnsley**	03.84	1983-88	201	0	0		

Dale Gordon (Norwich City), right, in action against Ian Snodin (Everton) Match Magazine

Bruce Grobbelaar (Liverpool & Zimbabwe) Match Magazine

Bryan Gunn (Norwich City) Match Magazine

Players Names	Birthplace	Date	Previous Club	League Club	Date Sign'd	Seasons Played	Career Record Apps	Sub	Gls	Pos.	Misc
UTCHER, Ron	Chester	25.09.56	App	**Chester C.**	01.74	1973	4	0	0	(F)	Twin brother of Paul/Brother of Graham
			Tr	**Luton T.**	06.74	1974-77	116	4	40		
			Tr	**Manchester C.**	08.78	1978	10	7	7		
			NAC Breda (Neth)	**Barnsley**	12.84	1984	18	1	6		
			Tr	**Oldham Ath**	07.85	1985-86	65	0	30		
			Tr	**Bradford C.**	03.87	1986-87	35	7	18		
			Tr	**Port Vale**	08.88	1988	39	2	17		
YFE, Tony	Carlisle	23.02.62	Penrith	**Carlisle U.**	09.87	1987-88	22	13	8	(F)	
GABBIADINI, Marco	Nottingham	20.01.68	App	**York C.**	09.85	1984-87	42	18	14	(F)	Brother of Ricardo/E U21-2
			Tr	**Sunderland**	09.87	1987-88	70	1	39		
GABBIADINI, Ricardo	Newport	11.03.70	YTS	**York C.** (YTS)	07.86	1987	0	1	0	(F)	Brother of Marco
			Tr	**Sunderland**	06.88						
GAGE, Kevin W.	Chiswick	21.04.64	App	**Wimbledon**	01.82	1980-86	135	33	15	(RB/M)	E Yth Int
			Tr	**Aston Villa**	07.87	1987-88	71	1	5		
GAGE, Wakely A.J.	Northampton	05.05.58	Desborough T.	**Northampton T.**	10.79	1979-84	215	3	17	(CD)	
			Tr	**Chester C.**	08.85	1985	17	0	1		
			Tr	**Peterborough U.**	11.85	1985-86	73	0	1		
			Tr	**Crewe Alex.**	06.87	1987-88	45	9	1		
GALE, A.P. (Tony)	Westminster	19.11.59	App	**Fulham**	08.77	1977-83	277	0	19	(CD)	E Yth Int/E U21-1
			Tr	**West Ham U.**	07.84	1984-88	158	2	2		
GALLACHER, Bernard	Johnstone	22.03.67	App	**Aston Villa**	03.85	1986-88	47	1	0	(LB)	
GALLAGHER, Jackie C.	Wisbech	06.04.58	March T.	**Lincoln C.**	02.76	1976	1	0	0	(F)	
			Kings Lynn	**Peterborough U.**	04.80	1979-80	11	2	1		
			Hong Kong	**Torquay U.**(N/C)	08.82	1982	38	4	7		
			Wisbech T.	**Peterborough U.**	08.85	1985-86	78	4	19		
			Tr	**Wolverhampton W.**	06.87	1987-88	10	17	4		
GALLIERS, Steve	Preston	21.08.57	Chorley	**Wimbledon**	06.77	1977-81	148	7	10	(M)	
			Tr	**Crystal Palace**	10.81	1981	8	5	0		
			Tr	**Wimbledon**	08.82	1982-87	145	1	5		
			L	**Bristol C.**	02.87	1986	9	0	0		
			Tr	**Bristol C.**	09.87	1987-88	65	3	6		
GALLOWAY, Mike	Oswestry	30.05.65	Jnrs	**Mansfield T.**	09.83	1983-85	39	15	3	(CD)	S Yth Int
			Tr	**Halifax T.**	02.86	1985-87	79	0	5		to Hearts 11.87
GALVIN, A. (Tony)	Huddersfield	12.07.56	Goole T.	**Tottenham H.**	01.78	1978-86	194	7	20	(W)	Brother of Chris/IR-28
			Tr	**Sheffield Wed.**	08.87	1987-88	21	7	1		
GAMBLE, S. Willie	Cottam (Nts)	05.03.68	App	**Lincoln C.**	01.86	1985-88	44	20	14	(F)	
GANNON, John S.	Wimbledon	18.12.66	App	**Wimbledon**	12.84	1985-87	13	3	2	(M)	
			L	**Crewe Alex.**	12.86	1986	14	1	0		
			L	**Sheffield U.**	02.89	1988	8	8	1		
GARDINER, Mark C.	Cirencester	25.12.66	App	**Swindon T.**	09.84	1983-86	7	3	1	(W)	
			Tr	**Torquay U.**	02.87	1986-87	37	12	4		
			Tr	**Crewe Alex.**	08.88	1988	37	1	11		
GARDNER, Stephen G.	Middlesbrough	03.07.68	App	**Manchester U.**	07.86					(CD)	
			Tr	**Burnley**	07.87	1987-88	85	1	0		
GARNER, Andy	Stonebroom (Dy)	08.03.66	App	**Derby Co.**	12.83	1983-87	48	23	17	(F)	
			Tr	**Blackpool**	08.88	1988	41	1	11		
GARNER, Darren J.	Plymouth	10.12.71	YTS	**Plymouth Arg.**	03.89	1988	1	0	0	(F)	
GARNER, Paul	Doncaster	01.12.55	App	**Huddersfield T.**	12.72	1972-75	96	0	2	(LB)	E Yth Int
			Tr	**Sheffield U.**	11.75	1975-83	248	3	7		
			L	**Gillingham**	09.83	1983	5	0	0		
			Tr	**Mansfield T.**	09.84	1984-88	102	9	8		
GARNER, Simon	Boston	23.11.59	App	**Blackburn Rov.**	11.77	1978-88	389	15	143	(F)	
GARNETT, Shaun M.	Wallasey	22.11.69	YTS	**Tranmere Rov.**	06.88	1987	0	1	0	(D)	
GARTON, W.F.(Billy)	Salford	15.03.65	App	**Manchester U.**	03.83	1984-88	39	2	0	(D)	
			L	**Birmingham C.**	03.86	1985	5	0	0		
GARWOOD, Jason	Birmingham	23.03.69	App	**Leicester C.**	03.87					(W)	
			L	**Northampton T.**	09.88	1988	5	1	0		
GASCOIGNE, Paul J.	Gateshead	27.05.67	App	**Newcastle U.**	05.85	1984-87	83	9	20	(M)	E U21-9/E-4/E 'B'
			Tr	**Tottenham H.**	07.88	1988	31	1	6		
GATES, Eric L.	Ferryhill	28.06.55	App	**Ipswich T.**	10.72	1973-84	267	29	73	(F)	Brother of Bill/E-2
			Tr	**Sunderland**	08.85	1985-88	129	16	37		
GATTING, Steve P.	Willesden	29.05.59	App	**Arsenal**	03.77	1978-80	50	8	5	(CD)	Brother of Mike (Cricketer)
			Tr	**Brighton & H.A.**	09.81	1981-88	251	3	18		
GAUGHAN, Steve E.	Doncaster	14.04.70	Hatfield Main	**Doncaster Rov.**	09.87	1987-88	22	16	2	(W)	
GAVIN, Mark W.	Baillieston	10.12.63	App	**Leeds U.**	12.81	1982-84	20	10	3	(LW)	
			L	**Hartlepool U.**	03.85	1984	7	0	0		
			Tr	**Carlisle U.**	07.85	1985	12	1	1		
			Tr	**Bolton W.**	03.86	1985-86	48	1	3		
			Tr	**Rochdale**	08.87	1987	23	0	6		
			Hearts	**Bristol C.**	10.88	1988	26	3	3		
GAVIN, Patrick J.	Hammersmith	05.06.67	Hanwell T.	**Gillingham**	03.89	1988	13	0	7	(F)	
GAYLE, Andrew K.	Manchester	17.09.70	YTS	**Oldham Ath.** (YTS)	07.87	1988	0	1	0	(F)	
GAYLE, Brian W.	Kingston	06.03.65	Tooting & Mitcham	**Wimbledon**	10.84	1984-87	76	7	3	(CD)	
			Tr	**Manchester C.**	07.88	1988	41	0	3		
GAYLE, Howard A.	Liverpool	18.05.58	Jnrs	**Liverpool**	11.77	1980	3	1	1	(W)	E U21-3
			L	**Fulham**	01.80	1979	14	0	0		
			L	**Newcastle U.**	11.82	1982	8	0	2		
			Tr	**Birmingham C.**	01.83	1982-83	45	1	9		
			Tr	**Sunderland**	08.84	1984-85	39	9	4		
			Dallas (USA)	**Stoke C.**	03.87	1986	4	2	2		
			Tr	**Blackburn Rov.**	07.87	1987-88	55	3	20		
GAYLE, John	Bromsgrove	30.07.64	Burton A.	**Wimbledon**	02.89	1988	2	0	0	(F)	
GAYLE, Marcus A.	Hammersmith	27.09.70	YTS	**Brentford** (YTS)	07.87	1988	0	3	0		
GAYNOR, Tommy	Limerick (Ire)	29.01.63	Limerick C.	**Doncaster Rov.**	12.86	1986-87	28	4	7	(F)	
			Tr	**Nottingham F.**	10.87	1987-88	26	5	7		

Players Names	Birthplace	Date	Previous Club	League Club	Date Sign'd	Seasons Played	Career Record Apps	Sub	Gls	Pos.	Misc
GEDDIS, David	Carlisle	12.03.58	App	**Ipswich T.**	08.75	1976-78	26	17	5	(F)	E Yth Int
			L	**Luton T.**	02.77	1976	9	4	4		
			Tr	**Aston Villa**	09.79	1979-82	43	4	12		
			L	**Luton T.**	12.82	1982	4	0	0		
			Tr	**Barnsley**	09.83	1983-84	45	0	24		
			Tr	**Birmingham C.**	12.84	1984-86	45	1	18		
			L	**Brentford**	11.86	1986	4	0	0		
			Tr	**Shrewsbury T.**	02.87	1986-88	36	3	10		
			Tr	**Swindon T.**	10.88	1988	8	2	3		
GEE, Philip J.	Pelsall	19.12.64	Gresley Rov	**Derby Co.**	09.85	1985-88	85	10	24	(F)	
GENNOE, Terry W.	Shrewsbury	16.03.53	Bricklayers Spts	**Bury**	06.73	1972-73	3	0	0	(G)	
			Tr	**Halifax T.**	05.75	1975-77	78	0	0		
			Tr	**Southampton**	02.78	1978-79	36	0	0		
			L	**Crystal Palace**	01.81	1980	3	0	0		
			Tr	**Blackburn Rov.**	08.81	1981-88	260	0	0		
GENOVESE, Domenico	Peterborough	02.02.61	Cambridge C.	**Peterborough U.**	03.88	1987-88	8	8	1	(F)	
GERNON, F.A.J.(Irvin)	Birmingham	30.12.62	App	**Ipswich T.**	01.80	1981-86	76	0	0	(FB)	E Yth Int/E U21-1
			L	**Northampton T.**	11.86	1986	9	0	0		
			Tr	**Gillingham**	03.87	1986-87	33	2	1		
			Tr	**Reading**	09.88	1988	18	4	0		
GIBBINS, Roger G.	Enfield	06.09.55	App	**Tottenham H.**	12.72					(M)	Son of Eddie/E Sch Int
			Tr	**Oxford U.**	08.75	1975	16	3	2		
			Tr	**Norwich C.**	06.76	1976-77	47	1	12		
			New England(USA)	**Cambridge U.**	09.79	1979-81	97	3	12		
			Tr	**Cardiff C.**	08.82	1982-85	135	4	17		
			Tr	**Swansea C.**	10.85	1985	35	0	6		
			Tr	**Newport Co.**	08.86	1986-87	79	0	8		
			Tr	**Torquay U.**	03.88	1987-88	32	1	5		
			Newport Co.	**Cardiff C.** (N/C)	03.89	1988	9	3	0		
GIBBS, Nigel J.	St. Albans	20.11.65	App	**Watford**	11.83	1983-88	146	3	2	(RB)	E U21-5/E Yth Int
GIBSON, Colin J.	Bridport	06.04.60	App	**Aston Villa**	04.78	1978-85	181	4	10	(LB/M)	E Sch Int/E U21-1
			Tr	**Manchester U.**	11.85	1985-88	69	4	8		
GIBSON, Terry B.	Walthamstow	23.12.62	App	**Tottenham H.**	01.80	1979-82	16	2	4	(F)	E Sch Int/E Yth Int
			Tr	**Coventry C.**	08.83	1983-85	97	1	43		
			Tr	**Manchester U.**	01.86	1985-86	14	9	1		
			Tr	**Wimbledon**	08.87	1987-88	33	1	11		
GIDMAN, John	Liverpool	10.01.54	Liverpool(App)	**Aston Villa**	08.71	1972-79	196	1	9	(RB)	E Yth Int/E U23-4/E-1
			Tr	**Everton**	10.79	1979-80	64	0	2		
			Tr	**Manchester U.**	08.81	1981-85	94	1	4		
			Tr	**Manchester C.**	10.86	1986-87	52	1	1		
			Tr	**Stoke C.**	08.88	1988	7	3	0		
			Tr	**Darlington**	02.89	1988	13	0	1		
GILBERT, David J.	Lincoln	22.06.63	App	**Lincoln C.**	06.81	1980-81	15	15	1	(M)	
			Tr	**Scunthorpe U.**	08.82	1982	1	0	0		
			Boston U.	**Northampton T.**	07.86	1986-88	120	0	21		
			Tr	**Grimsby T.**	03.89	1988	11	0	3		
GILBERT, W.A. (Billy)	Lewisham	10.11.59	App	**Crystal Palace**	12.76	1977-83	235	2	3	(CD)	E Sch Int/E Yth Int/E U21-11
			Tr	**Portsmouth**	06.84	1984-88	133	7	0		
GILKES, Michael E.	Hackney	20.07.65	Leicester C.(Jnrs)	**Reading**	07.84	1984-88	103	14	17	(W)	
GILL, A.G.D. (Tony)	Bradford	06.03.68	App	**Manchester U.**	03.86	1986-88	5	5	1	(FB)	
GILL, Gary	Middlesbrough	28.11.64	App	**Middlesbrough**	11.82	1983-88	68	8	2	(W)	
			L	**Hull C.**	12.83	1983	0	1	0		
GILLESPIE, Gary T.	Bonnybridge	05.07.60	Falkirk	**Coventry C.**	03.78	1978-82	171	1	6	(CD)	S U21-8/S-6
			Tr	**Liverpool**	07.83	1983-88	111	2	9		
GILLIGAN, Jimmy M.	Hammersmith	24.01.64	App	**Watford**	08.81	1981-84	18	9	6	(F)	E Yth Int
			L	**Lincoln C.**	10.82	1982	0	3	0		
			Tr	**Grimsby T.**	08.85	1985	19	6	4		
			Tr	**Swindon T.**	06.86	1986	13	4	5		
			L	**Newport Co.**	02.87	1986	4	1	1		
			Tr	**Lincoln C.**	03.87	1986	11	0	1		
			Tr	**Cardiff C.**	07.87	1987-88	92	0	34		
GITTENS, Jon	Birmingham	22.01.64	Paget Rangers	**Southampton**	10.85	1985-86	18	0	0	(CD)	
			Tr	**Swindon T.**	07.87	1987-88	56	2	1		
GLEASURE, Peter	Luton	08.10.60	App	**Millwall**	08.78	1980-82	55	0	0	(G)	
			Tr	**Northampton T.**	03.83	1982-88	282	0	0		
GLEGHORN, Nigel W.	Seaham	12.08.62	Seaham Red Star	**Ipswich T.**	08.85	1985-87	54	12	11	(W)	
			Tr	**Manchester C.**	08.88	1988	25	7	7		
GLENN, David A.	Wigan	30.11.62	App	**Wigan Ath.**	11.80	1980-82	68	4	4	(RB)	
			Tr	**Blackburn Rov.**	08.83	1983-84	24	0	0		
			Tr	**Chester C.**	07.85	1985-88	70	3	1		
GLOVER, Dean V.	West Bromwich	29.12.63	App	**Aston Villa**	12.81	1984-86	25	3	0	(CD/M)	
			L	**Sheffield U.**	10.86	1986	5	0	0		
			Tr	**Middlesbrough**	06.87	1987-88	44	6	5		
			Tr	**Port Vale**	02.89	1988	22	0	0		
GLOVER, E. Lee	Kettering	24.04.70	YTS	**Nottingham F.**	04.87	1987	17	3	3	(F)	S Yth Int/S U21-1
GODDARD, Karl E.	Leeds	29.12.67	App	**Manchester U.**	12.85					(LB)	E Sch Int
			Tr	**Bradford C.**	06.86	1986-88	67	5	0		
GODDARD, Paul	Harlington	12.10.59	App	**Q.P.R.**	07.77	1977-79	63	7	23	(F)	E U21-8/E-1
			Tr	**West Ham U.**	08.80	1980-86	159	11	54		
			Tr	**Newcastle U.**	11.86	1986-87	61	0	19		
			Tr	**Derby Co.**	08.88	1988	31	0	7		
GODDEN, A.L. (Tony)	Gillingham	02.08.55	Ashford T.	**West Bromwich A.**	08.75	1976-85	267	0	0	(G)	
			L	**Luton T.**	03.83	1982	12	0	0		
			L	**Walsall**	10.83	1983	19	0	0		
			Tr	**Chelsea**	03.86	1985-86	34	0	0		
			Tr	**Birmingham C.**	07.87	1987-88	29	0	0		
			L	**Bury**	12.88	1988	1	0	0		
GODFREY, Kevin	Kennington	24.02.60	App	**Leyton Orient**	03.77	1977-87	255	30	62	(W)	
			L	**Plymouth Arg.**	02.86	1985	7	0	1		
			Maidenhead U.	**Brentford**	10.88	1988	24	5	8		

Alan Hansen (Liverpool & Scotland) Match Magazine

John Hendrie (Newcastle United) Match Magazine

Richard Hill (Oxford United) Match Magazine

Andy Hinchcliffe (Manchester City) Match Magazine

Players Names	Birthplace	Date	Previous Club	League Club	Date Sign'd	Seasons Played	Career Record Apps	Sub	Gls	Pos.	Misc
GOLDSMITH, Craig S.W.	Peterborough	27.08.63	Mirrlees Blackstone	**Peterborough U.**	08.88	1988	34	6	6	(W)	
GOLDSMITH, Martin	Walsall	04.11.69	YTS	**Walsall**	08.88	1988	0	2	0	(F)	
GOODING, Mick C.	Newcastle	12.04.59	Bishop Auckland	**Rotherham U.**	07.79	1979-82	90	12	10	(M)	
			Tr	**Chesterfield**	12.82	1982	12	0	0		
			Tr	**Rotherham U.**	09.83	1983-86	149	7	32		
			Tr	**Peterborough U.**	08.87	1987-88	47	0	21		
			Tr	**Wolverhampton W.**	09.88	1988	30	1	4		
GOODISON, C. Wayne	Wakefield	23.09.64	App	**Barnsley**	09.82	1982-85	31	5	0	(FB)	
			Tr	**Crewe Alex.**	09.86	1986-88	90	4	1		
GOODMAN, Don R.	Leeds	09.05.66	Jnrs	**Bradford C.**	07.84	1983-86	65	5	14	(F)	
			Tr	**West Bromwich A.**	03.87	1986-88	74	12	24		
GOODWIN, Mark A.	Sheffield	23.02.60	App	**Leicester C.**	11.77	1977-80	69	22	8	(M)	
			Tr	**Notts Co.**	03.81	1980-86	226	11	24		
			Tr	**Walsall**	07.87	1987-88	59	9	2		
GOODWIN, Shaun L.	Rotherham	14.06.69	YTS	**Rotherham U.**	06.87	1987-88	35	9	4	(M)	
GOODYEAR, Clive	Lincoln	15.01.61	Lincoln Utd.	**Luton T.**	10.78	1979-83	85	5	4	(CD)	
			Tr	**Plymouth Arg.**	08.84	1984-86	99	7	5		
			Tr	**Wimbledon**	07.87	1987	21	1	0		
GORAM, Andy L.	Bury	13.04.64	W. Bromwich A. (App)	**Oldham Ath.**	08.81	1981-87	195	0	0	(G)	S U21-1/S-4/Son of Lewis to Hibernian 10.87
GORDON, Colin K.	Stourbridge	17.01.63	Oldbury U.	**Swindon T.**	10.84	1984-85	70	2	34	(F)	
			Tr	**Wimbledon**	06.86	1986	2	1	0		
			L	**Gillingham**	02.87	1986	4	0	2		
			Tr	**Reading**	07.87	1987-88	23	1	9		
			L	**Bristol C.**	03.88	1987	8	0	4		
			Tr	**Fulham**	10.88	1988	12	5	2		
GORDON, Dale A.	Great Yarmouth	09.01.67	App	**Norwich C.**	01.84	1984-88	118	11	17	(W)	E Sch Int/E Yth Int/E U21-4
GORE, Ian G.	Prescot	10.01.68	YTS	**Birmingham C.**	05.86					(D)	
			Southport	**Blackpool**	01.88	1988	19	2	0		
GORE, Shaun M.	West Ham	21.09.68	YTS	**Fulham**	06.86	1985-88	25	1	0	(D)	
GORMAN, Paul A.	Dublin	06.08.63	App	**Arsenal**	10.80	1981-83	5	1	0	(M)	
			Tr	**Birmingham C.**	06.84	1984	6	0	0		
			Tr	**Carlisle U.**	03.85	1984-88	135	11	7		
GORMAN, Paul M.	Macclesfield	18.09.68	YTS	**Doncaster Rov.**	07.87	1987-88	1	15	2	(F)	
GORMLEY, Eddie J.	Dublin	23.10.68	Bray W.	**Tottenham H.**	11.87					(M)	
			L	**Chesterfield**	11.88	1988	4	0	0		
GORTON, Andy W.	Salford	23.09.66	YTS	**Oldham Ath.**	07.84	1985-87	26	0	0	(G)	
			L	**Stockport Co.**	12.86	1986	14	0	0		
			L	**Tranmere Rov.**	05.88	1987	1	0	0		
			Tr	**Stockport Co.**	08.88	1988	34	0	0		
GOSNEY, Andrew R.	Southampton	08.11.63	App	**Portsmouth**	11.81	1981-88	23	0	0	(G)	E Yth Int
GOSS, Jeremy	Cyprus	11.05.65	YTS	**Norwich C.**	03.83	1983-87	22	7	2	(M)	
GOURLAY, Archie M.	Greenock	29.06.69	Morton	**Newcastle U.**	03.88	1988	0	1	0	(M)	
GRAHAM, Deiniol W.J.	Cannock	04.10.69	YTS	**Manchester U.**	10.87	1987	1	0	0	(F)	W Yth Int
GRAHAM, James	Glasgow	05.11.69	YTS	**Bradford C.**	09.88	1988	0	1	0	(M)	
GRAHAM, Mike A.	Lancaster	24.02.59	App	**Bolton W.**	02.77	1977-80	43	3	0	(RB)	
			Tr	**Swindon T.**	07.81	1981-84	141	0	1		
			Tr	**Mansfield T.**	07.85	1985-88	132	1	1		
			Tr	**Carlisle U.**	09.88	1988	44	0	2		
GRAHAM, Milton M.	Tottenham	02.11.62	Jnrs	**Bournemouth**	05.81	1981-84	54	19	12	(M)	
			Tr	**Chester C.**	08.85	1985-88	123	6	10		
GRAHAM, Tommy	Glasgow	31.03.58	Arthurlie	**Aston Villa**	04.78					(M)	
			Tr	**Barnsley**	12.78	1978-79	36	2	13		
			Tr	**Halifax T.**	10.80	1980-81	68	3	17		
			Tr	**Doncaster Rov.** (N/C)	08.82	1982	9	2	2		
			Tr	**Scunthorpe U.**	03.83	1982-85	102	7	21		
			Tr	**Scarborough**	(N/L)	1987-88	84	3	11		
GRAY, Andy A.	Lambeth	22.02.64	Dulwich Hamlet	**Crystal Palace**	11.84	1984-87	91	7	27	(M)	E U21-2
			Tr	**Aston Villa**	11.87	1987-88	34	3	4		
			Tr	**Q.P.R.**	02.89	1988	11	0	2		
GRAY, Andy M.	Glasgow	30.11.55	Dundee U.	**Aston Villa**	10.75	1975-78	112	1	54	(F)	S U23-4/S-20
			Tr	**Wolverhampton W.**	09.79	1979-83	130	3	38		
			Tr	**Everton**	11.83	1983-84	44	5	14		
			Tr	**Aston Villa**	07.85	1985-86	53	1	5		
			Tr	**Notts Co.**	08.87	1987	3	1	0		
			Tr	**West Bromwich A.**	09.87	1987-88	32	3	10		to Glasgow Rangers 9.88
GRAY, Frank T.	Glasgow	27.10.54	App	**Leeds U.**	11.71	1972-78	188	5	17	(LB)	S Sch Int/S U23-2/S-32
			Tr	**Nottingham F.**	08.79	1979-80	81	0	5		Brother of Eddie
			Tr	**Leeds U.**	05.81	1981-84	139	0	10		
			Tr	**Sunderland**	07.85	1985-88	118	28	8		
GRAY, Kevin J.	Sheffield	07.01.72	YTS	**Mansfield T.** (YTS)	08.88	1988	1	0	0	(CD)	
GRAY, Philip	Belfast	02.10.68	App	**Tottenham H.**	08.86	1986-88	1	2	0	(M)	
GRAY, Stuart	Withernsea	19.04.60	Withernsea YC	**Nottingham F.**	03.78	1980-82	48	1	3	(M)	
			L	**Bolton W.**	03.83	1982	10	0	0		
			Tr	**Barnsley**	08.83	1983-87	117	3	23		
			Tr	**Aston Villa**	11.87	1987-88	54	1	9		
GRAYSON, Simon D.	Sheffield	21.10.68	App	**Sheffield U.**	10.86					(F)	
			L	**Chesterfield**	11.87	1987	7	1	0		
			Tr	**Hartlepool U.**	04.88	1987-88	37	5	12		
GRAYSON, Simon N.	Ripon	16.12.69	YTS	**Leeds U.**	07.88	1987	2	0	0	(M)	
GREALISH, A.P. (Tony)	Paddington	21.09.56	App	**Leyton Orient**	07.74	1974-78	169	2	10	(M)	IR-44
			Tr	**Luton T.**	08.79	1979-80	78	0	2		
			Tr	**Brighton & H.A.**	07.81	1981-83	95	5	6		
			Tr	**West Bromwich A.**	03.84	1983-85	55	10	5		
			Tr	**Manchester C.**	10.86	1986	11	0	0		
			Tr	**Rotherham U.**	08.87	1987-88	74	3	7		
GREAVES, Steven R.	Chelsea	17.01.70	YTS	**Fulham**	07.88	1987	0	1	0	(FB)	

Players Names	Birthplace	Date	Previous Club	League Club	Date Sign'd	Seasons Played	Career Record Apps	Sub	Gls	Pos.	Misc
GREEN, John R.	Rotherham	07.08.58	App	**Rotherham U.**	03.76	1975-83	247	1	8	(CD)	
			Tr	**Scunthorpe U.**	09.83	1983-85	100	0	4		
			Tr	**Darlington**	10.85	1985-86	45	0	2		
			Tr	**Rotherham U.**	12.86	1986-88	84	1	3		
GREEN, Richard E.	Wolverhampton	22.11.67	YTS	**Shrewsbury T.**	07.86	1986-88	80	5	5	(D)	
GREEN, Ron R.	Birmingham	03.10.56	Alvechurch	**Walsall**	06.77	1977-83	163	0	0	(G)	
			Tr	**Shrewsbury T.**	06.84	1984	19	0	0		
			Tr	**Bristol Rov.**	02.85	1984-85	56	0	0		
			Tr	**Scunthorpe U.**	08.86	1986-87	78	0	0		
			Tr	**Wimbledon**	08.88	1988	4	0	0		
			L	**Shrewsbury T.**	09.88	1988	17	0	0		
			Tr	**Walsall**	03.89	1988	2	0	0		
GREENALL, Colin A.	Billinge	30.12.63	App	**Blackpool**	01.81	1980-86	179	4	9	(CD)	E Yth Int
			Tr	**Gillingham**	09.86	1986-87	62	0	5		
			Tr	**Oxford U.**	02.88	1987-88	52	0	2		
GREENOUGH, Ricky A.	Mexborough	30.05.61	Alfreton T.	**Chester C.**	01.85	1984-87	123	9	15	(D)	
			Tr	**Scarborough**	07.88						
			Tr	**York C.**	11.88	1988	26	0	1		
GREENWOOD, Nigel P.	Preston	27.11.66	App	**Preston N.E.**	09.84	1984-85	36	9	14	(F)	
			Tr	**Bury**	08.88	1986-88	65	25	19		
GREGORY, A.G.(Tony)	Doncaster	21.03.68	App	**Sheffield Wed**	01.86	1985-88	14	4	1	(M)	E Sch Int/E Yth Int
GREGORY, David S.	Sudbury	23.01.70	YTS	**Ipswich T.**	03.87	1988	0	2	0	(M)	
GRENFELL, Stephen J.	Enfield	27.10.66	App	**Tottenham H.**	08.84					(M/LB)	
			Tr	**Colchester U.**	10.86	1986-88	67	3	1		
GREW, Mark S.	Bilston	15.02.58	Jnrs	**West Bromwich A.**	06.76	1981-82	33	0	0	(G)	
			L	**Wigan Ath**	12.78	1978	4	0	0		
			Tr	**Leicester C.**	07.83	1983	5	0	0		
			L	**Oldham Ath.**	10.83	1983	5	0	0		
			Tr	**Ipswich T.**	03.84	1984	6	0	0		
			L	**Fulham**	09.85	1985	4	0	0		
			L	**West Bromwich A.**	01.86	1985	1	0	0		
			Tr	**Port Vale**	06.86	1986-88	81	0	0		
GREWCOCK, Neil	Leicester	26.04.62	App	**Leicester C.**	07.79	1979-80	7	1	1	(W)	
			Tr	**Gillingham**	03.82	1981-82	30	4	4		
			Shepshed Chart.	**Burnley**	06.84	1984-88	155	10	23		
GREYGOOSE, Dean	Thetford	18.12.64	App	**Cambridge U.**	11.82	1983-84	26	0	0	(G)	E Yth Int
			L	**Lincoln C.**	09.85	1985	6	0	0		
			Tr	**Leyton Orient**	12.85	1985	1	0	0		
			Tr	**Crystal Palace**	08.86						
			Tr	**Crewe Alex.**	08.87	1987-88	79	0	0		
GRIFFIN, Colin R.	Dudley	08.01.56	App	**Derby Co.**	01.74					(CD)	
			Tr	**Shrewsbury T.**	01.76	1975-88	402	4	7		
GRIFFITHS, Bryan	St. Helens	26.01.65	St. Helens T.	**Wigan Ath.**	11.88	1988	29	0	8	(W)	
GRIFFITHS, Carl B.	Welshpool	16.07.71	YTS	**Shrewsbury T.**	09.88	1988	17	11	6	(F)	W Yth Int
GRIMES, A. Ashley	Dublin	02.08.57	Bohemians	**Manchester U.**	03.77	1977-82	62	28	10	(LB)	IR 21-2/IR-17
			Tr	**Coventry C.**	08.83	1983	29	3	1		
			Tr	**Luton T.**	08.84	1984-88	85	2	3		
GRITT, Steve J.	Bournemouth	31.10.57	App	**Bournemouth**	10.75	1976	4	2	3	(M)	
			Tr	**Charlton Ath.**	07.77	1977-88	320	27	24		
GROBBELAAR, Bruce D.	Durban (SA)	06.10.57	Vancouver W. (Can)	**Crewe Alex.**(N/C)	12.79	1979	24	0	1	(G)	Zimbabwe Int
			Vancouver W. (Can)	**Liverpool**	03.81	1981-88	300	0	0		
GROCOCK, Chris R.	Grimsby	30.10.68	Jnrs	**Grimsby T.**	06.87	1985-88	18	25	1	(W)	
GROVES, Paul	Derby	28.02.66	Burton A.	**Leicester C.**	04.88	1987-88	7	9	1	(M)	
GROVES, Perry	City of London	19.04.65	App	**Colchester U.**	06.82	1981-86	142	14	26	(F)	
			Tr	**Arsenal**	09.86	1986-88	53	27	13		
GUMMER, Jason C.	Tredegar	27.10.67	YTS	**Cardiff C.**	07.85	1985-88	28	5	5	(M)	W Yth Int
			L	**Torquay U.**	03.89	1988	7	0	1		
GUNN, Bryan	Thurso	22.12.63	Aberdeen	**Norwich C.**	10.86	1986-88	104	0	0	(G)	S Sch Int/S Yth Int/S U21-8
GUNN, Bryn C.	Kettering	21.08.58	App	**Nottingham F.**	08.75	1975-84	129	2	1	(D)	
			L	**Shrewsbury T.**	11.85	1985	9	0	0		
			L	**Walsall**	01.86	1985	6	0	0		
			L	**Mansfield T.**	03.86	1985	5	0	0		
			Tr	**Peterborough U.**	08.86	1986-88	130	1	14		
GUSCOTT, Lindon	Lambeth	29.03.72	YTS	**Gillingham** (YTS)	06.88	1988	0	2	0	(F)	
GUTHRIE, Peter J.	Newcastle	10.10.61	Weymouth	**Tottenham H.**	01.88					(G)	
			L	**Swansea C.**	02.88	1987	14	0	0		
GWINNETT, Mel L.	Worcester	14.05.63	Stourbridge	**Peterborough U.**	05.81					(G)	
			Tr	**Hereford U.**(N/C)	09.82	1982	1	0	0		
			Gloucester C.	**Bradford C.**	06.84						
			Tr	**Exeter C.**	08.85	1985-88	46	0	0		
GYNN, Micky	Peterborough	19.08.61	App	**Peterborough U.**	04.79	1978-82	152	4	33	(M)	
			Tr	**Coventry C.**	08.83	1983-88	101	28	16		
HACKETT, Gary S.	Stourbridge	11.10.62	Bromsgrove Rov.	**Shrewsbury T.**	07.83	1983-86	142	8	17	(M)	
			Aberdeen	**Stoke C.**	03.88	1987-88	46	1	5		
HADDOCK, Peter M.	Newcastle	09.12.61	App	**Newcastle U.**	12.79	1981-85	53	4	0	(D)	
			L	**Burnley**	03.86	1985	7	0	0		
			Tr	**Leeds U.**	07.86	1986-88	56	7	1		
HAIG, Richard N.	Pontypridd	29.12.70	YTS	**Cardiff C.**(YTS)	06.87	1988	0	1	0	(M)	
HAIGH, Paul	Scarborough	04.05.58	App	**Hull C.**	06.75	1974-80	179	1	8	(D)	E U21-1
			Tr	**Carlisle U.**	11.80	1980-86	228	5	4		
			Tr	**Hartlepool U.**	07.87	1987-88	49	1	0		
HAINES, Ivan G.	Chatham	14.09.68	YTS	**Gillingham**	06.87	1987-88	10	3	0	(D)	
HALES, Kevin P.	Dartford	13.01.61	App	**Chelsea**	01.79	1979-82	18	2	2	(D/M)	
			Tr	**Leyton Orient**	08.83	1983-88	211	6	20		
HALL, Derek R.	Ashton-u-Lyne	05.01.65	App	**Coventry C.**	10.82	1982	1	0	0	(M)	
			Tr	**Torquay U.**	03.84	1983-84	55	0	6		
			Tr	**Swindon T.**	07.85	1985	9	1	0		
			Tr	**Southend U.**	08.86	1986-88	120	3	15		

Players Names	Birthplace	Date	Previous Club	League Club	Date Sign'd	Seasons Played	Career Record Apps	Sub	Gls	Pos.	Misc
HALL, Gareth D.	Croydon	20.03.69	App	**Chelsea**	05.86	1986-88	25	11	0	(RB)	W-4
HALL, Mark	Doncaster	11.05.70	YTS	**Doncaster Rov.**	06.88	1987-88	1	1	0	(RB)	
HALL, Wayne	Rotherham	25.10.68	Hatfield Main	**York C.** (N/C)	03.89	1988	0	2	0	(M)	
HALLWORTH, Jonathan G.	Stockport	26.10.65	App	**Ipswich T.**	05.83	1985-87	45	0	0	(G)	
			L	**Bristol Rov.**	01.85	1984	2	0	0		
			L	**Oldham Ath.**	02.89	1988	16	0	0		
HALPIN, John	Broxburn	15.11.61	Glasgow Celtic	**Carlisle U.**	10.84	1984-88	113	2	16	(LW)	
HALSALL, Mike	Bootle	21.07.61	App	**Liverpool**	05.79					(M)	
			Tr	**Birmingham C.**	03.83	1982-84	35	1	3		
			Tr	**Carlisle U.**	10.84	1984-86	92	0	11		
			Tr	**Grimsby T.**	02.87	1986	12	0	0		
			Tr	**Peterborough U.**	07.87	1987-88	87	0	5		
HAMILTON, David	South Shields	07.11.60	App	**Sunderland**	09.78					(M)	E Yth Int/Brother of Ian W.
			Tr	**Blackburn Rov.**	01.81	1980-85	104	10	7		
			L	**Cardiff C.**	03.85	1984	10	0	0		
			Tr	**Wigan Ath.**	07.86	1986-88	97	6	7		
HAMILTON, Gary J.	Glasgow	27.12.65	App	**Middlesbrough**	06.83	1982-88	217	12	25	(M)	S Yth Int
HAMILTON, Ian R.	Stevenage	14.12.67	App	**Southampton**	12.85					(W)	
			Tr	**Cambridge U.**	03.88	1987-88	23	1	1		
			Tr	**Scunthorpe U.**	12.88	1988	25	2	1		
HAMMOND, Nicky D.	Hornchurch	07.09.67	App	**Arsenal**	09.85					(G)	
			L	**Bristol Rov.**	08.86	1986	3	0	0		
			Tr	**Swindon T.**	06.87	1987	4	0	0		
HANCOCK, A.E. (Tony)	Manchester	31.01.67	Stockport Georgians	**Stockport Co.**	12.88	1988	2	10	5	(F)	
HANCOX, Paul A.	Manchester	22.07.70	YTS	**Rochdale** (YTS)	12.87	1987	0	2	0		
HANSBURY, Roger	Barnsley	26.01.55	App	**Norwich C.**	01.73	1974-80	78	0	0	(G)	
			L	**Cambridge U.**	11.77	1977	11	0	0		
			Eastern (HK)	**Burnley**	08.83	1983-84	83	0	0		
			Tr	**Cambridge U.**	07.85	1985	37	0	0		
			Tr	**Birmingham C.**	03.86	1986-88	56	0	0		
			L	**Sheffield U.**	10.87	1987	5	0	0		
			L	**Wolverhampton W.**	03.89	1988	3	0	0		
HANSEN, Alan D.	Alloa	13.06.55	Partick Thistle	**Liverpool**	04.77	1977-88	403	0	8	(CD)	S U23-3/S-26
HARBEY, Graham K.	Chesterfield	29.08.64	App	**Derby Co.**	08.82	1983-86	35	5	1	(LB)	
			Tr	**Ipswich T.**	07.87	1987-88	53	5	1		
HARDWICK, Steve	Mansfield	06.09.56	Jnrs	**Chesterfield**	07.74	1974-76	38	0	0	(G)	E Yth Int
			Tr	**Newcastle U.**	12.76	1977-82	92	0	0		
			Tr	**Oxford U.**	02.83	1982-87	156	0	0		
			L	**Crystal Palace**	03.86	1985	3	0	0		
			L	**Sunderland**	08.87	1987	6	0	0		
			Tr	**Huddersfield T.**	07.88	1988	46	0	0		
HARDY, Jason P.	Manchester	14.12.69	YTS	**Burnley**	07.88	1986-88	16	2	1	(FB)	
HARDYMAN, Paul G.	Portsmouth	11.03.64	Waterlooville	**Portsmouth**	07.83	1983-88	113	4	3	(LB)	E U21-2
HARFORD, Mick G.	Sunderland	12.02.59	Sunderland B.C.	**Lincoln C.**	07.77	1977-80	109	6	41	(F)	E-2/E 'B'
			Tr	**Newcastle U.**	12.80	1980	18	1	4		
			Tr	**Bristol C.**	08.81	1981	30	0	11		
			Tr	**Birmingham C.**	03.82	1981-84	92	0	25		
			Tr	**Luton T.**	12.84	1984-88	134	1	57		
HARKNESS, Steven	Carlisle	27.08.71	YTS	**Carlisle U.**	03.89	1988	12	1	0	(M)	
HARLE, David	Denaby	15.08.63	App	**Doncaster Rov.**	11.80	1979-81	48	13	3	(M)	E Yth Int
			Tr	**Exeter C.**	07.82	1982-83	42	1	6		
			Tr	**Doncaster Rov.**	09.83	1983-85	80	3	17		
			Tr	**Leeds U.**	12.85	1985	3	0	0		
			Tr	**Bristol C.**	03.86	1985-86	23	0	2		
			Tr	**Scunthorpe U.**	11.86	1986-88	88	1	10		
			Tr	**Peterborough U.**	03.89	1988	7	0	0		
HARPER, Alan	Liverpool	01.11.60	App	**Liverpool**	04.78					(M)	E Yth Int
			Tr	**Everton**	06.83	1983-87	103	24	4		
			Tr	**Sheffield Wed.**	07.88	1988	23	1	0		
HARPER, Stephen J.	Newcastle-u-Lyme	03.02.69	YTS	**Port Vale**	06.87	1987-88	16	12	2	(W)	
			Tr	**Preston N.E.**	03.89	1988	2	3	0		
HARRIS, Carl S.	Neath	03.11.56	App	**Leeds U.**	11.73	1974-81	123	30	26	(W)	W Sch Int/W U23-1/W-24
			Tr	**Charlton Ath.**	07.82	1982-84	73	3	7		
			Leeds U.(N/C)	**Bury**	12.85	1985-86	33	5	4		
			Cardiff C.(N/C)	**Rochdale**(N/C)	01.88	1987-88	24	1	3		
			Tr	**Exeter C.**	12.88	1988	11	5	1		
HARRIS, Jamie	Exeter	04.06.69	YTS	**Exeter C.**	08.86	1987-88	6	8	1	(F)	
HARRIS, Jason M.	Rochdale	26.12.69	YTS	**Burnley**	[illegible].88	1986	4	0	0	(M)	
HARRIS, Mark A.	Reading	15.07.63	Wokingham T.	**Crystal Palace**	02.88	1988	0	2	0	(CD)	
HARRISON, Frank N.	Eston	19.09.63	Guisborough T.	**Middlesbrough**	09.82					(LB)	
				Lincoln C.(N/C)	11.85	1985	0	1	0		
			Guiseley	**Halifax T.**	03.87	1986-88	45	0	1		
HARRISON, Wayne	Stockport	15.11.67	App	**Oldham Ath.**	12.84	1984	5	1	1	(F)	
			Tr	**Liverpool**	03.85						
			L	**Crewe Alex.**	12.88	1988	3	0	0		
HARROWER, Steven G.	Exeter	09.10.61	Dawlish	**Exeter C.**	01.84	1983-88	162	18	10	(W)	Son of William
HART, Nigel	Golborne	01.10.58		**Wigan Ath.**	08.78	1979	1	0	0	(CD)	Brother of Paul/Son of John
			Tr	**Leicester C.**	10.79						
			Tr	**Blackpool**	08.81	1981-82	36	1	0		
			Tr	**Crewe Alex.**	11.82	1982-86	139	3	10		
			Tr	**Bury**	02.87	1986-87	33	12	2		
			Tr	**Stockport Co.**	07.88	1988	37	1	2		
HART, Peter O.	Mexborough	14.08.57	App	**Huddersfield T.**	08.74	1973-79	208	2	7	(CD)	
			Tr	**Walsall**	08.80	1980-88	379	1	12		

David Hirst (Sheffield Wednesday) Match Magazine

Brian Horne (Millwall) Match Magazine

Mark Hughes (Manchester United & Wales) Match Magazine

Players Names	Birthplace	Date	Previous Club	League Club	Date Sign'd	Seasons Played	Career Record Apps	Sub	Gls	Pos.	Misc
HARTFORD, R. Asa	Clydebank	24.10.50	Jnrs	**West Bromwich A.**	11.67	1967-73	206	8	18	(M)	S U23-5/S U21-1/S-50
			Tr	**Manchester C.**	08.74	1974-78	184	1	22		
			Tr	**Nottingham F.**	07.79	1979	3	0	0		
			Tr	**Everton**	08.79	1979-81	81	0	6		
			Tr	**Manchester C.**	10.81	1981-83	75	0	7		
			Ft Lauderdale(USA)	**Norwich C.**	10.84	1984	28	0	2		
			Tr	**Bolton W.**	07.85	1985-86	81	0	8		
			Tr	**Stockport Co.**	06.87	1987-88	42	3	0		
			Tr	**Oldham Ath.**	03.89	1988	3	4	0		
HARVEY, Jimmy	Lurgan (NI)	02.05.58	Glenavon	**Arsenal**	08.77	1977-78	2	1	0	(M)	
			Tr	**Hereford U.**	03.80	1979-86	276	2	39		
			Tr	**Bristol C.**	03.87	1986-87	2	1	0		
			L	**Wrexham**	09.87	1987	6	0	0		
			Tr	**Tranmere Rov.**	10.87	1987-88	75	0	7		
HARVEY, Lee D.	Harlow	21.12.66	App	**Leyton Orient**	12.84	1983-88	54	33	10	(M)	E Yth Int
HARVEY, Richard G.	Letchworth	19.04.69	App	**Luton T.**	01.87	1986-88	16	1	0	(LB)	E Yth Int
HASLEGRAVE, Sean M.	Stoke	07.06.51	Jnrs	**Soke C.**	11.68	1970-75	106	7	5	(M)	
			Tr	**Nottingham F.**	07.76	1976	5	2	1		
			Tr	**Preston N.E.**	09.77	1977-80	111	2	2		
			Tr	**Crewe Alex.**	08.81	1981-82	78	4	1		
			Tr	**York C.**	07.83	1983-86	137	5	0		
			Tr	**Torquay U.**	08.87	1987-88	32	4	1		
HATELEY, Mark W.	Liverpool	07.11.61	App	**Coventry C.**	12.78	1978-82	86	7	25	(F)	E Yth Int/E U21-10/E-27/
			Tr	**Portsmouth**	06.83	1983	38	0	22		to A.C. Milan (Italy) 6.84
HATHAWAY, Ian	Wordsley	22.08.68	Bedworth U.	**Mansfield T.**	03.89	1988	4	8	1	(W)	
HAUSER, Thomas	West Germany	10.04.65	FC Basle (Switz)	**Sunderland**	02.89	1988	6	7	2	(F)	
HAWKE, Warren R.	Durham City	20.09.70	YTS	**Sunderland**	11.88	1988	1	3	0	(F)	
HAWKER, Phil N.	Solihull	07.12.62	App	**Birmingham C.**	06.80	1980-82	34	1	1	(D)	E Yth Int
			Tr	**Walsall**	12.82	1982-88	137	10	9		
HAWKINS, Nigel S.	Bristol	07.09.68	YTS	**Bristol C.**	02.87	1987-88	8	10	2	(F)	
HAWTIN, Craig S.	Buxton	29.03.70	YTS	**Chester C.**	09.88	1987-88	6	1	1	(RB)	
HAY, Alan B.	Dunfermline	28.11.58	Dundee	**Bolton W.**	03.77					(LB)	
			Tr	**Bristol C.**	07.78	1979-81	72	2	1		
			Tr	**York C.**	08.82	1982-85	147	3	3		
			Tr	**Tranmere Rov.**	08.86	1986	27	1	0		
			Hill of Beath	**York C.** (N/C)	12.88	1988	1	0	0		
			Tr	**Sunderland**	02.89	1988	1	0	0		
HAYCOCK, T. Paul	Sheffield	08.07.62	Burton A.	**Rotherham U.**	08.86	1986-88	75	19	22	(F)	
HAYES, Martin	Walthamstow	21.03.66	App	**Arsenal**	11.83	1985-88	62	28	23	(W)	E U21-2
HAYLOCK, Paul	Lowestoft	24.03.63	App	**Norwich C.**	01.81	1981-85	154	1	3	(RB)	
			Tr	**Gillingham**	08.86	1986-88	105	3	0		
HAZARD, Mike	Sunderland	05.02.60	App	**Tottenham H.**	02.78	1979-85	75	16	13	(M)	
			Tr	**Chelsea**	09.85	1985-88	65	3	9		
HAZEL, Desmond L.	Bradford	15.07.67	App	**Sheffield Wed.**	07.85	1987	5	1	0	(W)	
			L	**Grimsby T.**	10.86	1986	9	0	2		
			Tr	**Rotherham U.**	07.88	1988	39	3	6		
HAZEL, Ian	Merton	01.12.67	App	**Wimbledon**	12.85	1987-88	4	3	0	(M)	
			L	**Bristol Rov.**	02.89	1988	3	0	0		
HAZELL, R.J. (Bob)	Jamaica (WI)	14.06.59	App	**Wolverhampton W.**	05.77	1977-78	32	1	1	(CD)	E Yth Int/E U21-1/E 'B'
			Tr	**Q.P.R.**	09.79	1979-83	100	6	8		
			Tr	**Leicester C.**	09.83	1983-84	41	0	2		
			L	**Wolverhampton W.**	09.85	1985	1	0	0		
			Tr	**Luton T.**	08.86						
			Tr	**Reading**	11.86	1986	4	0	0		
			Tr	**Port Vale**	12.86	1986-88	81	0	1		
HEALD, Paul A.	Wath	20.09.68	YTS	**Sheffield U.**	06.87					(G)	
			Tr	**Leyton Orient**	11.88	1988	28	0	0		
HEARD, T. Pat	Hull	17.03.60	App	**Everton**	03.78	1978-79	10	1	0	(LB)	E Yth Int
			Tr	**Aston Villa**	10.79	1979-82	20	4	2		
			Tr	**Sheffield Wed.**	01.83	1982-84	22	3	3		
			Tr	**Newcastle U.**	09.84	1984	34	0	2		
			Tr	**Middlesbrough**	08.85	1985	25	0	2		
			Tr	**Hull C.**	03.86	1985-87	79	1	5		
			Tr	**Rotherham U.**	07.88	1988	28	2	4		
HEATH, Adrian P.	Stoke	11.01.61	App	**Stoke C.**	01.79	1978-81	94	1	16	(F)	E U21-8/Brother of Philip
			Tr	**Everton**	01.82	1981-88	206	20	71		to Espanol (Sp) 11.88
HEATH, Herbert	Wolverhampton	29.03.70	Walsall Wood	**Exeter C.** (N/C)	01.89	1988	3	2	0	(CD)	
HEATH, Philip A.	Stoke	24.11.64	App	**Stoke C.**	10.82	1982-87	144	12	17	(LW)	Brother of Adrian
			Tr	**Oxford U.**	06.88	1988	8	8	1		
HEATHCOTE, Michael	Kelloe (Dm)	10.09.65	Spennymoor U.	**Sunderland**	08.87	1987	0	1	0	(CD)	
			L	**Halifax T.**	12.87	1987	7	0	1		
HEBBERD, Trevor N.	Winchester	19.06.58	App	**Southampton**	06.76	1976-81	69	28	7	(M)	
			L	**Bolton W.**	09.81	1981	6	0	0		
			L	**Leicester C.**	11.81	1981	4	0	1		
			Tr	**Oxford U.**	03.82	1981-87	260	0	37		
			Tr	**Derby Co.**	08.88	1988	37	0	5		
HEDMAN, Rudi G.	Lambeth	16.11.64	Jnrs	**Colchester U.**	02.84	1983-88	166	10	10	(D)	
			Tr	**Crystal Palace**	12.88	1988	1	4	0		
HEDWORTH, Chris	Wallsend	05.01.64	App	**Newcastle U.**	01.82	1982-85	8	1	0	(D)	
			Tr	**Barnsley**	08.86	1986-87	19	6	0		
			Tr	**Halifax T.**	08.88	1988	11	0	0		
HELLIWELL, Ian	Rotherham	07.11.62	Matlock T.	**York C.**	10.87	1987-88	73	0	19	(F)	
HEMMING, Chris A.J.	Newcastle-u-Lyme	13.04.66	Jnrs	**Stoke C.**	04.84	1983-88	85	8	2	(D)	
			L	**Wigan Ath.**	01.89	1988	4	0	0		
HENDERSON, Mick R.	Newcastle	31.03.56	App	**Sunderland**	03.74	1975-78	81	3	2	(M)	
			Tr	**Watford**	11.79	1979-81	50	1	0		
			Tr	**Cardiff C.**	03.82	1981	11	0	0		
			Tr	**Sheffield U.**	08.82	1982-84	65	2	0		
			Tr	**Chesterfield**	01.85	1984-88	135	1	10		

Players Names	Birthplace	Date	Previous Club	League Club	Date Sign'd	Seasons Played	Career Record Apps	Sub	Gls	Pos.	Misc
HENDRIE, John G.	Lennoxtown	24.10.63	App	**Coventry C.**	05.81	1981-83	15	6	2	(RW)	
			L	**Hereford U.**	01.84	1983	6	0	0		
			Tr	**Bradford C.**	06.84	1984-87	173	0	46		
			Tr	**Newcastle U.**	06.88	1988	34	0	4		
HENDRIE, Paul F.	Glasgow	27.03.54	Kirkintilloch Rob Roy	**Birmingham C.**	03.72	1972-75	19	4	1	(W)	
			Portland T. (USA)	**Bristol Rov.**	09.77	1977-78	17	13	1		
			Tr	**Halifax T.**	07.79	1979-83	187	0	12		
			Tr	**Stockport Co.**	08.84	1984-88	114	7	6		
HENDRY, E. Colin J.	Keith	07.12.65	Dundee	**Blackburn Rov.**	03.87	1986-88	94	1	22	(CD)	
HENRY, A. (Tony)	Houghton le Spring	26.11.57	App	**Manchester C.**	12.74	1976-81	68	11	6	(M)	
			Tr	**Bolton W.**	09.81	1981-82	70	0	22		
			Tr	**Oldham Ath.**	03.83	1982-87	185	5	25		
			Tr	**Stoke C.**	11.87	1987-88	59	3	11		
HENRY, Charlie A.	Acton	13.02.62	App	**Swindon T.**	02.80	1980-88	200	23	26	(M)	
			L	**Torquay U.**	02.87	1986	6	0	1		
			L	**Northampton T.**	03.87	1986	4	0	1		
HENRY, Liburd A.	Dominica (WI)	29.08.67	Leytonstone & Ilford	**Watford**	11.87	1988	1	0	0	(F)	
			L	**Halifax T.**	09.88	1988	1	4	0		
HENRY, Nicky I.	Liverpool	21.02.69	YTS	**Oldham Ath.**	06.87	1987-88	17	6	0	(M)	
HENSHAW, Gary	Leeds	18.02.65	App	**Grimsby T.**	02.83	1983-86	46	4	9	(W)	
			Tr	**Bolton W.**	06.87	1987-88	39	13	4		
HEPPLE, John A.	Middlesbrough	12.03.70	YTS	**Sunderland**	07.87					(F)	
			L	**Hartlepool U.**	03.89	1988	1	1	0		
HERRERA, Roberto	Torquay	12.06.70	YTS	**Q.P.R.**	02.88	1988	0	2	0	(FB)	
HESFORD, Iain	Kenya	04.03.60	App	**Blackpool**	08.77	1977-82	202	0	0	(G)	E Yth Int/E U21-7/Son of Robert
			Tr	**Sheffield Wed.**	08.83						
			L	**Fulham**	01.85	1984	3	0	0		
			L	**Notts. Co.**	11.85	1985	10	0	0		
			Tr	**Sunderland**	08.86	1986-88	97	0	0		
			Tr	**Hull C.**	12.88	1988	22	0	0		
HETHERINGTON, R. Brent	Carlisle	06.12.61	Workington	**Carlisle U.**	08.87	1987-88	60	16	21	(F)	
HETZKE, Steve E.R.	Marlborough	03.06.55	App	**Reading**	06.73	1971-81	254	7	23	(CD)	
			Tr	**Blackpool**	07.82	1982-85	140	0	18		
			Tr	**Sunderland**	03.86	1985-86	31	0	0		
			Tr	**Chester C.**	06.87	1987	14	0	0		
			Tr	**Colchester U.**	03.88	1987-88	27	2	2		
HEWITT, Darren P.	Chichester	01.09.69	YTS	**Aldershot**	08.88	1988	0	2	0	(M)	
HEWITT, Jamie R.	Chesterfield	17.05.68	YTS	**Chesterfield**	04.86	1985-88	119	8	5	(RB)	
HIBBITT, Kenny	Bradford	03.01.51	App	**Bradford P.A.**	11.68	1967-68	13	2	0	(M)	Brother of Terry/E U23-1
			Tr	**Wolverhampton W.**	11.68	1968-83	446	19	88		
			Tr	**Coventry C.**	08.84	1984-85	42	5	4		
			Tr	**Bristol Rov.**	08.86	1986-88	51	2	5		
HICKS, Martin	Stratford-on-Avon	27.02.57	Stratford T.	**Charlton Ath.**	02.77					(CD)	
			Tr	**Reading**	02.78	1977-88	411	1	21		
HICKS, Stuart J.	Peterborough	30.05.67	YTS	**Peterborough U.**	07.84					(CD)	
			Wisbech T.	**Colchester U.**	03.88	1987-88	41	3	0		
HIGGINS, David A.	Liverpool	19.08.61	Eagle F.C.	**Tranmere Rov.**	08.83	1983-84	27	1	0	(RB)	
			Caernarfon T.	**Tranmere Rov.**	07.87	1987-88	74	2	2		
HIGGINS, Mark N.	Buxton	29.09.58	App	**Everton**	08.76	1976-83	150	2	6	(CD)	Son of John/E Sch Int/E Yth Int
			Retired	**Manchester U.**	12.85	1985	6	0	0		
			Tr	**Bury**	01.87	1986-88	67	1	0		
			Tr	**Stoke C.**	09.88	1988	33	0	1		
HIGNETT, Craig J.	Prescot	12.01.70	Liverpool (YTS)	**Crewe Alex.**	05.88	1988	1	0	0	(M)	
HILAIRE, Vince M.	Forest Hill	10.10.59	App	**Crystal Palace**	10.76	1976-83	239	16	29	(LW)	E Yth Int/E U21-9/E'B'
			Tr	**Luton T.**	07.84	1984	5	1	0		
			Tr	**Portsmouth**	11.84	1984-87	144	2	25		
			Tr	**Leeds U.**	07.88	1988	42	0	6		
HILDERSLEY, Ron	Kirkcaldy	06.04.65	App	**Manchester C.**	04.83	1982	1	0	0	(W)	
			L	**Chester C.**	01.84	1983	9	0	0		
			Tr	**Chester C.**	07.84	1984	5	4	0		
			Tr	**Rochdale**(N/C)	08.85	1985	12	4	0		
			Tr	**Preston N.E.**	06.86	1986-87	54	4	3		
			L	**Cambridge U.**	02.88	1987	9	0	3		
			Tr	**Blackburn Rov.**	07.88	1988	23	2	4		
HILDITCH, Mark W.	Royton	20.08.60	Jnrs	**Rochdale**	11.78	1977-82	184	13	40	(F)	
			Tr	**Tranmere Rov.**	08.83	1983-85	47	2	12		
			Altrincham	**Wigan Ath.**	09.86	1986-88	69	13	19		
HILEY, Scott P.	Plymouth	27.09.68	YTS	**Exeter C.**	08.86	1987-88	48	4	6	(M)	
HILL, Andy R.	Maltby	20.01.65	App	**Manchester U.**	01.83					(RB)	E Yth Int
			Tr	**Bury**	07.84	1984-88	206	0	8		
HILL, Colin F.	Uxbridge	12.11.63	App	**Arsenal**	08.81	1982-84	46	0	1	(D)	
			Maritimo (Portugal)	**Colchester U.**	10.87	1987-88	64	5	0		
HILL, David M.	Nottingham	06.06.66	YTS	**Scunthorpe U.**	02.85	1983-87	139	1	10	(LW)	
			Tr	**Ipswich T.**	07.88	1988	35	1	0		
HILL, Keith J.	Bolton	17.05.69	Jnrs	**Blackburn Rov.**	05.87	1987-88	14	2	2	(CD)	
HILL, Richard W.	Hinckley	20.09.63	Jnrs	**Leicester C.**	11.81					(M)	
			Nuneaton Bor.	**Northampton T.**	06.85	1985-86	86	0	46		
			Tr	**Watford**	05.87	1987	2	2	0		
			Tr	**Oxford U.**	09.87	1987-88	48	15	14		
HILL, Ricky A.	Paddington	05.03.59	App	**Luton T.**	05.76	1975-88	429	7	54	(M)	E Yth Int/E-3
HILLYARD, Ron W.	Rotherham	31.03.52	Jnrs	**York C.**	12.69	1969-73	61	0	0	(G)	
			L	**Hartlepool U.**	01.72	1971	23	0	0		
			Tr	**Gillingham**	07.74	1974-88	517	0	0		
HILTON, Paul	Oldham	08.10.59	Chadderton	**Bury**	07.78	1978-83	136	12	39	(CD)	
			Tr	**West Ham U.**	02.84	1983-88	47	13	7		
HIMSWORTH, Gary P.	Pickering	19.12.69	YTS	**York C.**	01.88	1987-88	58	5	4	(W)	
HINCHCLIFFE, Andy G.	Manchester	05.02.69	App	**Manchester C.**	08.86	1987-88	79	2	6	(LB)	E Yth Int/E U21-1

Kenny Jackett (Watford & Wales) Match Magazine

Players Names	Birthplace	Date	Previous Club	League Club	Date Sign'd	Seasons Played	Career Record Apps	Sub	Gls	Pos.	Misc
HINDMARCH, Rob	Morpeth	27.04.61	App	**Sunderland**	04.78	1977-83	114	1	2	(CD)	E Yth Int
			L	**Portsmouth**	12.83	1983	2	0	0		
			Tr	**Derby Co.**	07.84	1984-88	138	0	9		
HINE, Mark	Middlesbrough	18.05.64	Whitby T.	**Grimsby T.**	10.83	1984-85	20	2	1	(M)	
			Tr	**Darlington**	06.86	1986-88	126	2	8		
HINNIGAN, Joe P.	Liverpool	03.12.55	South Liverpool	**Wigan Ath.**	(N/L)	1978-79	66	0	10	(D)	
			Tr	**Sunderland**	02.80	1979-82	63	0	4		
			Tr	**Preston N.E.**	12.82	1982-83	51	1	8		
			Tr	**Gillingham**	08.84	1984-86	99	4	7		
			Tr	**Wrexham**	07.87	1987	28	1	1		
			Tr	**Chester C.**	08.88	1988	38	1	2		
HIRONS, Paul T.	Bath	06.03.71	Bristol C. (YTS)	**Torquay U.**	01.89	1988	1	4	0		
HIRST, David E.	Cudworth	07.12.67	App	**Barnsley**	11.85	1985	26	2	9	(F)	E Yth Int/E U21-4
			Tr	**Sheffield Wed.**	08.86	1986-88	60	17	16		
HITCHCOCK, Kevin J.	Canning Town	05.10.62	Barking	**Nottingham F.**	08.83					(G)	
			Tr	**Mansfield T.**	02.84	1983-87	182	0	0		
			Tr	**Chelsea**	03.88	1987-88	11	0	0		
HOBSON, Gordon	Sheffield	27.11.57	Sheffield Rangers	**Lincoln C.**	12.77	1977-84	260	12	73	(F)	
			Tr	**Grimsby T.**	06.85	1985-86	50	2	18		
			Tr	**Southampton**	11.86	1986-87	32	1	8		
			Tr	**Lincoln C.**	09.88	1988	32	0	15		
HOCKADAY, David	Billingham	09.11.57	Billingham Synth.	**Blackpool**	06.75	1976-82	131	16	24	(FB)	
			Tr	**Swindon T.**	08.83	1983-88	215	7	7		
HODDLE, Glenn	Hayes	27.10.57	App	**Tottenham H.**	04.57	1975-86	370	7	88	(M)	E Yth Int/E U21-12/E-49 to Monaco (Fr.) 7.87
HODDY, Kevin R.	Romford	06.01.68	App	**Fulham**	01.86	1986-88	13	9	1	(M)	
HODGE, Martin J.	Southport	04.02.59	App	**Plymouth Arg.**	02.77	1977-78	43	0	0	(G)	
			Tr	**Everton**	07.79	1979-80	25	0	0		
			L	**Preston N.E.**	12.81	1981	28	0	0		
			L	**Oldham Ath.**	07.82	1982	4	0	0		
			L	**Gillingham**	01.83	1982	4	0	0		
			L	**Preston N.E.**	02.83	1982	16	0	0		
			Tr	**Sheffield Wed.**	08.83	1983-87	197	0	0		
			Tr	**Leicester C.**	08.88	1988	19	0	0		
HODGE, Steve B.	Nottingham	25.10.62	App	**Nottingham F.**	10.80	1981-85	122	1	30	(M)	E U21-8/E-16
			Tr	**Aston Villa**	08.85	1985-86	53	0	12		
			Tr	**Tottenham H.**	12.86	1986-87	44	1	7		
			Tr	**Nottingham F.**	08.88	1988	33	1	7		
HODGES, David	Hereford	17.01.70	Jnrs	**Mansfield T.**	08.87	1986-88	59	5	6	(F)	
HODGES, Glyn P.	Streatham	30.04.63	App	**Wimbledon**	02.81	1980-86	200	32	49	(W)	W U21-3/W-8
			Tr	**Newcastle U.**	07.87	1987	7	0	0		
			Tr	**Watford**	10.87	1987-88	47	4	8		
HODGES, Kevin	Bridport	12.06.60	App	**Plymouth Arg.**	03.78	1978-88	406	20	74	(M)	
HODGSON, David J.	Gateshead	01.11.60	Jnrs	**Middlesbrough**	08.78	1978-81	116	9	16	(F)	E U21-6
			Tr	**Liverpool**	08.82	1982-83	21	7	4		
			Tr	**Sunderland**	08.84	1984-85	32	8	5		
			Tr	**Norwich C.**	07.86	1986	3	3	1		
			Jerez (Spain)	**Sheffield Wed.**	08.88	1988	6	5	1		
HODKINSON, Andy J.	Ashton-u-Lyne	04.11.65	Bolton W.(App)	**Oldham Ath.**	08.83	1983-84	4	1	1	(W)	E Sch Int
			Tr	**Stockport Co.**	08.85	1985-87	114	4	18		
			Tr	**Scunthorpe U.**	08.88	1988	38	3	8		
HODSON, Simeon P.	Lincoln	05.03.66	App	**Notts Co.**	03.84	1983-84	27	0	0	(RB)	
			Tr	**Charlton Ath.**	03.85	1984	5	0	0		
			Tr	**Lincoln C.**	01.86	1985-86	54	2	0		
			Tr	**Newport Co.**	08.87	1987	34	0	1		
			Tr	**West Bromwich A.**	03.88	1987-88	16	0	0		
HOGG, Graeme J.	Aberdeen	17.06.64	App	**Manchester U.**	06.82	1983-87	82	1	1	(CD)	S U21-4
			L	**West Bromwich A.**	11.87	1987	7	0	0		
			Tr	**Portsmouth**	08.88	1988	41	0	1		
HOLDEN, Andy I.	Flint	14.09.62	Rhyl	**Chester C.**	08.83	1983-86	100	0	17	(CD)	W U21-1/W-1
			Tr	**Wigan Ath.**	10.86	1986-88	48	1	4		
			Tr	**Oldham Ath.**	01.89	1988	13	0	4		
HOLDEN, Richard W.	Skipton	09.09.64	Carnegie College	**Burnley**(N/C)	03.86	1985	0	1	0	(LW)	
			Carnegie College	**Halifax T.**	09.86	1986-87	66	1	12		
			Tr	**Watford**	03.88	1987-88	42	0	8		
HOLDSWORTH, David G.	Walthamstow	08.11.68	App	**Watford**	11.86	1988	27	6	1	(CD)	E U21-1/Twin Brother of David
HOLDSWORTH, Dean C.	Walthamstow	08.11.68	App	**Watford**	11.86	1987-88	2	10	2	(F)	Twin Brother of David
			L	**Carlisle U.**	02.88	1987	4	0	1		
			L	**Port Vale**	03.88	1987	6	0	2		
			L	**Swansea C.**	08.88	1988	4	1	1		
			L	**Brentford**	10.88	1988	2	5	1		
HOLLOWAY, Ian S.	Kingswood	12.03.63	App	**Bristol Rov.**	03.81	1980-84	104	7	14	(W)	
			Tr	**Wimbledon**	07.85	1985	19	0	2		
			Tr	**Brentford**	03.86	1985-87	27	3	2		
			L	**Torquay U.**	01.87	1986	5	0	0		
			Tr	**Bristol Rov.**	08.87	1987-88	87	0	11		
HOLMES, Andrew J.	Stoke	07.01.69	App	**Stoke C.**	01.87	1987	1	1	0	(D)	
HOLMES Matthew J.E.	Luton	01.08.69	YTS	**Bournemouth**	08.88	1988	4	0	1	(M)	
			L	**Cardiff C.**	03.89	1988	0	1	0		
HOLMES, Micky A.	Blackpool	09.09.65	Yeadon C.	**Bradford C.**(N/C)	07.83	1984	0	5	0	(M)	
			Burnley (N/C)	**Wolverhampton W.**	11.85	1985-87	74	9	13		
			Tr	**Huddersfield T.**	07.88	1988	3	4	0		
			Tr	**Cambridge U.**	02.89	1988	7	4	0		
HOLMES, Paul	Chapeltown	18.02.68	App	**Doncaster Rov.**	02.86	1985-87	42	5	1	(FB)	Son of Albert
			Tr	**Torquay U.**	08.88	1988	19	6	0		
HOLSGROVE, Paul	Wellington	26.08.69	YTS	**Aldershot**	02.87	1987-88	0	3	0	(F)	
HONE, Mark J.	Croydon	31.03.68	Jnrs	**Crystal Palace**	07.85	1987-88	4	0	0	(D)	
HONOR, Christian R.	Bristol	05.06.68	App	**Bristol C.**	06.86	1985-88	40	6	0	(CD)	
			L	**Torquay U.**	11.86	1986	3	0	0		

Players Names	Birthplace	Date	Previous Club	League Club	Date Sign'd	Seasons Played	Career Record Apps	Sub	Gls	Pos.	Misc
HONOUR, Brian	Horden	16.02.64	App	**Darlington**	02.82	1981-83	59	15	4	(W)	
			Peterlee	**Hartlepool U.**	02.85	1984-88	164	9	11		
HOOLE, David J.	Chesterfield	16.10.70	YTS	**Chesterfield** (YTS)	08.87	1988	6	7	0	(M)	
HOOLICKIN, Gary J.	Middleton	29.10.57	App	**Oldham Ath.**	07.75	1976-86	209	2	2	(D)	Brother of Steve
HOOPER, Michael D.	Bristol	10.02.64	Mangotsfield	**Bristol C.**	01.84	1984	1	0	0	(G)	
			Tr	**Wrexham**	02.85	1984-85	34	0	0		
			Tr	**Liverpool**	10.85	1986-88	30	0	0		
HOOPER, Stuart R.J.	Lytham St. Annes	16.06.70	Jnrs	**Burnley**	07.88	1988	0	1	0	(F)	
HOPKINS, Jeff	Swansea	14.04.64	App	**Fulham**	09.81	1980-87	213	6	4	(CD)	W U21-2/W-14
			Tr	**Crystal Palace**	08.88	1988	43	0	0		
HOPKINS, Robert	Birmingham	25.10.61	App	**Aston Villa**	07.79	1979-82	1	2	1	(W)	
			Tr	**Birmingham C.**	03.83	1982-86	123	0	21		
			Tr	**Manchester C.**	08.86	1986	7	0	1		
			Tr	**West Bromwich A.**	10.86	1986-88	81	2	11		
			Tr	**Birmingham C.**	03.89	1988	9	0	0		
HORNE, Barry	St. Asaph	18.05.62	Rhyl	**Wrexham**	06.84	1984-86	136	0	17	(M)	W-8
			Tr	**Portsmouth**	07.87	1987-88	66	4	7		
			Tr	**Southampton**	03.89	1988	11	0	0		
HORNE, Brian S.	Billericay	05.10.67	App	**Millwall**	10.85	1986-88	113	0	0	(G)	E U21-3/E Yth Int
HORNER, Philip M.	Leeds	10.11.66	App	**Leicester C.**	11.84	1986-87	7	3	0	(CD)	E Yth Int
			L	**Rotherham U.**	03.86	1985	3	1	0		
			Tr	**Halifax T.**	08.88	1988	36	2	3		
HORRIX, Dean V.	Maidenhead	21.11.61	App	**Millwall**	04.79	1980-82	65	7	19	(F)	
			Tr	**Gillingham**	03.83	1982	7	7	0		
			Tr	**Reading**	08.83	1983-87	135	23	35		
			L	**Cardiff C.**	02.87	1986	9	0	3		
			Tr	**Millwall**	03.88	1987-88	5	5	1		
HOSKIN, J. Ashley	Accrington	27.03.68	App	**Burnley**	12.85	1985-88	72	16	11	(LW)	
HOTTE, Tim A.	Bradford	04.10.63	Arsenal (App)	**Huddersfield T.**	09.81	1981-82	14	2	4	(F)	
			Harrogate T.	**Halifax T.** (N/C)	08.85	1985	2	2	0		
			North Ferriby U.	**Hull C.**	10.87	1987-88	1	4	0		
			L	**York C.**	09.88	1988	1	1	0		
HOUCHEN, Keith M.	Middlesbrough	25.07.60	Chesterfield (Jnr.)	**Hartlepool U.**	02.78	1977-81	160	10	65	(F)	
			Tr	**Leyton Orient**	03.82	1981-83	74	2	20		
			Tr	**York C.**	03.84	1983-85	56	11	19		
			Tr	**Scunthorpe U.**	03.86	1985	9	0	2		
			Tr	**Coventry C.**	06.86	1986-88	43	11	7		to Hibernian 3.89
HOUGH, David J.	Crewe	20.02.66	App	**Swansea C.**	02.84	1983-88	126	23	8	(RB)	W Yth Int
HOUGHTON, Ray J.	Glasgow	09.01.62	Jnrs	**West Ham U.**	07.79	1981	0	1	0	(M)	IR-26
			Tr	**Fulham,**	07.82	1982-85	129	0	16		
			Tr	**Oxford U.**	09.85	1985-87	83	0	10		
			Tr	**Liverpool**	10.87	1987-88	64	2	12		
HOWARD, Mark E.	Kings Lynn	25.10.64	Kings Lynn	**Stockport Co.**	04.88	1987-88	12	6	2	(W)	
			L	**Cambridge U.**	03.89	1988	0	2	0		
HOWARD, Matthew J.	Watford	05.12.70	YTS	**Brentford** (YTS)	07.87	1987	0	1	0	(D)	
HOWARD, Terry	Stepney	26.02.66	App	**Chelsea**	02.84	1984-86	6	0	0	(D)	E Yth Int
			L	**Crystal Palace**	01.86	1985	4	0	0		
			L	**Chester C.**	01.87	1986	2	0	0		
			Tr	**Leyton Orient**	03.87	1986-88	99	0	9		
HOWELLS, David G.	Guildford	15.12.67	YTS	**Tottenham H.**	01.85	1985-88	17	23	4	(F)	E Yth Int
HOWEY, Stephen N.	Sunderland	26.10.71	YTS	**Newcastle U.** (YTS)	07.88	1988	0	1	0		
HOWLETT, Gary P.	Dublin	02.04.63	Home Farm	**Coventry C.**	11.80					(M)	IR Yth Int/IR-1
			Tr	**Brighton & H.A.**	08.82	1982-84	30	2	2		
			Tr	**Bournemouth**	12.84	1984-86	56	4	7		
			L	**Aldershot**	08.87	1987	1	0	0		
			L	**Chester C.**	12.87	1987	6	0	1		
			Tr	**York C.**	01.88	1987-88	38	3	6		
HOYLAND, Jamie W.	Sheffield	23.01.66	App	**Manchester C.**	11.83	1983-84	2	0	0	(M)	Son of Tommy/E Yth Int
			Tr	**Bury**	07.86	1986-88	123	3	19		
HUCKER, Peter I.	Hampstead	28.10.59	App	**Q.P.R.**	07.77	1980-85	160	0	0	(G)	E U21-2
			Tr	**Oxford U.**	02.87	1986-88	58	0	0		
			L	**West Bromwich A.**	01.88	1987	7	0	0		
HUGHES, Adrian	Billinge	19.12.70	YTS	**Preston N.E.**	03.89	1987-88	23	1	1	(CD)	
HUGHES, Darren J.	Prescot	06.10.65	App	**Everton**	10.83	1983-84	3	0	0	(LB)	
			Tr	**Shrewsbury T.**	06.85	1985-86	34	3	1		
			Tr	**Brighton & H.A.**	09.86	1986	26	0	2		
			Tr	**Port Vale**	09.87	1987-88	87	0	1		
HUGHES, Ken D.	Barmouth	09.01.66	Jnrs	**Crystal Palace**	08.85					(G)	
			Tr	**Shrewsbury T.**	07.86	1986-88	15	0	0		
HUGHES, L. Mark	Wrexham	01.11.63	App	**Manchester U.**	11.80	1983-85	85	4	37	(F)	W Sch Int/W U21-3/W-25
			Barcelona (Spain)	**Manchester U.**	07.88	1988	38	0	14		
HUGHES, Mark	Port Talbot	03.02.62	App	**Bristol Rov.**	02.80	1979-83	73	1	3	(CD)	Brother of Wayne/W Yth Int
			L	**Torquay U.**	12.82	1982	9	0	1		
			Tr	**Swansea C.**	07.84	1984	12	0	0		
			Tr	**Bristol C.**	02.85	1984-85	21	1	0		
			Tr	**Tranmere Rov.**	09.85	1985-88	124	3	2		
HUGHES, Michael E.	Larne (NI)	02.08.71	Jnrs	**Manchester C.**	08.88	1988	1	0	0	(W)	NI Yth Int/N I U21-1
HUGHES, Paul	Ashton-u-Lyne	19.12.68	YTS	**Bolton W.**	07.87	1987	11	0	0	(FB)	
HUGHES, Philip A.	Manchester	19.11.64	Manchester U. (App)	**Leeds U.**	01.83	1983-84	6	0	0	(G)	NI Yth Int/NI-3
			Tr	**Bury**	07.85	1985-87	80	0	0		
			Tr	**Wigan Ath.**	11.87	1987-88	47	0	0		
HUGHTON, Chris W.G.	Stratford	11.12.58	Jnrs	**Tottenham H.**	06.77	1979-88	285	4	12	(FB)	Brother of Henry/IR U21-1/IR-45
HULL, Alan E.	Southend	04.09.62	Barking	**Leyton Orient**	05.87	1987-88	39	14	10	(F)	Brother of Jeff
HULME, Kevin	Farnworth	02.12.67	Radcliffe Bor.	**Bury** (N/C)	03.89	1988	3	2	0	(F)	
HUMES, A. (Tony)	Blyth	19.03.66	App	**Ipswich T.**	05.83	1986-88	70	5	5	(CD)	

Players Names	Birthplace	Date	Previous Club	League Club	Date Sign'd	Seasons Played	Career Record Apps	Sub	Gls	Pos.	Misc
HUMPHREY, John	Paddington	31.01.61	App	**Wolverhampton W.**	01.79	1979-84	149	0	3	(RB)	
			Tr	**Charlton Ath.**	07.85	1985-88	156	0	3		
HUMPHRIES, Glenn	Hull	11.08.64	App	**Doncaster Rov.**	08.82	1980-87	174	6	8	(CD)	E Yth Int
			L	**Lincoln C.**	03.87	1986	9	0	0		
			Tr	**Bristol C.**	10.87	1987-88	44	2	0		
HUNT, David	Leicester	17.04.59	App	**Derby Co.**	04.77	1977	5	0	0	(M)	
			Tr	**Notts. Co.**	03.78	1977-86	331	5	28		
			Tr	**Aston Villa**	06.87	1987-88	12	1	0		
HUNTER, Geoff	Hull	27.10.59	App	**Manchester U.**	11.76					(M)	
			Tr	**Crewe Alex.**	08.79	1979-80	86	1	8		
			Tr	**Port Vale**	08.81	1981-86	218	3	15		
			Tr	**Wrexham**	08.87	1987-88	73	4	8		
HUNTER, Lee	Oldham	05.10.69	YTS	**Colchester U.**	06.88	1987-88	5	4	0	(M)	Son of Alan
HUNTER, Les	Middlesbrough	15.01.58	App	**Chesterfield**	08.75	1975-81	156	9	8	(CD)	
			Tr	**Scunthorpe U.**	07.82	1982-83	61	0	8		
			Tr	**Chesterfield**	01.84	1983-85	99	0	9		
			Tr	**Scunthorpe U.**	03.86	1985-86	49	0	5		
			Lincoln C.	**Chesterfield**	12.87	1987-88	31	0	3		
HURLOCK, Terry A.	Hackney	22.09.58	Leytonstone & Ilford	**Brentford**	08.80	1980-85	220	0	18	(M)	E 'B'
			Tr	**Reading**	02.86	1985-86	29	0	0		
			Tr	**Millwall**	02.87	1986-88	74	1	8		
HURLSTONE, Gary	Mexborough	25.04.63	Hatfield Main	**York C.**(N/C)	03.89	1988	1	1	0	(F)	
HUTCHINGS, Chris	Winchester	05.07.57	Harrow Bor.	**Chelsea**	07.80	1980-83	83	4	3	(FB)	
			Tr	**Brighton & H.A.**	11.83	1983-87	153	0	4		
			Tr	**Huddersfield T.**	12.87	1987-88	64	0	5		
HUTCHISON, Tommy	Cardenden	22.09.47	Alloa Ath.	**Blackpool**	02.68	1967-72	163	2	10	(LW)	S-17
			Tr	**Coventry C.**	10.72	1972-80	312	2	24		
			Tr	**Manchester C.**	10.80	1980-81	44	2	4		
			Hong Kong	**Burnley**	08.83	1983-84	92	0	4		
			Tr	**Swansea C.**	07.85	1985-88	126	7	7		
HYDE, Gary S.	Wolverhampton	28.12.69	YTS	**Darlington**	07.88	1987-88	31	7	3	(M)	
INCE, Paul E.C.	Ilford	21.10.67	YTS	**West Ham U.**	07.85	1986-88	65	6	7	(M)	E Yth Int/E U21-1
IRONSIDE, Ian	Sheffield	08.03.64	Jnrs	**Barnsley**	09.82					(G)	Son of Roy
			North Ferriby U.	**Scarborough**	03.88	1987-88	34	0	0		
IRVINE, Alan J.	Broxburn	29.11.62	Falkirk	**Liverpool**	11.86	1986	0	2	0	(F)	
			Dundee U.	**Shrewsbury T.**	02.88	1987-88	32	5	6		
IRWIN, Dennis J.	Cork (Ire)	31.10.65	App	**Leeds U.**	10.83	1983-85	72	0	1	(RB)	IR Yth Int/IR U21-1
			Tr	**Oldham Ath.**	05.86	1986-88	124	1	3		
ISAAC, Robert C.	Hackney	30.11.65	App	**Chelsea**	11.83	1984-86	9	0	0	(CD)	E Yth Int
			Tr	**Brighton & H.A.**	02.87	1986-88	30	0	0		
JACKETT, Kenny F.	Watford	05.01.62	App	**Watford**	01.80	1979-88	312	6	26	(M)	Son of Frank/W Yth Int/W U21-2/ W-31
JACKSON, Darren	Edinburgh	25.07.66	Meadowbank Th.	**Newcastle U.**	10.86	1986-88	53	16	7	(W)	to Dundee U. 12.88
JACKSON, Peter A.	Bradford	06.04.61	App	**Bradford C.**	04.79	1978-86	267	11	24	(CD)	
			Tr	**Newcastle U.**	10.86	1986-88	60	0	3		
			Tr	**Bradford C.**	09.88	1988	30	2	3		
JACOBS, Wayne G.	Sheffield	03.02.69	App	**Sheffield Wed.**	01.87	1987	5	1	0	(LB)	
			Tr	**Hull C.**	03.88	1987-88	39	0	0		
JAKUB, Yanek (Joe)	Falkirk	07.12.56	App	**Burnley**	12.73	1975-79	42	0	0	(M)	
			Tr	**Bury**	10.80	1980-86	262	3	27		
			AZ Alkamaar (Neth)	**Chester C.**	08.88	1988	42	0	1		
JAMES, Anthony C.	Sheffield	27.06.67	Gainsborough Trin.	**Lincoln C.**	08.88	1988	23	5	0	(D)	
JAMES, Julian C.	Tring	22.03.70	YTS	**Luton T.**	06.88	1987-88	1	3	0	(CD)	
JAMES, Leighton	Loughor	16.02.53	App	**Burnley**	02.70	1970-75	180	1	44	(LW)	W Sch Int/W U23-7/W-54
			Tr	**Derby Co.**	10.75	1975-77	67	1	15		
			Tr	**Q.P.R.**	10.77	1977-78	27	1	4		
			Tr	**Burnley**	09.78	1978-79	76	0	9		
			Tr	**Swansea C.**	04.80	1979-82	88	10	27		
			Tr	**Sunderland**	01.83	1982-83	50	2	4		
			Tr	**Bury**	08.84	1984	46	0	5		
			Tr	**Newport Co.**	08.85	1985	21	7	2		
			Tr	**Burnley**	08.86	1986-88	75	4	13		
JAMES, Robbie M.	Swansea	23.03.57	App	**Swansea C.**	04.74	1972-82	386	8	99	(M)	W U21-3/W-47
			Tr	**Stoke C.**	07.83	1983-84	48	0	6		
			Tr	**Q.P.R.**	10.84	1984-86	78	9	5		
			Tr	**Leicester C.**	06.87	1987	21	2	0		
			Tr	**Swansea C.**	01.88	1987-88	57	3	12		
JASPER, Dale W.	Croydon	14.01.64	App	**Chelsea**	01.82	1983-84	10	0	0	(M)	
			Tr	**Brighton & H.A.**	05.86	1986-87	44	5	6		
			Tr	**Crewe Alex.**	07.88	1988	38	1	1		
JEFFELS, Simon	Darton	18.01.66	App	**Barnsley**	01.84	1983-87	39	3	0	(CD)	E Yth Int
			L	**Preston N.E.**	10.87	1987	1	0	0		
			Tr	**Carlisle U.**	07.88	1988	28	1	0		
JEFFERS, John J.	Liverpool	05.10.68	App	**Liverpool**	10.86					(W)	
			Tr	**Port Vale**	12.88	1988	11	4	0		
JEFFREY, Michael R.	Liverpool	11.08.71	YTS	**Bolton W.**	02.89	1988	7	2	0	(F)	
JEMSON, Nigel B.	Preston	10.08.69	YTS	**Preston N.E.**	06.87	1985-87	28	4	8	(F)	
			Tr	**Nottingham F.**	03.88						
			L	**Bolton W.**	12.88	1988	4	1	0		
			L	**Preston N.E.**	03.89	1988	6	3	2		
JENKINSON, Leigh	Thorne	09.07.69	YTS	**Hull C.**	06.87	1987-88	8	6	1	(W)	
JEPSON, Ronnie F.	Stoke	12.05.63	Nantwich T.	**Port Vale** (N/C)	03.89	1988	1	1	0	(F)	
JEWELL, Paul	Liverpool	28.09.64	App	**Liverpool**	09.82					(F)	
			Tr	**Wigan Ath.**	12.84	1984-87	117	20	35		
			Tr	**Bradford C.**	07.88	1988	22	17	5		

Kevin Keen (West Ham United) Match Magazine

Ian Knight (Sheffield Wednesday) Match Magazine

Paul Lake (Manchester City) Match Magazine

Carl Leaburn (Charlton Athletic) Match Magazine

Players Names	Birthplace	Date	Previous Club	League Club	Date Sign'd	Seasons Played	Apps	Sub	Gls	Pos.	Misc
JOBLING, Kevin A.	Sunderland	01.01.68	App	**Leicester C.**	01.86	1986-87	4	5	0	(M)	
			Tr	**Grimsby T.**	02.88	1987-88	46	1	5		
JOBSON, Richard I.	Holderness	09.05.63	Burton A.	**Watford**	11.82	1982-84	26	2	4	(D)	
			Tr	**Hull C.**	02.85	1984-88	152	2	15		
JOHNROSE, Leonard	Preston	29.11.69	YTS	**Blackburn Rov.**	06.88	1987	0	1	0	(F)	
JOHNS, Nicky P.	Bristol	08.06.57	Minehead	**Millwall**	02.76	1976-77	50	0	0	(G)	Brother of Mark
			Tampa Bay (USA)	**Sheffield U.**	09.78	1978	1	0	0		
			Tr	**Charlton Ath.**	12.78	1978-87	288	0	0		
			Tr	**Q.P.R.**	12.87	1987-88	10	0	0		
JOHNSON, Alan K.	Wigan	19.02.71	YTS	**Wigan Ath.**	03.89	1988	4	4	1	(CD)	
JOHNSON, Gavin	Eye (Sk)	10.10.70	YTS	**Ipswich T.**	02.89	1988	4	0	0	(LB)	
JOHNSON, Ian	Newcastle	14.02.69	Gateshead	**Northampton T.**	11.87	1988	2	1	0	(CD)	
JOHNSON, Marvin A.	Wembley	29.10.68	App	**Luton T.**	10.86	1987-88	23	2	0	(CD)	
JOHNSON, Nigel M.	Rotherham	23.06.64	App	**Rotherham U.**	06.82	1982-84	89	0	1	(CD)	
			Tr	**Manchester C.**	06.85	1985	4	0	0		
			Tr	**Rotherham U.**	07.87	1987-88	49	0	2		
JOHNSON, Paul	Stoke	25.05.59	App	**Stoke C.**	05.77	1978-80	33	1	0	(LB)	
			Tr	**Shrewsbury T.**	05.81	1981-86	178	2	3		
			Tr	**York C.**	07.87	1987-88	83	0	1		
JOHNSON, Peter E.	Harrogate	05.10.58	App	**Middlesbrough**	10.76	1977-79	42	1	0	(LB)	
			Tr	**Newcastle U.**	10.80	1980	16	0	0		
			L	**Bristol C.**	09.82	1982	20	0	0		
			Tr	**Doncaster Rov.**	03.83	1982	12	0	0		
			Tr	**Darlington**	08.83	1983-84	89	0	2		
			Whitby T.	**Crewe Alex.** (N/C)	10.85	1985	8	0	0		
			Whitby T.	**Exeter C.** (N/C)	03.86	1985	5	0	0		
			Tr	**Southend U.**	08.86	1986-88	126	0	3		
JOHNSON, Robert S.	Bedford	22.02.62	App	**Luton T.**	08.79	1983-88	91	6	0	(FB)	
			L	**Lincoln C.**	08.83	1983	4	0	0		
JOHNSON, Steve A.	Liverpool	23.06.57	Altrincham	**Bury**	11.77	1977-82	139	15	52	(F)	
			Tr	**Rochdale**	08.83	1983	17	2	7		
			Tr	**Wigan Ath.**	02.84	1983-84	50	1	18		
			Tr	**Bristol C.**	03.85	1984-85	14	7	3		
			L	**Rochdale**	12.85	1985	3	3	1		
			L	**Chester C.**	03.86	1985	10	0	6		
			Tr	**Scunthorpe U.**	07.86	1986-87	59	13	20		
			Tr	**Chester C.**	08.88	1988	35	3	10		
JOHNSON, Tommy	Newcastle	15.01.71	YTS	**Notts Co.**	01.89	1988	6	4	4	(F)	
JOHNSTON, Maurice (Mo)	Glasgow	30.04.63	Partick Thistle	**Watford**	11.83	1983-84	37	1	23	(F)	S U21-3/S-27/to Celtic 10.84
JONES, Alex	Blackburn	27.11.64	App	**Oldham Ath.**	12.82	1982-84	8	1	0	(CD)	Son of George A.
			L	**Stockport Co.**	10.84	1984	3	0	0		
			Tr	**Preston N.E.**	06.86	1986-88	67	1	3		
JONES, Andy M.	Wrexham	09.01.63	Rhyl	**Port Vale**	06.85	1985-87	87	3	47	(F)	W 6
			Tr	**Charlton Ath.**	09.87	1987-88	23	11	10		
			L	**Port Vale**	02.89	1988	8	9	3		
JONES, David B.	Harrow	03.07.64	New Zealand	**Chelsea**	11.87					(F)	
			Barnet	**Bury**	09.88	1988	0	1	0		
			Barnet	**Leyton Orient**	12.88	1988	0	2	0		
			Barnet	**Burnley**	02.89	1988	4	0	0		
JONES, Gary	Huddersfield	06.04.69	Rossington Main	**Doncaster Rov.**	01.89	1988	9	8	2	(F)	
JONES, Joseph P.	Llandudno	04.03.55	Jnrs	**Wrexham**	01.73	1972-74	98	0	2	(D)	Brother of Frank/ W U23-4/W-72
			Tr	**Liverpool**	07.75	1975-77	72	0	3		
			Tr	**Wrexham**	10.78	1978-82	145	1	6		
			Tr	**Chelsea**	10.82	1982-84	76	2	2		
			Tr	**Huddersfield T.**	08.85	1985-86	67	1	3		
			Tr	**Wrexham**	08.87	1987-88	76	0	8		
JONES, Keith A.	Dulwich	14.10.65	App	**Chelsea**	08.83	1982-86	43	9	7	(M)	E Sch Int/E Yth Int
			Tr	**Brentford**	09.87	1987-88	74	2	4		
JONES, Linden	Tredegar	05.03.61	App	**Cardiff C.**	03.79	1978-83	142	3	2	(RB)	W U21-3
			Tr	**Newport Co.**	09.83	1983-86	141	0	5		
			Tr	**Reading**	07.87	1987-88	54	3	6		
JONES, Mark	Brownhills	04.01.68	App	**Walsall**	01.86	1987	6	2	0	(RB)	
			L	**Exeter C.**	11.88	1988	5	0	0		
JONES, Mark A.W.	Warley	22.10.61	App	**Aston Villa**	07.79	1981-83	24	0	0	(RB)	
			Tr	**Brighton & H.A.**	03.84	1983-84	9	0	0		
			Tr	**Birmingham C.**	10.84	1984-86	33	1	0		
			Tr	**Shrewsbury T.**	03.87						
			Tr	**Hereford U.**	06.87	1987-88	68	1	0		
JONES, Matthew L.	Chiswick	09.10.70	YTS	**Southend U.** (YTS)	07.87	1988	0	1	0		
JONES, Paul A.	Walsall	06.09.65	App	**Walsall**	09.83	1982-88	122	18	15	(M)	
			L	**Wrexham**	03.89	1988	5	0	0		
JONES, Paul B.	Ellesmere Port	13.05.53	App	**Bolton W.**	06.70	1970-82	440	4	37	(CD)	
			Tr	**Huddersfield T.**	07.83	1983-85	73	0	8		
			Tr	**Oldham Ath.**	12.85	1985-86	32	0	1		
			Tr	**Blackpool**	03.87	1986-87	31	6	0		
			Stalybridge Celtic	**Rochdale**	03.89	1988	14	0	2		
JONES, Philip A.	Liverpool	01.12.69	YTS	**Everton**	06.88	1987	0	1	0	(D)	
JONES, Richard J.	Pontypool	26.04.69	YTS	**Newport Co.**	07.87	1986-87	31	10	1	(M)	
			Tr	**Hereford U.**	08.88	1988	38	0	1		
JONES, Rob	Wrexham	05.11.71	YTS	**Crewe Alex.**	12.88	1987-88	16	8	1	(D)	
JONES, Tom	Aldershot	07.10.64	Aberdeen	**Swindon T.**	09.88	1988	40	0	6	(M)	
JONES, Vaughan	Tonyrefail	02.09.59	App	**Bristol Rov.**	09.77	1976-81	93	8	3	(D)	W Yth Int/W U21-2
			Tr	**Newport Co.**	08.82	1982-83	67	1	4		
			Tr	**Cardiff C.**	07.84	1984	11	0	0		
			Tr	**Bristol Rov.**	12.84	1984-88	174	3	6		

Players Names	Birthplace	Date	Previous Club	League Club	Date Sign'd	Seasons Played	Career Record Apps	Sub	Gls	Pos.	Misc
JONES, Vince	Watford	05.01.65	Wealdstone	**Wimbledon**	11.86	1986-88	77	0	9	(M)	
JONSSON, Siggi	Iceland	27.09.66	Akranes (Iceland)	**Sheffield Wed.**	02.85	1984-88	59	8	4	(M)	Iceland Int
			L	**Barnsley**	01.86	1985	5	0	0		
JORDAN, Joe	Carluke	15.12.51	Morton	**Leeds U.**	10.70	1971-77	139	30	35	(F)	S-52/S U23-1/A.C. Milan (Italy) 1980-83
			Tr	**Manchester U.**	01.78	1977-80	109	0	37		
			Verona (Italy)	**Southampton**	08.84	1984-86	48	0	12		
			Tr	**Bristol C.**	02.87	1986-88	38	18	8		
JOSEPH, Francis	Kilburn	06.03.60	Hillingdon Bor.	**Wimbledon**	11.80	1980-81	42	9	14	(F)	Brother of Roger
			Tr	**Brentford**	07.82	1982-86	103	7	44		
			L	**Wimbledon**	03.87	1986	2	3	1		
			Tr	**Reading**	07.87	1987	5	6	2		
			L	**Bristol Rov.**	01.88	1987	3	0	0		
			L	**Aldershot**	03.88	1987	9	1	2		
			Tr	**Sheffield U.**	07.88	1988	5	8	3		
			Tr	**Gillingham**	03.89	1988	10	5	1		
JOSEPH, Roger	Paddington	24.12.65	Southall	**Brentford**	10.84	1984-87	103	1	2	(RB)	Brother of Francis
			Tr	**Wimbledon**	08.88	1988	30	1	0		
JOYCE, Joe P.	Consett	18.03.61	Jnrs	**Barnsley**	11.79	1979-88	329	2	4	(RB)	
JOYCE, Sean W.	Doncaster	15.02.67	YTS	**Doncaster Rov.**	09.86	1985-87	39	2	2	(M)	
			L	**Exeter C.**	11.86	1986	1	0	0		
			Tr	**Torquay U.**	08.88	1988	27	3	3		
JOYCE, Warren G.	Oldham	20.01.65	Jnrs	**Bolton W.**	06.82	1982-87	180	4	17	(M)	Son of Walter
			Tr	**Preston N.E.**	10.87	1987-88	56	6	9		
JUDGE, Alan G.	Kingsbury	14.05.60	Jnrs	**Luton T.**	01.78	1979-82	11	0	0	(G)	
			Tr	**Reading**	09.82	1982-84	77	0	0		
			Tr	**Oxford U.**	12.84	1985-88	57	0	0		
			L	**Lincoln C.**	11.85	1985	2	0	0		
			L	**Cardiff C.**	10.87	1987	8	0	0		
JURYEFF, Ian M.	Gosport	24.11.62	App	**Southampton**	11.80	1983	0	2	0	(F)	
			L	**Mansfield T.**	03.84	1983	12	0	5		
			L	**Reading**	11.84	1984	7	0	1		
			Tr	**Leyton Orient**	02.85	1984-88	106	5	44		
			L	**Ipswich T.**	02.89	1988	0	2	0		
KAMARA, Alan	Sheffield	15.07.58	Kiveton Park	**York C.**	07.79	1979	10	0	0	(FB)	
			Tr	**Darlington**	06.80	1980-82	134	0	1		
			Burton Albion	**Scarborough**	11.87	1987-88	73	0	1		
KAMARA, Chris	Middlesbrough	25.12.57	App	**Portsmouth**	12.75	1975-76	56	7	7	(M)	
			Tr	**Swindon T.**	08.77	1977-80	133	14	21		
			Tr	**Portsmouth**	08.81	1981	11	0	0		
			Tr	**Brentford**	10.81	1981-84	150	2	28		
			Tr	**Swindon T.**	08.85	1985-87	86	1	6		
			Tr	**Stoke C.**	07.88	1988	38	0	4		
KASULE, Victor P.A.	Glasgow	28.05.65	Meadowbank Th.	**Shrewsbury T.**	01.88	1987-88	25	10	4	(W)	
KAY, John	Sunderland	29.01.64	App	**Arsenal**	08.81	1982-83	13	1	0	(RB)	
			Tr	**Wimbledon**	07.84	1984-86	63	0	2		
			L	**Middlesbrough**	01.85	1984	8	0	0		
			Tr	**Sunderland**	07.87	1987-88	57	0	0		
KEARNEY, Mark J.	Ormskirk	12.06.62	Marine	**Everton**	10.81					(W)	
			Tr	**Mansfield T.**	03.83	1982-88	187	2	26		
KEARNS, Ollie A.	Banbury	12.06.56	Banbury U.	**Reading**	03.77	1976-79	75	11	40	(F)	Brother of Mike
			Tr	**Oxford U.**	08.81	1981	9	9	4		
			Tr	**Walsall**	08.82	1982	31	7	11		
			Tr	**Hereford U.**	06.83	1983-87	166	4	58		
			Tr	**Wrexham**	12.87	1987-88	26	8	12		
KEELEY, Glenn M.	Barking	01.09.54	App	**Ipswich T.**	08.72	1972-73	4	0	0	(CD)	E Yth Int/Brother of Andy
			Tr	**Newcastle U.**	07.74	1974-75	43	1	2		
			Tr	**Blackburn Rov.**	08.76	1976-86	365	5	23		
			L	**Everton**	10.82	1982	1	0	0		
			Tr	**Oldham Ath**	08.87	1987	10	1	0		
			L	**Colchester U.**	02.88	1987	4	0	0		
			Tr	**Bolton W.**	09.88	1988	20	0	0		
KEELEY, John H.	Plaistow	27.07.61	App	**Southend U.**	07.79	1979-84	63	0	0	(G)	
			Chelmsford C.	**Brighton & H.A.**	08.86	1986-88	103	0	0		
KEEN, Kevin I.	Amersham	25.02.67	App	**West Ham U.**	03.84	1986-88	42	18	4	(M)	Son of Mike/E Yth Int/E Sch Int
KELLY, Alan T.	Preston	11.08.68	YTS	**Preston N.E.**	09.85	1985-87	54	0	0	(G)	Son of Alan J./IR Yth Int
KELLY, A.G. (Tony)	Prescot	01.10.64	App	**Liverpool**	09.82					(M)	
			Prescot Cables	**Wigan Ath.**	01.84	1983-85	98	3	15		
			Tr	**Stoke C.**	04.86	1985-86	33	3	4		
			Tr	**West Bromwich A.**	07.87	1987	26	0	1		
			L	**Chester C.**	09.88	1988	5	0	0		
			L	**Colchester U.**	10.88	1988	13	0	2		
			Tr	**Shrewsbury T.**	01.89	1988	19	1	5		
KELLY, David T.	Birmingham	25.11.65	Alvechurch	**Walsall**	12.83	1983-87	115	32	63	(F)	IR-3
			Tr	**West Ham U.**	08.88	1988	21	4	6		
KELLY, Gary A.	Preston	03.08.66	App	**Newcastle U.**	06.84	1986-88	49	0	0	(G)	Son of Alan J.
			L	**Blackpool**	10.88	1988	5	0	0		
KELLY, Gavin J.	Beverley	29.09.68	YTS	**Hull C.**	05.87	1988	3	0	0	(G)	
KELLY, John	Bebington	20.10.60	Cammell Laird	**Tranmere Rov.**	09.79	1979-81	55	9	9	(W)	Son of Noel/IR U21-1
			Tr	**Preston N.E.**	10.81	1981-84	120	10	27		
			Tr	**Chester C.**	08.85	1985-86	85	0	17		
			Tr	**Swindon T.**	06.87	1987	3	4	1		
			Tr	**Oldham Ath.**	11.87	1987-88	51	1	6		
KELLY, Mark D.	Blackpool	07.10.66		**Shrewsbury T.**	12.85					(LW)	
			Tr	**Cardiff C.**	06.87	1987-88	52	12	1		
KELLY, Mark J.	Sutton	27.11.69	YTS	**Portsmouth**	11.86	1987-88	16	15	1	(W)	E Yth Int/IR-2
KELLY, Norman	Belfast	10.10.70	YTS	**Oldham Ath.**(YTS)	07.87	1987-88	0	2	0	(M)	NI Yth Int

John Lukic (Arsenal) Match Magazine

Stuart McCall (Everton) Match Magazine

Alan McDonald (Q.P.R. & Northern Ireland) Match Magazine

Paul McGrath (Manchester United & Eire) Match Magazine

Players Names	Birthplace	Date	Previous Club	League Club	Date Sign'd	Seasons Played	Apps	Sub	Gls	Pos.	Misc
KELLY, Robert A.	Birmingham	21.12.64	App	**Leicester C.**	12.82	1983-86	17	7	1	(M)	
			L	**Tranmere Rov.**	12.84	1984	5	0	2		
			Tr	**Wolverhampton W.**	03.87	1986-88	13	3	2		
KELLY, Tom J.	Bellshill	28.03.64	Queen of South	**Hartlepool U.**	08.85	1985	14	1	0	(LB)	
			Tr	**Torquay U.**	07.86	1986-88	116	4	0		
KENDALL, Mark	Blackwood	20.09.58	App	**Tottenham H.**	07.76	1978-80	29	0	0	(G)	W Sch Int/W U21-1
			L	**Chesterfield**	11.79	1979	9	0	0		
			Tr	**Newport Co.**	09.80	1980-86	272	0	0		
			Tr	**Wolverhampton W.**	12.86	1986-88	106	0	0		
KENNEDY, Andy J.	Stirling	08.10.64	Hong Kong	**Birmingham C.**	03.85	1984-87	51	25	18	(F)	ex Glasgow Rangers
			L	**Sheffield U.**	03.87	1986	8	1	1		
			Tr	**Blackburn Rov.**	06.88	1988	23	2	10		
KENNEDY, Mick F.	Salford	09.04.61	App	**Halifax T.**	01.79	1978-79	74	2	4	(M)	IR-2
			Tr	**Huddersfield T.**	08.80	1980-81	80	1	9		
			Tr	**Middlesbrough**	08.82	1982-83	68	0	5		
			Tr	**Portsmouth**	06.84	1984-87	129	0	4		
			Tr	**Bradford C.**	01.88	1987-88	45	0	2		
			Tr	**Leicester C.**	03.89	1988	9	0	0		
KENT, Kevin J.	Stoke	19.03.65	App	**West Bromwich A.**	12.82	1983	1	1	0	(W)	
			Tr	**Newport Co.**	07.84	1984	23	10	1		
			Tr	**Mansfield T.**	08.85	1985-88	158	6	29		
KENWORTHY, A.D.(Tony)	Leeds	30.10.58	App	**Sheffield U.**	07.76	1975-85	281	5	34	(CD)	E Yth Int
			Tr	**Mansfield T.**	03.86	1985-88	97	2	0		
KEOWN, Martin R.	Oxford	24.07.66	App	**Arsenal**	01.84	1985	22	0	0	(CD)	E Yth Int/E U21-8
			L	**Brighton & H.A.**	02.85	1984-85	21	2	1		
			Tr	**Aston Villa**	06.86	1986-88	109	3	3		
KERNAGHAN, Alan N.	Otley	25.04.67	App	**Middlesbrough**	03.85	1984-88	49	36	7	(F)	
KERR, Dylan	Malta	14.01.67	South Africa	**Leeds U.**	01.89	1988	1	2	0	(FB)	
KERR, Paul A.	Portsmouth	09.06.64	App	**Aston Villa**	05.82	1983-86	16	8	3	(M)	
			Tr	**Middlesbrough**	01.87	1986-88	81	3	6		
KERRINS, Wayne M.	Brentwood	05.08.65	App	**Fulham**	08.83	1984-88	51	15	1	(M/FB)	Son of Pat
			L	**Port Vale**	03.85	1984	6	2	0		
			L	**Leyton Orient**	03.89	1988	3	0	0		
KERSLAKE, David	Stepney	19.06.66	App	**Q.P.R.**	06.83	1984-88	38	19	6	(M)	E Sch Int/E Yth Int/E U21-1
KETTERIDGE, Steve J.	Stevenage	07.11.59	Derby Co.(App)	**Wimbledon**	04.78	1978-84	229	8	32	(M)	
			Tr	**Crystal Palace**	08.85	1985-86	58	1	6		
			Tr	**Leyton Orient**	07.87	1987-88	26	5	2		
			L	**Cardiff C.**	10.88	1988	6	0	2		
KEVAN, David J.	Stranraer	31.08.68	App	**Notts Co.**	08.86	1985-88	81	5	3	(M)	
KILCLINE, Brian	Nottingham	07.05.62	App	**Notts Co.**	05.80	1979-83	156	2	9	(CD)	E U21-2
			Tr	**Coventry C.**	06.84	1984-88	148	0	24		
KIMBLE, Alan F.	Dagenham	06.08.66	Jnrs	**Charlton Ath.**	08.84	1984	6	0	0	(LB)	Twin brother of Garry
			L	**Exeter C.**	08.85	1985	1	0	0		
			Tr	**Cambridge U.**	08.86	1986-88	117	4	8		
KIMBLE, Garry L.	Dagenham	06.08.66	Jnrs	**Charlton Ath.**	08.84	1984	7	2	1	(LW)	Twin brother of Alan
			L	**Exeter C.**	08.85	1985	1	0	0		
			Tr	**Cambridge U.**	08.86	1986-87	39	2	2		
			Tr	**Doncaster Rov.**	10.87	1987-88	65	5	1		
KING, Andrew J.	Thatcham	30.03.70	Jnrs	**Reading**	06.88	1988	0	1	0	(F)	
KING, Philip G.	Bristol	28.12.67	App	**Exeter C.**	01.85	1984-85	24	3	0	(FB)	
			Tr	**Torquay U.**	07.86	1986	24	0	3		
			Tr	**Swindon T.**	02.87	1986-88	98	4	3		
KIRKHAM, Paul	Manchester	05.07.69	Manchester U.(YTS)	**Huddersfield T.**	09.87	1987	0	1	0	(F)	
KITE, Phil D.	Bristol	26.10.62	App	**Bristol Rov.**	10.80	1980-83	96	0	0	(G)	E Yth Int
			Tr	**Southampton**	08.84	1984-85	4	0	0		
			L	**Middlesbrough**	03.86	1985	2	0	0		
				Gillingham	02.87	1986-88	70	0	0		
KIWOMYA, Chris M.	Huddersfield	02.12.69	YTS	**Ipswich T.**	03.87	1988	16	10	2	(F)	Brother of Andy
KNIGHT, Alan E.	Balham	03.07.61	App	**Portsmouth**	03.79	1977-88	333	0	0	(G)	E Yth Int/E U21-2
KNIGHT, Ian J.	Hartlepool	26.10.66	App	**Barnsley**	10.84					(CD)	E U21-2
			Tr	**Sheffield Wed.**	08.85	1985-88	21	0	0		
KNIGHT, Keith	Cheltenham	16.02.69	Cheltenham T.	**Reading**	09.88	1988	25	4	7	(RW)	E Sch Int
KNILL, Alan R.	Slough	08.10.64	App	**Southampton**	10.82					(CD)	W Yth Int/W-I
			Tr	**Halifax T.**	07.84	1984-86	118	0	6		
			Tr	**Swansea C.**	08.87	1987-88	89	0	3		
KRISTENSEN, Bjorn	Denmark	10.10.63	Aarhus (Denmark)	**Newcastle U.**	03.89	1988	4	1	0	(D)	Danish Int
KRUSZYNSKI, Zbigniew	Poland	14.10.61	08 Homberg (WG)	**Wimbledon**	12.88	1988	13	3	0	(M)	
KUHL, Martin	Frimley	10.01.65	App	**Birmingham C.**	01.83	1982-86	103	8	5	(M)	
			Tr	**Sheffield U.**	03.87	1986-87	38	0	4		
			Tr	**Watford**	02.88	1987	4	0	0		
			Tr	**Portsmouth**	09.88	1988	31	1	1		
LAKE, Paul A.	Denton	28.10.68	YTS	**Manchester C.**	05.87	1986-88	70	4	6	(M)	EU21–4
LAMB, Alan	Gateshead	30.01.70	YTS	**Nottingham F.**	02.88					(F)	
			L	**Hereford U.**	03.89	1988	9	1	2		
LANE, Martin J.	Altrincham	12.04.61	Jnrs	**Manchester U.**	05.79					(LB)	
			Tr	**Chester C.**	08.82	1982-86	175	0	3		
			Tr	**Coventry C.**	01.87	1986-87	0	3	0		
			L	**Wrexham**	10.88	1988	6	0	0		
			Tr	**Chester C.**	01.89	1988	23	0	0		
LANGAN, David F.	Dublin	15.02.57	App	**Derby Co.**	02.75	1976-79	143	0	1	(RB)	IR-25
			Tr	**Birmingham C.**	07.80	1980-82	92	0	3		
			Tr	**Oxford U.**	08.84	1984-87	112	2	2		
			L	**Leicester C.**	10.87	1987	5	0	0		
			Tr	**Bournemouth**	12.87	1987	19	1	0		
			Tr	**Peterborough U.**	08.88	1988	18	1	0		

Players Names	Birthplace	Date	Previous Club	League Club	Date Sign'd	Seasons Played	Career Record Apps	Sub	Gls	Pos.	Misc
LANGE, A.S. (Tony)	West Ham	10.12.64	App	**Charlton Ath.**	12.82	1983-85	12	0	0	(G)	
			L	**Aldershot**	08.85	1985	7	0	0		
			Tr	**Aldershot**	07.86	1986-88	125	0	0		
LANGLEY, Kevin J.	St. Helens	24.05.64	App	**Wigan Ath.**	05.82	1981-85	156	4	6	(M)	
			Tr	**Everton**	07.86	1986	16	0	2		
			Tr	**Manchester C.**	03.87	1986	9	0	0		
			L	**Chester C.**	01.88	1987	9	0	0		
			Tr	**Birmingham C.**	03.88	1987-88	41	2	2		
LANGLEY, Richard J.	Lambeth	20.03.65	Corinthian Casuals	**Fulham**	11.86	1986-88	35	0	0	(D)	
LANGLEY, Tommy W.	Lambeth	08.02.58	App	**Chelsea**	04.75	1974-79	129	13	40	(F)	E Sch Int/E Yth Int/E U21-1
			Tr	**Q.P.R.**	08.80	1980	24	1	8		
			Tr	**Crystal Palace**	03.81	1980-82	54	5	9		
			AEK Athens (Greece)	**Coventry C.**	03.84	1983	2	0	0		
			Tr	**Wolverhampton W.**	07.84	1984	22	1	4		
			L	**Aldershot**	03.85	1984	16	0	4		
			Hong Kong	**Aldershot**	08.86	1986-87	80	1	21		
			Tr	**Exeter C.**	07.88	1988	14	7	2		
LAW, Brian J.	Merthyr Tydfil	01.01.70	App	**Q.P.R.**	08.87	1987-88	6	1	0	(D)	W Yth Int
LAW, Nicky	Greenwich	08.09.61	App	**Arsenal**	07.79					(D)	E Sch Int
			Tr	**Barnsley**	08.81	1981-85	113	1	1		
			Tr	**Blackpool**	08.85	1985-86	64	2	1		
			Tr	**Plymouth Arg.**	03.87	1986-87	37	1	5		
			Tr	**Notts Co.**	06.88	1988	42	2	4		
LAWRENCE, George R.	Kensington	14.09.62	App	**Southampton**	09.80	1981-82	7	3	1	(W)	
			L	**Oxford U.**	03.82	1981	15	0	4		
			Tr	**Oxford U.**	11.82	1982-84	63	0	21		
			Tr	**Southampton**	01.85	1984-86	58	12	11		
			Tr	**Millwall**	07.87	1987-88	26	2	4		
LAWS, Brian	Wallsend	14.10.61	App	**Burnley**	10.79	1979-82	125	0	12	(M)	
			Tr	**Huddersfield T.**	08.83	1983-84	56	0	1		
			Tr	**Middlesbrough**	03.85	1984-87	103	4	12		
			Tr	**Nottingham F.**	07.88	1988	20	2	1		
LE SAUX, Graeme P.	Jersey	17.10.68	St. Paul's (Jersey)	**Chelsea**	12.87	1988	0	1	0	(CD)	
LE TISSIER, Matt P.	Guernsey	14.10.68	App	**Southampton**	10.86	1986-88	43	28	15	(W)	E Yth Int
LEABURN, Carl W.	Lewisham	30.03.69	App	**Charlton Ath.**	03.87	1986-88	40	7	2	(F)	
LEADBITTER, Chris J.	Middlesbrough	17.10.67	App	**Grimsby T.**	09.85					(W)	
			Tr	**Hereford U.**	08.86	1986-87	32	4	1		
			Tr	**Cambridge U.**(N/C)	08.88	1988	27	4	6		
LEANING, Andy J.	Howden	18.05.63	Rowntree-Mackintosh	**York C.**	06.85	1985-86	69	0	0	(G)	
			Tr	**Sheffield U.**	05.87	1987	21	0	0		
			Tr	**Bristol C.**	09.88	1988	1	6	0		
LEE, Colin	Torquay	12.06.56	App	**Bristol C.**	06.74					(F/CD)	
			L	**Hereford U.**	11.74	1974	7	2	0		
			Tr	**Torquay U.**	01.77	1976-77	35	0	14		
			Tr	**Tottenham H.**	10.77	1977-79	57	5	18		
			Tr	**Chelsea**	01.80	1979-86	167	18	36		
			Tr	**Brentford**	07.87	1987-88	20	4	1		
LEE, David J.	Kingswood	26.11.69	YTS	**Chelsea**	06.88	1988	12	8	4	(M)	E Yth Int
LEE, David M.	Blackburn	05.11.67	YTS	**Bury**	08.86	1985-88	111	5	11	(W)	
LEE, Robert M.	West Ham	01.02.66	Jnrs	**Charlton Ath.**	07.83	1983-88	148	24	32	(W)	E U21-2
LEE, Sammy	Liverpool	07.02.59	App	**Liverpool**	04.76	1977-85	190	7	13	(M)	E Yth Int/E U21-6/E-14
			Tr	**Q.P.R.**	08.86	1986	29	1	0		to Osasuna (Sp.) 7.87
LEGG, Andrew	Neath	28.07.66		**Swansea C.**	08.88	1988	6	0	0	(W/FB)	
LEIGHTON, Jim	Johnstone	24.07.58	Aberdeen	**Manchester U.**	05.88	1988	38	0	0	(G)	S U21-1/S-50
LEISHMAN, Graham	Salford	00.04.68	Irlam T.	**Mansfield T.**	12.88	1988	6	6	1	(F)	
LEMON, Paul A.	Middlesbrough	03.06.66	App	**Sunderland**	05.84	1984-88	91	16	15	(W)	
			L	**Carlisle U.**	12.84	1984	2	0	0		
LENNON, Neil F.	Lurgan (NI)	25.06.71	YTS	**Manchester C.**(YTS)	11.87	1987	1	0	0	(RB)	
LEONARD, Gary A.	Newcastle	28.11.65	App	**West Bromwich A.**	11.83					(M)	
			Tr	**Shrewsbury T.**	07.85	1985-87	48	19	1		
			L	**Hereford U.**	03.88	1987	11	0	1		
			Tr	**Bury**	07.88	1988	4	5	1		
			Tr	**Stockport Co.**	03.89	1988	11	0	1		
LEONARD, Mark A.	St. Helens	27.09.62	Witton Albion	**Everton**	02.82					(F)	
			L	**Tranmere Rov.**	03.83	1982	6	1	0		
			Tr	**Crewe Alex.**	06.83	1983-84	51	3	15		
			Tr	**Stockport Co.**	02.85	1984-86	73	0	23		
			Tr	**Bradford C.**	09.86	1986-88	72	24	20		
LEONARD, Mike C.	Carshalton	09.05.59	Epsom & Ewell	**Halifax T.**	07.76	1976-79	69	0	0	(G)	
			Tr	**Notts Co.**	09.79	1979-88	204	0	0		
			Tr	**Chesterfield**	03.89	1988	16	0	0		
LEVER, Mark	Beverley	29.03.70	YTS	**Grimsby T.**	06.88	1987-88	37	1	2	(CD)	
LEWINGTON, Ray	Lambeth	07.09.56	App	**Chelsea**	02.74	1975-78	80	5	4	(M)	
			Vancouver W.(Canada)	**Wimbledon**	09.79	1979	23	0	0		
			Tr	**Fulham**	03.80	1979-84	172	2	20		
			Tr	**Sheffield U.**	07.85	1985	36	0	0		
			Tr	**Fulham**	07.86	1986-87	56	0	1		
LEWIS, Dudley K.	Swansea	17.11.62	App	**Swansea C.**	11.79	1980-88	228	2	2	(CD)	W Sch Int/W U21-9/W-1
LEWIS, Kevin	Hull	17.10.70	YTS	**Stoke C.**(YTS)	07.87	1987	0	1	0	(D)	
LEWIS, Micky	Birmingham	15.02.65	App	**West Bromwich A.**	02.82	1981-83	22	2	0	(M)	E Yth Int
			Tr	**Derby Co.**	11.84	1984-87	37	6	1		
			Tr	**Oxford U.**	08.88	1988	36	0	0		
LEWORTHY, David J.	Portsmouth	22.10.62	App	**Portsmouth**	09.80	1981	0	1	0	(F)	
			Fareham T.	**Tottenham H.**	08.84	1984-85	8	3	3		
			Tr	**Oxford U.**	12.85	1985-88	25	12	8		
			L	**Shrewsbury T.**	10.87	1987	6	0	3		
LEYDEN, Darren S.	Warley	20.02.70	YTS	**Torquay U.**	07.88	1988	7	2	0	(CD)	
LIGHTFOOT, Chris I.	Warrington	01.04.70	YTS	**Chester C.**	07.88	1987-88	46	6	7	(CD)	

Players Names	Birthplace	Date	Previous Club	League Club	Date Sign'd	Seasons Played	Career Record Apps	Sub	Gls	Pos.	Misc
LILLIS, Jason W.	Chatham	01.10.69	YTS	**Gillingham**	10.87	1987-88	15	14	3	(F)	
LILLIS, Mark A.	Manchester	17.01.60	Manchester C.(Jnr)	**Huddersfield T.**	07.78	1978-84	199	7	56	(F/M)	
			Tr	**Manchester C.**	06.85	1985	39	0	11		
			Tr	**Derby Co.**	08.86	1986-87	6	9	1		
			Tr	**Aston Villa**	09.87	1987-88	30	1	4		
LINEKER, Gary W.	Leicester	30.11.60	App	**Leicester C.**	11.78	1978-84	187	7	95	(F)	E-42/Footballer of Year 1986
			Tr	**Everton**	07.85	1985	41	0	30		to Barcelona(Spain) 7.86
LING, Martin	West Ham	15.07.66	App	**Exeter C.**	01.84	1982-85	109	7	14	(W)	
			Tr	**Swindon T.**	07.86	1986	2	0	0		
			Tr	**Southend U.**	10.86	1986-88	101	9	20		
LINIGHAN, Andy	Hartlepool	18.06.62	Jnrs	**Hartlepool U.**	09.80	1980-83	110	0	4	(CD)	Brother of David
			Tr	**Leeds U.**	05.84	1984-85	66	0	3		
			Tr	**Oldham Ath.**	01.86	1985-87	87	0	6		
			Tr	**Norwich C.**	03.88	1987-88	49	0	6		
LINIGHAN, David	Hartlepool	09.01.65	Jnrs	**Hartlepool U.**	03.82	1981-85	84	7	5	(CD)	Brother of Andy
			Tr	**Derby Co.**	08.86						
			Tr	**Shrewsbury T.**	12.86	1986-87	65	0	2		
			Tr	**Ipswich T.**	06.88	1988	40	1	2		
LISTER, Steve H.	Doncaster	18.11.61	App	**Doncaster Rov.**	05.79	1978-84	229	8	30	(M/CD)	
			Tr	**Scunthorpe U.**	07.85	1985-88	148	2	28		
LITCHFIELD, Peter	Manchester	27.07.56	Droylsden	**Preston N.E.**	01.79	1980-84	107	0	0	(G)	
			Tr	**Bradford C.**	07.85	1985-88	88	0	0		
			L	**Oldham Ath.**	10.88	1988	3	0	0		
LIVINGSTONE, Stephen	Middlesbrough	08.09.68	YTS	**Coventry C.**	07.86	1986-88	5	3	0	(F)	
LLEWELLYN, Andy D.	Bristol	22.02.66	App	**Bristol C.**	02.84	1982-88	144	12	3	(FB)	E Yth Int
LLOYD, Philip R.	Hemsworth	26.12.64	App	**Middlesbrough**	12.82					(CD)	
			Tr	**Barnsley**(N/C)	09.83						
			Tr	**Darlington**	03.84	1983-86	127	0	3		
			Tr	**Torquay U.**	08.87	1987-88	92	0	6		
LOCKER, Stephen	Ashington	05.11.70	Nottingham F. (YTS)	**Hartlepool U.**(YTS)	09.88	1988	0	1	0		
LOGAN, David	Middlesbrough	05.12.63	Whitby T.	**Mansfield T.**	06.84	1984-86	67	0	1	(LB)	
			Tr	**Northampton T.**	02.87	1986-87	39	2	1		
			Tr	**Halifax T.**	08.88	1988	3	0	0		
			Tr	**Stockport Co.**	10.88	1988	35	0	0		
LOMAX, Geoff W.	Droylsden	06.07.64	Jnrs	**Manchester C.**	07.81	1982-84	23	2	1	(D)	
			L	**Wolverhampton W.**	10.85	1985	5	0	0		
			Tr	**Carlisle U.**	12.85	1985-86	37	0	0		
			Tr	**Rochdale**	07.87	1987-88	70	1	0		
LONGDEN, D. Paul	Wakefield	28.09.62	App	**Barnsley**	09.80	1981-82	5	0	0	(LB)	
			Tr	**Scunthorpe U.**	08.83	1983-88	213	2	0		
LONGHURST, David J.	Northampton	15.01.65	App	**Nottingham F.**	01.83					(F)	
			Tr	**Halifax T.**	07.85	1985-86	85	0	24		
			Tr	**Northampton T.**	06.87	1987-88	34	3	7		
			Tr	**Peterborough U.**	10.88	1988	37	0	7		
LORAM, Mark J.	Paignton	13.08.67	Brixham Villa	**Torquay U.**	01.85	1984-85	50	2	8	(F)	
			Tr	**Q.P.R.**	05.86						
			Tr	**Torquay U.**	03.87	1986-88	85	10	17		
LORMOR, Anthony	Ashington	29.10.70	YTS	**Newcastle U.**	02.88	1987-88	6	2	3	(F)	
LOVE, Ian J.	Cardiff	01.03.58	Barry T.	**Swansea C.**	08.86	1986-88	33	8	9	(F)	
			Tr	**Torquay U.**	03.89	1988	8	1	0		
LOVELL, Steve J.	Swansea	16.07.60	App	**Crystal Palace**	08.77	1980-82	68	6	3	(F)	W Sch Int/W-6
			L	**Stockport Co.**	10.79	1979	12	0	0		
			Tr	**Millwall**	03.83	1982-85	143	3	44		
			L	**Swansea C.**	02.87	1986	2	0	1		
			Tr	**Gillingham**	02.87	1986-88	89	2	40		
LOWE, David A.	Liverpool	30.08.65	App	**Wigan Ath.**	06.83	1982-86	179	9	40	(RW)	E Yth Int/E U21-2
			Tr	**Ipswich T.**	06.87	1987-88	71	2	23		
LOWERY, A.W. (Tony)	Wallsend	06.07.61	Ashington	**West Bromwich A.**	03.81	1981	1	0	0	(M)	
			L	**Walsall**	02.82	1981	4	2	1		
			Tr	**Mansfield T.**	04.83	1982-88	230	0	20		
LOWNDES, Steve R.	Cwmbran	17.06.60	Jnrs	**Newport Co.**	10.77	1977-82	200	8	39	(W)	W U21-4/W-10
			Tr	**Millwall**	08.83	1983-85	95	1	16		
			Tr	**Barnsley**	08.86	1986-88	88	4	16		
LUCKETTI, Chris J.	Littleborough	28.09.71	YTS	**Rochdale**(YTS)	07.88	1988	1	0	0	(CD)	
LUKE, Noel E.	Birmingham	28.12.64	App	**West Bromwich A.**	04.82	1982-83	8	1	1	(W)	
			Tr	**Mansfield T.**	07.84	1984-85	41	9	9		
			Tr	**Peterborough U.**	08.86	1986-88	118	0	21		
LUKIC, John	Chesterfield	11.12.60	App	**Leeds U.**	12.78	1979-82	146	0	0	(G)	E Yth Int/E U21-7
			Tr	**Arsenal**	07.83	1983-88	185	0	0		
LUND, Gary J.	Grimsby	13.09.64	Jnrs	**Grimsby T.**	07.83	1983-85	47	13	24	(F)	E Yth Int/E U21-3
			Tr	**Lincoln C.**	08.86	1986	41	3	13		
			Tr	**Notts. Co.**	06.87	1987-88	69	13	28		
LUNDON, Sean	Liverpool	07.03.69	YTS	**Chester C.**	12.86	1986-88	39	1	2	(FB/W)	
LYNCH, Tommy	Limerick (Ire)	10.10.64	Limerick C.	**Sunderland**	08.88	1988	4	0	0	(M/LB)	
LYNEX, Steve C.	West Bromwich	23.01.58	App	**West Bromwich A.**	01.76					(W)	
			Shamrock Rov.	**Birmingham C.**	04.79	1978-80	28	18	10		
			Tr	**Leicester C.**	02.81	1980-86	200	13	57		
			L	**Birmingham C.**	10.86	1986	10	0	2		
			Tr	**West Bromwich A.**	03.87	1986-87	26	3	3		
			Tr	**Cardiff C.**	07.88	1988	34	2	0		
McALISTER, TOM G.	Clydebank	10.12.52	App	**Sheffield U.**	05.70	1971-75	63	0	0	(G)	
			Tr	**Rotherham U.**	01.76	1975-78	159	0	0		
			Tr	**Blackpool**	07.79	1979	16	0	0		
			Tr	**Swindon T.**	05.80	1980	1	0	0		
			L	**Bristol Rov.**	02.81	1980	13	0	0		
			Tr	**West Ham U.**	05.81	1981-88	85	0	0		
			L	**Colchester U.**	02.89	1988	20	0	0		
McALLISTER, Gary	Motherwell	25.12.64	Motherwell	**Leicester C.**	08.85	1985-88	156	2	36	(M)	

Joe McLaughlin (Chelsea) Match Magazine

Players Names	Birthplace	Date	Previous Club	League Club	Date Sign'd	Seasons Played	Career Record Apps	Sub	Gls	Pos.	Misc
McALLISTER, Kevin	Falkirk	08.11.62	Falkirk	**Chelsea**	05.85	1985-88	52	17	6	(W)	
McANDREW, A. (Tony)	Glasgow	11.04.56	App	**Middlesbrough**	08.73	1973-81	245	2	13	(CD)	
			Tr	**Chelsea**	09.82	1982-83	20	0	4		
			Tr	**Middlesbrough**	09.84	1984-85	66	0	2		
			Retired	**Darlington**	11.88	1988	11	0	0		
			Tr	**Hartlepool U.**	03.89	1988	4	0	0		
McATEER, Andy W.	Preston	24.04.61	App	**Preston N.E.**	04.79	1979-86	236	2	8	(LB)	
			Tr	**Blackpool**	12.86	1986-87	37	4	0		
			Tr	**Preston N.E.**	05.88	1988	11	2	1		
McAUGHTRIE, David	Cumnock	30.01.63	App	**Stoke C.**	01.81	1980-83	48	3	1	(CD)	
			Tr	**Carlisle U.**	07.84	1984	28	0	1		
			Tr	**York C.**	06.85	1985-86	64	0	1		
			Tr	**Darlington**	07.87	1987-88	36	3	0		
McAVENNIE, Frank	Glasgow	22.11.59	St. Mirren	**West Ham U.**	06.85	1985-87	85	0	33	(F)	S U21-5/S-5
			Glasgow Celtic	**West Ham U.**	03.89	1988	8	1	0		
McCALL, Steve H.	Carlisle	15.10.60	App	**Ipswich T.**	10.78	1979-86	249	8	7	(LB)	E Yth Int/E U21-6
			Tr	**Sheffield Wed.**	06.87	1987-88	7	0	0		
McCALL, Stuart M.	Leeds	10.06.64	App	**Bradford C.**	06.82	1982-87	235	3	37	(M)	E Yth Int/S U21-1/Son of Andy
			Tr	**Everton**	06.88	1988	29	4	0		
McCARRICK, Mark B.	Liverpool	04.02.62	Witton Albion	**Birmingham C.**	05.83	1983	12	3	0	(FB)	
			Tr	**Lincoln C.**	07.84	1984-85	42	2	0		
			Tr	**Crewe Alex**(N/C)	02.86	1985	10	1	0		
			Runcorn	**Tranmere Rov.**	08.87	1987-88	82	0	8		
McCARTHY, Mike J.	Barnsley	07.02.59	App	**Barnsley**	07.77	1977-83	272	0	7	(CD)	IR-36
			Tr	**Manchester C.**	12.83	1983-86	140	0	2		to Glasgow Celtic 5.87
McCARTHY, Sean C.	Bridgend	12.09.65	Bridgend T.	**Swansea C.**	10.85	1985-87	76	15	25	(F)	
			Tr	**Plymouth Arg.**	08.88	1988	37	1	8		
McCLAIR, Brian J.	Bellshill	08.12.63	Glasgow Celtic	**Manchester U.**	07.87	1987-88	78	0	34	(F)	S U21-8/S-10
McCLAREN, Steve	York	03.05.61	App	**Hull C.**	04.79	1979-84	171	7	16	(M)	
			Tr	**Derby Co.**	08.85	1985-87	23	2	0		
			L	**Lincoln C.**	02.87	1986	8	0	0		
			Tr	**Bristol C.**	02.88	1987-88	60	1	2		
McCLEAN, Christian A.	Colchester	17.10.63	Clacton T.	**Bristol Rov.**	03.88	1987-88	18	16	2	(F)	
McCLELLAND, John	Belfast	07.12.55	Portadown	**Cardiff C.**	02.74	1974	1	3	1	(CD)	NI-52
			Bangor City	**Mansfield T.**	05.78	1978-80	122	3	8		
			Glasgow Rangers	**Watford**	11.84	1984-88	184	0	3		
McCORD, Brian J.	Derby	24.08.68	App	**Derby Co.**	06.87	1987	1	0	0	(M)	
McCREERY, David	Belfast	16.09.57	App	**Manchester U.**	10.74	1974-78	48	38	7	(M)	NI Sch Int/NI U21-1/NI-63
			Tr	**Q.P.R.**	08.79	1979-80	56	1	4		
			Tulsa R.(USA)	**Newcastle U.**	10.82	1982-88	237	6	2		
McDERMOTT, Brian J.	Slough	08.04.61	App	**Arsenal**	02.79	1978-83	38	23	12	(F)	E Yth Int
			L	**Fulham**	03.83	1982	0	3	0		
			Tr	**Oxford U.**	12.84	1984-86	16	8	2		
			L	**Huddersfield T.**	10.86	1986	4	0	1		
			Tr	**Cardiff C.**	08.87	1987-88	49	2	8		
			Tr	**Exeter C.**	02.89	1988	19	0	1		
McDERMOTT, John	Middlesbrough	03.02.69	YTS	**Grimsby T.**	06.87	1986-88	70	9	1	(RB/M)	
McDONALD, Alan	Belfast	12.10.63	App	**Q.P.R.**	08.81	1983-88	164	4	8	(CD)	NI Yth Int/NI-22
			L	**Charlton Ath.**	03.83	1982	9	0	0		
MacDONALD, Gary	Middlesbrough	26.03.62	App	**Middlesbrough**	03.80	1980-83	40	13	5	(F)	
			Tr	**Carlisle U.**	07.84	1984	7	2	0		
			Tr	**Darlington**	10.84	1984-88	153	9	35		
McDONALD, Gavin J.	Salford	06.10.70	YTS	**Chesterfield** (YTS)	08.87	1988	5	7	1	(F)	
McDONALD, Ian C.	Barrow	10.05.53	App	**Barrow**	05.71	1970-71	30	5	2	(M)	
			Tr	**Workington**	02.73	1972-73	42	0	4		
			Tr	**Liverpool**	01.74						
			L	**Colchester U.**	02.75	1974	5	0	2		
			Tr	**Mansfield T.**	07.75	1975-76	47	9	4		
			Tr	**York C.**	11.77	1977-81	175	0	29		
			Tr	**Aldershot**	11.81	1981-88	340	0	49		
MacDONALD, John	Glasgow	15.04.61	Glasgow Rangers	**Charlton Ath.**	09.86	1986	2	0	0	(F)	S Sch Int/S Yth Int/SU21-8
			Tr	**Barnsley**	11.86	1986-88	84	6	19		
MacDONALD, Kevin D.	Inverness	22.12.60	Inverness Caledonian	**Leicester C.**	05.80	1980-84	133	5	8	(M)	
			Tr	**Liverpool**	11.84	1984-88	29	11	1		
			L	**Leicester C.**	12.87	1987	3	0	0		
McDONALD, Neil R.	Wallsend	02.11.65	App	**Newcastle U.**	02.83	1982-87	163	17	24	(RB)	E Sch Int/E Yth Int/EU21-5
			Tr	**Everton**	08.88	1988	22	3	1		
McDONALD, Robert R.	Hull	22.01.59	App	**Hull C.**	01.77	1976-79	17	8	2	(F)	
			PSV Eindhoven (Neth)	**Newcastle U.**	11.88	1988	6	4	1		
McDONOUGH, Darren K.	Belgium	07.11.62	App	**Oldham Ath.**	01.80	1980-86	178	5	14	(M)	
			Tr	**Luton T.**	09.86	1986-88	43	12	5		
McDONOUGH, Roy	Solihull	16.10.58	App	**Birmingham C.**	10.76	1976	2	0	1	(F)	
			Tr	**Walsall**	09.78	1978-80	76	6	15		
			Tr	**Chelsea**	10.80						
			Tr	**Colchester U.**	02.81	1980-82	89	4	24		
			Tr	**Southend U.**	08.83	1983	22	0	4		
			Tr	**Exeter C.**	01.84	1983-84	19	1	1		
			Tr	**Cambridge U.**	10.84	1984	30	2	5		
			Tr	**Southend U.**	08.85	1985-88	136	17	25		
McELHINNEY, Gerry A.	Derry (NI)	19.09.56	Distillery	**Bolton W.**	09.80	1980-84	107	2	2	(CD)	
			L	**Rochdale**	11.82	1982	20	0	1		
			Tr	**Plymouth Arg.**	01.85	1984-87	90	1	2		
			Tr	**Peterborough U.**	08.88	1988	33	0	1		
McEWAN, Stan	Wishaw	08.06.57	App	**Blackpool**	07.74	1974-81	204	10	24	(CD)	Brother of Billy
			Tr	**Exeter C.**	07.82	1982-83	65	0	15		
			Tr	**Hull C.**	03.84	1983-87	113	0	25		
			Tr	**Wigan Ath.**	12.87	1987-88	26	3	4		

Players Names	Birthplace	Date	Previous Club	League Club	Date Sign'd	Seasons Played	Career Record Apps	Sub	Gls	Pos.	Misc
McGARVEY, Scott T.	Glasgow	22.04.63	App	**Manchester U.**	04.80	1980-82	13	12	3	(F)	S-U21-4
			L	**Wolverhampton W.**	03.84	1983	13	0	2		
			Tr	**Portsmouth**	07.84	1984-85	17	6	6		
			L	**Carlisle U.**	01.86	1985	10	0	3		
			Tr	**Carlisle U.**	07.86	1986	25	0	8		
			Tr	**Grimsby T.**	03.87	1986-87	49	1	7		
			Tr	**Bristol C.**	09.88	1988	20	6	9		
McGEE, Paul	Dublin	17.05.68	Bohemians	**Colchester U.**	02.89	1988	3	0	0	(W)	
			Tr	**Wimbledon**	03.89	1988	1	0	1		
McGEENEY, Paddy M.	Sheffield	31.10.66	App	**Sheffield U.**	10.84	1984-85	15	1	0	(M)	
			L	**Rochdale**	11.86	1986	3	0	0		
			Tr	**Chesterfield**	08.87	1987-88	45	4	1		
McGINLAY, John	Inverness	08.04.64	Elgin C.	**Shrewsbury T.**	02.89	1988	14	2	5	(F)	
McGINLEY, John	Rowlands Gill	11.06.59	Gateshead	**Sunderland**	01.82	1981	3	0	0	(LW)	
			Charleroi (Bel.)	**Lincoln C.**	09.84	1984-86	69	2	11		
			Tr	**Rotherham U.**	09.86	1986	1	2	0		
			L	**Hartlepool U.**	01.87	1986	2	0	0		
			Tr	**Lincoln C.**	01.87	1986-88	36	5	7		
McGOLDRICK, Eddie J.P.	Corby	30.04.65	Nuneaton Bor.	**Northampton T.**	08.86	1986-88	97	10	9	(W)	
			Tr	**Crystal Palace**	01.89	1988	20	1	0		
McGRATH, Lloyd A.	Birmingham	24.02.65	App	**Coventry C.**	12.82	1983-88	108	3	3	(M)	E Yth Int/E U21-1
McGRATH, Paul	Ealing	04.12.59	St. Patricks Ath.	**Manchester U.**	04.82	1982-88	159	4	12	(CD)	IR-31
McGRORY, Shaun P.	Coventry	29.02.68	YTS	**Coventry C.**	07.86					(FB)	
			Tr	**Burnley**	07.87	1987-88	28	7	2		
McGUGAN, Paul J.	Glasgow	17.07.64	Glasgow Celtic	**Barnsley**	10.87	1987-88	47	2	2	(CD)	
McGUIRE, Doug J.	Bathgate	06.09.67	Glasgow Celtic (L)	**Sunderland**	03.88	1987	1	0	0	(M)	
			Glasgow Celtic	**Coventry C.**	08.88						
McILROY, Sammy B.	Belfast	02.08.54	App	**Manchester U.**	08.71	1971-81	320	22	57	(M)	NI-88
			Tr	**Stoke C.**	02.82	1981-84	132	1	14		
			Tr	**Manchester C.**	08.85	1985	12	0	1		
			Orgryte(Swe.)	**Manchester C.**	11.86	1986	1	0	0		
			Tr	**Bury**	03.87	1986-87	43	0	6		
			Madling(Austria)	**Bury**	08.88	1988	45	0	2		
McINALLY, Alan B.	Ayr	10.02.63	Glasgow Celtic	**Aston Villa**	07.87	1987-88	50	8	18	(F)	S-2
McINERNEY, Ian D.	Liverpool	26.01.64	Newcastle Blue Star	**Huddersfield T.**	08.88	1988	5	5	1	(W)	
McINTYRE, Joseph G.	Manchester	19.06.71	Port Vale (YTS)	**Rochdale** (YTS)	10.88	1988	2	2	0	(LB)	
McJANNET, W. Les	Cumnock	02.08.61	Jnrs	**Mansfield T.**	08.79	1979-81	73	1	0	(RB)	
			Matlock T.	**Scarborough**	08.87	1987-88	29	5	0		
			Tr	**Darlington**	12.88	1988	26	0	1		
McKELLAR, David N.	Irvine	22.05.56	App	**Ipswich T.**	03.74					(G)	
			Ardrossan Winton R.	**Derby Co.**	04.78	1978-79	41	0	0		
			Tr	**Brentford**	09.80	1980-81	84	0	0		
			Tr	**Carlisle U.**	08.83	1983-84	82	0	0		
			Hibernian	**Newcastle U.**	02.86	1985	10	0	0		
			Dunfermline Ath.(L)	**Hartlepool U.**	08.88	1988	5	0	0		
			Dunfermline Ath.	**Carlisle U.**	10.88	1988	34	0	0		
McKENNA, Ken M.	Birkenhead	02.07.60		**Tranmere Rov.**(N/C)	08.82	1982	2	2	0	(F)	
			Telford U.	**Tranmere Rov.**	08.87	1987-88	13	2	3		
McKENZIE, Ian E.	Wallsend	22.08.66	Newcastle U.(App)	**Barnsley**(N/C)	08.85	1985	1	0	0	(LB)	
			Tr	**Stockport Co.**	09.86	1986-88	51	8	0		
MACKENZIE, Steve	Romford	23.11.61	App	**Crystal Palace**	07.79					(M)	E Yth Int/E U21-3/E-'B'
			Tr	**Manchester C.**	07.79	1979-80	56	2	8		
			Tr	**West Bromwich A.**	08.81	1981-86	153	3	23		
			Tr	**Charlton Ath.**	08.87	1987-88	66	2	5		
McKERNON, Craig A.	Gloucester	23.02.68	App	**Mansfield T.**	02.86	1984-88	72	15	0	(M/RB)	
McKINNON, Robert	Glasgow	31.07.66	Rutherglen Glencairn	**Newcastle U.**	11.84	1985	1	0	0	(LB)	
			Tr	**Hartlepool U.**	07.86	1986-88	132	1	4		
McKNIGHT, Allen	Antrim (NI)	27.01.64	Glasgow Celtic	**West Ham U.**	07.88	1988	23	0	0	(G)	NI-10
MacLAREN, Ross	Edinburgh	14.04.62	Glasgow Rgrs (Jnrs)	**Shrewsbury T.**	08.80	1980-84	158	3	18	(CD)	
			Tr	**Derby Co.**	07.85	1985-87	113	9	4		
			Tr	**Swindon T.**	08.88	1988	37	0	4		
McLAUGHLIN, Joe	Greenock	02.06.60	Morton	**Chelsea**	06.83	1983-88	220	0	5	(CD)	S U21-10
McLEARY, Alan T.	Lambeth	06.10.64	App	**Millwall**	10.81	1982-88	186	14	5	(CD)	E Yth Int/E U21-1/E-'B'
McLOUGHLIN, Alan F.	Manchester	20.04.67	App	**Manchester U.**	04.85					(M)	
			Tr	**Swindon T.**	08.86	1986-88	40	3	3		
			L	**Torquay U.**	03.87	1986-87	21	3	4		
McLOUGHLIN, Paul B.	Bristol	23.12.63	Gisborne C.(NZ)	**Cardiff C.**	12.84	1984-85	40	9	4	(W)	
			Bristol C.(N/C)	**Hereford U.**	06.87	1987-88	72	2	14		
McMAHON, Steve	Liverpool	20.08.61	App	**Everton**	08.79	1980-82	99	1	11	(M)	E U21-6/E-5
			Tr	**Aston Villa**	05.83	1983-85	74	1	7		
			Tr	**Liverpool**	09.85	1985-88	128	1	23		
McMILLAN, L. Andy	South Africa	22.06.68	Hull C.(N/C)	**York C.**	10.87	1987-88	20	4	0	(FB)	
McMINN, Kevin (Ted)	Castle Douglas	28.09.62	Seville (Spain)	**Derby Co.**	02.88	1987-88	39	0	5	(W)	ex Glasgow Rangers
McNAB, Neil	Greenock	04.06.57	Morton	**Tottenham H.**	02.74	1973-78	63	9	3	(M)	S Sch Int/S U21-1
			Tr	**Bolton W.**	11.78	1978-79	33	2	4		
			Tr	**Brighton & H.A.**	02.80	1979-82	100	3	4		
			L	**Leeds U.**	12.82	1982	5	0	0		
			Tr	**Manchester C.**	07.83	1983-88	205	4	16		
McNALLY, Bernard A.	Shrewsbury	17.02.63	App	**Shrewsbury T.**	02.81	1980-88	278	4	23	(M)	NI-5
McNICHOL, Jim A.	Glasgow	09.06.58	Ipswich T.(App)	**Luton T.**	07.76	1976-78	13	2	0	(CD)	S U21-7
			Tr	**Brentford**	10.78	1978-83	151	4	22		
			Tr	**Exeter C.**	07.84	1984-85	87	0	10		
			Tr	**Torquay U.**	07.86	1986-88	124	0	13		
McPARLAND, Ian J.	Edinburgh	04.10.61	Ormiston Primrose	**Notts Co.**	12.80	1980-88	190	31	69	(F)	
			Tr	**Hull C.**	03.89	1988	11	0	1		

Neil McNab (Manchester City) Match Magazine

Lawrie Madden (Sheffield Wednesday) Match Magazine

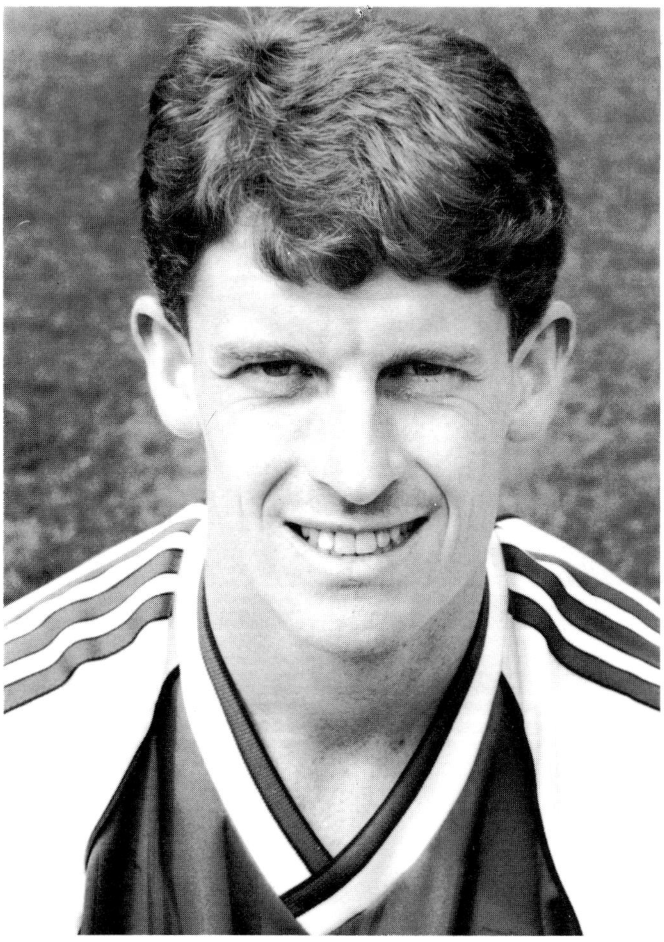

Brian Marwood (Arsenal & England) Match Magazine

Dave Mehmet (Maidstone United) Match Magazine

Players Names	Birthplace	Date	Previous Club	League Club	Date Sign'd	Seasons Played	Career Record Apps	Sub	Gls	Pos.	Misc
MacPHAIL, John	Dundee	07.12.55	Dundee	**Sheffield U.**	01.79	1979-82	135	0	7	(CD)	
			Tr	**York C.**	02.83	1982-85	141	1	24		
			Tr	**Bristol C.**	07.86	1986	26	0	1		
			Tr	**Sunderland**	07.87	1987-88	91	0	20		
McPHERSON, Keith A.	Greenwich	11.09.63	App	**West Ham U.**	09.81	1984	1	0	0	(CD)	
			L	**Cambridge U.**	09.85	1985	11	0	1		
			Tr	**Northampton T.**	01.86	1985-88	139	0	7		
McPHILLIPS, Terry	Manchester	01.10.68	Liverpool(YTS)	**Halifax T.**	09.87	1987-88	48	18	26	(F)	
McQUEEN, Tommy F.	Bellshill	01.04.63	Aberdeen	**West Ham U.**	03.87	1986-88	19	4	0	(LB)	
McSTAY, Willie	Hamilton	26.11.61	Glasgow Celtic	**Huddersfield T.**	03.87	1986-87	4	5	0	(D)	Brother of Paul
			Tr	**Notts Co.**	02.88	1987-88	33	9	1		(Celtic & Scotland)
MABBUTT, Gary V.	Bristol	23.08.61	App	**Bristol Rov.**	01.79	1978-81	122	9	10	(CD)	E Yth Int/E-13/E-'B'/EU21-5/
			Tr	**Tottenham H.**	08.82	1982-88	215	13	21		Son of Ray/Brother of Kevin
MACOWAT, Ian S.	Liverpool	19.11.65	App	**Everton**	11.83					(LB)	E Sch Int/E Yth Int
			Tr	**Gillingham**	01.85	1984-85	4	1	0		
			Tr	**Crewe Alex.**	07.86	1986-88	64	8	1		
MADDEN, Craig	Manchester	25.09.58	Northern Nomads	**Bury**	03.78	1977-85	278	19	129	(F)	
			Tr	**West Bromwich A.**	03.86	1985-86	10	2	3		
			Tr	**Blackpool**	02.87	1986-88	64	16	20		
MADDEN, David J.	Stepney	06.01.63	App	**Southampton**	01.81					(M)	
			L	**Bournemouth**	01.83	1982	5	0	0		
			Tr	**Arsenal**	08.83	1983	2	0	0		
			Tr	**Charlton Ath.**	06.84	1984	19	1	1		
			Los Angeles(USA)	**Reading**	11.87	1987	7	2	1		
			Tr	**Crystal Palace**	08.88	1988	17	2	5		
MADDEN, Lawrie D.	Hackney	28.09.55	Arsenal (N/C)	**Mansfield T.**(N/C)	03.75	1974-75	9	1	0	(CD)	
			Manchester Univ.	**Charlton Ath.**	03.78	1977-81	109	4	7		
			Tr	**Millwall**	03.82	1981-82	44	3	2		
			Tr	**Sheffield Wed.**	08.83	1983-88	191	1	2		
MADDISON, Neil S.	Darlington	02.10.69	YTS	**Southampton**	04.88	1988	3	2	2	(M)	
MADDIX, Danny S.	Ashford	11.10.67	App	**Tottenham H.**	07.85					(CD)	
			Tr	**Southend U.**	10.86	1986	2	0	0		
			Tr	**Q.P.R.**	07.87	1987-88	34	8	2		
MADDY, Paul M.	Cwmcarn	17.08.62	App	**Cardiff C.**	08.80	1980-82	35	8	3	(LM)	W U21-1
			L	**Hereford U.**	03.83	1982	9	0	1		
			Tr	**Swansea C.**	08.83	1983	18	2	3		
			Tr	**Hereford U.**	03.84	1983-85	75	2	16		
			Tr	**Brentford**	07.86	1986	29	2	5		
			Tr	**Chester C.**	07.87	1987	17	1	1		
			Tr	**Hereford U.**	03.88	1987-88	27	8	1		
MADRICK, Carl J.	Bolton	20.09.68	YTS	**Huddersfield T.**	06.87	1987	3	5	1	(F)	
			Tr	**Peterborough U.**	09.88	1988	3	5	0		
MAGUIRE, Gavin T.	Hammersmith	24.11.67	App	**Q.P.R.**	10.85	1986-88	33	7	0	(CD)	
			Tr	**Portsmouth**	12.88	1988	18	0	0		
MAGUIRE, Peter J.	Holmfirth	11.09.69	YTS	**Leeds U.**	07.88	1987	2	0	0	(F)	
MAIL, David	Bristol	12.09.62	App	**Aston Villa**	07.80					(CD)	
			Tr	**Blackburn Rov.**	01.82	1982-88	175	6	2		
MAIORANA, Guiliano	Cambridge	18.04.69	Histon	**Manchester U.**	11.88	1988	2	4	0	(LW)	
MALCOLM, Paul A.	Felling	11.12.64	App	**Newcastle U.**	12.82					(G)	
			Durham C.	**Rochdale**	09.84	1984	24	0	0		
			Tr	**Shrewsbury T.**	07.85						
			Tr	**Barnsley**	08.86	1986	3	0	0		
			Tr	**Doncaster Rov.**	07.88	1988	34	0	0		
MALKIN, Chris G.	Hoylake	04.06.67	Stork	**Tranmere Rov.**	07.87	1987-88	9	16	4	(F)	
MANUEL, W.A.J. (Billy)	Hackney	28.06.69	App	**Tottenham H.**	06.87					(M)	
			Tr	**Gillingham**	02.89	1988	13	4	1		
MARDENBOROUGH, Steve A.	Birmingham	11.09.64	App	**Coventry C.**	08.82					(F)	
			Tr	**Wolverhampton W.**	09.83	1983	9	0	1		
			L	**Cambridge U.**	02.84	1983	6	0	0		
			Tr	**Swansea C.**	07.84	1984	32	4	7		
			Tr	**Newport Co.**	07.85	1985-86	50	14	11		
			Tr	**Cardiff C.**	03.87	1986-87	18	14	1		
			Tr	**Hereford U.**	07.88	1988	20	7	0		
MARDON, Paul J.	Bristol	14.09.69	YTS	**Bristol C.**	01.88	1987-88	21	7	0	(CD)	
MARKER, Nick R.T.	Budleigh Salterton	03.05.65	App	**Exeter C.**	05.83	1981-87	196	6	3	(CD)	
			Tr	**Plymouth Arg.**	10.87	1987-88	68	1	7		
MARKS, Michael D.	Lambeth	23.03.68	App	**Millwall**	07.86	1986	36	0	10	(F)	
			L	**Mansfield T.**	01.88	1987	0	1	0		
			Tr	**Leyton Orient**	02.88	1987	3	0	0		
MARPLES, Chris	Chesterfield	03.08.64	Goole T.	**Chesterfield**	03.84	1984-86	84	0	0	(G)	Derbyshire Cricketer
			Tr	**Stockport Co.**	03.87	1986-87	57	0	0		
			Tr	**York C.**	07.88	1988	45	0	0		
MARSDEN, Chris	Sheffield	03.01.69	App	**Sheffield U.**	01.87	1987	13	3	1	(M)	
			Tr	**Huddersfield T.**	07.88	1988	10	4	1		
MARSH, Chris J.	Sedgley	14.01.70	YTS	**Walsall**	07.88	1987-88	3	13	0	(M)	
MARSH, Ian J.	Swansea	27.10.69	YTS	**Swansea C.**	07.88	1987	1	0	0	(LB)	
MARSH, Michael A.	Liverpool	21.07.69	Kirkby T.	**Liverpool**	08.87	1988	0	1	0	(F)	
MARSHALL, Colin	Glasgow	06.11.69	YTS	**Barnsley**	04.88	1988	0	1	0	(F)	
MARSHALL, Gary	Bristol	20.04.64	Shepton Mallet	**Bristol C.**	07.83	1983-87	48	20	7	(W)	
			L	**Torquay U.**	12.84	1984	7	0	1		
			Tr	**Carlisle U.**	07.88	1988	18	3	2		
MARSHALL, Ian P.	Oxford	20.03.66	App	**Everton**	03.84	1985-87	9	6	0	(CD)	
			Tr	**Oldham Ath.**	03.88	1987-88	51	0	4		
MARSHALL, John P.	Balham	18.08.64	App	**Fulham**	08.82	1983-88	184	10	17	(W/RB)	
MARTIN, Alvin E.	Bootle	29.07.58	App	**West Ham U.**	07.76	1977-88	341	2	23	(CD)	E Yth Int/E-17/E 'B'

Players Names	Birthplace	Date	Previous Club	League Club	Date Sign'd	Seasons Played	Career Record Apps	Sub	Gls	Pos.	Misc
MARTIN, David	East Ham	25.04.63	App	**Millwall**	05.80	1979-84	131	9	6	(D)	E Yth Int
			Tr	**Wimbledon**	09.84	1984-85	30	5	3		
			Tr	**Southend U.**	08.86	1986-88	103	7	4		
MARTIN, Dean	Halifax	09.09.67	App	**Halifax T.**	09.85	1986-88	86	2	6	(M)	
MARTIN, Lee A.	Hyde	05.02.68	YTS	**Manchester U.**	05.86	1987-88	20	5	1	(FB)	
MARTIN, Lee B.	Huddersfield	09.09.68	YTS	**Huddersfield T.**	06.87	1987	18	0	0	(G)	
MARTINDALE, David	Liverpool	09.04.64	Caernarfon T.	**Tranmere Rov.**	07.87	1987-88	54	12	5	(M)	
MARTYN, A. Nigel	St. Austell	11.08.66	St. Blazey	**Bristol Rov.**	08.87	1987-88	85	0	0	(G)	E U21-6
MARWOOD, Brian	Seaham	05.02.60	App	**Hull C.**	02.78	1979-83	154	4	51	(W)	E-1
			Tr	**Sheffield Wed.**	08.84	1984-87	125	3	27		
			Tr	**Arsenal**	03.88	1987-88	35	0	10		
MASKELL, Craig D.	Aldershot	10.04.68	App	**Southampton**	04.86	1985-86	2	4	1	(F)	
			Tr	**Huddersfield T.**	05.88	1988	46	0	28		
MATTHEWS, David	Hackney	20.11.65	App	**West Ham U.**	11.82					(F)	Son of Terry
			Basildon U.	**Walsall**	11.87						
			Tr	**Southend U.**	03.88	1988	1	5	0		
MATTHEWS, John M.	Camden	01.11.55	App	**Arsenal**	08.73	1974-77	38	7	2	(M)	
			Tr	**Sheffield U.**	08.78	1978-81	98	5	14		
			Tr	**Mansfield T.**	08.82	1982-83	70	2	6		
			Tr	**Chesterfield**	08.84	1984	38	0	1		
			Tr	**Plymouth Arg.**	08.85	1985-88	131	4	4		
MATTHEWS, Mike	Hull	25.09.60	App	**Wolverhampton W.**	10.78	1980-83	72	4	7	(M)	
			Tr	**Scunthorpe U.**	02.84	1983-85	56	2	5		
			North Ferriby U.	**Halifax T.**	09.86	1986-88	98	1	8		
			Tr	**Scarborough**	12.88	1988	7	0	1		
			Tr	**Stockport Co.**	02.89	1988	19	0	1		
MATTHEWS, Neil	Grimsby	19.09.66	App	**Grimsby T.**	09.84	1984-86	9	2	1	(F)	N I U21-1
			L	**Scunthorpe U.**	11.85	1985	1	0	0		
			L	**Halifax T.**	10.86	1986	9	0	2		
			L	**Bolton W.**	03.87	1986	1	0	0		
			Tr	**Halifax T.**	08.87	1987-88	61	5	17		
MATTHEWS, Neil P.	Manchester	03.12.67	App	**Blackpool**	12.85	1985-88	59	5	1	(RB)	
MATTHEWSON, Trevor	Sheffield	12.02.63	App	**Sheffield Wed.**	02.81	1980-82	3	0	0	(CD)	Nephew of Reg
			Tr	**Newport Co.**	10.83	1983-84	73	2	0		
			Tr	**Stockport Co.**	09.85	1985-86	79	1	0		
			Tr	**Lincoln C.**	(N/L)	1988	43	0	2		
MAUCHLEN, Alistair	Kilwinning	29.06.60	Motherwell	**Leicester C.**	08.85	1985-88	136	5	8	(M)	
MAUGE, Ronald C.	Islington	10.03.69	YTS	**Charlton Ath.**	07.87					(W)	
			Tr	**Fulham**	09.88	1988	12	1	0		
MAY, Andy M.	Bury	26.01.64	App	**Manchester C.**	01.82	1980-86	141	9	8	(M)	E U21-1
			Tr	**Huddersfield T.**	07.87	1987-88	72	1	5		
			L	**Bolton W.**	03.88	1987	9	1	2		
MAY, David	Oldham	24.06.70	YTS	**Blackburn Rov.**	06.88	1988	1	0	0	(CD)	
MAY, Larry C.	Sutton Coldfield	26.12.58	App	**Leicester C.**	12.76	1976-82	180	7	12	(CD)	
			Tr	**Barnsley**	09.83	1983-86	122	0	3		
			Tr	**Sheffield Wed.**	02.87	1986-87	30	1	1		
			Tr	**Brighton & H.A.**	09.88	1988	24	0	3		
MAZZON, Giorgio	Cheshunt	04.09.60	Hertford T.	**Tottenham H.**	04.79	1980-82	3	1	0	(D/M)	
			Tr	**Aldershot**	08.83	1983-88	184	11	6		
MEADE, Raphael J.	Islington	22.11.62	App	**Arsenal**	06.80	1981-84	25	16	14	(F)	
			Dundee U.	**Luton T.**	03.89	1988	2	2	0		
MEASHAM, Ian	Barnsley	14.12.64	App	**Huddersfield T.**	12.82	1984	17	0	0	(RB)	
			L	**Lincoln C.**	10.85	1985	6	0	0		
			L	**Rochdale**	03.86	1985	12	0	0		
			Tr	**Cambridge U.**	07.86	1986	46	0	0		
			Tr	**Burnley**	11.88	1988	30	0	1		
MEGSON, Gary J.	Manchester	02.05.59	App	**Plymouth Arg.**	05.77	1977-79	78	0	10	(M)	Son of Don
			Tr	**Everton**	12.79	1979-80	20	2	2		
			Tr	**Sheffield Wed.**	08.81	1981-83	123	0	13		
			Tr	**Nottingham F.**	08.84						
			Tr	**Newcastle U.**	11.84	1984-85	21	3	1		
			Tr	**Sheffield Wed.**	12.85	1985-87	107	3	12		
			Tr	**Manchester C.**	01.89	1988	22	0	1		
MEHEW, David S.	Camberley	29.10.67	Leeds U.(YTS)	**Bristol Rov.**	07.85	1985-88	68	6	25	(M)	
MEHMET, Dave	Camberwell	02.12.60	App	**Millwall**	12.77	1976-80	97	17	15	(M)	
			Tampa Bay R.(USA)	**Charlton Ath.**	01.82	1981-82	29	0	3		
			Tr	**Gillingham**	03.83	1982-85	128	4	39		
			Tr	**Millwall**	07.86	1986-87	17	1	1		
MELL, Stewart A.	Doncaster	15.10.57	Appleby Frodingham	**Doncaster Rov.**	02.80	1979-82	62	14	14	(F)	E Semi-pro Int 1985
			Tr	**Halifax T.**	07.83	1983	22	8	8		
			Burton Albion	**Scarborough**	(N/L)	1987-88	30	9	8		
MELLISH, Stuart M.	Hyde	19.11.69	YTS	**Rochdale**	07.88	1987-88	24	3	1	(M)	
MELROSE, Jim M.	Glasgow	07.10.58	Partick Thistle	**Leicester C.**	07.80	1980-82	57	15	21	(F)	S U21-8/S Sch Int/SF Lge Rep
			Tr	**Coventry C.**	09.82	1982	21	3	8		
			Glasgow Celtic (L)	**Wolverhampton W.**	09.84	1984	6	1	2		
			Glasgow Celtic	**Manchester C.**	11.84	1984-85	27	7	8		
			Tr	**Charlton Ath.**	03.86	1985-87	44	4	19		
			Tr	**Leeds U.**	09.87	1987	3	1	0		
			Tr	**Shrewsbury T.**	02.88	1987-88	22	8	3		
MELVILLE, Andrew R.	Swansea	29.11.68	YTS	**Swansea C.**	07.86	1985-88	119	10	17	(CD)	
MENDONCA, Clive P.	Sunderland	09.09.68	App	**Sheffield U.**	09.86	1986-87	8	5	4	(F)	
			L	**Doncaster Rov.**	02.88	1987	2	0	0		
			Tr	**Rotherham U.**	03.88	1987-88	9	9	3		
MERSON, Paul C.	Brent	20.03.68	App	**Arsenal**	11.85	1986-88	41	18	18	(F)	E Yth Int/E U21-3
			L	**Brentford**	01.87	1986	6	1	0		
METHVEN, Colin J.	India	10.12.55	East Fife	**Wigan Ath.**	10.79	1979-85	295	1	21	(CD)	
			Tr	**Blackpool**	07.86	1986-88	122	6	8		

Players Names	Birthplace	Date	Previous Club	League Club	Date Sign'd	Seasons Played	Career Record Apps	Sub	Gls	Pos.	Misc
MICKLEWHITE, Gary	Southwark	21.03.61	App	**Manchester U.**	03.78					(RW)	
			Tr	**Q.P.R.**	07.79	1980-84	97	9	11		
			Tr	**Derby Co.**	02.85	1984-88	138	11	25		
MILLAR, John	Coatbridge	08.12.66	Jnrs	**Chelsea**	08.84	1985-86	11	0	0	(FB)	
			L	**Northampton T.**	01.87	1986	1	0	0		
			Tr	**Blackburn Rov.**	07.87	1987-88	50	3	1		
MILLEN, Keith	Croydon	26.09.66	Jnrs	**Brentford**	08.84	1984-88	161	3	10	(CD)	
MILLER, Allan J.	Epping	9.03.70	YTS	**Arsenal**	05.88					(G)	E Yth Int/E U21-1
			L	**Plymouth Arg.**	11.88	1988	13	0	0		
MILLER, David B.	Burnley	08.01.64	App	**Burnley**	01.82	1982-84	27	5	3	(M/RB)	Son of Brian
			L	**Crewe Alex.**	03.83	1982	3	0	0		
			Tr	**Tranmere Rov.**	07.85	1985	25	4	1		
			Colne Dynamoes	**Preston N.E.**	12.86	1986-88	47	8	2		
			L	**Burnley**	02.89	1988	4	0	0		
MILLER, Ian	Perth	13.05.55	Jnrs	**Bury**	08.73	1973	9	6	0	(RW)	
			Tr	**Nottingham F.**	08.74						
			Tr	**Doncaster Rov.**	08.75	1975-77	124	0	14		
			Tr	**Swindon T.**	07.78	1978-80	123	4	9		
			Tr	**Blackburn Rov.**	08.81	1981-88	252	16	16		
MILLER, Kevin	Falmouth	15.03.69	Newquay	**Exeter C.** (N/C)	03.89	1988	3	0	0	(G)	
MILLER, Paul A.	Woking	31.01.68	Yeovil T.	**Wimbledon**	08.87	1987-88	20	3	5	(F)	
			L	**Newport Co.**	10.87	1987	6	0	2		
MILLER, Paul R.	Stepney	11.10.59	App	**Tottenham H.**	05.77	1978-86	206	2	7	(CD)	
			Tr	**Charlton Ath.**	02.87	1986-88	40	2	2		
			Tr	**Watford**	10.88	1988	20	0	1		
MILLIGAN, Michael J.	Manchester	20.02.67	YTS	**Oldham Ath.**	02.85	1985-88	120	1	10	(M)	Brother of Terry/IR U21-1
MILLS, Gary R.	Northampton	11.11.61	App	**Nottingham F.**	11.78	1978-81	50	8	8	(W)	E Sch Int/E Yth Int/E U21-2/ Son of Roly
			Seattle S.(USA)	**Derby Co.**	10.82	1982	18	0	2		
			Seattle S.(USA)	**Nottingham F.**	12.83	1983-86	63	16	4		
			Tr	**Notts Co.**	08.87	1987-88	75	0	8		
			Tr	**Leicester C.**	03.89	1988	13	0	0		
MILLS, Simon A.	Sheffield	16.08.64	App	**Sheffield Wed.**	08.82	1982-84	1	4	0	(M)	E Yth Int
			Tr	**York C.**	06.85	1985-87	97	2	5		
			Tr	**Port Vale**	12.87	1987-88	62	0	5		
MILNE, Ralph	Dundee	13.05.61	Dundee U.	**Charlton Ath.**	01.87	1986-87	19	3	0	(W)	S Yth Int/S U21-3
			Tr	**Bristol C.**	01.88	1987-88	29	1	6		
			Tr	**Manchester U.**	11.88	1988	19	3	3		
MILTON, Simon C.	Fulham	23.08.63	Bury Town	**Ipswich T.**	07.87	1987-88	32	11	11	(M)	
			L	**Exeter C.**	11.87	1987	2	0	3		
			L	**Torquay U.**	03.88	1987	4	0	1		
MIMMS, R.A. (Bob)	York	12.10.63	App	**Halifax T.**	08.81					(G)	E U21-3
			Tr	**Rotherham U.**	11.81	1981-84	83	0	0		
			Tr	**Everton**	06.85	1985-87	29	0	0		
			L	**Notts Co.**	03.86	1985	2	0	0		
			L	**Sunderland**	12.86	1986	4	0	0		
			L	**Blackburn Rov.**	01.87	1986	6	0	0		
			L	**Manchester C.**	09.87	1987	3	0	0		
			Tr	**Tottenham H.**	02.88	1987-88	33	0	0		
MINTO, Scott C	Heswall	06.08.71	YTS	**Charlton Ath.**	01.89	1988	1	2	0	(W)	
MIRANDINHA, (Da Silva, Francisco)	Brazil	02.07.59	Palmeiras (Brazil)	**Newcastle U.**	08.87	1987-88	47	7	20	(F)	Brazilian Int
MITCHELL, C. Brian	Stonehaven	16.07.63	Aberdeen	**Bradford C.**	02.87	1986-88	102	1	7	(RB)	
MITCHELL, David S.	Glasgow	13.06.62	Feyenoord (Neth)	**Chelsea**	12.88	1988	6	0	0	(F)	Australian Int
MITCHELL, Graham L.	Shipley	16.02.68	YTS	**Huddersfield T.**	06.86	1986-88	77	3	1	(CD/M)	
MOHAN, Nicky	Middlesbrough	06.10.70	Charlton Ath. (Jnr)	**Middlesbrough**	11.87	1988	5	1	0	(RB)	
MOLBY, Jan	Denmark	04.07.63	Ajax Amsterdam	**Liverpool**	08.84	1984-88	105	10	24	(M)	Danish Int
MONCUR, John F.	Stepney	22.09.66	App	**Tottenham H.**	08.84	1986-88	4	3	0	(M)	
			L	**Doncaster Rov.**	09.86	1986	4	0	0		
			L	**Cambridge U.**	03.87	1986	3	1	0		
			L	**Portsmouth**	03.89	1988	7	0	0		
MONEY, Richard	Lowestoft	13.10.55	Lowestoft T.	**Scunthorpe U.**	07.73	1973-77	165	8	4	(CD)	E 'B'
			Tr	**Fulham**	12.77	1977-79	106	0	3		
			Tr	**Liverpool**	04.80	1980	12	2	0		
			L	**Derby Co.**	12.81	1981	5	0	0		
			Tr	**Luton T.**	03.82	1981-82	44	0	1		
			Tr	**Portsmouth**	08.83	1983-85	17	0	0		
			Tr	**Scunthorpe U.**	10.85	1985-88	104	1	0		
MONINGTON, Mark D.	Bilsthorpe	21.10.70	Jnrs	**Burnley**	03.89	1988	6	2	1	(CD)	
MONKOU, Ken J.	Surinam	29.11.64	Feyenoord (Neth)	**Chelsea**	03.89	1988	0	2	0	(CD)	
MOONEY, Brian J.	Dublin	02.02.66	Home Farm	**Liverpool**	08.83					(W)	IR Yth Int
			L	**Wrexham**	12.85	1985	9	0	2		
			Tr	**Preston N.E.**	10.87	1987-88	72	2	9		
MOORE, David	Grimsby	17.12.59	App	**Grimsby T.**	12.77	1978-82	136	0	2	(RB)	Brother of Andy/Kevin
			Tr	**Carlisle U.**	08.83	1983	13	0	1		
			Tr	**Blackpool**	12.83	1983-86	114	1	1		
			Tr	**Grimsby T.**	12.86	1986-87	3	1	0		
			Tr	**Darlington**	08.88	1988	25	5	1		
MOORE, John	Consett	01.10.66	App	**Sunderland**	10.84	1984-87	4	11	1	(F)	
			L	**Newport Co.**	12.85	1985	2	0	0		
			L	**Darlington**	11.86	1986	2	0	1		
			L	**Mansfield T.**	03.87	1986	5	0	1		
			L	**Rochdale**	01.88	1987	10	0	2		
			Tr	**Hull C.**	06.88	1988	11	3	1		
			L	**Sheffield U.**	03.89	1988	4	1	0		
MOORE, Kevin T.	Grimsby	29.04.58	Jnrs	**Grimsby T.**	07.76	1976-86	397	3	27	(CD)	Brother of Andy/David/ E Sch Int
			Tr	**Oldham Ath.**	02.87	1986	13	0	1		
			Tr	**Southampton**	07.87	1987-88	60	0	6		

Mirandinha (Newcastle & Brazil)

Match Magazine

Players Names	Birthplace	Date	Previous Club	League Club	Date Sign'd	Seasons Played	Career Record Apps	Sub	Gls	Pos.	Misc
MOORE, Ronnie D.	Liverpool	29.01.53	Jnrs	**Tranmere Rov.**	05.71	1971-78	248	1	72	(F/CD)	
			Tr	**Cardiff C.**	02.79	1978-79	54	2	6		
			Tr	**Rotherham U.**	08.80	1980-83	124	1	51		
			Tr	**Charlton Ath.**	09.83	1983-84	60	2	13		
			Tr	**Rochdale**	07.85	1985	43	0	9		
			Tr	**Tranmere Rov.**	07.86	1986-88	75	0	6		
MORAN, Kevin B.	Dublin	29.04.56	Gaelic Football	**Manchester U.**	02.78	1978-87	228	3	21	(CD)	IR-44/to Sporting Gijon (Sp) 8.88
MORAN, Paul	Enfield	22.05.68	YTS	**Tottenham H.**	07.85	1986-88	14	8	1	(W)	
			L	**Portsmouth**	01.89	1988	3	0	0		
MORAN, Steve J.	Croydon	10.01.61	Jnrs	**Southampton**	08.79	1979-85	173	7	78	(F)	E U21-2
			Tr	**Leicester C.**	09.86	1986-87	35	8	14		
			Tr	**Reading**	11.87	1987-88	47	15	11		
MORGAN, Darren J.	Camberwell	05.11.67	App	**Millwall**	11.85	1986-88	27	6	1	(M)	W Yth Int
MORGAN, Gary	Consett	01.04.61	Berwick Rangers	**Darlington**	07.85	1985-88	146	0	3	(LB)	
MORGAN, Jonathan P.	Cardiff	10.07.70	YTS	**Cardiff C.**	07.88	1988	13	6	0	(M)	W Yth Int
MORGAN, Nick	East Ham	30.10.59	App	**West Ham U.**	11.77	1978-82	14	7	2	(F)	
			Tr	**Portsmouth**	03.83	1982-86	79	16	32		
			Tr	**Stoke C.**	11.86	1986-88	67	8	19		
MORGAN, Simon C.	Birmingham	05.09.66	YTS	**Leicester C.**	11.84	1985-88	133	10	2	(FB)	E U21-2
MORGAN, Stephen A.	Oldham	19.09.68	App	**Blackpool**	08.86	1985-88	99	7	9	(M/LB)	
MORGAN, Stephen J.	Wrexham	28.12.70	YTS	**Oldham Ath.** (YTS)	07.87	1987-88	1	1	0	(W)	W Yth Int
MORGAN, Trevor J.	Forest Gate	30.09.56	Leytonstone	**Bournemouth**	09.80	1980-81	53	0	13	(F)	
			Tr	**Mansfield T.**	11.81	1981	12	0	6		
			Tr	**Bournemouth**	03.82	1981-83	88	0	33		
			Tr	**Bristol C.**	03.84	1983-84	32	0	8		
			Tr	**Exeter C.**	11.84	1984-85	30	0	9		
			Tr	**Bristol Rov.**	09.85	1985-86	54	1	24		
			Tr	**Bristol C.**	01.87	1986	19	0	7		
			Tr	**Bolton W.**	06.87	1987-88	65	12	17		
MORLEY, A.W. (Tony)	Ormskirk	26.08.54	App	**Preston N.E.**	08.72	1972-75	78	6	15	(LW)	E Yth Int/E U23-1/E-6/E 'B'
			Tr	**Burnley**	02.76	1975-78	78	13	5		
			Tr	**Aston Villa**	06.79	1979-83	128	9	25		
			Tr	**West Bromwich A.**	12.83	1983-84	33	0	4		
			L	**Birmingham C.**	11.84	1984	4	0	3		
			Den Haag (Neth)	**West Bromwich A.**	08.87	1987	27	1	7		
			L	**Burnley**	10.88	1988	5	0	0		
MORLEY, Trevor W.	Nottingham	20.03.61	Nuneaton Bor.	**Northampton T.**	06.85	1985-87	107	0	39	(F)	E Semi-Pro Int/1984-5
			Tr	**Manchester C.**	01.88	1987-88	52	3	16		
MORRELL, Paul D.P.	Poole	23.03.61	Weymouth	**Bournemouth**	06.83	1983-88	231	4	6	(LB)	
MORRIS, Andy D.	Sheffield	17.11.67	Jnrs	**Rotherham U.**	07.85	1984-86	0	7	0	(F)	Brother of Neil
			Tr	**Chesterfield**	01.88	1987-88	49	3	9		
MORRIS, Chris B.	Newquay	24.12.63	Jnrs	**Sheffield Wed.**	10.82	1983-86	61	13	1	(FB)	E Sch Int/IR-14/to Celtic 8.87
MORRIS, Colin	Blyth	22.08.53	App	**Burnley**	08.71	1974-75	9	1	0	(RW)	
			Tr	**Southend U.**	01.77	1976-79	133	0	25		
			Tr	**Blackpool**	12.79	1979-81	87	0	26		
			Tr	**Sheffield U.**	02.82	1981-87	235	5	68		
			Tr	**Scarborough**	07.88	1988	20	3	3		
MORRIS, Mark	Chester	01.08.68	YTS	**Wrexham**	08.87	1985-88	11	0	0	(G)	
MORRIS, Mark J.	Morden	26.09.62	App	**Wimbledon**	09.80	1981-86	167	1	9	(CD)	
			L	**Aldershot**	09.85	1985	14	0	0		
			Tr	**Watford**	07.87	1987-88	42	0	1		
MORRIS, Neill A.	Sheffield	03.05.70	Doncaster Rov. (YTS)	**York C.**	09.88	1988	3	1	0	(F)	Brother of Andy
MORRIS, Ronnie	Birmingham	25.09.70	YTS	**Birmingham C.**	09.88	1987-88	3	8	0	(W)	
MORRISON, Andrew C.	Inverness	30.07.70	YTS	**Plymouth Arg.**	07.88	1987-88	2	1	0	(D)	
MORRISON, John	Kettering	27.07.70	YTS	**Torquay U.**	07.88	1988	13	5	0	(M)	
MORRISSEY, John J.(Jnr.)	Liverpool	08.03.65	App	**Everton**	03.83	1984	1	0	0	(RW)	Son of John (Snr.)/E Yth Int
			Tr	**Wolverhampton W.**	08.85	1985	5	5	1		
			Tr	**Tranmere Rov.**	10.85	1985-88	140	11	20		
MORTIMER, Paul H.	Kensington	08.05.68	Fulham (App)	**Charlton Ath.**	09.87	1987-88	41	4	5	(W)	E U21-1
MORTON, Neil	Congleton	21.12.68	YTS	**Crewe Alex.**	09.87	1986-88	18	13	1	(M)	
MOSES, Remi M.	Manchester	14.11.60	App	**West Bromwich A.**	11.78	1979-81	63	0	5	(M)	E U21-8
			Tr	**Manchester U.**	09.81	1981-87	143	7	7		
MOULDEN, Paul C.	Farnworth	06.09.67	App	**Manchester C.**	09.84	1985-88	48	16	18	(F)	E Yth Int/Son of Anthony
MOUNTFIELD, Derek N.	Liverpool	02.11.62	App	**Tranmere Rov.**	11.80	1980-81	26	0	1	(CD)	E U21-1
			Tr	**Everton**	06.82	1982-87	100	6	19		
			Tr	**Aston Villa**	06.88	1988	22	2	1		
MOVERLEY, Robert	Wakefield	18.01.69	YTS	**Bradford C.**	06.87					(G)	
			Tr	**Hartlepool U.**	12.88	1988	23	0	0		
MOWBRAY, A.M. (Tony)	Saltburn	22.11.63	App	**Middlesbrough**	11.81	1982-88	260	3	20	(CD)	E 'B'
MOWER, Kenny M.	Walsall	01.12.60	App	**Walsall**	11.78	1978-88	365	3	8	(LB)	
MOYES, David W.	Glasgow	25.04.63	Glasgow Celtic	**Cambridge U.**	10.83	1983-85	79	0	1	(CD)	
			Tr	**Bristol C.**	10.85	1985-87	83	0	6		
			Tr	**Shrewsbury T.**	10.87	1987-88	45	5	3		
MUDD, Paul A.	Hull	13.11.70	YTS	**Hull C.** (YTS)	07.88	1988	1	0	0	(FB)	
MUGGLETON, Carl D.	Leicester	13.09.68	App	**Leicester C.**	09.86	1988	3	0	0	(G)	
			L	**Chesterfield**	09.87	1987	17	0	0		
			L	**Blackpool**	02.88	1987	2	0	0		
			L	**Hartlepool U.**	10.88	1988	8	0	0		
MUIR, Ian J.	Coventry	05.05.63	App	**Q.P.R.**	09.80	1980	2	0	2	(F)	E Yth Int/E Sch Int
			L	**Burnley**	11.82	1982	1	1	1		
			Tr	**Birmingham C.**	08.83	1983	1	0	0		
			Tr	**Brighton & H.A.**	02.84	1983-84	3	1	0		
			L	**Swindon T.**	01.85	1984	2	0	0		
			Tr	**Tranmere Rov.**	07.85	1985-88	162	5	81		
MUMBY, Peter	Bradford	22.02.69	YTS	**Leeds U.**	07.87	1987-88	3	3	0	(F)	

Players Names	Birthplace	Date	Previous Club	League Club	Date Sign'd	Seasons Played	Career Record Apps	Sub	Gls	Pos.	Misc
MUNDEE, Denny W.J.	Swindon	10.10.68	Q.P.R. (App)	**Swindon T.**	08.86					(F)	
			Salisbury C.	**Bournemouth**	05.88	1988	1	1	0		
MUNGALL, Steve H.	Bellshill	22.05.58	Motherwell	**Tranmere Rov.**	07.79	1979-88	355	10	7	(D)	
MURPHY, Aidan J.	Manchester	17.09.67	App	**Manchester U.**	09.84					(M)	E Sch Int/E Yth Int
			L	**Lincoln C.**	10.86	1986	2	0	0		
			Tr	**Crewe Alex.**	05.87	1987-88	46	9	7		
MURRAY, Edward J.	Crosby	10.07.62	Stork	**Tranmere Rov.**	08.87	1987-88	11	16	1	(W)	
MURRAY, Malcolm	Buckie	26.07.64	Hearts	**Hull C.**	03.89	1988	6	2	0	(D)	
MUSSELWHITE, Paul S.	Portsmouth	22.12.68	App	**Portsmouth**(N/C)	12.86					(G)	
			Tr	**Scunthorpe U.**	03.88	1988	41	0	0		
MUSTOE, Robbie	Witney	28.08.68	Jnrs	**Oxford U.**	07.86	1986-88	42	11	3	(M)	
MUTCH, Andy T.	Liverpool	28.12.63	Southport	**Wolverhampton W.**	02.86	1985-88	144	3	58	(F)	E U21-1/E 'B'
MYCOCK, David C.	Todmorden	18.09.69	YTS	**Rochdale**	07.88	1987-88	19	3	0	(FB)	
NARBETT, Jonathan V.	Birmingham	21.11.68	App	**Shrewsbury T.**	09.86	1986-87	20	6	3	(M)	
			Tr	**Hereford U.**	10.88	1988	35	1	7		
NAUGHTON, Willie B.S.	Catrine (Ayrs)	20.03.62	App	**Preston N.E.**	03.80	1979-84	148	14	10	(LW)	
			Tr	**Walsall**	03.85	1984-88	139	12	16		
NAYIM AMAR, Mohamed	Morocco	05.11.66	Barcelona (Spain)	**Tottenham H.**	11.88	1988	8	3	2	(M)	
NAYLOR, Stuart W.	Wetherby	06.12.62	Yorkshire Amateurs	**Lincoln C.**	06.80	1981-85	49	0	0	(G)	E Yth Int/E 'B'
			L	**Peterborough U.**	02.83	1982	8	0	0		
			L	**Crewe Alex.**	10.83	1983-84	55	0	0		
			Tr	**West Bromwich A.**	02.86	1985-88	133	0	0		
NEAL, Phil G.	Irchester	29.02.51	App	**Northampton T.**	12.68	1968-74	182	4	29	(RB)	E-50
			Tr	**Liverpool**	10.74	1974-85	453	2	41		
			Tr	**Bolton W.**	12.85	1985-88	56	8	3		
NEBBELING, Gavin M.	South Africa	15.05.63	Arcadia Shep(SA)	**Crystal Palace**	08.81	1981-88	145	6	8	(CD)	
			L	**Northampton T.**	10.85	1985	11	0	0		
NEENAN, Joe P.	Manchester	17.03.59	App	**York C.**	03.77	1976-79	56	0	0	(G)	
			Tr	**Scunthorpe U.**	01.80	1979-84	191	0	0		
			L	**Burnley**	01.85	1984	9	0	0		
			Tr	**Burnley**	07.85	1985-86	81	0	0		
			Tr	**Peterborough U.**	07.87	1987-88	55	0	0		
			Tr	**Scarborough**	01.88	1987	6	0	0		
NEILL, Warren A.	Acton	21.11.62	App	**Q.P.R.**	09.80	1980-87	177	4	3	(RB)	E Sch Int
			Tr	**Portsmouth**	07.88	1988	43	0	0		
NELSON, Gary P.	Braintree	16.01.61	Jnrs	**Southend U.**	07.79	1979-82	106	23	17	(W)	
			Tr	**Swindon T.**	08.83	1983-84	78	1	7		
			Tr	**Plymouth Arg.**	07.85	1985-86	71	3	20		
			Tr	**Brighton & H.A.**	07.87	1987-88	88	0	36		
NEVILLE, Steve F.	Walthamstow	18.09.57	App	**Southampton**	09.75	1977	5	1	1	(W)	
			Tr	**Exeter C.**	09.78	1978-80	90	3	22		
			Tr	**Sheffield U.**	10.80	1980-81	40	9	6		
			Tr	**Exeter C.**	10.82	1982-84	89	3	27		
			Tr	**Bristol C.**	11.84	1984-87	128	6	40		
			Tr	**Exeter C.**	07.88	1988	38	0	14		
NEVIN, Pat K.F.	Glasgow	06.09.63	Clyde	**Chelsea**	07.83	1983-87	190	3	36	(RW)	S Yth Int/S U21-5/S-8
			Tr	**Everton**	07.88	1988	20	5	2		
NEWELL, Mike C.	Liverpool	27.01.65	Liverpool (Jnrs)	**Crewe Alex.**	09.83	1983	3	0	0	(F)	E U21-4
			Tr	**Wigan Ath.**	10.83	1983-85	64	8	25		
			Tr	**Luton T.**	01.86	1985-87	62	1	18		
			Tr	**Leicester C.**	09.87	1987-88	81	0	21		
NEWELL, Paul C.	Woolwich	23.02.69	YTS	**Southend U.**	06.87	1987-88	15	0	0	(G)	
NEWHOUSE, Aiden R.	Wallasey	23.05.72	Jnrs	**Chester C.** (YTS)	07.88	1987-88	14	12	2	(W)	E Sch Int
NEWMAN, Rob N.	Bradford-on-Avon	13.12.63	App	**Bristol C.**	10.81	1981-88	290	12	36	(FB/M)	
NEWSON, Mark J.	Stepney	07.12.60	App	**Charlton Ath.**	12.78					(D)	E Semi-pro Int 1984-5
			Maidstone U.	**Bournemouth**	05.85	1985-88	161	0	22		
NICHOLAS, Peter	Newport	10.11.59	App	**Crystal Palace**	12.76	1977-80	127	0	7	(M)	W Sch Int/W U21-3/W-59
			Tr	**Arsenal**	03.81	1980-82	57	3	1		
			Tr	**Crystal Palace**	10.83	1983-84	47	0	7		
			Tr	**Luton T.**	01.85	1984-86	102	0	1		
			Aberdeen	**Chelsea**	08.88	1988	39	0	2		
NICHOLSON, Shane M.	Newark	03.06.70	YTS	**Lincoln C.**	07.88	1986-88	38	3	1	(LB)	
NICOL, Paul J.	Scunthorpe	31.10.67	YTS	**Scunthorpe U.**	07.86	1986-88	51	6	1	(CD)	
NICOL, Steve	Irvine	11.12.61	Ayr U.	**Liverpool**	10.81	1982-88	175	9	25	(FB/M)	S U21-14/S-21
NIXON, Eric W.	Manchester	04.10.62	Curzon Ashton	**Manchester C.**	12.83	1985-87	58	0	0	(G)	
			L	**Wolverhampton W.**	08.86	1986	16	0	0		
			L	**Bradford C.**	11.86	1986	3	0	0		
			L	**Southampton**	12.86	1986	4	0	0		
			L	**Carlisle U.**	01.87	1986	16	0	0		
			L	**Tranmere Rov.**	03.88	1987	8	0	0		
			Tr	**Tranmere Rov.**	07.88	1988	45	0	0		
NIXON, Paul	Seaham	23.09.63	Seaham Red Star	**Bristol Rov.**	01.89	1988	0	1	0	(F)	New Zealand Int.
NOBBS, A. Keith	Bishop Auckland	19.09.61	App	**Middlesbrough**	09.79	1980	1	0	0	(RB)	
			Tr	**Halifax T.**	08.82	1982-83	87	0	1		
			Bishop Auckland	**Hartlepool U.**	08.85	1985-88	136	4	1		
NOGAN, Lee M.	Cardiff	21.05.69	YTS	**Oxford U.**	03.87	1987-88	4	2	0	(F)	
			L	**Brentford**	03.87	1986	10	1	2		
			L	**Southend U.**	09.87	1987	6	0	1		
NORMAN, A.J. (Tony)	Deeside	24.02.58	Jnrs	**Burnley**	08.76					(G)	W-3
			Tr	**Hull C.**	02.80	1979-88	372	0	0		
			Tr	**Sunderland**	12.88	1988	24	0	0		
NORRIS, Steve M.	Coventry	22.09.61	Telford U.	**Scarborough**	07.88	1988	27	4	9	(F)	

Derek Mountfield (Aston Villa) Match Magazine

Stuart Naylor (West Bromwich Albion) Match Magazine

Gary Parker (Nottingham Forest) Match Magazine

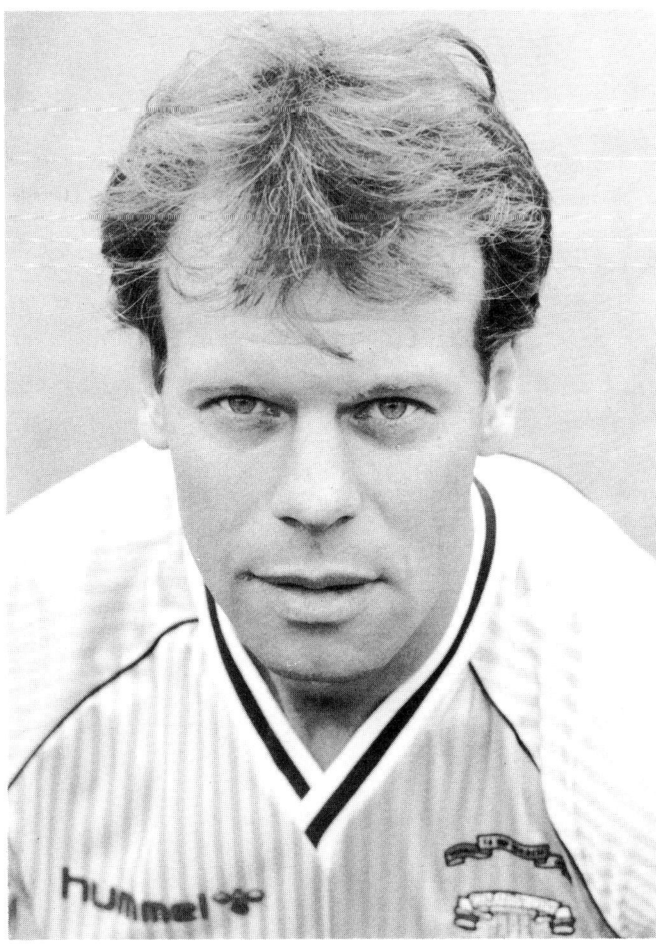

Trevor Peake (Coventry City) Match Magazine

Players Names	Birthplace	Date	Previous Club	League Club	Date Sign'd	Seasons Played	Career Record Apps	Sub	Gls	Pos.	Misc
NORTH, Marc V.	Ware	29.05.66	App	Luton T.	03.84	1985-86	11	7	3	(F)	Brother of Stacey
			L	Lincoln C.	03.85	1984	4	0	0		
			L	Scunthorpe U.	01.87	1986	4	1	2		
			L	Birmingham C.	03.87	1986	4	1	1		
			Tr	Grimsby T.	08.87	1987-88	64	3	17		
			Tr	Leicester C.	03.89	1988	1	7	1		
NORTH, Stacey S.	Luton	25.11.64	App	Luton T.	08.82	1983-87	24	1	0	(CD)	Brother of Marc/E Yth Int
			L	Wolverhampton W.	11.85	1985	3	0	0		
			Tr	West Bromwich A.	12.87	1987-88	64	0	0		
NORTON, David W.	Cannock	03.03.65	App	Aston Villa	03.83	1984-87	42	2	2	(RB)	E Yth Int
			Tr	Notts Co.	08.88	1988	8	0	0		
NORTON, Paul	Mexborough	17.09.69	Sheffield U. (YTS)	Hartlepool U.	08.88	1988	5	0	0	(G)	
NOTEMAN, Kevin S.	Preston	15.10.69	YTS	Leeds U.	06.88	1987	0	1	0	(F)	
NUGENT, Kevin P.	Edmonton	10.04.69	YTS	Leyton Orient	07.87	1987-88	12	2	3	(F)	
NUTTELL, Michael J.	Boston	22.11.68	YTS	Peterborough U.	08.87	1985-87	12	9	0	(F)	
			L	Crewe Alex.	12.87	1987	2	1	1		
			L	Carlisle U.	11.88	1988	1	2	0		
O'BRIEN, Liam F.	Dublin	05.09.64	Shamrock Rov.	Manchester U.	10.86	1986-88	16	15	2	(M)	IR-7
			Tr	Newcastle U.	11.88	1988	17	3	3		
O'CALLAGHAN, Kevin	Dagenham	19.10.61	App	Millwall	11.78	1978-79	15	5	3	(W)	IR-20
			Tr	Ipswich T.	01.80	1979-84	72	43	3		
			Tr	Portsmouth	01.85	1984-86	84	3	16		
			Tr	Millwall	06.87	1987-88	56	0	12		
O'CONNELL, Brendan	Lambeth	12.11.66	YTS	Portsmouth	07.85					(F)	
			Tr	Exeter C.	07.86	1986-87	73	8	20		
			Tr	Burnley	06.88	1988	42	1	13		
O'CONNOR, Mark A.	Southend	10.03.63	App	Q.P.R.	06.80	1981-82	2	1	0	(M)	
			L	Exeter C.	10.83	1983	38	0	1		
			Tr	Bristol Rov.	08.84	1984-85	79	1	10		
			Tr	Bournemouth	03.86	1985-88	110	12	12		
O'DOHERTY, Ken B.	Dublin	30.03.63	U.C. Dublin	Crystal Palace	02.85	1985-87	41	1	0	(D)	
			Tr	Huddersfield T.	06.88	1988	37	0	1		
O'DONNELL, Chris	Newcastle	26.05.68	App	Ipswich T.	06.85	1986-88	10	4	0	(D)	
			L	Northampton T.	01.88	1987	1	0	0		
O'DRISCOLL, Sean M.	Wolverhampton	01.07.57	Alvechurch	Fulham	11.79	1979-83	141	17	13	(W)	IR-3
			Tr	Bournemouth	02.84	1983-88	232	3	16		
O'HANLON, Kelham G.	Saltburn	16.05.62	App	Middlesbrough	05.80	1982-84	87	0	0	(G)	IR-1
			Tr	Rotherham U.	08.85	1985-88	172	0	0		
O'KEEFE, Eamon	Manchester	13.03.53	Stalybridge Celtic	Plymouth Arg.	02.74					(F)	IR-5/E Semi-Pro Int 1979
			Mossley	Everton	07.79	1979-81	26	14	6		
			Tr	Wigan Ath.	01.82	1981-82	56	2	25		
			Tr	Port Vale	07.83	1983-84	50	9	17		
			Tr	Blackpool	03.85	1984-86	33	3	23		
			Cork C.	Chester C.	03.89	1988	11	3	4		
O'KEEFE, J. Vince	Birmingham	02.04.57	Jnrs	Birmingham C.	07.75					(G)	
			Tr	Walsall	07.76						
			AP Leamington	Exeter C.	06.78	1978-79	53	0	0		
			Tr	Torquay U.	02.80	1979-81	108	0	0		
			Tr	Blackburn Rov.	08.82	1982-88	69	0	0		
			L	Bury	10.83	1983	2	0	0		
			L	Blackpool	12.86	1986	1	0	0		
			L	Blackpool	02.89	1988	6	0	0		
O'KELLY, Richard F.	West Bromwich	08.01.57	Alvechurch	Walsall	10.79	1980-85	189	15	55	(F)	
			Tr	Port Vale	07.86	1986-87	26	2	4		
			Tr	Walsall	01.88	1987	7	5	1		
			Tr	Grimsby T.	07.88	1988	38	1	10		
O'LEARY, David A.	Stoke Newington	02.05.58	App	Arsenal	07.75	1975-88	467	0	9	(CD)	IR-43
O'NEILL, Michael A.	Portadown (NI)	05.07.69	Coleraine	Newcastle U.	10.87	1987-88	36	12	15	(F)	NI-10
O'REGAN, Kieran	Cork (Ire)	09.11.63	Tramore Ath.	Brighton & H.A.	04.83	1982-86	69	17	2	(M/D)	IR-4
			Tr	Swindon T.	08.87	1987	23	3	1		
			Tr	Huddersfield T.	08.88	1988	36	0	2		
O'REILLY, Gary M.	Isleworth	21.03.61	Jnrs	Tottenham H.	09.79	1980-83	39	6	0	(CD)	IR Yth Int
			Tr	Brighton & H.A.	08.84	1984-86	78	1	3		
			Tr	Crystal Palace	01.87	1986-88	46	3	2		
O'RIORDAN, Donal J.	Dublin	14.05.57	App	Derby Co.	05.75	1976-77	2	4	1	(CD)	IR U21-1
			L	Doncaster Rov.	01.78	1977	2	0	0		
			Tulsa R. (USA)	Preston N.E.	10.78	1978-82	153	5	8		
			Tr	Carlisle U.	08.83	1983-84	84	0	18		
			Tr	Middlesbrough	08.85	1985	41	0	2		
			Tr	Grimsby T.	08.86	1986-87	86	0	16		
			Tr	Notts Co.	07.88	1988	40	3	3		
O'SHAUGHNESSY, Steve	Wrexham	13.10.67	YTS	Leeds U.	10.85					(M)	W Yth Int
			Tr	Bradford C.	11.85	1987	0	1	0		
			Tr	Rochdale	08.88	1988	38	3	6		
O'SHEA, Danny E.	Kennington	26.03.63	App	Arsenal	12.80	1982	6	0	0	(RB)	
			L	Charlton Ath.	02.84	1983	9	0	0		
			Tr	Exeter C.	08.84	1984	45	0	2		
			Tr	Southend U.	08.85	1985-88	116	2	12		
O'SHEA, Timothy J.	Pimlico	12.11.66	App	Tottenham H.	08.84	1986-87	1	2	0	(M)	IR Yth Int
			L	Newport Co.	10.86	1986	10	0	0		
			Tr	Leyton Orient	07.88	1988	7	2	1		
			Tr	Gillingham	02.89	1988	17	0	0		
OAKES, Keith B.	Bedworth	03.07.56	App	Peterborough U.	07.73	1972-77	48	14	2	(CD)	
			Tr	Newport Co.	09.78	1978-83	232	0	27		
			Tr	Gillingham	08.84	1984-86	84	2	7		
			Tr	Fulham	09.86	1986-87	76	0	3		
			Tr	Peterborough	08.88	1988	41	0	5		
OGDEN, Paul	Salford	16.10.69	Oldham Ath. (YTS)	Hartlepool U.	08.88	1988	7	3	0	(W)	

Players Names	Birthplace	Date	Previous Club	League Club	Date Sign'd	Seasons Played	Career Record Apps	Sub	Gls	Pos.	Misc
OGHANI, George W.	Manchester	02.09.60	Sheffield U. (Jnrs)	**Bury**	02.78					(F)	
			Hyde U.	**Bolton W.**	10.83	1983-86	86	13	27		
			L	**Wrexham**	03.87	1986	6	1	0		
			Tr	**Burnley**	06.87	1987-88	73	1	21		
OGILVIE, Gary F.	Dundee	16.11.67	Dundee	**Sunderland**	03.88	1988	0	1	0	(LB)	
OGLEY, Mark A.	Barnsley	10.03.67	App	**Barnsley**	03.85	1985-86	19	0	0	(D)	Son of Alan
			L	**Aldershot**	12.87	1987	6	2	0		
			Tr	**Carlisle U.**	03.88	1987-88	29	0	0		
OGRIZOVIC, Steve	Mansfield	12.09.57	Mansfield YC	**Chesterfield**	07.77	1977	16	0	0	(G)	
			Tr	**Liverpool**	11.77	1977-80	4	0	0		
			Tr	**Shrewsbury T.**	08.82	1982-83	84	0	0		
			Tr	**Coventry C.**	06.84	1984-88	204	0	0		
OLDFIELD, David C.	Australia	30.05.68	App	**Luton T.**	05.86	1987-88	21	8	4	(F)	
			Tr	**Manchester C.**	03.89	1988	8	3	3		
OLIVER, Gavin R.	Felling	06.09.62	App	**Sheffield Wed.**	08.80	1980-84	14	6	0	(CD)	
			L	**Tranmere Rov.**	01.83	1982	17	0	1		
			L	**Brighton & H.A.**	08.85	1985	15	1	0		
			Tr	**Bradford C.**	11.85	1985-88	148	1	2		
OLNEY, Ian D.	Luton	17.12.69	YTS	**Aston Villa**	07.88	1988	8	7	2	(F)	
OLSEN, Jesper	Denmark	20.03.61	Ajax Amsterdam	**Manchester U.**	07.84	1984-88	119	20	21	(LW)	Den Int/to Bordeaux (Fr) 11.88
OLSSON, Paul	Hull	24.12.65	App	**Hull C.**	12.83					(M)	
			Tr	**Exeter C.**	03.87	1986-87	38	5	2		
			Tr	**Scarborough**	08.88	1988	25	7	4		
ORD, Richard J.	Murton	03.03.70	YTS	**Sunderland**	07.87	1987-88	35	7	1	(CD)	
ORMONDROYD, Ian	Bradford	22.09.64	Thackley	**Bradford C.**	09.85	1985-88	72	15	20	(F)	
			L	**Oldham Ath.**	03.87	1986	8	2	1		
			Tr	**Aston Villa**	02.89	1988	9	3	1		
ORMSBY, Brendan T.C.	Birmingham	01.10.60	App	**Aston Villa**	10.78	1978-85	115	2	4	(CD)	E Sch Int/E Yth Int
			Tr	**Leeds U.**	02.86	1985-88	46	0	5		
OSBORNE, Steven C.	Middlesbrough	03.03.69	South Bank	**Peterborough U.**	03.89	1988	3	6	1	(M)	
OSBOURNE, C. Gary J.	Wolverhampton	22.10.69	YTS	**Shrewsbury T.**	07.88	1988	3	4	0	(FB)	
OSGOOD, Stephen	Bracknell	20.01.62	Newbury T.	**Aldershot**(N/C)	02.89	1988	1	0	0	(G)	
OSMAN, Russell C.	Repton (Dy)	14.02.59	App	**Ipswich T.**	03.76	1977-84	244	0	17	(CD)	Son of Rex/E-11/E Yth Int/ E U21-7
			Tr	**Leicester C.**	07.85	1985-87	108	0	8		
			Tr	**Southampton**	06.88	1988	36	0	0		
OUTHART, Anthony J.	Scarborough	17.09.63	Bridlington T.	**Scarborough**	11.87	1987-88	3	3	1	(F)	
OVERSON, Vince D.	Kettering	15.05.62	App	**Burnley**	11.79	1979-85	207	4	6	(CD)	Brother of Richard
			Tr	**Birmingham C.**	06.86	1986-88	112	0	1		
OWEN, Gordon	Barnsley	14.06.59	Jnrs	**Sheffield Wed.**	11.76	1977-82	32	15	5	(RW)	
			L	**Rotherham U.**	03.80	1979	9	0	0		
			L	**Doncaster Rov.**	11.82	1982	9	0	0		
			L	**Chesterfield**	03.83	1982	6	0	2		
			Tr	**Cardiff C.**	08.83	1983	38	1	14		
			Tr	**Barnsley**	08.84	1984-85	68	0	25		
			Tr	**Bristol C.**	08.86	1986-87	51	2	11		
			L	**Hull C.**	12.87	1987	3	0	0		
			Tr	**Mansfield T.**	01.88	1987-88	54	4	8		
OWERS, Adrian R.	Chelmsford	26.02.65	App	**Southend U.**	02.83	1982-84	18	9	0	(M)	
			Chelmsford C.	**Brighton & H.A.**	12.87	1987-88	30	3	4		
OWERS, Gary	Newcastle	03.10.68	App	**Sunderland**	10.86	1987-88	73	2	7	(M)	
PAGE, Don R.	Manchester	18.01.64	Runcorn	**Wigan Ath.**	03.89	1988	13	2	2	(F)	
PAINTER, Peter R	Wigan	26.01.71	YTS	**Chester C.** (YTS)	07.87	1987-88	5	5	1		
PALIN, Leigh G.	Worcester	12.09.65	App	**Aston Villa**	09.83					(M)	E Yth Int/Son of Grenville
			L	**Shrewsbury T.**	12.84	1984	2	0	0		
			Tr	**Nottingham F.**	11.85						
			Tr	**Bradford C.**	10.86	1986-88	65	6	10		
PALLISTER, Gary A.	Ramsgate	30.06.65	Billingham T.	**Middlesbrough**	11.84	1985-88	153	0	5	(CD)	E-2/E 'B'
			L	**Darlington**	10.85	1985	7	0	0		
PALMER, Carlton L.	Rowley Regis	05.12.65	YTS	**West Bromwich A.**	12.84	1985-88	114	7	4	(M)	E U21-3
			Tr	**Sheffield Wed.**	02.89	1988	13	0	1		
PALMER, Charlie A.	Aylesbury	10.07.63	App	**Watford**	07.81	1983	10	0	1	(RB)	
			Tr	**Derby Co.**	07.84	1984-85	51	0	2		
			Tr	**Hull C.**	02.87	1986-88	69	1	1		
			Tr	**Notts Co.**	02.89	1988	11	0	0		
PALMER, Roger N.	Manchester	30.01.59	App	**Manchester C.**	01.77	1977-80	22	9	9	(W)	
			Tr	**Oldham Ath.**	11.80	1980-88	346	3	113		
PARDEW, Alan S.	Wimbledon	18.07.61	Yeovil T.	**Crystal Palace**	03.87	1987-88	59	6	1	(M)	
PARIS, Alan D.	Slough	15.08.64	Slough T.	**Watford**	11.82					(RB)	
			Tr	**Peterborough U.**	08.85	1985-87	135	2	2		
			Tr	**Leicester C.**	07.88	1988	37	0	1		
PARKER, Gary S.	Oxford	07.09.65	App	**Luton T.**	05.83	1982-85	31	11	3	(M)	E Yth Int/E U21-3
			Tr	**Hull C.**	02.86	1985-87	82	2	8		
			Tr	**Nottingham F.**	03.88	1987-88	23	1	7		
PARKER, Martin T.	Exeter	18.10.70	YTS	**Exeter C.** (YTS)	07.87	1988	0	1	0	(M)	
PARKER, Paul A.	West Ham	04.04.64	App	**Fulham**	04.82	1980-86	140	13	2	(D)	E Yth Int/E-U21-8/E-3/E 'B'
			Tr	**Q.P.R.**	06.87	1987-88	76	0	0		
PARKES, Phil B.F.	Sedgley	08.08.50	Jnrs	**Walsall**	01.68	1968-69	52	0	0	(G)	E U23-6/E U21-1/E-1/E-'B'
			Tr	**Q.P.R.**	06.70	1970-78	344	0	0		
			Tr	**West Ham U.**	02.79	1978-88	322	0	0		
PARKIN, Brian	Birkenhead	12.10.65	Jnrs	**Oldham Ath.**	03.83	1983-84	6	0	0	(G)	
			Tr	**Crewe Alex.**	11.84	1984-87	98	0	0		
			Tr	**Crystal Palace**	06.88	1988	19	0	0		
PARKIN, Steve J.	Mansfield	07.11.65	App	**Stoke C.**	11.83	1982-88	104	9	5	(M/LB)	E Sch Int/E Yth Int/E U21-5
PARKIN, Tim J.	Penrith	31.12.57	App	**Blackburn Rov.**	03.76	1976-78	13	0	0	(CD)	
			FK Malmö (Sweden)	**Bristol Rov.**	08.81	1981-85	205	1	12		
			Tr	**Swindon T.**	07.86	1986-88	103	1	5		

Players Names	Birthplace	Date	Previous Club	League Club	Date Sign'd	Seasons Played	Apps	Sub	Gls	Pos.	Misc
PARKINSON, Gary	Middlesbrough	10.01.68	Everton (Jnr)	**Middlesbrough**	01.86	1986-88	117	3	2	(RB)	
PARKINSON, Joseph S.	Eccles	11.06.71	YTS	**Wigan Ath.**	03.89	1988	8	4	1	(M)	
PARKINSON, Philip J.	Chorley	01.12.67	App	**Southampton**	12.85					(W)	
			Tr	**Bury**	03.88	1987-88	44	3	1		
PARKS, A. (Tony)	Hackney	28.01.63	App	**Tottenham H.**	09.80	1981-87	37	0	0	(G)	
			L	**Oxford U.**	10.86	1986	5	0	0		
			L	**Gillingham**	09.87	1987	2	0	0		
			Tr	**Brentford**	08.88	1988	33	0	0		
PARRIS, George M.R.	Ilford	11.09.64	App	**West Ham U.**	09.82	1984-88	109	11	4	(LB/M)	E Sch Int
PASCOE, Colin J.	Port Talbot	09.04.65	App	**Swansea C.**	04.83	1982-87	167	7	39	(W)	W Yth Int/W U21-3/W-5
			Tr	**Sunderland**	03.88	1987-88	47	1	14		
PASHLEY, Terry	Chesterfield	11.10.56	App	**Burnley**	10.73	1975-77	16	2	0	(LB)	E Sch Int
			Tr	**Blackpool**	08.78	1978-82	201	0	7		
			Tr	**Bury**	08.83	1983-88	205	12	5		
PASKIN, W. John	Cape Town (SA)	01.02.62	Belgium	**West Bromwich A.**	08.88	1988	14	11	5	(F)	
PATERSON, Toby L.	Cresswell	15.05.71	YTS	**Halifax T.** (YTS)	07.87	1988	0	1	0		
PATES, Colin G.	Carshalton	10.08.61	App	**Chelsea**	07.79	1979-88	280	1	10	(CD)	E Yth Int
			Tr	**Charlton Ath.**	10.88	1988	20	1	0		
PATTERSON, Mark	Leeds	13.09.68	YTS	**Carlisle U.**	08.87	1986-87	19	3	0	(RB)	
			Tr	**Derby Co.**	11.87	1988	1	0	0		
PATTERSON, Mark A.	Darwen	24.05.65	App	**Blackburn Rov.**	05.83	1983-87	89	12	20	(W)	
			Tr	**Preston N.E.**	06.88	1988	42	0	15		
PAYNE, Lee J.	Luton	12.12.66	Barnet	**Newcastle U.**	09.88	1988	6	1	0	(LW)	
			Tr	**Reading**	03.89	1988	15	0	3		
PAYNE, Mark R.C.	Cheltenham	03.08.60	SC Cambuur (Neth)	**Stockport Co.**	08.88	1988	20	2	1	(F)	
PAYTON, Andrew P.	Whalley	03.10.67	YTS	**Hull C.**	05.86	1986-88	29	23	6	(M)	
PEACOCK, Darren	Bristol	03.02.68	YTS	**Newport Co.**	02.86	1985-87	24	4	0	(CD)	
			Tr	**Hereford U.**	03.89	1988	6	2	0		
PEACOCK, Gavin K.	Eltham	18.11.67	App	**Q.P.R.**	11.84	1986-87	7	10	1	(M)	Son of Keith/E Sch Int/E Yth Int
			L	**Gillingham**	10.87	1987	6	0	0		
			Tr	**Gillingham**	12.87	1987-88	63	1	11		
PEAKE, Andy M.	Market Harborough	01.11.61	App	**Leicester C.**	01.79	1978-84	141	6	13	(M)	E Yth Int/E U21-1
			Tr	**Grimsby T.**	08.85	1985-86	39	0	4		
			Tr	**Charlton Ath.**	09.86	1986-88	73	3	1		
PEAKE, Trevor	Nuneaton	10.02.57	Nuneaton Bor.	**Lincoln C.**	06.79	1979-82	171	0	7	(CD)	E Semi-Pro Int 1979
			Tr	**Coventry C.**	07.83	1983-88	206	1	5		
PEARCE, Chris L.	Newport	07.08.61	W'hampton W.(App)	**Blackburn Rov.**	10.79					(G)	W Sch Int
			L	**Rochdale**	08.80	1980	5	0	0		
			Tr	**Rochdale**	08.82	1982	36	0	0		
			Tr	**Port Vale**	06.83	1983-85	48	0	0		
			Tr	**Wrexham**	07.86	1986	25	0	0		
			Tr	**Burnley**	07.87	1987-88	85	0	0		
PEARCE, Graham C.	Hammersmith	08.07.59	Barnet	**Brighton & H.A.**	01.82	1982-85	87	1	2	(LB)	
			Tr	**Gillingham**	07.86	1986-87	65	0	0		
			Tr	**Brentford**	09.88	1988	11	7	0		
PEARCE, Stuart	Hammersmith	24.04.62	Wealdstone	**Coventry C.**	10.83	1983-84	51	0	4	(LB)	E U21-1/E-15
			Tr	**Nottingham F.**	06.85	1985-88	139	0	18		
PEARCEY, Jason	Leamington	23.07.71	YTS	**Mansfield T.** (YTS)	08.87	1988	1	0	0	(G)	
PEARS, Steve	Brandon	22.01.62	App	**Manchester U.**	01.79	1984	4	0	0	(G)	
			L	**Middlesbrough**	11.83	1983	12	0	0		
			Tr	**Middlesbrough**	07.85	1985-88	153	0	0		
PEARSON, John S.	Sheffield	01.09.63	App	**Sheffield Wed.**	05.81	1980-84	64	41	24	(F)	E Yth Int
			Tr	**Charlton Ath.**	05.85	1985-86	52	9	15		
			Tr	**Leeds U.**	01.87	1986-88	45	34	11		
PEARSON, Nigel G.	Nottingham	21.08.63	Heanor T.	**Shrewsbury T.**	11.81	1982-87	153	0	5	(CD)	
			Tr	**Sheffield Wed.**	10.87	1987-88	56	0	4		
PEARSON, Richard	Ulcombe (Ke)	18.10.70	YTS	**Gillingham** (YTS)	06.87	1988	2	1	0	(CD)	
PECKETT, Andy R.	Sheffield	19.09.69	YTS	**Doncaster Rov.**	06.88	1987-88	2	7	0	(M)	
PEER, Dean	Dudley	08.08.69	YTS	**Birmingham C.**	07.87	1986-88	16	3	1	(M)	
PEJIC, Mel	Newcastle-u-Lyme	27.04.59	Jnrs	**Stoke C.**	07.77	1979	1	0	0	(CD)	Brother of Mike
			Tr	**Hereford U.**	06.80	1980-88	309	4	7		
PEMBERTON, John M.	Oldham	18.11.64	Chadderton	**Rochdale** (N/C)	09.84	1984	1	0	0	(FB)	
			Tr	**Crewe Alex.**	03.85	1984-87	116	5	1		
			Tr	**Crystal Palace**	03.88	1987-88	42	2	1		
PENDER, John P.	Luton	19.11.63	App	**Wolverhampton W.**	11.81	1981-84	115	2	3	(CD)	IR Yth Int/IR U21-1
			Tr	**Charlton Ath.**	07.85	1985-87	41	0	0		
			Tr	**Bristol C.**	10.87	1987-88	73	0	3		
PENHALIGON, Gary	St. Austell	13.05.70	YTS	**Plymouth Arg.**	07.88	1988	1	0	0	(G)	
PENNEY, David M.	Wakefield	17.08.64	Pontefract Colly.	**Derby Co.**	09.85	1986-88	6	13	0	(F)	
PENNEY, Steve A.	Ballymena (NI)	16.01.64	Ballymena U.	**Brighton & H.A.**	11.83	1983-88	125	13	15	(W)	NI-17
PENNYFATHER, Glenn J.	Billericay	11.02.63	App	**Southend U.**	02.81	1980-87	231	7	36	(M)	
			Tr	**Crystal Palace**	11.87	1987-88	31	3	1		
PENRICE, Gary K.	Bristol	23.03.64	Mangotsfield	**Bristol Rov.**	11.84	1984-88	174	2	50	(F)	
PEPPER, Nigel C.	Rotherham	25.04.68	App	**Rotherham U.**	04.86	1985-88	20	6	0	(M)	
PERKS, Stephen J.	Bridgnorth	19.04.63	App	**Shrewsbury T.**	04.81	1984-88	165	0	0	(G)	
PERRY, Andy	Dulwich	28.12.62	Dulwich Hamlet	**Portsmouth**	11.86	1987	1	3	0	(F)	
			Tr	**Gillingham**	08.88	1988	8	5	0		
PERRY, Jason	Newport	02.04.70	Jnrs	**Cardiff C.**	08.87	1986-87	4	0	0	(D)	
PERRYMAN, Steve J.	Ealing	21.12.51	App	**Tottenham H.**	01.69	1969-85	653	2	31	(M)	E Sch Int/E Yth Int/E U23-17/E-1/ FWA Footballer of Year 1981-82
			Tr	**Oxford U.**	03.86	1985-86	17	0	0		
			Tr	**Brentford**	11.86	1986-88	41	9	0		

Chris Price (Aston Villa) Match Magazine

Trevor Putney (Norwich City) Match Magazine

Mike Quinn (Portsmouth) Match Magazine

Ian Redford (Ipswich Town) Match Magazine

Players Names	Birthplace	Date	Previous Club	League Club	Date Sign'd	Seasons Played	Career Record Apps	Sub	Gls	Pos.	Misc
PETERS, Gary D.	Carshalton	03.08.54	Guildford C.	**Reading**	05.75	1975-78	150	6	7	(D)	
			Tr	**Fulham**	08.79	1979-81	57	7	2		
			Tr	**Wimbledon**	07.82	1982-83	83	0	7		
			Tr	**Aldershot**	07.84	1984	17	0	1		
			Tr	**Reading**	02.85	1984-87	93	7	3		
			Tr	**Fulham** (N/C)	08.88	1988	7	2	2		
PEYTON, Gerry J.	Birmingham	20.05.56	Atherstone T.	**Burnley**	05.75	1975-76	30	0	0	(G)	IR-27
			Tr	**Fulham**	12.76	1976-85	345	0	0		
			L	**Southend U.**	09.83	1983	10	0	0		
			Tr	**Bournemouth**	07.86	1986-88	127	0	0		
PHELAN, Mike C.	Nelson	24.09.62	App	**Burnley**	07.80	1980-84	166	2	9	(M)	E Yth Int
			Tr	**Norwich C.**	07.85	1985-88	155	1	9		
PHELAN, Terry M.	Manchester	16.03.67	YTS	**Leeds U.**	08.84	1985	12	2	0	(LB)	IR Yth Int
			Tr	**Swansea C.**	07.86	1986	45	0	0		
			Tr	**Wimbledon**	07.87	1987-88	55	4	0		
PHILLIPS, David O.	West Germany	29.07.63	App	**Plymouth Arg.**	08.81	1981-83	65	8	15	(M)	W U21-3/W-22
			Tr	**Manchester C.**	08.84	1984-85	81	0	13		
			Tr	**Coventry C.**	06.86	1986-88	93	7	8		
PHILLIPS, Gary C.	St. Albans	20.09.61	Jnrs	**West Bromwich A.**	06.79					(G)	E Semi-Pro Int 1982
			Barnet	**Brentford**	12.84	1984-87	143	0	0		
			Tr	**Reading**	08.88	1988	24	0	0		
PHILLIPS, Ian A.	Edinburgh	23.04.59	Ipswich T. (App)	**Mansfield T.**	08.77	1977-78	18	5	0	(LB)	
			Tr	**Peterborough U.**	08.79	1979-81	97	0	3		
			Tr	**Northampton T.**	08.82	1982	42	0	1		
			Tr	**Colchester U.**	09.83	1983-86	150	0	8		
			Tr	**Aldershot**	08.87	1987-88	62	0	0		
PHILLIPS, Jimmy N.	Bolton	08.02.66	App	**Bolton W.**	08.83	1983-86	103	5	2	(LB)	
			Glasgow Rangers	**Oxford U.**	08.88	1988	45	0	3		
PHILLIPS, Les M.	Lambeth	07.01.63	App	**Birmingham C.**	08.80	1981-83	36	8	3	(M)	
			Tr	**Oxford U.**	03.84	1983-88	119	9	10		
PHILLIPS, Stuart G.	Halifax	30.12.61	App	**Hereford U.**	11.79	1977-87	285	8	83	(F)	
			Tr	**West Bromwich A.**	03.88	1987-88	15	0	4		
			Tr	**Swansea C.**	01.89	1988	4	2	0		
PHILLISKIRK, A. (Tony)	Sunderland	10.02.65	Sch	**Sheffield U.**	08.83	1983-87	62	18	20	(F)	E Sch Int
			L	**Rotherham U.**	10.86	1986	6	0	1		
			Tr	**Oldham Ath.**	07.88	1988	3	7	1		
			Tr	**Preston N.E.**	02.89	1988	13	1	6		
PHILPOTT, Lee	Barnet	21.02.70	YTS	**Peterborough U.**	07.88	1987-88	1	3	0	(M)	
PICKARD, Owen A.	Barnstaple	18.11.89	YTS	**Plymouth Arg.**	07.88	1988	1	1	0	(F)	
PICKERING, Mike J.	Heckmondwike	29.09.56	Jnrs	**Barnsley**	10.74	1974-76	100	0	1	(CD)	
			Tr	**Southampton**	06.77	1977-78	44	0	0		
			Tr	**Sheffield Wed.**	10.78	1978-82	106	4	1		
			L	**Norwich C.**	09.83	1983	0	1	0		
			L	**Bradford C.**	11.83	1983	4	0	0		
			L	**Barnsley**	12.83	1983	3	0	0		
			Tr	**Rotherham U.**	01.84	1983-85	102	0	1		
			Tr	**York C.**	07.86	1986	31	1	1		
			Tr	**Stockport Co.**	07.87	1987-88	15	1	0		
PICKERING, Nick	Newcastle	04.08.63	App	**Sunderland**	08.81	1981-85	177	2	18	(LM)	E Yth Int/E U21-15
			Tr	**Coventry C.**	01.86	1985-87	76	2	9		
			Tr	**Derby Co.**	08.88	1988	5	3	0		
PIKE, Geoff A.	Clapton	28.09.56	App	**West Ham U.**	09.74	1975-86	275	16	32	(M)	
			Tr	**Notts Co.**	07.87	1987-88	80	2	17		
PIKE, Martin R.	South Shields	21.10.64	App	**West Bromwich A.**	10.82					(LB)	
			Tr	**Peterborough U.**	08.83	1983-85	119	7	8		
			Tr	**Sheffield U.**	08.86	1986-88	125	1	5		
PILLING, Andrew J.	Wigan	30.06.69	YTS	**Preston N.E.** (YTS)	07.85	1985	1	0	0	(M)	
			Tr	**Wigan Ath.**	07.87	1987-88	54	5	5		
PINGEL, Frank	Denmark	09.05.64	Aarhus GF (Denmark)	**Newcastle U.**	01.89	1988	13	1	1	(F)	Danish Int
PISANTI, David	Israel	27.05.62	F.C. Köln (WG)	**Q.P.R.**	09.87	1987-88	16	6	0	(M)	
PITTMAN, Stephen	North Carolina(USA)	18.07.67	East Fife	**Shrewsbury T.**	03.89	1988	11	1	0	(LB)	
PLACE, Mark	Mansfield	16.11.69	YTS	**Mansfield T.**	07.88	1988	11	3	0	(D)	
PLASKETT, Stephen C.	Newcastle	24.04.71	YTS	**Hartlepool U.** (YTS)	03.89	1988	12	0	0	(RB)	
PLATNAUER, Nicky R.	Leicester	10.06.61	Bedford T.	**Bristol Rov.**	08.82	1982	21	3	7	(M/LB)	
			Tr	**Coventry C.**	08.83	1983-84	38	6	6		
			Tr	**Birmingham C.**	12.84	1984-85	23	5	2		
			L	**Reading**	01.86	1985	7	0	0		
			Tr	**Cardiff C.**	09.86	1986-88	110	5	6		
PLATT, David A.	Oldham	10.06.66	Chadderton	**Manchester U.**	07.84					(F)	E 'B'/E U21-3
			Tr	**Crewe Alex.**	01.85	1984-87	134	0	55		
			Tr	**Aston Villa**	02.88	1987-88	49	0	12		
PLUMMER, Calvin A.	Nottingham	14.02.63	App	**Nottingham F.**	02.81	1981-82	10	2	2	(W)	
			Tr	**Chesterfield**	12.82	1982	28	0	7		
			Tr	**Derby Co.**	08.83	1983	23	4	3		
			Tr	**Barnsley**	03.84	1983-86	41	13	6		
			Tr	**Nottingham F.**	12.86						
			Finland	**Nottingham F.**	10.87	1987	8	0	2		
			Tr	**Plymouth Arg.**	09.88	1988	17	6	1		
POINTON, Neil G.	Warsop	28.11.64	App	**Scunthorpe U.**	08.82	1981-85	159	0	2	(LB)	
			Tr	**Everton**	11.85	1985-88	76	7	4		
POLLARD, Gary	Staveley	30.12.59	Jnrs	**Chesterfield**	07.77	1977-82	83	4	1	(CD)	
			Tr	**Port Vale**	06.83	1983	18	0	0		
			Tr	**Mansfield T.**	07.84	1984-86	66	1	1		
			Tr	**Peterborough U.**	08.87	1987-88	20	0	0		
POLLARD, Kelly, J.	Chelmsford	17.11.71	YTS	**Colchester U.** (YTS)	07.88	1988	0	2	1	(F)	
POLSTON, Jonathan D.	Walthamstow	10.06.68	App	**Tottenham H.**	07.85	1986-88	6	5	0	(CD)	E Yth Int
POOLE, Gary J.	Stratford	11.09.67	Jnrs	**Tottenham H.**	07.85					(RB)	
			Tr	**Cambridge U.**	08.87		42	1	0		

Players Names	Birthplace	Date	Previous Club	League Club	Date Sign'd	Seasons Played	Career Record Apps	Sub	Gls	Pos.	Misc
POOLE, Kevin	Bromsgrove	21.07.63	App	**Aston Villa**	06.81	1984-86	28	0	0	(G)	
			L	**Northampton T.**	11.84	1984	3	0	0		
			Tr	**Middlesbrough**	08.87	1987-88	13	0	0		
PORTER, Andrew M.	Macclesfield	17.09.68	YTS	**Port Vale**	06.87	1986-88	16	5	1	(M)	
PORTER, Gary M.	Sunderland	06.03.66	App	**Watford**	03.84	1983-88	114	13	18	(M)	E Yth Int/E U21-12
POTTS, Steven J.	USA	07.05.67	App	**West Ham U.**	05.84	1984-88	39	7	0	(FB)	E Yth Int
POWELL, Chris G.R.	Lambeth	08.09.69	YTS	**Crystal Palace**	12.87	1988	2	1	0	(LB)	
POWELL, Cliff G.	Watford	21.02.68	App	**Watford**	02.86					(D)	
			L	**Hereford U.**	12.87	1987	7	0	0		
			Tr	**Sheffield U.**	03.88	1987-88	7	3	0		
			L	**Doncaster Rov.**	03.89	1988	4	0	0		
POWELL, Darryl A.	Lambeth	15.11.71	YTS	**Portsmouth**	12.88	1988	2	1	0	(F)	
PRATLEY, Richard G.	Banbury	12.01.63	Banbury U.	**Derby Co.**	07.83	1983-86	29	2	1	(CD)	
			L	**Scunthorpe U.**	03.84	1983	10	0	0		
			Tr	**Shrewsbury T.**	02.88	1987-88	37	2	0		
PREECE, Andy P.	Evesham	27.03.67	Evesham U.	**Northampton T.** (N/C)	08.88	1988	0	1	0	(F)	
PREECE, David W.	Bridgnorth	28.05.63	App	**Walsall**	07.80	1980-84	107	4	5	(LM)	E 'B'
			Tr	**Luton T.**	12.84	1984-88	114	1	4		
PREECE, Roger	Much Wenlock	09.06.69	Coventry C. (YTS)	**Wrexham**	08.86	1986-88	62	16	11	(M)	
PRESSMAN, Kevin P.	Fareham	06.11.67	App	**Sheffield Wed.**	11.85	1987-88	20	0	0	(G)	E Sch Int/E Yth Int/E U21-1
PRICE, Chris J.	Hereford	30.03.60	App	**Hereford U.**	01.78	1976-85	327	3	27	(RB)	
			Tr	**Blackburn Rov.**	07.86	1986-87	83	0	10		
			Tr	**Aston Villa**	05.88	1988	36	0	0		
PRIEST, Philip	Warley	09.09.66	App	**Chelsea**	09.83					(M)	E Sch Int/E Yth Int
			L	**Blackpool**	12.86	1986	1	0	0		
			L	**Brentford**	03.87	1986	3	2	1		
			Tr	**Shrewsbury T.**	07.87	1987-88	47	2	3		
PRINDIVILLE, Stephen A.	Harlow	26.12.68	App	**Leicester C.**	12.86	1987	0	1	0	(FB)	
			Tr	**Chesterfield**	06.88	1988	43	0	1		
PRIOR, Spencer J.	Southend	22.04.71	YTS	**Southend U.** (YTS)	07.87	1988	14	0	1	(CD)	
PRITCHARD, Howard K.	Cardiff	18.10.58	App	**Bristol C.**	08.76	1978-80	31	7	2	(W)	W Yth Int/W-1
			Tr	**Swindon T.**	08.81	1981-82	59	6	11		
			Tr	**Bristol C.**	08.83	1983-85	117	2	22		
			Tr	**Gillingham**	08.86	1986-87	84	4	20		
			Tr	**Walsall**	07.88	1988	36	4	6		
PROCTOR, Mark G.	Middlesbrough	30.01.61	App	**Middlesbrough**	09.78	1978-80	107	2	12	(M)	E Yth Int/E U21-4
			Tr	**Nottingham F.**	08.81	1981-82	60	4	5		
			Tr	**Sunderland**	03.83	1982-87	115	2	19		
			Tr	**Sheffield Wed.**	09.87	1987-88	59	0	4		
			Tr	**Middlesbrough**	03.89	1988	10	0	0		
PROUDLOCK, Paul	Hartlepool	25.10.65	Jnrs	**Hartlepool U.**	09.84	1984-85	8	7	0	(W)	
				Middlesbrough	11.86	1986-88	2	3	0		
			Tr	**Carlisle U.**	03.89	1988	10	0	3		
PRUDHOE, Mark	Washington	11.11.63	App	**Sunderland**	09.81	1982	7	0	0	(G)	
			L	**Hartlepool U.**	11.83	1983	3	0	0		
			Tr	**Birmingham C.**	09.84	1984	1	0	0		
			Tr	**Walsall**	02.86	1985-86	26	0	0		
			L	**Doncaster Rov.**	12.86	1986	5	0	0		
			L	**Grimsby T.**	03.87	1986	8	0	0		
			L	**Hartlepool U.**	08.87	1987	13	0	0		
			L	**Bristol C.**	11.87	1987	3	0	0		
			Tr	**Carlisle U.**	12.87	1987-88	34	0	0		
			Tr	**Darlington**	03.89	1988	12	0	0		
PUCKETT, David C.	Southampton	29.10.60	App	**Southampton**	10.78	1980-85	51	43	14	(F)	
			Tr	**Bournemouth**	07.86	1986-88	29	6	14		
			L	**Stoke C.**	03.88	1987	7	0	0		
			L	**Swansea C.**	11.88	1988	7	1	3		
			Tr	**Aldershot**	01.89	1988	21	0	11		
PUGH, Daral J.	Neath	05.06.61	App	**Doncaster Rov.**	12.78	1978-82	136	18	15	(W)	W U21-2
			Tr	**Huddersfield T.**	09.82	1982-84	52	32	7		
			Tr	**Rotherham U.**	07.85	1985-87	106	6	6		
			L	**Cambridge U.**	12.87	1987	6	0	1		
			Tr	**Torquay U.**	08.88	1988	26	3	0		
PULIS, A.R. (Tony)	Newport	16.01.58	App	**Bristol Rov.**	09.75	1975-80	78	7	3	(D/M)	
			Hong Kong	**Bristol Rov.**	06.82	1982-83	44	1	2		
			Tr	**Newport Co.**	07.84	1984-85	75	2	0		
			Tr	**Bournemouth**	08.86	1986-88	68	6	3		
PULLAN, Chris J.	Durham	14.12.67	Jnrs	**Watford**	07.86	1986-88	3	3	0	(M)	
			L	**Halifax T.**	02.89	1988	5	0	1		
PURDIE, Jon	Corby	22.02.67	App	**Arsenal**	01.85					(W)	E Sch Int
			Tr	**Wolverhampton W.**	07.85	1985-87	82	7	12		
			L	**Cambridge U.**	10.87	1987	7	0	2		
			Tr	**Oxford U.**	07.88	1988	5	6	0		
			L	**Brentford**	03.89	1988	5	1	0		
PURNELL, Philip	Bristol	16.09.64	Mangotsfield	**Bristol Rov.**	09.85	1985-88	102	8	20	(W)	
PUTNEY, Trevor A.	Harold Hill	11.02.61	Brentwood & Warley	**Ipswich T.**	09.80	1982-85	94	9	8	(M)	
			Tr	**Norwich C.**	06.86	1986-88	76	6	9		
PUTTNAM, David	Leicester	03.02.67	Leicester C.	**Leicester C.**	02.89	1988	2	1	0	(W)	
QUAMINA, Mark E.	Guyana	25.11.69	YTS	**Wimbledon**	07.88	1988	1	0	0	(M)	
QUINN, Jimmy M.	Belfast	18.11.59	Oswestry T.	**Swindon T.**	12.81	1981-83	34	15	10	(F)	NI-25
			Tr	**Blackburn Rov.**	08.84	1984-86	58	13	17		
			Tr	**Swindon T.**	12.86	1986-87	61	3	30		
			Tr	**Leicester C.**	06.88	1988	13	18	6		
			Tr	**Bradford C.**	03.89	1988	12	0	7		
QUINN, Mike	Liverpool	02.05.62	Derby Co. (App)	**Wigan Ath.**	09.79	1979-81	56	13	19	(F)	
			Tr	**Stockport Co.**	07.82	1982-83	62	1	39		
			Tr	**Oldham Ath.**	01.84	1983-85	78	2	34		
			Tr	**Portsmouth**	03.86	1986-88	115	6	54		
QUINN, Niall J.	Dublin	06.10.66	Jnrs	**Arsenal**	11.83	1985-88	53	8	12	(F)	IR Yth Int/IR-11

Steve Redmond (Manchester City) Match Magazine

Peter Reid (Q.P.R. & England) Match Magazine

Bryan Robson (Manchester United & England) Match Magazine

Players Names	Birthplace	Date	Previous Club	League Club	Date Sign'd	Seasons Played	Career Record Apps	Sub	Gls	Pos.	Misc
QUOW, Trevor	Peterborough	28.09.60	App	**Peterborough U.**	09.78	1978-85	191	12	17	(M)	
			Tr	**Gillingham**	08.86	1986-88	64	15	3		
			Tr	**Northampton T.**	01.89	1988	17	1	1		
RADFORD, Mark	Leicester	20.12.68	Jnrs	**Colchester U.**	05.87	1987-88	28	16	1	(M)	
RAFFELL, Stephen C.	Blyth	27.04.70	YTS	**Doncaster Rov.**	06.88	1987-88	22	5	0	(CD)	
RAMAGE, Craig D.	Derby	30.03.70	YTS	**Derby Co.**	07.88					(F)	
			L	**Wigan Ath.**	02.89	1988	10	0	2		
RAMSEY, Paul	Derry (NI)	03.09.62	App	**Leicester C.**	04.80	1980-88	227	4	10	(M/RB)	NI-14
RANDALL, Adrian J.	Amesbury	10.11.68	App	**Bournemouth**	08.86	1985-87	3	0	0	(M)	E Yth Int
			Tr	**Aldershot**	09.88	1988	37	0	2		
RANKINE, S. Mark	Doncaster	30.09.69	YTS	**Doncaster Rov.**	06.88	1987-88	60	4	13	(F)	
RANSHAW, Richard W.G.	Sleaford	17.04.70	YTS	**Lincoln C.** (N/C)	08.88	1988	0	1	0	(F)	
RANSON, Ray	St. Helens	12.06.60	App	**Manchester C.**	06.77	1978-83	181	2	1	(RB)	E Yth Int/E U21-10
			Tr	**Birmingham C.**	11.84	1984-88	136	1	0		
			Tr	**Newcastle U.**	12.88	1988	13	1	1		
RANTANEN, Jari J.	Finland	31.12.61	Gothenburg (Sweden)	**Leicester C.**	09.87	1987	10	3	3	(F)	Finnish Int
RATCLIFFE, Kevin	Deeside	12.11.60	App	**Everton**	11.78	1979-88	289	1	2	(CD)	W Sch Int/W U21-2/W-47
RATCLIFFE, Simon	Urmston	08.02.67	App	**Manchester U.**	02.85					(D)	E Sch Int/E Yth Int
			Tr	**Norwich C.**	06.87	1987	6	3	0		
			Tr	**Brentford**	01.89	1988	7	2	1		
RATHBONE, Mike J.	Birmingham	06.11.58	App	**Birmingham C.**	11.76	1976-78	17	3	0	(LB)	E Yth Int
			Tr	**Blackburn Rov.**	03.79	1978-86	270	3	2		
			Tr	**Preston N.E.**	07.87	1987-88	68	2	3		
RAVEN, Paul	Salisbury	28.07.70	Jnrs	**Doncaster Rov.**	06.88	1987-88	52	0	4	(CD)	E Sch Int
			Tr	**West Bromwich A.**	03.89	1988	3	0	0		
RAYNOR, Paul J.	Nottingham	29.04.66	App	**Nottingham F.**	04.84	1984	3	0	0	(F)	
			L	**Bristol Rov.**	03.85	1984	7	1	0		
			Tr	**Huddersfield T.**	08.85	1985-86	38	12	9		
			Tr	**Swansea C.**	03.87	1986-88	88	4	14		
			L	**Wrexham**	10.88	1988	6	0	0		
RECK, Sean M.	Oxford	05.05.67	App	**Oxford U.**	04.85	1986-88	11	3	0	(M)	
			L	**Newport Co.**	08.85	1985	15	0	0		
			L	**Reading**	03.86	1985	1	0	0		
REDFEARN, Neil D.	Dewsbury	20.06.65	Nottingham F.(App)	**Bolton W.**	06.82	1982-83	35	0	1	(M)	
			Tr	**Lincoln C.**	03.84	1983-85	96	4	13		
			Tr	**Doncaster Rov.**	08.86	1986	46	0	14		
			Tr	**Crystal Palace**	07.87	1987-88	57	0	10		
			Tr	**Watford**	11.88	1988	12	0	2		
REDFORD, Ian P.	Perth	05.04.60	Dundee U.	**Ipswich T.**	11.88	1988	22	2	2	(LW)	S Yth Int/S U21-6
REDMOND, Steve	Liverpool	02.11.67	App	**Manchester C.**	12.84	1985-88	127	2	3	(CD)	E Yth Int/E U21-12
REECE, Andy J.	Shrewsbury	05.09.62	Dudley T.	**Bristol Rov.**	08.87	1987-88	77	5	8	(M)	
REECE, Paul J.	Nottingham	16.07.68	App	**Stoke C.**	07.86	1986	2	0	0	(G)	
			Kettering T.	**Grimsby T.**	07.88	1988	14	0	0		
REED, Graham	Doncaster	24.06.61	App	**Barnsley**	06.79	1978-79	3	0	0	(RB)	
			Frickley Ath.	**Northampton T.**	06.85	1985-88	105	7	2		
REES, A.A. (Tony)	Merthyr Tydfil	01.08.64	App	**Aston Villa**	08.82					(F)	W Sch Int/W Yth Int/W U21-1/W-1
			Tr	**Birmingham C.**	07.83	1983-87	75	20	12		
			L	**Peterborough U.**	10.85	1985	5	0	2		
			L	**Shrewsbury T.**	03.86	1985	1	1	0		
			Tr	**Barnsley**	03.88	1987-88	27	4	3		
REES, Mark	Smethwick	13.10.61	App	**Walsall**	08.79	1978-88	181	49	36	(RW)	E Sch Int
			L	**Rochdale**	10.86	1986	2	1	0		
REES, Melvyn J.	Cardiff	25.01.67	YTS	**Cardiff C.**	09.84	1984-86	31	0	0	(G)	W Yth Int
			Tr	**Watford**	07.87	1987	3	0	0		
REEVES, Alan	Birkenhead	19.11.67	Heswall	**Norwich C.**	09.88					(CD)	Twin Brother of David
			L	**Gillingham**	02.89	1988	18	0	0		
REEVES, David	Birkenhead	19.11.67	Heswall	**Sheffield Wed.**	08.86	1988	8	9	2	(F)	Twin Brother of Alan
			L	**Scunthorpe U.**	12.86	1986	3	1	2		
			L	**Scunthorpe U.**	10.87	1987	6	0	4		
			L	**Burnley**	11.87	1987	16	0	8		
REGIS, Cyrille	French Guyana	09.02.58	Hayes	**West Bromwich A.**	05.77	1977-84	233	4	82	(F)	E U21-6/E-5/E 'B'
			Tr	**Coventry C.**	10.84	1984-88	168	2	39		
REID, Mark	Kilwinning	15.09.61	Glasgow Celtic	**Charlton Ath.**	05.85	1985-88	156	0	13	(LB)	S U21-2
REID, Nicky S.	Urmston	30.10.60	App	**Manchester C.**	10.78	1978-86	211	5	2	(D/M)	E U21-6
			Tr	**Blackburn Rov.**	07.87	1987-88	81	0	2		
REID, Paul R.	Warley	19.01.68	App	**Leicester C.**	01.86	1986-88	71	6	11	(W)	
REID, Peter	Huyton	20.06.56	App	**Bolton W.**	05.74	1974-82	222	3	23	(M)	E U21-6/E-13/PFA Player of Year 1984-85/Brother of Shaun
			Tr	**Everton**	12.82	1982-88	155	4	8		
			Tr	**Q.P.R.**	02.89	1988	14	0	1		
REID, Shaun	Huyton	13.10.65	YTS	**Rochdale**	09.83	1983-88	126	7	4	(M)	Brother of Peter
			L	**Preston N.E.**	12.85	1985	3	0	0		
			Tr	**York C.**	12.88	1988	24	0	2		
REID, Wesley A.	Lewisham	10.09.68	YTS	**Arsenal**	07.86					(M)	
			Tr	**Millwall**	06.87	1988	1	0	0		
REILLY, George G.	Bellshill	14.09.57	Corby T.	**Northampton T.**	06.76	1976-79	124	3	46	(F)	
			Tr	**Cambridge U.**	11.79	1979-82	136	2	36		
			Tr	**Watford**	08.83	1983-84	46	2	14		
			Tr	**Newcastle U.**	02.85	1984-85	31	0	10		
			Tr	**West Bromwich A.**	12.85	1985-87	42	1	9		
			Tr	**Cambridge U.**	07.88	1988	20	0	7		
RENNIE, David	Edinburgh	29.08.64	App	**Leicester C.**	05.82	1983-85	21	0	1	(CD)	S Yth Int
			Tr	**Leeds U.**	01.86	1985-88	95	6	5		
RHOADES-BROWN, Peter	Hampton	02.01.62	App	**Chelsea**	07.79	1979-83	86	10	4	(LW)	
			Tr	**Oxford U.**	01.84	1983-88	87	25	13		

Players Names	Birthplace	Date	Previous Club	League Club	Date Sign'd	Seasons Played	Career Record Apps	Sub	Gls	Pos.	Misc
RHODES, Andy C.	Askern	23.08.64	App	**Barnsley**	08.82	1983-84	36	0	0	(G)	
			Tr	**Doncaster Rov.**	10.85	1985-87	106	0	0		
			Tr	**Oldham Ath.**	03.88	1987-88	38	0	0		
RICE, Brian	Bellshill	11.10.63	Hibernian	**Nottingham F.**	08.85	1985-88	71	1	7	(LW)	S U21-1
			L	**Grimsby T.**	10.86	1986	4	0	0		
			L	**West Bromwich A.**	01.89	1988	2	1	0		
RICHARDS, Carl L.	Jamaica (WI)	01.12.60	Enfield	**Bournemouth**	07.86	1986-88	57	14	16	(F)	E Semi-Pro Int 1986
			Tr	**Birmingham C.**	10.88	1988	18	1	2		
RICHARDS, Steve C.	Dundee	24.10.61	App	**Hull C.**	10.79	1979-82	55	3	2	(CD)	
			Gainsborough Trin.	**York C.** (N/C)	12.84	1984	6	1	0		
			Tr	**Lincoln C.**	08.85	1985	21	0	0		
			Tr	**Cambridge U.** (N/C)	03.86	1985	4	0	2		
			Tr	**Scarborough**	(N/L)	1987-88	84	0	6		
RICHARDSON, Ian P.	Ely	09.05.64	App	**Watford**	05.82	1983-84	5	3	2	(F)	
			L	**Blackpool**	12.82	1982	4	1	2		
			L	**Rotherham U.**	02.85	1984	5	0	2		
			Tr	**Chester C.**	11.85	1985-86	31	4	10		
			Tr	**Scunthorpe U.**	10.86	1986-88	11	7	4		
RICHARDSON, Kevin	Newcastle	04.12.62	App	**Everton**	12.80	1981-86	95	14	16	(LM)	
			Tr	**Watford**	09.86	1986	39	0	2		
			Tr	**Arsenal**	08.87	1987-88	56	7	5		
RICHARDSON, Lee J.	Halifax	12.03.69	YTS	**Halifax T.**	07.87	1986-88	43	13	2	(M)	
			Tr	**Watford**	02.89	1988	9	0	0		
RICHARDSON, Nick	Halifax	11.04.67		**Halifax T.**	11.88	1988	4	3	0	(M)	
RICHARDSON, Steve E.	Slough	11.02.62	App	**Southampton**	02.80					(LB)	
			Tr	**Reading**	07.82	1982-88	249	3	2		
RIDEOUT, Paul D.	Bournemouth	14.08.64	App	**Swindon T.**	08.81	1980-82	90	5	38	(F)	E Sch Int/E Yth Int/E U21-5
			Tr	**Aston Villa**	06.83	1983-84	50	4	19		
			Bari (Italy)	**Southampton**	07.88	1988	20	4	6		
RILEY, David S.	Northampton	08.12.60	Keyworth U.	**Nottingham F.**	01.84	1983-86	7	5	2	(F)	
			L	**Darlington**	02.87	1986	6	0	2		
			L	**Peterborough U.**	07.87	1987	12	0	2		
			Tr	**Port Vale**	10.87	1987-88	73	1	11		
RILEY, Glyn	Barnsley	24.07.58	App	**Barnsley**	07.76	1974-81	102	28	16	(F)	
			L	**Doncaster Rov.**	12.79	1979	7	1	2		
			Tr	**Bristol C.**	08.82	1982-86	184	15	61		
			L	**Torquay U.**	09.87	1987	6	0	1		
			Tr	**Aldershot**	10.87	1987-88	48	10	5		
RIMMER, Neill	Liverpool	13.11.67	App	**Everton** (App)	04.84	1984	0	1	0	(M)	E Sch Int/E Yth Int
			Tr	**Ipswich T.**	08.85	1985-87	19	3	3		
			Tr	**Wigan Ath.**	07.88	1988	24	1	3		
RIMMER, Stuart A.	Southport	12.10.64	App	**Everton**	10.82	1981-83	3	0	0	(F)	E Yth Int
			Tr	**Chester C.**	01.85	1984-87	110	4	68		
			Tr	**Watford**	03.88	1987-88	10	0	1		
			Tr	**Notts Co.**	11.88	1988	3	1	2		
			Tr	**Walsall**	02.89	1988	20	0	8		
RING, Mike P.	Brighton	13.02.61	App	**Brighton & H.A.**	02.79	1981-83	1	4	0	(W)	
			Tr	**Hull C.**	07.84	1984-85	17	7	2		
			L	**Bolton W.**	03.86	1985	1	2	0		
			Tr	**Aldershot**	07.86	1986-88	53	26	16		
RIPLEY, Stuart E.	Middlesbrough	20.11.67	App	**Middlesbrough**	11.85	1984-88	126	6	16	(W)	E Yth Int/E U21-6
			L	**Bolton W.**	02.86	1985	5	0	1		
RITCHIE, Andy T.	Manchester	28.11.60	App	**Manchester U.**	12.77	1977-80	26	7	13	(F)	E Yth Int/E U21-1
			Tr	**Brighton & H.A.**	10.80	1980-82	82	7	23		
			Tr	**Leeds U.**	03.83	1982-86	127	9	40		
			Tr	**Oldham Ath.**	08.87	1987-88	66	1	33		
RIX, Graham	Doncaster	23.10.57	App	**Arsenal**	01.75	1976-87	338	13	41	(LM)	E U21-7/E-17
			L	**Brentford**	12.87	1987	6	0	0		to Caen (France) 5.88
ROBERTS, Alan	Newcastle	08.12.64	App	**Middlesbrough**	12.82	1982-85	28	10	2	(RW)	
			Tr	**Darlington**	09.85	1985-87	116	3	19		
			Tr	**Sheffield U.**	07.88	1988	25	4	2		
ROBERTS, Anthony M.	Bangor	04.08.69	YTS	**Q.P.R.**	07.87	1987	1	0	0	(G)	W Yth Int
ROBERTS, Brian L.F.	Manchester	06.11.55	App	**Coventry C.**	11.73	1975-83	209	6	1	(FB)	
			L	**Hereford U.**	02.75	1974	5	0	0		
			Tr	**Birmingham C.**	03.84	1983-88	173	4	0		
ROBERTS, Garreth W.	Hull	15.11.60	App	**Hull C.**	11.78	1978-88	365	5	47	(W)	W U21-1
ROBERTS, Graham P.	Southampton	03.07.59	Sholing	**Portsmouth** (N/C)	03.77					(CD)	E-6
			Weymouth	**Tottenham H.**	05.80	1980-86	200	9	23		
			Glasgow Rangers	**Chelsea**	08.88	1988	46	0	15		
ROBERTS, Iwan W.	Bangor	26.06.68	YTS	**Watford**	06.86	1985-88	32	22	9	(F)	W Yth Int
ROBERTS, Jeremy	Middlesbrough	24.11.66	Jnrs	**Hartlepool U.** (N/C)	12.83	1983	1	0	0	(G)	E Yth Int
			Tr	**Leicester C.**	07.84	1985	3	0	0		
			Luton T. (Trial)	**Darlington**	03.87	1986-87	29	0	0		
			Tr	**Brentford** (N/C)	09.88	1988	5	0	0		
ROBERTS, Jonathan W.	Ferndale	30.12.68	YTS	**Cardiff C.**	11.87	1987-88	9	0	0	(G)	W Yth Int
ROBERTS, Paul	West Ham	27.04.62	App	**Millwall**	04.79	1978-82	142	4	0	(RB)	
			Tr	**Brentford**	09.83	1983-84	61	1	0		
			Finland	**Swindon T.** (N/C)	09.85	1985	25	2	0		
			Tr	**Southend U.**	07.86	1986	38	0	0		
			Tr	**Aldershot**	08.87	1987	36	3	0		
			Leytonstone & Ilford	**Exeter C.** (N/C)	12.88	1988	3	0	0		
			Tr	**Southend U.**	01.89	1988	23	0	0		
ROBERTS, William J.	Bradford	09.04.63	Farsley Celtic	**Rochdale** (N/C)	11.88	1988	1	0	0	(F)	
ROBERTSON, Alistair	Linlithgow	09.09.52	App	**West Bromwich A.**	09.69	1969-85	504	2	8	(CD)	S Sch Int
			Tr	**Wolverhampton W.**	09.86	1986-88	102	0	0		
ROBERTSON, James	Gateshead	24.11.69	YTS	**Carlisle U.**	07.88	1987-88	9	3	0	(RB)	
ROBERTSON, John G.	Edinburgh	02.10.64	Hearts	**Newcastle U.**	04.88	1988	7	5	0	(F)	S U21-2/to Hearts 12.88
ROBINS, Mark G.	Ashton-u-Lyne	22.12.69	YTS	**Manchester U.**	12.86	1988	1	9	0	(F)	

Players Names	Birthplace	Date	Previous Club	League Club	Date Sign'd	Seasons Played	Career Record Apps	Sub	Gls	Pos.	Misc
ROBINSON, Colin R.	Birmingham	15.05.69	Mile Oak Rovers	**Shrewsbury T.**	11.82	1982-87	176	18	41	(F)	
			Tr	**Birmingham C.**	01.88	1987-88	34	3	6		
ROBINSON, David A.	Middlesbrough	14.01.65		**Hartlepool U.**	08.83	1983-85	64	2	1	(CD)	
			Tr	**Halifax T.**	08.86	1986-88	72	0	1		
ROBINSON, David J.	Newcastle	27.11.69	YTS	**Newcastle U.**	06.88	1988	0	1	0	(F)	
ROBINSON, Leslie	Shirebrook	01.03.67	Chesterfield (Jnrs)	**Mansfield T.**	10.84	1984-86	11	4	0	(M)	
			Tr	**Stockport Co.**	11.86	1986-87	67	0	3		
			Tr	**Doncaster Rov.**	03.88	1987-88	50	0	4		
ROBINSON, S. Liam	Bradford	29.12.65	Nottingham F. (App)	**Huddersfield T.**	01.84	1983-85	17	4	2	(F)	
			L	**Tranmere Rov.**	12.85	1985	4	0	3		
			Tr	**Bury**	07.86	1986-88	112	7	52		
ROBINSON, Mark J.	Rochdale	21.11.68	App	**West Bromwich A.**	11.86	1985-86	2	0	0	(M)	
			Tr	**Barnsley**	06.87	1987-88	16	5	2		
ROBINSON, Martin J.	Ilford	17.07.57	App	**Tottenham H.**	05.75	1975-77	5	1	2	(W)	
			Tr	**Charlton Ath.**	02.78	1977-84	218	10	58		
			L	**Reading**	09.82	1982	6	0	2		
			Tr	**Gillingham**	10.84	1984-86	91	5	23		
			Tr	**Southend U.**	07.87	1987-88	43	13	14		
ROBINSON, Michael A.	Sunderland	30.10.68	YTS	**Newcastle U.**	08.87					(FB)	
			Tr	**Darlington**	07.88	1988	0	1	0		
ROBINSON, Neil	Liverpool	20.04.57	App	**Everton**	05.74	1975-78	13	3	1	(RB/M)	
			Tr	**Swansea C.**	10.79	1979-84	114	9	7		
			Tr	**Grimsby T.**	09.84	1984-87	109	0	6		
			Tr	**Darlington**	07.88	1988	36	2	1		
ROBINSON, Philip J.	Stafford	06.01.67	App	**Aston Villa**	01.85	1986	2	1	1	(M)	
			Tr	**Wolverhampton W.**	06.87	1987-88	63	8	8		
ROBINSON, Ronnie	Sunderland	22.10.66	SC Vaux	**Ipswich T.**	10.84					(D)	
			SC Vaux	**Leeds U.**	11.85	1985-86	27	0	0		
			Tr	**Doncaster Rov.**	02.87	1986-88	76	2	5		
			Tr	**West Bromwich A.**	03.89	1988	1	0	0		
ROBSON, Bryan	Witton Gilbert (Dm)	11.01.57	App	**West Bromwich A.**	08.74	1974-81	194	4	39	(M)	E Yth Int/E U21-7/E-74/
			Tr	**Manchester U.**	10.81	1981-88	250	2	64		Brother of Gary
ROBSON, Gary	Chester-le-Street	06.07.65	App	**West Bromwich A.**	05.83	1982-88	88	20	10	(M)	Brother of Bryan
ROBSON, Mark A.	Newham	22.05.69	App	**Exeter C.**	12.86	1986	26	0	7	(LW)	
			Tr	**Tottenham H.**	07.87	1988	3	2	0		
			L	**Reading**	03.88	1987	5	2	0		
ROBSON, Stewart I.	Billericay	06.11.64	App	**Arsenal**	11.81	1981-86	150	1	16	(M)	E Yth Int/E U21-8
			Tr	**West Ham U.**	01.87	1986-88	61	0	3		
ROCASTLE, David	Lewisham	02.05.67	App	**Arsenal**	12.84	1985-88	127	3	15	(RW)	E U21-14/E-7
ROCHE, David	Newcastle	13.12.70	YTS	**Newcastle U.**	08.88	1988	0	2	0	(FB)	
ROCHE, Pat J.	Dublin	04.01.51	Shelbourne	**Manchester U.**	10.73	1974-81	46	0	0	(G)	IR-7
			Tr	**Brentford**	08.82	1982-83	71	0	0		
			Tr	**Halifax T.**	07.84	1984-88	184	0	0		
RODGER, Graham	Glasgow	01.04.67	App	**Wolverhampton W.**	08.83	1983	1	0	0	(CD)	E U21-4
			Tr	**Coventry C.**	02.85	1985-88	31	5	2		
RODGERSON, Ian	Hereford	09.04.66	Jnrs	**Hereford U.**	06.85	1985-87	95	5	6	(RB/M)	Son of Alan
			Tr	**Cardiff C.**	08.88	1988	39	1	0		
RODWELL, James R.	Lincoln	20.11.70	YTS	**Darlington** (YTS)	07.87	1988	1	0	0	(D)	
ROEDER, Glenn V.	Woodford	13.12.55	App	**Leyton Orient**	12.73	1974-77	107	8	4	(CD)	E 'B'
			Tr	**Q.P.R.**	08.78	1978-83	157	0	17		
			L	**Notts Co.**	11.83	1983	4	0	0		
			Tr	**Newcastle U.**	12.83	1983-88	193	0	9		
ROGERS, Lee J.	Doncaster	28.10.66	YTS	**Doncaster Rov.** (N/C)	07.84					(D)	
			Tr	**Chesterfield**	08.86	1986-88	99	4	0		
ROGERS, Lee M.	Bristol	08.04.67	App	**Bristol C.**	12.84	1984-86	30	0	0	(CD)	
			L	**Hereford U.**	03.87	1986	13	0	0		
			L	**York C.**	12.87	1987	5	2	0		
			Tr	**Exeter C.**	06.88	1988	45	0	0		
ROLPH, Andrew J.P.	Meriden	28.10.69	Mile Oak Rov.	**Chesterfield**	02.89	1988	4	8	1	(W)	
ROLPH, Darren G.	Romford	19.11.68	Kings Lynn	**Barnsley**	08.87	1987	1	1	0	(D)	
ROONEY, Simon A.	Manchester	10.07.70	YTS	**Blackpool**	06.88	1987-88	4	5	0	(F)	
ROSARIO, Robert M.	Hammersmith	04.03.66	Hillingdon Bor.	**Norwich C.**	12.83	1983-88	77	9	13	(F)	E U21-4
			L	**Wolverhampton W.**	12.85	1985	2	0	1		
ROSE, Kevin P.	Evesham	23.11.60	Ledbury T.	**Lincoln C.**	08.79					(G)	
			Ledbury T.	**Hereford U.**	03.83	1982-88	268	0	0		
ROSENIOR, Leroy De G.	Clapton	24.03.64	Jnrs	**Fulham**	08.82	1982-84	53	1	15	(F)	E Sch Int/E Yth Int
			Tr	**Q.P.R.**	08.85	1985-86	27	11	7		
			Tr	**Fulham**	06.87	1987	34	0	20		
			Tr	**West Ham U.**	03.88	1987-88	35	2	12		
ROSS, Michael P.	Southampton	02.09.71	YTS	**Portsmouth**	12.88	1988	0	1	0	(F)	
ROSTRON, J. Wilf	Sunderland	29.09.56	App	**Arsenal**	10.73	1974-76	12	5	2	(LB)	E Sch Int
			Tr	**Sunderland**	07.77	1977-79	75	1	17		
			Tr	**Watford**	10.79	1979-88	306	11	22		
			Tr	**Sheffield Wed.**	01.89	1988	7	0	0		
ROUGVIE, Doug	Ballingry (Fife)	24.05.56	Aberdeen	**Chelsea**	08.84	1984-86	74	0	3	(D)	S-1
			Tr	**Brighton & H.A.**	06.87	1987	35	0	2		
			Tr	**Shrewsbury T.**	08.88	1988	20	1	3		
			Tr	**Fulham**	02.89	1988	18	0	1		
ROWBOTHAM, Darren	Cardiff	22.10.66	Jnrs	**Plymouth Arg.**	11.84	1984-87	22	24	2	(M)	Brother of Jason
			Tr	**Exeter C.**	10.87	1987-88	65	3	22		
ROWBOTHAM, Jason	Cardiff	03.01.69	YTS	**Plymouth Arg.**	07.87	1987-88	8	1	0	(FB)	Brother of Darren
ROWELL, Gary	Seaham	06.06.57	App	**Sunderland**	07.74	1975-83	229	25	88	(W)	E U21-1/Son of John
			Tr	**Norwich C.**	08.84	1984	2	4	1		
			Tr	**Middlesbrough**	08.85	1985	27	0	10		
			Tr	**Brighton & H.A.**	08.86	1986-87	9	3	0		
			Tr	**Carlisle U.**	03.88	1987	7	0	0		
			Tr	**Burnley**	08.88	1988	8	10	1		

Robert Rosario (Norwich City) Match Magazine

Players Names	Birthplace	Date	Previous Club	League Club	Date Sign'd	Seasons Played	Career Record Apps	Sub	Gls	Pos.	Misc
RUDDOCK, Neil	Wandsworth	09.05.68	App	**Millwall**	03.86					(CD)	E Yth Int/E U21-3
			Tr	**Tottenham H.**	04.86	1986-87	7	2	0		
			Tr	**Millwall**	06.88	1988	0	2	1		
			Tr	**Southampton**	02.89	1988	13	0	3		
RUMBLE, Paul	Hemel Hempstead	14.03.69	App	**Watford**	03.87					(FB)	
			L	**Scunthorpe U.**	08.88	1988	8	0	1		
RUSH, Ian J.	St. Asaph	20.10.61	App	**Chester C.**	09.79	1978-79	33	1	14	(F)	W Sch Int/W U21-2/W-40
			Tr	**Liverpool**	04.80	1980-86	224	0	139		FWA & PFA Player of Year 1983-84
			Juventus (Italy)	**Liverpool**	08.88	1988	16	8	7		
RUSSELL, Colin	Liverpool	21.01.61	App	**Liverpool**	04.78	1980	0	1	0	(W)	
			Tr	**Huddersfield T.**	09.82	1982-83	64	2	23		
			L	**Stoke C.**	03.84	1983	11	0	2		
			Tr	**Bournemouth**	08.84	1984-85	65	3	14		
			Tr	**Doncaster Rov.**	07.86	1986-87	43	0	5		
			Tr	**Scarborough**	10.87	1987	12	1	2		
			Tr	**Wigan Ath.**	07.88	1988	8	0	3		
RUSSELL, Kevin J.	Portsmouth	06.12.66	Brighton & H.A.(App)	**Portsmouth**	10.84	1985-86	3	1	0	(F)	E Yth Int
			Tr	**Wrexham**	07.87	1987-88	84	0	43		
RUSSELL, Lee	Southampton	03.09.69	YTS	**Portsmouth**	07.88	1988	0	2	0	(FB)	
RUSSELL, Martin C.	Dublin	27.04.67	App	**Manchester U.**	04.84					(W)	IR Yth Int
			L	**Birmingham C.**	10.86	1986-88	3	2	0		
			Tr	**Leicester C.**	03.87	1986-87	13	7	0		
			Tr	**Scarborough**	02.89	1988	20	0	2		
RUSSELL, W.M. (Billy)	Glasgow	14.09.59	App	**Everton**	07.77					(RB)	S Yth Int
			Glasgow Celtic	**Doncaster Rov.**	07.79	1979-84	241	3	15		
			Tr	**Scunthorpe U.**	08.85	1985-87	113	4	7		
			Tr	**Rotherham U.**	08.88	1988	44	0	2		
RYAN, John B.	Ashton-u-Lyne	18.02.62	App	**Oldham Ath.**	02.80	1981-82	77	0	8	(LB)	E U21-1
			Tr	**Newcastle U.**	08.83	1983-84	28	0	1		
			Tr	**Sheffield Wed.**	09.84	1984	5	3	1		
			Tr	**Oldham Ath.**	08.85	1985-86	20	3	0		
			Tr	**Mansfield T.**	10.87	1987-88	53	9	1		
RYAN, Laurie J.	Watford	15.10.63	Dunstable	**Cambridge U.**	04.88	1987-88	36	5	12	(F)	
RYAN, Vaughan W.	Westminster	02.09.68	App	**Wimbledon**	08.86	1986-88	22	6	1	(M)	
			L	**Sheffield U.**	01.89	1988	2	1	0		
SADDINGTON, Nigel J.	Sunderland	09.12.65	S.C. Vaux.	**Doncaster Rov.**	09.84	1984	5	0	0	(CD)	
			Roker	**Sunderland**	01.86	1986	3	0	0		
			Tr	**Carlisle U.**	02.88	1987-88	53	0	5		
SAGE, Mel	Gillingham	24.03.64	App	**Gillingham**	03.82	1981-85	126	6	5	(RB)	
			Tr	**Derby Co.**	08.86	1986-88	54	1	3		
SALAKO, John A.	Nigeria	11.02.69	App	**Crystal Palace**	11.86	1986-88	35	28	1	(LW)	
SALATHIEL, D. Neil	Wrexham	10.11.62	Sheffield Wed. (Jnr)	**Wrexham** (N/C)	05.80	1980	4	0	0	(RB)	W Sch Int
			Tr	**Crewe Alex.**	06.81	1981-82	64	1	0		
			Arcadia Shep. (SA)	**Wrexham**	12.83	1983-88	208	1	3		
SALMAN, Danis M.M.	Cyprus	12.03.60	App	**Brentford**	08.77	1975-85	316	9	8	(D)	E Yth Int
			Tr	**Millwall**	08.86	1986-88	78	1	4		
SALMON, Mike B.	Leyland	14.07.64	Jnrs	**Blackburn Rov.**	10.81	1981	1	0	0	(G)	
			L	**Chester C.**	10.82	1982	16	0	0		
			Tr	**Stockport Co.**	08.83	1983-85	118	0	0		
			Tr	**Bolton W.**	07.86	1986	26	0	0		
			Tr	**Wrexham**	03.87	1986-88	100	0	0		
SAMWAYS, Mark	Doncaster	11.11.68	YTS	**Doncaster Rov.**	08.87	1987-88	23	0	0	(G)	
SAMWAYS, Vincent	Bethnal Green	27.10.68	App	**Tottenham H.**	10.85	1986-88	34	13	3	(M)	E Yth Int/E U21-5
SANCHEZ, Lawrie P.	Lambeth	22.10.59	Jnrs	**Reading**	09.78	1977-84	249	13	28	(M)	NI-2
			Tr	**Wimbledon**	12.84	1984-88	163	2	23		
SANDEMAN, Bradley R.	Northampton	24.02.70	YTS	**Northampton T.**	07.88	1987-88	8	16	1	(M)	
SANDFORD, Lee R.	Basingstoke	22.04.68	App	**Portsmouth**	12.85	1985-88	53	6	1	(LB)	E Yth Int
SANSOM, Kenny G.	Camberwell	26.09.58	App	**Crystal Palace**	12.75	1974-79	172	0	3	(LB)	E Sch Int/E Yth Int/E U21-8/E-86
			Tr	**Arsenal**	08.80	1980-87	314	0	6		
			Tr	**Newcastle U.**	12.88	1988	20	0	0		
SANSOME, Paul E.	New Addington	06.10.61	Crystal Palace (App)	**Millwall**	04.80	1981-87	156	0	0	(G)	
			Tr	**Southend U.**	03.88	1987-88	50	0	0		
SAUNDERS, Carl S.	Birmingham	26.11.64	Jnrs	**Stoke C.**	03.83	1982-88	118	24	22	(F/M)	
SAUNDERS, Dean N.	Swansea	21.06.64	App	**Swansea C.**	06.82	1983-84	42	7	12	(F)	W-13/Son of Roy
			L	**Cardiff C.**	03.85	1984	3	1	0		
			Tr	**Brighton & H.A.**	08.85	1985-86	66	6	20		
			Tr	**Oxford U.**	03.87	1986-88	57	2	21		
			Tr	**Derby Co.**	10.88	1988	30	0	14		
SAUNDERS, Steve J.P.	Warrington	21.09.64	App	**Bolton W.**	09.82	1983	3	0	0	(F)	
			Tr	**Crewe Alex.**	07.85	1985	15	7	1		
			Tr	**Preston N.E.** (N/C)	08.86						
			Northwich Vic.	**Grimsby T.**	08.87	1987-88	70	6	13		
SAUNDERS, Wesley	Sunderland	23.02.63	Jnrs	**Newcastle U.**	06.81	1981-84	79	0	0	(CD)	
			L	**Bradford C.**	03.85	1984	1	3	0		
			Tr	**Carlisle U.**	08.85	1985-87	97	0	11		To Dundee 2.88
SAVAGE, Rob J.	Liverpool	08.01.60	App	**Liverpool**	01.78					(M)	
			L	**Wrexham**	10.82	1982	27	0	10		
			Tr	**Stoke C.**	07.83	1983	5	2	0		
			Tr	**Bournemouth**	12.83	1983-86	80	2	18		
			Tr	**Bradford C.**	12.86	1986-87	11	0	0		
			Tr	**Bolton W.**	09.87	1987-88	78	1	11		
SAVILLE, Andy V.	Hull	12.12.64	Jnrs	**Hull C.**	09.83	1983-88	74	26	18	(F)	
			Tr	**Walsall**	03.89	1988	12	0	4		
SAYER, Andy C.	Brent	06.06.66	App	**Wimbledon**	06.84	1983-87	46	12	15	(F)	
			L	**Cambridge U.**	02.88	1987	2	3	0		
			Tr	**Fulham**	08.88	1988	19	9	10		
SCALES, John R.	Harrogate	04.07.66	Leeds U.(YTS)	**Bristol Rov.**	07.85	1985-86	68	4	2	(RB)	
			Tr	**Wimbledon**	07.87	1987-88	59	4	6		

Players Names	Birthplace	Date	Previous Club	League Club	Date Sign'd	Seasons Played	Career Record Apps	Sub	Gls	Pos.	Misc
SCHOFIELD, John D.	Barnsley	16.05.65	Gainsborough Trin.	**Lincoln C.**	11.88	1988	29	0	2	(M)	
SCOTT, Chris	Wallsend	11.09.63	Blyth Spartans	**Northampton T.**	07.87					(CD)	
			Tr	**Lincoln C.**	(N/L)	1988	4	0	0		
SCOTT, Ian	Radcliffe	20.09.67	App	**Manchester C.**	09.85	1987-88	20	4	3	(M)	E Sch Int
SCOTT, Ian R.	Otley	04.03.69	App	**Manchester U.**	03.87					(D)	
			Tr	**Stockport Co.**	09.87	1987-88	23	2	0		
SCOTT, Kevin W.	Easington	17.12.66	App	**Newcastle U.**	12.84	1986-88	36	0	2	(CD)	
SCOTT, Martin	Sheffield	07.01.68	App	**Rotherham U.**	01.86	1984-88	52	1	1	(LB)	
SCOTT, Peter R.	Notting Hill	01.10.63	App	**Fulham**	09.81	1981-88	167	7	21	(M)	
SCOTT, Robert	Bathgate	13.01.64	Whitburn Jnrs	**Colchester U.**	03.89	1988	12	0	5	(F)	
SCOTTING, Allen	Dartford	22.04.66	Charlton Ath. (Jnrs)	**Gillingham** (N/C)	02.84	1983	2	0	0	(FB)	
SEAGRAVES, Mark	Bootle	22.10.66	App	**Liverpool**	11.83					(D)	Brother of Chris/E Sch Int/E Yth Int
			L	**Norwich C.**	11.86	1986	3	0	0		
			Tr	**Manchester C.**	09.87	1987-88	34	6	0		
SEALEY, Les J.	Bethnal Green	29.09.57	App	**Coventry C.**	03.76	1976-82	158	0	0	(G)	Cousin of Alan
			Tr	**Luton T.**	08.83	1983-88	207	0	0		
			L	**Plymouth Arg.**	10.84	1984	6	0	0		
SEALY, A.J. (Tony)	Hackney	07.05.59	App	**Southampton**	05.77	1977-78	2	5	0	(F)	
			Tr	**Crystal Palace**	03.79	1978-80	16	8	5		
			L	**Port Vale**	02.80	1979	17	0	6		
			Tr	**Q.P.R.**	03.81	1980-83	57	6	18		
			L	**Port Vale**	02.82	1981	6	0	4		
			L	**Fulham**	12.83	1983	5	0	1		
			L	**Fulham**	08.84	1984	3	1	1		
			Tr	**Fulham**	01.85	1984-85	14	2	9		
			Tr	**Leicester C.**	09.85	1985-86	28	11	7		
			L	**Bournemouth**	03.87	1986	8	5	2		
			Sporting Lisbon (Port)	**Brentford** (N/C)	03.89	1988	11	1	4		
SEAMAN, David A.	Rotherham	19.09.63	App	**Leeds U.**	09.81					(G)	E U21-10/E-2
			Tr	**Peterborough U.**	08.82	1982-84	91	0	0		
			Tr	**Birmingham C.**	10.84	1984-85	75	0	0		
			Tr	**Q.P.R.**	08.86	1986-88	108	0	0		
SEDGLEY, Stephen P.	Enfield	26.05.68	App	**Coventry C.**	05.86	1986-88	81	3	3	(CD/M)	E U21-9
SEGERS, J.C.A. (Hans)	Netherlands	30.10.61	PSV Eindhoven	**Nottingham F.**	08.84	1984-87	58	0	0	(G)	
			L	**Stoke C.**	02.87	1986	1	0	0		
			L	**Sheffield U.**	11.87	1987	10	0	0		
			Tr	**Wimbledon**	09.88	1988	33	0	0		
SELLARS, Scott	Sheffield	27.11.65	App	**Leeds U.**	07.83	1982-85	72	4	12	(M)	E U21-3
			Tr	**Blackburn Rov.**	07.86	1986-88	114	6	13		
SENDALL, Richard A.	Stamford	10.07.67	Watford(App)	**Blackpool**	07.85	1985-86	6	5	0	(F)	
			Tr	**Carlisle U.**	07.88	1988	22	7	6		
SENIOR, Steve	Sheffield	15.05.63	App	**York C.**	05.81	1980-86	158	10	6	(RB)	
			L	**Darlington**	10.84	1984	5	0	0		
			Tr	**Northampton T.**	06.87	1987	1	3	0		
			Tr	**Wigan Ath.**	10.87	1987-88	64	2	3		
SENIOR, Trevor J.	Dorchester	28.11.61	Dorchester T.	**Portsmouth**	12.81	1981-82	11	0	2	(F)	
			L	**Aldershot**	03.83	1982	10	0	7		
			Tr	**Reading**	08.83	1983-86	164	0	102		
			Tr	**Watford**	07.87	1987	22	2	1		
			Tr	**Middlesbrough**	03.88	1987-88	9	1	2		
			Tr	**Reading**	10.88	1988	37	0	15		
SERTORI, Mark A.	Manchester	01.09.67		**Stockport Co.**	02.87	1986-87	3	1	0	(F)	
			Tr	**Lincoln C.**	N/L	1988	22	4	4		
SHAKESPEARE, Craig R.	Birmingham	26.10.63	App	**Walsall**	10.81	1982-88	276	8	45	(M)	
SHARP, Graeme M.	Glasgow	16.10.60	Dumbarton	**Everton**	04.80	1979-88	252	10	101	(F)	S U21-1/S-11
SHARPE, Lee S.	Birmingham	27.05.71	YTS	**Torquay U.**	05.88	1987	9	5	3	(LW)	E U21-1
			Tr	**Manchester U.**	05.88	1988	19	3	0		
SHAW, Adrian	Murton	13.04.66	App	**Nottingham F.**	12.83					(D/M)	
			Tr	**Halifax T.**	12.84	1984-87	95	5	1		
			Bridlington T.	**York C.** (N/C)	10.88	1988	5	0	0		
			Tr	**Chesterfield**	12.88	1988	24	1	1		
SHAW, Graham P.	Stoke	07.06.67	App	**Stoke C.**	06.85	1985-88	83	16	18	(F)	
SHAW, Richard E.	Brentford	11.09.68	App	**Crystal Palace**	09.86	1987-88	10	7	0	(FB)	
SHEARER, Alan	Newcastle	13.08.70	YTS	**Southampton**	04.88	1987-88	11	4	3	(F)	E Yth Int
SHEARER, David J.	Inverness	16.10.58	Inverness Clach.	**Middlesbrough**	01.78	1977-82	88	9	23	(F)	Brother of Duncan
			L	**Wigan Ath.**	03.80	1979	11	0	9		
			Tr	**Grimsby T.**	08.83	1983	1	3	0		
			Tr	**Gillingham**	08.84	1984-87	82	11	42		
			Tr	**Bournemouth**	10.87	1987	8	3	3		
			Tr	**Scunthorpe U.**	02.88	1987-88	16	0	7		
			Tr	**Darlington**	12.88	1988	6	1	0		
SHEARER, Duncan N.	Fort William	28.08.62	Inverness Clach.	**Chelsea**	11.83	1985	2	0	1	(F)	Brother of David
			Tr	**Huddersfield T.**	03.86	1985-87	80	3	38		
			Tr	**Swindon T.**	06.88	1988	33	3	14		
SHEARER, Peter A.	Coventry	04.02.67	App	**Birmingham C.**	02.85	1984	2	2	0	(M)	
			Tr	**Rochdale**	07.86	1986	1	0	0		
			Cheltenham T.	**Bournemouth**	03.89	1988	4	0	1		
SHEEDY, Kevin M.	Builth Wells	21.10.59	App	**Hereford U.**	10.76	1975-77	47	4	4	(LM)	IR U21-1/IR-22
			Tr	**Liverpool**	07.78	1980-81	1	2	0		
			Tr	**Everton**	08.82	1982-88	194	5	53		
SHEFFIELD, Jonathan	Bedworth	01.02.69	App	**Norwich C.**	02.87	1988	1	0	0	(G)	
SHELTON, Gary	Nottingham	21.03.58	App	**Walsall**	03.76	1975-77	12	12	0	(M)	E U21-1
			Tr	**Aston Villa**	01.78	1978-81	24	0	7		
			L	**Notts Co.**	03.80	1979	8	0	0		
			Tr	**Sheffield Wed.**	03.82	1981-86	195	3	18		
			Tr	**Oxford U.**	07.87	1987-88	60	5	1		
SHEPHERD, Anthony	Glasgow	16.11.66	Glasgow Celtic (L)	**Bristol C.**	12.88	1988	2	1	0	(M)	

Lawrie Sanchez (Wimbledon & Northern Ireland) Match Magazine

Kenny Sansom (Newcastle United & England) Match Magazine

Dean Saunders (Derby County & Wales) Match Magazine

Les Sealey (Luton Town) Match Magazine

Players Names	Birthplace	Date	Previous Club	League Club	Date Sign'd	Seasons Played	Career Record Apps	Sub	Gls	Pos.	Misc
SHERIDAN, John J.	Manchester	01.10.64	Manchester C.(Jnr)	**Leeds U.**	03.82	1982-88	225	5	47	(M)	IR Yth Int/IR-5
SHERINGHAM, Edward P. (Teddy)	Walthamstow	02.04.66	App	**Millwall**	01.84	1983-88	131	12	51	(F)	E Yth Int/E U21-1
			L	**Aldershot**	02.85	1984	4	1	0		
SHERWOOD, Steve	Selby	10.12.53	App	**Chelsea**	07.71	1971-75	16	0	0	(G)	Brother of Athlete John
			L	**Millwall**	10.73	1973	1	0	0		
			L	**Brentford**	01.74	1973-74	62	0	0		
			Tr	**Watford**	11.76	1976-86	211	0	1		
			Tr	**Grimsby T.**	07.87	1987-88	78	0	0		
SHERWOOD, Timothy A.	St. Albans	06.02.69	App	**Watford**	02.87	1987-88	23	9	2	(M)	
SHILTON, Peter L.	Leicester	18.09.49	App	**Leicester C.**	09.66	1965-74	286	0	1	(G)	E Sch Int/E Yth Int/E U23-13/E-109
			Tr	**Stoke C.**	11.74	1974-77	110	0	0		E F Lge Rep/PFA Player of Year
			Tr	**Nottingham F.**	09.77	1977-81	202	0	0		1977-8
			Tr	**Southampton**	08.82	1982-86	188	0	0		
			Tr	**Derby Co.**	07.87	1987-88	78	0	0		
SHINNERS, Paul	Westminster	08.01.59	Fisher Ath.	**Gillingham**	10.84	1984	1	3	0	(F)	
			L	**Colchester U.**	03.85	1984	6	0	1		
			Tr	**Leyton Orient**	07.85	1985-88	73	4	32		
SHIPLEY, George M.	Newcastle	07.03.59	App	**Southampton**	03.77	1979	2	1	0	(M)	
			L	**Reading**	03.79	1978	11	1	1		
			Tr	**Lincoln C.**	01.80	1979-84	229	1	42		
			Tr	**Charlton Ath.**	07.85	1985-86	61	0	6		
			Tr	**Gillingham**	08.87	1987-88	27	2	3		
SHIRTLIFF, Peter A.	Hoyland	06.04.61	App	**Sheffield Wed.**	10.78	1978-85	188	0	4	(CD)	Brother of Paul
			Tr	**Charlton Ath.**	07.86	1986-88	102	1	7		
SHORT, Chris M.	West Germany	09.05.70	Jnrs	**Scarborough**	07.88	1988	2	0	0	(D)	
SHORT, J. Craig	Bridlington	25.06.68	Pickering T.	**Scarborough**	10.87	1987-88	61	2	7	(CD)	
SHOTTON, Malcolm	Newcastle	16.02.57	App	**Leicester C.**	02.75					(CD)	
			Nuneaton Bor.	**Oxford U.**	05.80	1980-87	262	1	12		
			Tr	**Portsmouth**	08.87	1987	10	0	0		
			Tr	**Huddersfield T.**	02.88	1987-88	16	0	1		
			Tr	**Barnsley**	09.88	1988	35	2	5		
SHUTT, Carl S.	Sheffield	10.10.61	Spalding U.	**Sheffield Wed.**	05.85	1985-87	36	4	16	(F)	
			Tr	**Bristol C.**	10.87	1987-88	39	7	10		
			Tr	**Leeds U.**	03.89	1988	3	0	4		
SIDDALL, Barry	Ellesmere Port	12.09.54	App	**Bolton W.**	01.72	1972-76	137	0	0	(G)	E Yth Int
			Tr	**Sunderland**	09.76	1976-81	167	0	0		
			L	**Darlington**	10.80	1980	8	0	0		
			Tr	**Port Vale**	08.82	1982-84	81	0	0		
			L	**Blackpool**	10.83	1983	7	0	0		
			Tr	**Stoke C.**	01.85	1984-85	20	0	0		
			L	**Tranmere Rov.**	10.85	1985	12	0	0		
			L	**Manchester C.**	03.86	1985	6	0	0		
			Tr	**Blackpool**	08.86	1986-88	110	0	0		
SIMPSON, Fitzroy	Bradford-on-Avon	26.02.70	YTS	**Swindon T.**	07.88	1988	3	4	0	(F)	
SIMPSON, Paul D.	Carlisle	26.07.66	App	**Manchester C.**	08.83	1982-88	99	22	18	(LW)	E Yth Int/E U21-5
			Tr	**Oxford U.**	10.88	1988	24	1	8		
SIMS, Steve F.	Lincoln	02.07.57	App	**Leicester C.**	08.74	1975-78	78	1	3	(CD)	E U21-10/E 'B'/Son of Frank
			Tr	**Watford**	12.78	1978-83	150	2	4		
			Tr	**Notts Co.**	09.84	1984-86	85	0	5		
			Tr	**Watford**	10.86	1986	19	0	1		
			Tr	**Aston Villa**	06.87	1987-88	41	0	0		
SINCLAIR, Ronnie M.	Stirling	19.11.64	App	**Nottingham F.**	10.82					(G)	
			L	**Wrexham**	03.84	1983	11	0	0		
			Tr	**Leeds U.**	06.86	1986	8	0	0		
			L	**Halifax T.**	03.87	1986	4	0	0		
			L	**Halifax T.**	12.88	1988	10	0	0		
SINGLETON, Martin D.	Banbury	02.08.63	App	**Coventry C.**	01.81	1981-84	20	3	1	(M)	E Yth Int
			Tr	**Bradford C.**	12.84	1984-86	69	2	3		
			Tr	**West Bromwich A.**	12.86	1986-87	15	4	1		
			Tr	**Northampton T.**	11.87	1987-88	39	1	4		
SINNOTT, Lee	Pelsall	12.07.65	App	**Walsall**	11.82	1981-83	40	0	2	(D)	E Yth Int/E U21-1
			Tr	**Watford**	09.83	1983-86	71	7	2		
			Tr	**Bradford C.**	07.87	1987-88	84	0	3		
SINTON, Andy	Newcastle	19.03.66	App	**Cambridge U.**	04.83	1982-85	90	3	13	(M)	E Sch Int
			Tr	**Brentford**	12.85	1985-88	149	0	28		
			Tr	**Q.P.R.**	03.89	1988	10	0	3		
SITTON, John E.	Hackney	21.10.59	App	**Chelsea**	10.77	1978-79	11	2	0	(D)	
			Tr	**Millwall**	02.80	1979-80	43	2	1		
			Tr	**Gillingham**	09.81	1981-84	102	5	5		
			Tr	**Leyton Orient**	07.85	1985-88	108	1	5		
SKINNER, Justin	Hounslow	30.01.69	App	**Fulham**	11.86	1986-88	63	10	14	(M)	
SKIPPER, Peter D.	Hull	11.04.58	Schultz YC	**Hull C.**	02.79	1978-79	22	1	2	(CD)	
			L	**Scunthorpe U.**	02.80	1979	0	1	0		
			Tr	**Darlington**	05.80	1980-81	91	0	4		
			Tr	**Hull C.**	08.82	1982-88	264	1	17		
			Tr	**Oldham Ath.**	10.88	1988	27	0	1		
SLACK, Trevor C.	Peterborough	26.09.62	App	**Peterborough U.**	08.80	1980-85	201	1	18	(CD)	E Yth Int
			Tr	**Rotherham U.**	08.86	1986	14	1	1		
			Tr	**Grimsby T.**	08.87	1987	21	0	0		
			Tr	**Northampton T.**	02.88	1987	13	0	1		
			Tr	**Chesterfield**	09.88	1988	21	0	0		
SLATER, Stuart I.	Sudbury	27.03.69	App	**West Ham U.**	03.87	1987-88	16	4	1	(F)	
SLATTER, Neil J.	Cardiff	30.05.64	App	**Bristol Rov.**	05.82	1980-84	147	1	4	(D)	W Yth Int/W U21-6/W-20
			Tr	**Oxford U.**	07.85	1985-88	78	3	6		
SLAVEN, Bernie J.	Paisley	13.11.60	Albion Rov.	**Middlesbrough**	09.85	1985-88	158	1	61	(F)	
SMALLER, Paul A.	Scunthorpe	18.09.70	YTS	**Grimsby T.**(YTS)	08.88	1988	0	1	0	(CD)	
SMALLEY, Mark A.	Newark	02.01.65	App	**Nottingham F.**	01.83	1982-84	1	2	0	(CD)	E Yth Int
			L	**Birmingham C.**	03.86	1985	7	0	0		
			L	**Bristol Rov.**	08.86	1986	10	0	0		
			Tr	**Leyton Orient**	02.87	1986-88	58	3	4		

Players Names	Birthplace	Date	Previous Club	League Club	Date Sign'd	Seasons Played	Career Record Apps	Sub	Gls	Pos.	Misc
SMALLEY, Paul T.	Nottingham	17.11.66	App	**Notts Co.**	11.84	1985-87	112	6	0	(RB)	E Yth Int
			Tr	**Scunthorpe U.**	09.88	1988	39	0	1		
SMALLWOOD, Neil	York	03.12.66	Jnrs	**York C.**	06.85	1986-87	13	0	0	(G)	
			Tr	**Darlington**	08.88	1988	4	0	0		
SMART, Gary J.	Totnes	29.04.64	Wokingham T.	**Oxford U.**	07.88	1988	16	1	0	(FB)	
SMART, Jason	Rochdale	15.02.69	YTS	**Rochdale**	08.86	1985-88	116	1	4	(CD)	
SMEULDERS, John	Hackney	28.03.57	App	**Leyton Orient**	07.74					(G)	E Yth Int
			Tr	**Bournemouth**	07.79	1979-80	14	0	0		
			Weymouth	**Bournemouth**	01.84	1983-85	75	0	0		
			Tr	**Torquay U.**	07.86	1986	18	0	0		
			L	**Peterborough U.**	12.86	1986	1	0	0		
			Poole T.	**Bournemouth**	08.87	1987-88	9	0	0		
			L	**Brentford** (N/C)	10.88	1988	8	0	0		
SMILLIE, Neil	Barnsley	19.07.58	App	**Crystal Palace**	10.75	1976-81	71	12	7	(W)	Son of Ron
			L	**Brentford**	01.77	1976	3	0	0		
			Tr	**Brighton & H.A.**	08.82	1982-84	62	13	2		
			Tr	**Watford**	06.85	1985	10	6	3		
			L	**Reading**	12.86	1986	6	0	0		
			Tr	**Reading**	03.87	1986-87	32	1	0		
			Tr	**Brentford**	08.88	1988	25	3	2		
SMITH, Alan D.	Sheffield	07.12.66	App	**Sheffield Wed.**	12.84					(D)	
			Tr	**Darlington**	09.86	1986-88	26	5	1		
SMITH, Alan M.	Bromsgrove	21.11.62	Alvechurch	**Leicester C.**	06.82	1982-86	190	10	76	(F)	E Semi-Pro Int 1982/E-3
			Tr	**Arsenal**	05.87	1987-88	72	3	35		
SMITH, A. (Tony)	Sunderland	20.02.57	Jnrs	**Newcastle U.**	07.75	1977	1	1	0	(CD)	
			Tr	**Peterborough U.**	03.79	1978-81	68	0	5		
			Tr	**Halifax T.**	08.82	1982-83	81	2	3		
			Tr	**Hartlepool U.**	08.84	1984-88	200	0	8		
SMITH, Brian	Sheffield	27.10.66	App	**Sheffield U.**	10.84	1984-88	81	3	0	(D)	
			L	**Scunthorpe U.**	03.87	1986	6	0	1		
SMITH, Colin R.	Ruddington	03.11.58	Jnrs	**Nottingham F.**	06.77					(CD)	
			Tr	**Norwich C.**	08.82	1982	2	2	0		
			Hong Kong	**Cardiff C.**	10.83	1983-84	50	0	3		
			Tr	**Aldershot**	12.84	1984-88	163	2	4		
SMITH, David	Gloucester	29.03.68	YTS	**Coventry C.**	07.86	1987-88	48	3	7	(W)	E U21-7
SMITH, David A.	Sidcup	25.06.61	Welling U.	**Gillingham**	08.86	1986-88	90	14	10	(LW)	
SMITH, Dean	West Bromwich	19.03.71	YTS	**Walsall** (YTS)	10.87	1988	15	0	0	(CD)	
SMITH, Gareth S.	Leeds	09.04.71	YTS	**Halifax T.** (YTS)	07.87	1988	0	1	0		
SMITH, James	Johnstone	22.11.69	YTS	**Torquay U.**	07.88	1987-88	26	9	4	(M)	
SMITH, John	Liverpool	23.07.70	Jnrs	**Tranmere Rov.**	11.87	1988	1	1	0	(D)	
SMITH, Keith	Sheffield	17.10.63	Alfreton T.	**Exeter C.**	01.89	1988	2	13	2	(F)	
SMITH, Kevan	Eaglescliffe	13.12.59	Stockton	**Darlington**	09.79	1979-84	242	3	11	(CD)	
			Tr	**Rotherham U.**	07.85	1985-86	59	0	4		
			Tr	**Coventry C.**	12.86	1987	5	1	0		
			Tr	**York C.**	05.88	1988	30	1	5		
SMITH, Lindsay J.	Enfield	18.09.54	App	**Colchester U.**	03.72	1970-76	185	27	16	(CD)	
			L	**Charlton Ath.**	08.77	1977	1	0	0		
			L	**Millwall**	09.77	1977	4	1	0		
			Tr	**Cambridge U.**	10.77	1977-82	173	1	7		
			L	**Lincoln C.**	09.81	1981	5	0	0		
			Tr	**Plymouth Arg.**	10.82	1982-83	76	0	5		
			Tr	**Millwall**	07.84	1984-85	54	1	5		
			Tr	**Cambridge U.**	07.86	1986-88	102	0	16		
SMITH, Mark C.	Sheffield	21.03.60	App	**Sheffield Wed.**	03.78	1977-86	201	1	10	(CD)	E U21-5
			Tr	**Plymouth Arg.**	07.87	1987-88	76	0	6		
SMITH, Mark C.	Sheffield	19.12.61	Jnrs	**Sheffield U.**	08.80					(F)	
			Kettering T.	**Scunthorpe U.** (N/C)	09.85	1985	0	1	0		
			Kettering T.	**Rochdale**	07.88	1988	26	1	7		
			Tr	**Huddersfield T.**	02.89	1988	17	3	2		
SMITH, Michael K.	Hull	19.12.68	YTS	**Hull C.**	05.87	1988	9	3	1	(F)	
SMITH, Neil	Warley	10.02.70	YTS	**Shrewsbury T.**	07.88	1987	0	1	0	(M)	
SMITH, Nick L.	Berkeley (Glos)	28.01.69	YTS	**Southend U.**	07.87	1986-88	37	9	5	(M)	
SMITH, Paul M.	Rotherham	09.11.64	App	**Sheffield U.**	11.82	1982-85	29	7	1	(W)	
			L	**Stockport Co.**	08.85	1985	7	0	5		
			Tr	**Port Vale**	07.86	1986-87	42	2	7		
			Tr	**Lincoln C.**	(N/L)	1988	27	1	10		
SMITH, Paul S.	Brent	05.10.67	App	**Arsenal**	10.85					(W)	
			Tr	**Brentford**	08.87	1987	10	7	1		
			Tr	**Bristol Rov.**	07.88	1988	14	2	1		
			Tr	**Torquay U.**	03.89	1988	8	3	1		
SNODIN, Glyn	Rotherham	14.02.60	App	**Doncaster Rov.**	10.77	1976-84	288	21	61	(LB/LW)	Brother of Ian
			Tr	**Sheffield Wed.**	06.85	1985-86	51	8	1		
			Tr	**Leeds U.**	07.87	1987-88	66	4	10		
SNODIN, Ian	Rotherham	15.08.63	App	**Doncaster Rov.**	08.80	1979-84	181	7	25	(M/RB)	Brother of Glynn/E Yth Int/ E U21-4/E 'B'
			Tr	**Leeds U.**	05.85	1985-86	51	0	6		
			Tr	**Everton**	01.87	1986-88	67	3	2		
SOUTHALL, Neville	Llandudno	16.09.58	Winsford U.	**Bury**	06.80	1980	39	0	0	(G)	W-38/FWA Footballer of Year 1984-5
			Tr	**Everton**	07.81	1981-88	253	0	0		
			L	**Port Vale**	01.83	1982	9	0	0		
SPACKMAN, Nigel J.	Romsey	02.12.60	Andover T.	**Bournemouth**	05.80	1980-82	118	1	10	(M)	
			Tr	**Chelsea**	06.83	1983-86	139	2	12		
			Tr	**Liverpool**	02.87	1986-88	39	12	0		
			Tr	**Q.P.R.**	02.87	1988	16	0	1		
SPARHAM, Sean R.	Bexley	04.12.68	Jnrs	**Millwall**	05.87	1987-88	17	2	0	(LB)	
SPEARING, A. (Tony)	Romford	07.10.64	App	**Norwich C.**	10.82	1983-87	67	2	0	(LB)	E Yth Int
			L	**Stoke C.**	11.84	1984	9	0	0		
			L	**Oxford U.**	02.85	1984	5	0	0		
			Tr	**Leicester C.**	07.88	1988	36	0	0		

Players Names	Birthplace	Date	Previous Club	League Club	Date Sign'd	Seasons Played	Career Record Apps	Sub	Gls	Pos.	Misc
SPEED, Gary A.	Hawarden	08.09.69	YTS	**Leeds U.**	06.88	1988	1	0	0	(M)	
SPEEDIE, David R.	Glenrothes	20.02.60	Jnrs	**Barnsley**	10.78	1978-79	10	13	0	(F)	S U21-1/S-8
			Tr	**Darlington**	06.80	1980-81	88	0	21		
			Tr	**Chelsea**	06.82	1982-86	155	7	47		
			Tr	**Coventry C.**	07.87	1987-88	71	1	20		
SPINK, Nigel P.	Chelmsford	08.08.58	Chelmsford C.	**Aston Villa**	01.77	1979-88	211	0	0	(G)	E-1
SPOONER, Steve A.	Sutton	25.01.61	App	**Derby Co.**	12.78	1978-81	7	1	0	(M)	
			Tr	**Halifax T.**	12.81	1981-82	71	1	13		
			Tr	**Chesterfield**	07.83	1983-85	89	4	14		
			Tr	**Hereford U.**	07.86	1986-87	84	0	19		
			Tr	**York C.**	07.88	1988	31	0	5		
SPROSON, Phil J.	Stoke	13.10.59	Jnrs	**Port Vale**	12.77	1977-88	422	4	33	(CD)	Nephew of Roy
SPROSTON, Neil R.	Dudley	20.11.70	YTS	**Birmingham C.** (YTS)	07.87	1987	0	1	0	(D)	
STAFFORD, Clive A.	Ipswich	04.04.63	Diss T.	**Colchester U.**	02.89	1988	16	0	0	(FB)	
STAINROD, Simon A.	Sheffield	01.02.59	App	**Sheffield U.**	07.76	1975-78	59	8	14	(F)	E Yth Int
			Tr	**Oldham Ath.**	03.79	1978-80	69	0	21		
			Tr	**Q.P.R.**	11.80	1980-84	143	2	48		
			Tr	**Sheffield Wed.**	02.85	1984-85	8	7	2		
			Tr	**Aston Villa**	09.85	1985-87	58	5	16		
			Tr	**Stoke C.**	12.87	1987-88	27	1	6		to Strasbourg (Fr.) 02.89
STANCLIFFE, Paul I.	Sheffield	05.05.58	App	**Rotherham U.**	03.76	1975-82	285	0	8	(CD)	
			Tr	**Sheffield U.**	08.83	1983-88	235	0	12		
STANISLAUS, Roger E.P.	Hammersmith	02.11.68	YTS	**Arsenal**	07.86					(LB)	
			Tr	**Brentford**	09.87	1987-88	78	2	3		
STANLEY, Garry E.	Burton	04.03.54	App	**Chelsea**	03.71	1975-78	105	4	15	(M)	
			Tr	**Everton**	08.79	1979-80	52	0	1		
			Tr	**Swansea C.**	10.81	1981-83	60	12	4		
			Tr	**Portsmouth**	01.84	1983-85	43	4	1		
			Wichita (USA)	**Bristol C.**	08.88	1988	8	2	0		
STANNARD, Jim D.	Harold Hill	06.10.62	Ford U.	**Fulham**	06.80	1980-84	41	0	0	(G)	
			L	**Southend U.**	09.84	1984	6	0	0		
			L	**Charlton Ath.**	01.85	1984	1	0	0		
			Tr	**Southend U.**	03.85	1984-86	103	0	0		
			Tr	**Fulham**	08.87	1987-88	91	0	0		
STANT, Philip R.	Bolton	13.10.62	Army	**Reading** (N/C)	08.82	1982	3	1	2	(F)	
			Army	**Hereford U.**	11.86	1986-88	83	6	38		
STAPLETON, Frank A.	Dublin	10.07.56	App	**Arsenal**	09.73	1974-80	223	2	75	(F)	IR Yth Int/IR-69
			Tr	**Manchester U.**	08.81	1981-86	204	19	60		
			Ajax Amsterdam	**Derby Co.**	03.88	1987	10	0	1		to Le Havre (Fr) 9.88
STAPLETON, John R.	Manchester	30.09.69	W. Bromwich A.(YTS)	**Stockport Co.**	08.88	1988	1	0	0	(LB)	
STAPLETON, Simon J.	Oxford	10.12.68	App	**Portsmouth**	12.86					(RB)	
			Tr	**Bristol Rov.**	07.88	1988	4	1	0		
STARBUCK, Philip M.	Nottingham	24.11.68	App	**Nottingham F.**	08.86	1986-88	6	16	2	(F)	
			L	**Birmingham C.**	03.88	1987	3	0	0		
STATHAM, Brian	Zimbabwe	21.05.69	YTS	**Tottenham H.**	07.87	1987-88	20	4	0	(FB)	E U21-2
STATHAM, Derek J.	Wolverhampton	24.03.59	App	**West Bromwich A.**	01.77	1976-87	298	1	8	(LB)	E Yth Int/E U21-6/E 'B'/E-3
			Tr	**Southampton**	08.87	1987-88	64	0	2		
STAUNTON, Steve	Drogheda (Ire)	19.01.69	Dundalk	**Liverpool**	09.86	1988	17	4	0	(FB)	IR-5
			L	**Bradford C.**	11.87	1987	7	1	0		
STEEL, W. Jim	Dumfries	04.12.59	App	**Oldham Ath.**	12.77	1978-82	101	7	24	(F)	
			L	**Wigan Ath.**	11.82	1982	2	0	2		
			L	**Wrexham**	01.83	1982	9	0	6		
			Tr	**Port Vale**	03.83	1982-83	27	1	6		
			Tr	**Wrexham**	01.84	1983-87	164	0	51		
			Tr	**Tranmere Rov.**	11.87	1987-88	73	0	14		
STEELE, Timothy W.	Coventry	01.12.67	App	**Shrewsbury T.**	12.85	1985-88	41	20	5	(M)	
			Tr	**Wolverhampton W.**	02.89	1988	7	4	1		
STEIN, Brian	South Africa	19.10.57	Edgware T.	**Luton T.**	10.77	1977-87	378	10	127	(F)	E U21-3/E-1/Brother of Mark to Caen (Fr) 6.88
STEIN, E. Mark S.	South Africa	28.01.66	Jnrs	**Luton T.**	01.84	1983-87	41	13	19	(F)	E Yth Int/Brother of Brian
			L	**Aldershot**	01.86	1985	2	0	1		
			Tr	**Q.P.R.**	08.88	1988	19	12	4		
STEPHENS, Archie	Liverpool	19.05.54	Melksham T.	**Bristol Rov.**	08.81	1981-84	100	27	40	(F)	
			Tr	**Middlesbrough**	03.85	1984-87	87	5	24		
			Tr	**Carlisle U.**	12.87	1987-88	20	4	3		
			Tr	**Darlington**	03.89	1988	10	0	4		
STEPHENSON, Geoffrey	Tynemouth	28.04.70	YTS	**Grimsby T.**	07.88	1988	12	2	0	(FB)	
STEPHENSON, Paul	Wallsend	02.01.68	App	**Newcastle U.**	12.85	1985-88	58	3	1	(RW)	E Yth Int
			Tr	**Millwall**	11.88	1988	11	1	1		
STERLAND, Mel	Sheffield	01.10.61	App	**Sheffield Wed.**	10.79	1978-88	271	8	37	(RB)	E U21-7/E 'B'/E-1 to Glasgow Rangers 2.89
STERLING, Worrell R.	Bethnal Green	08.06.65	App	**Watford**	06.83	1982-88	82	12	14	(W)	
			Tr	**Peterborough U.**	03.89	1988	12	0	3		
STEVEN, Trevor M.	Berwick	21.09.63	App	**Burnley**	09.81	1980-82	74	2	11	(RW)	E Yth Int/E U21-2/E-25
			Tr	**Everton**	07.83	1983-88	210	4	48		
STEVENS, Gary A.	Hillingdon	30.03.62	App	**Brighton & H.A.**	10.79	1979-82	120	13	2	(RB/M)	E U21-8/E-7
			Tr	**Tottenham H.**	06.83	1983-88	136	4	6		
STEVENS, Gary M.	Birmingham	30.08.54	Evesham	**Cardiff C.**	09.78	1978-82	138	12	44	(F/CD)	
			Tr	**Shrewsbury T.**	09.82	1982-85	144	6	29		
			Tr	**Brentford**	07.86	1986	29	3	10		
			Tr	**Hereford U.**	03.87	1986-88	85	3	10		
STEVENS, M. Gary	Barrow	27.03.63	App	**Everton**	03.81	1981-87	207	1	9	(RB)	E U21-1/E-33 to Glasgow Rangers 7.88
STEVENS, Ian D.	Malta	21.10.66	YTS	**Preston N.E.**	11.84	1984-85	9	2	2	(F)	
			Lancaster C.	**Stockport Co.** (N/C)	10.86	1986	1	1	0		
			Lancaster C.	**Bolton W.**	03.87	1986-88	22	16	7		

David Seaman (Q.P.R. & England) Match Magazine

Scott Sellars (Blackburn Rovers) Match Magazine

Graeme Sharp (Everton & Scotland) Match Magazine

Glyn Snodin (Leeds United) Match Magazine

Players Names	Birthplace	Date	Previous Club	League Club	Date Sign'd	Seasons Played	Career Record Apps	Sub	Gls	Pos.	Misc
STEVENS, Keith H.	Merton	21.06.64	App	**Millwall**	06.81	1980-88	214	4	3	(RB)	
STEVENSON, Andrew J.	Scunthorpe	29.09.67	Jnrs	**Scunthorpe U.**	01.86	1985-88	29	14	0	(D)	
STEVENSON, Nigel C.A.	Swansea	02.11.58	App	**Swansea C.**	11.76	1975-86	247	12	15	(CD)	W U21-2/W-4
			L	**Cardiff C.**	10.85	1985	14	0	0		
			L	**Reading**	03.86	1985	3	0	0		
			Tr	**Cardiff C.**	08.87	1987-88	66	2	2		
STEWART, Ian E.	Belfast	10.09.61	Jnrs	**Q.P.R.**	05.80	1980-84	55	12	2	(LW)	NI Sch Int/NI-31
			L	**Millwall**	03.83	1982	10	1	3		
			Tr	**Newcastle U.**	08.85	1985-86	34	8	3		
			Tr	**Portsmouth**	07.87	1987	0	1	0		
			L	**Brentford**	02.88	1987	4	3	0		
			Tr	**Aldershot**	01.89	1988	21	1	0		
STEWART, Paul A.	Manchester	07.10.64	App	**Blackpool**	10.81	1981-86	188	13	56	(F)	E Yth Int/E U21-1/E 'B'
			Tr	**Manchester C.**	03.87	1986-87	51	0	27		
			Tr	**Tottenham H.**	06.88	1988	29	1	12		
STEWART, Ray S.M.	Perth	07.09.59	Dundee U.	**West Ham U.**	09.78	1979-88	339	1	62	(RB)	S Sch Int/S U21-12/S-7
STEWART, Robert A.	Broxburn	14.06.71	YTS	**Doncaster Rov.** (YTS)	07.87	1988	1	0	0	(M)	
STEWART, W.I. (Billy)	Liverpool	01.01.65	App	**Liverpool**	01.83					(G)	
			Tr	**Wigan Ath.**	07.84	1984-85	14	0	0		
			Tr	**Chester C.**	08.86	1986-88	102	0	0		
STILES, John C.	Manchester	06.05.64	Vancouver W. (Can)	**Leeds U.**	05.84	1984-88	49	16	2	(M)	Son of Nobby
STIMSON, Mark	Plaistow	27.12.67	YTS	**Tottenham H.**	07.85	1986-88	1	1	0	(FB)	
			L	**Leyton Orient**	03.88	1987	10	0	0		
			L	**Gillingham**	01.89	1988	18	0	0		
STOCKWELL, Mike T.	Chelmsford	14.02.65	App	**Ipswich T.**	12.82	1985-88	81	14	4	(FB)	
STOKES, Wayne D.	Wolverhampton	16.02.65	Coventry C.(App)	**Gillingham**	07.82	1982-83	2	1	0	(CD)	
				Stockport Co.	10.86	1986	17	1	1		
			Tr	**Hartlepool U.**	07.87	1987-88	61	0	2		
STONEHOUSE, Kevin	Bishop Auckland	20.09.59	Shildon	**Blackburn Rov.**	07.79	1979-82	77	8	27	(M)	
			Tr	**Huddersfield T.**	03.83	1982-83	20	2	4		
			Tr	**Blackpool**	03.84	1983-85	53	2	19		
			Tr	**Darlington**	07.87	1987-88	59	13	20		
			L	**Carlisle U.**	03.89	1988	0	3	0		
STORER, Stuart J.	Rugby	16.01.67	YTS	**Mansfield T.** (YTS)	08.83	1983	0	1	0	(RW)	
			VS Rugby	**Birmingham C.**	01.85	1985-86	5	3	0		
			Tr	**Everton**	03.87						
			L	**Wigan Ath.**	08.87	1987	9	3	0		
			Tr	**Bolton W.**	12.87	1987-88	22	16	3		
STOUTT, Stephen P.	Halifax	05.04.64		**Huddersfield T.** (N/C)	01.84	1983-84	6	0	0	(D)	
			Tr	**Wolverhampton W.**	04.85	1985-87	91	3	5		
			Tr	**Grimsby T.**	07.88	1988	2	0	1		
STOWELL, Mike	Preston	19.04.65	Leyland Motors	**Everton**	12.85					(G)	
			L	**Chester C.**	09.87	1987	14	0	0		
			L	**York C.**	12.87	1987	6	0	0		
			L	**Manchester C.**	01.88	1987	14	0	0		
			L	**Port Vale**	10.88	1988	7	0	0		
			L	**Wolverhampton W.**	03.89	1988	7	0	0		
STRACHAN, Gordon D.	Edinburgh	09.02.57	Aberdeen	**Manchester U.**	08.84	1984-87	155	5	33	(RM)	S-41/S U21-1
			Tr	**Leeds U.**	03.89	1988	11	0	3		
STREETE, Floyd A.	Jamaica (WI)	05.05.59	Rivet Spts(Aylesbury)	**Cambridge U.**	07.76	1976-82	111	14	19	(CD)	
			Utrecht (Neth)	**Derby Co.**	10.84	1984-85	35	0	0		
			Tr	**Wolverhampton W.**	10.85	1985-88	140	2	6		
STRINGFELLOW, Ian R.	Nottingham	08.05.69	App	**Mansfield T.**	08.86	1985-88	34	29	13	(F)	Nephew of Mike
STRODDER, Gary J.	Cleckheaton	01.04.65	App	**Lincoln C.**	04.83	1982-86	122	10	6	(CD)	Son of Colin
			Tr	**West Ham U.**	03.87	1986-88	43	6	1		
STUART, Mark R.	Hammersmith	15.12.66	Jnrs	**Charlton Ath.**	07.84	1984-88	89	18	28	(W)	
			Tr	**Plymouth Arg.**	11.88	1988	32	0	5		
STURRIDGE, Simon A.	Birmingham	09.12.69	YTS	**Birmingham C.**	07.88	1988	13	8	3	(F)	
SUCKLING, Perry J.	Leyton	12.10.65	App	**Coventry C.**	10.83	1982-83	27	0	0	(G)	E Yth Int/E U21-10
			Tr	**Manchester C.**	06.86	1986-87	39	0	0		
			Tr	**Crystal Palace**	01.88	1987-88	44	0	0		
SULLEY, Chris S.	Camberwell	03.12.59	App	**Chelsea**	12.77					(LB)	
			Tr	**Bournemouth**	03.81	1980-85	205	1	3		
			Dundee U.	**Blackburn Rov.**	03.87	1986-88	66	0	0		
SUMMERFIELD, Kevin	Walsall	07.01.59	App	**West Bromwich A.**	01.77	1978-81	5	4	4	(W)	E Yth Int
			Tr	**Birmingham C.**	05.82	1982	2	3	1		
			Tr	**Walsall**	12.82	1982-83	42	12	17		
			Tr	**Cardiff C.**	07.84	1984	10	0	1		
			Tr	**Plymouth Arg.**	12.84	1984-88	109	19	25		
SUSSEX, Andy R.	Enfield	23.11.64	App	**Leyton Orient**	11.82	1981-87	126	18	17	(W)	
			Tr	**Crewe Alex.**	06.88	1988	16	9	4		
SUTTON, David W.	Tarleton (Lancs.)	21.01.57	App	**Plymouth Arg.**	07.74	1973-77	60	1	0	(CD)	
			L	**Reading**	11.77	1977	9	0	0		
			Tr	**Huddersfield T.**	03.78	1977-83	242	0	11		
			Tr	**Bolton W.**	06.85	1985-87	98	0	4		
			Tr	**Rochdale**	08.88	1988	28	0	2		
SUTTON, Steve J.	Hartington	16.04.61	App	**Nottingham F.**	04.79	1980-88	169	0	0	(G)	
			L	**Mansfield T.**	03.81	1980	8	0	0		
			L	**Derby Co.**	01.85	1984	14	0	0		
SWAIN, Kenny M.	Birkenhead	28.01.52	Wycombe W.	**Chelsea**	08.73	1973-78	114	5	26	(FB)	
			Tr	**Aston Villa**	12,78	1978-82	148	0	4		
			Tr	**Nottingham F.**	10.82	1982-84	112	0	2		
			Tr	**Portsmouth**	07.85	1985-87	113	0	0		
			L	**West Bromwich A.**	02.88	1987	7	0	1		
			Tr	**Crewe Alex.**	08.88	1988	40	1	0		
SWAN, Peter H.	Leeds	28.09.66	YTS	**Leeds U.**	08.84	1985-88	43	6	11	(CD/F)	
			Tr	**Hull C.**	03.89	1988	11	0	1		
SWANN, Gary	York	11.04.62	App	**Hull C.**	04.80	1980-86	176	10	9	(M/FB)	
			Tr	**Preston N.E.**	11.86	1986-88	90	4	19		

Players Names	Birthplace	Date	Previous Club	League Club	Date Sign'd	Seasons Played	Career Record Apps	Sub	Gls	Pos.	Misc
SWEENEY, Paul	Glasgow	10.01.65	Raith Rov.	**Newcastle U.**	03.89	1988	6	2	0	(LB/M)	
SWINDLEHURST, Dave	Edgware	06.01.56	App	**Crystal Palace**	01.73	1973-79	221	16	73	(F)	E Yth Int/E U21-1
			Tr	**Derby Co.**	02.80	1979-82	110	0	29		
			Tr	**West Ham U.**	03.83	1982-84	52	9	16		
			Tr	**Sunderland**	08.85	1985-86	59	0	11		
			Cyprus	**Wimbledon** (N/C)	03.88	1987	2	0	0		
			Tr	**Colchester U.**	06.88	1988	12	0	5		
			L	**Peterborough U.**	12.88	1988	4	0	1		
SYMONS, Chris J.	Basingstoke	08.03.71	YTS	**Portsmouth**	12.88	1988	2	0	0	(CD)	W Yth Int
TAGGART, Gerald P.	Belfast	18.10.70	YTS	**Manchester C.**	07.89	1988	9	2	1	(CD)	NI Yth Int/NI U21-1
TAIT, Mick P.	Wallsend	30.09.56	App	**Oxford U.**	09.74	1974-76	61	3	23	(M)	
			Tr	**Carlisle U.**	10.77	1976-79	101	5	20		
			Tr	**Hull C.**	09.79	1979	29	4	3		
			Tr	**Portsmouth**	06.80	1980-86	228	12	31		
			Tr	**Reading**	08.87	1987-88	71	0	7		
TAIT, Paul R.	Sutton Coldfield	31.07.71	YTS	**Birmingham C.**	07.88	1987-88	6	5	0	(F)	
TALBOT, Brian E.	Ipswich	21.07.53	App	**Ipswich T.**	07.70	1973-78	177	0	25	(M)	E U21-1/E-6/E 'B'
			Tr	**Arsenal**	01.79	1978-84	245	9	40		
			Tr	**Watford**	06.85	1985-86	46	2	8		
			Tr	**Stoke C.**	10.86	1986-87	51	3	5		
			Tr	**West Bromwich A.**	01.88	1987-88	15	0	4		
TANKARD, Allen J.	Fleet	21.05.69	App	**Southampton**	05.87	1985-86	5	0	0	(LB)	E Yth Int
			Tr	**Wigan Ath.**	07.88	1988	31	2	1		
TANNER, Nick	Kingswood	24.05.65	Mangotsfield	**Bristol Rov.**	06.85	1985-87	104	3	3	(LB)	
			Tr	**Liverpool**	07.88	1988					
TAYLOR, Alan D.	Hinckley	14.11.53	Morecambe	**Rochdale**	05.73	1973-74	55	0	8	(F)	
			Tr	**West Ham U.**	11.74	1974-78	88	10	25		
			Tr	**Norwich C.**	08.79	1979	20	4	5		
			Vancouver W. (Can.)	**Cambridge U.**	10.80	1980-81	17	1	4		
			Vancouver W. (Can.)	**Hull C.** (N/C)	01.84	1983	13	1	3		
			Tr	**Burnley**	08.84	1984-85	60	4	23		
			Tr	**Bury**	06.86	1986-87	55	7	10		
				Norwich C.	09.88	1988	1	3	1		
TAYLOR, Alex	Baillieston	13.06.62	Hamilton Acad.	**Walsall**	08.88	1988	13	0	3	(W)	
TAYLOR, Jason S.	Wrexham	29.08.70	YTS	**Wrexham** (YTS)	09.87	1988	0	1	0		
TAYLOR, John P.	Norwich	24.10.64	Jnrs	**Colchester U.**	12.82					(F)	
			Sudbury T.	**Cambridge U.**	08.88	1988	34	6	12		
TAYLOR, Kevin	Wakefield	22.01.61	App	**Sheffield Wed.**	10.78	1978-83	118	7	21	(M)	
			Tr	**Derby Co.**	07.84	1984	22	0	2		
			Tr	**Crystal Palace**	03.85	1984-87	85	2	14		
			Tr	**Scunthorpe U.**	10.87	1987-88	74	2	13		
TAYLOR, Les	North Shields	04.12.56	App	**Oxford U.**	12.74	1974-80	219	0	15	(M)	
			Tr	**Watford**	11.80	1980-85	167	5	13		
			Tr	**Reading**	10.86	1986-88	69	6	3		
			L	**Colchester U.**	01.89	1988	14	2	0		
TAYLOR, P. Mark R.	Hartlepool	20.11.64		**Hartlepool U.**	01.84	1983-85	42	5	4	(LW)	
			L	**Crewe Alex.**	12.85	1985	3	0	0		
			Tr	**Blackpool**	08.86	1986-88	89	1	38		
TAYLOR, R. Mark	Birmingham	22.02.66	YTS	**Walsall**	07.84	1984-88	100	11	4	(FB)	
TAYLOR, Martin J.	Tamworth	09.12.66	Mile Oak Rovers	**Derby Co.**	07.86					(G)	
			L	**Carlisle U.**	09.87	1987	10	0	0		
			L	**Scunthorpe U.**	12.87	1987	8	0	0		
TAYLOR, R. (Bob)	Easington	03.02.67	Horden CW	**Leeds U.**	01.86	1985-88	33	9	8	(F)	
			Tr	**Bristol C.**	03.89	1988	12	0	8		
TAYLOR, Scott D.	Portsmouth	28.11.70	YTS	**Reading** (YTS)	07.87	1988	0	3	0		
TAYLOR, Shaun	Plymouth	26.03.63	Bideford	**Exeter C.**	12.86	1986-88	100	0	7	(CD)	
TAYLOR, Steve J.	Royton	18.10.55	App	**Bolton W.**	10.73	1974-77	34	6	16	(F)	
			L	**Port Vale**	10.75	1975	4	0	2		
			Tr	**Oldham Ath.**	10.77	1977-78	45	2	25		
			Tr	**Luton T.**	01.79	1978	15	5	1		
			Tr	**Mansfield T.**	07.79	1979	30	7	7		
			Tr	**Burnley**	07.80	1980-82	80	6	37		
			Tr	**Wigan Ath.**	08.83	1983	29	1	7		
			Tr	**Stockport Co.**	03.84	1983-84	26	0	8		
			Tr	**Rochdale**	11.84	1984-86	84	0	42		
			Tr	**Preston N.E.**	10.86	1986	5	0	2		
			Tr	**Burnley**	08.87	1987-88	38	7	6		
			Tr	**Rochdale**	03.89	1988	16	1	4		
TEALE, Shaun	Stockport	10.03.64	Weymouth	**Bournemouth**	01.89	1988	19	1	0	(CD)	E Semi Pro Int 1988
TEMPEST, Dale M.	Leeds	30.12.63	App	**Fulham**	12.81	1980-83	25	9	6	(F)	
			Tr	**Huddersfield T.**	08.84	1984-85	63	2	27		
			L	**Gillingham**	03.86	1985	9	0	4		
			Lokeren (Belgium)	**Colchester U.**	08.87	1987-88	69	8	18		
TERRY, Steve G.	Clapton	14.06.62	App	**Watford**	01.80	1979-87	160	0	14	(CD)	
			Tr	**Hull C.**	06.88	1988	33	0	1		
TESTER, Paul L.	Stroud	10.03.59	Cheltenham T.	**Shrewsbury T.**	07.83	1983-87	86	12	12	(LW)	
			L	**Hereford U.**	11.84	1984	4	0	0		
			Tr	**Hereford U.**	08.88	1988	40	4	6		
THACKERAY, Andy J.	Huddersfield	13.02.68	Jnrs	**Manchester C.**	02.86					(M)	
			Tr	**Huddersfield T.**	07.86	1986	2	0	0		
			Tr	**Newport Co.**	03.87	1986-87	53	1	4		
			Tr	**Wrexham**	07.88	1988	27	8	2		
THOMAS, Andy M.	Oxford	16.12.62	App	**Oxford U.**	12.80	1980-85	89	27	32	(M)	
			L	**Fulham**	12.82	1982	3	1	2		
			L	**Derby Co.**	03.83	1982	0	1	0		
			Tr	**Newcastle U.**	09.86	1986-87	24	7	6		
			Tr	**Bradford C.**	06.88	1988	15	8	5		
THOMAS, Dean	Bedworth	19.12.61	Nuneaton Bor.	**Wimbledon**	07.81	1981-83	57	0	8	(FB)	
			Fta. Dusseldorf (WG)	**Northampton T.**	08.88	1988	43	0	9		

Jim Stannard (Fulham) Match Magazine

Mike Stockwell (Ipswich Town) Match Magazine

Steve Sutton (Nottingham Forest) Match Magazine

Players Names	Birthplace	Date	Previous Club	League Club	Date Sign'd	Seasons Played	Career Record Apps	Sub	Gls	Pos.	Misc
THOMAS, Geoff R.	Manchester	05.08.64	Littleborough P.	**Rochdale** (N/C)	08.82	1982-83	10	1	1	(M)	
			Tr	**Crewe Alex.**	03.84	1983-86	120	5	21		
			Tr	**Crystal Palace**	06.87	1987-88	63	0	11		
THOMAS, Glen A.	Hackney	06.10.67	App	**Fulham**	10.85	1986-88	66	2	1	(FB)	
THOMAS, D. Gwyn	Swansea	26.09.57	App	**Leeds U.**	07.75	1974-83	79	10	3	(M)	W Sch Int/W U21-2
			Tr	**Barnsley**	03.84	1983-88	196	2	17		
THOMAS, John W.	Wednesbury	05.08.58		**Everton**	07.77					(F)	
			L	**Tranmere Rov.**	03.79	1978	10	1	2		
			L	**Halifax T.**	10.79	1979	5	0	0		
			Tr	**Bolton W.**	06.80	1980-81	18	4	6		
			Tr	**Chester C.**	08.82	1982	44	0	20		
			Tr	**Lincoln C.**	08.83	1983-84	56	11	18		
			Tr	**Preston N.E.**	06.85	1985-86	69	9	28		
			Tr	**Bolton W.**	07.87	1987-88	71	2	32		
THOMAS, Martin R.	Senghenydd	28.11.59	App	**Bristol Rov.**	09.77	1976-81	162	0	0	(G)	W Yth Int/W U21-2/W-1
			L	**Cardiff C.**	07.82	1982	15	0	0		
			L	**Southend U.**	02.83	1982	6	0	0		
			Tr	**Newcastle U.**	03.83	1982-87	118	0	0		
			L	**Middlesbrough**	10.84	1984	4	0	0		
			Tr	**Birmingham C.**	10.88	1988	36	0	0		
THOMAS, Michael L.	Lambeth	24.08.67	App	**Arsenal**	12.84	1986-88	81	5	15	(M)	E Yth Int/E U21-11/E-1
			L	**Portsmouth**	12.86	1986	3	0	0		
THOMAS, Micky R.	Newtown	07.07.54	Jnrs	**Wrexham**	05.72	1971-78	217	13	33	(W)	W U23-2/W-51
			Tr	**Manchester U.**	11.78	1978-80	90	0	11		
			Tr	**Everton**	08.81	1981	10	0	0		
			Tr	**Brighton & H.A.**	11.81	1981	18	2	0		
			Tr	**Stoke C.**	08.82	1982-83	57	0	14		
			Tr	**Chelsea**	01.84	1983-84	43	1	9		
			Tr	**West Bromwich A.**	09.85	1985	20	0	0		
			L	**Derby Co.**	03.86	1985	9	0	0		
			Wichita W. (USA)	**Shrewsbury T.**	08.88	1988	40	0	1		
THOMAS, Mitchell A.	Luton	02.10.64	App	**Luton T.**	08.82	1982-85	106	1	1	(LB)	E Yth Int/E U21-3
			Tr	**Tottenham H.**	07.86	1986-88	96	4	5		
THOMAS, Rod C.	Brent	10.10.70	YTS	**Watford**	05.88	1987-88	16	6	2	(W)	E Sch Int
THOMAS, Tony	Liverpool	12.07.71	YTS	**Tranmere Rov.**	02.89	1988	8	1	2	(M)	
THOMPSON, Andrew R.	Cannock	09.11.67	App	**West Bromwich A.**	11.85	1985-86	18	6	1	(M/LB)	
			Tr	**Wolverhampton W.**	11.86	1986-88	115	2	16		
THOMPSON, Chris D.	Walsall	24.01.60	App	**Bolton W.**	07.77	1979-82	66	7	18	(M)	E Yth Int
			L	**Lincoln C.**	03.83	1982	5	1	0		
			Tr	**Blackburn Rov.**	08.83	1983-85	81	4	24		
			Tr	**Wigan Ath.**	07.86	1986-87	67	7	12		
			Tr	**Blackpool**	07.88	1988	25	11	8		
THOMPSON, David G.	Ashington	20.11.68	App	**Millwall**	11.86	1987-88	18	2	1	(CD)	
THOMPSON, David S.	Manchester	27.05.62	North Withington	**Rochdale**	09.81	1981-85	147	8	13	(W)	
			Tr	**Notts Co.**	08.86	1986-87	52	3	8		
			Tr	**Wigan Ath.**	10.87	1987-88	69	0	10		
THOMPSON, Gary L.	Birmingham	07.10.59	App	**Coventry C.**	06.77	1977-82	127	7	38	(F)	E U21-6/Brother of Keith
			Tr	**West Bromwich A.**	02.83	1982-84	91	0	39		
			Tr	**Sheffield Wed.**	08.85	1985	35	1	7		
			Tr	**Aston Villa**	06.86	1986-88	56	4	17		
			Tr	**Watford**	12.88	1988	17	4	7		
THOMPSON, Keith A.	Birmingham	24.04.65	App	**Coventry C.**	01.83	1982-83	9	3	0	(W)	E Yth Int/Brother of Gary
			L	**Wimbledon**	10.83	1983	0	3	0		
			L	**Northampton T.**	03.85	1984	10	0	1		
			Real Oviedo (Spain)	**Coventry C.**	09.88	1988	2	7	1		
THOMPSON, Leslie	Cleethorpes	23.09.68	YTS	**Hull C.**	03.87	1987-88	11	3	2	(F)	
			L	**Scarborough**	12.88	1988	2	1	1		
THOMPSON, Neil	Beverley	02.10.63	Nottingham F.(App)	**Hull C.**	11.81	1981-82	29	2	0	(LB)	
			Tr	**Scarborough**	(N/L)	1987-88	87	0	15		
THOMPSON, Nigel D.	Leeds	01.03.67	App	**Leeds U.**	12.84	1983-86	6	1	0	(M)	
			L	**Rochdale**	08.87	1987	3	2	0		
			Tr	**Chesterfield**	03.88	1987-88	9	1	0		
THOMPSON, Richard J.	Bristol	11.04.69	Watford (Jnr)	**Newport Co.**	01.87	1987	10	3	2	(F)	
			Tr	**Torquay U.**	06.88	1988	11	4	3		
THOMPSON, Simon L.	Sheffield	27.02.70	YTS	**Rotherham U.**	06.88	1988	0	1	0	(M)	
THOMPSON, Steve J.	Oldham	02.11.64	App	**Bolton W.**	11.82	1982-88	237	6	38	(M)	
THOMPSON, Steve P.	Sheffield	28.07.55	Boston U.	**Lincoln C.**	04.80	1980-84	153	1	8	(CD)	
			Tr	**Charlton Ath.**	08.85	1985-87	95	0	0		
			Tr	**Leicester C.**	07.88						
			Tr	**Sheffield U.**	11.88	1988	20	0	1		
THOMPSTONE, Ian P.	Bury	17.07.71	YTS	**Manchester C.** (YTS)	06.87	1987	0	1	1	(M)	
THORN, Andy	Carshalton	12.11.66	YTS	**Wimbledon**	11.84	1984-87	106	1	2	(CD)	E U21-4
			Tr	**Newcastle U.**	08.88	1988	26	0	1		
THORNBER, Steve J.	Dewsbury	11.10.65	Jnrs	**Halifax T.**	01.83	1983-87	94	10	4	(M)	
			Tr	**Swansea C.**	08.88	1988	27	4	0		
THORPE, Adrian	Chesterfield	25.11.63		**Mansfield T.** (N/C)	08.82	1982	0	2	1	(W)	
			Heanor T.	**Bradford C.**	08.85	1985-87	9	8	1		
			L	**Tranmere Rov.**	11.86	1986	4	1	3		
			Tr	**Notts Co.**	11.87	1987-88	48	11	9		
THORPE, Andy	Stockport	15.09.60	Jnrs	**Stockport Co.**	08.78	1977-85	312	2	3	(D)	
			Tr	**Tranmere Rov.**	07.86	1986-87	51	2	0		
			Tr	**Stockport Co.**	01.88	1987-88	61	0	0		
THORSTVEDT, Erik	Norway	28.10.62	IFK Gothenberg (Swe)	**Tottenham H.**	12.88	1988	18	0	0	(G)	Norwegian Int
TILER, Carl	Sheffield	11.02.70	YTS	**Barnsley**	07.88	1987-88	4	1	1	(D)	
TILLSON, Andy	Huntingdon	30.06.66	Kettering T.	**Grimsby T.**	07.88	1988	44	1	2	(CD)	
TILSON, Steven	Wickford	27.07.66	Witham T.	**Southend U.**	02.89	1988	10	6	2	(M)	
TINKLER, John	Trimdon	24.08.68	Jnrs	**Hartlepool U.**	12.86	1986-88	54	6	3	(M)	

Players Names	Birthplace	Date	Previous Club	League Club	Date Sign'd	Seasons Played	Career Record Apps	Sub	Gls	Pos.	Misc
TINNION, Brian	Stanley	23.02.68	App	**Newcastle U.**	02.86	1986-88	30	2	2	(LB)	
			Tr	**Bradford C.**	03.89	1988	14	0	1		
TODD, Mark K.	Belfast	04.12.67	YTS	**Manchester U.**	08.85					(M)	
			Tr	**Sheffield U.**	06.87	1987-88	50	1	3		
TOMAN, J. Andy	Northallerton	07.03.62	Bishop Auckland	**Lincoln C.**	08.85	1985	21	3	4	(M)	
			Bishop Auckland	**Hartlepool U.**	01.87	1986-88	112	0	28		
TOMLINSON, Paul	Brierley Hill	22.02.64	Middlewood Rangers	**Sheffield U.**	06.83	1983-86	37	0	0	(G)	
			L	**Birmingham C.**	03.87	1986	11	0	0		
			Tr	**Bradford C.**	06.87	1987-88	80	0	0		
TOWNSEND, Andy D.	Maidstone	23.07.63	Weymouth	**Southampton**	01.85	1984-87	77	6	5	(M)	IR-4
			Tr	**Norwich C.**	08.88	1988	31	5	5		
TRACEY, Simon P.	Woolwich	09.12.67	App	**Wimbledon**	12.85	1988	1	0	0	(G)	
			Tr	**Sheffield U.**	10.88	1988	7	0	0		
TREACY, Darren P.	Lambeth	06.09.70	YTS	**Millwall**	02.89	1988	3	0	0	(M)	
TREVITT, Simon	Dewsbury	20.12.67	YTS	**Huddersfield T.**	06.86	1986-88	75	12	1	(RB)	
TREWICK, John	Bedlington	03.06.57	App	**West Bromwich A.**	07.74	1974-80	83	13	11	(M)	E Sch Int/E Yth Int
			Tr	**Newcastle U.**	12.80	1980-83	76	2	8		
			L	**Oxford U.**	01.84	1983	3	0	0		
			Tr	**Oxford U.**	08.84	1984-87	109	2	4		
			Tr	**Birmingham C.**	09.87	1987-88	35	2	0		
TROTTER, Michael	Hartlepool	27.10.69	YTS	**Middlesbrough**	11.87					(M)	
			L	**Doncaster Rov.**	11.88	1988	3	0	0		
TRUSSON, Mike S.	Northolt	26.05.59	App	**Plymouth Arg.**	01.77	1976-79	65	8	15	(M)	
			Tr	**Sheffield U.**	07.80	1980-83	125	1	31		
			Tr	**Rotherham U.**	12.83	1983-86	124	0	19		
			Tr	**Brighton & H.A.**	07.87	1987-88	34	3	2		
TUCKER, Gordon	Manchester	05.01.68	Derby Co. (N/C)	**Huddersfield T.**	07.87	1987-88	30	5	0	(CD)	
TUNKS, Roy W.	Worthing	21.01.51	App	**Rotherham U.**	03.68	1967-73	138	0	0	(G)	
			L	**York C.**	01.69	1968	4	0	0		
			Tr	**Preston N.E.**	11.74	1974-80	277	0	0		
			Tr	**Wigan Ath.**	11.81	1981-87	245	0	0		
			Tr	**Hartlepool U.**	07.88	1988	5	0	0		
			Tr	**Preston N.E.**	11.88	1988	23	0	0		
TUPLING, Stephen	Wensleydale	11.07.64	App	**Middlesbrough**	07.82					(M)	
			Tr	**Carlisle U.**	07.84	1984	1	0	0		
			Tr	**Darlington**	10.84	1984-86	105	6	8		
			Tr	**Newport Co.**	08.87	1987	30	3	2		
			Tr	**Cardiff C.**	08.88	1988	3	1	0		
			L	**Torquay U.**	09.88	1988	1	2	0		
			L	**Exeter C.**	01.89	1988	8	1	1		
TURNBULL, Lee M.	Stockton	27.09.67	YTS	**Middlesbrough**	09.85	1985-86	8	8	4	(M)	
			Tr	**Aston Villa**	08.87						
			Tr	**Doncaster Rov.**	11.87	1987-88	55	7	5		
TURNER, Chris R.	Sheffield	15.09.58	App	**Sheffield Wed.**	08.76	1976-78	91	0	0	(G)	E Yth Int
			L	**Lincoln C.**	10.78	1978	5	0	0		
			Tr	**Sunderland**	07.79	1979-84	195	0	0		
			Tr	**Manchester U.**	08.85	1985-87	64	0	0		
			Tr	**Sheffield Wed.**	09.88	1988	29	0	0		
TURNER, Paul E.	Cheshunt	13.11.68	App	**Arsenal**	07.86					(M)	
			Tr	**Cambridge U.**	09.87	1987-88	28	9	0		
TURNER, Philip	Sheffield	12.02.62	App	**Lincoln C.**	02.80	1979-85	239	2	19	(M)	
			Tr	**Grimsby T.**	08.86	1986-87	62	0	9		
			Tr	**Leicester C.**	02.88	1987-88	18	6	2		
			Tr	**Notts Co.**	03.89	1988	16	0	2		
TURNER, Robert P.	Hartlepool	18.09.66	App	**Huddersfield T.**	09.84	1984	0	1	0	(F)	
			Tr	**Cardiff C.**	07.85	1985-86	34	5	8		
			L	**Hartlepool U.**	10.86	1986	7	0	1		
			Tr	**Bristol Rov.**	12.86	1986-87	19	7	2		
			Tr	**Wimbledon**	12.87	1987-88	2	8	0		
			Tr	**Bristol C.**	01.89	1988	19	0	6		
TUTILL, Stephen A.	York	01.10.69	YTS	**York C.**	01.88	1987-88	41	2	1	(CD)	
TWENTYMAN, Geoff	Liverpool	10.03.59	Chorley	**Preston N.E.**	08.83	1983-85	95	3	4	(CD)	Son of Geoff (Sr)
			Tr	**Bristol Rov.**	08.86	1986-88	124	3	2		
TYNAN, Tommy E.	Liverpool	17.11.55	App	**Liverpool**	11.72					(F)	
			L	**Swansea C.**	10.75	1975	6	0	2		
			Tr	**Sheffield Wed.**	09.76	1976-78	89	2	31		
			Tr	**Lincoln C.**	10.78	1978	9	0	1		
			Tr	**Newport Co.**	02.79	1978-82	168	15	66		
			Tr	**Plymouth Arg.**	08.83	1983-84	80	0	43		
			Tr	**Rotherham U.**	07.85	1985-86	32	0	13		
			L	**Plymouth Arg.**	03.86	1985	9	0	9		
			Tr	**Plymouth Arg.**	09.86	1986-88	128	1	58		
UZZELL, John E.	Plymouth	31.03.59	App	**Plymouth Arg.**	03.77	1977-88	292	10	6	(D)	
VALENTINE, Peter	Huddersfield	16.04.63	App	**Huddersfield T.**	04.80	1981-82	19	0	1	(CD)	
			Tr	**Bolton W.**	07.83	1983-84	66	2	1		
			Tr	**Bury**	07.85	1985-88	161	3	8		
VAN DEN HAUWE, Pat W.R.	Belgium	16.12.60	App	**Birmingham C.**	08.78	1978-84	119	4	1	(D)	W-13
			Tr	**Everton**	09.84	1984-88	134	1	1		
VARADI, Imre	Paddington	08.07.59	Letchworth	**Sheffield U.**	04.78	1978	6	4	4	(F)	
			Tr	**Everton**	03.79	1979-80	22	4	6		
			Tr	**Newcastle U.**	08.81	1981-82	81	0	39		
			Tr	**Sheffield Wed.**	08.83	1983-84	72	4	33		
			Tr	**West Bromwich A.**	07.85	1985	30	2	9		
			Tr	**Manchester C.**	10.86	1986-88	56	9	26		
			Tr	**Sheffield Wed.**	09.88	1988	14	6	3		

Players Names	Birthplace	Date	Previous Club	League Club	Date Sign'd	Seasons Played	Career Record Apps	Sub	Gls	Pos.	Misc
VAUGHAN, John	Isleworth	26.06.64	App	**West Ham U.**	06.82					(G)	
			L	**Charlton Ath.**	03.85	1984	6	0	0		
			L	**Bristol Rov.**	09.85	1985	6	0	0		
			L	**Wrexham**	10.85	1985	4	0	0		
			L	**Bristol C.**	03.86	1985	2	0	0		
			Tr	**Fulham**	08.86	1986	44	0	0		
			L	**Bristol C.**	01.88	1987	3	0	0		
			Tr	**Cambridge U.**	06.88	1988	29	0	0		
VAUGHAN, Nigel M.	Caerleon	20.05.59	App	**Newport Co.**	05.77	1976-83	215	9	32	(M)	W U21-1/W-10
			Tr	**Cardiff C.**	09.83	1983-86	144	5	42		
			L	**Reading**	02.87	1986	5	0	1		
			Tr	**Wolverhampton W.**	08.87	1987-88	63	5	10		
VENISON, Barry	Consett	16.08.64	App	**Sunderland**	01.82	1981-85	169	4	2	(RB)	E Yth Int/E U21-10
			Tr	**Liverpool**	07.86	1986-88	63	3	0		
VENUS, Mark	Hartlepool	06.04.67	Jnrs	**Hartlepool U.** (N/C)	03.85	1984	4	0	0	(LB)	
			Tr	**Leicester C.**	09.85	1985-87	58	3	1		
			Tr	**Wolverhampton W.**	03.88	1987-88	35	4	0		
VEYSEY, Kenny J.	Hackney	08.06.67	Dawlish	**Torquay U.**	11.87	1988	25	0	0	(G)	
VICKERS, Stephen H.	Bishop Auckland	13.10.67	Spennymoor U.	**Tranmere Rov.**	09.85	1985-88	130	1	6	(CD)	
VINEY, Keith B.	Portsmouth	26.10.57	App	**Portsmouth**	10.75	1975-81	160	6	3	(LB)	
			Tr	**Exeter C.**	08.82	1982-88	270	0	8		
			L	**Bristol Rov.**	09.88	1988	2	1	0		
VINNICOMBE, Chris	Exeter	20.10.70	YTS	**Exeter C.** (YTS)	07.87	1988	21	4	0	(M)	
WADDLE, Chris R.	Felling	14.12.60	Tow Law T.	**Newcastle U.**	07.80	1980-84	169	1	46	(W)	E U21-1/E-44
			Tr	**Tottenham H.**	06.85	1985-88	137	1	33		
WADE, Bryan A.	Bath	25.06.63	Trowbridge T.	**Swindon T.**	05.85	1985-87	48	12	18	(F)	
			Tr	**Swansea C.**	08.88	1988	17	8	4		
WAITT, Mick H.	Hexham	25.06.60	Arnold Kingswell	**Notts Co.**	12.84	1984-86	71	11	27	(F)	
			Tr	**Lincoln C.**	(N/L)						
WAKENSHAW, Robbie A.	Ponteland	22.12.65	App	**Everton**	12.83	1983-84	2	1	1	(W)	E Yth Int
			Tr	**Carlisle U.**	09.85	1985	6	2	2		
			L	**Doncaster Rov.**	03.86	1985	8	0	3		
			Tr	**Rochdale**	09.86	1986	28	1	5		
			Tr	**Crewe Alex.**	06.87	1987-88	18	4	1		
WALFORD, Steve J.	Highgate	05.01.58	App	**Tottenham H.**	04.75	1975	1	1	0	(D)	E Yth Int
			Tr	**Arsenal**	08.77	1977-80	64	13	3		
			Tr	**Norwich C.**	03.81	1980-82	93	0	2		
			Tr	**West Ham U.**	08.83	1983-86	114	1	2		
			L	**Huddersfield T.**	10.87	1987	12	0	0		
			L	**Gillingham**	12.88	1988	4	0	0		
			L	**West Bromwich A.**	03.89	1988	3	1	0		
WALKER, Alan	Mossley	17.12.59		**Stockport Co.**	08.78					(CD)	
			Telford U.	**Lincoln C.**	10.83	1983-84	74	1	4		
			Tr	**Millwall**	07.85	1985-87	92	0	8		
			Tr	**Gillingham**	03.88	1987-88	29	0	1		
WALKER, Clive	Oxford	26.05.57	App	**Chelsea**	04.75	1976-83	168	30	60	(LW)	E Sch Int
			Tr	**Sunderland**	07.84	1984-85	48	2	10		
			Tr	**Q.P.R.**	12.85	1985-86	16	5	1		
			Tr	**Fulham**	10.87	1987-88	61	3	16		
WALKER, Des S.	Hackney	21.11.65	App	**Nottingham F.**	11.83	1983-88	152	4	0	(CD)	E U21-7/E-8
WALKER, Ray	North Shields	28.09.63	App	**Aston Villa**	09.81	1982-85	15	8	0	(M)	E Yth Int
			L	**Port Vale**	09.84	1984	15	0	1		
			Tr	**Port Vale**	07.86	1986-88	129	1	15		
WALLACE, David L. (Danny)	Greenwich	21.01.64	App	**Southampton**	01.82	1980-88	233	15	62	(W)	E U21-11/E Yth Int/E-1/ Brother of Ray/Rodney
WALLACE, Raymond G.	Greenwich	02.10.69	YTS	**Southampton**	04.88	1988	25	1	0	(FB)	Brother of Danny/Rodney/E U21-2
WALLACE, Rodney S.	Greenwich	02.10.69	YTS	**Southampton**	04.88	1987-88	41	12	13	(RW)	Brother of Danny/Ray/E U21-2
WALLER, David H.	Urmston	20.12.63		**Crewe Alex.**	01.82	1981-85	165	3	55	(F)	
			Tr	**Shrewsbury T.**	07.86	1986	11	0	3		
			Tr	**Chesterfield**	03.87	1987-88	74	2	37		
WALLING, Dean A.	Leeds	17.04.69	Leeds U. (App)	**Rochdale**	07.87	1987-88	34	12	5	(F)	
WALLINGTON, F. Mark	Sleaford	17.09.52	Jnrs	**Walsall**	10.71	1971	11	0	0	(G)	E Yth Int/E U23-2
			Tr	**Leicester C.**	03.72	1971-84	412	0	0		
			Tr	**Derby Co.**	07.85	1985-86	67	0	0		
			Tr	**Lincoln C.**	08.88	1988	38	0	0		
WALSH, Alan	Hartlepool	09.12.56	Horden C.W.	**Middlesbrough**	12.76	1977	0	3	0	(F)	
			Tr	**Darlington**	10.78	1978-83	245	6	87		
			Tr	**Bristol C.**	08.84	1984-88	215	3	77		
WALSH, Colin D.	Hamilton	22.07.62	App	**Nottingham F.**	08.79	1980-85	115	24	32	(M)	S U21-5/Brother of Derek
			Tr	**Charlton Ath**	09.86	1986-88	45	4	9		
			L	**Peterborough U.**	02.89	1988	5	0	1		
WALSH, Derek	Hamilton	24.10.67	App	**Everton**	10.84	1984	1	0	0	(M)	Brother of Colin
			Hamilton Acad.	**Carlisle U.**	08.88	1988	34	1	3		
WALSH, Gary	Wigan	21.03.68	App	**Manchester U.**	04.85	1986-87	30	0	0	(G)	E U21-2
WALSH, Ian P.	St. Davids	04.09.58	App	**Crystal Palace**	10.75	1976-81	101	16	23	(F)	W Sch Int/W U21-2/W-18
			Tr	**Swansea C.**	02.82	1981-83	32	5	11		
			Tr	**Barnsley**	07.84	1984-85	45	4	15		
			Tr	**Grimsby T.**	08.86	1986-87	36	5	13		
			Tr	**Cardiff C.**	01.88	1987-88	5	12	4		
WALSH, Mario M.	Paddington	19.01.66	App	**Portsmouth**	01.84					(F)	
			Tr	**Torquay U.**	01.85	1984-86	89	11	18		
			Tr	**Colchester U.**	08.87	1987-88	29	9	11		
WALSH, Mick C.	Manchester	20.06.56	Jnrs	**Bolton W.**	07.74	1974-80	169	8	4	(CD)	IR-5
			Tr	**Everton**	08.81	1981-82	20	0	0		
			L	**Norwich C.**	10.82	1982	5	0	0		
			L	**Burnley**	12.82	1982	3	0	0		
			Fort Lauderdale (USA)	**Manchester C.**	10.83	1983	3	1	0		
			Tr	**Blackpool**	02.84	1983-88	146	7	5		

Andy Townsend (Norwich City & Eire) Match Magazine

Players Names	Birthplace	Date	Previous Club	League Club	Date Sign'd	Seasons Played	Career Record Apps	Sub	Gls	Pos.	Misc
WALSH, Paul A.	Plumstead	01.10.62	App	**Charlton Ath.**	10.79	1979-81	85	2	24	(F)	E Yth Int/E U21-7/E-2
			Tr	**Luton T.**	07.82	1982-83	80	0	24		
			Tr	**Liverpool**	05.84	1984-87	63	14	25		
			Tr	**Tottenham H.**	02.88	1987-88	39	5	7		
WALSH, Steve	Preston	03.11.64	Jnrs	**Wigan Ath**	09.82	1982-85	123	3	4	(CD)	
			Tr	**Leicester C.**	06.86	1986-88	82	1	9		
WALTER, Dave W.	Holsworthy	03.09.61	Bideford	**Exeter C.**	11.88	1988	26	0	0	(G)	
WALTERS, Mark	Birmingham	02.06.64	App	**Aston Villa**	05.82	1981-87	168	13	39	(LW)	E Yth Int/E U21-9 to Glasgow Rangers 12.87
WALTERS, Steven P.	Plymouth	09.01.72	YTS	**Crewe Alex.**	03.89	1987-88	20	3	1	(M)	
WALTON, Mark A.	Merthyr Tydfil	01.06.69	Jnrs	**Luton T.**	02.87					(G)	
			Tr	**Colchester U.**	11.87	1987-88	40	0	0		
WALWYN, Keith I.	Jamaica (WI)	17.02.56	Winterton R.	**Chesterfield**	11.79	1980	3	0	2	(F)	
			Tr	**York C.**	07.81	1981-86	245	0	118		
			Tr	**Blackpool**	06.87	1987-88	51	18	16		
WARD, Anthony (Tony)	Warrington	04.04.70	YTS	**Everton**	06.88					(M)	
			L	**Doncaster Rov.**	12.88	1988	4	0	0		
WARD, Mark W.	Huyton	10.10.62	App	**Everton**	09.80					(RW)	E Semi-Pro Int 1983
			Northwich Vic.	**Oldham Ath.**	07.83	1983-84	84	0	12		
			Tr	**West Ham U.**	08.85	1985-88	146	0	7		
WARD, Paul T.	Fishburn	15.09.63	App	**Chelsea**	08.81					(M/FB)	
			Tr	**Middlesbrough**	09.82	1982-85	69	7	1		
			Tr	**Darlington**	09.85	1985-87	124	0	9		
			Tr	**Leyton Orient**	07.88	1988	25	0	1		
WARD, Peter	Durham	15.10.64	Chester-le-Street	**Huddersfield**	01.87	1986-88	24	13	2	(W)	
WARE, Paul D.	Congleton	07.11.70	YTS	**Stoke C.**	11.88	1987-88	10	2	1	(M)	
WARHURST, Paul	Stockport	26.09.69	YTS	**Manchester C.**	06.88					(D)	
			Tr	**Oldham Ath.**	10.88	1988	2	2	0		
WARK, John	Glasgow	04.08.57	App	**Ipswich T.**	08.74	1974-83	295	1	94	(M)	S U21-8/S-29/PFA Footballer of Year 1980-81
			Tr	**Liverpool**	03.84	1983-87	64	6	28		
			Tr	**Ipswich T.**	01.88	1987-88	46	2	13		
WARNER, John	Paddington	20.11.61	Burnham Ramblers	**Colchester U.** (N/C)	02.89	1988	7	8	3	(F)	
WARREN, Lee A.	Manchester	28.02.69	YTS	**Leeds U.**	07.87					(M)	
			Tr	**Rochdale**	10.87	1987	31	0	1		
			Tr	**Hull C.**	08.88	1988	27	1	0		
WASSALL, Darren P.J.	Birmingham	27.06.68	App	**Nottingham F.**	06.86	1987	2	1	0	(CD)	
			L	**Hereford U.**	10.87	1987	5	0	0		
			L	**Bury**	03.89	1988	7	0	1		
WATSON, Alex F.	Liverpool	06.04.68	App	**Liverpool**	05.85	1987-88	3	1	0	(CD)	Brother of David
WATSON, Andy A.	Leeds	01.04.67	Harrogate T.	**Halifax T.**	08.88	1988	42	3	5	(M)	
WATSON, David	Liverpool	20.11.61	Jnrs	**Liverpool**	05.79					(CD)	E U21-7/E-12/Brother of Alex
			Tr	**Norwich C.**	11.80	1980-85	212	0	11		
			Tr	**Everton**	08.86	1986-88	105	0	10		
WATSON, Tommy R.	Liverpool	29.09.69	YTS	**Grimsby T.**	06.88	1987-88	25	15	4	(M)	
WAUGH, Keith	Sunderland	27.10.56	App	**Sunderland**	07.74					(G)	
			Tr	**Peterborough U.**	07.76	1976-80	195	0	0		
			Tr	**Sheffield U.**	08.81	1981-84	[illegible]	0	0		
			L	**Cambridge U.**	11.84	1984	4	0	0		
			L	**Bristol C.**	12.84	1984	3	0	0		
			Tr	**Bristol C.**	07.85	1985-88	167	0	0		
WEATHERLY, C. Mark	Ramsgate	18.01.58	App	**Gillingham**	12.75	1974-88	408	49	46	(CD)	
WEBB, Alan R.	Telford	01.01.63	App	**West Bromwich A.**	01.80	1981-83	23	1	0	(RB)	
			L	**Lincoln C.**	03.84	1983	11	0	0		
			Tr	**Port Vale**	08.84	1984-88	166	3	2		
WEBB, Neil J.	Reading	30.07.63	App	**Reading**	11.80	1979-81	65	7	22	(M)	Son of Doug/E Yth Int/E U21-3/E-18/E-7
			Tr	**Portsmouth**	07.82	1982-84	123	0	34		
			Tr	**Nottingham F.**	06.85	1985-88	146	0	47		
WEBSTER, Simon P.	Hinckley	20.01.64	App	**Tottenham H.**	12.81	1982-83	2	1	0	(CD)	
			L	**Exeter C.**	11.83	1983	26	0	0		
			Tr	**Huddersfield T.**	02.85	1984-87	118	0	4		
			Tr	**Sheffield U.**	03.88	1987-88	17	0	3		
WEGERLE, Roy C.	South Africa	19.03.64	Tampa Bay (USA)	**Chelsea**	06.86	1986-87	15	8	3	(W)	
			L	**Swindon T.**	03.88	1987	7	0	1		
			Tr	**Luton T.**	07.88	1988	26	4	8		
WEIR, Peter R.	Johnstone	18.01.58	Aberdeen	**Leicester C.**	01.88	1987-88	26	2	2	(LW)	S-6/to St. Mirren 11.88
WELCH, Keith J.	Bolton	03.10.58	YTS	**Rochdale**	03.87	1986-88	116	0	0	(G)	
WELLS, Peter A.	Nottingham	13.08.56	App	**Nottingham F.**	10.74	1975-76	27	0	0	(G)	
			Tr	**Southampton**	12.76	1976-82	141	0	0		
			Tr	**Millwall**	02.83	1982-83	33	0	0		
			Tr	**Leyton Orient**	07.85	1985-88	148	0	0		
WEST, Colin	Wallsend	13.11.62	App	**Sunderland**	07.80	1981-84	88	14	21	(F)	
			Tr	**Watford**	03.85	1984-85	45	0	20		
			Glasgow Rangers	**Sheffield Wed.**	09.87	1987-88	40	5	8		
			Tr	**West Bromwich A.**	03.89	1988	17	0	8		
WEST, Colin W.	Middlesbrough	19.09.67	App	**Chelsea**	09.85	1986-87	8	8	4	(F)	E Yth Int
			L	**Swansea C.**	03.89	1988	14	0	3		
WEST, Gary	Scunthorpe	25.08.64	App	**Sheffield U.**	08.82	1982-84	75	0	2	(CD)	E Yth Int
			Tr	**Lincoln C.**	08.85	1985-86	83	0	4		
			Tr	**Gillingham**	07.87	1987-88	51	1	3		
			Tr	**Port Vale**	02.89	1988	11	3	1		
WESTLEY, Shane L.M.	Canterbury	16.06.65	App	**Charlton Ath.**	06.83	1983	8	0	0	(CD)	
			Tr	**Southend U.**	03.85	1984-88	142	2	10		
WESTON, Ian P.	Bristol	06.05.68	App	**Bristol Rov.**	05.86	1986-87	13	3	0	(M)	
			Tr	**Torquay U.**	09.88	1988	32	5	2		
WHARTON, Kenny	Newcastle	28.11.60	Grainger Park BC	**Newcastle U.**	01.79	1978-88	268	22	26	(LB/M)	
WHARTON, Sean R.	Newport	31.10.68	YTS	**Sunderland**	07.87	1988	1	0	0	(F)	

Players Names	Birthplace	Date	Previous Club	League Club	Date Sign'd	Seasons Played	Career Record Apps	Sub	Gls	Pos.	Misc
WHEELER, Paul	Caerphilly	03.01.65	App	**Bristol Rov.**	01.83					(F)	
			Aberaman	**Cardiff C.**	08.85	1985-88	72	29	10		
WHELAN, Ronnie A.	Dublin	25.09.61	Home Farm	**Liverpool**	10.79	1980-88	254	10	42	(M)	IR U21-1/IR-35
WHELLANS, Robert	Harrogate	14.02.69	YTS	**Bradford C.**	06.87					(F)	
			L	**Hartlepool U.**	12.87	1987	8	3	1		
WHISTON, Peter	Widnes	04.01.68		**Plymouth Arg.**	12.87	1988	1	1	0	(D)	
WHITE, David	Manchester	30.10.67	YTS	**Manchester C.**	10.85	1986-88	103	10	21	(RW)	E Yth Int/E U21-4
WHITE, Devan W.	Nottingham	02.03.64	Arnold	**Lincoln C.**	12.84	1984-85	21	8	4	(F)	
			Shepshed Chart.	**Bristol Rov.**	08.87	1987-88	70	9	20		
WHITE, Steve J.	Chipping Sodbury	02.01.59	Mangotsfield	**Bristol Rov.**	07.77	1977-79	46	4	20	(F)	E Sch Int
			Tr	**Luton T.**	12.79	1979-81	63	9	25		
			Tr	**Charlton Ath.**	07.82	1982	29	0	12		
			L	**Lincoln C.**	01.83	1982	2	1	0		
			L	**Luton T.**	02.83	1982	4	0	0		
			Tr	**Bristol Rov.**	08.83	1983-85	89	12	24		
			Tr	**Swindon T.**	07.86	1986-88	87	16	39		
WHITE, E. Winston	Leicester	26.10.58	App	**Leicester C.**	10.76	1976-78	10	2	1	(W)	
			Tr	**Hereford U.**	03.79	1978-82	169	6	21		
			Hong Kong	**Chesterfield** (N/C)	09.83	1983	0	1	0		
			Tr	**Port Vale** (N/C)	10.83	1983	0	1	0		
			Tr	**Stockport Co.** (N/C)	11.83	1983	4	0	1		
			Tr	**Bury**	12.83	1983-86	125	0	11		
			L	**Rochdale**	10.86	1986	4	0	0		
			Tr	**Colchester U.**	02.87	1986-88	64	1	8		
			Tr	**Burnley**	10.88	1988	30	5	5		
WHITEHEAD, Alan	Bury	20.11.56	Darwen	**Bury**	12.77	1977-80	98	1	13	(CD)	
			Tr	**Brentford**	08.81	1981-83	101	1	4		
			Tr	**Scunthorpe U.**	01.84	1983-86	106	2	8		
			Tr	**York C.**	10.86	1986-87	40	1	1		
			L	**Wigan Ath.**	03.87	1986	2	0	0		
			Tr	**Halifax T.**	08.88	1988	10	1	1		
WHITEHEAD, Clive R.	Birmingham	24.11.55	Northfield Jnrs	**Bristol C.**	08.73	1973-81	209	20	10	(RB/W)	E Yth Int
			Tr	**West Bromwich A.**	11.81	1981-86	157	11	6		
			L	**Wolverhampton W.**	01.86	1985	2	0	0		
			Tr	**Portsmouth**	06.87	1987-88	57	8	2		
WHITEHEAD, Philip M.	Halifax	17.12.69	YTS	**Halifax T.**	06.88	1986-88	23	0	0	(G)	
WHITEHOUSE, Dane L.	Sheffield	14.10.70	YTS	**Sheffield U.**	07.87	1988	3	2	0	(W)	
WHITEHURST, W. (Billy)	Thurnscoe	10.06.59	Mexborough Town	**Hull C.**	10.80	1980-85	176	17	47	(F)	
			Tr	**Newcastle U.**	12.85	1985-86	28	0	7		
			Tr	**Oxford U.**	10.86	1986-87	36	4	4		
			Tr	**Reading**	02.88	1987-88	17	0	8		
			Tr	**Sunderland**	09.88	1988	17	0	3		
			Tr	**Hull C.**	12.88	1988	21	0	5		
WHITESIDE, Norman	Belfast (NI)	07.05.65	App	**Manchester U.**	07.82	1981-88	193	13	47	(F)	NI Sch Int/NI-36
WHITLOCK, Mark	Portsmouth	14.03.61	App	**Southampton**	03.79	1981-85	55	6	1	(CD)	
			L	**Grimsby T.**	10.82	1982	7	1	0		
			L	**Aldershot**	03.83	1982	14	0	0		
			Tr	**Bournemouth**	07.86	1986-88	98	1	1		
			Tr	**Reading**	11.88	1988	16	1	0		
WHITLOW, Mike W.	Northwich	13.01.68	Witton A.	**Leeds U.**	11.88	1988	18	2	1	(W)	
WHITTON, Steve P.	East Ham	04.12.60	App	**Coventry C.**	09.78	1979-82	64	10	21	(F)	
			Tr	**West Ham U.**	07.83	1983-84	35	4	6		
			L	**Birmingham C.**	01.86	1985	8	0	3		
			Tr	**Birmingham C.**	08.86	1986-88	94	1	28		
			Tr	**Sheffield Wed.**	03.89	1988	12	0	3		
WHYTE, Chris A.	Islington	02.09.61	App	**Arsenal**	09.79	1981-85	86	4	8	(CD)	E U21-4
			L	**Crystal Palace**	08.84	1984	13	0	0		
			Los Angeles (USA)	**West Bromwich A.**	08.88	1988	40	0	3		
WIGLEY, Steve	Ashton-u-Lyne	15.10.61	Curzon Ashton	**Nottingham F.**	03.81	1982-85	69	13	2	(W)	
			Tr	**Sheffield U.**	10.85	1985-86	21	7	1		
			Tr	**Birmingham C.**	03.87	1986-88	87	0	3		
			Tr	**Portsmouth**	03.89	1988	11	0	0		
WIGNALL, Steve L.	Liverpool	17.09.54	Liverpool(Jnr)	**Doncaster Rov.**	03.72	1972-76	127	3	1	(CD)	Brother of David
			Tr	**Colchester U.**	09.77	1977-83	279	2	22		
			Tr	**Brentford**	08.84	1984-86	67	0	2		
			Tr	**Aldershot**	09.86	1986-88	107	2	3		
WILCOX, Russell	Hemsworth	25.03.64	App	**Doncaster Rov.** (App)	05.80	1980	1	0	0	(CD)	E Semi-Pro Int 1986
			Frickley Ath.	**Northampton T.**	08.86	1986-88	91	1	6		
WILDER, Chris J.	Chapeltown	23.09.67	App	**Southampton**	09.85					(RB)	
			Tr	**Sheffield U.**	08.86	1986-88	61	4	1		
WILKINS, Dean M.	Hillingdon	12.07.62	App	**Q.P.R.**	05.80	1980-82	1	5	0	(M)	Brother of Graham/Ray/Son of George
			Tr	**Brighton & H.A.**	08.83	1983	2	0	0		
			L	**Leyton Orient**	03.84	1983	10	0	0		
			PEC Zwolle (Neth)	**Brighton & H.A.**	07.87	1987-88	85	2	4		
WILKINS, Richard J.	Lambeth	28.05.65	Haverhill Rov.	**Colchester U.**	11.86	1986-88	107	2	19	(M)	
WILKINSON, Paul	Louth	30.10.64	App	**Grimsby T.**	10.82	1982-84	69	2	27	(F)	E U21-4
			Tr	**Everton**	03.85	1984-86	19	12	6		
			Tr	**Nottingham F.**	03.87	1986-87	32	2	5		
			Tr	**Watford**	08.88	1988	44	1	19		
WILKINSON, Stephen J.	Lincoln	01.09.68	App	**Leicester C.**	09.86	1986-88	3	4	1	(F)	
			L	**Crewe Alex.**	09.88	1988	3	2	2		
WILLIAMS, Adrian	Reading	16.08.71	YTS	**Reading**	03.89	1988	6	2	0	(FB)	
WILLIAMS, Andy	Birmingham	29.07.62	Solihull Bor.	**Coventry C.**	07.85	1985-86	3	6	0	(M)	
			Tr	**Rotherham U.**	10.86	1986-88	87	0	13		
			Tr	**Leeds U.**	11.88	1988	7	11	1		
WILLIAMS, Brett	Dudley	19.03.68	App	**Nottingham F.**	12.85	1985-88	20	0	0	(LB)	
			L	**Stockport Co.**	03.87	1986	2	0	0		
			L	**Northampton T.**	01.88	1987	3	1	0		

Chris Turner (Sheffield Wednesday) Match Magazine

Pat van den Hauwe (Everton & Wales) Match Magazine

Barry Venison (Liverpool) Match Magazine

Chris Waddle (Tottenham Hotspur & England) Match Magazine

Players Names	Birthplace	Date	Previous Club	League Club	Date Sign'd	Seasons Played	Career Record Apps	Sub	Gls	Pos.	Misc
WILLIAMS, Brian	Salford	05.11.55	App	**Bury**	04.73	1971-76	148	11	19	(LB/W)	
			Tr	**Q.P.R.**	07.77	1977	9	10	0		
			Tr	**Swindon T.**	06.78	1978-80	89	10	8		
			Tr	**Bristol Rov.**	07.81	1981-84	172	0	20		
			Tr	**Bristol C.**	07.85	1985-86	77	0	3		
			Tr	**Shrewsbury T.**	07.87	1987-88	62	3	1		
WILLIAMS, Darren	Birmingham	15.12.68	App	**Leicester C.**	12.86	1988	4	2	1	(W)	
WILLIAMS, David M.	Cardiff	11.03.55	Clifton Ath.	**Bristol Rov.**	08.75	1975-84	342	10	66	(M)	W Yth Int/W U21-1/W-5
			Tr	**Norwich C.**	07.85	1985-87	56	4	11		
WILLIAMS, David P.	Liverpool	18.09.68	YTS	**Oldham Ath.**	08.87					(G)	
			Tr	**Burnley**	03.88	1988	7	0	0		
WILLIAMS, Gareth J.	Cowes (IOW)	12.03.67	Gosport Bor.	**Aston Villa**	01.88	1987-88	2	0	0	(M)	
WILLIAMS, Gary	Wolverhampton	17.06.60	App	**Aston Villa**	06.78	1978-86	235	5	0	(FB)	
			L	**Walsall**	03.80	1979	9	0	0		
			Tr	**Leeds U.**	07.87	1987-88	39	0	3		
WILLIAMS, Gary	Nantwich	14.05.59	Jnrs	**Tranmere Rov.** (N/C)	09.76	1976	1	0	0	(M/FB)	
			Djurgaardens(Sweden)	**Blackpool**	08.80	1980	30	1	2		
			Tr	**Swindon T.**	08.81	1981	37	1	3		
			Tr	**Tranmere Rov.**	02.83	1982-88	163	11	16		
WILLIAMS, Gary A.	Bristol	08.06.63	App	**Bristol C.**	08.80	1980-83	98	2	1	(M/FB)	Son of Alan
			Portsmouth(trial)	**Swansea C.** (N/C)	01.85	1984	6	0	0		
			Bristol Rov.(trial)	**Oldham Ath.**	08.85	1985-88	44	12	12		
WILLIAMS, D. Geraint	Treorchy	05.01.62	App	**Bristol Rov.**	01.80	1980-84	138	3	8	(M)	W Yth Int/W U21-2/W-9
			Tr	**Derby Co.**	03.85	1984-88	168	1	7		
WILLIAMS, Jeremy S.	Didcot	24.03.60	App	**Reading**	03.78	1976-87	283	26	17	(RB/W)	
			Tr	**Gillingham**	08.88	1988	7	6	0		
WILLIAMS, W. John	Liverpool	03.10.60	Jnrs	**Tranmere Rov.**	10.79	1978-84	167	6	13	(CD)	
			Tr	**Port Vale**	07.85	1985-86	50	0	3		
			Tr	**Bournemouth**	12.86	1986-88	101	0	7		
WILLIAMS, Mike	Deeside	06.02.65	App	**Chester C.**	02.83	1981-83	30	4	4	(CD)	W Yth Int
			Tr	**Wrexham**	07.84	1984-88	159	6	3		
WILLIAMS, Neil J.F.	Waltham Abbey	23.10.64	App	**Watford**	08.82					(W/FB)	
			Tr	**Hull C.**	07.84	1984-87	75	16	9		
			Tr	**Preston N.E.**	07.88	1988	40	1	2		
WILLIAMS, Paul A.	Sheffield	08.09.63	Nuneaton Bor.	**Preston N.E.**	12.86	1986	1	0	0	(D/F)	
			Tr	**Newport Co.**	08.87	1987	26	0	3		
			Tr	**Sheffield U.**	03.88	1987-88	6	2	0		
WILLIAMS, Paul A.	London	16.08.65	Woodford T.	**Charlton Ath.**	02.87	1987-88	36	8	13	(F)	E U21-3
			L	**Brentford**	10.87	1987	7	0	3		
WILLIAMS, Paul L.	Liverpool	25.09.70	YTS	**Sunderland** (YTS)	07.87	1988	0	1	0	(W)	
WILLIAMS, Robert J.	Bridgend	09.10.68	YTS	**Oxford U.**	08.87					(FB)	
			Tr	**Hereford U.**	08.88	1988	5	0	0		
WILLIAMS, Steven B.	Mansfield	18.07.70	YTS	**Mansfield T.**	06.88	1986-88	4	7	0	(F)	
WILLIAMS, Steve C.	Hammersmith	12.07.58	App	**Southampton**	07.76	1975-84	277	1	18	(M)	E U21-14/E-6
			Tr	**Arsenal**	12.84	1984-87	93	2	4		
			Tr	**Luton T.**	08.88	1988	10	0	0		
WILLIAMS, Tommy E.	Winchburgh	18.12.57	App	**Leicester C.**	12.75	1977-85	236	5	10	(D)	
			Tr	**Birmingham C.**	08.86	1986-87	62	0	1		
			Tr	**Grimsby T.**	07.88	1988	19	0	0		
WILLIAMS, Wayne	Telford	17.11.63	App	**Shrewsbury T.**	11.81	1982-88	212	9	7	(RB)	
			L	**Northampton T.**	11.88	1988	3	0	1		
			Tr	**Northampton T.**	01.89	1988	23	0	0		
WILLIAMS, W.R. (Bill)	Littleborough	07.10.60	Ashe Labs	**Rochdale**	08.81	1981-84	89	6	2	(CD)	
			Tr	**Stockport Co.**	07.85	1985-88	104	0	1		
			Tr	**Manchester C.**	10.88	1988	0	1	0		
			Tr	**Stockport Co.**	12.88	1988	35	0	2		
WILLIAMSON, R. (Bobby)	Glasgow	13.08.61	Glasgow Rangers	**West Bromwich A.**	08.86	1986-87	40	13	11	(F)	
			Tr	**Rotherham U.**	07.88	1988	41	1	27		
WILLIS, Jim A.	Liverpool	12.07.68	Blackburn Rov.(YTS)	**Halifax T.**	08.86					(CD)	Brother of Paul
			Tr	**Stockport Co.**	12.87	1987	10	0	0		
			Tr	**Darlington**	03.88	1987-88	50	0	2		
WILLIS, Paul E.	Liverpool	24.01.70	YTS	**Halifax T.**	05.88	1987-88	1	4	0	(M)	Brother of Jim
			Tr	**Darlington** (YTS)	03.89	1988	1	1	1		
WILMOT, Rhys J.	Newport	21.02.62	App	**Arsenal**	02.80	1985-86	8	0	0	(G)	W Sch Int/W U21-6
			L	**Hereford U.**	03.83	1982	9	0	0		
			L	**Leyton Orient**	05.84	1984	46	0	0		
			L	**Swansea C.**	08.88	1988	16	0	0		
			L	**Plymouth Arg.**	03.89	1988	17	0	0		
WILSON, Andrew W.	Wigan	07.01.65		**Wigan Ath.**	08.87	1987-88	1	1	0	(M)	
WILSON, Clive A.	Manchester	13.11.61	Jnrs	**Manchester C.**	12.79	1981-86	107	2	9	(M/LB)	
			L	**Chester C.**	09.82	1982	21	0	2		
			Tr	**Chelsea**	05.87	1987-88	56	7	5		
WILSON, Danny J.	Wigan	01.01.60	Wigan Ath.	**Bury**	09.77	1977-79	87	3	8	(M)	NI-14
			Tr	**Chesterfield**	07.80	1980-82	100	0	13		
			Tr	**Nottingham F.**	01.83	1982	9	1	1		
			L	**Scunthorpe U.**	10.83	1983	6	0	3		
			Tr	**Brighton & H.A.**	11.83	1983-86	132	3	33		
			Tr	**Luton T.**	07.87	1987-88	75	0	17		
WILSON, David G.	Todmorden	20.03.69	App	**Manchester U.**	03.87	1988	0	4	0	(M)	
WILSON, Ian W.	Aberdeen	27.03.58	Elgin C.	**Leicester C.**	04.79	1979-87	277	8	17	(LM)	S-3
			Tr	**Everton**	09.87	1987-88	24	10	1		
WILSON, Kevin J.	Banbury	18.04.61	Banbury U.	**Derby Co.**	12.79	1979-84	106	16	30	(F)	NI-12
			Tr	**Ipswich T.**	01.85	1984-86	94	4	34		
			Tr	**Chelsea**	06.87	1987-88	59	12	17		
WILSON, Paul A.	Bradford	02.08.68	YTS	**Huddersfield T.**	06.86	1985-86	15	0	0	(LB)	
			Tr	**Norwich C.**	07.87						
			Tr	**Northampton T.**	02.88	1987-88	48	6	2		

Players Names	Birthplace	Date	Previous Club	League Club	Date Sign'd	Seasons Played	Career Record Apps	Sub	Gls	Pos.	Misc
WILSON, Phil	Hemsworth	16.10.60	App	**Bolton W.**	10.78	1979-80	35	4	4	(M)	
			Tr	**Huddersfield T.**	08.81	1981-86	229	4	16		
			Tr	**York C.**	08.87	1987-88	38	8	2		
WILSON, Robert J.	Kensington	05.06.61	App	**Fulham**	06.79	1979-84	168	7	34	(M)	
			Tr	**Millwall**	08.85	1985	28	0	12		
			Tr	**Luton T.**	08.86	1986-87	19	5	1		
			Tr	**Fulham**	09.87	1987-88	43	4	4		
WILSON, Terry	Broxburn	08.02.69	App	**Nottingham F.**	04.86	1987-88	57	6	6	(M)	S U21-4
WIMBLETON, Paul P.	Havant	13.11.64	App	**Portsmouth**	02.82	1981-83	5	5	0	(M)	E Sch Int
			Tr	**Cardiff C.**	08.86	1986-88	118	1	17		
WINDRIDGE, David H.	Atherstone	07.12.61	Jnrs	**Sheffield U.**	01.79					(W)	
			Tr	**Chesterfield**	03.80	1980-82	66	12	14		
			Tr	**Blackpool**	08.83	1983-86	87	14	18		
			Turkey	**Bury**	11.88	1988	1	0	0		
			Tr	**Rochdale**	01.89	1988	5	0	0		
WINSTANLEY, Mark A.	St. Helens	22.01.68	YTS	**Bolton W.**	07.86	1985-88	67	1	1	(CD)	
WINTER, Julian	Huddersfield	06.09.65	App	**Huddersfield T.**	09.83	1984-88	89	4	5	(M)	
			L	**Scunthorpe U.**	08.88	1988	4	0	0		
WINTERBURN, Nigel	Nuneaton	11.12.63	App	**Birmingham C.**	08.81					(LB)	E Yth Int/E U21-1
			Tr	**Wimbledon**	08.83	1983-86	164	1	8		
			Tr	**Arsenal**	05.87	1987-88	54	1	3		
WISE, Dennis F.	Kensington	16.12.66	Southampton(App)	**Wimbledon**	03.85	1984-88	92	8	18	(W)	E U21-1
WITHE, Chris	Liverpool	25.09.62	App	**Newcastle U.**	09.80	1980	2	0	0	(LB)	Brother of Peter
			Tr	**Bradford C.**	06.83	1983-87	141	2	2		
			Tr	**Notts Co.**	10.87	1987-88	80	0	3		
WITHE, Peter	Liverpool	30.08.51	Smith Coggins	**Southport**	11.70	1970-71	3	0	0	(F)	E-11/Brother of Chris
			Tr	**Barrow**	12.71	1971	1	0	0		
			Arcadia Shep.(SA)	**Wolverhampton W.**	11.73	1973-74	12	5	3		
			Tr	**Birmingham C.**	08.75	1975-76	35	0	9		
			Tr	**Nottingham F.**	09.76	1976-78	74	1	28		
			Tr	**Newcastle U.**	08.78	1978-79	76	0	25		
			Tr	**Aston Villa**	05.80	1980-84	182	0	74		
			Tr	**Sheffield U.**	07.85	1985-87	70	4	18		
			L	**Birmingham C.**	09.87	1987	8	0	2		
			Tr	**Huddersfield T.**(N/C)	07.88	1988	14	12	0		
WITHEY, Graham A.	Bristol	11.06.60	Bath C.	**Bristol Rov.**	08.82	1982	19	3	10	(F)	
			Tr	**Coventry C.**	08.83	1983-84	11	11	4		
			Tr	**Cardiff C.**	12.84	1984-85	27	0	7		
			Bath C.	**Bristol C.**	09.86	1986	1	1	0		
			Cheltenham T.	**Exeter C.**	07.88	1988	5	2	2		
WOOD, Darren	Derby	14.01.68	YTS	**Chesterfield**	06.87	1986-88	61	6	3	(CD)	
WOOD, Darren T.	Scarborough	09.06.64	App	**Middlesbrough**	07.81	1981-84	101	0	6	(RB/M)	E Sch Int
			Tr	**Chelsea**	09.84	1984-88	134	10	3		
			Tr	**Sheffield Wed.**	01.89	1988	7	1	0		
WOOD, George	Douglas (Lk.)	26.09.52	East Stirling	**Blackpool**	01.72	1971-76	117	0	0	(G)	S-4
			Tr	**Everton**	08.77	1977-79	103	0	0		
			Tr	**Arsenal**	08.80	1980-82	60	0	0		
			Tr	**Crystal Palace**	08.83	1983-87	192	0	0		
			Tr	**Cardiff C.**	01.88	1987-88	58	0	0		
WOOD, Paul	Oldham	20.03.70	YTS	**Sheffield U.**	09.88	1987	0	1	0	(M)	
			L	**Rochdale**	11.88	1988	2	3	0		
WOOD, Paul A.	Saltburn	01.11.64	App	**Portsmouth**	11.82	1983-86	25	22	7	(M)	
			Tr	**Brighton & H.A.**	08.87	1987-88	53	13	5		
WOOD, Steve A.	Bracknell	02.02.63	App	**Reading**	02.81	1979-86	216	3	9	(CD)	
			Tr	**Millwall**	06.87	1987-88	57	0	0		
WOOD, Trevor J.	Jersey	03.11.68	App	**Brighton & H.A.**	11.86					(G)	
			Tr	**Port Vale**	07.88	1988	2	0	0		
WOODCOCK, A.S. (Tony)	Nottingham	06.12.55	App	**Nottingham F.**	01.74	1973-79	125	4	36	(F)	E U21-2/E-42
			L	**Lincoln C.**	02.76	1975	2	2	1		
			L	**Doncaster Rov.**	09.76	1976	6	0	2		
			FC Köln(WG)	**Arsenal**	07.82	1982-85	129	2	56		to FC Köln 7.86
WOODS, Chris C.E.	Boston	14.11.59	App	**Nottingham F.**	12.76					(G)	E Yth Int/E U21-6/E-14
			Tr	**Q.P.R.**	07.79	1979-80	63	0	0		
			Tr	**Norwich C.**	03.81	1980-85	216	0	0		to Glasgow Rangers 6.86
WOODS, Neil S.	Bradford	30.07.66	App	**Doncaster Rov.**	08.83	1982-86	55	10	16	(F)	
			Glasgow Rangers	**Ipswich T.**	07.87	1987-88	12	8	4		
WOODS, Ray G.	Birkenhead	07.06.65	App	**Tranmere Rov.**	06.83	1982-84	9	5	2	(W)	
			Colne Dynamoes	**Wigan Ath.**	02.89	1988	5	3	0		
WOODTHORPE, Colin J.	Ellesmere Port	13.01.69	YTS	**Chester C.**	08.86	1986-88	108	1	5	(LB)	
WORSLEY, Graeme	Broadgreen	04.01.69	Bootle	**Shrewsbury T.**	03.89	1988	6	0	0	(RB)	
WORTHINGTON, Gary L.	Cleethorpes	10.11.66	App	**Manchester U.**	11.84					(F)	E Yth Int/Son of Dave
			Tr	**Huddersfield T.**	07.86						
			Tr	**Darlington**	07.87	1987-88	31	9	15		
WORTHINGTON, Nigel	Ballymena (NI)	04.11.61	Ballymena U.	**Notts Co.**	07.81	1981-83	62	5	4	(LB)	NI Yth Int/NI-25
			Tr	**Sheffield Wed.**	02.84	1983-88	167	1	2		
WRENCH, Mark N.	Warrington	27.09.69	YTS	**Wrexham**	09.88	1988	3	1	0	(FB)	
WRIGHT, Alan G.	Ashton-u-Lyne	28.09.71	Jnrs	**Blackpool**	04.89	1987-88	14	3	0	(M)	
WRIGHT, Darren J.	West Bromwich	14.03.68	YTS	**Wolverhampton W.**	07.85	1985	1	0	0	(FB)	
			Tr	**Wrexham**	08.86	1986-88	81	5	3		
WRIGHT, Ian E.	Woolwich	03.11.63	Greenwich Bor.	**Crystal Palace**	08.85	1985-88	135	18	63	(F)	
WRIGHT, Mark	Dorchester (Ox)	01.08.63	Jnrs	**Oxford U.**	08.80	1981	8	2	0	(CD)	E U21-4/E-22
			Tr	**Southampton**	03.82	1981-86	170	0	7		
			Tr	**Derby Co.**	08.87	1987-88	71	0	4		
WRIGHT, Tommy E.	Dunfermline	10.01.66	App	**Leeds U.**	01.83	1982-85	73	8	24	(W)	S Yth Int/S U21-1
			Tr	**Oldham Ath.**	10.86	1986-88	110	2	22		
WRIGHT, Tommy J.	Belfast	29.08.63	Linfield	**Newcastle U.**	01.88	1988	9	0	0	(G)	NI U21-1/NI-2

Players Names	Birthplace	Date	Previous Club	League Club	Date Sign'd	Seasons Played	Career Record Apps	Sub	Gls	Pos.	Misc
WRIGHTSON, Jeff G.	Newcastle	18.05.68	App	**Newcastle U.**	05.86	1986	3	1	0	(CD)	
			Tr	**Preston N.E.**	07.87	1987-88	59	4	0		
WYLDE, Rodger J.	Sheffield	08.03.54	App	**Sheffield Wed.**	07.71	1972-79	157	11	54	(F)	
			Tr	**Oldham Ath.**	02.80	1979-82	109	4	51		
			Sporting Lisbon(Port)	**Sunderland**	07.84	1984	8	3	3		
			Tr	**Barnsley**	12.84	1984-87	50	2	19		
			L	**Rotherham U.**	03.88	1987	6	0	1		
			Tr	**Stockport Co.**	07.88	1988	24	2	12		
WYNNE, Darren L.	St. Asaph	12.10.70	YTS	**Chester C.** (YTS)	07.87	1988	0	6	0		
YALLOP, Frank W.	Watford	04.04.64	App	**Ipswich T.**	01.82	1983-88	154	8	4	(RB)	E Yth Int
YATES, Dean R.	Leicester	26.10.67	App	**Notts Co.**	06.85	1984-88	181	0	21	(CD)	E U21-4
YATES, Mark J.	Birmingham	24.01.70	YTS	**Birmingham C.**	07.88	1987-88	17	6	3	(F)	
YATES, Steven	Bristol	29.01.70	YTS	**Bristol Rov.**	06.88	1986-88	37	0	0	(CD)	
YOUNG, Eric	Singapore	25.03.60	Slough T.	**Brighton & H.A.**	11.82	1983-86	126	0	10	(CD)	
			Tr	**Wimbledon**	07.87	1987-88	61	3	4		
YOUNG, Kevin	Sunderland	12.08.61	App	**Burnley**	05.79	1978-83	114	6	11	(LW)	
			L	**Torquay U.**	11.83	1983	3	0	1		
			L	**Port Vale**	12.83	1983	28	0	4		
			Tr	**Bury**	07.84	1984-86	85	3	10		to Utrecht (Neth) 11.86
YOUNG, Richard A.	Nottingham	18.10.68	YTS	**Notts Co.**	08.86	1986	18	17	5	(F)	
			Tr	**Southend U.**	08.87	1987-88	5	4	0		
			Tr	**Exeter C.**	03.89	1988	13	1	4		
ZELEM, Peter R.	Manchester	13.02.62	App	**Chester C.**	02.80	1980-84	124	5	15	(CD)	
			Tr	**Wolverhampton W.**	01.85	1984-86	45	0	1		
			Tr	**Preston N.E.**	03.87	1986	6	0	1		
			Tr	**Burnley**	08.87	1987-88	17	2	2		
ZONDERVAN, Romeo	Surinam	04.03.59	Twente Enschede	**West Bromwich A.**	03.82	1981-83	82	2	5	(M)	Neth Int
			Tr	**Ipswich T.**	03.84	1983-88	182	0	13		

Colin Walsh (Charlton Athletic)

Match Magazine

Paul Williams (Charlton Athletic) Match Magazine

Terry Wilson (Nottingham Forest) Match Magazine

Steve Wood (Millwall) Match Magazine

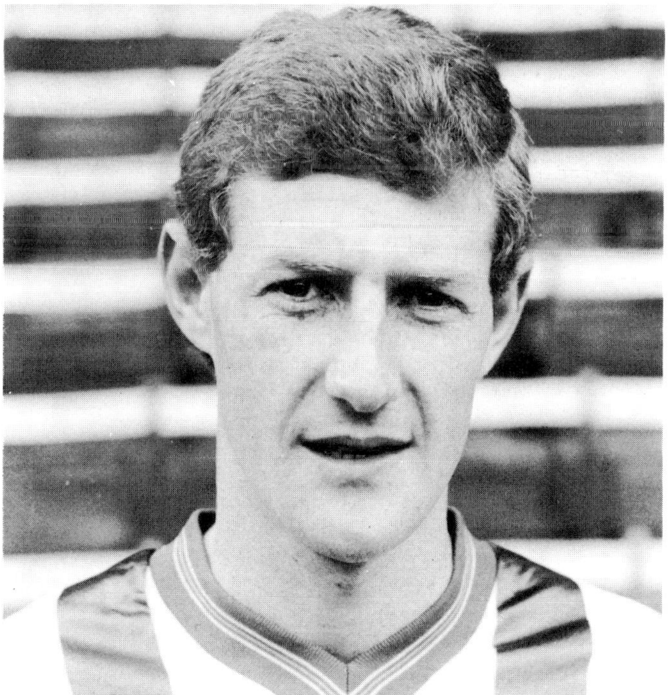

Nigel Worthington (Sheffield Wednesday & Northern Ireland) Match Magazine

Robson
Financial
Services
Limited

AVOID THE TRAP DOOR

WE BELIEVE THERE IS A HUGE TRAP DOOR UNDER THE WORLD'S STOCK MARKETS and sooner or later most people will fall through it, this means that carefully laid plans to provide pensions and savings will be devastated.

Robsons provide a unique Pension Management Service which not only gives opportunity of outstanding growth but at the same time provides a real chance of avoiding any major downturn. We believe the service we provide is unique.

Please contact:
Robson Financial Services Limited
6 Lovat Lane
London
EC3R 8DT

Tel: 01- 623 3495
Fax: 01- 623 0135

A FIMBRA MEMBER

AREA GRAPHICS LTD

Typesetters of Sporting Books and Magazines

Arden Press Way
Letchworth
Hertfordshire
SG6 1LH
Telephone
(0462) 670942

Don't consider sponsorship without considering sponsorship law.

For advice on sports, art, music and television sponsorship including contracts, financing of projects, tax, merchandising and licensing, copyright, trade marks, product endorsement, sales promotions, personal appearances and media regulations.
Please call Stephen or Michael Townley on 01- 251 2505.

Townleys

32 Sekforde Street,
London EC1R 0HH

FINAL WHISTLE

Football Antiques & Memorabilia

PRINTS • BOOKS • MEDALS
OBJET D'ART
COMMEMORATIVE WARE.
FROM FOOTBALL'S
GLORIOUS PAST

Tuesday - Friday 12-6pm.
Saturday 10am-2pm.

The Antique Market
Second Floor
13-25 Church Street
London NW8

tel. 01-262 3423

TUBE EDGEWARE ROAD
MARYLEBONE

THE ULTIMATE AUTHORITATIVE SPORTING ANNUALS

DON'T MISS

HUGMAN'S BRITISH BOXING YEARBOOK 1990
(£10.95) soft-back. 480 pages, 200 photographs.
The British Boxing publication. Produced in association
with the British Boxing Board of Control.
Published September 21st 1989.

HUGMAN'S INTERNATIONAL BOXING ANNUAL 1990
(£12.95) hard-back. 192 pages, 150 photographs.
International coverage, filled with colour action.
Review of the year, records and many other features.
Published September 21st 1989.

HUGMAN'S SWIMMING YEARBOOK 1990
(£10.95) soft-back.
The first ever comprehensive yearbook of British Swimming.
Produced in association with the Amateur Swimming Association.
Published November 3rd 1989.

HUGMAN'S CRICKET ANNUAL 1990
(£12.95) hard-back. 240 pages, 150 photographs.
Crammed full of facts and statistics, as well as plenty
of lively colour.
Produced with the Association of Cricket Statisticians.
Published 29th March 1990.

All available through your local bookshop or post-free (and the first 100
copies of each autographed by Barry Hugman) from our offices at:
24 Notting Hill Gate
London
W11 3JQ
Tel: 01-229 9944

Send your cheque or postal order made out to:
Hugman Sporting Publications Plc.

HUGMAN'S
SPORTING
PUBLICATIONS
LIMITED